Econometric Exercises, Volume 2

T0331981

Statistics

Building on the success of Abadir and Magnus' *Matrix Algebra* in the Econometric Exercises series, *Statistics* serves as a bridge between elementary and specialized statistics. Professors Abadir, Heijmans, and Magnus freely use matrix algebra to cover intermediate to advanced material. Each chapter contains a general introduction followed by a series of connected exercises which build up knowledge systematically. The characteristic feature of the book (and indeed the series) is that all exercises are fully solved. The authors present many new proofs of established results, along with new results, often involving shortcuts that resort to statistical conditioning arguments.

Karim Abadir is Emeritus Professor of Financial Econometrics at Imperial College London, and Distinguished Visiting Professor at the American University in Cairo. He was the Head of the Statistics Group at the University of York and Chair of Econometrics and Statistics joint between the Departments of Mathematics and Economics 1996-2005, then Chair of Financial Econometrics 2005-2017 at Imperial College London. He was a founding editor of the *Econometrics Journal* for 10 years.

Risto Heijmans (1940–2014) was Associate Professor in Econometrics at the former Institute of Actuarial Science and Econometrics of the University of Amsterdam. He taught in probability theory, statistics, and stochastic processes to students in actuarial science, econometrics, and operations research. He was an expert on asymptotic theory.

Jan R. Magnus worked at the London School of Economics from 1981 to 1996 and then at Tilburg University as Research Professor of Econometrics. In 2013 he moved to the Vrije Universiteit Amsterdam as Extraordinary Professor of Econometrics. Magnus is (co-)author of 8 books, and more than 100 scientific papers.

Econometric Exercises

General Editors:
Karim M. Abadir, *Imperial College Business School, Imperial College London, UK*
Jan R. Magnus, *Department of Econometrics and Operations Research, Vrije Universiteit Amsterdam, The Netherlands*
Peter C. B. Phillips, *Cowles Foundation for Research in Economics, Yale University, USA*

The volumes in Econometric Exercises are intended to be much more than a collection of several hundred solved exercises. Each book has a coherent and well-organized sequence of exercises in a specific field or sub-field of econometrics. Every chapter of a volume begins with a short technical introduction that emphasizes the main ideas and overviews the most relevant theorems and results, including applications and occasionally computer exercises. They are intended for undergraduates in econometrics with an introductory knowledge of statistics, for first and second year graduate students of econometrics, and for students and instructors from neighboring disciplines (e.g., statistics, political science, psychology and communications) with interests in econometric methods.

Titles in the Series (* = planned):

1 Matrix Algebra (K. M. Abadir and J. R. Magnus)
2 Statistics (K. M. Abadir, R. D. H. Heijmans, and J. R. Magnus)
3 Econometric Theory, I (P. Paruolo)*
4 Empirical Applications, I (A. van Soest and M. Verbeek)*
5 Econometric Theory, II*
6 Empirical Applications, II*
7 Bayesian Econometric Methods (G. Koop, D. J. Poirier, and J. L. Tobias)
7 Bayesian Econometric Methods 2nd edition (G. Koop, D. J. Poirier, J. L. Tobias, and J. Chan) *forthcoming*
* Time Series Econometrics, I
* Time Series Econometrics, II
* Microeconometrics
* Panel Data
* Nonlinear Models
* Nonparametrics and Semiparametrics
* Simulation-Based Econometrics
* Computational Methods
* Financial Econometrics
* Robustness
* Econometric Methodology

Website: www.cambridge.org/ECEX

Statistics

Karim M. Abadir
Imperial College Business School, Imperial College London, UK; and
Department of Mathematics and Department of Economics & Related Studies,
University of York, UK

Risto D. H. Heijmans†
Amsterdam School of Economics, University of Amsterdam, The Netherlands

Jan R. Magnus
Department of Econometrics and Operations Research,
Vrije Universiteit Amsterdam, The Netherlands

CAMBRIDGE
UNIVERSITY PRESS

† Deceased

CAMBRIDGE
UNIVERSITY PRESS

University Printing House, Cambridge CB2 8BS, United Kingdom

One Liberty Plaza, 20th Floor, New York, NY 10006, USA

477 Williamstown Road, Port Melbourne, VIC 3207, Australia

314–321, 3rd Floor, Plot 3, Splendor Forum, Jasola District Centre, New Delhi – 110025, India

79 Anson Road, #06–04/06, Singapore 079906

Cambridge University Press is part of the University of Cambridge.

It furthers the University's mission by disseminating knowledge in the pursuit of education, learning, and research at the highest international levels of excellence.

www.cambridge.org
Information on this title: www.cambridge.org/9780521822886
DOI: 10.1017/9781139016131

First published 2019

Printed in the United States of America by Sheridan Books, Inc., 2019

A catalogue record for this publication is available from the British Library.

ISBN 978-0-521-82288-6 Hardback
ISBN 978-0-521-53745-2 Paperback

To my lovely nephews and nieces: Maher, Sarah, Shahira, Karim, Christine. And to the loving memories of my father, Dr Maher Abadir, and my best friend, Dr Ashraf Mohsen. They used to enjoy a glass of whisky together. They may still do, if the ancients were right.

To Gawein.

To Gideon and Joyce, Hedda and Ralph, and to their amazing children.

Contents

List of exercises

Chapter 1: Probability

Chapter 14: Tests of hypotheses

Preface to the Series

The past two decades have seen econometrics grow into a vast discipline. Many different branches of the subject now happily coexist with one another. These branches interweave econometric theory and empirical applications, and bring econometric method to bear on a myriad of economic issues. Against this background, a guided treatment of the modern subject of econometrics in a series of volumes of worked econometric exercises seemed a natural and rather challenging idea.

The present series, *Econometric Exercises*, was conceived in 1995 with this challenge in mind. Now, almost a decade later it has become an exciting reality with the publication of the first installment of a series of volumes of worked econometric exercises. How can these volumes work as a tool of learning that adds value to the many existing textbooks of econometrics? What readers do we have in mind as benefiting from this series? What format best suits the objective of helping these readers learn, practice, and teach econometrics? These questions we now address, starting with our overall goals for the series.

Econometric Exercises is published as an organized set of volumes. Each volume in the series provides a coherent sequence of exercises in a specific field or subfield of econometrics. Solved exercises are assembled together in a structured and logical pedagogical framework that seeks to develop the subject matter of the field from its foundations through to its empirical applications and advanced reaches. As the Schaum Series has done so successfully for mathematics, the overall goal of *Econometric Exercises* is to develop the subject matter of econometrics through solved exercises, providing a coverage of the subject that begins at an introductory level and moves through to more advanced undergraduate and graduate level material.

Problem solving and worked exercises play a major role in every scientific subject. They are particularly important in a subject like econometrics where there is a rapidly growing literature of statistical and mathematical technique and an ever-expanding core to the discipline. As students, instructors, and researchers, we all benefit by seeing carefully worked-out solutions to problems that develop the subject and illustrate its methods and workings. Regular exercises and problem sets consolidate learning and reveal applications of textbook material. Clearly laid out solutions, paradigm answers, and alternate routes to solution all develop problem-solving skills. Exercises train students in clear analytical thinking and help them in preparing for tests and exams. Teachers, as well as students, find solved exercises useful in their classroom preparation and in designing problem sets, tests, and examinations. Worked problems and illustrative empirical applications appeal to researchers and professional economists wanting to learn about specific econometric techniques. Our intention for the *Econometric Exercises* series is to appeal to this wide range of potential users.

Each volume of the Series follows the same general template. Chapters begin with a short outline that emphasizes the main ideas and overviews the most relevant theorems and results. The introductions are followed by a sequential development of the material by solved examples and applications, and computer exercises where these are appropriate. All problems are solved and they are graduated in difficulty with solution techniques evolving in a logical, sequential fashion. Problems are asterisked when they require more creative solutions or reach higher levels of technical difficulty. Each volume is self-contained. There is some commonality in material across volumes in the Series in order to reinforce learning and to make each volume accessible to students and others who are working largely, or even completely, on their own.

Content is structured so that solutions follow immediately after the exercise is posed. This makes the text more readable and avoids repetition of the statement of the exercise when it is being solved. More importantly, posing the right question at the right moment in the development of a subject helps to anticipate and address future learning issues that students face. Furthermore, the methods developed in a solution and the precision and insights of the answers are often more important than the questions being posed. In effect, the inner workings of a good solution frequently provide benefit beyond what is relevant to the specific exercise.

Exercise titles are listed at the start of each volume, following the Table of Contents, so that readers may see the overall structure of the book and its more detailed contents. This organization reveals the exercise progression, how the exercises relate to one another, and where the material is heading. It should also tantalize readers with the exciting prospect of advanced material and intriguing applications.

The Series is intended for a readership that includes undergraduate students of econometrics with an introductory knowledge of statistics, first and second year graduate students of econometrics, as well as students and instructors from neighboring disciplines (like statistics, psychology, or political science) with interests in econometric methods. The volumes generally increase in difficulty as the topics become more specialized.

The early volumes in the Series (particularly those covering matrix algebra, statistics, econometric models, and empirical applications) provide a foundation to the study of econometrics. These volumes will be especially useful to students who are following the first year econometrics course sequence in North American graduate schools and need to prepare for graduate comprehensive examinations in econometrics and to write an applied econometrics paper. The early volumes will equally be of value to advanced undergraduates studying econometrics in Europe, to advanced undergraduates and honors students in the Australasian system, and to masters and doctoral students in general. Subsequent volumes will be of interest to professional economists, applied workers, and econometricians who are working with techniques in those areas, as well as students who are taking an advanced course sequence in econometrics and statisticians with interests in those topics.

The *Econometric Exercises* series is intended to offer an independent learning-by-doing program in econometrics and it provides a useful reference source for anyone wanting to learn more about econometric methods and applications. The individual volumes can be used in classroom teaching and examining in a variety of ways. For instance, instructors can work through some of the problems in class to demonstrate methods as they are introduced, they can illustrate theoretical material with some of the solved examples, and they can show real data applications of the methods by drawing on some of the empirical examples. For examining purposes, instructors may draw freely from the solved exercises in test preparation. The systematic development of the subject in individual volumes will make the material easily accessible both for students in revision and for instructors in test preparation.

In using the volumes, students and instructors may work through the material sequentially as part of a complete learning program, or they may dip directly into material where they are experiencing difficulty, in order to learn from solved exercises and illustrations. To promote intensive study, an instructor might announce to a class in advance of a test that some questions in the test will be selected from a certain chapter of one of the volumes. This approach encourages students to work through most of the exercises in a particular chapter by way of test preparation, thereby reinforcing classroom instruction.

As Series Editors, we welcome comments, criticisms, suggestions, and, of course, corrections from all our readers on each of the volumes in the Series as well as on the Series itself. We bid you as much happy reading and problem solving as we have had in writing and preparing this series.

York, Tilburg, New Haven
July 2004

Karim M. Abadir
Jan R. Magnus
Peter C. B. Phillips

Preface

This volume contains exercises in distribution theory, estimation, and inference. The abbreviated name of the volume should be taken in the context of the Series into which it fits. Since statistics is a very large subject, we expect that the reader has already followed an introductory statistics course. This volume covers intermediate to advanced material.

There are many outstanding books on second courses in statistics, or introductory statistical theory, as well as excellent advanced texts; see our reference list. However, the level between them is less well represented. Furthermore, the use of matrix algebra is typically relegated to some of the advanced texts. These are two of the gaps we aim to fill. We also present many new proofs of established results, in addition to new results, often involving shortcuts that resort to statistical conditioning arguments.

Along with *Matrix Algebra*, the first volume of the Series, this volume fulfills two different functions. It is of interest in its own right, but it also forms the basis on which subsequent, more specialized, volumes can build. As a consequence, not all the material of Part A is used in Part B, because the former contains many results in the important toolkit of distribution theory, which will be of use for later volumes in the Series.

In deciding which topic (and how much of it) to include, we have tried to balance the need for cohesion within one volume with the need for a wide foundation. There are inevitable omissions and incomplete coverage of more specialized material. Such topics are covered in later volumes.

At the beginning of each chapter, we introduce a topic and then follow with exercises on it. These introductions contain the basic concepts laying the ground for the exercises and briefly sketching how they hang together. The introduction does not attempt to list all the results from the exercises; instead, we try to give a broad flavor of the topic. At the end of each chapter we provide Notes, which contain some pointers to the literature and some comments about generalizations. They should be of interest even if the reader has not attempted all the exercises. We occasionally avoid formal details in an effort to stress ideas and methods, and we give references to details in the Notes.

We have chosen to pitch the standard level at readers who are not necessarily familiar with the elements of complex analysis. We have therefore added a star ($*$) more readily to exercises containing complex variables. Some introductory material on complex variables and other mathematical techniques (such as the Stieltjes integral) is collected in Appendix A. Readers intending to cover much of the book may find it useful to start with Appendix A as a background.

We have also given more hints to solutions in Part B, which is more advanced than Part A. As for specifics on coverage and course selections:

- The same chapter can be done at differing levels, leaving more difficult topics and exercises to further courses. This is particularly true for Part A, which is more encyclopedic than is needed to work through Part B.
- Chapter 10 (especially Section 10.3) is rather specialized.
- Sections 11.2 and 11.3 (sufficiency, ancillarity, et cetera) are not needed to proceed with much of the subsequent material, although they clarify choices that would otherwise seem arbitrary. The corresponding parts of the introduction to Chapter 11 may be skipped at a first reading, starting with the definition of sufficiency and ending with Basu's theorem.
- Section 14.3 and the corresponding parts of the introduction to Chapter 14 can also be skipped at a first reading, with the exception of the last exercise of that section, namely Exercise 14.39 on the asymptotic relative efficiency of tests, which is needed for Section 14.4.

We are grateful for constructive comments and assistance from Hendri Adriaens, Ramon van den Akker, Paul Bekker, Adel Beshai, Giovanni Caggiano, Pavel Čížek, Adriana Cornea-Madeira, Dmitry Danilov, Walter Distaso, Malena García Reyes, Liudas Giraitis, Angelica Gonzalez, David Hendry, Steve Lawford, Michel Lubrano, William Mikhail, Peter C. B. Phillips, Gaurav Saroliya, Ashoke Sinha, George Styan, Gabriel Talmain, Yubo Tao, Andrey Vasnev, Anna Woźniak, and the anonymous referees/readers. Special thanks go to Tassos Magdalinos and Paolo Paruolo for their many helpful comments. Karim is grateful to his former students on the course "Statistical Theory" at Exeter and York for their patience while some of these exercises were being tried out on them. Their constructive feedback has certainly made a difference. We also thank Susan Parkinson for her meticulous reading of our book, and Nicola Chapman, Karen Maloney, and their team at CUP.

To our great sadness our friend, colleague, and coauthor Risto Heijmans passed away in July 2014. We will miss his erudite wisdom in statistics and many other subjects, and above all his humour and zest for life.

London, Amsterdam Karim M. Abadir
September 2017 Jan R. Magnus

Part A

Probability and distribution theory

1

Probability

In this chapter, we introduce some elementary concepts of probability which will be required for the rest of this book. We start by introducing the notion of sets. *Sets* are collections of objects, such as numbers, which are called *elements* of the set. If an element x belongs to set A, we write $x \in A$; otherwise, $x \notin A$. The *empty set* $\varnothing$ contains no elements, while the *universal set* Ω contains all objects of a certain specified type. A set containing a single element is called a *singleton*. The *complement* of set A is the set of all objects in Ω but not included in A. It can be represented by $A^c := \{x : x \notin A\}$, which stands for "$x$ such that $x \notin A$". If a set A includes all the elements of another set B, the latter is called a *subset* of the former, and is denoted by $B \subseteq A$. The two sets may be equal, but if A contains further elements which are not in B, then B is a *proper subset* of A and this is denoted as $B \subset A$.

The *intersection* of two sets A and B is given by the elements belonging to both sets simultaneously, and is defined as $A \cap B := \{x : x \in A \text{ and } x \in B\}$. The collection of elements in set B but not in set A is $B \cap A^c$ and is denoted by $B \backslash A$. Sets A and B are *disjoint* if and only if $A \cap B = \varnothing$. The *union* of two sets is the collection of all elements in either set, and is defined by $A \cup B := \{x : x \in A \text{ or } x \in B\}$. Clearly,

$$A \cap B = B \cap A \quad \text{and} \quad A \cup B = B \cup A,$$

so that intersection and union possess the property of *commutativity*. The *distributive laws*

$$A \cup (B \cap C) = (A \cup B) \cap (A \cup C)$$

and

$$A \cap (B \cup C) = (A \cap B) \cup (A \cap C)$$

apply to sets. Finally, an important law of logic, when applied to sets, is *De Morgan's law* which states that

$$(A \cap B)^c = A^c \cup B^c$$

and

$$(A \cup B)^c = A^c \cap B^c;$$

see also Section A.1 in Appendix A. It can be extended to a *countable* collection of sets $A_1, A_2, \ldots$ (instead of just A, B), the adjective "countable" meaning that the A_i's can be enumerated by an index such as $i = 1, 2, \ldots, \infty$. Notice that countability does not necessarily mean that there is a finite number of A_i's (see the index i); rather it means that the set of natural numbers $\mathbb{N}$ is big enough to count all the A_i's.

Now consider the case when the objects in these sets are outcomes of a *random experiment*, one where chance could lead to a different outcome if the experiment were repeated. Then Ω is called the *sample space*, that is, the collection of all potential outcomes of the experiment.

Consider the most common example of an experiment: tossing a coin where the outcomes are a head (H) or a tail (T). Then the sample space is $\Omega = \{H, T\}$, namely head and tail. If the coin is to be tossed twice, then $\Omega = \{HH, TT, HT, TH\}$ where HT denotes a head followed by a tail.

An *event* A is a subset of Ω. For instance, $A = \{HT\}$ is an event in our last example. We also need to be able to talk about:

- the complement A^c of an event A, to discuss whether the event happens or not;
- the union $A_1 \cup A_2$ of two events A_1, A_2, to describe the event that one or the other (or both) happens;
- hence (by De Morgan's law) also the intersection $B_1 \cap B_2$ of two events B_1, B_2, this being the event where both happen simultaneously.

As will be seen in Chapter 2, the sample space Ω may be too big to have its elements enumerated by $i = 1, 2, \ldots$, so let us instead focus on some events of interest, $A_1, A_2, \ldots$, and define the following. A *sigma-algebra* (or *sigma-field*) of events, $\mathcal{F}$, is a collection of some events $A_i \subseteq \Omega$ (where $i = 1, 2, \ldots, \infty$) that satisfies:

- $\varnothing \in \mathcal{F}$;
- if $A \in \mathcal{F}$, then $A^c \in \mathcal{F}$;
- if $A_1, A_2, \dots \in \mathcal{F}$, then $A_1 \cup A_2 \cup \dots \in \mathcal{F}$.

To illustrate $\mathcal{F}$, recall the simplest case of tossing a coin once, leading to $\Omega = \{H, T\}$. Its largest sigma-algebra is the set of all subsets of Ω, called the *power set* and denoted by 2^Ω in general, and given by $\mathcal{F} = \{\varnothing, \{H\}, \{T\}, \Omega\}$ here; its smallest sigma-algebra is the trivial $\mathcal{F} = \{\varnothing, \Omega\}$, containing the *impossible event* $\varnothing$ (nothing happens) and the *certain event* Ω (either a head or a tail happens). Notice that $\mathcal{F}$ is a set whose elements are themselves sets, and that nonsingleton elements of $\mathcal{F}$ are *composite events*; for example, when tossing a coin twice, $\{\{HT\},\{TH\}\}$ is the composite event of getting one head and one tail regardless of the order in which this happens.

One can define a measure (or function) on this algebra, called *probability*, satisfying the axioms

$$\Pr(A_i) \geqslant 0 \text{ for } i = 1, 2, \ldots,$$
$$\Pr(A_1 \cup A_2 \cup \cdots) = \Pr(A_1) + \Pr(A_2) + \cdots,$$
$$\Pr(\Omega) = 1,$$

for any sequence of disjoint sets $A_1, A_2, \cdots \in \mathcal{F}$. The second axiom is called *countable additivity*, the property of countability having been built into the definition of $\mathcal{F}$ (on which probability is defined) though it is not always a property of Ω as will be illustrated in Chapter 2. These axioms imply that $\Pr(\varnothing) = 0$ and $\Pr(A_i) \in [0,1]$.

A *fair coin* is a coin having probability $\frac{1}{2}$ for each outcome. Typically, it is also implicitly assumed that the coin is to be tossed fairly, since a fair coin can be tossed unfairly by some professionals! Experiments can be conducted under different conditions (for example the coin need not be fair), so more than one probability measure can be defined on the same $\mathcal{F}$ and Ω. Often, probability can be interpreted as the frequency with which events would occur if the experiment were to be replicated ad infinitum. To sum up the features of the experiment, the *probability space* or *triplet* $(\Omega, \mathcal{F}, \Pr(\cdot))$ is used.

For any two elements of a sigma-algebra, say A and B, it follows (Exercise 1.5) that

$$\Pr(A \cup B) = \Pr(A) + \Pr(B) - \Pr(A \cap B).$$

There are two special cases worthy of attention where this formula can be simplified. First, two sets A and B are *mutually exclusive* (for example, $A =$ "raining tomorrow morning" and $B =$ "not raining tomorrow") if and only if the sets are disjoint, in which case $\Pr(A \cap B) = \Pr(\varnothing) = 0$ and hence $\Pr(A \cup B) = \Pr(A) + \Pr(B)$. Second, the sets A and B are *independent* (for example, $A =$ "you catch a cold" and $B =$ "your favorite program will be on TV") if and only if $\Pr(A \cap B) = \Pr(A)\Pr(B)$. If there are three sets A_1, A_2, A_3, we say that they are *pairwise independent* if and only if $\Pr(A_i \cap A_j) = \Pr(A_i)\Pr(A_j)$ for $i = 1, 2$ and $j > i$ (three combinations in all). They are *mutually* (or *jointly*) *independent* if and only if $\Pr(A_1 \cap A_2 \cap A_3) = \Pr(A_1)\Pr(A_2)\Pr(A_3)$. Pairwise independence does not necessarily lead to joint independence, as will be seen in Exercise 1.22. When using the term "independence" in the case of many events, we will mean joint independence unless stated otherwise.

If an event A were to occur, it may convey information about the possibility of realization of another uncertain event B. For example, suppose a teacher is waiting for her students in a lecture theater which has no windows. If several turn up holding wet umbrellas or coats (event A), it is likely that it's been raining outside (event B). The former event has conveyed some information about the latter, even though the latter couldn't be observed directly. The use of information in this way is called *conditioning*: the probability of B

being realized, if A were to occur, is denoted by $\Pr(B \mid A)$. When $\Pr(A) \neq 0$, this *conditional probability* is

$$\Pr(B \mid A) = \frac{\Pr(B \cap A)}{\Pr(A)}, \tag{1.1}$$

as will be seen and generalized in Exercise 1.25. The function $\Pr(B \mid A)$ satisfies the three defining properties of a probability measure on $\mathcal{F}$, which were given earlier.

The formula for conditional probability is important in many ways. First, we can obtain an alternative characterization of the independence of two events A and B as

$$\Pr(B \mid A) \equiv \frac{\Pr(B \cap A)}{\Pr(A)} = \frac{\Pr(B)\Pr(A)}{\Pr(A)} \equiv \Pr(B), \tag{1.2}$$

in which case event A conveys no information about event B, so conditioning on the former is superfluous: $\Pr(B \mid A) = \Pr(B)$. Notice that this definition of independence *seems* to treat A and B in different ways, unlike the earlier definition $\Pr(A \cap B) = \Pr(A)\Pr(B)$ which is symmetric in A and B. However, the same derivations as in (1.2), but with roles reversed, show that $\Pr(A \mid B) = \Pr(A)$ is also the case.

Second, one may apply the conditional factorization twice, when $\Pr(B) \neq 0$ as well, to get

$$\Pr(B \mid A) = \frac{\Pr(B \cap A)}{\Pr(A)} = \frac{\Pr(A \cap B)}{\Pr(A)} = \Pr(A \mid B)\frac{\Pr(B)}{\Pr(A)}, \tag{1.3}$$

which is one form of *Bayes' law*. Before extending this formula, let us introduce the following notation:

$$\bigcap_{i=1}^{n} A_i := A_1 \cap A_2 \cap \cdots \cap A_n$$

and

$$\bigcup_{i=1}^{n} A_i := A_1 \cup A_2 \cup \cdots \cup A_n$$

for the case of a sequence of sets $A_1, \ldots, A_n$. If one were to *partition* Ω, that is, to decompose Ω into a collection of some mutually disjoint subsets $C_1, \ldots, C_m$ such that

$$\Omega = \bigcup_{i=1}^{m} C_i$$

and $\Pr(C_i) \neq 0$ for all i, then

$$\Pr(B \mid A) = \Pr(A \mid B)\frac{\Pr(B)}{\sum_{i=1}^{m} \Pr(A \mid C_i)\Pr(C_i)}; \tag{1.4}$$

see Exercise 1.6. The sum

$$\sum_{i=1}^{m} \Pr(A \mid C_i)\Pr(C_i) \equiv \sum_{i=1}^{m} \Pr(A \cap C_i) = \Pr(A) \tag{1.5}$$

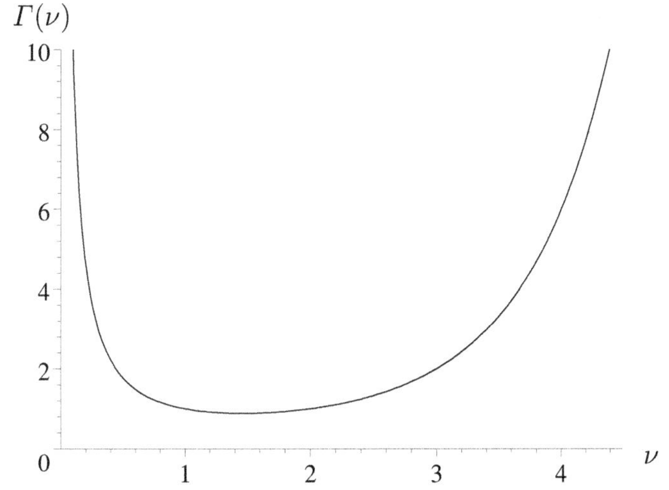

Figure 1.1. Gamma function, $\Gamma(\nu)$.

is sometimes called the *unconditional* (or *marginal*) *probability* of A, to stress the distinction from the conditional probability $\Pr(A \mid C_i)$. As an alternative to (1.3), a second form of Bayes' law occurs when A of (1.4) belongs to a sigma-algebra of events and $B = C_i$ for one specific i, for example, when $B = C_2$. Some illustrations are given in Section 1.2, in particular starting with Exercise 1.26.

Probabilities in this chapter and elsewhere often require computation of the *factorial function*, given by

$$n! = 1 \times 2 \times \cdots \times n$$

when n is a positive integer and $0! = 1$. We summarize this definition by

$$n! := \prod_{i=1}^{n} i, \qquad n = 0, 1, \ldots,$$

where empty products like $\prod_{i=1}^{0}$ are equal to 1, by mathematical convention, so $0! = 1$. This function refers to the number of ways in which n entities can be ordered. For example, there are $3 \times 2 \times 1 = 3!$ ways to order three individuals in a queue: there are three possible choices for assigning one of them to the head of the queue, two possibilities for the next in line, and finally only one remaining individual for the last position. The factorial function satisfies the recursion $n! = n \times (n-1)!$ for $n \in \mathbb{N}$, where $\mathbb{N}$ is the set of natural numbers $1, 2, \ldots$ We now introduce four extensions of this function.

First, the *gamma* (or *generalized factorial*) *function* is

$$\Gamma(\nu) := \int_0^{\infty} x^{\nu-1} \mathrm{e}^{-x} \, \mathrm{d}x, \qquad \nu > 0, \tag{1.6}$$

and satisfies the recursion $\Gamma(\nu) = (\nu - 1) \times \Gamma(\nu - 1)$ obtained by integrating by parts in (1.6); see Figure 1.1 for its plot. The definition of the function can be extended through this recursion for values of ν that are negative and not integers; however, we shall not need this in the current volume. When ν is a natural number, we obtain the factorial function: $\Gamma(\nu) = (\nu-1)!$. Another important special case of the gamma function is $\Gamma(\frac{1}{2}) = \sqrt{\pi}$, which is represented by the integral

$$\Gamma\left(\frac{1}{2}\right) = \int_0^\infty \mathrm{e}^{-x} \frac{\mathrm{d}x}{\sqrt{x}} = \sqrt{2}\int_0^\infty \mathrm{e}^{-y^2/2}\,\mathrm{d}y$$

by the change of variable $y = \sqrt{2x}$. This result will eventually be proved in Exercise 7.27. It allows the calculation of $\Gamma(n+\frac{1}{2})$ by recursion for all $n \in \mathbb{N}$.

Second, the *beta function* is defined by

$$B(\nu,\mu) := \frac{\Gamma(\nu)\Gamma(\mu)}{\Gamma(\nu+\mu)} = B(\mu,\nu),$$

and, when $\nu, \mu > 0$, we have two equivalent integral representations of the function,

$$B(\nu,\mu) = \int_0^1 x^{\nu-1}(1-x)^{\mu-1}\,\mathrm{d}x = \int_0^\infty \frac{y^{\nu-1}}{(1+y)^{\nu+\mu}}\,\mathrm{d}y,$$

by setting $x = y/(1+y)$.

The final two extensions are very closely linked and have an important probabilistic interpretation. For $j = 0, 1, \ldots$, the j (ordered) *permutations* of ν are

$$\mathrm{P}_j^\nu := \prod_{i=0}^{j-1}(\nu - i) = (\nu)(\nu-1)\cdots(\nu-j+1) = \frac{\Gamma(\nu+1)}{\Gamma(\nu-j+1)},$$

and the j (unordered) *combinations* of ν are

$$\binom{\nu}{j} := \frac{\prod_{i=0}^{j-1}(\nu-i)}{j!} = \frac{\Gamma(\nu+1)}{\Gamma(\nu-j+1)j!},$$

where $\binom{\cdot}{\cdot}$ is the symbol for the *binomial coefficient*, sometimes written as C_j^ν. These two functions are generally defined for $\nu \in \mathbb{R}$, which we will require later but not in this chapter. Here, we deal with the special case $\nu = n \in \mathbb{N}$ yielding

$$\frac{\Gamma(n+1)}{\Gamma(n-j+1)} = \frac{n!}{(n-j)!}.$$

In this case, the definition of binomial coefficients implies directly that

$$\binom{n}{j} = \frac{n!}{(n-j)!j!} = \binom{n}{n-j}. \tag{1.7}$$

Continuing with our earlier example of individuals in queues, suppose that we want to form a queue of $j = 3$ individuals from a group of n people, where $n \geqslant 3$. Then, we can do this in $n \times (n-1) \times (n-2) = \mathrm{P}_3^n$ ways. Now, suppose instead that we select the three individuals simultaneously and that ordering does not matter, for example because all three customers can be served simultaneously. Since there are 3! ways to rearrange any selection of three specific individuals, the number of ways to select three simultaneously is $\mathrm{P}_3^n/3! = \binom{n}{3}$. It is also equal to the number of ways to select $n-3$ individuals (or leave out three of them), $\binom{n}{n-3}$, a result implied more generally by (1.7). Generalizing these ideas to selecting $j_1, \dots, j_k$ individuals from respective groups of $n_1, \dots, n_k$ people, there are

$$\binom{n_1}{j_1} \cdots \binom{n_k}{j_k}$$

unordered selections; for example, selecting one from the set of two individuals $\{R, J\}$ and one from $\{K\}$, we can have $\binom{2}{1}\binom{1}{1} = 2$ (unordered) combinations: R, K or J, K. For ordered selections, we have as many as

$$\binom{n_1}{j_1} \cdots \binom{n_k}{j_k} \times (j_1 + \cdots + j_k)! = \mathrm{P}^{n_1}_{j_1} \cdots \mathrm{P}^{n_k}_{j_k} \times \frac{(j_1 + \cdots + j_k)!}{j_1! \cdots j_k!},$$

where $(j_1 + \cdots + j_k)!$ is the number of ways to order $j_1 + \cdots + j_k$ individuals. In the latter equation, we can interpret $\mathrm{P}^{n_\bullet}_{j_\bullet}$ as the number of ordered selections *within* each of the k groups, whereas

$$\frac{(j_1 + \cdots + j_k)!}{j_1! \cdots j_k!} \tag{1.8}$$

is the number of ways of allocating slots (say, in a queue of $j_1 + \cdots + j_k$) to groups, without distinction of the individuals within each group (by selecting j_1 simultaneously from group 1, and so on). Continuing with our last example, one from $\{\dagger, \dagger\}$ and one from $\{\star\}$ can be arranged in $(1+1)!/(1!1!) = 2$ ways, as $\dagger, \star$ or $\star, \dagger$. The factor in (1.8) is called the *multinomial coefficient* because it generalizes the binomial coefficient obtained when $k = 2$, which makes it particularly useful from Chapter 5 onwards.

The exercises in this chapter follow broadly the sequence of topics introduced earlier. We start with illustrations of random experiments and probabilities, then move on to conditioning. We conclude with a few exercises focusing on permutations and combinations.

1.1 Events and sets

Exercise 1.1 (Urn) An urn contains m red, m white, and m green balls ($m \geqslant 2$). Two balls are drawn at random, without replacement.
(a) What is the sample space?
(b) Define the events $A :=$ "drawing a green ball first" and $B :=$ "drawing at least one green ball". Express A and B as unions of elementary events.
(c) Also express $A \cap B$ and $A^c \cap B$ as unions of elementary events.

Solution
(a) Denote the red, white, and green balls by R, W, and G, respectively. Since the order matters, the sample space contains nine elements: $\Omega = \{RR, RW, RG, WR, WW, WG, GR, GW, GG\}$.
(b) $A = \{GR, GW, GG\}$ and $B = \{RG, WG, GR, GW, GG\}$.

(c) $A \cap B$ contains the elements that are in both A and B. Hence, $A \cap B = \{GR, GW, GG\}$. Notice that $A \cap B = A$ since A is a subset of B. $A^c \cap B$ contains the elements that are in B but not in A: $A^c \cap B = \{RG, WG\}$.

Exercise 1.2 (Urn, continued) Consider again the experiment of Exercise 1.1.
(a) Do the elements in the sample space have equal probability?
(b) Compute $\Pr(A)$ and $\Pr(B)$.
(c) Are A and B independent?

Solution
(a) If the two balls had been drawn with replacement, the sample space elements would have had equal probability $1/9$ each. However, without replacement, we have, for $i, j = R, W, G$,

$$\Pr(ii) = \frac{m}{3m} \times \frac{m-1}{3m-1} = \frac{m-1}{9m-3} < \frac{1}{9}$$

and, for $i \neq j$,

$$\Pr(ij) = \frac{m}{3m} \times \frac{m}{3m-1} = \frac{m}{9m-3} > \frac{1}{9}.$$

We see that both $\Pr(ii)$ and $\Pr(ij)$ approach $1/9$ when $m \to \infty$. Notice that we have adopted a shorthand notation that drops the braces around ij when it appears inside $\Pr(\cdot)$, a simplification used from now on.
(b) We have

$$\Pr(A) = \Pr(GR) + \Pr(GW) + \Pr(GG) = \frac{2m}{9m-3} + \frac{m-1}{9m-3} = \frac{1}{3}$$

and

$$\Pr(B) = \frac{4m}{9m-3} + \frac{m-1}{9m-3} = \frac{5m-1}{9m-3} > \frac{5}{9}.$$

The first result is also immediately obtained from $\Pr(A) = m/(3m)$.
(c) The two events are certainly not independent because A is a subset of B. As a result, $\Pr(A \cap B) = \Pr(A) > \Pr(A)\Pr(B)$.

Exercise 1.3 (Coin) Hedda tosses a fair coin four times.
(a) Give the sample space.
(b) What is the probability that she throws exactly three heads?
(c) What is the probability that she throws at least one head?
(d) What is the probability that the number of heads exceeds the number of tails?
(e) What is the probability that the number of heads equals the number of tails?

Solution
(a) Since each toss has two possible outcomes, there are $2^4 = 16$ sample elements and the sample space is $\Omega = \{HHHH, HHHT, HHTH, HTHH, THHH, TTHH, THTH,$

$THHT, HTHT, HTTH, HHTT, TTTH, TTHT, THTT, HTTT, TTTT\}$. All sample elements have equal probability $1/16$.
(b) $\Pr(\text{exactly three heads}) = (1/16) \times (\text{number of sample elements with exactly three heads}) = 4/16 = 1/4$.
(c) Counting the relevant elements of the sample space, we get $15/16$. Otherwise, we note that

$$\Pr(\text{at least one head}) = 1 - \Pr(\text{no heads}) = 1 - \frac{1}{16} = \frac{15}{16}.$$

(d) $5/16$.
(e) $6/16 = 3/8$.

*__Exercise 1.4 (Sum of two dice)__ Two fair dice are rolled once. What is the probability that the sum of the outcomes is i ($i = 2, \dots, 12$)?

Solution
Let x be the outcome of the roll of the first die and y that of the second die. Then

$$\Pr(x + y = i) = \sum_{j \in A_i} \Pr(x = j, y = i - j),$$

where

$$A_i = \{j : j \in \mathbb{N}, \quad 1 \leqslant j \leqslant 6, \quad 1 \leqslant i - j \leqslant 6\}, \qquad i = 2, \dots, 12.$$

Let n_i denote the number of elements in A_i. Then $n_i = 6 - |i - 7|$ and hence

$$\Pr(x + y = i) = \frac{6 - |i - 7|}{36}.$$

*__Exercise 1.5 (Probabilities of events: sums and implications)__ Let A and B be events. Show that:
(a) $\Pr(A \cap B^c) = \Pr(A) - \Pr(A \cap B)$;
(b) $\Pr(A \cup B) = 1 - \Pr(A^c \cap B^c)$;
(c) if $A \subset B$ then $\Pr(B) = \Pr(A) + \Pr(B \cap A^c)$, and interpret this in terms of what the statement "$A \Longrightarrow B$" means for the relation between $\Pr(A)$ and $\Pr(B)$;
(d) $\Pr(A \cup B) = \Pr(A) + \Pr(B) - \Pr(A \cap B)$;
(e) $\Pr(\text{exactly one of the events } A \text{ or } B \text{ occurs}) = \Pr(A) + \Pr(B) - 2\Pr(A \cap B)$.

Solution
We employ the facts that if $A_1 := A \cap B$ and $A_2 := A \cap B^c$, then $A_1 \cup A_2 = A$ and $A_1 \cap A_2 = \varnothing$; see Figure 1.2. We also recall that since $A_1 \cap A_2 = \varnothing$, it follows that $\Pr(A_1 \cup A_2) = \Pr(A_1) + \Pr(A_2)$.
(a) Using these facts, it follows that $\Pr(A) = \Pr(A \cap B) + \Pr(A \cap B^c)$.
(b) Since De Morgan's law gives $(A \cup B)^c = A^c \cap B^c$, it follows similarly that $\Pr(A \cup B) =$

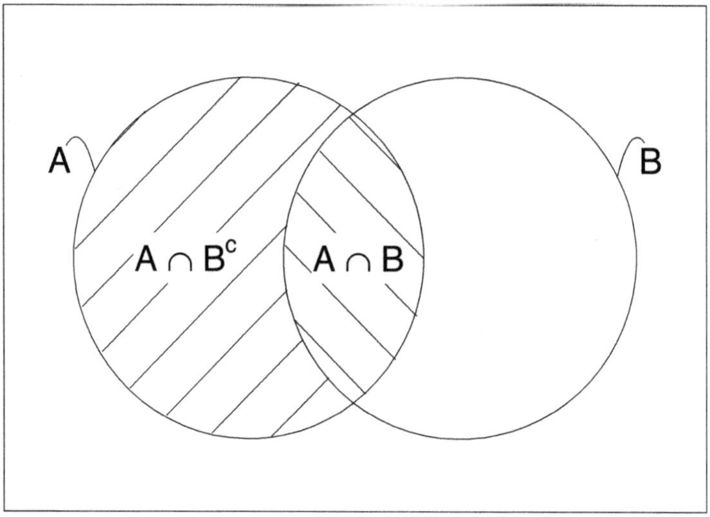

Figure 1.2. Decomposition of a set into two complements.

$1 - \Pr((A \cup B)^c) = 1 - \Pr(A^c \cap B^c)$.
(c) If A is a subset of B then $\Pr(A) = \Pr(A \cap B)$. Hence, using (a),

$$\Pr(B) = \Pr(B \cap A) + \Pr(B \cap A^c) = \Pr(A) + \Pr(B \cap A^c).$$

Therefore, "$A \Longrightarrow B$" (since A is a subset of B) leads to

$$\Pr(B) \geqslant \Pr(A),$$

by $\Pr(B \cap A^c) \geqslant 0$. The statement "$A \Longrightarrow B$" means that event A is sufficient but not necessary for B to hold: B can happen in other cases too, and is therefore at least as probable as A.
(d) Since A_2 and B are disjoint,

$$\Pr(A \cup B) = \Pr(A_2 \cup B) = \Pr(A_2) + \Pr(B) = \Pr(A) - \Pr(A \cap B) + \Pr(B)$$

by (a).
(e) The event that exactly one of A or B occurs is equal to the event $(A \cap B^c) \cup (A^c \cap B)$, a union of two disjoint sets; hence

$$\begin{aligned}\Pr((A \cap B^c) \cup (A^c \cap B)) &= \Pr(A \cap B^c) + \Pr(A^c \cap B) \\ &= \Pr(A) + \Pr(B) - 2\Pr(A \cap B),\end{aligned}$$

where (a) has been used twice in the last step.

Exercise 1.6 (Decomposition of measure on a set) Prove that if

$$\Omega = \bigcup_{i=1}^{m} C_i,$$

where $C_i \cap C_j = \varnothing$ for $i \neq j$, then $\Pr(A) = \sum_{i=1}^{m} \Pr(A \cap C_i)$.

Solution

We employ the same idea as in the preamble to the solution of Exercise 1.5. Let $A_i := A \cap C_i$. Then, the second distributive law given at the start of this chapter yields

$$\bigcup_{i=1}^{m} A_i = \bigcup_{i=1}^{m} (A \cap C_i) = A \cap \left(\bigcup_{i=1}^{m} C_i \right) = A \cap \Omega = A.$$

Together with $A_i \cap A_j = A \cap C_i \cap C_j = A \cap \varnothing = \varnothing$ for $i \neq j$, this gives

$$\Pr(A) = \Pr\left(\bigcup_{i=1}^{m} A_i \right) = \sum_{i=1}^{m} \Pr(A_i) = \sum_{i=1}^{m} \Pr(A \cap C_i).$$

Exercise 1.7 (Countable additivity: implied continuity) Continuing with the setup of the introduction, let $B_1, B_2, \dots$ and $D_1, D_2, \dots$ be events such that

$$B_1 \subseteq B_2 \subseteq \dots \quad \text{and} \quad D_1 \supseteq D_2 \supseteq \dots.$$

Prove that:
(a) $\Pr(\lim_{m\to\infty} B_m) = \lim_{m\to\infty} \Pr(B_m)$, that is, probability is a continuous function of the sets B_m;
(b) $\Pr(\lim_{m\to\infty} D_m) = \lim_{m\to\infty} \Pr(D_m)$.

Solution

(a) Define the sets

$$C_1 := B_1, \quad C_2 := B_2 \backslash B_1, \quad C_3 := B_3 \backslash B_2, \quad \dots,$$

where $C_1, C_2, \dots$ are disjoint (by $C_i = B_i \cap B_{i-1}^c$ for $i > 1$). Then, $B_m = \bigcup_{i=1}^{m} C_i$ and $\Pr(\lim_{m\to\infty} B_m) = \Pr\left(\bigcup_{i=1}^{\infty} C_i\right)$. The sets $C_1, C_2, \dots$ are indexed by i and the sequence is therefore countable, so

$$\Pr\left(\bigcup_{i=1}^{\infty} C_i \right) = \sum_{i=1}^{\infty} \Pr(C_i)$$

by the axiom of countable additivity of probability. Since $B_i = B_{i-1} \cup C_i$ and $B_{i-1} \cap C_i = \varnothing$ for $i > 1$, we have $\Pr(C_i) = \Pr(B_i) - \Pr(B_{i-1})$ and hence

$$\Pr\left(\lim_{m\to\infty} B_m \right) = \sum_{i=1}^{\infty} \Pr(C_i) = \Pr(B_1) + (\Pr(B_2) - \Pr(B_1)) + (\Pr(B_3) - \Pr(B_2)) + \dots = \lim_{m\to\infty} \Pr(B_m).$$

(b) Considering the complements $D_1^c \subseteq D_2^c \subseteq \dots$, we apply (a) to $B_m := D_m^c$. Using $\Pr(D_m) = 1 - \Pr(D_m^c)$ gives the required result. Noticc that the sets B_m are getting bigger, while D_m are decreasing (starting from a finite $\Pr(D_1)$), with

$$\bigcup_{m=1}^{\infty} B_m = \lim_{m\to\infty} B_m \quad \text{and} \quad \bigcap_{m=1}^{\infty} D_m = \lim_{m\to\infty} D_m,$$

so that $\lim_{m\to\infty} D_m$ and its subsets are events occurring in infinitely many of the sets $D_1, D_2, \ldots$ Notice also that countability is essential to the proof; otherwise, we could provide a counterexample as in the first footnote of Chapter 2.

Exercise 1.8 (Probabilities of events: products) Show that if A and B are events, then $\Pr(A \cap B) - \Pr(A)\Pr(B) = \Pr(A)\Pr(B^c) - \Pr(A \cap B^c)$.

Solution

We use the fact that $\Pr(A) = \Pr(A \cap B) + \Pr(A \cap B^c)$. Then

$$\begin{aligned}\Pr(A \cap B^c) - \Pr(A)\Pr(B^c) &= \Pr(A) - \Pr(A \cap B) - \Pr(A)(1 - \Pr(B)) \\ &= -\Pr(A \cap B) + \Pr(A)\Pr(B).\end{aligned}$$

Exercise 1.9 (The gambler) Hedda plays two games. The probability that she wins the first game is 0.8, the probability that she wins the second game is 0.6 and the probability that she wins both games is 0.5. Find the probability that Hedda wins:
(a) at least one game;
(b) exactly one game;
(c) neither game.

Solution

Let $S :=$ "Hedda wins first game" and $T :=$ "Hedda wins second game". We need to calculate the probability of the three events $A :=$ "Hedda wins at least one game", $B :=$ "Hedda wins exactly one game", and $C :=$ "Hedda wins neither game".
(a) $\Pr(A) = \Pr(S \cup T) = \Pr(S) + \Pr(T) - \Pr(S \cap T) = 0.8 + 0.6 - 0.5 = 0.9$.
(b) By Exercise 1.5(e), we find that $\Pr(B) = \Pr(S) + \Pr(T) - 2\Pr(S \cap T) = 0.8 + 0.6 - 2(0.5) = 0.4$.
(c) $\Pr(C) = 1 - \Pr(A) = 0.1$.

***Exercise 1.10 (Gambler's ruin)** Two players, Macho and Banco, play a game consisting of placing a sequence of independent bets. Each bet is worth a loss or a gain of 1 euro, and the whole game stops when one opponent has no money left. Macho has $m \in \mathbb{N}$ euros, while Banco has $b \in \mathbb{N}$ euros. The probability of winning each bet is given as 50%.
(a) Let p_n be the probability that Macho has n euros ($0 \leqslant n \leqslant m + b$) and that he goes on to win the game eventually. By linking p_n to p_{n-1} and p_{n+1}, solve for p_n.
(b) Calculate the probability, at the start of the game, that Macho wins the whole game. Is

it equal to the probability that Banco wins the game?

Solution

(a) There are two ways that this eventual win can happen. Macho can lose the current bet with 50% probability, then win the game eventually with probability given (by definition) by p_{n-1}. Alternatively, he can win the current bet with 50% probability, then go on to win the whole game with probability p_{n+1}. Therefore,

$$p_n = \frac{1}{2}p_{n-1} + \frac{1}{2}p_{n+1},$$

subject to the conditions that $p_0 = 0$ (he can't win the game if already ruined) and $p_{m+b} = 1$ (he won the game if the opponent is ruined). By rearrangement, this difference equation (see Section A.4.2) can be written as

$$p_{n+1} - p_n = p_n - p_{n-1}$$

and solved recursively as

$$\begin{aligned} p_{n+1} - p_n &= p_n - p_{n-1} \\ &= p_{n-1} - p_{n-2} \\ &\ \vdots \\ &= p_1 - p_0 = p_1. \end{aligned}$$

Since the difference between successive probabilities is p_1, it follows that $p_n = np_1$. We know that this succession of probabilities ends at $p_{m+b} = 1$, so $1 = p_{m+b} = (m+b)\,p_1$ implying that $p_1 = 1/(m+b)$ and

$$p_n = \frac{n}{m+b}.$$

(b) When Macho starts with m euros, the probability that he wins the game is $p_m = m/(m+b)$, so Banco wins with probability $1 - p_m = b/(m+b)$. The two probabilities are equal if and only if $m = b$. If Banco has more money ($b > m$), then he is more likely to win this game, even though each bet was a "fair" bet (50–50 chance).

Exercise 1.11 (Martingale betting) Now suppose that Macho has unlimited funds. He decides to play a different game with Banco. Each time he loses, he doubles the stake (the amount that he gambles) in the next bet, and he stops after his first win. Can Macho ever lose this game? What if the probability of winning each bet is $p < 50\%$?

Solution

Suppose that Macho gambles u units of currency in the first bet, and that he loses n bets and then wins the one after. His loss for the first n bets is

$$u\left(1 + 2 + 4 + \cdots + 2^{n-1}\right) = u\sum_{i=0}^{n-1} 2^i = u\left(2^n - 1\right)$$

by the geometric progression. He wins the next bet, which is worth $2^n u$, and has therefore won u in total (assuming that Banco has enough money to pay him!). This is true regardless of whether each bet was fair or not, as long as $p \neq 0$. The probability p does not enter the calculation or the resulting winnings, though it affects the random n.

Exercise 1.12 (Lost luggage) Sarah and Christine are travelling together, each with a suitcase. They carry a game which is made up of two components and which cannot be operated if one component is lost. They value this game above all else. Prove that they should put both components in the same suitcase. You may assume that the probability of losing a suitcase on their itinerary is $p \in (0,1)$ and that they are lost independently of each other.

Solution

The game is useless if a component is lost. If both components are in the same suitcase, then the probability of not being able to operate the game is p, which is the probability of losing one suitcase. If they separate the components into the two suitcases, then they need to work out the probability of losing either. Let A_i $(i = 1, 2)$ denote the event of losing suitcase i. Then, the probability of losing either suitcase is

$$\begin{aligned}\Pr(A_1 \cup A_2) &= \Pr(A_1) + \Pr(A_2) - \Pr(A_1 \cap A_2)\\ &= \Pr(A_1) + \Pr(A_2) - \Pr(A_1)\Pr(A_2) = 2p - p^2\end{aligned}$$

by the independence of A_1 and A_2, each with probability p. The stated advice follows since the difference in probabilities is $2p - p^2 - p = p - p^2 > 0$, by virtue of $p \in (0,1)$.

***Exercise 1.13 (Union–intersection)** Let $A_1, \dots, A_n$ be events. By induction, show that

$$\Pr\left(\bigcup_{i=1}^{n} A_i\right) = \sum_{i=1}^{n} \Pr(A_i) - \sum_{i<j\leqslant n} \Pr(A_i \cap A_j) + \sum_{i<j<k\leqslant n} \Pr(A_i \cap A_j \cap A_k)$$
$$+ \cdots + (-1)^{n+1} \Pr(A_1 \cap A_2 \cap \cdots \cap A_n).$$

Solution

We first verify graphically that the statement is correct for $n = 3$; see Figure 1.3. We see that $\Pr(A) = \Pr(E_1) + \Pr(E_4) + \Pr(E_5) + \Pr(E_7)$ and analogously for $\Pr(B)$ and $\Pr(C)$, their sum generating E_4, E_5, E_6 twice and E_7 three times. Also, $\Pr(A \cap B) = \Pr(E_4) + \Pr(E_7)$ and analogously for $\Pr(A \cap C)$ and $\Pr(B \cap C)$, their sum generating E_7 three times and no other repetitions. Finally, $\Pr(A \cap B \cap C) = \Pr(E_7)$. Hence, the result is true for $n = 3$.

We now prove the result formally. We know that $\Pr(A_1 \cup A_2) = \Pr(A_1) + \Pr(A_2) - \Pr(A_1 \cap A_2)$. Assume that the relation holds for some n. We will show that the relation

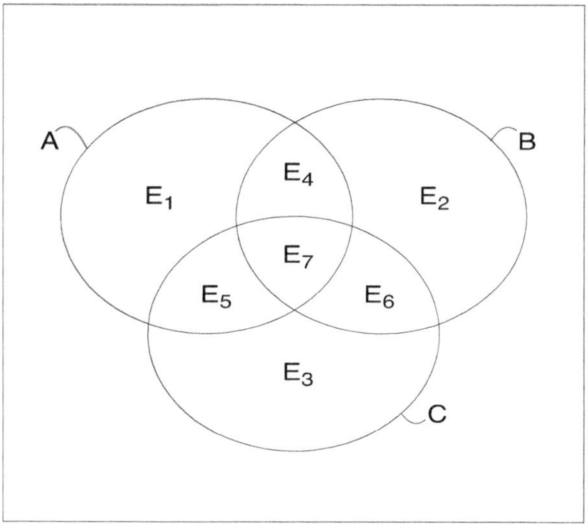

Figure 1.3. Decomposition of three sets into complementary parts.

then also holds for $n+1$. We have

$$\Pr\left(\bigcup_{i=1}^{n+1} A_i\right) = \Pr\left(\bigcup_{i=1}^{n} A_i \cup A_{n+1}\right)$$
$$= \Pr\left(\bigcup_{i=1}^{n} A_i\right) + \Pr(A_{n+1}) - \Pr\left(\left(\bigcup_{i=1}^{n} A_i\right) \cap A_{n+1}\right).$$

We now invoke the induction hypothesis twice. First,

$$\Pr\left(\bigcup_{i=1}^{n} A_i\right) = \sum_{i=1}^{n} \Pr(A_i) - \sum_{i<j\leqslant n} \Pr(A_i \cap A_j)$$
$$+ \sum_{i<j<k\leqslant n} \Pr(A_i \cap A_j \cap A_k) - \cdots,$$

where we note that there are $\binom{n}{m}$ terms in a sum containing the probability of intersection of m sets. Second,

$$\Pr\left(\left(\bigcup_{i=1}^{n} A_i\right) \cap A_{n+1}\right) = \Pr\left(\bigcup_{i=1}^{n} (A_i \cap A_{n+1})\right)$$
$$= \sum_{i=1}^{n} \Pr(A_i \cap A_{n+1}) - \sum_{i<j\leqslant n} \Pr(A_i \cap A_j \cap A_{n+1}) + \cdots$$
$$= \sum_{i<j=n+1} \Pr(A_i \cap A_j) - \sum_{i<j<k=n+1} \Pr(A_i \cap A_j \cap A_k) + \cdots.$$

Inserting the last two equations into the first gives the desired result.

***Exercise 1.14 (Bonferroni's inequalities)** By induction, show that

$$\Pr\left(\bigcup_{i=1}^{n} A_i\right) \leqslant \sum_{i=1}^{n} \Pr(A_i) \quad \textit{(Boole's inequality)},$$

$$\Pr\left(\bigcup_{i=1}^{n} A_i\right) \geqslant \sum_{i=1}^{n} \Pr(A_i) - \sum_{i<j\leqslant n} \Pr(A_i \cap A_j),$$

$$\Pr\left(\bigcup_{i=1}^{n} A_i\right) \leqslant \sum_{i=1}^{n} \Pr(A_i) - \sum_{i<j\leqslant n} \Pr(A_i \cap A_j) + \sum_{i<j<k\leqslant n} \Pr(A_i \cap A_j \cap A_k).$$

Solution

Let $C_n := \bigcup_{i=1}^{n} A_i$. Using the fact that

$$\Pr(A_1 \cup A_2) \leqslant \Pr(A_1) + \Pr(A_2),$$

we obtain

$$\Pr(C_{n+1}) = \Pr(C_n \cup A_{n+1}) \leqslant \Pr(C_n) + \Pr(A_{n+1}) \leqslant \sum_{i=1}^{n+1} \Pr(A_i),$$

proving the first inequality.

To prove the second inequality, we recall from Exercise 1.13 that

$$\Pr\left(\bigcup_{i=1}^{3} A_i\right) = \sum_{i=1}^{3} \Pr(A_i) - \sum_{i<j\leqslant 3} \Pr(A_i \cap A_j) + \Pr(A_1 \cap A_2 \cap A_3),$$

hence the inequality holds for $n = 3$ (it also holds trivially as an identity for $n = 2$). Assuming that the inequality holds for n, we have

$$\begin{aligned}\Pr(C_{n+1}) &= \Pr(C_n \cup A_{n+1}) = \Pr(A_{n+1}) + \Pr(C_n) - \Pr(C_n \cap A_{n+1}) \\ &\geqslant \sum_{i=1}^{n+1} \Pr(A_i) - \sum_{i<j\leqslant n} \Pr(A_i \cap A_j) - \Pr(C_n \cap A_{n+1}).\end{aligned}$$

Also, from Boole's inequality,

$$\Pr(C_n \cap A_{n+1}) = \Pr\left(\bigcup_{i=1}^{n} (A_i \cap A_{n+1})\right) \leqslant \sum_{i=1}^{n} \Pr(A_i \cap A_{n+1}),$$

and the result follows.

To prove the third inequality, we start by noting that it becomes an equality for $n = 3$ by Exercise 1.13, and that the same exercise shows that for $n = 4$ it holds as an inequality by omitting the last term which is $(-1)^{4+1} \Pr(A_1 \cap A_2 \cap \cdots \cap A_4) \leqslant 0$. Then, assuming that the inequality holds for n, we have

$$\begin{aligned}\Pr(C_{n+1}) &= \Pr(A_{n+1}) + \Pr(C_n) - \Pr(C_n \cap A_{n+1}) \\ &\leqslant \sum_{i=1}^{n+1} \Pr(A_i) - \sum_{i<j\leqslant n} \Pr(A_i \cap A_j) \\ &\quad + \sum_{i<j<k\leqslant n} \Pr(A_i \cap A_j \cap A_k) - \Pr(C_n \cap A_{n+1}),\end{aligned}$$

and the result follows from using the second inequality as

$$\begin{aligned}\Pr(C_n \cap A_{n+1}) &= \Pr\left(\bigcup_{i=1}^{n}(A_i \cap A_{n+1})\right) \\ &\geqslant \sum_{i=1}^{n} \Pr(A_i \cap A_{n+1}) - \sum_{i<j\leqslant n} \Pr(A_i \cap A_j \cap A_{n+1}).\end{aligned}$$

Compare Exercises 1.13 and 1.14, where the latter omits terms from the right-hand side of the former. You will notice a pattern: the first omitted term from the right-hand side of the equality in Exercise 1.13 has the same sign as the sum of all the omitted terms.

1.2 Conditioning and independence

Exercise 1.15 (Cards) A box contains four good cards and three bad cards. Eve draws a card and keeps it, then Adam draws a card from the remainder. Find the following probabilities:
(a) Pr(Eve's card is good);
(b) Pr(Adam's card is good | Eve's card is good);
(c) Pr(Adam's card is good | Eve's card is bad);
(d) Pr(Adam's card is good).

Solution
Let $A :=$ "Adam's card is good" and $E :=$ "Eve's card is good". Then:
(a) $\Pr(E) = 4/(4+3) = 4/7$;
(b) $\Pr(A \mid E) = 3/(3+4-1) = 1/2$;
(c) $\Pr(A \mid E^c) = 4/(4+3-1) = 2/3$;
(d) $\Pr(A) = \Pr(A \mid E)\Pr(E) + \Pr(A \mid E^c)\Pr(E^c) = (1/2)(4/7) + (2/3)(3/7) = 4/7$.
Hence, the order in which Adam and Eve draw the cards is irrelevant in this example.

Exercise 1.16 (Politics as usual?) An ambitious official notices that only 10% of accidents are caused by drunken drivers. He recommends more drinking as this will decrease the number of road accidents. When would he be right?

Solution
Let A be the event that an accident has happened, and D be the event that a driver is drunk. Then

$$\begin{aligned}\Pr(A) &= \Pr(A \mid D)\Pr(D) + \Pr(A \mid D^c)\,(1 - \Pr(D)) \\ &= (\Pr(A \mid D) - \Pr(A \mid D^c))\Pr(D) + \Pr(A \mid D^c).\end{aligned}$$

If we assume that $p_1 := \Pr(A \mid D)$ and $p_2 := \Pr(A \mid D^c)$ depend on biology rather than politics, then the politician can only play with $\Pr(D)$ in the equations above. Increasing it will reduce $\Pr(A)$ if and only if $p_1 < p_2$, which is not what research indicates!

Exercise 1.17 (Six dice) Six fair dice are rolled and the numbers that come up are multiplied. What is the probability that this product is:
(a) divisible by 5?
(b) not even?
(c) has last digit 5?

Solution
(a) To be divisible by 5 at least one of the six dice should have outcome 5, so the probability is $1 - (5/6)^6 \approx 0.665$.
(b) Let A denote the event that the product is odd (not even, that is, not divisible by 2). Then, A occurs if and only if all outcomes are odd and hence $\Pr(A) = (1/2)^6 \approx 0.016$. We see therefore that the probability of an even number is much larger than the probability of an odd number.
(c) Let B denote the event that the last digit of the product is 5. If the product is odd then the last digit is 5 unless all outcomes are 1 or 3. Hence, $\Pr(B \mid A) = 1-(2/3)^6$. Since B is a subset of A, we find $\Pr(B) = \Pr(B \cap A) = \Pr(B \mid A)\Pr(A) = \left(1 - (2/3)^6\right)(1/2)^6 = (1/2)^6 - (1/3)^6 \approx 0.014$.

Exercise 1.18 (Risky dice!) Maher and Kimo are playing a game of dice which has two variations.
(a) They each throw a die. Maher wins if he scores strictly more than Kimo, but Kimo wins otherwise.
(b) Maher throws two dice, but Kimo throws only one. The highest of the two scores of Maher is compared with the single score obtained by Kimo, and the same rule as in (a) applies for selecting the winner.
Work out the probability that Maher wins for each case, assuming the dice are fair. [Hint: For (b), use $\sum_{i=1}^{n} i^2 = \frac{1}{6}n\,(n+1)\,(2n+1)$, which is derived in Section A.4.1.]

Solution
(a) Let x be the score of Maher, and y that of Kimo. We need to work out $\Pr(x > y)$. We

know that $\Pr(x > y) = \Pr(x < y)$ as the dice are fair, and that

$$\Pr(x > y) + \Pr(x < y) + \Pr(x = y) = 1.$$

Now, $\Pr(x = y) = 6/36 = 1/6$, so that $2\Pr(x > y) = 5/6$ or $\Pr(x > y) = 5/12$.
(b) Let $x := \max\{x_1, x_2\}$ be the best score of Maher, and y be the single score of Kimo. We need

$$\Pr(x > y) = \sum_{v=1}^{6} \Pr(x > v \mid y = v) \Pr(y = v).$$

We can simplify this expression by noting that $\Pr(y = v) = 1/6$ and that, since the rolls of the dice are independent of each other, we can drop the conditioning on $y = v$. The required probability is therefore the average

$$\Pr(x > y) = \frac{1}{6} \sum_{v=1}^{6} \Pr(x > v) = \frac{1}{6} \sum_{v=1}^{6} (1 - \Pr(x \leqslant v)).$$

Now $\max\{x_1, x_2\} \leqslant v$ if and only if both $x_1 \leqslant v$ and $x_2 \leqslant v$; therefore

$$\begin{aligned}\Pr(x > y) &= \frac{1}{6} \sum_{v=1}^{6} (1 - \Pr(x_1 \leqslant v) \Pr(x_2 \leqslant v)) \\ &= \frac{1}{6} \sum_{v=1}^{6} \left(1 - \left(\frac{v}{6}\right)^2\right) = 1 - \frac{1}{6^3} \sum_{v=1}^{6} v^2 = \frac{125}{216}\end{aligned}$$

by the hint given in the question.

Exercise 1.19 (Independence) Show that A and B are independent events if and only if either of the following holds:
(a) A and B^c are independent;
(b) A^c and B^c are independent.

Solution
(a) A and B^c are independent if and only if $\Pr(A \cap B^c) = \Pr(A)\Pr(B^c)$. Now, since $\Pr(A) = \Pr(A \cap B) + \Pr(A \cap B^c)$ and, obviously, $\Pr(B) + \Pr(B^c) = 1$, it follows that A and B^c are independent if and only if $\Pr(A) - \Pr(A \cap B) = \Pr(A)(1 - \Pr(B))$; that is, if and only if $\Pr(A \cap B) = \Pr(A)\Pr(B)$.
(b) Since A and B are independent if and only if A and B^c are independent, it follows that B^c and A are independent if and only if B^c and A^c are independent.

***Exercise 1.20 (Exponential inequality)** Let $A_1, \dots, A_n$ be independent events. Show that

$$\Pr\left(\bigcap_{i=1}^{n} A_i^c\right) \leqslant \exp\left(-\sum_{i=1}^{n} \Pr(A_i)\right).$$

[Hint: First prove the inequality $\log(1-x) \leqslant -x$ for $0 \leqslant x < 1$.]

Solution

The inequality provided as a hint is a famous one. It follows directly by solving the optimization of $g(x) = \log(1-x) + x$ for x, the maximum being attained at $g(0) = 0$.

Now consider the inequality of the exercise. We may assume that $\Pr(A_i) < 1$ for all i, because if not then the left-hand side of the inequality is zero and the result is trivial. Further, since $A_1, \ldots, A_n$ are independent, so are $A_1^c, \ldots, A_n^c$, by Exercise 1.19. Thus,

$$\log\left(\Pr\left(\bigcap_{i=1}^{n} A_i^c\right)\right) = \log\left(\prod_{i=1}^{n} \Pr(A_i^c)\right)$$
$$= \sum_{i=1}^{n} \log(1 - \Pr(A_i)) \leqslant \sum_{i=1}^{n} -\Pr(A_i).$$

Exercise 1.21 (Independence is not a transitive relation) Give an example where events A and B are independent, events B and C are independent, but events A and C are not independent.

Solution

A trivial example is obtained when $C = A$. For another example, let $C = A^c$. Then, by Exercise 1.19, the independence of A and B is equivalent to the independence of B and C. However, it is clear that A is not independent of its complement C since $\Pr(A \cap C) = \Pr(\varnothing) = 0 \neq \Pr(A)\Pr(C)$ in general.

Exercise 1.22 (Pairwise independence does not imply joint independence) Suppose that, in an urn, there are four lottery tickets numbered 111, 221, 212, and 122. One ticket is drawn at random from the urn. Now consider the events A_i ($i = 1, 2, 3$) with A_i = "2 is in the i-th place". Use this to provide an example where events are pairwise independent, but not jointly independent.

Solution

We have $\Pr(A_i) = 1/2$ for $i = 1, 2, 3$ and $\Pr(A_i \cap A_j) = 1/4$ for all $i \neq j$. Hence, the three sets A_1, A_2, and A_3 are pairwise independent. But $\Pr(A_1 \cap A_2 \cap A_3) = 0 \neq (1/2) \times (1/2) \times (1/2)$. So the A_i's are not independent.

Exercise 1.23 (Mutually exclusive versus independent, 1) Let $\Pr(A) = 0.3$ and $\Pr(A \cup B) = 0.7$.

(a) For what value of $\Pr(B)$ are A and B mutually exclusive?

(b) For what value of $\Pr(B)$ are A and B independent?

Solution

For every A and B we have $\Pr(A \cup B) = \Pr(A) + \Pr(B) - \Pr(A \cap B)$, and hence, in this case, $\Pr(B) = \Pr(A \cap B) + 0.4$.

(a) A and B are mutually exclusive if and only if $\Pr(A \cap B) = 0$, that is, if and only if $\Pr(B) = 0.4$.

(b) A and B are independent if and only if $\Pr(A \cap B) = \Pr(A)\Pr(B)$, that is, if and only if $\Pr(B) = 4/7$.

Exercise 1.24 (Mutually exclusive versus independent, 2) Let A, B, and C be events such that $\Pr(A) = 1/4$, $\Pr(B) = 1/5$, and $\Pr(C) = 1/6$.

(a) Compute $\Pr(A \cup B \cup C)$ if A, B, and C are mutually exclusive.

(b) Compute $\Pr(A \cup B \cup C)$ if A, B, and C are independent.

Solution

We use the general relation $\Pr(A \cup B \cup C) = \Pr(A) + \Pr(B) + \Pr(C) - \Pr(A \cap B) - \Pr(A \cap C) - \Pr(B \cap C) + \Pr(A \cap B \cap C)$; see Exercise 1.13.

(a) A, B, and C are mutually exclusive if and only if $\Pr(A \cap B) = \Pr(A \cap C) = \Pr(B \cap C) = \Pr(A \cap B \cap C) = 0$. This occurs if and only if $\Pr(A \cup B \cup C) = 37/60$.

(b) A, B, and C are independent if and only if $\Pr(A \cap B) = \Pr(A)\Pr(B)$, $\Pr(A \cap C) = \Pr(A)\Pr(C)$, $\Pr(B \cap C) = \Pr(B)\Pr(C)$, and $\Pr(A \cap B \cap C) = \Pr(A)\Pr(B)\Pr(C)$. Hence, $\Pr(A \cup B \cup C) = 1/2$.

Exercise 1.25 (Sequential conditioning) Let $A_1, \dots, A_n$ be events. By induction, show that $\Pr(A_1 \cap \dots \cap A_n) = \Pr(A_1)\Pr(A_2 \mid A_1) \dots \Pr(A_n \mid A_{n-1} \cap \dots \cap A_1)$.

Solution

For $n = 2$, consider Figure 1.2. The event $B \mid A$ is represented by $B \cap A$ when A is considered as the given sample space (the new Ω), so that $\Pr(B \mid A)$ is $\Pr(B \cap A)$ relative to $\Pr(A)$. Next, assume that the statement holds for some n, and define $B := A_1 \cap \dots \cap A_n$. Then

$$\begin{aligned}\Pr(B \cap A_{n+1}) &= \Pr(B)\Pr(A_{n+1} \mid B)\\ &= \Pr(A_1 \cap \dots \cap A_n)\Pr(A_{n+1} \mid A_n \cap \dots \cap A_1)\\ &= \Pr(A_1)\Pr(A_2 \mid A_1) \cdots \Pr(A_n \mid A_{n-1} \cap \dots \cap A_1)\Pr(A_{n+1} \mid A_n \cap \dots \cap A_1)\end{aligned}$$

since the statement holds for n. This establishes that the statement holds for $n + 1$ too.

Exercise 1.26 (Thirty balls) A box contains 10 green balls, 6 black balls, and 14 red balls. Two balls are selected at random without replacement from the box.

(a) What is the probability that the second ball is red given that the first is red?

(b) What is the probability that both balls are red?

(c) What is the probability that the first ball is red given that the second is red?

(d) What is the probability that both balls have the same color?

Solution

(a) Let A_1 be the event that the first ball is red and A_2 the event that the second ball is red. If A_1 occurred, then 29 balls are left in the box of which 13 are red. Hence, $\Pr(A_2 \mid A_1) = 13/29$.

(b) $\Pr(A_1 \cap A_2) = \Pr(A_2 \mid A_1)\Pr(A_1) = (13/29)(14/30) = 91/435$.

(c) Here we have

$$\begin{aligned}\Pr(A_1 \mid A_2) &= \frac{\Pr(A_1 \cap A_2)}{\Pr(A_2)} = \frac{\Pr(A_2 \cap A_1)}{\Pr(A_2 \cap A_1) + \Pr(A_2 \cap A_1^c)} \\ &= \frac{\Pr(A_2 \cap A_1)}{\Pr(A_2 \cap A_1) + \Pr(A_2 \mid A_1^c)\Pr(A_1^c)} \\ &= \frac{91/435}{(91/435) + (14/29)(16/30)} = \frac{13}{29}.\end{aligned}$$

(d) Finally, the probability that both balls have the same color equals

$$\frac{10}{30} \times \frac{9}{29} + \frac{6}{30} \times \frac{5}{29} + \frac{14}{30} \times \frac{13}{29} = \frac{151}{435}.$$

Exercise 1.27 (Two boxes of balls) Box A contains six black and two white balls, while box B contains seven black and three white balls. A box is selected at random and a ball is drawn at random from the selected box.

(a) Find the probability of selecting a white ball.

(b) Suppose a black ball was drawn. What is the probability that it came from box A?

Solution

(a) Let $A :=$ "box A is selected" and $W :=$ "white ball is drawn", so that $A^c =$ "box B is selected" and $W^c =$ "black ball is drawn". Then,

$$\begin{aligned}\Pr(W) &= \Pr(W \cap A) + \Pr(W \cap A^c) \\ &= \Pr(W \mid A)\Pr(A) + \Pr(W \mid A^c)\Pr(A^c) \\ &= \frac{2}{8} \times \frac{1}{2} + \frac{3}{10} \times \frac{1}{2} = \frac{11}{40}.\end{aligned}$$

(b) The probability is

$$\Pr(A \mid W^c) = \frac{\Pr(A \cap W^c)}{\Pr(W^c)} = \frac{\Pr(W^c \mid A)\Pr(A)}{\Pr(W^c)} = \frac{(6/8)(1/2)}{29/40} = \frac{15}{29},$$

which is larger than $\frac{1}{2}$ because box A contains relatively more black balls (75%) than box B (70%).

***Exercise 1.28 (Change of mind?)** You are invited to play a game on a TV show. There are three boxes, only one of them containing a prize, and the show host knows which one it is (but you obviously don't). He asks you to select a box, without opening it. He then opens one of the two remaining boxes, showing you that it is empty. Only two boxes are left, one of them containing the prize. He asks you to choose a box again. Would you change your mind? What if the game consisted of 100 boxes instead of three, and the show host opened 98 boxes?

Solution

The box you chose at random is empty with probability 2/3 (case A) and contains the prize with probability 1/3 (case B). In case A, the host has no choice but to open the other empty box; while in case B he can open one of the two boxes. If your strategy is to switch, then you can only win in case A, and you do so with conditional (on being in case A) probability 1, hence with unconditional probability 2/3. If you persist with your original random choice, then you can only win in case B, and with probability 1/3. Hence, you should change.

This reasoning holds for the general case where the host shows you n boxes, then opens $n - 2$ empty boxes. In this case, the probabilities of a win without or with changing your mind are $1/n$ or $1 - 1/n$, respectively. For $n = 100$, not being stubborn is quite profitable (99% of the time)! The host has revealed a lot of information by opening 98 empty boxes, and persisting with your original choice makes no use of this information.

Exercise 1.29 (Rare disease) One in every 100 000 persons suffers from a rare disease. There is a test which, with a probability of 0.95, will be positive if you have the disease. However, if you don't have the disease the test will be positive with a probability of 0.005. If your test is positive, what is the probability that you actually have the disease? Comment on the implications of the result.

Solution

Let S be the event that you have the disease and T the event that the test is positive.

$$\Pr(S \mid T) = \frac{\Pr(S \cap T)}{\Pr(T)} = \frac{\Pr(T \mid S)\Pr(S)}{\Pr(T \mid S)\Pr(S) + \Pr(T \mid S^c)\Pr(S^c)}$$
$$= \frac{(0.95)(0.000\,01)}{(0.95)(0.000\,01) + (0.005)(0.999\,99)} \approx 0.002.$$

Notice that this probability is approximately

$$\Pr(S \mid T) \approx \frac{(0.95)(0.000\,01)}{(0.95)(0.000\,01) + 0.005} = \frac{95}{95 + 50\,000} \approx 0.002,$$

which has the following simple intuitive interpretation. On average, out of 10 million people taking the test, 100 of them will have the disease and 95 of them will test positive (the numerator of the last fraction), a small number indeed when compared to the false positives (approximately 0.5% of these 10 million). Testing positive has increased the (unfortunate) chance of having the disease from 1/100 000 to about 2/1000, but this is still a very low probability. If the test were repeated independently and there were no systematic biases, and if positive diagnoses were revealed again, then the probability of having the disease would again be increased. This can be an expensive procedure, whose cost and benefit should be analyzed. For example, it may be more beneficial to treat all cases showing symptoms without requiring the patients to take the test in the first place.

Exercise 1.30 (Two-headed coin) A box contains three coins, one of which has a head on both sides. The other two coins are normal and fair. A coin is chosen at random from the box and tossed three times.
(a) What is the probability of three heads?
(b) If a head turns up all three times, what is the probability that this is the two-headed coin?

Solution
Define the events $S :=$ "three heads come up in three tosses" and $T :=$ "selected coin has two heads". Then, $T^c =$ "selected coin is normal".
(a) $\Pr(S) = \Pr(S \mid T)\Pr(T) + \Pr(S \mid T^c)\Pr(T^c) = 1 \times (1/3) + (1/2)^3 \times (2/3) = 5/12$.
(b) $\Pr(T \mid S) = \Pr(S \mid T)\Pr(T)/\Pr(S) = 1 \times (1/3)/(5/12) = 4/5$.

***Exercise 1.31 (The secretary problem)** You wish to hire one secretary out of n candidates, interviewed in a random order. You do not have the address of any of the candidates, who leave immediately after the interview. Therefore, you have to make the decision to hire on the spot, before the chosen candidate leaves your office and before you see the remaining candidates. You know the rank of a candidate only relative to the ones seen previously, there are no possibilities of ties, and you'd rather have no secretary than have one that is not *the* best amongst the ones seen so far. Your strategy is to reject the first m candidates after seeing them, regardless of how good they are, and only after that do you recruit the one that is the best seen so far.
(a) Show that the probability of selecting the best candidate for any given m is $1/n$ for $m = 0$ and, for $m > 0$, it is

$$p_m = \frac{m}{n} \sum_{i=m+1}^{n} \frac{1}{i-1}.$$

[Hint: Write p_m as the sum of probabilities of success at the i-th interviewee, where $i > m$.]
(b) Assuming n is large, what is the optimal m and what is the corresponding probability of a success?

Solution
(a) Since the candidates are arranged randomly, the probability of selecting the best candidate is $1/n$ for $m = 0$. For $m > 0$, define $B_i :=$"i-th applicant is the best" and $H_i :=$"i-th

applicant is hired". Then, using Exercise 1.6, the required probability is

$$p_m = \sum_{i=m+1}^{n} \Pr(B_i \cap H_i) = \sum_{i=m+1}^{n} \Pr(B_i)\Pr(H_i \mid B_i) = \sum_{i=m+1}^{n} \frac{1}{n} \times \frac{m}{i-1},$$

where $\Pr(H_i \mid B_i)$ is equivalent to the probability that the best candidate before the i-th was among the m discarded ones that could not be recruited, hence is equal to $m/(i-1)$.
(b) The optimal m is the value which maximizes this probability. For n large and $(m/n) \to \phi$, where ϕ is the fraction of candidates discarded automatically, we can approximate the sum by the integral (see Section A.4 for more details)

$$p_m \to \phi \int_{\phi}^{1} \frac{\mathrm{d}u}{u} = -\phi \log(\phi)$$

which is optimized by solving

$$\frac{\mathrm{d}(-\phi \log(\phi))}{\mathrm{d}\phi} \equiv -\log(\phi) - 1 = 0,$$

the second derivative $-1/\phi < 0$ guaranteeing that this is a maximum. The optimal ϕ is therefore $\mathrm{e}^{-1} \approx 0.368$ and the corresponding probability of success is $-\mathrm{e}^{-1}\log(\mathrm{e}^{-1}) = \mathrm{e}^{-1}$. Recall that $p_0 = 1/n \to 0$, so that $\phi = 0$ is not optimal. Thus, the optimal strategy is for you to skip approximately the first 37% of candidates automatically, if you were lazy enough not to have noted down their addresses! Intuitively, you are less likely to succeed if you hire too early.

1.3 Factorials, permutations, and combinations

Exercise 1.32 (A random secretary) A secretary is blindfolded and asked to put n addressed letters in their corresponding n envelopes. All the letters and envelopes are of the same size and have no distinctive features apart from the addresses, and only one letter goes in one envelope. By applying Exercise 1.13, prove that the probability of at least one letter going in the correct envelope is

$$1 - \frac{1}{2!} + \frac{1}{3!} - \cdots + \frac{(-1)^{n+1}}{n!},$$

and find the limit of this probability as $n \to \infty$.

Solution
Let A_i $(i = 1, \ldots, n)$ denote the event that letter i gets put in the correct envelope. This

becomes a direct application of

$$\Pr\left(\bigcup_{i=1}^{n} A_i\right) = \sum_{i=1}^{n} \Pr(A_i) - \sum_{i<j\leqslant n} \Pr(A_i \cap A_j) + \sum_{i<j<k\leqslant n} \Pr(A_i \cap A_j \cap A_k)$$
$$+ \cdots + (-1)^{n+1} \Pr(A_1 \cap A_2 \cap \cdots \cap A_n)$$

of Exercise 1.13: its left-hand side is the probability that either of the A_i's occurs, and we need to calculate the right-hand side probabilities. The letters (and envelopes), all being identical, have an equal probability of being selected. The probability of the intersection of any m of the $A_\bullet$ sets is the probability of m matching letters and envelopes, with the remaining $n-m$ free to be shuffled (permuted) yielding the probability $(n-m)!/n!$, while each sum containing such a probability on the right-hand side of the displayed equation has $\binom{n}{m}$ terms (see Exercise 1.13). Thus,

$$\Pr\left(\bigcup_{i=1}^{n} A_i\right) = n\frac{(n-1)!}{n!} - \binom{n}{2}\frac{(n-2)!}{n!} + \binom{n}{3}\frac{(n-3)!}{n!}$$
$$+ \cdots + (-1)^{n+1}\binom{n}{n}\frac{(n-n)!}{n!}$$
$$= 1 - \frac{1}{2!} + \frac{1}{3!} + \cdots + \frac{(-1)^{n+1}}{n!}$$

as required. As $n \to \infty$, this is the series expansion of $1 - \exp(-1) \approx 0.632$.

***Exercise 1.33 (Pascal's triangle)** Let $n, j \in \mathbb{N}$ with $n > j$. Show that:
(a) $\binom{n}{j} = \binom{n-1}{j-1} + \binom{n-1}{j}$;
(b) $\sum_{i=0}^{n} (-1)^i \binom{n}{i} = 0$;
(c) $\sum_{i=0}^{n} \binom{2n}{2i} = 2^{2n-1}$;
(d) $\binom{m+n}{j} = \sum_{i\in A} \binom{m}{i}\binom{n}{j-i}$, where $m \in \mathbb{N}$ and $A := \{i : \max\{0, j-n\} \leqslant i \leqslant \min\{m, j\}\}$.

Solution
(a) We have

$$\binom{n-1}{j-1} + \binom{n-1}{j} = \frac{(n-1)!}{(j-1)!(n-j)!} + \frac{(n-1)!}{j!(n-1-j)!}$$
$$= \frac{j(n-1)! + (n-j)(n-1)!}{j!(n-j)!}$$
$$= \frac{n!}{j!(n-j)!} = \binom{n}{j}.$$

An alternative way to prove this relation is as follows. Suppose that there is a bag of n balls, where one is red and the rest are white. There are $\binom{n}{j}$ ways of choosing j balls,

without ordering. The red ball can be chosen in $\binom{1}{1}\binom{n-1}{j-1} = \binom{n-1}{j-1}$ ways, or not be chosen in $\binom{1}{0}\binom{n-1}{j} = \binom{n-1}{j}$ ways, adding up to $\binom{n}{j}$.
(b) The simplest proof is by letting $a = -1$ and $b = 1$ in the binomial expansion

$$(a+b)^n = \sum_{i=0}^{n} \binom{n}{i} a^i b^{n-i}.$$

Alternatively, let $S_n := \sum_{i=0}^{n}(-1)^i \binom{n}{i}$. Then, using (a) with the convention that $\binom{n-1}{-1} = \binom{n-1}{n} = 0$, we obtain

$$\begin{aligned} S_n &= \sum_{i=0}^{n}(-1)^i \binom{n-1}{i-1} + \sum_{i=0}^{n}(-1)^i \binom{n-1}{i} \\ &= \sum_{i=1}^{n}(-1)^i \binom{n-1}{i-1} + \sum_{i=0}^{n-1}(-1)^i \binom{n-1}{i} = -S_{n-1} + S_{n-1} = 0. \end{aligned}$$

(c) Again using (a), we find

$$\sum_{i=0}^{n} \binom{2n}{2i} = \sum_{i=0}^{n} \binom{2n-1}{2i-1} + \sum_{i=0}^{n} \binom{2n-1}{2i} = \sum_{j=-1}^{2n} \binom{2n-1}{j}$$

by combining the two sums. Since the first and last summands are zero, this becomes

$$\sum_{j=0}^{2n-1} \binom{2n-1}{j},$$

which equals 2^{2n-1} on choosing $a = b = 1$ in the binomial expansion.
(d) We follow the second approach used in (a). Suppose that there is a bag of $m + n$ balls, where m are red and n are white. There are $\binom{m+n}{j}$ ways of choosing j balls, without ordering. We can choose i red balls and $j - i$ white balls in $\binom{m}{i}\binom{n}{j-i}$ ways, without regard to ordering (see the introduction to this chapter). Summing over all the possible choices for i gives the required result.

Exercise 1.34 (How many drinks?) Suppose that you have n different liqueurs. How many types of mixtures can you create?

Solution
With each liqueur, you can decide to include it or exclude it from the mix, giving you $2 \times \cdots \times 2 = 2^n$ choices. Since the empty drink does not count, you have $2^n - 1$ possibilities, not necessarily all drinkable though! Note that we allow the n drinks that have only one liqueur, for the purists.

***Exercise 1.35 (How many events?)** Let Ω be a finite sample space. Show that the total number of events cannot be odd. What can the total number of events be? [Hint: Recall the power set, defined in the introduction to this chapter.]

Solution

Let Ω have $n < \infty$ sample points; hence, a fortiori, it is countable. As seen in the introduction to this chapter, an event is a collection of sample points. The space of events consists of the impossible event $\varnothing$, n events having precisely one sample point, $\binom{n}{i}$ events consisting of i sample points ($i = 2, \dots, n-1$), and the certain event consisting of all the sample points of Ω. So the total number of events is $\sum_{i=0}^{n}\binom{n}{i} = 2^n$ (choose $a = b = 1$ in the binomial expansion; see Exercise 1.33.) Notice that $2^n = 2 \times \cdots \times 2$ reflects the fact that, for each of the n sample points, there are two possibilities: inclusion or exclusion. So the total number of events in a finite sample space cannot be an odd number.

***Exercise 1.36 (The birthday)** Téta's birthday is on 12 June. She is teaching in a classroom containing n students.
(a) What is the probability that at least one of Téta's students has the same birthday as her?
(b) What is the probability that any two students have the same birthday?
(c) What is the probability that any two persons in this classroom have the same birthday?
(d) Compare the three probabilities for $n = 23$.
You may assume that the year is made up of 365 days (apologies to those born on 29 February!) and that birth is equally likely on any of these days.

Solution

(a) The probability that none of the students was born on 12 June, say p_1, is

$$p_1 = \prod_{i=1}^{n}\left(1 - \frac{1}{365}\right) = \left(1 - \frac{1}{365}\right)^n$$
$$= \exp\left(n \log\left(1 - \frac{1}{365}\right)\right) \approx \exp(-0.003n).$$

The required probability is $1 - p_1$.
(b) Let p_2 denote the probability that no two students have the same birthday. For $n > 365$, we have $p_2 = 0$. Otherwise,

$$p_2 = \frac{\mathrm{P}_n^{365}}{(365)^n} = \prod_{i=0}^{n-1}\frac{365-i}{365} = \prod_{i=0}^{n-1}\left(1 - \frac{i}{365}\right) = \exp\left(\sum_{i=0}^{n-1}\log\left(1 - \frac{i}{365}\right)\right).$$

We can use the approximation $\log(1-x) \approx -x$ for small x (the approximation would be inaccurate for very large classrooms) to get

$$p_2 \approx \exp\left(-\frac{1}{365}\sum_{i=0}^{n-1} i\right) = \exp\left(-\frac{n(n-1)}{730}\right)$$

by the sum of the first $n-1$ natural numbers

$$\sum_{i=0}^{n-1} i = \frac{n(n-1)}{2}.$$

The latter sum is worked out in Section A.4.1. The required probability is $1 - p_2$.
(c) For $n < 365$, the probability that no two persons (including Téta) have the same birthday, say p_3, is given by

$$p_3 = \prod_{i=0}^{n} \left(1 - \frac{i}{365}\right) = \exp\left(\sum_{i=0}^{n} \log\left(1 - \frac{i}{365}\right)\right)$$
$$\approx \exp\left(-\frac{1}{365}\sum_{i=0}^{n} i\right) = \exp\left(-\frac{n(n+1)}{730}\right),$$

and the required probability is $1 - p_3$.
(d) The exact probabilities, to two decimal places, are 0.06, 0.51, and 0.54, respectively. Clearly, the latter two are of a different order of magnitude from the first, because they do not require the two persons to be born on the same specific day, 12 June. The third must be higher than the second because we have one more person (the teacher) to include in the comparison of birthdays. The approximation formulae are not bad, giving 0.06, 0.50, and 0.53, respectively.

Notes

General references on probability include Billingsley (1995), Feller (1968, 1971), Grimmett and Stirzaker (2001), and Stirzaker (1994). From a more statistical perspective, we recommend Bain and Engelhardt (1992), Casella and Berger (2002), Hogg and Craig (1989), Mood, Graybill, and Boes (1974), and Mukhopadhyay (2000).

In the introduction, we have avoided a technical point which we summarize here. It will be mentioned again in the Notes to Chapter 5. If A is an event, then $A \subseteq \Omega$. However, the reverse implication is not necessarily true if Ω is not countable: not all subsets of Ω are necessarily events. This is a stronger statement than saying that the probability of some event in Ω is zero (which we will see in the discussion around (2.6) in the introduction to Chapter 2), since the previous sentence is about a subset of Ω that is not even an event (which is required for a probability measure to be defined).

In defining a sigma-algebra, we needed $i = 1, 2, \dots, \infty$. If the index i were finite ($i = 1, 2, \dots, n$ with $n < \infty$), we would end up with an *algebra*. This would not be sufficient to describe situations where, for example, the random experiment could go on indefinitely in principle. This is why we chose a sigma-algebra to define probabilities on.

The time path of the gamblers' winnings in Exercise 1.10 is a famous example of a random walk with absorbing barriers, a special case of Markov processes. The name "random walk" comes from the analogy of the time path with the trajectory of a drunk! Other random walks will appear in Exercise 4.23 (see the Notes to it) and in Part B. Exercise 1.11 is an example of a martingale gambling strategy. Exercise 1.14 is an illustration of *Bonferroni's inequalities*. More details on these subjects can be found in the general references listed above.

The first part of Exercise 1.28 is well known. It is the *Monty Hall problem*, in reference to the game show host who inspired the problem.

There are more complicated versions of Exercise 1.31, which is known as *the secretary problem* or *the bachelor's problem*. Ferguson (1989) provides an interesting account of open issues relating to this problem.

2

Random variables, probability distributions and densities

The previous chapter introduced the sample space Ω and an event space $\mathcal{F}$, with probability defined on the latter. Suppose that we attach a value to each outcome in Ω. For example, a gambler tossing a fair coin may get a *variable* payoff x, taking the values $x = 1$ for a tail (T) but $x = -1$ for a head (H). For any numerical constant $u \in \mathbb{R}$ (for example, $u = -1$), we will find that $x \leqslant u$ (for example, $x \leqslant -1$) is associated with an event in $\mathcal{F} = \{\varnothing, \{H\}, \{T\}, \Omega\}$:

for any $u \in (-\infty, -1)$, the event is $\varnothing$:	no event leads to $x \leqslant u$ for any $u \in (-\infty, -1)$,
for any $u \in [-1, 1)$, the event is $\{H\}$:	head (H) leads to $x \leqslant u$ for any $u \in [-1, 1)$,
for any $u \in [1, \infty)$, the event is Ω:	it is certain that $x \leqslant u$ for any $u \in [1, \infty)$.

Note that the winnings of the gambler are the variable x which is random and depends on the outcome of the toss (an element of Ω). For notational convenience, we suppress the dependence of x on the elements of Ω (some authors write it as the function $x(\omega)$, with $\omega \in \Omega$), but this dependence should not be forgotten and will occasionally be stressed later in this book. In general, we consider a *random variable* (r.v.) x to be a real-valued function of the elements of Ω such that, for any $u \in \mathbb{R}$, the relation $x \leqslant u$ identifies an event belonging to $\mathcal{F}$. Alternative names for a random variable include *stochastic* (or *nondeterministic*) *variable*, and *variate*.

Since the elements of $\mathcal{F}$ have probabilities attached to them, it is natural to ask for the corresponding probabilities that are implied for the variate x. The *cumulative distribution function* (abbreviated to c.d.f. or distribution function) of a variate x is $F_x(u) := \Pr(x \leqslant u)$, where u is a numerical constant. The case $x = u$ leads to the terminology that u is the *realization* of x, a term that we will use more loosely to refer to such values u in general. Recalling the example of our gambler tossing the fair coin,

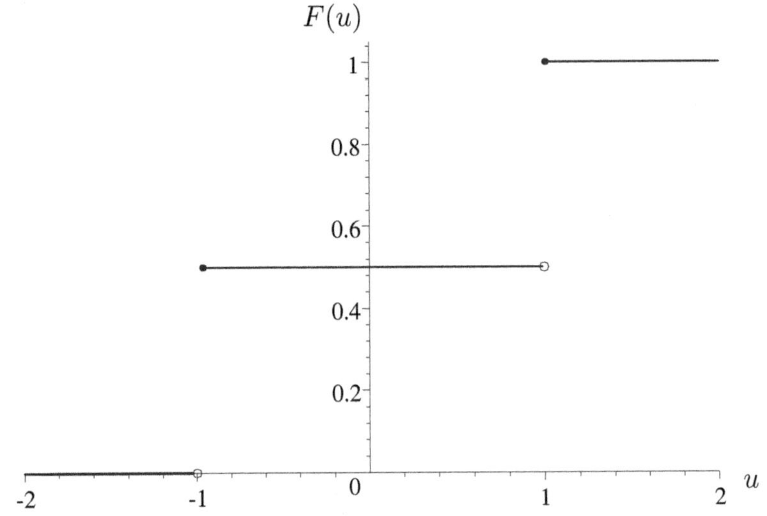

Figure 2.1. Distribution function for the example of coin tossing.

$$F_x(u) = \Pr(x \leqslant u) = \begin{cases} 0 & (u < -1), \\ \frac{1}{2} & (-1 \leqslant u < 1), \\ 1 & (u \geqslant 1), \end{cases} \tag{2.1}$$

which is plotted in Figure 2.1, this particular F_x being known as the *Rademacher distribution*. Clearly, the equality of two variates implies (but is not implied by) the equality of their c.d.f.s: there are other variates that have nothing to do with gambling but have the same c.d.f. (or probabilities) as in Figure 2.1! When no ambiguity arises about the variate in question, we drop the subscript x and write $F(u)$. We also write $x \in \mathcal{X} \subseteq \mathbb{R}$, where $\mathcal{X}$ is the set of all values of x where F increases. This set $\mathcal{X}$ is known as the *support* of the variate x. In the previous example, $\mathcal{X} = \{-1, 1\}$. When we have up to three variates, they are denoted by x, y, z with realizations u, v, w and supports $\mathcal{X}, \mathcal{Y}, \mathcal{Z}$, respectively. The general case will be handled in Chapter 5.

Define

$$F(u^-) := \lim_{h \to 0^+} F(u - h) = \lim_{h \downarrow 0} F(u - h),$$

$$F(u^+) := \lim_{h \to 0^+} F(u + h) = \lim_{h \downarrow 0} F(u + h),$$

where $h \to 0^+$ (or $h \downarrow 0$) indicates that h approaches 0 from the positive side (or h declines to 0). In the previous graph,

$$F(0^-) = F(0) = F(0^+) = \frac{1}{2}$$

since F is continuous at $u = 0$, but there is a jump at $u = 1$

$$F(1^-) = \frac{1}{2} < F(1) = F(1^+) = 1.$$

Also, the plot of the function F showed that it was nondecreasing, starting from 0 and ending at 1 as u increased in $\mathbb{R} \equiv (-\infty, \infty)$: we have $\Pr(x \leqslant u) \to 0$ as $u \to -\infty$ (since no $x \in \mathbb{R}$ can satisfy $x \leqslant -\infty$), and $\Pr(x \leqslant u) \to 1$ as $u \to \infty$ (since $x < \infty$ covers all the possibilities for $x \in \mathbb{R}$). This holds more generally, as the following definition shows.

For a function F to be a c.d.f., the following conditions need to hold:
(i) $\lim_{u \to -\infty} F(u) = 0$;
(ii) $\lim_{u \to \infty} F(u) = 1$;
(iii) $F(u^+) = F(u)$; and
(iv) $s < t$ implies $F(s) \leqslant F(t)$, which means that F is a nondecreasing function and

$$F(t) - F(s) \equiv \Pr(x \leqslant t) - \Pr(x \leqslant s)$$

is nonnegative if $s < t$, with

$$F(t) - F(s) = \Pr(s < x \leqslant t).$$

Notice that property (iii) means that $F(u^+) = \Pr(x \leqslant u)$, whereas the corresponding interpretation of $F(u^-)$ is obtained from[1]

$$\begin{aligned} F(u^-) &= F(u) - \left(F(u) - F(u^-)\right) \\ &= \Pr(x \leqslant u) - \lim_{h \to 0^+} \Pr(u - h < x \leqslant u) \\ &= \Pr(x \leqslant u) - \Pr(x = u) \\ &= \Pr(x < u). \end{aligned}$$

Another useful way of writing this is $\Pr(x = u) = F(u) - F(u^-)$.

Variates can be decomposed into different types. *Jordan's decomposition* splits any $F(u)$ into the convex combination of the c.d.f.s of a *discrete* variate and a *continuous* variate:

$$F(u) \equiv pF_{\mathrm{d}}(u) + (1 - p)F_{\mathrm{c}}(u),$$

where $p \in [0, 1]$ and F_{c} is a continuous function. The first component of the decomposition is given by $\sum_{t \leqslant u} \Pr(x = t)$ or, equivalently, the sum of all the jumps in the plot of F for all values of x up to u:

$$pF_{\mathrm{d}}(u) = \sum_{t \leqslant u} \left(F(t) - F(t^-)\right), \tag{2.2}$$

the points where F is continuous being omitted from the sum because they give $F(t) - F(t^-) = 0$ by the definition of continuity. (The jumps must be countable for $\sum_{t \leqslant u} \Pr(x = t)$ to be finite.) The second component of the decomposition of F is obtained as the remainder after deducting (2.2) from $F(u)$. When $p = 1$, the variate is said to be discrete; we have seen an example of such a function F_{d} earlier when we considered coin-tossing. For dis-

[1]This provides a simple example for which $\lim \Pr \neq \Pr \lim$, since the limit of $x \in (u - h, u]$ gives the empty set that has probability 0. The limit here is not taken over a countable sequence (since h is real-valued), unlike in Exercise 1.7.

crete variates, $f_x(u) := \Pr(x = u)$ is a *probability density function* (abbreviated to p.d.f. or density) and satisfies:
(i) $f_x(u) \geqslant 0$;
(ii) $\sum_{t \leqslant u} f_x(t) = F_x(u)$; and
(iii) $\sum_{t \in \mathcal{X}} f_x(t) = \lim_{u\to\infty} F_x(u) = 1$.
In other words: $\Pr(x = u)$ cannot be negative, $\Pr(x \leqslant u)$ is the sum of the probabilities (of the disjoint events) that $x = t$ for all $t \leqslant u$, and the sum of $\Pr(x = t)$ for all $t \in \mathcal{X}$ covers all the possibilities for the variate x. In the discrete case, $\mathcal{X}$ is countable, meaning that its elements can be enumerated (in correspondence with the natural numbers $\mathbb{N}$) and one may use sums like $\sum_{t\in\mathcal{X}}$ above. Our coin-tossing example illustrates a discrete variate with density

$$f_x(u) = F_x(u) - F_x(u^-) = \begin{cases} \frac{1}{2} & (u = -1), \\ \frac{1}{2} & (u = 1), \end{cases} \tag{2.3}$$

and $f_x(u) = 0$ elsewhere. This is sometimes abbreviated as $f_x(u) = \frac{1}{2} \times 1_{u\in\{-1,1\}}$, where $1_{\mathcal{K}}$ is the *indicator function* that returns 1 if condition $\mathcal{K}$ is satisfied and 0 otherwise. The definition of a p.d.f. for a continuous variate is more elaborate, and we now turn to an alternative decomposition for this purpose.

Lebesgue's decomposition splits any $F(u)$ into the convex combination of the c.d.f.s of a *singular* variate and an *absolutely continuous* variate, the latter c.d.f. being obtained as the absolutely continuous part (see Section A.4.3) of $F(u)$ and the former as the remainder. When the variate is absolutely continuous, its *probability density function* is an integrable function $f_x(u)$ satisfying:
(i) $f_x(u) \geqslant 0$;
(ii) $\int_{-\infty}^{u} f_x(t)\,\mathrm{d}t = F_x(u)$; and
(iii) $\int_{-\infty}^{\infty} f_x(t)\,\mathrm{d}t = \lim_{u\to\infty} F_x(u) = 1$.
For example, consider some radioactive material whose time to full decay is given by the variate $x \in \mathbb{R}_+$ with $\Pr(x > u) = \mathrm{e}^{-u}$. Hence, its c.d.f. is

$$F_x(u) = \Pr(x \leqslant u) = 1 - \Pr(x > u) = 1 - \mathrm{e}^{-u}$$

and is plotted in Figure 2.2. This gives rise to

$$\mathrm{e}^{-u} = 1 - F_x(u) = \int_{-\infty}^{\infty} f_x(t)\,\mathrm{d}t - \int_{-\infty}^{u} f_x(t)\,\mathrm{d}t = \int_{u}^{\infty} f_x(t)\,\mathrm{d}t \tag{2.4}$$

for $u \in \mathbb{R}_+$, and the integral equation $\mathrm{e}^{-u} = \int_u^{\infty} f_x(t)\,\mathrm{d}t$ can be used to infer the p.d.f.:

$$f_x(u) = \begin{cases} \mathrm{e}^{-u} & (u > 0), \\ 0 & (u \leqslant 0). \end{cases} \tag{2.5}$$

Formally, the p.d.f. arising from the integral equation $\int_{-\infty}^{u} f_x(t)\,\mathrm{d}t = F_x(u)$ of (ii) is not unique because f may be perturbed, at a countable set of points, by extra amounts which nevertheless integrate to zero; for example, see Exercise 2.5. By convention, we rule out such exceptions to the continuity of $f(u)$ and write $f(u) = \mathrm{d}F(u)/\mathrm{d}u$. Also, when

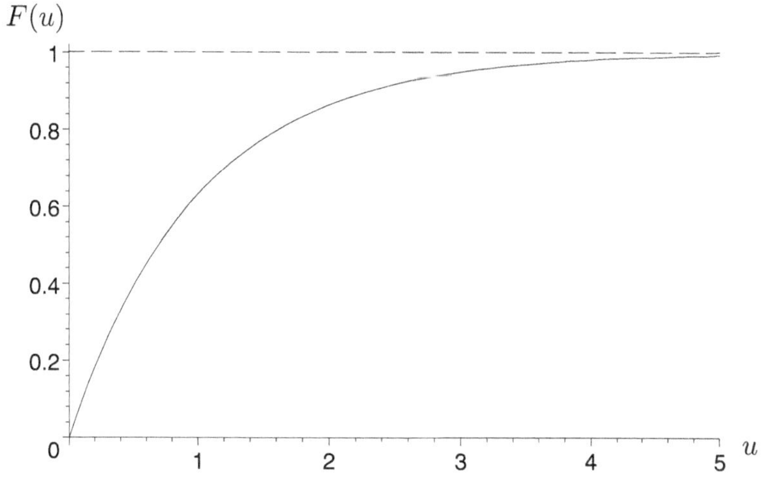

Figure 2.2. Distribution function for the example of radioactive decay.

computing $f(u) = \mathrm{d}F(u)/\mathrm{d}u$ we exclude the endpoints of the interval(s) making up the support $\mathcal{X}$ since F is not necessarily differentiable at these endpoints, and we set $f(u) = 0$ there, as we did in (2.5) for $u = 0$.

One should also be aware that, when F is a continuous c.d.f., we have

$$\Pr(x = u) \equiv F(u) - F(u^{-}) = 0 \tag{2.6}$$

for all $u \in \mathcal{X}$; namely, the probability is zero for a continuous variate x taking *exactly* the value u. Reverting to our example, the probability that the time to decay is exactly $1.11\ldots$ hours is zero: it is one of an infinite number of possibilities in the continuum of values of x in $\mathbb{R}_+$. By the same token, the description *with probability 1* (or *almost surely*, abbreviated by a.s.) is used to refer to an event happening always except for a set whose probability of occurrence is zero. This terminology is not the same as saying that the event will always happen. In our example of a continuous x, we had $\Pr(x \neq 1.11\ldots) = 1$ even though the extremely unlikely event that $x = 1.11\ldots$ was not ruled out because $f_x(1.11\ldots) = \mathrm{e}^{-1.11\ldots} > 0$. It may well be the case that $\Pr(A) = 0$ and $\Pr(\varnothing) = 0$ but that A is not the impossible event $\varnothing$ (empty set), as the previous example illustrates.

The two decompositions together imply that any c.d.f. can be decomposed into discrete, *singular continuous* (singular but not discrete), and absolutely continuous parts. Singular continuous variates are characterized by c.d.f.s satisfying all four rules defining a c.d.f., yet for which $\mathrm{d}F(u)/\mathrm{d}u = 0$ almost everywhere. Such variates are sometimes described as not possessing a density function on $\mathbb{R}$. Examples may seem contrived in this univariate setup, so we shall return to them in the multivariate case considered in later chapters, where they arise more naturally. Whenever no ambiguity arises, we shall drop the adjective "absolute" henceforth. Finally, to illustrate a variate that has discrete and continuous components, it is customary to think of the distribution of the levels of rainfall during a day: there is usually a positive probability of zero rain (hence a jump in the c.d.f. at zero), followed by a continuous distribution over positive levels of daily rainfall.

Regardless of whether the variate is discrete, its density is called the *Radon–Nikodym derivative* of the distribution function with respect to the measure on x, this being a counting measure for discrete x (recall that $\mathcal{X}$ is countable in this case) or the Lebesgue measure (length of intervals) for continuous x. In other words, the p.d.f. for discrete x is the change in the c.d.f. as x goes from one value in $\mathcal{X}$ to the next, while the p.d.f. for continuous x is the change in the c.d.f. as a result of x changing by an infinitesimal amount (the length of the interval Δx tends to 0). Some authors use *probability mass function*, p.m.f., to denote the density of a discrete variate. We prefer to use the unified p.d.f. terminology, even though a discrete variate is not "dense" (see Section A.3.1 for this term). This unified treatment of the p.d.f. will provide us with a convenient way of dealing with variates, especially in the following chapters. Another useful unifying approach is obtained by means of the *Stieltjes* (or *Riemann–Stieltjes*) *integral* of a function ψ with respect to F, denoted by $\int_{-\infty}^{\infty} \psi(u)\, \mathrm{d}F(u)$. For x an absolutely continuous variate, we have $\mathrm{d}F(u)/\,\mathrm{d}u = f(u)$ and $\int_{-\infty}^{\infty} \psi(u)\, \mathrm{d}F(u) = \int_{-\infty}^{\infty} \psi(u) f(u)\, \mathrm{d}u$; while x discrete yields

$$\int_{-\infty}^{\infty} \psi(u)\, \mathrm{d}F(u) = \sum_{u \in \mathcal{X}} \psi(u)(F(u) - F(u^-)) = \sum_{u \in \mathcal{X}} \psi(u) f(u)$$

since $F(u) - F(u^-) = 0$ (or $f(u) = 0$) when $u \notin \mathcal{X}$. Given the decompositions of c.d.f.s seen earlier, we can write $\int_{-\infty}^{\infty} \psi(u)\, \mathrm{d}F(u)$ in general as a convex combination of these two simpler formulations of the Stieltjes integral. Note that ψ need not be a continuous function. Illustrations can be found in the exercises, and more technical details in Section A.4.3.

Distribution functions imply properties for the corresponding variates. First, a variate x is *symmetric* (or *symmetrically distributed*) around c if and only if

$$\Pr(x \leqslant c - t) = \Pr(x \geqslant c + t) \quad \text{for all } t \in \mathbb{R}.$$

Using $F_x(u) = \Pr(x \leqslant u)$ and $F_x(u^-) = \Pr(x < u) = 1 - \Pr(x \geqslant u)$, we get the equivalent definition of symmetry as

$$F_x(c - t) + F_x(c + t^-) = 1 \quad \text{for all } t \in \mathbb{R}. \tag{2.7}$$

Notice that t will take values that are not necessarily in $\mathcal{X}$, if $\mathcal{X} \subset \mathbb{R}$. For x continuous, the condition reduces to $F_x(c - t) + F_x(c + t) = 1$ for all $t > 0$, which becomes $f_x(c - t) = f_x(c + t)$ upon differentiation with respect to t: the plot of the density to the right of $x = c$ is the mirror image of its plot to the left of $x = c$. (An illustration will be seen in Figure 4.3 in Exercise 4.14 below.) For x discrete, evaluating the defining equation of symmetry (2.7) once at t and once at t^+, then subtracting the two gives

$$\begin{aligned} 1 - 1 &= \left(F_x(c - t) + F_x(c + t^-)\right) - \left(F_x(c - t^+) + F_x(c + t)\right) \\ &= \left(F_x(c - t) - F_x(c - t^+)\right) - \left(F_x(c + t) - F_x(c + t^-)\right) \\ &\equiv f_x(c - t) - f_x(c + t); \end{aligned}$$

so $f_x(c+t) = f_x(c-t)$ again. The p.d.f. of the coin-tossing example in (2.3) provides one such illustration, being symmetric around $c = 0$. Notice in this example that (2.7) becomes $F_x(-t) + F_x(t^-) = 1$ and is satisfied for all t, whereas $F_x(-t) + F_x(t) = \frac{3}{2} \neq 1$ for $t = 1$; hence the importance of t^- in definition (2.7). In Exercise 2.7, we will show that symmetry means that the two different variates $x - c$ and $c - x$ have the same distribution.

Second, the α *quantile* of x is the smallest $q \in \mathcal{X}$ satisfying $F_x(q) \geqslant \alpha$, where α is some constant number $\alpha \in (0, 1)$ often expressed as a percentage, such as 10%. We sometimes denote the quantile by q_α when we wish to stress its connection to α. Continuous variates have c.d.f.s that contain no jumps in their plots, so the definition simplifies to finding the smallest $q \in \mathcal{X}$ satisfying $F_x(q) = \alpha$; for example, draw the horizontal line $F_x(u) = \alpha$ for any numerical value of α in Figure 2.2, and it will intersect the c.d.f. at q_α. If F is strictly increasing, as in this example, the quantile is just obtained by calculating the inverse function $q = F_x^{-1}(\alpha)$; flip Figure 2.2 to visualize q as a function of α (a convex F^{-1} in this case) and you get

$$\alpha = F_x(q) = 1 - \mathrm{e}^{-q} \implies q = -\log(1 - \alpha).$$

More generally, the smallest $q \in \mathcal{X}$ satisfying $F_x(q) \geqslant \alpha$ leads to the *quantile function* $q = Q_x(\alpha)$ as α varies. Clearly, since F is nondecreasing and continuous to the right, the "inverse" function Q will also be nondecreasing and continuous to the right. The extremities of the p.d.f. are called the *tails*, the upper tail (or right tail) of the density being the part corresponding to large upper values of u. Quantiles help us to assess the spread of these tails; for example, the 90% quantile of a continuous distribution satisfies $\Pr(x \leqslant q) = 0.9$, and a relatively "large" q here indicates a long upper tail of the density, while a substantial negative number for the 10% quantile indicates a long lower tail. (Illustrations will be seen in Exercise 4.14 below, especially in Figure 4.3.) Furthermore, the special case of $\alpha = 50\%$ gives rise to a solution q that is called the *median* and denoted by $q_{1/2}$ or $\operatorname{med}(x)$. The median is one indication of the center of the distribution of x, since there is about a 50% chance of realizations of x exceeding the median value.

Third, the *mode* of a distribution is the value $u_{\mathrm{M}} \in \mathcal{X}$ such that $f_x(u_{\mathrm{M}}) > f_x(u)$ for $u \in \mathcal{X}$ and in the neighborhood of u_{M}. Unlike the quantiles, the mode need not be unique, in which case one calls the corresponding distribution *multimodal*. More specifically, it is *bimodal* in the case of two modes, and so on. Also, the mode may not exist, for example, if all values of $x \in \mathcal{X}$ are equally probable.

We have encountered the basic decomposition of a c.d.f. in terms of a convex combination of c.d.f.s of different types. We now turn to the representation of a c.d.f. as a combination of c.d.f.s of the same type. Let x be a variate whose distribution depends on a changing parameter $\vartheta \in \Theta \subseteq \mathbb{R}$. For any given value θ of ϑ, we denote the density of x by $h(u \mid \theta)$ and its distribution by $H(u \mid \theta)$, the latter being shorthand for $\Pr(x \leqslant u \mid \vartheta = \theta)$ and sometimes also written as $H(u; \theta)$. Suppose that ϑ can be varied within Θ according to its own density $g(\theta)$ and distribution $G(\theta)$. Then, the mixed p.d.f. of x when ϑ varies discretely is

$$f_x(u) = \sum_{\theta \in \Theta} h(u \mid \theta) g(\theta)$$

and, when ϑ is continuous,

$$f_x(u) = \int_{\theta \in \Theta} h(u \mid \theta) g(\theta) \, d\theta;$$

both of these are subsumed by the Stieltjes integral

$$f_x(u) = \int_{-\infty}^{\infty} h(u \mid \theta) \, dG(\theta). \tag{2.8}$$

By Stieltjes-integrating both sides with respect to u, we obtain the mixed c.d.f.

$$F_x(u) = \int_{-\infty}^{\infty} H(u \mid \theta) \, dG(\theta). \tag{2.9}$$

We say that G is the *mixing distribution*, and F is the *G-mixture of H* (or just *mixed-H*). The reader may wish to investigate the analogy of mixing with Exercise 1.6; see also the discussion following (1.4) about conditional and unconditional probabilities. Notice that, in general, the functional forms F and H will differ from one another, but are of the same type (for example, continuous or discrete) regardless of the type of G.

The following exercises start by looking at the conditions for functions to be proper distribution or density functions, the relation between the two, and their properties. We then consider distributions of a variate constructed from another one, illustrating how some of them arise from random experiments; this topic will be revisited more extensively in Chapters 4 and 7, and will be used later. We finish by looking at some special distribution functions and their mixtures.

2.1 Distributions, densities, quantiles, and modes

Exercise 2.1 (To be or not to be?) Determine whether each of the following functions could be a c.d.f. over the domain indicated and, if so, find its Jordan decomposition as well as $\Pr(x = 0)$ and $\Pr(x = 1)$:
(a) $F(u) = e^{-u}$ $(0 \leqslant u < \infty)$;
(b) $F(u) = e^{u}$ $(-\infty < u \leqslant 0)$;
(c) $F(u) = 1 - e^{-u}$ $(-1 \leqslant u < \infty)$;

$$\text{(d) } F(u) = \begin{cases} 0.25e^{u} & (-\infty < u < 0), \\ 0.5 & (0 \leqslant u < 1), \\ 1 - e^{-u} & (1 \leqslant u < \infty). \end{cases}$$

Solution
(a) No; $F(u)$ is strictly decreasing, starting at 1 and declining to 0.

(b) Yes, because (i) $\lim_{u\to-\infty} F(u) = 0$, (ii) $\lim_{u\to\infty} F(u) = F(0) = 1$, (iii) $F(u)$ is a continuous function, and (iv) $F(s) < F(t)$ whenever $s < t$. The variate is continuous, so $\Pr(x = 0) = \Pr(x = 1) = 0$.
(c) No, because $F(u) < 0$ for $-1 \leqslant u < 0$.
(d) Yes, because (i) $\lim_{u\to-\infty} F(u) = 0$, (ii) $\lim_{u\to\infty} F(u) = 1$, (iii) $F(u)$ is a continuous function except at $u = 0$ and $u = 1$, where it is right-continuous, and (iv) $F(s) < F(t)$ whenever $s < t$. We have $\Pr(x = 0) = F(0) - F(0^-) = 0.5 - 0.25 = 0.25$, and $\Pr(x = 1) = F(1) - F(1^-) = 1 - \mathrm{e}^{-1} - 0.5 = 0.5 - \mathrm{e}^{-1}$. This c.d.f. decomposes into $F(u) = pF_{\mathrm{d}}(u) + (1-p)F_{\mathrm{c}}(u)$, where $p = \Pr(x = 1)$ and

$$F_{\mathrm{d}}(u) = \begin{cases} 0 & (-\infty < u < 0), \\ 0.25p^{-1} & (0 \leqslant u < 1), \\ 1 & (1 \leqslant u < \infty), \end{cases} \qquad F_{\mathrm{c}}(u) = \begin{cases} 0.25(1-p)^{-1}\mathrm{e}^{u} & (-\infty < u < 0), \\ 0.25(1-p)^{-1} & (0 \leqslant u < 1), \\ 1 - (1-p)^{-1}\mathrm{e}^{-u} & (1 \leqslant u < \infty), \end{cases}$$

the first component containing the two jumps of $F(u)$ while the second is continuous at those two points (and elsewhere).

Exercise 2.2 (Proper density functions: discrete) For each of the following functions $f(u)$ defined on $u \in \mathbb{N}$, find the value of c for which $f(u)$ is a p.d.f.:
(a) $f(u) = c2^u/u!$;
(b) $f(u) = cp^u$ $(0 < p < 1)$;
(c) $f(u) = c/(u(u+1))$;
(d) $f(u) = cp^u/u$ $(0 < p < 1)$.

Solution
Property (ii) of p.d.f.s, given in the introduction to this chapter, is needed only to link f to F. It is not needed to verify that some function is a proper density. Therefore, it remains to verify that $f(u) \geqslant 0$ for all u and that $\sum_{u=1}^{\infty} f(u) = 1$. Hence, we need $c > 0$ in all four cases. Further,
(a) $\sum_{u=1}^{\infty} 2^u/u! = \sum_{u=0}^{\infty} 2^u/u! - 1 = \mathrm{e}^2 - 1$ and hence $c = 1/(\mathrm{e}^2 - 1)$;
(b) $\sum_{u=1}^{\infty} p^u = p/(1-p)$, so that $c = (1-p)/p$;
(c) $\sum_{u=1}^{n} 1/(u(u+1)) = \sum_{u=1}^{n} (1/u - 1/(u+1)) = 1 - 1/(n+1) \to 1$ as $n \to \infty$, implying $c = 1$;
(d) $\sum_{u=1}^{\infty} p^u/u = \sum_{u=1}^{\infty} \int_0^p t^{u-1}\,\mathrm{d}t = \int_0^p \sum_{u=1}^{\infty} t^{u-1}\,\mathrm{d}t = \int_0^p 1/(1-t)\,\mathrm{d}t = -\log(1-p)$ and hence $c = -1/\log(1-p)$. The interchange of integral and sum is allowed because the sum is absolutely convergent for $p \in (0,1)$; see Section A.3. Note that this is a derivation of the series expansion of $\log(1-p)$, and that the series is valid more generally for $p \in (-1,1)$. When $p = -1$, the series representation is valid but is only conditionally convergent.

Exercise 2.3 (Proper density functions: continuous) For each of the following functions $f(u)$ defined on $u \in \mathbb{R}_+$, find the value of c for which $f(u)$ is a p.d.f.:

(a) $f(u) = cu^3 e^{-\lambda u}$;
(b) $f(u) = cu^{p-1} e^{-(\lambda u)^p}$;
where λ and p are both positive parameters.

Solution

(a) Using the transformation $v = \lambda u$, we have $\mathrm{d}v = \lambda\,\mathrm{d}u$ and

$$\int_0^\infty u^3 e^{-\lambda u}\,\mathrm{d}u = \frac{1}{\lambda^4}\int_0^\infty v^3 e^{-v}\,\mathrm{d}v = \frac{\Gamma(4)}{\lambda^4},$$

where we have used the definition of the gamma function given in Chapter 1. Hence, $c = \lambda^4/\Gamma(4) = \lambda^4/6 > 0$.
(b) We first calculate the c.d.f. $F(u)$. Let $h(u) := (\lambda u)^p$ and apply the transformation $v = (\lambda t)^p$, with $\mathrm{d}v = p\lambda^p t^{p-1}\,\mathrm{d}t$. Then

$$F(u) = c\int_0^u t^{p-1} e^{-(\lambda t)^p}\,\mathrm{d}t = \frac{c}{p\lambda^p}\int_0^{h(u)} e^{-v}\,\mathrm{d}v$$
$$= \frac{c}{p\lambda^p}\left[-e^{-v}\right]_0^{h(u)} = \frac{1-e^{-h(u)}}{p\lambda^p}c.$$

Since $h(u) \to \infty$ as $u \to \infty$, we must take $c = p\lambda^p$, so that $F(u) = 1 - e^{-h(u)}$.

Exercise 2.4 (Bounded p.d.f.) Let x be a positive continuous random variable with p.d.f. $f(u)$. If $f(u) \leqslant c$ for all $u > 0$, show that $\Pr(x \geqslant a) \geqslant 1 - ac$ for $a > 0$.

Solution

By definition,

$$1 = \int_0^\infty f(u)\,\mathrm{d}u$$
$$= \int_0^a f(u)\,\mathrm{d}u + \int_a^\infty f(u)\,\mathrm{d}u$$
$$\leqslant \int_0^a c\,\mathrm{d}u + \int_a^\infty f(u)\,\mathrm{d}u = ac + \Pr(x \geqslant a).$$

Hence, $\Pr(x \geqslant a) \geqslant 1 - ac$.

Exercise 2.5 (From c.d.f. to p.d.f. and quantiles) A continuous random variable x has the c.d.f.

$$F(u) = \begin{cases} 0 & (u < 1), \\ c(u - 2 + 1/u) & (1 \leqslant u < 2), \\ 1 & (u \geqslant 2). \end{cases}$$

(a) Compute c.
(b) What is the p.d.f. of x?

(c) Calculate the quantiles of x.

Solution

(a) Since $F(u)$ is continuous, we must have $F(1) = 0$ and $F(2) = 1$. The first condition is satisfied for any c, while the second implies that $c = 2$. Note, however, that if the continuity assumption were not made, then any choice of c such that $0 \leqslant c \leqslant 2$ would ensure that $F(u)$ is a distribution function.

(b) The p.d.f. $f(u)$ is obtained by differentiating $F(u)$. This gives $f(u) = 2(1 - 1/u^2)$ for $u \in (1, 2)$, and 0 for $u \notin (1, 2]$. Notice that the derivative does not exist at $u = 2$, its value being $3/2$ from the left but 0 from the right. As mentioned at the beginning of this chapter, we can define $f(2)$ to be any value satisfying the integral equation $\int_{-\infty}^{u} f(t)\, dt = F(u)$, which leaves open an infinite number of possible choices. For the sake of not introducing another discontinuity into $f(u)$, either $3/2$ or 0 will do. By convention, we define nonzero values of $f(u)$ only over open intervals, so we take the latter value of 0 for $f(2)$.

(c) We must solve $2(q - 2 + 1/q) = \alpha \in (0, 1)$ for $q \in (1, 2)$, which leads to the quadratic equation $2q^2 - (4 + \alpha)q + 2 = 0$. There are two solutions, but only one in the interval $q \in (1, 2)$ and increasing in α, namely the quantile function $q = \beta + \sqrt{\beta^2 - 1}$ where $\beta := 1 + \alpha/4$.

Exercise 2.6 (Symmetry and medians) Prove that any variate x, continuous or otherwise, satisfying $F_x(c + t^-) + F_x(c - t) = 1$ for all $t \in \mathbb{R}$, must have c as its median if $c \in \mathcal{X}$. Clarify the role of the condition $c \in \mathcal{X}$.

Solution

The variate x is by definition symmetrically distributed. Letting $t = 0$ in the condition for symmetry gives $F_x(c) = 1 - F_x(c^-)$. Substituting for F on the two sides by means of $F_x(c) = \Pr(x \leqslant c)$ and

$$1 - F_x(c^-) \equiv 1 - \Pr(x < c) = 1 - \Pr(x \leqslant c) + \Pr(x = c),$$

we get that the symmetry implies

$$\Pr(x \leqslant c) = \frac{1}{2} + \frac{1}{2} \Pr(x = c).$$

If $\Pr(x = c) = 0$, then $\Pr(x \leqslant c) = \frac{1}{2}$; and if $\Pr(x = c) > 0$, then $\Pr(x \leqslant c) > \frac{1}{2}$ but

$$\Pr(x < c) = \Pr(x \leqslant c) - \Pr(x = c) = \frac{1}{2} - \frac{1}{2} \Pr(x = c) < \frac{1}{2}.$$

Therefore, c is the smallest value satisfying $F_x(c) \geqslant \frac{1}{2}$, which is the definition of c as the median *if* c is part of the support of the distribution. There are instances of densities that are symmetric around a point which is not part of the support. For example, the coin-tossing example of the introduction to this chapter gives $\Pr(x = -1) = \Pr(x = +1) = \frac{1}{2}$ and hence a median of -1, although x is symmetric around $c = 0$. Notice also that, in this example, the median of $-x$ is also -1 and not 1, so

$$\operatorname{med}(-x) \neq -\operatorname{med}(x)$$

in general.

Exercise 2.7 (Symmetry and reflection) Let x be a variate with c.d.f. satisfying $F_x(c+t^-) + F_x(c-t) = 1$ for all $t \in \mathbb{R}$. Prove that $x - c$ and $c - x$ have the same distribution.

Solution
The c.d.f. of $x - c$ is

$$F_{x-c}(u) \equiv \Pr(x - c \leqslant u) = \Pr(x \leqslant c + u) \equiv F_x(c+u).$$

The c.d.f. of $c - x$ is

$$\begin{aligned} F_{c-x}(u) &\equiv \Pr(c - x \leqslant u) = \Pr(x \geqslant c - u) \\ &= 1 - \Pr(x < c - u) \equiv 1 - F_x\left((c-u)^-\right). \end{aligned}$$

Using $F_x((c+t)^-) = F_x(c+t^-) = 1 - F_x(c-t)$ where the last equality follows by symmetry, we get $F_{c-x}(u) = F_x(c+u)$. This is equal to $F_{x-c}(u)$ which was derived earlier, thus the two different variates $x - c$ and $c - x$ have the same distribution.

Exercise 2.8 (Mode: discrete) Calculate the modes of the densities in Exercise 2.2.

Solution
Consider the difference $D := \log(f(u+1)) - \log(f(u)) = \log(f(u+1)/f(u))$ or the ratio $R := f(u+1)/f(u)$ for $u \in \mathbb{N}$. Then:
(a) $R = 2/(u+1)$, which is 1 for $u = 1$, and < 1 otherwise. This implies that the density has $f(1) = f(2)$ and is monotonically decreasing thereafter. The density is therefore bimodal, with modes at $u = 1$ and $u = 2$.
(b) $R = p < 1$ for all $u \in \mathbb{N}$. The density is therefore monotonically decreasing from its mode at $u = 1$.
(c) $R = u/(u+2) < 1$, so the mode is at $u = 1$ in this case too.
(d) $R = pu/(u+1) < 1$, and again the mode is at $u = 1$.
The reader may wish to redo the exercise in terms of D, and see that the solutions are identical because $D = \log(R)$ is a monotonically increasing transformation. Notice that, in all cases, the scaling constant c plays no role in deciding the mode.

Exercise 2.9 (Mode: continuous) Calculate the modes of the densities in Exercise 2.3.

Solution
In contrast with Exercise 2.8, it is simpler to maximize $\log(f(u))$ rather than $f(u)$, although the solutions are identical. The reader may verify this by maximizing $f(u)$ instead

of $\log(f(u))$ and noticing, once more, that the scaling constant c will play no role. Here, differentiate $\log(f(u))$ and solve for $D := \mathrm{d}\log(f(u))/\mathrm{d}u = 0$, then check the second-order condition $D_2 := \mathrm{d}^2\log(f(u))/\mathrm{d}u^2 < 0$ for a maximum:
(a) $\log(f(u)) = \log(c) + 3\log(u) - \lambda u$ gives $D = 3/u - \lambda$ and $D_2 = -3/u^2 < 0$, so that $u = 3/\lambda$ is the mode.
(b) $\log(f(u)) = \log(c) + (p-1)\log(u) - (\lambda u)^p$ gives $D = (p-1)/u - p(\lambda u)^p/u$ and $D_2 = -(p-1)/u^2 - p(p-1)(\lambda u)^p/u^2$. The mode is $u = \lambda^{-1}(1-1/p)^{1/p}$ when the second-order condition is satisfied, namely, when $p - 1 > 0$. Otherwise, the mode is at $u = 0^+$ and the density is monotonically decreasing as u increases. Notice that this latter mode is at the edge of the support of the continuous variate x which is strictly positive.

2.2 Distribution of a variate constructed from another variate

Exercise 2.10 (Nonlinear transformation and randomness) Suppose that a random variable x can take the values -1 or $+1$ with equal probability. Derive the p.d.f.s of $z_1 := |x|$, $z_2 := x^2$, and $z_3 := |x-1|$.

Solution
$\Pr(z_1 = 1) = \Pr(x = -1 \text{ or } x = 1) = \Pr(x = -1) + \Pr(x = 1) = 1$, and $z_1 \neq 1$ gives a p.d.f. of 0. The p.d.f. is the same for z_2. Even though x is random, both z_1 and z_2 take the value 1 with probability 1. For z_3, we have $\Pr(z_3 = 2) = \Pr(z_3 = 0) = \frac{1}{2}$, and 0 otherwise.

***Exercise 2.11 (Maximum and minimum)** A box contains n pieces of paper numbered from 1 to n. Of these l are drawn at random and with replacement. Let x be the largest number drawn and y the smallest. Find:
(a) $F_x(u)$ and $f_x(u)$;
(b) $F_y(v)$ and $f_y(v)$.

Solution
(a) Let $x_1, \dots, x_l$ be the sample drawn. Then, first assuming that u is an integer in the interval $1 \leqslant u \leqslant n$,

$$\begin{aligned} F_x(u) &= \Pr(x \leqslant u) \\ &= \Pr(\text{all } l \text{ pieces drawn have a number} \leqslant u) \\ &= \Pr(x_1 \leqslant u, \dots, x_l \leqslant u) \\ &= \Pr(x_1 \leqslant u) \cdots \Pr(x_l \leqslant u) = (u/n)^l; \end{aligned}$$

an idea also used in Exercise 1.18(b). Let $\lfloor u \rfloor$ denotes the largest integer $\leqslant u$. Then, in general, $F_x(u) = 0$ for $u < 1$, $F_x(u) = 1$ for $u > n$, and $F_x(u) = (\lfloor u \rfloor/n)^l$ for $1 \leqslant u \leqslant n$ since x never takes noninteger values. It then follows that

$$f_x(u) = F_x(u) - F_x(u^-) = (u/n)^l - ((u-1)/n)^l$$

for $u = 1, \dots, n$, and is 0 otherwise.
(b) Similarly, for integer values of v,

$$\begin{aligned} F_y(v) &= \Pr(y \leqslant v) = 1 - \Pr(y > v) \\ &= 1 - \Pr(\text{all } l \text{ pieces drawn have a number} > v) \\ &= 1 - ((n-v)/n)^l, \end{aligned}$$

so that $F_y(v) = 1 - ((n - \lfloor v \rfloor)/n)^l$ for $1 \leqslant v \leqslant n$ in general (note that $n - \lfloor v \rfloor \neq \lfloor n - v \rfloor$), $F_y(v) = 0$ for $v < 1$, and $F_y(v) = 1$ for $v > n$. Hence,

$$f_y(v) = ((n - v + 1)/n)^l - ((n-v)/n)^l$$

for $v = 1, \dots, n$, and is 0 otherwise.

Exercise 2.12 (Maximum and minimum, continued) Now suppose that the pieces of paper are drawn without replacement and answer the same questions for $l \in \{1, \dots, n\}$.

Solution
(a) If u is an integer and $l \leqslant u$, we obtain

$$\begin{aligned} F_x(u) &= \Pr(x \leqslant u) \\ &= \Pr(\text{all } l \text{ pieces drawn have a number} \leqslant u) \\ &= \Pr(l \text{ drawn from the numbers } 1, \dots, u) = \binom{u}{l} \Big/ \binom{n}{l}. \end{aligned}$$

For $l > u$, we have that u cannot be the largest number and $F_x(u) = 0$. In general,

$$F_x(u) = \begin{cases} 0 & (u < l), \\ \binom{\lfloor u \rfloor}{l}/\binom{n}{l} & (l \leqslant u < n), \\ 1 & (u \geqslant n), \end{cases}$$

and

$$f_x(u) = \begin{cases} \left(\binom{u}{l} - \binom{u-1}{l}\right)/\binom{n}{l} & (u = 1, \dots, n), \\ 0 & (\text{elsewhere}). \end{cases}$$

(b) For v integer,

$$\begin{aligned} F_y(v) &= 1 - \Pr(y > v) \\ &= 1 - \Pr(l \text{ drawn from the numbers } v+1, \dots, n) = 1 - \binom{n-v}{l} \Big/ \binom{n}{l} \end{aligned}$$

if $l \leqslant n - v$, and $F_y(v) = 1$ if $l > n - v$. Hence, in general,

$$F_y(v) = \begin{cases} 0 & (v < 0), \\ 1 - \binom{n-\lfloor v \rfloor}{l} / \binom{n}{l} & (0 \leqslant v < n - l + 1), \\ 1 & (v \geqslant n - l + 1), \end{cases}$$

and

$$f_y(v) = \begin{cases} \left(\binom{n-v+1}{l} - \binom{n-v}{l}\right) / \binom{n}{l} & (v = 1, \dots, n), \\ 0 & \text{(elsewhere)}. \end{cases}$$

Exercise 2.13 (Boxing difference) The box of Exercise 2.11 again contains n pieces of paper numbered from 1 to n. Two pieces are drawn with replacement. Let x be the difference between the two numbers on the pieces. Give the p.d.f. of x.

Solution

Let x_1 denote the first number drawn from the box and x_2 the second. Then $x = x_1 - x_2$. For $0 \leqslant u \leqslant n - 1$, we find

$$\Pr(x = u) = \sum_{i=1}^{n-u} \Pr(x_1 = i + u, x_2 = i) = \frac{n-u}{n^2},$$

where there are $n - u$ equally probable events out of n^2 possibilities. The summation limits are given by the two relations $1 \leqslant i + u \leqslant n$ and $1 \leqslant i \leqslant n$, which reduce to $1 \leqslant i \leqslant n - u$ since we have assumed that $u \geqslant 0$.

Given the symmetry of the problem we also have, for $0 \leqslant u \leqslant n - 1$, $\Pr(x = -u) = (n - u)/n^2$ and hence in general, $\Pr(x = u) = (n - |u|)/n^2$.

***Exercise 2.14 (Seven-faced die)** We wish to construct a seven-faced die. We have one fair (six-faced) die and one fair coin with 1 on one side and 0 on the other. We roll the die and toss the coin once. Let x be the sum of the two numbers that come up; so x can take the values $1, 2, \dots, 7$ and can be thought of as a seven-faced die.

(a) Is the seven-faced die fair? [Hint: Obtain the p.d.f. of x.]

(b) Give the c.d.f. of x.

(c) Find $\Pr(x > 3)$.

(d) We now construct a new "coin" by letting $y = 0$ if x is even and $y = 1$ if x is odd. Is the new "coin" fair?

Solution

(a) Let x_1 denote the outcome of the die and x_2 the outcome of the coin, so that $x = x_1 + x_2$. There are $6 \times 2 = 12$ equally probable pairs (x_1, x_2). The events $x = 1$ and $x = 7$ can only be obtained in one way, while the other events can all be obtained in two ways. Hence, $\Pr(x = u) = 1/12$ for $u = 1$ or $u = 7$, and $\Pr(x = u) = 1/6$ for $2 \leqslant u \leqslant 6$. The seven-faced die is therefore not fair.

(b) We find the c.d.f. $F(u)$ from the p.d.f. $f(u)$ by using $F(u) = \Pr(x \leqslant u) = \sum_{i=1}^{\lfloor u \rfloor} f(i)$. Hence, $F(u) = 0$ for $u < 1$,

$$F(u) = \frac{1}{12} + \sum_{i=2}^{j} \frac{1}{6} = \frac{2j-1}{12}$$

for $j \leqslant u < j+1$ with $j = 1, \dots, 6$ (an alternative to using integer values of u), and $F(u) = 1$ for $u \geqslant 7$.
(c) $\Pr(x > 3) = 1 - F(3) = 1 - 5/12 = 7/12$.
(d) $\Pr(x \text{ odd}) = \Pr(x = 1 \text{ or } x = 3 \text{ or } x = 5 \text{ or } x = 7) = (1+2+2+1)/12 = 1/2$. Hence, the new "coin" is fair.

Exercise 2.15 (Seven-faced die, continued) Now assume that the coin in Exercise 2.14 is not fair, and answer the same questions.

Solution
Let $p := \Pr(x_2 = 1)$ and $q := \Pr(x_2 = 0) = 1 - p$.
(a) $\Pr(x = 1) = q/6$, $\Pr(x = 7) = p/6$, and, for $2 \leqslant u \leqslant 6$,

$$\Pr(x = u) = \Pr(x_1 = u, x_2 = 0) + \Pr(x_1 = u - 1, x_2 = 1) = (q + p)/6 = 1/6.$$

The seven-faced die is still not fair.
(b) $F(u) = 0$ for $u < 1$, $F(u) = (j - p)/6$ for $j \leqslant u < j+1$ $(j = 1, \dots, 6)$, and $F(u) = 1$ for $u \geqslant 7$.
(c) $\Pr(x > 3) = 1 - f(1) - f(2) - f(3) = 1 - q/6 - 2/6 = (4 - q)/6$.
(d) $\Pr(x \text{ odd}) = \Pr(x = 1 \text{ or } x = 3 \text{ or } x = 5 \text{ or } x = 7) = (q+1+1+p)/6 = 1/2$, hence the new "coin" is fair even when the original coin is not.

Exercise 2.16 (Change this uniform!) A continuous random variable x has p.d.f. $f_x(u) = \frac{1}{2}$ for $|u| < 1$ and 0 elsewhere. Obtain:
(a) the c.d.f. of x;
(b) the p.d.f. of $y := x^2$;
(c) the c.d.f. and p.d.f. of $z := |x|$.

Solution
(a) $F_x(u) = 0$ for $u < -1$. For $-1 \leqslant u < 1$, we find that

$$F_x(u) = \int_{-1}^{u} \frac{1}{2} \, \mathrm{d}t = \frac{u+1}{2},$$

and for $u \geqslant 1$, we have $F_x(u) = 1$.

(b) For $0 < v < 1$, we find that

$$\begin{aligned} F_y(v) &= \Pr(y \leqslant v) = \Pr\left(x^2 \leqslant v\right) \\ &= \Pr\left(-\sqrt{v} \leqslant x \leqslant \sqrt{v}\right) \\ &= \Pr\left(-\sqrt{v} < x \leqslant \sqrt{v}\right), \end{aligned}$$

the last step following by continuity of the variate y. The last expression is the difference

$$\begin{aligned} F_y(v) &= \Pr\left(x \leqslant \sqrt{v}\right) - \Pr\left(x \leqslant -\sqrt{v}\right) \\ &= F_x(\sqrt{v}) - F_x(-\sqrt{v}) \\ &= \frac{(\sqrt{v}+1) - (-\sqrt{v}+1)}{2} = \sqrt{v} \end{aligned}$$

from (a). Hence, the p.d.f. of v is $f_y(v) = 1/(2\sqrt{v})$ for $0 < v < 1$ and 0 elsewhere.
(c) Similarly, for $0 \leqslant w < 1$,

$$\begin{aligned} F_z(w) &= \Pr(z \leqslant w) = \Pr(|x| \leqslant w) \\ &= \Pr(-w \leqslant x \leqslant w) \\ &= \Pr(-w < x \leqslant w) = F_x(w) - F_x(-w) = w. \end{aligned}$$

Of course, $F_z(w) = 0$ for $w < 0$ and $F_z(w) = 1$ for $w \geqslant 1$. The p.d.f. is then $f_z(w) = 1$ for $0 < w < 1$ and 0 elsewhere.

Exercise 2.17 (Laplace p.d.f.) The continuous random variable x has p.d.f. $f_x(u) = \frac{1}{2}\mathrm{e}^{-|u|}$ for $u \in \mathbb{R}$. Obtain:
(a) the c.d.f. of x;
(b) the p.d.f. of $y := x^2$;
(c) the p.d.f. of $z := |x|$.

Solution
(a) We separate the cases $u \leqslant 0$ and $u > 0$. For $u \leqslant 0$ we have

$$F_x(u) = \int_{-\infty}^{u} \frac{1}{2}\mathrm{e}^{-|t|}\,\mathrm{d}t = \int_{-\infty}^{u} \frac{1}{2}\mathrm{e}^{t}\,\mathrm{d}t = \frac{1}{2}\mathrm{e}^{u}$$

and, for $u > 0$,

$$F_x(u) = \int_{-\infty}^{u} \frac{1}{2}\mathrm{e}^{-|t|}\,\mathrm{d}t = \frac{1}{2} + \int_{0}^{u} \frac{1}{2}\mathrm{e}^{-t}\,\mathrm{d}t = 1 - \frac{1}{2}\mathrm{e}^{-u}.$$

Notice that the variate is symmetric around the origin, so that $F_x(u) + F_x(-u) = 1$ for $u \in \mathbb{R}$.
(b) We find, for $v \geqslant 0$,

$$\begin{aligned} F_y(v) &= \Pr\left(-\sqrt{v} \leqslant x \leqslant \sqrt{v}\right) \\ &= \Pr\left(-\sqrt{v} < x \leqslant \sqrt{v}\right) = F_x(\sqrt{v}) - F_x(-\sqrt{v}) = 1 - \mathrm{e}^{-\sqrt{v}} \end{aligned}$$

and, for $v < 0$, $F_y(v) = 0$. The p.d.f. is therefore given by $f_y(v) = \mathrm{e}^{-\sqrt{v}}/(2\sqrt{v})$ for $v > 0$ and 0 otherwise.
(c) Similarly, for $w > 0$,

$$\begin{aligned} F_z(w) &= \Pr(|x| \leqslant w) = \Pr(-w \leqslant x \leqslant w) \\ &= \Pr(-w < x \leqslant w) = F_x(w) - F_x(-w) = 1 - \mathrm{e}^{-w}, \end{aligned}$$

and $F_z(w) = 0$ for $w \leqslant 0$. The p.d.f. is $f_z(w) = \mathrm{e}^{-w}$ for $w > 0$ and 0 elsewhere.

***Exercise 2.18 (Censorship, truncation, and hazard)** The continuous random variable x has p.d.f. $f_x(u) = \frac{1}{2}\mathrm{e}^{-|u|}$ for $u \in \mathbb{R}$.
(a) Give the c.d.f. and p.d.f. of the *left-censored variate* y defined by $y := x$ if $x > 0$ and $y := 0$ otherwise.
(b) Give the c.d.f. and p.d.f. of the *left-truncated variate* z defined by $z := x$ if $x > 0$ and z is unobserved otherwise.
(c) Obtain the density of z given that $z > w_0$.
(d) Evaluating the density in (c) as $z \to w_0^+$ gives the *hazard rate* of z. Show that it is equivalent to $-\mathrm{d}\log(1 - F_z(w_0))/\mathrm{d}w_0$ for any continuous variate, and that it is equal to a constant for the density given in this problem.

Solution
To fix ideas for (a) and (b), one possible example for x is the logarithm of the annual income of an individual. Then, y may be the taxable log(income), assuming incomes below one unit ($\log 1 = 0$) are not taxed, and z may be the log of the income reported to the tax authorities, assuming no reporting is required for incomes below one unit.
(a) We have $y \geqslant 0$, with c.d.f. $F_y(v) = 0$ for $v < 0$ and, for $v \geqslant 0$,

$$F_y(v) = \Pr(y \leqslant v) = \Pr(x \leqslant v) = F_x(v)$$

which we have as $1 - \mathrm{e}^{-v}/2$ from Exercise 2.17(a). The corresponding density is zero for $v < 0$, and $\mathrm{e}^{-v}/2$ for $v > 0$. For $v = 0$, recalling Jordan's decomposition, we get $\Pr(y = 0) = F_y(0) - F_y(0^-) = \frac{1}{2}$. This variate has a discrete component with nontrivial probability at $y = 0$.
(b) The realizations of the variate z occur if and only if $x > 0$, and we therefore have a positive variate whose c.d.f. for $w > 0$ is

$$\begin{aligned} F_z(w) &= \Pr(z \leqslant w) = \Pr(x \leqslant w \mid x > 0) = \frac{\Pr(x \leqslant w, x > 0)}{\Pr(x > 0)} \\ &= \frac{\Pr(x \leqslant w) - \Pr(x \leqslant 0)}{\Pr(x > 0)} = \frac{1 - \frac{1}{2}\mathrm{e}^{-w} - \frac{1}{2}}{\frac{1}{2}} = 1 - \mathrm{e}^{-w}. \end{aligned}$$

Notice that this is the c.d.f. of the variate from the example on radioactive material given in the introduction to this chapter and whose p.d.f. was derived as e^{-w} for $w \in \mathbb{R}_+$.

(c) By a similar argument to (b),

$$\Pr(z \leqslant w \mid z > w_0) = \frac{\Pr(z \leqslant w) - \Pr(z \leqslant w_0)}{1 - \Pr(z \leqslant w_0)} = \frac{F_z(w) - F_z(w_0)}{1 - F_z(w_0)}$$

for $w > w_0$. Substituting for F_z gives $\Pr(z \leqslant w \mid z > w_0) = 1 - \mathrm{e}^{w_0 - w}$. Differentiating with respect to w yields the density of z given that $z > w_0$:

$$\frac{f_z(w)}{1 - F_z(w_0)} = \mathrm{e}^{w_0 - w}.$$

Returning to our radioactivity example, this density indicates the following. Having survived until w_0, the density function of z over the rest of its lifetime is given by $\mathrm{e}^{w_0 - w}$, and it is the same exponential again but shifted by w_0. If a time w_0 has actually been reached with radioactivity still there, the clocks are set back to zero and the new time variable is $z - w_0$ (with realization $w - w_0$), which is not a very hopeful sign. This no-memory property will be revisited in some exercises in Chapter 4, starting with Exercise 4.12.

(d) The hazard rate is the function in (c) evaluated as $z \to w_0$ from above. It is also known as the *age-related failure rate* if the definition of z involves time, as in the previous example, and f_z would be the density of failures over time. Further commonplace examples include the probabilities of: death given that an individual has survived until w_0 (used in calculating life-insurance premia); the breakdown of a new machine given that it has functioned up to time w_0; finding employment given that a person has been unemployed for a period of length w_0; default on some obligation (such as a debt) given that no default has occurred up to time w_0.

The hazard rate is 1 for the variate whose conditional density is given in (c). More generally, hazards may vary with w_0, and we have

$$h(w_0) := \frac{f_z(w_0)}{1 - F_z(w_0)}.$$

Since both numerator and denominator are now functions of the same w_0,

$$h(w_0) = -\frac{\mathrm{d}\log(1 - F_z(w_0))}{\mathrm{d}w_0}$$

by continuity of the variate. This equation is equivalent to

$$1 - F_z(w_0) = \exp\left(-\int_0^{w_0} h(w)\,\mathrm{d}w\right)$$

for $w_0 > 0$. Notice the similarity of this exponential to the formula for continuous discounting by an instantaneous rate $h(w)$, used in economic theory. In statistics, the function $1 - F_z(w_0)$ is called the *survival function* because it gives $\Pr(z > w_0)$, and $h(w_0)$ is the relative (or percentage) change in the survival function as w_0 varies. (Taking logarithms transforms absolute scales into relative scales.)

2.3 Mixing of variates

Exercise 2.19 (Two-headed coin, continued) We consider the same box as in Exercise 1.30, which contains three coins, one of which has a head on both sides. The other two are normal fair coins. A coin is chosen at random and tossed three times. Find:
(a) the p.d.f. of the number of heads x;
(b) the c.d.f. of x.

Solution
(a) Let T be the event that the selected coin is two-headed and T^c the event that the selected coin is normal. Then,

$$\begin{aligned}\Pr(x = u) &= \Pr(x = u \mid T)\Pr(T) + \Pr(x = u \mid T^c)\Pr(T^c) \\ &= \frac{1}{3}\Pr(x = u \mid T) + \frac{2}{3}\Pr(x = u \mid T^c).\end{aligned}$$

Now, $\Pr(x = u \mid T)$ equals 1 for $u = 3$ and 0 otherwise, while $\Pr(x = u \mid T^c)$ equals $1/8$ for $u = 0$ or $u = 3$, and $3/8$ for $u = 1$ or $u = 2$. Hence, $\Pr(x = u)$ takes the values $1/12$, $1/4$, $1/4$, and $5/12$ for $u = 0, 1, 2, 3$, respectively.
(b) The c.d.f. $\Pr(x \leqslant u)$ then takes the values 0 for $u < 0$, $1/12$ for $0 \leqslant u < 1$, $1/3$ for $1 \leqslant u < 2$, $7/12$ for $2 \leqslant u < 3$, and 1 for $u \geqslant 3$.

Exercise 2.20 (Switching variate) Let x and y be two random variables. We toss a coin with $\Pr(\text{head}) = p$. Define a new random variable z such that $z := x$ if a head comes up and $z := y$ otherwise. Give the c.d.f. of z in terms of the c.d.f.s of x and y. If x and y are both continuous, what is the p.d.f. of z? How is the answer affected if x and y are both discrete?

Solution
Let H denote the event that a head comes up and H^c the event that a tail comes up. Then, we have

$$\begin{aligned}\Pr(z \leqslant w) &= \Pr(z \leqslant w \mid H)\Pr(H) + \Pr(z \leqslant w \mid H^c)\Pr(H^c) \\ &= pF_x(w) + (1-p)F_y(w).\end{aligned}$$

By differencing (with respect to w) for discrete z or differentiating for continuous z, the p.d.f. takes the same form, namely $f_z(w) = pf_x(w) + (1-p)f_y(w)$.

Exercise 2.21 (Switching variate, continued) In Exercise 2.20, let the variates be continuous and related by $y = 2c - x$, where $c \in \mathbb{R}$ is a constant. What is the c.d.f. of z? Comment on its functional form when x is symmetric around c.

Solution
The c.d.f. of z is

$$\begin{aligned}\Pr(z \leqslant w) &= p\Pr(x \leqslant w) + (1-p)\Pr(2c - x \leqslant w)\\ &= p\Pr(x \leqslant w) + (1-p)(1 - \Pr(x < 2c - w)).\end{aligned}$$

By continuity,

$$\begin{aligned}\Pr(z \leqslant w) &= p\Pr(x \leqslant w) + (1-p)(1 - \Pr(x \leqslant 2c - w))\\ &= pF_x(w) + (1-p)(1 - F_x(2c - w)).\end{aligned}$$

When x is symmetric around c, we have by definition $1 - F_x(2c - u) = F_x(u)$ for all $u \in \mathbb{R}$, so that the c.d.f. of z becomes $F_x(w)$. In other words, the distributions of x and z become identical. Note, however, that x and z are by no means identical variates. For example, when $c = 0$, the variate z can be chosen to switch from being x to $-x$, at the toss of a coin.

Exercise 2.22 (Symmetrizing a variate, via mixing) In Exercise 2.20, let $p = \frac{1}{2}$ and $y = -x$. What is the p.d.f. of z?

Solution
It is $f_z(w) = \frac{1}{2}(f_x(w) + f_x(-w)) = f_z(-w)$, which means that z is now symmetric regardless of the original p.d.f. of x. This symmetry is around zero, even if x was symmetric around some other point $c \neq 0$; compare with the second part of Exercise 2.21.

Exercise 2.23 (Kernels) Suppose that data x_i, $i = 1, \dots, n$, are obtained by repeated independent observations of a variate with continuous density $f(u)$. A smooth approximation of $f(u)$, say $\widehat{f}(u)$, may be obtained from the data by using a weighting function called a *kernel*; say

$$\widehat{f}(u) := \frac{1}{n\lambda}\sum_{i=1}^{n} K\left(\frac{u - x_i}{\lambda}\right),$$

where $\lambda > 0$ is the *smoothing parameter* and the kernel function K can be chosen as an arbitrary continuous density. Write $\widehat{f}(u)$ as a mixture of densities.

Solution
Define

$$h(u - x_i \mid \lambda) := \frac{1}{\lambda} K\left(\frac{u - x_i}{\lambda}\right), \quad i = 1, \dots, n,$$

where the scaling $1/\lambda$ indicates the concentration of the assigned weighting functions K around the points x_i. To show that $h(u - x_i \mid \lambda)$ is indeed a density function with respect to u, we must show that it is nonnegative everywhere and that it integrates to 1. The first property is established by the positivity of λ and the definition of K as a density function.

The second property is obtained as

$$\int_{-\infty}^{\infty} h(u - x_i \mid \lambda)\,\mathrm{d}u = \int_{-\infty}^{\infty} \frac{1}{\lambda} K\left(\frac{u - x_i}{\lambda}\right) \mathrm{d}u = \int_{-\infty}^{\infty} K(t)\,\mathrm{d}t = 1$$

by the change of variable $t = (u - x_i)/\lambda$ and hence $\mathrm{d}u = \lambda\,\mathrm{d}t$. The quantity $\widehat{f}(u)$ is then the average (mixture) of these $h(u - x_i \mid \lambda)$, with weights $1/n$ each.

Exercise 2.24 (Poisson mixture of exponentials) Let $x \in \mathbb{R}_+$ be a continuous variate with p.d.f. $p\mathrm{e}^{-pu}$, and $p \in \mathbb{N}$ varies according to the discrete density $\mathrm{e}^{-\lambda}\lambda^{p-1}/(p-1)!$, where $\lambda > 0$. Derive the mixed density of x by mixing p.d.f.s, then alternatively by mixing c.d.f.s.

Solution

The mixed variate has its p.d.f. defined over $x \in \mathbb{R}_+$, given by

$$f_x(u) = \sum_{p=1}^{\infty} p\mathrm{e}^{-pu} \frac{\mathrm{e}^{-\lambda}\lambda^{p-1}}{(p-1)!}.$$

To calculate the sum, change the index to $j = p - 1$. Then

$$f_x(u) = \mathrm{e}^{-u-\lambda} \sum_{j=0}^{\infty} (1 + j)\,\mathrm{e}^{-ju} \frac{\lambda^j}{j!} = \mathrm{e}^{-u-\lambda} \sum_{j=0}^{\infty} \frac{(\lambda\mathrm{e}^{-u})^j}{j!} + \mathrm{e}^{-u-\lambda} \sum_{j=1}^{\infty} j \frac{(\lambda\mathrm{e}^{-u})^j}{j!}$$

since the term with $j = 0$ in the second sum is 0. By using a new index $k = j - 1$ in the second sum, we obtain

$$\begin{aligned} f_x(u) &= \mathrm{e}^{-u-\lambda} \exp\left(\lambda\mathrm{e}^{-u}\right) + \lambda\mathrm{e}^{-2u-\lambda} \sum_{k=0}^{\infty} \frac{(\lambda\mathrm{e}^{-u})^k}{k!} \\ &= \mathrm{e}^{-u-\lambda} \exp\left(\lambda\mathrm{e}^{-u}\right) + \lambda\mathrm{e}^{-2u-\lambda} \exp\left(\lambda\mathrm{e}^{-u}\right) \\ &= \left(1 + \lambda\mathrm{e}^{-u}\right) \exp\left(-u - \lambda + \lambda\mathrm{e}^{-u}\right). \end{aligned}$$

The corresponding c.d.f. could have also been obtained by mixing the c.d.f.s $1 - \mathrm{e}^{-pu}$ with respect to p, as follows:

$$\begin{aligned} F_x(u) &= \sum_{p=1}^{\infty} \left(1 - \mathrm{e}^{-pu}\right) \frac{\mathrm{e}^{-\lambda}\lambda^{p-1}}{(p-1)!} = 1 - \sum_{p=1}^{\infty} \mathrm{e}^{-pu} \frac{\mathrm{e}^{-\lambda}\lambda^{p-1}}{(p-1)!} \\ &= 1 - \mathrm{e}^{-u-\lambda} \sum_{j=0}^{\infty} \frac{(\lambda\mathrm{e}^{-u})^j}{j!} = 1 - \exp\left(-u - \lambda + \lambda\mathrm{e}^{-u}\right). \end{aligned}$$

The p.d.f. obtained earlier is just the derivative with respect to u.

Exercise 2.25 (Gamma mixture of Poissons gives Nbin) Let x be a discrete variate defined over the nonnegative integers $0, 1, \ldots$ with p.d.f. $\mathrm{e}^{-p}p^u/u!$, and $p \in \mathbb{R}_+$ varies according to the continuous density $\lambda^\nu p^{\nu-1}\mathrm{e}^{-\lambda p}/\Gamma(\nu)$, where $\nu, \lambda > 0$. Derive the mixed density of x.

Solution

The mixed variate has its p.d.f. defined over $0, 1, \ldots$, given by

$$\begin{aligned}
f_x(u) &= \int_0^\infty \frac{\mathrm{e}^{-p}p^u}{u!}\frac{\lambda^\nu p^{\nu-1}\mathrm{e}^{-\lambda p}}{\Gamma(\nu)}\,\mathrm{d}p \\
&= \frac{\lambda^\nu}{u!\Gamma(\nu)(\lambda+1)^{u+\nu}}\int_0^\infty ((\lambda+1)p)^{u+\nu-1}\mathrm{e}^{-(\lambda+1)p}\,\mathrm{d}((\lambda+1)p) \\
&= \frac{\Gamma(u+\nu)\lambda^\nu}{u!\Gamma(\nu)(\lambda+1)^{u+\nu}} \\
&= \binom{u+\nu-1}{u}\frac{\lambda^\nu}{(\lambda+1)^{u+\nu}} \equiv \binom{u+\nu-1}{u}\beta^\nu(1-\beta)^u
\end{aligned}$$

by a change of variable $q = (\lambda+1)p$ and the definition of the gamma function, with $\beta := \lambda/(\lambda+1) \in (0, 1]$.

Exercise 2.26 (Chi-squared mixture of normals gives Student's t) Let $x \in \mathbb{R}$ be a continuous variate with p.d.f. $\exp\left(-u^2/(2m/p)\right)/\sqrt{2\pi m/p}$, where $m > 0$, and $p \in \mathbb{R}_+$ varies according to the continuous density $(p/2)^{m/2-1}\exp(-p/2)/(2\Gamma(m/2))$. Derive the mixed density of x.

Solution

The density of x is given by

$$\begin{aligned}
&\int_0^\infty \sqrt{\frac{p}{2\pi m}}\exp\left(-\frac{u^2p}{2m}\right)\frac{(p/2)^{m/2-1}}{2\Gamma(m/2)}\exp\left(-\frac{p}{2}\right)\mathrm{d}p \\
&\quad = \frac{1}{\sqrt{\pi m}\Gamma(m/2)}\int_0^\infty \exp\left(-\left(1+\frac{u^2}{m}\right)\frac{p}{2}\right)\left(\frac{p}{2}\right)^{(m-1)/2}\mathrm{d}\left(\frac{p}{2}\right) \\
&\quad = \frac{\Gamma((m+1)/2)}{\sqrt{\pi m}\Gamma(m/2)}\left(1+\frac{u^2}{m}\right)^{-(m+1)/2}
\end{aligned}$$

by a change of variable $q = (1+u^2/m)p/2$ and the definition of the gamma function. Note that the same proof applies if u is replaced by $u-\mu$ throughout, corresponding to a recentering of the variate x around μ instead of 0.

Notes

General references for this chapter are the same as for Chapter 1. Riesz and Sz.-Nagy (1955, pp. 48–49) and Billingsley (1995, pp. 407–409) give a good example of a singular continuous variate. In addition, we recommend the encyclopedic text Kendall and Stuart (1977) in which Stieltjes integrals are used for a unified treatment of discrete and continuous variates. Another possibility would be to use measure theory, but we do not assume knowledge of this topic for our volume. We also recommend the classic text by Rao (1973). The titles of the exercises in this chapter and the next contain names of distributions that will be introduced in detail in Chapter 4.

There is another Jordan decomposition, but in matrix algebra; for example, see Abadir and Magnus (2005). The difference in context from the decomposition seen in this chapter means that confusing the two is unlikely in the scalar case. We therefore do not use further qualifiers to distinguish them.

Exercises 2.1 and 2.5 were adapted from Bain and Engelhardt (1992, pp. 85, 86), and Exercise 2.2 is from Stirzaker (1994, p. 115). More on Exercise 2.23 can be found in Silverman (1986), which provides an excellent introduction to kernels and density estimation. We will explore this topic further in Chapter 13.

3

Expectations and their generating functions

In the previous chapter, we introduced distribution and density functions as two alternative methods to characterize the randomness of variates. In this chapter, we introduce the final method considered in this book, and relate it to the previous two.

The *moments* (or *raw moments*) of a random variable x are given by

$$\mu^{(j)} := \mathrm{E}\left(x^j\right) := \int_{-\infty}^{\infty} u^j \,\mathrm{d}F(u) = \begin{cases} \sum_{u\in\mathcal{X}} u^j f(u) & (x \text{ discrete}), \\ \int_{-\infty}^{\infty} u^j f(u)\,\mathrm{d}u & (x \text{ continuous}), \end{cases}$$

where F and f are the c.d.f. and p.d.f. of x, respectively, and j is the *order* of the moment. As the last equality shows, the j-th moment of x can be interpreted as the *weighted average* of the values that x^j can take, where the *weights* are given by the probability density function of x: a higher weight is assigned to more probable values. The symbol $\mathrm{E}(\cdot)$ represents the *expectation operator*, the random variable x^j is the *argument* of the expectation, and $\mathrm{E}\left(x^j\right)$ is the *expected value* (or *expectation* or *mean*) of x^j. Instead of writing $\mu^{(1)}$, it is typical to write just μ for the mean of x, which is a measure of the location of the center of the distribution of x; the notation $\mu^{(j)}$ indicates the mean of x^j for general j. It is usually assumed that $j \in \mathbb{N}$, but this is not necessary if x is positive with probability 1; see Exercises 3.5, 3.27(c), and 3.30 for illustrations. Sometimes, when we wish to stress that the expectation is taken with respect to the variate x, we use a subscript and write $\mathrm{E}_x(\cdot)$. Similarly, we may denote the mean of x by μ_x if we wish to distinguish it from the mean of another variate.

In an alternative description of the moments, they are calculated after centering the variate x around its mean. This provides the *central moments* of x:

$$\sigma^{(j)} := \mathrm{E}\left((x-\mu)^j\right) = \int_{-\infty}^{\infty} (u-\mu)^j \,\mathrm{d}F(u).$$

Central moments around any point other than μ can be defined similarly, though they are less commonly encountered. For $j = 1$,

$$\sigma^{(1)} = \int_{-\infty}^{\infty} u \, \mathrm{d}F(u) - \mu \int_{-\infty}^{\infty} \mathrm{d}F(u) = \mu - \mu \left[F(u)\right]_{-\infty}^{\infty} = \mu - \mu(1-0) = 0 \quad (3.1)$$

by the definition $\mu := \int_{-\infty}^{\infty} u \, \mathrm{d}F(u)$. Less trivial examples include the following:

- The *variance* of x, denoted by $\mathrm{var}(x)$, is equal to $\sigma^{(2)}$ which is usually written as σ^2 instead.[1] It measures the dispersion of the variate x or, viewed alternatively, the spread of the density of x. Its reciprocal is often called the *precision* of x. Its square root, σ, is known as the *standard deviation* of x and is measured in the same units as x. For example, we can consider incomes x in dollars or cents, in which case σ will also be calculated accordingly in dollars or cents. If we double σ then the *scale* of the variate is doubled, and similarly for multiplication by any factor λ; for example, $\lambda = 100$ in the case of converting from dollars to cents, and the values of x become a hundred times larger (this is a case of *scaling up* by 100). However, $\mathrm{var}(x)$ is location-invariant: shifting the graph of a distribution horizontally does not affect its dispersion or spread; see Exercise 3.15. When $\mu \neq 0$, the *coefficient of variation* σ/μ is a measure of relative variation that is scale-invariant.
- When $\mathrm{var}(x) \neq 0$, the *skewness* of x is $\sigma^{(3)}/\sigma^3$. It measures the excess of positive over negative deviations from μ. It is often said to measure the asymmetry of a density, but see Exercise 3.20. Skewness is invariant to changes in the location and scale of a variate.
- When $\mathrm{var}(x) \neq 0$, the *kurtosis* of x is $\sigma^{(4)}/\sigma^4$. It measures the thickness of the tails relative to the rest of a density. It is invariant to changes of location and scale. *Excess kurtosis* is defined as $\sigma^{(4)}/\sigma^4 - 3$, for a reason that will become apparent in Exercise 4.24 (see also Exercises 3.36 and 3.38 in this chapter).

If a variate is not singular continuous and has $\sigma^2 = 0$, then x has no variation almost surely, and it is therefore given by $x = \mu$ with probability 1. Such a variate is said to be *degenerate*.

There are instances of random variables x where "large" realizations u can arise too often, and the tail of the density does not decline fast enough. In this case, the integrals above can be unbounded and, if so, it is said that the moments do not exist. The condition for the existence of a moment of order j is

$$\int_{-\infty}^{\infty} |u|^j \, \mathrm{d}F(u) < \infty. \quad (3.2)$$

To illustrate why the absolute value of u is needed in (3.2), consider a variate with density

$$f(u) = \frac{1}{\pi(1+u^2)} \quad (u \in \mathbb{R}) \quad (3.3)$$

[1] Be careful that $\sigma^{(j)} = \sigma^j$ only for $j = 0$ or $j = 2$.

which has no moments of any order $j \in \mathbb{N}$ according to (3.2), because $\int_0^\infty u^j f(u)\,\mathrm{d}u = \infty$. If the absolute value were not present in (3.2), we would have the following dilemma:

- if all negative values of the random x are realized first, then $\int_{-\infty}^{\infty} u\,\mathrm{d}F(u) = -\infty$;
- if the realizations occur in the matched pairs $-u, u$, then $\int_{-\infty}^{\infty} u\,\mathrm{d}F(u) = 0$ (called the *Cauchy principal value*);
- if all positive values of x are realized first, then $\int_{-\infty}^{\infty} u\,\mathrm{d}F(u) = \infty$.

In fact, these three cases illustrate that *any* value between $-\infty$ and ∞ can be obtained for $\int_{-\infty}^{\infty} u\,\mathrm{d}F(u)$, which is why we need to have $|u|$ instead of u in the integrand of (3.2).[2] Since random variables do not occur in a predetermined order, an integral $\int_{-\infty}^{\infty} u\,\mathrm{d}F(u)$ that does not converge absolutely cannot have a unique value for a random series of $x = u$ values, and so $\mathrm{E}(x)$ does not exist in this case.

Exercise 3.25 will show that the existence of a moment of order $j+1 \in \mathbb{N}$ implies the existence of the moments of order $1, \dots, j$. Note that the variance did not exist in the case of (3.3), but we can still talk about the scale of this variate; for example, we can still change the scale of x by a factor λ. More details will follow in Exercises 3.15 and 3.16.

Since expectations are defined as integrals, they are *linear operators* possessing the following attractive properties:

$$\mathrm{E}\left(cg(x)\right) = c\,\mathrm{E}\left(g(x)\right), \quad c \neq 0 \text{ and nonrandom,}$$

$$\mathrm{E}\left(g(x) + h(x)\right) = \mathrm{E}\left(g(x)\right) + \mathrm{E}\left(h(x)\right), \quad \text{if the latter expectations exist,} \tag{3.4}$$

where g and h are any two functions. We have excluded $c = 0$ because $\mathrm{E}\left(cg(x)\right) = \mathrm{E}(0) = 0$, but $0 \times \mathrm{E}\left(g(x)\right)$ is not defined if $\mathrm{E}\left(g(x)\right)$ does not exist. Similarly, letting $h(x) := 1 - g(x)$ be a function whose expectation does not exist, $\mathrm{E}\left(g(x) + h(x)\right) = \mathrm{E}(1) = 1$ but $\mathrm{E}\left(g(x)\right) + \mathrm{E}\left(h(x)\right)$ is undefined. Note that (3.1) is now obtained more easily by means of these properties as

$$\mathrm{E}(x - \mu) = \mathrm{E}(x) - \mu = \mu - \mu = 0.$$

Also note that the expectation operator can be interchanged with other linear operators, assuming existence, except when they affect F or the limits of integration in addition to the integrand (see differentiating integrals by Leibniz' rule in Section A.4) or, in the case of limits (see the dominated convergence theorem in Section A.4.3), where some conditions are needed to make the interchange valid.

We now turn to an important result on a class of nonlinear transformations of expectations. *Jensen's inequality* states that if g is a convex function (see Section A.4.4 for a definition), then $g(\mathrm{E}(x)) \leqslant \mathrm{E}\left(g(x)\right)$ provided that both expectations exist. This is illustrated in Figure 3.1 when the variate x can take only one of two values, u_1 or u_2 with probability $\frac{1}{2}$ each, and the curve represents a convex function. The middle of the line

[2]One cannot rearrange terms in conditionally convergent series and integrals without risking a change in the result; see the discussion around (A.1) in Section A.3.2 for an illustration.

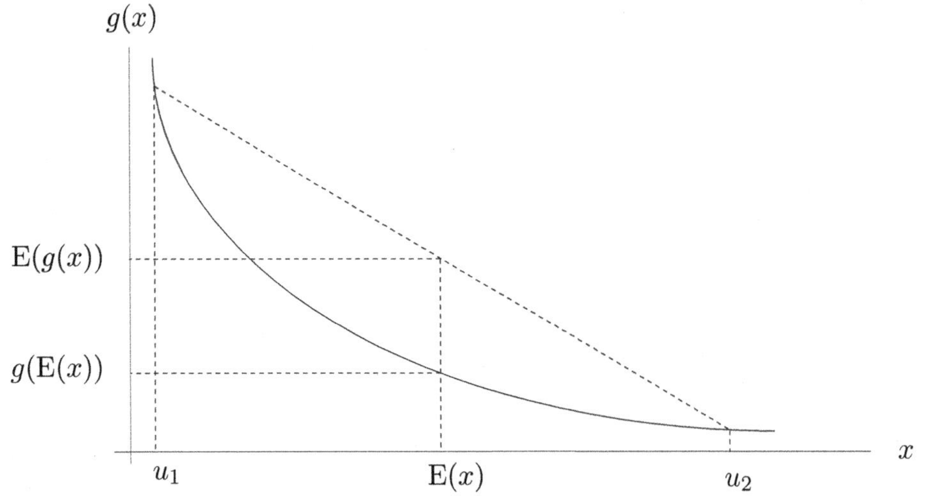

Figure 3.1. Jensen's inequality illustrated for a variate x that can take the values u_1 and u_2 only, with equal probabilities.

joining $g(u_1)$ and $g(u_2)$ is $\mathrm{E}(g(x)) = \frac{1}{2}g(u_1) + \frac{1}{2}g(u_2)$, and it exceeds the value of the function at the point $\mathrm{E}(x)$. Another example is the following. Since the function $g(x) = x^2$ is convex, Jensen's inequality gives $(\mathrm{E}(x))^2 \leqslant \mathrm{E}(x^2)$. This can be deduced by the following alternative route. Since $(x-\mu)^2 \geqslant 0$, its mean is $\mathrm{var}(x) := \mathrm{E}((x-\mu)^2) \geqslant 0$, the latter inequality implying that

$$\begin{aligned} 0 \leqslant \mathrm{E}\left((x-\mu)^2\right) &= \mathrm{E}\left(x^2 - 2\mu x + \mu^2\right) = \mathrm{E}\left(x^2\right) - 2\mu\,\mathrm{E}(x) + \mu^2 \\ &= \mathrm{E}\left(x^2\right) - (\mathrm{E}(x))^2, \end{aligned} \tag{3.5}$$

where the linearity of the expectation operator and the definition $\mu := \mathrm{E}(x)$ have been used in the last two steps, respectively. Inequalities other than Jensen's will be introduced in the exercises of this chapter (they are also contained in the Index under the main entry "inequality").

For any specific c.d.f. F, it can be tedious to have to recalculate the integral defining the moments every time a different j is desired. Furthermore, it would be convenient to summarize all the moments explicitly in a single function. This is the role played by "generating functions" in mathematics. The *moment-generating function* (m.g.f.) of a variate x is

$$m(t) := \mathrm{E}\left(\mathrm{e}^{tx}\right) = \int_{-\infty}^{\infty} \mathrm{e}^{tu}\,\mathrm{d}F(u),$$

where t is nonrandom and is defined to be real-valued and lying in an arbitrarily small open interval around the point $t = 0$, a choice that will be explained before the end of this paragraph. When there is some ambiguity about which variate is in question, we write $m_x(t)$. If the integral is bounded (finite-valued), the m.g.f. is said to exist, and we can integrate termwise the exponential series

$$m(t) \equiv \mathrm{E}\left(\sum_{j=0}^{\infty} \frac{t^j}{j!} x^j\right) = \sum_{j=0}^{\infty} \frac{t^j}{j!} \mathrm{E}\left(x^j\right).$$

We see that the coefficients of $t^j/j!$ are the required raw moments $\mu^{(j)}$. These can be obtained by expanding the function representing a particular $m(t)$, such as $m(t) = 1/(1-t)$, as a power series in t. Alternatively, the moments are obtained by differentiating the m.g.f. j times with respect to t, then setting $t = 0$:

$$m^{(j)}(0) := \left.\frac{\mathrm{d}^j \mathrm{E}\left(\mathrm{e}^{tx}\right)}{\mathrm{d}t^j}\right|_{t=0} = \mathrm{E}\left(x^j \mathrm{e}^{tx}\right)\big|_{t=0} = \mathrm{E}\left(x^j\right) \equiv \mu^{(j)}.$$

The two methods give the same answer.

A transformation of the m.g.f. into $\varkappa(t) := \log(m(t))$ gives the *cumulant-generating function* (c.g.f.) of x, and the value of the derivative $\varkappa^{(j)}(0)$ is called the j-th *cumulant* of x. Another related function, the *factorial-moment-generating function* (f.m.g.f.) of x is defined as

$$\varpi(\tau) := \mathrm{E}\left(\tau^x\right),$$

if the expectation exists. The nonrandom $\tau > 0$ is taken to lie in an arbitrarily small interval containing $\tau = 1$. Notice that

$$m(t) = \mathrm{E}\left(\mathrm{e}^{tx}\right) = \mathrm{E}\left(\left(\mathrm{e}^t\right)^x\right) = \varpi\left(\mathrm{e}^t\right)$$

and that the j-th *factorial moment* of x, defined by $\mathrm{E}\left(x(x-1)\dots(x-j+1)\right)$, is obtained as $\varpi^{(j)}(1)$; see Section A.4.1 for more on this moment. If x is discrete, $\varpi(\tau)$ is also known as the *probability-generating function* (p.g.f.) of x, since we can write in this case

$$\varpi(\tau) = \mathrm{E}\left(\tau^x\right) = \sum_{u \in \mathcal{X}} \Pr(x = u)\, \tau^u$$

and obtain $\Pr(x = u)$ as the coefficient of τ^u. Notice that probabilities themselves can be written in terms of expectations: we have

$$\Pr(A) = \sum_{i=1}^{m} \Pr(A \mid C_i) \Pr(C_i) = \mathrm{E}_C\left(\Pr(A \mid C)\right)$$

in the context of the decomposition following (1.4) (see also Exercise 1.6), and

$$f_x(u) = \mathrm{E}_\vartheta\left(h(u \mid \vartheta)\right) \quad \text{and} \quad F_x(u) = \mathrm{E}_\vartheta\left(H(u \mid \vartheta)\right) \tag{3.6}$$

in the context of mixing that was laid out in (2.8)–(2.9). Also, using the indicator function introduced in Chapter 2, we can write the more direct relation

$$\Pr(A) = \mathrm{E}\left(1_A\right),$$

where A is an event, a formulation that we will use in the proof of Exercise 3.12(a). This can be seen by writing out the integral for $\Pr(A)$ as in that exercise or by writing

$$\mathrm{E}(1_A) = 1 \times \Pr(A) + 0 \times \Pr(A^c) = \Pr(A).$$

We will revisit these ideas and give a more extensive treatment in Chapter 6.

When it exists, the m.g.f. of a variate identifies uniquely the corresponding c.d.f. associated with it. Unfortunately, the density $f(u) = \pi^{-1}(1+u^2)^{-1}$ seen earlier is an example where $\mathrm{E}\left(\mathrm{e}^{tx}\right)$ does not exist. The culprit term, e^{tx}, can become unbounded often enough to make the integral infinite. To solve this problem, define the *characteristic function* (c.f.) of x as

$$\varphi(\tau) := \mathrm{E}\left(\mathrm{e}^{\mathrm{i}\tau x}\right), \tag{3.7}$$

where $\mathrm{i} = \sqrt{-1}$ is the imaginary unit (see Section A.2) and $\tau \in \mathbb{R}$. Such a function will always exist because

$$\mathrm{e}^{\mathrm{i}\tau x} = \cos(\tau x) + \mathrm{i}\sin(\tau x)$$

is always bounded for real-valued τx and, thus, so is its mean. Knowing the c.f. of a variate for all $\tau \in \mathbb{R}$ identifies uniquely its c.d.f. for all $x \in \mathbb{R}$, and vice versa. For the case of a continuous variate, the c.f. of x is the *Fourier transform* of its p.d.f., following from (3.7) as

$$\mathcal{F}_\tau\{f(u)\} := \int_{-\infty}^{\infty} \mathrm{e}^{\mathrm{i}\tau u} f(u)\,\mathrm{d}u = \varphi(\tau), \tag{3.8}$$

where the subscript τ indicates the parameter of the transformation. This transform operator possesses an inverse given by

$$f(u) = \mathcal{F}_u^{-1}\{\varphi(\tau)\} := \frac{1}{2\pi}\int_{-\infty}^{\infty} \mathrm{e}^{-\mathrm{i}u\tau}\varphi(\tau)\,\mathrm{d}\tau, \tag{3.9}$$

where u is now the parameter of the *inverse Fourier transform* of the function $\varphi(\tau)$. In general, for variates that are not necessarily continuous,

$$\varphi(\tau) = \int_{-\infty}^{\infty} \mathrm{e}^{\mathrm{i}\tau u}\,\mathrm{d}F(u) \tag{3.10}$$

and

$$F(u) = \frac{1}{2} + \frac{1}{2\pi}\int_0^{\infty} \frac{\mathrm{e}^{\mathrm{i}u\tau}\varphi(-\tau) - \mathrm{e}^{-\mathrm{i}u\tau}\varphi(\tau)}{\mathrm{i}\tau}\,\mathrm{d}\tau;$$

the formulae (3.8) and (3.9) are obtained by differentiating $F(u)$ with respect to u. Formulae for obtaining p.d.f.s or c.d.f.s by Fourier inversion are called *inversion theorems*. Notice that the definition of $\varphi(\tau)$ in terms of $F(u)$ implies the following properties: $\varphi(0) = 1$, $\varphi(-\tau)$ and $\varphi(\tau)$ are complex conjugates (hence the last integrand above is real), $\varphi(\tau)$ is a continuous function of τ, and $|\varphi(\tau)| \leqslant \mathrm{E}\left(\left|\mathrm{e}^{\mathrm{i}\tau x}\right|\right) = \mathrm{E}(1) = 1$.

The exercises of this chapter investigate moments, their relation to distribution and density functions, and their generating functions, respectively.

3.1 Calculating the moments

Exercise 3.1 (Boxing mean) A box contains n pieces of paper numbered from 1 to n. Of these l are drawn at random and with replacement; see Exercise 2.11. Let x be the largest number drawn and y the smallest. For $l = 2$, compute the mean and the variance of: (a) x; and (b) y. [Hint: In Section A.4.1, we derive $\sum_{i=1}^{n} i = n(n+1)/2$, $\sum_{i=1}^{n} i^2 = n(n+1)(2n+1)/6$, and $\sum_{i=1}^{n} i^3 = n^2(n+1)^2/4$.]

Solution

(a) From Exercise 2.11 we know that

$$f_x(u) = \left(\frac{u}{n}\right)^2 - \left(\frac{u-1}{n}\right)^2 = \frac{2u-1}{n^2} \qquad (u = 1, \dots, n).$$

Hence,

$$\begin{aligned}
\mathrm{E}(x) &= \sum_{u=1}^{n} u f_x(u) = \frac{1}{n^2} \sum_{u=1}^{n} u(2u-1) \\
&= \frac{2}{n^2} \sum_{u=1}^{n} u^2 - \frac{1}{n^2} \sum_{u=1}^{n} u \\
&= \frac{2}{n^2} \times \frac{1}{6} n(n+1)(2n+1) - \frac{1}{n^2} \times \frac{1}{2} n(n+1) = \frac{(n+1)(4n-1)}{6n}
\end{aligned}$$

and

$$\begin{aligned}
\mathrm{E}\left(x^2\right) &= \sum_{u=1}^{n} u^2 f_x(u) = \frac{1}{n^2} \sum_{u=1}^{n} u^2(2u-1) \\
&= \frac{2}{n^2} \sum_{u=1}^{n} u^3 - \frac{1}{n^2} \sum_{u=1}^{n} u^2 \\
&= \frac{2}{n^2} \left(\frac{n(n+1)}{2}\right)^2 - \frac{1}{n^2} \times \frac{1}{6} n(n+1)(2n+1) \\
&= \frac{(n+1)(3n^2+n-1)}{6n}.
\end{aligned}$$

It follows that

$$\mathrm{var}(x) = \mathrm{E}\left(x^2\right) - (\mathrm{E}(x))^2 = \frac{(n+1)(2n^3-2n^2+n-1)}{36n^2}.$$

(b) In a similar fashion we find

$$f_y(v) = \left(\frac{n-v+1}{n}\right)^2 - \left(\frac{n-v}{n}\right)^2 = \frac{2(n-v)+1}{n^2} = \frac{2}{n} - f_x(v),$$

and similar derivations yield

$$\mathrm{E}(y) = \frac{(n+1)(2n+1)}{6n}, \quad \mathrm{E}\left(y^2\right) = \frac{(n+1)(n^2+n+1)}{6n},$$

$$\mathrm{var}(y) = \frac{(n+1)(n-1)(2n^2+1)}{36n^2}.$$

In fact, we could have found $\mathrm{E}(y)$ and $\mathrm{var}(y)$ in a simpler way by noting that $\mathrm{E}(x+y) = n+1$ and $\mathrm{var}(y) = \mathrm{var}(x)$, because of the symmetry of the minimum and maximum in this case.

Exercise 3.2 (St. Petersburg paradox) Suppose that a fair coin is tossed repeatedly, until a tail is obtained. When a tail occurs, you are given a prize depending on how many tosses, x, it took to reach this outcome. More specifically, you are paid 2^{x-1}. What is the expected value of this payment?

Solution

Since the coin is fair, the probability of a tail at each toss is $\frac{1}{2}$. The tosses are independent, so the probability of a tail at the u-th toss is given by

$$p_u = \left(\frac{1}{2}\right)^u$$

for $u \in \mathbb{N}$. The expected value of the payment is therefore

$$\sum_{u=1}^{\infty} 2^{u-1} p_u = \sum_{u=1}^{\infty} \frac{2^{u-1}}{2^u} = \frac{1}{2} \sum_{u=1}^{\infty} 1 = \infty.$$

How much would you pay for this gamble?! (See the Notes at the end of the chapter.)

Exercise 3.3 (Desperately unlucky: aren't we all?) You wish to compare your experience with $x-1$ other gamblers who have faced, independently, an identical gamble to yours. You decide to keep increasing x until you find a gambler with a bigger loss (or smaller gain) than yours. Show that $\mathrm{E}(x) = \infty$.

Solution

Since the gambles are independent and identical, the probability of your being the biggest loser in a group containing $x-1$ other gamblers is $1/u$ for any given $x = u$. Therefore, this is the probability that you would have to look for more than $u-1$ gamblers to find one who has worse luck than you:

$$\Pr(x > u-1) = \frac{1}{u}$$

for $u \in \mathbb{N}$. This implies that

$$\Pr(x = u) = \Pr(x > u-1) - \Pr(x > u) = \frac{1}{u} - \frac{1}{u+1} = \frac{1}{u(u+1)},$$

which is the density seen in Exercise 2.2(c). The corresponding expectation is

$$\mathrm{E}(x) = \sum_{u=1}^{\infty} u \frac{1}{u(u+1)} = \sum_{u=1}^{\infty} \frac{1}{u+1}.$$

By the change of index $v = u + 1$,

$$\mathrm{E}(x) = \sum_{v=2}^{\infty} \frac{1}{v} = -1 + \sum_{v=1}^{\infty} \frac{1}{v} = -1 - \log(0^+) = \infty$$

by the logarithmic expansion of $\log(1-p)$ in Exercise 2.2(d) as $p \to 1^-$, or see Section A.3.2. Informally, summing v^{-1} gives a result of the same order of magnitude as $\int w^{-1}\,\mathrm{d}w = \log(w)$, hence divergent as $w \to \infty$; see Section A.4.1 for more on summation operators.

The result $\mathrm{E}(x) = \infty$ means that, on average, you would have to consult infinitely many gamblers to find someone unluckier than yourself! By the way, the same logic applies to all of our gamblers when they assess their luck.

Exercise 3.4 (Mean of a variate and its inverse) A discrete random variable $x \in \mathbb{N}$ has p.d.f. $f(u) = 6/(\pi^2 u^2)$. Compute $\mathrm{E}(x)$ and $\mathrm{E}(1/x)$, showing that $\mathrm{E}(1/x) \neq 1/\mathrm{E}(x)$.

Solution

We have

$$\mathrm{E}(x) = \frac{6}{\pi^2} \sum_{u=1}^{\infty} \frac{1}{u} = -\frac{6}{\pi^2} \log\left(0^+\right) = \infty$$

by the logarithmic expansion. However,

$$\mathrm{E}\left(\frac{1}{x}\right) = \frac{6}{\pi^2} \sum_{u=1}^{\infty} \frac{1}{u^3}.$$

This series of positive terms is convergent to a finite positive constant; see the convergence criteria in Section A.3.2. As in the previous exercise, by an informal analogy with integrals, the sum is of order $1/u^2$ and hence finite. Furthermore, its calculation reveals that $\mathrm{E}(1/x) \approx 0.731$, hence the required inequality.

Exercise 3.5 (Gamma moments) The random variable $x \in \mathbb{R}_+$ has p.d.f. $f(u) = \lambda^\nu u^{\nu-1} \mathrm{e}^{-\lambda u} / \Gamma(\nu)$ where $\nu, \lambda > 0$.

(a) Show that $\mathrm{E}(x^p) = \Gamma(p+\nu) / (\Gamma(\nu)\lambda^p)$.

(b) Show that $\mathrm{E}(1/x) \neq 1/\mathrm{E}(x)$.

Solution

(a) The expectation is now written as an integral. Using the transformation $v = \lambda u$ with

$\mathrm{d}v = \lambda\,\mathrm{d}u$, we find that

$$\mathrm{E}(x^p) = \int_0^\infty \frac{\lambda^\nu u^{p+\nu-1}\mathrm{e}^{-\lambda u}}{\Gamma(\nu)}\,\mathrm{d}u = \frac{1}{\lambda^p \Gamma(\nu)} \int_0^\infty v^{p+\nu-1}\mathrm{e}^{-v}\,\mathrm{d}v = \frac{\Gamma(p+\nu)}{\lambda^p \Gamma(\nu)},$$

by the definition of the gamma function (see Chapter 1) with $p + \nu > 0$.
(b) The ratio of gamma functions in (a) is the permutation defined in Chapter 1. For $p = 1$, we have $\mathrm{E}(x) = \nu/\lambda$. For $p = -1$ and $\nu > 1$, we have $\mathrm{E}(1/x) = \lambda/(\nu - 1)$. For $p = -1$ and $0 < \nu \leqslant 1$, the integral in (a) is not equal to the gamma function (whose integral definition requires $p + \nu > 0$) and is infinite. Hence, $\mathrm{E}(1/x) > 1/\mathrm{E}(x)$. Note that, in general, the inverse function $g(x) := 1/x$ is a convex function over $x \in \mathbb{R}_+$, and Jensen's inequality applies to it.

Exercise 3.6 (Change this uniform back!) Compute the mean and variance of the random variables x, x^2, and $|x|$ of Exercise 2.16, where we had the p.d.f. $f_x(u) = \frac{1}{2}$ for $|u| < 1$ and 0 elsewhere.

Solution
We could obtain the expectation and variance from the three density functions of x, y, and z in Exercise 2.16. It is easier, however, to compute

$$\mathrm{E}(x) = \int_{-1}^{1} \frac{1}{2} u\,\mathrm{d}u = \frac{1}{4}\left[u^2\right]_{-1}^{1} = 0,$$

$$\mathrm{E}(|x|) = \int_{-1}^{1} \frac{1}{2}|u|\,\mathrm{d}u = \int_0^1 u\,\mathrm{d}u = \frac{1}{2},$$

$$\mathrm{E}(x^2) = \int_{-1}^{1} \frac{1}{2}u^2\,\mathrm{d}u = \int_0^1 u^2\,\mathrm{d}u = \frac{1}{3},$$

$$\mathrm{E}(x^4) = \int_{-1}^{1} \frac{1}{2}u^4\,\mathrm{d}u = \int_0^1 u^4\,\mathrm{d}u = \frac{1}{5}.$$

Then,

$$\mathrm{E}(x) = 0, \quad \mathrm{var}(x) = \mathrm{E}(x^2) = \frac{1}{3},$$

$$\mathrm{E}(x^2) = \frac{1}{3}, \quad \mathrm{var}(x^2) = \mathrm{E}(x^4) - (\mathrm{E}(x^2))^2 = \frac{1}{5} - \frac{1}{9} = \frac{4}{45},$$

$$\mathrm{E}(|x|) = \frac{1}{2}, \quad \mathrm{var}(|x|) = \mathrm{E}(x^2) - (\mathrm{E}(|x|))^2 = \frac{1}{3} - \frac{1}{4} = \frac{1}{12}.$$

Notice that $\mathrm{E}(|x|) > \mathrm{E}(x)$ since x can be negative while $|x|$ is never negative, and $\mathrm{var}(|x|) < \mathrm{var}(x)$ since x is allowed to vary more widely than $|x|$.

3.2 Equality and inequality relations for moments and distributions

Exercise 3.7 (Absolutely variable!) Show that:
(a) $\mathrm{E}(|x|) \geqslant |\mathrm{E}(x)|$;
(b) $\operatorname{var}(|x|) \leqslant \operatorname{var}(x)$; interpret the latter result.

Solution
The simple example of $\Pr(x = -1) = \Pr(x = 1) = \frac{1}{2}$ illustrates the inequalities. Now to the general proof.
(a) The first inequality follows from

$$|\mathrm{E}(x)| = \left| \int_{-\infty}^{\infty} u \, \mathrm{d}F(u) \right| \leqslant \int_{-\infty}^{\infty} |u| \, \mathrm{d}F(u) = \mathrm{E}(|x|),$$

which can also be illustrated with Exercise 3.6. Note that equality holds when (for $x \in \mathcal{X}$) one of $\mathcal{X} \subseteq \mathbb{R}_{0,+}$ or $\mathcal{X} \subseteq \mathbb{R}_{0,-}$ holds. Alternatively, by the triangle inequality,

$$|\mathrm{E}(x)| = \left| \int_{-\infty}^{0} u \, \mathrm{d}F(u) + \int_{0}^{\infty} u \, \mathrm{d}F(u) \right| \leqslant \left| \int_{-\infty}^{0} u \, \mathrm{d}F(u) \right| + \int_{0}^{\infty} u \, \mathrm{d}F(u) = \mathrm{E}(|x|)$$

implies that equality holds if and only if either $\int_{-\infty}^{0} u \, \mathrm{d}F(u) = 0$ or $\int_{0}^{\infty} u \, \mathrm{d}F(u) = 0$.
(b) Since

$$\operatorname{var}(x) = \mathrm{E}\left(x^2\right) - \left(\mathrm{E}(x)\right)^2,$$
$$\operatorname{var}(|x|) = \mathrm{E}\left(x^2\right) - \left(\mathrm{E}(|x|)\right)^2,$$

and $\mathrm{E}(|x|) \geqslant |\mathrm{E}(x)|$ from (a), the result follows. If x takes both negative and positive values with nonnegligible probabilities, its variability is reduced by merging the two sides of its distribution into one side only, which is what taking the absolute value does.

Exercise 3.8 (Triangular array of probabilities) Let x be a random variable defined on the positive integers. Prove that $\mathrm{E}(x) = \sum_{i=1}^{\infty} \Pr(x \geqslant i)$.

Solution
We have

$$\begin{aligned}\sum_{i=1}^{\infty} \Pr(x \geqslant i) &= \Pr(x \geqslant 1) + \Pr(x \geqslant 2) + \Pr(x \geqslant 3) + \cdots \\ &= \Pr(x = 1) + \Pr(x = 2) + \Pr(x = 3) + \cdots \\ &\qquad\qquad\quad\; + \Pr(x = 2) + \Pr(x = 3) + \cdots \\ &\qquad\qquad\qquad\qquad\qquad\; + \Pr(x = 3) + \cdots;\end{aligned}$$

hence,

$$\sum_{i=1}^{\infty} \Pr(x \geqslant i) = \sum_{i=1}^{\infty} i \Pr(x = i) = \mathrm{E}(x).$$

*__Exercise 3.9 (Integrating c.d.f.s, for the moments)__ Assume that $\mathrm{E}\left(x^j\right)$ exists for some $j \in \mathbb{N}$. Prove that

$$\mathrm{E}\left(x^j\right) = j \int_0^\infty u^{j-1}(1 - F(u))\,\mathrm{d}u - j \int_{-\infty}^0 u^{j-1} F(u)\,\mathrm{d}u,$$

leading to the two special cases

$$\mathrm{E}(x) = \int_0^\infty (1 - F(u))\,\mathrm{d}u - \int_{-\infty}^0 F(u)\,\mathrm{d}u$$

and

$$\mathrm{var}(x) = 2 \int_0^\infty u(1 - F(u) + F(-u))\,\mathrm{d}u - (\mathrm{E}(x))^2.$$

Solution
Write

$$\mathrm{E}\left(x^j\right) = \int_{-\infty}^\infty u^j\,\mathrm{d}F(u) = \int_{-\infty}^0 u^j\,\mathrm{d}F(u) + \int_0^\infty u^j\,\mathrm{d}F(u),$$

where u^j is continuous at $u = 0$, thus allowing us to split the Stieltjes integral over two intervals; see Section A.4.3. Now, integrating by parts,

$$\begin{aligned}\int_{-\infty}^0 u^j\,\mathrm{d}F(u) &= \left[u^j F(u)\right]_{-\infty}^0 - j \int_{-\infty}^0 u^{j-1} F(u)\,\mathrm{d}u \\ &= -\lim_{u\to-\infty} u^j F(u) - j \int_{-\infty}^0 u^{j-1} F(u)\,\mathrm{d}u\end{aligned}$$

and

$$\begin{aligned}\int_0^\infty u^j\,\mathrm{d}F(u) &= -\left[u^j (1 - F(u))\right]_0^\infty + j \int_0^\infty u^{j-1}(1 - F(u))\,\mathrm{d}u \\ &= -\lim_{u\to\infty} u^j (1 - F(u)) + j \int_0^\infty u^{j-1}(1 - F(u))\,\mathrm{d}u.\end{aligned}$$

By the existence of $\mathrm{E}\left(x^j\right)$, these two limits are finite. Furthermore, they are zero (hence yielding the required result) because

$$0 \leqslant \lim_{u\to-\infty} |u|^j F(u) = \lim_{u\to-\infty} |u|^j \int_{-\infty}^u \mathrm{d}F(t) \leqslant \lim_{u\to-\infty} \int_{-\infty}^u |t|^j\,\mathrm{d}F(t) = 0$$

and

$$0 \leqslant \lim_{u\to\infty} u^j (1 - F(u)) = \lim_{u\to\infty} u^j \int_u^\infty \mathrm{d}F(t) \leqslant \lim_{u\to\infty} \int_u^\infty t^j\,\mathrm{d}F(t) = 0.$$

The special cases of the mean and variance follow directly, and the first implies Exercise 3.8:

$$\mathrm{E}(x) = \int_0^\infty (1 - F(u))\,\mathrm{d}u = \int_0^\infty \Pr(x > u)\,\mathrm{d}u = \sum_{i=1}^{\infty} \Pr(x \geqslant i),$$

since $\Pr(x > u)$ is a step function over intervals of unit length.

***Exercise 3.10 (Stochastic dominance)** A variate x is said to *stochastically dominate* another variate y if $\Pr(x > t) \geqslant \Pr(y > t)$ for all $t \in \mathbb{R}$, that is, $F_x(t) \leqslant F_y(t)$. This is also known as *first-order stochastic dominance*, with strict dominance applying if, in addition, $\Pr(x > t) > \Pr(y > t)$ for some $t \in \mathbb{R}$.
(a) Let x stochastically dominate y. Prove that $\mathrm{E}(x) \geqslant \mathrm{E}(y)$, using Exercise 3.9, but that $\mathrm{var}(x)$ need not be larger than $\mathrm{var}(y)$, assuming these moments exist.
(b) Let g be any continuous function whose first derivative is positive everywhere, and whose expectations with respect to x and y exist. Prove that $\mathrm{E}(g(x)) \geqslant \mathrm{E}(g(y))$ if and only if x stochastically dominates y.

Solution
(a) By Exercise 3.9,

$$\begin{aligned}\mathrm{E}(x) - \mathrm{E}(y) &= \int_0^\infty (F_y(t) - F_x(t))\,\mathrm{d}t - \int_{-\infty}^0 (F_x(t) - F_y(t))\,\mathrm{d}t \\ &= \int_{-\infty}^\infty (F_y(t) - F_x(t))\,\mathrm{d}t \geqslant 0\end{aligned}$$

since $F_x(t) \leqslant F_y(t)$ for all $t \in \mathbb{R}$. For the variances, we only need a counterexample. Let y take the values -1 and 1 with probability $\frac{1}{2}$ each, and let $x = 1$ with probability 1. Then, x stochastically dominates y, but $\mathrm{var}(x) = 0$ and

$$\mathrm{var}(y) = \mathrm{E}\left((y-0)^2\right) = \frac{1}{2}(-1)^2 + \frac{1}{2}(1)^2 = 1.$$

(b) We start by commenting that (b) is compatible with the counterexample for the variances in part (a), since the two variates did not have the same mean there. Now to the proof. The "if" part follows the steps of Exercise 3.9, exploiting the continuity of g to split the Stieltjes integrals that are the expectations of g. Integrating by parts and using the existence of $\mathrm{E}(g(x))$ and $\mathrm{E}(g(y))$,

$$\int_{-\infty}^0 g(t)\,\mathrm{d}F(t) = [g(t)\,F(t)]_{-\infty}^0 - \int_{-\infty}^0 g'(t)\,F(t)\,\mathrm{d}t = -\int_{-\infty}^0 g'(t)\,F(t)\,\mathrm{d}t$$

and $\int_0^\infty g(t)\,\mathrm{d}F(t) = \int_0^\infty g'(t)\,(1 - F(t))\,\mathrm{d}t$. Hence,

$$\begin{aligned}\mathrm{E}(g(x)) - \mathrm{E}(g(y)) &= \int_0^\infty g'(t)\,(F_y(t) - F_x(t))\,\mathrm{d}t - \int_{-\infty}^0 g'(t)\,(F_x(t) - F_y(t))\,\mathrm{d}t \\ &= \int_{-\infty}^\infty g'(t)\,(F_y(t) - F_x(t))\,\mathrm{d}t,\end{aligned}$$

which is nonnegative since $g'(t) > 0$ and $F_y(t) \geqslant F_x(t)$ for all $t \in \mathbb{R}$.

The "only if" part is proved by contradiction (see Section A.1). Suppose that $\mathrm{E}(g(x)) \geqslant \mathrm{E}(g(y))$ or, equivalently, $\int_{-\infty}^{\infty} g'(t)(F_y(t) - F_x(t))\,\mathrm{d}t \geqslant 0$, but that $F_y(t_0) < F_x(t_0)$ for a value $t_0 \in \mathbb{R}$. Now c.d.f.s are right-continuous, $F(t^+) = F(t)$, which implies that we must have $F_y(t) < F_x(t)$ over some interval $(t_0, t_0 + \epsilon)$ of length $\epsilon > 0$. We need to show that there exists a function g that satisfies our assumptions but contradicts $\int_{-\infty}^{\infty} g'(t)(F_y(t) - F_x(t))\,\mathrm{d}t \geqslant 0$. This is achieved by choosing any continuous g such that g' is sufficiently large in the interval $(t_0, t_0 + \epsilon)$ to make $\int_{-\infty}^{\infty} g'(t)(F_y(t) - F_x(t))\,\mathrm{d}t$ become negative, that is,

$$\int_{(t_0,t_0+\epsilon)} g'(t)\,|F_y(t) - F_x(t)|\,\mathrm{d}t > \int_{\mathbb{R}\setminus(t_0,t_0+\epsilon)} g'(t)(F_y(t) - F_x(t))\,\mathrm{d}t.$$

Note that since $\mathrm{E}(g(x))$ and $\mathrm{E}(g(y))$ are both finite, $\int_{\mathbb{R}\setminus(t_0,t_0+\epsilon)} g'(t)(F_y(t) - F_x(t))\,\mathrm{d}t$ is finite and therefore the required "large" g' is finite over $(t_0, t_0 + \epsilon)$.

***Exercise 3.11 (Quantile function and moments)** Let $Q_x(\alpha)$ be the quantile function of a variate x, defined in Chapter 2 as the smallest $Q_x(\alpha) \in \mathcal{X}$ satisfying $F_x(Q_x(\alpha)) \geqslant \alpha$. Prove that:

(a) $\mathrm{E}(x) = \int_0^1 Q_x(\alpha)\,\mathrm{d}\alpha$;

(b) $\mathrm{var}(x) = \int_0^1 (Q_x(\alpha) - \mathrm{E}(x))^2\,\mathrm{d}\alpha$.

Solution

(a) We have

$$\mathrm{E}(x) = \int_{-\infty}^{\infty} u\,\mathrm{d}F_x(u) = \int_A u\,\mathrm{d}F_x(u)$$

where A is the set of points for which F is strictly increasing. For each finite $u \in A$ there exists $Q_x(\alpha) = u$ for some $\alpha \in (0,1)$ because, if the c.d.f. does not increase at a point u (as is the case in A^c), then a value smaller than u is the quantile corresponding to this value of $F_x(u)$. Using $u = Q_x(\alpha) \in A$ in the integral gives

$$\mathrm{E}(x) = \int_A Q_x(\alpha)\,\mathrm{d}F_x(Q_x(\alpha)).$$

If there is no jump (discontinuity) in the c.d.f., then $F_x(Q_x(\alpha)) = \alpha$ by definition for all $\alpha \in (0,1)$ and we have the required result by

$$\int_A Q_x(\alpha)\,\mathrm{d}F_x(Q_x(\alpha)) = \int_0^1 Q_x(\alpha)\,\mathrm{d}\alpha.$$

If there is a jump at some point u, then its contribution to $\mathrm{E}(x)$ is $u\Pr(x = u)$, which we can show to be identical to its contribution to $\int Q_x(\alpha)\,\mathrm{d}\alpha$: since $Q_x(\alpha) = u$ for

$\alpha \in (F_x(u^-), F_x(u))$,

$$\int_{F_x(u^-)}^{F_x(u)} Q_x(\alpha)\, \mathrm{d}\alpha = u \int_{F_x(u^-)}^{F_x(u)} \mathrm{d}\alpha = u\left(F_x(u) - F_x(u^-)\right) = u \Pr(x = u).$$

The required result follows by combining the two cases as in Jordan's decomposition.
(b) Write

$$\begin{aligned}\int_0^1 (Q_x(\alpha) - \mathrm{E}(x))^2\, \mathrm{d}\alpha &= \int_0^1 Q_x(\alpha)^2\, \mathrm{d}\alpha - 2\,\mathrm{E}(x) \int_0^1 Q_x(\alpha)\, \mathrm{d}\alpha + (\mathrm{E}(x))^2 \int_0^1 \mathrm{d}\alpha \\ &= \int_0^1 Q_x(\alpha)^2\, \mathrm{d}\alpha - 2(\mathrm{E}(x))^2 + (\mathrm{E}(x))^2 \\ &= \int_0^1 Q_x(\alpha)^2\, \mathrm{d}\alpha - (\mathrm{E}(x))^2.\end{aligned}$$

Using the same reasoning as in (a) gives $\int_0^1 Q_x(\alpha)^2\, \mathrm{d}\alpha = \mathrm{E}(x^2)$. Similar relations apply to the higher-order moments.

Exercise 3.12 (Inequalities linking probability to expectation) For $x \in \mathcal{X}$, assume that the following expectations exist, and that $a > 0$ and $c \geqslant 0$ are nonrandom.
(a) Let $g(u) \geqslant 0$ for all $u \in \mathcal{X}$. Show that $\mathrm{E}(g(x))/a \geqslant \Pr(g(x) \geqslant a)$.
(b) Prove *Markov's inequality*, $\mathrm{E}(|x|)/a \geqslant \Pr(|x| \geqslant a)$.
(c) Prove *Chebyshev's inequality*, $\mathrm{E}(x^2)/a^2 \geqslant \Pr(|x| \geqslant a)$.
(d) Show that $\mathrm{E}((x+c)^2)/(a+c)^2 \geqslant \Pr(x \geqslant a)$. Can you derive a sharper inequality than this one?
(e) Prove *Chernoff's inequality*, $\mathrm{e}^{-ac} m_x(c) \geqslant \Pr(x \geqslant a)$, where the function m_x is the m.g.f. of x. Show that the sharpest inequality that this implies for $m_x(c) = \exp(c^2/2)$ is $\Pr(x \geqslant a) \leqslant \exp(-a^2/2)$.
(f) Let $h(u)$ be an even function, that is, $h(u) = h(-u)$. Assume further that it satisfies $h(u) \geqslant 0$ and that $h(u)$ increases for $u > 0$. Show that $\mathrm{E}(h(x))/h(a) \geqslant \Pr(|x| \geqslant a)$.

Solution
(a) Defining $A := \{x : g(x) \geqslant a\} \subseteq \mathcal{X}$ and recalling that $g(x) \geqslant 0$ for all $x \in \mathcal{X}$, we combine these into $g(x) \geqslant a 1_{x \in A}$ for all $x \in \mathcal{X}$. Taking expectations on both sides of the last inequality gives the required result, since $\mathrm{E}(1_{x\in A}) = \Pr(x \in A) = \Pr(g(x) \geqslant a)$. Since $\Pr(g(x) \geqslant a) \geqslant \Pr(g(x) > a)$, the stated inequality is sharper (more informative) than that obtained by using $\{x : g(x) > a\}$. Note that an alternative proof can be obtained by defining $B := \{u : g(u) \geqslant a\}$ and using

$$\Pr(g(x) \geqslant a) = \int_{u \in B} \mathrm{d}F(u) \leqslant \int_{u \in B} \frac{g(u)}{a}\, \mathrm{d}F(u),$$

since $g(u)/a \geqslant 1$ in B. As $g(u) \geqslant 0$ for all $u \in \mathcal{X}$, we get

$$\int_{u \in B} g(u)\,\mathrm{d}F(u) \leqslant \int_{u \in \mathcal{X}} g(u)\,\mathrm{d}F(u) = \mathrm{E}\left(g(x)\right)$$

and the result follows. (As an aide-mémoire on which way these inequalities go, recall that probabilities are in $[0, 1]$ while expectations can be unbounded.)
(b) Choose $g(u) = |u|$ and apply (a).
(c) Choose $g(u) = u^2$ and write a^2 instead of a.
(d) Chebyshev's inequality gives

$$\begin{aligned}\frac{\mathrm{E}\left((x+c)^2\right)}{(a+c)^2} &\geqslant \Pr\left(|x+c| \geqslant a+c\right)\\ &= \Pr\left(x+c \geqslant a+c\right) + \Pr\left(-x-c \geqslant a+c\right)\\ &= \Pr\left(x \geqslant a\right) + \Pr\left(-x-c \geqslant a+c\right).\end{aligned}$$

The inequality stated in the question drops the second term, and is therefore not as sharp as Chebyshev's.
(e) Since $\Pr(x \geqslant a) = \Pr(\mathrm{e}^{cx} \geqslant \mathrm{e}^{ca})$ for $c \geqslant 0$, the inequality follows by using $g(x) = \mathrm{e}^{cx}$ in (a). Substituting $m_x(c) = \exp\left(c^2/2\right)$ gives $\Pr(x \geqslant a) \leqslant \exp\left(-ac + c^2/2\right)$, and the right-hand side is minimized with respect to $c \geqslant 0$ by choosing $c = a$. The variate possessing this m.g.f. is called a *standard normal* and will be encountered frequently from now on.
(f) $\Pr(|x| \geqslant a) = \Pr(h(|x|) \geqslant h(a))$ because h is monotone increasing when its argument is positive. Since $h(|x|) = h(x)$, the inequality follows from (a) again.

Exercise 3.13 (A bound for existence) Prove that

$$\mathrm{E}\left(|x|\right) \leqslant \sum_{i=1}^{\infty} \Pr\left(|x| \geqslant i-1\right),$$

where we assume that the series converges (otherwise the bound on $\mathrm{E}(|x|)$ would be uninformative).

Solution
Since $|x| < i$ for all $|x| \in [i-1, i)$,

$$\begin{aligned}\mathrm{E}\left(|x|\right) &\leqslant \sum_{i=1}^{\infty} i \Pr\left(i-1 \leqslant |x| < i\right) = \sum_{i=1}^{\infty} i\left(\Pr\left(|x| \geqslant i-1\right) - \Pr\left(|x| \geqslant i\right)\right)\\ &= \sum_{i=1}^{\infty} \Pr\left(|x| \geqslant i-1\right)\\ &\quad + \sum_{i=1}^{\infty} (i-1)\Pr\left(|x| \geqslant i-1\right) - \sum_{i=1}^{\infty} i \Pr\left(|x| \geqslant i\right),\end{aligned}$$

where the separation of the first series is allowed because it is assumed to be absolutely convergent; see Section A.3. The required result follows because the last two series are identical and cancel out, term by term, since

$$\sum_{i=1}^{\infty}(i-1)\Pr(|x| \geqslant i-1) = 0 + \sum_{i=2}^{\infty}(i-1)\Pr(|x| \geqslant i-1) = \sum_{j=1}^{\infty} j\Pr(|x| \geqslant j)$$

by the change of index $j = i - 1$.

Exercise 3.14 (Jensen's inequality) Let g be a real-valued convex function, and suppose that $\mu := \mathrm{E}(x)$ and $\mathrm{E}(g(x))$ exist. You may assume that there exists a line $a + bx$, with constants $a, b \in \mathbb{R}$, such that $g(\mu) = a + b\mu$ and $g(x) \geqslant a + bx$ for all x. For example, in Figure 3.1, there exists a tangent to g at the point μ such that the tangent lies below the function. Prove that:
(a) $g(\mu) \leqslant \mathrm{E}(g(x))$;
(b) $\mathrm{E}(\log(x)) \leqslant \log(\mu)$ if $\Pr(x > 0) = 1$;
(c) $\sum_{i=1}^n p_i u_i \geqslant \prod_{i=1}^n u_i^{p_i}$, where $u_i, p_i > 0$ and $\sum_{i=1}^n p_i = 1$.

Solution
(a) Taking expectations on both sides of $g(x) \geqslant a + bx$ gives $\mathrm{E}(g(x)) \geqslant a + b\mu = g(\mu)$, as required. Notice that if the function $g(x)$ is strictly convex, $g(x) > a + bx$ everywhere except at $x = \mu$, and the equality in Jensen's relation holds if and only if $\Pr(x = \mu) = 1$. The latter condition will be detailed further in Exercise 10.16(c) in connection with sequences. Again using Figure 3.1 for illustration, as the distance between u_1 and u_2 shrinks to zero, we get $\Pr(x = \mu) = 1$ and $\mathrm{E}(g(x)) = g(\mu)$.
(b) Since $\mathrm{d}^2\log(u)/\mathrm{d}u^2 = -1/u^2 < 0$, it follows (see Section A.4.4) that $-\log(u)$ is a strictly convex function of u and hence that $-\mathrm{E}(\log(x)) \geqslant -\log(\mathrm{E}(x))$.
(c) Define the random variable x such that $\Pr(x = u_i) = p_i$. Then, $\mathrm{E}(x) = \sum_{i=1}^n p_i u_i$ and

$$\mathrm{E}(\log(x)) = \sum_{i=1}^{n} p_i \log(u_i) = \log\left(\prod_{i=1}^{n} u_i^{p_i}\right);$$

hence, using (b),

$$\log\left(\sum_{i=1}^{n} p_i u_i\right) \geqslant \log\left(\prod_{i=1}^{n} u_i^{p_i}\right).$$

Since $\log(u)$ is an increasing function, the result follows. (Taking $p_i = 1/n$ gives the inequality relating the arithmetic and geometric means.)

Exercise 3.15 (Location and scale) The variate y is defined in terms of another variate x by $y := \alpha + \lambda x$, where $\alpha \in \mathbb{R}$ and $\lambda \in \mathbb{R}\backslash\{0\}$ are nonrandom. Prove that $\mathrm{E}(y) = \alpha + \lambda\mathrm{E}(x)$ and derive the relation between the j-th central (around the mean) moments of y and of x.

Solution

The first result follows directly by the linearity of the expectation operator. For the second,

$$\mathrm{E}\left((y-\mathrm{E}(y))^j\right)=\mathrm{E}\left((\alpha+\lambda x-\alpha-\lambda\mathrm{E}(x))^j\right)=\lambda^j\,\mathrm{E}\left((x-\mathrm{E}(x))^j\right).$$

Notice that this implies that the variance is location-invariant, that is, it is unaffected by α.

Exercise 3.16 (Location and scale in c.d.f.s) Suppose that the c.d.f. of a random variable x has the form

$$F(u)=H\left(\frac{u-\alpha}{\lambda}\right),$$

where $\lambda>0$ and H is a function that makes F a proper distribution. Show that:
(a) if α is increased by c, then so are the mean (if it exists), modes (if they exist), and median;
(b) if λ is multiplied by $k\neq 0$, then $\operatorname{var}(x)$ (if it exists) is multiplied by k^2.

Solution

(a) Denote the new and old means by ν and μ, respectively. Then, the new mean is given by

$$\begin{aligned}\nu&=\int_{-\infty}^{\infty}u\,\mathrm{d}H\left(\frac{u-\alpha-c}{\lambda}\right)\\&=\int_{-\infty}^{\infty}(t+c)\,\mathrm{d}H\left(\frac{t-\alpha}{\lambda}\right)=\mu+c\left[H\left(\frac{t-\alpha}{\lambda}\right)\right]_{-\infty}^{\infty}=\mu+c,\end{aligned}$$

where the change of variable $t=u-c$ has been used. For the median, the solution for the smallest u satisfying

$$H\left(\frac{u-\alpha-c}{\lambda}\right)\geqslant\frac{1}{2}$$

is again related by a difference of c to the solution for the smallest t satisfying

$$H\left(\frac{t-\alpha}{\lambda}\right)\geqslant\frac{1}{2}.$$

Finally, the same relation holds between the local maximizers of the implied p.d.f.s.
(b) First, we show that $\operatorname{var}(x)$ is unaffected by an alteration of α (the location parameter) to any other value $\alpha+c$; see also Exercise 3.15. Using the change of variable $t=u-c$ as in (a), we have the new variance

$$\operatorname{var}(x)=\int_{-\infty}^{\infty}(u-\nu)^2\,\mathrm{d}H\left(\frac{u-\alpha-c}{\lambda}\right)=\int_{-\infty}^{\infty}(t+c-\nu)^2\,\mathrm{d}H\left(\frac{t-\alpha}{\lambda}\right)$$

where the last integral can be seen to be identical to the old variance, once it is noticed that $\mu=\nu-c$ from (a). We can therefore set $\alpha=0$, without loss of generality, when investigating the central moments of x. For this purpose, when $j=1,2$ and if λ is multiplied by

k, denoting the new and old raw moments by $\nu^{(j)}$ and $\mu^{(j)}$, respectively, we have

$$\nu^{(j)} = \int_{-\infty}^{\infty} w^j \, \mathrm{d}H\left(\frac{w}{k\lambda}\right) = k^j \int_{-\infty}^{\infty} u^j \, \mathrm{d}H\left(\frac{u}{\lambda}\right) = k^j \mu^{(j)}$$

by the change of variable $u = w/k$. Effectively, we have shown that multiplying λ by k is tantamount to a change of random variables from x to $z = kx$. The result for the variance follows since $\mathrm{var}(z) = \mathrm{E}\left(z^2\right) - (\mathrm{E}\,(z))^2$.

Exercise 3.17 (Moments around different locations!) Let x be a random variable with finite first two moments. Show that

$$\mathrm{E}\left((x-c)^2\right) = \mathrm{var}(x) + (\mathrm{E}\,(x) - c)^2$$

for any $c \in \mathbb{R}$.

Solution

Write $\mu := \mathrm{E}\,(x)$ and expand the quadratic:

$$\begin{aligned}(x-c)^2 &= (x-\mu+\mu-c)^2 \\ &= (x-\mu)^2 + (\mu-c)^2 + 2\,(\mu-c)\,(x-\mu)\,.\end{aligned}$$

Now we can take expectations on both sides of the equality and use the linearity of the operator E:

$$\mathrm{E}\left((x-c)^2\right) = \mathrm{E}\left((x-\mu)^2\right) + (\mu-c)^2 + 2\,(\mu-c)\,\mathrm{E}\,(x-\mu)$$

since $\mu - c$ is nonrandom. We get the required result because $x - \mu$ is centered around 0:

$$\mathrm{E}\,(x-\mu) = \mathrm{E}\,(x) - \mu \equiv 0.$$

This proof is constructive and "from first principles". There is an alternative proof that verifies the desired result by making use of

$$\mathrm{E}\left(y^2\right) = \mathrm{var}(y) + (\mathrm{E}\,(y))^2\,,$$

a relation that was obtained in (3.5). By letting $y := x - c$, then using $\mathrm{var}(x-c) = \mathrm{var}(x)$ (location-invariance from Exercise 3.15) and $\mathrm{E}(x-c) = \mathrm{E}(x) - c$, we get the required result.

*__Exercise 3.18 (LS versus LAD)__ Let x be a random variable with finite first two moments.

(a) Derive c to minimize $\mathrm{E}\left((x-c)^2\right)$, known as the solution of the *least squares* (LS) problem.

(b) If the median of x satisfies $F(q) = \frac{1}{2}$, show that $c = q$ minimizes $\mathrm{E}\,(|x-c|)$, known as the solution of the *least absolute deviations* (LAD) problem. What if $F(q) > \frac{1}{2}$?

(c) Show that the mean and the median can never be more than one standard deviation apart.

Solution

(a) By Exercise 3.17,

$$\mathrm{E}\left((x-c)^2\right) = \mathrm{var}(x) + (\mathrm{E}(x) - c)^2 .$$

The result follows by noting that c appears only in the nonnegative $(\mathrm{E}(x) - c)^2$, which is minimized by setting $c = \mathrm{E}(x)$.

Alternatively, we can differentiate the objective function as

$$\frac{\mathrm{d}}{\mathrm{d}c}\left(\mathrm{E}\left(x^2\right) - 2c\,\mathrm{E}(x) + c^2\right) = -2\,\mathrm{E}(x) + 2c$$

and solve for the value of c that makes it 0. This gives $c = \mathrm{E}(x)$, which is indeed a minimum since the second derivative of the function is $2 > 0$.

(b) For any chosen constant a, since $|x - a|$ is a continuous function, we can split the expectation (see Section A.4.3) as

$$\begin{aligned}\mathrm{E}(|x-a|) &= \int_{-\infty}^{a} (a-u)\,\mathrm{d}F(u) + \int_{a}^{\infty} (u-a)\,\mathrm{d}F(u) \\ &= \int_{-\infty}^{q} (a-u)\,\mathrm{d}F(u) + 2\int_{q}^{a} (a-u)\,\mathrm{d}F(u) + \int_{q}^{\infty} (u-a)\,\mathrm{d}F(u).\end{aligned}$$

When $a = q$, the middle integral vanishes. Applying this formula twice, with $a = c$ and $a = q$, respectively, gives

$$\begin{aligned}&\mathrm{E}(|x-c|) - \mathrm{E}(|x-q|) \\ &= \int_{-\infty}^{q} (c-q)\,\mathrm{d}F(u) + 2\int_{q}^{c} (c-u)\,\mathrm{d}F(u) + \int_{q}^{\infty} (q-c)\,\mathrm{d}F(u) \\ &= (c-q)[F(u)]_{-\infty}^{q} + 2\int_{q}^{c} (c-u)\,\mathrm{d}F(u) + (q-c)[F(u)]_{q}^{\infty} \\ &= (c-q)(2F(q)-1) + 2\int_{q}^{c} (c-u)\,\mathrm{d}F(u).\end{aligned}$$

If $F(q) = \frac{1}{2}$, then this reduces to $2\int_q^c (c-u)\,\mathrm{d}F(u)$, which is always nonnegative for the following reason. For $q < c$, the integrand $c - u$ is positive and so is the differential. For $q > c$, both are negative so the product is positive. Choosing $c = q$ minimizes the integral by making it zero.

If $F(q) > \frac{1}{2}$, the variate cannot be continuous. Integration by parts gives

$$\begin{aligned}\mathrm{E}(|x-c|) - \mathrm{E}(|x-q|) &= (c-q)(2F(q)-1) + 2\left([(c-u)F(u)]_q^c + \int_q^c F(u)\,\mathrm{d}u\right) \\ &= (c-q)(2F(q)-1) + 2\left((q-c)F(q) + \int_q^c F(u)\,\mathrm{d}u\right) \\ &= q - c + 2\int_q^c F(u)\,\mathrm{d}u = \int_q^c (2F(u)-1)\,\mathrm{d}u,\end{aligned}$$

which, incidentally, is valid for $F(q) = \frac{1}{2}$ as well. Since q is the smallest u satisfying $F(u) \geqslant \frac{1}{2}$ but $F(q) > \frac{1}{2}$, we must have $F(q^-) < \frac{1}{2}$. Hence, $F(u) > \frac{1}{2}$ for $u > q$, and $F(u) < \frac{1}{2}$ for $u < q$. In either case, the integral is positive and hence is minimized at $c = q$.

(c) The distance between the mean $\mathrm{E}(x)$ and median q is

$$\begin{aligned} |\mathrm{E}(x) - q| &= |\mathrm{E}(x - q)| \leqslant \mathrm{E}(|x - q|) \\ &\leqslant \mathrm{E}(|x - \mu|) \qquad \text{(by part (b))} \\ &\leqslant \sqrt{\mathrm{E}\left((x-\mu)^2\right)} \qquad \text{(by Jensen's inequality),} \end{aligned}$$

where $\mathrm{E}\left((x-\mu)^2\right) \equiv \mathrm{var}(x)$. Notice that the last inequality need not be strict, even if $\sigma > 0$; for example, it becomes an equality if you take $x - \mu = \pm 1$ with equal probability. For the last inequality to be strict, it is the variance of $|x - \mu|$ (not of $x - \mu$) that needs to be nonzero.

Exercise 3.19 (Symmetry and mean) Let x be symmetric around c. Prove that $c = \mathrm{E}(x)$ if the latter exists. Prove also that, if $c \in \mathcal{X}$, then its mean equals its median.

Solution

We saw in Exercise 2.7 that $x - c$ and $c - x$ have the same distribution, by the symmetry of x. Then

$$\mathrm{E}(x - c) = \mathrm{E}(c - x) \equiv -\mathrm{E}(x - c),$$

an equation of the form $a = -a$ implying $a = 0$, that is, $\mathrm{E}(x - c) = 0$ and hence $\mathrm{E}(x) = c$. Equality of the mean and median, subject to the stated conditions, follows from Exercise 2.6.

***Exercise 3.20 (Symmetry and skewness)** Assume that the skewness $\sigma^{(3)}/\sigma^3$ of a variate x exists. Prove that symmetry implies that $\sigma^{(3)} = 0$, but that the converse does not hold.

Solution

Exercise 3.19 implies that $x - \mu$ and $\mu - x$ have the same distribution. Therefore,

$$\mathrm{E}\left((x-\mu)^3\right) = \mathrm{E}\left((\mu - x)^3\right).$$

But

$$\mathrm{E}\left((x-\mu)^3\right) \equiv \mathrm{E}\left((-1)^3(\mu - x)^3\right) = -\mathrm{E}\left((\mu - x)^3\right),$$

hence $\mathrm{E}\left((\mu - x)^3\right) = -\mathrm{E}\left((\mu - x)^3\right)$ and we get $\mathrm{E}\left((\mu - x)^3\right) = 0$. In fact, the same proof can be used to show that all odd-order central moments are zero: $\sigma^{(2j+1)} = 0$ for $j \in \mathbb{N}$.

To prove that $\sigma^{(3)} = 0$ does not imply symmetry, it is sufficient to provide a counterexample. We choose a variate x whose p.d.f. (which will also be used in the next exercise) is an equally weighted mixture of two densities with different functional forms but with raw moments $-\mu^{(1)}, -\mu^{(3)}$ and $\mu^{(1)}, \mu^{(3)}$ respectively, so that $\mathrm{E}(x) = 0 = \mathrm{E}(x^3)$ but the density is not symmetric around $\mu = 0$. One such choice is

$$f(u) = \frac{1}{2}\left(1_{u\in\mathbb{R}_-}\mathrm{e}^u\right) + \frac{1}{2}\left(1_{u\in(1-\sqrt{5},1+\sqrt{5})}\frac{1}{2\sqrt{5}}\right) \equiv 1_{u\in\mathbb{R}_-}\frac{\mathrm{e}^u}{2} + 1_{u\in(1-\sqrt{5},1+\sqrt{5})}\frac{1}{4\sqrt{5}},$$

where the terms in the each of the two parentheses are proper densities. The result is not symmetric around zero since $f(u) \neq f(-u)$. On the other hand, the density in the first component has mean

$$\int_{-\infty}^{0} u\mathrm{e}^u \,\mathrm{d}u = -\int_0^\infty v\mathrm{e}^{-v}\,\mathrm{d}v = -\Gamma(2) = -1! = -1$$

by the change of variable $v = -u$ and the definition of the gamma function (see Chapter 1), while the second's mean is the midpoint of its symmetric density

$$\frac{(1-\sqrt{5}) + (1+\sqrt{5})}{2} = 1;$$

hence $\mathrm{E}(x) = \frac{1}{2}(-1) + \frac{1}{2}(1) = 0$. Furthermore,

$$\begin{aligned}\mathrm{E}\left(x^3\right) &= \frac{1}{2}\int_{-\infty}^{0} u^3\mathrm{e}^u\,\mathrm{d}u + \frac{1}{2}\int_{1-\sqrt{5}}^{1+\sqrt{5}} u^3\frac{1}{2\sqrt{5}}\,\mathrm{d}u \\ &= -\frac{1}{2}\Gamma(4) + \frac{1}{2}\frac{\left[u^4\right]_{1-\sqrt{5}}^{1+\sqrt{5}}}{8\sqrt{5}} = -\frac{3!}{2} + \frac{1}{2}\frac{\left(1+\sqrt{5}\right)^4 - \left(1-\sqrt{5}\right)^4}{8\sqrt{5}}.\end{aligned}$$

Using the binomial expansion twice and collecting terms, we obtain

$$(a+b)^4 - (a-b)^4 = 2\sum_{j \text{ odd}}\binom{4}{j}a^j b^{4-j} = 8ab^3 + 8a^3b$$

because terms with even values of j cancel out, and with $a = 1$ and $b = \sqrt{5}$ we get

$$\mathrm{E}\left(x^3\right) = -3 + \frac{1}{2}\frac{5\sqrt{5}+\sqrt{5}}{\sqrt{5}} = 0.$$

Exercise 3.21 (A myth amiss) There is a famous myth in statistics: that unimodal distributions where $\sigma^{(3)} > 0$ will have mode < median < mean. Prove that these inequalities are incorrect. [Hint: Use the type of density in the counterexample of Exercise 3.20.]

Solution

We start by showing that the first inequality is incorrect. In Exercise 3.20, we have both the mean and mode as 0, but numerical calculation of

$$F(u) = \frac{\mathrm{e}^{\min\{0,u\}}}{2} + 1_{u>1-\sqrt{5}}\frac{\min\left\{1+\sqrt{5},u\right\} - 1 + \sqrt{5}}{4\sqrt{5}}$$

reveals that the median is approximately $-\frac{1}{4}$ (it is obviously negative since more than half the density lies to the left of $u = 0$). Allocating slightly less probability to the lower end of the density, one can substantially increase the mean and skewness but not alter the median by as much. The mode is unchanged. As a result, we have a counterexample where the median is less than the mode, in spite of the positive skew. For example, replacing e^u by $2e^{2u}$ gives $\mu = \frac{1}{4}, \sigma^{(3)} = \frac{47}{32} > 0$, and a median of approximately -0.14.

For the second inequality, we alter the flat (or uniform) component of the density to have

$$1_{u\in\mathbb{R}_-}\frac{e^u}{2} + 1_{u\in(-\epsilon,2+\epsilon)}\frac{1}{4+4\epsilon},$$

where $\epsilon > 0$ and small. The components have means of opposite sign, giving $\mu = 0$. The mode is at 0, as before. The median is smaller than the mean and mode because $\Pr(x < 0) > \frac{1}{2}$, but the skewness is negative because of the long lower tail of the exponential function:

$$\begin{aligned}\sigma^{(3)} &= \int_{-\infty}^{0} \frac{e^u}{2} u^3 \, du + \int_{-\epsilon}^{2+\epsilon} \frac{1}{4+4\epsilon} u^3 \, du = -\frac{\Gamma(4)}{2} + \left[\frac{u^4}{16(1+\epsilon)}\right]_{-\epsilon}^{2+\epsilon} \\ &= -3 + \frac{((1+\epsilon)+1)^4 - ((1+\epsilon)-1)^4}{16(1+\epsilon)} = -3 + \frac{1+(1+\epsilon)^2}{2} = -2 + \frac{1}{2}\epsilon^2 + \epsilon\end{aligned}$$

which is negative for ϵ small. In other words, the mirror image of that density,

$$1_{u\in\mathbb{R}_+}\frac{e^{-u}}{2} + 1_{u\in(-2-\epsilon,\epsilon)}\frac{1}{4+4\epsilon},$$

has $\sigma^{(3)} > 0$, but mean $=$ mode $<$ median, in violation of the second inequality of the myth.

Finally, we can make the mean less than the mode by shifting the flat component of the last density slightly to the left, so none of the $\binom{3}{2} = 3$ relations holds!

3.3 Generating functions and the properties of moments

Exercise 3.22 (Central versus raw moment-generation) Differentiating j times the m.g.f. $m_x(t)$, then setting $t = 0$ gives the j-th raw moment of x. Derive the corresponding function to which applying the same operation gives the j-th central moment of x.

Solution

To obtain the central moments, one applies the same procedure to $e^{-t\mu}m_x(t)$, where $\mu := E(x)$. To see this, write

$$e^{-t\mu}m_x(t) = e^{-t\mu}\,E\left(e^{tx}\right) = E\left(e^{t(x-\mu)}\right),$$

the last step following as $e^{-t\mu}$ is nonrandom. Expanding the exponential and using the existence of $m_x(t)$, as in the introduction to this chapter,

$$\mathrm{E}\left(\mathrm{e}^{t(x-\mu)}\right) = \mathrm{E}\left(\sum_{j=0}^{\infty} \frac{t^j}{j!}(x-\mu)^j\right) = \sum_{j=0}^{\infty} \frac{t^j}{j!}\mathrm{E}\left((x-\mu)^j\right),$$

which generates the central moments $\mathrm{E}\left((x-\mu)^j\right)$.

***Exercise 3.23 (Symmetry and c.f.s)** Let x be a variate which is symmetrically distributed around c and has the c.f. $\varphi(\tau)$. Show that $g(\tau) := \mathrm{e}^{-\mathrm{i}\tau c}\varphi(\tau)$ is a real-valued even function of τ.

Solution

By the definition of c.f.s,

$$g(\tau) = \mathrm{e}^{-\mathrm{i}\tau c}\,\mathrm{E}\left(\mathrm{e}^{\mathrm{i}\tau x}\right) = \mathrm{E}\left(\mathrm{e}^{\mathrm{i}\tau(x-c)}\right).$$

The symmetry of x around c implies that $x - c$ and $c - x$ have the same distribution (by Exercise 2.7), hence

$$g(\tau) = \mathrm{E}\left(\mathrm{e}^{\mathrm{i}\tau(x-c)}\right) = \mathrm{E}\left(\mathrm{e}^{\mathrm{i}\tau(c-x)}\right) = g(-\tau),$$

proving that g is an even function. Now, $\mathrm{e}^{\mathrm{i}a} = \cos(a) + \mathrm{i}\sin(a)$, with imaginary part $\mathrm{Im}\left(\mathrm{e}^{\mathrm{i}a}\right) = \sin(a) = -\sin(-a)$ for $a \in \mathbb{R}$, hence

$$\mathrm{Im}\left(g(\tau)\right) = \mathrm{E}\left(\sin\left(\tau(x-c)\right)\right) = -\mathrm{E}\left(\sin\left(\tau(c-x)\right)\right) = -\mathrm{Im}\left(g(-\tau)\right)$$

for $\tau \in \mathbb{R}$. But we have just established that $g(-\tau) = g(\tau)$; therefore, the last equation becomes $\mathrm{Im}\left(g(\tau)\right) = -\mathrm{Im}\left(g(\tau)\right)$ and we infer that $\mathrm{Im}\left(g(\tau)\right) = 0$.

Exercise 3.24 (Pareto moments) A random variable x has p.d.f.

$$f(u) = \begin{cases} pu^{-p-1} & (1 < u < \infty), \\ 0 & (\text{elsewhere}), \end{cases}$$

where $p > 0$.
(a) Show that the m.g.f. $m(t)$ does not exist.
(b) For what values of p does $\mathrm{E}\left(x^3\right)$ exist?

Solution

(a) We use the fact that $\mathrm{e}^{tu} \geqslant (tu)^j/j!$ for $j = 0, 1, \ldots$ and $t \geqslant 0$. Then, for $j = p + 1$,

$$\begin{aligned} m(t) &= \mathrm{E}\left(\mathrm{e}^{tx}\right) \\ &= p\int_1^{\infty} \frac{\mathrm{e}^{tu}}{u^{p+1}}\,\mathrm{d}u \geqslant \frac{p}{(p+1)!}\int_1^{\infty} \frac{(tu)^{p+1}}{u^{p+1}}\,\mathrm{d}u = \frac{pt^{p+1}}{(p+1)!}\int_1^{\infty}\mathrm{d}u = \infty. \end{aligned}$$

(b) The expectation takes the form

$$\mathrm{E}\left(x^3\right) = p\int_1^{\infty} u^{-(p-2)}\,\mathrm{d}u = \frac{-p}{p-3}\left[u^{-(p-3)}\right]_1^{\infty} = \frac{p}{p-3}$$

if $p > 3$. The integral does not exist otherwise, including in the case $p = 3$ where

$$\mathrm{E}\left(x^3\right) = 3\int_1^{\infty} \frac{\mathrm{d}u}{u} = 3\left[\log\left(u\right)\right]_1^{\infty} = \infty.$$

Exercise 3.25 (High-order implies low-order: existence of moments) Prove that the existence of the raw moment of order $j + 1$ of a variate x implies the existence of its raw moment of order j, where $j \in \mathbb{N}$. Hence, prove that the existence of $\mathrm{E}\left(x^j\right)$ implies the existence of $\mathrm{E}\left((x-c)^j\right)$ for all $|c| < \infty$.

Solution

For any $j \in \mathbb{N}$, we have $\mathrm{E}\left(|x|^j\right) = I_1 + I_2$ where

$$I_1 := \int_{|u|\leqslant 1} |u|^j\,\mathrm{d}F(u) \leqslant \int_{|u|\leqslant 1} \mathrm{d}F(u) = F(1) - F(-1) \leqslant 1$$

and

$$I_2 := \int_{|u|>1} |u|^j\,\mathrm{d}F(u).$$

Interval-splitting is allowed since $|u|^j$ is a continuous function at $u = 1$; see Section A.4.3. Demonstrating the existence of $\mathrm{E}\left(x^j\right)$ is now the same as showing that I_2 is finite, so

$$\int_{|u|>1} |u|^j\,\mathrm{d}F(u) \leqslant \int_{|u|>1} |u|^{j+1}\,\mathrm{d}F(u) < \infty$$

gives the first result. Notice that the latter inequality gives the essence of this proof: the existence of a moment of order $j+1$ implies that the p.d.f. must decline at a rate faster than $|u|^{j+2}$ as $|u| \to \infty$ and, a fortiori, lower-order moments will then exist. This was illustrated in Exercise 3.24(b).

For the second result, we write

$$\mathrm{E}\left(|x-c|^j\right) = \int_{-\infty}^{c} (c-u)^j\,\mathrm{d}F(u) + \int_{c}^{\infty} (u-c)^j\,\mathrm{d}F(u).$$

By the binomial expansion $(u-c)^j = \sum_{i=0}^{j}\binom{j}{i}u^{j-i}(-c)^i$, and by the existence of raw moments of orders $\leqslant j$, the second result is proved. The result is intuitive: a finite location shift (by c) does not affect the existence of a moment of x.

Notice that this exercise implies that we could have disposed of the assumption of the existence of the first moment of x in Exercise 3.17. It would have been sufficient to assume the existence of the second moment of x.

***Exercise 3.26 (Existence of m.g.f. or moments?)** Show that the existence of all moments of a variate is a necessary condition for its m.g.f. to exist. (This condition is not sufficient, as we shall see in the next exercise.)

Solution

We prove necessity by the contrapositive method (see Section A.1). We will demonstrate that if moments exist only up to finite integer order $j-1$, then the m.g.f. does not exist. By definition we have

$$m(t) = \mathrm{E}\left(\mathrm{e}^{tx}\right) = \int_{-\infty}^{0} \mathrm{e}^{tu}\, \mathrm{d}F(u) + \int_{0}^{\infty} \mathrm{e}^{tu}\, \mathrm{d}F(u),$$

and splitting the Stieltjes integral into two is allowed because of the continuity of the exponential function at $u=0$. We need to show that $m(t)$ does not exist in some open interval containing 0. Since $\mathrm{E}\left(|x|^j\right)$ does not exist (by the definition of existence), at least one of the two integrals

$$I_1 := \int_{-\infty}^{0} |u|^j\, \mathrm{d}F(u) \quad \text{or} \quad I_2 := \int_{0}^{\infty} u^j\, \mathrm{d}F(u)$$

must be infinite. For $t<0$,

$$\int_{0}^{\infty} \mathrm{e}^{tu}\, \mathrm{d}F(u) \leqslant \int_{0}^{\infty} \mathrm{d}F(u) = 1 - F(0) < \infty$$

but

$$\int_{-\infty}^{0} \mathrm{e}^{tu}\, \mathrm{d}F(u) \geqslant \int_{-\infty}^{0} \frac{|tu|^j}{j!}\, \mathrm{d}F(u) = \frac{|t|^j}{j!} I_1.$$

For $t>0$,

$$\int_{-\infty}^{0} \mathrm{e}^{tu}\, \mathrm{d}F(u) \leqslant \int_{-\infty}^{0} \mathrm{d}F(u) = F(0) < \infty$$

but

$$\int_{0}^{\infty} \mathrm{e}^{tu}\, \mathrm{d}F(u) \geqslant \int_{0}^{\infty} \frac{(tu)^j}{j!}\, \mathrm{d}F(u) = \frac{t^j}{j!} I_2.$$

Therefore, the unboundedness of either I_1 or I_2 implies that $m(t)$ does not exist in an open neighborhood of $t=0$.

Exercise 3.27 (Log-normal moments) Let x be a real positive variate, with p.d.f.

$$f_x(u) = \frac{1}{2u\sqrt{2\pi}} \mathrm{e}^{-(\log(u))^2/8}.$$

(a) Show that $y := \log(x)$ is distributed over the whole real line, with p.d.f.

$$f_y(v) = \frac{1}{2\sqrt{2\pi}} \mathrm{e}^{-v^2/8}.$$

(b) Show that the m.g.f. of y is equal to e^{2t^2}.

(c) Find $\mathrm{E}(x^p)$ for $p \in \mathbb{R}$. What does this imply for the m.g.f. of x?

Solution

(a) Since

$$F_y(v) = \Pr(y \leqslant v) = \Pr(\log(x) \leqslant v) = \Pr(x \leqslant \mathrm{e}^v) = F_x(\mathrm{e}^v),$$

we find that

$$f_y(v) = \frac{\mathrm{d}}{\mathrm{d}v}F_y(v) = \frac{\mathrm{d}}{\mathrm{d}v}F_x(\mathrm{e}^v) = \mathrm{e}^v f_x(\mathrm{e}^v) = \frac{1}{2\sqrt{2\pi}}\mathrm{e}^{-v^2/8}.$$

(b) By definition,

$$\begin{aligned} m_y(t) = \mathrm{E}\left(\mathrm{e}^{ty}\right) &= \frac{1}{2\sqrt{2\pi}}\int_{-\infty}^{\infty} \mathrm{e}^{tv-v^2/8}\,\mathrm{d}v \\ &= \frac{1}{2\sqrt{2\pi}}\int_{-\infty}^{\infty} \mathrm{e}^{-((v-4t)^2-16t^2)/8}\,\mathrm{d}v = \frac{\mathrm{e}^{2t^2}}{2\sqrt{2\pi}}\int_{-\infty}^{\infty} \mathrm{e}^{-(v-4t)^2/8}\,\mathrm{d}v. \end{aligned}$$

By using the transformation $w = v - 4t$ with $\mathrm{d}w = \mathrm{d}v$,

$$m_y(t) = \frac{\mathrm{e}^{2t^2}}{2\sqrt{2\pi}}\int_{-\infty}^{\infty} \mathrm{e}^{-w^2/8}\,\mathrm{d}w = \mathrm{e}^{2t^2}\int_{-\infty}^{\infty} f_y(w)\,\mathrm{d}w = \mathrm{e}^{2t^2}.$$

(c) For *any* positive variate z and any real power p,

$$\mathrm{E}(z^p) = \mathrm{E}\left(\mathrm{e}^{p\log(z)}\right) = m_{\log(z)}(p).$$

Applying this result here, the expectation of x^p is found by using (b):

$$\mathrm{E}(x^p) = m_y(p) = \mathrm{e}^{2p^2}.$$

This implies that the terms in the "moment-generating" sum $\sum_{j=0}^{\infty}\mathrm{E}\left(x^j\right)t^j/j!$ diverge as $j \to \infty$. More formally,

$$\mathrm{E}\left(\mathrm{e}^{tx}\right) = \mathrm{E}\left(\mathrm{e}^{t\mathrm{e}^y}\right) = \frac{1}{2\sqrt{2\pi}}\int_{-\infty}^{\infty} \mathrm{e}^{t\mathrm{e}^v - v^2/8}\,\mathrm{d}v$$

has a positive integrand everywhere, and is furthermore unbounded as $v \to \infty$ when $t > 0$. Although all the moments of x exist, the m.g.f. does not exist because the moments increase too fast as j increases.

***Exercise 3.28 (Fake moments)** Show that none of the three functions $g_1(t) := \mathrm{e}^{-t^2/2}$, $g_2(t) := \frac{1}{2}\mathrm{e}^{-t}$, and $g_3(t) := \mathrm{e}^{-|t|}$ is an m.g.f. Can they be c.f.s? Can $g_4(t) := \mathrm{e}^{\mathrm{i}t^2}$ be a c.f.?

Solution

For g_1, we have $g_1''(t) = (t^2-1)g_1(t)$, so that $g_1''(0) = -g_1(0) = -1$. If g_1 were an m.g.f., this would imply that $\mathrm{E}\left(x^2\right) < 0$, a contradiction. However, we saw in Exercise 3.27(b) that m.g.f.s of the type $m_y(\tau) = g_1(2\tau/\mathrm{i})$ exist. Since $g_1(t) = m_y(\mathrm{i}t/2) = \mathrm{E}\left(\mathrm{e}^{\mathrm{i}ty/2}\right)$, it follows that $g_1(t)$ is the c.f. of $y/2$, where y is the variate from Exercise 3.27.

For g_2, we see that $g_2(0) = \frac{1}{2}$, while $\mathrm{E}\left(\mathrm{e}^{0\times x}\right) = \mathrm{E}(1) = 1$. Thus, g_2 is neither an m.g.f. nor a c.f.

Since g_3 is not differentiable at 0, it cannot be an m.g.f. Notice that this also implies that, if this function were a c.f., the moments of the corresponding variate would not exist. To establish that it is a c.f., we Fourier-invert it to check that it gives rise to a proper p.d.f.:

$$\begin{aligned}
h(u) &= \frac{1}{2\pi}\int_{-\infty}^{\infty} \mathrm{e}^{-|t|-\mathrm{i}tu}\,\mathrm{d}t = \frac{1}{2\pi}\left(\int_{-\infty}^{0} \mathrm{e}^{(1-\mathrm{i}u)t}\,\mathrm{d}t + \int_{0}^{\infty} \mathrm{e}^{(-1-\mathrm{i}u)t}\,\mathrm{d}t\right) \\
&= \frac{1}{2\pi}\left(\left[\frac{\mathrm{e}^{(1-\mathrm{i}u)t}}{1-\mathrm{i}u}\right]_{-\infty}^{0} - \left[\frac{\mathrm{e}^{(-1-\mathrm{i}u)t}}{1+\mathrm{i}u}\right]_{0}^{\infty}\right) \\
&= \frac{1}{2\pi}\left(\frac{1}{1-\mathrm{i}u} + \frac{1}{1+\mathrm{i}u}\right) = \frac{1}{\pi\left(1+u^2\right)}
\end{aligned}$$

since $\mathrm{e}^{-\mathrm{i}ut}$ is bounded as $|t| \to \infty$ and $\mathrm{i}^2 = -1$. This is the *Cauchy density* seen in (3.3) of the introduction to this chapter, and it does not possess moments of any order.

Finally, $g_4(t)$ cannot be a c.f. because $g_4(-t)$ equals $g_4(t)$ rather than being its complex conjugate (namely $\mathrm{e}^{-\mathrm{i}t^2}$).

***Exercise 3.29 (Expansion of c.f.s and existence of moments)** Show that

$$\left|\mathrm{e}^{\mathrm{i}t} - \sum_{j=0}^{k-1} \frac{(\mathrm{i}t)^j}{j!}\right| \leqslant \frac{|t|^k}{k!}$$

for $t \in \mathbb{R}$. Hence show that, if the k-th moment of x exists, its c.f. has the expansion

$$\varphi_x(\tau) = \sum_{j=0}^{k} \frac{(\mathrm{i}\tau)^j}{j!}\mathrm{E}\left(x^j\right) + o(\tau^k)$$

as $\tau \to 0$. (A function $g(\tau)$ having $\lim_{\tau\to 0} g(\tau)/\tau^\alpha = 0$ is said to be of *order of magnitude smaller than* τ^α as $\tau \to 0$, which is written as $g(\tau) = o(\tau^\alpha)$; see Section A.3.4 for more details.)

Solution

For $k \geqslant 1$, we have

$$g_k(t) := \mathrm{e}^{\mathrm{i}t} - \sum_{j=0}^{k-1} \frac{(\mathrm{i}t)^j}{j!} = \sum_{j=k}^{\infty} \frac{(\mathrm{i}t)^j}{j!} = \sum_{j=k-1}^{\infty} \frac{\mathrm{i}\int_0^t (\mathrm{i}s)^j\,\mathrm{d}s}{j!} = \mathrm{i}\int_0^t g_{k-1}(s)\,\mathrm{d}s.$$

We will show that the required result follows by induction. For $k = 1$,

$$|g_1(t)| = \left|\mathrm{e}^{\mathrm{i}t} - 1\right| = \left|\mathrm{i}\int_0^t \mathrm{e}^{\mathrm{i}s}\,\mathrm{d}s\right| = \left|\int_0^t \mathrm{e}^{\mathrm{i}s}\,\mathrm{d}s\right| \leqslant \int_0^{|t|} \left|\mathrm{e}^{\mathrm{i}s}\right|\mathrm{d}s = |t|,$$

since $|\mathrm{i}| = 1$ and $\left|\mathrm{e}^{\mathrm{i}s}\right| = 1$ for $s \in \mathbb{R}$. Assume that the result $|g_k(t)| \leqslant |t|^k/k!$ holds for some k. Then

$$|g_{k+1}(t)| = \left|\int_0^t g_k(s)\,\mathrm{d}s\right| \leqslant \int_0^{|t|} |g_k(s)|\,\mathrm{d}s \leqslant \int_0^{|t|} \frac{s^k}{k!}\,\mathrm{d}s = \frac{|t|^{k+1}}{(k+1)!},$$

so the result holds for $k+1$ as well, as required. This type of inequality will be used in another guise in Exercise 10.37.

We saw in Exercise 3.25 that the existence of the k-th moment implies the existence of all lower-order moments. Since

$$\frac{\varphi_x(\tau+h)-\varphi_x(\tau)}{h} = \mathrm{E}\left(\mathrm{e}^{\mathrm{i}\tau x}\frac{\mathrm{e}^{\mathrm{i}hx}-1}{h}\right),$$

we have

$$\left|\frac{\varphi_x(\tau+h)-\varphi_x(\tau)}{h}\right| \leqslant \mathrm{E}\left(\left|\mathrm{e}^{\mathrm{i}\tau x}\right|\left|\frac{\mathrm{e}^{\mathrm{i}hx}-1}{h}\right|\right) = \mathrm{E}\left(\left|\frac{\mathrm{e}^{\mathrm{i}hx}-1}{h}\right|\right) \leqslant \mathrm{E}\left(|x|\right) < \infty$$

by $\left|\mathrm{e}^{\mathrm{i}hx}-1\right| \leqslant |hx|$ for all $h \in \mathbb{R}$ from the first part (with $k=1$) and by the existence of $\mathrm{E}\left(x\right)$, respectively. The dominated convergence theorem (see Section A.4.3) implies that the derivative exists and is given by

$$\varphi_x'(\tau) := \lim_{h\to 0}\frac{\varphi_x(\tau+h)-\varphi_x(\tau)}{h} = \mathrm{E}\left(\mathrm{e}^{\mathrm{i}\tau x}\lim_{h\to 0}\frac{\mathrm{e}^{\mathrm{i}hx}-1}{h}\right) = \mathrm{E}\left(\mathrm{i}x\mathrm{e}^{\mathrm{i}\tau x}\right),$$

which is a continuous function of τ. The proof for general k follows as in the first part of the exercise. Hence, Taylor-expanding around $\tau = 0$, we obtain

$$\varphi_x(\tau) = \sum_{j=0}^{k}\frac{\tau^j\varphi_x^{(j)}(0)}{j!} + r_k(\tau) = \sum_{j=0}^{k}\frac{(\mathrm{i}\tau)^j}{j!}\mathrm{E}\left(x^j\right) + r_k(\tau),$$

where the remainder

$$r_k(\tau) := \varphi_x(\tau) - \sum_{j=0}^{k}\frac{\tau^j\varphi_x^{(j)}(0)}{j!}$$

can be differentiated k times and the continuity of the k-th derivative of φ implies that $r_k^{(k)}(\tau) = o(1)$ as $\tau \to 0$, hence $r_k(\tau) = o(\tau^k)$.

Exercise 3.30 (Inverse moments) Suppose that $x \in \mathbb{R}_+$ and that its m.g.f. $m(t)$ exists. Assuming that $\mathrm{E}\left(x^{-\nu}\right)$ exists for a given $\nu \in \mathbb{R}_+$, show that it is obtained from $\int_0^\infty \tau^{\nu-1}m(-\tau)\,\mathrm{d}\tau/\Gamma(\nu)$.

Solution

The m.g.f. is defined for all $t<0$, because $tx<0$ implies $\mathrm{e}^{tx}<1$ so that $m(t) = \mathrm{E}\left(\mathrm{e}^{tx}\right)$

is bounded. The required integral is

$$\int_0^\infty \tau^{\nu-1} m(-\tau)\,\mathrm{d}\tau = \int_0^\infty \tau^{\nu-1}\,\mathrm{E}\left(\mathrm{e}^{-\tau x}\right)\mathrm{d}\tau = \mathrm{E}\left(\int_0^\infty \tau^{\nu-1}\mathrm{e}^{-\tau x}\,\mathrm{d}\tau\right)$$
$$= \mathrm{E}\left(x^{-\nu}\int_0^\infty t^{\nu-1}\mathrm{e}^{-t}\,\mathrm{d}t\right) = \mathrm{E}\left(x^{-\nu}\right)\Gamma(\nu),$$

where the exchange of integral and expectation is allowed by the existence conditions (see Section A.3.5), and the change of variable $t = \tau x$ is used.

Exercise 3.31 (m.g.f.: discrete) Suppose that x is a discrete random variable with m.g.f.

$$m(t) = \frac{1}{8}\mathrm{e}^{t} + \frac{1}{2}\mathrm{e}^{2t} + \frac{3}{8}\mathrm{e}^{8t}.$$

(a) Compute $\mathrm{E}(x)$ and $\mathrm{var}(x)$.
(b) Give the p.d.f. of x.

Solution

(a) We find that

$$\mathrm{E}(x) = m'(0) = \frac{1}{8} + 1 + 3 = \frac{33}{8},$$
$$\mathrm{E}\left(x^2\right) = m''(0) = \frac{1}{8} + 2 + 24 = \frac{209}{8},$$

and hence $\mathrm{var}(x) = 583/64$.
(b) The probability-generating function of x is

$$\varpi(\tau) = m(\log(\tau)) = \frac{1}{8}\tau + \frac{1}{2}\tau^2 + \frac{3}{8}\tau^8,$$

so the p.d.f. is given by $\Pr(x = 1) = 1/8$, $\Pr(x = 2) = 1/2$, and $\Pr(x = 8) = 3/8$.

Exercise 3.32 (m.g.f.: continuous) Suppose that a continuous random variable x has p.d.f. $f(u) = 3u^2$ for $0 < u < 1$ and 0 otherwise.
(a) Derive the m.g.f. of x.
(b) Obtain $\Pr(|x - \mu| \leqslant k\sigma)$ for $k > 0$.

Solution

(a) By successive integration by parts, we obtain

$$m(t) = \int_0^1 3u^2\mathrm{e}^{tu}\,\mathrm{d}u = \left[\frac{3u^2}{t}\mathrm{e}^{tu}\right]_0^1 - \int_0^1 \frac{6u}{t}\mathrm{e}^{tu}\,\mathrm{d}u$$
$$= \frac{3}{t}\mathrm{e}^{t} - \left[\frac{6u}{t^2}\mathrm{e}^{tu}\right]_0^1 + \frac{6}{t^2}\int_0^1 \mathrm{e}^{tu}\,\mathrm{d}u = \frac{3}{t}\mathrm{e}^{t} - \frac{6}{t^2}\mathrm{e}^{t} + \frac{6}{t^3}\mathrm{e}^{t} - \frac{6}{t^3}.$$

As it stands, $m(t)$ is not expressed in a convenient form, since we are interested in its behavior around $t = 0$. For this purpose, we use the series definition of the exponential function, before integrating:

$$m(t) = \mathrm{E}\left(\mathrm{e}^{tx}\right) = \mathrm{E}\left(\sum_{i=0}^{\infty} \frac{t^i}{i!} x^i\right)$$

$$= \int_0^1 \sum_{i=0}^{\infty} \frac{t^i}{i!} u^i f(u)\,\mathrm{d}u = 3 \sum_{i=0}^{\infty} \frac{t^i}{i!} \int_0^1 u^{i+2}\,\mathrm{d}u = 3 \sum_{i=0}^{\infty} \frac{t^i}{i!(i+3)}.$$

(b) We need to start by working out the variance σ^2 of x. Using the last representation of $m(t)$ and differentiating j times, we see that at $t = 0$, $m^{(j)}(0) = 3/(j+3)$, and hence that $m'(0) = 3/4$ and $m''(0) = 3/5$. This implies that $\mu = 3/4$ and $\sigma^2 = 3/5 - (3/4)^2 = 3/80$.

Since $F(u) = 0$ for $u \leqslant 0$, $F(u) = u^3$ for $0 < u < 1$, and $F(u) = 1$ for $u \geqslant 1$, we have

$$\Pr\left(|x - \mu| \leqslant k\sigma\right) = \Pr\left(\mu - k\sigma \leqslant x \leqslant \mu + k\sigma\right) = F(\mu + k\sigma) - F(\mu - k\sigma).$$

Given the values of μ and σ here,

$$\Pr\left(|x - \mu| \leqslant k\sigma\right) = \begin{cases} (\mu + k\sigma)^3 - (\mu - k\sigma)^3 & (0 < k \leqslant (1-\mu)/\sigma), \\ 1 - (\mu - k\sigma)^3 & ((1-\mu)/\sigma < k \leqslant \mu/\sigma), \\ 1 & (k > \mu/\sigma), \end{cases}$$

$$= \begin{cases} \frac{3}{1600}\sqrt{15}(k^3 + 90k) & (0 < k \leqslant \frac{\sqrt{15}}{3}), \\ \frac{1}{1600}(3\sqrt{15}k^3 - 135k^2 + 135\sqrt{15}k + 925) & (\frac{\sqrt{15}}{3} < k \leqslant \sqrt{15}), \\ 1 & (k > \sqrt{15}). \end{cases}$$

Exercise 3.33 (Binomial, Poisson, and geometric moments) Let x be a variate with f.m.g.f. $\varpi(t)$.

(a) If x follows the *binomial distribution*

$$\Pr(x = u) = \binom{n}{u} p^u (1-p)^{n-u} \quad (u \in \{0, 1, \dots, n\}, \quad p \in [0, 1]),$$

derive $\varpi(t)$, then use it to show that $\mathrm{E}(x) = np$ and $\mathrm{var}(x) = np(1-p)$. Also, derive $\mathrm{E}\left(x^3\right)$.

(b) If x follows the *Poisson distribution*

$$\Pr(x = u) = \mathrm{e}^{-\lambda} \frac{\lambda^u}{u!} \quad (u \in \mathbb{Z}_{0,+}, \quad \lambda \in \mathbb{R}_+),$$

derive $\varpi(t)$, then show that $\mathrm{E}(x) = \lambda = \mathrm{var}(x)$. Also, derive $\mathrm{E}\left(x^3\right)$.

(c) If x follows the *geometric distribution*

$$\Pr(x = u) = p(1-p)^u \quad (u \in \mathbb{Z}_{0,+}, \quad p \in (0, 1]).$$

derive $\varpi(t)$, then obtain $\mathrm{E}(x)$ and $\mathrm{var}(x)$.

Solution

(a) We have

$$\varpi(t) = \mathrm{E}\left(t^x\right) = \sum_{u=0}^{n} t^u \binom{n}{u} p^u (1-p)^{n-u} = \sum_{u=0}^{n} \binom{n}{u} (pt)^u (1-p)^{n-u} = (pt+1-p)^n$$

by using the binomial expansion. Hence,

$$\varpi'(t) = np(pt+1-p)^{n-1}, \quad \varpi''(t) = n(n-1)p^2(pt+1-p)^{n-2},$$
$$\varpi'''(t) = n(n-1)(n-2)p^3(pt+1-p)^{n-3},$$

so that, at $t = 1$,

$$\mathrm{E}\left(x\right) = \varpi'(1) = np, \quad \mathrm{E}\left(x(x-1)\right) = \varpi''(1) = n(n-1)p^2,$$
$$\mathrm{E}\left(x(x-1)(x-2)\right) = \varpi'''(1) = n(n-1)(n-2)p^3,$$

with $\varpi'''(1) = \mathrm{E}\left(x^3\right) - 3\,\mathrm{E}\left(x^2\right) + 2\,\mathrm{E}\left(x\right)$. It follows that

$$\mathrm{E}\left(x\right) = np, \quad \mathrm{E}\left(x^2\right) = n(n-1)p^2 + np, \quad \mathrm{var}(x) = np(1-p),$$
$$\mathrm{E}\left(x^3\right) = n(n-1)(n-2)p^3 + 3n(n-1)p^2 + np.$$

(b) In a similar way, we find

$$\varpi(t) = \sum_{u=0}^{\infty} \frac{\mathrm{e}^{-\lambda}(\lambda t)^u}{u!} = \mathrm{e}^{-\lambda}\mathrm{e}^{\lambda t} = \mathrm{e}^{-\lambda(1-t)},$$

implying that $\varpi^{(k)}(t) = \lambda^k \mathrm{e}^{-\lambda(1-t)}$ and so $\varpi^{(k)}(1) = \lambda^k$; hence

$$\mathrm{E}\left(x\right) = \varpi'(1) = \lambda, \quad \mathrm{E}\left(x(x-1)\right) = \varpi''(1) = \lambda^2,$$
$$\mathrm{E}\left(x(x-1)(x-2)\right) = \varpi'''(1) = \lambda^3.$$

This gives

$$\mathrm{E}\left(x\right) = \lambda, \quad \mathrm{E}\left(x^2\right) = \lambda^2 + \lambda, \quad \mathrm{var}(x) = \lambda,$$
$$\mathrm{E}\left(x^3\right) = \lambda^3 + 3\lambda^2 + \lambda.$$

(c) Define $q := 1 - p$. For $|qt| < 1$,

$$\varpi(t) = \mathrm{E}\left(t^x\right) = \sum_{u=0}^{\infty} p(qt)^u = \frac{p}{1-qt}.$$

Now

$$\varpi'(t) = \frac{pq}{(1-qt)^2}, \quad \varpi''(t) = \frac{2pq^2}{(1-qt)^3},$$

implying $\varpi'(1) = q/p$ and $\varpi''(1) = 2(q/p)^2$. Hence, $\mathrm{E}\left(x\right) = \varpi'(1) = q/p$,

$$\mathrm{E}\left(x^2\right) = \mathrm{E}\left(x(x-1)\right) + \mathrm{E}\left(x\right) = \varpi''(1) + \varpi'(1) = 2\frac{q^2}{p^2} + \frac{q}{p},$$

and $\mathrm{var}(x) = (q/p)^2 + q/p = q/p^2$.

Notice that, in the three examples of this problem, it is easier to calculate the mean indirectly from the f.m.g.f., rather than by direct computation of $\mathrm{E}(x) = \sum_{u\in\mathcal{X}} u \Pr(x = u)$.

Exercise 3.34 (m.g.f. or f.m.g.f.?) A random variable x has p.d.f.

$$f(u) = 2^{-(u+1)} \quad (u = 0, 1, 2, \dots).$$

(a) Derive $m(t)$ and $\varpi(t)$.
(b) Compute $\mathrm{E}(x^3)$.

Solution

(a) For all $t < \log 2$ we have $\mathrm{e}^t/2 < 1$ and hence

$$m(t) = \mathrm{E}\left(\mathrm{e}^{tx}\right) = \sum_{u=0}^{\infty} \mathrm{e}^{tu} 2^{-(u+1)} = \frac{1}{2}\sum_{u=0}^{\infty}\left(\frac{\mathrm{e}^t}{2}\right)^u = \frac{1}{2} \times \frac{1}{1-\mathrm{e}^t/2} = \frac{1}{2-\mathrm{e}^t}.$$

Similarly, for all t such that $|t| < 2$,

$$\varpi(t) = \mathrm{E}\left(t^{x}\right) = \sum_{u=0}^{\infty} t^{u} 2^{-(u+1)} = \frac{1}{2}\sum_{u=0}^{\infty}\left(\frac{t}{2}\right)^u = \frac{1}{2} \times \frac{1}{1-t/2} = \frac{1}{2-t}.$$

(b) Notice that $\varpi(t)$ is easier to use here than $m(t)$. We have

$$\varpi'(t) = \frac{1}{(2-t)^2}, \quad \varpi''(t) = \frac{2}{(2-t)^3}, \quad \varpi'''(t) = \frac{6}{(2-t)^4}.$$

Hence, $\mathrm{E}(x) = \varpi'(1) = 1$, $\mathrm{E}(x^2) = \varpi''(1) + \mathrm{E}(x) = 2 + 1 = 3$, and $\mathrm{E}(x^3) = \varpi'''(1) + 3\,\mathrm{E}(x^2) - 2\,\mathrm{E}(x) = 6 + 9 - 2 = 13$.

***Exercise 3.35 (Normal functions, for the moment!)** The standard-normal variate $x \in \mathbb{R}$ has a p.d.f. defined by

$$\phi(u) := \frac{1}{\sqrt{2\pi}}\mathrm{e}^{-u^2/2},$$

and its c.d.f. is denoted by $\Phi(u)$; see also Exercises 3.12(e) and 3.27. Derive:
(a) the m.g.f. of $|x|$, and $\mathrm{E}(|x|)$;
(b) the m.g.f. of $y = x^2$.

Solution

(a) We have

$$\begin{aligned} m_{|x|}(t) &= \mathrm{E}\left(\mathrm{e}^{t|x|}\right) = \frac{1}{\sqrt{2\pi}}\int_{-\infty}^{\infty} \mathrm{e}^{t|u|-u^2/2}\,\mathrm{d}u = \frac{2}{\sqrt{2\pi}}\int_{0}^{\infty} \mathrm{e}^{tu-u^2/2}\,\mathrm{d}u \\ &= \frac{2}{\sqrt{2\pi}}\int_{0}^{\infty} \mathrm{e}^{-((u-t)^2-t^2)/2}\,\mathrm{d}u = \frac{2}{\sqrt{2\pi}}\mathrm{e}^{t^2/2}\int_{0}^{\infty} \mathrm{e}^{-(u-t)^2/2}\,\mathrm{d}u, \end{aligned}$$

where the third equality follows from the symmetry of the integrand around 0. By the change of variable $w = u - t$, we have

$$m_{|x|}(t) = \frac{2}{\sqrt{2\pi}} e^{t^2/2} \int_{-t}^{\infty} e^{-w^2/2} \, dw = 2e^{t^2/2}(1 - \Phi(-t)) = 2e^{t^2/2}\Phi(t)$$

using the symmetry of x around zero, that is, $\phi(u) = \phi(-u)$. Hence, $\mathrm{E}(|x|) = m'_{|x|}(0) = 2\phi(0) = \sqrt{2/\pi}$.
(b) We have

$$m_y(t) = \frac{1}{\sqrt{2\pi}} \int_{-\infty}^{\infty} e^{tu^2 - u^2/2} \, du = \frac{1}{\sqrt{2\pi}} \int_{-\infty}^{\infty} e^{-u^2(1-2t)/2} \, du,$$

where $t < \frac{1}{2}$. Making the transformation $w = u\sqrt{1-2t}$ with $dw = \sqrt{1-2t}\, du$, we obtain

$$m_y(t) = \frac{1}{\sqrt{1-2t}} \times \frac{1}{\sqrt{2\pi}} \int_{-\infty}^{\infty} e^{-w^2/2} \, dw = \frac{1}{\sqrt{1-2t}}.$$

Exercise 3.36 (Cumulants: first four and a tilt!) Let x be a variate with c.g.f. $\varkappa(t)$.
(a) Show that $\varkappa'(0) = \mathrm{E}(x)$.
(b) Show that $\varkappa''(0) = \mathrm{var}(x)$.
(c) Derive $\varkappa^{(3)}(0)$ and $\varkappa^{(4)}(0)$.
(d) Show that $f_y(v) := \exp(tv - \varkappa(t)) f_x(v)$ is a proper density function (it is called an *exponentially tilted density*), for any given t such that $\varkappa(t)$ exists, and that

$$\varkappa_y(s) = \varkappa(s+t) - \varkappa(t);$$

hence $\mathrm{E}(y) = \varkappa'(t)$ and $\mathrm{var}(y) = \varkappa''(t)$.

Solution
(a) By definition,

$$\varkappa'(t) = \frac{d}{dt} \log(m(t)) = \frac{m'(t)}{m(t)}.$$

Hence, $\varkappa'(0) = m'(0)/m(0) = m'(0) = \mathrm{E}(x)$.
(b) Using (a), we have

$$\varkappa''(t) = \frac{m''(t)m(t) - (m'(t))^2}{(m(t))^2},$$

and hence

$$\varkappa''(0) = m''(0) - (m'(0))^2 = \mathrm{E}(x^2) - (\mathrm{E}(x))^2 = \mathrm{var}(x).$$

In fact, we could have defined the centered variate $z := x - \mathrm{E}(x)$ having $\mathrm{E}(z) = 0$ but whose central moments are identical to those of x. From Exercise 3.22, the c.g.f. of z is

$$\log\left(e^{-t\,\mathrm{E}(x)} m(t)\right) = -t\,\mathrm{E}(x) + \varkappa(t),$$

so, apart from the first cumulant (the mean), the two variates will have identical higher-order c.g.f. derivatives and hence cumulants. We could therefore have treated $\varkappa^{(j)}(0)$ as if it were the j-th cumulant of z for $j > 1$, and used $\mathrm{E}(z) = 0$ to obtain

$$\varkappa''(0) = m''(0) - (m'(0))^2 = \mathrm{E}\left(z^2\right) - 0 = \mathrm{var}(z),$$

where $\mathrm{var}(z) = \mathrm{var}(x)$. We will do so henceforth.
(c) From (b),

$$\varkappa^{(3)}(t) = \frac{m^{(3)}(t)m(t) + m''(t)m'(t) - 2m''(t)m'(t)}{(m(t))^2} - 2m'(t)\frac{m''(t)m(t) - (m'(t))^2}{(m(t))^3}$$

and $m'(0) = 0$ for z gives

$$\varkappa^{(3)}(0) = \mathrm{E}\left(z^3\right) = \mathrm{E}\left((x - \mathrm{E}(x))^3\right).$$

Finally, differentiating and then omitting terms containing $m'(0)$ below,

$$\begin{aligned}\varkappa^{(4)}(0) &= \frac{m^{(4)}(0)m(0) - m''(0)m''(0)}{(m(0))^2} - 2m''(0)\frac{m''(0)m(0)}{(m(0))^3} \\ &= \mathrm{E}\left(z^4\right) - 3\left(\mathrm{var}(z)\right)^2 = \mathrm{E}\left((x - \mathrm{E}(x))^4\right) - 3\left(\mathrm{var}(x)\right)^2.\end{aligned}$$

Notice that the excess kurtosis of x is simply the scaled fourth cumulant $\varkappa^{(4)}(0)/\left(\mathrm{var}(x)\right)^2$.
(d) To ensure that the function is a proper density, we need to check the two conditions. First, we have $\exp(tv - \varkappa(t)) \geqslant 0$ and $f_x(v) \geqslant 0$. Second, if x is a continuous variate, the density of y integrates to 1 because

$$\begin{aligned}\int_{-\infty}^{\infty} \exp(tv - \varkappa(t)) f_x(v)\,\mathrm{d}v &= \exp(-\varkappa(t)) \int_{-\infty}^{\infty} \exp(tv)\, f_x(v)\,\mathrm{d}v \\ &= \exp(-\varkappa(t))\,\mathrm{E}_x(\exp(tx)) = \exp(-\varkappa(t))\, m_x(t) = 1.\end{aligned}$$

The same reasoning applies for x discrete, using a sum instead of an integral. The c.g.f. of y is

$$\begin{aligned}\varkappa_y(s) = \log\left(\mathrm{E}_y\left(\mathrm{e}^{sy}\right)\right) &= \log\left(\mathrm{e}^{-\varkappa(t)} \int_{-\infty}^{\infty} \mathrm{e}^{(s+t)v} f_x(v)\,\mathrm{d}v\right) \\ &= -\varkappa(t) + \log\left(\mathrm{E}_x\left(\mathrm{e}^{(s+t)x}\right)\right) = \varkappa(s+t) - \varkappa(t),\end{aligned}$$

and similarly for y discrete. The required moments follow from (a) and (b). The procedure of augmenting $f_x(v)$ with the exponential term $\exp(tv - \varkappa(t))$, which depends on the additional parameter t as well as on the argument v, can be related to the construction of a family of distributions to be encountered in (4.4), Exercise 11.15, and Section 14.3. See further properties of tilting in Exercise 7.34 and their uses in Exercise 10.41.

Exercise 3.37 (Cumulants: example) Assume that the p.d.f. of x is

$$f(u) = \begin{cases} e^{-(u+2)} & (-2 < u < \infty), \\ 0 & (\text{elsewhere}). \end{cases}$$

Compute its c.g.f. $\varkappa(t)$ and use this result to determine the first four cumulants.

Solution

We first compute $m(t)$ as follows:

$$m(t) = \int_{-2}^{\infty} e^{tu-u-2}\, du = e^{-2} \int_{-2}^{\infty} e^{-u(1-t)}\, du = \frac{-e^{-2}}{1-t} \left[e^{-u(1-t)} \right]_{-2}^{\infty} = \frac{e^{-2t}}{1-t}$$

for $t < 1$. We thus obtain $\varkappa(t) = \log(m(t)) = -\log(1-t) - 2t$, and this yields

$$\mathrm{E}(x) = \varkappa'(0) = \left. \frac{1}{1-t} \right|_{t=0} - 2 = -1,$$

$$\mathrm{var}(x) = \varkappa''(0) = \left. \frac{1}{(1-t)^2} \right|_{t=0} = 1,$$

$$\varkappa^{(3)}(0) = \left. \frac{2}{(1-t)^3} \right|_{t=0} = 2,$$

$$\varkappa^{(4)}(0) = \left. \frac{6}{(1-t)^4} \right|_{t=0} = 6.$$

The results confirm that the density is positively skewed, having a relatively long upper tail which is also thick (positive excess kurtosis). As an alternative derivation, $\varkappa^{(j)}(0)$ can be obtained from the logarithmic expansion of the c.g.f. as the coefficient of $t^j/j!$ in

$$\varkappa(t) = -\log(1-t) - 2t = -2t + \sum_{j=1}^{\infty} \frac{t^j}{j},$$

that is, $(j-1)!$ for $j > 1$.

Exercise 3.38 (Location and scale in cumulants) Let x be a variate with c.g.f. $\varkappa(t)$, and define $y := \alpha + \lambda x$, where $\alpha \in \mathbb{R}$ and $\lambda \in \mathbb{R}\backslash\{0\}$ are nonrandom.

(a) Show that the c.g.f. of y is $\varkappa_y(t) = \alpha t + \varkappa_x(\lambda t)$.

(b) Show that $\varkappa_y^{(j)}(0)$ is unaffected by α for $j > 1$.

(c) Show that $\varkappa_y'(0) = \alpha + \varkappa_x'(0)$ and that $\varkappa_y^{(j)}(0) = \lambda^j \varkappa_x^{(j)}(0)$ for $j > 1$.

(d) Assume that $\varkappa_x(t) = \frac{1}{2}t^2$. Show that $\varkappa_y'(0) = \alpha$, $\varkappa_y''(0) = \lambda^2$, and $\varkappa_y^{(j)}(0) = 0$ for $j > 2$.

Solution

(a) This follows as in Exercise 3.22:

$$m_y(t) = \mathrm{E}\left(e^{ty}\right) = \mathrm{E}\left(e^{t(\alpha+\lambda x)}\right) = e^{\alpha t}\, \mathrm{E}\left(e^{\lambda t x}\right) = e^{\alpha t} m_x(\lambda t),$$

and taking the logarithm of the m.g.f. gives the c.g.f. and the required result.
(b) Since α appears only in the term that is linear in t, differentiating with respect to t more than once makes α vanish. This is also obvious from the fact that, in $y := \alpha + \lambda x$, the α affects location only; hence it affects only $\varkappa_y'(0)$.
(c) This follows by the chain rule, since

$$\frac{\mathrm{d}\varkappa_y(t)}{\mathrm{d}t} = \alpha + \frac{\mathrm{d}\varkappa_x(\lambda t)}{\mathrm{d}t} = \alpha + \lambda \frac{\mathrm{d}\varkappa_x(\lambda t)}{\mathrm{d}(\lambda t)}$$

and repeating the operation $j-1$ times gives the required result.
(d) This is the c.g.f. of the standard normal variate introduced in Exercise 3.12(e) and seen a few times since then. Clearly, $\varkappa_x''(0) = 1$ and $\varkappa_x^{(j)}(0) = 0$ for $j > 2$. Applying (c) gives the required result for y.

Notes

General references for this chapter are the same as for Chapter 2. For an introduction to Fourier and related transforms, one may consult Spiegel (1965). Exercise 2.18 introduced truncated variates. A study of their c.f.s can be found in Abadir and Magdalinos (2002) for the general case, including truncated normal variates.

Exercise 3.3 and other "bad luck" phenomena are analyzed in Feller (1971, pp. 15–17). In Exercise 3.2, we saw that the expected value of the gamble is infinite. In spite of this, most people would not pay a finite large amount of money to enter this game! This is why it became known as the St. Petersburg paradox. Its resolution is by means of utility functions, a familiar notion for economists. See also the Notes to Chapter 11. Utility functions can also be interpreted as the subject of Exercise 3.10(b): it is customary to think of the function g as representing utility, and F_x, F_y as two different income distributions whose inequality is being compared. The result of the exercise can be proved more generally for g continuous and increasing, but not necessarily differentiable.

It is not the case that $\mathrm{E}(x_1/x_2) = \mathrm{E}(x_1)/\mathrm{E}(x_2)$ in general. Simple examples were given in Exercises 3.4 and 3.5, and the general case follows from Exercise 3.14 (Jensen's inequality). Nevertheless, Exercise 10.36 will show that, under some conditions, the difference between $\mathrm{E}(x_1/x_2)$ and $\mathrm{E}(x_1)/\mathrm{E}(x_2)$ is not large. See also the Notes to Chapter 8 for a special case where the equality holds exactly. Another exception will be seen in Exercise 11.29(f) where x_1/x_2 is independent of x_2.

An alternative method of solution to Exercise 3.18(b) could have been to differentiate $\int_m^c (2F(u)-1)\,\mathrm{d}u$ by Leibniz' rule (see Section A.4), giving rise to the first-order condition $2F(c) - 1 = 0$. However, one has to be careful with interpreting this in the case where $F(m) > \frac{1}{2}$, and with the second-order condition. We prefer the derivations presented in the exercise.

There are various other measures of skewness, which are less commonly used. They include Karl Pearson's first and second measures, respectively,

$$\frac{\text{mean} - \text{mode}}{\text{standard deviation}} \quad \text{and} \quad \frac{3\,(\text{mean} - \text{median})}{\text{standard deviation}}.$$

The latter lies in the interval $[-3, 3]$, as can be deduced from Exercise 3.18(c). If one of these two measures of skewness is adopted then, in the myth discussed in Exercise 3.21, one inequality is a tautology but the other will still not hold (as shown in the counterexample). If the reader is uncomfortable about the uniform component being flat and/or the exponential providing only a half-mode, then these can be altered slightly without changing the counterexample. For example, subject to rescaling the densities to integrate to 1, we can add an arbitrarily small slope to the uniform and/or make the density continuous at any point by having a steep line join it up to the next point. For further details, see Abadir (2005). See also the counterexample of Stoyanov (1997, p. 50), in the case where the sign of the skewness is not restricted.

Knowing all the moments of a random variable does *not* necessarily identify its distribution uniquely. To achieve this in general, we need further to know the c.f. that generates all these moments. For example, there is more than one distribution having all the moments of order $j \in \mathbb{N}$ that are found in Exercise 3.27(c); see Grimmett and Stirzaker (2001, p. 211) for other distributions sharing the same moments.

If the m.g.f. exists, then it is an analytic function (it satisfies the Cauchy–Riemann equations) and is thus differentiable infinitely many times in an open neighborhood of $t = 0$ in the complex plane; see Section A.3.4 and the Notes to Appendix A. As a result, $\varphi(\tau) = m(\mathrm{i}\tau)$ is also analytic and the expansion of Exercise 3.29 can be taken to infinitely many terms ($k = \infty$).

One can always construct a distribution function having any prespecified finite $\mu \in \mathbb{R}$ and $\sigma \in \mathbb{R}_+$, for any values of μ and σ. However, this does not extend to higher-order moments. If the distribution satisfies all the rules introduced in the previous chapter, then the matrix whose typical element is $\mu^{(i+j-2)}$ must have nonnegative leading principal minors. The first minor is $\mu^{(0)} \equiv 1 > 0$, and the second implies that $\sigma^2 \geqslant 0$, which is trivially satisfied. However, the third implies that the square of the skewness cannot exceed the kurtosis minus 1. This is an implication of Hamburger's (1920) moment problem.

Finally, characteristic functions have one more property that is not used in the rest of this book. It is known as the *positive semidefinite property*: for $\boldsymbol{A} := (\varphi(\tau_j - \tau_i))$, the Hermitian form $\boldsymbol{s}^*\boldsymbol{A}\boldsymbol{s}$ is nonnegative for all complex vectors $\boldsymbol{s}$ and real scalars τ_i, τ_j. This arises from the following reasoning. Since $\varphi(-\tau)$ and $\varphi(\tau)$ are complex conjugates, the matrix is Hermitian since $(\varphi(\tau_j - \tau_i))^* = (\varphi(\tau_j - \tau_i))$; hence $(\boldsymbol{s}^*\boldsymbol{A}\boldsymbol{s})^* = \boldsymbol{s}^*\boldsymbol{A}\boldsymbol{s}$, which is therefore real. Furthermore,

$$\boldsymbol{s}^*\boldsymbol{A}\boldsymbol{s} = \sum_{i,j} s_i^* \operatorname{E}\left(\mathrm{e}^{\mathrm{i}(\tau_j - \tau_i)x}\right) s_j = \operatorname{E}\left(\left(\sum_i s_i \mathrm{e}^{\mathrm{i}\tau_i x}\right)^* \left(\sum_j s_j \mathrm{e}^{\mathrm{i}\tau_j x}\right)\right) = \operatorname{E}\left(\left|\sum_i s_i \mathrm{e}^{\mathrm{i}\tau_i x}\right|^2\right),$$

which is nonnegative. A continuous function φ is a c.f. if and only if it satisfies this property and $\varphi(0) = 1$, a result known as *Bochner's theorem*; see Chapter 19 of Feller (1971) for a proof.

4

Special univariate distributions

So far, we have studied the properties of general distributions of one-dimensional variates and have applied them to special distributions in some of the exercises. This chapter is an unusual one, in that it seems like an extended appendix, yet it is an essential ingredient at the heart of statistics. Here, we collect the special distributions most often encountered and relate them to one another. In many instances, distributions which are special cases of others have been included, nevertheless, because of their importance in statistics. Some of these distributions arise out of natural phenomena or have attractive special properties which are explored in the exercises.

We denote by $z \sim \mathrm{D}_{\mathcal{Z}}(\boldsymbol{\theta})$ a random variable $z \in \mathcal{Z}$ varying according to some *distribution* (or *law*) D which depends on a vector of parameters $\boldsymbol{\theta} \in \Theta$, where Θ is the *parameter space* over which the distribution is defined. When the support is unambiguous, the subscript $\mathcal{Z}$ is dropped. We sometimes also require the use of a subscript for the distribution when denoting its quantile; for example, $\mathrm{D}_{0.05}$ represents the 5% quantile of distribution D. Thus, the 5% quantile of the normal is $\mathrm{N}_{0.05} \approx -1.645$ (to three decimal places), because $\Pr(z < -1.645) \approx 5\%$ for a normal distribution. The first type of subscript is a set, whereas the latter is a real number from the interval $[0, 1]$, so no ambiguities should arise. From Chapter 6 onwards, we will introduce multivariate distributions, which may also require the use of subscripts to denote the dimension of the variate, a natural number (it is 1 here); hence there is still no scope for ambiguity.

Table 4.1: Distributions for discrete variates z.

	p.d.f. $f_z(w)$	domain	c.f. $\varphi_z(\tau)$
Uniform, discrete: $\mathrm{U}_{\{n,m\}}$	$\dfrac{1}{m-n+1}$	$w \in \{n, n+1, \dots, m\}$, $n, m \in \mathbb{Z}$, with $m \geqslant n$, $\mu = \frac{n+m}{2}$, $\sigma^2 = \frac{(m-n+1)^2-1}{12}$	$\dfrac{e^{in\tau} - e^{i(m+1)\tau}}{(m-n+1)(1-e^{i\tau})}$
Binomial: $\mathrm{Bin}(n,p)$	$\binom{n}{w} p^w (1-p)^{n-w}$	$w \in \{0, 1, \dots, n\}$, $n \in \mathbb{N}$, $p \in [0,1]$, $\mu = np$, $\sigma^2 = np(1-p)$	$\left(1 + \left(e^{i\tau} - 1\right) p\right)^n$
Bernoulli: $\mathrm{Ber}(p)$	$p^w (1-p)^{1-w}$	$w \in \{0, 1\}$, $p \in [0,1]$, $\mu = p$, $\sigma^2 = p(1-p)$	$1 + \left(e^{i\tau} - 1\right) p$
Negative binomial: $\mathrm{Nbin}(\nu, p)$	$\binom{w+\nu-1}{w} p^\nu (1-p)^w$	$w \in \mathbb{Z}_{0,+}$, $\nu \in \mathbb{R}_+$, $p \in (0,1]$, $\mu = (p^{-1}-1)\nu$, $\sigma^2 = p^{-1}\mu$	$\left(p^{-1} + \left(1 - p^{-1}\right) e^{i\tau}\right)^{-\nu}$
Geometric: $\mathrm{Geo}(p)$	$p(1-p)^w$	$w \in \mathbb{Z}_{0,+}$, $p \in (0,1]$, $\mu = p^{-1} - 1$, $\sigma^2 = p^{-1}\mu$	$\left(p^{-1} + \left(1 - p^{-1}\right) e^{i\tau}\right)^{-1}$
Hypergeometric: $\mathrm{Hyp}(m, k, n)$	$\dfrac{\binom{k}{w}\binom{m-k}{n-w}}{\binom{m}{n}}$	$w \in \{0, 1, \dots, n\}$, $n \in \{1, 2, \dots, m\}$, $k \in \{0, 1, \dots, m\}$, $m \in \mathbb{N}$, $\mu = kn/m$, σ^2 given in (4.2)	$\sum_{j=0}^{n} \dfrac{\binom{k}{j}\binom{n}{j}}{\binom{m}{j}} \left(e^{i\tau} - 1\right)^j$
Poisson: $\mathrm{Poi}(\lambda)$	$\dfrac{e^{-\lambda}\lambda^w}{w!}$	$w \in \mathbb{Z}_{0,+}$, $\mu = \sigma^2 = \lambda \in \mathbb{R}_+$	$\exp\left(\lambda\left(e^{i\tau} - 1\right)\right)$

A *random sample* of values of z can be obtained by repeated independent drawings (or observations) from the same $\mathrm{D}_{\mathcal{Z}}(\boldsymbol{\theta})$. This is often written as $z_i \sim \mathrm{IID}_{\mathcal{Z}}(\boldsymbol{\theta})$, where $i = 1, \ldots, n$, and is the abbreviation of "the z_i's are *independently and identically distributed* (or i.i.d.) as $\mathrm{D}_{\mathcal{Z}}(\boldsymbol{\theta})$". There is some redundancy in this notation, in the sense that the distributions are clearly identical over i whenever $\mathcal{Z}$ and $\boldsymbol{\theta}$ are not varying with i. For this reason, when drawing from $\mathrm{N}(\mu, \sigma^2)$, the *normal distribution with mean* μ *and variance* σ^2, we write $z_i \sim \mathrm{IN}(\mu, \sigma^2)$, where $i = 1, \ldots, n$, dropping the "identical" from $\mathrm{IIN}(\mu, \sigma^2)$. We denote sequences, which are ordered sets, just as we denoted sets: with braces (curly brackets). Ordered sequences $\{z_1, \ldots, z_n\}$ are summarized as $\{z_i\}_{i=1}^n$ or, dropping the index i, simply $\{z_n\}$. We therefore also use the shorthand notation $\{z_n\} \sim \mathrm{IID}_{\mathcal{Z}}(\boldsymbol{\theta})$. As in Chapter 1, we warn that pairwise independence does not necessarily lead to joint independence. When using the term "independence" in the case of a sample, we will mean joint independence, unless stated otherwise.

In the tables of this chapter, the name and notation for a distribution are followed by its p.d.f., its domain of definition, and the alternative description in terms of its c.f. when the latter is known. Whenever they are expressible in concise form, the mean μ and variance σ^2 also appear, either directly as parameters or as functions of the parameters of the p.d.f. (these parameters may have a physical interpretation and so are not always replaced by μ or σ^2, even if it would be correct to do so). The exception is if these two moments do not exist, or if they are too cumbersome to display in the table. We use p for probability in the discrete case, but p for power in the continuous case where we also use α, β for location, λ for scaling, and ν (or n, m) for the shape of the density.

In Table 4.1, we list the most important distributions for discrete variates. We can rewrite the p.d.f. of $\mathrm{Nbin}(\nu, p)$ by means of

$$\begin{aligned}\binom{w+\nu-1}{w} &= \frac{(w+\nu-1)(w+\nu-2)\cdots(\nu+1)(\nu)}{w!}\\ &= (-1)^w \frac{(-\nu)(-\nu-1)\cdots(-\nu-w+2)(-\nu-w+1)}{w!}\\ &= (-1)^w \binom{-\nu}{w},\end{aligned} \tag{4.1}$$

where $-\nu$ explains the qualifier N (negative) in Nbin. The relation of $\mathrm{Nbin}(\nu, p)$ to $\mathrm{Bin}(n, p)$ is explored in Exercise 4.4.

The c.f. of the hypergeometric distribution follows from its p.d.f., and it is obtained as

$$\mathrm{E}\left(\mathrm{e}^{\mathrm{i}\tau z}\right) = \sum_{w=0}^{n} \frac{\binom{k}{w}\binom{m-k}{n-w}}{\binom{m}{n}} \mathrm{e}^{\mathrm{i}\tau w},$$

which is not in a convenient form for calculating derivatives in the neighborhood (short for "an arbitrarily small open neighborhood") of $\mathrm{e}^0 = 1$. However, this c.f. (called the *Gauss hypergeometric function*, a special case of the hypergeometric function defined in the Notes to this chapter) satisfies an identity which allows us to rewrite it as stated in the table; see also the comment at the end of Exercise 4.11(b). The corresponding m.g.f. exists and is obtained as $\varphi(t/\mathrm{i})$; hence, Table 4.1 implies the m.g.f.

$$m(t) = 1 + \frac{kn}{m}\left(\mathrm{e}^t - 1\right) + \frac{k(k-1)n(n-1)}{2m(m-1)}\left(\mathrm{e}^t - 1\right)^2 + \cdots,$$

which gives $\mu = kn/m$ and

$$\sigma^2 = \left(\frac{kn}{m} + \frac{k(k-1)n(n-1)}{m(m-1)}\right) - \mu^2 = \frac{kn}{m}\left(1 - \frac{k}{m}\right)\frac{m-n}{m-1}. \tag{4.2}$$

Further moments can be obtained similarly. In Table 4.1, all the m.g.f.s corresponding to the listed c.f.s exist, and some were derived earlier; for example, see Exercise 3.33. This is not always the case for the next table, as we will see. But first we note that, for the Poi(λ), not just the mean and variance but *all* cumulants are equal to λ; see Exercise 3.36 for the interpretation of the first few cumulants in terms of moments. This follows from expanding the Poisson's c.g.f. (obtained from Table 4.1) as

$$\varkappa(t) = \log\left(\varphi(t/\mathrm{i})\right) = \lambda\left(\mathrm{e}^t - 1\right) = \lambda\sum_{j=1}^{\infty}\frac{t^j}{j!},$$

or from $\varkappa^{(j)}(0) = \lambda$ for all $j \in \mathbb{N}$. Given that the m.g.f. exists, this property identifies a Poisson variate, just as Exercise 3.38(d) shows that a normal variate is identified by the property $\varkappa^{(j)}(0) = 0$ for all $j > 2$.

In Table 4.2, we list the most important distributions for continuous variates, some of which will be plotted in Exercise 4.14. Usually, special cases are listed after their more general counterparts, but there are instances of two generalizations where one is not a special case of the other; for example, the GG and noncentral χ^2 generalize the central χ^2 in different ways. A few of these distributions have further generalizations, which are not covered here. Straightforward modifications (for example, location shifts or logarithmic versions such as the fat-tailed log-gamma or log-logistic) have usually not been listed either, nor have two-sided extensions. For example, the *two-sided generalized gamma* variate $x \in \mathbb{R}$ has a density that can be generated from $z := |x| \sim \mathrm{GG}(\nu, p, \lambda)$ and then tossing a fair coin to choose the sign of x, giving $f_x(u) = \frac{1}{2}f_z(|u|)$ for $u \in \mathbb{R}$; this follows from Exercise 2.22 since $f_z(w) = 0$ when $w < 0$. When $\nu p = 1$, this density is known as the *generalized error density* (GED).

Some distributions in Table 4.2 are known under alternative names: the continuous uniform as *rectangular*, the normal as *Gaussian*, the Laplace as *double exponential*. We have included the *generalized inverse gamma* (for which $p < 0$) in our definition of the generalized gamma. (Note that we use IG for inverse Gaussian, not inverse gamma which is subsumed into GG.) An important related distribution is the *generalized extreme value* (GEV), with p.d.f.

$$\frac{\lambda\exp\left(-\left(1 - \frac{\lambda(w-\alpha)}{p}\right)^p\right)}{\left(1 - \frac{\lambda(w-\alpha)}{p}\right)^{1-p}} \qquad \left(\lambda \in \mathbb{R}_+,\ p^{-1} \in \mathbb{R},\ 1 - \lambda(w-\alpha)p^{-1} \in \mathbb{R}_+\right) \tag{4.3}$$

and corresponding c.d.f. $\exp\left(-\left(1-\lambda\left(w-\alpha\right)/p\right)^{p}\right)$. Exercise 4.28 shows that this is essentially a generalized gamma distribution, apart from a location shift by α when $p^{-1} \neq 0$. The qualifier "generalized" in GEV is there because it encompasses all three types of extreme-value distributions. Such distributions arise when considering extreme events, such as river flooding or stock market crashes. The Type I distribution is the Gumbel, obtained by letting $p^{-1} \to 0$ in the GEV c.d.f.; upon differentiating with respect to w, we obtain the formula in Table 4.2 where the listed constant $\gamma := -\,\mathrm{d}\log(\Gamma(w))/\,\mathrm{d}w\,|_{w=1} \approx 0.577$ is *Euler's gamma*. Extreme-value distribution Types II and III are also called, respectively, Fréchet ($p < 0$) and Weibull ($p > 0$, then take $\alpha = -p/\lambda$ in GEV and redefine w as $-w$ and $(\lambda/p)^p$ as λ to get the p.d.f. in Table 4.2). The sampling setup that leads to these three distributions will be analyzed in Chapter 10 of Part B.

Whenever the support $\mathcal{Z}$ is an interval of infinite length, but with $\mathcal{Z} \subset \mathbb{R}$, we have standardized it to be $\mathbb{R}_+$ except in the Pareto case where $\mathcal{Z}$ has to be a proper subset of $\mathbb{R}_+$. (A Pareto defined on $\mathbb{R}_+$ is called a *shifted Pareto*.) The term *standardized* (or *standard*) *distribution* $\mathrm{D.}(\cdot)$ is typically used when the variate has $\sigma = 1$ (or scaling $\lambda = 1$ if σ does not exist), and support satisfying one of the following:

- $w \in (0, 1)$ for intervals of finite length;
- $w \in \mathbb{R}_+$ for intervals of infinite length but which are proper subsets of $\mathbb{R}$; or
- z is centered around 0 when $w \in \mathbb{R}$.

Important examples include: the *standard beta* $\mathrm{Beta}_{(0,1)}(p, q)$, denoted by $\mathrm{Beta}(p, q)$; and the *standard normal* $\mathrm{N}(0, 1)$, whose p.d.f. is denoted by $\phi(w)$ and c.d.f. by $\Phi(w)$, already seen a few times, mainly in Exercises 3.12(e) and 3.35. In the density of $\mathrm{Beta}(p, q)$, the factor $B(p, q)$ is the beta function of Chapter 1. The *standard Cauchy* has parameters $\alpha = 0$ for location (or centering) and $\lambda = 1$ for scale, where we have been careful not to use the terms "mean" and "standard deviation" (or "variance") which do not exist for this variate, as discussed in the introduction to Chapter 3. This distribution is equivalent to Student's $\mathrm{t}(1)$, as can be verified from the equality of the two densities. Note that the scale parameter λ is used instead of σ in the log-normal (see the reason why in Exercise 4.14(b)), Cauchy, and inverse gamma (GG when $p < 0$) to *increase* the spread of the variate as λ increases, unlike in the remaining cases of Table 4.2.

Note that $\chi^2(n) = \mathrm{GG}\left(\frac{1}{2}n, 1, \frac{1}{2}\right)$, and that any positive m or n (called *degrees of freedom*) are allowed in χ^2, F, and t, but it is often the case in applications and in published tables of quantiles that $m, n \in \mathbb{N}$. By f_{D} denoting the p.d.f. of a distribution D, the noncentral χ^2 and F have an attractive representation in terms of the mixtures of densities introduced in Chapter 2. For example, the noncentral $\chi^2(n, \delta)$ is the mixture of central $\chi^2(2j + n)$ such that $j \in \mathbb{Z}_{0,+}$ varies according to the mixing $\mathrm{Poi}(\delta/2)$ p.d.f. $\exp(-\delta/2)\,(\delta/2)^j/j!$. The same applies to the corresponding c.f.s, as seen in the χ^2 case by applying

$$\exp\left(\frac{\mathrm{i}\delta\tau}{1-2\mathrm{i}\tau}\right) = \exp\left(-\frac{\delta}{2}\right)\exp\left(\frac{\delta}{2\left(1-2\mathrm{i}\tau\right)}\right) = \exp\left(-\frac{\delta}{2}\right)\sum_{j=0}^{\infty}\frac{(\delta/2)^j}{j!}\left(1-2\mathrm{i}\tau\right)^{-j}.$$

Table 4.2: Distributions for continuous variates z.

	p.d.f. $f_z(w)$	domain	c.f. $\varphi_z(\tau)$
Beta: $\mathrm{Beta}_{(\alpha,\beta)}(p,q)$	$\frac{(w-\alpha)^{p-1}(\beta-w)^{q-1}}{B(p,q)(\beta-\alpha)^{p+q-1}}$	$w \in (\alpha,\beta)$, $\alpha < \beta \in \mathbb{R}$, $p,q \in \mathbb{R}_+$, $\mu = \frac{\alpha q+\beta p}{q+p}$, $\sigma^2 = \frac{pq(\beta-\alpha)^2}{(p+q+1)(p+q)^2}$	$\mathrm{e}^{\mathrm{i}\alpha\tau} \sum_{j=0}^{\infty} \frac{\binom{-p}{j}(\mathrm{i}(\beta-\alpha)\tau)^j}{\binom{-p-q}{j} j!}$
Uniform, continuous: $\mathrm{U}_{(\alpha,\beta)}$	$\frac{1}{\beta-\alpha}$	$w \in (\alpha,\beta)$, $\alpha < \beta \in \mathbb{R}$, $\mu = \frac{\alpha+\beta}{2}$, $\sigma^2 = \frac{(\beta-\alpha)^2}{12}$	$\frac{\mathrm{e}^{\mathrm{i}\beta\tau} - \mathrm{e}^{\mathrm{i}\alpha\tau}}{\mathrm{i}(\beta-\alpha)\tau}$
Normal: $\mathrm{N}(\mu,\sigma^2)$	$\frac{1}{\sigma\sqrt{2\pi}} \exp\left(-\frac{(w-\mu)^2}{2\sigma^2}\right)$	$w,\mu \in \mathbb{R}$, $\sigma \in \mathbb{R}_+$	$\exp\left(\mathrm{i}\mu\tau - \frac{\sigma^2\tau^2}{2}\right)$
Inverse Gaussian: $\mathrm{IG}(\mu,\sigma^2)$	$\sqrt{\frac{\mu^3}{2\pi w^3\sigma^2}} \exp\left(-\frac{\mu(w-\mu)^2}{2\sigma^2 w}\right)$	$w,\mu,\sigma \in \mathbb{R}_+$	$\exp\left(\frac{\mu^2}{\sigma^2} - \frac{\mu^2}{\sigma^2}\sqrt{1-\frac{2\mathrm{i}\sigma^2\tau}{\mu}}\right)$
Log-normal: $\mathrm{LN}(\alpha,\lambda^2)$	$\frac{1}{w\lambda\sqrt{2\pi}} \exp\left(-\frac{(\log(w)-\alpha)^2}{2\lambda^2}\right)$	$w,\lambda \in \mathbb{R}_+$, $\alpha \in \mathbb{R}$; $\mathrm{E}(z^\tau) = \exp\left(\alpha\tau + \frac{\lambda^2\tau^2}{2}\right)$	no known solution to integral needed for c.f. [and $\nexists$ m.g.f.]
Gumbel: $\mathrm{Gum}(\alpha,\lambda)$	$\lambda \exp\left(-\lambda(w-\alpha) - \mathrm{e}^{-\lambda(w-\alpha)}\right)$	$w,\alpha \in \mathbb{R}$, $\lambda = \frac{\pi}{\sigma\sqrt{6}} \in \mathbb{R}_+$, $\mu = \alpha + \frac{\gamma}{\lambda}$ (see Note for γ)	$\mathrm{e}^{\mathrm{i}\alpha\tau}\Gamma\left(1-\mathrm{i}\lambda^{-1}\tau\right)$
Generalized gamma: $\mathrm{GG}(\nu,p,\lambda)$	$\frac{\lvert p\rvert\lambda^\nu w^{\nu p-1}}{\Gamma(\nu)} \exp(-\lambda w^p)$	$w,\nu,\lambda \in \mathbb{R}_+$, $p \in \mathbb{R}\setminus\{0\}$, $\mu = \lambda^{-\frac{1}{p}} \frac{\Gamma\left(\nu+\frac{1}{p}\right)}{\Gamma(\nu)}$ if $\nu > -\frac{1}{p}$	$\sum_{j=0}^{\infty} \frac{\Gamma(\nu+j/p)(\mathrm{i}\lambda^{-1/p}\tau)^j}{\Gamma(\nu)\, j!}$, $p \in \mathbb{R}_+$. [$\nexists$ m.g.f. for $p \in \mathbb{R}_-$]
Weibull: $\mathrm{Wei}(p,\lambda)$	$\lambda p w^{p-1} \exp(-\lambda w^p)$	$w,p,\lambda \in \mathbb{R}_+$, $\mu = \lambda^{-1/p}\Gamma(1+1/p)$	$\sum_{j=0}^{\infty} \frac{\Gamma(1+j/p)(\mathrm{i}\lambda^{-1/p}\tau)^j}{j!}$
Gamma: $\mathrm{Gam}(\nu,\lambda)$	$\frac{\lambda^\nu w^{\nu-1}}{\Gamma(\nu)} \exp(-\lambda w)$	$w,\nu,\lambda \in \mathbb{R}_+$, $\mu = \sigma^2\lambda = \frac{\nu}{\lambda}$	$\left(1-\mathrm{i}\lambda^{-1}\tau\right)^{-\nu}$
Chi-squared (χ^2): $\chi^2(n)$	$\frac{(w/2)^{\frac{n}{2}-1}}{2\Gamma\left(\frac{n}{2}\right)} \exp\left(-\frac{w}{2}\right)$	$w,n \in \mathbb{R}_+$, $\mu = \frac{\sigma^2}{2} = n$	$(1-2\mathrm{i}\tau)^{-n/2}$

continued

Noncentral χ^2: $\chi^2(n,\delta)$	$\mathrm{e}^{-\delta/2}\sum_{j=0}^{\infty}\frac{(\delta/2)^j}{j!}f_{\chi^2(2j+n)}(w)$ $=\frac{(w/2)^{\frac{n}{2}-1}}{2}\mathrm{e}^{-(\delta+w)/2}\sum_{j=0}^{\infty}\frac{(\delta w/4)^j}{j!\Gamma\left(j+\frac{n}{2}\right)}$	$w,n,\delta\in\mathbb{R}_+$, $\mu=n+\delta$, $\sigma^2=2n+4\delta$	$\mathrm{e}^{-\delta/2}\sum_{j=0}^{\infty}\frac{(\delta/2)^j}{j!}\varphi_{\chi^2(2j+n)}(\tau)$ $=(1-2\mathrm{i}\tau)^{-n/2}\exp\left(\frac{\mathrm{i}\delta\tau}{1-2\mathrm{i}\tau}\right)$
Exponential: $\mathrm{Expo}(\lambda)$	$\lambda\exp(-\lambda w)$	$w,\lambda\in\mathbb{R}_+$, $\mu=\sigma^2\lambda=\frac{1}{\lambda}$	$\left(1-\mathrm{i}\lambda^{-1}\tau\right)^{-1}$
Laplace: $\mathrm{Lap}(\mu,\lambda)$	$\frac{\lambda}{2}\exp(-\lambda\lvert w-\mu\rvert)$	$w,\mu\in\mathbb{R}$, $\lambda=\frac{\sqrt{2}}{\sigma}\in\mathbb{R}_+$	$\frac{\mathrm{e}^{\mathrm{i}\mu\tau}}{1+\lambda^{-2}\tau^2}$
Logistic: $\mathrm{Lgst}(\mu,\sigma^2)$	$\frac{\pi}{\sigma\sqrt{48}}\left(\cosh\left(\frac{\pi(w-\mu)}{\sigma\sqrt{12}}\right)\right)^{-2}$	$w,\mu\in\mathbb{R}$, $\sigma\in\mathbb{R}_+$	$\frac{\sigma\tau\sqrt{3}\mathrm{e}^{\mathrm{i}\mu\tau}}{\sinh\left(\sigma\tau\sqrt{3}\right)}$
Noncentral F: $\mathrm{F}(m,n,\delta)$	$\mathrm{e}^{-\delta/2}\sum_{j=0}^{\infty}\frac{(\delta/2)^j}{j!}\frac{m}{2j+m}f_{\mathrm{F}(2j+m,n)}\left(\frac{mw}{2j+m}\right)$ $=\frac{m}{n}\mathrm{e}^{-\delta/2}\sum_{j=0}^{\infty}\frac{(\delta/2)^j\left(\frac{m}{n}w\right)^{j+\frac{m}{2}-1}}{B\left(j+\frac{m}{2},\frac{n}{2}\right)j!\left(1+\frac{m}{n}w\right)^{j+\frac{m+n}{2}}}$	$w,m,n,\delta\in\mathbb{R}_+$, $\mu=\frac{n(m+\delta)}{m(n-2)}$ if $n>2$	$\mathrm{e}^{-\delta/2}\sum_{j=0}^{\infty}\frac{(\delta/2)^j}{j!}\varphi_{\mathrm{F}(2j+m,n)}\left(\frac{2j+m}{m}\tau\right)$ [$\nexists$ m.g.f. for $n<\infty$]
Fisher–Snedecor F: $\mathrm{F}(m,n)$	$\frac{\frac{m}{n}\left(\frac{m}{n}w\right)^{\frac{m}{2}-1}}{B\left(\frac{m}{2},\frac{n}{2}\right)\left(1+\frac{m}{n}w\right)^{\frac{m+n}{2}}}$	$w,m,n\in\mathbb{R}_+$, $\mu=\frac{n}{n-2}$ if $n>2$	c.f. expressible in terms of hypergeometric functions [and $\nexists$ m.g.f. for $n<\infty$]
Noncentral t: $\mathrm{t}(n,\delta)$	$f_{\mathrm{t}(n)}(w)\,\mathrm{e}^{-\delta^2/2}\sum_{j=0}^{\infty}\frac{\Gamma\left(\frac{j+n+1}{2}\right)}{\Gamma\left(\frac{n+1}{2}\right)j!}\left(\frac{\delta w\sqrt{2}}{\sqrt{n+w^2}}\right)^j$	$w,\delta\in\mathbb{R}$, $n\in\mathbb{R}_+$, $\mu=\frac{\sqrt{n}\Gamma\left(\frac{n-1}{2}\right)}{\sqrt{2}\Gamma\left(\frac{n}{2}\right)}\delta$ if $n>1$	c.f. expressible in terms of hypergeometric functions [and $\nexists$ m.g.f. for $n<\infty$]
Student's t: $\mathrm{t}(n)$	$\frac{\Gamma\left(\frac{n+1}{2}\right)}{\sqrt{\pi n}\Gamma\left(\frac{n}{2}\right)\left(1+\frac{w^2}{n}\right)^{\frac{n+1}{2}}}$	$w\in\mathbb{R}$, $n\in\mathbb{R}_+$, $\mu=0$ if $n>1$	c.f. expressible in terms of hypergeometric functions [and $\nexists$ m.g.f. for $n<\infty$]
Cauchy: $\mathrm{Cau}(\alpha,\lambda)$	$\frac{1}{\pi\lambda\left(1+\left(\frac{w-\alpha}{\lambda}\right)^2\right)}$	$w,\alpha\in\mathbb{R}$, $\lambda\in\mathbb{R}_+$, [$\nexists\,\mathrm{E}(z^j)$ for $j\in\mathbb{N}$]	$\mathrm{e}^{\mathrm{i}\alpha\tau-\lambda\lvert\tau\rvert}$ [$\nexists$ m.g.f.]
Pareto: $\mathrm{Par}_{(\alpha,\infty)}(p)$	$\frac{p\alpha^p}{w^{p+1}}$	$w-\alpha,\alpha,p\in\mathbb{R}_+$, $\mu=\frac{p\alpha}{p-1}$ if $p>1$	$p(-\mathrm{i}\alpha\tau)^p\,\Gamma(-p,-\mathrm{i}\alpha\tau)$ [$\nexists$ m.g.f.]

Note: for the Gumbel, $\gamma\equiv 0.577216\ldots$ is Euler's gamma; while for the Pareto, $\Gamma(\cdot,\cdot)$ is the incomplete gamma function of Exercise 4.20.

Series expansions are not unique, as will be illustrated for $\Phi(w)$ in Exercises 4.21 and 10.40, the latter being nonconvergent. See also Exercise 4.11. The series in Table 4.2 are absolutely convergent for finite parameter and argument values, with one exception. For some parameter values of GG and Weibull, the listed series representation of $\varphi(\tau)$ is convergent only in the neighborhood of $\tau = 0$, which is what is required for calculating $\varphi^{(j)}(0)$. One should be careful that, when the c.f. is given but the m.g.f. does not exist, one should not differentiate too many times to get high-order "moments" that do not exist. For example, when $p < 0$ in GG, one may use the stated c.f. for obtaining the j-th moment as the coefficient of $(\mathrm{i}\tau)^j/j!$ in the expansion, so long as $j < -\nu p$ but not for larger j. A similar comment applies to the last entry of Table 4.2, where the c.f. $\Gamma(\cdot,\cdot)$ is the *incomplete gamma function*, which is also used to compute the c.d.f. of gamma variates; see Exercise 4.20.

There exist many classifications of distributions. We now consider three of the most prominent.

In Part B of this volume, important results on the optimality of some statistical procedures will be proved in generality for a class of variates z whose p.d.f. belongs to a special family. Let m be the dimension of the vector $\boldsymbol{\theta} \in \Theta$. Then, a p.d.f. $f(w)$ belongs to the *exponential family* (or *exponential class*) if there exists a factorization

$$f(w) = g_0(\boldsymbol{\theta})h_0(w)\exp\left(\sum_{l=1}^{j} g_l(\boldsymbol{\theta})h_l(w)\right), \tag{4.4}$$

where the functions $h_{\bullet}$ depend on w only, and the *natural parameters* defined for $l = 1, \dots, j$ by

$$\nu_l := g_l(\boldsymbol{\theta}) \quad \text{and} \quad \boldsymbol{\nu} := (\nu_1, \dots, \nu_j)' \in \Upsilon$$

are functions of $\boldsymbol{\theta}$ alone and so is $g_0(\boldsymbol{\theta})$; the *natural parameterization* of the family is

$$f(w) = m_0(\boldsymbol{\nu})h_0(w)\exp\left(\boldsymbol{\nu}'\boldsymbol{h}(w)\right) \tag{4.5}$$

with $\boldsymbol{h}(w) := (h_1(w), \dots, h_j(w))'$. (The prime after vectors denotes their transpose, in the last case transforming from a row to a column vector. Note that a prime at the end of a vector function as in $\boldsymbol{h}(\cdot)'$ denotes the transpose of the vector, whereas $\boldsymbol{h}'(\cdot)$ denotes a derivative of the function.) As an example of (4.4), $\mathrm{N}(\mu, \sigma^2)$ has $\boldsymbol{\theta} = (\mu, \sigma^2)'$ and

$$\begin{aligned} f(w) &= \frac{1}{\sqrt{2\pi\sigma^2}}\exp\left(\frac{-w^2 + 2\mu w - \mu^2}{2\sigma^2}\right) \\ &= \left(\frac{1}{\sqrt{2\pi\sigma^2}}\exp\left(\frac{-\mu^2}{2\sigma^2}\right)\right)\left(w^0\right)\exp\left(\left(\frac{-1}{2\sigma^2}\right)\left(w^2\right) + \left(\frac{\mu}{\sigma^2}\right)(w)\right) \end{aligned} \tag{4.6}$$

such that $j = 2 = m$. Clearly, the functions g and h need not be uniquely defined, and it is their mere existence which allows membership of the exponential class. In the above example, we could have written instead

$$f(w) = \left(\frac{1}{\sqrt{2\pi\sigma^2}} \exp\left(\frac{-\mu^2}{2\sigma^2}\right)\right)\left(w^0\right) \exp\left(\left(\frac{-1}{2\sigma^2}\right)\left(w^2+w\right) + \left(\frac{1+2\mu}{2\sigma^2}\right)(w)\right).$$

The exponential-family classification applies to discrete as well as to continuous variates, and subsumes many of the p.d.f.s in the tables; see Exercise 4.37. An example of such a discrete variate is Geo(p), where $\theta = p$ and

$$f(w) = p(1-p)^w = (p)\left(w^0\right) \mathrm{e}^{(\log(1-p))(w)}, \tag{4.7}$$

which satisfies the general definition (4.4), with $j = 1 = m$. From the first term of the logarithmic expansion in Section A.3.2, $\log(1-p) \approx -p$ for small p, and the geometric density (4.7) can be viewed as the discrete analogue of Expo(p); see also Exercises 4.12 and 4.13 for the no-memory property that they share. We define the exponential family (4.4) to be *regular* if the following conditions are satisfied:
(i) the support of z does not depend on $\boldsymbol{\theta}$;
(ii) the $g_l(\boldsymbol{\theta})$ are continuous and functionally independent for all $\boldsymbol{\theta} \in \Theta$, and $m_0(\boldsymbol{\nu}) > 0$ defines a j-dimensional open set for $\boldsymbol{\nu}$ that coincides with the set Υ; and
(iii) either

(a) for discrete variates, the $h_l(w)$ are linearly independent functions of the discrete w, or

(b) for continuous variates, $h_0(w)$ is continuous and the derivatives $h_l'(w)$ are linearly independent continuous functions.

The linear independence of h_l or of its first derivative ensures that the family is in *reduced form*; otherwise some of the j components would be redundant and the sum could be compressed into a smaller one. The reason for considering derivatives in the continuous case is that the mean-value theorem (see Section A.3.4 since here w is a scalar) can be used to compress the sum if the h_l' are not linearly independent. The strong requirement of functional independence of the g_l is needed to prevent an equivalent reformulation of $\boldsymbol{\theta}$ that would make the functions linearly dependent. Typically $m = j$ for a regular exponential, while $m < j$ leads to a *curved exponential*. For example, N(μ, μ^2) is a curved exponential with $m = 1 < j = 2$ and $\mu \in \mathbb{R}$ is not the two-dimensional space required in condition (ii) above, unlike the regular case of N(μ, σ^2) defined over the open two-dimensional $\Theta = \mathbb{R} \times \mathbb{R}_+$ and $\Upsilon = \mathbb{R}_- \times \mathbb{R}$ (the latter follows from (4.6)). Points may be deleted from Θ if necessary to achieve the open set needed to regularize the family, but this may not always be feasible in the case of discrete z. Further comparisons of m and j will be encountered from Chapter 11 onwards.

Each distribution carries an inherent amount of information, which can also be used for classification purposes. Measures of information include the *Tsallis entropy* and *Rényi entropy* defined, respectively, by

$$\frac{1}{p}\left(1 - \mathrm{E}\left[(f(z))^p\right]\right) \quad \text{and} \quad -\frac{1}{p}\log\left(\mathrm{E}\left[(f(z))^p\right]\right), \tag{4.8}$$

where we take $p > -1$. The case $p = 0$ yields the *Shannon entropy* (or simply *the entropy*) given by $-\operatorname{E}[\log(f(z))]$ or $-\int_{-\infty}^{\infty}\log(f(w))\,\mathrm{d}F(w)$; see Exercise 4.38. Note that the random term inside the expectation is the p.d.f. with the random variable z (not its realization w) as its argument. Entropy means disorder. Variates with the highest entropies are going to have the least "memory" (compare Exercises 4.12 and 4.41) and be the least informative (see Exercise 4.40 where the density implies that all outcomes are equally likely). A related measure of how much one p.d.f. differs relative to another is given by the *Kullback–Leibler information criterion* (KLIC) or *Kullback–Leibler divergence*:

$$\mathrm{KL}(f_z, f_x) := \operatorname{E}_z\left(\log\left(\frac{f_z(z)}{f_x(z)}\right)\right) = \int_{-\infty}^{\infty}\log\left(\frac{f_z(w)}{f_x(w)}\right)\mathrm{d}F_z(w).$$

For example, we may wish to assess how far away (in terms of information) the standard Laplace density is located relative to the standard normal. We note that $\operatorname{E}_z(\cdot)$ indicates that the expectation is taken with respect to the variate z, not x, and that the arguments of the expectations are random functions rather than their realizations. We also note that the KLIC is not a measure which is symmetric with respect to x and z, that is, $\mathrm{KL}(f_z, f_x) \neq \mathrm{KL}(f_x, f_z)$ in general.

Another important class of distributions is defined, this time by its c.f. instead of its density function. Its natural justification will arise in later chapters, in connection with sums of i.i.d. variates and limit theorems. First, we define the distribution of a variate z to be *infinitely divisible* if its c.f. $\varphi_z(\tau)$ can be decomposed into the product of n identical c.f.s $\varphi_y(\tau)$ for any $n \in \mathbb{N}$, that is, if

$$\varphi_z(\tau) = \prod_{i=1}^{n}\varphi_y(\tau) \equiv (\varphi_y(\tau))^n.$$

We will see in the introduction to Chapter 6 that this statement is equivalent to $z = \sum_{i=1}^{n} y_i$, where y_i is an i.i.d. sequence drawn from the distribution of y. An important special case is the *compound Poisson* whose c.f. is $\varphi_z(\tau) = \exp(\lambda\varphi_x(\tau) - \lambda)$, where $\lambda \geqslant 0$ and $\varphi_x(\tau)$ is the c.f. of some other variate x. It follows from $\varphi_z(\tau)$ that z is infinitely divisible into other compound Poisson c.f.s $\varphi_y(\tau) = \exp(l\varphi_x(\tau) - l)$ which have parameter $l := \lambda/n$ instead of λ. An alternative representation, in terms of x, can be obtained from the following expansion:

$$\varphi_z(\tau) = \mathrm{e}^{\lambda\varphi_x(\tau)-\lambda} = \mathrm{e}^{-\lambda}\sum_{m=0}^{\infty}\frac{\lambda^m}{m!}(\varphi_x(\tau))^m.$$

We recognize this as the c.f. of a Poisson mixture of a variate $\xi := \sum_{j=1}^{m} x_j$, where the x_j are i.i.d. drawings from the distribution of x, and $m \sim \mathrm{Poi}(\lambda)$. Examples include the Poisson itself when x is degenerate ($\varphi_x(\tau) = \mathrm{e}^{\mathrm{i}c\tau}$ where c is nonrandom as in Exercise 3.23), the gamma (see the expansion in Exercise 4.20), and the negative binomial (compare with gamma's c.f. or expand the integrand in Exercise 2.25). The large-n equivalence of the infinite divisibility decomposition and the compound Poisson representation will be proved in Chapter 10.

In the definition of infinite divisibility, if we were to require further that the distribution of y differs from that of z only by an arbitrary location and by a specific scaling of $n^{-1/p}$, namely

$$\varphi_z(\tau) = \mathrm{e}^{\mathrm{i}\alpha_n\tau} \prod_{i=1}^{n} \varphi_z(n^{-1/p}\tau) \equiv \mathrm{e}^{\mathrm{i}\alpha_n\tau} \left(\varphi_z(n^{-1/p}\tau)\right)^n$$

for some constants $\alpha_n \in \mathbb{R}$ and $p \in (0, 2]$, then z would have a *stable (or Lévy–Khinchine) distribution* with *index* (or *characteristic exponent*) p. Only one function φ_z satisfies this equality, and it is given by

$$\varphi_z(\tau) = \exp\left(\mathrm{i}\alpha\tau - |\lambda\tau|^p \left(1 + \mathrm{i}\nu\widetilde{p}\frac{\tau}{|\tau|}\right)\right), \tag{4.9}$$

where

$$\widetilde{p} := \begin{cases} -\tan\left(\frac{\pi}{2}p\right) & (p \neq 1), \\ \frac{2}{\pi}\log|\tau| & (p = 1), \end{cases}$$

and $\tau = 0$ gives $\tau/|\tau| = \mathrm{sgn}(\tau) = 0$. The roles of the various parameters are as follows: $\alpha \in \mathbb{R}$ for location, $\lambda \in [0, \infty)$ for scale, $\nu \in [-1, 1]$ for asymmetry. Stable distributions, which are denoted by $z \sim \mathrm{S}^p(\alpha, \lambda, \nu)$, have two notable special cases:[1] $\mathrm{N}(\alpha, 2\lambda^2)$ when $p = 2$, and $\mathrm{Cau}(\alpha, \lambda)$ when $p = 1$ and $\nu = 0$. When $\lambda = 0$, we have $\varphi_z(\tau) = \exp(\mathrm{i}\alpha\tau)$ and, by Exercise 3.23, z becomes a degenerate variate satisfying $z = \alpha$ with probability 1. Notable exclusions are the Poisson and the log-normal (see the method in Exercise 4.44), which are infinitely divisible but not stable. Two general properties of stable laws are that they have infinite variances (hence fat-tailed p.d.f.s) for $p \neq 2$, and have bell-shaped p.d.f.s (hence are continuous and unimodal). This bell shape will be symmetric when either $\nu = 0$ or $p = 2$.

The exercises of this chapter investigate the distributions given in the tables and their relation to one another, when a link exists. We follow as closely as is feasible the order given by the listing in the tables. We then consider some classifications of densities, and how our special distributions fit in.

4.1 Discrete distributions

Exercise 4.1 (Discrete uniforms!) Let x be a discrete random variable that is uniformly distributed over the set $\{0, 1, \dots, k-1\}$. Compute $\mathrm{E}(x)$ and $\mathrm{var}(x)$. [Hint: In Section A.4.1, we derive $\sum_{i=1}^{n} i = n(n+1)/2$ and $\sum_{i=1}^{n} i^2 = n(n+1)(2n+1)/6$.]

[1] We reserve the subscripts of $\mathrm{S}_\bullet$ for other uses, mentioned at the start of this chapter; hence the use of the superscript in S^p, where p is the characteristic exponent of the stable law.

Solution
We find

$$\mathrm{E}(x) = \sum_{u=0}^{k-1} \frac{u}{k} = \frac{1}{k} \times \frac{(k-1)k}{2} = \frac{k-1}{2}$$

and

$$\mathrm{E}\left(x^2\right) = \sum_{u=0}^{k-1} \frac{u^2}{k} = \frac{1}{k} \times \frac{(k-1)k(2k-1)}{6} = \frac{1}{6}(k-1)(2k-1).$$

Hence,

$$\mathrm{var}(x) = \frac{1}{6}(k-1)(2k-1) - \left(\frac{k-1}{2}\right)^2 = \frac{k^2-1}{12}.$$

Exercise 4.2 (Unimodal bin?) Let x be binomially distributed with parameters n and p. Show that $\Pr(x = u)$ increases monotonically until it reaches it largest value and then decreases monotonically. Does this imply that the p.d.f. is unimodal?

Solution
For $u \in \{1, 2, \dots, n\}$, we have the ratio

$$R := \frac{\Pr(x = u)}{\Pr(x = u - 1)} = \frac{\binom{n}{u} p^u (1-p)^{n-u}}{\binom{n}{u-1} p^{u-1} (1-p)^{n-u+1}} = \frac{(n-u+1)p}{u(1-p)}.$$

Hence, $\Pr(x = u)$ increases for $R > 1$ and decreases for $R < 1$, that is, it increases for $u < (n+1)p$ and decreases for $u > (n+1)p$.

If there is a $u \in \{1, 2, \dots, n\}$ which solves $u = (n+1)p$, then $R = 1$ and the p.d.f. is bimodal. If not, then it is unimodal.

Exercise 4.3 (Binomial representation: the drug) A standard drug is known to cure 80% of patients suffering from a disease. A new drug cures 85 patients out of 100 in a trial. What is the probability that the old drug would have cured 85 or more of these patients? [Hint: Consider the curing of one patient as a drawing from the Bernoulli distribution (binary Yes/No outcome), then combine the results for 100 patients.]

Solution
Define a random variable y_i which takes the value 1 if the new drug cures patient i (successful outcome) and 0 otherwise. Then y_i follows a Bernoulli distribution with parameter p, the percentage of patients cured by the new drug. The new drug is better if $p > 0.8$, but we don't actually observe p.

We have a sample of $n = 100$ patients, so that our variates are $y_1, \dots, y_{100}$, with realizations $v_1, \dots, v_{100}$. We know that $\sum_{i=1}^{100} v_i = 85$, but we need to derive the general distribution of the variate $z := \sum_{i=1}^{n} y_i \in \{0, 1, \dots, n\}$. Assume that the y_i's are independent, for example because the disease is not contagious and/or because the sample was randomly selected from different locations. For any realization w, there are $\binom{n}{w}$ possible combinations of patients, and the probability of observing each of these combinations is

$$\left(\prod_{i=1}^{w} p\right) \times \left(\prod_{i=w+1}^{n} (1-p)\right) = p^w (1-p)^{n-w}$$

by the independence of each patient from the others. Then $z \sim \text{Bin}(n, p)$. The binomial is therefore the general distribution of the sum (or number of successes) of a repeated Bernoulli trial.

If $p = 0.8$, then the probability that 85 or more out of 100 patients in a trial are cured is $\sum_{w=85}^{100} \binom{100}{w} (0.8)^w (0.2)^{100-w} \approx 0.129$, which is not a high probability. It seems that the new drug is better. A more rigorous formulation of this last statement will be given in the final two chapters, where the topics of confidence intervals and the testing of hypotheses are tackled.

Exercise 4.4 (If you don't succeed, try and try again (Nbin take 2)) Consider the following two stories.

(a) Sarah throws eggs at a bad musician who will give up if and only if three eggs have hit him. For each throw, the probability of a successful hit is 0.6. You may assume that no-one else in the audience has eggs, and that Sarah is the best shot of them all. Compute the probability that exactly n eggs will be required to stop the musician from playing. What is the probability that fewer than six eggs will be required? (Sarah needs to know how many eggs to buy from the shop!)

(b) There are k different types of coupon in boxes for sale, and every box contains one coupon. The probability that a box contains coupon i is $1/k$. It is assumed that there are infinitely many boxes, or that your purchases are sufficiently small, so that the probability $1/k$ is not affected by what you do. What is the expected number of boxes you have to buy (at random) so that you possess at least one of each type of coupon?

Solution

(a) Sarah will require n eggs if two out of the previous $n-1$ eggs hit their target *and* the n-th is a hit too (the last one *has* to be a hit: it finishes the game!). Defining this joint probability as the product of the probabilities of two independent events, with the probability of one success as $p = 0.6$, we have

$$\begin{aligned} \Pr(n \text{ throws}) &= p \times f_{\text{Bin}(n-1,p)}(2) \\ &= p \binom{n-1}{2} p^2 (1-p)^{n-1-2} = \binom{n-1}{2} (0.6)^3 (0.4)^{n-3}. \end{aligned}$$

Noting that $\binom{n-1}{2} = \binom{n-1}{n-3}$, from Table 4.1 we can identify the distribution of the random number of throws in excess of three (that is, $n-3$ here) whose realization is $w = 0, 1, \ldots$ (think of w as the number of failures to hit the target). It is the negative binomial $\text{Nbin}(\nu, p)$

where $\nu = 3$. This is the general distribution for trying over and above ν times, until ν successes are achieved, the geometric distribution being the special case where $\nu = 1$. See also Exercise 4.17.

The probability that fewer than six eggs will be required by Sarah is

$$\sum_{n=3}^{5} \binom{n-1}{2} (0.6)^3 (0.4)^{n-3} = \sum_{w=0}^{5-3} \binom{w+2}{2} (0.6)^3 (0.4)^w \approx 0.683,$$

where $w = 0$ denotes the perfect score of exactly three throws. She'd better improve her aim (practice a few days to change p), or buy more eggs, to have a better chance than 68.3%!

(b) The first box gives you one coupon. Let the random variable x_1 be the number of boxes you have to buy in order to get a coupon which is different from the first one. As we saw in (a), a geometric p.d.f. arises for the number of required attempts in excess of 1, so $x_1 - 1$ is a geometric random variable with $p_1 = (k-1)/k$. Once you have two different coupons, let x_2 be the number of boxes you have to buy in order to get a coupon which is different from the first two. Then $x_2 - 1$ is a geometric random variable with $p_2 = (k-2)/k$. Proceeding in this way, the number of boxes you need to buy equals $x = 1 + x_1 + x_2 + \cdots + x_{k-1}$. Since a $\operatorname{Geo}(p)$ has mean $p^{-1} - 1$, we have $\operatorname{E}(x_i) = p_i^{-1} = k/(k-i)$ and the expected number of boxes you have to buy is

$$\sum_{i=0}^{k-1} k/(k-i) = k \sum_{j=1}^{k} 1/j.$$

The last step follows by reversing the index i into $j = k - i$.

Exercise 4.5 (Hypergeometric cards) Five cards are drawn without replacement from an ordinary deck of 52 cards. Compute the probability of

(a) exactly two aces;
(b) exactly two kings;
(c) fewer than two aces;
(d) at least two aces.

Solution

(a) The number of different ways of choosing two aces is $\binom{4}{2}$, the number of different ways of choosing five cards is $\binom{52}{5}$, and the number of different ways of choosing three cards other than an ace is $\binom{48}{3}$. Since all possible samples having two aces are equally likely, the probability of exactly two aces is $\binom{4}{2}\binom{48}{3}/\binom{52}{5} \approx 0.040$. Notice that this is the probability given by $u = 2$ in $\operatorname{Hyp}(52, 4, 5)$, which is the general distribution for sampling without replacement: in $\operatorname{Hyp}(m, k, n)$, we use m for the maximum of the population (52 cards), k for a characteristic of some in this population (aces), and n for the sample (5 cards are drawn).

(b) Same as (a).

(c) $\sum_{u=0}^{1}\binom{4}{u}\binom{48}{5-u}/\binom{52}{5} \approx 0.958$.
(d) The answer is 1 minus the answer to (c), because the two events are complements. Hence, the probability is approximately 0.042. Verify that drawing three or four aces occurs only once in about every 570 draws (on average), that is, with probability approximately equal to 0.175%.

Exercise 4.6 (Hyper employees) An office has 10 employees, three men and seven women. Four are chosen at random to attend a course on office efficiency.
(a) What is the probability that an equal number of men and women is chosen?
(b) What is the probability that more women than men are chosen?

Solution
(a) Let x denote the number of women chosen. Then

$$\Pr(x=2) = \frac{\binom{7}{2}\binom{3}{2}}{\binom{10}{4}} = \frac{3}{10}.$$

(b) The desired probability is

$$\Pr(x=3) + \Pr(x=4) = \frac{\binom{7}{3}\binom{3}{1}}{\binom{10}{4}} + \frac{\binom{7}{4}}{\binom{10}{4}} = \frac{2}{3}.$$

Exercise 4.7 (Capture–recapture) A species of shark happens to be living in a large salt lake where they have no predators (such as humans). They are known to live long, not reproduce very often, and not prey on each other. This population contains m individuals; however, Shahira does not know how big the population is. She decides to catch a number k of them at randomly selected locations, depths, and times of the day. She then tags them and releases them. A few days later, she returns and catches n sharks at random.
(a) What is the probability that, among these n sharks, u are tagged?
(b) What is the expected number of tagged sharks and their variance?
(c) What is the value of u that maximizes the probability in (a), and how does it relate to the moments in (b)?
(d) Suppose instead that Shahira were to carry on recapturing sharks until she gets ν tagged sharks. The number of sharks to be recaptured would then become a random variable, say z. Show that $z-\nu \in \{0, 1, \dots m-k\}$ has the *negative hypergeometric* distribution Hyp$(-k-1, -\nu, m-k)$. (The name follows because the last two parameters are negative, analogously to the story of Exercise 4.4 where trials occur until a required number of successes has been achieved. See also Exercise 7.37.)

Solution
(a) Shahira is drawing at random, without replacement, from a population of m individuals, of whom k are tagged. There are $\binom{m}{n}$ ways of drawing n sharks, $\binom{k}{u}$ ways of drawing u

tagged sharks, and $\binom{m-k}{n-u}$ ways of drawing $n-u$ untagged sharks. Therefore, defining the variate x to be the number of recaptured tagged sharks,

$$\Pr(x = u) = \frac{\binom{k}{u}\binom{m-k}{n-u}}{\binom{m}{n}},$$

which is a hypergeometric distribution.
(b) The mean and variance of $\text{Hyp}(m, k, n)$ are derived in the introduction to this chapter, giving

$$\mathrm{E}(x) = \frac{nk}{m} \qquad \text{and} \qquad \operatorname{var}(x) = \frac{nk}{m}\left(1 - \frac{k}{m}\right)\frac{m-n}{m-1}.$$

These results have a natural interpretation. If the expected number of tagged sharks were to be caught (meaning that $u = \mathrm{E}(x) \in \mathbb{N}$), then the population m could simply be calculated as the ratio $k/(u/n)$, where k is the number of tags Shahira successfully applied in the first capture and u/n is the proportion of tagged sharks that she calculated from the second capture. Also, since $p := k/m$ is the proportion of tagged sharks in the lake, we have $\mathrm{E}(x) = np$ (she *expects* to catch this in recaptures) and

$$\operatorname{var}(x) = np(1-p)\frac{m-n}{m-1}.$$

For n small relative to m, the latter is approximately $np(1-p)$. Compare these moments to those of the binomial in Table 4.1.
(c) To find the maximum probability as u varies, consider the ratio

$$R := \frac{\Pr(x = u)}{\Pr(x = u-1)} = \frac{\binom{k}{u}\binom{m-k}{n-u}}{\binom{k}{u-1}\binom{m-k}{n-u+1}} = \frac{(k-u+1)(n-u+1)}{u(m-k-n+u)}.$$

Hence, as x increases from $u-1$ to u, the probability increases if $R > 1$. That is, it increases if $u < c$, where

$$c := \frac{(n+1)(k+1)}{m+2}.$$

It decreases if $u > c$, and is unchanged if $u = c$. If $c \notin \mathbb{N}$, then the most likely number of tagged sharks in the recapture is the integer part of c. If $c \in \mathbb{N}$, then $x = c-1$ and $x = c$ are equally likely.

For n and k large (hence m large too), we have $c \approx \mathrm{E}(x)$. More generally, $c \in (\mathrm{E}(x), \mathrm{E}(x)+1)$ since

$$\frac{(n+1)(k+1)}{m+2} - \frac{nk}{m} = \frac{m + (mn + mk - 2nk)}{m(m+2)} > 0$$

by $m \geqslant \max\{n, k\} > 0$, and

$$\frac{(n+1)(k+1)}{m+2} - \left(\frac{nk}{m} + 1\right) = \frac{-m - (m-n)(m-k) - nk}{m(m+2)} < 0.$$

(d) By working out, in the same way as in Exercise 4.4, the joint probability that $\nu - 1$ out of $w-1$ sharks are tagged *and* the w-th is tagged, we obtain

$$\Pr(z=w) = \frac{k}{m} \times \frac{\binom{k-1}{\nu-1}\binom{m-k}{w-\nu}}{\binom{m-1}{w-1}}.$$

The marginal probability that the w-th shark is tagged is k/m, while the second factor is the conditional probability. Unlike in Exercise 4.4, the trials here are not independent since Shahira is sampling without replacement from a finite population, hence the need for conditioning. The probability can be rewritten as

$$\begin{aligned}\Pr(z=w) &= \frac{(w-1)!\,(m-w)!k!\,(m-k)!}{(\nu-1)!\,(k-\nu)!\,(w-\nu)!\,(m-k-w+\nu)!m!}\\ &= \frac{\binom{w-1}{w-\nu}\binom{m-w}{m-k-w+\nu}}{\binom{m}{m-k}} = \frac{\binom{-\nu}{w-\nu}\binom{\nu-k-1}{m-k-w+\nu}}{\binom{-k-1}{m-k}} \qquad (w-\nu \in \{0,1,\dots m-k\}),\end{aligned}$$

the last step following from (4.1). This reveals that $z-\nu \sim \text{Hyp}(-k-1,-\nu,m-k)$.

Exercise 4.8 (Poisson decomposition) The number of people entering a shop on a certain day follows a Poisson distribution with parameter λ. A person entering the shop is female with probability p (thus male with probability $q := 1-p$), and people arrive independently. What is the distribution of the number of women entering the shop?

Solution

Let x denote the number of women, y the number of men, and z the total number of persons entering the shop. Then, we have

$$\begin{aligned}\Pr(x=u, y=v) &= \Pr(x=u \mid z=u+v)\Pr(z=u+v)\\ &= \binom{u+v}{u} p^u q^v \frac{\lambda^{u+v}\mathrm{e}^{-\lambda}}{(u+v)!}.\end{aligned}$$

The first probability is obtained from the binomial distribution, which gives the possible ways that u females can arrive out of $u+v$ people, without particular interest in distinguishing the order of arrivals *within* genders. Expanding the binomial symbol and rearranging, the joint probability factors as follows:

$$\begin{aligned}\Pr(x=u, y=v) &= \frac{(p\lambda)^u\mathrm{e}^{-p\lambda}}{u!} \times \frac{(q\lambda)^v\mathrm{e}^{-q\lambda}}{v!}\\ &= f_{\text{Poi}(p\lambda)}(u) \times f_{\text{Poi}(q\lambda)}(v) = \Pr(x=u) \times \Pr(y=v),\end{aligned}$$

where we see that the number of women and the number of men have independent Poisson distributions with parameters $p\lambda$ and $q\lambda$, respectively, with the two arrival means adding up to $p\lambda + q\lambda = \lambda$. Notice that we have not assumed at the outset that x or y are Poisson. It is therefore remarkable that we find the Poisson total z decomposing into two Poissons. We will revisit this type of decomposition in the introduction to Chapter 8 and in Exercise 8.7.

Exercise 4.9 (Poisson limit of binomial) Let x be a binomially distributed random variable with parameters n and p. Let $\lambda = np$. For fixed λ, show that, as $n \to \infty$ (and hence $p \to 0$),

$$\Pr(x = u) \to \frac{1}{u!}\lambda^u \mathrm{e}^{-\lambda}.$$

Solution

Since x is binomially distributed, we have $\Pr(x = u) = \binom{n}{u} p^u q^{n-u}$, where $q := 1 - p$. Replacing p by λ/n, we obtain

$$\begin{aligned}\Pr(x = u) &= \binom{n}{u}\left(\frac{\lambda}{n}\right)^u\left(1 - \frac{\lambda}{n}\right)^{n-u} \\ &= \frac{n}{n} \times \frac{n-1}{n} \cdots \frac{n-u+2}{n} \times \frac{n-u+1}{n} \times \frac{\lambda^u}{u!}\left(1 - \frac{\lambda}{n}\right)^{n-u}.\end{aligned}$$

Now, as $n \to \infty$, we get $(1 - \lambda/n)^n \to \mathrm{e}^{-\lambda}$ and the result follows. This shows that we can use the Poisson distribution as an approximation to the binomial distribution in cases where n is large, p is small, and np is neither large nor small.

Exercise 4.10 (Binomial complements' c.d.f.s) Suppose that x follows a $\text{Bin}(n, p)$ distribution and y follows a $\text{Bin}(n, q)$ distribution, where $p + q = 1$. Show that

$$\Pr(x \leqslant u) = 1 - \Pr(y \leqslant n - u - 1).$$

Solution

Using the binomial p.d.f., we start by writing the corresponding c.d.f. as $\Pr(x \leqslant u) = \sum_{j=0}^{u} \binom{n}{j} p^j q^{n-j}$ and

$$\Pr(y \leqslant n - u - 1) = \sum_{i=0}^{n-u-1} \binom{n}{i} q^i p^{n-i} = \sum_{j=u+1}^{n} \binom{n}{j} p^j q^{n-j}$$

using the change of index $j = n - i$ and

$$\binom{n}{j} = \frac{n!}{j!(n-j)!} = \binom{n}{n-j}.$$

The result follows from

$$\Pr(x \leqslant u) + \Pr(y \leqslant n - u - 1) = \sum_{j=0}^{n} \binom{n}{j} p^j q^{n-j} = (p + q)^n = 1,$$

namely by the fact that the binomial probabilities add up to 1. It can also be restated as

$$\Pr(x \leqslant u) = \Pr(y \geqslant n - u)$$

since integer y implies that $\Pr(y \leqslant n-u-1) = \Pr(y < n-u)$.

***Exercise 4.11 (Binomial, beta, and Student's t c.d.f.s)** The c.d.f. of the binomial has more than one representation.
(a) Prove that, for $u < n$,

$$\sum_{k=0}^{u} \binom{n}{k} p^k (1-p)^{n-k} = (n-u)\binom{n}{u} \int_0^{1-p} t^{n-u-1}(1-t)^u \, dt,$$

thus establishing an integral representation for the c.d.f. of the binomial.
(b) The integral representation of the *incomplete beta function* is

$$I_v(r,s) := \frac{1}{B(r,s)} \int_0^v t^{r-1}(1-t)^{s-1} \, dt,$$

where $r, s \in \mathbb{R}_+$ and $v \in (0,1)$. Work out two series representations for $I_v(r,s)$, hence obtaining explicitly the c.d.f. of the standard Beta(p,q). [Hint: Use the binomial expansion.] Show that the series in (a) is a special case.
(c) Using the incomplete beta function, obtain the c.d.f. of Student's t.

Solution
(a) Let $h_L(p)$ denote the left-hand side of the equality as a function of p, and let $h_R(p)$ denote the right-hand side. Then, differentiating h_L with respect to p,

$$h_L'(p) = \sum_{k=1}^{u} k\binom{n}{k} p^{k-1}(1-p)^{n-k} - \sum_{k=0}^{u} (n-k)\binom{n}{k} p^k (1-p)^{n-k-1}.$$

Changing the indexation of the first sum, and expanding the binomials,

$$\begin{aligned} h_L'(p) &= \sum_{k=0}^{u-1} \frac{n!}{k!(n-k-1)!} p^k (1-p)^{n-k-1} - \sum_{k=0}^{u} \frac{n!}{k!(n-k-1)!} p^k (1-p)^{n-k-1} \\ &= -\frac{n!}{u!(n-u-1)!} p^u (1-p)^{n-u-1} = -(n-u)\binom{n}{u}(1-p)^{n-u-1} p^u. \end{aligned}$$

However, this is also the derivative of h_R, by Leibniz' rule (see Section A.4). Hence, $h_L(p) = h_R(p) + c$ with c some constant not depending on p. Letting $p = 1$ shows that $h_L(1) = h_R(1) = 0$ for $u < n$, hence $c = 0$.
(b) The integral seen earlier is a special case of the c.d.f. of the standard beta given by $I_v(r,s)$. We have

$$\frac{1}{B(r,s)} \int_v^1 t^{r-1}(1-t)^{s-1} \, dt = \frac{1}{B(r,s)} \int_0^{1-v} (1-\tau)^{r-1} \tau^{s-1} \, d\tau = I_{1-v}(s,r)$$

by the change of variable $\tau = 1-t$ and $B(r,s) = B(s,r)$. Furthermore, the beta density function integrates to 1. Therefore, $I_v(r,s) + I_{1-v}(s,r) = 1$.

We now work out the integral explicitly in terms of its series representation. Expanding the binomial $(1-t)^{s-1}$,

$$\begin{aligned} I_v(r,s) &= \frac{1}{B(r,s)} \int_0^v \sum_{k=0}^{\infty} \binom{s-1}{k} (-1)^k t^{k+r-1}\, \mathrm{d}t \\ &= \frac{1}{B(r,s)} \sum_{k=0}^{\infty} \binom{s-1}{k} (-1)^k \int_0^v t^{k+r-1}\, \mathrm{d}t \\ &= \frac{1}{B(r,s)} \sum_{k=0}^{\infty} \binom{s-1}{k} (-1)^k \left[\frac{t^{k+r}}{k+r}\right]_0^v = \frac{v^r}{B(r,s)} \sum_{k=0}^{\infty} \binom{s-1}{k} \frac{(-v)^k}{k+r} \end{aligned}$$

since $k+r>0$. Swapping the integral and sum is allowed because the sum is absolutely convergent over the interval of integration. When $s \in \mathbb{N}$, this series terminates after s terms because $\binom{s-1}{k} = (s-1)(s-2)\dots(s-k)/k!$ will have a zero numerator (put $k = s, s+1, \dots$). A similar comment can be made about the case where $r \in \mathbb{N}$ *after* exploiting $I_v(r,s) + I_{1-v}(s,r) = 1$ and writing the alternative representation

$$I_v(r,s) = 1 - I_{1-v}(s,r) = 1 - \frac{(1-v)^s}{B(r,s)} \sum_{k=0}^{\infty} \binom{r-1}{k} \frac{(v-1)^k}{k+s}.$$

We can now specialize the incomplete beta function to the case of the binomial c.d.f. seen in (a). By

$$(n-u)\binom{n}{u} = \frac{(n-u)n!}{(n-u)!u!} = \frac{n!}{(n-u-1)!u!} = \frac{\Gamma(n+1)}{\Gamma(n-u)\Gamma(u+1)} = \frac{1}{B(n-u,u+1)},$$

we confirm that $I_{1-p}(n-u, u+1)$ is the integral in (a).

In the case where r or s is a natural number, $I_v(r,s)$ has yet another formulation as a series. For example, when $s \in \mathbb{N}$ and $v \neq 0$, the change of variable $\tau = t/v$ and the same methods as before give

$$\begin{aligned} I_v(r,s) &= \frac{v^r}{B(r,s)} \int_0^1 \tau^{r-1}(1-v\tau)^{s-1}\, \mathrm{d}\tau \\ &= \frac{v^r}{B(r,s)} \int_0^1 \tau^{r-1}\left((1-v) + v(1-\tau)\right)^{s-1} \mathrm{d}\tau \\ &= \frac{v^r}{B(r,s)} \sum_{k=0}^{s-1} \binom{s-1}{k} (1-v)^k v^{s-k-1} \int_0^1 \tau^{r-1}(1-\tau)^{s-k-1}\, \mathrm{d}\tau \\ &\equiv \frac{v^r}{B(r,s)} \sum_{k=0}^{s-1} \binom{s-1}{k} (1-v)^k v^{s-k-1} B(r, s-k) \\ &= \sum_{k=0}^{s-1} \binom{r+s-1}{k} (1-v)^k v^{r+s-k-1} \end{aligned}$$

by the definition of the beta and binomial functions. This gives the required special series for $I_{1-p}(n-u, u+1)$. Incidentally, the identity between this last form and the first form

for $I_v(r,s)$ is an application of an identity satisfied by Gauss hypergeometric functions. It hinges on an integral representation being expanded in two different ways.
(c) By the symmetry of the p.d.f. of Student's t, its c.d.f. is

$$F_{\mathrm{t}}(v) = \frac{1}{2} + \operatorname{sgn}(v) \int_0^{|v|} \frac{\Gamma\left(\frac{n+1}{2}\right)}{\sqrt{\pi n}\,\Gamma\left(\frac{n}{2}\right)\left(1+\frac{w^2}{n}\right)^{\frac{n+1}{2}}} \,\mathrm{d}w.$$

By the change of variable $u = 1/\left(1+w^2/n\right)$ (or $w = \sqrt{n}\sqrt{u^{-1}-1}$),

$$\begin{aligned} F_{\mathrm{t}}(v) &= \frac{1}{2} + \frac{\operatorname{sgn}(v)\,\Gamma\left(\frac{n+1}{2}\right)}{2\sqrt{\pi}\,\Gamma\left(\frac{n}{2}\right)} \int_{1/(1+v^2/n)}^{1} \frac{u^{\frac{n}{2}-1}}{\sqrt{1-u}} \,\mathrm{d}u \\ &= \frac{1}{2} + \frac{\operatorname{sgn}(v)}{2}\left(1 - F_{\mathrm{Beta}\left(\frac{n}{2},\frac{1}{2}\right)}\left(\frac{1}{1+v^2/n}\right)\right) \\ &= \frac{1}{2} + \frac{\operatorname{sgn}(v)}{2}\left(1 - I_{n/(n+v^2)}\left(\frac{n}{2},\frac{1}{2}\right)\right) \\ &= \frac{1}{2} + \frac{\operatorname{sgn}(v)}{2} I_{v^2/(n+v^2)}\left(\frac{1}{2},\frac{n}{2}\right). \end{aligned}$$

Note that the special case $\mathrm{t}(1)$ is the Cauchy c.d.f., and the integral simplifies to $\frac{1}{2} + \frac{1}{\pi}\tan^{-1}(v)$; see also Exercise 4.35.

Exercise 4.12 (Forgetful pair) Show that the geometric and exponential distributions have the *no-memory property*: $\Pr(x \geqslant v + w \mid x \geqslant v) = \Pr(x \geqslant w)$ for every $v, w \in \mathcal{X}$.

Solution
For the geometric distribution, let $q := 1 - p \in [0, 1)$. For any $u \in \mathbb{Z}_{0,+}$,

$$\Pr(x \geqslant u) = \sum_{i=u}^{\infty} pq^i = pq^u(1 + q + q^2 + \cdots) = \frac{pq^u}{1-q} = q^u;$$

hence

$$\Pr(x \geqslant v + w \mid x \geqslant v) = \frac{\Pr(x \geqslant v + w)}{\Pr(x \geqslant v)} = \frac{q^{v+w}}{q^v} = q^w = \Pr(x \geqslant w).$$

For the exponential distribution,

$$\Pr(x \geqslant u) = \lambda \int_u^{\infty} \mathrm{e}^{-\lambda v} \,\mathrm{d}v = \mathrm{e}^{-\lambda u};$$

hence

$$\Pr(x \geqslant v + w \mid x \geqslant v) = \frac{\mathrm{e}^{-\lambda(v+w)}}{\mathrm{e}^{-\lambda v}} = \mathrm{e}^{-\lambda w} = \Pr(x \geqslant w).$$

Notice the parallel result that these distributions imply: in both cases, the hazard rate (defined in Exercise 2.18) is a constant that does not depend on the realization of x. In other words, for these two distributions, the failure rate is independent of age.

***Exercise 4.13 (Forgetful Geo)** Let $x \in \mathbb{Z}_{0,+}$. Show that the only distribution of x with the no-memory property is the geometric distribution. [Hint: Use this property to relate $\Pr(x \geqslant u)$ to $\Pr(x \geqslant u-1)$.]

Solution
Let $p := \Pr(x = 0)$. Then

$$\Pr(x \geqslant 1) = 1 - \Pr(x = 0) = 1 - p,$$

because $x \in \mathbb{Z}_{0,+}$. Any distribution with the no-memory property must satisfy

$$\Pr(x \geqslant v + w) = \Pr(x \geqslant v)\Pr(x \geqslant w)$$

for any $v, w \in \mathcal{X}$. Choosing $v = 1$ and $u = v + w \geqslant 1$,

$$\Pr(x \geqslant u) = \Pr(x \geqslant 1)\Pr(x \geqslant u-1) = (1-p)\Pr(x \geqslant u-1).$$

This equation provides us with a recursive formula to calculate $\Pr(x \geqslant u)$ in terms of $\Pr(x \geqslant u-1)$:

$$\Pr(x \geqslant u) = (1-p)\Pr(x \geqslant u-1) = (1-p)^2\Pr(x \geqslant u-2) = \cdots = (1-p)^u.$$

Hence,

$$\begin{aligned}\Pr(x = u) &= \Pr(x \geqslant u) - \Pr(x \geqslant u+1)\\ &= (1-p)^u - (1-p)^{u+1} = p(1-p)^u,\end{aligned}$$

which identifies the required distribution as geometric.

4.2 Continuous distributions

Exercise 4.14 (Picture this!) Plot the following densities, commenting on how their appearance is affected by the parameter values:
(a) $\text{Beta}(1,1)$, $\text{Beta}\left(\frac{3}{2},\frac{5}{4}\right)$, and $\text{Beta}\left(\frac{3}{2},\frac{1}{2}\right)$;
(b) $\text{IG}(1,1)$ and $\text{LN}(\alpha,\lambda^2)$, where you should choose α,λ such that $\mu = 1 = \sigma$;
(c) $\text{N}(0,1)$, $\text{N}(0,2)$, and $\text{Cau}(0,1)$;
(d) $\chi^2(1)$, $\chi^2(2)$, and $\chi^2(4)$;
(e) $\chi^2(4)$, $\chi^2(4,3)$, and $\chi^2(4,9)$.

Solution
(a) In Figure 4.1, we see that Beta(1,1) is just a uniform distribution over (0,1), and that any Beta(p,q) with either $p = 1$ or $q = 1$ is going to have a nonzero $f(0^+)$ or $f(1^-)$, respectively. As we increase both p and q, the density goes to zero at both ends, as Beta($\frac{3}{2},\frac{5}{4}$) suggests. Finally, the density of Beta($\frac{3}{2},\frac{1}{2}$) becomes infinite as w tends to the upper edge

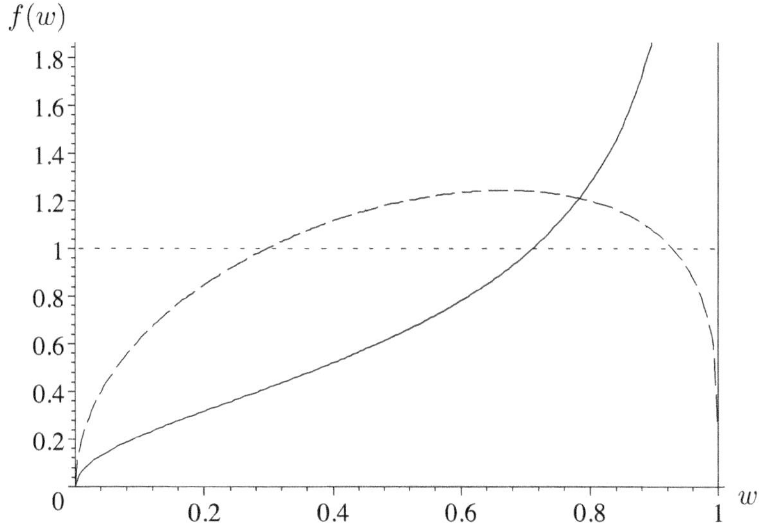

Figure 4.1. Beta densities: Beta(1,1), dotted line; Beta($\frac{3}{2}, \frac{5}{4}$), dashed line; Beta($\frac{3}{2}, \frac{1}{2}$), solid line.

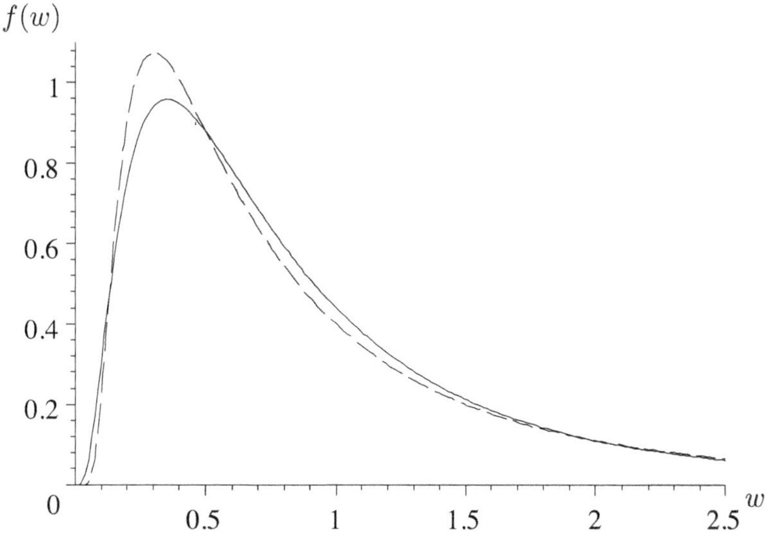

Figure 4.2. IG(1,1), dashed line; LN($-\frac{1}{2}\log 2, \log 2$), solid line.

of its support (depicted for convenience by another vertical axis at $w = 1$), because $q < 1$.
(b) From Table 4.2, we know that $z \sim \text{LN}(\alpha, \lambda^2)$ has $\text{E}(z^j) = \exp(\alpha j + \lambda^2 j^2/2)$, from which we need to solve $1 = \text{E}(z) = \exp(\alpha + \lambda^2/2)$ and

$$1 = \text{E}(z^2) - (\text{E}(z))^2 = \exp(2\alpha + 2\lambda^2) - 1;$$

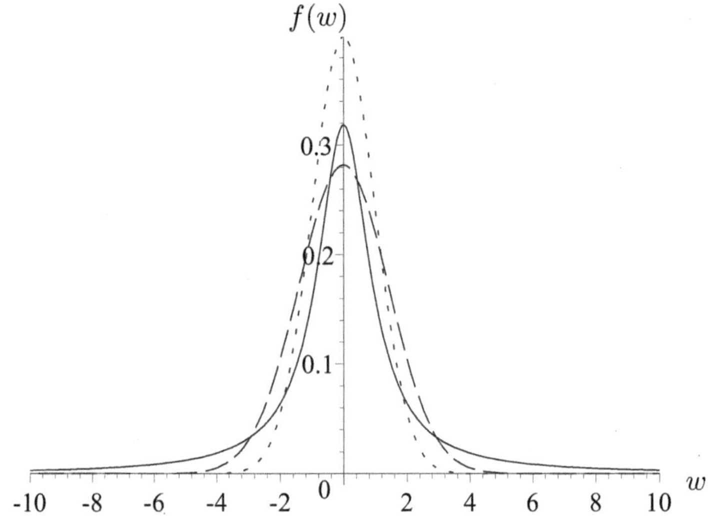

Figure 4.3. $\mathrm{N}(0,1)$, dotted line; $\mathrm{N}(0,2)$, dashed line; $\mathrm{Cau}(0,1)$, solid line.

or, equivalently, $1 = \exp\left(2\alpha + \lambda^2\right)$ and $2 = \exp\left(2\alpha + 2\lambda^2\right)$. Dividing the last two equations gives

$$\frac{2}{1} = \frac{\exp\left(2\alpha + 2\lambda^2\right)}{\exp\left(2\alpha + \lambda^2\right)} = \exp\left(\lambda^2\right),$$

hence $\lambda = \sqrt{\log 2}$. Accordingly,

$$1 = \exp\left(2\alpha + \lambda^2\right) = 2\exp\left(2\alpha\right)$$

solves $\alpha = -\frac{1}{2}\log 2 = -\log\sqrt{2}$. Hence, $z \sim \mathrm{LN}(-\frac{1}{2}\log 2, \log 2)$ is a variate with unit mean and unit variance, while $\log(z)$ is a normal with mean $-\frac{1}{2}\log 2$ and variance $\log 2$ by the logarithmic relation between the two variates shown in Exercise 3.27; compare also the two densities in Table 4.2. This is why we write $z \sim \mathrm{LN}\left(\alpha, \lambda^2\right)$ rather than $\mathrm{LN}\left(\mu, \sigma^2\right)$: the moments of z are not the arguments of LN (which are the moments of $\log(z)$). Notice how Jensen's inequality applies to $\mathrm{E}\left(\log\left(z\right)\right) < \log\left(\mathrm{E}\left(z\right)\right) = 0$, a relation that we will make more precise in Exercise 8.6(b). Note also that a change of the variable of integration gives the log-normal c.d.f. as

$$F_z\left(w\right) = \Phi\left(\frac{\log\left(w\right) - \alpha}{\lambda}\right)$$

and hence its median as $\exp\left(\alpha\right)$, smaller than the mean $\exp\left(\alpha + \lambda^2/2\right)$ but larger than the mode $\exp\left(\alpha - \lambda^2\right)$ obtained by maximizing $\log f_z\left(w\right)$; compare Exercise 3.21.

We can see in Figure 4.2 that the inverse Gaussian is slightly more concentrated that the log-normal with comparable mean and variance 1. This was reflected in the higher-order moments of the log-normal in Exercise 3.27(c). Compare also the rates of decay of the two densities, as $w \to \infty$ in Table 4.2.

(c) In Figure 4.3, as the variance increases, the normal distribution becomes more spread

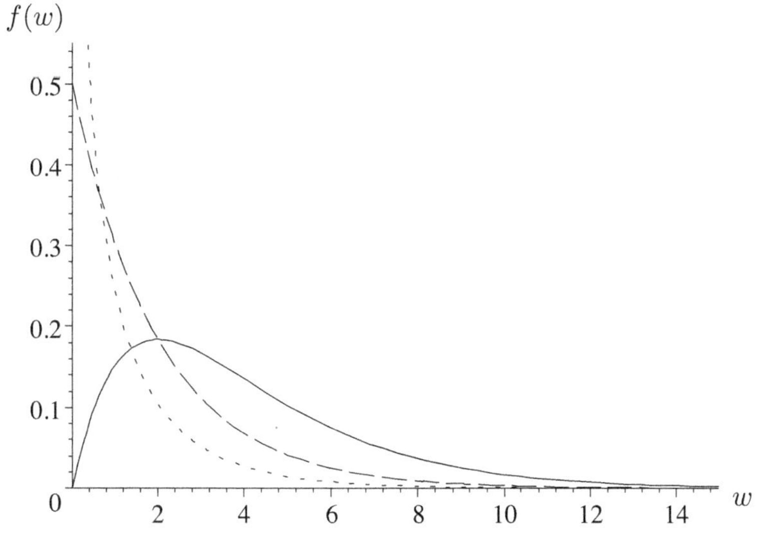

Figure 4.4. Central χ^2 densities: $\chi^2(1)$, dotted line; $\chi^2(2)$, dashed line; $\chi^2(4)$, solid line.

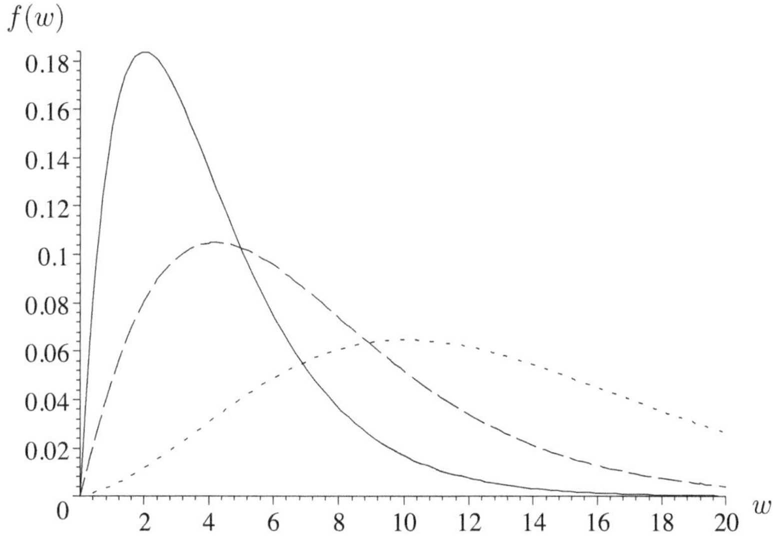

Figure 4.5. Central and noncentral χ^2 densities: $\chi^2(4)$, solid line; $\chi^2(4, 3)$, dashed line; $\chi^2(4, 9)$, dotted line.

out. However, in comparison with the Cauchy which does not possess finite moments of any order, most of the distribution is well contained within a small interval. Notice how the standard Cauchy's tails still continue to be substantial for large w, whereas the normals' tails decay exponentially fast. Notice also that the densities intersect each other: they all integrate to 1, but Cauchy's long tail contributes a large component to the c.d.f. (the area

under the p.d.f.) relative to the normal which has to compensate with a larger integral value elsewhere. Both distributions are symmetric around 0 (they have a mirror image on either side of the vertical axis) and bell-shaped. Contrast this, for example, with the log-normal of part (b): transformations like $\exp(\cdot)$ alter the symmetry of variates.
(d) In Figure 4.4, the χ^2 with degrees of freedom less than 2 has a density tending to ∞ at the origin, while the $\chi^2(2)$ has density $\frac{1}{2}$ as $w \to 0^+$. Otherwise, the density is bell-shaped, tending to zero at both ends, and its "center of gravity" (mean, median, or mode) shifts to the right as the degrees of freedom n increase in $\chi^2(n)$. As $n \to \infty$, Exercise 10.32(a) will prove that the density looks increasingly like that of a normal variate.
(e) The same $\chi^2(4)$ has been plotted in Figure 4.5, but the scaling of the axes has been changed. We see that an increase in the noncentrality parameter from 0 (for a central χ^2) to 9 shifts the center of the density to the right, and flattens it (so that it still integrates to 1). The distributions are still bell-shaped.

Exercise 4.15 (Forget about fatigue) The time z (in hours) until failure of a particular battery follows an exponential distribution.
(a) Derive $\Pr(z > 10)$.
(b) After c hours the battery is still functioning. Find the conditional probability that the battery functions for at least another h hours. In other words, find $\Pr(z \geqslant c + h \mid z \geqslant c)$. What do you notice?

Solution
Let $f_z(w) = \lambda e^{-\lambda w}$ for $w > 0$. Then:
(a) $\Pr(z > 10) = \int_{10}^{\infty} \lambda e^{-\lambda w} \, dw = e^{-10\lambda}$;
(b) the conditional probability is

$$\Pr(z \geqslant c + h \mid z \geqslant c) = \frac{\Pr(z \geqslant c + h)}{\Pr(z \geqslant c)} = \frac{e^{-\lambda(c+h)}}{e^{-\lambda c}} = e^{-\lambda h} = \Pr(z \geqslant h).$$

We see that the conditional probability does not depend on c, this being an illustration of the no-memory property in Exercise 4.12.

Exercise 4.16 (Gamma-time and Poisson-arrival representations) For the shop of Exercise 4.8, derive the distribution of the time for which the shop attendant has to wait until the next customer arrives. What is the distribution of the time until n customers have arrived?

Solution
Use $z \in \mathbb{R}_+$ here to denote the waiting time in minutes, with w its realization (the time actually waited), while taking $x \sim \text{Poi}(\lambda)$ to be the distribution of the number of customer arrivals. Since λ is the mean of the arrivals, we see that $r := \lambda/w$ is the mean arrival rate (arrivals per unit of time) or *intensity* parameter. Then, the probability of $x = 0$ arrivals is given by the Poisson p.d.f. evaluated at 0 as e^{-rw}. The event $x = 0$ means that the shop

attendant has to wait more than w minutes (for all w) for an arrival, so $\Pr(z > w) = e^{-rw}$ as well. The c.d.f. of z is therefore $1 - e^{-rw}$ and its p.d.f. is obtained as Expo(r) by differentiation with respect to w.

Similarly, the probability of $x < n$ arrivals is given by the Poisson c.d.f. at $n-1$,

$$\Pr(x \leqslant n-1) = \sum_{u=0}^{n-1} \Pr(x = u) = \sum_{u=0}^{n-1} \frac{(rw)^u e^{-rw}}{u!},$$

which is also the probability that the shop attendant has to wait more than w minutes for the n-th arrival, given by $\Pr(z > w)$. The p.d.f. of z is therefore obtained by differentiating $\Pr(z \leqslant w) = 1 - \Pr(z > w)$ with respect to w, and the result is

$$\begin{aligned}
&-\sum_{u=0}^{n-1} \frac{ur(rw)^{u-1}e^{-rw}}{u!} + \sum_{u=0}^{n-1} \frac{r(rw)^u e^{-rw}}{u!} \\
&= -\sum_{u=1}^{n-1} \frac{r(rw)^{u-1}e^{-rw}}{(u-1)!} + \sum_{u=0}^{n-1} \frac{r(rw)^u e^{-rw}}{u!} \\
&= -\sum_{j=0}^{n-2} \frac{r(rw)^{j}e^{-rw}}{j!} + \sum_{u=0}^{n-1} \frac{r(rw)^u e^{-rw}}{u!} \\
&= \frac{r(rw)^{n-1}e^{-rw}}{(n-1)!} = \frac{r^n w^{n-1} e^{-rw}}{\Gamma(n)},
\end{aligned}$$

which we recognize as the p.d.f. of a Gam(n, r) variate. Notice that this derivation implies the identity

$$\sum_{u=0}^{n-1} \frac{(rw)^u e^{-rw}}{u!} = 1 - \int_0^w \frac{r^n t^{n-1} e^{-rt}}{\Gamma(n)} \, dt$$

relating the c.d.f. of a Poisson variate to the c.d.f. of a gamma variate when $n \in \mathbb{N}$.

Exercise 4.17 (Nbin representation, take 1 again) In the shop of Exercise 4.8, suppose instead that the rate of arrival is not fixed. Assume that people arrive according to a Poi(p), and that the parameter p representing the mean of arrivals varies according to a Gam(ν, λ) distribution. Work out the distribution of the arrival of customers in this shop.

Solution

This was worked out in Exercise 2.25, and the result is the Nbin$(\nu, \lambda/(\lambda+1))$ distribution. Notice that ν need not be an integer here, unlike in the Nbin representation in Exercise 4.4.

***Exercise 4.18 (Uniform representation)** The variates x and y are independent and have the same exponential density function. Define $z := x/(x+y) \in (0, 1)$.

(a) By using the mixing decomposition of c.d.f.s in Chapter 2, show that the c.d.f. of z is

$$F_z(w) = \int_0^\infty \Pr\left(x \leqslant \frac{w}{1-w}v\right) \mathrm{d}F_y(v).$$

(b) Hence show that z is uniformly distributed.

Solution

(a) The c.d.f. is

$$F_z(w) = \Pr(z \leqslant w) = \Pr\left(\frac{x}{x+y} \leqslant w\right) = \Pr(x \leqslant w(x+y)) = \Pr(x(1-w) \leqslant wy)$$

$$= \Pr\left(x \leqslant \frac{w}{1-w}y\right) = \int_0^\infty \Pr\left(x \leqslant \frac{w}{1-w}v \,\middle|\, y = v\right) \mathrm{d}F_y(v)$$

by the mixing decomposition of Chapter 2. Note that, using the terminology of Chapter 3 and (3.6), this is the expectation (with respect to y) of the conditional probability. By the independence of x and y, the conditional and unconditional probabilities are equal, and we obtain the stated result.

(b) Using $\mathrm{d}F_y(v) = f_y(v)\,\mathrm{d}v$ and the exponential densities of x and y,

$$F_z(w) = \int_0^\infty \left(\int_0^{wv/(1-w)} \lambda \mathrm{e}^{-\lambda u}\,\mathrm{d}u\right) \lambda \mathrm{e}^{-\lambda v}\,\mathrm{d}v = \int_0^\infty \left(1 - \mathrm{e}^{-\frac{\lambda w v}{1-w}}\right) \lambda \mathrm{e}^{-\lambda v}\,\mathrm{d}v$$

$$= \int_0^\infty \lambda \mathrm{e}^{-\lambda v}\,\mathrm{d}v - \lambda \int_0^\infty \exp\left(-\left(\lambda + \frac{\lambda w}{1-w}\right)v\right) \mathrm{d}v$$

$$= 1 - \lambda \int_0^\infty \exp\left(-\frac{\lambda v}{1-w}\right) \mathrm{d}v = 1 - \frac{\lambda(1-w)}{\lambda} = w.$$

By differentiating $F_z(w)$, we see that z has a uniform distribution on $(0,1)$.

Exercise 4.19 (Gamma patience!) The shop attendant of Exercise 4.16 wants to calculate the distribution of the waiting time until five customers arrive, and he knows that the mean arrival rate is 1/5. Compute the c.d.f. of $\mathrm{Gam}(4, 1/5)$.

Solution

Using successive integration by parts,

$$F(w) = \frac{1}{5^4 3!} \int_0^w t^3 \mathrm{e}^{-t/5}\,\mathrm{d}t = \left[-\frac{5^{-3} t^3 \mathrm{e}^{-t/5}}{3!}\right]_0^w + \int_0^w \frac{5^{-3} t^2 \mathrm{e}^{-t/5}}{2}\,\mathrm{d}t$$

$$= -\frac{5^{-3} w^3 \mathrm{e}^{-w/5}}{3!} - \frac{5^{-2} w^2 \mathrm{e}^{-w/5}}{2} + \int_0^w 5^{-2} t \mathrm{e}^{-t/5}\,\mathrm{d}t$$

$$= -\frac{5^{-3} w^3 \mathrm{e}^{-w/5}}{3!} - \frac{5^{-2} w^2 \mathrm{e}^{-w/5}}{2} - 5^{-1} w \mathrm{e}^{-w/5} - \mathrm{e}^{-w/5} + 1.$$

Exercise 4.20 (Gamma c.d.f.) The integral representation of the *incomplete gamma function* is

$$\Gamma(\nu, w) := \int_w^{\infty} \tau^{\nu-1} \mathrm{e}^{-\tau} \, \mathrm{d}\tau = \Gamma(\nu) - \int_0^w \tau^{\nu-1} \mathrm{e}^{-\tau} \, \mathrm{d}\tau$$

for $\nu > 0$. Obtain its series representation and use it to express explicitly the c.d.f. of $x \sim \mathrm{GG}(\nu, p, \lambda)$. [Hint: Expand the exponential in the latter integral.]

Solution

For $p > 0$, the c.d.f. of $\mathrm{GG}(\nu, p, \lambda)$ is

$$\Pr(x \leqslant u) = \int_0^u \frac{p\lambda^{\nu} t^{\nu p-1}}{\Gamma(\nu)} \mathrm{e}^{-\lambda t^p} \, \mathrm{d}t = \int_0^{\lambda u^p} \frac{\tau^{\nu-1}}{\Gamma(\nu)} \mathrm{e}^{-\tau} \, \mathrm{d}\tau$$

by the change of variable $\tau = \lambda t^p$ (with $\tau^{-1} \, \mathrm{d}\tau = pt^{-1} \, \mathrm{d}t$); and, for $p < 0$,

$$\Pr(x \leqslant u) = \int_u^0 \frac{p\lambda^{\nu} t^{\nu p-1}}{\Gamma(\nu)} \mathrm{e}^{-\lambda t^p} \, \mathrm{d}t = \int_{\lambda u^p}^{\infty} \frac{\tau^{\nu-1}}{\Gamma(\nu)} \mathrm{e}^{-\tau} \, \mathrm{d}\tau$$

since $\lambda(0^+)^p = \infty$ for negative p. These integrals are related to the incomplete gamma function, which satisfies the integration-by-parts recursion

$$\Gamma(\nu + 1, w) = \nu \Gamma(\nu, w) + w^{\nu} \mathrm{e}^{-w},$$

where

$$\Gamma(1, w) = \int_w^{\infty} \mathrm{e}^{-\tau} \, \mathrm{d}\tau = \mathrm{e}^{-w}.$$

When $\nu \in \mathbb{N}$, this recursion generalizes the first formula in Exercise 4.19, giving rise to the identity at the end of the solution to Exercise 4.16 and implying that the c.d.f. of a $\mathrm{Poi}(\lambda)$ variate is $\Gamma(n + 1, \lambda)/n!$. However, the general expression for any $\nu \in \mathbb{R}_+$ is obtained by expanding the exponential and integrating termwise over the finite interval $(0, w)$:

$$\Gamma(\nu, w) = \Gamma(\nu) - \sum_{j=0}^{\infty} \frac{(-1)^j}{j!} \int_0^w \tau^{j+\nu-1} \, \mathrm{d}\tau = \Gamma(\nu) - w^{\nu} \sum_{j=0}^{\infty} \frac{(-w)^j}{j!(j + \nu)}$$

since $j + \nu > 0$. The convergence of this series is as rapid as the exponential series, as will be illustrated in Exercise 4.22.

The c.d.f. is therefore $1 - \Gamma(\nu, \lambda u^p)/\Gamma(\nu)$ for $p > 0$, and $\Gamma(\nu, \lambda u^p)/\Gamma(\nu)$ for $p < 0$. This can be combined into

$$1_{p>0} - \mathrm{sgn}(p) \frac{\Gamma(\nu, \lambda u^p)}{\Gamma(\nu)}.$$

Incidentally, the incomplete gamma function and the hypergeometric c.f. (mentioned in the introduction to this chapter) are both special cases of the hypergeometric function defined in the Notes to this chapter.

*__Exercise 4.21 (Normal c.d.f.)__ Derive two alternative explicit formulae for the c.d.f. of $x \sim \text{N}(0,1)$.

Solution

The density is symmetric about its mean, 0, so that $\Phi(0) = \frac{1}{2}$. As before, expanding the exponential and then integrating termwise over a finite interval gives

$$\Phi(u) := \int_{-\infty}^{u} e^{-t^2/2} \frac{dt}{\sqrt{2\pi}} = \Phi(0) + \int_{0}^{u} e^{-t^2/2} \frac{dt}{\sqrt{2\pi}}$$

$$= \frac{1}{2} + \int_0^u \sum_{j=0}^{\infty} \frac{(-t^2/2)^j}{j!} \frac{dt}{\sqrt{2\pi}} = \frac{1}{2} + \frac{u}{\sqrt{2\pi}} \sum_{j=0}^{\infty} \frac{(-u^2/2)^j}{j!(2j+1)}.$$

The reader may wish to verify that this series is expressible as

$$\Phi(u) = \frac{1+\operatorname{sgn}(u)}{2} - \frac{\operatorname{sgn}(u)}{2\sqrt{\pi}} \Gamma\left(\frac{1}{2}, \frac{u^2}{2}\right)$$

in terms of the incomplete gamma function.

An alternative (yet equivalent) form for $\Phi(u)$ can be obtained by expanding the same integral differently. By the symmetry around 0 of the standard normal p.d.f.,

$$\Phi(u) = \frac{1}{2} + \int_0^u e^{-t^2/2} \frac{dt}{\sqrt{2\pi}} = \frac{1}{2} + \frac{1}{2} \int_{-u}^{u} e^{-t^2/2} \frac{dt}{\sqrt{2\pi}}$$

$$= \frac{1}{2} + \frac{e^{-u^2/2}}{2} \int_{-u}^{u} e^{(u^2-t^2)/2} \frac{dt}{\sqrt{2\pi}} = \frac{1}{2} + \frac{\phi(u)}{2} \int_{-u}^{u} e^{(u-t)(u+t)/2} \, dt$$

$$= \frac{1}{2} + \frac{\phi(u)}{2} \int_{-u}^{u} \sum_{j=0}^{\infty} \frac{(u-t)^j (u+t)^j}{j! 2^j} \, dt.$$

This integral can be worked out by means of the definition of the $\text{Beta}_{(-u,u)}(j+1, j+1)$ density as

$$\Phi(u) = \frac{1}{2} + \frac{\phi(u)}{2} \sum_{j=0}^{\infty} \frac{B(j+1, j+1)(2u)^{2j+1}}{j! 2^j} = \frac{1}{2} + u\phi(u) \sum_{j=0}^{\infty} \frac{j!(2u^2)^j}{(2j+1)!}$$

since $\Gamma(j+1) = j!$. One may simplify the expression further. Since

$$\frac{j! 2^j}{(2j+1)!} = \frac{\left(\prod_{i=1}^j i\right)\left(\prod_{i=1}^j 2\right)}{\prod_{k=1}^{2j+1} k} = \frac{\prod_{i=1}^j (2i)}{\left(\prod_{i=1}^j (2i+1)\right) \prod_{i=1}^j (2i)} = \frac{1}{2^j \prod_{i=1}^j \left(i + \frac{1}{2}\right)}$$

$$= \frac{\Gamma\left(\frac{3}{2}\right)}{2^j \left(\prod_{i=1}^j \left(i+\frac{1}{2}\right)\right) \Gamma\left(\frac{3}{2}\right)} = \frac{\Gamma\left(\frac{3}{2}\right)}{2^j \Gamma\left(j + \frac{3}{2}\right)}$$

by the recurrence identity $\Gamma(\nu+1)=\nu\Gamma(\nu)$, and

$$\Gamma\left(\frac{3}{2}\right)=\frac{1}{2}\Gamma\left(\frac{1}{2}\right)=\frac{\sqrt{\pi}}{2},$$

we get

$$\Phi(u)=\frac{1}{2}+u\phi(u)\frac{\sqrt{\pi}}{2}\sum_{j=0}^{\infty}\frac{(u^2/2)^j}{\Gamma\left(j+\frac{3}{2}\right)}.$$

Exercise 4.22 (Normal numbers) Suppose that $x \sim$ N(3, 0.16). Using the formulae in Exercise 4.21, find the following probabilities exactly to four decimal places:
(a) $\Pr(x>3)$;
(b) $\Pr(x>3.3)$;
(c) $\Pr(2.8 \leqslant x \leqslant 3.1)$.

Solution

Let $z=(x-3)/0.4$. Then $\mathrm{E}(z)=3-3=0$ and $\mathrm{var}(z)=0.16/(0.4)^2=1$, so that $z \sim$ N(0,1).
(a) Since x is distributed symmetrically around 3, $\Pr(x>3)=0.5$.
(b) We have $\Pr(x>3.3)=\Pr(z>0.75)=\Pr(z<-0.75)$ by the symmetry of z, and

$$\Phi(-0.75)=0.5-\frac{0.75}{\sqrt{2\pi}}\sum_{j=0}^{\infty}\frac{(-(0.75)^2/2)^j}{j!(2j+1)}$$
$$\approx 0.5-(0.299\,21-0.028\,05+0.002\,37-0.000\,16+0.000\,01)\approx 0.2266,$$

where one should be careful not to round the intermediate numbers to four decimal places before adding them up (otherwise we would have obtained 0.2267, which is not correct). Notice how fast this "infinite" series converges to any fixed required precision, actually at the same rate as the series $\mathrm{e}^w=\sum_{j=0}^{\infty}w^j/j!$ which can be used to calculate the exponential function for w not too large. The other formula for $\Phi(u)$ gives

$$\Phi(-0.75)=0.5-0.75\frac{\mathrm{e}^{-(0.75)^2/2}}{\sqrt{2\pi}}\sum_{j=0}^{\infty}\frac{((0.75)^2/2)^j}{\left(\frac{3}{2}\right)\cdots\left(j+\frac{1}{2}\right)}$$
$$\approx 0.5-(0.225\,85+0.042\,35+0.004\,76+0.000\,38+0.000\,02)\approx 0.2266,$$

where, for $j=0$, the empty product $\prod_{i=1}^{0}\left(i+\frac{1}{2}\right)=1$ by mathematical convention. This result corresponds to the normal c.d.f. value found in the usual published tables. The formulae of Exercise 4.21 can be used to obtain these values to a higher precision if needed.

(c) Since $\Pr(2.8 \leqslant x \leqslant 3.1) = \Pr(-0.5 \leqslant z \leqslant 0.25)$, we have

$$\Phi(0.25) - \Phi(-0.5) = \frac{1}{\sqrt{2\pi}} \sum_{j=0}^{\infty} \frac{(-0.5)^j}{j!(2j+1)} \left((0.25)^{2j+1} - (-0.5)^{2j+1}\right)$$

$$\approx 0.299\,21 - 0.009\,35 + 0.000\,32 - 0.000\,01 \approx 0.2902.$$

Exercise 4.23 (Pricing a financial option) Suppose that an investor possesses at time t some *European call option*, a piece of paper giving her the right (but not the obligation) to buy one share of a company at a fixed price k (called the *strike price*) m months later. The time $T := t + m > t$ is called the *expiration date*, and the option becomes worthless after that. Suppose that the interest rate (or time-value of money) is zero, and that the stock pays no dividends. Denote by x_t and c_t the share and call-option prices, respectively, at time t. Assume that there exists at time t some probability density for the final x_T, denoted by $f_{x_T}(u)$, with respect to which expectations can be taken to evaluate the option, and that $c_t = \mathrm{E}_t(\max\{0, x_T - k\})$, where E_t denotes the expectation taken at time t.
(a) Show that

$$\left.\frac{\mathrm{d}^2 c_t}{\mathrm{d}k^2}\right|_{k=u} = f_{x_T}(u).$$

(b) Assuming that $z := x_T/x_t \sim \mathrm{LN}(-\sigma^2 m/2, \sigma^2 m)$, where $x_t \in \mathbb{R}_+$, derive the *Black–Scholes–Merton* formula $c_t = x_t \Phi(d_1) - k\Phi(d_2)$ with

$$d_1 := \frac{\log(x_t/k) + \sigma^2 m/2}{\sigma\sqrt{m}} \quad \text{and} \quad d_2 := \frac{\log(x_t/k) - \sigma^2 m/2}{\sigma\sqrt{m}}.$$

Solution
(a) The quantity $\max\{0, x_T - k\}$ is the intrinsic value of the option, evaluating the savings that the investor can make by exercising her option at time T. This value can fluctuate dramatically in percentage terms (for example, from 0 to any number is an infinitely large increase), much more so than the underlying share price. We have

$$c_t = \mathrm{E}_t(\max\{0, x_T - k\}) = \int_k^{\infty} (u - k) f_{x_T}(u)\,\mathrm{d}u.$$

Differentiating by means of Leibniz' rule (see Section A.4),

$$\frac{\mathrm{d}c_t}{\mathrm{d}k} = (k - k) f_{x_T}(k) - \int_k^{\infty} f_{x_T}(u)\,\mathrm{d}u = -(1 - F_{x_T}(k)),$$

where F_{x_T} is the c.d.f. corresponding to f_{x_T}. Differentiating once more, we obtain

$$\frac{\mathrm{d}^2 c_t}{\mathrm{d}k^2} = f_{x_T}(k),$$

which gives the required result upon evaluating the derivative at $k = u$.
(b) Since x_t is already known at time t, it is nonrandom and

$$c_t = x_t \operatorname{E}_t\left(\max\left\{0, \frac{x_T}{x_t} - \frac{k}{x_t}\right\}\right).$$

The only remaining random variable is $z := x_T/x_t$, which is log-normal and whose density gives

$$\begin{aligned} c_t = {} & x_t \int_{k/x_t}^{\infty} \frac{w}{w\sqrt{2\pi\sigma^2 m}} \exp\left(-\frac{\left(\log(w) + \sigma^2 m/2\right)^2}{2\sigma^2 m}\right) \mathrm{d}w \\ & - x_t \frac{k}{x_t} \int_{k/x_t}^{\infty} \frac{1}{w\sqrt{2\pi\sigma^2 m}} \exp\left(-\frac{\left(\log(w) + \sigma^2 m/2\right)^2}{2\sigma^2 m}\right) \mathrm{d}w. \end{aligned}$$

By the change of variable $v = \log(w)$,

$$\begin{aligned} c_t = {} & x_t \int_{\log(k/x_t)}^{\infty} \frac{1}{\sqrt{2\pi\sigma^2 m}} \exp\left(-\frac{\left(v + \sigma^2 m/2\right)^2}{2\sigma^2 m}\right) \mathrm{e}^{v} \, \mathrm{d}v \\ & - k \int_{\log(k/x_t)}^{\infty} \frac{1}{\sqrt{2\pi\sigma^2 m}} \exp\left(-\frac{\left(v + \sigma^2 m/2\right)^2}{2\sigma^2 m}\right) \mathrm{d}v, \end{aligned}$$

where in the first integral we can simplify the product of exponents by means of

$$\left(v + \sigma^2 m/2\right)^2 - 2\sigma^2 m v = \left(v - \sigma^2 m/2\right)^2.$$

Using $1 - \Phi(d) = \Phi(-d)$ gives the required result.

As noted at the end of the solution of Exercise 2.18, taking logarithms transforms absolute scales into relative (percentage) scales. Roughly speaking, if we plotted $\log(x_t)$ against time t (the horizontal axis), equal distances on the vertical axis would denote equal *percentage* changes in x_t. More formally, the logarithmic transformation allows small changes to be expressed in percentages of the original variate:

$$\log(x_t) - \log(x_{t-1}) = \log(x_t/x_{t-1}) = \log\left(1 + \frac{x_t - x_{t-1}}{x_{t-1}}\right) \approx \frac{x_t - x_{t-1}}{x_{t-1}}$$

by the logarithmic expansion (see Section A.3.2) when the percentage $(x_t - x_{t-1})/x_{t-1}$ is small. See Exercise 10.35 for a related transformation.

Exercise 4.24 (Normal moments) Let $z \sim \mathrm{N}(0,1)$. Compute $\operatorname{E}\left(z^j\right)$ for $j \in \mathbb{N}$. Hence, show that the excess kurtosis of a normal variate is zero (or $\operatorname{E}\left(z^4\right) = 3$) and $\operatorname{E}\left(z^6\right) = 15$.

Solution

We provide two solutions. The first uses the moment-generating function of z,

$$m(t) = \frac{1}{\sqrt{2\pi}} \int_{-\infty}^{\infty} \mathrm{e}^{tw} \mathrm{e}^{-w^2/2} \, \mathrm{d}w = \frac{1}{\sqrt{2\pi}} \mathrm{e}^{t^2/2} \int_{-\infty}^{\infty} \mathrm{e}^{-(w-t)^2/2} \, \mathrm{d}w = \mathrm{e}^{t^2/2},$$

where we have used the fact that the $\mathrm{N}(t,1)$ distribution integrates to 1. Expanding the exponential,

$$m(t) = \sum_{i=0}^{\infty} \frac{(t^2/2)^i}{i!} = \sum_{i=0}^{\infty} \frac{t^{2i}}{2^i i!} = \sum_{i=0}^{\infty} \frac{(2i)!}{2^i i!} \times \frac{t^{2i}}{(2i)!},$$

hence

$$\mathrm{E}\left(z^{2k+1}\right) = 0 \quad \text{and} \quad \mathrm{E}\left(z^{2k}\right) = \frac{(2k)!}{2^k k!} = 1 \times 3 \times 5 \times \cdots \times (2k-1).$$

The second solution uses only basic properties of the expectation:

$$\mathrm{E}\left(z^j\right) = \frac{1}{\sqrt{2\pi}} \int_{-\infty}^{\infty} w^j \mathrm{e}^{-w^2/2} \,\mathrm{d}w.$$

Since $h(w) := w^{2k+1}\mathrm{e}^{-w^2/2}$ is an odd function of w (that is, $h(-w) = -h(w)$), it follows that $\mathrm{E}\left(z^{2k+1}\right) = 0$. Regarding the even moments, we find

$$\mathrm{E}\left(z^{2k}\right) = \frac{1}{\sqrt{2\pi}} \int_{-\infty}^{\infty} w^{2k}\mathrm{e}^{-w^2/2} \,\mathrm{d}w = \frac{2}{\sqrt{2\pi}} \int_{0}^{\infty} w^{2k}\mathrm{e}^{-w^2/2} \,\mathrm{d}w.$$

By the transformation $u = w^2/2$ with $\mathrm{d}u = w\,\mathrm{d}w$,

$$\mathrm{E}\left(z^{2k}\right) = \frac{2^k}{\sqrt{\pi}} \int_{0}^{\infty} u^{k-1/2}\mathrm{e}^{-u} \,\mathrm{d}u = \frac{2^k}{\sqrt{\pi}} \Gamma\left(k + \frac{1}{2}\right).$$

Since $\Gamma\left(\frac{1}{2}\right) = \sqrt{\pi}$ and $\Gamma(\nu+1) = \nu\Gamma(\nu)$,

$$\Gamma\left(k+\frac{1}{2}\right) = \left(k-\frac{1}{2}\right)\left(k-\frac{3}{2}\right)\cdots\left(\frac{1}{2}\right)\Gamma\left(\frac{1}{2}\right)$$
$$= \left(\frac{2k-1}{2}\right)\left(\frac{2k-3}{2}\right)\cdots\left(\frac{1}{2}\right)\sqrt{\pi},$$

and the same result follows.

***Exercise 4.25 (Noncentral $\chi^2(1,\delta)$ representation)** Let $x \sim \mathrm{N}(\mu, \sigma^2)$. Show that $y := x^2/\sigma^2$ has the $\chi^2(1, \mu^2/\sigma^2)$ distribution.

Solution

We know that $z := x/\sigma \sim \mathrm{N}(\mu/\sigma, 1)$. We can find the c.d.f. of y as follows:

$$F_y(v) = \Pr(y \leqslant v) = \Pr\left(z^2 \leqslant v\right) = \Pr\left(-\sqrt{v} \leqslant z \leqslant \sqrt{v}\right)$$
$$= \Pr\left(-\frac{\mu}{\sigma} - \sqrt{v} \leqslant z - \frac{\mu}{\sigma} \leqslant -\frac{\mu}{\sigma} + \sqrt{v}\right)$$
$$= \Phi\left(-\frac{\mu}{\sigma} + \sqrt{v}\right) - \Phi\left(-\frac{\mu}{\sigma} - \sqrt{v}\right).$$

By differentiating $F_y(v)$ with respect to v, we obtain

$$\begin{aligned}
f_y(v) &= \frac{1}{2\sqrt{v}}\phi\left(-\frac{\mu}{\sigma}+\sqrt{v}\right)+\frac{1}{2\sqrt{v}}\phi\left(-\frac{\mu}{\sigma}-\sqrt{v}\right)\\
&= \frac{1}{2\sqrt{2\pi v}}\left(\mathrm{e}^{-\frac{1}{2}\left(-\frac{\mu}{\sigma}+\sqrt{v}\right)^2}+\mathrm{e}^{-\frac{1}{2}\left(-\frac{\mu}{\sigma}-\sqrt{v}\right)^2}\right)\\
&= \frac{\mathrm{e}^{-\frac{1}{2}\left(\frac{\mu^2}{\sigma^2}+v\right)}}{2\sqrt{2\pi v}}\left(\mathrm{e}^{\frac{\mu}{\sigma}\sqrt{v}}+\mathrm{e}^{-\frac{\mu}{\sigma}\sqrt{v}}\right) \equiv \frac{\mathrm{e}^{-\frac{1}{2}\left(\frac{\mu^2}{\sigma^2}+v\right)}\cosh\left(\frac{\mu}{\sigma}\sqrt{v}\right)}{\sqrt{2\pi v}}.
\end{aligned}$$

Now consider the general p.d.f. of a $\chi^2(n,\delta)$ from Table 4.2. Setting $n = 1$ there and simplifying gives the p.d.f. of a $\chi^2(1,\delta)$ as

$$\begin{aligned}
\mathrm{e}^{-\delta/2}\sum_{j=0}^{\infty}\frac{(\delta/2)^j}{j!}\frac{(v/2)^{j-\frac{1}{2}}}{2\Gamma\left(j+\frac{1}{2}\right)}\mathrm{e}^{-v/2} &= \frac{\mathrm{e}^{-\delta/2-v/2}}{\sqrt{2v}}\sum_{j=0}^{\infty}\frac{(\delta v/4)^j}{j!\Gamma\left(j+\frac{1}{2}\right)}\\
&= \frac{\mathrm{e}^{-\delta/2-v/2}}{\sqrt{2\pi v}}\sum_{j=0}^{\infty}\frac{(\delta v)^j}{(2j)!} \equiv \frac{\mathrm{e}^{-\delta/2-v/2}}{\sqrt{2\pi v}}\cosh\left(\sqrt{\delta v}\right)
\end{aligned}$$

since the derivations in Exercise 4.24 showed that $(2j)! = 2^{2j}j!\Gamma(j+1/2)/\sqrt{\pi}$. This is our $f_y(v)$, with $\delta = \mu^2/\sigma^2$, identifying our density as that of a $\chi^2(1,\mu^2/\sigma^2)$ variate. Note that its corresponding c.d.f. F_y was derived at the start of the solution in terms of the standard normal c.d.f. Φ.

We offer a second solution, which uses the fact that the moment-generating function of a $\chi^2(n,\delta)$-distributed variate is $(1-2t)^{-n/2}\exp(\delta t/(1-2t))$. Then, since $z := x/\sigma \sim \mathrm{N}(\mu/\sigma, 1)$, we obtain

$$\begin{aligned}
m_y(t) = \mathrm{E}\left(\mathrm{e}^{ty}\right) = \mathrm{E}\left(\mathrm{e}^{tz^2}\right) &= \frac{1}{\sqrt{2\pi}}\int_{-\infty}^{\infty}\mathrm{e}^{tw^2-\frac{1}{2}\left(w-\frac{\mu}{\sigma}\right)^2}\,\mathrm{d}w\\
&= \frac{1}{\sqrt{2\pi}}\mathrm{e}^{-\frac{\mu^2}{2\sigma^2}}\int_{-\infty}^{\infty}\mathrm{e}^{\left(t-\frac{1}{2}\right)w^2+\frac{\mu}{\sigma}w}\,\mathrm{d}w\\
&= \frac{1}{\sqrt{2\pi}}\exp\left(-\frac{\mu^2}{2\sigma^2}-\frac{\mu^2}{4\sigma^2(t-1/2)}\right)\\
&\quad\times\int_{-\infty}^{\infty}\exp\left(\left(t-\frac{1}{2}\right)\left(w+\frac{\mu}{2\sigma(t-1/2)}\right)^2\right)\mathrm{d}w
\end{aligned}$$

by completing the square in the exponent. The final integral can be worked out from the density of an

$$\mathrm{N}\left(\frac{\mu}{2\sigma\left(\frac{1}{2}-t\right)}, \frac{1}{1-2t}\right)$$

variate, with $t < \frac{1}{2}$. This yields

$$m_y(t) = \frac{\exp\left(-\frac{\mu^2}{2\sigma^2}\left(1 + \frac{1}{2t-1}\right)\right)}{\sqrt{1-2t}} = (1-2t)^{-1/2} \exp\left(\frac{\mu^2}{\sigma^2} \times \frac{t}{1-2t}\right),$$

which we recognize as the m.g.f. of the $\chi^2(1, \mu^2/\sigma^2)$ distribution.

Exercise 4.26 (Beta and gamma moments) Obtain $\mathrm{E}\left(x^k\right)$ for k any positive real number, inferring the mean and the variance when:
(a) $x \sim \mathrm{Beta}(p, q)$;
(b) $x \sim \mathrm{Gam}(\nu, \lambda)$.

Solution
(a) The variate x is positive with probability 1, and we obtain its k-th moment for $k \in \mathbb{R}_+$ as

$$\mathrm{E}\left(x^k\right) = \frac{\Gamma(p+q)}{\Gamma(p)\Gamma(q)} \int_0^1 u^{p+k-1}(1-u)^{q-1}\,\mathrm{d}u$$
$$= \frac{\Gamma(p+q)}{\Gamma(p)\Gamma(q)} \times \frac{\Gamma(p+k)\Gamma(q)}{\Gamma(p+q+k)} = \frac{\Gamma(p+q)}{\Gamma(p+q+k)} \times \frac{\Gamma(p+k)}{\Gamma(p)}.$$

Using $\Gamma(\nu+1) = \nu\Gamma(\nu)$,

$$\mathrm{E}(x) = \frac{p}{p+q}, \quad \mathrm{E}\left(x^2\right) = \frac{p(p+1)}{(p+q)(p+q+1)}, \quad \mathrm{var}(x) = \frac{pq}{(p+q)^2(p+q+1)}.$$

(b) As before,

$$\mathrm{E}\left(x^k\right) = \frac{\lambda^\nu}{\Gamma(\nu)} \int_0^\infty u^{\nu+k-1}\mathrm{e}^{-\lambda u}\,\mathrm{d}u$$
$$= \frac{\lambda^\nu}{\Gamma(\nu)} \times \frac{\Gamma(\nu+k)}{\lambda^{\nu+k}} = \frac{\Gamma(\nu+k)}{\lambda^k\Gamma(\nu)}.$$

Hence,

$$\mathrm{E}(x) = \frac{\nu}{\lambda}, \quad \mathrm{E}\left(x^2\right) = \frac{\nu(\nu+1)}{\lambda^2}, \quad \mathrm{var}(x) = \frac{\nu}{\lambda^2}.$$

Exercise 4.27 (Gamma inverse moments) Derive the inverse moments $\mathrm{E}\left(x^{-j}\right)$ of $\mathrm{Gam}(\nu, \lambda)$ using Exercise 3.30, and state the condition for their existence. Compare your formula with the result in Exercise 4.26(b).

Solution
By the formula in Exercise 3.30 and the $\mathrm{Gam}(\nu, \lambda)$ m.g.f. from Table 4.2, we have

$$\mathrm{E}\left(x^{-j}\right) = \frac{1}{\Gamma(j)} \int_0^\infty \tau^{j-1}\left(1 + \frac{\tau}{\lambda}\right)^{-\nu} \mathrm{d}\tau = \frac{\lambda^j}{\Gamma(j)} \int_0^\infty t^{j-1}(1+t)^{-\nu}\,\mathrm{d}t,$$

using the change of variable $t = \tau/\lambda$. The integral representation of the beta function (see the introduction to Chapter 1) implies

$$\mathrm{E}\left(x^{-j}\right) = \frac{\lambda^j B(j, \nu - j)}{\Gamma(j)} = \frac{\lambda^j \Gamma(\nu - j)}{\Gamma(\nu)}$$

for $\nu - j > 0$. The result also follows from integrating the F-density, a connection that will be made clearer in Exercise 4.31. The formula we have just derived for $\mathrm{E}\left(x^{-j}\right)$ agrees with that in Exercise 4.26(b). The existence requirement here is that $j < \nu$, which allows any real $j \in (-\infty, \nu)$.

***Exercise 4.28 (Generalized extreme value c.d.f.)** Derive the GEV c.d.f. from its p.d.f.

$$f_z(w) = \frac{\lambda \exp\left(-\left(1 - \frac{\lambda(w-\alpha)}{p}\right)^p\right)}{\left(1 - \frac{\lambda(w-\alpha)}{p}\right)^{1-p}} \qquad (\lambda \in \mathbb{R}_+,\ p^{-1} \in \mathbb{R},\ 1-\lambda(w-\alpha)p^{-1} \in \mathbb{R}_+),$$

and show the relation of GEV variates to the generalized gamma. [Hint: Consider the three cases $p < 0, p > 0$, and $p^{-1} \to 0$.]

Solution

Three different cases arise. If $p < 0$, then $w \in (\alpha + p/\lambda, \infty)$ and the c.d.f. of z is

$$\int_{\alpha+p/\lambda}^{w} \frac{\lambda \exp\left(-\left(1 - \frac{\lambda(t-\alpha)}{p}\right)^p\right)}{\left(1 - \frac{\lambda(t-\alpha)}{p}\right)^{1-p}} \mathrm{d}t = \left[\exp\left(-\left(1 - \frac{\lambda(t-\alpha)}{p}\right)^p\right)\right]_{\alpha+p/\lambda}^{w}$$

$$= \exp\left(-\left(1 - \frac{\lambda(w-\alpha)}{p}\right)^p\right),$$

as $\exp\left(-(0^+)^p\right) = \exp\left(-(\infty)^{-p}\right) = 0$ for $p < 0$. To find the link with GG, consider the variate $y := \lambda^{-1} - (z - \alpha)p^{-1} \in \mathbb{R}_+$ which has c.d.f.

$$\Pr(y \leqslant v) = \Pr\left(\lambda^{-1} - (z - \alpha)p^{-1} \leqslant v\right) = \Pr\left(z \leqslant \alpha + p\lambda^{-1} - pv\right)$$

since multiplying both sides of the inequality by $-p > 0$ does not change it. As a result, we get

$$\Pr(y \leqslant v) = \exp\left(-\left(1 - \frac{\lambda\left((\alpha + p\lambda^{-1} - pv) - \alpha\right)}{p}\right)^p\right) = \exp\left(-(\lambda v)^p\right). \quad (4.10)$$

By differentiating with respect to v, we get the p.d.f. $-p\lambda^p v^{p-1} \exp\left(-(\lambda v)^p\right)$, which is a $\mathrm{GG}(1, p, \lambda^p)$ density.

If $p > 0$, then $w \in (-\infty, \alpha + p/\lambda)$ and the c.d.f. of z is

$$\int_{-\infty}^{w} \frac{\lambda \exp\left(-\left(1-\frac{\lambda(t-\alpha)}{p}\right)^{p}\right)}{\left(1-\frac{\lambda(t-\alpha)}{p}\right)^{1-p}} dt = \left[\exp\left(-\left(1-\frac{\lambda(t-\alpha)}{p}\right)^{p}\right)\right]_{-\infty}^{w}$$
$$= \exp\left(-\left(1-\frac{\lambda(w-\alpha)}{p}\right)^{p}\right)$$

since $\exp(-(\infty)^p) = 0$ for $p > 0$. The variate $y = \lambda^{-1} - (z-\alpha)p^{-1} \in \mathbb{R}_+$ is now negatively related to z and has c.d.f.

$$\begin{aligned}\Pr(y \leqslant v) &= \Pr\left(\lambda^{-1} - (z-\alpha)\,p^{-1} \leqslant v\right) \\ &= \Pr\left(z \geqslant \alpha + p\lambda^{-1} - pv\right) = 1 - \exp\left(-(\lambda v)^p\right), \qquad (4.11)\end{aligned}$$

and the corresponding p.d.f. is $p\lambda^p v^{p-1} \exp(-(\lambda v)^p)$. We recognize it from Table 4.2 as a Weibull density, that is, a $\mathrm{GG}(1, p, \lambda^p)$ density.

Finally, we can choose to let $p^{-1} \to 0^-$ or $p^{-1} \to 0^+$ and use the logarithmic expansion (see Section A.3.2):

$$\left(1-\frac{c}{p}\right)^{p} = \exp\left(p \log\left(1-\frac{c}{p}\right)\right) = \exp\left(p\left(-\frac{c}{p}-\frac{c^2}{2p^2}-\dots\right)\right) \to \exp(-c).$$

We get $w \in \mathbb{R}$ and the c.d.f. of z becomes $\exp(-\exp(-\lambda(w-\alpha)))$, identifying a Gumbel variate. By defining $y := \exp(-\lambda z) \in \mathbb{R}_+$, we have

$$\begin{aligned}\Pr(y \leqslant v) &= \Pr(\exp(-\lambda z) \leqslant v) = \Pr\left(z \geqslant -\lambda^{-1}\log(v)\right) \\ &= 1 - \exp\left(-\mathrm{e}^{-\lambda(-\lambda^{-1}\log(v)-\alpha)}\right) \\ &= 1 - \exp\left(-\mathrm{e}^{\lambda\alpha+\log(v)}\right) = 1 - \exp\left(-\mathrm{e}^{\lambda\alpha} v\right),\end{aligned}$$

which is the c.d.f. of an $\mathrm{Expo}(\mathrm{e}^{\lambda\alpha})$ variate. Alternatively, the variate $y := \exp(-z) \in \mathbb{R}_+$ has the c.d.f.

$$\begin{aligned}\Pr(y \leqslant v) &= \Pr(\exp(-z) \leqslant v) = \Pr(z \geqslant -\log(v)) \\ &= 1 - \exp\left(-\mathrm{e}^{-\lambda(-\log(v)-\alpha)}\right) = 1 - \exp\left(-\mathrm{e}^{\lambda\alpha} v^{\lambda}\right), \qquad (4.12)\end{aligned}$$

and the corresponding p.d.f. is $\lambda \mathrm{e}^{\lambda\alpha} v^{\lambda-1} \exp\left(-\mathrm{e}^{\lambda\alpha} v^{\lambda}\right)$, which is a $\mathrm{GG}(1, \lambda, \mathrm{e}^{\lambda\alpha})$ density.

In addition, comparing (4.12) with (4.11), we have that z is Gumbel if and only if e^{-z} is Weibull. Similarly, comparing (4.12) with (4.10), we have that z is Gumbel if and only if e^{z} is a Fréchet defined on $\mathbb{R}_+$.

***Exercise 4.29 (Fourier, Laplace, and Cauchy: les trois mousquetaires!)** The variate x has a Laplace distribution. Derive its characteristic function. Comment on its relation to the Cauchy p.d.f. when both distributions are centered around 0.

Solution

The c.f. is obtained as

$$\varphi(\tau) = \mathrm{E}\left(\mathrm{e}^{\mathrm{i}\tau x}\right) = \int_{-\infty}^{\infty} \frac{\lambda}{2} \mathrm{e}^{\mathrm{i}\tau u - \lambda|u-\mu|}\,\mathrm{d}u = \frac{\mathrm{e}^{\mathrm{i}\tau\mu}}{2} \int_{-\infty}^{\infty} \mathrm{e}^{\mathrm{i}\tau v/\lambda - |v|}\,\mathrm{d}v$$

by the change of variable $v = (u-\mu)\lambda$. This is the same type of integral as in Exercise 3.28, giving

$$\varphi(\tau) = \frac{\mathrm{e}^{\mathrm{i}\tau\mu}}{1 + \lambda^{-2}\tau^2}.$$

When $\mu = 0$ in the Laplace distribution, and $\alpha = 0$ in the Cauchy distribution, the two variates are centered around 0. The Cauchy p.d.f. (resp. c.f.) is essentially the Laplace c.f. (resp. p.d.f.) after rescaling the p.d.f. so that it integrates to 1. In other words, apart from the scaling factor 2π, the functions $\lambda \mathrm{e}^{-\lambda|u|}/2$ and $1/(1 + \lambda^{-2}\tau^2)$ form a Fourier-transform pair. The latter has very long tails (decaying hyperbolically) relative to the former (decaying exponentially). This is a general feature of Fourier pairs: if one has long tails, then the other has short tails. There is one striking exception to this rule in Table 4.2, namely the standard normal p.d.f. and c.f. pair, which are both of the form $\mathrm{e}^{-t^2/2}$, up to a scaling constant.

Exercise 4.30 (Logistic identity) Let x have the p.d.f.

$$f(u) = \frac{\lambda \mathrm{e}^{\lambda(u-\alpha)}}{(1 + \mathrm{e}^{\lambda(u-\alpha)})^2} \qquad (u, \alpha \in \mathbb{R}, \lambda \in \mathbb{R}_+).$$

(a) Show that this is the logistic p.d.f., and that it is symmetric around α.
(b) Determine the c.d.f. of x, and its inverse $u = F^{-1}(p)$ for $p \in [0, 1]$.
(c) Obtain $\Pr(|x - \alpha| \leqslant 1)$.

Solution

(a) By taking the exponential in the numerator into the denominator, we have

$$f(u) = \frac{\lambda}{\mathrm{e}^{-\lambda(u-\alpha)}(1 + \mathrm{e}^{\lambda(u-\alpha)})^2} = \frac{\lambda}{(\mathrm{e}^{-\lambda(u-\alpha)/2} + \mathrm{e}^{\lambda(u-\alpha)/2})^2} = \frac{\lambda}{\left(2\cosh\left(\frac{\lambda}{2}(u-\alpha)\right)\right)^2}.$$

This is the same as the logistic p.d.f. in Table 4.2, with $\alpha = \mu$ and $\lambda = \pi/(\sigma\sqrt{3})$. Since $\cosh(\cdot)$ is an even function,

$$f(\alpha - u) = \frac{\lambda}{\left(2\cosh\left(\frac{\lambda}{2}(-u)\right)\right)^2} = \frac{\lambda}{\left(2\cosh\left(\frac{\lambda}{2}(u)\right)\right)^2} = f(\alpha + u)$$

and x is symmetric around its mean α.
(b) The c.d.f. is

$$F(u) = \int_{-\infty}^{u} \frac{\lambda \mathrm{e}^{\lambda(t-\alpha)}}{(1 + \mathrm{e}^{\lambda(t-\alpha)})^2}\,\mathrm{d}t = \left[\frac{\mathrm{e}^{\lambda(t-\alpha)}}{1 + \mathrm{e}^{\lambda(t-\alpha)}}\right]_{-\infty}^{u} = \frac{\mathrm{e}^{\lambda(u-\alpha)}}{1 + \mathrm{e}^{\lambda(u-\alpha)}},$$

which could also be written as $1/(1+e^{-\lambda(u-\alpha)})$ or $[1+\tanh(\lambda(u-\alpha)/2)]/2$; see Section A.3.3. Note that in the case $\alpha = 0$ and $\lambda = 1$, often encountered in practice, we have $\sigma^2 = \pi^2/3 \approx 3.290 \neq 1$. The inverse of the c.d.f., the quantile function, is obtained by inverting the relation

$$\frac{1}{1+e^{-\lambda(u-\alpha)}} = p.$$

This is achieved by the steps

$$1+e^{-\lambda(u-\alpha)} = \frac{1}{p} \iff -\lambda(u-\alpha) = \log\left(\frac{1}{p}-1\right) \iff u = \alpha - \lambda^{-1}\log\left(\frac{1-p}{p}\right).$$

The function $\log(p/(1-p))$ is known as the *logit* transformation, mapping $[0,1]$ to $\mathbb{R}$.
(c) We find

$$\begin{aligned}\Pr(|x-\alpha| \leqslant 1) &= \Pr(-1 \leqslant x-\alpha \leqslant 1) = \Pr(\alpha-1 \leqslant x \leqslant 1+\alpha)\\ &= F(1+\alpha) - F(\alpha-1) = \frac{e^{\lambda}}{1+e^{\lambda}} - \frac{e^{-\lambda}}{1+e^{-\lambda}} = \frac{e^{\lambda}-1}{e^{\lambda}+1} = \tanh\left(\frac{\lambda}{2}\right).\end{aligned}$$

Exercise 4.31 (F is one-to-one with beta) Let $x \sim F(m,n)$ and define $z := (m/n)x$. Show that $y := z/(1+z) \sim \text{Beta}\left(\frac{m}{2},\frac{n}{2}\right)$.

Solution
We have

$$\Pr(z \leqslant w) = \Pr\left(x \leqslant \tfrac{n}{m}w\right) = \int_0^{\frac{n}{m}w} \frac{\left(\frac{m}{n}u\right)^{\frac{m}{2}-1}}{B\left(\frac{m}{2},\frac{n}{2}\right)\left(1+\frac{m}{n}u\right)^{\frac{m+n}{2}}}\,d\left(\tfrac{m}{n}u\right)$$

from the density of $F(m,n)$ in Table 4.2. By the change of variable

$$v = \frac{\frac{m}{n}u}{1+\frac{m}{n}u}, \quad \text{hence } \tfrac{m}{n}u = \frac{v}{1-v} \equiv \frac{1}{v^{-1}-1},$$

we get

$$\begin{aligned}\Pr(z \leqslant w) &= \int_0^{\frac{w}{1+w}} \frac{\left(\frac{v}{1-v}\right)^{\frac{m}{2}-1}}{B\left(\frac{m}{2},\frac{n}{2}\right)\left(1+\frac{v}{1-v}\right)^{\frac{m+n}{2}}}\,d\left(\frac{1}{v^{-1}-1}\right)\\ &= \int_0^{\frac{w}{1+w}} \frac{\left(\frac{v}{1-v}\right)^{\frac{m}{2}-1}}{B\left(\frac{m}{2},\frac{n}{2}\right)\left(\frac{1}{1-v}\right)^{\frac{m+n}{2}}}\,\frac{v^{-2}}{(v^{-1}-1)^2}\,dv\\ &= \int_0^{\frac{w}{1+w}} \frac{v^{\frac{m}{2}-1}(1-v)^{\frac{n}{2}-1}}{B\left(\frac{m}{2},\frac{n}{2}\right)}\,dv \equiv \Pr\left(y \leqslant \frac{w}{1+w}\right)\end{aligned}$$

where the variate y has the Beta$\left(\frac{m}{2}, \frac{n}{2}\right)$ density, and its c.d.f. is given in Exercise 4.11.

Exercise 4.32 (Noncentral F representation) Let $x \sim \chi^2(m, \delta)$ be independently distributed from $y \sim \chi^2(n)$. Derive the p.d.f. of $z := (nx)/(my)$.

Solution

The c.d.f. of z is

$$F(w) = \Pr\left(\frac{nx}{my} \leqslant w\right) = \Pr\left(x \leqslant \frac{wm}{n} y\right).$$

We can obtain this probability by the mixing argument used in Exercise 4.18 and the independence of x and y as

$$F(w) = \int_0^{\infty} \int_{-\infty}^{wmv/n} \mathrm{e}^{-\delta/2} \sum_{j=0}^{\infty} \frac{\left(\frac{\delta}{2}\right)^j}{j!} \frac{\left(\frac{u}{2}\right)^{\frac{2j+m}{2}-1} \exp\left(-\frac{u}{2}\right)}{2\Gamma\left(\frac{2j+m}{2}\right)} \mathrm{d}u \frac{\left(\frac{v}{2}\right)^{\frac{n}{2}-1} \exp\left(-\frac{v}{2}\right)}{2\Gamma\left(\frac{n}{2}\right)} \mathrm{d}v.$$

Using Leibniz' rule (see Section A.4) to differentiate with respect to w,

$$f(w) = \int_0^{\infty} \frac{mv}{n} \mathrm{e}^{-\delta/2} \sum_{j=0}^{\infty} \frac{\left(\frac{\delta}{2}\right)^j}{j!} \frac{\left(\frac{mwv}{2n}\right)^{\frac{2j+m}{2}-1} \exp\left(-\frac{mwv}{2n}\right)}{2\Gamma\left(\frac{2j+m}{2}\right)} \frac{\left(\frac{v}{2}\right)^{\frac{n}{2}-1} \exp\left(-\frac{v}{2}\right)}{2\Gamma\left(\frac{n}{2}\right)} \mathrm{d}v$$

$$= \mathrm{e}^{-\delta/2} \sum_{j=0}^{\infty} \frac{\left(\frac{\delta}{2}\right)^j}{j!} \frac{m}{n} \left(\frac{mw}{n}\right)^{\frac{2j+m}{2}-1} \int_0^{\infty} \frac{\left(\frac{v}{2}\right)^{\frac{2j+m+n}{2}-1} \exp\left(-\left(1+\frac{mw}{n}\right)\frac{v}{2}\right)}{\Gamma\left(\frac{2j+m}{2}\right)\Gamma\left(\frac{n}{2}\right)} \mathrm{d}\left(\frac{v}{2}\right).$$

By the change of variable $t = (1 + mw/n)\, v/2 \in \mathbb{R}_+$ (since $v, w \in \mathbb{R}_+$) and the integral definition of $\Gamma\left((2j + m + n)/2\right)$, we get

$$f(w) = \mathrm{e}^{-\delta/2} \sum_{j=0}^{\infty} \frac{\left(\frac{\delta}{2}\right)^j}{j!} \frac{\frac{m}{n}\left(\frac{mw}{n}\right)^{\frac{2j+m}{2}-1}}{\left(1+\frac{mw}{n}\right)^{\frac{2j+m+n}{2}}} \int_0^{\infty} \frac{t^{\frac{2j+m+n}{2}-1} \exp(-t)}{\Gamma\left(\frac{2j+m}{2}\right)\Gamma\left(\frac{n}{2}\right)} \mathrm{d}t$$

$$= \mathrm{e}^{-\delta/2} \sum_{j=0}^{\infty} \frac{\left(\frac{\delta}{2}\right)^j}{j!} \frac{\frac{m}{n}\left(\frac{mw}{n}\right)^{\frac{2j+m}{2}-1}}{B\left(\frac{2j+m}{2}, \frac{n}{2}\right)\left(1+\frac{mw}{n}\right)^{\frac{2j+m+n}{2}}},$$

which is the p.d.f. of a noncentral F(m, n, δ) variate. Notice that this representation and that in Exercise 4.31 together imply Exercise 4.18, the uniform being the special case Beta$(1, 1)$. Notice also that the special case $\delta = 0$ gives rise here to $z^{-1} \sim$ F(n, m) by the same derivations.

Exercise 4.33 (Noncentral t^2 and F) Let $x \sim$ t(n, δ) and $y := x^2$. Show that $y \sim$ F$(1, n, \delta^2)$.

Solution

The c.d.f. of y is $F(v) = \Pr(y \leqslant v) = \Pr(x^2 \leqslant v) = \Pr(-\sqrt{v} \leqslant x \leqslant \sqrt{v})$. Therefore, we have

$$F(v) = \int_{-\sqrt{v}}^{\sqrt{v}} \frac{\mathrm{e}^{-\delta^2/2}}{\sqrt{\pi n}\left(1+\frac{u^2}{n}\right)^{\frac{n+1}{2}}} \sum_{j=0}^{\infty} \frac{\Gamma\left(\frac{j+n+1}{2}\right)}{\Gamma\left(\frac{n}{2}\right) j!} \left(\frac{\delta u\sqrt{2/n}}{\sqrt{1+\frac{u^2}{n}}}\right)^j \mathrm{d}u$$

$$= \frac{\mathrm{e}^{-\delta^2/2}}{\sqrt{\pi n}} \sum_{j=0}^{\infty} \frac{\Gamma\left(\frac{j+n+1}{2}\right)\left(\delta\sqrt{\frac{2}{n}}\right)^j}{\Gamma\left(\frac{n}{2}\right) j!} \int_{-\sqrt{v}}^{\sqrt{v}} \frac{u^j}{\left(1+\frac{u^2}{n}\right)^{\frac{j+n+1}{2}}} \mathrm{d}u.$$

Using Leibniz' rule (see Section A.4) to differentiate with respect to v yields

$$f(v) = \frac{\mathrm{e}^{-\delta^2/2}}{\sqrt{\pi n}} \sum_{j=0}^{\infty} \frac{\Gamma\left(\frac{j+n+1}{2}\right)\left(\delta\sqrt{\frac{2}{n}}\right)^j}{\Gamma\left(\frac{n}{2}\right) j!} \frac{(\sqrt{v})^j + (-\sqrt{v})^j}{2\sqrt{v}\left(1+\frac{v}{n}\right)^{\frac{j+n+1}{2}}}$$

$$= \frac{\mathrm{e}^{-\delta^2/2}}{\sqrt{\pi n v}} \sum_{k=0}^{\infty} \frac{\Gamma\left(\frac{2k+n+1}{2}\right)\left(\frac{2}{n}\delta^2 v\right)^k}{\Gamma\left(\frac{n}{2}\right)(2k)!\left(1+\frac{v}{n}\right)^{\frac{2k+n+1}{2}}},$$

since the terms where j is odd drop out. Recall Exercise 4.24, which showed that $(2k)! = 2^{2k}k!\Gamma\left(k+\frac{1}{2}\right)/\sqrt{\pi}$, so that rearranging the terms in the p.d.f. gives

$$f(v) = \mathrm{e}^{-\delta^2/2} \sum_{k=0}^{\infty} \frac{\left(\frac{\delta^2}{2}\right)^k}{k!} \frac{\frac{1}{n}\left(\frac{1}{n}v\right)^{\frac{2k+1}{2}-1}}{B\left(\frac{n}{2},\frac{2k+1}{2}\right)\left(1+\frac{1}{n}v\right)^{\frac{2k+n+1}{2}}},$$

which is the p.d.f. of an $\mathrm{F}(1, n, \delta^2)$ variate. Notice that the densities of the noncentral t and a location-shifted t are very different. Exercise 4.32 and the present exercise indicate how the former arises (by a shifted numerator of t) and that it is not symmetric in general; for the latter, see Exercise 2.26 (the whole ratio is shifted).

Exercise 4.34 (F and t moments) Calculate the moments $\mathrm{E}\left(z^j\right)$ for $z \sim \mathrm{F}(m,n)$, stating the conditions for their existence. What do these conditions imply for the existence of moments for Student's t?

Solution

Let $y \sim \chi^2(n)$ where $n \in \mathbb{R}_+$. Then,

$$\mathrm{E}\left(y^j\right) = \int_0^{\infty} v^j \frac{v^{n/2-1}\mathrm{e}^{-v/2}}{2^{n/2}\Gamma(n/2)} \mathrm{d}v$$

$$= \frac{1}{2^{n/2}\Gamma(n/2)} \int_0^{\infty} v^{(2j+n)/2-1}\mathrm{e}^{-v/2}\,\mathrm{d}v$$

$$= \frac{1}{2^{n/2}\Gamma(n/2)} 2^{(2j+n)/2}\Gamma\left(\frac{2j+n}{2}\right) = \frac{2^j\Gamma(n/2+j)}{\Gamma(n/2)},$$

provided that $2j+n > 0$. Now, let $x \sim \chi^2(m)$ where $m \in \mathbb{R}_+$, and assume that x and y are independent. Then the random variable $z := (n/m)(x/y)$ follows an $\mathrm{F}(m,n)$ distribution by Exercise 4.32 and, using the independence of x and y, we have

$$\begin{aligned}\mathrm{E}\left(z^j\right) &= (n/m)^j\,\mathrm{E}\left(x^j\right)\mathrm{E}\left(y^{-j}\right)\\ &= \left(\frac{n}{m}\right)^j \frac{2^j\Gamma(m/2+j)}{\Gamma(m/2)} \times \frac{2^{-j}\Gamma(n/2-j)}{\Gamma(n/2)} = \frac{\Gamma(m/2+j)}{m^j\Gamma(m/2)} \times \frac{n^j\Gamma(n/2-j)}{\Gamma(n/2)},\end{aligned}$$

provided that $-m/2 < j < n/2$. Exercise 4.33 implies the equivalence of $z \sim \mathrm{F}(1,n)$ and $(\mathrm{t}(n))^2$, so the k-th moment of t exists if and only if $\mathrm{E}\left(z^{k/2}\right)$ exists, namely when $-1 < k < n$. This can also be obtained directly from $\int_{-\infty}^{\infty} |w|^k \left(1+w^2/n\right)^{-(n+1)/2} \mathrm{d}w < \infty$ if and only if $k > -1$ and $k - n - 1 < -1$.

Exercise 4.35 (Cauchy representation) Suppose that $x \sim \mathrm{N}(0,1)$ and is independent of $y \sim \mathrm{N}(0,1)$.
(a) Derive the density and distribution functions of $z := x/y$.
(b) What is the density function of z^{-1}?

Solution
(a) The c.d.f. of z is

$$\begin{aligned}F(w) &= \Pr\left(\frac{x}{y} \leqslant w\right) = \Pr\left(\frac{x}{y} \leqslant w, y > 0\right) + \Pr\left(\frac{x}{y} \leqslant w, y < 0\right)\\ &= \Pr\left(x \leqslant wy, y > 0\right) + \Pr\left(x \geqslant wy, y < 0\right)\end{aligned}$$

since $\Pr(y = 0) = 0$ by continuity. We can obtain these probabilities by the mixing argument used in Exercise 4.18 and the independence of x and y (with p.d.f.s $\phi(u)$ and $\phi(v)$ respectively) as

$$F(w) = \int_0^{\infty}\int_{-\infty}^{wv} \phi(u)\,\mathrm{d}u\,\phi(v)\,\mathrm{d}v + \int_{-\infty}^{0}\int_{wv}^{\infty} \phi(u)\,\mathrm{d}u\,\phi(v)\,\mathrm{d}v.$$

Using Leibniz' rule (see Section A.4) to differentiate with respect to w yields

$$f(w) = \int_0^{\infty} \phi(v)\phi(wv)v\,\mathrm{d}v - \int_{-\infty}^{0} \phi(v)\phi(wv)v\,\mathrm{d}v = 2\int_0^{\infty} \phi(v)\phi(wv)v\,\mathrm{d}v,$$

since ϕ is an even function. Substituting for ϕ and making the change of variable $t = v^2/2$ (with $\mathrm{d}t = v\,\mathrm{d}v$),

$$f(w) = \frac{1}{\pi}\int_0^{\infty} \mathrm{e}^{-v^2(1+w^2)/2} v\,\mathrm{d}v = \frac{1}{\pi}\int_0^{\infty} \mathrm{e}^{-t(1+w^2)}\,\mathrm{d}t = \frac{1}{\pi}\frac{1}{1+w^2},$$

which is the p.d.f. of a Cauchy variate. The corresponding c.d.f. is obtained by noting that the density is symmetric around 0, and

$$F(w) = \int_{-\infty}^{w} \frac{1}{\pi}\frac{1}{1+t^2}\,\mathrm{d}t = \frac{1}{2} + \frac{1}{\pi}\int_0^{w} \frac{1}{1+t^2}\,\mathrm{d}t = \frac{1}{2} + \frac{1}{\pi}\tan^{-1}(w);$$

see also Exercise 4.11(c). As an alternative expression for F, we have

$$F(w) = 1 - \frac{1}{\pi}\int_{w}^{\infty} \frac{1}{1+t^2}\,\mathrm{d}t = 1 - \frac{\cot^{-1}(w)}{\pi} = \frac{\cot^{-1}(-w)}{\pi}.$$

(b) The density function of $z^{-1} = y/x$ could be obtained by the same method, and it is clearly also Cauchy since the new numerator (y) and denominator (x) are still independent $\mathrm{N}(0,1)$ variates. Notice, however, that the two variates z and z^{-1} are certainly not identical, even though they possess the same density function. They even have the same standard Cauchy densities as $-z$ and $-z^{-1}$, respectively, since $-x \sim \mathrm{N}(0,1)$ independently of y.

Exercise 4.36 (Normal limit of Student's t) Let $x \sim \mathrm{t}(n)$. Using

$$\lim_{\nu\to\infty} \frac{\Gamma(\nu+a)}{\nu^{a-b}\Gamma(\nu+b)} = 1$$

from Section A.3.4, show that $\Pr(x \leqslant u) \to \Phi(u)$ as $n \to \infty$.

Solution

From the density of Student's t, we have the c.d.f.

$$\Pr(x \leqslant u) = \int_{-\infty}^{u} \frac{\Gamma\left(\frac{n+1}{2}\right)}{\sqrt{\pi n}\,\Gamma\left(\frac{n}{2}\right)\left(1+\frac{t^2}{n}\right)^{\frac{n+1}{2}}}\,\mathrm{d}t,$$

where we will assume $n > 1$ henceforth. Since the lower tail of the Cauchy (the case of $n = 1$) dominates $\mathrm{t}(n)$ for some $t < t_0$ (t_0 finite), there exists a function integrable over $\int_{-\infty}^{t_0} + \int_{t_0}^{u}$ and dominating the $\mathrm{t}(n)$ density. The dominated convergence theorem (see Section A.4.3) implies that we can therefore interchange the limit and integral signs:

$$\begin{aligned}
\lim_{n\to\infty} \Pr(x \leqslant u) &= \frac{1}{\sqrt{2\pi}}\int_{-\infty}^{u} \lim_{n\to\infty} \frac{\Gamma\left(\frac{n+1}{2}\right)}{\left(\frac{n}{2}\right)^{1/2}\Gamma\left(\frac{n}{2}\right)} \lim_{n\to\infty}\left(1+\frac{t^2}{n}\right)^{-\frac{n+1}{2}} \mathrm{d}t \\
&= \frac{1}{\sqrt{2\pi}}\int_{-\infty}^{u} \lim_{n\to\infty} \exp\left(-\frac{n+1}{2}\times\frac{t^2}{n}\right)\mathrm{d}t \\
&= \frac{1}{\sqrt{2\pi}}\int_{-\infty}^{u} \exp\left(-\frac{t^2}{2}\right)\mathrm{d}t = \Phi(u).
\end{aligned}$$

4.3 Classifications: exponential family, information, stability

Exercise 4.37 (A big family, exponentially!) Consider the definition of the exponential family of densities in (4.4).

(a) Which of the densities in Tables 4.1 and 4.2 belong to the exponential family?

(b) Is your answer altered if some of the parameters are known fixed constants (such as $m = 2$)?
(c) What if these fixed constants are the support?

Solution
(a) Consider the tables without imposing restrictions on the parameters (such as the standardizations $\mu = 0$ or $\lambda = 1$). By applying the definition of an exponential-family p.d.f., the following are excluded because some parameter cannot be factored out from the functions of w: uniform discrete, binomial, negative binomial, hypergeometric, beta, uniform continuous, Gumbel, generalized gamma, Weibull, noncentral χ^2, Laplace, logistic, F, noncentral F, t, noncentral t, Cauchy, Pareto. Note that densities defined over a parameter-dependent interval have an indicator function that combines w and the parameters in a nonseparable way, like the continuous uniform's $1_{w\in(\alpha,\beta)}(\beta-\alpha)^{-1}$.
(b) First, m/n times an $\mathrm{F}(m,n)$ variate, and $n^{-1/2}$ times a $\mathrm{t}(n)$ variate, are members of the family. Furthermore, if we take some parameters to have a known constant value, as is the case in sampling situations, then the family is larger and we can allow back: binomial (known n), negative binomial (known ν), F (known m, n), t (known n). If we know p in the generalized gamma or in the Weibull, then they are welcome to join the family. The case of knowing λ in the Gumbel density or μ in the Laplace density would also be allowed, but these scaling and centering parameters are not usually known in practice.
(c) Let us start with the simplest case. Apart from the indicator function mentioned in (a), the rest of the density factors as per the exponential-class definition for the two uniform distributions and the Pareto. For this reason, they are sometimes called *nonregular* exponential: they violate only the regularity condition that the support should not depend on the parameters. Fixing the support to a known constant makes them regular, and similarly for the beta. The standard beta defined on (0,1) is a regular exponential, but its general form with support (α, β) is not exponential, regular or otherwise: one cannot factor $(w-\alpha)^{p-1}$ into the product of separate functions of w and α, for general p, and similarly for $(\beta - w)^{q-1}$. Note that it is straightforward to show that the standard Pareto $\mathrm{Par}_{(1,\infty)}(p)$ variate is obtained by taking $\exp(z)$ where $z \sim \mathrm{Expo}(p)$, hence the link with the exponential family.

Exercise 4.38 (Shannon's entropy) Assuming the expectations are finite, derive Shannon's entropy by letting $p \to 0$ in:
(a) the Tsallis entropy $p^{-1}\left(1 - \mathrm{E}\left[(f(z))^p\right]\right)$;
(b) the Rényi entropy $-p^{-1}\log\left(\mathrm{E}\left[(f(z))^p\right]\right)$.

Solution
(a) The definition of a c.d.f. gives $\int_{-\infty}^{\infty} \mathrm{d}F(w) = 1$, which we use to replace the constant 1

in this entropy's definition. Letting $p \to 0$,

$$\lim_{p\to 0}\frac{1}{p}\left(\int_{-\infty}^{\infty} \mathrm{d}F(w) - \int_{-\infty}^{\infty} (f(w))^p \,\mathrm{d}F(w)\right) = \int_{-\infty}^{\infty} \lim_{p\to 0}\frac{1-(f(w))^p}{p}\,\mathrm{d}F(w).$$

Interchange of the integral and limit operators is allowed by the dominated convergence theorem, since the integrand satisfies $|1-(f(w))^p| < 1$ for p sufficiently small and

$$\int_{-\infty}^{\infty} 1\,\mathrm{d}F(w) = \mathrm{E}(1) = 1$$

is finite. Using the exponential expansion as follows,

$$\begin{aligned}\lim_{p\to 0}\frac{1-(f(w))^p}{p} &= \lim_{p\to 0}\frac{1-\mathrm{e}^{p\log(f(w))}}{p} = -\lim_{p\to 0}\sum_{j=1}^{\infty}\frac{p^{j-1}(\log(f(w)))^j}{j!}\\ &= -\log(f(w)),\end{aligned}$$

we obtain Shannon's entropy as the limit of the Tsallis entropy. The same limit could have been obtained by l'Hôpital's rule (See Section A.3.4) instead of the exponential expansion.
(b) Similarly,

$$\frac{-\log(\mathrm{E}[(f(z))^p])}{p} = \frac{-\log\left(\mathrm{E}\left(\mathrm{e}^{p\log(f(z))}\right)\right)}{p}.$$

Using l'Hôpital's rule,

$$\begin{aligned}\lim_{p\to 0}\frac{-\log\left(\mathrm{E}\left(\mathrm{e}^{p\log(f(z))}\right)\right)}{p} &= \left.\frac{-\mathrm{dE}\left(\mathrm{e}^{p\log(f(z))}\right)/\mathrm{d}p}{\mathrm{E}[(f(z))^p]}\right|_{p=0}\\ &= \left.\frac{-\mathrm{E}\left[\log(f(z))\,\mathrm{e}^{p\log(f(z))}\right]}{\mathrm{E}[(f(z))^p]}\right|_{p=0} = -\mathrm{E}[\log(f(z))].\end{aligned}$$

Exercise 4.39 (Entropy, location, and scale) Derive the Shannon entropy of $x \sim \mathrm{N}(\mu, \sigma^2)$, showing how it is affected by the variance σ^2. Is this a general feature of entropies?

Solution
The $\mathrm{N}(\mu, \sigma^2)$ distribution has entropy

$$\begin{aligned}-\mathrm{E}\left(\log\left(\frac{\mathrm{e}^{-(x-\mu)^2/(2\sigma^2)}}{\sigma\sqrt{2\pi}}\right)\right) &= \mathrm{E}\left(\frac{(x-\mu)^2}{2\sigma^2}\right) + \mathrm{E}\left(\log\left(\sigma\sqrt{2\pi}\right)\right)\\ &= \frac{\mathrm{var}(x)}{2\sigma^2} + \log\left(\sigma\sqrt{2\pi}\right) = \frac{1}{2} + \log\left(\sigma\sqrt{2\pi}\right),\end{aligned}$$

which is not affected by the location of x (since μ does not appear in the result) but increases with $\mathrm{var}(x)$. This dependence on the variance is not necessarily a general feature of entropies. For example, a variate x with $\Pr(x = \pm 1) = \frac{1}{2}$ has the same entropy as another one y with $\Pr(y = \pm 2) = \frac{1}{2}$, even though $\mathrm{var}(y) = 4\,\mathrm{var}(x)$. Entropy quantifies the relative uncertainty of outcomes, rather than the spread of the distribution per se. In fact, the counterexample we have just given applies to all discrete variates, because their entropies

$$E_x := -\sum_{u \in \mathcal{X}} \Pr(x = u) \log(\Pr(x = u))$$

are unaffected by changes of location and scale for x: if $y := \alpha + \lambda x$, then

$$E_y := -\sum_{u \in \mathcal{X}} \Pr(y = \alpha + \lambda u) \log(\Pr(y = \alpha + \lambda u)) = E_x.$$

We will encounter more on this topic in Exercises 7.33 and 8.12.

Exercise 4.40 (Most disorderly uniform) Derive the maximum-entropy density function for any variate $x \in \{0, 1, \dots, n\}$.

Solution

For a discrete variate, defining $q_j := \Pr(x = j)$ and the vector $\boldsymbol{q} := (q_1, \dots, q_n)'$, we can write the entropy as

$$S(\boldsymbol{q}) := -\sum_{j=0}^{n} q_j \log(q_j) = -\left(1 - \sum_{j=1}^{n} q_j\right) \log\left(1 - \sum_{j=1}^{n} q_j\right) - \sum_{j=1}^{n} q_j \log(q_j)$$

since the sum of probabilities is $\sum_{j=0}^{n} q_j = 1$. Differentiating partially with respect to each q_k, for $k = 1, \dots, n$, gives

$$\begin{aligned}\frac{\partial S(\boldsymbol{q})}{\partial q_k} &= \log\left(1 - \sum_{j=1}^{n} q_j\right) + \frac{1 - \sum_{j=1}^{n} q_j}{1 - \sum_{j=1}^{n} q_j} - \log(q_k) - \frac{q_k}{q_k} \\ &= \log\left(1 - \sum_{j=1}^{n} q_j\right) - \log(q_k) = \log(q_0) - \log(q_k).\end{aligned}$$

Solving $\partial S(\boldsymbol{q})/\partial q_k = 0$ gives $q_0 = q_k$ as the optimum solution, namely the uniform distribution with $q_k = 1/(n+1)$. Checking the second-order condition requires the calculation of

$$\frac{\partial^2 S(\boldsymbol{q})}{\partial q_k \partial q_m} = -\frac{1}{1 - \sum_{j=1}^{n} q_j} - \frac{\partial \log(q_k)}{\partial q_m} = \begin{cases} -q_0^{-1} - q_k^{-1} & (k = m), \\ -q_0^{-1} & (k \neq m). \end{cases}$$

At the optimum, all probabilities are equal and we get

$$\left.\frac{\partial^2 S(\boldsymbol{q})}{\partial \boldsymbol{q} \partial \boldsymbol{q}'}\right|_{q_\bullet = 1/(n+1)} = -(n+1) \begin{pmatrix} 2 & 1 & \dots & 1 \\ 1 & 2 & \dots & 1 \\ \vdots & \vdots & & \vdots \\ 1 & 1 & \dots & 2 \end{pmatrix} = -(n+1)\left(\boldsymbol{I}_n + \boldsymbol{\imath}\boldsymbol{\imath}'\right),$$

where $\boldsymbol{I}_n$ is the identity matrix of order n and $\boldsymbol{\imath}$ is a vector of ones. The matrix is negative definite because, for any $\boldsymbol{b} \neq \mathbf{0}_n$, we have

$$-(n+1)\,\boldsymbol{b}'\left(\boldsymbol{I}_n + \boldsymbol{\imath}\boldsymbol{\imath}'\right)\boldsymbol{b} = -(n+1)\left(\boldsymbol{b}'\boldsymbol{b} + \left(\boldsymbol{b}'\boldsymbol{\imath}\right)^2\right) < 0.$$

The solution is therefore a maximum. Intuitively, the maximum-entropy (or least informative) distribution is the distribution where anything can happen with equal probability. This result extends to the case of a continuous uniform distribution, by the method in Exercise 4.41.

***Exercise 4.41 (Most disorderly: mean and variance)** Let x be a continuous variate. Derive the maximum-entropy density:
(a) when $x \in \mathbb{R}_+$ and x has a preassigned (chosen constant) mean μ;
(b) when $x \in \mathbb{R}$ and x has preassigned mean μ and variance σ^2.

Solution
(a) For a continuous variate on $\mathbb{R}_+$, we can define the entropy as $-\int_0^\infty f(u)\log(f(u))\,\mathrm{d}u$. We wish to maximize the entropy subject to the two conditions that $\int_0^\infty f(u)\,\mathrm{d}u = 1$ and $\int_0^\infty uf(u)\,\mathrm{d}u = \mu$. Thus, we define the Lagrangian (see Section A.4.5)

$$\begin{aligned} S(f) := & -\int_0^\infty f(u)\log(f(u))\,\mathrm{d}u \\ & + \lambda_0\left(1 - \int_0^\infty f(u)\,\mathrm{d}u\right) + \lambda_1\left(\mu - \int_0^\infty uf(u)\,\mathrm{d}u\right). \end{aligned}$$

One has to be careful here: as in Exercise 4.40, we differentiate with respect to the p.d.f. *at every point* u. Differentiating with respect to f at a given u (denoted by the shorthand $\partial S(f)/\partial f$), we obtain

$$\frac{\partial S(f)}{\partial f} = -\left(\log(f(u)) + 1 + \lambda_0 + \lambda_1 u\right),$$

and setting this to zero yields the solution $f(u) = \mathrm{e}^{-1-\lambda_0-\lambda_1 u}$. This solution could be perturbed at a countable set of points without affecting the optimality, but this would give us a discontinuous p.d.f., which we have ruled out by convention in the introduction to Chapter 2. From $u \in \mathbb{R}_+$, we recognize this as the density of Expo(λ_1) with $\mathrm{e}^{-1-\lambda_0} = \lambda_1$. Alternatively, the constraints give

$$1 = \int_0^\infty \mathrm{e}^{-1-\lambda_0-\lambda_1 u}\,\mathrm{d}u = \mathrm{e}^{-1-\lambda_0}\left[\frac{\mathrm{e}^{-\lambda_1 u}}{-\lambda_1}\right]_0^\infty = \frac{\mathrm{e}^{-1-\lambda_0}}{\lambda_1},$$

where we note that $\lambda_1 > 0$ (otherwise $f(u) \to \infty$ as $u \to \infty$), and

$$\mu = \int_0^\infty u\mathrm{e}^{-1-\lambda_0-\lambda_1 u}\,\mathrm{d}u = \mathrm{e}^{-1-\lambda_0}\left[\frac{u\mathrm{e}^{-\lambda_1 u}}{-\lambda_1}\right]_0^\infty - \mathrm{e}^{-1-\lambda_0}\left[\frac{\mathrm{e}^{-\lambda_1 u}}{\lambda_1^2}\right]_0^\infty = \frac{\mathrm{e}^{-1-\lambda_0}}{\lambda_1^2}$$

using integration by parts. The two constraints therefore imply that the Lagrange multipliers are $\lambda_1 = \mu^{-1} = \mathrm{e}^{-1-\lambda_0}$, and we have $f(u) = \lambda_1\mathrm{e}^{-\lambda_1 u}$ as required.

The two alternative derivations show that, once we restrict our attention to solutions f

that are density functions (with some mean denoted by μ), we need not solve the constraints directly to obtain f. Therefore, $\partial^2 S(f)/\partial f^2 = -f(u)^{-1} < 0$ is sufficient to show that entropy is maximized when f is taken to be a density.
(b) Let $\nu := \sigma^2 + \mu^2$. Proceeding as before,

$$S(f) := -\int_{-\infty}^{\infty} f(u)\log(f(u))\,\mathrm{d}u + \lambda_0\left(1 - \int_{-\infty}^{\infty} f(u)\,\mathrm{d}u\right)$$
$$+ \lambda_1\left(\mu - \int_{-\infty}^{\infty} uf(u)\,\mathrm{d}u\right) + \lambda_2\left(\nu - \int_{-\infty}^{\infty} u^2 f(u)\,\mathrm{d}u\right).$$

Differentiating with respect to f gives

$$\frac{\partial S(f)}{\partial f} = -\left(\log(f(u)) + 1 + \lambda_0 + \lambda_1 u + \lambda_2 u^2\right),$$

and the optimum is achieved at

$$f(u) = \mathrm{e}^{-1-\lambda_0-\lambda_1 u-\lambda_2 u^2} = \exp\left(-1 - \lambda_0 + \frac{\lambda_1^2}{4\lambda_2}\right)\exp\left(-\lambda_2\left(u + \frac{\lambda_1}{2\lambda_2}\right)^2\right),$$

where we recognize the normal distribution with variance $1/(2\lambda_2)$ and mean $-\lambda_1/(2\lambda_2)$. Once we restrict attention to solutions f that are density functions, the second-order condition is as in (a).

***Exercise 4.42 (Jeffreys' divergence)** There are two conditions for a function to be a *semimetric*:
(i) it should be symmetric in its arguments (for example the distance between a and b equals the distance between b and a);
(ii) it should be nonnegative, being zero if and only if its arguments are equal (for example the distance between a and b is zero if and only if $b = a$) with probability 1.
Consider $\mathrm{KL}(f_x, f_z) := \int_{-\infty}^{\infty} \log(f_x(u)/f_z(u))\,\mathrm{d}F_x(u)$.
(a) Symmetrize $\mathrm{KL}(f_x, f_z)$. [Hint: Consider $\mathrm{KL}(f_z, f_x)$ too.]
(b) Show that both $\mathrm{KL}(f_x, f_z)$ and the symmetrized function are nonnegative, and determine when they are zero. [Hint: Write the KLIC as an expectation, then use Jensen's inequality.]

Solution
(a) We know that $\mathrm{KL}(f_x, f_z) := \int_{-\infty}^{\infty} \log(f_x(u)/f_z(u))\,\mathrm{d}F_x(u) \neq \mathrm{KL}(f_z, f_x)$ in general. However,

$$\delta(f_x, f_z) := \mathrm{KL}(f_x, f_z) + \mathrm{KL}(f_z, f_x) = \mathrm{KL}(f_z, f_x) + \mathrm{KL}(f_x, f_z) = \delta(f_z, f_x),$$

which is the required function that symmetrizes KLIC. This function is known as *Jeffreys' divergence*. More explicitly,

$$\mathrm{KL}(f_z, f_x) = \int_{-\infty}^{\infty} \log\left(\frac{f_z(u)}{f_x(u)}\right)\mathrm{d}F_z(u) = -\int_{-\infty}^{\infty} \log\left(\frac{f_x(u)}{f_z(u)}\right)\mathrm{d}F_z(u)$$

and

$$\delta(f_x, f_z) = \int_{-\infty}^{\infty} \log\left(\frac{f_x(u)}{f_z(u)}\right) \mathrm{d}(F_x(u) - F_z(u))$$
$$= \int_{-\infty}^{\infty} \log\left(\frac{f_z(u)}{f_x(u)}\right) \mathrm{d}(F_z(u) - F_x(u)) = \delta(f_z, f_x).$$

(b) One can write the KLIC as a difference of two entropies,

$$\mathrm{KL}(f_x, f_z) = -\int_{-\infty}^{\infty} \log(f_z(u))\,\mathrm{d}F_x(u) - \left(-\int_{-\infty}^{\infty} \log(f_x(u))\,\mathrm{d}F_x(u)\right),$$

where the former integral is called a *cross-entropy* and is larger than the latter (the "disorder" of a distribution with respect to itself is less than its "disorder" with respect to another distribution). To prove this, we start by applying Jensen's inequality:

$$\mathrm{KL}(f_x, f_z) = \mathrm{E}_x\left(-\log\left(\frac{f_z(x)}{f_x(x)}\right)\right) \geqslant -\log\left(\mathrm{E}_x\left(\frac{f_z(x)}{f_x(x)}\right)\right)$$

because $-\log(\cdot)$ is a strictly convex function, which also implies (see the proof of Exercise 3.14(a)) that the inequality will simplify to an equality if and only if $f_x(x)/f_z(x)$ is degenerate. Since densities have to integrate or add up to 1, this degenerate proportionality of the densities is equivalent to saying that $f_x(x) = f_z(x)$ with probability 1 (as x varies). Now, the inequality can be simplified by noting that

$$\log\left(\mathrm{E}_x\left(\frac{f_z(x)}{f_x(x)}\right)\right) = \log\left(\sum_{u\in\mathcal{X}}\left(\frac{f_z(u)}{f_x(u)}\right) f_x(u)\right) = \log\left(\sum_{u\in\mathcal{X}} f_z(u)\right) = \log 1 = 0$$

in the discrete case, and

$$\log\left(\mathrm{E}_x\left(\frac{f_z(x)}{f_x(x)}\right)\right) = \log\left(\int_{-\infty}^{\infty} f_z(u)\,\mathrm{d}u\right) = \log 1 = 0$$

in the continuous case. This implies that KLIC $\geqslant 0$, with equality holding if and only if $f_x(x) = f_z(x)$ with probability 1. By definition, the same inequality applies to $\delta(f_x, f_z)$.

Exercise 4.43 (Hellinger distance) Define the *Hellinger distance* between f_z and f_x as

$$\mathrm{H}(f_z, f_x) := \left(\int_{-\infty}^{\infty} \left(\sqrt{f_z(w)} - \sqrt{f_x(w)}\right)^2 \mathrm{d}w\right)^{1/2},$$

where it is assumed that z and x are continuous variates.

(a) Show that $\mathrm{H}(f_z, f_x)^2 = 2 - 2\int_{-\infty}^{\infty} \sqrt{f_z(w) f_x(w)}\,\mathrm{d}w$.

(b) Assume that f_z and f_x are defined on the same support $\mathcal{Z}$, and that

$$\left|\frac{f_z(w) - f_x(w)}{f_z(w)}\right| < \epsilon$$

(where $\epsilon > 0$ is a small constant) for all $w \in \mathcal{Z}$ except for a countable subset where $|f_z(w) - f_x(w)| < \infty$. Show that $\mathrm{KL}(f_z, f_x) = 2\mathrm{H}(f_z, f_x)^2 + O(\epsilon^3)$. (A function $g(\epsilon)$

having a bounded $\lim_{\epsilon\to c} g(\epsilon)/\epsilon^{\alpha}$ is said to be of *order of magnitude at most* ϵ^{α}, as $\epsilon \to c$; this is written as $g(\epsilon) = O(\epsilon^{\alpha})$. See Section A.3.4 for more details.)

Solution

(a) Expanding the quadratic and using the fact that these densities integrate to 1,

$$\begin{aligned} \mathrm{H}(f_z, f_x)^2 &= \int_{-\infty}^{\infty} \left(f_z(w) + f_x(w) - 2\sqrt{f_z(w) f_x(w)} \right) \mathrm{d}w \\ &= 2 - 2\int_{-\infty}^{\infty} \sqrt{f_z(w) f_x(w)}\, \mathrm{d}w. \end{aligned}$$

Notice that the function H is symmetric in its arguments, unlike the KLIC.

(b) By the definition of the KLIC for continuous variates,

$$\mathrm{KL}(f_z, f_x) = \int_{\mathcal{Z}} \log\left(\frac{f_z(w)}{f_x(w)}\right) f_z(w)\, \mathrm{d}w = -2\int_{\mathcal{Z}} \log\left(\frac{\sqrt{f_x(w)}}{\sqrt{f_z(w)}}\right) f_z(w)\, \mathrm{d}w.$$

The binomial expansion shows that

$$\sqrt{\frac{f_x(w)}{f_z(w)}} = \left(1 + \frac{f_x(w) - f_z(w)}{f_z(w)}\right)^{1/2} = 1 + O\left(\frac{f_x(w) - f_z(w)}{f_z(w)}\right) = 1 + O(\epsilon);$$

thus the argument of the logarithm is in the neighborhood of 1. By $\log(1+a) = a - a^2/2 + O(a^3)$ for small a (see Section A.3.2), we have

$$\begin{aligned} \mathrm{KL}(f_z, f_x) &= -2\int_{\mathcal{Z}} \left(\frac{\sqrt{f_x(w)}}{\sqrt{f_z(w)}} - 1\right) f_z(w)\, \mathrm{d}w + \int_{\mathcal{Z}} \left(\frac{\sqrt{f_x(w)}}{\sqrt{f_z(w)}} - 1\right)^2 f_z(w)\, \mathrm{d}w \\ &\quad + \int_{\mathcal{Z}} O(\epsilon^3) f_z(w)\, \mathrm{d}w \\ &= -2\int_{\mathcal{Z}} \left(\sqrt{f_x(w) f_z(w)} - f_z(w)\right) \mathrm{d}w \\ &\quad + \int_{\mathcal{Z}} \left(f_x(w) - 2\sqrt{f_x(w) f_z(w)} + f_z(w)\right) \mathrm{d}w + \int_{\mathcal{Z}} O(\epsilon^3) f_z(w)\, \mathrm{d}w. \end{aligned}$$

Using (a) for the first integral, the definition of $\mathrm{H}(f_z, f_x)$ for the second, and the dominated convergence theorem for the third,

$$\mathrm{KL}(f_z, f_x) = \left[\left(\mathrm{H}(f_z, f_x)^2 - 2\right) + 2\right] + \mathrm{H}(f_z, f_x)^2 + O(\epsilon^3) = 2\mathrm{H}(f_z, f_x)^2 + O(\epsilon^3).$$

Notice that the Hellinger distance is well defined even if the supports of z and x differ, a case where the KLIC can become infinite (it deems the two densities to be infinitely different if the difference in supports has a positive probability).

***Exercise 4.44 (Unstable gamma)** Let $z \sim \mathrm{Gam}(\nu, \lambda)$.

(a) Prove that z is infinitely divisible.

(b) Show that z is not stable.

Solution

(a) Not only is gamma infinitely divisible, but also its c.f. decomposes into the product of gamma c.f.s with the same scaling parameter:

$$\varphi_z(\tau) = (1 - \mathrm{i}\lambda^{-1}\tau)^{-\nu} = \prod_{i=1}^{n}(1 - \mathrm{i}\lambda^{-1}\tau)^{-\nu/n},$$

the product of n Gam$(\nu/n, \lambda)$ c.f.s. This is, nevertheless, not sufficient to achieve distributional stability, as we will now see.

(b) Rewrite the definition of a stable variate z as

$$\mathrm{e}^{-\mathrm{i}\alpha_n\tau}\varphi_z(\tau) = \left(\varphi_z\left(n^{-1/p}\tau\right)\right)^n$$

or

$$\mathrm{e}^{-\mathrm{i}\alpha_n\tau/n}(1 - \mathrm{i}\lambda^{-1}\tau)^{-\nu/n} = \mathrm{E}\left(\mathrm{e}^{\mathrm{i}\tau\left(n^{-1/p}z\right)}\right).$$

This equality implies the following. Apart from an arbitrary location shift, which should actually be set to 0 here so that the variates remain defined over $\mathbb{R}_+$, there should exist a $p \in (0, 2]$ such that $n^{-1/p}z \sim$ Gam$(\nu/n, \lambda)$. This equality cannot be satisfied because it can be verified, by either the gamma c.f. or the c.d.f. in Exercise 4.20, that $n^{-1/p}z \sim$ Gam$(\nu, n^{1/p}\lambda)$: this cannot be turned into a Gam$(\nu/n, \lambda)$ for any $p \in (0, 2]$ and general n. The former distribution is about rescaling Gam(ν, λ) into $n^{1/p}\lambda$, whereas the latter is about reshaping it into ν/n. We give a simple illustration of the latter impossibility, which will be encountered in more detail in Exercise 7.3: the sum of two independent $\chi^2(1)$ variates will be seen to be a $\chi^2(2)$, but Figure 4.4 shows that no amount of rescaling or recentering of the latter's p.d.f. can make it look like a $\chi^2(1)$ density which is infinite at the origin. Note that, for discrete variates, we would have an additional concern about keeping the same support for the scaled sum as for the original variates (for example, integers).

Notes

An outstanding encyclopedic reference for special univariate distributions can be found in the volumes by Johnson, Kotz, and Kemp (1993), and Johnson, Kotz, and Balakrishnan (1994, 1995). We have not listed all the special cases that can be found in the literature, such as the *arc-sine distribution* defined as Beta$\left(\frac{1}{2}, \frac{1}{2}\right)$, or the Rademacher (seen in the introduction to Chapter 2) defined as $2x - 1$ with $x \sim$ Ber$\left(\frac{1}{2}\right)$. The reader should be aware that the notation varies. For example, we use Gam(ν, λ) while some authors use $\Gamma(\lambda, \nu)$ or $\Gamma(\alpha, \beta)$ with $\beta := 1/\lambda$. We have also avoided using the symbol $\Gamma(\cdot, \cdot)$, preferring instead Gam$(\cdot, \cdot)$ to denote the gamma distribution. The reason is that the former is already in use to denote the incomplete gamma function; see, for example, Exercise 4.20. Like the function Φ of Exercise 4.21, the incomplete gamma has the alternative representation

$$\Gamma(\nu, w) = \Gamma(\nu) - w^{\nu} \mathrm{e}^{-w} \sum_{j=0}^{\infty} \frac{w^j}{\prod_{i=0}^{j} (\nu + i)}.$$

The c.d.f.s derived in this chapter (also the c.f.s and noncentral p.d.f.s in Table 4.2, and the series in Section A.3.3) can all be written in terms of the *hypergeometric function*

$${}_pF_q(a_1, \dots, a_p; c_1, \dots, c_q; w) := \sum_{j=0}^{\infty} \frac{\prod_{k=1}^{p} (\Gamma(j + a_k)/\Gamma(a_k))}{\prod_{k=1}^{q} (\Gamma(j + c_k)/\Gamma(c_k))} \frac{w^j}{j!}, \tag{4.13}$$

where

$$\frac{\Gamma(j+b)}{\Gamma(b)} = \prod_{i=0}^{j-1} (b+i) = (-1)^j \, \mathrm{P}_j^{-b}.$$

An encyclopedic reference for hypergeometric functions can be found in Erdélyi (1953, 1955). An introduction containing further references and applications, including details on calculating divergent series, can be found in Abadir (1999). For continuous variates, series expansions of a quantile function or inverse c.d.f. $q = F^{-1}(\alpha)$ can be obtained by means of Cornish–Fisher inversions; see, for example, Johnson, Kotz, and Balakrishnan (1994).

The practical use of some distributions may not be illustrated in this volume, if the applications are quite specialized. For example, the inverse Gaussian is useful in time series analysis, stochastic processes, and mathematical finance. A version of it is used to describe the probability that a barrier is reached for the first time (called *first passage time*) by a stochastic process with identical (for equal time increments) and independent Gaussian increments, called *Brownian motion* or *Wiener process*; for example, see Etheridge (2002, p. 61). Brownian motion arises as the continuous-time limit of the random walk that we shall analyze in Exercise 10.42, with $n \to \infty$ there. The reader is referred to Etheridge (2002) or Černý (2004) for more details on this topic and on Exercise 4.23, or see Hull (1989) for a less mathematical introduction. In part (b) of that exercise, $\log(z) \sim \mathrm{N}\left(-\sigma^2 m/2, \sigma^2 m\right)$ arose because x_t follows a geometric Brownian motion, which is not quite the same as $\log(x_t)$ being a Brownian motion. The difference in the means arises, in a dynamic context, from the Itô term of stochastic calculus: the usual chain rule of deterministic calculus has to be modified for an extra variance-related term when dealing with differentials of functions of normal variates, unless the variate is degenerate as in the delta method of Exercise 10.20. That the variance is $\sigma^2 m$ is explained by the variance of the increments of random walks obtained in the derivations of Exercise 10.42(b).

The sampling was random in Exercise 4.4, but not in Exercise 4.7(d). The contrast between these two sampling setups will be tackled in Section 9.1, especially in Exercises 9.8 and 9.9.

The property introduced in Exercise 4.12 is really a *conditional* no-memory property, but the adjective is often dropped when the context is clear. In the case of stochastic processes or time series it is best to retain this adjective, because the unconditional memory may also be of interest.

In Exercise 4.29, we noted that Fourier pairs of functions have tails whose lengths are inversely related. This has great significance in mathematical physics too, where the position and the momentum of a particle form such a pair. A famous version of *Heisenberg's uncertainty principle* states that we cannot measure accurately both position and momentum: if one is measured accurately, the other one is not. Malley and Hornstein (1993) and Barndorff-Nielsen, Gill, and Jupp (2003) introduce some of the concepts of quantum theory (where randomness and uncertainty play a key role) from a statistical viewpoint.

Some continuous distributions arise as limits of others. This will be explored in Chapter 10 and illustrated in Exercise 10.32. For the time being, Exercise 4.36 worked out that $\mathrm{t}(n)$ tends to a normal as $n \to \infty$, something that is also clear from the published tables of quantiles. It is possible, but rather elaborate for this volume, to work out the next terms in an expansion of the c.d.f. of $\mathrm{t}(n)$ in terms of n^{-j}, where $j = 0, 1, \dots$ and n is large. This is done by combining two expansions: a generalization of the exercise's expansion of the ratio of gamma functions (such as in Section A.3.4) and

$$\left(1+\frac{t^2}{n}\right)^{-\frac{n+1}{2}} = \exp\left(\log\left(1+\frac{t^2}{n}\right)^{-\frac{n+1}{2}}\right) = \exp\left(-\frac{n+1}{2}\log\left(1+\frac{t^2}{n}\right)\right)$$

$$= \exp\left(-\frac{t^2}{2}\left(1+\frac{1}{n}\right)\sum_{j=0}^{\infty}\frac{\left(-t^2/n\right)^j}{j+1}\right).$$

Terms up to a particular order of magnitude in n can be selected from the product of the two expansions. Continuing with the theme of limits, we have two further comments to make. We defined $\mathrm{GG}(\nu, p, \lambda)$ with $p \neq 0$ for convenience only. If we were to allow $p \to 0$ in $\mathrm{GG}(\nu, p, \lambda)$, and take $\lambda = \nu \to \infty$ with $|p|\sqrt{\nu} \to 1/c$ (where $c \in \mathbb{R}_+$ and finite), we would get $\mathrm{LN}(0, c^2)$. Finally, we have defined the GEV distribution (4.3) in terms of p rather than its reciprocal, as it has a connection with the power p of $\mathrm{Par}(p)$ which will be explored in Part B, especially in Chapter 10.

A classic reference for information measures in statistics is Kullback (1959). Note that $\delta(f_x, f_z)$ of Exercise 4.42 is a semimetric but not a metric (a measure of distance) because in general it does not satisfy the triangle inequality. For a counterexample using the Poisson density, see Kullback (1959, p. 35). On the other hand, Hellinger's distance is a metric by virtue of its definition as a norm. For statistical applications of Hellinger's distance, see Beran (1977). For some uses of the KLIC, see Chapters 6–8 and 12–14 in the present text.

5

Joint distributions and densities

The need for this chapter arises once we start considering the realistic case of more than one variate at a time, the *multivariate* case. We have already started dealing with this topic (in disguise) in the introductions to conditioning and mixing in Chapters 1 and 2, and in some exercises using these ideas in Chapter 4.

Let

$$\boldsymbol{x} := \begin{pmatrix} x_1 \\ \vdots \\ x_m \end{pmatrix}$$

be a *random vector*, a vector of random variables, with support $\mathcal{X} \subseteq \mathbb{R}^m$. Denoting again a transpose by a prime, we write the realization of the row vector $\boldsymbol{x}'$ as $\boldsymbol{w}' := (w_1, \dots, w_m)$. We reserve boldface $\boldsymbol{u}$ and $\boldsymbol{v}$ for their traditional use in regression analysis (for example in Chapter 13), hence our choice of $\boldsymbol{w}$ as the realization of $\boldsymbol{x}$. With m up to 3, we can write $\boldsymbol{w} := (u, v, w)'$ as the realization of $\boldsymbol{x} := (x, y, z)'$ to avoid unnecessary subscripts. If some ambiguity arises when using $\mathcal{X}$ for the support of $\boldsymbol{x}$ as well as x, we can avoid this by subscripting the support with the relevant variable. If we have n random vectors, we use $\boldsymbol{x}_i$ and $\boldsymbol{w}_i$, with $i = 1, \dots, n$. With n up to 3, we write $\boldsymbol{x}, \boldsymbol{y}, \boldsymbol{z}$ with realizations $\boldsymbol{w}_{\boldsymbol{x}}, \boldsymbol{w}_{\boldsymbol{y}}, \boldsymbol{w}_{\boldsymbol{z}}$, in which case the elements of $\boldsymbol{x}$ must now be denoted by $x_1, x_2, \dots$, even if $m \leqslant 3$, and likewise for $\boldsymbol{y}$ and $\boldsymbol{z}$. For variates having a special notation, such as the sample mean $\overline{\boldsymbol{x}}$ to be seen later, we write $\boldsymbol{w}_{\overline{\boldsymbol{x}}}$ for the realization.

We need to define the probability functions associated with the vector variate $\boldsymbol{x}$. The joint event

$$\{x_1 : x_1 \leqslant w_1\} \cap \dots \cap \{x_m : x_m \leqslant w_m\} \tag{5.1}$$

is written more compactly as $\{\boldsymbol{x} : \boldsymbol{x} \leqslant \boldsymbol{w}\}$, where the vector inequality is meant to apply element-by-element. The variate $\boldsymbol{x}$ has the *joint c.d.f.*

$$F_{\boldsymbol{x}}(\boldsymbol{w}) := \Pr(\boldsymbol{x} \leqslant \boldsymbol{w}).$$

Clearly, this probability is a one-dimensional function of a vector. For example, we have a single number for the probability of the composite event that the temperature is $\leqslant 5°\text{C}$ *and* that it will snow within the hour. Now suppose instead that we consider the probability that the temperature is anything $\leqslant \infty$ and that it will snow: this is simply the probability that it will snow! In general, (5.1) implies that the relation of the joint c.d.f. to our earlier individual c.d.f.s, which are called *marginal c.d.f.s*, is

$$\begin{aligned} F_{x_1}(w_1) &:= \Pr(x_1 \leqslant w_1) = \Pr(x_1 \leqslant w_1, x_2 \leqslant \infty, \dots, x_m \leqslant \infty) \\ &\equiv F_{\boldsymbol{x}}(w_1, \infty, \dots, \infty) \end{aligned} \tag{5.2}$$

since we are restricting only x_1, to satisfy $x_1 \leqslant w_1$, while the remaining variates are unrestricted. The process of obtaining marginal from joint c.d.f.s is called *marginalization* with respect to $x_2, \dots, x_m$. A relation similar to (5.2) applies to the other $j = 2, \dots, m$ components of $\boldsymbol{x}$. Also, one could obtain the joint distribution of a subset of $\boldsymbol{x}$, rather than just x_1. For example, partitioning $\boldsymbol{x}' = (\boldsymbol{x}_1', \boldsymbol{x}_2')$ with dimensions $k > 0$ and $m - k > 0$, respectively, we have

$$F_{\boldsymbol{x}_1}(\boldsymbol{w}_1) \equiv F_{\boldsymbol{x}_1}(w_1, \dots, w_k) = F_{\boldsymbol{x}}(w_1, \dots, w_k, \infty, \dots, \infty).$$

When there is no ambiguity, we abbreviate $F_{x_j}(w_j)$ to $F_j(w_j)$, and $F_{\boldsymbol{x}}(\boldsymbol{w})$ to $F(\boldsymbol{w})$.

The joint c.d.f. obeys certain rules which generalize the four rules in Chapter 2, namely:
(i) $F(\boldsymbol{w}) = 0$ if *any* of the m arguments is $-\infty$;
(ii) $F(\boldsymbol{w}) = 1$ if *all* the m arguments are ∞;
(iii) $F(\dots, w_j^+, \dots) := \lim_{h\to 0^+} F(\dots, w_j + h, \dots) = F(\dots, w_j, \dots)$ for all j; and
(iv) for all real constants $s_j < t_j$,

$$\Pr(s_1 < x_1 \leqslant t_1, \dots, s_m < x_m \leqslant t_m) \equiv \left[[F(w_1, \dots, w_m)]_{s_1}^{t_1} \dots\right]_{s_m}^{t_m} \geqslant 0.$$

For the case $m = 2$, the latter condition becomes

$$\begin{aligned} \left[[F(w_1, w_2)]_{s_1}^{t_1}\right]_{s_2}^{t_2} &= [F(t_1, w_2) - F(s_1, w_2)]_{s_2}^{t_2} \\ &= F(t_1, t_2) - F(s_1, t_2) - (F(t_1, s_2) - F(s_1, s_2)) \\ &= F(t_1, t_2) + F(s_1, s_2) - F(s_1, t_2) - F(t_1, s_2) \geqslant 0. \end{aligned}$$

The condition effectively requires the nonnegativity of the joint probability that x_j ($j = 1, \dots, m$) are in nonempty intervals, in other words, that $\boldsymbol{x}$ falls in a hyperrectangle (an m-dimensional generalization of a rectangle). This leads us to the following definition of a p.d.f.

Let $F_{\boldsymbol{x}}(\boldsymbol{w}^-) := \lim_{\boldsymbol{h}\to \boldsymbol{0}_m^+} F_{\boldsymbol{x}}(\boldsymbol{w} - \boldsymbol{h}) = \Pr(\boldsymbol{x} < \boldsymbol{w})$, where the signs in the superscript of the vector $\boldsymbol{w}$ will be used with this meaning in this book, unless stated otherwise (such as in the case of the generalized inverse of a matrix in Chapters 12 and 14). The *joint p.d.f.*

for a discrete vector variate is $f_{\boldsymbol{x}}(\boldsymbol{w}) := \Pr(\boldsymbol{x} = \boldsymbol{w}) = F_{\boldsymbol{x}}(\boldsymbol{w}) - F_{\boldsymbol{x}}(\boldsymbol{w}^-)$ and satisfies three conditions similar to those in Chapter 2:
(i) $f_{\boldsymbol{x}}(\boldsymbol{w}) \geqslant 0$;
(ii) $\sum_{\boldsymbol{t}\leqslant\boldsymbol{w}} f_{\boldsymbol{x}}(\boldsymbol{t}) = F_{\boldsymbol{x}}(\boldsymbol{w})$; and
(iii) $\sum_{\boldsymbol{t}\in\mathcal{X}} f_{\boldsymbol{x}}(\boldsymbol{t}) = F_{\boldsymbol{x}}(\infty, \dots, \infty) = 1$.
For an absolutely continuous vector variate, the p.d.f. is

$$f_{\boldsymbol{x}}(\boldsymbol{w}) := \frac{\partial^m}{\partial w_1 \dots \partial w_m} F_{\boldsymbol{x}}(\boldsymbol{w})$$

and satisfies:
(i) $f_{\boldsymbol{x}}(\boldsymbol{w}) \geqslant 0$;
(ii) $\int_{\boldsymbol{t}\leqslant\boldsymbol{w}} f_{\boldsymbol{x}}(\boldsymbol{t})\, \mathrm{d}\boldsymbol{t} = F_{\boldsymbol{x}}(\boldsymbol{w})$; and
(iii) $\int_{\boldsymbol{t}\in\mathcal{X}} f_{\boldsymbol{x}}(\boldsymbol{t})\, \mathrm{d}\boldsymbol{t} = F_{\boldsymbol{x}}(\infty, \dots, \infty) = 1$, where we have used the notation

$$\int_{\boldsymbol{t}\leqslant\boldsymbol{w}} f_{\boldsymbol{x}}(\boldsymbol{t})\, \mathrm{d}\boldsymbol{t} \equiv \int_{-\infty}^{w_1} \dots \int_{-\infty}^{w_m} f_{\boldsymbol{x}}(\boldsymbol{t})\, \mathrm{d}t_m \dots \mathrm{d}t_1$$

for the m-dimensional integrals. These integrals can be calculated one at a time, or in a different order, because they are absolutely convergent to the finite value of the c.d.f.; see Section A.3.5. The equivalence of these alternative calculations will be illustrated in Sections 5.2 and 5.3.

We can obtain the *marginal p.d.f.s* in the discrete case by differencing the corresponding marginal c.d.f., or in the continuous case by differentiating it; for example, differencing (5.2) gives

$$\begin{aligned} f_{x_1}(w_1) &= F_{\boldsymbol{x}}(w_1, \infty, \dots, \infty) - F_{\boldsymbol{x}}(w_1^-, \infty, \dots, \infty) \\ &= \sum_{t_1\leqslant w_1} \left(\sum_{t_2\leqslant\infty} \dots \sum_{t_m\leqslant\infty} f_{\boldsymbol{x}}(\boldsymbol{t}) \right) - \sum_{t_1\leqslant w_1^-} \left(\sum_{t_2\leqslant\infty} \dots \sum_{t_m\leqslant\infty} f_{\boldsymbol{x}}(\boldsymbol{t}) \right) \\ &= \sum_{t_2\leqslant\infty} \dots \sum_{t_m\leqslant\infty} f_{\boldsymbol{x}}(w_1, t_2, \dots, t_m), \end{aligned}$$

or differentiating it gives

$$\begin{aligned} f_{x_1}(w_1) &= \frac{\mathrm{d}}{\mathrm{d}w_1} F_{\boldsymbol{x}}(w_1, \infty, \dots, \infty) = \frac{\mathrm{d}}{\mathrm{d}w_1} \int_{-\infty}^{w_1} \int_{-\infty}^{\infty} \dots \int_{-\infty}^{\infty} f_{\boldsymbol{x}}(\boldsymbol{t})\, \mathrm{d}t_m \dots \mathrm{d}t_2\, \mathrm{d}t_1 \\ &= \int_{-\infty}^{\infty} \dots \int_{-\infty}^{\infty} f_{\boldsymbol{x}}(w_1, t_2, \dots, t_m)\, \mathrm{d}t_m \dots \mathrm{d}t_2 \end{aligned}$$

by Leibniz' rule for differentiating integrals (see Section A.4). These two equations also show that a marginal p.d.f. can be obtained from the joint p.d.f. by summing or integrating over all the possible values of the remaining variates. Care is often needed with the domain of definition of the p.d.f., and the corresponding simplification of the limits of summation or integration over the values where $f_{\boldsymbol{x}} \neq 0$ (that is, over $\mathcal{X}$), as will be seen in the exercises.

As in Chapter 2, if we wish to stress that the distribution depends on a parameter vector $\boldsymbol{\theta}$, we write $F_{\boldsymbol{x}}(\boldsymbol{w}; \boldsymbol{\theta})$ or $F_{\boldsymbol{x}}(\boldsymbol{w} \mid \boldsymbol{\theta})$. Also, as before, we resort to the unifying notation of the Stieltjes integral of a function ψ with respect to $F_{\boldsymbol{x}}$:

$$\int_{\mathbb{R}^m} \psi(\boldsymbol{w})\,\mathrm{d}F_{\boldsymbol{x}}(\boldsymbol{w}) = \begin{cases} \sum_{\boldsymbol{x}\in\mathcal{X}} \psi(\boldsymbol{w}) f_{\boldsymbol{x}}(\boldsymbol{w}) & (\boldsymbol{x} \text{ discrete}), \\ \int_{\boldsymbol{x}\in\mathcal{X}} \psi(\boldsymbol{w}) f_{\boldsymbol{x}}(\boldsymbol{w})\,\mathrm{d}\boldsymbol{w} & (\boldsymbol{x} \text{ continuous}); \end{cases} \tag{5.3}$$

where $\mathrm{d}F_{\boldsymbol{x}}(\boldsymbol{w})$ is interpreted as $\partial_{w_1} \dots \partial_{w_m} F_{\boldsymbol{x}}(\boldsymbol{w})$ and the subscript of the partial differentials denotes the variable changing while the others are kept fixed, for instance, giving $f_{\boldsymbol{x}}(\boldsymbol{w})\,\mathrm{d}w_m \dots \mathrm{d}w_1$ in the continuous case. This is the notation commonly used in statistics, though it is not ideal from a mathematical point of view: our $\mathrm{d}F_{\boldsymbol{x}}(\boldsymbol{w})$ should not be confused with the total differential $\sum_{j=1}^{m} (\partial F_{\boldsymbol{x}}(\boldsymbol{w})/\partial w_j)\,\mathrm{d}w_j$.

From the above discussion of joint and marginal probability functions, we see that one can always deduce the latter from the former. The reverse is, however, not true, as will be illustrated in some of the exercises such as Exercises 5.9 and 5.13. Before we can explain why, we need to explore further the meaning of a joint probability function, which has been rather abstract so far. The key to interpreting these functions is in Chapter 1. Take $m = 2$, the *bivariate* case. Then, the joint c.d.f. is

$$F_{x,y}(u, v) = \Pr(x \leqslant u, y \leqslant v) = \Pr(x \leqslant u \mid y \leqslant v) \Pr(y \leqslant v)$$

by conditioning. The conditional probability simplifies to $\Pr(x \leqslant u)$ for all u, v if and only if x is independent of y, in which case

$$F_{x,y}(u, v) = \Pr(x \leqslant u) \Pr(y \leqslant v) \equiv F_x(u) F_y(v),$$

and accordingly $f_{x,y}(u, v) = f_x(u) f_y(v)$ for all u, v. However, it is often the case that y (for example a person's income) conveys some information about x (for example this person's expenditure), or vice versa. If so, then a knowledge of all the marginal functions is not sufficient to allow us to deduce their joint behavior and interactions. Indeed, the main purpose of studying a joint distribution is to identify such dependence between the variates. Apart from the very last exercises of this chapter, we defer an explicit treatment of measures of dependence to the next chapter. We now turn to examples (and counterexamples) for joint densities and distributions, starting with the discrete case. We warn, as in Exercise 1.22, that pairwise independence does not necessarily lead to joint independence; see Exercises 5.17 and 5.18 below. When using the term "independence" in the multivariate case, we will mean joint independence unless stated otherwise.

5.1 Multivariate discrete

Exercise 5.1 (Multi cards) From an ordinary deck of cards, four cards are drawn with replacement. Define $\boldsymbol{x} := (x, y, z)'$, where x = number of hearts, y = number of diamonds, and z = number of spades. Obtain:
(a) the joint p.d.f. $f(u, v, w)$;
(b) $f_{x,y}(u, v)$;
(c) the marginal densities;

(d) $\Pr(x + y = i)$ for all i.

Solution

(a) Using the multinomial formula in the introduction to Chapter 1, there are

$$\frac{4!}{u!v!w!(4-u-v-w)!}$$

ways to order the selection of u hearts, v diamonds, w spades, and $(4-u-v-w)$ clubs from the four possible types (groups) of cards. Furthermore, each type has probability $\frac{1}{4}$ of being selected in each draw. The result is the *multinomial distribution*: for $\boldsymbol{w} := (u, v, w)' \geqslant \mathbf{0}$ and $u + v + w \leqslant 4$,

$$\begin{aligned} f(\boldsymbol{w}) &= \Pr(\boldsymbol{x} = \boldsymbol{w}) \\ &= \frac{4!}{u!v!w!(4-u-v-w)!}\left(\frac{1}{4}\right)^u\left(\frac{1}{4}\right)^v\left(\frac{1}{4}\right)^w\left(\frac{1}{4}\right)^{4-u-v-w} \\ &= \frac{3}{32u!v!w!(4-u-v-w)!}. \end{aligned}$$

(b) We can derive the bivariate density by marginalizing with respect to z:

$$\begin{aligned} f_{x,y}(u, v) &= \sum_{w=0}^{4-u-v} f(u, v, w) = \frac{3}{32u!v!}\sum_{w=0}^{4-u-v}\frac{1}{w!(4-u-v-w)!} \\ &= \frac{3}{32u!v!(4-u-v)!}\sum_{w=0}^{4-u-v}\binom{4-u-v}{w} \\ &= \frac{3}{32u!v!(4-u-v)!}(1+1)^{4-u-v} = \frac{3}{2^{u+v+1}u!v!(4-u-v)!} \end{aligned}$$

by the binomial expansion. Alternatively, we can use the fact that (x, y) also has a multinomial distribution with three possible outcomes:

$$\begin{aligned} f_{x,y}(u, v) &= \frac{4!}{u!v!(4-u-v)!}\left(\frac{1}{4}\right)^u\left(\frac{1}{4}\right)^v\left(\frac{1}{2}\right)^{4-u-v} \\ &= \frac{3}{2^{u+v+1}u!v!(4-u-v)!}. \end{aligned}$$

(c) By definition, all three random variables have a $\text{Bin}(4, 1/4)$ distribution. This is a special case of the following more general result. If $(x_1, \dots, x_m)$ has a multinomial distribution with parameters $(n, p_1, \dots, p_m)$, then the marginal distribution of any of the x_j variables is binomial with parameters n and p_j. Furthermore, any subset $(x_1, \dots, x_k)$ has a multinomial density.

(d) This is the event of drawing hearts or diamonds: their total is $x + y$ and the event has

$p = \frac{1}{2}$. We obtain a binomial density with $n = 4$ and $p = \frac{1}{2}$,

$$\Pr(x + y = i) = \frac{4!}{i!(4-i)!}\left(\frac{1}{2}\right)^i\left(1 - \frac{1}{2}\right)^{4-i} = \frac{3}{2i!(4-i)!}$$

for $i \in \{0, 1, \dots, n\}$, and 0 otherwise.

Exercise 5.2 (Hyper cards) Six cards are drawn without replacement from an ordinary deck of 52 cards. Define $\boldsymbol{x} := (x, y, z)'$, where x = the number of hearts, y = the number of diamonds, and z = the number of black cards. For $i = 0, 1, \dots, 6$, calculate:
(a) $\Pr(x = 2, z = i)$;
(b) $\Pr(x + y = i)$.

Solution
(a) Because the cards are drawn without replacement, we obtain a *multivariate hypergeometric density*. (If the cards had been drawn with replacement we would have obtained the multinomial density.) Thus,

$$\begin{aligned}\Pr(x = 2, z = i; n = 6) &= \Pr(\boldsymbol{x} = (2, 4 - i, i)') \\ &= \frac{\binom{13}{2}\binom{13}{4-i}\binom{26}{i}}{\binom{52}{6}} \qquad (i = 0, 1, \dots, 4).\end{aligned}$$

and $\Pr(x = 2, z = 5; n = 6) = \Pr(x = 2, z = 6; n = 6) = 0$.
(b) This is simply the probability of drawing i red cards and $6 - i$ black cards. The hypergeometric distribution gives

$$\Pr(x + y = i) = \frac{\binom{26}{i}\binom{26}{6-i}}{\binom{52}{6}} \qquad (i = 0, 1, \dots, 6).$$

We conclude that the marginal densities of a multivariate hypergeometric density are hypergeometric.

Exercise 5.3 (Multinomial–Pareto) Let $x_1, \dots, x_n$ be a random sample from the Pareto p.d.f.

$$f(u) = \begin{cases} 3u^{-4} & (u > 1), \\ 0 & (u \leqslant 1). \end{cases}$$

For the j-th observation, event i occurs if $i < x_j \leqslant i + 1$ for $i = 1, 2, 3$, and event 4 occurs if $x_j > 4$. Let z_i := number of times that event i occurs, and let w be a positive integer. Obtain:
(a) $\Pr(z_1 + z_4 > w)$;
(b) $\Pr(z_1 = w, z_4 = 2)$.

Solution
We are dealing with a multinomial distribution with four possible outcomes, and with pa-

rameters n and $p_1, \dots, p_4$, where

$$p_i = \Pr(i < x \leqslant i+1) = \int_i^{i+1} 3u^{-4}\,\mathrm{d}u = i^{-3} - (i+1)^{-3}$$

for $i = 1, 2, 3$, and $p_4 = \int_4^\infty 3u^{-4}\,\mathrm{d}u = 4^{-3}$.
(a) Define a new random variable $y := z_1 + z_4$. As in Exercise 5.1, y has a binomial distribution with parameters n and $p = p_1 + p_4$. Thus,

$$\Pr(z_1 + z_4 = v) = \binom{n}{v}(p_1+p_4)^v(1-p_1-p_4)^{n-v} = \binom{n}{v}\left(\frac{57}{64}\right)^v\left(\frac{7}{64}\right)^{n-v},$$

and hence

$$\Pr(z_1 + z_4 > w) = \sum_{v=w+1}^{n}\binom{n}{v}\left(\frac{57}{64}\right)^v\left(\frac{7}{64}\right)^{n-v} \qquad (1 \leqslant w \leqslant n-1).$$

(b) As in Exercise 5.1, we use the fact that (z_1, z_4) follows a multinomial distribution with parameters n, p_1, and p_4. Therefore, for $0 \leqslant w \leqslant n-2$,

$$\Pr(z_1 = w, z_4 = 2) = \frac{n!}{w!2!(n-w-2)!}\left(\frac{7}{8}\right)^w\left(\frac{1}{64}\right)^2\left(\frac{7}{64}\right)^{n-w-2}.$$

Exercise 5.4 (Multinomial–exponential) Let $x_1, \dots, x_n$ be a random sample from an exponential distribution with expectation 1. We define $\boldsymbol{y} := (y_1, y_2, y_3)'$, where y_1 is the number of sample values between 1 and 2, y_2 is the number of sample values between 3 and 4, and y_3 is the number of sample values greater than 6. Calculate:
(a) $\Pr(\boldsymbol{y} = \boldsymbol{w})$;
(b) $\Pr(y_1 + y_2 = i)$.

Solution
(a) If x follows an exponential distribution with expectation 1, then

$$\Pr(a < x < b) = \int_a^b \mathrm{e}^{-t}\,\mathrm{d}t = \mathrm{e}^{-a} - \mathrm{e}^{-b}$$

for $0 < a < b$. Let

$$p_1 = \Pr(1 < x < 2) = \frac{\mathrm{e}-1}{\mathrm{e}^2}, \quad p_2 = \Pr(3 < x < 4) = \frac{\mathrm{e}-1}{\mathrm{e}^4},$$
$$p_3 = \Pr(x > 6) = \mathrm{e}^{-6}, \quad p_4 = 1 - p_1 - p_2 - p_3.$$

We are dealing with a multinomial distribution, and hence

$$\Pr(\boldsymbol{y} = \boldsymbol{w}) = \frac{n!}{\left(\prod_{i=1}^3 w_i!\right)(n - \boldsymbol{w}'\boldsymbol{\imath})!}\left(\prod_{i=1}^3 p_i^{y_i}\right)p_4^{n-\boldsymbol{w}'\boldsymbol{\imath}}$$

for $\boldsymbol{w} \geqslant \mathbf{0}$ and $\boldsymbol{w}'\boldsymbol{\imath} \leqslant n$, with $\boldsymbol{\imath} := (1, 1, 1)'$.

(b) We are now dealing with a binomial distribution, and hence

$$\Pr(y_1 + y_2 = i) = \binom{n}{i} (p_1 + p_2)^i (p_3 + p_4)^{n-i} \quad (i = 0, 1, \dots, n).$$

Exercise 5.5 (Negative "p.d.f.") Give an example of a function satisfying all the rules for a c.d.f. given in the introduction except (iv).

Solution

We can take the simplest bivariate case, $m = 2$. One such function is

$$H(u, v) = \begin{cases} 0 & (u < 0, v < 0), \\ p_1 & (u \geqslant 0, v < 0), \\ p_2 & (u < 0, v \geqslant 0), \\ 1 & (u \geqslant 0, v \geqslant 0), \end{cases}$$

where $p_1, p_2 \in (0, 1]$ and $p_1 + p_2 > 1$. This definition covers all four quadrants of the u, v space. In spite of this function being monotone increasing from 0 to 1 in its arguments, and being continuous to the right at any point, its corresponding "p.d.f." can become negative: for any $u, v < 0$, we have

$$H(0, 0) + H(u, v) - H(0, v) - H(u, 0) = 1 - p_1 - p_2 < 0,$$

which violates condition (iv).

If this function had been a proper c.d.f., then

$$\begin{aligned} \Pr(x = 0, y = 0) &= \Pr(0^- < x \leqslant 0, 0^- < y \leqslant 0) \\ &= H(0, 0) + H(0^-, 0^-) - H(0, 0^-) - H(0^-, 0) \\ &= 1 - p_1 - p_2 \end{aligned}$$

would have been nonnegative.

5.2 Bivariate continuous

Exercise 5.6 (Bivariate beta, 1) The joint p.d.f. of (x, y) is

$$f(u, v) = \begin{cases} cu^{p-1}(1-u)^{q-1}v^{r-1}(1-v)^{s-1} & (0 < u < 1,\ 0 < v < 1), \\ 0 & (\text{elsewhere}), \end{cases}$$

where $p, q, r, s > 0$. Obtain:

(a) c and the marginal densities;

(b) the joint c.d.f. $F(u, v)$.

Solution

(a) We have

$$1 = \int_0^1 \int_0^1 cu^{p-1}(1-u)^{q-1}v^{r-1}(1-v)^{s-1}\,du\,dv$$
$$= c\left(\int_0^1 u^{p-1}(1-u)^{q-1}\,du\right)\left(\int_0^1 v^{r-1}(1-v)^{s-1}\,dv\right) = cB(p,q)B(r,s),$$

so that $c^{-1} = B(p,q)B(r,s)$. The marginal densities are obtained directly by noting that x and y are independent, since the joint density factorizes into the product of the marginal standard Beta(p,q) and Beta(r,s) densities.

(b) By the independence of x and y, the joint distribution factors into the product of the marginal ones. More specifically, looking at the distinct cases for x and y, we obtain

$$F(u,v) = \Pr(x \leqslant u, y \leqslant v) = \begin{cases} 0 & (u \leqslant 0 \text{ or } v \leqslant 0), \\ I_u(p,q)I_v(r,s) & (0 < u < 1,\ 0 < v < 1), \\ I_u(p,q) & (0 < u < 1,\ v \geqslant 1), \\ I_v(r,s) & (0 < v < 1,\ u \geqslant 1), \\ 1 & (u \geqslant 1,\ v \geqslant 1), \end{cases}$$

where $I_{\bullet}(\cdot,\cdot)$ is the incomplete beta function of Exercise 4.11. The c.d.f. is zero if *either* $u \leqslant 0$ or $v \leqslant 0$, since the probability that $x \leqslant 0$ is zero regardless of what happens to y, and vice versa. By contrast, the c.d.f. is 1 when *both* $u \geqslant 1$ and $v \geqslant 1$, since not all possibilities (or possible events) have been exhausted when either $x < 1$ or $y < 1$.

***Exercise 5.7 (Bivariate beta, 2)** The joint p.d.f. of (x, y) is

$$f(u,v) = \begin{cases} 3u^2 & (0 < u < 1,\ 0 < v < 1), \\ 0 & (\text{elsewhere}). \end{cases}$$

(a) Calculate $\Pr(x/y \leqslant w)$ for $w \in \mathbb{R}$.
(b) Calculate $\Pr(x + y \leqslant w)$ for $w \in \mathbb{R}$.

Solution

(a) The support of x/y is $\mathbb{R}_+$. Let us consider $0 < w \leqslant 1$ first. Then, $\Pr(x/y \leqslant w) = \Pr(x \leqslant wy)$, where $wy < 1$, and the mixing argument already used in Section 4.2 leads to

$$\Pr(x \leqslant wy) = \int_0^1 \int_0^{wv} 3u^2\,du\,dv$$
$$= \int_0^1 \left[u^3\right]_0^{wv} dv = w^3 \int_0^1 v^3\,dv = w^3\left[\frac{v^4}{4}\right]_0^1 = \frac{w^3}{4}.$$

If $w > 1$ then, in the previous equation, the upper limit of integration for u should not be allowed to exceed $wv = 1$ since u cannot exceed 1. Instead, an easier way to tackle this difficulty is to first rewrite $\Pr(x/y \leqslant w) = \Pr(y \geqslant x/w)$, where $x/w < 1$; then we have

$$\Pr(y \geqslant x/w) = \int_0^1 \int_{u/w}^1 3u^2 \, dv \, du$$
$$= \int_0^1 3u^2 \left(1 - \frac{u}{w}\right) du = \left[u^3 - \frac{3}{4w}u^4\right]_0^1 = 1 - \frac{3}{4w}.$$

Hence,

$$\Pr(x/y \leqslant w) = \begin{cases} 0 & (w \leqslant 0), \\ \frac{1}{4}w^3 & (0 < w \leqslant 1), \\ 1 - \frac{3}{4}w^{-1} & (1 < w < \infty). \end{cases}$$

(b) The support of $x + y$ is $(0, 2)$. We have $\Pr(x + y \leqslant w) = \Pr(y \leqslant w - x)$, and here too we consider the two nontrivial possibilities. If $0 < w \leqslant 1$,

$$\Pr(x + y \leqslant w) = \int_0^w \int_0^{w-u} 3u^2 \, dv \, du$$
$$= \int_0^w 3u^2(w - u) \, du = w^4 - \frac{3}{4}w^4 = \frac{1}{4}w^4;$$

and, if $1 < w \leqslant 2$,

$$\Pr(x + y \leqslant w) = 1 - \Pr(x + y > w) = 1 - \Pr(y > w - x)$$
$$= 1 - \int_{w-1}^1 \int_{w-u}^1 3u^2 \, dv \, du,$$

where the limits of the outer integral for x ensure that $w - x \leqslant 1$, giving

$$\Pr(x + y \leqslant w) = 1 - \int_{w-1}^1 3u^2(1 - w + u) \, du$$
$$= 1 - \left[(1 - w)u^3 + \frac{3}{4}u^4\right]_{w-1}^1 = \frac{1}{4} + (w - 1) - \frac{1}{4}(w - 1)^4.$$

Hence,

$$\Pr(x + y \leqslant w) = \begin{cases} 0 & (w \leqslant 0), \\ \frac{1}{4}w^4 & (0 < w \leqslant 1), \\ \frac{1}{4} + w - 1 - \frac{1}{4}(w - 1)^4 & (1 < w \leqslant 2), \\ 1 & (w > 2). \end{cases}$$

Exercise 5.8 (Dirichlet density) The joint p.d.f. of (x, y) is

$$f(u, v) = \begin{cases} cu^2v^2 & (u > 0,\ v > 0,\ u + v < 2), \\ 0 & (\text{elsewhere}). \end{cases}$$

(a) Compute c and derive the marginal densities.
(b) Derive $\Pr(x + y \leqslant w)$.

Solution

(a) To compute c, we use the beta density to find

$$\int_0^2 \int_0^{2-u} u^2 v^2 \,\mathrm{d}v \,\mathrm{d}u = \frac{1}{3}\int_0^2 u^2 (2-u)^3 \,\mathrm{d}u = \frac{1}{3} \times \frac{\Gamma(3)\,\Gamma(4)}{\Gamma(7)} 2^{7-1} = \frac{16}{45},$$

and hence $c = 45/16$. The p.d.f. of x is

$$f_x(u) = \frac{45}{16} u^2 \int_0^{2-u} v^2 \,\mathrm{d}v = \frac{15}{16} u^2 (2-u)^3$$

for $0 < u < 2$ and 0 elsewhere. Since the joint density $f(u, v)$ is symmetric in its arguments, the marginal $f_y(v)$ takes the same form as $f_x(u)$. Note that, even though the marginals are beta, the joint density is not a bivariate beta because of the support of (x, y), unlike in Exercises 5.6 and 5.7.

(b) For $0 < w < 2$,

$$\begin{aligned}\Pr(x + y \leqslant w) &= \frac{45}{16} \int_0^w u^2 \int_0^{w-u} v^2 \,\mathrm{d}v \,\mathrm{d}u \\ &= \frac{15}{16} \int_0^w u^2 (w-u)^3 \,\mathrm{d}u = \frac{15}{16} \frac{\Gamma(3)\,\Gamma(4)}{\Gamma(7)} w^{7-1} = \frac{1}{64} w^6.\end{aligned}$$

The probability is zero for $w \leqslant 0$ and is 1 for $w \geqslant 2$.

Exercise 5.9 (Bivariate cubic) The joint p.d.f. of (x, y) is

$$f(u, v) = \begin{cases} cu(u+v)^2 & (0 < u < v < 1), \\ 0 & (\text{elsewhere}). \end{cases}$$

(a) Compute c and derive the marginal densities. Can you infer the joint density back from the two marginals?

(b) Derive $\Pr(x + y < 1)$.

Solution

(a) We have

$$\begin{aligned}\int_0^1 \int_u^1 u(u+v)^2 \,\mathrm{d}v \,\mathrm{d}u &= \int_0^1 \frac{u}{3} \left[(u+v)^3\right]_u^1 \mathrm{d}u = \int_0^1 \frac{u}{3} \left((1+u)^3 - 8u^3\right) \mathrm{d}u \\ &= \left(\left[\frac{u(1+u)^4}{12} \right]_0^1 - \frac{1}{12} \int_0^1 (1+u)^4 \,\mathrm{d}u \right) - \frac{8}{15} \left[u^5\right]_0^1 \\ &= \frac{16}{12} - \frac{32}{60} + \frac{1}{60} - \frac{8}{15} = \frac{17}{60},\end{aligned}$$

and hence $c = 60/17$. Notice that the same domain of integration would be covered by $\int_0^1 \int_0^v u(u+v)^2 \,\mathrm{d}u \,\mathrm{d}v$.

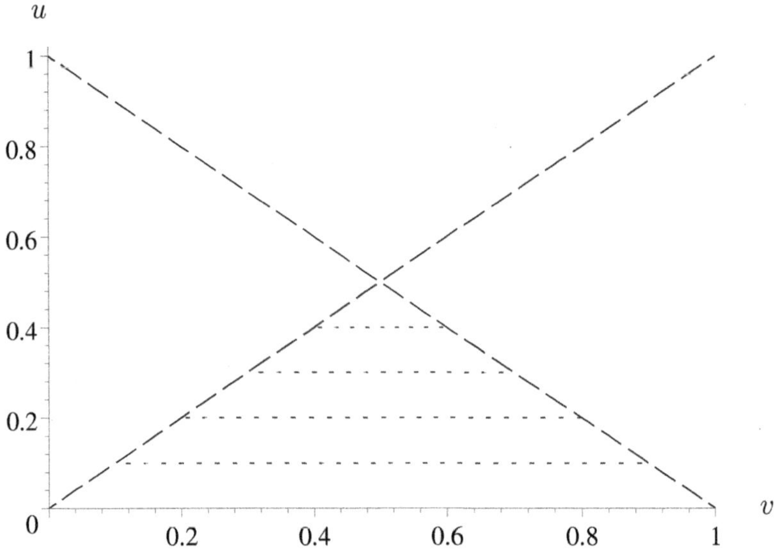

Figure 5.1. The domain of integration defined by $u + v < 1$ and $0 < u < v < 1$.

The marginal densities are found as follows:

$$f_x(u) = \frac{60u}{17} \int_u^1 (u+v)^2 \, dv = \frac{20u}{17} \left((1+u)^3 - 8u^3\right)$$

for $0 < u < 1$ and 0 elsewhere; and

$$f_y(v) = \frac{60}{17} \int_0^v u(u+v)^2 \, du = \frac{20}{17} \left(\left[u(u+v)^3\right]_0^v - \int_0^v (u+v)^3 \, du \right)$$

$$= \frac{20}{17} \left[(u+v)^3 \left(u - \frac{u+v}{4} \right) \right]_0^v = \frac{20}{17} \left(4v^4 + \frac{v^4}{4} \right) = 5v^4$$

for $0 < v < 1$ and 0 elsewhere. The product of the two densities is not equal to the original joint density, so the variates are not independent. We cannot recover the joint density function knowing only the marginals. Furthermore, from the marginals we cannot determine uniquely the domain of definition of the joint density.

(b) We need to define the limits of a double integral over $u + v < 1$ and satisfying $0 < u < v < 1$. In other words, we need to find the intersection of these two sets. Figure 5.1 displays this area as the dotted triangle that looks like a pyramid seen from its side. Algebraically, starting with the latter restriction, if u is to go from 0 to v, then $u + v < 1$ gives $v < \frac{1}{2}$ (the left half of the triangle). But this is not the only solution set. If $v > \frac{1}{2}$, then u must satisfy $u < 1 - v$ (the right half of the triangle). The variates are continuous, so that

$\Pr(y = \frac{1}{2}) = 0$, and we omit this case. Then,

$$\Pr(x + y < 1) = \int_0^{1/2} \int_0^{v} f(u, v)\, du\, dv + \int_{1/2}^{1} \int_0^{1-v} f(u, v)\, du\, dv$$

$$= \frac{20}{17} \int_0^{1/2} \left[(u+v)^3 \left(u - \frac{u+v}{4} \right) \right]_0^v dv + \frac{20}{17} \int_{1/2}^{1} \left[(u+v)^3 \left(u - \frac{u+v}{4} \right) \right]_0^{1-v} dv$$

$$= 5 \int_0^{1/2} v^4\, dv + \frac{20}{17} \int_{1/2}^{1} \left(\left(1 - v - \frac{1}{4} \right) + \frac{v^4}{4} \right) dv$$

$$= \left[v^5 \right]_0^{1/2} + \frac{20}{17} \left[\frac{3v}{4} - \frac{v^2}{2} + \frac{v^5}{20} \right]_{1/2}^{1} = \frac{1}{32} + \frac{31}{544} = \frac{3}{34}.$$

Exercise 5.10 (Gamma marginals) The joint p.d.f. of (x, y) is

$$f(u, v) = \begin{cases} \lambda^2 e^{-\lambda v} & (0 < u < v < \infty), \\ 0 & (\text{elsewhere}), \end{cases}$$

where $\lambda > 0$. Derive the marginal densities.

Solution

For $u > 0$,

$$f_x(u) = \lambda^2 \int_u^{\infty} e^{-\lambda v}\, dv = \lambda e^{-\lambda u},$$

and 0 elsewhere. Similarly, for $v > 0$,

$$f_y(v) = \lambda^2 e^{-\lambda v} \int_0^{v} du = \lambda^2 v e^{-\lambda v},$$

and 0 elsewhere.

Exercise 5.11 (GG marginals) The joint p.d.f. of (x, y) is:

$$f(u, v) = \begin{cases} c v e^{-v^2} & (0 < u < v < \infty), \\ 0 & (\text{elsewhere}). \end{cases}$$

(a) Compute c.
(b) Derive $f_x(u)$ and $f_y(v)$.

Solution

(a) We have

$$\int_0^{\infty} \int_u^{\infty} v e^{-v^2}\, dv\, du = -\frac{1}{2} \int_0^{\infty} \left[e^{-v^2} \right]_u^{\infty} du = \frac{1}{2} \int_0^{\infty} e^{-u^2}\, du = \frac{1}{2} \times \frac{\sqrt{2\pi}\sqrt{\frac{1}{2}}}{2} = \frac{\sqrt{\pi}}{4},$$

using the fact that $N(0, \frac{1}{2})$ is symmetric around 0 and integrates to 1. Hence, $c = 4/\sqrt{\pi}$.

Since the domain of integration is the area below the 45° line $u = v$ when v is on the horizontal axis (as in Figure 5.1), we could have written the same double integral here as $\int_0^\infty \int_0^v v\mathrm{e}^{-v^2}\, \mathrm{d}u\, \mathrm{d}v$, but its evaluation would have required an extra step.

(b) Using (a) we obtain

$$f_x(u) = \frac{4}{\sqrt{\pi}} \int_u^\infty v\mathrm{e}^{-v^2}\, \mathrm{d}v = \frac{2}{\sqrt{\pi}} \mathrm{e}^{-u^2}$$

for $u > 0$ and 0 elsewhere. Also,

$$f_y(v) = \frac{4}{\sqrt{\pi}} \int_0^v v\mathrm{e}^{-v^2}\, \mathrm{d}u = \frac{4}{\sqrt{\pi}} v^2 \mathrm{e}^{-v^2}$$

for $v > 0$ and 0 elsewhere.

5.3 Trivariate continuous

Exercise 5.12 (Trivariate quadratic, 1) The joint p.d.f. of (x, y, z) is

$$f(u, v, w) = \begin{cases} cu^2 & (0 < u < v < w < 1), \\ 0 & (\text{elsewhere}). \end{cases}$$

(a) Compute c.
(b) Derive $f_{x,y}(u, v)$ and $f_{x,z}(u, w)$.
(c) Derive $f_y(v)$ and $f_z(w)$.

Solution

(a) Since

$$\begin{aligned} \int_0^1 u^2 \int_u^1 \int_v^1 \mathrm{d}w\, \mathrm{d}v\, \mathrm{d}u &= \int_0^1 u^2 \int_u^1 (1 - v)\, \mathrm{d}v\, \mathrm{d}u \\ &= \frac{1}{2} \int_0^1 u^2 (1 - u)^2\, \mathrm{d}u = \frac{\Gamma(3)\Gamma(3)}{2\Gamma(6)} = \frac{1}{60}, \end{aligned}$$

we have $c = 60$. Note carefully the limits of integration.

(b) To find the density of (x, y), we integrate $f(u, v, w)$ over z. This gives

$$f_{x,y}(u, v) = 60u^2 \int_v^1 \mathrm{d}w = 60u^2(1 - v)$$

for $0 < u < v < 1$ and 0 elsewhere. Similarly,

$$f_{x,z}(u, w) = 60u^2 \int_u^w \mathrm{d}v = 60u^2(w - u)$$

for $0 < u < w < 1$ and 0 elsewhere.

(c) Finally, using (b),

$$f_y(v) = 60(1-v)\int_0^v u^2 \,\mathrm{d}u = 20(1-v)v^3$$

for $0 < v < 1$ and 0 elsewhere; and

$$f_z(w) = 60\int_0^w u^2(w-u)\,\mathrm{d}u = 60\,\frac{\Gamma(3)\Gamma(2)w^4}{\Gamma(5)} = 5w^4$$

for $0 < w < 1$ and 0 elsewhere.

Exercise 5.13 (Trivariate quadratic, 2) The joint p.d.f. of (x, y, z) is

$$f(u,v,w) = \begin{cases} cu^2v^2 & (0 < u < v < w < 1), \\ 0 & (\text{elsewhere}). \end{cases}$$

(a) Compute c.
(b) Derive $f_{x,z}(u,w)$, $f_{x,y}(u,v)$, and $f_{y,z}(v,w)$.
(c) Using the results from (b), obtain $f_x(u)$, $f_y(v)$, and $f_z(w)$.
(d) Is z independent of (x,y)? Is it independent of y?

Solution

(a) We have

$$\begin{aligned} c^{-1} &= \int_0^1\int_u^1\int_v^1 u^2v^2 \,\mathrm{d}w\,\mathrm{d}v\,\mathrm{d}u = \int_0^1 u^2\int_u^1 v^2(1-v)\,\mathrm{d}v\,\mathrm{d}u \\ &= \int_0^1 u^2\left[\frac{1}{3}v^3 - \frac{1}{4}v^4\right]_u^1 \mathrm{d}u = \int_0^1 u^2\left(\frac{1}{12} - \frac{1}{3}u^3 + \frac{1}{4}u^4\right)\mathrm{d}u \\ &= \frac{1}{36} - \frac{1}{18} + \frac{1}{28} = \frac{1}{126}, \end{aligned}$$

and hence $c = 126$.

(b) Using (a), we thus obtain, for $0 < u < w < 1$,

$$f_{x,z}(u,w) = 126u^2\int_u^w v^2\,\mathrm{d}v = 42u^2(w^3 - u^3),$$

and 0 elsewhere. Next, for $0 < u < v < 1$,

$$f_{x,y}(u,v) = 126u^2v^2\int_v^1 \mathrm{d}w = 126u^2v^2(1-v)$$

and 0 elsewhere. Finally, for $0 < v < w < 1$,

$$f_{y,z}(v,w) = 126v^2\int_0^v u^2\,\mathrm{d}u = 42v^5,$$

and 0 elsewhere.

(c) We use the results obtained in (b). Then, each of the three marginal densities can be obtained in two ways. For example, for $0 < u < 1$, we have

$$f_x(u) = 42u^2 \int_u^1 (w^3 - u^3)\,dw \quad \text{or} \quad f_x(u) = 126u^2 \int_u^1 v^2(1-v)\,dv.$$

In either case, $f_x(u) = (21/2)u^2(1 - 4u^3 + 3u^4)$ for $0 < u < 1$ and 0 elsewhere. Next, for $0 < v < 1$,

$$f_y(v) = 126v^2(1-v) \int_0^v u^2\,du \quad \text{or} \quad f_y(v) = 42v^5 \int_v^1 dw,$$

which gives $f_y(v) = 42v^5(1-v)$ for $0 < v < 1$ and 0 elsewhere. Finally,

$$f_z(w) = 42 \int_0^w u^2(w^3 - u^3)\,du \quad \text{or} \quad f_z(w) = 42 \int_0^w v^5\,dv,$$

so that $f_z(w) = 7w^6$ for $0 < w < 1$ and 0 elsewhere.
(d) The joint density function of (x, y, z) does not depend on the realization w of z. One may therefore be tempted to conclude that z is independent of (x, y), but this is not the case because here $f_z(w)f_{x,y}(u, v) \neq f(u, v, w)$. Furthermore, the domain of definition of $f(u, v, w)$ shows the interaction (inequality) of w with u and v. The same logic can also be used to show that $f_{y,z}(v, w) = 42v^5$ does not imply the independence of z from y.

Exercise 5.14 (Bivariate and beta) The joint p.d.f. of (x, y, z) is

$$f(u, v, w) = \begin{cases} 72u(1-v)w^2 & (0 < u < v < 1,\ 0 < w < 1), \\ 0 & \text{(elsewhere)}. \end{cases}$$

(a) Derive $f_{x,y}(u, v)$ and $f_{x,z}(u, w)$.
(b) Derive the marginal densities of x, y, and z.
(c) Is z independent of (x, y)? Is it independent of x?

Solution
(a) By integrating $f(u, v, w)$ over w, we find

$$f_{x,y}(u, v) = 72u(1-v) \int_0^1 w^2\,dw = 24u(1-v)$$

for $0 < u < v < 1$ and 0 elsewhere. Similarly, by integrating $f(u, v, w)$ over v,

$$f_{x,z}(u, w) = 72uw^2 \int_u^1 (1-v)\,dv = 36u(1-u)^2w^2$$

for $0 < u < 1, 0 < w < 1$ and 0 elsewhere.
(b) Using the results in (a), we can obtain the first marginal density in two ways since, for $0 < u < 1$,

$$f_x(u) = 24u \int_u^1 (1-v)\,dv \quad \text{and also} \quad f_x(u) = 36u(1-u)^2 \int_0^1 w^2\,dw.$$

In either case, $f_x(u) = 12u(1-u)^2$ for $0 < u < 1$ and 0 elsewhere. The other two marginal densities are

$$f_y(v) = 24(1-v)\int_0^v u\,\mathrm{d}u = 12v^2(1-v)$$

for $0 < v < 1$ and 0 elsewhere; and

$$f_z(w) = 36w^2 \int_0^1 u(1-u)^2\,\mathrm{d}u = 3w^2$$

for $0 < w < 1$ and 0 elsewhere.
(c) Notice that w is unrelated to u and v in the domain of definition of the density, unlike in Exercise 5.13. The joint density $f(u, v, w)$ factors into $f_{x,y}(u, v)f_z(w)$, which was clear from the outset. The independence of z and x follows in the same way from $f_{x,z}(u, w)$; see also Exercise 5.18.

Exercise 5.15 (Bivariate and uniform) The joint p.d.f. of (x, y, z) is

$$f(u, v, w) = \begin{cases} cuv^2 & (0 < u < v < 1,\ 0 < w < 1), \\ 0 & (\text{elsewhere}). \end{cases}$$

(a) Compute c, $f_y(v)$, and $f_z(w)$.
(b) Derive the c.d.f. $F_{x,y}(u, v)$.

Solution
(a) We first compute c. Since

$$\begin{aligned}\int_0^1\int_u^1\int_0^1 uv^2\,\mathrm{d}w\,\mathrm{d}v\,\mathrm{d}u &= \int_0^1 u\int_u^1 v^2\,\mathrm{d}v\,\mathrm{d}u \\ &= \frac{1}{3}\int_0^1 u(1-u^3)\,\mathrm{d}u = \frac{1}{6} - \frac{1}{15} = \frac{1}{10},\end{aligned}$$

we find $c = 10$. Next,

$$f_y(v) = 10v^2 \int_0^v u\int_0^1 \mathrm{d}w\,\mathrm{d}u = 5v^4$$

for $0 < v < 1$ and 0 elsewhere. Clearly, $z \sim \mathrm{U}_{(0,1)}$ is independent of (x, y), since its domain of definition does not depend on them and the joint density factorizes into $1 \times f_{x,y}(u, v)$.
(b) The joint density of (x, y) is $f_{x,y}(u, v) = 10uv^2$ for $0 < u < v < 1$ and 0 elsewhere. To find the c.d.f., we have to distinguish between different cases where each argument (u or v) does or does not fall within the support of the p.d.f.. First, if $0 < u < v < 1$,

$$\begin{aligned}F_{x,y}(u, v) &= 10\int_0^u\int_s^v st^2\,\mathrm{d}t\,\mathrm{d}s \\ &= \frac{10}{3}\int_0^u s(v^3 - s^3)\,\mathrm{d}s = \frac{10}{6}u^2v^3 - \frac{10}{15}u^5 = \frac{u^2}{3}(5v^3 - 2u^3).\end{aligned}$$

Next, if $0 < u < 1, v \geqslant 1$, then

$$F_{x,y}(u,v) = F_{x,y}(u,1) = \frac{u^2}{3}(5 - 2u^3),$$

and, if $0 < v < 1, u \geqslant v$, then

$$F_{x,y}(u,v) = F_{x,y}(v,v) = v^5.$$

Finally, $F_{x,y}(u,v) = 0$ if either $u \leqslant 0$ or $v \leqslant 0$, and $F_{x,y}(u,v) = 1$ if both $u \geqslant 1$ and $v \geqslant 1$.

5.4 Distribution functions and independence of variates

Exercise 5.16 (Probability of equality for continuous independent) Let x, y be two independent continuous variates. Show that $\Pr(x = y) = 0$. What if only one of the variates is continuous? [Hint: Use the mixing decomposition first introduced in Chapter 2 to derive the c.d.f. of $z := x - y$.]

Solution
For $z := x - y$, we have

$$\Pr(z \leqslant w) = \Pr(x \leqslant y + w) = \int_{-\infty}^{\infty} \Pr(x \leqslant v + w \mid y = v) \, \mathrm{d}F_y(v)$$

as in, for example, some of the exercises in Section 4.2 and Exercise 5.7. The independence of x, y gives $\Pr(z \leqslant w) = \int_{-\infty}^{\infty} \Pr(x \leqslant v + w) \, \mathrm{d}F_y(v)$. Then,

$$\begin{aligned}\Pr(x = y) &= \Pr(z = 0) = \Pr(z \leqslant 0) - \Pr(z < 0) \\ &= \int_{-\infty}^{\infty} (\Pr(x \leqslant v) - \Pr(x < v)) \, \mathrm{d}F_y(v) = 0\end{aligned}$$

since $\Pr(x \leqslant v) = \Pr(x < v)$ by the continuity of x. The proof makes use of the continuity of only one of the variates (the roles of x, y may be reversed if needed), so the result also applies to the case where only one of the variates is continuous.

Exercise 5.17 (Joint independence) Let $\boldsymbol{x} := (x_1, \dots, x_m)'$ have the joint density $f(\boldsymbol{w})$. Prove that $f(\boldsymbol{w}) = \prod_{j=1}^{m} f_j(w_j)$ for all $\boldsymbol{w}$ if and only if all the nonoverlapping subsets of $\boldsymbol{x}$ are mutually independent.

Solution
Recall the sequential conditioning that was introduced in Chapter 1 (see Exercise 1.25),

and use it to write the joint distribution as

$$\begin{aligned}\Pr(x_1 \leqslant w_1, \dots, x_m \leqslant w_m) \\ = \Pr(x_1 \leqslant w_1) \prod_{j=2}^{m} \Pr\left(x_j \leqslant w_j \mid x_{j-1} \leqslant w_{j-1}, \dots, x_1 \leqslant w_1\right).\end{aligned}$$

The conditioning terms can be dropped (sequentially) if and only if x_j is independent of $(x_{j-1}, \dots, x_1)$ for any ordering of the m variates, in which case we can write the equivalent form of the c.d.f.:

$$F(\boldsymbol{w}) = \prod_{j=1}^{m} F_j(w_j).$$

The Radon–Nikodym derivative of both sides is the required result. Alternatively, one may difference or differentiate both sides to get the p.d.f. in the discrete or continuous cases, respectively.

There are a few things to stress here. First, the independence of x_j from $(x_{j-1}, \dots, x_1)$ is a stronger requirement than the independence of x_j from x_i, for all $i < j$, as will be shown in Exercise 5.18; see also Chapter 1. Second, this independence has to hold for *any* choice of $j-1$ components to condition on. Third, the factorization into the product of marginals has to hold for all $\boldsymbol{w}$, and this implies that the domains of definition for the marginal densities must all be unrelated; that is, $\mathcal{X}$ factors into the Cartesian product of $\mathcal{X}_j$, where $\mathcal{X}_j$ is the support for x_j.

***Exercise 5.18 (Subset independence)** Let $\boldsymbol{x} := (x_1, \dots, x_m)'$, with $m > 2$ and joint distribution $F(\boldsymbol{w})$. Prove that

$$F(\boldsymbol{w}) = F_1(w_1) \times F_{2,\dots,m}(w_2, \dots, w_m) \quad \text{(for all } \boldsymbol{w}\text{)}$$

is a sufficient but not a necessary condition for

$$\begin{gathered} x_1 \text{ independent of } x_2, \\ \vdots \\ x_1 \text{ independent of } x_m; \end{gathered}$$

in other words, that the vector $(x_2, \dots, x_m)$ is jointly independent of x_1 implies, but is not implied by, x_1 being *pairwise* independent of each of $x_2, \dots, x_m$.

Solution

The sufficiency proof is easy, since

$$F(\boldsymbol{w}) = F_1(w_1) \times F_{2,\dots,m}(w_2, \dots, w_m)$$

implies that

$$\begin{aligned} F_{1,j}(w_1, w_j) &= F(w_1, \infty, \dots, \infty, w_j, \infty, \dots, \infty) \\ &= F_1(w_1) \times F_{2,\dots,m}(\infty, \dots, \infty, w_j, \infty, \dots, \infty) = F_1(w_1) \times F_j(w_j) \end{aligned}$$

for $j = 2, \ldots, m$. Pairwise independence, however, does not imply joint independence: see the counterexample in Exercise 1.22. The relation

$$F_{1,j}(w_1, w_j) = F_1(w_1) \times F_j(w_j)$$

implies a factorization of $F(w_1, \infty, \ldots, \infty, w_j, \infty, \ldots, \infty)$, but there is no reason why it should imply anything about a factorization of the general $F(\boldsymbol{w})$ where more than two elements of $\boldsymbol{w}$ can be simultaneously finite.

Exercise 5.19 (Copulas) Define implicitly the *copula function* C by

$$F(\boldsymbol{w}) = C(F_1(w_1), \ldots, F_m(w_m)),$$

where $F(\boldsymbol{w})$ is the c.d.f. of $\boldsymbol{x}$ and $F_j(w_j)$ are its marginals, $j = 1, \ldots, m$. It is the function representing the dependence structure, by transforming the m separate marginals into a joint distribution. Prove that:
(a) $C = 0$ if any of its arguments is 0;
(b) $C(a, 1, \ldots, 1) = a$;
(c) C is nondecreasing in any one of its arguments;
(d) $[[C(a_1, \ldots, a_m)]_{s_1}^{t_1} \ldots]_{s_m}^{t_m} \geqslant 0$ for $s_j, t_j \in [0, 1]$ and $s_j < t_j$;
(e) the joint independence of $\boldsymbol{x}$ is equivalent to $C(a_1, \ldots, a_m) = \prod_{j=1}^{m} a_j$.

Solution
(a) The arguments of C are marginal c.d.f.s. If the j-th argument is zero, then the event $\{x_j : x_j \leqslant w_j\}$ has zero probability and, a fortiori, the composite event $\{\boldsymbol{x} : \boldsymbol{x} \leqslant \boldsymbol{w}\}$ has $\Pr(\boldsymbol{x} \leqslant \boldsymbol{w}) = 0$.
(b) If $F_j(w_j) = 1$ for $j = 2, \ldots, m$, then $\Pr(x_j > w_j) = 0$ and the event

$$\{x_1 : x_1 > w_1\} \cup \{x_2 : x_2 > w_2\} \cup \cdots \cup \{x_m : x_m > w_m\}$$

has the same probability as $\{x_1 : x_1 > w_1\}$. In other words,

$$1 - F(\boldsymbol{w}) = 1 - F_1(w_1)$$

and $F_1(w_1) = F(\boldsymbol{w}) = C(F_1(w_1), 1, \ldots, 1)$ as required.
(c) Recall that any specific marginal $F_j(w_j) := \Pr(x_j \leqslant w_j)$ is a nondecreasing function of w_j, and that the joint $F(\boldsymbol{w})$ is also a nondecreasing function of w_j, other things being equal. Therefore, an increase in the j-th argument of the function C occurs only if (that is, it implies that) w_j increases, which in turn has a nondecreasing effect on the joint c.d.f. $F(\boldsymbol{w}) = C(\cdot)$.
(d) This follows by the same logic as in (c), coupled with property (iv) of c.d.f.s given in the introduction to this chapter, namely that the probability of $\boldsymbol{x}$ falling in a hyperrectangle is nonnegative.
(e) This follows from Exercise 5.17. Deviations from independence can be measured by how far the C function is from the product form $\prod_{j=1}^{m} a_j$, which is known as the *independence copula*. In fact, for continuous variates, the implicit definition of the copula can be

differentiated (by the chain rule) to yield

$$f(\boldsymbol{w}) = c(F_1(w_1), \dots, F_m(w_m)) \prod_{j=1}^{m} f_j(w_j),$$

where

$$c(a_1, \dots, a_m) := \frac{\partial^m}{\partial a_1 \dots \partial a_m} C(a_1, \dots, a_m)$$

measures the extent of deviation from $\prod_{j=1}^{m} f_j(w_j)$, the independence factorization of $f(\boldsymbol{w})$. Further properties will be established in Exercise 7.40.

Notes

General references for this chapter are the same as for Chapter 2. For further results on the copulas of Exercise 5.19, see Schweizer and Sklar (1983), Joe (1997), and Nelsen (1999).

In this chapter and the next, some joint densities (that do not factor into products of independent marginals) have elaborate names which we have not used in labeling the corresponding exercises. This is because of the different (and usually not nested) ways that dependence structures can be modeled. For example, the "gamma marginals" of Exercise 5.10 is known as *McKay's bivariate gamma*, to distinguish it from other types of bivariate gamma distributions, of which there are many. Also, Exercise 5.8 introduces a special and scaled case of the *standard Dirichlet* density

$$f_{\boldsymbol{x}}(\boldsymbol{w}) = \frac{\Gamma(\sum_{i=1}^{m+1} p_i)}{\prod_{i=1}^{m+1} \Gamma(p_i)} \left(\prod_{i=1}^{m} w_i^{p_i - 1} \right) \left(1 - \sum_{i=1}^{m} w_i \right)^{p_{m+1}-1}$$

for $\boldsymbol{w} > \mathbf{0}_m$, $\boldsymbol{\imath}_m' \boldsymbol{w} < 1$, and $\boldsymbol{p} > \mathbf{0}_{m+1}$, with $f_{\boldsymbol{x}}(\boldsymbol{w}) = 0$ otherwise; it generalizes the standard beta differently from the "bivariate beta" of Exercises 5.6 and 5.7. See Johnson, Kotz, and Balakrishnan (1997) and Kotz, Balakrishnan, and Johnson (2000) for more details. Other examples include "quadratic" densities, which belong to inverse Pareto variates in disguise! For an example of the construction of densities with dependent domains of definition, see Exercise 7.17. Finally, the multivariate generalization of the exponential family of Chapter 4 will be studied in Exercise 11.15, rather than in Chapters 5 and 6.

The last sentence of the solution of Exercise 5.17 has touched on an issue that we will not explore further in this volume, regarding the definition of a joint probability space. We direct the interested reader to the references in the Notes to Chapter 1, where we have also mentioned a related point. The summary of the point at issue is the following. A probability space $(\Omega, \mathcal{F}, \Pr(\cdot))$ is said to be *complete* if all subsets of events having zero probability (see the discussion around (2.6) in the introduction to Chapter 2) are also events. To define a joint probability may require a completion of the space by finding the smallest sigma field of joint events $\mathcal{F}_1 \times \mathcal{F}_2 \times \cdots$.

6

Conditioning, dependence, and joint moments

In this chapter, we consider how to measure the extent of the dependence between variates, exploiting the additional information contained in joint (rather than just marginal) distribution and density functions. For this multivariate context, we also generalize the third description of randomness seen earlier, namely moments and their generating functions, which we then use to measure dependence.

We start with the bivariate case. Define $\boldsymbol{x} := (x, y)' \in \mathcal{X}$, with joint distribution function $F_{x,y}(u, v)$. The probability $F_{y|x=u}(v) := \Pr(y \leqslant v \mid x = u)$ is called the *c.d.f. of y given* (or *conditional on*) x, sometimes also denoted by $F_y(v \mid x = u)$, and it satisfies

$$F_{x,y}(u, v) = \Pr(x \leqslant u, y \leqslant v) = \begin{cases} \sum_{t \leqslant u} \Pr(y \leqslant v \mid x = t) f_x(t) & (x \text{ discrete}), \\ \int_{t \leqslant u} \Pr(y \leqslant v \mid x = t) f_x(t)\,\mathrm{d}t & (x \text{ continuous}), \end{cases}$$

$$= \int_{t \leqslant u} F_{y|x=t}(v)\,\mathrm{d}F_x(t). \tag{6.1}$$

The comment about integral equations made after (2.5) applies here too for $F_{y|x=t}(v)$ in the continuous case, bearing in mind that we also need any conditional c.d.f. to obey the usual four rules for a proper distribution as a function of its argument v for all types of variates (Exercise 6.25). The special case of the independence of y from x simplifies

$$F_{y|x=u}(v) = \Pr(y \leqslant v \mid x = u) = \Pr(y \leqslant v) = F_y(v)$$

for all u, v. Note that, in the conditional c.d.f. introduced in (6.1), x is presumed to take the single value $x = t$, rather than $x \leqslant t$. We have already seen (6.1) for $u \to \infty$ in Chapter 2 when we introduced the concept of mixing, in which case we obtained the *marginal* or *unconditional c.d.f.* $F_{x,y}(\infty, v) = F_y(v)$.

Differencing (for a discrete r.v.) or differentiating (for a continuous r.v.) both sides of (6.1) with respect to u, v gives the corresponding $f_{y|x=u}(v)$, called the *p.d.f. of y given x*

(or *of y conditional on x*) as

$$f_{x,y}(u,v) = f_{y|x=u}(v) f_x(u), \tag{6.2}$$

with the interpretation that $f_{y|x=u}(v) = \Pr(y = v \mid x = u)$ in the case of discrete y, whereas $f_{y|x=u}(v) = \mathrm{d}F_{y|x=u}(v)/\mathrm{d}v$ in the case of continuous y (see Exercise 6.26 for x, y continuous). Notice that this is a p.d.f. for the variate y which, if continuous, has $\Pr(y = v \mid \cdot) = 0$. It would therefore not be correct to equate $f_{y|x=u}(v)$ to $\Pr(y = v \mid x = u)$ in the continuous case. (In fact, one should also be cautious in interpreting the conditioning on events having probability 0, if $x = u$ is such an event, as Exercise 7.20 will illustrate in the next chapter.) It follows from (6.2) that the random variable $y \mid x = u$ is almost surely unique if $f_x(u) \neq 0$, and the conditional density $f_{y|x=u}(u)$ cannot be determined if $f_x(u) = 0$. The reason for the qualifier "almost surely" is the issue of the uniqueness of solutions to integral equations, as discussed following (2.5).

Like its c.d.f. counterpart, the conditional p.d.f. obeys all the rules of a proper density function. The *marginal* or *unconditional p.d.f.*, $f_y(v)$, is obtained by taking the mean of $f_{y|x=u}(v)$ over all possible outcomes u, namely

$$f_y(v) = \mathrm{E}_x\left(f_{y|x}(v)\right) = \int_{-\infty}^{\infty} f_{y|x=u}(v)\,\mathrm{d}F_x(u), \tag{6.3}$$

where $\mathrm{E}_x(\cdot)$ indicates that the expectation is taken with respect to x; again, see the discussion of mixing in Chapter 2 and its reformulation in (3.6). Observe that the argument of the expectation is $f_{y|x}(v)$, which is a function of the random x, unlike in $f_{y|x=u}(v)$ where x is fixed to the value u. We will normally abbreviate $f_{y|x=u}(v)$ to $f_{y|u}(v)$, unless there is potential for misunderstanding, and similarly for the conditional c.d.f.s. Another common notation is $f_y(v \mid x = u)$ or $f_y(v \mid u)$. Note that, like (6.1), the formulation (6.3) applies to any combination of types of variates; for example, x discrete and y continuous.

We can generalize the definitions of conditional distributions and densities to the multivariate case. Partition the transpose of the m-dimensional vector variate $\boldsymbol{x}$ into $\boldsymbol{x}' := (\boldsymbol{x}_1', \boldsymbol{x}_2')$ with dimensions $k > 0$ and $m - k > 0$, and its realization $\boldsymbol{w}' := (\boldsymbol{w}_1', \boldsymbol{w}_2')$ accordingly. Then, $F_{\boldsymbol{x}_2|\boldsymbol{w}_1}(\boldsymbol{w}_2) := \Pr(\boldsymbol{x}_2 \leqslant \boldsymbol{w}_2 \mid \boldsymbol{x}_1 = \boldsymbol{w}_1)$. The case of discrete $\boldsymbol{x}$ gives $f_{\boldsymbol{x}_2|\boldsymbol{w}_1}(\boldsymbol{w}_2) = \Pr(\boldsymbol{x}_2 = \boldsymbol{w}_2 \mid \boldsymbol{x}_1 = \boldsymbol{w}_1)$, while $\boldsymbol{x}$ absolutely continuous gives

$$f_{\boldsymbol{x}_2|\boldsymbol{w}_1}(\boldsymbol{w}_2) = \frac{\partial^{m-k}}{\partial w_{k+1} \dots \partial w_m} F_{\boldsymbol{x}_2|\boldsymbol{w}_1}(\boldsymbol{w}_2).$$

The marginal or unconditional counterparts are obtained by taking the mean of the conditional $f_{\boldsymbol{x}_2|\boldsymbol{x}_1}(\boldsymbol{w}_2)$ over all possible values $\boldsymbol{x}_1 = \boldsymbol{w}_1$.

It remains for us to extend the multivariate definitions to moments and their generating functions. The expectation of the vector variate $\boldsymbol{x}$ is

$$\mathrm{E}(\boldsymbol{x}) \equiv \mathrm{E}\begin{pmatrix} x_1 \\ \vdots \\ x_m \end{pmatrix} := \begin{pmatrix} \mathrm{E}(x_1) \\ \vdots \\ \mathrm{E}(x_m) \end{pmatrix}.$$

This vector is usually denoted by $\boldsymbol{\mu}$ with typical element μ_i, and is said to exist if all m univariate means exist. This does not conflict with the notation we use for the j-th raw moment of component x_i, written as $\mu_i^{(j)}$. The definition implies that, using the transpose operator,

$$(\mathrm{E}(\boldsymbol{x}))' = (\mathrm{E}(x_1), \ldots, \mathrm{E}(x_m)) = \mathrm{E}(\boldsymbol{x}'),$$

and similarly for the interchange of $\mathrm{E}(\cdot)$ with the linear sum and trace $\mathrm{tr}(\cdot)$ operators (see Exercises 6.3 and 6.6 for illustrations); but see the proviso in the discussion after (3.4) for exceptions relating to interchanges of linear operators. This brings us to the formulation of $\mathrm{E}(\boldsymbol{x})$ in terms of $F_{\boldsymbol{x}}$: the mean vector is obtained as $\int_{\boldsymbol{w}\in\mathbb{R}^m} \boldsymbol{w}\, \mathrm{d}F_{\boldsymbol{x}}(\boldsymbol{w})$, or

$$\mathrm{E}(\boldsymbol{x}) = \begin{pmatrix} \mathrm{E}(x_1) \\ \vdots \\ \mathrm{E}(x_m) \end{pmatrix} = \begin{pmatrix} \int_{-\infty}^{\infty} w_1\, \mathrm{d}F_1(w_1) \\ \vdots \\ \int_{-\infty}^{\infty} w_m\, \mathrm{d}F_m(w_m) \end{pmatrix},$$

where the last equality shows that, in the case of the mean, there is nothing to be gained from knowledge of the interaction of the elements of $\boldsymbol{x}$ through the joint c.d.f. (as opposed to knowing simply the marginal c.d.f.s). This is no longer the case for any higher-order moment. The $m \times m$ symmetric matrix of the second central moments, often denoted by $\boldsymbol{\Sigma}$ with typical element σ_{ij} (with $\sigma_i^2 := \sigma_{ii}$ for the diagonal), is

$$\begin{aligned}
\mathrm{var}(\boldsymbol{x}) &:= \mathrm{E}\left((\boldsymbol{x}-\boldsymbol{\mu})(\boldsymbol{x}-\boldsymbol{\mu})'\right) \\
&= \mathrm{E}\left[\begin{pmatrix} x_1-\mu_1 \\ \vdots \\ x_m-\mu_m \end{pmatrix}\left(x_1-\mu_1, \ldots, x_m-\mu_m\right)\right] \\
&= \begin{pmatrix} \mathrm{E}\left[(x_1-\mu_1)(x_1-\mu_1)\right] & \ldots & \mathrm{E}\left[(x_1-\mu_1)(x_m-\mu_m)\right] \\ \vdots & & \vdots \\ \mathrm{E}\left[(x_m-\mu_m)(x_1-\mu_1)\right] & \ldots & \mathrm{E}\left[(x_m-\mu_m)(x_m-\mu_m)\right] \end{pmatrix},
\end{aligned}$$

where $(\boldsymbol{x}-\boldsymbol{\mu})(\boldsymbol{x}-\boldsymbol{\mu})'$ is the *outer product* of the vector $(\boldsymbol{x}-\boldsymbol{\mu})$ with itself.[1] The variance is also expressible as $\int_{\boldsymbol{w}\in\mathbb{R}^m} (\boldsymbol{w}-\boldsymbol{\mu})(\boldsymbol{w}-\boldsymbol{\mu})'\, \mathrm{d}F_{\boldsymbol{x}}(\boldsymbol{w})$. The diagonal elements are the familiar $\mathrm{E}\left((x_i-\mu_i)^2\right) = \mathrm{var}(x_i)$. The off-diagonal elements are the *covariances* of the elements of $\boldsymbol{x}$ and are denoted by $\mathrm{cov}(x_i, x_j) := \mathrm{E}\left((x_i-\mu_i)(x_j-\mu_j)\right)$. Covariances are defined for vectors too:

$$\begin{aligned}
\mathrm{cov}(\boldsymbol{x}_1, \boldsymbol{x}_2) &:= \mathrm{E}\left((\boldsymbol{x}_1-\boldsymbol{\mu}_1)(\boldsymbol{x}_2-\boldsymbol{\mu}_2)'\right) \\
&= \mathrm{E}\left(\boldsymbol{x}_1\boldsymbol{x}_2' - \boldsymbol{\mu}_1\boldsymbol{x}_2' - \boldsymbol{x}_1\boldsymbol{\mu}_2' + \boldsymbol{\mu}_1\boldsymbol{\mu}_2'\right) \\
&= \mathrm{E}\left(\boldsymbol{x}_1\boldsymbol{x}_2'\right) - \boldsymbol{\mu}_1\mathrm{E}\left(\boldsymbol{x}_2'\right) - \mathrm{E}(\boldsymbol{x}_1)\boldsymbol{\mu}_2' + \boldsymbol{\mu}_1\boldsymbol{\mu}_2' = \mathrm{E}\left(\boldsymbol{x}_1\boldsymbol{x}_2'\right) - \boldsymbol{\mu}_1\boldsymbol{\mu}_2'.
\end{aligned}$$

[1]We actually define the variance as the expectation of an outer product, regardless of whether the variate is a column or a row vector, so we have $\mathrm{var}(\boldsymbol{x}') = \mathrm{var}(\boldsymbol{x})$ as the same $m \times m$ matrix.

Note that this is also equal to either $\mathrm{E}((\boldsymbol{x}_1-\boldsymbol{\mu}_1)\boldsymbol{x}_2')$ or $\mathrm{E}\left(\boldsymbol{x}_1(\boldsymbol{x}_2-\boldsymbol{\mu}_2)'\right)$, and is expressible as $\int_{\boldsymbol{w}\in\mathbb{R}^m}(\boldsymbol{w}_1-\boldsymbol{\mu}_1)(\boldsymbol{w}_2-\boldsymbol{\mu}_2)'\,\mathrm{d}F_{\boldsymbol{x}}(\boldsymbol{w})$.[2] Similar derivations imply the linearity property (when these moments exist):

$$\operatorname{cov}(\boldsymbol{x}_1+\boldsymbol{A}\boldsymbol{y}_1,\boldsymbol{x}_2)=\operatorname{cov}(\boldsymbol{x}_1,\boldsymbol{x}_2)+\operatorname{cov}(\boldsymbol{A}\boldsymbol{y}_1,\boldsymbol{x}_2)=\operatorname{cov}(\boldsymbol{x}_1,\boldsymbol{x}_2)+\boldsymbol{A}\operatorname{cov}(\boldsymbol{y}_1,\boldsymbol{x}_2)$$

for $\boldsymbol{x}_1$ of the same dimension as $\boldsymbol{A}\boldsymbol{y}_1$ with $\boldsymbol{A}$ nonrandom. A large and positive (resp. negative) $\operatorname{cov}(x_i,x_j)$ arises if a large $(x_i-\mu_i)$ is associated often enough with a large $(x_j-\mu_j)$ of the same (resp. opposite) sign. The covariance is closer to zero if no such associations exist. There are two limitations to this simple measure of dependence, and these are now tackled.

First, like variances (see Exercise 3.15), covariances are location-invariant but not scale-invariant. Defining $\boldsymbol{y}:=100\boldsymbol{x}$ (for example, changing the units from meters to centimeters) gives

$$\begin{aligned}\operatorname{var}(\boldsymbol{y})&=\mathrm{E}\left((\boldsymbol{y}-\mathrm{E}(\boldsymbol{y}))(\boldsymbol{y}-\mathrm{E}(\boldsymbol{y}))'\right)\\&=\mathrm{E}\left((100)^2(\boldsymbol{x}-\mathrm{E}(\boldsymbol{x}))(\boldsymbol{x}-\mathrm{E}(\boldsymbol{x}))'\right)=(100)^2\operatorname{var}(\boldsymbol{x}),\end{aligned}$$

where all the elements of the matrix $\operatorname{var}(\boldsymbol{x})$ have been rescaled by $(100)^2$. Since the diagonal elements (variances) have been rescaled to the same extent as the off-diagonal elements (covariances), one could obtain the location-invariant *and* scale-invariant *correlation coefficient*

$$\operatorname{corr}(x_i,x_j):=\frac{\operatorname{cov}(x_i,x_j)}{\sqrt{\operatorname{var}(x_i)\times\operatorname{var}(x_j)}}\qquad(\operatorname{var}(x_i),\operatorname{var}(x_j)\neq 0),$$

also denoted by ρ_{x_i,x_j} or $\rho_{i,j}$, dropping the subscript of ρ altogether when the context is clear; however, we use corr instead of ρ when the argument is too elaborate to display in a subscript. The variance matrix introduced earlier can be rewritten in terms of correlations, in such a way that the typical element is $\rho_{ij}\sigma_i\sigma_j$. Correlation measures the strength of the relation between the linear functions $(x_i-\mu_i)$ and $(x_j-\mu_j)$ on a standardized scale of $[-100\%,100\%]$. The bound $|\rho|\leqslant 1$ is the statistical formulation of the *Cauchy–Schwarz inequality* (Exercise 6.20), and a linear relation holds with probability 1 between x_i and x_j whenever $|\rho|=1$, in which case x_i,x_j are said to be *perfectly correlated* or *collinear*. More generally, the magnitude of ρ indicates the strength of the linear relation, while the sign of ρ indicates whether the variates are positively or negatively related. The case $\rho=0$ indicates the absence of a linear relation between the variates, which are then said to be *uncorrelated* or *orthogonal*. The geometrical terms "collinear" and "orthogonal" will be clarified at the end of Exercise 6.20, where we will also see that $\rho^2\leqslant 1$ or

$$(\operatorname{cov}(x_i,x_j))^2\leqslant\operatorname{var}(x_i)\operatorname{var}(x_j)$$

[2]Contrasting with the previous footnote, $\operatorname{cov}(\boldsymbol{x}_2,\boldsymbol{x}_1)=(\operatorname{cov}(\boldsymbol{x}_1,\boldsymbol{x}_2))'\neq\operatorname{cov}(\boldsymbol{x}_1,\boldsymbol{x}_2)$ in general. This matrix is not even square when $k\neq m-k$. Therefore, the ordering of the arguments $\boldsymbol{x}_1$ and $\boldsymbol{x}_2$ of $\operatorname{cov}(\boldsymbol{x}_1,\boldsymbol{x}_2)$ matters when these are different vectors.

implies that $\text{cov}(x_i, x_j)$ is finite whenever the variances of x_i, x_j exist (Exercise 6.3 extends this inequality to show that $\text{var}(\boldsymbol{x})$ is positive semidefinite.) Note that the Cauchy–Schwarz inequality bounds a moment of the joint distribution by moments of the marginals. If one variate is degenerate, say $x_i = \mu_i$ almost surely, then

$$\text{cov}(x_i, x_j) \equiv \mathrm{E}\left((x_i - \mu_i)(x_j - \mu_j)\right) = 0$$

since $(x_i - \mu_i) = 0$ with probability 1. In this case, $\text{var}(x_i) = 0$ also, but we take $\rho_{ij} = 0$ by convention.

Second, we have already alluded to the fact that only the linear relation of x_i to x_j is measured in $\mathrm{E}\left((x_i - \mu_i)(x_j - \mu_j)\right)$ where the powers of $(x_i - \mu_i)$ and $(x_j - \mu_j)$ are 1. Linear independence does not preclude other forms of dependence; see Exercises 6.13 and 6.29, the latter giving an alternative representation for covariances. We have seen that $\text{cov}(x_i, x_j) = \mathrm{E}(x_i x_j) - \mathrm{E}(x_i)\,\mathrm{E}(x_j)$, so

$$\text{cov}(x_i, x_j) = 0 \iff \mathrm{E}(x_i x_j) = \mathrm{E}(x_i)\,\mathrm{E}(x_j).$$

The latter factorization of expectations is necessary (*if* these moments exist) but not sufficient for the independence of x_i and x_j. In general, it is not enough for the first moment of $\prod_{i=1}^m x_i$ to satisfy

$$\mathrm{E}\left(\prod_{i=1}^m x_i\right) = \prod_{i=1}^m \mathrm{E}(x_i)$$

for the x_i's to be independent. This brings us to the topic of higher-order multivariate moments, m.g.f.s, and c.f.s.

Letting $\boldsymbol{\tau} := (\tau_1, \dots, \tau_m)'$, the *joint c.f.* of $\boldsymbol{x}$ is defined by

$$\varphi_{\boldsymbol{x}}(\boldsymbol{\tau}) := \mathrm{E}\left(\mathrm{e}^{\mathrm{i}\boldsymbol{\tau}'\boldsymbol{x}}\right) = \mathrm{E}\left(\mathrm{e}^{\mathrm{i}\tau_1 x_1 + \dots + \mathrm{i}\tau_m x_m}\right) = \int_{\boldsymbol{w}\in\mathbb{R}^m} \mathrm{e}^{\mathrm{i}\boldsymbol{\tau}'\boldsymbol{w}}\,\mathrm{d}F_{\boldsymbol{x}}(\boldsymbol{w}), \tag{6.4}$$

and the *joint m.g.f.* is $m_{\boldsymbol{x}}(\boldsymbol{t}) := \mathrm{E}(\mathrm{e}^{\boldsymbol{t}'\boldsymbol{x}})$ when the expectation exists. As in the univariate case, the moments are obtained by differentiating the m.g.f.; for example, the first two are

$$\left.\frac{\partial m_{\boldsymbol{x}}(\boldsymbol{t})}{\partial \boldsymbol{t}}\right|_{\boldsymbol{t}=\mathbf{0}} = \mathrm{E}\left(\frac{\partial \mathrm{e}^{\boldsymbol{t}'\boldsymbol{x}}}{\partial \boldsymbol{t}}\right)\Bigg|_{\boldsymbol{t}=\mathbf{0}} = \mathrm{E}\left(\boldsymbol{x}\mathrm{e}^{\boldsymbol{t}'\boldsymbol{x}}\right)\Big|_{\boldsymbol{t}=\mathbf{0}} = \mathrm{E}(\boldsymbol{x})$$

and, since $\boldsymbol{t}'\boldsymbol{x} = \sum_{i=1}^m t_i x_i = \boldsymbol{x}'\boldsymbol{t}$,

$$\left.\frac{\partial^2 m_{\boldsymbol{x}}(\boldsymbol{t})}{\partial \boldsymbol{t}\,\partial \boldsymbol{t}'}\right|_{\boldsymbol{t}=\mathbf{0}} = \left.\frac{\partial\,\mathrm{E}\left(\boldsymbol{x}\mathrm{e}^{\boldsymbol{x}'\boldsymbol{t}}\right)}{\partial \boldsymbol{t}'}\right|_{\boldsymbol{t}=\mathbf{0}} = \mathrm{E}\left(\boldsymbol{x}\boldsymbol{x}'\mathrm{e}^{\boldsymbol{t}'\boldsymbol{x}}\right)\Big|_{\boldsymbol{t}=\mathbf{0}} = \mathrm{E}(\boldsymbol{x}\boldsymbol{x}');$$

see Section A.4 for vector derivatives. The c.f. is in one-to-one correspondence with the p.d.f. and c.d.f., as in the scalar case. When $\boldsymbol{x}$ is a continuous variate,

$$f_{\boldsymbol{x}}(\boldsymbol{w}) = \mathcal{F}_{\boldsymbol{w}}^{-1}\{\varphi_{\boldsymbol{x}}(\boldsymbol{\tau})\} := (2\pi)^{-m}\int_{\boldsymbol{\tau}\in\mathbb{R}^m} \mathrm{e}^{-\mathrm{i}\boldsymbol{\tau}'\boldsymbol{w}}\varphi_{\boldsymbol{x}}(\boldsymbol{\tau})\,\mathrm{d}\boldsymbol{\tau}.$$

The *marginal c.f.* of x_1 is obtained as

$$\varphi_1(\tau_1) := \mathrm{E}\left(\mathrm{e}^{\mathrm{i}\tau_1 x_1}\right) = \mathrm{E}\left(\mathrm{e}^{\mathrm{i}\tau_1 x_1 + 0\times x_2 + \cdots + 0\times x_m}\right) = \varphi_{\boldsymbol{x}}\left(\tau_1, 0, \ldots, 0\right).$$

Independence is characterized by the factorization of joint into marginal probabilities (p.d.f. or c.d.f.), and the same applies to the equivalent c.f. formulation:

$$\varphi_{\boldsymbol{x}}(\boldsymbol{\tau}) = \prod_{i=1}^{m} \varphi_i(\tau_i).$$

Otherwise, one should use *conditional c.f.s* or *conditional moments*, these being the same expectations but calculated with conditional c.d.f.s. We will see in Exercise 6.28 how conditioning leads to the *law of iterated expectations* (LIE), which states that, for any two functions g and h,

$$\mathrm{E}\left(g(x)h(x,y)\right) = \mathrm{E}_x\left[g(x)\,\mathrm{E}_{y|x}\left(h(x,y)\right)\right], \tag{6.5}$$

assuming the expectations exist, and where $\mathrm{E}_{y|x}(\cdot)$ denotes the expectation taken with respect to the conditional distribution of $y \mid x$. In other words, when averaging with respect to two variables, fix one (x) and take the average, *then* average with respect to the variable that was initially fixed (x). Notice the use of $y \mid x$ as in (6.3), not $y \mid x = u$ as in (6.2). An alternative notation to $\mathrm{E}_{y|x}(h(x,y))$ is $\mathrm{E}(h(x,y) \mid x)$, but in the latter case it is implicit which variate we take expectations with respect to; see Exercise 6.47(b) for an illustration where care is needed because of this. Both notations apply also to conditional variances and covariances; for example, we will use subscripts for var just as we do for E. If x and y are independent, and if h depends only on y, *then* the LIE becomes

$$\mathrm{E}\left(g(x)h(y)\right) = \mathrm{E}_x\left[g(x)\,\mathrm{E}_{y|x}\left(h(y)\right)\right] = \mathrm{E}_x\left[g(x)\,\mathrm{E}_y\left(h(y)\right)\right] = \mathrm{E}_x\left(g(x)\right)\mathrm{E}_y\left(h(y)\right),$$

which is also implied directly by the factorization of the joint probability into marginal probabilities. Important relations arise from the LIE, such as

$$\mathrm{var}\left(h\left(y\right)\right) = \mathrm{E}_x\left(\mathrm{var}_{y|x}(h\left(y\right))\right) + \mathrm{var}_x\left(\mathrm{E}_{y|x}\left(h\left(y\right)\right)\right);$$

thus, the variance is the average of the conditional variances, plus the variance of the conditional averages. This will be particularly useful not only here but also in Chapter 11.

Conditional covariances can be a powerful tool in attributing linear dependence within the components of a vector. Partition the m-dimensional $\boldsymbol{x}' := (\boldsymbol{x}_1', \boldsymbol{x}_2')$ into $k \geqslant 2$ and $m - k > 0$ components, and let y and z be two elements of $\boldsymbol{x}_1$. Then, the *conditional correlation coefficient*

$$\rho_{y,z|\boldsymbol{x}_2} \equiv \mathrm{corr}\left(y, z \mid \boldsymbol{x}_2\right) := \frac{\mathrm{cov}\left(y, z \mid \boldsymbol{x}_2\right)}{\sqrt{\mathrm{var}\left(y \mid \boldsymbol{x}_2\right) \times \mathrm{var}\left(z \mid \boldsymbol{x}_2\right)}} \tag{6.6}$$

measures the linear relation between y and z, after accounting for the influence of $\boldsymbol{x}_2$ on both variates; see Exercises 6.18, 6.19, and 6.51. (We avoid the more precise but cumbersome notation $\mathrm{corr}((y,z) \mid \boldsymbol{x}_2)$ which stresses that both variates are conditioned on $\boldsymbol{x}_2$.) This is different from $\mathrm{corr}(y, z \mid \boldsymbol{w}_2)$, which measures the linear relation between y and z when $\boldsymbol{x}_2$ is presumed to be known as $\boldsymbol{x}_2 = \boldsymbol{w}_2$, a point mentioned earlier in connection with (6.3) and (6.5).

When m is small, one may visualize some of the dependence between variates by examining their bivariate densities. The *contour plot* of a bivariate density $f_{x,y}(u,v)$ for continuous (x,y) is a plot of the *iso-probability contours* defined by $f_{x,y}(u,v) = \alpha$ for a succession of values $\alpha_1 > \cdots > \alpha_j > 0$. These contours are similar to the wiggly lines in weather maps, or to two-dimensional maps of mountains. An illustration is given in Exercise 6.1.

If the iso-probability contours are circles, or more generally hyperspheres (spheres in m dimensions), then we say that the variate is spherically distributed. Formally, a variate $\boldsymbol{x}$ is *spherically distributed* if $\boldsymbol{x}$ and $\boldsymbol{T}\boldsymbol{x}$ have identical distributions for any orthogonal matrix $\boldsymbol{T}$. The reason is that rotating the vector $\boldsymbol{x}$ or permuting its elements, by premultiplying it with an orthogonal matrix, leaves the location of the iso-probability contours unchanged. Since the contours are spheres, the density varies if and only if there is a change in the value of the inner product $\boldsymbol{w}'\boldsymbol{w}$. Clearly, $\boldsymbol{w}'\boldsymbol{T}'\boldsymbol{T}\boldsymbol{w} = \boldsymbol{w}'\boldsymbol{w}$ for all orthogonal $\boldsymbol{T}$, even if $\boldsymbol{T} \neq \boldsymbol{I}_m$ (the symbol $\boldsymbol{I}_m$ denotes the identity matrix of order m).

A more general class of densities for $\boldsymbol{x}$ is obtained if the iso-probability contours are ellipses centered around a point $\boldsymbol{c}$, with the orientation of the ellipse showing the direction of the relation between the components of $\boldsymbol{x}$. A nonsingular *elliptically distributed* (or *elliptically contoured*) variate $\boldsymbol{x} \sim \text{EC}(\boldsymbol{c}, \boldsymbol{A})$ is one whose p.d.f. depends on the realization $\boldsymbol{w}$ only through $(\boldsymbol{w}-\boldsymbol{c})' \boldsymbol{A}^{-1} (\boldsymbol{w}-\boldsymbol{c})$, where $\boldsymbol{A}$ is a positive definite matrix of constant parameters that provide weights for the squared norm of $(\boldsymbol{w}-\boldsymbol{c})$. Generally, a quadratic form like

$$(\boldsymbol{w}_1 - \boldsymbol{w}_2)' (\text{var}(\boldsymbol{x}))^{-1} (\boldsymbol{w}_1 - \boldsymbol{w}_2)$$

is called the *Mahalanobis distance* between $\boldsymbol{w}_1$ and $\boldsymbol{w}_2$. The extent of the difference between two realizations of $\boldsymbol{x}$ depends on how volatile the variate is. For example, inflating $\text{var}(\boldsymbol{x})$ by a factor $\alpha > 1$ and $(\boldsymbol{w}_1 - \boldsymbol{w}_2)$ by $\sqrt{\alpha}$, we get an unchanged "statistical" distance between the two realizations even though they are further apart, and this is so because the distribution of $\boldsymbol{x}$ is now more spread out but the relative positions of the two new realizations are unchanged.

We write $\text{EC}_m(\boldsymbol{c}, \boldsymbol{A})$ when we wish to display the dimension m of $\boldsymbol{x}$. If the mean of $\boldsymbol{x} \sim \text{EC}(\boldsymbol{c}, \boldsymbol{A})$ exists, it is given by $\boldsymbol{c}$; see Exercises 6.49 and 7.31. If the variance of $\boldsymbol{x}$ exists, it is *proportional* to $\boldsymbol{A}$; see Exercise 7.31. Examples of $\text{EC}_m(\boldsymbol{c}, \boldsymbol{A})$ densities include the *multivariate t*:

$$f_{\boldsymbol{x}}(\boldsymbol{w}) = \frac{\Gamma\left(\frac{\nu+m}{2}\right) |\boldsymbol{A}|^{-1/2}}{(\pi\nu)^{m/2}\, \Gamma\left(\frac{\nu}{2}\right) \left(1 + \frac{1}{\nu}(\boldsymbol{w}-\boldsymbol{c})' \boldsymbol{A}^{-1} (\boldsymbol{w}-\boldsymbol{c})\right)^{(\nu+m)/2}}, \tag{6.7}$$

where ν is the number of degrees of freedom; $\nu = 1$ gives the *multivariate Cauchy*, whose moments do not exist. Using the idiosyncratic shorthand $\text{t}(\nu)$ for t with ν degrees of freedom, we will show in Exercise 6.50 that the variance of the $\text{t}(\nu)$ in (6.7) is $\frac{\nu}{\nu-2}\boldsymbol{A}$ (*not* $\boldsymbol{A}$) when $\nu > 2$, similarly to the univariate case. As in Exercise 4.36, it is straightforward to take the limit as $\nu \to \infty$ to get

$$f_{\boldsymbol{x}}(\boldsymbol{w}) = \frac{|\boldsymbol{A}|^{-1/2}}{(2\pi)^{m/2}} \exp\left(-\frac{1}{2}(\boldsymbol{w}-\boldsymbol{c})' \boldsymbol{A}^{-1}(\boldsymbol{w}-\boldsymbol{c})\right),$$

which is the p.d.f. of a nonsingular *multivariate normal*, denoted by $\boldsymbol{x} \sim \mathrm{N}(\boldsymbol{c}, \boldsymbol{A})$ or $\boldsymbol{x} \sim \mathrm{N}_m(\boldsymbol{c}, \boldsymbol{A})$, where $\boldsymbol{A}$ is nonsingular. As before, for the standard case $\boldsymbol{x} \sim \mathrm{N}(\boldsymbol{0}, \boldsymbol{I}_m)$, we denote the density by $\phi(\boldsymbol{w})$ and the distribution by $\Phi(\boldsymbol{w})$. This variate will be analyzed in detail in Chapter 8. Denoting a multivariate $\mathrm{t}(\nu)$ by $\boldsymbol{z} \sim \mathrm{EC}(\boldsymbol{c}, \boldsymbol{A})$, it arises when $\boldsymbol{x} \sim \mathrm{N}(\boldsymbol{c}, \boldsymbol{A})$ is divided by an independent variate $\sqrt{y/\nu}$ having $y \sim \chi^2(\nu)$, which can be verified by methods to be introduced in the next chapter; for example, see Exercise 7.30 where we will also find out how

$$\frac{1}{m}(\boldsymbol{z}-\boldsymbol{c})' \boldsymbol{A}^{-1}(\boldsymbol{z}-\boldsymbol{c}) \sim \mathrm{F}(m, \nu) \tag{6.8}$$

compares with the univariate case of $\mathrm{t}^2(\nu) = \mathrm{F}(1, \nu)$ from Exercise 4.33. As it has become clear from recent examples, the notation $\mathrm{EC}_m(\boldsymbol{c}, \boldsymbol{A})$ is incomplete in some sense (a completion will be given in the solution of Exercise 7.31(a) of Chapter 7). It refers to a whole *class* of distributions rather than a single specific distribution, and this should be kept in mind. When we wish to indicate that two variates have the same *type* of elliptical distribution, for example both are multivariate t (possibly with different parameters), we will say so explicitly.

The exercises in this chapter start with illustrations of a special bivariate density, then move on to analyzing properties of multivariate moments and dependence. The focus is later shifted to conditioning, first in theory then in practice. Conditioning and dependence are analyzed further in the last few exercises. In addition to its conventional uses, conditioning is a very useful dimension-reduction device, simplifying the mathematical derivations and giving them a statistical interpretation.

6.1 Moments and dependence

Exercise 6.1 (Bivariate normal pictures) Let $m = 2$ and $\boldsymbol{x} := (x, y)'$, with realization $\boldsymbol{w} := (u, v)'$, mean $\boldsymbol{\mu} := (\mu_1, \mu_2)'$, and variance

$$\boldsymbol{\Sigma} := \begin{pmatrix} \sigma_1^2 & \rho\sigma_1\sigma_2 \\ \rho\sigma_1\sigma_2 & \sigma_2^2 \end{pmatrix} \qquad (|\rho| < 1 \text{ and } \sigma_1, \sigma_2 > 0).$$

(a) Express the density of the nonsingular bivariate normal in terms of these scalar parameters.
(b) Plot this density function for the case $\boldsymbol{\mu} = \boldsymbol{0}$ and $\boldsymbol{\Sigma} = \boldsymbol{I}_2$, and obtain the contour plots for $f(\boldsymbol{w}) = 0.05, 0.10, 0.15$. Briefly comment on the plots, on their relation to elliptical distributions, and on the implied conditional densities.

(c) Answer (b) again for $\boldsymbol{\mu} = \mathbf{0}$ and

$$\boldsymbol{\Sigma} = \begin{pmatrix} 1 & \frac{1}{2} \\ \frac{1}{2} & 1 \end{pmatrix}.$$

Solution

(a) Since

$$\boldsymbol{\Sigma}^{-1} = \frac{1}{\sigma_1^2 \sigma_2^2 (1 - \rho^2)} \begin{pmatrix} \sigma_2^2 & -\rho\sigma_1\sigma_2 \\ -\rho\sigma_1\sigma_2 & \sigma_1^2 \end{pmatrix},$$

we get

$$\begin{aligned} f(\boldsymbol{w}) &= (2\pi)^{-m/2} |\boldsymbol{\Sigma}|^{-1/2} \exp\left(-\frac{1}{2}(\boldsymbol{w} - \boldsymbol{\mu})' \boldsymbol{\Sigma}^{-1} (\boldsymbol{w} - \boldsymbol{\mu})\right) \\ &= \frac{1}{2\pi\sigma_1\sigma_2\sqrt{1 - \rho^2}} \exp(-Q/2) \end{aligned}$$

where

$$Q = \frac{\sigma_2^2 (u - \mu_1)^2 - 2\rho\sigma_1\sigma_2 (u - \mu_1)(v - \mu_2) + \sigma_1^2 (v - \mu_2)^2}{\sigma_1^2 \sigma_2^2 (1 - \rho^2)}.$$

(b) The density in Figure 6.1 is a perfectly symmetric bell, which is invariant to any rotation of the plane given by the (u, v) axes. This is an example of a spherically distributed variate, as the contour plot in Figure 6.2 also clearly shows. The innermost circle is the one where combinations of u and v give a p.d.f. of 0.15, whereas for the outermost circle the p.d.f. is 0.05 and we start proceeding into the tails of the density. Each contour can be visualized as arising from Figure 6.1 by taking a "horizontal" cut or slice, parallel to the (u, v) axes' plane, giving a fixed reading on the vertical axis $f(u, v)$. The conditional density of y is given by $f_{y|u}(v) = f(u, v)/f_x(u)$. The numerator of this ratio can be represented in Figure 6.1 by fixing x to a particular value of u, for example $x = -1$, then taking a slice parallel to the (v, f) axes' plane. Each slice is represented in Figure 6.1 by a mesh line. The conditional density is then obtained by rescaling (dividing) that slice by the fixed value $f_x(u)$. In the first figure of this exercise, all the parallel mesh lines look the same and are identical once rescaled, because x and y are independent and

$$\begin{aligned} f_{y|u}(v) = \frac{f(u, v)}{f_x(u)} &= \frac{(2\pi)^{-1} \exp\left(-\frac{1}{2}(u^2 + v^2)\right)}{f_x(u)} \\ &= \frac{\left((2\pi)^{-1/2} \exp\left(-\frac{1}{2}u^2\right)\right)\left((2\pi)^{-1/2} \exp\left(-\frac{1}{2}v^2\right)\right)}{f_x(u)} \\ &= (2\pi)^{-1/2} \exp\left(-\frac{1}{2}v^2\right) = \phi(v), \end{aligned}$$

where ϕ denotes the standard normal density function.

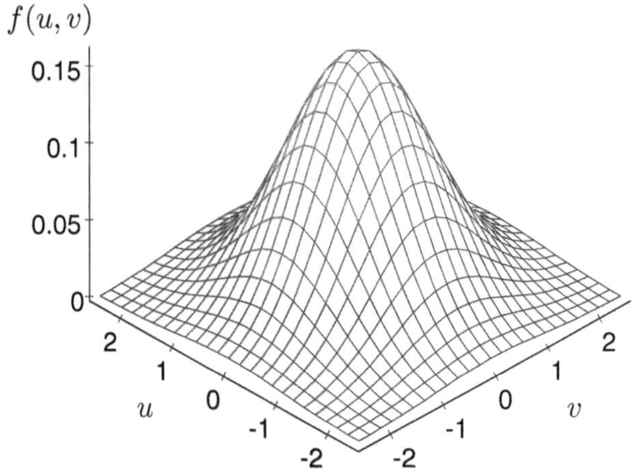

Figure 6.1. Bivariate standard normal.

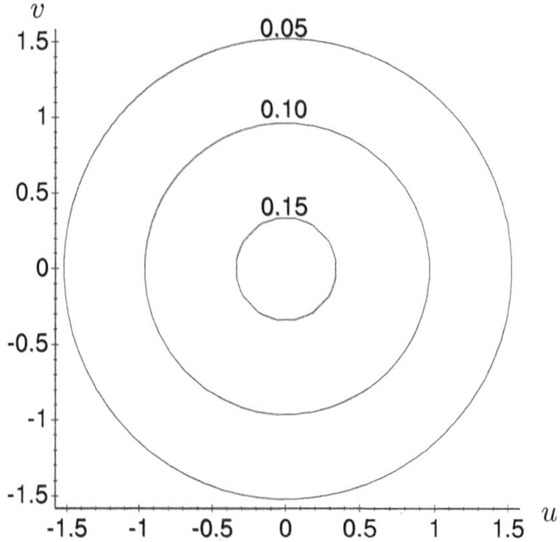

Figure 6.2. Contour plot for bivariate standard normal, with values of $f(u, v) = 0.15, 0.10, 0.05$.

(c) We showed in the introduction that the independence of x and y implies that $\text{cov}(x, y) = 0$ (hence $\rho = 0$). By its contrapositive (see Section A.1), if $\rho \neq 0$, then x and y are not independent. For the second $\boldsymbol{\Sigma}$, the variates are not independent because

$$\rho = \frac{\text{cov}(x, y)}{\sqrt{\text{var}(x) \times \text{var}(y)}} = \frac{1}{2}$$

and there exists at least a linear relation. The density in Figure 6.3 is no longer invariant to rotations, since the bell is not perfectly shaped. A large value of u is more probable (a higher value of f in the graph) to coexist with a large value of v, which indicates a positive relation between x and y. Furthermore, the location of the conditionals $f_{y|u}(v)$ now shifts to the right (to higher v) as u increases: there is a positive linear relation between the

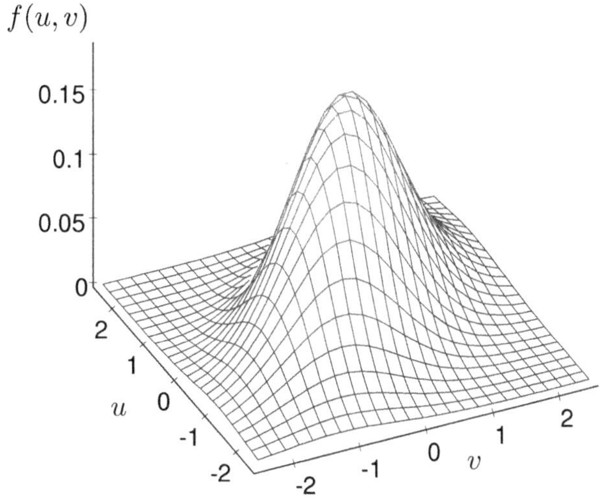

Figure 6.3. Bivariate normal with standard marginals but $\rho = +\frac{1}{2}$.

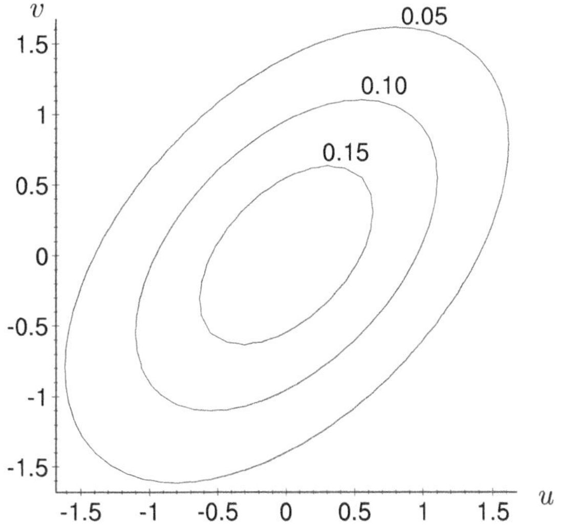

Figure 6.4. Contour plot for bivariate normal with standard marginals but $\rho = +\frac{1}{2}$, and values of $f(u, v) = 0.15, 0.10, 0.05$.

two variates x and y (we shall quantify this in Exercise 6.51 and Chapter 8). This can be seen equally clearly in Figure 6.4, where the direction of the ellipses reflects the positive correlation. This bivariate density is not spherical: rotation of the ellipses by 90° would alter the correlation from positive to negative:

$$\begin{aligned}\operatorname{var}(\boldsymbol{T}\boldsymbol{x}) &= \mathrm{E}\left((\boldsymbol{T}\boldsymbol{x})(\boldsymbol{T}\boldsymbol{x})'\right) - \mathrm{E}(\boldsymbol{T}\boldsymbol{x})\,\mathrm{E}(\boldsymbol{T}\boldsymbol{x})' \\ &= \boldsymbol{T}\,\mathrm{E}\left(\boldsymbol{x}\boldsymbol{x}'\right)\boldsymbol{T}' - \boldsymbol{T}\,\mathrm{E}(\boldsymbol{x})\,\mathrm{E}\left(\boldsymbol{x}'\right)\boldsymbol{T}' \\ &= \boldsymbol{T}\left(\mathrm{E}\left(\boldsymbol{x}\boldsymbol{x}'\right) - \mathrm{E}(\boldsymbol{x})\,\mathrm{E}\left(\boldsymbol{x}'\right)\right)\boldsymbol{T}' = \boldsymbol{T}\boldsymbol{\Sigma}\boldsymbol{T}' \neq \boldsymbol{\Sigma}\end{aligned}$$

and, now letting $\boldsymbol{T}$ be the orthogonal matrix of counterclockwise rotation by 90°, we have

$$\operatorname{var}(\boldsymbol{T}\boldsymbol{x}) = \operatorname{var}\left(\begin{pmatrix}\cos 90^\circ & -\sin 90^\circ\\ \sin 90^\circ & \cos 90^\circ\end{pmatrix}\begin{pmatrix}x\\ y\end{pmatrix}\right) = \operatorname{var}\left(\begin{pmatrix}0 & -1\\ 1 & 0\end{pmatrix}\begin{pmatrix}x\\ y\end{pmatrix}\right)$$
$$= \begin{pmatrix}0 & -1\\ 1 & 0\end{pmatrix}\begin{pmatrix}1 & \frac{1}{2}\\ \frac{1}{2} & 1\end{pmatrix}\begin{pmatrix}0 & -1\\ 1 & 0\end{pmatrix}' = \begin{pmatrix}-\frac{1}{2} & -1\\ 1 & \frac{1}{2}\end{pmatrix}\begin{pmatrix}0 & 1\\ -1 & 0\end{pmatrix} = \begin{pmatrix}1 & -\frac{1}{2}\\ -\frac{1}{2} & 1\end{pmatrix}.$$

The vector $\boldsymbol{x}$ is, nevertheless, elliptically distributed in both cases, as one could have also guessed from the functional form of $f(\boldsymbol{w})$.

***Exercise 6.2 (Shots on target)** George is firing at a fixed target at the center of an extremely large sheet of paper. You may take this target to be the origin $\mathbf{0}_2$ of a plane. Assume that the p.d.f. of shots hitting a point is a continuous function depending only on the distance of this point from the central target. Assume also that the vertical errors from the targeted point are distributed independently of the horizontal errors, and that both are continuously distributed. Prove that the density of the shots on the paper is a bivariate normal. [Hint: Write the joint density in terms of the coordinates of any point on the paper, then use the independence of the two coordinates and the fact that the only continuous function satisfying $g(w_1)g(w_2) = g(w_1 + w_2)$ is $g(w) = \exp(aw)$; see Hamel's equation at the end of Section A.2.]

Solution

Let any point on the paper be represented by the vector $\boldsymbol{x} := (x, y)'$, whose random distance from the origin is $\sqrt{x^2 + y^2}$. Since the distribution varies continuously as a function of this distance only, we obtain that $\boldsymbol{x}$ is spherically distributed with density $f_{x,y}(u, v) = h(u^2 + v^2)$ for some continuous function h. Also, x and y being independently distributed, we have

$$h(u^2 + v^2) = f_x(u) f_y(v).$$

The marginal density functions f_x and f_y are also related to h by the initializations

$$h(0) = f_x(0) f_y(0), \quad h(u^2) = f_x(u) f_y(0), \quad h(v^2) = f_x(0) f_y(v),$$

or equivalently

$$h(0) = f_x(0) f_y(0), \quad \frac{h(u^2)}{h(0)} = \frac{f_x(u)}{f_x(0)}, \quad \frac{h(v^2)}{h(0)} = \frac{f_y(v)}{f_y(0)},$$

where $f_x(0), f_y(0) \neq 0$ since the target $\mathbf{0}_2$ must have nonzero density if it is to be hit! Combining these relations,

$$\frac{h(u^2 + v^2)}{h(0)} = \frac{f_x(u) f_y(v)}{f_x(0) f_y(0)} = \frac{h(u^2)}{h(0)} \times \frac{h(v^2)}{h(0)}.$$

This equation tells us that $g(w) := h(w)/h(0)$, defined for $w \geqslant 0$, is a function satisfying $g(w_1)g(w_2) = g(w_1 + w_2)$. There is only one continuous solution to g, and it is given by the exponential function $g(w) = \exp(aw)$, so that $h(u^2)/h(0) = \exp(au^2)$. Accordingly, $f(u) = f(0)\exp(au^2)$ for both f_x and f_y, which turn out to be identical marginals (*not* by assumption). This marginal density is the $\mathrm{N}(0,\sigma^2)$ density, with $\sigma^2 = -1/(2a) > 0$, and the joint density is therefore the bivariate normal. The reader may wish to verify this spherical density by throwing darts at Figure 6.2!

Exercise 6.3 (Variance of linear combinations)
(a) Prove that $\operatorname{var}(ax+by) = a^2\operatorname{var}(x) + b^2\operatorname{var}(y) + 2ab\operatorname{cov}(x,y)$, and its multivariate generalization $\operatorname{var}(\boldsymbol{a}'\boldsymbol{x}) = \boldsymbol{a}'\operatorname{var}(\boldsymbol{x})\,\boldsymbol{a}$, where $\boldsymbol{a}$ is a vector of arbitrary constants.
(b) Give two implications of this result.

Solution
(a) We prove the general case first, as the use of matrix algebra makes it easier. Since 1×1 quantities and their transposes are identical, $\boldsymbol{a}'\boldsymbol{x} = \boldsymbol{x}'\boldsymbol{a}$ and

$$\begin{aligned}\operatorname{var}(\boldsymbol{a}'\boldsymbol{x}) &= \mathrm{E}\left[(\boldsymbol{a}'\boldsymbol{x} - \mathrm{E}(\boldsymbol{a}'\boldsymbol{x}))\,(\boldsymbol{x}'\boldsymbol{a} - \mathrm{E}(\boldsymbol{x}'\boldsymbol{a}))\right]\\ &= \boldsymbol{a}'\,\mathrm{E}\left[(\boldsymbol{x} - \mathrm{E}(\boldsymbol{x}))\,(\boldsymbol{x} - \mathrm{E}(\boldsymbol{x}))'\right]\boldsymbol{a} = \boldsymbol{a}'\operatorname{var}(\boldsymbol{x})\,\boldsymbol{a}.\end{aligned}$$

Letting $\boldsymbol{a} = (a,b)'$ and $\boldsymbol{x} = (x,y)'$ gives the required special case. Alternatively,

$$\begin{aligned}\operatorname{var}(ax+by) &= \mathrm{E}\left[(ax+by-\mathrm{E}(ax+by))^2\right]\\ &= \mathrm{E}\left[(a(x-\mathrm{E}(x)) + b(y-\mathrm{E}(y)))^2\right].\end{aligned}$$

Expanding the quadratic gives

$$\begin{aligned}\operatorname{var}(ax+by) &= \mathrm{E}\left[a^2(x-\mathrm{E}(x))^2 + b^2(y-\mathrm{E}(y))^2 + 2ab(x-\mathrm{E}(x))(y-\mathrm{E}(y))\right]\\ &= a^2\operatorname{var}(x) + b^2\operatorname{var}(y) + 2ab\operatorname{cov}(x,y).\end{aligned}$$

Another illustration of the flexibility introduced by matrices will be seen in Exercise 6.4.
(b) Two other important results follow from (a). First, since $\operatorname{var}(\boldsymbol{a}'\boldsymbol{x}) \geqslant 0$ for any $\boldsymbol{a}$, then $\boldsymbol{a}'\operatorname{var}(\boldsymbol{x})\,\boldsymbol{a} \geqslant 0$ too, which is why $\operatorname{var}(\boldsymbol{x})$ is by definition a positive semidefinite matrix. Second, if there exists a nontrivial ($\boldsymbol{a} \neq \boldsymbol{0}$) linear combination $\boldsymbol{a}'\boldsymbol{x}$ which has zero variance, then some components of $\boldsymbol{x}$ are linearly dependent with probability 1; for example, if $y := 2x+3$, then $\operatorname{var}(2x-y) = 0$. If, in addition, $\boldsymbol{x}$ is a continuous variate, then it is called singular continuous and $\operatorname{var}(\boldsymbol{x})$ is a singular matrix. This illustrates the definition of singular variates introduced in Chapter 2. Notice that we do not require $\boldsymbol{x}$ itself to be a constant with probability 1, but rather that there exists a combination $\boldsymbol{a}'\boldsymbol{x}$ which satisfies this condition.

Exercise 6.4 (Life is simpler with the matrix!) Let

$$\begin{aligned}y_1 &:= 4 + x_1 + 2x_2\\ y_2 &:= 5 + x_1 + x_2,\end{aligned}$$

where x_1 and x_2 are two i.i.d. variates, with mean 0 and variance 1. Derive the mean, variance, and covariance of y_1 and y_2, first without and then with matrices.

Solution

Taking expectations in the definition of y_1 and y_2, we get

$$\mathrm{E}(y_1) = 4 + \mathrm{E}(x_1) + 2\,\mathrm{E}(x_2) = 4$$

and

$$\mathrm{E}(y_2) = 5 + \mathrm{E}(x_1) + \mathrm{E}(x_2) = 5.$$

The variances are given by

$$\mathrm{var}(y_1) = \mathrm{var}(x_1 + 2x_2) = \mathrm{var}(x_1) + 4\,\mathrm{var}(x_2) + 4\,\mathrm{cov}(x_1, x_2) = 1 + 4 + 0 = 5$$

and

$$\mathrm{var}(y_2) = \mathrm{var}(x_1 + x_2) = \mathrm{var}(x_1) + \mathrm{var}(x_2) + 2\,\mathrm{cov}(x_1, x_2) = 1 + 1 + 0 = 2.$$

Finally,

$$\begin{aligned}
\mathrm{cov}(y_1, y_2) &= \mathrm{E}((y_1 - 4)(y_2 - 5)) \\
&= \mathrm{E}((x_1 + 2x_2)(x_1 + x_2)) \\
&= \mathrm{E}\left(x_1^2 + 3x_1x_2 + 2x_2^2\right) \\
&= \mathrm{var}(x_1) + 3\,\mathrm{cov}(x_1, x_2) + 2\,\mathrm{var}(x_2) \\
&= 1 + 0 + 2 = 3.
\end{aligned}$$

The result is much easier to obtain, especially when the dimensions increase beyond 2, by writing $\boldsymbol{y} := \boldsymbol{c} + \boldsymbol{A}'\boldsymbol{x}$ for

$$\begin{pmatrix} y_1 \\ y_2 \end{pmatrix} = \begin{pmatrix} 4 \\ 5 \end{pmatrix} + \begin{pmatrix} 1 & 2 \\ 1 & 1 \end{pmatrix} \begin{pmatrix} x_1 \\ x_2 \end{pmatrix}.$$

Then,

$$\mathrm{E}(\boldsymbol{y}) = \mathrm{E}(\boldsymbol{c}) + \mathrm{E}\left(\boldsymbol{A}'\boldsymbol{x}\right) = \boldsymbol{c} + \boldsymbol{A}'\,\mathrm{E}(\boldsymbol{x}) = \boldsymbol{c} = \begin{pmatrix} 4 \\ 5 \end{pmatrix}$$

since $\mathrm{E}(\boldsymbol{x}) = \boldsymbol{0}$, and

$$\mathrm{var}(\boldsymbol{y}) = \mathrm{var}\left(\boldsymbol{A}'\boldsymbol{x}\right) = \boldsymbol{A}'\,\mathrm{var}(\boldsymbol{x})\,\boldsymbol{A} = \boldsymbol{A}'\boldsymbol{I}_2\boldsymbol{A} = \boldsymbol{A}'\boldsymbol{A} = \begin{pmatrix} 1 & 2 \\ 1 & 1 \end{pmatrix} \begin{pmatrix} 1 & 1 \\ 2 & 1 \end{pmatrix} = \begin{pmatrix} 5 & 3 \\ 3 & 2 \end{pmatrix}.$$

Exercise 6.5 (Moments around different locations: multivariate) Let $\boldsymbol{x}$ be an $m \times 1$ random vector with finite first two moments. Show that

$$\mathrm{E}\left((\boldsymbol{x} - \boldsymbol{c})(\boldsymbol{x} - \boldsymbol{c})'\right) = \mathrm{var}(\boldsymbol{x}) + (\mathrm{E}(\boldsymbol{x}) - \boldsymbol{c})(\mathrm{E}(\boldsymbol{x}) - \boldsymbol{c})'$$

for any nonrandom $\boldsymbol{c} \in \mathbb{R}^m$.

Solution

This is the multivariate version of Exercise 3.17. Let $\boldsymbol{\mu} := \mathrm{E}(\boldsymbol{x})$. Then

$$\begin{aligned}(\boldsymbol{x}-\boldsymbol{c})(\boldsymbol{x}-\boldsymbol{c})' &= ((\boldsymbol{x}-\boldsymbol{\mu})+(\boldsymbol{\mu}-\boldsymbol{c}))\,((\boldsymbol{x}-\boldsymbol{\mu})+(\boldsymbol{\mu}-\boldsymbol{c}))' \\ &= (\boldsymbol{x}-\boldsymbol{\mu})\,(\boldsymbol{x}-\boldsymbol{\mu})' + (\boldsymbol{\mu}-\boldsymbol{c})\,(\boldsymbol{\mu}-\boldsymbol{c})' \\ &\quad + (\boldsymbol{x}-\boldsymbol{\mu})\,(\boldsymbol{\mu}-\boldsymbol{c})' + (\boldsymbol{\mu}-\boldsymbol{c})\,(\boldsymbol{x}-\boldsymbol{\mu})'.\end{aligned}$$

By the linearity of expectations and $\mathrm{E}\,(\boldsymbol{x}-\boldsymbol{\mu}) \equiv \mathbf{0}$, we have

$$\mathrm{E}\left((\boldsymbol{\mu}-\boldsymbol{c})\,(\boldsymbol{x}-\boldsymbol{\mu})'\right) = (\boldsymbol{\mu}-\boldsymbol{c})\,\mathrm{E}\,(\boldsymbol{x}-\boldsymbol{\mu})' = \mathbf{O}$$

since $\boldsymbol{\mu}$ and $\boldsymbol{c}$ are nonrandom, and similarly $\mathrm{E}\left((\boldsymbol{x}-\boldsymbol{\mu})\,(\boldsymbol{\mu}-\boldsymbol{c})'\right) = \mathbf{O}$. Therefore,

$$\mathrm{E}\left((\boldsymbol{x}-\boldsymbol{c})(\boldsymbol{x}-\boldsymbol{c})'\right) = \mathrm{E}\left((\boldsymbol{x}-\boldsymbol{\mu})\,(\boldsymbol{x}-\boldsymbol{\mu})'\right) + (\boldsymbol{\mu}-\boldsymbol{c})\,(\boldsymbol{\mu}-\boldsymbol{c})' + \mathbf{O}.$$

The result follows by using the definitions of $\boldsymbol{\mu}$ and $\mathrm{var}(\boldsymbol{x})$.

Exercise 6.6 (Moments of linear and quadratic transformations) Let $\boldsymbol{y} := \boldsymbol{c} + \boldsymbol{A}'\boldsymbol{x}$, where $\boldsymbol{c}$ and $\boldsymbol{A}$ are nonrandom, $\mathrm{E}\,(\boldsymbol{x}) = \mathbf{0}_n$, and $\mathrm{var}\,(\boldsymbol{x}) = \boldsymbol{\Sigma}$. Derive $\mathrm{E}\,(\boldsymbol{y})$, $\mathrm{var}\,(\boldsymbol{y})$, $\mathrm{E}\,(\boldsymbol{y}\boldsymbol{y}')$, and $\mathrm{E}\,(\boldsymbol{y}'\boldsymbol{y})$.

Solution

Taking expectations on both sides of the definition of $\boldsymbol{y}$, we have

$$\mathrm{E}\,(\boldsymbol{y}) = \mathrm{E}\,(\boldsymbol{c}) + \mathrm{E}\left(\boldsymbol{A}'\boldsymbol{x}\right) = \boldsymbol{c} + \boldsymbol{A}'\,\mathrm{E}\,(\boldsymbol{x}) = \boldsymbol{c}.$$

Then $\boldsymbol{y} - \mathrm{E}\,(\boldsymbol{y}) = \boldsymbol{A}'\boldsymbol{x}$ implies that

$$\begin{aligned}\mathrm{var}\,(\boldsymbol{y}) &= \mathrm{E}\left((\boldsymbol{y}-\mathrm{E}\,(\boldsymbol{y}))\,(\boldsymbol{y}-\mathrm{E}\,(\boldsymbol{y}))'\right) \\ &= \mathrm{E}\left(\left(\boldsymbol{A}'\boldsymbol{x}\right)\left(\boldsymbol{A}'\boldsymbol{x}\right)'\right) = \boldsymbol{A}'\,\mathrm{E}\left(\boldsymbol{x}\boldsymbol{x}'\right)\boldsymbol{A} = \boldsymbol{A}'\boldsymbol{\Sigma}\boldsymbol{A}\end{aligned}$$

since $\mathrm{E}\,(\boldsymbol{x}) = \mathbf{0}$. By $\mathrm{var}\,(\boldsymbol{y}) = \mathrm{E}\,(\boldsymbol{y}\boldsymbol{y}') - \mathrm{E}\,(\boldsymbol{y})\,\mathrm{E}\,(\boldsymbol{y})' = \mathrm{E}\,(\boldsymbol{y}\boldsymbol{y}') - \boldsymbol{c}\boldsymbol{c}'$, we infer that

$$\mathrm{E}\left(\boldsymbol{y}\boldsymbol{y}'\right) = \boldsymbol{c}\boldsymbol{c}' + \boldsymbol{A}'\boldsymbol{\Sigma}\boldsymbol{A}.$$

Finally, since $\boldsymbol{y}'\boldsymbol{y} = \mathrm{tr}\,(\boldsymbol{y}'\boldsymbol{y}) = \mathrm{tr}\,(\boldsymbol{y}\boldsymbol{y}')$ and the trace function is just the addition of the diagonal elements of a matrix,

$$\mathrm{E}\left(\boldsymbol{y}'\boldsymbol{y}\right) = \mathrm{E}\left(\mathrm{tr}\left(\boldsymbol{y}\boldsymbol{y}'\right)\right) = \mathrm{tr}\left(\mathrm{E}\left(\boldsymbol{y}\boldsymbol{y}'\right)\right) = \mathrm{tr}\left(\boldsymbol{c}\boldsymbol{c}' + \boldsymbol{A}'\boldsymbol{\Sigma}\boldsymbol{A}\right) = \boldsymbol{c}'\boldsymbol{c} + \mathrm{tr}\left(\boldsymbol{A}'\boldsymbol{\Sigma}\boldsymbol{A}\right).$$

Note that the dimensions of $\boldsymbol{y}$ and $\boldsymbol{x}$ were not assumed to be the same, so that $\boldsymbol{A}$ could be any $n \times m$ matrix.

***Exercise 6.7 (Quadratic forms: variance)** Let $x_1, \dots, x_n$ be an i.i.d. sequence, with

$$\mathrm{E}\,(x_i) = 0, \quad \mathrm{E}(x_i^2) = 1, \quad \gamma := \mathrm{E}\left(x_i^3\right), \quad \kappa := \mathrm{E}\left(x_i^4\right) - 3,$$

for all $i = 1, \dots, n$. Define $\boldsymbol{x} := (x_1, \dots, x_n)'$.

(a) Show that

$$\operatorname{var}\left(\boldsymbol{x}'\boldsymbol{B}\boldsymbol{x}\right) = \kappa \operatorname{tr}\left((\operatorname{dg}\boldsymbol{B})^2\right) + 2\operatorname{tr}\left(\boldsymbol{B}^2\right),$$

where $\boldsymbol{B}$ is a symmetric $n \times n$ matrix and $\operatorname{dg}\boldsymbol{B} := \operatorname{diag}(b_{11},\dots,b_{nn})$ is a diagonal matrix that contains the diagonal elements of $\boldsymbol{B}$.
(b) Let $\boldsymbol{y} := \boldsymbol{c} + \boldsymbol{A}'\boldsymbol{x}$, where $\boldsymbol{c}$ and $\boldsymbol{A}$ are nonrandom. Show that

$$\operatorname{var}\left(\boldsymbol{y}'\boldsymbol{y}\right) = 4\boldsymbol{c}'\boldsymbol{A}'\boldsymbol{A}\boldsymbol{c} + 4\gamma\boldsymbol{c}'\boldsymbol{A}'\left(\operatorname{dg}\boldsymbol{Q}\right)\boldsymbol{\imath} + \kappa\operatorname{tr}\left((\operatorname{dg}\boldsymbol{Q})^2\right) + 2\operatorname{tr}\left(\boldsymbol{Q}^2\right),$$

where $\boldsymbol{Q} := \boldsymbol{A}\boldsymbol{A}'$ and $\boldsymbol{\imath} := (1,\dots,1)'$.

Solution
(a) By writing $\mathrm{E}(\boldsymbol{x}) = \mathbf{0}$ and $\operatorname{var}(\boldsymbol{x}) = \boldsymbol{I}_n$, we have $\mathrm{E}(\boldsymbol{x}\boldsymbol{x}') = \operatorname{var}(\boldsymbol{x}) + \mathrm{E}(\boldsymbol{x})\mathrm{E}(\boldsymbol{x})' = \boldsymbol{I}_n$ and, as in Exercise 6.6,

$$\mathrm{E}\left(\boldsymbol{x}'\boldsymbol{B}\boldsymbol{x}\right) = \mathrm{E}\left(\operatorname{tr}\left(\boldsymbol{x}'\boldsymbol{B}\boldsymbol{x}\right)\right) = \mathrm{E}\left(\operatorname{tr}\left(\boldsymbol{B}\boldsymbol{x}\boldsymbol{x}'\right)\right) = \operatorname{tr}\left(\boldsymbol{B}\,\mathrm{E}\left(\boldsymbol{x}\boldsymbol{x}'\right)\right) = \operatorname{tr}(\boldsymbol{B}).$$

Then,

$$\begin{aligned}\operatorname{var}\left(\boldsymbol{x}'\boldsymbol{B}\boldsymbol{x}\right) &= \mathrm{E}\left(\left(\boldsymbol{x}'\boldsymbol{B}\boldsymbol{x}\right)^2\right) - (\operatorname{tr}(\boldsymbol{B}))^2 \\ &= \mathrm{E}\left(\left(\sum_i b_{ii}x_i^2 + \sum_{i\neq j} b_{ij}x_ix_j\right)\left(\sum_s b_{ss}x_s^2 + \sum_{s\neq t} b_{st}x_sx_t\right)\right) - (\operatorname{tr}(\boldsymbol{B}))^2.\end{aligned}$$

Expanding the product and taking expectations, the terms $\sum_i\sum_{s\neq t}$ and $\sum_{i\neq j}\sum_s$ drop out because independence of the x's implies that

$$\mathrm{E}\left(x_i^2x_sx_t\right) = \begin{cases}\mathrm{E}\left(x_i^3\right)\mathrm{E}(x_t) & (i = s \neq t),\\ \mathrm{E}\left(x_i^3\right)\mathrm{E}(x_s) & (i = t \neq s),\\ \mathrm{E}\left(x_i^2\right)\mathrm{E}(x_s)\mathrm{E}(x_t) & (i \neq s \neq t),\end{cases}$$

where we can use $\mathrm{E}(x_\bullet) = 0$, and similarly for the term $\sum_{i\neq j}\sum_{s\neq t}$ unless $s = i \neq j = t$ or $t = i \neq j = s$. Hence,

$$\begin{aligned}\operatorname{var}\left(\boldsymbol{x}'\boldsymbol{B}\boldsymbol{x}\right) &= \sum_i b_{ii}^2\,\mathrm{E}\left(x_i^4\right) + \sum_{i\neq s} b_{ii}b_{ss}\,\mathrm{E}\left(x_i^2x_s^2\right) + 2\sum_{i\neq j} b_{ij}^2\,\mathrm{E}\left(x_i^2x_j^2\right) - (\operatorname{tr}(\boldsymbol{B}))^2 \\ &= (3+\kappa)\sum_i b_{ii}^2 + \sum_{i\neq s} b_{ii}b_{ss} + 2\sum_{i\neq j} b_{ij}^2 - (\operatorname{tr}(\boldsymbol{B}))^2,\end{aligned}$$

by the independence of the x's implying $\mathrm{E}\left(x_i^2x_s^2\right) = \mathrm{E}\left(x_i^2\right)\mathrm{E}\left(x_s^2\right)$ for $i \neq s$. Collecting terms,

$$\begin{aligned}\operatorname{var}\left(\boldsymbol{x}'\boldsymbol{B}\boldsymbol{x}\right) &= \kappa\sum_i b_{ii}^2 + \sum_{i,s} b_{ii}b_{ss} + 2\sum_{i,j} b_{ij}^2 - \left(\sum_i b_{ii}\right)^2 \\ &= \kappa\sum_i b_{ii}^2 + 2\sum_{i,j} b_{ij}^2 = \kappa\operatorname{tr}\left((\operatorname{dg}\boldsymbol{B})^2\right) + 2\operatorname{tr}\left(\boldsymbol{B}^2\right),\end{aligned}$$

the last step following by the symmetry of $\boldsymbol{B}$.
(b) By the relation of $\boldsymbol{y}$ to $\boldsymbol{x}$, Exercise 6.6 gives us $\mathrm{E}(\boldsymbol{y}'\boldsymbol{y}) = \boldsymbol{c}'\boldsymbol{c} + \operatorname{tr}(\boldsymbol{Q})$. Notice that we have not assumed that $\boldsymbol{A}$ is square. However, $\boldsymbol{Q}$ is now more restricted than $\boldsymbol{B}$ of (a), as it is taken here to be of the form $\boldsymbol{Q} = \boldsymbol{A}\boldsymbol{A}'$, hence positive semidefinite rather than just symmetric. Substituting for $\boldsymbol{y}$,

$$\begin{aligned}\operatorname{var}(\boldsymbol{y}'\boldsymbol{y}) &= \mathrm{E}\left(\left((\boldsymbol{c}' + \boldsymbol{x}'\boldsymbol{A})(\boldsymbol{c} + \boldsymbol{A}'\boldsymbol{x}) - \boldsymbol{c}'\boldsymbol{c} - \operatorname{tr}\boldsymbol{Q}\right)^2\right) \\ &= \mathrm{E}\left(\left(2\boldsymbol{c}'\boldsymbol{A}'\boldsymbol{x} + (\boldsymbol{x}'\boldsymbol{Q}\boldsymbol{x} - \operatorname{tr}\boldsymbol{Q})\right)^2\right)\end{aligned}$$

by $\boldsymbol{c}'\boldsymbol{A}'\boldsymbol{x} = \boldsymbol{x}'\boldsymbol{A}\boldsymbol{c}$, since 1×1 quantities and their transposes are identical. Expanding the quadratic and using $\mathrm{E}(\boldsymbol{x}) = \boldsymbol{0}$,

$$\operatorname{var}(\boldsymbol{y}'\boldsymbol{y}) = 4\,\mathrm{E}\left((\boldsymbol{c}'\boldsymbol{A}'\boldsymbol{x})^2\right) + 4\,\mathrm{E}(\boldsymbol{c}'\boldsymbol{A}'\boldsymbol{x}\boldsymbol{x}'\boldsymbol{Q}\boldsymbol{x}) + \mathrm{E}\left((\boldsymbol{x}'\boldsymbol{Q}\boldsymbol{x} - \operatorname{tr}\boldsymbol{Q})^2\right).$$

We already have the last expectation from (a). For the first,

$$\mathrm{E}\left((\boldsymbol{c}'\boldsymbol{A}'\boldsymbol{x})^2\right) = \mathrm{E}(\boldsymbol{c}'\boldsymbol{A}'\boldsymbol{x}\boldsymbol{x}'\boldsymbol{A}\boldsymbol{c}) = \boldsymbol{c}'\boldsymbol{A}'\,\mathrm{E}(\boldsymbol{x}\boldsymbol{x}')\,\boldsymbol{A}\boldsymbol{c} = \boldsymbol{c}'\boldsymbol{A}'\boldsymbol{I}_n\boldsymbol{A}\boldsymbol{c} = \boldsymbol{c}'\boldsymbol{A}'\boldsymbol{A}\boldsymbol{c}.$$

For the second, since $\mathrm{E}(x_i x_j x_k) = 0$ unless $i = j = k$,

$$\begin{aligned}\mathrm{E}(\boldsymbol{c}'\boldsymbol{A}'\boldsymbol{x}\boldsymbol{x}'\boldsymbol{Q}\boldsymbol{x}) &= \boldsymbol{c}'\boldsymbol{A}'\,\mathrm{E}\left(\boldsymbol{x}\sum_{i=1}^{n}\sum_{j=1}^{n} q_{ij}x_i x_j\right) \\ &= \boldsymbol{c}'\boldsymbol{A}'\,\mathrm{E}\begin{pmatrix} q_{11}x_1^3 \\ \vdots \\ q_{nn}x_n^3 \end{pmatrix} = \gamma\boldsymbol{c}'\boldsymbol{A}'\begin{pmatrix} q_{11} \\ \vdots \\ q_{nn} \end{pmatrix} = \gamma\boldsymbol{c}'\boldsymbol{A}'(\operatorname{dg}\boldsymbol{Q})\,\boldsymbol{\imath}.\end{aligned}$$

The result follows by adding the three expectations. Notice that the skewness γ now appears in this result when the centering of the variate is $\boldsymbol{c} \neq \boldsymbol{0}$, unlike in part (a).

Exercise 6.8 (Quadratic forms: symmetry) Define $\boldsymbol{x} := (x_1, \dots, x_n)'$ and let $\boldsymbol{B}$ be an $n \times n$ real matrix. Show that $\boldsymbol{x}'\boldsymbol{B}\boldsymbol{x} = \boldsymbol{x}'\boldsymbol{B}_{\mathrm{s}}\boldsymbol{x}$, where $\boldsymbol{B}_{\mathrm{s}} := \frac{1}{2}(\boldsymbol{B} + \boldsymbol{B}')$ is symmetric even if $\boldsymbol{B}$ is not. What does this imply for the formula of $\operatorname{var}(\boldsymbol{x}'\boldsymbol{B}\boldsymbol{x})$ in Exercise 6.7?

Solution
We have

$$\boldsymbol{x}'\boldsymbol{B}_{\mathrm{s}}\boldsymbol{x} = \frac{1}{2}\boldsymbol{x}'(\boldsymbol{B} + \boldsymbol{B}')\boldsymbol{x} = \frac{1}{2}\boldsymbol{x}'\boldsymbol{B}\boldsymbol{x} + \frac{1}{2}\boldsymbol{x}'\boldsymbol{B}'\boldsymbol{x} = \frac{1}{2}\boldsymbol{x}'\boldsymbol{B}\boldsymbol{x} + \frac{1}{2}(\boldsymbol{x}'\boldsymbol{B}\boldsymbol{x})' = \boldsymbol{x}'\boldsymbol{B}\boldsymbol{x}$$

again since the 1×1 variable and its transpose are identical. Alternatively, we can do the following. Any matrix can be written as the sum of a symmetric and a skew-symmetric component:

$$\boldsymbol{B} = \frac{1}{2}(\boldsymbol{B} + \boldsymbol{B}') + \frac{1}{2}(\boldsymbol{B} - \boldsymbol{B}').$$

Defining $z := \boldsymbol{x}'(\boldsymbol{B} - \boldsymbol{B}')\boldsymbol{x}$, we have that

$$z' = \boldsymbol{x}'\left(\boldsymbol{B}' - \boldsymbol{B}\right)\boldsymbol{x} = -\boldsymbol{x}'\left(\boldsymbol{B} - \boldsymbol{B}'\right)\boldsymbol{x} = -z,$$

which implies that z is identically zero (since $z = z'$ is a 1×1 quantity). Therefore, only the symmetric component of $\boldsymbol{B}$ matters for quadratic forms.

Exercise 6.9 (Skewed difference) Let x and y be independent variates, with $\mathrm{E}(x) = \mathrm{E}(y) = 0$. Show that

$$\mathrm{E}\left(x^3\right) - \mathrm{E}\left(y^3\right) = \mathrm{E}\left((x-y)^3\right),$$

assuming that these moments exist. How is this relation affected if x and y are allowed to have nonzero means?

Solution
By the binomial expansion,

$$\begin{aligned}\mathrm{E}\left((x-y)^3\right) &= \mathrm{E}\left(x^3 - 3x^2y + 3xy^2 - y^3\right)\\ &= \mathrm{E}\left(x^3\right) - 3\,\mathrm{E}\left(x^2\right)\mathrm{E}(y) + 3\,\mathrm{E}(x)\,\mathrm{E}\left(y^2\right) - \mathrm{E}\left(y^3\right),\end{aligned}$$

where we have used the independence of x and y to write $\mathrm{E}\left(x^i y^j\right) = \mathrm{E}\left(x^i\right)\mathrm{E}\left(y^j\right)$. The required result follows by $\mathrm{E}(x) = \mathrm{E}(y) = 0$.

If, instead, $\mathrm{E}(x) = \mu_x$ and $\mathrm{E}(y) = \mu_y$, then the equality applies to central rather than raw moments. The third central moment of $x - y$ is

$$\sigma_{x-y}^{(3)} := \mathrm{E}\left(((x-y) - (\mu_x - \mu_y))^3\right) = \mathrm{E}\left(((x-\mu_x) - (y-\mu_y))^3\right).$$

Defining $z_1 := x - \mu_x$ and $z_2 := y - \mu_y$, then applying the first part of the exercise gives

$$\sigma_{x-y}^{(3)} = \sigma_x^{(3)} - \sigma_y^{(3)}.$$

Exercise 6.10 (Covariance of sum and difference) Let x and y be random variables with finite second moments. Show that $\mathrm{cov}(x+y, x-y) = 0$ if and only if $\mathrm{var}(x) = \mathrm{var}(y)$.

Solution
We have

$$\begin{aligned}\mathrm{cov}(x+y, x-y) &= \mathrm{cov}(x,x) - \mathrm{cov}(x,y) + \mathrm{cov}(y,x) - \mathrm{cov}(y,y)\\ &= \mathrm{var}(x) - \mathrm{var}(y),\end{aligned}$$

and the identity follows. Note that $x + y$ need not be independent of $x - y$ (for example they both depend on x), even though their covariance is zero. This will be illustrated in Exercise 7.13.

Exercise 6.11 (Covariance of sums or differences in random sample) Let (x, y) have a bivariate distribution with finite second moments, and suppose we take a random sample $(x_1, y_1), \dots, (x_n, y_n)$. Show that $\operatorname{cov}(x_i \pm x_j, y_i \pm y_j) = 2\operatorname{cov}(x, y)$ for $i \neq j$, and hence that $\operatorname{corr}(x_i \pm x_j, y_i \pm y_j) = \operatorname{corr}(x, y)$.

Solution
We have

$$\begin{aligned}\operatorname{cov}(x_i - x_j, y_i - y_j) &= \operatorname{cov}(x_i, y_i) + \operatorname{cov}(x_j, y_j) - \operatorname{cov}(x_j, y_i) - \operatorname{cov}(x_i, y_j) \\ &= \operatorname{cov}(x_i, y_i) + \operatorname{cov}(x_j, y_j)\end{aligned}$$

by the independence of the data for $i \neq j$. Since the data are also identically distributed, $\operatorname{cov}(x_i, y_i) = \operatorname{cov}(x_j, y_j)$ and we get $\operatorname{cov}(x_i - x_j, y_i - y_j) = 2\operatorname{cov}(x, y)$. The same result holds for the sum instead of the difference of the data. It also implies that $\operatorname{var}(x_i \pm x_j) = 2\operatorname{var}(x)$ and similarly for y, hence that the scale-invariant correlation is unchanged: $\operatorname{corr}(x_i \pm x_j, y_i \pm y_j) = \operatorname{corr}(x, y)$.

Exercise 6.12 (Correlation and linear dependence) Let $y := ax + b$, where $a, b \in \mathbb{R}$ are nonrandom. Calculate the correlation ρ between x and y, assuming their second moments exist and are nonzero.

Solution
If $y = ax + b$, then $\operatorname{cov}(x, y) = \operatorname{cov}(x, ax + b) = a\operatorname{var}(x)$ and $\operatorname{var}(y) = \operatorname{var}(ax + b) = a^2 \operatorname{var}(x)$, so that

$$\rho = \frac{a\operatorname{var}(x)}{\sqrt{\operatorname{var}(x)\, a^2 \operatorname{var}(x)}} = \frac{a}{|a|} = \operatorname{sgn}(a).$$

For $a \neq 0$ we have a correlation of $+1$ or -1, depending on the sign of a. This result and its converse will be proved more generally in Exercise 6.20. When $a = 0$, the variates do not co-vary and $\rho = 0$ by convention.

Exercise 6.13 (Correlation and nonlinear dependence) Let $y := x^2$, where x is symmetrically distributed around 0. Calculate the correlation ρ between x and y, assuming the second moment of y exists.

Solution
The existence of $\mathrm{E}(y^2)$ implies that $\mathrm{E}(x^j)$ exists for $j \leqslant 4$, by Exercise 3.25. We know that

$$\operatorname{cov}(x, y) = \operatorname{cov}\left(x, x^2\right) = \mathrm{E}\left(x^3\right) - \mathrm{E}(x)\,\mathrm{E}\left(x^2\right).$$

By Exercise 3.20, symmetry implies that central odd-order moments are zero, so $\mathrm{E}(x) = \mathrm{E}\left(x^3\right) = 0$ and hence $\operatorname{cov}(x, y) = 0$ here. The correlation is therefore zero. This is true even though y is exactly equal to x^2 for all values of x, and therefore x and y are certainly not independent. This result arises because the dependence between y and x is nonlinear, whereas ρ measures linear dependence only.

Exercise 6.14 (Covariance of even functions and linear forms) Let $\boldsymbol{x}$ be a symmetrically distributed random vector with $\mathrm{E}(\boldsymbol{x}) = \mathbf{0}$, and let $\boldsymbol{b}$ be a conformable vector of constants. Show that $\boldsymbol{b}'\boldsymbol{x}$ and $h(\boldsymbol{x})$ are uncorrelated for any even function h, assuming the moments exist.

Solution

Using $\mathrm{E}(\boldsymbol{x}) = \mathbf{0}$ and $\operatorname{cov}(\boldsymbol{x}, y) = \mathrm{E}((\boldsymbol{x} - \mathrm{E}(\boldsymbol{x}))\, y)$,

$$\operatorname{cov}\left(\boldsymbol{b}'\boldsymbol{x}, h(\boldsymbol{x})\right) = \boldsymbol{b}'\,\mathrm{E}(\boldsymbol{x}h(\boldsymbol{x})) - \boldsymbol{b}'\,\mathrm{E}(\boldsymbol{x})\,\mathrm{E}(h(\boldsymbol{x})) = \boldsymbol{b}'\,\mathrm{E}(\boldsymbol{x}h(\boldsymbol{x})).$$

Now, for *any* distribution that is symmetric around the origin, $\boldsymbol{x}$ and $-\boldsymbol{x}$ have the same distribution (see Exercise 2.7) and hence the same moments if they exist. Therefore,

$$\begin{aligned}\mathrm{E}(\boldsymbol{x}h(\boldsymbol{x})) &= \frac{1}{2}\mathrm{E}(\boldsymbol{x}h(\boldsymbol{x})) + \frac{1}{2}\mathrm{E}(-\boldsymbol{x}h(-\boldsymbol{x})) \\ &= \frac{1}{2}\mathrm{E}(\boldsymbol{x}h(\boldsymbol{x})) - \frac{1}{2}\mathrm{E}(\boldsymbol{x}h(-\boldsymbol{x})) = \mathbf{0}\end{aligned}$$

since $h(-\boldsymbol{x}) = h(\boldsymbol{x})$ by the definition of even functions. We have used this notion implicitly in Exercise 6.13 and more explicitly in Exercise 3.19.

Exercise 6.15 (Normal's covariance with nonlinear functions) Let $x \sim \mathrm{N}(\mu, \sigma^2)$. Show that $\operatorname{cov}(x, h(x)) = \sigma^2\,\mathrm{E}(h'(x))$ when the two expectations exist and h is a function that is differentiable once.

Solution

We shall use integration by parts. We have

$$\begin{aligned}\operatorname{cov}(x, h(x)) = \mathrm{E}((x-\mu)\,h(x)) &= \frac{1}{\sigma\sqrt{2\pi}}\int_{-\infty}^{\infty} h(u)\,(u-\mu)\exp\left(-\frac{(u-\mu)^2}{2\sigma^2}\right)\mathrm{d}u \\ &= \frac{-\sigma^2}{\sigma\sqrt{2\pi}}\left[h(u)\exp\left(-\frac{(u-\mu)^2}{2\sigma^2}\right)\right]_{-\infty}^{\infty} \\ &\quad - \frac{-\sigma^2}{\sigma\sqrt{2\pi}}\int_{-\infty}^{\infty} h'(u)\exp\left(-\frac{(u-\mu)^2}{2\sigma^2}\right)\mathrm{d}u.\end{aligned}$$

The latter integral is $\sigma^2\,\mathrm{E}(h'(x))$, by definition, and the required equality holds when $g(u) := h(u)\exp\left(-(u-\mu)^2/(2\sigma^2)\right)$ satisfies $\lim_{u\to\pm\infty} g(u) = 0$. Suppose that this last condition were not the case. Then, $\int_{-\infty}^{\infty} |(u-\mu)\,g(u)|\,\mathrm{d}u$ would be infinite and the expectation $\mathrm{E}((x-\mu)\,h(x))$ would not exist. This has been ruled out by assumption, thus implying $\lim_{u\to\pm\infty} g(u) = 0$. Results along similar lines can be obtained for some densities other than the normal.

Exercise 6.16 (Absolutely mean!) Show the following weighted-average decomposition:

$$\mathrm{E}(|y|) = \Pr(y > 0)\,\mathrm{E}(y \mid y > 0) + \Pr(y < 0)\,\mathrm{E}(-y \mid y < 0).$$

Simplify the formula if $\Pr(y > 0) = \Pr(y < 0)$. What if y is symmetric around 0?

Solution
For $w \geqslant 0$,

$$\begin{aligned} F_{|y|}(w) &\equiv \Pr(|y| \leqslant w) \\ &= \Pr(y > 0)\Pr(y \leqslant w \mid y > 0) + \Pr(y < 0)\Pr(-y \leqslant w \mid y < 0) + \Pr(y = 0) \\ &\equiv \Pr(y > 0)\,F_{y|y>0}(w) + \Pr(y < 0)\,F_{-y|y<0}(w) + \Pr(y = 0), \end{aligned}$$

and we get

$$\begin{aligned} \mathrm{E}(|y|) &= \int_0^{\infty} w\,\mathrm{d}F_{|y|}(w) \\ &= \Pr(y > 0)\int_0^{\infty} w\,\mathrm{d}F_{y|y>0}(w) + \Pr(y < 0)\int_0^{\infty} w\,\mathrm{d}F_{-y|y<0}(w) + 0 \\ &= \Pr(y > 0)\,\mathrm{E}(y \mid y > 0) + \Pr(y < 0)\,\mathrm{E}(-y \mid y < 0), \end{aligned}$$

as required. This result was derived from first principles, but it can be obtained alternatively by means of the LIE, by defining $x := \mathrm{sgn}(y)$ and writing out $\mathrm{E}_x(\mathrm{E}_{y|x}(|y|))$ explicitly.

Now suppose that y is symmetric around 0. Let $p := \Pr(y > 0) = \Pr(y < 0) \leqslant \frac{1}{2}$. Then

$$\mathrm{E}(|y|) = p\,(\mathrm{E}(y \mid y > 0) - \mathrm{E}(y \mid y < 0)).$$

Furthermore, if y is symmetric around zero, then $\mathrm{E}(y \mid y > 0) = \mathrm{E}(-y \mid y < 0)$ since y and $-y$ have the same distribution (see Exercise 2.7) and

$$\mathrm{E}(|y|) = 2p\,\mathrm{E}(y \mid y > 0).$$

Exercise 6.17 (Conditioning on which function?) Assuming the moments exist, show that:
(a) if $h(x)$ is an invertible function for all $x \in \mathcal{X}$, then $\mathrm{E}(y \mid h(x)) = \mathrm{E}(y \mid x)$;
(b) $\mathrm{E}(y \mid h(x)) \neq \mathrm{E}(y \mid x)$ in general.

Solution
(a) Since the function is invertible, $h(x) = h(u)$ if and only if $x = u$.
(b) We can provide a counterexample to the equality. Take $h(x) = x^2$, where $x = \mathrm{sgn}(y)$ with y symmetrically distributed around 0 and $\Pr(y = 0) = 0$. Then, since $x^2 = 1$ regard-

less of y, we have on the one hand

$$\mathrm{E}\left(y \mid x^2\right) = \mathrm{E}\left(y\right) = 0$$

by the symmetry of y and the existence of the moment. On the other hand, since x determines the sign of y, we have

$$\mathrm{E}\left(y \mid x\right) = x\,\mathrm{E}\left(|y|\right),$$

the symmetry of y implying that $\mathrm{E}\left(y \mid y > 0\right) = -\mathrm{E}\left(y \mid y < 0\right)$; see Exercise 6.16 with $p = \frac{1}{2}$. Since $\Pr\left(x = 0\right) = \Pr\left(y = 0\right) = 0$, we have $\mathrm{E}\left(y \mid x\right) \neq 0$ almost surely, so differing from $\mathrm{E}\left(y \mid x^2\right)$.

Exercise 6.18 (Conditioning can be upsetting, for dependence) Let $\boldsymbol{x} := (x, y, z)'$ and assume that the variance of $\boldsymbol{x}$ exists.
(a) Suppose that y depends on x and z, but that x and z are independent. Show that, when conditioning on y, the variates x and z can become dependent on one another.
(b) Suppose that $z = g\left(y\right)$ and $y = h\left(x\right)$, where the two functions are nondegenerate (not identically equal to a constant). Prove that x and z are not independent, but that they become independent when conditioning on y.

Solution
(a) As an example, take $y = x/z$ with x and z independent, and $\Pr\left(z = 0\right) = 0$. Then,

$$\begin{aligned}\rho_{z,x|y} &= \frac{\operatorname{cov}\left(z, x \mid y\right)}{\sqrt{\operatorname{var}\left(z \mid y\right)\operatorname{var}\left(x \mid y\right)}} = \frac{\operatorname{cov}\left(z, zy \mid y\right)}{\sqrt{\operatorname{var}\left(z \mid y\right)\operatorname{var}\left(zy \mid y\right)}}\\ &= \frac{y\operatorname{cov}\left(z, z \mid y\right)}{\sqrt{\operatorname{var}\left(z \mid y\right)y^2\operatorname{var}\left(z \mid y\right)}} = \operatorname{sgn}\left(y\right)\end{aligned}$$

when $\operatorname{var}\left(z \mid y\right) \neq 0$. In fact, fixing y makes x proportional to z (even though x and z were unrelated at the outset), with Exercise 6.12 implying perfect correlation. Notice that we used the general result that $\rho_{z,z|y} = 1$ regardless of y, as long as the variate $z \mid y$ is not degenerate.
(b) The fact that x and z are not independent follows from $z = g\left(y\right) = g\left(h\left(x\right)\right)$. Now, conditioning on y fixes z and $h\left(x\right)$, so that z is trivially independent of $h\left(x\right)$. Notice that z becomes a constant when we condition on y, but that x need not be fixed. To show that x can still be random, take the function $h\left(x\right) := x^2$. It allows x to take either of the values $\pm\sqrt{y}$, whatever the fixed value of y.

Exercise 6.19 (Partial may reveal all) Let $\boldsymbol{x} := (x, y, z)'$, where the variance of $\boldsymbol{x}$ exists and is nonsingular. Suppose that $y := xh\left(z\right)$ with $\Pr\left(h\left(z\right) = 0\right) = 0$ for some function h depending on z only.
(a) Derive $\rho_{x,y|z}$ and $\rho_{y,z|x}$.
(b) If $\left|\rho_{y,z|x}\right| = 1$ with probability 1, what can you infer about $h\left(z\right)$ and y?

Solution

(a) We have

$$\rho_{x,y|z} = \frac{\operatorname{cov}(x, xh(z) \mid z)}{\sqrt{\operatorname{var}(x \mid z)\operatorname{var}(xh(z) \mid z)}} = \frac{h(z)\operatorname{var}(x \mid z)}{\sqrt{\operatorname{var}(x \mid z)\, h(z)^2 \operatorname{var}(x \mid z)}} = \operatorname{sgn}(h(z)),$$

where $\operatorname{var}(x \mid z) \neq 0$ because the vector $\boldsymbol{x}$ is a nonsingular variate. Since $\Pr(h(z) = 0) = 0$, we get $|\rho_{x,y|z}| = 1$ with probability 1, regardless of the value taken by $\rho_{x,y}$. This is because, given z, the variates x and $y := xh(z)$ are proportional. Similarly,

$$\rho_{y,z|x} = \frac{\operatorname{cov}(xh(z), z \mid x)}{\sqrt{\operatorname{var}(xh(z) \mid x)\operatorname{var}(z \mid x)}} = \frac{\operatorname{sgn}(x)\operatorname{cov}(h(z), z \mid x)}{\sqrt{\operatorname{var}(h(z) \mid x)\operatorname{var}(z \mid x)}} = \operatorname{sgn}(x)\,\rho_{z,h(z)|x}.$$

(b) If $|\rho_{y,z|x}| = 1$, then $|\rho_{z,h(z)|x}| = 1$ by (a). Therefore, conditionally on x, the function $h(z)$ is linear and has a nonzero slope with probability 1, and the result holds unconditionally too since $h(z)$ does not depend on x. Also, since $y := xh(z)$, we have $y = (a + bz)x$ for some constants $a \in \mathbb{R}$, $b \in \mathbb{R}\backslash\{0\}$ and such that $\Pr(z = -a/b) = 0$.

*__Exercise 6.20 (Cauchy–Schwarz: expectations version)__ Let $\operatorname{var}(x)$ and $\operatorname{var}(y)$ be positive and finite. Prove that $|\rho_{x,y}| \leqslant 1$, where the equality holds if and only if y is a linear transformation of x with probability 1.

Solution

Consider the arbitrary linear combinations $y + \alpha x$ where $\alpha \in \mathbb{R}$ is unspecified but nonrandom. Then, for all α, we have

$$0 \leqslant \operatorname{var}(y + \alpha x) = \operatorname{var}(y) + 2\alpha \operatorname{cov}(x, y) + \alpha^2 \operatorname{var}(x)$$

by Exercise 6.3. This is a quadratic function of α, which is nonnegative everywhere if and only if the discriminant is nonpositive (the case of no distinct real roots for α), that is,

$$D := (2\operatorname{cov}(x, y))^2 - 4(\operatorname{var}(x))(\operatorname{var}(y)) \leqslant 0.$$

Notice that the inequality implies that the covariance is finite if the variances exist. We now need to make use of the existence of the variances for defining the ratio in $\rho_{x,y}$. Using the definition of $\rho_{x,y}$, this inequality becomes $\rho_{x,y}^2 \leqslant 1$.

The equality $\rho_{x,y}^2 = 1$ holds if and only if $D = 0$, that is,

$$\operatorname{var}(y) = (\operatorname{cov}(x, y))^2 / \operatorname{var}(x),$$

which we can use to rewrite the quadratic function as

$$\operatorname{var}(y + \alpha x) \equiv \operatorname{var}(y) + 2\alpha \operatorname{cov}(x, y) + \alpha^2 \operatorname{var}(x) = \left(\frac{\operatorname{cov}(x, y)}{\operatorname{var}(x)} + \alpha\right)^2 \operatorname{var}(x).$$

This gives the repeated root $\alpha_1 := -\operatorname{cov}(x, y) / \operatorname{var}(x)$ that makes this function 0, hence

$$\operatorname{var}(y + \alpha_1 x) = 0,$$

which shows that $\rho_{x,y}^2 = 1$ is equivalent to saying that $y + \alpha_1 x$ is constant (y is a linear transformation of x) with probability 1.

The Cauchy–Schwarz inequality is a mathematical result that applies also to sequences of nonrandom variables. The same method as that employed in Exercise 3.14(c) can be used (with $p_i = 1/n$) to show that, for any two n-dimensional nonzero real vectors $\boldsymbol{u}$ and $\boldsymbol{v}$,

$$\frac{\frac{1}{n}\sum_{i=1}^n u_i v_i}{\sqrt{\left(\frac{1}{n}\sum_{i=1}^n u_i^2\right) \times \left(\frac{1}{n}\sum_{i=1}^n v_i^2\right)}} = \frac{\boldsymbol{u}'\boldsymbol{v}}{\|\boldsymbol{u}\| \times \|\boldsymbol{v}\|} \equiv \cos\theta \in [-1, 1],$$

where θ is defined as the angle between the vectors $\boldsymbol{u}$ and $\boldsymbol{v}$. We have $\rho = \pm 1$ if and only if $\boldsymbol{u}$ and $\boldsymbol{v}$ are collinear. Orthogonality of the two vectors gives $\rho = 0$.

***Exercise 6.21 (Multiple correlation)** Partition the m-dimensional $\boldsymbol{x}' := (x_1, \boldsymbol{x}_2')$ into one and $m - 1 > 0$ components, and accordingly its variance matrix as

$$\boldsymbol{\Sigma} := \begin{pmatrix} \sigma_{11} & \boldsymbol{\sigma}_{21}' \\ \boldsymbol{\sigma}_{21} & \boldsymbol{\Sigma}_{22} \end{pmatrix},$$

and assume that it is positive definite. The *canonical correlation coefficient* between x_1 and $\boldsymbol{x}_2$ is defined as

$$\rho_{x_1,\boldsymbol{x}_2}^{\max} := \max_{\boldsymbol{b}\in\mathbb{R}^{m-1}} \rho_{x_1,\boldsymbol{b}'\boldsymbol{x}_2}.$$

Using the Cauchy–Schwarz inequality, prove that this definition yields the *multiple correlation coefficient* $(\boldsymbol{\sigma}_{21}'\boldsymbol{\Sigma}_{22}^{-1}\boldsymbol{\sigma}_{21}/\sigma_{11})^{1/2}$ as the solution to the maximization, and hence obtain $\boldsymbol{b}$. (The notation $\overline{R}$ is also used for $\rho^{\max}$, but we prefer to use $\overline{\rho}$ instead if necessary, reserving R for sample counterparts.)

Solution

The canonical correlation coefficient measures the maximal correlation that any linear combination $\boldsymbol{b}'\boldsymbol{x}_2$ can achieve with x_1. This correlation is clearly not negative, because we have $\operatorname{corr}(x_1, -\boldsymbol{b}'\boldsymbol{x}_2) = -\operatorname{corr}(x_1, \boldsymbol{b}'\boldsymbol{x}_2)$ and $\max\{-\rho, \rho\} \geqslant 0$. As in the derivations of Exercise 6.3,

$$\rho_{x_1,\boldsymbol{b}'\boldsymbol{x}_2} := \frac{\operatorname{cov}(x_1, \boldsymbol{b}'\boldsymbol{x}_2)}{\sqrt{\operatorname{var}(x_1)\operatorname{var}(\boldsymbol{b}'\boldsymbol{x}_2)}} = \frac{\boldsymbol{b}'\boldsymbol{\sigma}_{21}}{\sqrt{\sigma_{11}\boldsymbol{b}'\boldsymbol{\Sigma}_{22}\boldsymbol{b}}} = \frac{\left(\boldsymbol{b}'\boldsymbol{\Sigma}_{22}^{1/2}\right)\left(\boldsymbol{\Sigma}_{22}^{-1/2}\boldsymbol{\sigma}_{21}\right)}{\sqrt{\sigma_{11}\boldsymbol{b}'\boldsymbol{\Sigma}_{22}\boldsymbol{b}}},$$

where $\boldsymbol{\Sigma}_{22}^{1/2}$ is the unique symmetric square root of $\boldsymbol{\Sigma}$. Applying the Cauchy–Schwarz inequality $\boldsymbol{u}'\boldsymbol{v} \leqslant \|\boldsymbol{u}\| \times \|\boldsymbol{v}\|$ to the vectors $\boldsymbol{u} := \boldsymbol{\Sigma}_{22}^{1/2}\boldsymbol{b}$ and $\boldsymbol{v} := \boldsymbol{\Sigma}_{22}^{-1/2}\boldsymbol{\sigma}_{21}$,

$$\rho_{x_1,\boldsymbol{b}'\boldsymbol{x}_2} \leqslant \rho_{x_1,\boldsymbol{x}_2}^{\max} = \frac{\left\|\boldsymbol{\Sigma}_{22}^{1/2}\boldsymbol{b}\right\| \times \left\|\boldsymbol{\Sigma}_{22}^{-1/2}\boldsymbol{\sigma}_{21}\right\|}{\sqrt{\sigma_{11}\boldsymbol{b}'\boldsymbol{\Sigma}_{22}\boldsymbol{b}}} = \frac{\left\|\boldsymbol{\Sigma}_{22}^{-1/2}\boldsymbol{\sigma}_{21}\right\|}{\sqrt{\sigma_{11}}} = \sqrt{\frac{\boldsymbol{\sigma}_{21}'\boldsymbol{\Sigma}_{22}^{-1}\boldsymbol{\sigma}_{21}}{\sigma_{11}}}.$$

The inequality becomes an equality if and only if the nonrandom vectors $\boldsymbol{u}$ and $\boldsymbol{v}$ are collinear, that is, $\boldsymbol{\Sigma}_{22}^{1/2}\boldsymbol{b}$ is proportional to $\boldsymbol{\Sigma}_{22}^{-1/2}\boldsymbol{\sigma}_{21}$. Choosing $\boldsymbol{b} = \boldsymbol{\Sigma}_{22}^{-1}\boldsymbol{\sigma}_{21}$ achieves this, since correlation is invariant to scale (or proportionality factors). Note that the vector $\boldsymbol{\Sigma}_{22}^{-1}\boldsymbol{\sigma}_{21}$ generalizes the slope coefficient $-\alpha_1 := \operatorname{cov}(x, y) / \operatorname{var}(x)$ of Exercise 6.20.

Exercise 6.22 (Correlation matrix) Let $\boldsymbol{x} := (x_1, \dots, x_m)'$ have variance $\boldsymbol{\Sigma}$, and define the correlations $\rho_{ij} := \sigma_{ij}/\sqrt{\sigma_{ii}\sigma_{jj}}$.
(a) Prove that the correlation matrix $\boldsymbol{R} := (\rho_{ij})$ is positive semidefinite.
(b) If $\rho_{ij} = \rho$ (a constant) for all $i \neq j$, prove that $\rho \geqslant -1/(m-1)$.

Solution
(a) Consider the transformation $y_i = x_i/\sqrt{\sigma_{ii}}$ $(i = 1, \dots, m)$. Then, $\operatorname{var}(y_i) = 1$ and $\operatorname{cov}(y_i, y_j) = \rho_{ij}$ for $i \neq j$. The correlation matrix $\boldsymbol{R}$ is therefore a variance matrix, and hence positive semidefinite by Exercise 6.3.
(b) This is an *equicorrelation matrix*, which can be written as

$$\boldsymbol{R} = (1-\rho)\,\boldsymbol{I}_m + \rho\boldsymbol{\imath}\boldsymbol{\imath}'$$

with $\boldsymbol{\imath} := (1, \dots, 1)'$. Since $\boldsymbol{R}$ is positive semidefinite, $\boldsymbol{a}'\boldsymbol{R}\boldsymbol{a} \geqslant 0$ for all $m \times 1$ vectors $\boldsymbol{a}$. Choosing $\boldsymbol{a} = \boldsymbol{\imath}$ implies that $m + (m^2 - m)\rho \geqslant 0$, and hence that $\rho \geqslant -1/(m-1)$. The choice of $\boldsymbol{a}$ may seem arbitrary, but it arises as follows. Substituting for $\boldsymbol{R}$ in $\boldsymbol{a}'\boldsymbol{R}\boldsymbol{a} \geqslant 0$,

$$\boldsymbol{a}'\boldsymbol{a}\,(1-\rho) + \rho\boldsymbol{a}'\boldsymbol{\imath}\boldsymbol{\imath}'\boldsymbol{a} \geqslant 0.$$

Rearranging,

$$\left(\frac{\boldsymbol{a}'\boldsymbol{\imath}\boldsymbol{\imath}'\boldsymbol{a}}{\boldsymbol{a}'\boldsymbol{a}} - 1\right)\rho \geqslant -1$$

for all $\boldsymbol{a} \neq \boldsymbol{0}$, where $\boldsymbol{a}'\boldsymbol{\imath}\boldsymbol{\imath}'\boldsymbol{a}/\boldsymbol{a}'\boldsymbol{a}$ is the *Rayleigh quotient* of the matrix $\boldsymbol{\imath}\boldsymbol{\imath}'$. Now, the matrix $\boldsymbol{\imath}\boldsymbol{\imath}'$ has rank 1. Therefore, $m-1$ of its eigenvalues are zero. Since the trace of a matrix equals the sum of its eigenvalues, the nonzero eigenvalue is equal to $\operatorname{tr}(\boldsymbol{\imath}\boldsymbol{\imath}') = \boldsymbol{\imath}'\boldsymbol{\imath} = m$. The Rayleigh quotient is bounded above by the largest eigenvalue, m. It reaches this value when $\boldsymbol{a}$ is chosen to be the eigenvector corresponding to m by solving

$$(\boldsymbol{\imath}\boldsymbol{\imath}')\,\boldsymbol{a} = m\boldsymbol{a},$$

to get $\boldsymbol{a} = \boldsymbol{\imath}$. This gives

$$\rho \geqslant -\frac{1}{\frac{\boldsymbol{a}'\boldsymbol{\imath}\boldsymbol{\imath}'\boldsymbol{a}}{\boldsymbol{a}'\boldsymbol{a}} - 1} = -\frac{1}{m-1}$$

as required.

An alternative solution is obtained by writing

$$\boldsymbol{R} = (1-\rho)\,(\boldsymbol{I}_m - \boldsymbol{M}) + (1 + (m-1)\,\rho)\,\boldsymbol{M},$$

where $\boldsymbol{M} := m^{-1}\boldsymbol{\imath}\boldsymbol{\imath}'$ is idempotent and so is $\boldsymbol{I}_m - \boldsymbol{M}$. They are simultaneously diagonalizable in the form $\operatorname{diag}(1, \mathbf{O})$ and $\operatorname{diag}(0, \boldsymbol{I}_{m-1})$, respectively, so the eigenvalues of $\boldsymbol{R}$ are $1-\rho$ and $1 + (m-1)\,\rho$, and these must be nonnegative since idempotent matrices are positive semidefinite. The latter restriction yields $\rho \geqslant -1/(m-1)$.

Exercise 6.23 (Overall variation) Let the $m \times 1$ random vector y have the variance $\boldsymbol{\Sigma}$. Two scalar measures of overall variation are often encountered in multivariate analysis. The first is the *generalized variance* $|\boldsymbol{\Sigma}|$, and the second is the *total variance* (or sum of the variances) $\operatorname{tr}(\boldsymbol{\Sigma})$.
(a) Prove that

$$|\boldsymbol{\Sigma}| \leqslant |\mathrm{dg}\,\boldsymbol{\Sigma}| \leqslant \left(\frac{1}{m}\operatorname{tr}(\boldsymbol{\Sigma})\right)^m,$$

where $|\mathrm{dg}\,\boldsymbol{\Sigma}|$ is the product of the variances.
(b) When do these relations hold as equalities?

Solution
(a) The second inequality is a direct application of the arithmetic–geometric mean inequality of Exercise 3.14(c), obtained by taking $u_i = \sigma_i^2$ and $p_i = 1/m$ there (and replacing n by m). For the first inequality, if $\boldsymbol{\Sigma}$ is singular, then $|\boldsymbol{\Sigma}| = 0$ and

$$|\mathrm{dg}\,\boldsymbol{\Sigma}| = \prod_{i=1}^{m} \sigma_i^2 \geqslant 0.$$

Otherwise, if $\boldsymbol{\Sigma}$ is nonsingular, then it is positive definite and we can define the matrix of correlations as

$$\boldsymbol{R} := (\mathrm{dg}\,\boldsymbol{\Sigma})^{-1/2}\,\boldsymbol{\Sigma}\,(\mathrm{dg}\,\boldsymbol{\Sigma})^{-1/2},$$

where the diagonal elements of $\boldsymbol{R}$ are 1. Denoting the eigenvalues of $\boldsymbol{R}$ by $\lambda_i > 0$ (the sign following from Exercise 6.22(a)), we have

$$|\boldsymbol{R}| = \prod_{i=1}^{m} \lambda_i \leqslant \left(\frac{1}{m}\sum_{i=1}^{m} \lambda_i\right)^m = \left(\frac{1}{m}\operatorname{tr}(\boldsymbol{R})\right)^m = \left(\frac{m}{m}\right)^m = 1,$$

where the arithmetic–geometric mean inequality has been used again. Since

$$1 \geqslant |\boldsymbol{R}| = \frac{|\boldsymbol{\Sigma}|}{|\mathrm{dg}\,\boldsymbol{\Sigma}|},$$

we have the required first inequality.
(b) The first equality holds if $\boldsymbol{\Sigma}$ is singular and at least one of its diagonal elements is zero. If $\boldsymbol{\Sigma}$ is nonsingular, both inequalities hinge on the arithmetic–geometric mean inequality applied to λ_i and σ_i^2, respectively, and so they become equalities if and only if all the λ_i or all the σ_i^2 are equal, respectively, as the proof of Exercise 3.14 indicates. We now spell out the implications for $\boldsymbol{\Sigma}$ of these two conditions.

First, in the case of $\lambda_i = \lambda$ for all i, the symmetry of $\boldsymbol{R}$ means that it is orthogonally decomposable by means of some orthogonal matrix $\boldsymbol{T}$, and so $\boldsymbol{R} = \boldsymbol{T}(\lambda \boldsymbol{I}_m)\boldsymbol{T}' = \lambda \boldsymbol{I}_m$. The diagonal of $\boldsymbol{R}$ is 1, so we must have $\lambda = 1$. The inequality $|\boldsymbol{\Sigma}| \leqslant |\mathrm{dg}\,\boldsymbol{\Sigma}|$ provides a measure of how close $\boldsymbol{\Sigma}$ is to diagonality. Second, in the case of $\sigma_i = \sigma$ for all i, all that is required is that the diagonal elements of $\boldsymbol{\Sigma}$ be equal. Finally, taking the two conditions together, we have that

$$|\boldsymbol{\Sigma}| = \left(\frac{1}{m}\operatorname{tr}(\boldsymbol{\Sigma})\right)^m$$

if and only if $\boldsymbol{\Sigma} = \sigma^2 \boldsymbol{I}_m$. The inequality of generalized and total variances measures how far $\boldsymbol{\Sigma}$ is from a scalar matrix $\sigma^2 \boldsymbol{I}_m$ (see the relation of elliptical to spherical distributions).

Exercise 6.24 (Characteristic functions: matrix variates) Suppose we have the $m \times m$ random matrix $\boldsymbol{Z}$. We could obtain the joint c.f. of its m^2 elements by stacking its columns into the $m^2 \times 1$ vector $\boldsymbol{z} := \operatorname{vec}(\boldsymbol{Z})$, using the vec (or vectorizing) operator, and proceeding as in the introduction to this chapter. Suppose, however, that we wish to keep $\boldsymbol{Z}$ in its original format. Show that:
(a) the c.f. of $\boldsymbol{Z}$ can be written as $\varphi_{\boldsymbol{Z}}(\boldsymbol{T}) = \mathrm{E}(\operatorname{etr}(\mathrm{i}\boldsymbol{T}'\boldsymbol{Z}))$, where $\boldsymbol{T}$ is a nonrandom $m \times m$ matrix and $\operatorname{etr}(\cdot) \equiv \exp(\operatorname{tr}(\cdot))$;
(b) $\varphi_{\boldsymbol{Z}}(\boldsymbol{T}) = \mathrm{E}(\operatorname{etr}(\mathrm{i}\boldsymbol{T}_{\mathrm{s}}\boldsymbol{Z}_{\mathrm{s}} - \mathrm{i}\boldsymbol{T}_{\mathrm{a}}\boldsymbol{Z}_{\mathrm{a}}))$, where we define $\boldsymbol{T}_{\mathrm{s}} := \frac{1}{2}(\boldsymbol{T} + \boldsymbol{T}')$ and $\boldsymbol{T}_{\mathrm{a}} := \frac{1}{2}(\boldsymbol{T} - \boldsymbol{T}')$, and similarly for $\boldsymbol{Z}$.
(c) $\varphi_{\boldsymbol{Z}}(\boldsymbol{T}) = \mathrm{E}(\operatorname{etr}(\mathrm{i}\boldsymbol{T}_{\mathrm{s}}\boldsymbol{Z}))$ if $\boldsymbol{Z}$ is symmetric.

Solution
(a) Writing $\boldsymbol{t} := \operatorname{vec}(\boldsymbol{T})$,

$$\varphi_{\boldsymbol{Z}}(\boldsymbol{T}) := \mathrm{E}\left(\exp\left(\mathrm{i}\sum_{j=1}^{m}\sum_{k=1}^{m} t_{jk}z_{jk}\right)\right) = \mathrm{E}\left(\exp\left(\mathrm{i}\boldsymbol{t}'\boldsymbol{z}\right)\right) = \mathrm{E}\left(\operatorname{etr}\left(\mathrm{i}\boldsymbol{T}'\boldsymbol{Z}\right)\right).$$

(b) Any $m \times m$ matrix can be written as the sum of a symmetric and a skew-symmetric (or anti-symmetric) component, so here we write $\boldsymbol{T} = \boldsymbol{T}_{\mathrm{s}} + \boldsymbol{T}_{\mathrm{a}}$ and similarly $\boldsymbol{Z} = \boldsymbol{Z}_{\mathrm{s}} + \boldsymbol{Z}_{\mathrm{a}}$. Therefore,

$$\begin{aligned}\boldsymbol{T}'\boldsymbol{Z} &= (\boldsymbol{T}_{\mathrm{s}} + \boldsymbol{T}_{\mathrm{a}})'(\boldsymbol{Z}_{\mathrm{s}} + \boldsymbol{Z}_{\mathrm{a}}) \\ &= \boldsymbol{T}_{\mathrm{s}}'\boldsymbol{Z}_{\mathrm{s}} + \boldsymbol{T}_{\mathrm{a}}'\boldsymbol{Z}_{\mathrm{a}} + \boldsymbol{T}_{\mathrm{s}}'\boldsymbol{Z}_{\mathrm{a}} + \boldsymbol{T}_{\mathrm{a}}'\boldsymbol{Z}_{\mathrm{s}} \\ &= \boldsymbol{T}_{\mathrm{s}}\boldsymbol{Z}_{\mathrm{s}} - \boldsymbol{T}_{\mathrm{a}}\boldsymbol{Z}_{\mathrm{a}} + \boldsymbol{T}_{\mathrm{s}}\boldsymbol{Z}_{\mathrm{a}} - \boldsymbol{T}_{\mathrm{a}}\boldsymbol{Z}_{\mathrm{s}},\end{aligned}$$

as $\boldsymbol{T}_{\mathrm{s}}' = \boldsymbol{T}_{\mathrm{s}}$ and $\boldsymbol{T}_{\mathrm{a}}' = -\boldsymbol{T}_{\mathrm{a}}$. Now, since $\operatorname{tr}(\boldsymbol{A}) = \operatorname{tr}(\boldsymbol{A}')$ for any square matrix $\boldsymbol{A}$, we have

$$\operatorname{tr}(\boldsymbol{T}_{\mathrm{s}}\boldsymbol{Z}_{\mathrm{a}}) = \operatorname{tr}\left((\boldsymbol{T}_{\mathrm{s}}\boldsymbol{Z}_{\mathrm{a}})'\right) = \operatorname{tr}\left(\boldsymbol{Z}_{\mathrm{a}}'\boldsymbol{T}_{\mathrm{s}}'\right) = -\operatorname{tr}(\boldsymbol{Z}_{\mathrm{a}}\boldsymbol{T}_{\mathrm{s}}) = -\operatorname{tr}(\boldsymbol{T}_{\mathrm{s}}\boldsymbol{Z}_{\mathrm{a}}),$$

as $\operatorname{tr}(\boldsymbol{AB}) = \operatorname{tr}(\boldsymbol{BA})$. Hence, $\operatorname{tr}(\boldsymbol{T}_{\mathrm{s}}\boldsymbol{Z}_{\mathrm{a}}) = 0$. Similarly, $\operatorname{tr}(\boldsymbol{T}_{\mathrm{a}}\boldsymbol{Z}_{\mathrm{s}}) = 0$, and the result follows.
(c) If $\boldsymbol{Z}$ is symmetric, then $\boldsymbol{Z}_{\mathrm{a}} = \frac{1}{2}(\boldsymbol{Z} - \boldsymbol{Z}') = \frac{1}{2}(\boldsymbol{Z} - \boldsymbol{Z}) = \mathbf{O}$ and $\boldsymbol{Z}_{\mathrm{s}} = \boldsymbol{Z}$, so the result follows. Note that there are only $m(m+1)/2$ distinct elements in a symmetric matrix $\boldsymbol{Z}$, and their joint c.f. is

$$\mathrm{E}\left(\exp\left(\mathrm{i}\sum_{j=1}^{m}\sum_{k=1}^{j} \tau_{jk}z_{jk}\right)\right),$$

with the correspondences $\tau_{jj} = t_{jj}$ but $\tau_{jk} = t_{jk} + t_{kj}$ for $k < j$. For convenience, when $\boldsymbol{Z}$ is symmetric (such as later in Section 9.2), we relabel these and define henceforth the c.f. as

$$\varphi_{\boldsymbol{Z}}(\boldsymbol{T}) := \mathrm{E}\left(\exp\left(\mathrm{i}\sum_{j=1}^{m}\sum_{k=1}^{j} t_{jk} z_{jk}\right)\right) = \mathrm{E}\left(\exp\left(\mathrm{i}\,\mathrm{vech}(\boldsymbol{T})'\,\mathrm{vech}(\boldsymbol{Z})\right)\right)$$

where $\boldsymbol{T}$ is lower triangular and vech $(\boldsymbol{T})$ denotes the vector containing t_{jk} for only $j \geqslant k$ (vech is known as the "half-vec" operator).

6.2 Conditional distributions and expectations, theory

Exercise 6.25 (Proper conditionals) Prove that conditional c.d.f.s and p.d.f.s obey the usual rules of their unconditional counterparts.

Solution

We need to prove this only for conditional c.d.f.s, since the result for the corresponding p.d.f. follows immediately from its definition as the Radon–Nikodym derivative of the conditional distribution function.

Partition an m-dimensional vector variate $\boldsymbol{x}$ into $\boldsymbol{x}' := (\boldsymbol{x}_1', \boldsymbol{x}_2')$ with dimensions $k > 0$ and $m - k > 0$, and its realization $\boldsymbol{w}' := (\boldsymbol{w}_1', \boldsymbol{w}_2')$ accordingly. Then, by writing $F_{\boldsymbol{x}_2|\boldsymbol{w}_1}(\boldsymbol{w}_2)$ as $\Pr(\boldsymbol{x}_2 \leqslant \boldsymbol{w}_2 \mid \boldsymbol{x}_1 = \boldsymbol{w}_1)$, the conditional c.d.f. satisfies:
(i) $F_{\boldsymbol{x}_2|\boldsymbol{w}_1}(\boldsymbol{w}_2) = 0$ if any of the $m - k$ components of $\boldsymbol{w}_2$ is $-\infty$;
(ii) $F_{\boldsymbol{x}_2|\boldsymbol{w}_1}(\infty, \dots, \infty) = 1$;
(iii) for $F_{\boldsymbol{x}_2|\boldsymbol{w}_1}(\boldsymbol{w}_2^+) := \lim_{\boldsymbol{h}\to\boldsymbol{0}_{m-k}^+} F_{\boldsymbol{x}_2|\boldsymbol{w}_1}(\boldsymbol{w}_2 + \boldsymbol{h})$,

$$F_{\boldsymbol{x}_2|\boldsymbol{w}_1}(\boldsymbol{w}_2^+) = \frac{\Pr(\boldsymbol{x}_1 = \boldsymbol{w}_1, \boldsymbol{x}_2 \leqslant \boldsymbol{w}_2^+)}{\Pr(\boldsymbol{x}_1 = \boldsymbol{w}_1)} = \frac{\Pr(\boldsymbol{x}_1 = \boldsymbol{w}_1, \boldsymbol{x}_2 \leqslant \boldsymbol{w}_2)}{\Pr(\boldsymbol{x}_1 = \boldsymbol{w}_1)} = F_{\boldsymbol{x}_2|\boldsymbol{w}_1}(\boldsymbol{w}_2);$$

(iv) for all real constant $(m - k)$-dimensional vectors satisfying $\boldsymbol{s} < \boldsymbol{t}$,

$$\left[\left[F_{\boldsymbol{x}_2|\boldsymbol{w}_1}(\boldsymbol{w}_2)\right]_{s_1}^{t_1} \cdots\right]_{s_{m-k}}^{t_{m-k}} = \Pr(\boldsymbol{s} < \boldsymbol{x}_2 \leqslant \boldsymbol{t} \mid \boldsymbol{x}_1 = \boldsymbol{w}_1) \geqslant 0.$$

It is therefore a proper distribution function. (We have used $\boldsymbol{x}_1 = \boldsymbol{w}_1$ as a shorthand in the continuous case, as will be clarified in Exercise 6.26.)

Exercise 6.26 (Conditionals for continuous variates) Show that if (x, y) is continuous with joint p.d.f. $f(u, v)$, then

$$f_{y|x=u}(v) = \frac{\mathrm{d}}{\mathrm{d}v} \lim_{h\to 0^+} \Pr(y \leqslant v \mid u \leqslant x \leqslant u + h).$$

Solution

First of all, notice that division by h is not required in this formula, unlike when we take the derivative of some function:

$$\frac{\mathrm{d}}{\mathrm{d}u} g(u) = \lim_{h \to 0} \frac{g(u+h) - g(u)}{h}.$$

Here we condition on $x = u$, hence $h \to 0^+$ in $\Pr(y \leqslant v \mid u \leqslant x \leqslant u+h)$. The only differentiation in this exercise is with respect to v and not u. We have

$$\Pr(y \leqslant v \mid u \leqslant x \leqslant u+h) = \frac{\Pr(y \leqslant v, u \leqslant x \leqslant u+h)}{\Pr(u \leqslant x \leqslant u+h)}$$

$$= \frac{\int_{-\infty}^{v} \int_{u}^{u+h} f(s,t)\,\mathrm{d}s\,\mathrm{d}t}{\int_{u}^{u+h} f_x(s)\,\mathrm{d}s}.$$

Now if $h \to 0^+$, then *both* numerator and denominator tend to 0, since $\Pr(x = u) = 0$ for continuous x. Invoking l'Hôpital's rule gives

$$\lim_{h \to 0^+} \Pr(y \leqslant v \mid u \leqslant x \leqslant u+h) = \lim_{h \to 0^+} \frac{\frac{\mathrm{d}}{\mathrm{d}h} \int_{-\infty}^{v} \int_{u}^{u+h} f(s,t)\,\mathrm{d}s\,\mathrm{d}t}{\frac{\mathrm{d}}{\mathrm{d}h} \int_{u}^{u+h} f_x(s)\,\mathrm{d}s}$$

$$= \lim_{h \to 0^+} \frac{\int_{-\infty}^{v} f(u+h,t)\,\mathrm{d}t}{f_x(u+h)} = \frac{\int_{-\infty}^{v} f(u,t)\,\mathrm{d}t}{f_x(u)},$$

using Leibniz' rule to differentiate the integrals. Differentiating both sides with respect to v and using $f_{y|x=u}(v) = f(u,v)/f_x(u)$ gives the desired result.

Exercise 6.27 (Conditioning both ways) Let $f(u,v)$ be the joint p.d.f. of (x,y), with $f_x(u)$, $f_y(v)$ as the marginal densities and $f_{x|v}(u)$, $f_{y|u}(v)$ as the conditional densities. Suppose there exists a constant v_0 such that $f_{y|u}(v_0) \neq 0$ for all $u \in \mathbb{R}$. Show that

$$f(u,v) = c \times \frac{f_{y|u}(v) f_{x|v_0}(u)}{f_{y|u}(v_0)},$$

where c is a constant.

Solution

By definition, we have $f(u,v) = f_{y|u}(v) f_x(u)$ and also $f(u,v) = f_{x|v}(u) f_y(v)$, where one should note that the conditioning is on the *realizations* u and v. Hence, for $v = v_0$,

$$f_{y|u}(v_0) f_x(u) = f_{x|v_0}(u) f_y(v_0).$$

Letting $c = f_y(v_0)$ and multiplying both sides by $f_{y|u}(v)$, the result follows.

***Exercise 6.28 (The LIE)** Let x and y be two random variables.

(a) By using the definition $\mathrm{d}F_{x,y}(u,v) = \partial_v \partial_u F_{x,y}(u,v)$ that was given in the introduction to Chapter 5, show that

$$\mathrm{d}F_{x,y}(u,v) = \left(\mathrm{d}F_{y|u}(v)\right)\left(\mathrm{d}F_x(u)\right).$$

(b) Prove that

$$\mathrm{E}\left(g(x)h(y)\right) = \mathrm{E}_x\left(g(x)\,\mathrm{E}_{y|x}\left(h(y)\right)\right),$$

assuming the expectations exist.
(c) How would the formula in (b) change if h were a function of both x and y, namely $h\left(x,y\right)$? How would it change if the left-hand side to be decomposed were $\mathrm{E}_{x,y|z}(\psi(x,y,z))$, where z is a third variate?
(d) Show that (b) implies that

$$\mathrm{var}\left(h\left(y\right)\right) = \mathrm{E}_x\left(\mathrm{var}_{y|x}(h\left(y\right))\right) + \mathrm{var}_x\left(\mathrm{E}_{y|x}\left(h\left(y\right)\right)\right).$$

Hence show that $\mathrm{var}\left(h\left(y\right)\right) \geqslant \mathrm{E}_x\left(\mathrm{var}_{y|x}(h\left(y\right))\right)$ and $\mathrm{var}\left(h\left(y\right)\right) \geqslant \mathrm{var}_x\left(\mathrm{E}_{y|x}(h\left(y\right))\right)$, and interpret these inequalities.

Solution

(a) Since the joint c.d.f. factorizes into $F_{x,y}(u,v) = \int_{t\leqslant u} F_{y|x=t}(v)\,\mathrm{d}F_x(t)$, taking differentials on both sides gives

$$\begin{aligned}
\mathrm{d}F_{x,y}(u,v) &= \partial_v\partial_u F_{x,y}(u,v)\\
&= \partial_v\partial_u\left(\int_{-\infty}^{u} F_{y|x=t}(v)\,\mathrm{d}F_x(t)\right)\\
&= \partial_v\left(F_{y|u}(v)\,\mathrm{d}F_x(u)\right) = \left(\mathrm{d}F_{y|u}(v)\right)\left(\mathrm{d}F_x(u)\right),
\end{aligned}$$

where the differential of the integral follows as in Leibniz' rule. For example, the case of x,y continuous gives $f_{y|u}(v)f_x(u)\,\mathrm{d}u\,\mathrm{d}v$, which can also be seen from

$$\mathrm{d}F_{x,y}(u,v) = f_{x,y}\left(u,v\right)\mathrm{d}u\,\mathrm{d}v = f_{y|u}(v)f_x(u)\,\mathrm{d}u\,\mathrm{d}v.$$

(b) First note that, even if x,y were continuous, the functions g or h need not be so. This is why a derivation using Stieltjes integrals is preferable to considering the possible combination of cases for x,y and their functions g,h. Applying (a) to the definition of expectations,

$$\begin{aligned}
\mathrm{E}\left(g(x)h(y)\right) &= \int_{-\infty}^{\infty}\int_{-\infty}^{\infty} g(u)h(v)\,\mathrm{d}F_{x,y}(u,v)\\
&= \int_{-\infty}^{\infty}\int_{-\infty}^{\infty} g(u)h(v)\left(\mathrm{d}F_{y|u}(v)\right)\left(\mathrm{d}F_x(u)\right)\\
&= \int_{-\infty}^{\infty} g(u)\left(\int_{-\infty}^{\infty} h(v)\,\mathrm{d}F_{y|u}(v)\right)\mathrm{d}F_x(u)\\
&= \int_{-\infty}^{\infty} g(u)\,\mathrm{E}_{y|u}\left(h(y)\right)\mathrm{d}F_x(u) = \mathrm{E}_x\left(g(x)\,\mathrm{E}_{y|x}\left(h(y)\right)\right).
\end{aligned}$$

Notice how the subscript of the conditional expectation has changed in the last step, just as

the argument of the function g has.
(c) Following the same steps as in (b) leads to

$$\mathrm{E}\left(g(x)h(x,y)\right)=\int_{-\infty}^{\infty}g(u)\,\mathrm{E}_{y|u}\left(h(u,y)\right)\mathrm{d}F_x(u)=\mathrm{E}_x\left(g(x)\,\mathrm{E}_{y|x}\left(h(x,y)\right)\right)$$

and

$$\mathrm{E}_{x,y|z}\left(\psi\left(x,y,z\right)\right)=\mathrm{E}_{x|z}\left(\mathrm{E}_{y|x,z}\left(\psi\left(x,y,z\right)\right)\right),$$

assuming the expectations exist. The last result shows that conditioning successively on two nested sets of variables $\{z\}\subset\{x,z\}$ (as on the right-hand side), we can combine the two expectations into a single expectation conditioned on the smaller of the two sets (as on the left-hand side).
(d) Using the definition of variances and the law of iterated expectations, twice, and the shorthand $h\equiv h\left(y\right)$,

$$\begin{aligned}\mathrm{E}_x\left[\mathrm{var}_{y|x}(h)\right]&=\mathrm{E}_x\left[\mathrm{E}_{y|x}\left(h^2\right)-\left(\mathrm{E}_{y|x}\left(h\right)\right)^2\right]\\&=\mathrm{E}\left(h^2\right)-\mathrm{E}_x\left[\left(\mathrm{E}_{y|x}\left(h\right)\right)^2\right]\\&=\mathrm{var}\left(h\right)+\left(\mathrm{E}\left(h\right)\right)^2-\mathrm{var}_x\left(\mathrm{E}_{y|x}\left(h\right)\right)-\left(\mathrm{E}_x\left[\mathrm{E}_{y|x}\left(h\right)\right]\right)^2\\&=\mathrm{var}\left(h\right)-\mathrm{var}_x\left(\mathrm{E}_{y|x}\left(h\right)\right),\end{aligned}$$

and the nonnegativity of variances implies the inequalities, as required. The inequalities reflect the fact that conditioning exploits information about y which may be contained in x, thus reducing the variability of $h\left(y\right)$ or, at worst, leaving it unchanged. Two special cases arise. First, if $\mathrm{E}_{y|x}\left(h\left(y\right)\right)$ is not a function of x (see Exercise 6.47) with probability 1, then $\mathrm{var}_x\left(\mathrm{E}_{y|x}\left(h\left(y\right)\right)\right)=0$ and the first inequality becomes an equality. Second, the same happens to the second inequality if $\mathrm{var}_{y|x}(h\left(y\right))=0$ with probability 1, that is, if x accounts almost surely for all the variability in $h\left(y\right)$.

***Exercise 6.29 (Covariance as a measure of divergence between joint and marginal c.d.f.s)** Assuming moments of order 2 exist, show that

$$\mathrm{cov}(x,y)=\int_{-\infty}^{\infty}\int_{-\infty}^{\infty}\left(F_{x,y}(u,v)-F_x(u)F_y(v)\right)\mathrm{d}u\,\mathrm{d}v.$$

[Hint: Rewrite the covariance by means of the LIE, then use Exercise 3.9 and (6.1).]

Solution

We start by remarking that this formula shows quite clearly that independence ($F_{x,y}(u,v)=F_x(u)F_y(v)$ for all u,v) implies $\mathrm{cov}(x,y)=0$, but that the converse is not true: the integrand can be nonzero with cancelling terms such that $\mathrm{cov}(x,y)=0$.

By the LIE,

$$\mathrm{cov}(x,y)=\mathrm{E}_x\,\mathrm{E}_{y|x}\left(x\left(y-\mathrm{E}\left(y\right)\right)\right)=\mathrm{E}_x\left(x\left(\mathrm{E}_{y|x}\left(y\right)-\mathrm{E}\left(y\right)\right)\right),$$

and Exercise 3.9 gives

$$\begin{aligned}
&\mathrm{E}_{y|x}(y) - \mathrm{E}(y) \\
&= \int_0^\infty \left(1 - F_{y|x}(v)\right) \mathrm{d}v - \int_{-\infty}^0 F_{y|x}(v)\,\mathrm{d}v - \left(\int_0^\infty (1 - F_y(v))\,\mathrm{d}v - \int_{-\infty}^0 F_y(v)\,\mathrm{d}v\right) \\
&= \int_0^\infty \left(F_y(v) - F_{y|x}(v)\right) \mathrm{d}v + \int_{-\infty}^0 \left(F_y(v) - F_{y|x}(v)\right) \mathrm{d}v = \int_{-\infty}^\infty \left(F_y(v) - F_{y|x}(v)\right) \mathrm{d}v;
\end{aligned}$$

hence

$$\begin{aligned}
\operatorname{cov}(x, y) &= \mathrm{E}_x\left(x \int_{-\infty}^\infty \left(F_y(v) - F_{y|x}(v)\right) \mathrm{d}v\right) \\
&= \int_{-\infty}^\infty u \int_{-\infty}^\infty \left(F_y(v) - F_{y|x=u}(v)\right) \mathrm{d}v\,\mathrm{d}F_x(u) \\
&= \int_{-\infty}^\infty \int_{-\infty}^\infty u\left(F_y(v) - F_{y|x=u}(v)\right) \mathrm{d}F_x(u)\,\mathrm{d}v,
\end{aligned}$$

where swapping the integrals is allowed by the existence of the expectation or absolute convergence of the double integral; see Section A.3.5. Integrating by parts with respect to u is allowable by the existence assumption (see Section A.4.3) and, using

$$\int_{t\leqslant u} \left(F_y(v) - F_{y|x=t}(v)\right) \mathrm{d}F_x(t) = F_y(v)F_x(u) - F_{x,y}(u, v)$$

from (6.1), we get

$$\begin{aligned}
\operatorname{cov}(x, y) = &\int_{-\infty}^\infty \left[u\left(F_y(v)F_x(u) - F_{x,y}(u, v)\right)\right]_{-\infty}^\infty \mathrm{d}v \\
&- \int_{-\infty}^\infty \int_{-\infty}^\infty \left(F_y(v)F_x(u) - F_{x,y}(u, v)\right) \mathrm{d}u\,\mathrm{d}v.
\end{aligned}$$

The proof of Exercise 3.9 gives the details required to show that

$$\begin{aligned}
&\left[u\left(F_x(u)F_y(v) - F_{x,y}(u, v)\right)\right]_{u=-\infty}^\infty \\
&= \lim_{u\to\infty} \left(u\left(1 \times F_y(v) - F_{x,y}(\infty, v)\right)\right) - \lim_{u\to-\infty} \left(u\left(0 \times F_y(v) - 0\right)\right) = 0
\end{aligned}$$

with $F_x(\infty) = 1$, $F_{x,y}(\infty, v) = F_y(v)$, $F_x(-\infty) = 0$, and $F_{x,y}(-\infty, v) = 0$.

Exercise 6.30 (Conditional information) The Kullback–Leibler information criterion for the multivariate case is $\mathrm{KL}(f_{\boldsymbol{x}}, f_{\boldsymbol{z}}) := \mathrm{E}_{\boldsymbol{x}}\left(\log(f_{\boldsymbol{x}}(\boldsymbol{x})/f_{\boldsymbol{z}}(\boldsymbol{x}))\right)$, where $\boldsymbol{x}$ and $\boldsymbol{z}$ are of the same dimension. For $\boldsymbol{x}' := (\boldsymbol{x}_1', \boldsymbol{x}_2')$ and accordingly $\boldsymbol{z}' := (\boldsymbol{z}_1', \boldsymbol{z}_2')$, we define

$$\mathrm{KL}_{2|1}\left(f_{\boldsymbol{x}_2|\boldsymbol{x}_1=\boldsymbol{w}_1}, f_{\boldsymbol{z}_2|\boldsymbol{z}_1=\boldsymbol{w}_1}\right) := \mathrm{E}_{\boldsymbol{x}_2}\left(\log\left(\frac{f_{\boldsymbol{x}_2|\boldsymbol{x}_1=\boldsymbol{w}_1}(\boldsymbol{x}_2)}{f_{\boldsymbol{z}_2|\boldsymbol{z}_1=\boldsymbol{w}_1}(\boldsymbol{x}_2)}\right)\right)$$

and

$$\begin{aligned}\mathrm{KL}\left(f_{x_2|x_1}, f_{z_2|z_1=x_1}\right) &:= \mathrm{E}_{x_1}\left(\mathrm{KL}_{2|1}\left(f_{x_2|x_1}, f_{z_2|z_1=x_1}\right)\right)\\ &\equiv \mathrm{E}\left(\log\left(\frac{f_{x_2|x_1}(x_2)}{f_{z_2|z_1=x_1}(x_2)}\right)\right).\end{aligned}$$

Note that the former of these two expressions is a function of w_1 but the latter is not, and that the former is effectively a conditional expectation (the conditioning being in the argument of the operator E_{x_2}, not in its subscript). Prove and interpret:
(a) independence of x_1 from x_2, and of z_1 from z_2, implies the decomposition $\mathrm{KL}(f_x, f_z) = \mathrm{KL}(f_{x_1}, f_{z_1}) + \mathrm{KL}(f_{x_2}, f_{z_2})$;
(b) $\mathrm{KL}(f_x, f_z) \geqslant \mathrm{KL}(f_{x_1}, f_{z_1})$, with equality if and only if $\mathrm{KL}\left(f_{x_2|x_1}, f_{z_2|z_1=x_1}\right) = 0$;
(c) $\mathrm{KL}(f_x, f_z) \geqslant \mathrm{KL}\left(f_{x_2|x_1}, f_{z_2|z_1=x_1}\right)$, with equality if and only if $\mathrm{KL}(f_{x_1}, f_{z_1}) = 0$.

Solution

By the law of iterated expectations and by the definition of conditional densities,

$$\begin{aligned}\mathrm{KL}\left(f_x, f_z\right) &= \mathrm{E}_{x_1}\left(\mathrm{E}_{x_2|x_1}\left(\log\left(\frac{f_x(x)}{f_z(x)}\right)\right)\right)\\ &= \mathrm{E}_{x_1}\left(\mathrm{E}_{x_2|x_1}\left(\log\left(\frac{f_{x_2|x_1}(x_2)f_{x_1}(x_1)}{f_{z_2|z_1=x_1}(x_2)f_{z_1}(x_1)}\right)\right)\right).\end{aligned}$$

We can therefore decompose the KLIC into

$$\begin{aligned}\mathrm{KL}\left(f_x, f_z\right) &= \mathrm{E}_{x_1}\left(\mathrm{E}_{x_2|x_1}\left(\log\left(\frac{f_{x_2|x_1}(x_2)}{f_{z_2|z_1=x_1}(x_2)}\right)\right)\right) + \mathrm{E}_{x_1}\left(\log\left(\frac{f_{x_1}(x_1)}{f_{z_1}(x_1)}\right)\right)\\ &= \mathrm{E}\left(\log\left(\frac{f_{x_2|x_1}(x_2)}{f_{z_2|z_1=x_1}(x_2)}\right)\right) + \mathrm{E}\left(\log\left(\frac{f_{x_1}(x_1)}{f_{z_1}(x_1)}\right)\right)\\ &= \mathrm{KL}\left(f_{x_2|x_1}, f_{z_2|z_1=x_1}\right) + \mathrm{KL}\left(f_{x_1}, f_{z_1}\right).\end{aligned}$$

Result (a) is obtained since independence leads to $f_{x_2|x_1} = f_{x_2}$ and $f_{z_2|z_1=x_1} = f_{z_2}$. In this case, the total information about the dissimilarity of x and z can be decomposed into the sum of individual information about the corresponding components, and there are no interaction terms between these components. For results (b) and (c), we recall from Exercise 4.42 that KL is nonnegative, and the stated inequalities follow. Notice that $\mathrm{KL}(f_{x_2|x_1}, f_{z_2|z_1=x_1}) = 0$ implies that $\mathrm{KL}_{2|1}(f_{x_2|x_1}, f_{z_2|z_1=x_1}) = 0$ with probability 1, because the latter is nonnegative and has to average to 0 as x_1 varies.

We now interpret the inequalities in (b) and (c) in terms of the roles of x_1 versus $x_2 \mid x_1$ in conveying information about the divergence between x and z. The joint information is not less than the marginal information or conditional information, with equalities occurring whenever x_1 (case (b)) or $x_2 \mid x_1$ (case (c)) contains all the information about the dissimilarity of x and z. Notice that $\mathrm{KL}(f_{x_1}, f_{z_1}) = 0$ does not mean that x_1 contains no information about divergences, since it actually does contribute to the explanatory power of $x_2 \mid x_1$; it means that x_1 contains information only insofar as it affects x_2.

6.3 Conditional distributions and expectations, practice

Exercise 6.31 (Multinomials: conditioning) A fair die is cast n times. Let x_i denote the number of times that i comes up, $i = 1, 2, \ldots, 6$. Derive $\Pr(x_1 + x_6 = s \mid x_5 = t)$.

Solution
We start by deriving the joint p.d.f. of the two variates in the required conditional probability. Define $z_1 := x_1 + x_6$, $z_2 := x_5$, and $z_3 := x_2 + x_3 + x_4$, with realizations $w_1, w_2, w_3 \geqslant 0$ where $w_3 = n - w_1 - w_2$. We get the multinomial distribution

$$\Pr(z_1 = w_1, z_2 = w_2) = \frac{n!}{w_1!w_2!w_3!}\left(\frac{2}{6}\right)^{w_1}\left(\frac{1}{6}\right)^{w_2}\left(\frac{3}{6}\right)^{w_3}.$$

Hence,

$$\Pr(z_1 = s \mid z_2 = t) = \frac{\Pr(z_1 = s, z_2 = t)}{\Pr(z_2 = t)} = \frac{\frac{n!}{s!t!(n-s-t)!}\left(\frac{1}{3}\right)^s\left(\frac{1}{6}\right)^t\left(\frac{1}{2}\right)^{n-s-t}}{\binom{n}{t}\left(\frac{1}{6}\right)^t\left(\frac{5}{6}\right)^{n-t}}$$
$$= \frac{(n-t)!}{s!(n-t-s)!}\left(\frac{2}{5}\right)^s\left(\frac{3}{5}\right)^{n-t-s},$$

and we conclude that the distribution of $(x_1 + x_6 = s \mid x_5 = t)$ is $\text{Bin}(n - t, 2/5)$.

Exercise 6.32 (Multinomials: conditioning the other way) Suppose that

$$\Pr(x_1 = u_1, x_2 = u_2) = \frac{n!}{u_1!u_2!(n - u_1 - u_2)!}p_1^{u_1}p_2^{u_2}(1 - p_1 - p_2)^{n-u_1-u_2},$$

where the u_i (for $i = 1, 2$) are integers satisfying $0 \leqslant u_i \leqslant n$ and $0 \leqslant u_1 + u_2 \leqslant n$, with $0 < p_i < 1$ and $0 < p_1 + p_2 < 1$. Show that

$$\Pr(x_1 = s \mid x_1 + x_2 = t) = \binom{t}{s}\left(\frac{p_1}{p_1 + p_2}\right)^s\left(\frac{p_2}{p_1 + p_2}\right)^{t-s} \quad (s = 0, 1, \ldots, t).$$

Solution
We know that

$$\Pr(x_1 = s \mid x_1 + x_2 = t) = \frac{\Pr(x_1 = s, x_2 = t - s)}{\Pr(x_1 + x_2 = t)}.$$

The numerator is equal to

$$\Pr(x_1 = s, x_2 = t - s) = \frac{n!}{s!(t-s)!(n - s - (t - s))!}p_1^s p_2^{t-s}(1 - p_1 - p_2)^{n-t}$$

and the denominator is

$$\Pr(x_1 + x_2 = t) = \binom{n}{t}(p_1 + p_2)^t(1 - p_1 - p_2)^{n-t}.$$

Dividing numerator by denominator gives the result.

Exercise 6.33 (The LIE: numbers) The population of the variates x and y is composed of five equally probable values of (x, y), given by

$$(1,2), \quad (1,3), \quad (2,2), \quad (2,3), \quad (2,5).$$

Calculate $\mathrm{E}(y)$ and $\mathrm{var}(y)$ by means of the LIE, and check that they are identical to the moments when calculated unconditionally.

Solution

We note that $x = 1$ or $x = 2$. First, we have

$$\mathrm{E}_{y|x=1}(y) = \frac{2+3}{2} = \frac{5}{2} \quad \text{and} \quad \mathrm{E}_{y|x=2}(y) = \frac{2+3+5}{3} = \frac{10}{3},$$

with $\Pr(x = 1) = 2/5$ and $\Pr(x = 2) = 3/5$ giving the weighted average

$$\mathrm{E}(y) = \left(\frac{5}{2}\right)\frac{2}{5} + \left(\frac{10}{3}\right)\frac{3}{5} = 3.$$

This is also what we get directly as

$$\mathrm{E}(y) = (2+3+2+3+5)\frac{1}{5} = 3.$$

Second, we need

$$\mathrm{var}(y) = \mathrm{var}_x\left(\mathrm{E}_{y|x}(y)\right) + \mathrm{E}_x\left(\mathrm{var}_{y|x}(y)\right).$$

We have

$$\mathrm{var}_{y|x=1}(y) = \left(2^2 + 3^2\right)\frac{1}{2} - \left(\frac{5}{2}\right)^2 = \frac{1}{4},$$

$$\mathrm{var}_{y|x=2}(y) = \left(2^2 + 3^2 + 5^2\right)\frac{1}{3} - \left(\frac{10}{3}\right)^2 = \frac{14}{9},$$

hence

$$\mathrm{E}_x\left(\mathrm{var}_{y|x}(y)\right) = \left(\frac{1}{4}\right)\frac{2}{5} + \left(\frac{14}{9}\right)\frac{3}{5} = \frac{31}{30}.$$

Now,

$$\mathrm{var}_x\left(\mathrm{E}_{y|x}(y)\right) = \left(\frac{5}{2}\right)^2\frac{2}{5} + \left(\frac{10}{3}\right)^2\frac{3}{5} - 3^2 = \frac{1}{6},$$

hence $\mathrm{var}(y) = 36/30 = 6/5$. This matches the unconditional

$$\mathrm{var}(y) = \left(2^2 + 3^2 + 2^2 + 3^2 + 5^2\right)\frac{1}{5} - 3^2 = \frac{6}{5}.$$

Exercise 6.34 (Gamma marginals: conditioning) The joint p.d.f. of (x, y) is

$$f(u, v) = \begin{cases} \mathrm{e}^{-v} & (0 < u < v < \infty), \\ 0 & \text{(elsewhere)}. \end{cases}$$

(a) Derive $f_{y|u}(v)$, $\mathrm{E}_{y|u}(y)$, and $\mathrm{E}_{y|u}(y^2)$.
(b) Use the results from (a) to evaluate $\mathrm{var}(y)$.

Solution
(a) We first obtain the marginal density of x as

$$f_x(u) = \int_u^\infty \mathrm{e}^{-v}\,\mathrm{d}v = \mathrm{e}^{-u}$$

for $u > 0$ and 0 elsewhere, that is, a standard exponential. Hence,

$$f_{y|u}(v) = \mathrm{e}^{-(v-u)}$$

for $v > u$ and 0 elsewhere. In other words, we can generate the joint density by first taking $x \sim$ Expo(1), then y as another exponential (with parameter 1) but shifted by $x = u$ (thus the support of y is (u, ∞)).

Making the transformation $t = v - u$ with $\mathrm{d}t = \mathrm{d}v$, the required expectations are

$$\mathrm{E}_{y|u}(y) = \int_u^\infty v\mathrm{e}^{-(v-u)}\,\mathrm{d}v = \int_0^\infty (t+u)\,\mathrm{e}^{-t}\,\mathrm{d}t = 1 + u$$

and

$$\mathrm{E}_{y|u}(y^2) = \int_u^\infty v^2\mathrm{e}^{-(v-u)}\,\mathrm{d}v = \int_0^\infty \left(t^2 + 2ut + u^2\right)\mathrm{e}^{-t}\,\mathrm{d}t = 2 + 2u + u^2,$$

using properties of the exponential distribution with parameter 1.
(b) We have

$$\mathrm{var}_{y|u}(y) = \mathrm{E}_{y|u}(y^2) - \left(\mathrm{E}_{y|u}(y)\right)^2 = u^2 + 2u + 2 - (u+1)^2 = 1$$

and, by Exercise 6.28,

$$\mathrm{var}(y) = \mathrm{var}_x\left(\mathrm{E}_{y|x}(y)\right) + \mathrm{E}_x\left(\mathrm{var}_{y|x}(y)\right) = \mathrm{var}(1+x) + \mathrm{E}(1) = 1 + 1 = 2$$

since x is exponentially distributed with parameter 1.

Exercise 6.35 (Gamma marginals: conditioning the other way) The joint p.d.f. of (x, y) is given by

$$f(u, v) = \begin{cases} \lambda^2\mathrm{e}^{-\lambda v} & (0 < u < v < \infty), \\ 0 & \text{(elsewhere)}, \end{cases}$$

where $\lambda > 0$. Derive $\mathrm{E}_{x|v}(x)$, $\mathrm{cov}(x, 4x - y)$, and $\rho_{x,x+y}$.

Solution

We start by working out both marginal densities for later use:

$$f_x(u) = \lambda^2 \int_u^\infty e^{-\lambda v} \, dv = \lambda e^{-\lambda u} \quad (u > 0)$$

and

$$f_y(v) = \lambda^2 e^{-\lambda v} \int_0^v du = \lambda^2 v e^{-\lambda v} \quad (v > 0).$$

We note that $x \sim$ Expo(λ) with

$$\mathrm{E}(x) = \frac{1}{\lambda}, \quad \mathrm{var}(x) = \frac{1}{\lambda^2},$$

and that $y \sim$ Gam(2, λ) with

$$\mathrm{E}(y) = \frac{2}{\lambda}, \quad \mathrm{var}(y) = \frac{2}{\lambda^2}.$$

Next, we find the conditional density

$$f_{x|v}(u) = \frac{f(u,v)}{f_y(v)} = \frac{1}{v} \quad (0 < u < v)$$

and conclude that $\mathrm{E}_{x|v}(x) = \int_0^v (u/v) \, du = v/2$, so that the conditional expectation is linear in v. As in the previous exercise, we note that the factorization allows us to generate the variates, but in the reverse order to previously, using $y \sim$ Gam(2, λ) and then $x \mid y = v$ as a uniform on $(0, v)$.

For the remainder of the exercise, we need $\mathrm{cov}(x, y)$. We start with

$$\mathrm{E}(xy) = \int_0^\infty u \int_u^\infty \lambda^2 v e^{-\lambda v} \, dv \, du = \int_0^\infty u \varGamma(2, \lambda u) \, du,$$

where the incomplete gamma function is defined in Exercise 4.20 as

$$\varGamma(2, \lambda u) = \varGamma(1, \lambda u) + \lambda u e^{-\lambda u} = e^{-\lambda u} + \lambda u e^{-\lambda u}.$$

This gives

$$\mathrm{E}(xy) = \int_0^\infty \left(u + \lambda u^2\right) e^{-\lambda u} \, du = \frac{1}{\lambda^2} + \frac{2}{\lambda^2} = \frac{3}{\lambda^2}$$

by the scaling factors of the $\mathrm{Gam}(2, \lambda)$ and $\mathrm{Gam}(3, \lambda)$ densities, or alternatively by the expectations of λ^{-1} times Expo(λ) and Gam(2, λ). We can now work out

$$\mathrm{cov}(x, y) = \mathrm{E}(xy) - \frac{1}{\lambda} \times \frac{2}{\lambda} = \frac{1}{\lambda^2},$$

giving

$$\mathrm{cov}(x, 4x - y) = 4 \, \mathrm{var}(x) - \mathrm{cov}(x, y) = \frac{3}{\lambda^2}$$

and

$$\rho_{x,x+y} = \frac{\operatorname{cov}(x, x+y)}{\sqrt{\operatorname{var}(x) \times \operatorname{var}(x+y)}}$$

$$= \frac{\operatorname{var}(x) + \operatorname{cov}(x,y)}{\sqrt{\operatorname{var}(x)\left(\operatorname{var}(x) + \operatorname{var}(y) + 2\operatorname{cov}(x,y)\right)}} = \frac{2/\lambda^2}{\sqrt{(1/\lambda^2)(5/\lambda^2)}} = \frac{2}{\sqrt{5}},$$

where it can be seen that the correlation coefficient is scale-invariant and thus free of λ.

Exercise 6.36 (Bivariate beta: conditioning) The joint p.d.f. of (x, y) is given by

$$f(u,v) = \begin{cases} \frac{1}{16}uv^3 & (0 < u < 2,\ 0 < v < 2), \\ 0 & \text{(elsewhere)}. \end{cases}$$

(a) Derive $\operatorname{E}_{x|y}(x)$ and $\operatorname{var}_{x|y}(x)$ and use these to compute $\operatorname{var}(x)$.
(b) Evaluate $\operatorname{E}\left(x^2(2-y)^3\right)$.

Solution
(a) First, we obtain the marginal density of y as

$$f_y(v) = \frac{v^3}{16}\int_0^2 u \, du = \frac{v^3}{8}$$

for $0 < v < 2$ and 0 elsewhere. The conditional density of x is

$$f_{x|v}(u) = \frac{uv^3}{16} \times \frac{8}{v^3} = \frac{1}{2}u$$

for $0 < u < 2$ and 0 elsewhere. Note that the conditional density does not depend on v in this problem. Hence,

$$\operatorname{E}_{x|y}(x) = \frac{1}{2}\int_0^2 u^2 \, du = \frac{4}{3}.$$

Similarly, $\operatorname{E}_{x|y}(x^2) = 2$, so that $\operatorname{var}_{x|y}(x) = 2/9$. Since neither $\operatorname{E}_{x|y}(x)$ nor $\operatorname{E}_{x|y}(x^2)$ depends on y, we find that $\operatorname{var}(x) = \operatorname{var}_{x|y}(x) = 2/9$. In fact, x and y are independent, so these results should come as no surprise.
(b) Since x and y are independent we write

$$\operatorname{E}\left(x^2(2-y)^3\right) = \operatorname{E}\left(x^2\right)\operatorname{E}\left((2-y)^3\right) = 2\int_0^2 \frac{(2-v)^3 v^3}{8} \, dv = \frac{2^7 B(4,4)}{4} = \frac{8}{35},$$

by the integral of the beta density.

Exercise 6.37 (Dirichlet: conditioning) The joint p.d.f. of x and y is given by

$$f(u,v) = \begin{cases} \frac{45}{16}u^2v^2 & (u > 0,\ v > 0,\ u + v < 2), \\ 0 & \text{(elsewhere)}. \end{cases}$$

(a) Derive $f_{x|v}(u)$.
(b) Compute $\operatorname{cov}(x, y)$.

(c) Evaluate $\mathrm{E}\left(x^2 y\right)$ by using $f_y(v)$ and $f_{x|v}(u)$ only.

Solution

(a) To calculate $f_{x|v}(u)$ we work out

$$f_y(v) = \frac{45}{16} v^2 \int_0^{2-v} u^2 \, \mathrm{d}u = \frac{15}{16} v^2 (2-v)^3$$

for $0 < v < 2$ and 0 elsewhere. Hence,

$$f_{x|v}(u) = \frac{(45/16)\, u^2 v^2}{(15/16) v^2 (2-v)^3} = \frac{3u^2}{(2-v)^3}$$

for $0 < u < 2 - v$ and 0 elsewhere.

(b) We may calculate the covariance directly by double integration, but it is easier to use the following indirect route. First, we calculate

$$\mathrm{E}_{x|y}\left(x\right) = \int_0^{2-y} \frac{3u^3}{(2-y)^3} \, \mathrm{d}u = \frac{3}{(2-y)^3} \left[\frac{1}{4} u^4\right]_0^{2-y} = \frac{3}{4}(2-y).$$

Hence, $\mathrm{E}\left(x\right) = \mathrm{E}_y\left(\mathrm{E}_{x|y}(x)\right) = 3/2 - (3/4)\,\mathrm{E}\left(y\right)$. Because of the symmetry of the density function in its arguments, $\mathrm{E}\left(x\right)$ and $\mathrm{E}\left(y\right)$ must be the same, so that $\mathrm{E}\left(x\right) = \mathrm{E}\left(y\right) = 6/7$. Also,

$$\begin{aligned} \mathrm{E}\left(xy\right) &= \mathrm{E}_y\left(y\, \mathrm{E}_{x|y}\left(x\right)\right) = \mathrm{E}\left(\frac{3}{4} y(2-y)\right) \\ &= \frac{45}{64} \int_0^2 v^3 (2-v)^4 \, \mathrm{d}v = 180 B(4,5) = \frac{9}{14}. \end{aligned}$$

Hence, $\mathrm{cov}(x,y) = 9/14 - (6/7)^2 = -9/98$.

(c) Finally,

$$\mathrm{E}_{x|v}\left(x^2\right) = \int_0^{2-v} \frac{3u^4}{(2-v)^3} \, \mathrm{d}u = \frac{3}{5(2-v)^3} \left[u^5\right]_0^{2-v} = \frac{3}{5}(2-v)^2,$$

implying that

$$\begin{aligned} \mathrm{E}\left(x^2 y\right) &= \mathrm{E}_y\left(y\, \mathrm{E}_{x|y}\left(x^2\right)\right) = \mathrm{E}\left(\frac{3}{5} y(2-y)^2\right) \\ &= \frac{9}{16} \int_0^2 v^3 (2-v)^5 \, \mathrm{d}v = 3^2 2^5 B(4,6) = \frac{4}{7}. \end{aligned}$$

***Exercise 6.38 (Uniform disk)** The joint p.d.f. of (x, y) is given by

$$f(u,v) = \begin{cases} \frac{1}{\pi} & (u^2 + v^2 < 1), \\ 0 & \text{(elsewhere)}, \end{cases}$$

that is, x, y are *uniformly distributed over the unit disk* $x^2 + y^2 < 1$.

(a) Show that $\mathrm{cov}\left(x, y\right) = 0$.

(b) Show that x and y are not independent.

Solution

(a) Notice that this is a spherical density: the value of $f(u,v)$ is a function of u^2+v^2 only. The marginal density of x is

$$f_x(u) = \frac{1}{\pi}\int_{-\sqrt{1-u^2}}^{\sqrt{1-u^2}} \mathrm{d}v = \frac{2\sqrt{1-u^2}}{\pi}$$

for $-1 < u < 1$ and 0 elsewhere, which is a beta density. The expectation of x is

$$\mathrm{E}\,(x) = \frac{2}{\pi}\int_{-1}^{1} u\sqrt{1-u^2}\,\mathrm{d}u = 0$$

since $u\sqrt{1-u^2}$ is an odd function of u. Because of the symmetry of the joint density function in u and v, we also have $\mathrm{E}\,(y) = 0$. Then, letting

$$h(u) := \int_{-\sqrt{1-u^2}}^{\sqrt{1-u^2}} v\,\mathrm{d}v,$$

we obtain

$$\begin{aligned}\mathrm{cov}\,(x,y) = \mathrm{E}\,(xy) &= \frac{1}{\pi}\int_{-1}^{0} uh(u)\,\mathrm{d}u + \frac{1}{\pi}\int_{0}^{1} uh(u)\,\mathrm{d}u \\ &= -\frac{1}{\pi}\int_{0}^{1} th(-t)\,\mathrm{d}t + \frac{1}{\pi}\int_{0}^{1} uh(u)\,\mathrm{d}u = 0,\end{aligned}$$

where we have used the transformation $t = -u$ and the fact that $h(-t) = h(t)$.

(b) Both $f_x(u)$ and $f_y(v)$ have the same domain of definition, $(-1,1)$, but

$$\{(u,v) : u^2+v^2 < 1\} \neq \{(u,v) : -1 < u < 1, -1 < v < 1\}$$

and hence x and y are not independent, even though $\mathrm{cov}\,(x,y) = 0$. This can also be seen through the conditional density

$$f_{y|x=u}(v) = \frac{1}{2\sqrt{1-u^2}},$$

which depends on u. Notice that y is uniformly distributed when conditioning on $x = u$, although the *marginal* density of y is not uniform (it is a symmetric beta that peaks at zero, as follows from (a), making small $|y|$ most probable unconditionally).

Exercise 6.39 (Bivariate and beta: conditioning) The joint p.d.f. of (x,y,z) is given by

$$f(u,v,w) = \begin{cases} 72u(1-v)w^2 & (0 < u < v < 1,\ 0 < w < 1), \\ 0 & (\text{elsewhere}). \end{cases}$$

Derive $f_{x|v}(u)$, then obtain $\mathrm{E}_{x|v}\,(x)$ and $\mathrm{cov}\,(x,y)$.

Solution

We first integrate over w and obtain $f_{x,y}(u,v)$ as

$$f_{x,y}(u,v) = 72u(1-v)\int_0^1 w^2\,\mathrm{d}w = 24u(1-v)$$

for $0 < u < v < 1$ and 0 elsewhere. We use this density to find the marginal density

$$f_y(v) = 24(1-v)\int_0^v u\,\mathrm{d}u = 12v^2(1-v)$$

for $0 < v < 1$ and 0 elsewhere. Hence,

$$f_{x|v}(u) = \frac{2}{v^2}u$$

for $0 < u < v$ and 0 elsewhere. Using the conditional density we obtain

$$\mathrm{E}_{x|v}(x) = \int_0^v \frac{2u^2}{v^2}\,\mathrm{d}u = \frac{2}{3}v.$$

To calculate the covariance we need the expectation of y,

$$\mathrm{E}(y) = 12\int_0^1 v^3(1-v)\,\mathrm{d}v = 12B(4,2) = \frac{3}{5},$$

and of y^2,

$$\mathrm{E}\left(y^2\right) = 12\int_0^1 v^4(1-v)\,\mathrm{d}v = 12B(5,2) = \frac{2}{5}.$$

Hence,

$$\begin{aligned}\operatorname{cov}(x,y) &= \mathrm{E}\left[(x-\mathrm{E}(x))(y-\mathrm{E}(y))\right] = \mathrm{E}_y\left[(y-\mathrm{E}(y))\,\mathrm{E}_{x|y}(x-\mathrm{E}(x))\right]\\ &= \mathrm{E}_y\left[(y-\mathrm{E}(y))\left(\frac{2}{3}y - \mathrm{E}_y\left(\frac{2}{3}y\right)\right)\right]\\ &= \frac{2}{3}\mathrm{E}\left((y-\mathrm{E}(y))^2\right) = \frac{2}{3}\left(\mathrm{E}\left(y^2\right) - (\mathrm{E}(y))^2\right) = \frac{2}{75}.\end{aligned}$$

Exercise 6.40 (Trivariate quadratic: conditioning) The joint p.d.f. of (x,y,z) is

$$f(u,v,w) = \begin{cases} 126u^2v^2 & (0 < u < v < w < 1),\\ 0 & (\text{elsewhere}).\end{cases}$$

(a) Derive $f_{x|w}(u)$.
(b) Evaluate $\operatorname{cov}(x,z)$.

Solution

(a) First, we have

$$f_{x,z}(u,w) = 126u^2\int_u^w v^2\,\mathrm{d}v = 42u^2(w^3-u^3) \quad (0 < u < w < 1).$$

It then follows that

$$f_z(w) = 42\int_0^w u^2(w^3-u^3)\,\mathrm{d}u = 42\left[u^3\left(\frac{w^3}{3}-\frac{u^3}{6}\right)\right]_0^w = 7w^6 \quad (0<w<1).$$

Hence,

$$f_{x|w}(u) = \frac{6u^2(w^3-u^3)}{w^6} \quad (0<u<w).$$

(b) We find that

$$\mathrm{E}_{x|w}(x) = \int_0^w \frac{6u^3(w^3-u^3)}{w^6}\,\mathrm{d}u = \frac{6}{w^6}\left[\frac{1}{4}u^4w^3 - \frac{1}{7}u^7\right]_0^w = \frac{9}{14}w,$$

and hence

$$\mathrm{E}(xz) = \mathrm{E}_z\left(z\,\mathrm{E}_{x|z}(x)\right) = \frac{9}{14}\mathrm{E}\left(z^2\right) = \frac{9}{2}\int_0^1 w^8\,\mathrm{d}w = \frac{1}{2}.$$

Also,

$$\mathrm{E}(z) = 7\int_0^1 w^7 = \frac{7}{8}, \qquad \mathrm{E}(x) = \mathrm{E}_z\left(\mathrm{E}_{x|z}(x)\right) = \mathrm{E}_z\left(\frac{9}{14}z\right) = \frac{9}{14}\times\frac{7}{8} = \frac{9}{16}.$$

Hence, $\mathrm{cov}(x,z) = (1/2)-(7/8)(9/16) = 1/128$.

***Exercise 6.41 (Multivariate t: conditioning)** Partition the m-dimensional vector variate $\boldsymbol{x}$ into $\boldsymbol{x}' := (\boldsymbol{x}_1', \boldsymbol{x}_2') \sim \mathrm{EC}(\mathbf{0}, \boldsymbol{A})$, where $\boldsymbol{A} = \mathrm{diag}(\boldsymbol{A}_{11}, \boldsymbol{A}_{22})$ with dimensions $k>0$ and $m-k>0$. Assuming further that the distribution of $\boldsymbol{x}$ is $\mathrm{t}(\nu)$, prove that $\boldsymbol{x}_1$ is also $\mathrm{t}(\nu)$ and that, in this case of a block-diagonal $\boldsymbol{A}$, we have that $\boldsymbol{x}_2 \mid \boldsymbol{x}_1$ is $\mathrm{t}(\nu+k)$.

Solution

Omitting the constants of proportionality that do not depend on $\boldsymbol{w}$, the joint density is

$$f_{\boldsymbol{x}}(\boldsymbol{w}) \propto \left(1+\frac{1}{\nu}\boldsymbol{w}'\boldsymbol{A}^{-1}\boldsymbol{w}\right)^{-(\nu+m)/2} = \left(1+\frac{1}{\nu}\left(\boldsymbol{w}_1'\boldsymbol{A}_{11}^{-1}\boldsymbol{w}_1 + \boldsymbol{w}_2'\boldsymbol{A}_{22}^{-1}\boldsymbol{w}_2\right)\right)^{-(\nu+m)/2}$$

$$= \left(1+\frac{\boldsymbol{w}_2'\boldsymbol{A}_{22}^{-1}\boldsymbol{w}_2}{\nu+\boldsymbol{w}_1'\boldsymbol{A}_{11}^{-1}\boldsymbol{w}_1}\right)^{-(\nu+m)/2}\left(1+\frac{1}{\nu}\boldsymbol{w}_1'\boldsymbol{A}_{11}^{-1}\boldsymbol{w}_1\right)^{-(\nu+m)/2}$$

$$= \left(1+\boldsymbol{w}_2'\left(\left(\nu+\boldsymbol{w}_1'\boldsymbol{A}_{11}^{-1}\boldsymbol{w}_1\right)\boldsymbol{A}_{22}\right)^{-1}\boldsymbol{w}_2\right)^{-(\nu+m)/2}\left(1+\frac{1}{\nu}\boldsymbol{w}_1'\boldsymbol{A}_{11}^{-1}\boldsymbol{w}_1\right)^{-(\nu+m)/2}.$$

Before we can claim that this is a factorization into conditional and marginal densities, we need to make sure that the factor containing $\boldsymbol{w}_2$ is a proper conditional density, since $\boldsymbol{w}_1$ appears in both factors. The conditional density is a multivariate t because of its functional form; see (6.7). Since $\boldsymbol{w}_2$ is of order $m-k$, the power $\nu+m$ indicates that we have $\nu+m-(m-k) = \nu+k$ degrees of freedom, hence that

$$f_{\boldsymbol{x}_2|\boldsymbol{x}_1=\boldsymbol{w}_1}(\boldsymbol{w}_2) \propto \left|\boldsymbol{C}_{\boldsymbol{w}_1}\right|^{-1/2}\left(1+\frac{1}{\nu+k}\boldsymbol{w}_2'\boldsymbol{C}_{\boldsymbol{w}_1}^{-1}\boldsymbol{w}_2\right)^{-(\nu+m)/2}$$

with

$$\boldsymbol{C}_{\boldsymbol{w}_1} := \frac{\nu + \boldsymbol{w}_1' \boldsymbol{A}_{11}^{-1} \boldsymbol{w}_1}{\nu + k} \boldsymbol{A}_{22}.$$

Using

$$|\boldsymbol{C}_{\boldsymbol{w}_1}|^{1/2} = \left(\frac{\nu + \boldsymbol{w}_1' \boldsymbol{A}_{11}^{-1} \boldsymbol{w}_1}{\nu + k} \right)^{(m-k)/2} |\boldsymbol{A}_{22}|^{1/2} \propto \left(1 + \frac{1}{\nu} \boldsymbol{w}_1' \boldsymbol{A}_{11}^{-1} \boldsymbol{w}_1 \right)^{(m-k)/2},$$

we get

$$f_{\boldsymbol{x}}(\boldsymbol{w}) \propto \frac{|\boldsymbol{C}_{\boldsymbol{w}_1}|^{-1/2}}{\left(1 + \frac{1}{\nu+k} \boldsymbol{w}_2' \boldsymbol{C}_{\boldsymbol{w}_1}^{-1} \boldsymbol{w}_2 \right)^{(\nu+m)/2}} \times \left(1 + \frac{1}{\nu} \boldsymbol{w}_1' \boldsymbol{A}_{11}^{-1} \boldsymbol{w}_1 \right)^{-(\nu+k)/2}.$$

Apart from constants which do not depend on $\boldsymbol{w}$, the two multiplicative factors are now $\mathrm{t}(\nu + k)$ and $\mathrm{t}(\nu)$ densities, respectively, the latter following as the dimension of $\boldsymbol{w}_1$ is k. There are three features to note. First, the marginal density of $\boldsymbol{x}_1$ has the same number of degrees of freedom ν as the joint density of $\boldsymbol{x}$, something that we will prove more generally in Exercises 6.49(a) and 7.31(b). Second, both the conditional and marginal variates are centered around the origin, the former because of the block-diagonality of $\boldsymbol{A}$, something that we will encounter in more detail in Exercise 6.51. Third, the block-diagonality of $\boldsymbol{A}$ nevertheless does *not* imply that $\boldsymbol{x}_2$ is independent of $\boldsymbol{x}_1$ (the density of $\boldsymbol{x}_2 \mid \boldsymbol{x}_1 = \boldsymbol{w}_1$ contains $\boldsymbol{w}_1$); further discussion of this will be seen in Exercise 6.51(c).

Exercise 6.42 (Normal's truncation and censorship) Let $y := \max\{c, x + \mu\}$ and $x \sim \mathrm{N}(0, \sigma^2)$. Define $d := (c - \mu)/\sigma$ as the quantile (standardized point) of truncation or censorship, and $h := \phi(d)/(1 - \Phi(d))$ as the normal's hazard rate (in general, $h^{-1} \equiv (1 - F(d))/f(d)$ is known as *Mills' ratio*); see Exercise 2.18 for definitions. Prove:
(a) $\mathrm{E}(y \mid x + \mu > c) = \mu + \sigma h$;
(b) $\mathrm{var}(y \mid x + \mu > c) = \sigma^2 (1 - (h - d) h)$;
(c) $\mathrm{E}(y) = \Phi(d) c + (1 - \Phi(d)) (\mu + \sigma h)$;
(d) $\mathrm{var}(y) = \sigma^2 (1 - \Phi(d)) \left(1 - (h - d) h + (h - d)^2 \Phi(d)\right)$.
Notice that $y \mid y > c$ (or equivalently $y \mid x + \mu > c$) is a truncated variate, while y is a censored variate.

Solution
(a) Let us rewrite $y = \max\{c, z\}$, where $z := x + \mu \sim \mathrm{N}(\mu, \sigma^2)$. Then, $\mathrm{E}(y \mid z > c) = \mathrm{E}(z \mid z > c)$ and, since the density of $z \mid z > c$ is

$$f_{z|z>c}(w) = \frac{f_z(w)}{\Pr(z > c)} = \frac{f_z(w)}{\Pr((z - \mu)/\sigma > d)} = \frac{f_z(w)}{1 - \Phi(d)}$$

for $z > c$ and 0 otherwise, we get

$$\begin{aligned} \mathrm{E}(z \mid z > c) &= \frac{1}{(1-\Phi(d))\,\sigma\sqrt{2\pi}} \int_c^\infty w \exp\left(-\frac{(w-\mu)^2}{2\sigma^2}\right) \mathrm{d}w \\ &= \frac{1}{(1-\Phi(d))\,\sqrt{2\pi}} \int_d^\infty (\mu + \sigma t) \exp\left(-t^2/2\right) \mathrm{d}t \end{aligned}$$

on standardizing using $t = (w-\mu)/\sigma$. Using the definitions of $\phi(d)$ and $\Phi(d)$,

$$\begin{aligned} \mathrm{E}(z \mid z > c) &= \frac{\mu}{1-\Phi(d)} \int_d^\infty \frac{\exp\left(-t^2/2\right)}{\sqrt{2\pi}} \mathrm{d}t + \frac{\sigma}{1-\Phi(d)} \int_d^\infty \frac{t\exp\left(-t^2/2\right)}{\sqrt{2\pi}} \mathrm{d}t \\ &= \mu - \frac{\sigma}{1-\Phi(d)} \left[\frac{\exp\left(-t^2/2\right)}{\sqrt{2\pi}}\right]_d^\infty = \mu + \sigma h. \end{aligned}$$

(b) As in (a),

$$\begin{aligned} \mathrm{var}(y \mid z > c) &= \frac{1}{(1-\Phi(d))\,\sigma\sqrt{2\pi}} \int_c^\infty (w - (\mu+\sigma h))^2 \exp\left(-\frac{(w-\mu)^2}{2\sigma^2}\right) \mathrm{d}w \\ &= \frac{\sigma^2}{(1-\Phi(d))\,\sqrt{2\pi}} \int_d^\infty (t-h)^2 \exp\left(-t^2/2\right) \mathrm{d}t. \end{aligned}$$

Expanding as $(t-h)^2 = t^2 + h^2 - 2ht$ and integrating as before,

$$\mathrm{var}(y \mid z > c) = \frac{\sigma^2}{1-\Phi(d)} \int_d^\infty \frac{t^2\exp\left(-t^2/2\right)}{\sqrt{2\pi}} \mathrm{d}t + \sigma^2 h^2 - 2\sigma^2 h^2.$$

Now, integration by parts gives

$$\begin{aligned} \int_d^\infty \frac{t^2\exp\left(-t^2/2\right)}{\sqrt{2\pi}} \mathrm{d}t &= -\left[\frac{t\exp\left(-t^2/2\right)}{\sqrt{2\pi}}\right]_d^\infty + \int_d^\infty \frac{\exp\left(-t^2/2\right)}{\sqrt{2\pi}} \mathrm{d}t \\ &= d\phi(d) + (1-\Phi(d)), \end{aligned}$$

hence

$$\mathrm{var}(y \mid z > c) = \sigma^2 (dh + 1) - \sigma^2 h^2 = \sigma^2 \left(1 + dh - h^2\right).$$

(c) First, $z \leqslant c$ (hence $y = c$) with probability

$$\Pr(z \leqslant c) = \Pr\left(\frac{z-\mu}{\sigma} \leqslant d\right) = \Phi(d).$$

Second, $z > c$ with probability $1 - \Phi(d)$, in which case (a) tells us that $\mathrm{E}(y \mid z > c) = \mu + \sigma h$. The unconditional $\mathrm{E}(y)$ is obtained from the LIE (or as in the proof of Exercise 6.16) as

$$\begin{aligned} \mathrm{E}(y) &= \Pr(z \leqslant c)\,\mathrm{E}(y \mid z \leqslant c) + \Pr(z > c)\,\mathrm{E}(y \mid z > c) \\ &= \Phi(d)c + (1-\Phi(d))\,(\mu + \sigma h). \end{aligned}$$

(d) For the variance, we will use the LIE again:

$$\operatorname{var}(y) = \operatorname{var}_z(\mathrm{E}_{y|z}(y)) + \mathrm{E}_z(\operatorname{var}_{y|z}(y)).$$

The second term is easy to work out as before, because

$$\begin{aligned}\mathrm{E}_z(\operatorname{var}_{y|z}(y)) &= \Phi(d)\operatorname{var}(y \mid z \leqslant c) + (1-\Phi(d))\operatorname{var}(y \mid z > c)\\ &= \Phi(d)\operatorname{var}(c) + (1-\Phi(d))\operatorname{var}(y \mid z > c)\\ &= 0 + \sigma^2(1-\Phi(d))(1-(h-d)\,h),\end{aligned}$$

where the last variance follows from (b). For the first term of $\operatorname{var}(y)$,

$$\begin{aligned}\operatorname{var}_z(\mathrm{E}_{y|z}(y)) &= \mathrm{E}_z\left[\left[\mathrm{E}_{y|z}(y) - \mathrm{E}_z(\mathrm{E}_{y|z}(y))\right]^2\right] = \mathrm{E}_z\left[\left[\mathrm{E}_{y|z}(y) - \mathrm{E}(y)\right]^2\right]\\ &= \mathrm{E}_z\left[\left[\mathrm{E}_{y|z}(y) - \Phi(d)c - (1-\Phi(d))(\mu+\sigma h)\right]^2\right],\end{aligned}$$

where we can use $\mathrm{E}_{y|z\leqslant c}(y) = c$ and $\mathrm{E}_{y|z>c}(y) = \mu + \sigma h$ to get

$$\begin{aligned}\operatorname{var}_z(\mathrm{E}_{y|z}(y)) &= \Phi(d)\left[c - \Phi(d)c - (1-\Phi(d))(\mu+\sigma h)\right]^2\\ &\quad + (1-\Phi(d))\left[\mu + \sigma h - \Phi(d)c - (1-\Phi(d))(\mu+\sigma h)\right]^2\\ &= \Phi(d)(1-\Phi(d))^2(c-\mu-\sigma h)^2 + (1-\Phi(d))\Phi(d)^2(-c+\mu+\sigma h)^2\\ &= \Phi(d)(1-\Phi(d))(c-\mu-\sigma h)^2(1-\Phi(d)+\Phi(d))\\ &= \Phi(d)(1-\Phi(d))(\sigma d-\sigma h)^2,\end{aligned}$$

where the last step follows from the definition of d. Adding this result to the result for $\mathrm{E}_z(\operatorname{var}_{y|z}(y))$ gives the required expression for $\operatorname{var}(y)$.

6.4 Conditional distributions and dependence

Exercise 6.43 (Properties of error terms) Define

$$\varepsilon := y - \mathrm{E}_{y|x}(y),$$

which is the difference between y and what we expect it to be if we know x, hence the terminology *error term*. Assuming the expectations exist, show that:

(a) $\mathrm{E}_{y|x}(\varepsilon) = 0$;
(b) $\operatorname{var}_{y|x}(\varepsilon) = \operatorname{var}_{y|x}(y)$;
(c) $\mathrm{E}(\varepsilon) = 0$;
(d) $\operatorname{var}(\varepsilon) = \mathrm{E}_x\left(\operatorname{var}_{y|x}(y)\right)$;
(e) $\operatorname{cov}(\varepsilon, x) = 0$;
(f) $\operatorname{cov}(\varepsilon, \mathrm{E}_{y|x}(y)) = 0$;
(g) $\operatorname{cov}(\varepsilon, h(x)) = 0$ for any function h whose expectation exists.

Solution

(a) Since $\varepsilon = y - \mathrm{E}_{y|x}(y)$, we find that $\mathrm{E}_{y|x}(\varepsilon) = \mathrm{E}_{y|x}(y) - \mathrm{E}_{y|x}(y) = 0$.
(b) $\operatorname{var}_{y|x}(\varepsilon) = \operatorname{var}_{y|x}(y - \mathrm{E}_{y|x}(y))$ and, since $\mathrm{E}_{y|x}(y)$ is a function of x which is held constant when taking $\operatorname{var}_{y|x}(\cdot)$, we have $\operatorname{var}_{y|x}(y - \mathrm{E}_{y|x}(y)) = \operatorname{var}_{y|x}(y)$.
(c) $\mathrm{E}(\varepsilon) = \mathrm{E}_x\left(\mathrm{E}_{y|x}(\varepsilon)\right) = \mathrm{E}(0) = 0$.
(d) By Exercise 6.28(d), $\operatorname{var}(\varepsilon) = \mathrm{E}_x\left(\operatorname{var}_{y|x}(\varepsilon)\right) + \operatorname{var}_x(\mathrm{E}_{y|x}(\varepsilon)) = \mathrm{E}_x\left(\operatorname{var}_{y|x}(y)\right)$, by (b) and (a), respectively.
(e)–(g) All three are obtained as

$$\begin{aligned}\operatorname{cov}(\varepsilon, h(x)) &= \mathrm{E}(\varepsilon h(x)) - \mathrm{E}(\varepsilon)\,\mathrm{E}(h(x)) \\ &= \mathrm{E}(\varepsilon h(x)) = \mathrm{E}_x\left(h(x)\,\mathrm{E}_{y|x}(\varepsilon)\right) = \mathrm{E}(h(x) \times 0) = 0.\end{aligned}$$

Exercise 6.44 (Linear conditional expectation) Consider two random variables x and y with $\mathrm{E}(x) = \mu_1$, $\mathrm{E}(y) = \mu_2$, $\operatorname{var}(x) = \sigma_1^2$, $\operatorname{var}(y) = \sigma_2^2$, and correlation coefficient ρ. If $\mathrm{E}_{y|u}(y)$ is a linear function of u, then show that

$$\mathrm{E}_{y|x}(y) = \mu_2 + \rho\sigma_2\frac{x - \mu_1}{\sigma_1} \quad \text{and} \quad \mathrm{E}_x\left(\operatorname{var}_{y|x}(y)\right) = (1 - \rho^2)\sigma_2^2 \leqslant \sigma_2^2.$$

Solution

By assumption, $\mathrm{E}_{y|u}(y) = \alpha + \beta u$ for some α and β. Hence,

$$\mu_2 = \mathrm{E}_x\left(\mathrm{E}_{y|x}(y)\right) = \alpha + \beta\,\mathrm{E}(x) = \alpha + \beta\mu_1$$

and

$$\mathrm{E}(xy) = \mathrm{E}_x\left(x\,\mathrm{E}_{y|x}(y)\right) = \alpha\,\mathrm{E}(x) + \beta\,\mathrm{E}\left(x^2\right) = \alpha\mu_1 + \beta(\sigma_1^2 + \mu_1^2).$$

Also,

$$\mathrm{E}(xy) = \operatorname{cov}(x, y) + \mu_1\mu_2 = \rho\sigma_1\sigma_2 + \mu_1\mu_2.$$

Equating the two expressions for $\mathrm{E}(xy)$ gives

$$\alpha\mu_1 + \beta(\sigma_1^2 + \mu_1^2) = \rho\sigma_1\sigma_2 + \mu_1\mu_2.$$

Together with the first equation, $\mu_2 = \alpha + \beta\mu_1$, this gives us two equations with two unknowns (α and β) whose solution is

$$\beta = \frac{\rho\sigma_2}{\sigma_1}, \qquad \alpha = \mu_2 - \frac{\rho\sigma_2}{\sigma_1}\mu_1.$$

Finally, since $\operatorname{var}(y) = \mathrm{E}_x\left(\operatorname{var}_{y|x}(y)\right) + \operatorname{var}_x(\mathrm{E}_{y|x}(y))$, we obtain

$$\mathrm{E}_x\left(\operatorname{var}_{y|x}(y)\right) = \sigma_2^2 - \operatorname{var}\left(\mu_2 + \frac{\rho\sigma_2}{\sigma_1}(x - \mu_1)\right) = \sigma_2^2 - \rho^2\sigma_2^2 = (1 - \rho^2)\sigma_2^2.$$

Exercise 6.45 (Linear conditional expectation, restricted) For two random variables x and y, the following four moment restrictions are given: $\mathrm{E}(y) = 1$, $\mathrm{var}(x) = 1$, $\mathrm{E}_{y|u}(y) = 1 + u$, and $\mathrm{E}_x\left(\mathrm{var}_{y|x}(y)\right) = 2$. Evaluate $\mathrm{E}(x)$, $\mathrm{var}(y)$, and ρ.

Solution

There are two first moments ($\mathrm{E}(x)$ and $\mathrm{E}(y)$), and three second moments ($\mathrm{var}(x)$, $\mathrm{var}(y)$, and ρ). However, we have only four restrictions. Nevertheless, we can obtain all the moments. In a sense, the linearity of the conditional moment counts for two restrictions. Since

$$\mathrm{E}(y) = \mathrm{E}_x\left(\mathrm{E}_{y|x}(y)\right) = \mathrm{E}(1 + x) = 1 + \mathrm{E}(x),$$

we find that $\mathrm{E}(x) = 0$. Next, since

$$\mathrm{var}(y) = \mathrm{E}_x\left(\mathrm{var}_{y|x}(y)\right) + \mathrm{var}_x\left(\mathrm{E}_{y|x}(y)\right),$$

we find that $\mathrm{var}(y) = 2 + \mathrm{var}(x) = 3$. Finally, from Exercise 6.44 we have

$$\mathrm{E}_{y|u}(y) = \mathrm{E}(y) + \rho\sqrt{\frac{\mathrm{var}(y)}{\mathrm{var}(x)}}(u - \mathrm{E}(x)),$$

which gives $\rho = 1/\sqrt{3}$.

*__Exercise 6.46 (Best predictors)__ Consider a random vector (x, y) with known p.d.f. $f(u, v)$ and finite second-order moments. A single draw is made. You are told the value of x that was drawn. Then you are asked to predict the value of y that accompanied this value of x. You are free to choose any function of x, say $h(x)$, as your predictor. The "best" predictor is the one which minimizes $\mathrm{E}\left[(y - h(x))^2\right]$.

(a) Show that the best predictor of y is $h(x) = \mathrm{E}_{y|x}(y)$, assuming the expectation exists. Some authors use this property to *define* the conditional expectation. [Hint: Expand $(y - \mathrm{E}_{y|x}(y) + \mathrm{E}_{y|x}(y) - h(x))^2$.]

(b) Show that $\mathrm{E}(y)$ is not as good a predictor as $\mathrm{E}_{y|x}(y)$.

(c) Show that the best *linear* predictor of y is $h(x) = a + bx$, where

$$a = \mathrm{E}(y) - b\,\mathrm{E}(x) \qquad \text{and} \qquad b = \frac{\mathrm{cov}(x, y)}{\mathrm{var}(x)},$$

assuming that $\mathrm{var}(x) > 0$.

Solution

(a) Let

$$z_1 := y - \mathrm{E}_{y|x}(y), \qquad z_2 := y - h(x), \qquad z_3 := \mathrm{E}_{y|x}(y) - h(x),$$

and notice that z_3 is a function of x but not of y. Then,

$$\mathrm{E}\left(z_2^2\right) = \mathrm{E}\left((z_1 + z_3)^2\right) = \mathrm{E}\left(z_1^2\right) + 2\,\mathrm{E}(z_3 z_1) + \mathrm{E}\left(z_3^2\right) = \mathrm{E}\left(z_1^2\right) + \mathrm{E}\left(z_3^2\right),$$

because $\mathrm{E}(z_3 z_1) = \mathrm{E}_x\left(z_3\,\mathrm{E}_{y|x}(z_1)\right) = 0$. Hence, $\mathrm{E}\left(z_2^2\right)$ is minimized with respect to the

choice of function h when $\mathrm{E}\left(z_3^2\right) = 0$, that is, when $z_3 = 0$ with probability 1.
(b) Since

$$\mathrm{E}\left[(y - \mathrm{E}(y))^2\right] = \operatorname{var}(y) = \mathrm{E}_x\left(\operatorname{var}_{y|x}(y)\right) + \operatorname{var}_x\left(\mathrm{E}_{y|x}(y)\right)$$

and

$$\mathrm{E}\left[\left(y - \mathrm{E}_{y|x}(y)\right)^2\right] = \mathrm{E}_x\left[\mathrm{E}_{y|x}\left[\left(y - \mathrm{E}_{y|x}(y)\right)^2\right]\right] = \mathrm{E}_x\left(\operatorname{var}_{y|x}(y)\right),$$

the ranking of predictors follows since $\operatorname{var}_x\left(\mathrm{E}_{y|x}(y)\right) \geqslant 0$. Intuitively, if we know x, it is not a good idea to throw away this information (by not conditioning on x), so $\mathrm{E}_{y|x}(y)$ is at least as good a predictor as $\mathrm{E}(y)$; recall the example about rain and the teacher, seen before (1.1). If $\mathrm{E}_{y|x}(y)$ does not depend on x, then $\operatorname{var}_x\left(\mathrm{E}_{y|x}(y)\right) = 0$ and the two predictors are equally good.
(c) We wish to minimize $S := \mathrm{E}\left((y - a - bx)^2\right)$ with respect to the unknowns a and b. Differentiating gives

$$\frac{\partial S}{\partial a} = -2\,\mathrm{E}(y - a - bx) \quad \text{and} \quad \frac{\partial S}{\partial b} = -2\,\mathrm{E}(x(y - a - bx)).$$

The interchange of derivative and expectation is allowed since f does not vary with a, b (recall Leibniz' rule). Setting the partial derivatives equal to zero gives the best a and b as $a = \mathrm{E}(y) - b\,\mathrm{E}(x)$ and

$$\begin{aligned} 0 &= \mathrm{E}(x(y - a - bx)) = \mathrm{E}\left[x\left(y - (\mathrm{E}(y) - b\,\mathrm{E}(x)) - bx\right)\right] \\ &= \mathrm{E}\left[x\left(y - \mathrm{E}(y)\right) - bx\left(x - \mathrm{E}(x)\right)\right] = \operatorname{cov}(x, y) - b\operatorname{var}(x), \end{aligned}$$

as required. The second-order conditions

$$\frac{\partial^2 S}{\partial a^2} = 2 > 0, \qquad \frac{\partial^2 S}{\partial b^2} = 2\,\mathrm{E}\left(x^2\right) > 0, \qquad \frac{\partial^2 S}{\partial a \partial b} = 2\,\mathrm{E}(x)$$

imply that

$$\begin{vmatrix} 2 & 2\,\mathrm{E}(x) \\ 2\,\mathrm{E}(x) & 2\,\mathrm{E}\left(x^2\right) \end{vmatrix} = 4\operatorname{var}(x) > 0$$

and thus confirm that the obtained a, b give the best (not worst!) predictor. The formula for the optimal b could have been predicted from the proof of Exercise 6.20. Its multivariate generalization is the $\boldsymbol{b}$ of Exercise 6.21. The result also implies the following: if it is known that the conditional expectation is linear, then the best predictor has the formulae for a and b derived here. We will revisit these issues in the context of regression in Chapter 13.

***Exercise 6.47 (Mean-independence)** We say that y is *mean-independent* of x if $\mathrm{E}_{y|x}(y)$ exists and does not depend on x with probability 1. If y is mean-independent of x, show that:
(a) $\mathrm{E}_{y|x}(y) = \mathrm{E}(y)$ with probability 1;
(b) y is mean-independent of $h(x)$, where h is a function such that $\mathrm{E}(y \mid h(x))$ exists;
(c) y is uncorrelated with x, if the second moments exist;

(d) y is uncorrelated with $h(x)$, if the second moments exist;
(e) x is not necessarily mean-independent of y.

Solution
(a) $\mathrm{E}(y) = \mathrm{E}_x\left(\mathrm{E}_{y|x}(y)\right) = \mathrm{E}_x(1)\,\mathrm{E}_{y|x}(y)$, because the event that $\mathrm{E}_{y|x}(y)$ depends on x has probability zero, thus allowing us to factor the iterated expectation into a product.
(b) If h is an invertible function, then $\mathrm{E}(y \mid h(x) = h(u)) = \mathrm{E}(y \mid x = u)$ and the result follows. If h is not invertible, then there is a set $A_w \subseteq \mathcal{X}$ where the equality $h(u) = w$ holds for all $u \in A_w$. In this case, the condition $z := h(x) = w$ still allows x to vary randomly within A_w, and

$$\mathrm{E}(y \mid h(x) = w) = \mathrm{E}_{x,y|h(x)=w}(y) = \mathrm{E}_{x \in A_w}\left(\mathrm{E}_{y|x}(y)\right);$$

see Exercise 6.28(c) or think of the last expression as a weighted average as x varies within A_w. Notice that the notations $\mathrm{E}(y \mid h(x) = w)$ and $\mathrm{E}_{y|h(x)=w}(y)$ are not equivalent here, because h allows x to vary in A_w and hence the subscript y is incomplete (x also varies). Now y is mean-independent of x, so the inner expectation does not depend on x with probability 1, hence

$$\mathrm{E}(y \mid h(x) = w) = \mathrm{E}_{x \in A_w}(1)\,\mathrm{E}_{y|x}(y) = \mathrm{E}_{y|x}(y) = \mathrm{E}(y),$$

where the last step follows by (a).
(c) Let $z := \mathrm{E}_{y|x}(y)$. Then,

$$\mathrm{E}(z) \equiv \mathrm{E}_x\left(\mathrm{E}_{y|x}(y)\right) = \mathrm{E}(y)$$

and

$$\mathrm{E}(xz) \equiv \mathrm{E}_x\left(x\,\mathrm{E}_{y|x}(y)\right) = \mathrm{E}(xy).$$

Hence, $\mathrm{cov}(x, y) = \mathrm{cov}(x, z)$, which is zero since mean-independence indicates that z is a finite constant with probability 1.
(d) It follows from (b) that y is mean-independent of $h(x)$. Hence, by (c), y is uncorrelated with $h(x)$.
(e) Suppose that (x, y) can take three values, $(1, -1)$, $(0, 0)$, and $(1, 1)$, each with probability $1/3$. Then, $\mathrm{E}_{y|u}(y) = 0$ for every u, but $\mathrm{E}_{x|v}(x)$ equals 1 for $|v| = 1$ and 0 for $v = 0$, thus depending on v.

Exercise 6.48 (Mean-independence, continued) Consider the four statements:
(i) y and x are independent.
(ii) y is uncorrelated with $\mathrm{E}_{y|x}(y)$.
(iii) y is mean-independent of x.
(iv) y is uncorrelated with x.
Show that (i) $\Longrightarrow$ (ii) $\Longrightarrow$ (iii) $\Longrightarrow$ (iv), assuming that the moments exist.

Solution

(i) $\Longrightarrow$ (ii): Independence implies that $\mathrm{E}_{y|x}(y) = \mathrm{E}(y)$. Hence, $\mathrm{cov}\left(y, \mathrm{E}_{y|x}(y)\right) = \mathrm{cov}(y, \mathrm{E}(y)) = 0$.

(ii) $\Longrightarrow$ (iii): Let $z := \mathrm{E}_{y|x}(y)$. Then, $\mathrm{cov}(z, y - z) = 0$ by Exercise 6.43(f). By assumption, $\mathrm{cov}(z, y) = 0$. Hence, $\mathrm{var}(z) = 0$ and z is a constant (namely $\mathrm{E}(y)$) with probability 1.

(iii) $\Longrightarrow$ (iv): This follows from Exercise 6.47(c).

Exercise 6.49 (Ellipticals' linear transformations) Let $\boldsymbol{y} := \boldsymbol{a} + \boldsymbol{B}\boldsymbol{x}$, where $\boldsymbol{x} \sim \mathrm{EC}_m(\boldsymbol{c}, \boldsymbol{A})$ and $\boldsymbol{B}$ is invertible (hence square). Show that:

(a) $\boldsymbol{y}$ is also elliptical of the same type as $\boldsymbol{x}$, and $\boldsymbol{y} \sim \mathrm{EC}_m(\boldsymbol{a} + \boldsymbol{B}\boldsymbol{c}, \boldsymbol{B}\boldsymbol{A}\boldsymbol{B}')$;

(b) $\mathrm{E}(\boldsymbol{x}) = \boldsymbol{c}$ when the expectation exists. [Hint: Choose $\boldsymbol{y}$ such that its density is centered around $\boldsymbol{0}$.]

Solution

(a) We remind the reader of Exercise 3.16 for a univariate parallel. The density of $\boldsymbol{x}$ varies only with the realization of $(\boldsymbol{x} - \boldsymbol{c})' \boldsymbol{A}^{-1} (\boldsymbol{x} - \boldsymbol{c})$. We can express this quadratic form in terms of $\boldsymbol{y}$, using the definition of $\boldsymbol{y}$, as

$$
\begin{aligned}
(\boldsymbol{x} - \boldsymbol{c})' \boldsymbol{A}^{-1} (\boldsymbol{x} - \boldsymbol{c}) &= (\boldsymbol{x} - \boldsymbol{c})' \boldsymbol{B}' \left(\boldsymbol{B}\boldsymbol{A}\boldsymbol{B}'\right)^{-1} \boldsymbol{B} (\boldsymbol{x} - \boldsymbol{c}) \\
&= (\boldsymbol{B}\boldsymbol{x} - \boldsymbol{B}\boldsymbol{c})' \left(\boldsymbol{B}\boldsymbol{A}\boldsymbol{B}'\right)^{-1} (\boldsymbol{B}\boldsymbol{x} - \boldsymbol{B}\boldsymbol{c}) \\
&= (\boldsymbol{y} - \boldsymbol{a} - \boldsymbol{B}\boldsymbol{c})' \left(\boldsymbol{B}\boldsymbol{A}\boldsymbol{B}'\right)^{-1} (\boldsymbol{y} - \boldsymbol{a} - \boldsymbol{B}\boldsymbol{c}),
\end{aligned}
$$

whose realizations will fully characterize the p.d.f. of $\boldsymbol{y}$. Therefore, $\boldsymbol{y}$ is elliptical with parameters as stated. Furthermore, the two identical quadratic forms enter the p.d.f. through the same function, so $\boldsymbol{x}$ and $\boldsymbol{y}$ are ellipticals of the same type. The two densities only differ by a constant factor of proportionality that makes the densities integrate to 1; see Exercise 6.41 for an illustration. This factor will be studied explicitly in the next chapter.

(b) Taking $\boldsymbol{a} = -\boldsymbol{c}$ and $\boldsymbol{B} = \boldsymbol{I}_m$ in (a), we get $\boldsymbol{y} \sim \mathrm{EC}_m(\boldsymbol{0}, \boldsymbol{A})$ and similarly $-\boldsymbol{y} \sim \mathrm{EC}_m(\boldsymbol{0}, \boldsymbol{A})$. The two densities are identical, so $\mathrm{E}(\boldsymbol{y}) = \mathrm{E}(-\boldsymbol{y})$ and hence $\mathrm{E}(\boldsymbol{y}) = \boldsymbol{0}$. Note that the density varies only with realizations of $\boldsymbol{y}'\boldsymbol{A}^{-1}\boldsymbol{y}$, which is an even function of $\boldsymbol{y}$. Substituting for the definition of $\boldsymbol{y}$ in terms of $\boldsymbol{x}$ gives

$$
\boldsymbol{0} = \mathrm{E}(\boldsymbol{y}) = \mathrm{E}(\boldsymbol{a} + \boldsymbol{B}\boldsymbol{x}) = \boldsymbol{a} + \boldsymbol{B}\,\mathrm{E}(\boldsymbol{x}) = -\boldsymbol{c} + \mathrm{E}(\boldsymbol{x}),
$$

and rearranging yields the required result.

Exercise 6.50 (Multivariate t: variance) Let $\boldsymbol{x} \sim \mathrm{EC}_m(\boldsymbol{0}, \boldsymbol{A})$. Assume further that $\boldsymbol{x}$ is multivariate $\mathrm{t}(\nu)$. Show that its variance is $\frac{\nu}{\nu-2}\boldsymbol{A}$ when $\nu > 2$.

Solution

Defining $\boldsymbol{y} := \boldsymbol{A}^{-1/2}\boldsymbol{x}$, we have $\mathrm{var}(\boldsymbol{x}) = \boldsymbol{A}^{1/2}\,\mathrm{var}(\boldsymbol{y})\boldsymbol{A}^{1/2}$. If we can show that $\mathrm{var}(\boldsymbol{y}) = \frac{\nu}{\nu-2}\boldsymbol{I}_m$, then we are done.

Exercise 6.49(a) implies that $\boldsymbol{y} \sim \mathrm{EC}(\mathbf{0}, \boldsymbol{I}_m)$ and is also multivariate $\mathrm{t}(\nu)$, albeit with the standardized $\boldsymbol{I}_m$ instead of $\boldsymbol{A}$. Its univariate marginals are also standard $\mathrm{t}(\nu)$ by Exercise 6.41. Hence, the variances of these marginals are all $\frac{\nu}{\nu-2}$, as in Chapter 4, the existence condition being $\nu > 2$. The covariances are all zero, since the integrand in

$$\mathrm{E}(y_i y_j) = \int_{\mathbb{R}^2} v_i v_j \frac{\Gamma\left(\frac{\nu+2}{2}\right)}{\pi\nu\Gamma\left(\frac{\nu}{2}\right)\left(1 + \frac{1}{\nu}\left(v_i^2 + v_j^2\right)\right)^{(\nu+2)/2}} \mathrm{d}v_i \, \mathrm{d}v_j$$

is an odd function of v_i and v_j, and hence zero. (A similar type of symmetry argument was used in Exercise 6.14, and even earlier in Exercise 3.19.)

*__Exercise 6.51 (Ellipticals' linear conditional expectation)__ Partition the m-dimensional vector variate $\boldsymbol{x}$ into $\boldsymbol{x}' := (\boldsymbol{x}_1', \boldsymbol{x}_2')$ with dimensions $k > 0$ and $m - k > 0$, and its realization $\boldsymbol{w}' := (\boldsymbol{w}_1', \boldsymbol{w}_2')$ similarly. Let $\boldsymbol{x} \sim \mathrm{EC}(\boldsymbol{c}, \boldsymbol{A})$, where $\boldsymbol{c}$ is partitioned in the same way as $\boldsymbol{x}$, and the symmetric $\boldsymbol{A}$ correspondingly as

$$\boldsymbol{A} := \begin{pmatrix} \boldsymbol{A}_{11} & \boldsymbol{A}_{12} \\ \boldsymbol{A}_{21} & \boldsymbol{A}_{22} \end{pmatrix}.$$

Define $\boldsymbol{A}_{22|1} := \boldsymbol{A}_{22} - \boldsymbol{A}_{21}\boldsymbol{A}_{11}^{-1}\boldsymbol{A}_{12}$, whose inverse is the last diagonal block of $\boldsymbol{A}^{-1}$; see Section A.4. (An alternative notation for $\boldsymbol{A}_{22|1}$ is $\boldsymbol{A}_{22\cdot 1}$.)
(a) By using Exercise 6.49, prove that $\boldsymbol{x}_2 \mid \boldsymbol{x}_1 \sim \mathrm{EC}\left(\boldsymbol{c}_{2|1}, \boldsymbol{A}_{22|1}\right)$, where

$$\boldsymbol{c}_{2|1} := \boldsymbol{c}_2 + \boldsymbol{A}_{21}\boldsymbol{A}_{11}^{-1}(\boldsymbol{x}_1 - \boldsymbol{c}_1),$$

and hence that $\mathrm{E}_{\boldsymbol{x}_2|\boldsymbol{x}_1}(\boldsymbol{x}_2) = \boldsymbol{c}_{2|1}$ when the conditional mean exists. [Hint: Choose a transformation $\boldsymbol{y} := \boldsymbol{a} + \boldsymbol{B}\boldsymbol{x}$ such that $\boldsymbol{B}\boldsymbol{A}\boldsymbol{B}'$ is block-diagonal.]
(b) When does mean-independence of $\boldsymbol{x}_2$ from $\boldsymbol{x}_1$ occur, and how does this condition relate to spherical distributions?
(c) Is mean-independence sufficient to guarantee independence? Illustrate your answer with the multivariate t density of Exercise 6.41 when the mean is assumed to exist.
(d) Assume that the variance of $\boldsymbol{x}$ exists and is therefore proportional to $\boldsymbol{A}$ (to be proved in Exercise 7.31(c) in generality), with the corresponding precision matrix being proportional to $\boldsymbol{\Pi} := \boldsymbol{A}^{-1}$. Show that the correlation of x_i with x_j $(i \neq j)$ conditional on the rest of $\boldsymbol{x}$ is

$$\frac{-\pi_{ij}}{\sqrt{\pi_{ii}\pi_{jj}}},$$

where $\pi_{\boldsymbol{\cdot}}$ are the elements of $\boldsymbol{\Pi}$.

Solution
(a) Define

$$\boldsymbol{B} := \begin{pmatrix} \boldsymbol{I}_k & \mathrm{O} \\ -\boldsymbol{A}_{21}\boldsymbol{A}_{11}^{-1} & \boldsymbol{I}_{m-k} \end{pmatrix},$$

where $|\boldsymbol{B}| = 1 \neq 0$. Then, $\boldsymbol{y} := \boldsymbol{B}(\boldsymbol{x}-\boldsymbol{c})$ can be written as

$$\boldsymbol{y} = \begin{pmatrix} \boldsymbol{I}_k & \mathbf{O} \\ -\boldsymbol{A}_{21}\boldsymbol{A}_{11}^{-1} & \boldsymbol{I}_{m-k} \end{pmatrix} \begin{pmatrix} \boldsymbol{x}_1 - \boldsymbol{c}_1 \\ \boldsymbol{x}_2 - \boldsymbol{c}_2 \end{pmatrix} = \begin{pmatrix} \boldsymbol{x}_1 - \boldsymbol{c}_1 \\ \boldsymbol{x}_2 - \boldsymbol{c}_2 - \boldsymbol{A}_{21}\boldsymbol{A}_{11}^{-1}(\boldsymbol{x}_1 - \boldsymbol{c}_1) \end{pmatrix}.$$

Exercise 6.49 shows that $\boldsymbol{y}$ is elliptically distributed around $\mathbf{0}_m$, with weighting matrix

$$\boldsymbol{B}\boldsymbol{A}\boldsymbol{B}' = \begin{pmatrix} \boldsymbol{I}_k & \mathbf{O} \\ -\boldsymbol{A}_{21}\boldsymbol{A}_{11}^{-1} & \boldsymbol{I}_{m-k} \end{pmatrix} \begin{pmatrix} \boldsymbol{A}_{11} & \boldsymbol{A}_{12} \\ \boldsymbol{A}_{21} & \boldsymbol{A}_{22} \end{pmatrix} \begin{pmatrix} \boldsymbol{I}_k & -\boldsymbol{A}_{11}^{-1}\boldsymbol{A}_{12} \\ \mathbf{O} & \boldsymbol{I}_{m-k} \end{pmatrix}$$

$$= \begin{pmatrix} \boldsymbol{A}_{11} & \boldsymbol{A}_{12} \\ \mathbf{O} & \boldsymbol{A}_{22|1} \end{pmatrix} \begin{pmatrix} \boldsymbol{I}_k & -\boldsymbol{A}_{11}^{-1}\boldsymbol{A}_{12} \\ \mathbf{O} & \boldsymbol{I}_{m-k} \end{pmatrix} = \begin{pmatrix} \boldsymbol{A}_{11} & \mathbf{O} \\ \mathbf{O} & \boldsymbol{A}_{22|1} \end{pmatrix},$$

where $\boldsymbol{A}_{22|1} := \boldsymbol{A}_{22} - \boldsymbol{A}_{21}\boldsymbol{A}_{11}^{-1}\boldsymbol{A}_{12}$. The density of $\boldsymbol{y}$ is therefore fully characterized by the realizations of

$$(\boldsymbol{y}_1', \boldsymbol{y}_2') \begin{pmatrix} \boldsymbol{A}_{11} & \mathbf{O} \\ \mathbf{O} & \boldsymbol{A}_{22|1} \end{pmatrix}^{-1} \begin{pmatrix} \boldsymbol{y}_1 \\ \boldsymbol{y}_2 \end{pmatrix} = \boldsymbol{y}_1'\boldsymbol{A}_{11}^{-1}\boldsymbol{y}_1 + \boldsymbol{y}_2'\boldsymbol{A}_{22|1}^{-1}\boldsymbol{y}_2$$

which will vary if and only if $\boldsymbol{y}_2'\boldsymbol{A}_{22|1}^{-1}\boldsymbol{y}_2$ changes, since we have conditioned on $\boldsymbol{y}_1 := \boldsymbol{x}_1 - \boldsymbol{c}_1$. As a result, the density of $\boldsymbol{y}_2$, given $\boldsymbol{x}_1$, is $\mathrm{EC}_{m-k}(\mathbf{0}, \boldsymbol{A}_{22|1})$, and the distribution for $\boldsymbol{x}_2 = \boldsymbol{y}_2 + \boldsymbol{c}_2 + \boldsymbol{A}_{21}\boldsymbol{A}_{11}^{-1}(\boldsymbol{x}_1 - \boldsymbol{c}_1)$ follows by Exercise 6.49(a). The expectation follows by Exercise 6.49(b). The reader is encouraged to compare these results with the bivariate formulae of Exercises 6.44 and 6.46(c). The conditional expectation is linear in $\boldsymbol{x}_1$, and this is illustrated in the discussion of Figure 6.3 in Exercise 6.1.

(b) The special case $\boldsymbol{A} = \mathrm{diag}(\boldsymbol{A}_{11}, \boldsymbol{A}_{22})$ implies the mean-independence of $\boldsymbol{x}_1$ from $\boldsymbol{x}_2$, and the converse is also true since $\boldsymbol{x}_2$ is not a singular variate. Also, mean-independence turns out to be a symmetric relation here: the mean-independence of $\boldsymbol{x}_1$ from $\boldsymbol{x}_2$ is equivalent to the mean-independence of $\boldsymbol{x}_2$ from $\boldsymbol{x}_1$. The case $\boldsymbol{A} = \mathrm{diag}(\boldsymbol{A}_{11}, \boldsymbol{A}_{22})$ reduces to a spherical distribution if we have the stronger requirement that $\boldsymbol{A}_{11}$ and $\boldsymbol{A}_{22}$ are scalar matrices (matrices of the form $\lambda\boldsymbol{I}$), so sphericity is sufficient but not necessary for mean-independence within the class of elliptical densities.

(c) The mean-independence of $\boldsymbol{x}_1$ and $\boldsymbol{x}_2$ is equivalent to $\boldsymbol{A}_{21} = \mathbf{O}$, regardless of $\boldsymbol{c}$. Therefore, we can use the variate in Exercise 6.41 (where $\boldsymbol{c} = \mathbf{0}$) to answer this part of the question. In the joint density of $\boldsymbol{x}$ there, we could not separate $\boldsymbol{w}_1'\boldsymbol{A}_{11}^{-1}\boldsymbol{w}_1$ completely out of the conditional density. Therefore, the components $\boldsymbol{x}_1$ and $\boldsymbol{x}_2$ need not be mutually independent, even when $\boldsymbol{A}_{12} = \mathbf{O}$. In fact, even if $\boldsymbol{A} = \boldsymbol{I}_m$, the multivariate t density does not factor into the product of univariate t densities, unlike in Exercise 6.1(b) for the normal. The normal distribution happens to be the only elliptical where independence and no-correlation coincide, as will be seen in Exercise 8.10. Also, unlike the special case of the normal which we will explore in Chapter 8, the even-order moments of $\boldsymbol{x}_2 \mid \boldsymbol{x}_1$ will be functions of $\boldsymbol{x}_1'\boldsymbol{A}_{11}^{-1}\boldsymbol{x}_1$, hence depending on $\boldsymbol{x}_1$ in addition to $\boldsymbol{A}$. If the variance of the conditional distribution exists, it will be *proportional* to $\boldsymbol{A}_{22|1}$, with the 1×1 constant $\boldsymbol{x}_1'\boldsymbol{A}_{11}^{-1}\boldsymbol{x}_1$ entering the factor of proportionality in general.

(d) Using the setup of the earlier parts of the exercise, let $\boldsymbol{x}_2$ be $(x_i, x_j)'$. Then, (a) shows that the variance of $\boldsymbol{x}_2 \mid \boldsymbol{x}_1$ is proportional to $\boldsymbol{A}_{22|1}$, whose inverse is the last block of

A^{-1}. (We will revisit the topic of the conditioning and inversion of partitioned matrices in Section 12.3.) Writing

$$A_{22|1} = \begin{pmatrix} v_{ii} & v_{ij} \\ v_{ij} & v_{jj} \end{pmatrix},$$

the conditional correlation is given as usual by $\rho := v_{ij}/\sqrt{v_{ii}v_{jj}}$ which is invariant to scale (or proportionality). Inverting this matrix, we obtain

$$A_{22|1}^{-1} = \frac{1}{v_{ii}v_{jj} - v_{ij}^2} \begin{pmatrix} v_{jj} & -v_{ij} \\ -v_{ij} & v_{ii} \end{pmatrix}$$

and the result in terms of the $\pi_{\boldsymbol{\cdot}}$ follows. Note that the point where we required elliptical variates here was in calling $A_{22|1}$ the conditional variance (proportionally so), a formula that need not apply to other distributions.

Exercise 6.52 (Joint independence, by c.f.) Prove that the joint c.f. factorizes into the product of the marginals, $\varphi_{x}(\tau) = \prod_{i=1}^{m} \varphi_i(\tau_i)$, if and only if all the nonoverlapping subsets of x are mutually independent.

Solution

This exercise can be viewed as a continuation of Exercise 5.17, because of the one-to-one correspondence between c.d.f.s (or p.d.f.s) and c.f.s, namely

$$\varphi_{x}(\tau) = \int_{w \in \mathbb{R}^m} e^{i\tau' w}\, dF_{x}(w).$$

Independence occurs if and only if $F_{x}(w) = \prod_{i=1}^{m} F_i(w_i)$ for all w, in which case

$$\varphi_{x}(\tau) = \int_{w \in \mathbb{R}^m} e^{i\tau' w}\, d\left(\prod_{i=1}^{m} F_i(w_i)\right) = \int_{-\infty}^{\infty} \dots \int_{-\infty}^{\infty} e^{i(\tau_1 w_1 + \dots + \tau_m w_m)} \prod_{i=1}^{m} (dF_i(w_i))$$
$$= \prod_{i=1}^{m} \left(\int_{-\infty}^{\infty} e^{i\tau_i w_i}\, dF_i(w_i)\right) = \prod_{i=1}^{m} \varphi_i(\tau_i).$$

Exercise 6.53 (Joint independence, by cumulants' additivity) Prove that the *joint c.g.f.* $\varkappa_{x}(t) := \log(\mathrm{E}(\exp(t'x)))$ factorizes into the sum of the marginals $\sum_{i=1}^{m} \varkappa_i(t_i)$, when these c.g.f.s exist, if and only if all the nonoverlapping subsets of x are mutually independent. How does this result relate to Exercise 6.9?

Solution

By Exercise 6.52, independence is equivalent to $\varphi_{x}(\tau) = \prod_{i=1}^{m} \varphi_i(\tau_i)$. By the existence of the c.g.f.s $\varkappa_{\boldsymbol{x}}(\boldsymbol{t})$ and $\varkappa_i(t_i)$ in an arbitrarily small open neighborhood of $\boldsymbol{t} = \mathbf{0}_m$,

$$\begin{aligned}\varkappa_{\boldsymbol{x}}(\boldsymbol{t}) &\equiv \log\left(\mathrm{E}\left(\prod_{i=1}^{m} \mathrm{e}^{t_i x_i}\right)\right)\\ &= \log\left(\prod_{i=1}^{m} \mathrm{E}\left(\mathrm{e}^{t_i x_i}\right)\right) \qquad \text{(if and only if independence)}\\ &\equiv \sum_{i=1}^{m} \log\left(\mathrm{E}\left(\mathrm{e}^{t_i x_i}\right)\right) \equiv \sum_{i=1}^{m} \varkappa_i(t_i).\end{aligned}$$

One important implication is obtained by setting $t_2 = at_1$, where $a \in \mathbb{R}$ is nonrandom, and choosing the remaining $t_i = 0$. This tells us that any j-th order cumulant of $x_1 + ax_2$ is equal to the sum of the j-th order cumulants of x_1 and of ax_2, if x_1 and x_2 are independent. When $j = 2$, we get $\mathrm{var}(x_1 + ax_2) = \mathrm{var}(x_1) + \mathrm{var}(ax_2)$. When $j = 3$, set $a = -1$ and use the result of Exercise 3.36(c) that $\varkappa^{(3)}(0)$ is the third central moment of the variate, then the outcome is Exercise 6.9.

Notes

General references for this chapter are the same as for Chapter 2; for more specialized references on multivariate analysis, we cite Anderson (1984), Mardia, Kent, and Bibby (1979) and Muirhead (1982).

The idea behind Exercise 6.2 has an interesting history, which is clarified in Hoffmann-Jørgensen (1994, p. 294). See also Rao (1973, pp. 158–159).

Exercise 6.18 illustrates how conditional dependence can differ from unconditional dependence. In fact, the *paradox of Yule and Simpson* is a case where conditioning reverses the sign of the dependence; for example, see Cox and Wermuth (2003) for conditions under which the reversal will not happen. See also Exercise 13.9. Here are a couple of practical examples of the paradox. The percentage of workers injured at their workplace may increase over time, at the national level, and yet these percentages may be decreasing within each region of that country. This could happen if the regions' populations were growing at different rates, and regions with a high percentage of accidents had become predominant in that country. A similar story could be told about the price index of sold houses. For example, the index could be falling in a weak market if owners of expensive properties can afford not to sell them. In this case, the average price of a property sold is less than usual because fewer expensive properties are being sold, even if properties' prices (within each segment of the market) are not falling.

For alternative proofs of the Cauchy–Schwarz inequality of Exercise 6.20, see our companion volume, Abadir and Magnus (2005). Those proofs do not make use of random variables. Other inequalities in Abadir and Magnus (2005) can be similarly interpreted in terms of moments of random variables. See that volume also for more details on the eigenvalues and eigenvectors of the equicorrelation matrix of Exercise 6.22(b), and for the derivation of the bounds of the Rayleigh quotient. Exercise 6.24 uses the vec and vech operators, which are also studied in that volume.

At the end of Exercise 6.28(a) (and after (5.3)), we have implicitly used Cauchy's rule of invariance to write a differential version of Leibniz' rule in the continuous case; see Chapter 13 of Abadir and Magnus (2005) for the former rule. We have not presented the full details of the Stieltjes derivations, opting instead to focus on the ideas.

Conditional expectation can also be defined with respect to sigma-fields that are subsets of $\mathcal{F}$. In this case, the *tower property* states that repeated conditioning with respect to nested sigma-fields is equal (with probability 1) to conditioning only once with respect to the smallest of these fields, and that the ordering of the sequence of conditioning fields does not matter. We saw an example while proving Exercise 6.28(c). As an extreme case, the expectation of a variate, conditional on the largest sigma-field, is the variate itself; and conditioning further on a smaller field gives the property stated above. The smallest conditioning set overrides the others. For more details, see Billingsley (1995, p. 448). It is an idea that we will see in another guise in Exercise 12.39.

In Exercise 6.46, we derive the best predictor for the special bivariate case. Its existence and uniqueness was established more generally under the name "projection theorem" in Chapter 3 of Abadir and Magnus (2005).

Though our definition of mean-independence is more general than that of Goldberger (1991), the simple example of Exercise 6.47(e) is due to him.

In Exercise 6.51(a), the decomposition of $\boldsymbol{A}$ that leads to the block-diagonal matrix $\operatorname{diag}\left(\boldsymbol{A}_{11}, \boldsymbol{A}_{22|1}\right)$ is a well-known method. The matrix $\boldsymbol{A}_{22|1}$ is known as the Schur complement of $\boldsymbol{A}_{11}$; see Section A.4 or Abadir and Magnus (2005). Also, if we are willing to assume the existence of the variance of $\boldsymbol{x}$, then the linearity of the conditional expectations arises if and only if $\boldsymbol{x}$ is elliptical; see Nimmo-Smith (1979) and Hardin (1982).

As introduced in (6.6) and used subsequently, the conditional correlation (or covariance) between two distinct variates y, z measures the linear relation between them, after accounting for the influence of $\boldsymbol{x}$ on both variates. If this were done after accounting for only the *linear* influence of $\boldsymbol{x}$ on both variates, we would obtain the *partial correlation* (or *partial covariance*) instead. The partial correlation is commonly denoted by $\rho_{y,z\cdot\boldsymbol{x}}$ instead of $\rho_{y,z|\boldsymbol{x}}$, and similarly the partial variance matrices by $\boldsymbol{\Sigma}_{22\cdot1}$. Because of the linear projection involved in defining partial variance matrices, the formula obtained in Exercise 6.51(d) applies in general to the partial correlations for *any* distribution whose required moments exist. For more on the relation between partial and conditional correlations, see Baba, Shibata, and Sibuya (2004).

7

Functions of random variables

Let $\boldsymbol{x}$ be an $m \times 1$ variate with a known distribution. Suppose that $\boldsymbol{x}$ is transformed into a new $n \times 1$ variate defined by $\boldsymbol{y} := \boldsymbol{g}(\boldsymbol{x}) \in \mathcal{Y}$, for example, by the linear transformation

$$\begin{pmatrix} y_1 \\ y_2 \end{pmatrix} = \begin{pmatrix} c_1 - x_1 + x_2 \\ c_2 + x_1 + x_2 \end{pmatrix} = \begin{pmatrix} c_1 \\ c_2 \end{pmatrix} + \begin{pmatrix} -1 & 1 \\ 1 & 1 \end{pmatrix} \begin{pmatrix} x_1 \\ x_2 \end{pmatrix},$$

where c_1, c_2 are nonrandom. How can we express the randomness of $\boldsymbol{y}$ in terms of the (known) distribution of $\boldsymbol{x}$? Three main methods of describing this randomness are available, as in the case of the original variate $\boldsymbol{x}$.

First, the *m.g.f.* (or *c.f.*) *technique* transforms the known m.g.f. (or c.f.) of $\boldsymbol{x}$ into one for $\boldsymbol{y}$, thus identifying the distribution of $\boldsymbol{y}$. For example, suppose that we know that x has the m.g.f. $m_x(t) = \exp\left(\frac{1}{2}t^2\right)$. Define $y := \mu + \sigma x$, with nonrandom parameters $\mu \in \mathbb{R}$ and $\sigma \in \mathbb{R}_+$. The m.g.f. of this new variate is

$$\begin{aligned} m_y(\tau) &= \mathrm{E}\left(\mathrm{e}^{\tau(\mu+\sigma x)}\right) = \mathrm{e}^{\mu\tau}\,\mathrm{E}\left(\mathrm{e}^{\sigma\tau x}\right) \\ &= \mathrm{e}^{\mu\tau} m_x(\sigma\tau) = \mathrm{e}^{\mu\tau+(\sigma\tau)^2/2}, \end{aligned}$$

which identifies it (from Table 4.2 for example) as $y \sim \mathrm{N}(\mu, \sigma^2)$. In general, if we have already worked out $\mathrm{E}(\mathrm{e}^{\boldsymbol{t}'\boldsymbol{x}})$, where $\boldsymbol{t}$ is a nonrandom $n \times 1$ vector, we may be able to infer

$$m_{\boldsymbol{y}}(\boldsymbol{\tau}) = \mathrm{E}_{\boldsymbol{y}}\left(\mathrm{e}^{\boldsymbol{\tau}'\boldsymbol{y}}\right) = \mathrm{E}_{\boldsymbol{x}}\left(\mathrm{e}^{\boldsymbol{\tau}'\boldsymbol{g}(\boldsymbol{x})}\right)$$

without having to recalculate the expectation with respect to $\boldsymbol{y}$.

Second, the *c.d.f. technique* employs a similar idea by linking the distribution functions of $\boldsymbol{x}$ and $\boldsymbol{y}$. We have

$$F_{\boldsymbol{y}}(\boldsymbol{w}_{\boldsymbol{y}}) = \Pr(\boldsymbol{y} \leqslant \boldsymbol{w}_{\boldsymbol{y}}) = \Pr(\boldsymbol{g}(\boldsymbol{x}) \leqslant \boldsymbol{w}_{\boldsymbol{y}}).$$

This inequality defines a set $A := \{\boldsymbol{x} : \boldsymbol{g}(\boldsymbol{x}) \leqslant \boldsymbol{w}_{\boldsymbol{y}} \text{ and } \boldsymbol{x} \in \mathcal{X}\}$, which could be used to express the required probability $\Pr(A)$ in terms of the known c.d.f. of $\boldsymbol{x}$. Continuing with our earlier example, we know that $x \sim \mathrm{N}(0,1)$, so the distribution function of y is given by

$$\begin{aligned} F_y(w_y) &= \Pr(y \leqslant w_y) = \Pr(\mu + \sigma x \leqslant w_y) \\ &= \Pr\left(x \leqslant \frac{w_y - \mu}{\sigma}\right) = \Phi\left(\frac{w_y - \mu}{\sigma}\right), \end{aligned}$$

where Φ is the standard normal distribution function and here $A = \{x : x \leqslant (w_y - \mu)/\sigma\}$. This is a special case of Exercise 3.16 on location and scale in c.d.f.s. It is a simple example where the transformation is invertible, and we could write $x = g^{-1}(y)$. We will see later in this chapter more elaborate examples where the function g need not be invertible. Also, one has to be careful that, even if $m = n$ and $\boldsymbol{g}$ is invertible, it is not correct to rewrite the inequality in set A as either $\boldsymbol{x} \leqslant \boldsymbol{g}^{-1}(\boldsymbol{w_y})$ or $\boldsymbol{x} \geqslant \boldsymbol{g}^{-1}(\boldsymbol{w_y})$ when $m > 1$. For example,

$$\begin{pmatrix} -1 & 1 \\ 1 & 0 \end{pmatrix} \begin{pmatrix} x_1 \\ x_2 \end{pmatrix} \leqslant \begin{pmatrix} 0 \\ 0 \end{pmatrix} \tag{7.1}$$

is not equivalent to either of

$$\begin{pmatrix} x_1 \\ x_2 \end{pmatrix} \leqslant \begin{pmatrix} 0 \\ 0 \end{pmatrix} \quad \text{or} \quad \begin{pmatrix} x_1 \\ x_2 \end{pmatrix} \geqslant \begin{pmatrix} 0 \\ 0 \end{pmatrix},$$

because the three regions of the plane $\mathbb{R}^2$ defined by these three vector inequalities are all different.

Third, the *p.d.f. technique* asks the same question again, but in terms of the density functions. One needs to treat the two cases of discrete and continuous variates separately. Recall the different definitions of the *two* types of p.d.f.s in terms of *the* c.d.f., seen in earlier chapters.

For discrete $\boldsymbol{y}$,

$$f_{\boldsymbol{y}}(\boldsymbol{w_y}) = \Pr(\boldsymbol{y} = \boldsymbol{w_y}) = \Pr(\boldsymbol{g}(\boldsymbol{x}) = \boldsymbol{w_y}).$$

This equality defines a set of values $B := \{\boldsymbol{x} : \boldsymbol{g}(\boldsymbol{x}) = \boldsymbol{w_y} \text{ and } \boldsymbol{x} \in \mathcal{X}\}$ for which it is satisfied, and which can express the required probability $f_{\boldsymbol{y}}(\boldsymbol{w_y}) = \Pr(B)$ in terms of the known p.d.f. of $\boldsymbol{x}$. When $\boldsymbol{x}$ too is discrete, this becomes

$$f_{\boldsymbol{y}}(\boldsymbol{w_y}) = \sum_{\boldsymbol{w_x} \in B} \Pr(\boldsymbol{x} = \boldsymbol{w_x}) = \sum_{\boldsymbol{w_x} \in B} f_{\boldsymbol{x}}(\boldsymbol{w_x}),$$

which relates the two p.d.f.s. For example, if $y = x^2$ and y is a discrete variate, then x is discrete and

$$\begin{aligned} f_y(w_y) &= \Pr(y = w_y) = \Pr(x^2 = w_y) = \Pr(x = \sqrt{w_y}) + \Pr(x = -\sqrt{w_y}) \\ &= f_x(\sqrt{w_y}) + f_x(-\sqrt{w_y}) \end{aligned} \tag{7.2}$$

for $w_y \in \mathcal{Y}$, and $f_y(w_y) = 0$ otherwise. Notice that it is not necessarily the case that $\boldsymbol{x}$ is discrete when $\boldsymbol{y}$ is discrete. For example, the transformation $y = \lfloor x \rfloor$ returns the integer value of x, so y is discrete even if x is not.

For continuous $\boldsymbol{y}$, we assume that the function $\boldsymbol{g}(\boldsymbol{x})$ is continuously differentiable (implying that $\boldsymbol{x}$ is continuous too) and that $n = m$. This latter condition should not be seen as restrictive, since we may always augment the case $n < m$ with some identities. For example, the transformation $y = x_1 + x_2$, which has $n = 1$ and $m = 2$, can be rewritten as

$$\begin{pmatrix} y_1 \\ y_2 \end{pmatrix} = \begin{pmatrix} 1 & 1 \\ 0 & 1 \end{pmatrix} \begin{pmatrix} x_1 \\ x_2 \end{pmatrix},$$

where the dimensions of $\boldsymbol{x}$ and the augmented $\boldsymbol{y}$ are now the same, after using the identity mapping of $y_2 = x_2$. The marginal density of $y_1 = x_1 + x_2$ can then be obtained by integrating y_2 out of the joint density of (y_1, y_2). We further require the augmented transformation to be nonsingular, that is, the *Jacobian matrix*

$$\frac{\partial \boldsymbol{x}}{\partial \boldsymbol{y}'} \equiv \begin{pmatrix} \frac{\partial x_1}{\partial \boldsymbol{y}'} \\ \vdots \\ \frac{\partial x_m}{\partial \boldsymbol{y}'} \end{pmatrix} \equiv \begin{pmatrix} \frac{\partial x_1}{\partial y_1} & \cdots & \frac{\partial x_1}{\partial y_m} \\ \vdots & & \vdots \\ \frac{\partial x_m}{\partial y_1} & \cdots & \frac{\partial x_m}{\partial y_m} \end{pmatrix}$$

should have a determinant satisfying $|\partial \boldsymbol{x}/\partial \boldsymbol{y}'| \neq 0$ for some $\boldsymbol{x} \in \mathcal{X}$, where $|\partial \boldsymbol{x}/\partial \boldsymbol{y}'|$ is the *Jacobian* of the transformation. Notice the statistical tradition of calling this the Jacobian of the transformation $\boldsymbol{x} \mapsto \boldsymbol{y}$, rather than that of $\boldsymbol{y} \mapsto \boldsymbol{x}$ as in mathematics. The role of the assumption $|\partial \boldsymbol{x}/\partial \boldsymbol{y}'| \neq 0$ is to rule out having redundant variates in the vector $\boldsymbol{y}$. For example, we rule out augmenting

$$\begin{pmatrix} y_1 \\ y_2 \end{pmatrix} = \begin{pmatrix} 1 & 1 & 1 \\ 1 & 1 & -1 \end{pmatrix} \begin{pmatrix} x_1 \\ x_2 \\ x_3 \end{pmatrix}$$

by adding $y_3 = x_3$, that is, we rule out

$$\begin{pmatrix} y_1 \\ y_2 \\ y_3 \end{pmatrix} = \begin{pmatrix} 1 & 1 & 1 \\ 1 & 1 & -1 \\ 0 & 0 & 1 \end{pmatrix} \begin{pmatrix} x_1 \\ x_2 \\ x_3 \end{pmatrix}.$$

Doing so would make y_3 redundant, since $y_1 - y_2 = 2x_3$ and thus x_3 is already determined by y_1 and y_2. Instead, one may use $y_3 = x_1$ or $y_3 = x_2$ to avoid a singular Jacobian matrix.

We are now in a position to state the *transformation theorem* for continuous variates. We start with the simple case of invertible functions, where we can write $\boldsymbol{x} = \boldsymbol{g}^{-1}(\boldsymbol{y})$, then we conclude with the general situation of $\boldsymbol{y} = \boldsymbol{g}(\boldsymbol{x})$ being piecewise invertible (that is, invertible within each component of some partition of $\mathcal{X}$). For the first situation, we have

$$f_{\boldsymbol{y}}(\boldsymbol{w}_{\boldsymbol{y}}) = \left| \det \left(\frac{\partial \boldsymbol{g}^{-1}(\boldsymbol{w}_{\boldsymbol{y}})}{\partial \boldsymbol{w}_{\boldsymbol{y}}'} \right) \right| f_{\boldsymbol{x}}\left(\boldsymbol{g}^{-1}(\boldsymbol{w}_{\boldsymbol{y}})\right) \qquad (\boldsymbol{w}_{\boldsymbol{y}} \in \mathcal{Y}), \tag{7.3}$$

where $\partial \boldsymbol{g}^{-1}(\boldsymbol{w}_{\boldsymbol{y}}) / \partial \boldsymbol{w}_{\boldsymbol{y}}'$ is $\partial \boldsymbol{x}/\partial \boldsymbol{y}'$ evaluated at $\boldsymbol{y} = \boldsymbol{w}_{\boldsymbol{y}}$ and $\boldsymbol{x} = \boldsymbol{g}^{-1}(\boldsymbol{w}_{\boldsymbol{y}})$, the use of an absolute value in (7.3) ensuring that probabilities are not negative. We use the term *Jacobian factor* for the absolute value of the determinant. This result will be proved in

Exercise 7.32.

To illustrate this theorem, suppose we have

$$\boldsymbol{y} = \boldsymbol{c} + \boldsymbol{A}\boldsymbol{x},$$

where $\boldsymbol{c}$ is a nonrandom vector and $\boldsymbol{A}$ is an invertible matrix of constants, altering the location and scale of $\boldsymbol{x}$, respectively. Then, the inverse function is $\boldsymbol{x} = \boldsymbol{A}^{-1}(\boldsymbol{y} - \boldsymbol{c})$ and $\partial\boldsymbol{x}/\partial\boldsymbol{y}' = \boldsymbol{A}^{-1}$; see Section A.4. It follows that, whatever the density function of $\boldsymbol{x}$, the density function of $\boldsymbol{y}$ is

$$f_{\boldsymbol{y}}(\boldsymbol{w}_{\boldsymbol{y}}) = \frac{1}{|\det \boldsymbol{A}|} f_{\boldsymbol{x}}\left(\boldsymbol{A}^{-1}(\boldsymbol{w}_{\boldsymbol{y}} - \boldsymbol{c})\right).$$

Recall that $\boldsymbol{A}$ is nonsingular, so its determinant is nonzero. The knowledge of a particular density $f_{\boldsymbol{x}}$ implies immediate knowledge of the corresponding $f_{\boldsymbol{y}}$. This is the multivariate counterpart of Exercise 3.16 for densities of continuous variates. An important special case of this linear transformation is the *convolution of* $\boldsymbol{x}$ when one element of $\boldsymbol{y}$ is given by $\sum_{i=1}^{m} x_i$ or $\boldsymbol{\imath}_m'\boldsymbol{x}$ (where $\boldsymbol{\imath}_m$ is the m-dimensional vector of ones, which we sometimes write simply as $\boldsymbol{\imath}$). The joint density of

$$\boldsymbol{y} = \begin{pmatrix} 1 & \boldsymbol{\imath}_{m-1}' \\ \boldsymbol{0} & \boldsymbol{I}_{m-1} \end{pmatrix} \boldsymbol{x}$$

is

$$f_{\boldsymbol{y}}(\boldsymbol{w}_{\boldsymbol{y}}) = f_{\boldsymbol{x}}\left(\begin{pmatrix} 1 & -\boldsymbol{\imath}_{m-1}' \\ \boldsymbol{0} & \boldsymbol{I}_{m-1} \end{pmatrix} \boldsymbol{w}_{\boldsymbol{y}}\right) \tag{7.4}$$

by the formula for the partitioned inverse (or by $x_1 = y_1 - \sum_{i=2}^{m} y_i$). The marginal density of the sum $\boldsymbol{\imath}_m'\boldsymbol{x}$ is given by integrating (7.4) with respect to $(w_{y_2}, \dots, w_{y_m})$ over $\mathbb{R}^{m-1}$. For example, in the case of $m = 2$, we get

$$f_{x_1+x_2}(v_1) = \int_{-\infty}^{\infty} f_{x_1,x_2}(v_1 - v_2, v_2)\, \mathrm{d}v_2.$$

In the case where $\boldsymbol{x}$ has components that are jointly independent, it is simplest to use the c.f. technique to obtain the convolution's c.f.:

$$\varphi_y(\tau) := \mathrm{E}\left(\mathrm{e}^{\mathrm{i}\tau y}\right) \equiv \mathrm{E}\left(\mathrm{e}^{\mathrm{i}\tau(x_1+\dots+x_m)}\right) = \mathrm{E}\left(\mathrm{e}^{\mathrm{i}\tau x_1}\right)\cdots\mathrm{E}\left(\mathrm{e}^{\mathrm{i}\tau x_m}\right) \equiv \prod_{i=1}^{m} \varphi_{x_i}(\tau);$$

the reader is referred back to Chapter 4 for a discussion of important special cases, such as that of infinite divisibility. This will be useful for working out the properties of the *sample mean* (or *average*) of the i.i.d. sequence $x_1, \dots, x_m$, defined by

$$\overline{x} := \frac{1}{m}\sum_{i=1}^{m} x_i,$$

which is a measure of the central location in the sample. For completeness, we also define the *sample variance*, which assesses the spread or dispersion of the data, by

$$s^2 := \frac{1}{m-1}\sum_{i=1}^{m}(x_i-\overline{x})^2 = \frac{1}{m-1}\sum_{i=1}^{m}x_i^2 - \frac{m}{m-1}\overline{x}^2,$$

where the last equality will be established in the proof of Exercise 7.16(d) (we assume that $m > 1$ whenever we talk about s^2). Both functions will be justified and analyzed more fully in Chapter 9. Another important function of this random sample is the following. Let y_i denote the i-th smallest observation in a sample, so we have $y_1 \leqslant \cdots \leqslant y_m$ where $y_1 = \min_i\{x_i\}$ and $y_m = \max_i\{x_i\}$. These ordered y_i's are called *order statistics*, and they are the sample counterparts of the i/m quantile. We define the sample *midrange* (a measure of central location) as $\frac{1}{2}(y_1 + y_m)$, and its *range* (a measure of its spread) as $y_m - y_1$.

We now turn to the general case where the function does not possess a unique inverse over all of $\boldsymbol{x} \in \mathcal{X}$, but is invertible (with probability 1) within each of the subsets $\mathcal{X}_i$ of some partition $\bigcup_{i=1}^{p}\mathcal{X}_i = \mathcal{X}$. Note that the term "partition" implies that the sets $\mathcal{X}_i$ are nonoverlapping (see Chapter 1). Then,

$$f_{\boldsymbol{y}}(\boldsymbol{w_y}) = \sum_{i=1}^{p}\left|\det\left(\frac{\partial \boldsymbol{g}_i^{-1}(\boldsymbol{w_y})}{\partial \boldsymbol{w}_{\boldsymbol{y}}'}\right)\right| f_{\boldsymbol{x}}\left(\boldsymbol{g}_i^{-1}(\boldsymbol{w_y})\right) \qquad (\boldsymbol{w_y} \in \mathcal{Y}), \tag{7.5}$$

where $\boldsymbol{g}_i^{-1}(\boldsymbol{w_y})$ is the inverse function within the partition $\mathcal{X}_i$. For example, if $y = x^2$ where $x \in \mathbb{R}$ is continuous, we partition $\mathbb{R}$ into $x = \sqrt{y} \geqslant 0$ and $x = -\sqrt{y} < 0$. Then, $\left|\mathrm{d}(\pm\sqrt{y})/\mathrm{d}y\right| = 1/(2\sqrt{y})$ and we have the p.d.f.

$$f_y(w_y) = \frac{1}{2\sqrt{w_y}}f_x\left(\sqrt{w_y}\right) + \frac{1}{2\sqrt{w_y}}f_x\left(-\sqrt{w_y}\right) \tag{7.6}$$

for $w_y > 0$, which is to be contrasted with (7.2). We can check (7.6) by the c.d.f. technique as follows. To start, we write

$$\begin{aligned} F_y(w_y) &= \Pr(y \leqslant w_y) = \Pr\left(x^2 \leqslant w_y\right) = \Pr\left(x \in \left[-\sqrt{w_y}, \sqrt{w_y}\right]\right) \\ &= \Pr\left(x \leqslant \sqrt{w_y}\right) - \Pr\left(x < -\sqrt{w_y}\right) = F_x\left(\sqrt{w_y}\right) - F_x\left(-\sqrt{w_y}\right), \end{aligned}$$

where the last step follows from $\Pr\left(x < -\sqrt{w_y}\right) = \Pr\left(x \leqslant -\sqrt{w_y}\right)$ since x is a continuous variate. This leads to (7.6) upon differentiating $F_y(w_y)$:

$$\begin{aligned} \frac{\mathrm{d}}{\mathrm{d}w_y}F_x\left(\pm\sqrt{w_y}\right) &= \frac{\mathrm{d}}{\mathrm{d}w_y}\int_{-\infty}^{\pm\sqrt{w_y}} f_x(u)\,\mathrm{d}u \\ &= f_x\left(\pm\sqrt{w_y}\right)\frac{\mathrm{d}\left(\pm\sqrt{w_y}\right)}{\mathrm{d}w_y} = \pm\frac{f_x\left(\pm\sqrt{w_y}\right)}{2\sqrt{w_y}}, \end{aligned}$$

where we have used Leibniz' rule. We could also interpret $F_y(w_y)$ as follows:

$$\begin{aligned} F_y(w_y) &= \Pr\left(x \in \left(0, \sqrt{w_y}\right)\right) + \Pr\left(x \in \left(-\sqrt{w_y}, 0\right)\right) \\ &= \int_0^{\sqrt{w_y}} f_x(u)\,\mathrm{d}u + \int_{-\sqrt{w_y}}^{0} f_x(u)\,\mathrm{d}u \end{aligned}$$

and the corresponding p.d.f. $f_y(w_y)$ is obtained by differentiating the integral over each of the two partitions of $\mathcal{X}$. This illustrates why (7.5) is made up of a sum of the usual formula (7.3) over the p partitions of $\mathcal{X}$.

Some results from earlier chapters could have been derived alternatively by means of the transformation theorem. This is especially true of Chapter 4, where we derived representations of variates as functions of other variates. Here, we apply the three techniques of transformation to special distributions, exploring their properties and relations in a way that continues the developments of Chapter 4. As examples of commonly used functions, we consider sums, powers, and products. We also analyze alternative coordinate representations of a vector, and the relation between these coordinates. When the vector is a random variable, we work out the implied relation between the distributions of the coordinates. We conclude by investigating the distribution of the order statistics, and how they relate to the distribution of the original variate. Even when the data are i.i.d., order statistics are *not* i.i.d., as we shall see in Exercise 7.35; for example, the largest observation always exceeds any other, and therefore they cannot have the same distribution. They are also not linear functions of the data; for example,

$$\max\{x_1, x_2\} = \frac{1}{2}(x_1 + x_2) + \frac{1}{2}|x_1 - x_2|, \tag{7.7}$$

which is not linear because of the presence of the absolute-value function. Also, unlike the mean, the midrange is not a linear function of the data when there are more than two observations. Finally, in Exercise 7.38, we generalize the very important result that $F_z(z) \sim \mathrm{U}_{(0,1)}$ for *any* continuous variate z. Note that the argument of the c.d.f. is the random variable itself, rather than its realization w, and the random function $F_z(z)$ is known as the *probability integral transform* (PIT); for example, for $z \sim \text{Expo}(1)$,

$$F_z(z) = 1 - \mathrm{e}^{-z} \sim \mathrm{U}_{(0,1)}.$$

The result is itself a direct consequence of the transformation theorem: the random variable $x := F_z(z)$ has realizations $u = F_z(w) \in (0,1)$ and p.d.f.

$$f_x(u) = \frac{1}{|\mathrm{d}u/\mathrm{d}w|} f_z(w) = \frac{f_z(w)}{|\mathrm{d}F_z(w)/\mathrm{d}w|} = \frac{f_z(w)}{|f_z(w)|} = 1,$$

subject to the understanding that, for all $u \in (0,1)$, the "inverse" $w = F_z^{-1}(u)$ is the quantile function introduced in Chapter 2 (to guarantee that $f_z(w) \neq 0$ for all $u \in (0,1)$).

7.1 Linear, univariate, and other elementary transformations

Exercise 7.1 (Bin and Nbin representations, one more take!) Prove that:
(a) repeated independent Bernoulli trials x_i, $i = 1, \ldots, n$, give rise to the binomial distribution for $\sum_{i=1}^{n} x_i$;
(b) independent drawings from a geometric distribution leads to their sum being a negative binomial.

Solution

(a) In Exercise 4.3, we proved the first part by using the p.d.f., so we now provide an alternative proof. Let $y := \sum_{i=1}^{n} x_i$, where the x_i are independent Bernoulli trials from $\text{Ber}(p)$. Then, the c.f. of y is

$$\varphi_y(\tau) = \mathrm{E}\left(\mathrm{e}^{\mathrm{i}\tau(x_1+\cdots+x_n)}\right) = \prod_{i=1}^{n} \mathrm{E}\left(\mathrm{e}^{\mathrm{i}\tau x_i}\right)$$

by the independence of x_i, $i = 1, \dots, n$. Substituting for the c.f. of the Bernoulli x_i variates,

$$\varphi_y(\tau) = \prod_{i=1}^{n} \left(1 + \left(\mathrm{e}^{\mathrm{i}\tau} - 1\right) p\right) = \left(1 + \left(\mathrm{e}^{\mathrm{i}\tau} - 1\right) p\right)^n,$$

which identifies y as a $\text{Bin}(n, p)$.

(b) Similarly, if the x_i are independent $\text{Geo}(p)$, then

$$\varphi_y(\tau) = \prod_{i=1}^{n} \mathrm{E}\left(\mathrm{e}^{\mathrm{i}\tau x_i}\right) = \prod_{i=1}^{n} \left(p^{-1} + \left(1 - p^{-1}\right) \mathrm{e}^{\mathrm{i}\tau}\right)^{-1} = \left(p^{-1} + \left(1 - p^{-1}\right) \mathrm{e}^{\mathrm{i}\tau}\right)^{-n},$$

which again identifies y as an $\text{Nbin}(n, p)$. See also Exercises 4.4 and 4.17.

Exercise 7.2 (Chebyshev's inequality, revisited) There exist many forms of Chebyshev's inequality, the one stated in Exercise 3.12 being $\mathrm{E}\left(x^2\right)/a^2 \geqslant \Pr\left(|x| \geqslant a\right)$ for $a > 0$ and nonrandom.

(a) If x is a random variable with mean μ and variance σ^2, show that Chebyshev's inequality can be written as

$$\Pr\left(|x - \mu| < a\sigma\right) \geqslant 1 - \frac{1}{a^2} \qquad (a > 0).$$

(b) A fair coin is tossed n times, and x is the number of heads. Show that

$$\Pr\left(0.4 < \frac{x}{n} < 0.6\right) \geqslant \frac{3}{4}$$

if $n \geqslant 100$.

Solution

(a) Define $y := x - \mu$ with $\mathrm{E}\left(y^2\right) = \text{var}(y) = \sigma^2$. Using Exercise 3.12, we obtain

$$\Pr\left(|y| < a\sigma\right) = 1 - \Pr\left(|y| \geqslant a\sigma\right) \geqslant 1 - \frac{\mathrm{E}\left(y^2\right)}{a^2\sigma^2} = 1 - \frac{1}{a^2}.$$

(b) Let $y_i = 1$ if the i-th toss comes up heads and 0 otherwise. Then, $y_i \sim \text{Ber}(\frac{1}{2})$ and $x = \sum_{i=1}^{n} y_i \sim \text{Bin}(n, \frac{1}{2})$. Hence, $\mathrm{E}(x) = n/2$ and $\text{var}(x) = n/4$. Using (a),

$$\Pr\left(0.4n < x < 0.6n\right) = \Pr\left(|x - 0.5n| < 0.1n\right) = \Pr\left(|x - \mu| < a\sigma\right)$$

for $a^2 = n/25$, hence

$$\Pr(0.4n < x < 0.6n) \geqslant 1 - \frac{1}{a^2} = 1 - \frac{25}{n} \geqslant \frac{3}{4}.$$

***Exercise 7.3 (Reproduction)** A distribution $\mathrm{D}(\boldsymbol{\theta})$ is said to be *reproductive* if there exist nontrivial cases for which

$$x_1 \sim \mathrm{D}(\boldsymbol{\theta}_1) \quad \text{and} \quad x_2 \sim \mathrm{D}(\boldsymbol{\theta}_2) \quad \text{implies} \quad a_1 x_1 + a_2 x_2 \sim \mathrm{D}(\boldsymbol{\theta}_3),$$

where x_1 and x_2 are independent, $\mathrm{D}(\cdot)$ is the same distribution throughout, and a_1, a_2 are nonzero constants which may depend on $\boldsymbol{\theta}_1, \boldsymbol{\theta}_2, \boldsymbol{\theta}_3$.
(a) Prove that $\mathrm{N}(\mu, \sigma^2)$, $\mathrm{Cau}(\alpha, \lambda)$, $\mathrm{Gam}(\nu, \lambda)$, $\chi^2(n, \delta)$, $\mathrm{IG}(\mu, \sigma^2)$ are reproductive, by using the c.f.s to find a nontrivial solution for $a_1, a_2, \boldsymbol{\theta}_1, \boldsymbol{\theta}_2, \boldsymbol{\theta}_3$ in each case. Show how the result for $\chi^2(n, \delta)$ implies that, for $x_i \sim \mathrm{IN}(\mu_i, 1)$ and $i = 1, \ldots, n$, we have $\sum_{i=1}^n x_i^2 \sim \chi^2(n, \delta)$ with $\delta := \sum_{i=1}^n \mu_i^2$.
(b) Is $\mathrm{U}_{(\alpha,\beta)}$ reproductive?
(c) Compare the reproductive property with that of infinite divisibility.

Solution
Define $x_3 := a_1 x_1 + a_2 x_2$. We need to solve

$$\begin{aligned}\varphi_{\mathrm{D}(\boldsymbol{\theta}_3)}(\tau) &\equiv \mathrm{E}\left(\mathrm{e}^{\mathrm{i}\tau(a_1 x_1 + a_2 x_2)}\right) \\ &= \mathrm{E}\left(\mathrm{e}^{\mathrm{i}a_1 \tau x_1}\right)\mathrm{E}\left(\mathrm{e}^{\mathrm{i}a_2 \tau x_2}\right) \equiv \varphi_{\mathrm{D}(\boldsymbol{\theta}_1)}(a_1\tau)\,\varphi_{\mathrm{D}(\boldsymbol{\theta}_2)}(a_2\tau).\end{aligned}$$

(a) For $\mathrm{N}(\mu, \sigma^2)$, we need to solve

$$\exp\left(\mathrm{i}\mu_3\tau - \frac{\sigma_3^2\tau^2}{2}\right) = \exp\left(\mathrm{i}\mu_1 a_1\tau - \frac{\sigma_1^2 a_1^2\tau^2}{2}\right)\exp\left(\mathrm{i}\mu_2 a_2\tau - \frac{\sigma_2^2 a_2^2\tau^2}{2}\right).$$

Equating the coefficients of τ on each side gives $\mu_3 = a_1\mu_1 + a_2\mu_2$, and similarly for τ^2 gives $\sigma_3^2 = a_1^2\sigma_1^2 + a_2^2\sigma_2^2$. Here, a_1 and a_2 can take any value in $\mathbb{R}$. This proves that arbitrary linear combinations of two independent normals are normal. The formulae for the mean and variance of the sum, μ_3 and σ_3^2, are in accordance with the general principles of Chapter 6.

For $\mathrm{Cau}(\alpha, \lambda)$,

$$\exp(\mathrm{i}\alpha_3\tau - \lambda_3|\tau|) = \exp(\mathrm{i}\alpha_1 a_1\tau - \lambda_1|a_1\tau|)\exp(\mathrm{i}\alpha_2 a_2\tau - \lambda_2|a_2\tau|)$$

implies that $\alpha_3 = a_1\alpha_1 + a_2\alpha_2$ and $\lambda_3 = |a_1|\,\lambda_1 + |a_2|\,\lambda_2$, where one should be careful with the wording since the mean and variance do not exist for this distribution. Notice that taking

$$a_1 = a_2 = \frac{1}{2}, \quad \alpha_1 = \alpha_2 = 0, \quad \lambda_1 = \lambda_2 = 1$$

shows that the sample mean of two $\mathrm{Cau}(0,1)$ is also $\mathrm{Cau}(0,1)$; see the stable laws in Chapter 4.

For $\mathrm{Gam}(\nu, \lambda)$, we require that

$$\left(1-\mathrm{i}\lambda_3^{-1}\tau\right)^{-\nu_3} = \left(1-\mathrm{i}\lambda_1^{-1}a_1\tau\right)^{-\nu_1}\left(1-\mathrm{i}\lambda_2^{-1}a_2\tau\right)^{-\nu_2},$$

implying that $\nu_3 = \nu_1 + \nu_2$ and $\lambda_3^{-1} = \lambda_2^{-1}a_2 = \lambda_1^{-1}a_1$ as a solution. This implies, for example, that the sum of a $\mathrm{Gam}(\nu_1, \lambda)$ and a $\mathrm{Gam}(\nu_2, \lambda)$ is $\mathrm{Gam}(\nu_1+\nu_2, \lambda)$.

Similarly, for $\chi^2(n, \delta)$, solving

$$\frac{\exp\left(\mathrm{i}\delta_3\tau/\left(1-2\mathrm{i}\tau\right)\right)}{\left(1-2\mathrm{i}\tau\right)^{n_3/2}} = \frac{\exp\left(\mathrm{i}\delta_1 a_1\tau/\left(1-2\mathrm{i}a_1\tau\right)\right)}{\left(1-2\mathrm{i}a_1\tau\right)^{n_1/2}} \times \frac{\exp\left(\mathrm{i}\delta_2 a_2\tau/\left(1-2\mathrm{i}a_2\tau\right)\right)}{\left(1-2\mathrm{i}a_2\tau\right)^{n_2/2}}$$

gives $n_3 = n_1 + n_2$, $a_1 = a_2 = 1$, and $\delta_3 = \delta_1 + \delta_2$, so that the sum of a $\chi^2(n_1, \delta_1)$ and a $\chi^2(n_2, \delta_2)$ is $\chi^2(n_1+n_2, \delta_1+\delta_2)$. Together with Exercise 4.25, this implies that, for $x_i \sim \mathrm{IN}(\mu_i, 1)$ and $i = 1, \dots, n$, we have $\sum_{i=1}^n x_i^2 \sim \chi^2(n, \delta)$ with $\delta := \sum_{i=1}^n \mu_i^2$.

For $\mathrm{IG}(\mu, \sigma^2)$,

$$\begin{aligned}
&\exp\left(\frac{\mu_3^2}{\sigma_3^2} - \frac{\mu_3^2}{\sigma_3^2}\sqrt{1-\frac{2\mathrm{i}\sigma_3^2\tau}{\mu_3}}\right)\\
&= \exp\left(\frac{\mu_1^2}{\sigma_1^2} - \frac{\mu_1^2}{\sigma_1^2}\sqrt{1-\frac{2\mathrm{i}\sigma_1^2 a_1\tau}{\mu_1}}\right)\exp\left(\frac{\mu_2^2}{\sigma_2^2} - \frac{\mu_2^2}{\sigma_2^2}\sqrt{1-\frac{2\mathrm{i}\sigma_2^2 a_2\tau}{\mu_2}}\right)\\
&= \exp\left(\frac{\mu_1^2}{\sigma_1^2} + \frac{\mu_2^2}{\sigma_2^2} - \frac{\mu_1^2}{\sigma_1^2}\sqrt{1-\frac{2\mathrm{i}\sigma_1^2 a_1\tau}{\mu_1}} - \frac{\mu_2^2}{\sigma_2^2}\sqrt{1-\frac{2\mathrm{i}\sigma_2^2 a_2\tau}{\mu_2}}\right)
\end{aligned}$$

yields

$$\frac{\mu_3^2}{\sigma_3^2} = \frac{\mu_1^2}{\sigma_1^2} + \frac{\mu_2^2}{\sigma_2^2} \quad \text{and} \quad \frac{\sigma_3^2}{\mu_3} = \frac{\sigma_1^2 a_1}{\mu_1} = \frac{\sigma_2^2 a_2}{\mu_2},$$

which gives us three equations in $a_1, a_2, \mu_3, \sigma_3$, with a solution in terms of a_1:

$$a_2 = \frac{\mu_2\sigma_1^2}{\mu_1\sigma_2^2}a_1, \quad \mu_3 = a_1\frac{\sigma_1^2}{\mu_1}\left(\frac{\mu_1^2}{\sigma_1^2}+\frac{\mu_2^2}{\sigma_2^2}\right), \quad \sigma_3^2 = \left(a_1\frac{\sigma_1^2}{\mu_1}\right)^2\left(\frac{\mu_1^2}{\sigma_1^2}+\frac{\mu_2^2}{\sigma_2^2}\right).$$

From considerations of symmetry (of forms), we may wish to fix $a_1 = \mu_1/\sigma_1^2$ so that $a_2 = \mu_2/\sigma_2^2$ and we have

$$\mu_3 = \frac{\mu_1^2}{\sigma_1^2} + \frac{\mu_2^2}{\sigma_2^2} \quad \text{and} \quad \sigma_3^2 = \mu_3.$$

An alternative special case arises when x_1 and x_2 are both drawn from the same $\mathrm{IG}(\mu, \sigma^2)$. Then, the three equations imply $\frac{1}{2}(x_1+x_2) \sim \mathrm{IG}(\mu, \frac{1}{2}\sigma^2)$, where the formula for mean and variance are as anticipated from the general theory.

(b) For $\mathrm{U}_{(\alpha,\beta)}$,

$$\frac{\mathrm{e}^{\mathrm{i}\beta_3\tau}-\mathrm{e}^{\mathrm{i}\alpha_3\tau}}{\mathrm{i}\,(\beta_3-\alpha_3)\,\tau}=\frac{\mathrm{e}^{\mathrm{i}\beta_1 a_1\tau}-\mathrm{e}^{\mathrm{i}\alpha_1 a_1\tau}}{\mathrm{i}\,(\beta_1-\alpha_1)\,a_1\tau}\times\frac{\mathrm{e}^{\mathrm{i}\beta_2 a_2\tau}-\mathrm{e}^{\mathrm{i}\alpha_2 a_2\tau}}{\mathrm{i}\,(\beta_2-\alpha_2)\,a_2\tau}$$

possesses no solution where powers of τ can be equated on both sides of the equality, apart from the trivial one where either (but not both) $a_1 \to 0$ or $a_2 \to 0$. See also Exercise 7.13 where the (triangular) density of $x_1 + x_2$ is worked out.
(c) The distribution which $\mathrm{D}(\cdot)$ reproduces is of the same type $\mathrm{D}(\cdot)$. In *this* sense, reproduction is more restrictive than infinite divisibility (but not as restrictive as stability). However, reproduction allows different parameters $a_1 \neq a_2$ and $\boldsymbol{\theta}_1 \neq \boldsymbol{\theta}_2$, so a_1x_1 and a_2x_2 need not be identically distributed, something that is ruled out by infinite divisibility. There is also a subtle difference in focus between the two concepts: reproduction is about cumulating variates (x_1 and x_2 getting together and producing x_3), whereas infinite divisibility is about decomposing a variate into components. To illustrate, we take two examples. Exercise 7.1 implies that an $\mathrm{Nbin}(\nu, p)$ variate can be decomposed into m independent $\mathrm{Nbin}(\nu/m, p)$ variates for any $\nu/m \in \mathbb{R}_+$ (hence any $m \in \mathbb{N}$); see also Exercise 4.8 for the Poisson. Cumulating and decomposing variates is equivalent in this case. However, $\mathrm{Bin}(n, p)$ can be decomposed as $\mathrm{Bin}(n/m, p)$ if and only if $n/m \in \mathbb{N}$, which is certainly not possible for any arbitrary $m \in \mathbb{N}$. If reproduction had been defined in terms of decompositions, $\mathrm{Bin}(1, p)$ would have failed the criterion.

Exercise 7.4 (Quantiles are not additive) An individual owns two assets. The returns on them are independent and each distributed as $x_i \sim \mathrm{N}(\mu, \sigma^2), i = 1, 2$, with $\sigma > 0$. Obtain the 5% quantile of the average returns $\overline{x}$ that she makes on the assets, comparing it to 5% quantile of each asset.

Solution
As follows from Exercise 7.3(a),

$$\overline{x} := \frac{1}{2}\,(x_1 + x_2) \sim \mathrm{N}\left(\mu, \frac{\sigma^2}{2}\right).$$

Diversification of the assets in her portfolio has reduced volatility and hence risk. We will see this phenomenon, more generally, in Exercises 7.15 and 7.16 and then in the next three chapters, showing that $\mathrm{var}(\overline{x})$ declines at a rate of $1/n$ as the number of components n of $\overline{x}$ increases. When the variances of the components $x_1, x_2, \ldots$ differ, the optimal combination is not $\overline{x}$, but rather the weighted average, as we will show in Exercise 11.2 and more generally in Exercise 13.12.

As seen in the introduction to Chapter 4, the 5% quantile of the standard normal $z \sim \mathrm{N}(0, 1)$ is -1.645 (to three decimal places) since $\Pr(z < -1.645) \approx 5\%$. Therefore, the 5% quantile of x_i ($i = 1, 2$) is $q := \mu - 1.645\sigma$, whereas for $\overline{x}$ it is

$$\mu - 1.645\frac{\sigma}{\sqrt{2}} \approx \mu - 1.163\sigma > q,$$

again a manifestation of the reduction in risk. As a result, we can see that quantiles are *not* additive: even though x_1 and x_2 have identical quantiles, their average has a different one. In the context of the distribution of losses, these quantiles are called *value at risk* (VaR).

Exercise 7.5 (Adding or mixing?) Let $x_1 \sim \mathrm{N}(-1,1)$ independently of $x_2 \sim \mathrm{N}(1,1)$. Obtain the density of the mixed x_j if $\Pr(j=1) = \Pr(j=2) = \frac{1}{2}$.

Solution
From Chapter 2, the mixed density is

$$f_x(u) = \frac{1}{2}\frac{\mathrm{e}^{-(u+1)^2/2}}{\sqrt{2\pi}} + \frac{1}{2}\frac{\mathrm{e}^{-(u-1)^2/2}}{\sqrt{2\pi}} = \frac{\mathrm{e}^{-u^2/2}}{\sqrt{2\pi\mathrm{e}}}\left(\frac{\mathrm{e}^{-u}+\mathrm{e}^{u}}{2}\right) = \frac{\mathrm{e}^{-u^2/2}}{\sqrt{2\pi\mathrm{e}}}\cosh(u).$$

This is the average of the densities, a concept which is totally different from the density of the average $\frac{1}{2}(x_1+x_2) \sim \mathrm{N}(0,\frac{1}{2})$. Reproduction is not mixing!

Exercise 7.6 (Forgetful Expo, again) Let $x \in \mathbb{R}_+$ and $\{x_1, x_2, x_3\}$ be a random sample from the exponential density $f_x(u) = \lambda\mathrm{e}^{-\lambda u}$ with $\lambda > 0$. What is the probability that $x_1 > x_2 + x_3$?

Solution
Let $y := x_2 + x_3 \in \mathbb{R}_+$. Since Expo($\lambda$) is the special case Gam$(1,\lambda)$, Exercise 7.3 implies that $f_y(v) = \lambda^2 v\mathrm{e}^{-\lambda v}$ for $v > 0$. Using the same idea as in Exercise 4.18,

$$\begin{aligned}\Pr(x_1 > x_2 + x_3) &= \Pr(x_1 > y)\\ &= \int_0^\infty \Pr(x_1 > v \mid y = v) f_y(v)\,\mathrm{d}v = \int_0^\infty \Pr(x_1 > v) f_y(v)\,\mathrm{d}v\end{aligned}$$

since y depends on x_2, x_3 but is independent of x_1, hence

$$\begin{aligned}\Pr(x_1 > x_2 + x_3) &= \int_0^\infty f_y(v)\left(\int_v^\infty f_x(u)\,\mathrm{d}u\right)\mathrm{d}v\\ &= \int_0^\infty \lambda^2 v\mathrm{e}^{-\lambda v}\int_v^\infty \lambda\mathrm{e}^{-\lambda u}\,\mathrm{d}u\,\mathrm{d}v = \lambda^2\int_0^\infty v\mathrm{e}^{-2\lambda v}\,\mathrm{d}v = \lambda^2\frac{1}{(2\lambda)^2} = \frac{1}{4}.\end{aligned}$$

Another proof makes use of the exponential's no-memory property, introduced in Exercise 4.12. We have

$$\begin{aligned}\Pr(x_1 > x_2 + x_3) = &\Pr(x_1 > x_2 + x_3 \mid x_1 > x_2)\Pr(x_1 > x_2)\\ &+ \Pr(x_1 > x_2 + x_3 \mid x_1 < x_2)\Pr(x_1 < x_2)\end{aligned}$$

by the continuity of the variates implying $\Pr(x_1 = x_2) = 0$ for independent x_1, x_2 (see Exercise 5.16). Since the no-memory property implies that $\Pr(x_1 > x_2 + x_3 \mid x_1 > x_2) = \Pr(x_1 > x_3)$, and since the two inequalities $x_1 > x_2 + x_3$ and $x_1 < x_2$ cannot occur simultaneously,

$$\Pr(x_1 > x_2 + x_3) = \Pr(x_1 > x_3)\Pr(x_1 > x_2) + 0 \times \Pr(x_1 < x_2).$$

Since x_1 and x_3 are independently and identically distributed (and continuous), $\Pr(x_1 > x_3) = \frac{1}{2}$. By the same argument, $\Pr(x_1 > x_2) = \frac{1}{2}$. This gives $\Pr(x_1 > x_2 + x_3) = \frac{1}{4}$.

Exercise 7.7 (Uniform representation: exponential and Laplace, again) The p.d.f. of $x \in \mathbb{R}$ is given by

$$f_x(u) = \frac{1}{2}\mathrm{e}^{-|u|}.$$

(a) Find the p.d.f. of $y := |x|$.
(b) If $z := 0$ when $x \leqslant 0$, and $z := 1$ when $x > 0$, find the p.d.f. of z.
(c) If $z := \mathrm{e}^{-|x|}$, find the p.d.f. of z.

Solution
(a) The c.d.f. of y is

$$\begin{aligned}\Pr(y \leqslant v) &= \Pr(|x| \leqslant v) = \Pr(-v \leqslant x \leqslant v)\\ &= \int_{-v}^{0} \frac{1}{2}\mathrm{e}^{u}\,\mathrm{d}u + \int_{0}^{v} \frac{1}{2}\mathrm{e}^{-u}\,\mathrm{d}u = \left[\frac{1}{2}\mathrm{e}^{u}\right]_{-v}^{0} - \left[\frac{1}{2}\mathrm{e}^{-u}\right]_{0}^{v}\\ &= \frac{1}{2} - \frac{1}{2}\mathrm{e}^{-v} - \frac{1}{2}\mathrm{e}^{-v} + \frac{1}{2} = 1 - \mathrm{e}^{-v}.\end{aligned}$$

Hence, $f_y(v) = \mathrm{e}^{-v}$ for $v > 0$ and 0 elsewhere, which is in agreement with Exercise 2.17(c). Alternatively, the transformation theorem can be applied after partitioning $\mathcal{X}$ into $x = y > 0$ and $x = -y < 0$, yielding

$$f_y(v) = \frac{1}{2}\mathrm{e}^{-v} + \frac{1}{2}\mathrm{e}^{-v} = \mathrm{e}^{-v}.$$

(b) $\Pr(z = 0) = \Pr(z = 1) = \frac{1}{2}$.
(c) Since $z \in (0, 1)$ and $y = |x| = -\log(z)$, transforming from y to z gives

$$f_z(w) = \frac{1}{w}\mathrm{e}^{-(-\log(w))} = 1,$$

which is the p.d.f. of the standard uniform. This representation of the uniform distribution can also be proved by the PIT, as will be seen in Exercise 7.39(b), and it is an alternative to the representation in Exercise 4.18. Two further representations will be given in Exercises 7.25 and 7.26.

Exercise 7.8 (Disjoint sets and additive probabilities) If $x \in \mathbb{R}$ is a continuous variate with known c.d.f. F_x, derive the c.d.f. of:
(a) $z := -|x|$;
(b) $y := |x|$.

Solution

(a) Clearly $z \leqslant 0$, giving

$$F_z(w) = \Pr(z \leqslant w) = \Pr(-|x| \leqslant w) = \Pr(|x| \geqslant -w) = \Pr(x \geqslant -w) + \Pr(x \leqslant w)$$

for $w \leqslant 0$, and $F_z(w) = 1$ for $w > 0$. The reason why we could decompose $\Pr(|x| \geqslant -w)$ into the sum of two probabilities is that the sets $\{x : x \geqslant -w\}$ and $\{x : x \leqslant w\}$ are disjoint, because $w \leqslant 0$. Continuity of the variate x implies that $\Pr(x \geqslant -w) = \Pr(x > -w)$ and hence

$$F_z(w) = 1 - \Pr(x \leqslant -w) + \Pr(x \leqslant w) = 1 - F_x(-w) + F_x(w)$$

for $w \leqslant 0$, and $F_z(w) = 1$ for $w > 0$. Note that $F_z(0) = 1 - F_x(0) + F_x(0) = 1$. As a check on the answer, a proper c.d.f. will always satisfy the four defining conditions in Chapter 2: (i) $\lim_{w\to-\infty} F_z(w) = 1 - 1 + 0 = 0$, (ii) $\lim_{w\to\infty} F_z(w) = 1$ since $w > 0$, (iii) $F_z(w^+) = F_z(w)$ by the continuity of F_x, and (iv) $s < t$ implies $F_z(s) \leqslant F_z(t)$, since $F_x(w)$ and $-F_x(-w)$ are both nondecreasing in w.

(b) There are two alternative solutions. First, from $y = -z \geqslant 0$ and the continuity of the variate,

$$\begin{aligned} F_y(v) &= \Pr(y \leqslant v) = \Pr(-z \leqslant v) = \Pr(z \geqslant -v) \\ &= 1 - F_z(-v) = F_x(v) - F_x(-v) \end{aligned}$$

for $v \geqslant 0$, and $F_y(v) = 0$ for $v < 0$. Second,

$$F_y(v) = \Pr(y \leqslant v) = \Pr(|x| \leqslant v) = \Pr(-v \leqslant x \leqslant v),$$

where we should *not* write $\Pr(|x| \leqslant v)$ in terms of the sets $\{x : x \geqslant -v\}$ and $\{x : x \leqslant v\}$ in the additive way we used in (a), because $v \geqslant 0$ and thus the two sets are not disjoint. The continuity of x gives

$$F_y(v) = \Pr(-v < x \leqslant v) = \Pr(x \leqslant v) - \Pr(x \leqslant -v) = F_x(v) - F_x(-v)$$

for $v \geqslant 0$.

Exercise 7.9 (Transformed by the three methods) The continuous variate $\boldsymbol{x} \in \mathbb{R}^m$ has c.f. $\varphi_{\boldsymbol{x}}$, c.d.f. $F_{\boldsymbol{x}}$, and p.d.f. $f_{\boldsymbol{x}}$. Let $\boldsymbol{y} := -2\boldsymbol{x}$. Find the c.f., c.d.f., and p.d.f. of $\boldsymbol{y}$, each by a different method. Show that all three methods imply the same answer for $f_{\boldsymbol{y}}$.

Solution

The c.f. of $\boldsymbol{y}$ is

$$\varphi_{\boldsymbol{y}}(\boldsymbol{\tau}) = \mathrm{E}\left(\mathrm{e}^{\mathrm{i}\boldsymbol{\tau}'\boldsymbol{y}}\right) = \mathrm{E}\left(\mathrm{e}^{\mathrm{i}\boldsymbol{\tau}'(-2\boldsymbol{x})}\right) = \mathrm{E}\left(\mathrm{e}^{\mathrm{i}(-2\boldsymbol{\tau})'\boldsymbol{x}}\right) = \varphi_{\boldsymbol{x}}(-2\boldsymbol{\tau}).$$

Its c.d.f. is

$$F_{\boldsymbol{y}}(\boldsymbol{w}) = \Pr(\boldsymbol{y} \leqslant \boldsymbol{w}) = \Pr(-2\boldsymbol{x} \leqslant \boldsymbol{w})$$
$$= \Pr\left(\boldsymbol{x} \geqslant -\frac{1}{2}\boldsymbol{w}\right) = 1 - \Pr\left(\boldsymbol{x} < -\frac{1}{2}\boldsymbol{w}\right) = 1 - F_{\boldsymbol{x}}\left(-\frac{1}{2}\boldsymbol{w}\right)$$

by the continuity of $\boldsymbol{x}$. Finally, the transformation theorem requires that

$$\left|\det\left(\frac{\partial \boldsymbol{x}}{\partial \boldsymbol{y}'}\right)\right| = \left|\det\left(-\frac{1}{2}\boldsymbol{I}_m\right)\right| = \left|(-2)^{-m}\right| = 2^{-m}$$

and we have

$$f_{\boldsymbol{y}}(\boldsymbol{w}) = 2^{-m} f_{\boldsymbol{x}}\left(-\frac{1}{2}\boldsymbol{w}\right).$$

To verify this last result using the $F_{\boldsymbol{y}}$ we have derived, continuity of the variate implies that

$$f_{\boldsymbol{y}}(\boldsymbol{w}) = \frac{\partial^m}{\partial w_1 \dots \partial w_m} F_{\boldsymbol{y}}(\boldsymbol{w}) = \frac{\partial^m}{\partial w_1 \dots \partial w_m}\left(1 - F_{\boldsymbol{x}}\left(-\frac{1}{2}\boldsymbol{w}\right)\right)$$
$$= \frac{\partial^m}{\partial w_1 \dots \partial w_m}\left(\int_{-w_1/2}^{\infty} \cdots \int_{-w_m/2}^{\infty} f_{\boldsymbol{x}}(u_1, \dots, u_m)\, \mathrm{d}u_m \dots \mathrm{d}u_1\right)$$
$$= f_{\boldsymbol{x}}\left(-\frac{w_1}{2}, \dots, -\frac{w_m}{2}\right) \prod_{i=1}^{m}\left(-1 \times \frac{\mathrm{d}(-\frac{1}{2}w_i)}{\mathrm{d}w_i}\right) = 2^{-m} f_{\boldsymbol{x}}\left(-\frac{1}{2}\boldsymbol{w}\right)$$

by repeated use of Leibniz' rule. To verify that the derived $\varphi_{\boldsymbol{y}}$ also implies the same $f_{\boldsymbol{y}}$, we write

$$\varphi_{\boldsymbol{y}}(\boldsymbol{\tau}) = \varphi_{\boldsymbol{x}}(-2\boldsymbol{\tau}) = \int_{-\infty}^{\infty} \cdots \int_{-\infty}^{\infty} \mathrm{e}^{\mathrm{i}(-2u_1\tau_1 - \dots - 2u_m\tau_m)} f_{\boldsymbol{x}}(u_1, \dots, u_m)\, \mathrm{d}u_m \dots \mathrm{d}u_1$$
$$= \int_{\infty}^{-\infty} \cdots \int_{\infty}^{-\infty} \mathrm{e}^{\mathrm{i}(w_1\tau_1 + \dots + w_m\tau_m)} f_{\boldsymbol{x}}\left(-\frac{w_1}{2}, \dots, -\frac{w_m}{2}\right) \mathrm{d}\left(-\frac{w_m}{2}\right) \dots \mathrm{d}\left(-\frac{w_1}{2}\right)$$

by the change of variables $w_i = -2u_i$, and rearranging yields

$$\varphi_{\boldsymbol{y}}(\boldsymbol{\tau}) = \int_{-\infty}^{\infty} \cdots \int_{-\infty}^{\infty} \mathrm{e}^{\mathrm{i}(w_1\tau_1 + \dots + w_m\tau_m)} \left(2^{-m} f_{\boldsymbol{x}}\left(-\frac{w_1}{2}, \dots, -\frac{w_m}{2}\right)\right) \mathrm{d}w_m \dots \mathrm{d}w_1,$$

which is the c.f. of an m-dimensional variate with density function $2^{-m} f_{\boldsymbol{x}}\left(-\frac{1}{2}\boldsymbol{w}\right)$.

Exercise 7.10 (Convolution of dependents) The joint p.d.f. of (x, y) is given by

$$f_{x,y}(u, v) = \begin{cases} \mathrm{e}^{-v} & (0 < u < v < \infty), \\ 0 & (\text{elsewhere}). \end{cases}$$

(a) Obtain the joint p.d.f. of (x, z), where $z := x + y$.
(b) Find the marginal p.d.f. of z.

Solution

(a) The transformation from $(x, y) \equiv (x, z - x)$ to (x, z) has Jacobian factor

$$\begin{vmatrix} 1 & 0 \\ -1 & 1 \end{vmatrix} = 1.$$

Hence,

$$f_{x,z}(u, w) = \begin{cases} e^{-(w-u)} & (0 < u < \frac{1}{2}w), \\ 0 & \text{(elsewhere)}. \end{cases}$$

The new domain of definition arises because $v = w - u$ has been substituted into $0 < u < v$.
(b) The p.d.f. of z is

$$f_z(w) = \int_0^{w/2} e^{-(w-u)} \, du = \left[e^{-(w-u)} \right]_0^{w/2} = e^{-w/2} \left(1 - e^{-w/2}\right) \qquad (w > 0).$$

Exercise 7.11 (Convolution of bivariate exponential) The joint p.d.f. of (x, y) is given by

$$f_{x,y}(u, v) = \begin{cases} 4e^{-2(u+v)} & (u > 0, \ v > 0), \\ 0 & \text{(elsewhere)}. \end{cases}$$

Find the p.d.f. of $z := x + y$.

Solution

Consider the transformation from $(x, y) \equiv (x, z - x)$ to (x, z). The Jacobian factor equals 1 and hence

$$f_{x,z}(u, w) = \begin{cases} 4e^{-2w} & (0 < u < w), \\ 0 & \text{(elsewhere)}. \end{cases}$$

Note carefully the new domain of definition of the density function. The marginal density is

$$f_z(w) = \int_0^w 4e^{-2w} \, du = \begin{cases} 4we^{-2w} & (w > 0), \\ 0 & \text{(elsewhere)}. \end{cases}$$

Exercise 7.12 (Convolution, conditional expectation, and derivative of log-density) Let $z := x + y$, where x, y are independent continuous variates with supports over $\mathbb{R}$.
(a) Prove that the marginal density of z can be written as $f_z(w) = \mathrm{E}_{x|z=w}(f_y(z - x))$.
(b) Prove that

$$\frac{\mathrm{d} \log (f_z(w))}{\mathrm{d}w} = \mathrm{E}_{x|z=w} \left(\frac{\mathrm{d} \log (f_x(x))}{\mathrm{d}x} \right).$$

(c) Would the relation in (b) also hold if the supports of x and y were $\mathbb{R}_+$?

Solution

(a) From the definition of a convolution, we have

$$f_z(w) = \int_{-\infty}^{\infty} f_x(u)\, f_y(w-u)\, \mathrm{d}u = \mathrm{E}_{x|z=w}\left(f_y(z-x)\right),$$

where the independence of x and y has been used to factor $f_{x,y}$ into the product in the integrand.

(b) Since the limits of integration in (a) do not depend on w,

$$\frac{\mathrm{d}f_z(w)}{\mathrm{d}w} = \frac{\mathrm{d}}{\mathrm{d}w}\int_{-\infty}^{\infty} f_x(u)\, f_y(w-u)\, \mathrm{d}u = \int_{-\infty}^{\infty} f_x(u)\, \frac{\partial f_y(w-u)}{\partial w}\, \mathrm{d}u.$$

Integrating by parts with respect to u,

$$\begin{aligned}\frac{\mathrm{d}f_z(w)}{\mathrm{d}w} &= -\left[f_x(u)\, f_y(w-u)\right]_{-\infty}^{\infty} + \int_{-\infty}^{\infty} \frac{\mathrm{d}f_x(u)}{\mathrm{d}u} f_y(w-u)\, \mathrm{d}u \\ &= 0 + \int_{-\infty}^{\infty} \frac{\mathrm{d}\log(f_x(u))}{\mathrm{d}u} f_x(u)\, f_y(w-u)\, \mathrm{d}u \\ &= \int_{-\infty}^{\infty} \frac{\mathrm{d}\log(f_x(u))}{\mathrm{d}u} f_{x,z}(u,w)\, \mathrm{d}u\end{aligned}$$

by the independence of x, y and the transformation theorem. We have also used the idea that the densities must tend to 0 as their arguments tend to $\pm\infty$, otherwise they would not integrate to a finite value. Dividing both sides by $f_z(w)$ gives the required result.

(c) The relation need not hold if the supports are not $\mathbb{R}$. For example, we need to ensure that $f_x(u)\, f_y(w-u) \to 0$ at the edges of the support for x, when integrating by parts as we have done. More fundamentally, when $x, y \in \mathbb{R}_+$, the domain of integration for u would become $0 < u < w$, thus depending on w, and we cannot interchange the differentiation and integration freely (see Leibniz' rule) for any arbitrary f_x and f_y.

Exercise 7.13 (Convoluting two rectangulars gives a triangular) Consider a random sample z_1 and z_2 from a standard uniform (rectangular) distribution. Let $x := z_1 - z_2$ and $y := z_1 + z_2$.

(a) Derive $f_{x,y}(u, v)$.

(b) Derive the marginal densities of x and y.

(c) Show that $\mathrm{cov}(x, y) = 0$. Are x and y independent?

Solution

(a) Since $z_1 = (x + y)/2$ and $z_2 = (y - x)/2$, the Jacobian factor of the transformation from (z_1, z_2) to (x, y) is

$$\begin{vmatrix} \frac{1}{2} & \frac{1}{2} \\ -\frac{1}{2} & \frac{1}{2} \end{vmatrix} = \frac{1}{2}.$$

The region where the p.d.f. takes positive values is given by $0 < \frac{1}{2}(u + v) < 1$ and

$0 < \frac{1}{2}(v-u) < 1$, so

$$f_{x,y}(u,v) = \begin{cases} \frac{1}{2} & (0 < \frac{1}{2}(u+v) < 1 \quad \text{and} \quad 0 < \frac{1}{2}(v-u) < 1), \\ 0 & \text{(elsewhere)}. \end{cases}$$

There are two possible ways of rewriting the domain of definition of this density in order to separate u from v. The first formulation is $-u < v < 2-u$ and $u < v < 2+u$, leading to $\max\{-u,u\} < v < \min\{2-u, 2+u\}$ and $-1 < u < 1$. Since

$$\max\{a,b\} = \frac{a+b}{2} + \left|\frac{a-b}{2}\right| \quad \text{and} \quad \min\{a,b\} = \frac{a+b}{2} - \left|\frac{a-b}{2}\right|,$$

this is equivalent to $-1 < u < 1$ and $|u| < v < 2-|u|$. The second formulation is $-v < u < 2-v$ and $v-2 < u < v$, leading to $\max\{-v, v-2\} < u < \min\{2-v, v\}$ with $0 < v < 2$. This is equivalent to $0 < v < 2$ and $|1-v|-1 < u < 1-|1-v|$.
(b) The marginal densities are

$$f_x(u) = \frac{1}{2}\int_{|u|}^{2-|u|} dv = \begin{cases} 1-|u| & (|u| < 1), \\ 0 & \text{(elsewhere)}, \end{cases}$$

and

$$f_y(v) = \frac{1}{2}\int_{|1-v|-1}^{1-|1-v|} du = \begin{cases} 1-|1-v| & (0 < v < 2), \\ 0 & \text{(elsewhere)}. \end{cases}$$

Both marginal densities have a triangular shape when plotted, centered around $x = 0$ and $y = 1$, respectively. Even though z_1 and z_2 are rectangular and all values are equally likely, their difference x is more likely to be near the center of the distribution than other values. The reason is that $x \approx 0$ arises from more combinations of z_1 and z_2 than, say, the extreme $x \approx 1$. A similar story can be told for y. This "central" tendency of sums will be revisited in Chapter 10. See also Exercise 7.22(c) for a discussion of products.
(c) As seen in Exercise 6.10 (subject to relabeling of the variates), irrespective of the distribution of z_1 and z_2, we have $\text{cov}(x,y) = \text{var}(z_1) - \text{var}(z_2)$. This is zero if z_1 and z_2 have the same variance, as is the case here. However, comparing (a) and (b) shows that x and y are not independent.

Exercise 7.14 (Convoluted but normal!) The joint p.d.f. of $(x,y) \in \mathbb{R}^2$ is given by

$$f_{x,y}(u,v) = \frac{1}{2\pi}\mathrm{e}^{-\left(u^2+(v-u)^2\right)/2}.$$

(a) Obtain the p.d.f. of $z := x - y$.
(b) Are z and x independent?

Solution
(a) We first determine the p.d.f. of (x,z). Consider the transformation from $(x,y) \equiv$

$(x, x - z)$ to (x, z) with Jacobian

$$\begin{vmatrix} 1 & 0 \\ 1 & -1 \end{vmatrix} = -1.$$

Then

$$f_{x,z}(u, w) = \frac{|-1|}{2\pi} \mathrm{e}^{-(u^2+w^2)/2}.$$

The p.d.f. of z is

$$f_z(w) = \frac{1}{2\pi} \mathrm{e}^{-w^2/2} \int_{-\infty}^{\infty} \mathrm{e}^{-u^2/2} \, \mathrm{d}u = \frac{1}{\sqrt{2\pi}} \mathrm{e}^{-w^2/2}.$$

(b) Since $f_x(u) = (1/\sqrt{2\pi})\mathrm{e}^{-u^2/2}$, it follows that $f_{x,z}(u, w) = f_x(u) f_z(w)$ over $\mathbb{R}^2$, and hence x and z are independent. This was also clear from the relation of the $f_{x,z}$ derived here to the formula for the bivariate normal density seen, for example, in Exercise 6.1.

Exercise 7.15 (Convoluted normals: orthogonality) Let $x_1, \dots, x_n$ be a random sample from an $\mathrm{N}(0, 1)$ distribution. Define $z_1 := \sum_{i=1}^n \alpha_i x_i$ and $z_2 := \sum_{i=1}^n \beta_i x_i$.
(a) Find the distribution of z_1.
(b) Show that z_1 and z_2 are independent if and only if $\sum_{i=1}^n \alpha_i \beta_i = 0$.
(c) How would the results in (a) and (b) be affected if x_i were drawn independently from the more general $\mathrm{N}(\mu_i, \sigma_i^2)$?

Solution
(a) The moment-generating function of z_1 is

$$m_{z_1}(t) = \mathrm{E}\left(\mathrm{e}^{t z_1}\right) = \mathrm{E}\left(\mathrm{e}^{\sum_{i=1}^n t \alpha_i x_i}\right) = \mathrm{E}\left(\prod_{i=1}^n \mathrm{e}^{t \alpha_i x_i}\right) = \prod_{i=1}^n \mathrm{E}\left(\mathrm{e}^{t \alpha_i x_i}\right)$$

by the independence of the x_i's. Then,

$$m_{z_1}(t) = \prod_{i=1}^n m_{x_i}(\alpha_i t) = \prod_{i=1}^n \mathrm{e}^{\alpha_i^2 t^2/2} = \mathrm{e}^{(t^2/2)\sum_{i=1}^n \alpha_i^2},$$

which is the m.g.f. of $\mathrm{N}(0, \sum_{i=1}^n \alpha_i^2)$. Hence, $z_1 \sim \mathrm{N}(0, \sum_{i=1}^n \alpha_i^2)$ and, similarly, $z_2 \sim \mathrm{N}(0, \sum_{i=1}^n \beta_i^2)$. Linear combinations of independent normals are therefore normal too.
(b) We know, from Chapter 6, that z_1 and z_2 are independent if and only if $m_{z_1,z_2}(t_1, t_2) = m_{z_1}(t_1) m_{z_2}(t_2)$. Now,

$$\begin{aligned} m_{z_1,z_2}(t_1, t_2) &= \mathrm{E}\left(\exp\left(t_1 \sum_{i=1}^n \alpha_i x_i + t_2 \sum_{i=1}^n \beta_i x_i\right)\right) \\ &= \mathrm{E}\left(\exp\left(\sum_{i=1}^n (t_1 \alpha_i + t_2 \beta_i) x_i\right)\right) \end{aligned}$$

and, using the independence of the x_i's,

$$m_{z_1,z_2}(t_1,t_2) = \prod_{i=1}^{n} \mathrm{E}\left(\exp\left((t_1\alpha_i + t_2\beta_i)x_i\right)\right)$$
$$= \prod_{i=1}^{n} \exp\left(\frac{(t_1\alpha_i + t_2\beta_i)^2}{2}\right)$$
$$= \exp\left(\frac{t_1^2}{2}\sum_{i=1}^{n}\alpha_i^2 + \frac{t_2^2}{2}\sum_{i=1}^{n}\beta_i^2 + t_1t_2\sum_{i=1}^{n}\alpha_i\beta_i\right).$$

The m.g.f. factorizes if and only if $\sum_{i=1}^{n}\alpha_i\beta_i = 0$. Notice that, as a general result,

$$\mathrm{cov}(z_1,z_2) \equiv \sum_{i=1}^{n}\sum_{j=1}^{n}\alpha_i\beta_j\,\mathrm{cov}(x_i,x_j) = \sum_{i=1}^{n}\alpha_i\beta_i\,\mathrm{var}(x_i)$$

when $\mathrm{cov}(x_i,x_j) = 0$ for $i \neq j$. Applied to the current context, we have $\mathrm{cov}(z_1,z_2) = \sum_{i=1}^{n}\alpha_i\beta_i$, hence the m.g.f. factorizes if and only if $\mathrm{cov}(z_1,z_2) = 0$. We will revisit this orthogonality condition in the next chapter.

(c) This part generalizes the result about the normal distribution in Exercise 7.3. First, by the independence of the x_i's,

$$m_{z_1}(t_1) = \mathrm{E}\left(\exp\left(t_1\sum_{i=1}^{n}\alpha_i x_i\right)\right)$$
$$= \prod_{i=1}^{n} m_{x_i}(t_1\alpha_i\sigma_i) = \exp\left(t_1\sum_{i=1}^{n}\alpha_i\mu_i + \frac{t_1^2}{2}\sum_{i=1}^{n}\alpha_i^2\sigma_i^2\right),$$

hence $z_1 = \sum_{i=1}^{n}\alpha_i x_i \sim \mathrm{N}(\sum_{i=1}^{n}\alpha_i\mu_i, \sum_{i=1}^{n}\alpha_i^2\sigma_i^2)$. Then

$$m_{z_1,z_2}(t_1,t_2) = \mathrm{E}\left(\exp\left(\sum_{i=1}^{n}(t_1\alpha_i + t_2\beta_i)x_i\right)\right) = \prod_{i=1}^{n}\mathrm{E}\left(\exp\left((t_1\alpha_i + t_2\beta_i)x_i\right)\right)$$
$$= \prod_{i=1}^{n}\exp\left(\mu_i(t_1\alpha_i + t_2\beta_i) + \frac{\sigma_i^2}{2}(t_1^2\alpha_i^2 + t_2^2\beta_i^2 + 2t_1t_2\alpha_i\beta_i)\right)$$
$$= m_{z_1}(t_1)\,m_{z_2}(t_2)\exp\left(t_1t_2\sum_{i=1}^{n}\sigma_i^2\alpha_i\beta_i\right).$$

Hence, z_1 and z_2 are independent if and only if $\sum_{i=1}^{n}\sigma_i^2\alpha_i\beta_i = 0$, that is, if and only if $\mathrm{cov}(z_1,z_2) = 0$ as before. As in (b), in the case of two normal variates z_1 and z_2, independence coincides with lack of correlation; see the discussion in Exercise 6.51(c).

Exercise 7.16 (Helmert's transformation) Let $x_1,\dots,x_n$ be a random sample from the standard normal distribution. Let $\boldsymbol{A}$ be the $n \times n$ matrix

$$\boldsymbol{A} := \begin{pmatrix} \frac{1}{\sqrt{n}} & \frac{1}{\sqrt{n}} & \frac{1}{\sqrt{n}} & \cdots & \frac{1}{\sqrt{n}} \\ \frac{1}{\sqrt{2}} & -\frac{1}{\sqrt{2}} & 0 & \cdots & 0 \\ \frac{1}{\sqrt{6}} & \frac{1}{\sqrt{6}} & -\frac{2}{\sqrt{6}} & \cdots & 0 \\ \vdots & \vdots & \vdots & & \vdots \\ \frac{1}{\sqrt{n(n-1)}} & \frac{1}{\sqrt{n(n-1)}} & \frac{1}{\sqrt{n(n-1)}} & \cdots & -\frac{(n-1)}{\sqrt{n(n-1)}} \end{pmatrix},$$

where the first row is given by $(1/\sqrt{n})\boldsymbol{\imath}'$, and the j-th row ($j \geqslant 2$) by

$$\boldsymbol{a}_j' = \left(\frac{1}{\sqrt{j(j-1)}}, \dots, \frac{1}{\sqrt{j(j-1)}}, -\frac{j-1}{\sqrt{j(j-1)}}, 0, \dots, 0\right)$$

such that $a_{jj} = -(j-1)/\sqrt{j(j-1)}$. Let

$$\overline{x} := \frac{1}{n}\sum_{i=1}^{n} x_i \quad \text{and} \quad s^2 := \frac{1}{n-1}\sum_{i=1}^{n}(x_i - \overline{x})^2.$$

Now define $\boldsymbol{y} := \boldsymbol{A}\boldsymbol{x}$, where $\boldsymbol{x} := (x_1, \dots, x_n)'$, a transformation known as *Helmert's transformation*.

(a) Show that $\boldsymbol{A}$ is an orthogonal matrix.

(b) Show that $y_1, \dots, y_n$ are independent and standard-normally distributed.

(c) Show that $\overline{x} = y_1/\sqrt{n}$.

(d) Show that $(n-1)s^2 = \sum_{i=2}^{n} y_i^2 \sim \chi^2(n-1)$.

(e) Are $\overline{x}$ and s^2 independent? What if $x_1, \dots, x_n$ were a random sample from $\mathrm{N}(\mu, \sigma^2)$?

Solution

(a) The inner product of the j-th row with itself is

$$\boldsymbol{a}_j'\boldsymbol{a}_j = \left(\sum_{i=1}^{j-1}\left(\frac{1}{\sqrt{j(j-1)}}\right)^2\right) + \left(\frac{j-1}{\sqrt{j(j-1)}}\right)^2 = \frac{j-1}{j(j-1)} + \frac{(j-1)^2}{j(j-1)} = 1$$

for $j > 1$, and $\boldsymbol{a}_1'\boldsymbol{a}_1 = \frac{1}{n}\boldsymbol{\imath}'\boldsymbol{\imath} = 1$. Also, for $j > 1$,

$$\boldsymbol{a}_j'\boldsymbol{a}_1 = \frac{1}{\sqrt{n}}\left(\left(\sum_{i=1}^{j-1}\frac{1}{\sqrt{j(j-1)}}\right) - \frac{j-1}{\sqrt{j(j-1)}}\right) = 0$$

and, for $1 < k < j$,

$$\boldsymbol{a}_j'\boldsymbol{a}_k = \left(\sum_{i=1}^{k-1}\frac{1}{\sqrt{jk(j-1)(k-1)}}\right) - \frac{k-1}{\sqrt{jk(j-1)(k-1)}} = 0.$$

Hence, $\boldsymbol{A}'\boldsymbol{A} = \boldsymbol{I}_n$ and $\boldsymbol{A}$ is orthogonal.

(b) By the independence of the components of $\boldsymbol{x}$, its density is

$$\prod_{i=1}^{n} \phi\left(w_{x_i}\right) = \prod_{i=1}^{n} \left(\frac{1}{\sqrt{2\pi}} \mathrm{e}^{-w_{x_i}^2/2}\right) = \frac{\exp\left(-\frac{1}{2}\sum_{i=1}^{n} w_{x_i}^2\right)}{(2\pi)^{n/2}} = (2\pi)^{-n/2} \mathrm{e}^{-\boldsymbol{w}_x' \boldsymbol{w}_x/2},$$

where $\boldsymbol{w}_x := (w_{x_1}, \dots, w_{x_n})'$. To apply the transformation theorem, we note that $|\boldsymbol{A}| = \pm 1$ since the matrix is orthogonal, and that $\boldsymbol{x} = \boldsymbol{A}^{-1}\boldsymbol{y} = \boldsymbol{A}'\boldsymbol{y}$ (implying also that $\boldsymbol{x}'\boldsymbol{x} = \boldsymbol{y}'\boldsymbol{A}\boldsymbol{A}'\boldsymbol{y} = \boldsymbol{y}'\boldsymbol{y}$). Hence, the transformation from $\boldsymbol{x}$ to $\boldsymbol{y}$ is given by

$$f_{\boldsymbol{y}}\left(\boldsymbol{w}_{\boldsymbol{y}}\right) = |\pm 1|(2\pi)^{-n/2}\mathrm{e}^{-\boldsymbol{w}_{\boldsymbol{y}}'\boldsymbol{A}\boldsymbol{A}'\boldsymbol{w}_{\boldsymbol{y}}/2} = (2\pi)^{-n/2}\mathrm{e}^{-\boldsymbol{w}_{\boldsymbol{y}}'\boldsymbol{w}_{\boldsymbol{y}}/2}.$$

The result is not surprising once we recall that $\boldsymbol{x} \sim \mathrm{N}(\mathbf{0}, \boldsymbol{I}_n)$ is spherically distributed (see Chapter 6) and hence its density is invariant to orthogonal transformations.
(c) By definition, $\overline{x} = n^{-1}\sum_{i=1}^{n} x_i = n^{-1}\boldsymbol{\imath}'\boldsymbol{x} = y_1/\sqrt{n}$.
(d) We have

$$\begin{aligned}(n-1)s^2 &= \sum_{i=1}^{n}\left(x_i^2 - 2\overline{x}x_i + \overline{x}^2\right) = \sum_{i=1}^{n} x_i^2 - 2\overline{x}n\left(\frac{1}{n}\sum_{i=1}^{n} x_i\right) + \overline{x}^2\sum_{i=1}^{n} 1 \\ &= \sum_{i=1}^{n} x_i^2 - n\overline{x}^2 = \sum_{i=1}^{n} y_i^2 - n\left(\frac{1}{\sqrt{n}}y_1\right)^2 = \sum_{i=2}^{n} y_i^2,\end{aligned}$$

which is a general result that holds for any distribution of $\boldsymbol{x}$. Since the y_i's are i.i.d. $\mathrm{N}(0,1)$-distributed, it follows that the y_i^2 $(i = 1, \dots, n)$ are i.i.d. $\chi^2(1)$ by Exercise 4.25. Hence, $(n-1)s^2 = \sum_{i=2}^{n} y_i^2 \sim \chi^2(n-1)$ by using the reproductive property in Exercise 7.3(a).
(e) We have shown that $\overline{x}$ depends only on y_1, and s^2 depends only on $y_2, \dots, y_n$. Since the y_i's are independent, $\overline{x}$ and s^2 are independent. More generally, let $z_i := (x_i - \mu)/\sigma$. Then $z_i \sim \mathrm{N}(0,1)$ as assumed earlier and, since z_i and x_i are related by a deterministic transformation, the same logic applies as before. More specifically, define $\overline{z} := n^{-1}\sum_{i=1}^{n} z_i = (\overline{x} - \mu)/\sigma$ and

$$s_z^2 := \frac{1}{n-1}\sum_{i=1}^{n}(z_i - \overline{z})^2 = \frac{1}{n-1}\sum_{i=1}^{n}\left(\frac{x_i - \overline{x}}{\sigma}\right)^2 = \frac{s^2}{\sigma^2}.$$

This gives $\overline{x} = \mu + \sigma\overline{z}$ and $s^2 = \sigma^2 s_z^2$, hence

$$\overline{x} = \mu + \frac{\sigma y_1}{\sqrt{n}} \quad \text{and} \quad s^2 = \sigma^2\sum_{i=2}^{n} y_i^2,$$

where we see that $\overline{x}$ depends only on y_1, while s^2 depends only on $y_2, \dots, y_n$. This establishes that $\overline{x}$ and s^2 are independent. It also shows that $(n-1)\,s^2/\sigma^2 \sim \chi^2(n-1)$.

Exercise 7.17 (Convoluted into gammas) The joint density of (x, y) is given by

$$f_{x,y}(u, v) = \frac{\lambda^{2n}}{(2n-3)!}u(v-u)^{2n-3}\mathrm{e}^{-\lambda v}$$

for $0 < u < v < \infty$ and $\lambda > 0$.

(a) Derive the p.d.f. of $z := y - x$.
(b) Are x and z independent?

Solution
(a) Consider the transformation from $(x, y) \equiv (x, x + z)$ to (x, z) with Jacobian factor

$$\begin{vmatrix} 1 & 0 \\ 1 & 1 \end{vmatrix} = 1.$$

The joint p.d.f. of (x, z) is

$$f_{x,z}(u, w) = \frac{\lambda^{2n}}{(2n-3)!} u w^{2n-3} \mathrm{e}^{-\lambda(u+w)}$$

for $u > 0$ and $w > 0$. Hence, for $w > 0$,

$$f_z(w) = \frac{\lambda^{2n}}{(2n-3)!} w^{2n-3} \mathrm{e}^{-\lambda w} \int_0^\infty u \mathrm{e}^{-\lambda u} \, \mathrm{d}u = \frac{\lambda^{2n-2}}{(2n-3)!} w^{2n-3} \mathrm{e}^{-\lambda w}$$

by the fact that the gamma density integrates to 1.
(b) Also, for $u > 0$,

$$f_x(u) = u \mathrm{e}^{-\lambda u} \int_0^\infty \frac{1}{(2n-3)!} \lambda^{2n} w^{2n-3} \mathrm{e}^{-\lambda w} \, \mathrm{d}w = \lambda^2 u \mathrm{e}^{-\lambda u}.$$

Hence, x and z are independent. This can also be seen from

$$f_{x|w}(u) = \frac{f_{x,z}(u, w)}{f_z(w)} = \lambda^2 u \mathrm{e}^{-\lambda u}$$

for $u, w > 0$, which does not depend on w.

Notice that this exercise clarifies the construction, in the previous two chapters, of densities with dependent domains of definition. Even though x and y are *not* independent, we can start from a pair of independent variates x and z, then transform z.

7.2 Products and ratios

Exercise 7.18 (Properties of the gamma distribution) Let $\nu, \lambda > 0$ and let the p.d.f. of $x \in \mathbb{R}_+$ be given by

$$f_x(u) = \frac{\lambda^\nu u^{\nu-1} \mathrm{e}^{-\lambda u}}{\Gamma(\nu)}.$$

Let $x_1, \ldots, x_n$ be a random sample of size $n > 1$ from this distribution.
(a) Show that the p.d.f. of $z := \sum_{i=1}^n x_i$ is given by $f_z(w) = \lambda^{n\nu} w^{n\nu-1} \mathrm{e}^{-\lambda w} / \Gamma(n\nu)$ for $w > 0$, and 0 elsewhere.
(b) Give the joint p.d.f. of x_1 and $z - x_1$.
(c) Give the joint p.d.f. of x_1/z and z, showing that x_1/z and z are independent. What is

the marginal distribution of x_1/z?

Solution

(a) We provide two solutions. The first solution uses the moment-generating function of the Gam(ν, λ) distribution,

$$m_x(t) = \int_0^\infty \frac{\lambda^\nu u^{\nu-1} e^{-\lambda u + tu}}{\Gamma(\nu)} du = \left(\frac{\lambda}{\lambda - t}\right)^\nu,$$

provided that $t < \lambda$. By the independence of the x_i's, we obtain $m_z(t) = (\lambda/(\lambda - t))^{n\nu}$, which is the m.g.f. of a Gam$(n\nu, \lambda)$ distribution. See also Exercise 7.3.

The second solution uses induction. The statement is obviously true for $n = 1$. Assume that the statement is true for $n - 1$. Then, letting $z_n := \sum_{i=1}^n x_i$, we have

$$f_{z_{n-1}}(w_{n-1}) = \frac{\lambda^{(n-1)\nu} w_{n-1}^{(n-1)\nu-1} e^{-\lambda w_{n-1}}}{\Gamma((n-1)\nu)}.$$

The Jacobian factor of the transformation from $(z_{n-1}, x_n) \equiv (z_n - x_n, x_n)$ to (z_n, x_n) is

$$\begin{vmatrix} 1 & 0 \\ -1 & 1 \end{vmatrix} = 1$$

and, by the independence of z_{n-1} from x_n,

$$f_{x_n, z_n}(u_n, w_n) = \frac{\lambda^{(n-1)\nu}(w_n - u_n)^{(n-1)\nu-1} e^{-\lambda(w_n - u_n)}}{\Gamma((n-1)\nu)} \times \frac{\lambda^\nu u_n^{\nu-1} e^{-\lambda u_n}}{\Gamma(\nu)}$$

for $0 < u_n < w_n$, implying the marginal density

$$f_{z_n}(w_n) = \frac{\lambda^{n\nu} e^{-\lambda w_n}}{\Gamma(\nu)\Gamma((n-1)\nu)} \int_0^{w_n} u_n^{\nu-1}(w_n - u_n)^{(n-1)\nu-1} du_n = \frac{\lambda^{n\nu} w_n^{n\nu-1} e^{-\lambda w_n}}{\Gamma(n\nu)}$$

by the fact that the beta density integrates to 1.

(b) Let $y_1 := z - x_1 \in \mathbb{R}_+$, which is independent of $x_1 \in \mathbb{R}_+$. Using (a), we obtain

$$f_{x_1, y_1}(u_1, v_1) = \frac{\lambda^\nu u_1^{\nu-1} e^{-\lambda u_1}}{\Gamma(\nu)} \times \frac{\lambda^{(n-1)\nu} v_1^{(n-1)\nu-1} e^{-\lambda v_1}}{\Gamma((n-1)\nu)}.$$

(c) Let $y := x_1/z$ and consider the transformation from $(x_1, y_1) \equiv (yz, (1-y)z)$ to (y, z). The Jacobian factor is

$$\begin{vmatrix} z & y \\ -z & 1-y \end{vmatrix} = z.$$

Hence,

$$\begin{aligned} f_{y,z}(v, w) &= \frac{w\lambda^{n\nu}(vw)^{\nu-1} e^{-\lambda vw} ((1-v)w)^{(n-1)\nu-1} e^{-\lambda(1-v)w}}{\Gamma(\nu)\Gamma((n-1)\nu)} \\ &= \frac{v^{\nu-1}(1-v)^{(n-1)\nu-1}\lambda^{n\nu} w^{n\nu-1} e^{-\lambda w}}{\Gamma(\nu)\Gamma((n-1)\nu)} \qquad (0 < v < 1,\ w > 0). \end{aligned}$$

The marginal density is thus

$$f_y(v) = \frac{v^{\nu-1}(1-v)^{(n-1)\nu-1}}{\Gamma(\nu)\,\Gamma((n-1)\nu)} \int_0^\infty \lambda^{n\nu} w^{n\nu-1} \mathrm{e}^{-\lambda w}\, \mathrm{d}w$$
$$= \frac{\Gamma(n\nu)}{\Gamma(\nu)\,\Gamma((n-1)\nu)} v^{\nu-1}(1-v)^{(n-1)\nu-1} \qquad (0 < v < 1),$$

which is a Beta$(\nu, (n-1)\nu)$, and the required independence follows from (a). The results in (b) and (c) would, of course, be the same if x_1 were replaced by any of the other x_i's.

Exercise 7.19 (Gamma, χ^2, and F) For $\nu, \lambda > 0$, the p.d.f. of $x \in \mathbb{R}_+$ is given by

$$f_x(u) = \frac{\lambda^\nu u^{\nu-1} \mathrm{e}^{-\lambda u}}{\Gamma(\nu)}.$$

(a) Show that $2\lambda x \sim \chi^2(2\nu)$.
(b) Let $x_1, \dots, x_n$ be a random sample from $f_x(u)$. Define $z_1 := \sum_{i=1}^m x_i$ and $z_2 := \sum_{i=m+1}^n x_i$, where $0 < m < n$. Obtain $\Pr(z_1/(z_1+z_2) \leqslant q)$ for $0 < q < 1$ by means of the F distribution.

Solution
(a) Let $y := 2\lambda x$. Then, $\mathrm{d}x/\mathrm{d}y = 1/(2\lambda) > 0$ and hence

$$f_y(v) = \frac{1}{2\lambda} \times \frac{\lambda^\nu u^{\nu-1} \mathrm{e}^{-\lambda u}}{\Gamma(\nu)} = \frac{v^{\nu-1}\mathrm{e}^{-v/2}}{2^\nu \Gamma(\nu)},$$

which is the p.d.f. of the χ^2 distribution with 2ν degrees of freedom.
(b) We have

$$\Pr\left(\frac{z_1}{z_1+z_2} \leqslant q\right) = \Pr\left(\frac{z_1+z_2}{z_1} \geqslant \frac{1}{q}\right) = \Pr\left(\frac{z_2}{z_1} \geqslant \frac{1}{q} - 1\right)$$
$$= \Pr\left(\frac{2\lambda z_2}{2\lambda z_1} \geqslant \frac{1-q}{q}\right).$$

Now, $2\lambda z_1$ and $2\lambda z_2$ are sums of m and $n-m$ independent $\chi^2(2\nu)$ variables, respectively, and are therefore $\chi^2(2\nu m)$ and $\chi^2(2\nu(n-m))$ by Exercise 7.18. Moreover, they are independent, so that

$$z := \frac{m}{n-m} \times \frac{2\lambda z_2}{2\lambda z_1} \sim \mathrm{F}(2\nu(n-m), 2\nu m)$$

by Exercise 4.32. Hence,

$$\Pr\left(\frac{z_1}{z_1+z_2} \leqslant q\right) = \Pr\left(\frac{n-m}{m} z \geqslant \frac{1-q}{q}\right) = \Pr\left(z \geqslant \frac{m}{n-m} \times \frac{1-q}{q}\right).$$

This is not surprising, given the connections already highlighted in Exercises 7.18 and 4.31.

Exercise 7.20 (Conditioning on the difference or on the ratio?) Let x_1 and x_2 be independent Expo(λ) variates, and define

$$y_1 := x_1 + x_2, \quad y_2 := x_1/x_2, \quad y_3 := x_1 - x_2.$$

(a) Obtain the density of $y_1 \mid y_2 = v_2$.
(b) Obtain the density of $y_1 \mid y_3 = v_3$.
(c) Show that $f_{y_1|y_2=1}(v_1) \neq f_{y_1|y_3=0}(v_1)$ even though $y_2 = 1$ and $y_3 = 0$ are identical conditions. Explain this apparent contradiction in terms of the definition of conditional densities in Exercise 6.26.

Solution
(a) We will show that this follows from Exercise 7.18. First, Exercise 7.18(c) shows that y_1 is distributed independently of y_1/x_2. From

$$y_2 = \frac{x_1}{x_2} = \frac{y_1}{x_2} - 1,$$

we find that y_1 is also independent of y_2. Second, Exercise 7.18(a) tells us that $y_1 \sim \text{Gam}(2, \lambda)$ independently of y_2, hence

$$f_{y_1|y_2=v_2}(v_1) = f_{y_1}(v_1) = \lambda^2 v_1 e^{-\lambda v_1}$$

for $v_1 > 0$ and 0 otherwise.
(b) We start by noting that $\text{cov}(y_1, y_3) = 0$ by the general formula in Exercise 6.10. However, y_1 is not independent of y_3, as we will see. Since

$$x_1 = \frac{y_1 + y_3}{2} \quad \text{and} \quad x_2 = \frac{y_1 - y_3}{2},$$

with Jacobian

$$\begin{vmatrix} \frac{1}{2} & \frac{1}{2} \\ \frac{1}{2} & -\frac{1}{2} \end{vmatrix} = -\frac{1}{2},$$

the joint density of y_1 and y_3 is

$$f_{y_1,y_3}(v_1, v_3) = \frac{1}{2}\left(\lambda e^{-\lambda(v_1+v_3)/2}\right)\left(\lambda e^{-\lambda(v_1-v_3)/2}\right) = \frac{\lambda^2}{2} e^{-\lambda v_1}$$

for $v_1 > \max\{-v_3, v_3\}$ and 0 otherwise. Note that $\max\{-v_3, v_3\} = |v_3|$ by (7.7). The marginal density of y_3 is therefore

$$f_{y_3}(v_3) = \int_{|v_3|}^{\infty} \frac{\lambda^2}{2} e^{-\lambda v_1}\, dv_1 = \left[-\frac{\lambda}{2} e^{-\lambda v_1}\right]_{|v_3|}^{\infty} = \frac{\lambda}{2} e^{-\lambda |v_3|}.$$

Note that $y_3 \in \mathbb{R}$ and that we have just shown it to have a Laplace density (see Table 4.2). The required conditional density is therefore

$$f_{y_1|y_3=v_3}(v_1) = \lambda e^{-\lambda(v_1 - |v_3|)}$$

for $v_1 > |v_3|$ and 0 otherwise. This resulting density can be interpreted in terms of the no-memory property of exponentials, by the same method as that used in Exercise 7.6.

(c) The conditions $y_2 = 1$ and $y_3 = 0$ are identical, both implying $x_1 = x_2$, but

$$f_{y_1|y_2=1}(v_1) = \lambda^2 v_1 \mathrm{e}^{-\lambda v_1} \quad \text{while} \quad f_{y_1|y_3=0}(v_1) = \lambda \mathrm{e}^{-\lambda v_1}.$$

As we warned in the introduction to Chapter 6, after (6.2), conditioning on events having probability 0 has to be done with caution. Exercise 6.26 gave the precise meaning of such conditional densities. The two alternative events on which we condition when writing

$$y_2 := x_1/x_2 = 1 \quad \text{and} \quad y_3 := x_1 - x_2 = 0$$

are, respectively,

$$\{x_2 \leqslant x_1 \leqslant (1+h)x_2\} \quad \text{and} \quad \{x_2 \leqslant x_1 \leqslant x_2 + h\}$$

for $h \to 0^+$. These two sets (hence the sigma-fields) are not the same.

Exercise 7.21 (Bivariate linear: product's p.d.f.) The joint p.d.f. of (x, y) is given by

$$f_{x,y}(u,v) = \begin{cases} 2(u+v) & (0 < u < v < 1), \\ 0 & (\text{elsewhere}). \end{cases}$$

Let $z := xy$.
(a) Give the joint density of (x, z).
(b) Obtain the p.d.f. of z.
(c) Obtain the p.d.f. of x.
(d) Are x and z independent?

Solution
(a) Since $y = z/x$, the Jacobian factor of the transformation from (x, y) to (x, z) is

$$\begin{vmatrix} 1 & 0 \\ -zx^{-2} & x^{-1} \end{vmatrix} = \frac{1}{x}.$$

Hence,

$$f_{x,z}(u,w) = \begin{cases} 2\left(1 + w/u^2\right) & (0 < u^2 < w < u < 1), \\ 0 & (\text{elsewhere}). \end{cases}$$

(b) Since $w < 1$, we have $w < u < \sqrt{w} < 1$ and the density of z is

$$f_z(w) = 2\int_w^{\sqrt{w}} \left(1 + \frac{w}{u^2}\right) \mathrm{d}u = 2\left[u - \frac{w}{u}\right]_w^{\sqrt{w}} = \begin{cases} 2(1-w) & (0 < w < 1), \\ 0 & (\text{elsewhere}). \end{cases}$$

(c) We can obtain the p.d.f. of x from $f_{x,y}(u,v)$ or from $f_{x,z}(u,w)$. Thus,

$$\begin{aligned} f_x(u) &= \int_u^1 f_{x,y}(u,v)\,\mathrm{d}v = 2\int_u^1 (u+v)\,\mathrm{d}v \\ &= 2u(1-u) + 1 - u^2 = \begin{cases} 1 + 2u - 3u^2 & (0 < u < 1), \\ 0 & (\text{elsewhere}). \end{cases} \end{aligned}$$

Alternatively,

$$\begin{aligned} f_x(u) &= \int_{u^2}^{u} f_{x,z}(u,w)\,\mathrm{d}w = 2\int_{u^2}^{u}\left(1+\frac{w}{u^2}\right)\mathrm{d}w \\ &= \left[2w+\frac{w^2}{u^2}\right]_{u^2}^{u} = \begin{cases} 1+2u-3u^2 & (0<u<1), \\ 0 & (\text{elsewhere}). \end{cases} \end{aligned}$$

(d) As seen in the previous two chapters, it is enough to consider the domain of definition of the density in (a) to realize that x and z are not independent.

***Exercise 7.22 (Product of normals)** Let x, y be an independent sample from an $\mathrm{N}(0,1)$ distribution.

(a) Obtain the m.g.f. of xy.

(b) Show that the p.d.f. of $2xy$ is the same as the p.d.f. of $x^2 - y^2$.

(c) Prove that the p.d.f. of $2xy$ is infinite at the origin, and interpret this result.

(d) Derive the p.d.f. of ξ^2, where $\xi := \min\{x, y\}$.

Solution

(a) We use the law of iterated expectations, exploiting the independence of x and y,

$$\begin{aligned} m_{xy}(t) &= \mathrm{E}_x\left(\mathrm{E}_{y|x}\left(\mathrm{e}^{txy}\right)\right) = \mathrm{E}_x\left(\mathrm{E}_y\left(\mathrm{e}^{txy}\right)\right) = \mathrm{E}_x\left(m_y\left(tx\right)\right) \\ &= \mathrm{E}_x\left(\mathrm{e}^{t^2x^2/2}\right) = \frac{1}{\sqrt{2\pi}}\int_{-\infty}^{\infty} \mathrm{e}^{-u^2(1-t^2)/2}\,\mathrm{d}u = \frac{1}{\sqrt{1-t^2}} \qquad (|t|<1). \end{aligned}$$

(b) We give two solutions. The simplest is to note that

$$x^2 - y^2 = 2\frac{x-y}{\sqrt{2}}\frac{x+y}{\sqrt{2}} = 2\eta_1\eta_2,$$

where η_1 and η_2 are independent $\mathrm{N}(0,1)$ by Exercise 7.15. The p.d.f. of $2\eta_1\eta_2$ (hence x^2-y^2) is the same as the p.d.f. of $2xy$. In the second solution, we calculate the m.g.f.s of $2xy$ and x^2-y^2, showing that they are equal. We have

$$\begin{aligned} m_{x^2-y^2}(t) &= \mathrm{E}\left(\mathrm{e}^{tx^2-ty^2}\right) = \frac{1}{2\pi}\int_{-\infty}^{\infty}\int_{-\infty}^{\infty} \mathrm{e}^{-u^2/2+tu^2-v^2/2-tv^2}\,\mathrm{d}u\,\mathrm{d}v \\ &= \frac{1}{\sqrt{2\pi}}\int_{-\infty}^{\infty} \mathrm{e}^{-u^2(1-2t)/2}\,\mathrm{d}u \frac{1}{\sqrt{2\pi}}\int_{-\infty}^{\infty} \mathrm{e}^{-v^2(1+2t)/2}\,\mathrm{d}v \\ &= \frac{1}{\sqrt{1-2t}}\frac{1}{\sqrt{1+2t}} = \frac{1}{\sqrt{1-4t^2}} \qquad (4t^2<1), \end{aligned}$$

and $m_{2xy}(t) = \mathrm{E}\left(\mathrm{e}^{2txy}\right) = m_{xy}(2t) = 1/\sqrt{1-4t^2}$ from (a).

(c) By the inversion theorem of Chapter 3,

$$f_{2xy}(0) = \frac{1}{2\pi}\int_{-\infty}^{\infty} m_{2xy}(\mathrm{i}t)\,\mathrm{d}t = \frac{1}{2\pi}\int_{-\infty}^{\infty}\frac{1}{\sqrt{1+4t^2}}\,\mathrm{d}t = \left[\frac{\sinh^{-1}(2t)}{4\pi}\right]_{-\infty}^{\infty} = \infty.$$

The product of two independent standard normals is heavily centered around the origin. Its

p.d.f. has a discontinuity at the origin, but is nevertheless integrable, since all c.d.f.s are finite. We saw a result with a similar interpretation, in the context of sums, in Exercise 7.13(b). Furthermore, this result is made clearer once one recalls from (b) that the density of $2xy$ is the same as the density of $x^2 - y^2$, and that x^2 and y^2 are independent $\chi^2(1)$ variates whose density tends to infinity at the origin; see Figure 4.4 of Exercise 4.14(d).
(d) Since $\min\{x, y\} > c$ whenever both $x > c$ and $y > c$,

$$F_\xi(w_\xi) = \Pr(\min\{x, y\} \leqslant w_\xi) = 1 - \Pr(\min\{x, y\} > w_\xi)$$
$$= 1 - \Pr(x > w_\xi)\Pr(y > w_\xi) = 1 - (\Pr(x > w_\xi))^2 .$$

Hence, the c.d.f. of $z := \xi^2$ is given by

$$F_z(w) = \Pr(\xi^2 \leqslant w) = \Pr(-\sqrt{w} \leqslant \xi \leqslant \sqrt{w}) = F_\xi(\sqrt{w}) - F_\xi(-\sqrt{w})$$
$$= 1 - (\Pr(x > \sqrt{w}))^2 - 1 + (\Pr(x > -\sqrt{w}))^2$$
$$= (\Pr(x > -\sqrt{w}))^2 - (\Pr(x > \sqrt{w}))^2.$$

If $\Phi(u)$ denotes the c.d.f. of the $\mathrm{N}(0, 1)$ distribution and $\phi(u)$ its p.d.f., then, using the fact that $\Phi(-u) + \Phi(u) = 1$ for all u,

$$F_z(w) = (1 - \Phi(-\sqrt{w}))^2 - (1 - \Phi(\sqrt{w}))^2$$
$$= (\Phi(\sqrt{w}))^2 - (1 - \Phi(\sqrt{w}))^2 = 2\Phi(\sqrt{w}) - 1.$$

This is the c.d.f. of a $\chi^2(1)$ variate seen in the solution of Exercise 4.25. To confirm this,

$$f_z(w) = 2\frac{\mathrm{d}\Phi(\sqrt{w})}{\mathrm{d}\sqrt{w}}\frac{\mathrm{d}\sqrt{w}}{\mathrm{d}w} = w^{-1/2}\phi(\sqrt{w}) = \frac{1}{\sqrt{2\pi w}}\mathrm{e}^{-w/2},$$

which is the $\chi^2(1)$ density.

An alternative solution can be obtained. By continuity, $\Pr(x = y) = 0$ (Exercise 5.16) and

$$F_z(w) = \Pr(\xi^2 \leqslant w)$$
$$= \Pr(x^2 \leqslant w \mid x < y)\Pr(x < y) + \Pr(y^2 \leqslant w \mid y < x)\Pr(y < x)$$
$$= \frac{1}{2}\Pr(x^2 \leqslant w \mid x < y) + \frac{1}{2}\Pr(y^2 \leqslant w \mid y < x)$$
$$= \Pr(x^2 \leqslant w \mid x < y),$$

by symmetry of the problem in x and y. The result follows from $x^2 \sim \chi^2(1)$, if we can dispose of the condition $x < y$. To do this, we use the independence of x and y again to write

$$\Pr(x^2 \leqslant w \mid x < y) = \Pr(x^2 \leqslant w \mid x > y),$$

hence

$$\begin{aligned} F_z(w) &= \frac{1}{2}\left(\Pr(x^2 \leqslant w \mid x < y) + \Pr(x^2 \leqslant w \mid x > y)\right) \\ &= \frac{1}{2}\left(\frac{\Pr(x^2 \leqslant w, x < y)}{\Pr(x < y)} + \frac{\Pr(x^2 \leqslant w, x > y)}{\Pr(x > y)}\right) \\ &= \Pr(x^2 \leqslant w, x < y) + \Pr(x^2 \leqslant w, x > y) = \Pr(x^2 \leqslant w), \end{aligned}$$

the last equality following from the definition of the marginal c.d.f. of x^2, seen as early as in (1.5).

Exercise 7.23 (Products of log-normals) Let $x_1, \dots, x_n$ be a random sample from the $\mathrm{N}(\mu, \sigma^2)$ distribution, and define $y_i := \mathrm{e}^{x_i}$. Derive:
(a) the p.d.f. of y_i;
(b) the p.d.f.s of $\prod_{i=1}^n y_i$ and $\prod_{i=1}^n y_i^\alpha$;
(c) the p.d.f. of y_1/y_2;
(d) $\mathrm{E}\left(\prod_{i=1}^n y_i\right)$.

Solution
(a) Since $x_i = \log(y_i)$, we have $\mathrm{d}x_i/\mathrm{d}y_i = 1/y_i$, and hence

$$f_{y_i}(v) = \frac{1}{v} f_{x_i}(\log(v)) = \frac{1}{\sigma v\sqrt{2\pi}} \exp\left(-\frac{(\log(v) - \mu)^2}{2\sigma^2}\right) \qquad (0 < v < \infty),$$

which is the p.d.f. of a log-normal distribution, so $y_i \sim \mathrm{LN}(\mu, \sigma^2)$. Notice that μ and σ^2 are the mean and variance of x_i, rather than those of y_i.
(b) Let $z := \prod_{i=1}^n y_i = \exp(\sum_{i=1}^n x_i)$. Since $\sum_{i=1}^n x_i \sim \mathrm{N}(n\mu, n\sigma^2)$ by Exercise 7.15, we find that

$$f_z(w) = \frac{1}{\sigma w\sqrt{2\pi n}} \exp\left(-\frac{(\log(w) - n\mu)^2}{2n\sigma^2}\right).$$

More generally, $z := \prod_{i=1}^n y_i^\alpha = \exp(\alpha \sum_{i=1}^n x_i)$ has

$$f_z(w) = \frac{1}{|\alpha|\sigma w\sqrt{2\pi n}} \exp\left(-\frac{(\log(w) - n\alpha\mu)^2}{2n\alpha^2\sigma^2}\right)$$

for $\alpha \neq 0$.
(c) We have

$$\frac{y_1}{y_2} = \mathrm{e}^{x_1 - x_2} \quad \text{where} \quad x_1 - x_2 \sim \mathrm{N}(0, 2\sigma^2),$$

and hence

$$f_{y_1/y_2}(w) = \frac{1}{2\sigma w\sqrt{\pi}} \mathrm{e}^{-(\log(w))^2/4\sigma^2}.$$

(d) Let $z := \sum_{i=1}^{n} x_i \sim \mathrm{N}(n\mu, n\sigma^2)$. Then,

$$\mathrm{E}\left(\prod_{i=1}^{n} y_i\right) = \mathrm{E}\left(\exp\left(\sum_{i=1}^{n} x_i\right)\right) = \mathrm{E}\left(\exp(z)\right) = m_z(1) = \exp\left(n\mu + n\sigma^2/2\right)$$

from the formula for the normal m.g.f.

***Exercise 7.24 (Distribution of ratios, via c.f.s)** Let x_1, x_2 be any two continuous variates with c.f. $\varphi(\tau_1, \tau_2)$ and satisfying $\Pr(x_2 > 0) = 1$. Define the variate $z := x_1/x_2$ and let $x_w := x_1 - w x_2$.

(a) Derive the c.f. of the variate x_w in terms of the original c.f. of x_1, x_2.

(b) Prove that $[F_{x_w}(u)]_0^\infty = 1 - F_z(w)$.

(c) By using the inversion theorem for $F_{x_w}(0)$, prove the *Gurland–Geary formula*

$$f_z(w) = \frac{1}{2\pi \mathrm{i}} \int_{-\infty}^{\infty} \left. \frac{\partial \varphi(\tau_1, \tau_2)}{\partial \tau_2} \right|_{\tau_2 = -w\tau_1} \mathrm{d}\tau_1.$$

(d) Assuming that $\mathrm{E}\left(z^j\right)$ exists for some $j \in \mathbb{N}$, prove that

$$\mathrm{E}\left(z^j\right) = \frac{1}{(j-1)!} \int_0^\infty \left. \frac{\partial^j \varphi(-\mathrm{i}\tau_1, \mathrm{i}\tau_2)}{\partial \tau_1^j} \right|_{\tau_1 = 0} \tau_2^{j-1} \, \mathrm{d}\tau_2.$$

(e) Assuming that $\mathrm{E}\left(x_1^j / x_2^\nu\right)$ exists for some $j \in \mathbb{N}$ and $\nu \in \mathbb{R}_+$, prove that

$$\mathrm{E}\left(x_1^j / x_2^\nu\right) = \frac{1}{\Gamma(\nu)} \int_0^\infty \left. \frac{\partial^j \varphi(-\mathrm{i}\tau_1, \mathrm{i}\tau_2)}{\partial \tau_1^j} \right|_{\tau_1 = 0} \tau_2^{\nu-1} \, \mathrm{d}\tau_2.$$

Solution

(a) $\mathrm{E}\left(\exp\left(\mathrm{i}\tau x_w\right)\right) = \mathrm{E}\left(\exp\left(\mathrm{i}\tau\left(x_1 - w x_2\right)\right)\right) = \varphi(\tau, -w\tau)$.

(b) $F_z(w) = \Pr(x_1/x_2 \leqslant w) = \Pr(x_w \leqslant 0) = F_{x_w}(0)$ and, by definition, $F_{x_w}(\infty) = 1$. Subtracting the former from the latter gives the result.

(c) Since we have the c.f. of x_w from (a), the inversion theorem of Chapter 3 gives

$$\begin{aligned} F_{x_w}(0) &= \frac{1}{2} - \frac{1}{2\pi \mathrm{i}} \int_0^\infty \frac{\varphi(\tau, -w\tau) - \varphi(-\tau, w\tau)}{\tau} \, \mathrm{d}\tau \\ &= \frac{1}{2} - \frac{1}{2\pi \mathrm{i}} \int_{-\infty}^\infty \frac{\varphi(\tau, -w\tau)}{\tau} \, \mathrm{d}\tau. \end{aligned}$$

From (b), we have $F_z(w) = F_{x_w}(0)$, so that differentiating the previous equation with respect to w gives

$$\begin{aligned} f_z(w) = \frac{\mathrm{d}F_{x_w}(0)}{\mathrm{d}w} &= -\frac{1}{2\pi \mathrm{i}} \int_{-\infty}^\infty \frac{\partial}{\partial w}\left(\frac{\varphi(\tau, -w\tau)}{\tau}\right) \mathrm{d}\tau \\ &= \frac{1}{2\pi \mathrm{i}} \int_{-\infty}^\infty \left. \frac{\partial \varphi(\tau_1, \tau_2)}{\partial \tau_2} \right|_{\tau_2 = -w\tau_1} \mathrm{d}\tau_1 \end{aligned}$$

by the chain rule.
(d) The shortest derivation of this result is obtained by following the route of Exercise 3.30. We have

$$\begin{aligned}
&\frac{1}{(j-1)!}\int_0^\infty \left.\frac{\partial^j \varphi(-\mathrm{i}\tau_1, \mathrm{i}\tau_2)}{\partial \tau_1^j}\right|_{\tau_1=0} \tau_2^{j-1}\,\mathrm{d}\tau_2 \\
&= \frac{1}{(j-1)!}\int_0^\infty \left.\frac{\partial^j \mathrm{E}\left(\exp\left(\tau_1 x_1 - \tau_2 x_2\right)\right)}{\partial \tau_1^j}\right|_{\tau_1=0} \tau_2^{j-1}\,\mathrm{d}\tau_2 \\
&= \frac{1}{(j-1)!}\int_0^\infty \mathrm{E}\left(x_1^j \exp\left(-\tau_2 x_2\right)\right) \tau_2^{j-1}\,\mathrm{d}\tau_2 \\
&= \frac{1}{(j-1)!}\mathrm{E}\left(x_1^j \int_0^\infty \exp\left(-\tau_2 x_2\right) \tau_2^{j-1}\,\mathrm{d}\tau_2\right),
\end{aligned}$$

where the existence of the moment allows the interchange of integral and expectation; see Section A.3.5. The result follows directly by the integral representation of the gamma function and $\Pr(x_2 > 0) = 1$.
(e) This follows as in (d).

7.3 General transformations, including geometrical and ordering

Exercise 7.25 (Box–Müller transformation) Let x_1 and x_2 be a random sample from the standard uniform distribution. Consider the *Box–Müller transformation*,

$$\begin{pmatrix} y_1 \\ y_2 \end{pmatrix} := \sqrt{-2\log(x_1)}\begin{pmatrix} \cos(2\pi x_2) \\ \sin(2\pi x_2) \end{pmatrix}.$$

Show that y_1 and y_2 are independent standard-normal random variables.

Solution
We have

$$y_1^2 + y_2^2 = -2\log(x_1) \quad \text{and} \quad y_2/y_1 = \tan(2\pi x_2).$$

Hence, we can solve for x_1 and x_2, obtaining

$$x_1 = \mathrm{e}^{-(y_1^2+y_2^2)/2} \quad \text{and} \quad x_2 = \frac{1}{2\pi}\tan^{-1}(y_2/y_1).$$

Using the fact that $\mathrm{d}(\tan^{-1}(z))/\,\mathrm{d}z = 1/(1+z^2)$, we find the Jacobian of the transformation from (x_1, x_2) to (y_1, y_2):

$$\begin{vmatrix} -y_1\mathrm{e}^{-(y_1^2+y_2^2)/2} & -y_2\mathrm{e}^{-(y_1^2+y_2^2)/2} \\ -\dfrac{y_2}{2\pi y_1^2} \times \dfrac{1}{1+y_2^2/y_1^2} & \dfrac{1}{2\pi y_1} \times \dfrac{1}{1+y_2^2/y_1^2} \end{vmatrix} = -\frac{1}{2\pi}\mathrm{e}^{-(y_1^2+y_2^2)/2},$$

leading to

$$f_{y_1,y_2}(v_1,v_2) = \frac{1}{2\pi}\mathrm{e}^{-(v_1^2+v_2^2)/2} = \phi(v_1)\,\phi(v_2),$$

where it is easy to see that y_1 and y_2 are independent and identically distributed standard normals. When we look back at the standard bivariate normal contour plots of Figure 6.2, we realize that we have obtained here the rectangular coordinates (y_1, y_2) of any point (or vector) $\boldsymbol{y}$ from its polar coordinates, namely its squared length $\|\boldsymbol{y}\|^2 = y_1^2 + y_2^2 = -2\log(x_1)$ and its angle $\tan^{-1}(y_2/y_1) = 2\pi x_2$; see also Section A.2. Clearly, the angle is uniformly distributed over $(0, 2\pi)$, since Figure 6.2 shows that all random rotation of the circles are equally likely: they all leave the contours unchanged and give rise to the same value of the density function. The uniformity of x_1 follows by noting that the density is linear-exponential in $v_1^2 + v_2^2$ and recalling Exercise 7.7(c). Finally, the support $\mathbb{R}^2$ of $\boldsymbol{y}$ follows from the logarithmic relation $y_1^2 + y_2^2 = -2\log(x_1)$ as $x_1 \to 0^+$ or 1^-, and from the signs of the trigonometric functions in the definition of $\boldsymbol{y}$.

***Exercise 7.26 (Marsaglia–Bray transformation)** Let x_1 and x_2 be uniformly distributed over the unit disk, with joint density

$$f_{x_1,x_2}(u_1,u_2) = \begin{cases} \frac{1}{\pi} & (u_1^2 + u_2^2 < 1), \\ 0 & (\text{elsewhere}), \end{cases}$$

where we stress that x_1 and x_2 are not independent because $x_1^2 + x_2^2 < 1$; see Exercise 6.38. Consider the *Marsaglia–Bray transformation*,

$$\begin{pmatrix} y_1 \\ y_2 \end{pmatrix} := \sqrt{\frac{-2\log(x_1^2 + x_2^2)}{x_1^2 + x_2^2}} \begin{pmatrix} x_1 \\ x_2 \end{pmatrix}.$$

Show that y_1 and y_2 are independent standard-normal random variables.

Solution

We first note that using the Marsaglia–Bray transformation, there is only one series to calculate (the logarithmic function is a series), whereas the Box–Müller transformation involves two (logarithm and cosine, the sine being obtained from $\sin^2 = 1 - \cos^2$). For the series representations of these functions, see Section A.3.3.

We have

$$y_1^2 + y_2^2 = -2\log(x_1^2 + x_2^2) = -2\log(x_1^2\,(1 + y_2^2/y_1^2))$$

since $y_2/y_1 = x_2/x_1$. Hence,

$$x_1^2 = \frac{\exp\left(-(y_1^2 + y_2^2)/2\right)}{1 + y_2^2/y_1^2} = y_1^2 \frac{\exp\left(-(y_1^2 + y_2^2)/2\right)}{y_1^2 + y_2^2}.$$

Now differentiating the first equality gives

$$
\begin{aligned}
2x_1 \frac{\partial x_1}{\partial y_1} &= 2\frac{y_2^2}{y_1^3} \frac{\exp\left(-(y_1^2+y_2^2)/2\right)}{\left(1+y_2^2/y_1^2\right)^2} - \frac{y_1 \exp\left(-(y_1^2+y_2^2)/2\right)}{1+y_2^2/y_1^2} \\
&= \left(\frac{2y_2^2/y_1^2}{y_1^2+y_2^2} - 1\right) y_1 x_1^2
\end{aligned}
$$

and

$$
\begin{aligned}
2x_1 \frac{\partial x_1}{\partial y_2} &= -2\frac{y_2}{y_1^2} \frac{\exp\left(-(y_1^2+y_2^2)/2\right)}{\left(1+y_2^2/y_1^2\right)^2} - \frac{y_2 \exp\left(-(y_1^2+y_2^2)/2\right)}{1+y_2^2/y_1^2} \\
&= -\left(\frac{2}{y_1^2+y_2^2} + 1\right) y_2 x_1^2.
\end{aligned}
$$

Differentiating both sides of $x_2 = x_1 (y_2/y_1)$ gives

$$
\frac{\partial x_2}{\partial y_2} = \frac{x_1}{y_1} + \frac{y_2}{y_1}\frac{\partial x_1}{\partial y_2} \quad \text{and} \quad \frac{\partial x_2}{\partial y_1} = \frac{y_2}{y_1}\frac{\partial x_1}{\partial y_1} - \frac{x_1 y_2}{y_1^2}.
$$

Therefore,

$$
\begin{aligned}
\det\left(\frac{\partial(x_1,x_2)}{\partial(y_1,y_2)'}\right) &= \frac{\partial x_1}{\partial y_1}\frac{\partial x_2}{\partial y_2} - \frac{\partial x_1}{\partial y_2}\frac{\partial x_2}{\partial y_1} \\
&= \frac{\partial x_1}{\partial y_1}\left(\frac{x_1}{y_1} + \frac{y_2}{y_1}\frac{\partial x_1}{\partial y_2}\right) - \frac{\partial x_1}{\partial y_2}\left(\frac{y_2}{y_1}\frac{\partial x_1}{\partial y_1} - \frac{x_1 y_2}{y_1^2}\right) \\
&= \frac{x_1}{y_1}\frac{\partial x_1}{\partial y_1} + \frac{x_1 y_2}{y_1^2}\frac{\partial x_1}{\partial y_2} \\
&= \left(\frac{y_2^2/y_1^2}{y_1^2+y_2^2} - \frac{1}{2}\right) x_1^2 - \left(\frac{1}{y_1^2+y_2^2} + \frac{1}{2}\right)\frac{y_2^2}{y_1^2} x_1^2 \\
&= -\frac{1+y_2^2/y_1^2}{2} x_1^2 = -\frac{\exp\left(-(y_1^2+y_2^2)/2\right)}{2}.
\end{aligned}
$$

The transformation theorem implies that

$$
\begin{aligned}
f_{\boldsymbol{y}}(v_1,v_2) &= \left|\det\left(\frac{\partial(u_1,u_2)}{\partial(v_1,v_2)'}\right)\right| f_{\boldsymbol{x}}(u_1,u_2) = \frac{1}{\pi}\left|\det\left(\frac{\partial(u_1,u_2)}{\partial(v_1,v_2)'}\right)\right| \\
&= \frac{\exp\left(-(v_1^2+v_2^2)/2\right)}{2\pi} = \phi(v_1)\phi(v_2).
\end{aligned}
$$

The domain of $\boldsymbol{y}$ follows from the logarithmic relation $\|\boldsymbol{y}\|^2 = -2\log(\|\boldsymbol{x}\|^2)$ (given at the start of the solution) as $\|\boldsymbol{x}\| \to 0^+$ or 1^-, with $\operatorname{sgn}(y_i) = \operatorname{sgn}(x_i)$ for $i = 1,2$.

Exercise 7.27 (Constant of integration: normal p.d.f.) By using the transformation theorem, prove that:
(a) $\int_{-\infty}^{\infty} \mathrm{e}^{-v^2/2}\,\mathrm{d}v = \sqrt{2\pi}$;
(b) $\Gamma(\frac{1}{2}) = \sqrt{\pi}$.

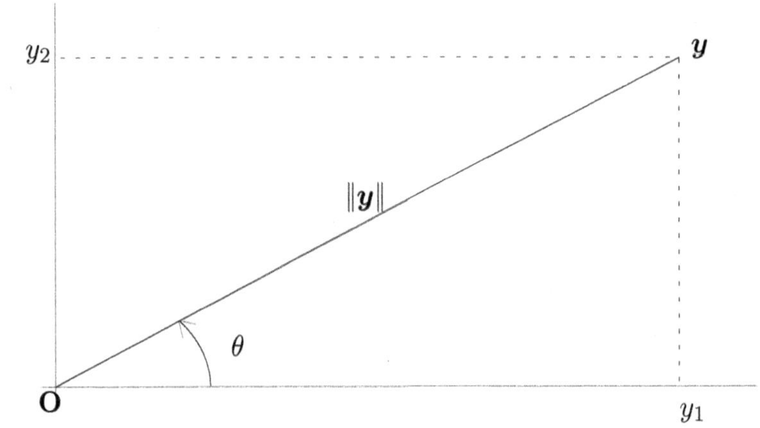

Figure 7.1. Rectangular and polar coordinates of $\boldsymbol{y}$.

Solution

(a) The proof follows from the discussion at the end of Exercise 7.25. Consider the density $f_y(v) := \alpha^{-1}\exp(-v^2/2)$ defined for $y \in \mathbb{R}$, with $\alpha > 0$, and let y_1 and y_2 be a random sample drawn from it, with joint density

$$f_{y_1,y_2}(v_1, v_2) = \alpha^{-2}\exp\left(-(v_1^2 + v_2^2)/2\right).$$

Now transform from rectangular coordinates $\boldsymbol{y} := (y_1, y_2)'$ to polar ones $\boldsymbol{z} := (\theta, \|\boldsymbol{y}\|)'$ by means of

$$y_1 = z_2\cos(z_1) \quad \text{and} \quad y_2 = z_2\sin(z_1),$$

where $z_1 := \tan^{-1}(y_2/y_1) \in (0, 2\pi)$ is the angle of the vector $\boldsymbol{y}$ and $z_2 := \sqrt{y_1^2 + y_2^2} = \|\boldsymbol{y}\| \in \mathbb{R}_+$ is its length; see Figure 7.1. The Jacobian is

$$\begin{vmatrix} -z_2\sin(z_1) & \cos(z_1) \\ z_2\cos(z_1) & \sin(z_1) \end{vmatrix} = -z_2(\sin(z_1))^2 - z_2(\cos(z_1))^2 = -z_2,$$

giving the joint density

$$f_{z_1,z_2}(w_1, w_2) = w_2\alpha^{-2}\mathrm{e}^{-w_2^2/2},$$

where w_1 does not appear on the right-hand side and z_1 is thus uniformly distributed over $(0, 2\pi)$ with density $1/(2\pi)$, independently of z_2. We can now work out the scaling constant α, more easily than from f_{y_1,y_2}, by integrating over the domain of z_1 and z_2:

$$\begin{aligned} 1 &= \int_0^\infty \int_0^{2\pi} f_{z_1,z_2}(w_1, w_2)\,\mathrm{d}w_1\,\mathrm{d}w_2 \\ &= \alpha^{-2}\int_0^{2\pi} \mathrm{d}w_1 \int_0^\infty w_2\mathrm{e}^{-w_2^2/2}\,\mathrm{d}w_2 = -\alpha^{-2}\left[w_1\right]_0^{2\pi}\left[\mathrm{e}^{-w_2^2/2}\right]_0^\infty = \frac{2\pi}{\alpha^2}, \end{aligned}$$

whose solution is $\alpha = \sqrt{2\pi}$. This result can also be proved as an application of Exercise

7.29 below. Note that Table 4.2 identifies $z_2 \sim \text{Wei}(2, \frac{1}{2})$.

We offer another proof, given by Laplace in 1812, which avoids using the transformation theorem. Given

$$\int_0^\infty e^{-\lambda s}\, ds = \frac{1}{\lambda} \quad \text{and} \quad \int_0^\infty \frac{dt}{1+t^2} = \left[\tan^{-1}(t)\right]_0^\infty = \frac{\pi}{2},$$

we have

$$\frac{1}{2}\int_0^\infty \int_0^\infty e^{-s(1+t^2)}\, ds\, dt = \frac{1}{2}\int_0^\infty \frac{dt}{1+t^2} = \frac{\pi}{4}.$$

Now consider the same double integral again, making the transformation from t to $v = t\sqrt{s}$. Then,

$$\begin{aligned}\frac{1}{2}\int_0^\infty \int_0^\infty e^{-s(1+t^2)}\, dt\, ds &= \frac{1}{2}\int_0^\infty s^{-1/2} e^{-s} \int_0^\infty e^{-v^2}\, dv\, ds \\ &= \left(\int_0^\infty e^{-u^2}\, du\right)\left(\int_0^\infty e^{-v^2}\, dv\right)\end{aligned}$$

by the transformation $s = u^2$. The last two integrals are identical, and their product is equal to $\pi/4$ from the preceding equation. Therefore,

$$\int_0^\infty e^{-u^2}\, du = \sqrt{\frac{\pi}{4}}.$$

Making the change of variable $u = v/\sqrt{2}$ here, we get

$$\sqrt{\frac{\pi}{4}} = \int_0^\infty e^{-v^2/2} \frac{dv}{\sqrt{2}} = \frac{1}{2}\int_{-\infty}^\infty e^{-v^2/2} \frac{dv}{\sqrt{2}};$$

hence $\int_{-\infty}^\infty e^{-v^2/2}\, dv = \sqrt{2\pi}$.

(b) From (a), we have

$$\int_0^\infty e^{-v^2/2}\, dv = \frac{\sqrt{2\pi}}{2} = \sqrt{\frac{\pi}{2}}.$$

By the change of variable $s = v^2/2$, so that $ds = v\, dv = \sqrt{2s}\, dv$, the last equation becomes

$$\sqrt{\pi} = \sqrt{2}\int_0^\infty \frac{e^{-s}}{\sqrt{2s}}\, ds = \Gamma\left(\frac{1}{2}\right).$$

***Exercise 7.28 (Rotation of an elementary vector: Jacobian)** For $j = 1, 2, \dots, m-1$ with $m > 1$, define $\theta_j \in [0, 2\pi)$,

$$\boldsymbol{T}_j := \begin{pmatrix} \cos(\theta_j) & -\sin(\theta_j) \\ \sin(\theta_j) & \cos(\theta_j) \end{pmatrix}, \qquad \boldsymbol{A}_j := \begin{pmatrix} \boldsymbol{I}_{j-1} & \mathbf{O} & \mathbf{O} \\ \mathbf{O} & \boldsymbol{T}_j & \mathbf{O} \\ \mathbf{O} & \mathbf{O} & \boldsymbol{I}_{m-j-1} \end{pmatrix}.$$

(a) Show that any nonzero real-valued m-dimensional vector $\boldsymbol{y}$ can be written as

$$\begin{pmatrix} y_1 \\ y_2 \\ \vdots \\ y_{m-1} \\ y_m \end{pmatrix} = \|\boldsymbol{y}\| \begin{pmatrix} \cos(\theta_1) \\ \cos(\theta_2)\sin(\theta_1) \\ \vdots \\ \cos(\theta_{m-1})\sin(\theta_{m-2})\cdots\sin(\theta_1) \\ \sin(\theta_{m-1})\sin(\theta_{m-2})\cdots\sin(\theta_1) \end{pmatrix},$$

and interpret the two sides of this equation. [Hint: Consider the product $\boldsymbol{A}_{m-1}\cdots\boldsymbol{A}_1\boldsymbol{e}_1$, where $\boldsymbol{e}_1 := (1,0,\dots,0)'$ denotes the first elementary vector.]
(b) Prove that the Jacobian of the transformation from $\boldsymbol{y}$ to $\boldsymbol{z} := (\theta_1,\dots,\theta_{m-1},\|\boldsymbol{y}\|)'$ is

$$D := \det\left(\frac{\partial \boldsymbol{y}}{\partial \boldsymbol{z}'}\right) = (-\|\boldsymbol{y}\|)^{m-1}\prod_{i=1}^{m-2}(\sin(\theta_i))^{m-i-1}.$$

Solution
(a) The normalized vector $\|\boldsymbol{y}\|^{-1}\boldsymbol{y}$ has unit length, by $\left\|\|\boldsymbol{y}\|^{-1}\boldsymbol{y}\right\| = \|\boldsymbol{y}\|^{-1}\|\boldsymbol{y}\| = 1$. It resides on the unit sphere, and so does $\boldsymbol{e}_1$. The product $\boldsymbol{A}_{m-1}\cdots\boldsymbol{A}_1\boldsymbol{e}_1$ corresponds to a succession of rotations, starting from the fixed point $\boldsymbol{e}_1$ (which lies on the y_1-axis), by $m-1$ angles from $m-1$ perpendicular axes, all the rotations taking place along the unit sphere. Therefore, by choosing the appropriate $\theta_1,\dots,\theta_{m-1}$, we can rewrite any $\boldsymbol{y}$ as

$$\boldsymbol{y} = \|\boldsymbol{y}\|\,\boldsymbol{A}_{m-1}\cdots\boldsymbol{A}_1\boldsymbol{e}_1.$$

Any other arbitrary fixed point could have been used instead of $\boldsymbol{e}_1$ to represent $\boldsymbol{y}$, but the angles and the length would have been different. Successive multiplication by the matrices $\boldsymbol{A}_j$ gives

$$\boldsymbol{A}_1\boldsymbol{e}_1 = \begin{pmatrix} \cos(\theta_1) & -\sin(\theta_1) & \boldsymbol{0}' \\ \sin(\theta_1) & \cos(\theta_1) & \boldsymbol{0}' \\ \boldsymbol{0} & \boldsymbol{0} & \boldsymbol{I}_{m-2} \end{pmatrix}\begin{pmatrix} 1 \\ 0 \\ \boldsymbol{0} \end{pmatrix} = \begin{pmatrix} \cos(\theta_1) \\ \sin(\theta_1) \\ \boldsymbol{0} \end{pmatrix},$$

$$\boldsymbol{A}_2\boldsymbol{A}_1\boldsymbol{e}_1 = \begin{pmatrix} 1 & 0 & 0 & \boldsymbol{0}' \\ 0 & \cos(\theta_2) & -\sin(\theta_2) & \boldsymbol{0}' \\ 0 & \sin(\theta_2) & \cos(\theta_2) & \boldsymbol{0}' \\ \boldsymbol{0} & \boldsymbol{0} & \boldsymbol{0} & \boldsymbol{I}_{m-3} \end{pmatrix}\begin{pmatrix} \cos(\theta_1) \\ \sin(\theta_1) \\ \boldsymbol{0} \end{pmatrix} = \begin{pmatrix} \cos(\theta_1) \\ \cos(\theta_2)\sin(\theta_1) \\ \sin(\theta_2)\sin(\theta_1) \\ \boldsymbol{0} \end{pmatrix},$$

and so on. Formally, this should be proved by induction but we shall not do so here, choosing instead to show the pattern by the first few rotations.

The vector $(y_1,\dots,y_m)'$ represents the point $\boldsymbol{y}$ in terms of rectangular coordinates, while $\|\boldsymbol{y}\|$ times the right-hand side is the "polar" representation of the same point; compare to the two-dimensional case seen in Exercise 7.27. Strictly speaking, the mathematical name is *spherical representation* (because of the successive rotations along a sphere) rather than polar. However the adjective "spherical" is used in statistics to refer to distributions, and is therefore best avoided here.

(b) The Jacobian is

$$D = \begin{vmatrix} -y_1 \tan(\theta_1) & 0 & \dots & 0 & y_1/\|\boldsymbol{y}\| \\ y_2 \cot(\theta_1) & -y_2 \tan(\theta_2) & \dots & 0 & y_2/\|\boldsymbol{y}\| \\ \vdots & \vdots & & \vdots & \vdots \\ y_{m-1} \cot(\theta_1) & y_{m-1} \cot(\theta_2) & \dots & -y_{m-1} \tan(\theta_{m-1}) & y_{m-1}/\|\boldsymbol{y}\| \\ y_m \cot(\theta_1) & y_m \cot(\theta_2) & \dots & y_m \cot(\theta_{m-1}) & y_m/\|\boldsymbol{y}\| \end{vmatrix},$$

where expressions such as $y_m \cot(\theta_{m-1})$ are a convenient shorthand for

$$\|\boldsymbol{y}\| \cos(\theta_{m-1}) \sin(\theta_{m-2}) \cdots \sin(\theta_1)$$

for any value of the θ's, including values yielding a zero product. In order to evaluate the determinant, we add λ_1 times the first column to the m-th column, then λ_2 times the second column to the m-th column, and so on until we add λ_{m-1} times the $(m-1)$-th column to the m-th column. We choose λ_j ($j = 1, \dots, m-1$) such that the j-th element in the m-th column reduces to 0 after all the additions are carried out; we will show that

$$\lambda_j = \frac{\cot(\theta_j)}{\|\boldsymbol{y}\| \prod_{i=1}^{j-1} (\sin(\theta_i))^2}.$$

This is so because $(\cot(\theta_k))^2 = (\sin(\theta_k))^{-2} - 1$ implies

$$\begin{aligned} \|\boldsymbol{y}\| \sum_{k=1}^{j-1} \lambda_k \cot(\theta_k) &= \sum_{k=1}^{j-1} \frac{\cot(\theta_k)}{\prod_{i=1}^{k-1} (\sin(\theta_i))^2} \cot(\theta_k) \\ &= \sum_{k=1}^{j-1} \frac{1}{\prod_{i=1}^{k} (\sin(\theta_i))^2} - \sum_{k=1}^{j-1} \frac{1}{\prod_{i=1}^{k-1} (\sin(\theta_i))^2} \\ &= \sum_{l=2}^{j} \frac{1}{\prod_{i=1}^{l-1} (\sin(\theta_i))^2} - \sum_{k=1}^{j-1} \frac{1}{\prod_{i=1}^{k-1} (\sin(\theta_i))^2} = \frac{1}{\prod_{i=1}^{j-1} (\sin(\theta_i))^2} - 1 \\ &= \|\boldsymbol{y}\| \lambda_j \tan(\theta_j) - 1, \end{aligned}$$

(which also holds for $j = m$), hence

$$D = \begin{vmatrix} -y_1 \tan(\theta_1) & 0 & \dots & 0 & 0 \\ y_2 \cot(\theta_1) & -y_2 \tan(\theta_2) & \dots & 0 & 0 \\ \vdots & \vdots & & \vdots & \vdots \\ y_{m-1} \cot(\theta_1) & y_{m-1} \cot(\theta_2) & \dots & -y_{m-1} \tan(\theta_{m-1}) & 0 \\ y_m \cot(\theta_1) & y_m \cot(\theta_2) & \dots & y_m \cot(\theta_{m-1}) & y_m \lambda_m \tan(\theta_m) \end{vmatrix}$$

$$= \frac{y_m \prod_{j=1}^{m-1} (-y_j \tan(\theta_j))}{\|\boldsymbol{y}\| \prod_{j=1}^{m-1} (\sin(\theta_j))^2} = \frac{y_m}{\|\boldsymbol{y}\| \prod_{j=1}^{m-1} \sin(\theta_j)} \prod_{j=1}^{m-1} \frac{-y_j}{\cos(\theta_j)}.$$

By the definitions $y_m = \|\boldsymbol{y}\| \prod_{j=1}^{m-1} \sin(\theta_j)$ and $y_j = \|\boldsymbol{y}\| \cos(\theta_j) \prod_{i=1}^{j-1} \sin(\theta_i)$ for $j < m$, we get $D = (-\|\boldsymbol{y}\|)^{m-1} \prod_{j=1}^{m-1} \prod_{i=1}^{j-1} \sin(\theta_i)$. The result follows by expanding the double sum and collecting powers of $\sin(\theta_1)$, then $\sin(\theta_2)$, and so on.

Exercise 7.29 (Rectangular to polar) Let $\boldsymbol{y}$ be spherically distributed with density function $f_{\boldsymbol{y}}(\boldsymbol{w}_{\boldsymbol{y}}) = h(\boldsymbol{w}_{\boldsymbol{y}}'\boldsymbol{w}_{\boldsymbol{y}})$ for some appropriate function h.
(a) Using the polar representation of the vector $\boldsymbol{y}$, given in Exercise 7.28, derive the joint p.d.f. of $\boldsymbol{z} := (\theta_1, \ldots, \theta_{m-1}, \|\boldsymbol{y}\|)'$, commenting on the distributions of its components.
(b) Assuming $\Pr(\boldsymbol{y} = \boldsymbol{0}) = 0$, prove that $\boldsymbol{x} := \|\boldsymbol{y}\|^{-1}\boldsymbol{y}$ is distributed independently of $\|\boldsymbol{y}\|$.
(c) Prove that $\boldsymbol{x}$ is distributed uniformly on the unit sphere, that is, it can take values only on the unit sphere and its density is invariant to rotations.

Solution
(a) This follows immediately by using the transformation theorem, and taking the absolute value of the Jacobian in Exercise 7.28(b). We get

$$f_{\boldsymbol{z}}(\boldsymbol{w}) = \left(w_m^{m-1}\prod_{i=1}^{m-2}|\sin(w_i)|^{m-i-1}\right)h\left(w_m^2\right)$$
$$= \left(\prod_{i=1}^{m-2}|\sin(w_i)|^{m-i-1}\right)\left(w_{m-1}^0\right)\left(w_m^{m-1}h\left(w_m^2\right)\right),$$

where $w_j \in (0, 2\pi)$ for $j < m$, and $w_m \in \mathbb{R}_+$. We can see that the density factors into a product of terms containing only one component of $\boldsymbol{w}$ at a time. This means that the components are jointly independent, with densities proportional (so that each p.d.f. integrates to 1) to these factors. This generalizes the two-dimensional case of Exercise 7.27(a). Notice that θ_{m-1} is uniformly distributed over $(0, 2\pi)$ because its density is proportional to the constant $w_{m-1}^0 = 1$, but that the other angles are *not* uniformly distributed. In fact, their densities peak at $\pi/2$ and $3\pi/2$, indicating the following. Whatever is the angle θ_{m-1}, the most likely next rotation by $\boldsymbol{A}_{m-2}$ (of Exercise 7.28) transforms the point to one that is in an orthogonal position, in order to preserve spherical symmetry. It is like the movement of the air in the final stages of inflating a round ball!
(b) The vector $\boldsymbol{x} := \|\boldsymbol{y}\|^{-1}\boldsymbol{y}$ is numerically invariant to changing the length of $\boldsymbol{y}$ by any factor $\lambda \in \mathbb{R}_+$, that is, $\|\lambda\boldsymbol{y}\|^{-1}\lambda\boldsymbol{y} = \|\boldsymbol{y}\|^{-1}\boldsymbol{y}$. Therefore, $\boldsymbol{x}$ is independent of $\|\boldsymbol{y}\|$.
(c) From Exercise 7.28(a), the normalized vector $\boldsymbol{x} := \|\boldsymbol{y}\|^{-1}\boldsymbol{y}$ varies on the unit sphere. Alternatively,

$$\|\boldsymbol{x}\| = \left\|\|\boldsymbol{y}\|^{-1}\boldsymbol{y}\right\| = \|\boldsymbol{y}\|^{-1}\|\boldsymbol{y}\| = 1,$$

so $\boldsymbol{x}$ is always on the unit sphere. Now, we give the proof of uniformity. Since $\boldsymbol{y}$ is spherically distributed, the distributions of $\boldsymbol{y}$ and $\boldsymbol{T}\boldsymbol{y}$ coincide for all orthogonal matrices $\boldsymbol{T}$. This implies that the distributions of $\|\boldsymbol{y}\|^{-1}\boldsymbol{y}$ and $\|\boldsymbol{T}\boldsymbol{y}\|^{-1}\boldsymbol{T}\boldsymbol{y}$ coincide. The former is $\boldsymbol{x}$ and the latter is

$$\|\boldsymbol{T}\boldsymbol{y}\|^{-1}\boldsymbol{T}\boldsymbol{y} = (\boldsymbol{y}'\boldsymbol{T}'\boldsymbol{T}\boldsymbol{y})^{-1/2}\boldsymbol{T}\boldsymbol{y} = (\boldsymbol{y}'\boldsymbol{y})^{-1/2}\boldsymbol{T}\boldsymbol{y} = \boldsymbol{T}\left(\|\boldsymbol{y}\|^{-1}\boldsymbol{y}\right) = \boldsymbol{T}\boldsymbol{x},$$

so the distributions of x and Tx coincide, implying that x is also spherically distributed. Because x is always on the unit sphere and its density is invariant to rotations, it is uniformly distributed on this sphere.

Exercise 7.30 (Robustness of F to dependence and nonnormality) Let the $n \times 1$ vector y be spherically distributed, with $\Pr(y = 0) = 0$ and $n > 1$.
(a) Defining $z_1 := \sum_{i=1}^{m} y_i^2$ and $z_2 := \sum_{i=m+1}^{n} y_i^2$, where $m < n$, show that

$$z := \frac{m}{n-m} \times \frac{z_2}{z_1} \sim \mathrm{F}(n-m, m).$$

(b) Assume further that y is multivariate t with ν degrees of freedom. Show that we have $\Pr(y'y \leqslant w) = F(w/n)$, where F is the c.d.f. of a $\mathrm{F}(n, \nu)$ variate. [Hint: Recall from Exercise 6.41 that $y_1 \sim \mathrm{t}(\nu)$, and from Exercise 4.33 that $y_1^2 \sim \mathrm{F}(1, \nu)$.]

Solution
(a) This is an immediate consequence of applying Exercise 7.29 to Exercise 7.19, as we will show. Since all spherical variates y, normal or otherwise, possess the property that $\|y\|^{-1} y$ is distributed uniformly on the unit sphere, the distribution of

$$z = \frac{m \sum_{i=m+1}^{n} y_i^2}{(n-m)\sum_{i=1}^{m} y_i^2} = \frac{m \sum_{i=m+1}^{n} (y_i/\|y\|)^2}{(n-m)\sum_{i=1}^{m} (y_i/\|y\|)^2}$$

is the same for all spherical y. The common distribution has been worked out for the case of a spherical normal in Exercise 7.19 as $\mathrm{F}(n-m, m)$. Spherically distributed variates include ones whose moments do not necessarily exist, such as the multivariate *standard* Cauchy (take $A = I$ in the multivariate Cauchy of Chapter 6 to get a spherical distribution). They also allow the components of y to be dependent, even when uncorrelated, the exception being the normal distribution; see the discussion in Exercise 6.51(c). Here, we do not require independence.
(b) This follows from writing $y'y = \sum_{i=1}^{n} y_i^2$, where $y_i^2 \sim \mathrm{F}(1, \nu)$, and using Exercise 7.19 again to obtain $n^{-1}\sum_{i=1}^{n} y_i^2 \sim \mathrm{F}(n, \nu)$. Incidentally, retracing our steps backwards from here, given the univariate t representation in terms of the χ^2 and the normal, we confirm the representation of the multivariate t that was given in the discussion before (6.8).

***Exercise 7.31 (Ellipticals' c.f.)** Consider the $m \times 1$ vector $x \sim \mathrm{EC}(c, A)$, where A is positive definite.
(a) Prove that the c.f. is $\varphi_x(\tau) = \exp(\mathrm{i}\tau' c)\, h(\tau' A \tau)$ for some continuous function h satisfying $h(0) = 1$. [Hint: Transform x into a spherical variate, then use Exercise 7.29(c) and the fact that the inner product of two unit-length vectors depends only on the angle between them.]
(b) Prove that all the marginal distributions of x are elliptical, and of the same elliptical type as x.
(c) If the mean and variance of x exist, show that they are c and $-2h'(0)A$, respectively.

Solution

(a) By Exercise 6.49, we have that $y := A^{-1/2}(x - c) \sim \text{EC}(0_m, I_m)$, where $A^{1/2}$ is the unique symmetric square root of A. Hence, y is spherical. The c.f. of y is

$$\varphi_y(t) = \text{E}\left(e^{it'y}\right) = \text{E}\left(e^{i\|t\|\left(\|t\|^{-1}t\right)'\left(\|y\|^{-1}y\right)\|y\|}\right).$$

Since the inner product of two unit-length vectors is equal to the cosine of the angle between them, it follows that $(\|t\|^{-1}t)'(\|y\|^{-1}y)$ is a function of only the angle between $\|t\|^{-1}t$ and $\|y\|^{-1}y$. By Exercise 7.29, the latter vector is uniformly distributed on the unit sphere (all rotations are equally likely), so that the expectation is invariant to the angle between the two vectors, whatever the chosen deterministic t. After taking expectations, we are left with a function of $\|t\|$ only, say $h\left(\|t\|^2\right)$ because $\|t\| \geqslant 0$. Then

$$\begin{aligned}\varphi_x(\tau) &= \text{E}\left(e^{i\tau'x}\right) = \text{E}\left(e^{i\tau'(c+A^{1/2}y)}\right) = e^{i\tau'c}\,\text{E}\left(e^{i\tau'A^{1/2}y}\right)\\ &= e^{i\tau'c}\varphi_y\left(A^{1/2}\tau\right) = e^{i\tau'c}h\left(\tau'A^{1/2}A^{1/2}\tau\right) = e^{i\tau'c}h\left(\tau'A\tau\right)\end{aligned}$$

as required. We have $h(0) = 1$ because $\varphi_x(0) = h(0)$ and $\varphi_x(0) \equiv \text{E}\left(e^0\right)$. Continuity follows (as do other features) from the properties of c.f.s, seen as early as in the introduction to Chapter 3. For example, in the case of the normal distribution, we have $h(s) := \exp(-s/2)$, where $s := \tau'A\tau$; this will be studied in detail in Chapter 8. Recall the comment after (6.8) about the incompleteness of the notation $\text{EC}(c, A)$: the uniqueness of c.f.s means that the function h can complete the description of the distribution of $\text{EC}(c, A)$ as $\text{EC}(c, A, h)$ if needed.

(b) Let $x' := (x_1', x_2')$ and partition c, τ, and A accordingly. The marginal c.f. of x_2 is

$$\varphi_{x_2}(\tau_2) = \text{E}\left(e^{i(0',\tau_2')x}\right) = \exp\left(i\tau_2'c_2\right)h\left(\tau_2'A_{22}\tau_2\right),$$

which is the c.f. of an elliptical variate with parameters c_2 and A_{22}. Furthermore, the c.f. of x_2 is of the same functional form as that of x. The proof is generally valid for any subset of x: we may first rearrange the elements of x by premultiplying it with a permutation matrix (the result is still an elliptical variate, by Exercise 6.49), before selecting the relevant subset.

(c) In general, if the first two moments exist, then

$$\left.\frac{\partial\varphi_x(\tau)}{\partial\tau}\right|_{\tau=0} = \text{E}\left.\left(\frac{\partial e^{i\tau'x}}{\partial\tau}\right)\right|_{\tau=0} = \text{E}\left.\left(ix e^{i\tau'x}\right)\right|_{\tau=0} = i\,\text{E}(x)$$

and, by $\tau'x = x'\tau$,

$$\left.\frac{\partial^2\varphi_x(\tau)}{\partial\tau\partial\tau'}\right|_{\tau=0} = \left.\frac{\partial\,\text{E}\left(ix e^{ix'\tau}\right)}{\partial\tau'}\right|_{\tau=0} = \text{E}\left.\left(i^2 xx' e^{i\tau'x}\right)\right|_{\tau=0} = -\text{E}\left(xx'\right),$$

as in the introduction to Chapter 6. Therefore, for $\varphi_x(\tau) = \exp(i\tau'c)\,h(\tau'A\tau)$, we have

$$i\,\text{E}(x) = \left.\left(ih\left(\tau'A\tau\right)c + 2h'\left(\tau'A\tau\right)A\tau\right)e^{i\tau'c}\right|_{\tau=0} = ih(0)\,c = ic,$$

confirming Exercise 6.49(b), and

$$-\mathrm{E}\left(\boldsymbol{x}\boldsymbol{x}'\right) = \left.\frac{\partial\left(\left(\mathrm{i}h\left(\boldsymbol{\tau}'\boldsymbol{A}\boldsymbol{\tau}\right)\boldsymbol{c}+2h'\left(\boldsymbol{\tau}'\boldsymbol{A}\boldsymbol{\tau}\right)\boldsymbol{A}\boldsymbol{\tau}\right)\mathrm{e}^{\mathrm{i}\boldsymbol{\tau}'\boldsymbol{c}}\right)}{\partial\boldsymbol{\tau}'}\right|_{\boldsymbol{\tau}=\mathbf{0}}$$

$$= 2h'(0)\,\boldsymbol{A} + (\mathrm{i}h(0)\,\boldsymbol{c})\,\mathrm{i}\boldsymbol{c}' = 2h'(0)\,\boldsymbol{A} - \boldsymbol{c}\boldsymbol{c}'.$$

Using $\operatorname{var}(\boldsymbol{x}) = \mathrm{E}(\boldsymbol{x}\boldsymbol{x}') - \mathrm{E}(\boldsymbol{x})\,\mathrm{E}(\boldsymbol{x}')$ gives the required result. See the method in Exercise 3.22 for an alternative route to calculating $\operatorname{var}(\boldsymbol{x})$. Note that $h(s) = \exp(-s/2)$ gives $-2h'(0) = 1$, which will be useful for the normal distribution.

***Exercise 7.32 (Transformation theorem)** Prove the transformation theorem when $\boldsymbol{y} = \boldsymbol{g}(\boldsymbol{x})$ is an invertible function over $\boldsymbol{x} \in \mathcal{X}$:
(a) first for $m = 1$;
(b) then, by induction, for the general case.
[Hint: Use conditional densities in (b).]

Solution
(a) First, assume that $g(x)$ is an increasing function. By the c.d.f. method,

$$F_y(w_y) = \Pr(y \leqslant w_y) = \Pr\left(x \leqslant g^{-1}(w_y)\right) = \int_{-\infty}^{g^{-1}(w_y)} f_x(s)\,\mathrm{d}s.$$

Differentiating both sides with respect to w_y, by Leibniz' rule, gives the required result. Alternatively, the change of variable of integration $t = g(s)$ gives

$$F_y(w_y) = \int_{-\infty}^{w_y} f_x\left(g^{-1}(t)\right)\mathrm{d}g^{-1}(t) = \int_{-\infty}^{w_y} f_x\left(g^{-1}(t)\right)\frac{\mathrm{d}g^{-1}(t)}{\mathrm{d}t}\,\mathrm{d}t,$$

which identifies $f_y(t)$ as the integrand. Notice that the Jacobian is evaluated at $(x, y) = (s, t)$. A variant of this alternative approach will be used in the vector case, later in the proof.

Second, for $g(x)$ a decreasing function,

$$F_y(w_y) = \Pr(y \leqslant w_y) = \Pr\left(x \geqslant g^{-1}(w_y)\right) = 1 - \int_{-\infty}^{g^{-1}(w_y)} f_x(s)\,\mathrm{d}s,$$

and we get the required result by differentiating both sides. Notice that $\mathrm{d}g^{-1}(w_y)/\mathrm{d}w_y$ is negative in this case, because the function (and hence its inverse) is decreasing in its argument, which explains the appearance of the absolute value in the transformation theorem.
(b) We now assume that the relation holds for some m, where $m \geqslant 1$, and prove it for $m+1$. We decompose the joint density into the product of the marginal density for the last component times the conditional density for the first m components. Define the $(m+1)\times m$ matrix $\boldsymbol{C}_1$ and the $(m+1)\times 1$ vector $\boldsymbol{c}_2$ by

$$\boldsymbol{I}_{m+1} = \begin{pmatrix} \boldsymbol{I}_m & \mathbf{0}_m \\ \mathbf{0}_m' & 1 \end{pmatrix} = (\boldsymbol{C}_1, \boldsymbol{c}_2),$$

so that they select the blocks of $\boldsymbol{x}$ as

$$\boldsymbol{x} := \begin{pmatrix} x_1 \\ \vdots \\ x_m \\ x_{m+1} \end{pmatrix} = \begin{pmatrix} \boldsymbol{C}_1' \boldsymbol{x} \\ \boldsymbol{c}_2' \boldsymbol{x} \end{pmatrix},$$

and similarly for the other vectors. We have

$$\begin{aligned} F_{\boldsymbol{y}}\left(\boldsymbol{w}_{\boldsymbol{y}}\right) &= \int_{\boldsymbol{g}(\boldsymbol{s}) \leqslant \boldsymbol{w}_{\boldsymbol{y}}} f_{\boldsymbol{x}}\left(\boldsymbol{s}\right) \mathrm{d}\boldsymbol{s} \\ &= \int \int_{\boldsymbol{g}(\boldsymbol{s}) \leqslant \boldsymbol{w}_{\boldsymbol{y}}} f_{\boldsymbol{c}_2'\boldsymbol{x}}\left(\boldsymbol{c}_2'\boldsymbol{s}\right) f_{\boldsymbol{C}_1'\boldsymbol{x} | \boldsymbol{c}_2'\boldsymbol{s}}\left(\boldsymbol{C}_1'\boldsymbol{s}\right) \mathrm{d}\left(\boldsymbol{C}_1'\boldsymbol{s}\right) \mathrm{d}\left(\boldsymbol{c}_2'\boldsymbol{s}\right). \end{aligned}$$

We have to be careful that, in general, $\boldsymbol{g}\left(\boldsymbol{x}\right) \leqslant \boldsymbol{y}$ is *not* the same as either of $\boldsymbol{x} \leqslant \boldsymbol{g}^{-1}\left(\boldsymbol{y}\right)$ or $\boldsymbol{x} \geqslant \boldsymbol{g}^{-1}\left(\boldsymbol{y}\right)$ in the vector case, as seen in the introduction. The transformation theorem holds for variates of dimensions 1 (by proof) and m (by the induction assumption), so it can be applied to both densities in this formula. We now need to work out the Jacobians of the two transformations

$$\boldsymbol{c}_2'\boldsymbol{x} \mapsto \boldsymbol{c}_2'\boldsymbol{y} \quad \text{and} \quad \boldsymbol{C}_1'\boldsymbol{x}\ \left(\text{given } \boldsymbol{c}_2'\boldsymbol{x}\right) \mapsto \boldsymbol{C}_1'\boldsymbol{y}\ \left(\text{given } \boldsymbol{c}_2'\boldsymbol{y}\right),$$

where $\boldsymbol{x} = \boldsymbol{g}^{-1}\left(\boldsymbol{y}\right)$, then evaluate them at $\left(\boldsymbol{x}, \boldsymbol{y}\right) = \left(\boldsymbol{s}, \boldsymbol{t}\right)$, as in (a), and substitute them into the last formula for $F_{\boldsymbol{y}}(\boldsymbol{w}_{\boldsymbol{y}})$.

To obtain the Jacobians of these transformations, a Taylor-series linearization near the point $\boldsymbol{y} = \boldsymbol{t}$ gives $\boldsymbol{x} = \boldsymbol{g}^{-1}\left(\boldsymbol{y}\right) = \boldsymbol{g}^{-1}\left(\boldsymbol{t}\right) + \boldsymbol{A}\left(\boldsymbol{y} - \boldsymbol{t}\right) + \boldsymbol{r}$, where

$$\boldsymbol{A} := \begin{pmatrix} \boldsymbol{A}_{11} & \boldsymbol{a}_{12} \\ \boldsymbol{a}_{21}' & a_{22} \end{pmatrix} = \frac{\partial \boldsymbol{g}^{-1}\left(\boldsymbol{t}\right)}{\partial \boldsymbol{t}'}$$

and $\boldsymbol{r}$ contains the remainder terms. This linearization can be rewritten as $\boldsymbol{z} := \boldsymbol{A}\boldsymbol{y}$, where $\boldsymbol{z}$ differs from $\boldsymbol{x}$ by a constant and by $\boldsymbol{r}$. For the first integral in $F_{\boldsymbol{y}}(\boldsymbol{w}_{\boldsymbol{y}})$, the Jacobian is simply

$$\left.\frac{\partial x_{m+1}}{\partial y_{m+1}}\right|_{\boldsymbol{y}=\boldsymbol{t}} = \frac{\partial z_{m+1}}{\partial y_{m+1}} = a_{22}.$$

For the second integral, matters are more elaborate because of the dependence of the integral on $\boldsymbol{c}_2'\boldsymbol{s}$ (or s_{m+1}). We write

$$\boldsymbol{A}^{-1} = \begin{pmatrix} \boldsymbol{B}_{11} & \boldsymbol{b}_{12} \\ \boldsymbol{b}_{21}' & b_{22} \end{pmatrix},$$

where $\boldsymbol{B}_{11} = (\boldsymbol{A}_{11} - \frac{1}{a_{22}}\boldsymbol{a}_{12}\boldsymbol{a}_{21}')^{-1}$. Then, $\boldsymbol{C}_1'\boldsymbol{A}^{-1} = (\boldsymbol{B}_{11}, \boldsymbol{b}_{12})$, and hence

$$\boldsymbol{C}_1'\boldsymbol{y} = \boldsymbol{C}_1'\boldsymbol{A}^{-1}\boldsymbol{z} = \boldsymbol{B}_{11}\boldsymbol{C}_1'\boldsymbol{z} + \boldsymbol{b}_{12}\boldsymbol{c}_2'\boldsymbol{z}.$$

Since we have conditioned on $\boldsymbol{c}_2'\boldsymbol{x}$ (or x_{m+1}) in the second integral of $F_{\boldsymbol{y}}(\boldsymbol{w}_{\boldsymbol{y}})$, it can be treated as a constant when calculating the Jacobian, and so

$$\left.\frac{\partial\left(C_1'x\right)}{\partial\left(C_1'y\right)'}\right|_{y=t}=\frac{\partial\left(C_1'z\right)}{\partial\left(C_1'y\right)'}=B_{11}^{-1}.$$

Substituting both Jacobians into $F_y(w_y)$ yields

$$\begin{aligned}F_y\left(w_y\right)&=\int_{t\leqslant w_y}\left|a_{22}\right| f_{c_2'x}\left(c_2'g^{-1}\left(t\right)\right)\left|\det B_{11}^{-1}\right| f_{C_1'x|c_2'g^{-1}(t)}\left(C_1'g^{-1}\left(t\right)\right)\mathrm{d}t\\&=\int_{t\leqslant w_y}\left|\det A\right| f_x\left(g^{-1}\left(t\right)\right)\mathrm{d}t,\end{aligned}$$

where the last step follows since $f_{c_2'x}\left(c_2's\right) f_{C_1'x|c_2's}\left(C_1's\right)=f_x\left(s\right)$ and

$$a_{22}\det B_{11}^{-1}=a_{22}\det\left(A_{11}-\frac{1}{a_{22}}a_{12}a_{21}'\right)=\det A\equiv\det\left(\frac{\partial g^{-1}\left(t\right)}{\partial t'}\right);$$

see Section A.4 for the determinant of a partitioned matrix. The result follows by differentiating both sides of $F_y(w_y)$ with respect to w_y, which is equivalent to evaluating the integrand at $t=w_y$. Notice that we have assumed implicitly that $a_{22}\neq 0$ and $\left|B_{11}^{-1}\right|\neq 0$. This is not a restrictive assumption since, for $|A|\neq 0$, we can always find a permutation of the elements of x or y to achieve this, for example, by reordering

$$\begin{pmatrix}y_1\\y_2\end{pmatrix}=\begin{pmatrix}-1&1\\1&0\end{pmatrix}\begin{pmatrix}x_1\\x_2\end{pmatrix}\quad\text{into}\quad\begin{pmatrix}y_2\\y_1\end{pmatrix}=\begin{pmatrix}1&0\\-1&1\end{pmatrix}\begin{pmatrix}x_1\\x_2\end{pmatrix}.$$

The absolute value of the determinant of a permutation (hence orthogonal) matrix is always 1, so the result is unaltered.

We can interpret the transformation theorem in a similar way to Leibniz' rule. The Jacobian factor provides the change in the volume of the domain covered by the limits of integration of x as y changes infinitesimally: the determinant is the volume of the parallelotope formed by the vectors $\partial x_i/\partial y'$, evaluated at $y=w_y$ and $x=g^{-1}\left(w_y\right)$.

Exercise 7.33 (Transformation and information) Let x and z be m-dimensional continuous vector variates. Define $\mathrm{KL}(f_x,f_z):=\mathrm{E}_x\left(\log\left(f_x\left(x\right)/f_z\left(x\right)\right)\right)$ and the transformation $y:=g\left(x\right)$ such that g is a deterministic, continuously differentiable, and invertible function.

(a) Prove that $\mathrm{KL}(f_x,f_z)=\mathrm{KL}\left(f_{g(x)},f_{g(z)}\right)$, so that the KLIC is invariant to transformations of variates.

(b) Show that the entropies $\mathrm{E}\left(-\log\left(f_x\left(x\right)\right)\right)$ and $\mathrm{E}\left(-\log\left(f_y\left(y\right)\right)\right)$ are generally not equal, illustrating the case $m=1$ with the entropies of two normally distributed variates.

Solution

(a) By definition,

$$\mathrm{KL}(f_{g(x)},f_{g(z)}):=\mathrm{E}\left(\log\left(\frac{f_{g(x)}\left(y\right)}{f_{g(z)}\left(y\right)}\right)\right),$$

then the transformation theorem gives

$$\mathrm{KL}(f_{\boldsymbol{g}(\boldsymbol{x})}, f_{\boldsymbol{g}(\boldsymbol{z})}) = \mathrm{E}\left(\log\left(\frac{\left|\det\left(\frac{\partial \boldsymbol{g}^{-1}(\boldsymbol{y})}{\partial \boldsymbol{y}'}\right)\right| f_{\boldsymbol{x}}\left(\boldsymbol{g}^{-1}\left(\boldsymbol{y}\right)\right)}{\left|\det\left(\frac{\partial \boldsymbol{g}^{-1}(\boldsymbol{y})}{\partial \boldsymbol{y}'}\right)\right| f_{\boldsymbol{z}}\left(\boldsymbol{g}^{-1}\left(\boldsymbol{y}\right)\right)}\right)\right)$$

$$= \mathrm{E}\left(\log\left(\frac{f_{\boldsymbol{x}}(\boldsymbol{x})}{f_{\boldsymbol{z}}(\boldsymbol{x})}\right)\right) \equiv \mathrm{KL}(f_{\boldsymbol{x}}, f_{\boldsymbol{z}}).$$

(b) However,

$$\mathrm{E}\left(\log\left(f_{\boldsymbol{g}(\boldsymbol{x})}\left(\boldsymbol{y}\right)\right)\right) = \mathrm{E}\left(\log\left(\left|\det\left(\frac{\partial \boldsymbol{g}^{-1}\left(\boldsymbol{y}\right)}{\partial \boldsymbol{y}'}\right)\right| f_{\boldsymbol{x}}\left(\boldsymbol{g}^{-1}\left(\boldsymbol{y}\right)\right)\right)\right)$$

$$= \mathrm{E}\left(\log\left(f_{\boldsymbol{x}}\left(\boldsymbol{x}\right)\right)\right) + \mathrm{E}\left(\log\left|\det\left(\frac{\partial \boldsymbol{g}^{-1}\left(\boldsymbol{y}\right)}{\partial \boldsymbol{y}'}\right)\right|\right),$$

where the last expectation need not always be equal to zero (it is zero when $\boldsymbol{x}$ and $\boldsymbol{y}$ differ only in location, $\boldsymbol{y} = \boldsymbol{a} + \boldsymbol{x}$). For example, Exercise 4.39 showed that the $\mathrm{N}(\mu, \sigma^2)$ distribution has entropy

$$-\mathrm{E}\left(\log\left(\frac{\mathrm{e}^{-(x-\mu)^2/(2\sigma^2)}}{\sigma\sqrt{2\pi}}\right)\right) = \frac{1}{2} + \log\left(\sigma\sqrt{2\pi}\right).$$

As we transform $\mathrm{N}(\mu_1, \sigma_1^2)$ into $\mathrm{N}(\mu_2, \sigma_2^2)$, the entropy is unchanged if $\sigma_1^2 = \sigma_2^2$. Otherwise, it changes by $\log(\sigma_2\sqrt{2\pi}) - \log\left(\sigma_1\sqrt{2\pi}\right) = \log(\sigma_2/\sigma_1)$.

Exercise 7.34 (Exponential tilting of a sum) Let x be a variate with c.g.f. $\varkappa(t)$, and let $f_y\left(v\right) := \exp\left(tv - \varkappa\left(t\right)\right) f_x\left(v\right)$ be its exponentially tilted density, as encountered in Exercise 3.36(d). Suppose that we have a random sample $x_1, \ldots, x_n$ and define $z := \sum_{i=1}^n x_i$ which can be tilted by the same parameter t into ζ. Show that:
(a) $f_\zeta(w) = \exp\left(tw - n\varkappa\left(t\right)\right) f_z(w)$;
(b) $\varkappa_\zeta(s) = n\left(\varkappa_x(s+t) - \varkappa_x(t)\right)$;
(c) tilting $z := \sum_{i=1}^n x_i$ into ζ is equivalent to tilting each x_i into y_i and then summing them.

Solution
We prove the exercise for $n > 1$, since for the case $n = 1$ the three results are true by Exercise 3.36(d).
(a) Tilting the density of z requires its c.g.f.

$$\varkappa_z(t) := \log\left(\mathrm{E}\left(\mathrm{e}^{t\sum_{i=1}^n x_i}\right)\right) = \log\left(\prod_{i=1}^n \mathrm{E}\left(\mathrm{e}^{tx_i}\right)\right) \equiv \sum_{i=1}^n \log\left(\mathrm{E}\left(\mathrm{e}^{tx_i}\right)\right)$$

$$= \sum_{i=1}^n \varkappa(t) = n\varkappa(t)$$

by the i.i.d. assumption for the sample of x's. The required result follows by the definition of tilting.

(b) This follows from applying the c.g.f. of z in (a) to Exercise 3.36(d).

(c) As seen in the discussion of convolutions in this chapter's introduction, the Jacobian for the transformation from $(x_1, x_2, \dots, x_n)$ to $(z, x_2, \dots, x_n)$ is 1, and similarly for $(y_1, y_2, \dots, y_n)$ to $(\sum_{i=1}^n y_i, y_2, \dots, y_n)$. Tilting z in the joint density of $(z, x_2, \dots, x_n)$ produces the factor

$$\exp\left(tw - n\varkappa(t)\right)$$

because of the c.g.f. in (a). Tilting each x_i into y_i instead, the density of $\boldsymbol{y}$ is the density of $\boldsymbol{x}$ multiplied by the factor

$$\prod_{i=1}^n \exp\left(tv_i - \varkappa(t)\right) = \exp\left(t\sum_{i=1}^n v_i - n\varkappa(t)\right),$$

where $\sum_{i=1}^n v_i$ is the realization of $\sum_{i=1}^n y_i$, as required.

***Exercise 7.35 (Distributions of order statistics)** Let $x_1, \dots, x_n$ be a random sample of size $n > 1$ from a continuous variate x with density function f. Let y_i denote the i-th order statistic. Show that:

(a) the c.d.f. of y_i is $F_{y_i}(v_i) = \sum_{k=i}^n \binom{n}{k} (F(v_i))^k (1 - F(v_i))^{n-k}$, and its p.d.f. is

$$f_{y_i}(v_i) = \frac{n!}{(i-1)!(n-i)!} f(v_i) \left(F(v_i)\right)^{i-1} \left(1 - F(v_i)\right)^{n-i};$$

(b) for $v_1 < v_n$, we have the joint p.d.f.

$$f_{y_1, y_n}(v_1, v_n) = n(n-1) f(v_1) f(v_n) \left(F(v_n) - F(v_1)\right)^{n-2};$$

(c) for $i < j$ and $v_i < v_j$, we have the joint p.d.f.

$$f_{y_i, y_j}(v_i, v_j) = \frac{n! f(v_i) f(v_j) \left(F(v_i)\right)^{i-1} \left(F(v_j) - F(v_i)\right)^{j-i-1} \left(1 - F(v_j)\right)^{n-j}}{(i-1)!\,(j-i-1)!\,(n-j)!};$$

(d) for $v_1 < \dots < v_n$, we have the joint p.d.f.

$$f_{y_1, \dots, y_n}(v_1, \dots, v_n) = n! f(v_1) \dots f(v_n).$$

[Hints: First, recall how Exercise 4.3 was proved. Then, for (a), recall the identity in Exercise 4.11(a). For the rest, you may wish to consider quantities like $\Pr(v_i < y_i \leqslant v_i + \Delta v_i)/\Delta v_i$, where $\Delta v_i \to 0^+$.]

Solution

(a) The c.d.f. of y_i is

$$\Pr(y_i \leqslant v_i) = \Pr(\text{at least } i \text{ of the } x\text{'s} \leqslant v_i) = \sum_{k=i}^n \Pr(\text{exactly } k \text{ of the } x\text{'s} \leqslant v_i).$$

The event $\{\text{exactly one } x \leqslant v_i\}$ is a Bernoulli trial with probability of success $\Pr(x \leqslant v_i) = F(v_i)$ and, repeating this over a sample of n independent draws from x, we get a binomial density; see Exercise 4.3. Therefore,

$$F_{y_i}(v_i) \equiv \Pr(y_i \leqslant v_i) = \sum_{k=i}^{n} \binom{n}{k} (F(v_i))^k (1 - F(v_i))^{n-k},$$

which is also valid for discrete variates x; see Exercise 2.11 for an illustration.

This sum is the complement of a binomial c.d.f. for $k \sim \text{Bin}(n, p)$, where $p := F(v_i)$; more specifically, $\Pr(y_i \leqslant v_i) = \Pr(k \geqslant i) = 1 - \Pr(k \leqslant i - 1)$. By Exercise 4.11(a), this c.d.f. can be written as

$$\Pr(y_i \leqslant v_i) = 1 - (n - i + 1) \binom{n}{i-1} \int_0^{1-F(v_i)} t^{n-i} (1 - t)^{i-1} \, \mathrm{d}t.$$

Then, differentiating by Leibniz' rule gives the required result for continuous variates. Alternatively, differentiating $F_{y_i}(v_i)$ directly with respect to v_i and simplifying the sums gives the required density.

(b) We proceed in the same manner as in (a). The c.d.f. is

$$\begin{aligned}\Pr(y_1 \leqslant v_1, y_n \leqslant v_n) &= \sum_{k=1}^{n} \Pr(k \text{ of the } x\text{'s} \leqslant v_1 \text{ and all } x\text{'s} \leqslant v_n) \\ &= \sum_{k=1}^{n} \Pr(k \text{ of the } x\text{'s} \leqslant v_1 \text{ and } n-k \text{ lie in the interval } (v_1, v_n]).\end{aligned}$$

Since $\Pr(x \leqslant v_1) = F(v_1)$ and $\Pr(x \in (v_1, v_n]) = F(v_n) - F(v_1)$, and the events can be combined in $\binom{n}{k}$ ways (compare Exercise 4.3), we have

$$\begin{aligned}\Pr(y_1 \leqslant v_1, y_n \leqslant v_n) &= \sum_{k=1}^{n} \binom{n}{k} (F(v_1))^k (F(v_n) - F(v_1))^{n-k} \\ &= \left(\sum_{k=0}^{n} \binom{n}{k} (F(v_1))^k (F(v_n) - F(v_1))^{n-k} \right) - (F(v_n) - F(v_1))^n \\ &= (F(v_1) + F(v_n) - F(v_1))^n - (F(v_n) - F(v_1))^n \\ &= (F(v_n))^n - (F(v_n) - F(v_1))^n,\end{aligned}$$

which is also valid for discrete variates x. Partial differentiation with respect to v_1 and v_n gives the required result for continuous variates.

(c) A derivation along the lines in (b) is possible. However, we will consider the following alternative route. Since we are interested only in the density for continuous variates, we can use the fact that

$$\begin{aligned}f_{y_i, y_j}(v_i, v_j) &= \frac{\partial^2 F_{y_i, y_j}(v_i, v_j)}{\partial v_i \partial v_j} \\ &= \lim_{\Delta v_i, \Delta v_j \to 0^+} \frac{\Pr(v_i < y_i \leqslant v_i + \Delta v_i, v_j < y_j \leqslant v_j + \Delta v_j)}{\Delta v_i \Delta v_j}.\end{aligned}$$

Since $\Pr(y_i = y_j) = 0$ for continuous variates, $\Delta v_i, \Delta v_j \to 0^+$ implies that the composite event $v_i < y_i \leqslant v_i + \Delta v_i$ and $v_j < y_j \leqslant v_j + \Delta v_j$ is equivalent to

$$i-1 \text{ of the } x\text{'s in } (-\infty, v_i], \quad \text{one in } (v_i, v_i + \Delta v_i], \quad j-i-1 \text{ in } (v_i + \Delta v_i, v_j],$$
$$\text{one in } (v_j, v_j + \Delta v_j], \quad n-j \text{ in } (v_j + \Delta v_j, \infty).$$

We now have five intervals, so we need to resort to the multinomial instead of the binomial, giving the required probability as

$$\frac{n!}{(i-1)!\,1!\,(j-i-1)!\,1!\,(n-j)!} p_1^{i-1}\, p_2\, p_3^{j-i-1}\, p_4\, p_5^{n-j},$$

where

$$p_1 := F(v_i), \quad p_2 := F(v_i + \Delta v_i) - F(v_i), \quad p_3 := F(v_j) - F(v_i + \Delta v_i),$$
$$p_4 := F(v_j + \Delta v_j) - F(v_j), \quad p_5 := 1 - F(v_j + \Delta v_j).$$

Taking the limit, we get

$$\begin{aligned} f_{y_i, y_j}(v_i, v_j) &= \frac{n!\,(F(v_i))^{i-1}\,(F(v_j) - F(v_i))^{j-i-1}\,(1 - F(v_j))^{n-j}}{(i-1)!\,(j-i-1)!\,(n-j)!} \\ &\quad \times \lim_{\Delta v_i, \Delta v_j \to 0^+} \frac{(F(v_i + \Delta v_i) - F(v_i))\,(F(v_j + \Delta v_j) - F(v_j))}{\Delta v_i \Delta v_j} \\ &= \frac{n!\,(F(v_i))^{i-1}\,(F(v_j) - F(v_i))^{j-i-1}\,(1 - F(v_j))^{n-j}}{(i-1)!\,(j-i-1)!\,(n-j)!} f(v_i) f(v_j). \end{aligned}$$

(d) By the same reasoning as in (c), we consider the probability that exactly one value of x falls in each of the intervals $(v_i, v_i + \Delta v_i]$ for $i = 1, \dots, n$. Taking the limit as $\Delta v_i \to 0^+$ for all i gives the result. Note the important fact that, even though the joint density factors into separate terms for each v_i, the order statistics are not independent because the domain of definition is interdependent since $v_1 < \cdots < v_n$.

Exercise 7.36 (Ordered exponentials) Let $x_1, \dots, x_n$ be a random sample of $x \sim \text{Expo}(\lambda)$, and let $y_1, \dots, y_n$ be the corresponding order statistics.
(a) Show that $y_1 \sim \text{Expo}(\lambda n)$.
(b) Derive the p.d.f. of the sample range $z := y_n - y_1$.
(c) Let $n = 3$. Show that $y_1, y_2 - y_1, y_3 - y_2$ are independent, and that $y_{i+1} - y_i \sim \text{Expo}(\lambda\,(n-i))$ for $i = 1, 2$.

Solution
(a) Let $f(u) = \lambda \mathrm{e}^{-\lambda u}$ with c.d.f. $F(u) = 1 - \mathrm{e}^{-\lambda u}$. From Exercise 7.35(a) we know that

$$\begin{aligned} f_{y_1}(v_1) &= \frac{n!}{(n-1)!0!} f(v_1)(F(v_1))^0 (1 - F(v_1))^{n-1} \\ &= n\lambda \mathrm{e}^{-\lambda v_1} \left(\mathrm{e}^{-\lambda v_1}\right)^{n-1} = n\lambda \mathrm{e}^{-n\lambda v_1} \end{aligned}$$

for $v_1 > 0$, which is also an exponential density but with parameter $n\lambda$.

(b) From Exercise 7.35(b) we know that, for $v_1 < v_n$ and $n > 1$,

$$\begin{aligned} f_{y_1,y_n}(v_1, v_n) &= n(n-1)f(v_1)f(v_n)\left(F(v_n) - F(v_1)\right)^{n-2} \\ &= n(n-1)\lambda^2 \mathrm{e}^{-\lambda v_1}\mathrm{e}^{-\lambda v_n}\left(\mathrm{e}^{-\lambda v_1} - \mathrm{e}^{-\lambda v_n}\right)^{n-2} \\ &= n(n-1)\lambda^2 \mathrm{e}^{-n\lambda v_1}\mathrm{e}^{-\lambda(v_n - v_1)}\left(1 - \mathrm{e}^{-\lambda(v_n - v_1)}\right)^{n-2}. \end{aligned}$$

Now consider the transformation from (y_1, y_n) to (y_1, z). The Jacobian factor is 1 and hence

$$f_{y_1,z}(v_1, w) = n(n-1)\lambda^2 \mathrm{e}^{-n\lambda v_1}\mathrm{e}^{-\lambda w}\left(1 - \mathrm{e}^{-\lambda w}\right)^{n-2} \qquad (v_1 > 0, w > 0).$$

From this joint density, we obtain the marginal density

$$\begin{aligned} f_z(w) &= n(n-1)\lambda^2 \mathrm{e}^{-\lambda w}\left(1 - \mathrm{e}^{-\lambda w}\right)^{n-2} \int_0^\infty \mathrm{e}^{-n\lambda v_1}\, \mathrm{d}v_1 \\ &= (n-1)\lambda \mathrm{e}^{-\lambda w}\left(1 - \mathrm{e}^{-\lambda w}\right)^{n-2} \qquad (w > 0). \end{aligned}$$

Alternatively, $f_{y_1,z}$ and (a) give the same result without integration.
(c) We start by stressing that y_1, y_2, y_3 are not independent, even if $y_1, y_2 - y_1, y_3 - y_2$ are independent in this special exponential case where the no-memory property is key. Transforming the density in Exercise 7.35(d) to

$$z_1 := y_1, \quad z_2 := y_2 - y_1, \quad z_3 := y_3 - y_2,$$

we have a lower triangular Jacobian matrix with ones on the diagonal. Therefore, for $w_1, w_2, w_3 > 0$,

$$\begin{aligned} f_{z_1,z_2,z_3}(w_1, w_2, w_3) &= 3!f(w_1)f(w_1 + w_2)f(w_1 + w_2 + w_3) \\ &= 3!\lambda^3 \exp\left(-3\lambda w_1 - 2\lambda w_2 - \lambda w_3\right) \\ &= 3\lambda \exp\left(-3\lambda w_1\right) 2\lambda \exp\left(-2\lambda w_2\right) \lambda \exp\left(-\lambda w_3\right) \end{aligned}$$

and the result follows.

Exercise 7.37 (Extremists) This exercise illustrates again the link between some of the discrete distributions of Chapter 4, this time within the context of an extreme event.
(a) Suppose that an extreme event (such as a flood or a market crash) occurs with probability p in a given period. Define $x = 1$ if it occurs, and $x = 0$ otherwise. What is the distribution of x?
(b) For the extreme event in (a), what is the probability of k occurrences in a random sample of size n?
(c) Continuing with the same story, what is the probability that you have to wait for $w + k$ observations before k of these events occur?
(d) Let $x_1, \ldots, x_n$ be a random sample of size $n > 1$ from a continuous variate x with density function f, and let y_i denote the i-th order statistic. Suppose that we were to en-

large our sample to $n + m$. What is the probability that l of these extra m observations will exceed some previous record, say the j-th largest among the previous n observations, y_{n-j+1}, where $1 \leqslant j \leqslant n$? [Hint: Start with the required probability conditionally on $y_{n-j+1} = v$, then use the density of y_{n-j+1} from Exercise 7.35(a) to work out the unconditional probability.]

Solution

Parts (a)–(c) are Exercises 4.3 and 4.4 in another guise.

(a) This is a Bernoulli variate, with p.d.f.

$$f(u) = p^u (1-p)^{1-u} \qquad (u = 0, 1, \quad 0 \leqslant p \leqslant 1).$$

(b) Repeating a Bernoulli trial n independent times, the number of extremes has the binomial p.d.f.

$$f(k) = \binom{n}{k} p^k (1-p)^{n-k} \qquad (k = 0, 1, \ldots, n, \quad 0 \leqslant p \leqslant 1).$$

(c) There are two cases to consider. If $p \neq 0$, to achieve k of these events we now need a random number of trials $z + k$, and z is the number of failures to have such an event. The p.d.f. of z is the negative binomial

$$f(w) = \binom{w+k-1}{w} p^k (1-p)^w \qquad (w = 0, 1, \ldots, \quad 0 < p \leqslant 1).$$

If $p = 0$, there is no chance of the event ever happening, which is why we exclude $p = 0$ from consideration in this part.

(d) The occurrence of one extreme is now defined as the event that $x_{n+i} > y_{n-j+1}$ for some $i \in \{1, \ldots, m\}$. Suppose that we start by taking a given $y_{n-j+1} = v$. By the independence of the m new observations, this is a repeated Bernoulli trial. If we use z to denote the number of successes of the inequality $x_{n+i} > v$, we have $z \sim \text{Bin}(m, 1 - F(v))$ since $\Pr(x > v) = 1 - F(v)$. This is the conditional distribution of z, given $y_{n-j+1} = v$, and in Chapter 6 it was shown that the unconditional density is obtained as the expectation of the conditional density as y_{n-j+1} varies: $f_z = \mathrm{E}_y\left(f_{z|y}\right)$. (Here, z is discrete and y is continuous.) Using the binomial density of $z \mid v$ and the density of y_{n-j+1} from Exercise 7.35(a),

$$\begin{aligned} f_z(l) &= \int_{-\infty}^{\infty} \left(\binom{m}{l} (1 - F(v))^l F(v)^{m-l} \right) \\ &\quad \times \left(\frac{n!}{(n-j)!(j-1)!} f(v) F(v)^{n-j} (1 - F(v))^{j-1} \right) \mathrm{d}v \\ &= \frac{n! m!}{l!(j-1)!(n-j)!\,(m-l)!} \int_{-\infty}^{\infty} (1 - F(v))^{l+j-1} F(v)^{n+m-l-j} \, \mathrm{d}F(v) \end{aligned}$$

for $l = 0, 1, \ldots, m$. Now consider the change of variable $u = F(v) \in [0, 1]$. This simplifies the integral to

$$\begin{aligned} f_z(l) &= \frac{n!m!}{l!(j-1)!(n-j)!\,(m-l)!}\int_0^1 (1-u)^{l+j-1}\,u^{n+m-l-j}\,\mathrm{d}u \\ &= \frac{(l+j-1)!\,(n+m-l-j)!n!m!}{l!(j-1)!(n-j)!\,(m-l)!\,(n+m)!} \\ &= \frac{\binom{l+j-1}{l}\binom{n+m-l-j}{m-l}}{\binom{n+m}{m}} = \frac{\binom{-j}{l}\binom{j-n-1}{m-l}}{\binom{-n-1}{m}} \end{aligned}$$

by the standard beta integral (see Chapter 1) or the integral of the standard beta density (see Table 4.2), and relations such as

$$\binom{l+j-1}{l} = (-1)^l\binom{-j}{l}$$

from (4.1). This p.d.f. is the negative hypergeometric $z \sim \text{Hyp}(-n-1,-j,m)$ seen in Exercise 4.7(d). Notice the invariance of this density of z with respect to the underlying density f of the data x: the result holds for *any* continuous variate, a type of "invariance" result that will be revisited in Chapter 10 in the context of $n \to \infty$. To illustrate this, when $m = 2$ and $j = 1$, $f_z(l)$ gives

$$\Pr(z=0) = \frac{n}{n+2},\quad \Pr(z=1) = \frac{2n}{(n+1)(n+2)},\quad \Pr(z=2) = \frac{2}{(n+1)(n+2)},$$

for any continuous variate. These probabilities add up to 100%, with $z = 0$ (no exceedance of previous record) the most likely event when $n \geqslant m = 2$ here. This simple result matches very closely the observed outcomes when stock returns follow a random walk like that assumed in Exercise 4.23(b) and the Note to it.

***Exercise 7.38 (Uniform and beta, from continuous c.d.f.s: the PIT)** Let z be a continuous random variable with p.d.f. $f(w)$ and c.d.f. $F(w)$. Consider the random sample $z_1,\dots,z_n$, with corresponding order statistics $y_1,\dots,y_n$. Show that $F(y_i)$ follows a Beta($i, n-i+1$) distribution, where we stress that the argument y_i of $F(\cdot)$ is random. [Hint: Start by establishing that $F(z) \sim \text{U}_{(0,1)}$, then use it in Exercise 7.35(a).]

Solution

We start with the easiest case, where $F(w)$ is strictly increasing, rather than simply non-decreasing. Then, $F(w) = p \in (0,1)$ implies the existence of the inverse function $w = F^{-1}(p)$, and we have

$$\Pr(F(z) \leqslant p) = \Pr\left(z \leqslant F^{-1}(p)\right) \equiv F\left(F^{-1}(p)\right) = p,$$

which we recognize as the c.d.f. of a standard uniform variate, regardless of the functional form of F. This implies that $F(y_1),\dots,F(y_n)$ are the order statistics from a standard uniform distribution and thus, by Exercise 7.35(a),

$$f_{F(y_i)}(p_i) = \begin{cases} \frac{n!}{(n-i)!(i-1)!} p_i^{i-1}(1-p_i)^{n-i} & (0 < p_i < 1), \\ 0 & (\text{elsewhere}), \end{cases}$$

which is a Beta$(i, n-i+1)$ density. We now turn to the more general case where $F(w)$ is nondecreasing.

Recall the general definition of the p quantile as being the smallest w satisfying $F(w) \geqslant p$, the case here being one of a continuous c.d.f. where the inequality becomes an equality. We define the quantile function $Q(p)$ as the smallest w satisfying $F(w) = p$. Then,

$$\begin{aligned} \Pr(F(z) \leqslant p) &= \Pr(z \leqslant Q(p)) + \Pr(z \in \text{interval where } F(z) \text{ is constant at } p) \\ &= \Pr(z \leqslant Q(p)) \equiv F(Q(p)) = F(w) = p, \end{aligned}$$

which identifies the c.d.f. of $F(z)$ as the standard uniform. The distribution of $F(y_i)$ follows as before.

Exercise 7.39 (Representation of continuous r.v.s in terms of uniforms, via the PIT) In Exercise 7.38, it was established that $F_z(z) \sim \mathrm{U}_{(0,1)}$ for any continuous variate z having c.d.f. F_z. Letting $x \sim \mathrm{U}_{(0,1)}$, use the PIT to show that:
(a) $\cot(\pi x)$ is a standard Cauchy variate;
(b) $-\log(x)$ is a standard exponential variate.

Solution

(a) We saw in Exercise 4.35 that a Cauchy variate can be represented as a ratio of two independent standard normals, and that its c.d.f. is

$$F_z(w) = \frac{\cot^{-1}(-w)}{\pi} = 1 - \frac{\cot^{-1}(w)}{\pi}.$$

Here, we give a representation in terms of a transformed uniform variate, instead of two normal variates. There are two possible routes to the same result. The first is to solve

$$x = F_z(z)$$

using the first expression for the c.d.f. as $x = \cot^{-1}(-z)/\pi$, hence $-z = \cot(\pi x)$. Since z is standard Cauchy, then so is $-z$. Therefore, $\cot(\pi x)$ is standard Cauchy. The second route uses the fact that if $x \sim \mathrm{U}_{(0,1)}$ then $1 - x \sim \mathrm{U}_{(0,1)}$ also. Using the second form of F_z to solve

$$1 - x = 1 - \frac{\cot^{-1}(z)}{\pi},$$

we get $z = \cot(\pi x)$.

(b) We saw this result earlier in Exercise 7.7, but here we use the PIT shortcut (no pun intended!). Let $z \in \mathbb{R}_-$ have the c.d.f. $F_z(w) = \exp(w)$ for $w \in \mathbb{R}_-$ and $F_z(w) = 1$ elsewhere, that is, $-z$ is a standard exponential. Solving $x = F_z(z) \equiv \exp(z)$ tells us that z has the same distribution as $\log(x)$. Therefore, $-\log(x)$ is a standard exponential variate.

Exercise 7.40 (Copula's uniqueness for continuous variates) Define implicitly the copula function C by

$$F(\boldsymbol{w}) = C(F_1(w_1), \dots, F_m(w_m)),$$

where $F(\boldsymbol{w})$ is the c.d.f. of $\boldsymbol{z}$ and $F_j(w_j)$ are its marginals, $j = 1, \dots, m$. Assuming that $\boldsymbol{z}$ is a continuous variate, derive the explicit formula for C.

Solution

Exercise 7.38 showed that $F_j(z_j) \sim \mathrm{U}_{(0,1)}$ for *any* continuous z_j, and that the quantile function $Q_j(p_j) = w_j$ satisfies $F_j(Q_j(p_j)) = p_j$ for all $p_j \in (0,1)$ uniquely. Substituting for $\boldsymbol{w}$ into the implicit definition of a copula,

$$F(Q_1(p_1), \dots, Q_m(p_m)) = C(F_1(Q_1(p_1)), \dots, F_m(Q_m(p_m))) = C(p_1, \dots, p_m).$$

In other words, $C(p_1, \dots, p_m) = F(Q_1(p_1), \dots, Q_m(p_m))$ uniquely for all $p_j \in (0,1)$, which is the formula for C in terms of the quantile functions ("inverse" c.d.f.s) $Q_j(p_j)$. The argument of C can be interpreted as the realization of m standard-uniform variates, regardless of what type of continuous variates the z_j's are, thus defining C independently of the marginal distributions. Recall that Exercise 5.19 demonstrated that the copula is a c.d.f. mapping $[0,1]^m \to [0,1]$.

Notes

General references for this chapter are the same as for Chapter 6.

Helmert's matrix (Exercise 7.16) has $(1/\sqrt{n})\boldsymbol{\imath}'$ as its first row, and the remainder are linearly independent vectors orthogonal to $\boldsymbol{\imath}$. Therefore, by Exercise 8.74 of our companion volume, Abadir and Magnus (2005), Helmert's matrix can be used to diagonalize equicorrelation matrices (defined in Exercise 6.22).

Section 7.1 presupposes knowledge of the underlying distribution when (say) x is transformed into y. In a context more general than that of Taylor expansions, Abadir and Cornea-Madeira (2018) derived expansions formulating the expectations of y in terms of the expectations of x, when the distributions of these variates are not known.

Exercise 7.20 is due to Grimmett and Stirzaker (2001, p. 111). Similar warnings can be found in Billingsley (1995, p. 441).

The p.d.f. of the product of normals (mentioned in Exercise 7.22) was derived by Craig (1936) and its c.d.f. in Abadir (1993b, Theorem 3.1(b), p. 193). Meng (2005, p. 147) extended Exercise 7.24(e) to the case when j is not an integer by splitting it into an integer and a remainder, then integrating the c.f. one more time to cope with the latter part. The same paper gives various applications of the formula, showing how it can succeed more easily than direct approaches to obtaining the moments, in difficult problems where the c.f. is easily available but the p.d.f. is not.

The "statistical" proof (which uses the conditioning shortcut) of the transformation theorem in Exercise 7.32 is from Abadir and Magnus (2007), where some historical background is also given. Earlier proofs (for arbitrary mathematical functions) typically resorted to advanced results in calculus, on differential forms and changes of variables of integration; for example, see Rudin (1976, Chapter 10). They are lengthier and more elaborate than is needed to transform statistical density functions for continuous variates.

The transformations of Section 7.3 are very useful for generating random variables by simulation, starting from uniform variates that are relatively easily to generate. There are two prominent approaches to doing so. First, if $x \sim \mathrm{U}_{(0,1)}$ then we can generate any continuous y-variate having c.d.f. F_y from $F_y^{-1}(x)$ when F_y^{-1} is known explicitly. This was illustrated in Exercise 7.39. Second, an alternative approach would be to use (bivariate) transformations as in Exercise 7.26.

8

The multivariate normal and functions thereof

Before concluding the first part of this book, we need to take a closer look at the multivariate normal distribution, which will arise repeatedly later on. There are natural phenomena that give rise to it; for example, see Exercise 6.2. It will also be very useful in dealing with large-sample theory, the "asymptotic theory" of later chapters.

We have seen in Exercise 7.15 that linear combinations of independent normals are also normal, but is this still the case if the components of the sum are not independent? The answer is negative, in general. Exercise 2.22 implies a counterexample: let $x \sim \mathrm{N}(0,1)$ and toss a fair coin to define

$$z := \begin{cases} -x & \text{if a tail comes up} \\ x & \text{if a head comes up.} \end{cases}$$

The unconditional (or mixed) density of z is

$$f_z(w) = \frac{1}{2}\phi(-w) + \frac{1}{2}\phi(w) = \frac{1}{2}\phi(w) + \frac{1}{2}\phi(w) = \phi(w),$$

hence $z \sim \mathrm{N}(0,1)$. However, the linear combination $z + x$ is such that

$$z + x = \begin{cases} 0 & \text{if a tail comes up} \\ 2x & \text{if a head comes up,} \end{cases}$$

which is not a normal variate (unconditionally) because $\Pr(z + x = 0) = \frac{1}{2}$, that is, the c.d.f. F_{z+x} has a jump at the origin. The *nonlinear* dependence linking z and x is responsible for this result.

This leads us to the following definition, where linearity plays a crucial role. An $m \times 1$ vector $\boldsymbol{x}$ is said to have a *multivariate* (or *joint*) *normal* distribution, denoted by $\boldsymbol{x} \sim \mathrm{N}(\boldsymbol{\mu}, \boldsymbol{\Sigma})$ or $\boldsymbol{x} \sim \mathrm{N}_m(\boldsymbol{\mu}, \boldsymbol{\Sigma})$, if and only if any arbitrary linear combination $\boldsymbol{a}'\boldsymbol{x}$ is normally distributed, where $\boldsymbol{a} \in \mathbb{R}^m$ is nonrandom. This definition should be treated carefully. There are cases where two normal variates need not be jointly normal, as we saw in the previous paragraph. Another illustration of this pitfall will be given in Exercise 8.9, where uncorrelated normals could be dependent. This cautioning aside, we shall usually drop the adjective "joint", unless doing so leads to ambiguity.

Exercise 8.5 will show that our definition of the multivariate normal is equivalent to the variate possessing the characteristic function

$$\varphi_{\boldsymbol{x}}(\boldsymbol{\tau}) = \exp\left(\mathrm{i}\boldsymbol{\mu}'\boldsymbol{\tau} - \frac{1}{2}\boldsymbol{\tau}'\boldsymbol{\Sigma}\boldsymbol{\tau}\right).$$

Furthermore, when $\boldsymbol{\Sigma}$ is nonsingular, the definition implies the density function defined (without proof) in Chapter 6, and to be derived in Exercise 8.8(b) in this chapter, namely

$$f_{\boldsymbol{x}}(\boldsymbol{w}) = (2\pi)^{-m/2} |\boldsymbol{\Sigma}|^{-1/2} \exp\left(-\frac{1}{2}(\boldsymbol{w}-\boldsymbol{\mu})'\boldsymbol{\Sigma}^{-1}(\boldsymbol{w}-\boldsymbol{\mu})\right). \tag{8.1}$$

The nonsingular normal is therefore a special case of elliptical distributions, for which we have already derived a number of results. For example, Exercise 8.13 will show that partitioning

$$\boldsymbol{x} = \begin{pmatrix} \boldsymbol{x}_1 \\ \boldsymbol{x}_2 \end{pmatrix}, \quad \boldsymbol{\mu} = \begin{pmatrix} \boldsymbol{\mu}_1 \\ \boldsymbol{\mu}_2 \end{pmatrix}, \quad \boldsymbol{\Sigma} = \begin{pmatrix} \boldsymbol{\Sigma}_{11} & \boldsymbol{\Sigma}_{12} \\ \boldsymbol{\Sigma}_{21} & \boldsymbol{\Sigma}_{22} \end{pmatrix},$$

where $\boldsymbol{x}_1$ and $\boldsymbol{x}_2$ have dimensions $k > 0$ and $m - k > 0$, respectively, yields

$$\boldsymbol{x}_1 \mid \boldsymbol{x}_2 \sim \mathrm{N}(\boldsymbol{\mu}_1 + \boldsymbol{\Sigma}_{12}\boldsymbol{\Sigma}_{22}^{-1}(\boldsymbol{x}_2 - \boldsymbol{\mu}_2), \boldsymbol{\Sigma}_{11|2});$$

here the conditional variance is $\boldsymbol{\Sigma}_{11|2} := \boldsymbol{\Sigma}_{11} - \boldsymbol{\Sigma}_{12}\boldsymbol{\Sigma}_{22}^{-1}\boldsymbol{\Sigma}_{21}$, which is the Schur complement (see Section A.4) of $\boldsymbol{\Sigma}_{22}$. The alternative notation $\boldsymbol{\Sigma}_{11\cdot 2}$ exists; see the Notes to Chapter 6. Note that $\boldsymbol{\Sigma}_{11|2}^{-1}$ is the first diagonal block of the partitioned inverse of $\boldsymbol{\Sigma}$, and that

$$|\boldsymbol{\Sigma}| = |\boldsymbol{\Sigma}_{22}| \times |\boldsymbol{\Sigma}_{11|2}|.$$

If an elliptically distributed variate possesses a finite mean, then its conditional expectation is linear; see Exercise 6.51. This feature applies to the special case of the normal, as we have just seen. However, the normal has another feature not shared by ellipticals in general: $\boldsymbol{x}_1 \mid \boldsymbol{x}_2$ has a conditional variance that is independent of $\boldsymbol{x}_2$.

Many results mentioned earlier are made possible by a transformation that we saw in Exercise 6.49, in the general setup of elliptical distributions, and that we will repeat here. Let $\boldsymbol{z} \sim \mathrm{N}(\boldsymbol{0}, \boldsymbol{I}_n)$ and define $\boldsymbol{y} := \boldsymbol{\mu} + \boldsymbol{A}'\boldsymbol{z}$, where $\boldsymbol{\mu}$ and $\boldsymbol{A}$ are nonrandom and $\boldsymbol{A}$ is $n \times m$. We will prove in Exercise 8.8(a) that the linear transformation of $\boldsymbol{z}$ into $\boldsymbol{y}$ yields a new set of joint normals, $\boldsymbol{y} \sim \mathrm{N}_m(\boldsymbol{\mu}, \boldsymbol{A}'\boldsymbol{A})$, where $\boldsymbol{A}'\boldsymbol{A}$ is square but possibly singular (for example if $m > n$). Many results follows from this, such as the density in (8.1). Exercise 8.10 will also use this transformation to show that this multivariate normal is the *only* elliptical distribution where zero correlation (hence lack of a linear relation) between the components implies their complete independence! This is another reflection of the close connection between the multivariate normal and linearity.

We will also be interested in quadratic forms of the type $\boldsymbol{z}'\boldsymbol{B}\boldsymbol{z}$ or $\boldsymbol{y}'\boldsymbol{B}\boldsymbol{y}$, where we will assume without loss of generality (see Exercise 6.8) that $\boldsymbol{B}$ is symmetric. We also assume that $\boldsymbol{B}$ is nonrandom, unless stated otherwise. Some features of general quadratic forms have been worked out in Exercises 6.6 and 6.7. Let us specialize the result of the latter to $\boldsymbol{z} \sim \mathrm{N}(\mathbf{0}, \boldsymbol{I}_n)$, where $\gamma := \mathrm{E}\left(z_i^3\right) = 0$ and $\kappa := \mathrm{E}\left(z_i^4\right) - 3 = 0$ (by Exercise 4.24): defining $\boldsymbol{y} := \boldsymbol{\mu} + \boldsymbol{A}'\boldsymbol{z}$ gives

$$\operatorname{var}\left(\boldsymbol{z}'\boldsymbol{B}\boldsymbol{z}\right) = 2\operatorname{tr}\left(\boldsymbol{B}^2\right) \quad \text{and} \quad \operatorname{var}\left(\boldsymbol{y}'\boldsymbol{y}\right) = 4\boldsymbol{\mu}'\boldsymbol{A}'\boldsymbol{A}\boldsymbol{\mu} + 2\operatorname{tr}\left(\boldsymbol{Q}^2\right),$$

where $\boldsymbol{Q} := \boldsymbol{A}\boldsymbol{A}'$. These results can be used indirectly too. For example, define $\boldsymbol{x} := \boldsymbol{\Sigma}^{1/2}\boldsymbol{z}$, where $\boldsymbol{\Sigma}^{1/2}$ is the unique symmetric square root of the positive definite matrix $\boldsymbol{\Sigma}$. Then $\boldsymbol{x} \sim \mathrm{N}\left(\mathbf{0}, \boldsymbol{\Sigma}\right)$ and

$$\begin{aligned}\operatorname{var}\left(\boldsymbol{x}'\boldsymbol{B}\boldsymbol{x}\right) &= \operatorname{var}\left(\boldsymbol{z}'\boldsymbol{\Sigma}^{1/2}\boldsymbol{B}\boldsymbol{\Sigma}^{1/2}\boldsymbol{z}\right) = 2\operatorname{tr}\left(\left(\boldsymbol{\Sigma}^{1/2}\boldsymbol{B}\boldsymbol{\Sigma}^{1/2}\right)^2\right)\\ &= 2\operatorname{tr}\left(\boldsymbol{\Sigma}^{1/2}\boldsymbol{B}\boldsymbol{\Sigma}\boldsymbol{B}\boldsymbol{\Sigma}^{1/2}\right) = 2\operatorname{tr}\left(\left(\boldsymbol{B}\boldsymbol{\Sigma}\right)^2\right)\end{aligned}$$

for any arbitrary symmetric (possibly singular) matrix $\boldsymbol{B}$. This result can be generalized to the covariance of two quadratic forms by means of

$$\mathrm{E}\left(\boldsymbol{x}'\boldsymbol{B}\boldsymbol{x}\right) = \mathrm{E}\left(\operatorname{tr}\left(\boldsymbol{B}\boldsymbol{x}\boldsymbol{x}'\right)\right) = \operatorname{tr}\left(\boldsymbol{B}\,\mathrm{E}\left(\boldsymbol{x}\boldsymbol{x}'\right)\right) = \operatorname{tr}\left(\boldsymbol{B}\boldsymbol{\Sigma}\right)$$

and Exercise 8.35, where a special case gives rise to the fourth-order moments of the multivariate normal. Covariances for related nonlinear functions have already been analyzed in Exercise 6.14 for variates that are not necessarily normal, and in Exercise 6.15 for univariate normals.

There are two striking results which have not been mentioned so far, and which are connected to one another. First, *Cramér's deconvolution theorem* states that for $y := x_1 + x_2$, where x_1 and x_2 are independent variates, we have the following equivalence: y is normal *if and only if* x_1 and x_2 are both normal. See Exercise 8.7 for a proof that assumes the m.g.f.s of x_1 and x_2 exist. For discrete variates, there is a parallel to this result, relying on the Poisson distribution instead of the normal. It is due to Raikov, and we saw it in Exercise 4.8.

The second striking result is in Exercise 8.34, and its proof depends on Cramér's deconvolution theorem. From earlier chapters, we know that if $\{x_n\} \sim \mathrm{IN}(\mu, \sigma^2)$ (so independent *and* identical normals), then $\overline{x} := n^{-1}\sum_{i=1}^n x_i \sim \mathrm{N}(\mu, \sigma^2/n)$ independently of $\sum_{i=1}^n (x_i - \overline{x})^2/\sigma^2 \sim \chi^2(n-1)$. Now let x_i ($i = 1, \dots, n$, where $2 \leqslant n < \infty$) be independent but not necessarily identically distributed: it turns out that the reverse implication is also true! Furthermore, when $n \geqslant 3$, a less restrictive version of this reverse implication is possible: if $\overline{x} \sim \mathrm{N}(\mu, \sigma^2/n)$ and $\sum_{i=1}^n (x_i - \overline{x})^2/\sigma^2 \sim \chi^2(n-1)$ (where the normal is not assumed to be independent of the χ^2), then $\{x_n\} \sim \mathrm{IN}(\mu, \sigma^2)$.

The exercises in this chapter are broadly divided into two categories, one describing properties of the multivariate normal and the other working out the implied properties of quadratic functions of normals. The exercises are predominantly about the normal distribution, but occasionally also about the class of ellipticals to which some properties readily extend.

8.1 Properties of the multivariate normal

Exercise 8.1 (Mahalanobis distances) Evaluate c, $\boldsymbol{\mu}$, and $\boldsymbol{\Sigma}$ for the following normal densities:
(a) $c\exp(-\frac{1}{2}(u-1)^2-\frac{1}{2}(v-2)^2)$;
(b) $c\exp(-\frac{1}{2}\left(u^2+v^2+4w^2+2uw-2u-4w+\frac{4}{3}\right))$;
(c) $c\exp(-\frac{1}{2}\left(2u^2+2v^2+w^2-2uv-2vw+2u+2w+6\right))$;
(d) $c\exp(-\frac{1}{2}\left(u^2+v^2+4u-6v+13\right))$;
(e) $c\exp(-\frac{1}{2}\left(2u^2+v^2+2uv-22u-14v+65\right))$.

Solution
Write the m-dimensional normal density as

$$f(\boldsymbol{w}) = c\exp\left(-\frac{1}{2}(\boldsymbol{w}-\boldsymbol{\mu})'\boldsymbol{\Sigma}^{-1}(\boldsymbol{w}-\boldsymbol{\mu})\right)$$

with $c=(2\pi)^{-m/2}|\boldsymbol{\Sigma}|^{-1/2}$. Then, first calculating $\boldsymbol{\mu}$ and $\boldsymbol{\Sigma}^{-1}$, we find
(a)

$$\boldsymbol{\mu}=\begin{pmatrix}1\\2\end{pmatrix},\quad \boldsymbol{\Sigma}^{-1}=\begin{pmatrix}1&0\\0&1\end{pmatrix},\quad \boldsymbol{\Sigma}=\begin{pmatrix}1&0\\0&1\end{pmatrix},\quad c=\frac{1}{2\pi};$$

(b)

$$\boldsymbol{\mu}=\begin{pmatrix}2/3\\0\\1/3\end{pmatrix},\quad \boldsymbol{\Sigma}^{-1}=\begin{pmatrix}1&0&1\\0&1&0\\1&0&4\end{pmatrix},\quad \boldsymbol{\Sigma}=\frac{1}{3}\begin{pmatrix}4&0&-1\\0&3&0\\-1&0&1\end{pmatrix},\quad c=(2\pi)^{-3/2}\sqrt{3};$$

(c)

$$\boldsymbol{\mu}=\begin{pmatrix}-2\\-3\\-4\end{pmatrix},\quad \boldsymbol{\Sigma}^{-1}=\begin{pmatrix}2&-1&0\\-1&2&-1\\0&-1&1\end{pmatrix},\quad \boldsymbol{\Sigma}=\begin{pmatrix}1&1&1\\1&2&2\\1&2&3\end{pmatrix},\quad c=(2\pi)^{-3/2};$$

(d)

$$\boldsymbol{\mu}=\begin{pmatrix}-2\\3\end{pmatrix},\quad \boldsymbol{\Sigma}^{-1}=\begin{pmatrix}1&0\\0&1\end{pmatrix},\quad \boldsymbol{\Sigma}=\begin{pmatrix}1&0\\0&1\end{pmatrix},\quad c=\frac{1}{2\pi};$$

(e)

$$\boldsymbol{\mu}=\begin{pmatrix}4\\3\end{pmatrix},\quad \boldsymbol{\Sigma}^{-1}=\begin{pmatrix}2&1\\1&1\end{pmatrix},\quad \boldsymbol{\Sigma}=\begin{pmatrix}1&-1\\-1&2\end{pmatrix},\quad c=\frac{1}{2\pi}.$$

Exercise 8.2 (Independent normal increments) Let $(x, y, z)'$ be trivariate normal with mean $\mathbf{0}$. Assume that $\operatorname{var}(x) = 1$, $\operatorname{var}(x - y) = 1$, and $\operatorname{var}(z - y) = 1$ and that x, $x - y$, and $z - y$ are independent. Evaluate the variance matrix of (x, y, z).

Solution

We have to solve six equations with six unknowns:

$$\begin{aligned}
\operatorname{var}(x) &= 1, \\
\operatorname{var}(x-y) &= \operatorname{var}(x) + \operatorname{var}(y) - 2\operatorname{cov}(x,y) = 1, \\
\operatorname{var}(z-y) &= \operatorname{var}(z) + \operatorname{var}(y) - 2\operatorname{cov}(z,y) = 1, \\
\operatorname{cov}(x, x-y) &= \operatorname{var}(x) - \operatorname{cov}(x,y) = 0, \\
\operatorname{cov}(x, z-y) &= \operatorname{cov}(x,z) - \operatorname{cov}(x,y) = 0, \\
\operatorname{cov}(x-y, z-y) &= \operatorname{cov}(x,z) - \operatorname{cov}(x,y) - \operatorname{cov}(y,z) + \operatorname{var}(y) = 0.
\end{aligned}$$

We obtain the variance matrix

$$\boldsymbol{\Sigma} = \begin{pmatrix} 1 & 1 & 1 \\ 1 & 2 & 2 \\ 1 & 2 & 3 \end{pmatrix}.$$

Alternatively, the problem states directly that

$$\begin{pmatrix} x \\ x-y \\ z-y \end{pmatrix} = \begin{pmatrix} 1 & 0 & 0 \\ 1 & -1 & 0 \\ 0 & -1 & 1 \end{pmatrix} \begin{pmatrix} x \\ y \\ z \end{pmatrix} \sim \mathrm{N}(\mathbf{0}, \boldsymbol{I}_3),$$

whereupon premultiplying both sides by the inverse of the square matrix gives that $(x, y, z)'$ is normal with mean $\mathbf{0}$ and variance as follows:

$$\begin{pmatrix} 1 & 0 & 0 \\ 1 & -1 & 0 \\ 0 & -1 & 1 \end{pmatrix}^{-1} \begin{pmatrix} 1 & 0 & 0 \\ 0 & 1 & 0 \\ 0 & 0 & 1 \end{pmatrix} \begin{pmatrix} 1 & 1 & 0 \\ 0 & -1 & -1 \\ 0 & 0 & 1 \end{pmatrix}^{-1} = \begin{pmatrix} 1 & 0 & 0 \\ 1 & -1 & 0 \\ 1 & -1 & 1 \end{pmatrix} \begin{pmatrix} 1 & 1 & 1 \\ 0 & -1 & -1 \\ 0 & 0 & 1 \end{pmatrix} = \begin{pmatrix} 1 & 1 & 1 \\ 1 & 2 & 2 \\ 1 & 2 & 3 \end{pmatrix}.$$

Exercise 8.3 (Covariance of sum and difference: normals) Let (x, y) follow a bivariate normal distribution with variance matrix $\boldsymbol{\Sigma}$. If $x + 2y$ and $x - 2y$ are independent, what can be said about $\boldsymbol{\Sigma}$?

Solution

There is one restriction, namely that $\operatorname{cov}(x + 2y, x - 2y) = 0$, which we expand into

$$\operatorname{var}(x) - 2\operatorname{cov}(x,y) + 2\operatorname{cov}(y,x) - 4\operatorname{var}(y) = \operatorname{var}(x) - 4\operatorname{var}(y) = 0.$$

Therefore, the variance matrix takes the form

$$\boldsymbol{\Sigma} = \sigma^2 \begin{pmatrix} 4 & 2\rho \\ 2\rho & 1 \end{pmatrix},$$

where ρ is the correlation between x and y.

Exercise 8.4 (Normal's definition: moments) Let $\boldsymbol{x} \sim \mathrm{N}_m(\boldsymbol{\mu}, \boldsymbol{\Sigma})$. Show that $\boldsymbol{a}'\boldsymbol{x} \sim \mathrm{N}(\boldsymbol{a}'\boldsymbol{\mu}, \boldsymbol{a}'\boldsymbol{\Sigma}\boldsymbol{a})$ for all nonrandom $\boldsymbol{a} \in \mathbb{R}^m$.

Solution

By definition of the joint normal, $\boldsymbol{a}'\boldsymbol{x}$ is normally distributed. Therefore, all we need to do is to derive the first two moments of $\boldsymbol{a}'\boldsymbol{x}$, then the normal distribution of $\boldsymbol{a}'\boldsymbol{x}$ is fully specified. First, we have

$$\mathrm{E}\left(\boldsymbol{a}'\boldsymbol{x}\right) = \boldsymbol{a}' \mathrm{E}\left(\boldsymbol{x}\right) = \boldsymbol{a}'\boldsymbol{\mu}$$

as $\boldsymbol{a}$ is nonrandom. Second, using the fact that $\boldsymbol{a}'\boldsymbol{x} = \boldsymbol{x}'\boldsymbol{a}$ since both are 1×1,

$$\begin{aligned} \mathrm{var}\left(\boldsymbol{a}'\boldsymbol{x}\right) &= \mathrm{E}\left(\left(\boldsymbol{a}'\boldsymbol{x} - \boldsymbol{a}'\boldsymbol{\mu}\right)^2\right) = \mathrm{E}\left(\left(\boldsymbol{a}'\boldsymbol{x} - \boldsymbol{a}'\boldsymbol{\mu}\right)\left(\boldsymbol{x}'\boldsymbol{a} - \boldsymbol{\mu}'\boldsymbol{a}\right)\right) \\ &= \boldsymbol{a}' \mathrm{E}\left(\left(\boldsymbol{x} - \boldsymbol{\mu}\right)\left(\boldsymbol{x} - \boldsymbol{\mu}\right)'\right)\boldsymbol{a} = \boldsymbol{a}' \mathrm{var}\left(\boldsymbol{x}\right)\boldsymbol{a} = \boldsymbol{a}'\boldsymbol{\Sigma}\boldsymbol{a}. \end{aligned}$$

Exercise 8.5 (Normal's definition: m.g.f.) Derive the m.g.f. of $\boldsymbol{x} \sim \mathrm{N}_m(\boldsymbol{\mu}, \boldsymbol{\Sigma})$, and use it to obtain $\mathrm{E}\left(\boldsymbol{x}\right)$ and $\mathrm{var}\left(\boldsymbol{x}\right)$.

Solution

As seen in Exercise 8.4, the joint normal satisfies $\boldsymbol{a}'\boldsymbol{x} \sim \mathrm{N}(\boldsymbol{a}'\boldsymbol{\mu}, \boldsymbol{a}'\boldsymbol{\Sigma}\boldsymbol{a})$ for all nonrandom $\boldsymbol{a} \in \mathbb{R}^m$, and this univariate normal $\boldsymbol{a}'\boldsymbol{x}$ has a known m.g.f.; see, for example, Chapter 4. Hence,

$$\mathrm{E}\left(\mathrm{e}^{\boldsymbol{a}'\boldsymbol{x}}\right) = m_{\boldsymbol{a}'\boldsymbol{x}}\left(1\right) = \mathrm{e}^{\boldsymbol{a}'\boldsymbol{\mu} + \frac{1}{2}\boldsymbol{a}'\boldsymbol{\Sigma}\boldsymbol{a}},$$

where $m_{\boldsymbol{a}'\boldsymbol{x}}\left(t\right)$ is the m.g.f. of $\boldsymbol{a}'\boldsymbol{x}$. So, the joint m.g.f. of $\boldsymbol{x}$ is

$$m_{\boldsymbol{x}}\left(\boldsymbol{t}\right) := \mathrm{E}\left(\mathrm{e}^{\boldsymbol{t}'\boldsymbol{x}}\right) = \mathrm{e}^{\boldsymbol{t}'\boldsymbol{\mu} + \frac{1}{2}\boldsymbol{t}'\boldsymbol{\Sigma}\boldsymbol{t}}$$

for $\boldsymbol{t} \in \mathbb{R}^m$.

The moments are obtained from the joint m.g.f. by differentiation. For the mean,

$$\mathrm{E}\left(\boldsymbol{x}\right) = \left.\frac{\partial m_{\boldsymbol{x}}\left(\boldsymbol{t}\right)}{\partial \boldsymbol{t}}\right|_{\boldsymbol{t}=\mathbf{0}} = \left.\left(\boldsymbol{\mu} + \boldsymbol{\Sigma}\boldsymbol{t}\right)\mathrm{e}^{\boldsymbol{t}'\boldsymbol{\mu} + \frac{1}{2}\boldsymbol{t}'\boldsymbol{\Sigma}\boldsymbol{t}}\right|_{\boldsymbol{t}=\mathbf{0}} = \boldsymbol{\mu}.$$

For the variance, we could differentiate twice to obtain $\mathrm{E}\left(\boldsymbol{x}\boldsymbol{x}'\right)$, then subtract $\mathrm{E}\left(\boldsymbol{x}\right)\mathrm{E}\left(\boldsymbol{x}\right)'$, as in Exercise 7.31(c). However, Exercise 3.22 gives us a shortcut for generating central moments, namely by differentiating $\mathrm{E}\left(\mathrm{e}^{\boldsymbol{t}'(\boldsymbol{x}-\boldsymbol{\mu})}\right) = m_{\boldsymbol{x}}\left(\boldsymbol{t}\right)\mathrm{e}^{-\boldsymbol{t}'\boldsymbol{\mu}}$ instead of $m_{\boldsymbol{x}}\left(\boldsymbol{t}\right)$.

Therefore,

$$\operatorname{var}(\boldsymbol{x}) = \left.\frac{\partial^2 \left(\mathrm{e}^{\frac{1}{2}\boldsymbol{t}'\boldsymbol{\Sigma}\boldsymbol{t}}\right)}{\partial \boldsymbol{t}\partial \boldsymbol{t}'}\right|_{\boldsymbol{t}=\boldsymbol{0}} = \left.\frac{\partial \left(\boldsymbol{t}'\boldsymbol{\Sigma}\mathrm{e}^{\frac{1}{2}\boldsymbol{t}'\boldsymbol{\Sigma}\boldsymbol{t}}\right)}{\partial \boldsymbol{t}}\right|_{\boldsymbol{t}=\boldsymbol{0}}$$
$$= \left.\left(\boldsymbol{\Sigma}\mathrm{e}^{\frac{1}{2}\boldsymbol{t}'\boldsymbol{\Sigma}\boldsymbol{t}} + \boldsymbol{\Sigma}\boldsymbol{t}\boldsymbol{t}'\boldsymbol{\Sigma}\mathrm{e}^{\frac{1}{2}\boldsymbol{t}'\boldsymbol{\Sigma}\boldsymbol{t}}\right)\right|_{\boldsymbol{t}=\boldsymbol{0}} = \boldsymbol{\Sigma}.$$

Exercise 8.6 (Normal m.g.f.'s convexity) Let x_1 and x_2 be two jointly normal variates.
(a) Show that $\log\left(\mathrm{E}\left(\mathrm{e}^{x_1+x_2}\right)\right) = \mathrm{E}(x_1+x_2) + \frac{1}{2}\operatorname{var}(x_1+x_2)$.
(b) How does (a) relate to Jensen's inequality?

Solution
(a) Since $y := x_1 + x_2$ is univariate normal,

$$\mathrm{E}\left(\mathrm{e}^{y}\right) = m_y(1) = \exp\left(\mathrm{E}(y) + \frac{1}{2}\operatorname{var}(y)\right),$$

and taking the logarithm gives the required result. Clearly, the derivations generalize to the sum of more than two variates.
(b) Recalling that $\exp(\cdot)$ is a convex function, (a) can be restated as

$$\mathrm{E}\left(\mathrm{e}^{y}\right) = \mathrm{e}^{\mathrm{E}(y)} \times \exp\left(\frac{1}{2}\operatorname{var}(y)\right) \geqslant \mathrm{e}^{\mathrm{E}(y)}$$

since $\operatorname{var}(y) \geqslant 0$. The relation $\mathrm{E}\left(\mathrm{e}^{y}\right) \geqslant \mathrm{e}^{\mathrm{E}(y)}$ can be viewed as a direct application of Jensen's inequality. In the case of a normal variate, we are able to quantify exactly the extent of the difference between the two sides. Notice that $\mathrm{E}(y)$ and $\operatorname{var}(y)$ differ by a factor $-\frac{1}{2}$ whenever $\mathrm{E}(\mathrm{e}^{y}) = 1$, and that e^{y} is a log-normal variate. This explains the factor linking the two log-normal parameters of Exercise 4.14(b).

***Exercise 8.7 (Cramér's deconvolution theorem)** Let x_1 and x_2 be independent variates having m.g.f.s $m_1(t_1)$ and $m_2(t_2)$, respectively, and define $y := x_1 + x_2$. Prove that y is normal if and only if x_1 and x_2 are both normal. [Hint: For the "only if" part, write the c.f. of y in terms of the c.f.s of x_1 and x_2, and use the bound for the c.f. of (say) x_2 to infer an inequality for the c.f. of x_1.]

Solution
The "if" part is easy to prove; see, for example, Exercise 7.15. The "only if" part is less obvious. We will assume that $y \sim \mathrm{N}(0,1)$, without loss of generality (the usual extension to $\mu + \sigma y$ applies). Then, the c.f. of y is

$$\mathrm{e}^{-t^2/2} = \mathrm{E}\left(\mathrm{e}^{\mathrm{i}ty}\right) = \mathrm{E}\left(\mathrm{e}^{\mathrm{i}t(x_1+x_2)}\right) = \mathrm{E}\left(\mathrm{e}^{\mathrm{i}tx_1}\right)\mathrm{E}\left(\mathrm{e}^{\mathrm{i}tx_2}\right) \equiv m_1(\mathrm{i}t)\, m_2(\mathrm{i}t),$$

where the factorization follows by the independence of x_1 and x_2. Note that, for t real-valued,

$$\left|\mathrm{E}\left(\mathrm{e}^{\mathrm{i}tx_2}\right)\right| \leqslant \mathrm{E}\left(\left|\mathrm{e}^{\mathrm{i}tx_2}\right|\right) = \mathrm{E}(1) = 1,$$

so we have $\mathrm{e}^{-t^2/2} \leqslant |m_1(\mathrm{i}t)|$ or equivalently

$$-2\log|m_1(\mathrm{i}t)| \leqslant t^2.$$

Since the m.g.f. of x_1 exists, all the derivatives of $m_1(\mathrm{i}t)$ are finite at $t = 0$ (by Exercise 3.26) and therefore $\log|m_1(\mathrm{i}t)|$ has the representation $\sum_{j=0}^{\infty} \alpha_j(\mathrm{i}t)^j$. For the displayed inequality to hold for general t, the power of t in this series cannot exceed 2. Hence,

$$\log|m_1(\mathrm{i}t)| = \alpha_1 \mathrm{i}t - \alpha_2 t^2$$

and there is no constant term in the polynomial because $m_1(0) = \mathrm{E}(\mathrm{e}^0) = 1$, by definition. We can restrict the coefficients further, but this is not required here. What we have shown is that $m_1(t) = \exp\left(\alpha_1 t + \alpha_2 t^2\right)$, which establishes normality for x_1. By the symmetry of the argument, x_2 is also normal.

Exercise 8.8 (Joint normals from independent ones) Let $z_1, \dots, z_n$ be a random sample from the $\mathrm{N}(0,1)$ distribution. Define $\boldsymbol{z} := (z_1, \dots, z_n)'$ and $\boldsymbol{y} := \boldsymbol{c} + \boldsymbol{A}'\boldsymbol{z}$, where $\boldsymbol{c}$ and $\boldsymbol{A}$ are nonrandom.
(a) What is the distribution of $\boldsymbol{y}$? What is the marginal distribution of any subset of $\boldsymbol{y}$?
(b) Let $\boldsymbol{A}$ be a nonsingular $n \times n$ matrix. Derive the p.d.f. of $\boldsymbol{y}$.
(c) Hence prove that y_i and y_j are independent if and only if $\operatorname{cov}(y_i, y_j) = 0$.

Solution
(a) We proceed in three steps to address the first question. First, if $z \sim \mathrm{N}(0,1)$ then $m_z(t) = \exp(\frac{1}{2}t^2)$. Second, by the independence of $z_1, \dots, z_n$,

$$m_{\boldsymbol{z}}(\boldsymbol{t}) \equiv \mathrm{E}\left(\mathrm{e}^{\sum_{i=1}^n t_i z_i}\right) \equiv \mathrm{E}\left(\prod_{i=1}^n \mathrm{e}^{t_i z_i}\right) = \prod_{i=1}^n \mathrm{E}\left(\mathrm{e}^{t_i z_i}\right) \equiv \prod_{i=1}^n m_{z_i}(t_i),$$

and hence $m_{\boldsymbol{z}}(\boldsymbol{t}) = \prod_{i=1}^n \exp(\frac{1}{2}t_i^2) = \exp(\frac{1}{2}\boldsymbol{t}'\boldsymbol{t})$. This identifies $\boldsymbol{z}$ as $\mathrm{N}(\boldsymbol{0}, \boldsymbol{I}_n)$, by Exercise 8.5. Third, if $\boldsymbol{y} = \boldsymbol{c} + \boldsymbol{A}'\boldsymbol{z}$, then

$$\begin{aligned} m_{\boldsymbol{y}}(\boldsymbol{t}) &= \mathrm{E}\left(\mathrm{e}^{\boldsymbol{t}'\boldsymbol{y}}\right) = \mathrm{E}\left(\mathrm{e}^{\boldsymbol{t}'(\boldsymbol{c}+\boldsymbol{A}'\boldsymbol{z})}\right) \\ &= \mathrm{e}^{\boldsymbol{t}'\boldsymbol{c}}\,\mathrm{E}\left(\mathrm{e}^{(\boldsymbol{A}\boldsymbol{t})'\boldsymbol{z}}\right) = \mathrm{e}^{\boldsymbol{t}'\boldsymbol{c}} m_{\boldsymbol{z}}(\boldsymbol{A}\boldsymbol{t}) = \mathrm{e}^{\boldsymbol{t}'\boldsymbol{c}+\frac{1}{2}\boldsymbol{t}'\boldsymbol{A}'\boldsymbol{A}\boldsymbol{t}}, \end{aligned}$$

which we identify (from Exercise 8.5) as the m.g.f. of a normal variate with mean $\boldsymbol{c}$ and variance $\boldsymbol{A}'\boldsymbol{A}$. This means that $\boldsymbol{y} \sim \mathrm{N}(\boldsymbol{\mu}, \boldsymbol{\Sigma})$, where $\boldsymbol{\mu} = \boldsymbol{c}$ and $\boldsymbol{\Sigma} = \boldsymbol{A}'\boldsymbol{A}$ is a positive semidefinite matrix.

Finally, in this part of the exercise, we have not assumed that $\boldsymbol{A}$ is a square matrix. We can therefore take $\boldsymbol{A}'$ to be an $m \times n$ selection matrix ($m < n$), that is, a column-permutation of the matrix $(\boldsymbol{I}_m, \mathbf{O})$, and the implication is that any subset of $\boldsymbol{y}$ is also

normally distributed. By the relation of normal to elliptical variates, the two results of (a) are in agreement with Exercises 6.49(a) and 7.31(b), respectively.
(b) We first obtain the p.d.f. of $\boldsymbol{z}$. Since the z_i's are independent, we have

$$f_{\boldsymbol{z}}(\boldsymbol{w}) = \prod_{i=1}^{n} \left(\frac{1}{\sqrt{2\pi}} \mathrm{e}^{-\frac{1}{2}w_i^2} \right) = (2\pi)^{-n/2} \mathrm{e}^{-\frac{1}{2}\boldsymbol{w}'\boldsymbol{w}} \equiv \phi(\boldsymbol{w}).$$

Next, consider the transformation from $\boldsymbol{z}$ to $\boldsymbol{y}$. Since $\boldsymbol{z} = \boldsymbol{A}'^{-1}(\boldsymbol{y} - \boldsymbol{\mu})$ with $\partial \boldsymbol{z}/\partial \boldsymbol{y}' = \boldsymbol{A}'^{-1}$, the transformation theorem gives us

$$\begin{aligned} f_{\boldsymbol{y}}(\boldsymbol{w_y}) &= (2\pi)^{-n/2} \left| \det \boldsymbol{A}^{-1} \right| \exp\left(-\frac{1}{2} (\boldsymbol{w_y} - \boldsymbol{\mu})' \boldsymbol{A}^{-1} \boldsymbol{A}'^{-1} (\boldsymbol{w_y} - \boldsymbol{\mu}) \right) \\ &= (2\pi)^{-n/2} (\det \boldsymbol{\Sigma})^{-1/2} \exp\left(-\frac{1}{2} (\boldsymbol{w_y} - \boldsymbol{\mu})' \boldsymbol{\Sigma}^{-1} (\boldsymbol{w_y} - \boldsymbol{\mu}) \right) \end{aligned}$$

by $\det \boldsymbol{\Sigma} = \det(\boldsymbol{A}'\boldsymbol{A}) = (\det \boldsymbol{A})^2 > 0$.
(c) From (a), we know that the bivariate distribution of (y_i, y_j) is also normal for $i \neq j$. Hence, for a nonsingular normal distribution,

$$\begin{aligned} & f_{y_i,y_j}(w_i, w_j) \\ &= \frac{1}{2\pi} \begin{vmatrix} \sigma_{ii} & \sigma_{ij} \\ \sigma_{ij} & \sigma_{jj} \end{vmatrix}^{-1/2} \exp\left(-\frac{1}{2} \left(w_i - \mu_i, w_j - \mu_j \right) \begin{pmatrix} \sigma_{ii} & \sigma_{ij} \\ \sigma_{ij} & \sigma_{jj} \end{pmatrix}^{-1} \begin{pmatrix} w_i - \mu_i \\ w_j - \mu_j \end{pmatrix} \right) \\ &= \frac{1}{2\pi\sqrt{\sigma_{ii}\sigma_{jj} - \sigma_{ij}^2}} \\ &\quad \times \exp\left(-\frac{\sigma_{jj}(w_i - \mu_i)^2 - 2\sigma_{ij}(w_i - \mu_i)(w_j - \mu_j) + \sigma_{ii}(w_j - \mu_j)^2}{2\left(\sigma_{ii}\sigma_{jj} - \sigma_{ij}^2\right)} \right), \end{aligned}$$

and

$$f_{y_i}(w_i) = \frac{1}{\sqrt{2\pi\sigma_{ii}}} \exp\left(-\frac{(w_i - \mu_i)^2}{2\sigma_{ii}} \right), \quad f_{y_j}(w_j) = \frac{1}{\sqrt{2\pi\sigma_{jj}}} \exp\left(-\frac{(w_j - \mu_j)^2}{2\sigma_{jj}} \right).$$

Hence, $f_{y_i,y_j}(w_i, w_j) = f_{y_i}(w_i) f_{y_j}(w_j)$ for all w_i, w_j if and only if $\sigma_{ij} = 0$.

Exercise 8.9 (Independence and correlation: mixed normals) Consider the bivariate normal distribution with $\mathrm{E}(z_1) = \mathrm{E}(z_2) = 0$, $\mathrm{var}(z_1) = \mathrm{var}(z_2) = 1$, and $\mathrm{cov}(z_1, z_2) = \rho$; hence,

$$f_{z_1,z_2}(u, v; \rho) = \frac{1}{2\pi\sqrt{1-\rho^2}} \exp\left(-\frac{u^2 - 2\rho uv + v^2}{2(1-\rho^2)} \right),$$

where we explicitly write ρ as a parameter that is a given in the argument of $f(\cdot)$. Now, define a mixed-normal p.d.f.

$$f_{x,y}(u,v) := \frac{1}{2} f_{z_1,z_2}(u,v;\rho) + \frac{1}{2} f_{z_1,z_2}(u,v;-\rho).$$

In the notation of Chapter 2, this $f_{x,y}$ means that $z_1 = (x \mid \varrho)$ and $z_2 = (y \mid \varrho)$, where $\varrho = \pm\rho$ with equal probability.
(a) Show that the marginal distributions of $f_{x,y}(u,v)$ are both standard normal.
(b) Show that $\operatorname{cov}(x,y) = 0$, but that x and y are not independent.
(c) How can this result be reconciled with Exercise 8.8?

Solution
(a) For the marginal distributions, we obtain

$$\begin{aligned} f_x(u) &= \int_{-\infty}^{\infty} f_{x,y}(u,v)\,\mathrm{d}v = \frac{1}{2}\int_{-\infty}^{\infty} f_{z_1,z_2}(u,v;\rho)\,\mathrm{d}v + \frac{1}{2}\int_{-\infty}^{\infty} f_{z_1,z_2}(u,v;-\rho)\,\mathrm{d}v \\ &= \frac{1}{2} f_{z_1}(u) + \frac{1}{2} f_{z_1}(u) = \frac{1}{\sqrt{2\pi}}\mathrm{e}^{-u^2/2}, \end{aligned}$$

and similarly for $f_y(v)$. Hence, x and y are both standard normals, even though the joint distribution $f_{x,y}$ is not bivariate normal.
(b) We have

$$\begin{aligned} \operatorname{cov}(x,y) &= \mathrm{E}(xy) \\ &= \frac{1}{2}\int_{-\infty}^{\infty}\int_{-\infty}^{\infty} uv\, f_{z_1,z_2}(u,v;\rho)\,\mathrm{d}u\,\mathrm{d}v + \frac{1}{2}\int_{-\infty}^{\infty}\int_{-\infty}^{\infty} uv\, f_{z_1,z_2}(u,v;-\rho)\,\mathrm{d}u\,\mathrm{d}v \\ &= \frac{1}{2}\rho - \frac{1}{2}\rho = 0, \end{aligned}$$

but $f_{x,y}(u,v) \neq f_x(u) f_y(v)$.
(c) In Exercise 8.8(c), we showed that if $\boldsymbol{x} \sim \mathrm{N}(\boldsymbol{\mu}, \boldsymbol{\Sigma})$ and $\operatorname{cov}(x_i, x_j) = 0$, then x_i and x_j are independent. Here we have shown that even if $x_i \sim \mathrm{N}(\mu_i, \sigma_{ii})$, $x_j \sim \mathrm{N}(\mu_j, \sigma_{jj})$, and $\operatorname{cov}(x_i, x_j) = 0$, then it does not necessarily follow that x_i and x_j are independent. The *joint* distribution of (x_i, x_j) must be normal, not just the two marginals.

Exercise 8.10 (Independence and correlation: ellipticals) Let $\boldsymbol{x} \sim \mathrm{EC}(\boldsymbol{c}, \boldsymbol{A})$, where $\boldsymbol{A} = \operatorname{diag}(a_1, \dots, a_m)$ is positive definite. Prove that $x_1, \dots, x_m$ are independent if and only if $\boldsymbol{x} \sim \mathrm{N}(\boldsymbol{c}, \alpha\boldsymbol{A})$ for some constant $\alpha > 0$.

Solution
We have that $\boldsymbol{y} := \boldsymbol{A}^{-1/2}(\boldsymbol{x} - \boldsymbol{c}) \sim \mathrm{EC}(\boldsymbol{0}, \boldsymbol{I}_m)$ by Exercise 6.49, so we may prove the exercise for $\boldsymbol{y}$ instead of $\boldsymbol{x}$, or assume that $\boldsymbol{c} = \boldsymbol{0}$ and $\boldsymbol{A} = \boldsymbol{I}_m$. The "if" part is a direct consequence of Exercise 8.8(c). The "only if" part follows from extending the equations of Exercise 6.2 to m variates. This shows that the multivariate normal is the only elliptical distribution where zero correlation and independence coincide; see also the discussion in

Exercise 6.51(c). This is a remarkable property of the multivariate normal: the absence of a linear relation (correlation) between the components is equivalent to the absence of *any* relation!

Exercise 8.11 (Subset independence: normals) Let $\boldsymbol{x} := (x_1, \dots, x_m)'$ with $m > 2$ and joint distribution $F(\boldsymbol{w})$. Exercise 5.18 showed that the vector $(x_2, \dots, x_m)$ being jointly independent of x_1 is a sufficient but not a necessary condition for x_1 to be pairwise independent of x_j $(j = 2, \dots, m)$. Prove that, in the specific case where $\boldsymbol{x}$ has a nonsingular normal distribution, the factorization

$$F(\boldsymbol{w}) = F_1(w_1) \times F_{2,\dots,m}(w_2, \dots, w_m), \quad \text{for all } \boldsymbol{w},$$

is both sufficient and necessary for x_1 to be pairwise independent of x_j $(j = 2, \dots, m)$.

Solution

Sufficiency follows directly from Exercise 5.18. For the "necessary" part of the proof, we note that if x_1 is independent of x_j $(j = 2, \dots, m)$, then

$$\operatorname{cov}\left(x_1, \sum_{j=2}^{m} a_j x_j\right) = \sum_{j=2}^{m} a_j \operatorname{cov}(x_1, x_j) = 0$$

for arbitrary nonrandom a_j. Now, $\boldsymbol{x}$ being jointly normal, any linear combination of its components is also normal, and the lack of correlation that we found implies independence. Therefore, $(x_2, \dots, x_m)$ is jointly independent of x_1. Notice that this is a result which need not hold for nonnormal distributions; the reason for this is that the nonsingular joint normal has the property that the absence of a linear relation is equivalent to independence. Notice also the condition for nonsingularity, which has allowed us to use p.d.f.s and c.d.f.s; otherwise, one should use the m.g.f. through which joint normality is defined in generality, as will be illustrated in Exercise 8.31 for functions of $\boldsymbol{x}$ that may have a singular distribution.

Exercise 8.12 (Information divergence between independent normals) Let $\boldsymbol{x}_1 \sim \mathrm{N}_m(\boldsymbol{\mu}_1, \boldsymbol{\Sigma})$ and $\boldsymbol{x}_2 \sim \mathrm{N}_m(\boldsymbol{\mu}_2, \boldsymbol{\Sigma})$, where the common variance matrix is positive definite, and recall the definition $\mathrm{KL}(f_{\boldsymbol{x}_1}, f_{\boldsymbol{x}_2}) := \mathrm{E}_{\boldsymbol{x}_1}(\log(f_{\boldsymbol{x}_1}(\boldsymbol{x}_1)/f_{\boldsymbol{x}_2}(\boldsymbol{x}_1)))$. Derive and compare $\mathrm{KL}(f_{\boldsymbol{x}_1}, f_{\boldsymbol{x}_2})$ and $\mathrm{KL}(f_{\boldsymbol{x}_2}, f_{\boldsymbol{x}_1})$.

Solution

Since

$$f_{\boldsymbol{x}_1}(\boldsymbol{w}_1) = (2\pi)^{-m/2} |\boldsymbol{\Sigma}|^{-1/2} \exp\left(-\frac{1}{2} (\boldsymbol{w}_1 - \boldsymbol{\mu}_1)' \boldsymbol{\Sigma}^{-1} (\boldsymbol{w}_1 - \boldsymbol{\mu}_1)\right)$$

and similarly for $\boldsymbol{x}_2$, we have

$$\mathrm{KL}\left(f_{\boldsymbol{x}_1}, f_{\boldsymbol{x}_2}\right) = \mathrm{E}_{\boldsymbol{x}_1}\left(\log\left(\frac{\exp\left(-\frac{1}{2}\left(\boldsymbol{x}_1-\boldsymbol{\mu}_1\right)'\boldsymbol{\Sigma}^{-1}\left(\boldsymbol{x}_1-\boldsymbol{\mu}_1\right)\right)}{\exp\left(-\frac{1}{2}\left(\boldsymbol{x}_1-\boldsymbol{\mu}_2\right)'\boldsymbol{\Sigma}^{-1}\left(\boldsymbol{x}_1-\boldsymbol{\mu}_2\right)\right)}\right)\right)$$

$$= \mathrm{E}_{\boldsymbol{x}_1}\left(\log\left(\frac{\exp\left(\boldsymbol{x}_1'\boldsymbol{\Sigma}^{-1}\boldsymbol{\mu}_1-\frac{1}{2}\boldsymbol{\mu}_1'\boldsymbol{\Sigma}^{-1}\boldsymbol{\mu}_1\right)}{\exp\left(\boldsymbol{x}_1'\boldsymbol{\Sigma}^{-1}\boldsymbol{\mu}_2-\frac{1}{2}\boldsymbol{\mu}_2'\boldsymbol{\Sigma}^{-1}\boldsymbol{\mu}_2\right)}\right)\right)$$

using $\boldsymbol{\mu}_1'\boldsymbol{\Sigma}^{-1}\boldsymbol{x}_1 = (\boldsymbol{\mu}_1'\boldsymbol{\Sigma}^{-1}\boldsymbol{x}_1)'$ since they are both 1×1 quantities. Simplifying, then taking expectations,

$$\mathrm{KL}\left(f_{\boldsymbol{x}_1}, f_{\boldsymbol{x}_2}\right) = \mathrm{E}_{\boldsymbol{x}_1}\left(\boldsymbol{x}_1'\boldsymbol{\Sigma}^{-1}\left(\boldsymbol{\mu}_1-\boldsymbol{\mu}_2\right)+\frac{1}{2}\boldsymbol{\mu}_2'\boldsymbol{\Sigma}^{-1}\boldsymbol{\mu}_2-\frac{1}{2}\boldsymbol{\mu}_1'\boldsymbol{\Sigma}^{-1}\boldsymbol{\mu}_1\right)$$

$$= \boldsymbol{\mu}_1'\boldsymbol{\Sigma}^{-1}\left(\boldsymbol{\mu}_1-\boldsymbol{\mu}_2\right)+\frac{1}{2}\boldsymbol{\mu}_2'\boldsymbol{\Sigma}^{-1}\boldsymbol{\mu}_2-\frac{1}{2}\boldsymbol{\mu}_1'\boldsymbol{\Sigma}^{-1}\boldsymbol{\mu}_1$$

$$= \frac{1}{2}\left(\boldsymbol{\mu}_1-\boldsymbol{\mu}_2\right)'\boldsymbol{\Sigma}^{-1}\left(\boldsymbol{\mu}_1-\boldsymbol{\mu}_2\right).$$

The KLIC is exceptionally symmetric in this case, where the two vectors are normal and are mutually independent, and we have $\mathrm{KL}(f_{\boldsymbol{x}_2}, f_{\boldsymbol{x}_1}) = \mathrm{KL}(f_{\boldsymbol{x}_1}, f_{\boldsymbol{x}_2})$. It is also proportional to the Mahalanobis distance between the two vectors $\boldsymbol{\mu}_1$ and $\boldsymbol{\mu}_2$.

Exercise 8.13 (Conditional normal distribution) Let $\boldsymbol{x} \sim \mathrm{N}_m(\boldsymbol{\mu}, \boldsymbol{\Sigma})$, where $\boldsymbol{\Sigma}$ is positive definite. Partition $\boldsymbol{x}' := (\boldsymbol{x}_1', \boldsymbol{x}_2')$, where $\boldsymbol{x}_1$ and $\boldsymbol{x}_2$ have dimensions $k > 0$ and $m - k > 0$, respectively. Derive the conditional distribution (given in the introduction to the chapter) of $\boldsymbol{x}_1 \mid \boldsymbol{x}_2$:
(a) for $m = 2$;
(b) for general $m \geqslant 2$.

Solution
(a) For $m = 2$, we write $\boldsymbol{\Sigma}$ and its inverse as

$$\boldsymbol{\Sigma} = \begin{pmatrix}\sigma_1^2 & \rho\sigma_1\sigma_2\\ \rho\sigma_1\sigma_2 & \sigma_2^2\end{pmatrix}, \qquad \boldsymbol{\Sigma}^{-1} = \frac{1}{\sigma_1^2\sigma_2^2(1-\rho^2)}\begin{pmatrix}\sigma_2^2 & -\rho\sigma_1\sigma_2\\ -\rho\sigma_1\sigma_2 & \sigma_1^2\end{pmatrix}.$$

We also define $\mu_{1|2} := \mu_1 + (\rho\sigma_1/\sigma_2)(w_2 - \mu_2)$ and $\sigma_{11|2} := \sigma_1^2(1-\rho^2)$, where w_2 is the realization of x_2. The joint density of x_1 and x_2 is

$$f_{x_1,x_2}(w_1, w_2)$$

$$\propto \exp\left(-\frac{1}{2\sigma_1^2\sigma_2^2(1-\rho^2)}\begin{pmatrix}w_1-\mu_1\\ w_2-\mu_2\end{pmatrix}'\begin{pmatrix}\sigma_2^2 & -\rho\sigma_1\sigma_2\\ -\rho\sigma_1\sigma_2 & \sigma_1^2\end{pmatrix}\begin{pmatrix}w_1-\mu_1\\ w_2-\mu_2\end{pmatrix}\right)$$

$$= \exp\left(-\frac{\sigma_2^2\left(w_1-\mu_1\right)^2-2\rho\sigma_1\sigma_2\left(w_1-\mu_1\right)\left(w_2-\mu_2\right)+\sigma_1^2\left(w_2-\mu_2\right)^2}{2\sigma_1^2\sigma_2^2\left(1-\rho^2\right)}\right),$$

where the factor of proportionality is not shown, and the marginal density of x_2 is

$$f_{x_2}(w_2) \propto \exp\left(-\frac{(w_2-\mu_2)^2}{2\sigma_2^2}\right).$$

Hence, the required conditional density is

$$f_{x_1|x_2=w_2}(w_1) = \frac{f_{x_1,x_2}(w_1,w_2)}{f_{x_2}(w_2)} \propto \exp\left(-\frac{1}{2}Q\right)$$

where

$$\begin{aligned} Q &= -\frac{(w_2-\mu_2)^2}{\sigma_2^2} + \frac{\sigma_2^2(w_1-\mu_1)^2 - 2\rho\sigma_1\sigma_2(w_1-\mu_1)(w_2-\mu_2) + \sigma_1^2(w_2-\mu_2)^2}{\sigma_1^2\sigma_2^2(1-\rho^2)} \\ &= \frac{(w_1-\mu_1)^2 - 2\rho\sigma_1(w_1-\mu_1)(w_2-\mu_2)/\sigma_2 + \rho^2\sigma_1^2((w_2-\mu_2)/\sigma_2)^2}{\sigma_1^2(1-\rho^2)} \\ &= \frac{((w_1-\mu_1) - \rho\sigma_1(w_2-\mu_2)/\sigma_2)^2}{\sigma_1^2(1-\rho^2)} = \frac{(w_1-\mu_{1|2})^2}{\sigma_{11|2}}, \end{aligned}$$

which identifies $x_1 \mid x_2 = w_2$ as a normal variate with mean $\mu_{1|2}$ and variance $\sigma_{11|2}$. Notice from $\sigma_{11|2} = \sigma_1^2(1-\rho^2) \leqslant \sigma_1^2$ that conditioning reduces the variance σ_1^2 by the factor $1-\rho^2$, as expected from Exercise 6.46 for example. If $\rho = 0$, there is no variance reduction because x_1 is independent of x_2.

(b) The result for the general m-dimensional case follows once one recalls that the nonsingular normal is a special case of the elliptical distribution, whose conditional distribution has been worked out in Exercise 6.51 and moments in Exercise 7.31(c). Notice that the joint density factors into

$$\begin{aligned} f_{\boldsymbol{x}}(\boldsymbol{w}) &= \frac{\exp\left(-\frac{1}{2}(\boldsymbol{w}_1-\boldsymbol{\mu}_{1|2})'\boldsymbol{\Sigma}_{11|2}^{-1}(\boldsymbol{w}_1-\boldsymbol{\mu}_{1|2})\right)}{(2\pi)^{k/2}\left|\boldsymbol{\Sigma}_{11|2}\right|^{1/2}} \\ &\quad\times \frac{\exp\left(-\frac{1}{2}(\boldsymbol{w}_2-\boldsymbol{\mu}_2)'\boldsymbol{\Sigma}_2^{-1}(\boldsymbol{w}_2-\boldsymbol{\mu}_2)\right)}{(2\pi)^{(m-k)/2}\left|\boldsymbol{\Sigma}_{22}\right|^{1/2}}, \end{aligned}$$

where $\boldsymbol{\mu}_{1|2} := \boldsymbol{\mu}_1 - \boldsymbol{\Sigma}_{12}\boldsymbol{\Sigma}_{22}^{-1}(\boldsymbol{w}_2-\boldsymbol{\mu}_2)$, since the transformation of $\boldsymbol{x}$ to $\boldsymbol{y}$ of Exercise 6.51(a) has unit Jacobian ($|\boldsymbol{B}| = 1$ there).

Exercise 8.14 (Conditional normal numbers) Let $(x_1,\dots,x_4)'$ follow a normal distribution with mean **0** and variance

$$\boldsymbol{\Sigma} = \begin{pmatrix} 4 & 0 & 2 & 1 \\ 0 & 4 & 0 & 2 \\ 2 & 0 & 4 & 1 \\ 1 & 2 & 1 & 4 \end{pmatrix}.$$

(a) Evaluate $\mathrm{E}_{x_1|x_3=1,x_4=0}(x_1)$ and $\mathrm{var}_{x_1|x_3=1,x_4=0}(x_1)$.

(b) Let $z_1 := ax_1 + bx_3$ and $z_2 := ax_2 + cx_4$. For which a, b, c are z_1 and z_2 independent?

Solution
(a) Let $(\boldsymbol{x}_1', \boldsymbol{x}_2')'$ be jointly normal with mean $\mathbf{0}$ and variance matrix

$$\boldsymbol{\Sigma} = \begin{pmatrix} \boldsymbol{\Sigma}_{11} & \boldsymbol{\Sigma}_{12} \\ \boldsymbol{\Sigma}_{21} & \boldsymbol{\Sigma}_{22} \end{pmatrix}.$$

Then, we know that

$$\mathrm{E}_{\boldsymbol{x}_1|\boldsymbol{x}_2}(\boldsymbol{x}_1) = \boldsymbol{\Sigma}_{12}\boldsymbol{\Sigma}_{22}^{-1}\boldsymbol{x}_2, \qquad \mathrm{var}_{\boldsymbol{x}_1|\boldsymbol{x}_2}(\boldsymbol{x}_1) = \boldsymbol{\Sigma}_{11} - \boldsymbol{\Sigma}_{12}\boldsymbol{\Sigma}_{22}^{-1}\boldsymbol{\Sigma}_{21}.$$

Letting $\boldsymbol{x}_1 := (x_1)$ and $\boldsymbol{x}_2 := (x_3, x_4)'$, we have

$$\boldsymbol{\Sigma}_{12}\boldsymbol{\Sigma}_{22}^{-1} = (2, 1)\begin{pmatrix} 4 & 1 \\ 1 & 4 \end{pmatrix}^{-1} = (2, 1)\begin{pmatrix} \frac{4}{15} & -\frac{1}{15} \\ -\frac{1}{15} & \frac{4}{15} \end{pmatrix} = \left(\tfrac{7}{15}, \tfrac{2}{15}\right),$$

hence

$$\mathrm{E}_{x_1|x_3=1,x_4=0}(x_1) = \left(\tfrac{7}{15}, \tfrac{2}{15}\right)\begin{pmatrix} 1 \\ 0 \end{pmatrix} = \frac{7}{15}$$

and

$$\mathrm{var}_{x_1|x_3=1,x_4=0}(x_1) = 4 - \left(\tfrac{7}{15}, \tfrac{2}{15}\right)\begin{pmatrix} 2 \\ 1 \end{pmatrix} = \frac{44}{15}.$$

(b) The two random variables are independent when their covariance is zero. Now,

$$\begin{aligned} &\mathrm{cov}(ax_1 + bx_3, ax_2 + cx_4) \\ &\quad = a^2\,\mathrm{cov}(x_1, x_2) + ac\,\mathrm{cov}(x_1, x_4) + ab\,\mathrm{cov}(x_2, x_3) + bc\,\mathrm{cov}(x_3, x_4) \\ &\quad = 0 + ac + 0 + bc = c(a + b). \end{aligned}$$

Hence, independence occurs when $c = 0$ or when $a = -b$.

Exercise 8.15 (Normals' variance via conditionals) Let $(x, y)'$ follow a bivariate normal distribution with mean $\mathbf{0}$ and variance $\boldsymbol{\Sigma}$. Assume that $\mathrm{var}(x + 2y) = 17$, that $x - 2y$ and $x + y$ are independent, and that $\mathrm{E}_{x|y=1}(x) = \frac{1}{2}$. Compute $\boldsymbol{\Sigma}$.

Solution
Apart from the usual symmetry requirement, there are three restrictions on $\boldsymbol{\Sigma}$, namely

$$\mathrm{var}(x) + 4\,\mathrm{cov}(x, y) + 4\,\mathrm{var}(y) = 17,$$

$$\mathrm{var}(x) - \mathrm{cov}(x, y) - 2\,\mathrm{var}(y) = 0,$$

$$\frac{\mathrm{cov}(x, y)}{\mathrm{var}(y)} = \frac{1}{2},$$

where the last equality follows from the formula for the conditional normal. Hence,

$$\boldsymbol{\Sigma} = \begin{pmatrix} 5 & 1 \\ 1 & 2 \end{pmatrix}.$$

Exercise 8.16 (Normals' parameters via conditionals) Let (x, y) follow a bivariate normal distribution, such that $x \sim \mathrm{N}(\mu, \sigma^2)$ and $y \mid x \sim \mathrm{N}(x, \sigma^2)$. Find the parameters of this bivariate distribution.

Solution
First, $\mathrm{E}(y) = \mathrm{E}_x(\mathrm{E}_{y|x}(y)) = \mathrm{E}(x) = \mu$. Next, from Exercise 6.28,

$$\mathrm{var}(y) = \mathrm{E}_x(\mathrm{var}_{y|x}(y)) + \mathrm{var}_x(\mathrm{E}_{y|x}(y)) = \sigma^2 + \sigma^2 = 2\sigma^2,$$

and

$$\mathrm{E}(xy) = \mathrm{E}_x(x\,\mathrm{E}_{y|x}(y)) = \mathrm{E}(x^2) = \mu^2 + \sigma^2.$$

Hence,

$$\mathrm{cov}(x, y) = \mathrm{E}(xy) - \mathrm{E}(x)\,\mathrm{E}(y) = \mu^2 + \sigma^2 - \mu^2 = \sigma^2.$$

We thus obtain

$$\begin{pmatrix} x \\ y \end{pmatrix} \sim \mathrm{N}\left(\begin{pmatrix} \mu \\ \mu \end{pmatrix}, \begin{pmatrix} \sigma^2 & \sigma^2 \\ \sigma^2 & 2\sigma^2 \end{pmatrix}\right).$$

Exercise 8.17 (Conditional on normal's square) Let (x, y) follow a bivariate normal distribution with $\mathrm{E}(x) = \mathrm{E}(y) = 0$ and $\mathrm{var}(x) = \mathrm{var}(y) = 1$. Derive the distribution of $x \mid y^2$.

Solution
Let $z := y^2$. We first find the c.d.f. of (x, z).

$$\begin{aligned} F_{x,z}(u, w) &:= \Pr(x \leqslant u, z \leqslant w) \\ &= \Pr(x \leqslant u, -\sqrt{w} \leqslant y \leqslant \sqrt{w}) \\ &= \frac{1}{2\pi\sqrt{1-\rho^2}} \int_{-\infty}^{u} \int_{-\sqrt{w}}^{\sqrt{w}} \exp\left(-\frac{t^2 - 2\rho t v + v^2}{2(1-\rho^2)}\right) \mathrm{d}v\, \mathrm{d}t. \end{aligned}$$

Using Leibniz' rule twice,

$$\begin{aligned} f_{x,z}(u, w) &= \frac{\partial^2}{\partial u \partial w} \Pr(x \leqslant u, z \leqslant w) \\ &= \frac{1}{2\pi\sqrt{1-\rho^2}} \frac{\partial}{\partial w} \int_{-\sqrt{w}}^{\sqrt{w}} \exp\left(-\frac{u^2 \quad 2\rho u v + v^2}{2(1-\rho^2)}\right) \mathrm{d}v \\ &= \frac{1}{2\pi\sqrt{1-\rho^2}} \frac{\mathrm{e}^{-w/2}}{2\sqrt{w}} \left(\mathrm{e}^{h(\rho)} + \mathrm{e}^{h(-\rho)}\right), \end{aligned}$$

where

$$h(\rho) := -\frac{(u - \rho\sqrt{w})^2}{2(1-\rho^2)}.$$

Notice the relation of $h(\rho)$ to the formula for the conditional normal. Also, since $z \sim \chi^2(1)$ by Exercise 4.25,

$$f_z(w) = \frac{1}{\sqrt{2\pi w}} \mathrm{e}^{-w/2}.$$

Hence,

$$f_{x|z=w}(u) = \frac{\mathrm{e}^{h(\rho)} + \mathrm{e}^{h(-\rho)}}{2\sqrt{2\pi}\sqrt{1-\rho^2}}$$

and

$$f_{x|y^2}(u) = \frac{\exp\left(-\frac{(u-\rho|y|)^2}{2(1-\rho^2)}\right) + \exp\left(-\frac{(u+\rho|y|)^2}{2(1-\rho^2)}\right)}{2\sqrt{2\pi}\sqrt{1-\rho^2}} = \frac{\exp\left(-\frac{u^2+\rho^2 y^2}{2(1-\rho^2)}\right)\cosh\left(\frac{\rho u y}{1-\rho^2}\right)}{\sqrt{2\pi}\sqrt{1-\rho^2}},$$

where we use y instead of $|y|$ in the argument of cosh because it is an even function.

Exercise 8.18 (Correlation of normal's squares) Let (x, y) follow a bivariate normal distribution with $\mathrm{E}(x) = \mathrm{E}(y) = 0$ and $\mathrm{var}(x) = \mathrm{var}(y) = 1$. Let $\rho := \mathrm{corr}(x, y)$. Show that $\mathrm{corr}(x^2, y^2) = \rho^2$.

Solution
The formula for the conditional normal implies that $x \mid y \sim \mathrm{N}(\rho y, 1-\rho^2)$. Also, since $y \sim \mathrm{N}(0,1)$, we have $\mathrm{E}(y^2) = 1$ and $\mathrm{E}(y^4) = 3$, the latter having been derived in Exercise 4.24. Now, using $\mathrm{E}_{x|y}(x^2) = \mathrm{var}_{x|y}(x) + (\mathrm{E}_{x|y}(x))^2$, we obtain

$$\begin{aligned}\mathrm{E}(x^2y^2) &= \mathrm{E}(y^2\,\mathrm{E}_{x|y}(x^2)) = \mathrm{E}(y^2(1-\rho^2+\rho^2y^2)) \\ &= (1-\rho^2)\,\mathrm{E}(y^2) + \rho^2\,\mathrm{E}(y^4) = 1-\rho^2+3\rho^2 = 1+2\rho^2.\end{aligned}$$

This, together with $\mathrm{E}(x^2) = \mathrm{E}(y^2) = 1$, implies that $\mathrm{cov}(x^2, y^2) = 2\rho^2$. The variance of a $\chi^2(1)$ gives $\mathrm{var}(x^2) = \mathrm{var}(y^2) = 2$, implying that $\mathrm{corr}(x^2, y^2) = \rho^2$.

Exercise 8.19 (Fourth-order moments: normals) Let $\boldsymbol{x} := (x_1, \dots, x_4)'$ follow a normal distribution with mean $\mathbf{0}$ and positive definite variance $\boldsymbol{\Sigma}$. Prove that:
(a) $\mathrm{var}(x_1^2) = 2\sigma_{11}^2$;
(b) $\mathrm{cov}(x_1^2, x_1x_2) = 2\sigma_{11}\sigma_{12}$;
(c) $\mathrm{cov}(x_1^2, x_2^2) = 2\sigma_{12}^2$;
(d) $\mathrm{E}(x_1^2x_2^2) = 2\sigma_{12}^2 + \sigma_{11}\sigma_{22}$;
(e) $\mathrm{E}(x_1^2x_2x_3) = 2\sigma_{12}\sigma_{13} + \sigma_{11}\sigma_{23}$;
(f) $\mathrm{E}(x_1x_2x_3x_4) = \sigma_{12}\sigma_{34} + \sigma_{13}\sigma_{24} + \sigma_{14}\sigma_{23}$;

(g) for $i, j, k, l \in \{1, 2, 3, 4\}$,

$$\mathrm{E}\left(x_i x_j x_k x_l\right) = \sigma_{ij}\sigma_{kl} + \sigma_{ik}\sigma_{jl} + \sigma_{il}\sigma_{jk} \quad \text{and} \quad \operatorname{cov}\left(x_i x_j, x_k x_l\right) = \sigma_{ik}\sigma_{jl} + \sigma_{il}\sigma_{jk}.$$

[Hint: Use iterated expectations and the moments of conditional normals.]

Solution

(a) $\operatorname{var}\left(x_1^2\right) = \mathrm{E}\left(x_1^4\right) - \left(\mathrm{E}\left(x_1^2\right)\right)^2 = 3\sigma_{11}^2 - \sigma_{11}^2 = 2\sigma_{11}^2$.

(b) $\operatorname{cov}\left(x_1^2, x_1 x_2\right) = \mathrm{E}\left(x_1^3 x_2\right) - \mathrm{E}\left(x_1^2\right)\mathrm{E}\left(x_1 x_2\right)$. To work out the first expectation, we use the LIE and $\mathrm{E}_{x_2|x_1}\left(x_2\right) = (\sigma_{12}/\sigma_{11})x_1$ from the formula for the conditional normal, hence

$$\begin{aligned}\operatorname{cov}\left(x_1^2, x_1 x_2\right) &= \mathrm{E}_{x_1}\left(x_1^3\,\mathrm{E}_{x_2|x_1}\left(x_2\right)\right) - \sigma_{11}\sigma_{12}\\ &= \frac{\sigma_{12}}{\sigma_{11}}\mathrm{E}_{x_1}\left(x_1^4\right) - \sigma_{11}\sigma_{12} = 3\sigma_{11}\sigma_{12} - \sigma_{11}\sigma_{12} = 2\sigma_{11}\sigma_{12}.\end{aligned}$$

(c) This follows from Exercise 8.18. Let $y_1 := x_1/\sqrt{\sigma_{11}}$ and $y_2 := x_2/\sqrt{\sigma_{22}}$, both having unit variance and correlation $\rho = \operatorname{cov}(x_1, x_2)/\sqrt{\sigma_{11}\sigma_{22}} = \sigma_{12}/\sqrt{\sigma_{11}\sigma_{22}}$. Then

$$\operatorname{cov}\left(x_1^2, x_2^2\right) = \sigma_{11}\sigma_{22}\operatorname{cov}\left(y_1^2, y_2^2\right) = 2\sigma_{11}\sigma_{22}\left(\frac{\sigma_{12}}{\sqrt{\sigma_{11}\sigma_{22}}}\right)^2 = 2\sigma_{12}^2.$$

(d) We know that

$$\operatorname{cov}\left(x_1^2, x_2^2\right) = \mathrm{E}\left(x_1^2 x_2^2\right) - \mathrm{E}\left(x_1^2\right)\mathrm{E}\left(x_2^2\right) = \mathrm{E}\left(x_1^2 x_2^2\right) - \sigma_{11}\sigma_{22},$$

and substituting from (c) into the left-hand side gives $\mathrm{E}\left(x_1^2 x_2^2\right) = \sigma_{11}\sigma_{22} + 2\sigma_{12}^2$. Note that this implies that

$$\operatorname{var}\left(x_1 x_2\right) = \mathrm{E}\left(x_1^2 x_2^2\right) - \left(\mathrm{E}\left(x_1 x_2\right)\right)^2 = \sigma_{11}\sigma_{22} + \sigma_{12}\sigma_{21},$$

where we see a symmetry in the permutation of the subscripts.

(e) We have $\mathrm{E}\left(x_1^2 x_2 x_3\right) = \mathrm{E}_{x_1}\left(x_1^2\,\mathrm{E}_{x_2,x_3|x_1}\left(x_2 x_3\right)\right)$. The distribution of $x_2, x_3 \mid x_1$ has a variance matrix that is independent of x_1, namely

$$\begin{pmatrix}\sigma_{22} & \sigma_{23}\\ \sigma_{23} & \sigma_{33}\end{pmatrix} - \frac{1}{\sigma_{11}}\begin{pmatrix}\sigma_{12}\\ \sigma_{13}\end{pmatrix}\left(\sigma_{12}, \sigma_{13}\right).$$

Therefore, the conditional (on x_1) covariance of x_2 and x_3 is the off-diagonal element, $\sigma_{23} - \sigma_{12}\sigma_{13}/\sigma_{11}$, and

$$\begin{aligned}\mathrm{E}\left(x_1^2 x_2 x_3\right) &= \mathrm{E}_{x_1}\left(x_1^2\left(\operatorname{cov}_{x_2,x_3|x_1}\left(x_2, x_3\right) + \mathrm{E}_{x_2|x_1}\left(x_2\right) \times \mathrm{E}_{x_3|x_1}\left(x_3\right)\right)\right)\\ &= \mathrm{E}_{x_1}\left(x_1^2\left(\sigma_{23} - \frac{\sigma_{12}\sigma_{13}}{\sigma_{11}} + \frac{\sigma_{12}}{\sigma_{11}}x_1 \times \frac{\sigma_{13}}{\sigma_{11}}x_1\right)\right)\\ &= \sigma_{11}\sigma_{23} - \sigma_{12}\sigma_{13} + \frac{\sigma_{12}\sigma_{13}}{\sigma_{11}^2}\mathrm{E}\left(x_1^4\right)\\ &= \sigma_{11}\sigma_{23} - \sigma_{12}\sigma_{13} + 3\sigma_{12}\sigma_{13} = 2\sigma_{12}\sigma_{13} + \sigma_{11}\sigma_{23}.\end{aligned}$$

(f) The solution is easy to guess from the succession of earlier results in this exercise, as hinted at the end of (d), but we now need to prove it! Write $\boldsymbol{x}' := (\boldsymbol{x}_1', \boldsymbol{x}_2')$, where $\boldsymbol{x}_1' := (x_1, x_2)$ and $\boldsymbol{x}_2' := (x_3, x_4)$. Then, as in (e), we have

$$\begin{aligned}
\mathrm{E}\left(x_1x_2x_3x_4\right) &= \mathrm{E}_{x_1,x_2}\left(x_1x_2 \,\mathrm{E}_{x_3,x_4|x_1,x_2}\left(x_3x_4\right)\right) \\
&= \mathrm{E}_{\boldsymbol{x}_1}\left(x_1x_2 \,\mathrm{E}_{\boldsymbol{x}_2|\boldsymbol{x}_1}\left((1,0)\,\boldsymbol{x}_2\boldsymbol{x}_2'\begin{pmatrix}0\\1\end{pmatrix}\right)\right) \\
&= \mathrm{E}_{\boldsymbol{x}_1}\left((x_1x_2,0)\left(\mathrm{var}_{\boldsymbol{x}_2|\boldsymbol{x}_1}\left(\boldsymbol{x}_2\right) + \mathrm{E}_{\boldsymbol{x}_2|\boldsymbol{x}_1}\left(\boldsymbol{x}_2\right)\mathrm{E}_{\boldsymbol{x}_2|\boldsymbol{x}_1}\left(\boldsymbol{x}_2\right)'\right)\right)\begin{pmatrix}0\\1\end{pmatrix} \\
&= \mathrm{E}\left((x_1x_2,0)\left(\boldsymbol{\Sigma}_{22|1} + \boldsymbol{\Sigma}_{21}\boldsymbol{\Sigma}_{11}^{-1}\boldsymbol{x}_1\boldsymbol{x}_1'\boldsymbol{\Sigma}_{11}^{-1}\boldsymbol{\Sigma}_{12}\right)\right)\begin{pmatrix}0\\1\end{pmatrix} \\
&= (\sigma_{12},0)\,\boldsymbol{\Sigma}_{22|1}\begin{pmatrix}0\\1\end{pmatrix} + (1,0)\,\boldsymbol{\Sigma}_{21}\boldsymbol{\Sigma}_{11}^{-1}\,\mathrm{E}\left(x_1x_2\boldsymbol{x}_1\boldsymbol{x}_1'\right)\boldsymbol{\Sigma}_{11}^{-1}\boldsymbol{\Sigma}_{12}\begin{pmatrix}0\\1\end{pmatrix}.
\end{aligned}$$

Now

$$\mathrm{E}\left(x_1x_2\boldsymbol{x}_1\boldsymbol{x}_1'\right) = \mathrm{E}\begin{pmatrix}x_1^3x_2 & x_1^2x_2^2\\ x_1^2x_2^2 & x_1x_2^3\end{pmatrix} = \begin{pmatrix}3\sigma_{11}\sigma_{12} & 2\sigma_{12}^2+\sigma_{11}\sigma_{22}\\ 2\sigma_{12}^2+\sigma_{11}\sigma_{22} & 3\sigma_{12}\sigma_{22}\end{pmatrix},$$

where the diagonal follows from the proof of (b), and the off-diagonal elements from (d). Using $\boldsymbol{\Sigma}_{22|1} = \boldsymbol{\Sigma}_{22} - \boldsymbol{\Sigma}_{21}\boldsymbol{\Sigma}_{11}^{-1}\boldsymbol{\Sigma}_{12}$, we get

$$\begin{aligned}
&\mathrm{E}\left(x_1x_2x_3x_4\right) \\
&= \sigma_{12}\sigma_{34} \\
&\quad - (1,0)\,\boldsymbol{\Sigma}_{21}\boldsymbol{\Sigma}_{11}^{-1}\left(\sigma_{12}\boldsymbol{\Sigma}_{11} - \begin{pmatrix}3\sigma_{11}\sigma_{12} & 2\sigma_{12}^2+\sigma_{11}\sigma_{22}\\ 2\sigma_{12}^2+\sigma_{11}\sigma_{22} & 3\sigma_{12}\sigma_{22}\end{pmatrix}\right)\boldsymbol{\Sigma}_{11}^{-1}\boldsymbol{\Sigma}_{12}\begin{pmatrix}0\\1\end{pmatrix} \\
&= \sigma_{12}\sigma_{34} + (1,0)\,\boldsymbol{\Sigma}_{21}\boldsymbol{\Sigma}_{11}^{-1}\begin{pmatrix}2\sigma_{11}\sigma_{12} & \sigma_{12}^2+\sigma_{11}\sigma_{22}\\ \sigma_{12}^2+\sigma_{11}\sigma_{22} & 2\sigma_{12}\sigma_{22}\end{pmatrix}\boldsymbol{\Sigma}_{11}^{-1}\boldsymbol{\Sigma}_{12}\begin{pmatrix}0\\1\end{pmatrix} \\
&= \sigma_{12}\sigma_{34} + (1,0)\,\boldsymbol{\Sigma}_{21}\boldsymbol{\Sigma}_{11}^{-1}\begin{pmatrix}\sigma_{11} & \sigma_{12}\\ \sigma_{12} & \sigma_{22}\end{pmatrix}\begin{pmatrix}\sigma_{12} & \sigma_{22}\\ \sigma_{11} & \sigma_{12}\end{pmatrix}\boldsymbol{\Sigma}_{11}^{-1}\boldsymbol{\Sigma}_{12}\begin{pmatrix}0\\1\end{pmatrix} \\
&= \sigma_{12}\sigma_{34} + (1,0)\,\boldsymbol{\Sigma}_{21}\boldsymbol{\Sigma}_{11}^{-1}\begin{pmatrix}\sigma_{11} & \sigma_{12}\\ \sigma_{12} & \sigma_{22}\end{pmatrix}\begin{pmatrix}0 & 1\\ 1 & 0\end{pmatrix}\begin{pmatrix}\sigma_{11} & \sigma_{12}\\ \sigma_{12} & \sigma_{22}\end{pmatrix}\boldsymbol{\Sigma}_{11}^{-1}\boldsymbol{\Sigma}_{12}\begin{pmatrix}0\\1\end{pmatrix},
\end{aligned}$$

where we notice that there is a permutation matrix in the middle. Substituting for $\boldsymbol{\Sigma}_{11}$ and $\boldsymbol{\Sigma}_{12}$, then simplifying,

$$\begin{aligned}
\mathrm{E}\left(x_1x_2x_3x_4\right) &= \sigma_{12}\sigma_{34} + (1,0)\begin{pmatrix}\sigma_{13} & \sigma_{23}\\ \sigma_{14} & \sigma_{24}\end{pmatrix}\begin{pmatrix}0 & 1\\ 1 & 0\end{pmatrix}\begin{pmatrix}\sigma_{13} & \sigma_{14}\\ \sigma_{23} & \sigma_{24}\end{pmatrix}\begin{pmatrix}0\\1\end{pmatrix} \\
&= \sigma_{12}\sigma_{34} + \left(\sigma_{13},\sigma_{23}\right)\begin{pmatrix}0 & 1\\ 1 & 0\end{pmatrix}\begin{pmatrix}\sigma_{14}\\ \sigma_{24}\end{pmatrix} = \sigma_{12}\sigma_{34} + \sigma_{13}\sigma_{24} + \sigma_{14}\sigma_{23},
\end{aligned}$$

where we notice the combination of the subscripts.

(g) The first result follows from (d)–(f), $\mathrm{E}(x_1^4) = 3\sigma_{11}^2$, and $\mathrm{E}(x_1^3x_2) = 3\sigma_{11}\sigma_{12}$ from the proof of (b). The second, for covariances, follows by subtracting $\mathrm{E}(x_i x_j)\mathrm{E}(x_k x_l) = \sigma_{ij}\sigma_{kl}$.

As a general comment on this exercise, all the results can be obtained by two alternative methods which do not require conditioning. First, Exercise 8.35 below will give the covariance of two quadratic forms in $\boldsymbol{x}$, and this can be specialized to the cases above. Second, Exercise 8.20 will now show that the moments can also be obtained directly by differentiating the moment-generating function of $\boldsymbol{x}$.

***Exercise 8.20 (Fourth-order moments: ellipticals)** Let $\boldsymbol{x} := (x_1, x_2)' \sim \mathrm{EC}(\mathbf{0}, \boldsymbol{A})$, with c.f. $\varphi_{\boldsymbol{x}}(\boldsymbol{\tau}) = h(\boldsymbol{\tau}'\boldsymbol{A}\boldsymbol{\tau})$ and positive definite variance $\boldsymbol{\Sigma} := -2h'(0)\boldsymbol{A}$ assumed finite. (These results were derived in Exercise 7.31.) Assume also that $\mathrm{E}\left(x_1^j x_2^{4-j}\right)$ exists for all $j = 0, \dots, 4$, and let $\kappa := \mathrm{E}\left(x_1^4/\sigma_{11}^2\right) - 3$. Prove that:

(a) $\mathrm{var}\left(x_1^2\right) = (2+\kappa)\sigma_{11}^2$;

(b) $\mathrm{cov}\left(x_1^2, x_1 x_2\right) = (2+\kappa)\sigma_{11}\sigma_{12}$;

(c) $\mathrm{E}\left(x_1^4/\sigma_{11}^2\right) = \mathrm{E}\left(x_2^4/\sigma_{22}^2\right) = 3h''(0)/(h'(0))^2$;

(d) $\mathrm{E}\left(x_1^2 x_2^2\right) = \left(2\sigma_{12}^2 + \sigma_{11}\sigma_{22}\right)(1+\kappa/3)$;

(e) for $i, j, k, l \in \{1, 2\}$,

$$\mathrm{E}(x_i x_j x_k x_l) = (\sigma_{ij}\sigma_{kl} + \sigma_{ik}\sigma_{jl} + \sigma_{il}\sigma_{jk})(1+\kappa/3)$$

and $\mathrm{cov}(x_i x_j, x_k x_l) = \mathrm{E}(x_i x_j x_k x_l) - \sigma_{ij}\sigma_{kl}$.

Solution

(a) $\mathrm{var}\left(x_1^2\right) = \mathrm{E}\left(x_1^4\right) - \left(\mathrm{E}\left(x_1^2\right)\right)^2 = (3+\kappa)\sigma_{11}^2 - \sigma_{11}^2 = (2+\kappa)\sigma_{11}^2$.

(b) Using the ellipticals' linear conditionals (Exercise 6.51) and the proportionality of $\boldsymbol{\Sigma}$ to $\boldsymbol{A}$, we have $\mathrm{E}_{x_2|x_1}(x_2) = (\sigma_{12}/\sigma_{11})x_1$. Then, using the LIE,

$$\begin{aligned}\mathrm{cov}\left(x_1^2, x_1 x_2\right) &= \mathrm{E}\left(x_1^3 x_2\right) - \mathrm{E}\left(x_1^2\right)\mathrm{E}(x_1 x_2) = \mathrm{E}_{x_1}\left(x_1^3\,\mathrm{E}_{x_2|x_1}(x_2)\right) - \sigma_{11}\sigma_{12} \\ &= \frac{\sigma_{12}}{\sigma_{11}}\mathrm{E}_{x_1}\left(x_1^4\right) - \sigma_{11}\sigma_{12} = (3+\kappa)\sigma_{11}\sigma_{12} - \sigma_{11}\sigma_{12} = (2+\kappa)\sigma_{11}\sigma_{12}.\end{aligned}$$

(c) Define $(y_1, y_2) := (x_1/\sqrt{\sigma_{11}}, x_2/\sqrt{\sigma_{22}})$, which is elliptical of the same type as $\boldsymbol{x}$ (by Exercise 6.49) and has variance

$$\boldsymbol{\Omega} := \begin{pmatrix} 1 & \rho \\ \rho & 1 \end{pmatrix},$$

with $\rho := \sigma_{12}/\sqrt{\sigma_{11}\sigma_{22}}$. We have $\mathrm{E}\left(y_1^4\right) = \mathrm{E}\left(x_1^4/\sigma_{11}^2\right) = 3+\kappa$, and we will show that the same equality holds for y_2 and that $3+\kappa = 3h''(0)/(h'(0))^2$. The marginal distributions of y_1 and y_2 have the same κ, because they are of the same type, by Exercise 7.31(b). This is seen by setting $\tau_2 = 0$, which gives

$$\varphi_{y_1}(\tau_1) = h\left(-\frac{1}{2h'(0)}\tau_1^2\right)$$

by Exercise 7.31(c) and y_1 having unit variance. The same holds for y_2. Recalling that

$\varphi_{y_1}(\tau_1) \equiv \mathrm{E}\left(\mathrm{e}^{\mathrm{i}\tau_1 y_1}\right)$, differentiating it four times with respect to τ_1, then setting $\tau_1 = 0$, gives $\mathrm{E}\left(y_1^4\right)$ since $\mathrm{i}^4 = 1$. (See Exercise 3.36(c) for an alternative route.) We have

$$\varphi'_{y_1}(\tau_1) = -\frac{\tau_1}{h'(0)} h'\left(-\frac{\tau_1^2}{2h'(0)}\right),$$

$$\varphi''_{y_1}(\tau_1) = -\frac{1}{h'(0)} h'\left(-\frac{\tau_1^2}{2h'(0)}\right) + \frac{\tau_1^2}{(h'(0))^2} h''\left(-\frac{\tau_1^2}{2h'(0)}\right),$$

$$\begin{aligned}\varphi'''_{y_1}(\tau_1) = &\frac{\tau_1}{(h'(0))^2} h''\left(-\frac{\tau_1^2}{2h'(0)}\right)\\ &+\frac{2\tau_1}{(h'(0))^2} h''\left(-\frac{\tau_1^2}{2h'(0)}\right) - \frac{\tau_1^3}{(h'(0))^3} h'''\left(-\frac{\tau_1^2}{2h'(0)}\right).\end{aligned}$$

Differentiating the last expression, and setting $\tau_1 = 0$, gives

$$\varphi^{(4)}_{y_1}(0) = \frac{1}{(h'(0))^2} h''(0) + \frac{2}{(h'(0))^2} h''(0) = \frac{3h''(0)}{(h'(0))^2}$$

as required. Notice that we did not force *both* x_1 and x_2 to have the same kurtosis in the statement of the question: it is an equality that follows automatically from the c.f. of joint ellipticals. For example, the multivariate t has a common κ for all its marginals, and the joint normal has the same $\kappa = 0$ for all its marginals.

(d) Differentiating the c.f. of (y_1, y_2) twice with respect to each of τ_1 and τ_2, then setting $\boldsymbol{\tau} = \mathbf{0}_2$, we get $\mathrm{E}\left(y_1^2 y_2^2\right)$ since $\mathrm{i}^4 = 1$. As in the proof of Exercise 7.31(c),

$$\frac{\partial^2 \varphi(\boldsymbol{\tau})}{\partial \boldsymbol{\tau} \partial \boldsymbol{\tau}'} = \frac{h''\left(-\frac{1}{2h'(0)}\boldsymbol{\tau}'\boldsymbol{\Omega}\boldsymbol{\tau}\right)}{(h'(0))^2}\boldsymbol{\Omega}\boldsymbol{\tau}\boldsymbol{\tau}'\boldsymbol{\Omega} - \frac{h'\left(-\frac{1}{2h'(0)}\boldsymbol{\tau}'\boldsymbol{\Omega}\boldsymbol{\tau}\right)}{h'(0)}\boldsymbol{\Omega}.$$

Since we have already differentiated twice with respect to τ_2, we can set $\tau_2 = 0$ and select the last element of the Hessian:

$$\begin{aligned}\left.\frac{\partial^2 \varphi(\boldsymbol{\tau})}{\partial \tau_2^2}\right|_{\tau_2=0} &= \frac{h''\left(-\frac{\tau_1^2}{2h'(0)}\right)}{(h'(0))^2}(0,1)\begin{pmatrix}1 & \rho\\ \rho & 1\end{pmatrix}\begin{pmatrix}\tau_1^2 & 0\\ 0 & 0\end{pmatrix}\begin{pmatrix}1 & \rho\\ \rho & 1\end{pmatrix}\begin{pmatrix}0\\ 1\end{pmatrix} - \frac{h'\left(-\frac{\tau_1^2}{2h'(0)}\right)}{h'(0)}\\ &= \frac{h''\left(-\frac{\tau_1^2}{2h'(0)}\right)}{(h'(0))^2}(\rho,1)\begin{pmatrix}\tau_1^2 & 0\\ 0 & 0\end{pmatrix}\begin{pmatrix}\rho\\ 1\end{pmatrix} - \frac{h'\left(-\frac{\tau_1^2}{2h'(0)}\right)}{h'(0)}\\ &= \frac{\rho^2\tau_1^2 h''\left(-\frac{\tau_1^2}{2h'(0)}\right) - h'(0)\,h'\left(-\frac{\tau_1^2}{2h'(0)}\right)}{(h'(0))^2}.\end{aligned}$$

It remains for us to differentiate this expression twice with respect to τ_1, then set $\tau_1 = 0$.

We get

$$\begin{aligned}
&\mathrm{E}\left(y_1^2 y_2^2\right) \\
&= \frac{1}{\left(h'(0)\right)^2} \frac{\partial}{\partial \tau_1}\left(-\frac{\rho^2 \tau_1^3}{h'(0)} h'''\left(-\frac{\tau_1^2}{2h'(0)}\right) + \left(1+2\rho^2\right)\tau_1 h''\left(-\frac{\tau_1^2}{2h'(0)}\right)\right)\Bigg|_{\tau_1=0} \\
&= \left(1+2\rho^2\right)\frac{h''(0)}{\left(h'(0)\right)^2}.
\end{aligned}$$

Since $\kappa + 3 = 3h''(0)/\left(h'(0)\right)^2$ from (c), the result follows by using $\rho = \sigma_{12}/\sqrt{\sigma_{11}\sigma_{22}}$ and $\mathrm{E}\left(x_1^2 x_2^2\right) = \sigma_{11}\sigma_{22}\,\mathrm{E}\left(y_1^2 y_2^2\right)$.
(e) This follows from (c), (d), and $\mathrm{E}(x_1^3 x_2) = (3+\kappa)\,\sigma_{11}\sigma_{12}$ from the proof of (b).

Exercise 8.21 (Normals' correlation via conditional probability) Let $\boldsymbol{x} := (x_1, x_2)'$ follow a normal distribution with

$$\mathrm{E}(\boldsymbol{x}) = \begin{pmatrix} 5 \\ 10 \end{pmatrix}, \qquad \mathrm{var}(\boldsymbol{x}) = \begin{pmatrix} 1 & 5\rho \\ 5\rho & 25 \end{pmatrix}.$$

You are told that $\Pr(4 < x_2 < 16 \mid x_1 = 5) = 0.954$, and you know that $\Phi(2) \approx 0.977$. Compute ρ.

Solution

Let y denote the random variable $x_2 \mid (x_1 = 5)$. Then, by the formula for the conditional normal,

$$y \sim \mathrm{N}(10, 25(1-\rho^2)) \quad \text{and} \quad z := \frac{y-10}{5\sqrt{1-\rho^2}} \sim \mathrm{N}(0,1).$$

Hence,

$$\begin{aligned}
0.954 &= \Pr(4 < y < 16) \\
&= \Pr\left(\frac{-6}{5\sqrt{1-\rho^2}} < z < \frac{6}{5\sqrt{1-\rho^2}}\right) = 2\Phi\left(\frac{6}{5\sqrt{1-\rho^2}}\right) - 1.
\end{aligned}$$

It follows that $\Phi(6/(5\sqrt{1-\rho^2})) = 0.977$, that is, $6/(5\sqrt{1-\rho^2}) \approx 2$. Therefore, $\rho \approx \pm 0.8$. The information we have is conditional on x_1 being exactly equal to its mean value of 5, so we cannot determine whether ρ is positive or negative.

***Exercise 8.22 (Normal's quadrant probability is one-to-one with correlation)** Let $(x, y)'$ follow a bivariate normal distribution with mean **0** and correlation ρ. Write $\alpha := \Pr(x > 0, y > 0)$.
(a) If $\mathrm{var}(x) = \mathrm{var}(y) = 1$, show that $\rho = \sin\left(2\pi(\alpha - 1/4)\right)$. [Hint: Start by expressing α as a probability-integral depending on ρ, differentiate the expression, then solve the differential equation (this is an indirect way of solving the integral).]
(b) Show that this result holds even when $\mathrm{var}(x) = \mathrm{var}(y) = 1$ is not satisfied.

Solution

(a) We need to express ρ in terms of α. We first express α in terms of ρ. Let $h(\rho) := \alpha = \Pr(x > 0, y > 0)$. Then

$$\begin{aligned}
h(\rho) &= \frac{1}{2\pi\sqrt{1-\rho^2}} \int_0^\infty \int_0^\infty \exp\left(-\frac{1}{2}\left(\frac{u^2 - 2\rho uv + v^2}{1-\rho^2}\right)\right) \mathrm{d}v \, \mathrm{d}u \\
&= \frac{1}{2\pi\sqrt{1-\rho^2}} \int_0^\infty \int_0^\infty \exp\left(-\frac{1}{2}\left(\frac{(1-\rho^2)u^2 + (v-\rho u)^2}{1-\rho^2}\right)\right) \mathrm{d}v \, \mathrm{d}u \\
&= \frac{1}{2\pi\sqrt{1-\rho^2}} \int_0^\infty \mathrm{e}^{-u^2/2} \int_0^\infty \exp\left(-\frac{1}{2}\left(\frac{v-\rho u}{\sqrt{1-\rho^2}}\right)^2\right) \mathrm{d}v \, \mathrm{d}u \\
&= \frac{1}{2\pi} \int_0^\infty \mathrm{e}^{-u^2/2} \int_{-\rho u/\sqrt{1-\rho^2}}^\infty \mathrm{e}^{-w^2/2} \, \mathrm{d}w \, \mathrm{d}u
\end{aligned}$$

by the transformation from (u, v) to (u, w) with $w = (v - \rho u)/\sqrt{1-\rho^2}$ and Jacobian factor $\sqrt{1-\rho^2}$. Notice the relation of w to the conditional normal. Now define

$$g(u, \rho) := \int_{-\rho u/\sqrt{1-\rho^2}}^\infty \mathrm{e}^{-w^2/2} \, \mathrm{d}w$$

whose derivative with respect to ρ is

$$\frac{\partial g(u, \rho)}{\partial \rho} = (1-\rho^2)^{-3/2} u \exp\left(-\frac{\rho^2 u^2}{2(1-\rho^2)}\right).$$

The derivative of $h(\rho)$ is

$$\begin{aligned}
h'(\rho) &= \frac{1}{2\pi} \int_0^\infty \mathrm{e}^{-u^2/2} \frac{\partial g(u, \rho)}{\partial \rho} \, \mathrm{d}u \\
&= \frac{(1-\rho^2)^{-3/2}}{2\pi} \int_0^\infty u\mathrm{e}^{-u^2/2} \exp\left(-\frac{\rho^2 u^2}{2(1-\rho^2)}\right) \mathrm{d}u \\
&= \frac{(1-\rho^2)^{-3/2}}{2\pi} \int_0^\infty u \exp\left(-\frac{u^2}{2(1-\rho^2)}\right) \mathrm{d}u \\
&= -\frac{(1-\rho^2)^{-1/2}}{2\pi} \left[\exp\left(-\frac{u^2}{2(1-\rho^2)}\right)\right]_0^\infty = \frac{(1-\rho^2)^{-1/2}}{2\pi}.
\end{aligned}$$

This implies that

$$\alpha = h(\rho) = \frac{1}{2\pi} \int \frac{\mathrm{d}\rho}{\sqrt{1-\rho^2}} + c = \frac{1}{2\pi} \sin^{-1}(\rho) + c,$$

where c is a constant of integration; see Section A.3.3 for the expression of $\sin^{-1}$ in terms of log. Since $\rho = 0$ implies $\alpha = \Pr(x > 0, y > 0) = 1/4$, we find that $c = 1/4$ and the result follows.

A similar proof can be obtained by first showing that the bivariate density here satisfies $\partial f(u,v)/\partial\rho = \partial^2 f(u,v)/(\partial u \partial v)$, then calculating

$$h'(\rho) = \frac{1}{2\pi\sqrt{1-\rho^2}}\left[\mathrm{e}^{-u^2/2}\left[\exp\left(-\frac{1}{2}\left(\frac{v-\rho u}{\sqrt{1-\rho^2}}\right)^2\right)\right]_0^\infty\right]_0^\infty = \frac{1}{2\pi\sqrt{1-\rho^2}}$$

and proceeding as before. A different solution could also be provided, making use of the method of the exercises at the start of Section 7.3, in which coordinates are changed before the double integral is worked out.

(b) Let $z_1 := \sigma_1 x$ and $z_2 := \sigma_2 y$. The quantity

$$\Pr(z_1 > 0, z_2 > 0) = \Pr(x > 0, y > 0) = \alpha$$

is invariant to the rescaling of the variates, and we know (by construction in Chapter 6) that so is ρ. As a consequence, part (a) applies also to (z_1, z_2).

8.2 Quadratic forms for the multivariate normal

Exercise 8.23 (Product of normals: dependents' case) Let $(x, y)'$ follow a bivariate normal distribution with mean $\mathbf{0}$. Assume that $\operatorname{var}(x) = \operatorname{var}(y) = 1$ and $\operatorname{cov}(x, y) = \rho$. Derive the m.g.f. of xy.

Solution

We find the m.g.f. of xy through the conditional distribution of $x \mid y$. Since $x \mid y \sim \mathrm{N}(\rho y, 1-\rho^2)$, which has a known m.g.f. (see Section 8.1 or Table 4.2), we have

$$\begin{aligned} m_{xy}(t) &= \mathrm{E}\left(\mathrm{e}^{txy}\right) = \mathrm{E}_y\left(\mathrm{E}_{x|y}\left(\mathrm{e}^{txy}\right)\right) = \mathrm{E}_y(m_{x|y}(ty)) \\ &= \mathrm{E}\left(\exp\left(t\rho y^2 + \frac{1}{2}t^2y^2(1-\rho^2)\right)\right) \\ &= \mathrm{E}\left(\exp\left(y^2(t\rho + \frac{1}{2}t^2(1-\rho^2))\right)\right) \\ &= m_{y^2}(\tau) \qquad \left(\tau := t\rho + \frac{1}{2}t^2(1-\rho^2)\right) \\ &= (1-2\tau)^{-1/2} \qquad \left(\tau < \frac{1}{2}\right), \end{aligned}$$

where we have used the fact that $y^2 \sim \chi^2(1)$. Hence,

$$m_{xy}(t) = \frac{1}{\sqrt{1-2\left(\rho t + \frac{1}{2}(1-\rho^2)t^2\right)}},$$

which should be compared with Exercise 7.22(a) where x and y were independent.

Exercise 8.24 (Quadratic form: cumulants)
(a) Let $\boldsymbol{x} \sim \mathrm{N}_m(\mathbf{0}, \boldsymbol{I}_m)$ and $\boldsymbol{\Lambda} := \operatorname{diag}(\lambda_1, \dots, \lambda_m)$, where the λ's are real and nonrandom. Prove that the j-th cumulant of $\boldsymbol{x}'\boldsymbol{\Lambda}\boldsymbol{x}$ is $2^{j-1}(j-1)!\operatorname{tr}(\boldsymbol{\Lambda}^j)$ for $j \in \mathbb{N}$.
(b) Let $\boldsymbol{x} \sim \mathrm{N}_m(\mathbf{0}, \boldsymbol{\Sigma})$, with $\boldsymbol{\Sigma}$ positive definite. Prove that the j-th cumulant of $\boldsymbol{x}'\boldsymbol{C}\boldsymbol{x}$ is $2^{j-1}(j-1)!\operatorname{tr}((\boldsymbol{C}\boldsymbol{\Sigma})^j)$ for $j \in \mathbb{N}$.

Solution
(a) We have $y := \boldsymbol{x}'\boldsymbol{\Lambda}\boldsymbol{x} = \sum_{i=1}^m \lambda_i x_i^2$. The components of $\boldsymbol{x}$ are mutually independent, so Exercise 6.53 implies that $\varkappa_y(t) = \sum_{i=1}^m \varkappa_{\lambda_i x_i^2}(t)$. Now, Exercise 3.38(c) shows that

$$\varkappa^{(j)}_{\lambda_i x_i^2}(0) = \lambda_i^j \varkappa^{(j)}_{x_i^2}(0),$$

and it remains for us to work out the j-th cumulant of $x_i^2 \sim \chi^2(1)$. Expanding the c.g.f. of a $\chi^2(1)$ variate (see, for example, the c.f. in Table 4.2), we obtain

$$-\frac{1}{2}\log(1-2t) = \frac{1}{2}\sum_{j=1}^{\infty}\frac{(2t)^j}{j};$$

hence the j-th cumulant of x_i^2 is the coefficient of $t^j/j!$, namely $2^{j-1}(j-1)!$. See also Exercise 3.37. The stated result follows from

$$\varkappa_y^{(j)}(0) = \sum_{i=1}^m \lambda_i^j \varkappa^{(j)}_{x_i^2}(0) = 2^{j-1}(j-1)!\sum_{i=1}^m \lambda_i^j = 2^{j-1}(j-1)!\operatorname{tr}(\boldsymbol{\Lambda}^j)$$

since $\boldsymbol{\Lambda}$ is diagonal.
(b) Let $\boldsymbol{z} := \boldsymbol{\Sigma}^{-1/2}\boldsymbol{x}$, where $\boldsymbol{\Sigma}^{1/2}$ is the symmetric square root of $\boldsymbol{\Sigma}$. Then, $\boldsymbol{z} \sim \mathrm{N}(\mathbf{0}, \boldsymbol{I}_m)$ and $y := \boldsymbol{x}'\boldsymbol{C}\boldsymbol{x} = \boldsymbol{z}'\boldsymbol{B}\boldsymbol{z}$, where $\boldsymbol{B} := \boldsymbol{\Sigma}^{1/2}\boldsymbol{C}\boldsymbol{\Sigma}^{1/2}$. Since $\boldsymbol{B}$ is symmetric, there exists an orthogonal matrix $\boldsymbol{T}$ ($\boldsymbol{T}'\boldsymbol{T} = \boldsymbol{I}_m$) such that $\boldsymbol{B} = \boldsymbol{T}\boldsymbol{\Lambda}\boldsymbol{T}'$, where $\boldsymbol{\Lambda}$ is a diagonal matrix containing the real eigenvalues of $\boldsymbol{B}$. Now,

$$y = \boldsymbol{z}'\boldsymbol{B}\boldsymbol{z} = \boldsymbol{z}'\boldsymbol{T}\boldsymbol{\Lambda}\boldsymbol{T}'\boldsymbol{z}$$

and, since $\boldsymbol{T}'\boldsymbol{z} \sim \mathrm{N}(\mathbf{0}, \boldsymbol{I}_m)$ by $\boldsymbol{T}'\boldsymbol{T} = \boldsymbol{I}_m$, we can use the result obtained in (a). Using

$$\operatorname{tr}(\boldsymbol{\Lambda}^j) = \operatorname{tr}((\boldsymbol{T}'\boldsymbol{B}\boldsymbol{T})^j) = \operatorname{tr}(\boldsymbol{B}^j) = \operatorname{tr}((\boldsymbol{\Sigma}^{1/2}\boldsymbol{C}\boldsymbol{\Sigma}^{1/2})^j) = \operatorname{tr}((\boldsymbol{C}\boldsymbol{\Sigma})^j)$$

gives the stated result. For a generalization of this result, see the next exercise.

***Exercise 8.25 (Quadratic form: m.g.f.)** Let $\boldsymbol{x} \sim \mathrm{N}_m(\boldsymbol{\mu}, \boldsymbol{\Sigma})$. Derive the m.g.f. of $\boldsymbol{x}'\boldsymbol{C}\boldsymbol{x}$:
(a) when $\boldsymbol{\Sigma} = \boldsymbol{I}_m$;
(b) when $\boldsymbol{\Sigma}$ is positive definite.

Solution
(a) Since $\boldsymbol{C}$ is symmetric there exists an orthogonal matrix $\boldsymbol{T}$ ($\boldsymbol{T}'\boldsymbol{T} = \boldsymbol{I}_m$) such that $\boldsymbol{T}'\boldsymbol{C}\boldsymbol{T} = \boldsymbol{\Lambda}$, where $\boldsymbol{\Lambda} = \operatorname{diag}(\lambda_1, \dots, \lambda_m)$ is a diagonal matrix of the eigenvalues of $\boldsymbol{C}$.

Letting $\boldsymbol{y} := \boldsymbol{T}'\boldsymbol{x}$, we have $\boldsymbol{x}'\boldsymbol{C}\boldsymbol{x} = (\boldsymbol{T}\boldsymbol{y})'\boldsymbol{C}(\boldsymbol{T}\boldsymbol{y}) = \boldsymbol{y}'(\boldsymbol{T}'\boldsymbol{C}\boldsymbol{T})\boldsymbol{y} = \boldsymbol{y}'\boldsymbol{\Lambda}\boldsymbol{y}$. Denoting $\boldsymbol{a} := \boldsymbol{T}'\boldsymbol{\mu}$ and using $\operatorname{var}(\boldsymbol{y}) = \boldsymbol{T}'\operatorname{var}(\boldsymbol{x})\boldsymbol{T} = \boldsymbol{I}_m$, we have $\boldsymbol{y} \sim \mathrm{N}(\boldsymbol{a}, \boldsymbol{I}_m)$. The variates $y_1^2, \dots, y_m^2$ are independently distributed, and Exercise 4.25 tells us that $y_i^2 \sim \chi^2(1, a_i^2)$ with m.g.f. obtainable from Table 4.2 as

$$m_{y_i^2}(t) = \frac{1}{\sqrt{1-2t}} \exp\left(\frac{a_i^2 t}{1-2t}\right) = \frac{1}{\sqrt{1-2t}} \exp\left(-\frac{a_i^2}{2}\left(1 - \frac{1}{1-2t}\right)\right),$$

where $t < \frac{1}{2}$. Hence,

$$\begin{aligned} m_{\boldsymbol{x}'\boldsymbol{C}\boldsymbol{x}}(t) &= \mathrm{E}\left(\mathrm{e}^{t\boldsymbol{x}'\boldsymbol{C}\boldsymbol{x}}\right) = \mathrm{E}\left(\mathrm{e}^{t\boldsymbol{y}'\boldsymbol{\Lambda}\boldsymbol{y}}\right) = \mathrm{E}\left(\mathrm{e}^{t\sum_{i=1}^m \lambda_i y_i^2}\right) \\ &= \mathrm{E}\left(\prod_{i=1}^m \mathrm{e}^{t\lambda_i y_i^2}\right) = \prod_{i=1}^m \mathrm{E}\left(\mathrm{e}^{t\lambda_i y_i^2}\right), \end{aligned}$$

the last step following from the independence of the y_i $(i = 1, \dots, m)$. Now, by the definition $\mathrm{E}(\mathrm{e}^{t\lambda_i y_i^2}) = m_{y_i^2}(t\lambda_i)$ and $\boldsymbol{T}' = \boldsymbol{T}^{-1}$, we get

$$\begin{aligned} m_{\boldsymbol{x}'\boldsymbol{C}\boldsymbol{x}}(t) &= \prod_{i=1}^m \left(\frac{1}{\sqrt{1-2t\lambda_i}} \exp\left(-\frac{a_i^2}{2}\right) \exp\left(\frac{a_i^2/2}{1-2t\lambda_i}\right)\right) \\ &= |\boldsymbol{I}_m - 2t\boldsymbol{\Lambda}|^{-1/2} \exp\left(-\frac{1}{2}\boldsymbol{a}'\boldsymbol{a} + \frac{1}{2}\boldsymbol{a}'\left(\boldsymbol{I}_m - 2t\boldsymbol{\Lambda}\right)^{-1}\boldsymbol{a}\right) \\ &= |\boldsymbol{T}(\boldsymbol{I}_m - 2t\boldsymbol{\Lambda})\boldsymbol{T}'|^{-1/2} \exp\left(-\frac{1}{2}\boldsymbol{a}'\boldsymbol{T}'\boldsymbol{T}\boldsymbol{a} + \frac{1}{2}\boldsymbol{a}'\boldsymbol{T}'\left(\boldsymbol{T}\left(\boldsymbol{I}_m - 2t\boldsymbol{\Lambda}\right)\boldsymbol{T}'\right)^{-1}\boldsymbol{T}\boldsymbol{a}\right) \\ &= |\boldsymbol{I}_m - 2t\boldsymbol{C}|^{-1/2} \exp\left(-\frac{1}{2}\boldsymbol{\mu}'\boldsymbol{\mu} + \frac{1}{2}\boldsymbol{\mu}'\left(\boldsymbol{I}_m - 2t\boldsymbol{C}\right)^{-1}\boldsymbol{\mu}\right), \end{aligned}$$

where $t\lambda_i < \frac{1}{2}$ for $i = 1, \dots, m$ and we have used $|\boldsymbol{T}\boldsymbol{Q}| = |\boldsymbol{Q}\boldsymbol{T}|$ for any conformable $\boldsymbol{Q}$. These m conditions on t can be reformulated in terms of only two of them. If $\max_i\{\lambda_i\} > 0$, then we require that $t < 1/(2\max_i\{\lambda_i\})$. If $\min_i\{\lambda_i\} < 0$, then we require that $t > 1/(2\min_i\{\lambda_i\})$.

(b) Define $\boldsymbol{z} := \boldsymbol{\Sigma}^{-1/2}\boldsymbol{x} \sim \mathrm{N}(\boldsymbol{\Sigma}^{-1/2}\boldsymbol{\mu}, \boldsymbol{I}_m)$, where $\boldsymbol{\Sigma}^{1/2}$ is the symmetric square root of $\boldsymbol{\Sigma}$. Let $\boldsymbol{B} := \boldsymbol{\Sigma}^{1/2}\boldsymbol{C}\boldsymbol{\Sigma}^{1/2}$. Then $\boldsymbol{x}'\boldsymbol{C}\boldsymbol{x} = \boldsymbol{z}'\boldsymbol{B}\boldsymbol{z}$. We have the latter's m.g.f. from (a) as

$$\begin{aligned} &|\boldsymbol{I}_m - 2t\boldsymbol{B}|^{-1/2} \exp\left(-\frac{1}{2}\boldsymbol{\mu}'\boldsymbol{\Sigma}^{-1/2}\boldsymbol{\Sigma}^{-1/2}\boldsymbol{\mu} + \frac{1}{2}\boldsymbol{\mu}'\boldsymbol{\Sigma}^{-1/2}\left(\boldsymbol{I}_m - 2t\boldsymbol{B}\right)^{-1}\boldsymbol{\Sigma}^{-1/2}\boldsymbol{\mu}\right) \\ &= |\boldsymbol{I}_m - 2t\boldsymbol{\Sigma}^{1/2}\boldsymbol{C}\boldsymbol{\Sigma}^{1/2}|^{-1/2} \\ &\quad \times \exp\left(-\frac{1}{2}\boldsymbol{\mu}'\boldsymbol{\Sigma}^{-1}\boldsymbol{\mu} + \frac{1}{2}\boldsymbol{\mu}'\boldsymbol{\Sigma}^{-1/2}\left(\boldsymbol{I}_m - 2t\boldsymbol{\Sigma}^{1/2}\boldsymbol{C}\boldsymbol{\Sigma}^{1/2}\right)^{-1}\boldsymbol{\Sigma}^{-1/2}\boldsymbol{\mu}\right) \\ &= |\boldsymbol{\Sigma}|^{1/2}|\boldsymbol{\Sigma} - 2t\boldsymbol{\Sigma}\boldsymbol{C}\boldsymbol{\Sigma}|^{-1/2} \exp\left(-\frac{1}{2}\boldsymbol{\mu}'\boldsymbol{\Sigma}^{-1}\boldsymbol{\mu} + \frac{1}{2}\boldsymbol{\mu}'\left(\boldsymbol{\Sigma} - 2t\boldsymbol{\Sigma}\boldsymbol{C}\boldsymbol{\Sigma}\right)^{-1}\boldsymbol{\mu}\right) \end{aligned}$$

where, now denoting the eigenvalues of $\boldsymbol{B}$ (not $\boldsymbol{C}$) by λ_i, we require $t\lambda_i < \frac{1}{2}$ for $i =$

$1, \dots, m$. Note that $|\boldsymbol{\Sigma}|^{1/2}|\boldsymbol{\Sigma} - 2t\boldsymbol{\Sigma}\boldsymbol{C}\boldsymbol{\Sigma}|^{-1/2} = |\boldsymbol{I}_m - 2t\boldsymbol{C}\boldsymbol{\Sigma}|^{-1/2}$ can be used to rewrite the result. Also, this result generalizes Exercise 8.24, the relation becoming apparent from the identity $\log|\boldsymbol{I}_n - \boldsymbol{A}| = -\sum_{j=1}^{\infty} \frac{1}{j}\operatorname{tr}(\boldsymbol{A}^j)$ where the spectral radius of $\boldsymbol{A}$ is less than 1.

Exercise 8.26 (Quadratic form and dependents' product) Derive the m.g.f. of Exercise 8.23 by simplifying the m.g.f. in Exercise 8.25.

Solution
Exercise 8.23 defines

$$\begin{pmatrix} x \\ y \end{pmatrix} \sim \mathrm{N}\left(\begin{pmatrix} 0 \\ 0 \end{pmatrix}, \begin{pmatrix} 1 & \rho \\ \rho & 1 \end{pmatrix}\right)$$

and requires the m.g.f. of

$$xy \equiv (x, y)\begin{pmatrix} 0 & \frac{1}{2} \\ \frac{1}{2} & 0 \end{pmatrix}\begin{pmatrix} x \\ y \end{pmatrix}.$$

Identifying

$$\boldsymbol{x} = \begin{pmatrix} x \\ y \end{pmatrix}, \quad \boldsymbol{\mu} = \begin{pmatrix} 0 \\ 0 \end{pmatrix}, \quad \boldsymbol{\Sigma} = \begin{pmatrix} 1 & \rho \\ \rho & 1 \end{pmatrix}, \quad \boldsymbol{C} = \begin{pmatrix} 0 & \frac{1}{2} \\ \frac{1}{2} & 0 \end{pmatrix},$$

where we see that $2\boldsymbol{C}$ is a permutation matrix, then substituting into the last formula of Exercise 8.25 gives

$$\begin{aligned} m_{\boldsymbol{x}'\boldsymbol{C}\boldsymbol{x}}(t) &= |\boldsymbol{I}_2 - 2t\boldsymbol{C}\boldsymbol{\Sigma}|^{-1/2} \\ &= \left|\begin{pmatrix} 1 & 0 \\ 0 & 1 \end{pmatrix} - 2t\begin{pmatrix} 0 & \frac{1}{2} \\ \frac{1}{2} & 0 \end{pmatrix}\begin{pmatrix} 1 & \rho \\ \rho & 1 \end{pmatrix}\right|^{-1/2} = \left|\begin{pmatrix} 1 & 0 \\ 0 & 1 \end{pmatrix} - t\begin{pmatrix} \rho & 1 \\ 1 & \rho \end{pmatrix}\right|^{-1/2} \\ &= \begin{vmatrix} 1-\rho t & -t \\ -t & 1-\rho t \end{vmatrix}^{-1/2} = \frac{1}{\sqrt{(1-\rho t)^2 - t^2}} = \frac{1}{\sqrt{1 - 2\left(\rho t + \frac{1}{2}(1-\rho^2)t^2\right)}}, \end{aligned}$$

where t is restricted by $2\rho t + (1-\rho^2)t^2 < 1$.

Exercise 8.27 (Quadratic form and independents' product) Let $\boldsymbol{x} \sim \mathrm{N}(\boldsymbol{0}, \boldsymbol{I}_n)$. Show that $z := \sum_{i<j} x_i x_j$ has the c.d.f.

$$\Pr(z \leqslant w) = \Pr\left(\chi^2(1) - \frac{1}{n-1}\chi^2(n-1) \leqslant \frac{2w}{n-1}\right),$$

where the two χ^2 variates are independent.

Solution
Let $\overline{x}$ be the mean of the random sample $x_1, \dots, x_n$ and s^2 its sample variance. Then we

can write

$$2z = \sum_{i \neq j} x_i x_j = \left(\sum_{i=1}^{n} x_i \right)^2 - \sum_{i=1}^{n} x_i^2$$
$$= (n\overline{x})^2 - \left((n-1) s^2 + n\overline{x}^2 \right) = (n-1) \left(n\overline{x}^2 - s^2 \right).$$

Exercise 7.16 on Helmert's transformation has shown that $(n-1)s^2 \sim \chi^2(n-1)$ independently of $\sqrt{n}\overline{x} \sim \mathrm{N}(0,1)$ and hence of $n\overline{x}^2 \sim \chi^2(1)$. This gives the required result.

A second solution is obtained by writing $z = \boldsymbol{x}'\boldsymbol{A}\boldsymbol{x}$, where $\boldsymbol{A} := \frac{1}{2}(\boldsymbol{\imath}\boldsymbol{\imath}' - \boldsymbol{I}_n)$ is a matrix having all off-diagonal elements equal to $\frac{1}{2}$ and zeros on the diagonal. The eigenvalues of $\boldsymbol{\imath}\boldsymbol{\imath}'$ are 0 ($n-1$ times) and n (once), so that the eigenvalues of $\boldsymbol{A}$ are $\lambda_1 = (n-1)/2$ and $\lambda_2 = \cdots = \lambda_n = -1/2$. Now, let $\boldsymbol{T}'\boldsymbol{A}\boldsymbol{T} = \boldsymbol{\Lambda}$, where $\boldsymbol{\Lambda}$ is the diagonal matrix of eigenvalues of $\boldsymbol{A}$ and $\boldsymbol{T}$ is orthogonal. From $\boldsymbol{y} := \boldsymbol{T}'\boldsymbol{x} \sim \mathrm{N}(\boldsymbol{0}, \boldsymbol{I}_n)$, we have

$$z = \boldsymbol{x}'\boldsymbol{A}\boldsymbol{x} = \boldsymbol{y}'\boldsymbol{\Lambda}\boldsymbol{y} = \frac{n-1}{2} \left(y_1^2 - \frac{1}{n-1} \sum_{i=2}^{n} y_i^2 \right),$$

and the result follows.

Exercise 8.28 (Quadratic form and χ^2 distribution, 1) Let $\boldsymbol{x} \sim \mathrm{N}_m(\boldsymbol{\mu}, \boldsymbol{\Sigma})$, where $\boldsymbol{\Sigma}$ is positive definite. Prove that:
(a) $(\boldsymbol{x} - \boldsymbol{\mu})' \boldsymbol{\Sigma}^{-1} (\boldsymbol{x} - \boldsymbol{\mu}) \sim \chi^2(m)$;
(b) $\boldsymbol{x}'\boldsymbol{\Sigma}^{-1}\boldsymbol{x} \sim \chi^2(m, \delta)$, where $\delta := \boldsymbol{\mu}'\boldsymbol{\Sigma}^{-1}\boldsymbol{\mu}$.

Solution
(a) Define $\boldsymbol{y} := \boldsymbol{\Sigma}^{-1/2} (\boldsymbol{x} - \boldsymbol{\mu}) \sim \mathrm{N}(\boldsymbol{0}, \boldsymbol{I}_m)$. Then

$$z := (\boldsymbol{x} - \boldsymbol{\mu})' \boldsymbol{\Sigma}^{-1} (\boldsymbol{x} - \boldsymbol{\mu}) = \boldsymbol{y}'\boldsymbol{y} = \sum_{i=1}^{m} y_i^2 \sim \chi^2(m).$$

Note that $(\boldsymbol{x} - \boldsymbol{\mu})' \boldsymbol{\Sigma}^{-1} (\boldsymbol{x} - \boldsymbol{\mu}) = w$, where $w > 0$, defines an ellipsoid (or an ellipse for $m = 2$). For $m = 2$, we have an illustration in Figure 6.4 of Exercise 6.1. Also, $\Pr(z \leqslant w)$ is the area, under the bivariate normal curve of Figure 6.3, which lies within the ellipse defined by $z = w$. This area is given by the χ^2 distribution.
(b) Define $\boldsymbol{y} := \boldsymbol{\Sigma}^{-1/2}\boldsymbol{x} \sim \mathrm{N}(\boldsymbol{c}, \boldsymbol{I}_m)$, where $\boldsymbol{c} := \boldsymbol{\Sigma}^{-1/2}\boldsymbol{\mu}$. Then

$$\boldsymbol{x}'\boldsymbol{\Sigma}^{-1}\boldsymbol{x} = \boldsymbol{y}'\boldsymbol{y} = \sum_{i=1}^{m} y_i^2 \sim \chi^2(m, \delta),$$

where $\delta := \sum_{i=1}^{m} c_i^2 = \boldsymbol{c}'\boldsymbol{c} = \boldsymbol{\mu}'\boldsymbol{\Sigma}^{-1}\boldsymbol{\mu}$, by Exercise 7.3(a).

Exercise 8.29 (Quadratic form and χ^2 distribution, 2) Let $\boldsymbol{x} \sim \mathrm{N}_m(\boldsymbol{\mu}, \boldsymbol{\Sigma})$, where $\boldsymbol{\Sigma}$ is positive definite. Show that $\boldsymbol{x}'\boldsymbol{C}\boldsymbol{x}$ follows a $\chi^2(r, \delta)$ distribution if and only if $\boldsymbol{C}\boldsymbol{\Sigma} = \boldsymbol{C}\boldsymbol{\Sigma}\boldsymbol{C}\boldsymbol{\Sigma}$, in which case $r = \mathrm{rk}(\boldsymbol{C})$ and $\delta = \boldsymbol{\mu}'\boldsymbol{\Sigma}^{-1/2}\boldsymbol{C}\boldsymbol{\Sigma}^{-1/2}\boldsymbol{\mu}$.

Solution

Again, assume first that $\boldsymbol{\Sigma} = \boldsymbol{I}_m$. Then, we need to show that $\boldsymbol{x}'\boldsymbol{C}\boldsymbol{x} \sim \chi^2(r, \delta)$ if and only if $\boldsymbol{C}$ is idempotent ($\boldsymbol{C} = \boldsymbol{C}\boldsymbol{C}$). Now, by Exercise 8.25, the m.g.f. of $\boldsymbol{x}'\boldsymbol{C}\boldsymbol{x}$ is

$$m_{\boldsymbol{x}'\boldsymbol{C}\boldsymbol{x}}(t) = \frac{1}{\prod_{i=1}^m (1-2t\lambda_i)^{1/2}} \exp\left(-\frac{1}{2}\boldsymbol{\mu}'\boldsymbol{\mu} + \frac{1}{2}\boldsymbol{\mu}'\left(\boldsymbol{I}_m - 2t\boldsymbol{C}\right)^{-1}\boldsymbol{\mu}\right),$$

where $\lambda_1, \dots, \lambda_m$ are the eigenvalues of $\boldsymbol{C}$. We also know that the m.g.f. of a $\chi^2(r, \delta)$ is

$$m_{\chi^2(r,\delta)}(t) = \frac{1}{(1-2t)^{r/2}} \exp\left(\frac{\delta t}{1-2t}\right).$$

By equating the same functions of t (powers or exponentials) in both m.g.f.s, we must have

$$\prod_{i=1}^m (1-2t\lambda_i) = (1-2t)^r$$

and

$$\frac{1}{2}\boldsymbol{\mu}'\left(\left(\boldsymbol{I}_m - 2t\boldsymbol{C}\right)^{-1} - \boldsymbol{I}_m\right)\boldsymbol{\mu} = \frac{\delta t}{1-2t}.$$

The first equality occurs if and only if r of the λ_i are equal to 1 and the remaining λ_i are 0. That is, if and only if $\boldsymbol{C}$ is idempotent of rank r. If so, then the only thing that the last equality does is to define δ. To work this out, recall that $t < 1/(2\max_i\{\lambda_i\}) = 1/2$ and use the geometric progression to expand

$$\frac{1}{2}\left(\left(\boldsymbol{I}_m - 2t\boldsymbol{C}\right)^{-1} - \boldsymbol{I}_m\right) = \frac{1}{2}\sum_{j=1}^{\infty}(2t\boldsymbol{C})^j = \frac{1}{2}\sum_{j=1}^{\infty}(2t)^j\,\boldsymbol{C},$$

where the last equality arises because $\boldsymbol{C}$ is idempotent. Collecting terms,

$$\frac{1}{2}\sum_{j=1}^{\infty}(2t)^j = -\frac{1}{2} + \frac{1}{2}\sum_{j=0}^{\infty}(2t)^j = \frac{1}{2}\left(-1 + \frac{1}{1-2t}\right) = \frac{t}{1-2t}$$

identifies δ as $\boldsymbol{\mu}'\boldsymbol{C}\boldsymbol{\mu}$.

If $\boldsymbol{\Sigma}$ is not the identity matrix, then the result follows by considering $\boldsymbol{z} := \boldsymbol{\Sigma}^{-1/2}\boldsymbol{x} \sim \mathrm{N}(\boldsymbol{\Sigma}^{-1/2}\boldsymbol{\mu}, \boldsymbol{I}_m)$ and defining $\boldsymbol{B} := \boldsymbol{\Sigma}^{1/2}\boldsymbol{C}\boldsymbol{\Sigma}^{1/2}$ as before. Then, $\boldsymbol{x}'\boldsymbol{C}\boldsymbol{x} = \boldsymbol{z}'\boldsymbol{B}\boldsymbol{z}$ and this follows a $\chi^2(r, \delta)$ distribution if and only if $\boldsymbol{B}$ is idempotent, that is, if and only if $\boldsymbol{C}\boldsymbol{\Sigma} = \boldsymbol{C}\boldsymbol{\Sigma}\boldsymbol{C}\boldsymbol{\Sigma}$ (hence $\boldsymbol{C}\boldsymbol{\Sigma}$ is idempotent). The ranks of $\boldsymbol{B}$ and $\boldsymbol{C}$ are the same, since $\boldsymbol{\Sigma}$ is of full rank.

Exercise 8.30 (Quadratic and linear forms) Let $\boldsymbol{x} \sim \mathrm{N}(\boldsymbol{0}, \boldsymbol{I}_m)$. Show that $\boldsymbol{b}'\boldsymbol{x}$ and $\boldsymbol{x}'\boldsymbol{C}\boldsymbol{x}$ are uncorrelated, but not independent in general.

Solution

Since the x_i are independent, with $\mathrm{E}(x_i) = \mathrm{E}(x_i^3) = 0$, we see that

$$\mathrm{cov}(\boldsymbol{b}'\boldsymbol{x}, \boldsymbol{x}'\boldsymbol{C}\boldsymbol{x}) = \sum_{ijk} b_i c_{jk}\,\mathrm{E}(x_i x_j x_k) = 0,$$

because $\mathrm{E}(x_i x_j x_k) = 0$ for all i, j, k (this can be proved alternatively by Exercise 6.14). But, for example, x_i and x_i^2 are not independent. The condition for independence will be derived in the next exercise.

Exercise 8.31 (Quadratic and linear forms: m.g.f.) Let $\boldsymbol{x} \sim \mathrm{N}_n(\boldsymbol{\mu}, \boldsymbol{\Sigma})$, where $\boldsymbol{\Sigma}$ is positive definite. Let $\boldsymbol{C}$ be a symmetric $n \times n$ matrix and $\boldsymbol{B}$ be an $n \times m$ matrix.
(a) Derive the joint moment-generating function of $(\boldsymbol{B}'\boldsymbol{x}, \boldsymbol{x}'\boldsymbol{C}\boldsymbol{x})$.
(b) Show that $\boldsymbol{B}'\boldsymbol{x}$ and $\boldsymbol{x}'\boldsymbol{C}\boldsymbol{x}$ are independent if and only if $\boldsymbol{C\Sigma B} = \mathbf{O}$.

Solution

We start by noting that the relation of m to n has been left intentionally unspecified: we have not required that $m \leqslant n$ or any such condition. If $m > n$, then the m-dimensional vector $\boldsymbol{B}'\boldsymbol{x}$ has a singular distribution. See also the comment at the end of Exercise 8.11.
(a) Assume first that $\boldsymbol{\Sigma} = \boldsymbol{I}_n$. Then

$$\begin{aligned} m_{\boldsymbol{B}'\boldsymbol{x},\boldsymbol{x}'\boldsymbol{C}\boldsymbol{x}}(\boldsymbol{s}, t) &= \mathrm{E}\left(\exp\left(\boldsymbol{s}'\boldsymbol{B}'\boldsymbol{x} + t\boldsymbol{x}'\boldsymbol{C}\boldsymbol{x}\right)\right) \\ &= \frac{1}{(2\pi)^{n/2}} \int_{\mathbb{R}^n} \exp\left(\boldsymbol{s}'\boldsymbol{B}'\boldsymbol{x} + t\boldsymbol{x}'\boldsymbol{C}\boldsymbol{x}\right) \exp\left(-\frac{1}{2}(\boldsymbol{x}-\boldsymbol{\mu})'(\boldsymbol{x}-\boldsymbol{\mu})\right) \mathrm{d}\boldsymbol{x} \\ &= \frac{\mathrm{e}^{-\frac{1}{2}\boldsymbol{\mu}'\boldsymbol{\mu}}}{(2\pi)^{n/2}} \int_{\mathbb{R}^n} \exp\left(-\frac{1}{2}\left(\boldsymbol{x}'(\boldsymbol{I}_n - 2t\boldsymbol{C})\boldsymbol{x} - 2(\boldsymbol{B}\boldsymbol{s}+\boldsymbol{\mu})'\boldsymbol{x}\right)\right) \mathrm{d}\boldsymbol{x}. \end{aligned}$$

Defining $\boldsymbol{\Omega} := (\boldsymbol{I}_n - 2t\boldsymbol{C})^{-1}$ and $\boldsymbol{\delta} := \boldsymbol{\Omega}(\boldsymbol{B}\boldsymbol{s}+\boldsymbol{\mu})$, then completing the quadratic form in the exponential gives

$$\begin{aligned} m_{\boldsymbol{B}'\boldsymbol{x},\boldsymbol{x}'\boldsymbol{C}\boldsymbol{x}}(\boldsymbol{s}, t) &= \frac{\mathrm{e}^{-\frac{1}{2}\boldsymbol{\mu}'\boldsymbol{\mu}}}{(2\pi)^{n/2}} \int_{\mathbb{R}^n} \exp\left(-\frac{1}{2}\left(\boldsymbol{x}'\boldsymbol{\Omega}^{-1}\boldsymbol{x} - 2\boldsymbol{\delta}'\boldsymbol{\Omega}^{-1}\boldsymbol{x}\right)\right) \mathrm{d}\boldsymbol{x} \\ &= \frac{\mathrm{e}^{-\frac{1}{2}\boldsymbol{\mu}'\boldsymbol{\mu}}}{(2\pi)^{n/2}} \int_{\mathbb{R}^n} \exp\left(-\frac{1}{2}\left((\boldsymbol{x}-\boldsymbol{\delta})'\boldsymbol{\Omega}^{-1}(\boldsymbol{x}-\boldsymbol{\delta}) - \boldsymbol{\delta}'\boldsymbol{\Omega}^{-1}\boldsymbol{\delta}\right)\right) \mathrm{d}\boldsymbol{x} \\ &= |\boldsymbol{\Omega}|^{1/2} \exp\left(-\frac{1}{2}\boldsymbol{\mu}'\boldsymbol{\mu} + \frac{1}{2}\boldsymbol{\delta}'\boldsymbol{\Omega}^{-1}\boldsymbol{\delta}\right) \\ &= |\boldsymbol{I}_n - 2t\boldsymbol{C}|^{-1/2} \exp\left(-\frac{1}{2}\boldsymbol{\mu}'\boldsymbol{\mu} + \frac{1}{2}(\boldsymbol{B}\boldsymbol{s}+\boldsymbol{\mu})'(\boldsymbol{I}_n - 2t\boldsymbol{C})^{-1}(\boldsymbol{B}\boldsymbol{s}+\boldsymbol{\mu})\right), \end{aligned}$$

using the fact that the density of $\mathrm{N}_n(\boldsymbol{\delta}, \boldsymbol{\Omega})$ integrates to 1.

In the general case, we define

$$\boldsymbol{z} := \boldsymbol{\Sigma}^{-1/2}\boldsymbol{x} \sim \mathrm{N}(\boldsymbol{\Sigma}^{-1/2}\boldsymbol{\mu}, \boldsymbol{I}_n), \qquad \boldsymbol{A} := \boldsymbol{\Sigma}^{1/2}\boldsymbol{B}, \qquad \boldsymbol{Q} := \boldsymbol{\Sigma}^{1/2}\boldsymbol{C}\boldsymbol{\Sigma}^{1/2},$$

so that $\boldsymbol{B}'\boldsymbol{x} = \boldsymbol{A}'\boldsymbol{z}$ and $\boldsymbol{x}'\boldsymbol{C}\boldsymbol{x} = \boldsymbol{z}'\boldsymbol{Q}\boldsymbol{z}$. Then

$$
\begin{aligned}
&m_{\boldsymbol{B}'\boldsymbol{x},\boldsymbol{x}'\boldsymbol{C}\boldsymbol{x}}(\boldsymbol{s},t) = m_{\boldsymbol{A}'\boldsymbol{z},\boldsymbol{z}'\boldsymbol{Q}\boldsymbol{z}}(\boldsymbol{s},t)\\
&\quad = |\boldsymbol{I}_n - 2t\boldsymbol{Q}|^{-1/2}\\
&\qquad \times \exp\left(-\frac{1}{2}\boldsymbol{\mu}'\boldsymbol{\Sigma}^{-1}\boldsymbol{\mu} + \frac{1}{2}\left(\boldsymbol{A}\boldsymbol{s} + \boldsymbol{\Sigma}^{-1/2}\boldsymbol{\mu}\right)'(\boldsymbol{I}_n - 2t\boldsymbol{Q})^{-1}\left(\boldsymbol{A}\boldsymbol{s} + \boldsymbol{\Sigma}^{-1/2}\boldsymbol{\mu}\right)\right)\\
&\quad = |\boldsymbol{I}_n - 2t\boldsymbol{C}\boldsymbol{\Sigma}|^{-1/2}\\
&\qquad \times \exp\left(-\frac{1}{2}\boldsymbol{\mu}'\boldsymbol{\Sigma}^{-1}\boldsymbol{\mu} + \frac{1}{2}(\boldsymbol{\Sigma}\boldsymbol{B}\boldsymbol{s} + \boldsymbol{\mu})'(\boldsymbol{\Sigma} - 2t\boldsymbol{\Sigma}\boldsymbol{C}\boldsymbol{\Sigma})^{-1}(\boldsymbol{\Sigma}\boldsymbol{B}\boldsymbol{s} + \boldsymbol{\mu})\right).
\end{aligned}
$$

(b) Independence of the two quadratic forms occurs when the joint m.g.f. factors into the product of the marginals. The determinant in $m_{\boldsymbol{B}'\boldsymbol{x},\boldsymbol{x}'\boldsymbol{C}\boldsymbol{x}}(\boldsymbol{s},t)$ depends only on t, so the exponential is the remaining expression where we require the separation of terms in $\boldsymbol{s}$ and t. As seen in Exercise 8.29, expanding as

$$(\boldsymbol{\Sigma} - 2t\boldsymbol{\Sigma}\boldsymbol{C}\boldsymbol{\Sigma})^{-1} = \boldsymbol{\Sigma}^{-1}(\boldsymbol{I}_n - 2t\boldsymbol{\Sigma}\boldsymbol{C})^{-1} = \boldsymbol{\Sigma}^{-1}\sum_{j=0}^{\infty}(2t\boldsymbol{\Sigma}\boldsymbol{C})^j$$

and substituting into the exponential shows that terms involving the product of $\boldsymbol{C}$ with $\boldsymbol{B}$ will vanish if and only if $\boldsymbol{C}\boldsymbol{\Sigma}\boldsymbol{B} = \mathbf{O}$. Notice the sequence of matrices, $(\boldsymbol{\Sigma}\boldsymbol{C})^2 = \boldsymbol{\Sigma}\boldsymbol{C}\boldsymbol{\Sigma}\boldsymbol{C}$ and so on, that leads to this condition.

Exercise 8.32 (Quadratic and linear forms: numbers) Let $(x, y)'$ be bivariate normally distributed with mean $\mathbf{0}$ and variance $\boldsymbol{\Sigma}$. Assume that $\operatorname{var}(x + 2y) = 16$, that $x - 2y$ and $x + y$ are independent, and that $x + 2y$ and $x^2 - 2xy + y^2$ are independent. Find:
(a) $\boldsymbol{\Sigma}$;
(b) the expectation and variance of $x^2 + 4xy + 4y^2$.

Solution
(a) Let

$$\boldsymbol{\Sigma} = \begin{pmatrix} a & b \\ b & c \end{pmatrix}, \quad \boldsymbol{C} = \begin{pmatrix} 1 & -1 \\ -1 & 1 \end{pmatrix}, \quad \boldsymbol{b} = \begin{pmatrix} 1 \\ 2 \end{pmatrix}.$$

We have three pieces of information:

$$
\begin{aligned}
\operatorname{var}(x + 2y) &= \operatorname{var}(x) + 4\operatorname{var}(y) + 4\operatorname{cov}(x, y) = a + 4c + 4b = 16,\\
\operatorname{cov}(x - 2y, x + y) &= \operatorname{var}(x) - 2\operatorname{var}(y) - \operatorname{cov}(x, y) = a - 2c - b = 0,
\end{aligned}
$$

$$\boldsymbol{C}\boldsymbol{\Sigma}\boldsymbol{b} = \begin{pmatrix} 1 & -1 \\ -1 & 1 \end{pmatrix}\begin{pmatrix} a + 2b \\ b + 2c \end{pmatrix} = \begin{pmatrix} a + b - 2c \\ -(a + b - 2c) \end{pmatrix} = \begin{pmatrix} 0 \\ 0 \end{pmatrix}.$$

Solving the three equations gives $a = 16/3$, $b = 0$, and $c = 8/3$, implying that x and y are independent but not identically distributed.

(b) Let $\boldsymbol{B} = \begin{pmatrix} 1 & 2 \\ 2 & 4 \end{pmatrix}$, so that $x^2 + 4xy + 4y^2 = \boldsymbol{x}'\boldsymbol{B}\boldsymbol{x}$. Then

$$\mathrm{E}(\boldsymbol{x}'\boldsymbol{B}\boldsymbol{x}) = \mathrm{E}\left(\operatorname{tr}\left(\boldsymbol{B}\boldsymbol{x}\boldsymbol{x}'\right)\right) = \operatorname{tr}\left(\boldsymbol{B}\boldsymbol{\Sigma}\right) = \frac{8}{3}\operatorname{tr}\left(\begin{pmatrix} 1 & 2 \\ 2 & 4 \end{pmatrix}\begin{pmatrix} 2 & 0 \\ 0 & 1 \end{pmatrix}\right) = \frac{16}{3}\operatorname{tr}\begin{pmatrix} 1 & 1 \\ 2 & 2 \end{pmatrix} = 16$$

and, as discussed in the introduction to this chapter,

$$\operatorname{var}(\boldsymbol{x}'\boldsymbol{B}\boldsymbol{x}) = 2\operatorname{tr}\left((\boldsymbol{B}\boldsymbol{\Sigma})^2\right) = 2\left(\frac{16}{3}\right)^2\operatorname{tr}\left(\begin{pmatrix} 1 & 1 \\ 2 & 2 \end{pmatrix}\begin{pmatrix} 1 & 1 \\ 2 & 2 \end{pmatrix}\right) = 512.$$

Notice that $\boldsymbol{B}\boldsymbol{\Sigma}$ is singular, hence $\operatorname{tr}(\boldsymbol{B}\boldsymbol{\Sigma})$ equals its nonzero eigenvalue and $\operatorname{tr}\left((\boldsymbol{B}\boldsymbol{\Sigma})^2\right)$ is the square of this eigenvalue.

Alternatively, since $x^2 + 4xy + 4y^2 = (x + 2y)^2$ and $(x + 2y) \sim \mathrm{N}(0, a + 4b + 4c)$, we see that $(x + 2y)^2/(a + 4b + 4c) \sim \chi^2(1)$. It follows that $\mathrm{E}((x + 2y)^2) = a + 4b + 4c = 16$ and $\operatorname{var}((x + 2y)^2) = 2(a + 4b + 4c)^2 = 512$.

Exercise 8.33 (Quadratic and linear forms: more numbers) Let $(x_1, \dots, x_4)'$ follow a normal distribution with mean **0** and variance

$$\boldsymbol{\Sigma} = \begin{pmatrix} 4 & 0 & 2 & 1 \\ 0 & 4 & 0 & 2 \\ 2 & 0 & 4 & 1 \\ 1 & 2 & 1 & 4 \end{pmatrix}.$$

(a) Find the conditional distribution of $x_1 \mid (x_3 = 1, x_4 = 0)$.
(b) Give the values of a, b, and c for which the two random variables $ax_1 + bx_3$ and $ax_2 + cx_4$ are independent.
(c) Let $y := (15x_2^2 + 12x_3^2 + 16x_4^2 + 4x_2x_3 - 16x_2x_4 - 8x_3x_4)/44$. Find the distribution of y.
(d) For which values of a and b are $ax_1 + bx_3$ and y independent?

Solution

(a) Since the joint distribution of (x_1, x_3, x_4) is given by

$$\begin{pmatrix} x_1 \\ x_3 \\ x_4 \end{pmatrix} \sim \mathrm{N}\left(\begin{pmatrix} 0 \\ 0 \\ 0 \end{pmatrix}, \begin{pmatrix} 4 & 2 & 1 \\ 2 & 4 & 1 \\ 1 & 1 & 4 \end{pmatrix}\right),$$

we can use the formula for the conditional normal to find

$$(x_1 \mid x_3 = 1, x_4 = 0) \sim \mathrm{N}\left((2, 1)\begin{pmatrix} 4 & 1 \\ 1 & 4 \end{pmatrix}^{-1}\begin{pmatrix} 1 \\ 0 \end{pmatrix}, 4 - (2, 1)\begin{pmatrix} 4 & 1 \\ 1 & 4 \end{pmatrix}^{-1}\begin{pmatrix} 2 \\ 1 \end{pmatrix}\right).$$

Since

$$(2, 1)\begin{pmatrix} 4 & 1 \\ 1 & 4 \end{pmatrix}^{-1} = (2, 1)\begin{pmatrix} \frac{4}{15} & -\frac{1}{15} \\ -\frac{1}{15} & \frac{4}{15} \end{pmatrix} = \left(\tfrac{7}{15}, \tfrac{2}{15}\right),$$

we get the $\mathrm{N}\left(\frac{7}{15}, \frac{44}{15}\right)$ conditional distribution.
(b) We have

$$\begin{aligned}
&\operatorname{cov}(ax_1 + bx_3, ax_2 + cx_4)\\
&\quad = a^2 \operatorname{cov}(x_1, x_2) + ac \operatorname{cov}(x_1, x_4) + ab \operatorname{cov}(x_2, x_3) + bc \operatorname{cov}(x_3, x_4)\\
&\quad = ac + bc = 0,
\end{aligned}$$

and hence $a = -b$ or $c = 0$.
(c) We write y as a quadratic form:

$$y = \frac{1}{44}\left(x_2, x_3, x_4\right)\begin{pmatrix} 15 & 2 & -8\\ 2 & 12 & -4\\ -8 & -4 & 16\end{pmatrix}\begin{pmatrix} x_2\\ x_3\\ x_4\end{pmatrix}.$$

Since the joint distribution of (x_2, x_3, x_4) is given by

$$\begin{pmatrix} x_2\\ x_3\\ x_4\end{pmatrix} \sim \mathrm{N}\left(\begin{pmatrix} 0\\ 0\\ 0\end{pmatrix}, \begin{pmatrix} 4 & 0 & 2\\ 0 & 4 & 1\\ 2 & 1 & 4\end{pmatrix}\right),$$

we obtain

$$\boldsymbol{C\Sigma} = \frac{1}{44}\begin{pmatrix} 15 & 2 & -8\\ 2 & 12 & -4\\ -8 & -4 & 16\end{pmatrix}\begin{pmatrix} 4 & 0 & 2\\ 0 & 4 & 1\\ 2 & 1 & 4\end{pmatrix} = \begin{pmatrix} 1 & 0 & 0\\ 0 & 1 & 0\\ 0 & 0 & 1\end{pmatrix}.$$

Since $\boldsymbol{C\Sigma} = \boldsymbol{I}_3$, we have that $(\boldsymbol{C\Sigma})^2 = \boldsymbol{C\Sigma}$ and hence, by Exercise 8.29, $y \sim \chi^2(3)$.
(d) We have

$$ax_1 + bx_3 = \left(a, 0, b, 0\right)\begin{pmatrix} x_1\\ x_2\\ x_3\\ x_4\end{pmatrix}, \quad y = \frac{1}{44}\left(x_1, x_2, x_3, x_4\right)\begin{pmatrix} 0 & 0 & 0 & 0\\ 0 & 15 & 2 & -8\\ 0 & 2 & 12 & -4\\ 0 & -8 & -4 & 16\end{pmatrix}\begin{pmatrix} x_1\\ x_2\\ x_3\\ x_4\end{pmatrix}.$$

Hence, using the result of Exercise 8.31, the linear form and the quadratic form are independent if and only if the following product is zero:

$$\frac{1}{44}\begin{pmatrix} 0 & 0 & 0 & 0\\ 0 & 15 & 2 & -8\\ 0 & 2 & 12 & -4\\ 0 & -8 & -4 & 16\end{pmatrix}\begin{pmatrix} 4 & 0 & 2 & 1\\ 0 & 4 & 0 & 2\\ 2 & 0 & 4 & 1\\ 1 & 2 & 1 & 4\end{pmatrix}\begin{pmatrix} a\\ 0\\ b\\ 0\end{pmatrix} = \frac{1}{44}\begin{pmatrix} 0\\ -4a\\ 20a + 44b\\ 8a\end{pmatrix}.$$

This occurs if and only if both a and b are zero. Hence, there are only trivial values (the linear form vanishes) for which the linear form and the quadratic form are independent.

***Exercise 8.34 (Normal sample's moments: an equivalence)** Let $\boldsymbol{x} := (x_1, \dots, x_n)'$ be a vector of independent (but not necessarily identically distributed) components, where $2 \leqslant n < \infty$. Define $\overline{x} := n^{-1}\sum_{i=1}^n x_i$ and $z := \sum_{i=1}^n (x_i - \overline{x})^2$.
(a) Show that $\boldsymbol{x} \sim \mathrm{N}(\mu\boldsymbol{\imath}, \sigma^2 \boldsymbol{I}_n)$ implies that $\overline{x}$ and z are independent.

(b) Show that $\boldsymbol{x} \sim \mathrm{N}(\mu\boldsymbol{\imath}, \sigma^2\boldsymbol{I}_n)$ implies that $\overline{x} \sim \mathrm{N}(\mu, \sigma^2/n)$ and $z/\sigma^2 \sim \chi^2(n-1)$.
(c) For $n \geqslant 3$, prove that if both $\overline{x} \sim \mathrm{N}(\mu, \sigma^2/n)$ and $z/\sigma^2 \sim \chi^2(n-1)$, then $\boldsymbol{x} \sim \mathrm{N}(\mu\boldsymbol{\imath}, \sigma^2\boldsymbol{I}_n)$. [Hint: Use Cramér's deconvolution theorem, then find the mean and variance of x_i implied by Exercise 8.29.]
(d) Why is the statement in (c) not necessarily true for $n = 2$? What additional conditions are needed to make it hold for $n = 2$?

Solution
(a) Let $\overline{x} = \boldsymbol{b}'\boldsymbol{x}$ and $z = \sum_{i=1}^{n} x_i^2 - n\overline{x}^2 = \boldsymbol{x}'\boldsymbol{C}\boldsymbol{x}$, where $\boldsymbol{b} := \frac{1}{n}\boldsymbol{\imath}$ and $\boldsymbol{C} := \boldsymbol{I}_n - \frac{1}{n}\boldsymbol{\imath}\boldsymbol{\imath}'$. Then, by Exercise 8.31, $\overline{x}$ and z are independent if and only if $\boldsymbol{C}\boldsymbol{\Sigma}\boldsymbol{b} = \boldsymbol{0}$, that is, if and only if $\boldsymbol{C}\boldsymbol{b} = \boldsymbol{0}$. We have

$$\boldsymbol{C}\boldsymbol{b} = \left(\boldsymbol{I}_n - \frac{1}{n}\boldsymbol{\imath}\boldsymbol{\imath}'\right)\left(\frac{1}{n}\boldsymbol{\imath}\right) = \frac{1}{n}\boldsymbol{\imath} - \frac{1}{n^2}\boldsymbol{\imath}\boldsymbol{\imath}'\boldsymbol{\imath} = \boldsymbol{0},$$

which establishes the result. Note that $\boldsymbol{C} = \boldsymbol{C}^2$ implies $z = (\boldsymbol{C}\boldsymbol{x})'(\boldsymbol{C}\boldsymbol{x})$, where $\boldsymbol{C}\boldsymbol{x}$ is the vector of "de-meaned" values $x_i - \overline{x}$.
(b) The result for $\overline{x}$ follows as a special case of Exercise 7.15. Alternatively, recall that linear combinations of normals are also normal, with

$$\mathrm{E}\left(\frac{1}{n}\boldsymbol{\imath}'\boldsymbol{x}\right) = \frac{1}{n}\boldsymbol{\imath}'\,\mathrm{E}(\boldsymbol{x}) = \frac{1}{n}\boldsymbol{\imath}'(\mu\boldsymbol{\imath}) = \mu$$

and

$$\mathrm{var}\left(\frac{1}{n}\boldsymbol{\imath}'\boldsymbol{x}\right) = \left(\frac{1}{n}\boldsymbol{\imath}\right)'\mathrm{var}(\boldsymbol{x})\left(\frac{1}{n}\boldsymbol{\imath}\right) = \frac{\sigma^2\boldsymbol{\imath}'\boldsymbol{\imath}}{n^2} = \frac{\sigma^2}{n}.$$

For z/σ^2, we note that $\boldsymbol{C}$ is idempotent with

$$\mathrm{tr}(\boldsymbol{C}) = \mathrm{tr}\left(\boldsymbol{I}_n - \frac{1}{n}\boldsymbol{\imath}\boldsymbol{\imath}'\right) = n - \frac{1}{n}\boldsymbol{\imath}'\boldsymbol{\imath} = n - 1$$

and rank equal to the trace. Then $\sigma^{-2}z = \boldsymbol{x}'(\sigma^{-2}\boldsymbol{C})\boldsymbol{x} \sim \chi^2(n-1)$ by Exercise 8.29.
(c) For $n < \infty$, Cramér's deconvolution theorem (see, for example, Exercise 8.7) can be used $n-1$ times to tell us that $\overline{x} \sim \mathrm{N}(\mu, \sigma^2/n)$ decomposes into the sum of n independent normals, so that $\boldsymbol{\Sigma} := \mathrm{var}(\boldsymbol{x})$ is a diagonal matrix satisfying $\mathrm{tr}(\boldsymbol{\Sigma}) = n\sigma^2$. However, that theorem does not require the components of the decomposition to have identical variances and means, and we need to derive these two results, respectively. First, $\boldsymbol{x}'(\sigma^{-2}\boldsymbol{C})\boldsymbol{x} \sim \chi^2(n-1)$ implies, by Exercise 8.29, that $\boldsymbol{C} = \sigma^{-2}\boldsymbol{C}\boldsymbol{\Sigma}\boldsymbol{C}$. Since $\boldsymbol{C} = \boldsymbol{C}^2$, we have $\boldsymbol{C}\boldsymbol{D}\boldsymbol{C} = \mathbf{O}$, where

$$\boldsymbol{D} \equiv \mathrm{diag}(d_1, \dots, d_n) := \boldsymbol{I}_n - \sigma^{-2}\boldsymbol{\Sigma}$$

with $\mathrm{tr}(\boldsymbol{D}) = n - \sigma^{-2}(n\sigma^2) = 0$. Now

$$\boldsymbol{C}\boldsymbol{D}\boldsymbol{C} = \left(\boldsymbol{I}_n - \frac{1}{n}\boldsymbol{\imath}\boldsymbol{\imath}'\right)\left(\boldsymbol{D} - \frac{1}{n}\boldsymbol{D}\boldsymbol{\imath}\boldsymbol{\imath}'\right) = \boldsymbol{D} - \frac{1}{n}\boldsymbol{D}\boldsymbol{\imath}\boldsymbol{\imath}' - \frac{1}{n}\boldsymbol{\imath}\boldsymbol{\imath}'\boldsymbol{D} + \frac{1}{n^2}\boldsymbol{\imath}\boldsymbol{\imath}'\boldsymbol{D}\boldsymbol{\imath}\boldsymbol{\imath}'$$

and, using $\boldsymbol{\imath}'\boldsymbol{D}\boldsymbol{\imath} = \mathrm{tr}(\boldsymbol{D}) = 0$, the i-th diagonal element of $\boldsymbol{C}\boldsymbol{D}\boldsymbol{C}$ is $(1 - 2/n)d_i$. For

$n \geqslant 3$, the equation $\boldsymbol{CDC} = \mathbf{O}$ thus gives $d_i = 0$ for $i = 1, \dots, n$, and hence $\boldsymbol{\Sigma} = \sigma^2 \boldsymbol{I}_n$. Second, to obtain the mean, Exercise 8.29 tells us that the noncentrality parameter of $\boldsymbol{x}' \left(\sigma^{-2}\boldsymbol{C}\right) \boldsymbol{x}$ is given by $\boldsymbol{\mu}'\boldsymbol{\Sigma}^{-1/2} \left(\sigma^{-2}\boldsymbol{C}\right) \boldsymbol{\Sigma}^{-1/2}\boldsymbol{\mu}$. Since our quadratic form has a central χ^2 distribution and $\boldsymbol{\Sigma} = \sigma^2 \boldsymbol{I}_n$, we obtain $\boldsymbol{C\mu} = \mathbf{0}$ and hence $\boldsymbol{\mu} = \boldsymbol{\imath\imath}'\boldsymbol{\mu}/n$. Then $\mathrm{E}(\boldsymbol{x}) = \mu\boldsymbol{\imath}$ follows since $\mu = \mathrm{E}\left(\overline{x}\right) = \mathrm{E}\left(\boldsymbol{\imath}'\boldsymbol{x}/n\right) = \boldsymbol{\imath}'\boldsymbol{\mu}/n$.
(d) When $n = 2$,

$$\boldsymbol{C} = \frac{1}{2}\begin{pmatrix} 1 & -1 \\ -1 & 1 \end{pmatrix}$$

and

$$\begin{aligned}\boldsymbol{CDC} &= \frac{1}{4}\begin{pmatrix} 1 & -1 \\ -1 & 1 \end{pmatrix}\begin{pmatrix} d_1 & 0 \\ 0 & d_2 \end{pmatrix}\begin{pmatrix} 1 & -1 \\ -1 & 1 \end{pmatrix} \\ &= \frac{1}{4}\begin{pmatrix} d_1 & -d_2 \\ -d_1 & d_2 \end{pmatrix}\begin{pmatrix} 1 & -1 \\ -1 & 1 \end{pmatrix} = \frac{d_1 + d_2}{4}\begin{pmatrix} 1 & -1 \\ -1 & 1 \end{pmatrix}.\end{aligned}$$

Equating the latter to zero provides no further information on the variance of the two normal components of $\boldsymbol{x}$, beyond what is already known from $\operatorname{tr}(\boldsymbol{D}) = 0$. In this case, result (c) does not hold.

As a counterexample, let

$$\begin{pmatrix} x_1 \\ x_2 \end{pmatrix} \sim \mathrm{N}\left(\begin{pmatrix} 0 \\ 0 \end{pmatrix}, \begin{pmatrix} \frac{1}{2} & 0 \\ 0 & \frac{3}{2} \end{pmatrix}\right).$$

Then, it is still the case that $\overline{x} \sim \mathrm{N}(0, \frac{1}{2})$ and

$$z = \frac{1}{2}\left(x_1, x_2\right)\begin{pmatrix} 1 & -1 \\ -1 & 1 \end{pmatrix}\begin{pmatrix} x_1 \\ x_2 \end{pmatrix} = \frac{1}{2}\left(x_1 - x_2\right)^2 \sim \chi^2(1).$$

However, $\operatorname{cov}(x_1 + x_2, x_1 - x_2) = \operatorname{var}(x_1) - \operatorname{var}(x_2) \neq 0$, so that $\overline{x}$ is not independent of z. We will now show that assuming the independence of $\overline{x}$ and z makes the statement in (c) hold for $n = 2$ also.

Independence of the linear form $\boldsymbol{\imath}'\boldsymbol{x}/n$ and the quadratic form $\boldsymbol{x}'\boldsymbol{Cx}/\sigma^2$ occurs if and only if $\boldsymbol{C\Sigma\imath} = \mathbf{0}$, by Exercise 8.31(b). For $n = 2$, setting

$$\frac{1}{2}\begin{pmatrix} 1 & -1 \\ -1 & 1 \end{pmatrix}\begin{pmatrix} \sigma_1^2 & 0 \\ 0 & \sigma_2^2 \end{pmatrix}\begin{pmatrix} 1 \\ 1 \end{pmatrix} = \frac{1}{2}\begin{pmatrix} \sigma_1^2 - \sigma_2^2 \\ \sigma_2^2 - \sigma_1^2 \end{pmatrix}$$

equal to zero, we get $\sigma_1^2 = \sigma_2^2$.

Exercise 8.35 (Quadratic forms: covariance)
(a) If $\boldsymbol{x} \sim \mathrm{N}_m(\mathbf{0}, \boldsymbol{I}_m)$, prove that

$$\mathrm{E}(\boldsymbol{x}'\boldsymbol{Bx} \times \boldsymbol{x}'\boldsymbol{Cx}) = \operatorname{tr}(\boldsymbol{B})\operatorname{tr}(\boldsymbol{C}) + 2\operatorname{tr}(\boldsymbol{BC}).$$

(b) If $\boldsymbol{x} \sim \mathrm{N}_m(\mathbf{0}, \boldsymbol{\Sigma})$, where $\boldsymbol{\Sigma}$ is positive definite, prove that

$$\mathrm{E}(\boldsymbol{x}'\boldsymbol{Bx} \times \boldsymbol{x}'\boldsymbol{Cx}) = \operatorname{tr}(\boldsymbol{B\Sigma})\operatorname{tr}(\boldsymbol{C\Sigma}) + 2\operatorname{tr}(\boldsymbol{B\Sigma C\Sigma}).$$

(c) If $\boldsymbol{x} \sim \mathrm{N}_m(\mathbf{0}, \boldsymbol{\Sigma})$, where $\boldsymbol{\Sigma}$ is positive definite, prove that

$$\mathrm{E}(x_1 x_2 x_3 x_4) = \sigma_{12}\sigma_{34} + \sigma_{13}\sigma_{24} + \sigma_{14}\sigma_{23}.$$

Solution

(a) We write

$$\boldsymbol{x}'\boldsymbol{B}\boldsymbol{x} \times \boldsymbol{x}'\boldsymbol{C}\boldsymbol{x} = \sum_{i,j=1}^{m} \sum_{s,t=1}^{m} b_{ij} c_{st} x_i x_j x_s x_t,$$

so that

$$\begin{aligned}\mathrm{E}(\boldsymbol{x}'\boldsymbol{B}\boldsymbol{x} \times \boldsymbol{x}'\boldsymbol{C}\boldsymbol{x}) &= \sum_{i,j=1}^{m} \sum_{s,t=1}^{m} b_{ij} c_{st}\, \mathrm{E}(x_i x_j x_s x_t) \\ &= \sum_{i=1}^{m} b_{ii} c_{ii}\, \mathrm{E}(x_i^4) + \sum_{i \neq j} (b_{ii} c_{jj} + b_{ij} c_{ij} + b_{ij} c_{ji})\, \mathrm{E}(x_i^2 x_j^2)\end{aligned}$$

by the independence of the x's, as in the proof of Exercise 6.7(a).

By $\mathrm{E}(x_i^2 x_j^2) = \mathrm{E}(x_i^2)\,\mathrm{E}(x_j^2) = 1$ when $i \neq j$,

$$\begin{aligned}\mathrm{E}(\boldsymbol{x}'\boldsymbol{B}\boldsymbol{x} \times \boldsymbol{x}'\boldsymbol{C}\boldsymbol{x}) &= 3\sum_{i=1}^{m} b_{ii} c_{ii} + \sum_{i \neq j} (b_{ii} c_{jj} + b_{ij} c_{ij} + b_{ij} c_{ji}) \\ &= \sum_{i,j} (b_{ii} c_{jj} + b_{ij} c_{ij} + b_{ij} c_{ji}) \\ &= \mathrm{tr}(\boldsymbol{B})\,\mathrm{tr}(\boldsymbol{C}) + 2\,\mathrm{tr}(\boldsymbol{B}\boldsymbol{C})\end{aligned}$$

by the symmetry of $\boldsymbol{B}$ and $\boldsymbol{C}$.

(b) Let $\boldsymbol{z} := \boldsymbol{\Sigma}^{-1/2}\boldsymbol{x}$, where $\boldsymbol{\Sigma}^{1/2}$ is the symmetric square root of $\boldsymbol{\Sigma}$. Then, $\boldsymbol{z} \sim \mathrm{N}(\mathbf{0}, \boldsymbol{I}_m)$ and, since $\boldsymbol{\Sigma}^{1/2}\boldsymbol{B}\boldsymbol{\Sigma}^{1/2}$ and $\boldsymbol{\Sigma}^{1/2}\boldsymbol{C}\boldsymbol{\Sigma}^{1/2}$ are symmetric, we can use (a) to get

$$\begin{aligned}\mathrm{E}(\boldsymbol{x}'\boldsymbol{B}\boldsymbol{x} \times \boldsymbol{x}'\boldsymbol{C}\boldsymbol{x}) &= \mathrm{E}(\boldsymbol{z}'\boldsymbol{\Sigma}^{1/2}\boldsymbol{B}\boldsymbol{\Sigma}^{1/2}\boldsymbol{z} \times \boldsymbol{z}'\boldsymbol{\Sigma}^{1/2}\boldsymbol{C}\boldsymbol{\Sigma}^{1/2}\boldsymbol{z}) \\ &= \mathrm{tr}(\boldsymbol{\Sigma}^{1/2}\boldsymbol{B}\boldsymbol{\Sigma}^{1/2})\,\mathrm{tr}(\boldsymbol{\Sigma}^{1/2}\boldsymbol{C}\boldsymbol{\Sigma}^{1/2}) \\ &\quad + 2\,\mathrm{tr}(\boldsymbol{\Sigma}^{1/2}\boldsymbol{B}\boldsymbol{\Sigma}^{1/2}\boldsymbol{\Sigma}^{1/2}\boldsymbol{C}\boldsymbol{\Sigma}^{1/2}) \\ &= \mathrm{tr}(\boldsymbol{B}\boldsymbol{\Sigma})\,\mathrm{tr}(\boldsymbol{C}\boldsymbol{\Sigma}) + 2\,\mathrm{tr}(\boldsymbol{B}\boldsymbol{\Sigma}\boldsymbol{C}\boldsymbol{\Sigma}).\end{aligned}$$

Notice that $\mathrm{tr}(\boldsymbol{B}\boldsymbol{\Sigma}) = \mathrm{E}(\boldsymbol{x}'\boldsymbol{B}\boldsymbol{x})$ and $\mathrm{tr}(\boldsymbol{C}\boldsymbol{\Sigma}) = \mathrm{E}(\boldsymbol{x}'\boldsymbol{C}\boldsymbol{x})$, so that the covariance is equal to $2\,\mathrm{tr}(\boldsymbol{B}\boldsymbol{\Sigma}\boldsymbol{C}\boldsymbol{\Sigma})$ and $\boldsymbol{B}\boldsymbol{\Sigma}\boldsymbol{C} = \mathbf{O}$ yields zero correlation (independence will be analyzed in Exercise 8.36).

(c) We only need to consider $m = 4$, since the marginal distribution of $(x_1, x_2, x_3, x_4)'$ is invariant to the rest of $\boldsymbol{x}$. Let $\boldsymbol{B} := \frac{1}{2}(\boldsymbol{e}_1\boldsymbol{e}_2' + \boldsymbol{e}_2\boldsymbol{e}_1')$ and $\boldsymbol{C} := \frac{1}{2}(\boldsymbol{e}_3\boldsymbol{e}_4' + \boldsymbol{e}_4\boldsymbol{e}_3')$, where $\boldsymbol{e}_i$ is the i-th column of $\boldsymbol{I}_4$. Both $\boldsymbol{B}$ and $\boldsymbol{C}$ are symmetric. Then $\boldsymbol{x}'\boldsymbol{B}\boldsymbol{x} = x_1 x_2$ and

$\boldsymbol{x}'\boldsymbol{C}\boldsymbol{x} = x_3 x_4$, and the result in (b) implies that

$$\begin{aligned} \mathrm{E}(x_1x_2x_3x_4) &= \mathrm{E}(\boldsymbol{x}'\boldsymbol{B}\boldsymbol{x} \times \boldsymbol{x}'\boldsymbol{C}\boldsymbol{x}) = \operatorname{tr}(\boldsymbol{B}\boldsymbol{\Sigma})\operatorname{tr}(\boldsymbol{C}\boldsymbol{\Sigma}) + 2\operatorname{tr}(\boldsymbol{B}\boldsymbol{\Sigma}\boldsymbol{C}\boldsymbol{\Sigma}) \\ &= \frac{1}{4}\operatorname{tr}((\boldsymbol{e}_1\boldsymbol{e}_2' + \boldsymbol{e}_2\boldsymbol{e}_1')\boldsymbol{\Sigma})\operatorname{tr}((\boldsymbol{e}_3\boldsymbol{e}_4' + \boldsymbol{e}_4\boldsymbol{e}_3')\boldsymbol{\Sigma}) \\ &\quad + \frac{1}{2}\operatorname{tr}((\boldsymbol{e}_1\boldsymbol{e}_2' + \boldsymbol{e}_2\boldsymbol{e}_1')\boldsymbol{\Sigma}(\boldsymbol{e}_3\boldsymbol{e}_4' + \boldsymbol{e}_4\boldsymbol{e}_3')\boldsymbol{\Sigma}) \\ &= \boldsymbol{e}_1'\boldsymbol{\Sigma}\boldsymbol{e}_2\boldsymbol{e}_3'\boldsymbol{\Sigma}\boldsymbol{e}_4 + \boldsymbol{e}_1'\boldsymbol{\Sigma}(\boldsymbol{e}_3\boldsymbol{e}_4' + \boldsymbol{e}_4\boldsymbol{e}_3')\boldsymbol{\Sigma}\boldsymbol{e}_2 \\ &= \sigma_{12}\sigma_{34} + \sigma_{13}\sigma_{24} + \sigma_{14}\sigma_{23}. \end{aligned}$$

We saw this result in Exercises 8.19 and 8.20.

Exercise 8.36 (Quadratic forms: independence) Let $\boldsymbol{x} \sim \mathrm{N}_m(\boldsymbol{\mu}, \boldsymbol{\Sigma})$, where $\boldsymbol{\Sigma}$ is positive definite.
(a) Obtain the joint moment-generating function of $(\boldsymbol{x}'\boldsymbol{B}\boldsymbol{x}, \boldsymbol{x}'\boldsymbol{C}\boldsymbol{x})$.
(b) Show that $\boldsymbol{x}'\boldsymbol{B}\boldsymbol{x}$ and $\boldsymbol{x}'\boldsymbol{C}\boldsymbol{x}$ are independent if and only if $\boldsymbol{B}\boldsymbol{\Sigma}\boldsymbol{C} = \mathbf{O}$. [Hint: Use the *Craig–Sakamoto lemma* of matrix algebra, which says that for two symmetric matrices $\boldsymbol{A}_1$ and $\boldsymbol{A}_2$, we have

$$\boldsymbol{A}_1\boldsymbol{A}_2 = \mathbf{O} \iff |\boldsymbol{I}_m - k_1\boldsymbol{A}_1| \times |\boldsymbol{I}_m - k_2\boldsymbol{A}_2| = |\boldsymbol{I}_m - k_1\boldsymbol{A}_1 - k_2\boldsymbol{A}_2|$$

for all real-valued scalars k_1 and k_2.]

Solution
(a) By writing

$$m(t_1, t_2) = \mathrm{E}(\exp(t_1\boldsymbol{x}'\boldsymbol{B}\boldsymbol{x} + t_2\boldsymbol{x}'\boldsymbol{C}\boldsymbol{x})) = \mathrm{E}(\exp(\boldsymbol{x}'(t_1\boldsymbol{B} + t_2\boldsymbol{C})\boldsymbol{x})),$$

we can use the m.g.f. previously derived in Exercise 8.25. Hence,

$$\begin{aligned} m(t_1, t_2) &= |\boldsymbol{I}_m - 2t_1\boldsymbol{B}\boldsymbol{\Sigma} - 2t_2\boldsymbol{C}\boldsymbol{\Sigma}|^{-1/2} \\ &\quad \times \exp\left(-\frac{1}{2}\boldsymbol{\mu}'\boldsymbol{\Sigma}^{-1}\boldsymbol{\mu} + \frac{1}{2}\boldsymbol{\mu}'\left(\boldsymbol{\Sigma} - 2\boldsymbol{\Sigma}(t_1\boldsymbol{B} + t_2\boldsymbol{C})\boldsymbol{\Sigma}\right)^{-1}\boldsymbol{\mu}\right). \end{aligned}$$

(b) Independence of the two quadratic forms occurs when the joint m.g.f. factors into the product of the marginals. We shall need the Craig–Sakamoto lemma here. Letting $\boldsymbol{A}_1 = \boldsymbol{\Sigma}^{1/2}\boldsymbol{B}\boldsymbol{\Sigma}^{1/2}$ and $\boldsymbol{A}_2 = \boldsymbol{\Sigma}^{1/2}\boldsymbol{C}\boldsymbol{\Sigma}^{1/2}$, we can factor the determinant in the m.g.f. if and only if $\boldsymbol{\Sigma}^{1/2}\boldsymbol{B}\boldsymbol{\Sigma}\boldsymbol{C}\boldsymbol{\Sigma}^{1/2} = \mathbf{O}$, that is, $\boldsymbol{B}\boldsymbol{\Sigma}\boldsymbol{C} = \mathbf{O}$. Finally, as seen in Exercise 8.29, we can use the expansion

$$\begin{aligned} \left(\boldsymbol{\Sigma} - 2\boldsymbol{\Sigma}(t_1\boldsymbol{B} + t_2\boldsymbol{C})\boldsymbol{\Sigma}\right)^{-1} &= \boldsymbol{\Sigma}^{-1}\left(\boldsymbol{I}_m - 2\boldsymbol{\Sigma}(t_1\boldsymbol{B} + t_2\boldsymbol{C})\right)^{-1} \\ &= \boldsymbol{\Sigma}^{-1}\sum_{j=0}^{\infty}\left(2\boldsymbol{\Sigma}(t_1\boldsymbol{B} + t_2\boldsymbol{C})\right)^j, \end{aligned}$$

subject to the usual conditions on t_1 and t_2. Terms involving the product $t_1 \times t_2$ will vanish identically if and only if

$$(\boldsymbol{\Sigma}(t_1\boldsymbol{B}+t_2\boldsymbol{C}))^2 = t_1^2\boldsymbol{\Sigma B\Sigma B} + t_2^2\boldsymbol{\Sigma C\Sigma C},$$

that is, if and only if $\boldsymbol{B\Sigma C} = \mathbf{O}$. Should this happen, then

$$\begin{aligned}(\boldsymbol{\Sigma} - 2\boldsymbol{\Sigma}(t_1\boldsymbol{B}+t_2\boldsymbol{C})\boldsymbol{\Sigma})^{-1} &= \boldsymbol{\Sigma}^{-1}\sum_{j=0}^{\infty}\left((2t_1\boldsymbol{\Sigma B})^j + (2t_2\boldsymbol{\Sigma C})^j\right)\\ &= (\boldsymbol{\Sigma} - 2t_1\boldsymbol{\Sigma B\Sigma})^{-1} + (\boldsymbol{\Sigma} - 2t_2\boldsymbol{\Sigma C\Sigma})^{-1}\end{aligned}$$

and the exponential of the m.g.f. also factors into the product of separate exponential functions of t_1 and t_2. This completes the factorization of $m(t_1, t_2)$.

Exercise 8.37 (Robustness of F, again) Let $\boldsymbol{y}$ be an $n \times 1$ vector which is spherically distributed, with $\Pr(\boldsymbol{y} = \mathbf{0}) = 0$, and define $\boldsymbol{B}$ and $\boldsymbol{C}$ to be $n \times n$ idempotent matrices of positive rank and satisfying $\boldsymbol{BC} = \mathbf{O}$.

(a) Show that

$$z := \frac{\operatorname{rk}(\boldsymbol{C})}{\operatorname{rk}(\boldsymbol{B})} \times \frac{\boldsymbol{y}'\boldsymbol{B}\boldsymbol{y}}{\boldsymbol{y}'\boldsymbol{C}\boldsymbol{y}} \sim \mathrm{F}(\operatorname{rk}(\boldsymbol{B}), \operatorname{rk}(\boldsymbol{C})).$$

(b) Assume further that $\boldsymbol{y}$ is multivariate t with ν degrees of freedom. Show that the c.d.f. of the quadratic form $\boldsymbol{y}'\boldsymbol{B}\boldsymbol{y}$ is $\Pr(\boldsymbol{y}'\boldsymbol{B}\boldsymbol{y} \leqslant w) = F(w/\operatorname{rk}(\boldsymbol{B}))$, where F denotes the c.d.f. of an $\mathrm{F}(\operatorname{rk}(\boldsymbol{B}), \nu)$ variate here. How do you reconcile this F distribution, which arises from a quadratic form, with the χ^2 distribution that arises from quadratic forms in normals?

Solution

(a) We proved a special case of this result in Exercise 7.30. By Exercise 7.29, all spherical variates $\boldsymbol{y}$, normal or otherwise, have $\|\boldsymbol{y}\|^{-1}\boldsymbol{y}$ distributed uniformly on the unit sphere. By writing

$$z = \frac{\operatorname{rk}(\boldsymbol{C})}{\operatorname{rk}(\boldsymbol{B})} \times \frac{\left(\|\boldsymbol{y}\|^{-1}\boldsymbol{y}\right)'\boldsymbol{B}\left(\|\boldsymbol{y}\|^{-1}\boldsymbol{y}\right)}{\left(\|\boldsymbol{y}\|^{-1}\boldsymbol{y}\right)'\boldsymbol{C}\left(\|\boldsymbol{y}\|^{-1}\boldsymbol{y}\right)},$$

we see that z depends on $\boldsymbol{y}$ only though $\|\boldsymbol{y}\|^{-1}\boldsymbol{y}$. We shall therefore be able to apply known results on quadratic forms for $\mathrm{N}(\mathbf{0}, \boldsymbol{I}_n)$ variates, without loss of generality, to all sphericals. Exercise 8.29 implies that

$$\boldsymbol{y}'\boldsymbol{B}\boldsymbol{y} \sim \chi^2(\operatorname{rk}(\boldsymbol{B})) \quad \text{and} \quad \boldsymbol{y}'\boldsymbol{C}\boldsymbol{y} \sim \chi^2(\operatorname{rk}(\boldsymbol{C})),$$

while Exercise 8.36 implies that they are independently distributed if and only if $\boldsymbol{BC} = \mathbf{O}$. The representation of an F variate in terms of the ratio of independent χ^2 variates was proved in Exercise 4.32, which establishes our result.

(b) The matrix $\boldsymbol{B}$ is symmetric idempotent, so $\boldsymbol{B} = \boldsymbol{T}\operatorname{diag}(\boldsymbol{I}_r, \mathbf{O})\boldsymbol{T}'$, where $\boldsymbol{T}$ is orthogonal and $r := \operatorname{rk}(\boldsymbol{B})$. Then, defining $\boldsymbol{x} := \boldsymbol{T}'\boldsymbol{y}$, its distribution is the same as $\boldsymbol{y}$, since

$\boldsymbol{x}'\boldsymbol{x} = \boldsymbol{y}'\boldsymbol{y}$ and the Jacobian factor is $|\det \boldsymbol{T}| = 1$. Therefore, $\boldsymbol{x}$ is multivariate t with ν degrees of freedom, and

$$\boldsymbol{y}'\boldsymbol{B}\boldsymbol{y} = \boldsymbol{y}'\boldsymbol{T}\,\mathrm{diag}\,(\boldsymbol{I}_r, \mathbf{O})\,\boldsymbol{T}'\boldsymbol{y} = \boldsymbol{x}'\,\mathrm{diag}\,(\boldsymbol{I}_r, \mathbf{O})\,\boldsymbol{x} = \sum_{i=1}^{r} x_i^2,$$

where $x_i^2 \sim \mathrm{F}(1, \nu)$ and $r^{-1}\sum_{i=1}^{r} x_i^2 \sim \mathrm{F}(r, \nu)$ by the reproductive property of χ^2 (the numerator of F). Hence, $\boldsymbol{y}'\boldsymbol{B}\boldsymbol{y}/\operatorname{rk}(\boldsymbol{B}) \sim \mathrm{F}(\operatorname{rk}(\boldsymbol{B}), \nu)$ as required.

There are two ways to establish the relation in the question, both of which require letting $\nu \to \infty$: one way is through the components $\boldsymbol{y}$ of the quadratic form, and another is through the distribution of the form z. The first way follows directly from the multivariate normal being the limit of t when $\nu \to \infty$ (see the discussion following (6.7)), in which case $\boldsymbol{y} \sim \mathrm{N}(\mathbf{0}, \boldsymbol{I}_n)$ and the $\chi^2(r)$ distribution of $\boldsymbol{y}'\boldsymbol{B}\boldsymbol{y}$ follows from Exercise 8.29. The second way will follow in Exercise 10.32(d).

Exercise 8.38 (Quadratic forms: orthogonal projections) Let $\boldsymbol{x} \sim \mathrm{N}(\mathbf{0}, \boldsymbol{I}_m)$ and let $\boldsymbol{A}$ be an $m \times k$ matrix of rank k. Let $\boldsymbol{P} := \boldsymbol{A}(\boldsymbol{A}'\boldsymbol{A})^{-1}\boldsymbol{A}'$ and $\boldsymbol{M} := \boldsymbol{I}_m - \boldsymbol{P}$. Obtain the distribution of $\boldsymbol{x}'\boldsymbol{P}\boldsymbol{x}$ and of $\boldsymbol{x}'\boldsymbol{M}\boldsymbol{x}$, and show that they are independent.

Solution

The matrices $\boldsymbol{P}$ and $\boldsymbol{M}$ are both idempotent, so that Exercise 8.29 applies. We have

$$\boldsymbol{P}^2 = \boldsymbol{A}(\boldsymbol{A}'\boldsymbol{A})^{-1}\boldsymbol{A}'\boldsymbol{A}(\boldsymbol{A}'\boldsymbol{A})^{-1}\boldsymbol{A}' = \boldsymbol{A}(\boldsymbol{A}'\boldsymbol{A})^{-1}\boldsymbol{A}' = \boldsymbol{P},$$

with

$$\operatorname{rk}(\boldsymbol{P}) = \operatorname{tr}(\boldsymbol{P}) = \operatorname{tr}\left(\boldsymbol{A}(\boldsymbol{A}'\boldsymbol{A})^{-1}\boldsymbol{A}'\right) = \operatorname{tr}\left((\boldsymbol{A}'\boldsymbol{A})^{-1}\boldsymbol{A}'\boldsymbol{A}\right) = \operatorname{tr}(\boldsymbol{I}_k) = k.$$

Similarly,

$$\boldsymbol{M}^2 = (\boldsymbol{I}_m - \boldsymbol{P})(\boldsymbol{I}_m - \boldsymbol{P}) = \boldsymbol{I}_m - \boldsymbol{P} - \boldsymbol{P} + \boldsymbol{P}^2 = \boldsymbol{I}_m - \boldsymbol{P} = \boldsymbol{M}$$

by $\boldsymbol{P}^2 = \boldsymbol{P}$, and

$$\operatorname{rk}(\boldsymbol{M}) = \operatorname{tr}(\boldsymbol{M}) = \operatorname{tr}(\boldsymbol{I}_m) - \operatorname{tr}(\boldsymbol{P}) = m - k.$$

Hence, $\boldsymbol{x}'\boldsymbol{P}\boldsymbol{x} \sim \chi^2(k)$ and $\boldsymbol{x}'\boldsymbol{M}\boldsymbol{x} \sim \chi^2(m-k)$.

To establish the independence of the two quadratic forms, Exercise 8.36 tells us that the only thing we have to show is that $\boldsymbol{M}\boldsymbol{P} = \mathbf{O}$. Now, since $\boldsymbol{P}$ is idempotent,

$$\boldsymbol{M}\boldsymbol{P} = (\boldsymbol{I}_m - \boldsymbol{P})\boldsymbol{P} = \boldsymbol{P} - \boldsymbol{P}^2 = \boldsymbol{P} - \boldsymbol{P} = \mathbf{O},$$

and the result follows. There is a geometrical interpretation of this result: using the fact that $\boldsymbol{P}$ and $\boldsymbol{M}$ are symmetric and idempotent, we can rewrite the quadratic forms as $(\boldsymbol{P}\boldsymbol{x})'(\boldsymbol{P}\boldsymbol{x})$ and $(\boldsymbol{M}\boldsymbol{x})'(\boldsymbol{M}\boldsymbol{x})$, where the normally distributed vectors $\boldsymbol{P}\boldsymbol{x}$ and $\boldsymbol{M}\boldsymbol{x}$ are orthogonal and hence independent.

***Exercise 8.39 (Quadratic forms: decompositions)** Let $\boldsymbol{x} \sim \mathrm{N}_m(\mathbf{0}, \boldsymbol{\Sigma})$, with $\boldsymbol{\Sigma}$ positive definite. Define $y_1 := \boldsymbol{x}'\boldsymbol{B}\boldsymbol{x}$, $y_2 := \boldsymbol{x}'\boldsymbol{C}\boldsymbol{x}$, and $y := y_1 + y_2$, with $r_1 := \operatorname{rk}(\boldsymbol{B})$,

$r_2 := \operatorname{rk}(\boldsymbol{C})$, and $r := \operatorname{rk}(\boldsymbol{B}+\boldsymbol{C})$. Assuming that $y \sim \chi^2(r)$, prove that:
(a) if $y_1 \sim \chi^2(r_1)$ and $y_2 \sim \chi^2(r_2)$, then y_1 and y_2 are independent and $r = r_1 + r_2$;
(b) if y_1 and y_2 are independent, then $y_1 \sim \chi^2(r_1)$, $y_2 \sim \chi^2(r_2)$, and $r = r_1 + r_2$;
(c) if $r = r_1 + r_2$, then $y_1 \sim \chi^2(r_1)$, $y_2 \sim \chi^2(r_2)$, and y_1 and y_2 are independent. [Hint: For any symmetric $m \times m$ matrix $\boldsymbol{B}$, we have $\operatorname{rk}(\boldsymbol{B}) + \operatorname{rk}(\boldsymbol{I}_m - \boldsymbol{B}) \geqslant m$, with equality if and only if $\boldsymbol{B}^2 = \boldsymbol{B}$.]

Solution

Again we assume first that $\boldsymbol{\Sigma} = \boldsymbol{I}_m$. In the general case, we would define $\boldsymbol{z} := \boldsymbol{\Sigma}^{-1/2}\boldsymbol{x}$, $\boldsymbol{Q}_1 := \boldsymbol{\Sigma}^{1/2}\boldsymbol{B}\boldsymbol{\Sigma}^{1/2}$, and $\boldsymbol{Q}_2 := \boldsymbol{\Sigma}^{1/2}\boldsymbol{C}\boldsymbol{\Sigma}^{1/2}$ and apply the results to $\boldsymbol{z}$, $\boldsymbol{Q}_1$, and $\boldsymbol{Q}_2$. Notice that we will effectively establish the equivalence of the following statements:
(i) $y_1 \sim \chi^2(r_1)$ and $y_2 \sim \chi^2(r_2)$,
(ii) y_1 and y_2 are independent,
(iii) $r = r_1 + r_2$,
since any one of them implies the other two when we assume $y \sim \chi^2(r)$.
(a) From the given distributions of y_1, y_2, and y, we infer (using Exercise 8.29) that $\boldsymbol{B}^2 = \boldsymbol{B}$, $\boldsymbol{C}^2 = \boldsymbol{C}$, and $(\boldsymbol{B}+\boldsymbol{C})^2 = \boldsymbol{B}+\boldsymbol{C}$. It follows that $\boldsymbol{BC} = -\boldsymbol{CB}$, that is, $\boldsymbol{BC}$ is skew-symmetric. Premultiplying both sides by $\boldsymbol{B}$ and using the fact that $\boldsymbol{B}^2 = \boldsymbol{B}$, we get

$$\boldsymbol{BC} = -\boldsymbol{BCB}.$$

The right-hand side is a symmetric matrix, by the symmetry of $\boldsymbol{B}$ and $\boldsymbol{C}$, so the product $\boldsymbol{BC}$ must be symmetric too. For $\boldsymbol{BC}$ to be symmetric and skew-symmetric at the same time, it must be $\mathbf{O}$, which establishes the independence of the quadratic forms y_1 and y_2 (by Exercise 8.36). For the ranks, we observe that

$$\operatorname{rk}(\boldsymbol{B}+\boldsymbol{C}) = \operatorname{tr}(\boldsymbol{B}+\boldsymbol{C}) = \operatorname{tr}(\boldsymbol{B}) + \operatorname{tr}(\boldsymbol{C}) = \operatorname{rk}(\boldsymbol{B}) + \operatorname{rk}(\boldsymbol{C})$$

since the rank of an idempotent matrix is equal to its trace.
(b) Since $\boldsymbol{CB} = \mathbf{O}$ (by independence) and $\boldsymbol{B}+\boldsymbol{C}$ is idempotent (by $y \sim \chi^2(r)$), we have

$$\boldsymbol{B}^2 = (\boldsymbol{B}+\boldsymbol{C})\boldsymbol{B} = (\boldsymbol{B}+\boldsymbol{C})^2\boldsymbol{B} = \boldsymbol{B}^3,$$

that is, $\boldsymbol{B}^2(\boldsymbol{I}_m - \boldsymbol{B}) = \mathbf{O}$ and hence $(\boldsymbol{I}_m - \boldsymbol{B})\boldsymbol{B}^2(\boldsymbol{I}_m - \boldsymbol{B}) = \mathbf{O}$. This implies that $\boldsymbol{B}(\boldsymbol{I}_m - \boldsymbol{B}) = \mathbf{O}$ and hence $\boldsymbol{B}^2 = \boldsymbol{B}$. It follows that $y_1 \sim \chi^2(r_1)$. In the same way, we can prove that $\boldsymbol{C}^2 = \boldsymbol{C}$ and $y_2 \sim \chi^2(r_2)$. The rank equality then follows as in (a).
(c) Define $\boldsymbol{Q} := \boldsymbol{I}_m - (\boldsymbol{B}+\boldsymbol{C})$. Now, $y \sim \chi^2(r)$ implies that $\boldsymbol{B}+\boldsymbol{C}$ is idempotent, and so $\operatorname{rk}(\boldsymbol{Q}) = m - r$. Since $r = r_1 + r_2$, we have $\operatorname{rk}(\boldsymbol{Q}) = m - r_1 - r_2$ and

$$\operatorname{rk}(\boldsymbol{I}_m - \boldsymbol{B}) = \operatorname{rk}(\boldsymbol{C}+\boldsymbol{Q}) \leqslant \operatorname{rk}(\boldsymbol{C}) + \operatorname{rk}(\boldsymbol{Q}) = m - r_1 = m - \operatorname{rk}(\boldsymbol{B}).$$

Accordingly, $\operatorname{rk}(\boldsymbol{I}_m - \boldsymbol{B}) + \operatorname{rk}(\boldsymbol{B}) \leqslant m$. But we know that it is always true that $\operatorname{rk}(\boldsymbol{B}) + \operatorname{rk}(\boldsymbol{I}_m - \boldsymbol{B}) \geqslant m$, so $\operatorname{rk}(\boldsymbol{B}) + \operatorname{rk}(\boldsymbol{I}_m - \boldsymbol{B}) = m$ and hence $\boldsymbol{B}^2 = \boldsymbol{B}$ by the hint in the question. In the same way, we have $\boldsymbol{C}^2 = \boldsymbol{C}$. This implies that y_1 and y_2 are χ^2-distributed (by Exercise 8.29) and, from (a), y_1 and y_2 are independent.

***Exercise 8.40 (Quadratic forms: complementarity)** Let $\boldsymbol{x} \sim \mathrm{N}(\mathbf{0}, \sigma^2 \boldsymbol{I}_m)$. Define $y_1 := \boldsymbol{x}'\boldsymbol{B}\boldsymbol{x}$, $y_2 := \boldsymbol{x}'\boldsymbol{C}\boldsymbol{x}$, and $y := y_1 + y_2$. Assume that $y_1/\sigma^2 \sim \chi^2(r_1)$ and $y/\sigma^2 \sim \chi^2(r)$ for some $r_1, r \in \mathbb{N}$, and that $\boldsymbol{C}$ is positive semidefinite.
(a) Show that y_1 and y_2 are independent. [Hint: Consider the orthogonal diagonalization of $\boldsymbol{B}+\boldsymbol{C}$, say $\boldsymbol{T}'(\boldsymbol{B}+\boldsymbol{C})\boldsymbol{T}$, and work out the restrictions implied for $\boldsymbol{T}'\boldsymbol{B}\boldsymbol{T}$ and $\boldsymbol{T}'\boldsymbol{C}\boldsymbol{T}$.]
(b) Hence, show that $y_2/\sigma^2 \sim \chi^2(r_2)$, where $r_2 = r - r_1 = \mathrm{rk}(\boldsymbol{C})$.

Solution
(a) We can set $\sigma^2 = 1$ without loss of generality, since we could redefine $(1/\sigma)\boldsymbol{x}$ and proceed. The assumptions imply (by Exercise 8.29) that $\boldsymbol{B}$ and $\boldsymbol{B}+\boldsymbol{C}$ are idempotent of ranks r_1 and r, respectively, and hence also positive semidefinite. We have the orthogonal diagonalization

$$\boldsymbol{T}'(\boldsymbol{B}+\boldsymbol{C})\boldsymbol{T} = \begin{pmatrix} \boldsymbol{I}_r & \mathbf{O} \\ \mathbf{O} & \mathbf{O} \end{pmatrix}, \qquad \boldsymbol{T}'\boldsymbol{T} = \boldsymbol{I}_m.$$

Now consider the two matrices

$$\boldsymbol{T}'\boldsymbol{B}\boldsymbol{T} = \begin{pmatrix} \boldsymbol{B}_1 & \boldsymbol{B}_2 \\ \boldsymbol{B}_2' & \boldsymbol{B}_3 \end{pmatrix}, \qquad \boldsymbol{T}'\boldsymbol{C}\boldsymbol{T} = \begin{pmatrix} \boldsymbol{C}_1 & \boldsymbol{C}_2 \\ \boldsymbol{C}_2' & \boldsymbol{C}_3 \end{pmatrix}.$$

Since both matrices are positive semidefinite, the submatrices $\boldsymbol{B}_3$ and $\boldsymbol{C}_3$ are also positive semidefinite. But since $\boldsymbol{B}_3 + \boldsymbol{C}_3 = \mathbf{O}$, it follows that $\boldsymbol{B}_3 = \boldsymbol{C}_3 = \mathbf{O}$. Further, since $\boldsymbol{B}$ is idempotent, so is $\boldsymbol{T}'\boldsymbol{B}\boldsymbol{T}$, and we have

$$\begin{pmatrix} \boldsymbol{B}_1 & \boldsymbol{B}_2 \\ \boldsymbol{B}_2' & \mathbf{O} \end{pmatrix} = \boldsymbol{T}'\boldsymbol{B}\boldsymbol{T} = (\boldsymbol{T}'\boldsymbol{B}\boldsymbol{T})^2 = \begin{pmatrix} \boldsymbol{B}_1^2 + \boldsymbol{B}_2\boldsymbol{B}_2' & \boldsymbol{B}_1\boldsymbol{B}_2 \\ \boldsymbol{B}_2'\boldsymbol{B}_1 & \boldsymbol{B}_2'\boldsymbol{B}_2 \end{pmatrix}.$$

This shows that $\boldsymbol{B}_2'\boldsymbol{B}_2 = \mathbf{O}$ and hence that $\boldsymbol{B}_2 = \mathbf{O}$. Then, by $\boldsymbol{B}_2 + \boldsymbol{C}_2 = \mathbf{O}$, we get $\boldsymbol{C}_2 = \mathbf{O}$ as well. We thus find

$$\boldsymbol{T}'\boldsymbol{B}\boldsymbol{T} = \begin{pmatrix} \boldsymbol{B}_1 & \mathbf{O} \\ \mathbf{O} & \mathbf{O} \end{pmatrix}, \qquad \boldsymbol{T}'\boldsymbol{C}\boldsymbol{T} = \begin{pmatrix} \boldsymbol{C}_1 & \mathbf{O} \\ \mathbf{O} & \mathbf{O} \end{pmatrix},$$

with $\boldsymbol{B}_1 + \boldsymbol{C}_1 = \boldsymbol{I}_r$. Hence, $\boldsymbol{B}_1\boldsymbol{C}_1 = \boldsymbol{B}_1(\boldsymbol{I}_r - \boldsymbol{B}_1) = \boldsymbol{B}_1 - \boldsymbol{B}_1^2 = \mathbf{O}$, since $\boldsymbol{B}_1$ is idempotent. This implies that $(\boldsymbol{T}'\boldsymbol{B}\boldsymbol{T})(\boldsymbol{T}'\boldsymbol{C}\boldsymbol{T}) = \mathbf{O}$ and hence that $\boldsymbol{B}\boldsymbol{C} = \mathbf{O}$. Therefore, y_1 and y_2 are independent.
(b) This follows from Exercise 8.39(b).

Exercise 8.41 (Quadratic forms: complementarity versus independence) Let $y_1 \sim \chi^2(r_1)$ be independent of $y \sim \chi^2(r)$, where $r > r_1$ and $r_1, r \in \mathbb{N}$. Show that $y_2 := y - y_1$ does not follow a χ^2 distribution.

Solution

We have the m.g.f. of y_2 as

$$\begin{aligned} m_{y_2}(t) &= \mathrm{E}(\mathrm{e}^{ty_2}) = \mathrm{E}(\mathrm{e}^{t(y-y_1)}) = \mathrm{E}(\mathrm{e}^{ty})\,\mathrm{E}(\mathrm{e}^{-ty_1}) \\ &= m_y(t)m_{y_1}(-t) = (1-2t)^{-r/2}(1+2t)^{-r_1/2}. \end{aligned}$$

This can be written as a power of $(1-2t)$ only when $t=0$ but not in any neighborhood of $t=0$, and it is therefore not the m.g.f. of a χ^2 variate. For example, in Exercise 8.40, the variates y and y_1 could not be independent.

***Exercise 8.42 (Cochran's theorem)** Let $x_1, \dots, x_n$ be a random sample from the $\mathrm{N}(0,1)$ distribution. Suppose $\boldsymbol{C}_1, \dots, \boldsymbol{C}_k$ are positive semidefinite $n \times n$ matrices satisfying $\sum_{j=1}^k \boldsymbol{C}_j = \boldsymbol{I}_n$. Define $y_j := \boldsymbol{x}'\boldsymbol{C}_j\boldsymbol{x}$ and $r_j := \mathrm{rk}(\boldsymbol{C}_j)$. Show that the following statements are all equivalent to one another:
(i) $y_j \sim \chi^2(r_j)$, for $j = 1, \dots, k$;
(ii) y_i and y_j are independent, for all $i \neq j$;
(iii) $\sum_{j=1}^k r_j = n$.

Solution

We need to prove only two equivalences; the third will then follow by transitivity. Note that $y := \sum_{j=1}^k y_j = \boldsymbol{x}'\boldsymbol{x} \sim \chi^2(n)$.

(i)$\Longrightarrow$(ii): This follows by induction from Exercise 8.39. Alternatively, Exercise 8.29 tells us that $y_j \sim \chi^2(r_j)$ is equivalent to $\boldsymbol{C}_j$ being idempotent of rank r_j, and so we can use this additional information about all the $\boldsymbol{C}_j$ to simplify the proof of Exercise 8.39. Squaring both sides of the equation $\sum_j \boldsymbol{C}_j = \boldsymbol{I}_n$ gives $\sum_j \boldsymbol{C}_j + \sum_{i\neq j} \boldsymbol{C}_i\boldsymbol{C}_j = \boldsymbol{I}_n$ or, equivalently, $\sum_{i\neq j} \boldsymbol{C}_i\boldsymbol{C}_j = \mathbf{O}$. Taking traces on both sides gives $\sum_{i\neq j} \mathrm{tr}(\boldsymbol{C}_i\boldsymbol{C}_j) = 0$. But $\boldsymbol{C}_i$ being idempotent implies that

$$\mathrm{tr}(\boldsymbol{C}_i\boldsymbol{C}_j) = \mathrm{tr}(\boldsymbol{C}_i^2\boldsymbol{C}_j^2) = \mathrm{tr}(\boldsymbol{C}_i\boldsymbol{C}_j^2\boldsymbol{C}_i) \geqslant 0,$$

and the previous sum can be satisfied if and only if $\mathrm{tr}(\boldsymbol{C}_i\boldsymbol{C}_j^2\boldsymbol{C}_i) = 0$ for all $i \neq j$. This gives $\boldsymbol{C}_i\boldsymbol{C}_j = \mathbf{O}$ and establishes the independence of y_i and y_j by Exercise 8.36.

(ii)$\Longrightarrow$(i): Exercise 8.36 tells us that y_i and y_j $(i \neq j)$ are independent if and only if $\boldsymbol{C}_i\boldsymbol{C}_j = \mathbf{O}$. As a result, raising $\sum_j \boldsymbol{C}_j = \boldsymbol{I}_n$ to any natural number m and then taking the trace, we get $\sum_j \mathrm{tr}(\boldsymbol{C}_j^m) = n$. For $\boldsymbol{C}_j$ positive semidefinite, this equality can hold for all $m \in \mathbb{N}$ if and only if all the eigenvalues of $\boldsymbol{C}_j$ are either 0 or 1, that is, the $\boldsymbol{C}_j$ are idempotent, which we know is equivalent to $y_j \sim \chi^2(r_j)$ by Exercise 8.29.

(i)$\Longrightarrow$(iii): If $y_j \sim \chi^2(r_j)$, then $\boldsymbol{C}_j$ is idempotent and

$$\sum_{j=1}^k r_j = \sum_{j=1}^k \mathrm{rk}(\boldsymbol{C}_j) = \sum_{j=1}^k \mathrm{tr}(\boldsymbol{C}_j) = \mathrm{tr}\left(\sum_{j=1}^k \boldsymbol{C}_j\right) = \mathrm{tr}(\boldsymbol{I}_n) = n$$

as required.

(iii)$\Longrightarrow$(i): Let $\boldsymbol{B} := \boldsymbol{C}_2 + \cdots + \boldsymbol{C}_k$. Now

$$\operatorname{rk}(\boldsymbol{B}) + \operatorname{rk}(\boldsymbol{C}_1) \geqslant \operatorname{rk}(\boldsymbol{B} + \boldsymbol{C}_1) = \operatorname{rk}(\boldsymbol{I}_n) = n,$$

hence $\operatorname{rk}(\boldsymbol{B}) \geqslant n - r_1$. But

$$\operatorname{rk}(\boldsymbol{B}) \leqslant \sum_{j=2}^{k} \operatorname{rk}(\boldsymbol{C}_j) = n - r_1.$$

Therefore, $\operatorname{rk}(\boldsymbol{B}) = n - r_1$ and Exercise 8.39(c) gives $y_1 \sim \chi^2(r_1)$. In the same way, we have $y_j \sim \chi^2(r_j)$ for all j.

Notes

General references for this chapter are the same as for Chapter 6. The specialized nature of this chapter means that we have relied on quite a bit of matrix algebra, especially Section 8.2 and particularly Exercises 8.36, 8.39, and 8.40. For more on this topic, see our companion volume, Abadir and Magnus (2005), and references therein.

The result of Exercise 8.20(e) is generally true for more than two variables, and can be written in matrix notation as

$$\operatorname{var}(\boldsymbol{x} \otimes \boldsymbol{x}) = 2\left(1 + \frac{\kappa}{3}\right) \boldsymbol{N}_k \left(\boldsymbol{\Sigma} \otimes \boldsymbol{\Sigma}\right) + \frac{\kappa}{3} \left(\operatorname{vec} \boldsymbol{\Sigma}\right) \left(\operatorname{vec} \boldsymbol{\Sigma}\right)' \tag{8.2}$$

or

$$\operatorname{E}(\boldsymbol{x}\boldsymbol{x}' \otimes \boldsymbol{x}\boldsymbol{x}') = \left(1 + \frac{\kappa}{3}\right) \left(2\boldsymbol{N}_k \left(\boldsymbol{\Sigma} \otimes \boldsymbol{\Sigma}\right) + \left(\operatorname{vec} \boldsymbol{\Sigma}\right) \left(\operatorname{vec} \boldsymbol{\Sigma}\right)'\right),$$

where $\boldsymbol{N}_k$ is the symmetrizer matrix; see Section 11.2 of Abadir and Magnus (2005) for the normal case. Compare with Exercise 6.7 but keep in mind that, within the class of elliptical distributions, the concepts of independence and no-correlation coincide only for the normal case (Exercise 8.10).

The deconvolution theorems of Cramér and Raikov can be found in Feller (1971) or Loève (1977). Cramér's theorem is actually more general than is stated in Exercise 8.7, because it does not presume the existence of m.g.f.s for x_1 and x_2, at the cost of a further complication of the proof. In our proof, we have used (without needing to resort to the language of complex analysis) the fact that the existence of the m.g.f. implies that it is analytic (it satisfies the Cauchy–Riemann equations) and is thus differentiable infinitely many times in an open neighborhood of $t = 0$ in the complex plane; see Section A.3.4 and the Notes to Appendix A. However, if one did not assume the existence of m.g.f.s, then one would require some theorem from complex function theory. One such requisite would be the "principle of isolated zeros" or the "uniqueness theorem for analytic functions". Another alternative requisite would be "Hadamard's factorization theorem", used in Loève (1977, p. 284).

The solutions we chose for Exercises 8.7 and 8.34 are to be found in Abadir and Magnus (2004a). We assume the full generality of Cramér's result in our statement of Exercise

8.34(c). A version of Exercise 8.34(d) is proved by a different approach in Theorem 6 of Zinger (1958). There, the independence of $\overline{x}$ and z is assumed, but not the normality of $\boldsymbol{x}$. In fact, for $2 \leqslant n < \infty$, the normality of $\boldsymbol{x}$ is obtained there as a result of one of two alternative assumptions: that the components of $\boldsymbol{x}$ are pairwise identically distributed or are decomposable further as i.i.d. variates.

Characterization theory is the study of the properties that characterize a distribution (or a class of distributions) uniquely. The results of Exercises 8.7, 8.10, and 8.34 are examples for the case of the normal. For a list of others, see Johnson, Kotz, and Balakrishnan (1994). Another famous example is the characterization theorem of Darmois and Skitovič: for $x_1, \dots, x_n$ an independent sequence, if $y_1 := \sum_{i=1}^n a_i x_i$ is independent of $y_2 := \sum_{i=1}^n b_i x_i$ when $a_i, b_i \neq 0$ $(i = 1, \dots, n)$, then each x_i is normally distributed.

The joint m.g.f. of Exercise 8.36(a) is a starting point for many important results in statistics. One such result is the distribution of the ratio of dependent quadratic forms, since many estimators and tests in statistics can be so written. By applying Exercise 7.24, either numerically or analytically, it is possible to obtain the distribution and moments of the required ratios. A useful case was derived analytically in Ghazal (1994). See also his Corollary 1 for a special case where the expectation of the ratio of quadratic forms equals the ratio of the expectations (compare the related comment in the Notes to Chapter 3).

Exercises 8.39–8.42 can be extended to general $\mathrm{N}(\boldsymbol{\mu}, \boldsymbol{\Sigma})$ and noncentral χ^2 variates, as was done in earlier exercises which were less elaborate. Graybill and Marsaglia (1957) gave a number of such results. See also Chapter 8 of Abadir and Magnus (2005) for the mathematical aspects of spectral decompositions and idempotents.

Part B

Estimation and inference

9

Sample statistics and their distributions

Up to now, we have dealt with various foundational aspects of random variables and their distributions. We have occasionally touched on how these variates can arise in practice. In the second part of this book, we start analyzing in more detail how these variates are connected with sampling situations, how we can estimate the parameters of their distributions (which are typically unknown in practice), and how to conduct inference regarding these estimates and their magnitudes. This chapter starts with the first of these three aims.

In Chapter 4, we defined a random sample of x to be one obtained by repeated independent drawings from a particular distribution $\mathrm{D}_{\mathcal{X}}(\boldsymbol{\theta})$. We usually do not know the parameter vector $\boldsymbol{\theta}$, and we wish to gain information on it through this sample. We resort to sampling because it would be too expensive (and usually impossible) to collect data on the whole *population* under study, namely the group of all objects described by this variate x.

A *statistic* is a function of the observations in the sample. This function must not depend on any unknowns, and should be computable from the sample alone. For example, for $x_1, \dots, x_n$ a random sample of x, the sample mean (or average) $\overline{x} := n^{-1} \sum_{i=1}^{n} x_i$ is a statistic. It is the sample analogue of $\mu := \mathrm{E}(x)$. More generally, for $j \in \mathbb{N}$, the j-th *raw sample moment* $n^{-1} \sum_{i=1}^{n} x_i^j$ is the sample analogue of the population's j-th raw moment $\mathrm{E}\left(x^j\right)$. If μ were known, then the j-th *central sample moment* would be $n^{-1} \sum_{i=1}^{n} (x_i - \mu)^j$. In practice, μ is typically unknown and is replaced by the sample mean and, for $j = 2$, we get the sample variance

$$s^2 := \frac{1}{n-1} \sum_{i=1}^{n} (x_i - \overline{x})^2 .$$

Exercise 9.4(a) will show that equivalent expressions for s^2 include the following:

$$s^2 = \frac{1}{n-1} \left(\sum_{i=1}^{n} x_i^2 - n\overline{x}^2 \right) = \frac{1}{n-1} \left(\sum_{i=1}^{n} (x_i - \mu)^2 - n (\overline{x} - \mu)^2 \right).$$

We shall assume that $n > 1$ whenever we are talking about s^2. The division factor $n-1$ is used instead of n for a reason that will be explained in Exercises 9.4(c) and 9.16(b). For the time being, we just note that we have "lost" one sample point, as far as s^2 is concerned, because we have had to estimate μ by $\overline{x}$. Both statistics were briefly encountered in Chapter 7. We call $x_i - \overline{x}$ the *de-meaned* (or *centered*) *observations*, already considered in Exercises 7.16 and 8.34. We will analyze this operation further, especially in Exercises 9.4 and 9.16. In parallel with the other main measures of location introduced in Chapter 2, we define the following two. The *sample mode* is the most frequent value in the sample. The *sample median* is the middle value in the ranked observations (if n is odd), or the average of the two middle values (if n is even). It is often denoted by $\widehat{q}_{1/2}$ or $\widehat{\text{med}}(x)$, because of its connection to the population's median $q_{1/2}$ or $\text{med}(x)$, with a hat denoting the sample counterpart. Occasionally, we may denote it by $\widetilde{x}$, in contrast with the sample mean $\overline{x}$.

For an m-dimensional vector variate $\boldsymbol{x}$, the mean of a random sample $\boldsymbol{x}_1, \ldots, \boldsymbol{x}_n$ is the vector

$$\overline{\boldsymbol{x}} := \frac{1}{n} \sum_{i=1}^{n} \boldsymbol{x}_i$$

and the sample variance $\boldsymbol{S} = (s_{jk})$ is the matrix

$$\boldsymbol{S} := \frac{1}{n-1} \sum_{i=1}^{n} (\boldsymbol{x}_i - \overline{\boldsymbol{x}})(\boldsymbol{x}_i - \overline{\boldsymbol{x}})',$$

where s_{jk} is the *sample covariance* between the j-th and k-th variables in $\boldsymbol{x}_i$; see Exercise 9.5(b) for the derivation of the equivalent expressions

$$\begin{aligned}\boldsymbol{S} &= \frac{1}{n-1} \left(\sum_{i=1}^{n} \boldsymbol{x}_i \boldsymbol{x}_i' - n \overline{\boldsymbol{x}}\, \overline{\boldsymbol{x}}' \right) \\ &= \frac{1}{n-1} \left(\sum_{i=1}^{n} (\boldsymbol{x}_i - \boldsymbol{\mu})(\boldsymbol{x}_i - \boldsymbol{\mu})' - n (\overline{\boldsymbol{x}} - \boldsymbol{\mu})(\overline{\boldsymbol{x}} - \boldsymbol{\mu})' \right).\end{aligned}$$

We will also consider the *sample correlation*

$$\widehat{\rho}_{jk} := \frac{s_{jk}}{\sqrt{s_{jj} s_{kk}}},$$

abbreviated to $\widehat{\rho}$ when there is no ambiguity. The symbol r_{jk} is used occasionally as an alternative to $\widehat{\rho}_{jk}$, or $\widehat{\text{corr}}(x_j, x_k)$ with x_j, x_k a shorthand for the j-th and k-th variables in $\boldsymbol{x}_i$, respectively.[1] Like its population counterpart ρ, the sample correlation satisfies $\widehat{\rho} \in [-1, 1]$, as follows directly by the same method as that of Exercise 6.20. Like ρ that measures the

[1] Some authors use $\widehat{\text{var}}(x_j)$ and $\widehat{\text{cov}}(x_j, x_k)$ for s_{jj} and s_{jk}, respectively. We do not do so here, choosing instead $\widehat{\text{var}}(x) := n^{-1} \sum_i (x_i - \overline{x})^2$ and similarly for $\widehat{\text{cov}}(x_j, x_k)$ for a reason that will become apparent when we estimate variance matrices in Chapter 12, in particular in Exercise 12.17. The choice of n or $n-1$ as divisor of (co)variances does not affect the scale-invariant $\widehat{\text{corr}}(x_j, x_k)$.

strength of the linear relation between x_j and x_k in the population, the sample's $\widehat{\rho}$ measures how close the data are to falling on a straight line in a plot of the sequence of points $(x_j, x_k)_i$ for $i = 1, \dots, n$. We shall elaborate on this issue further when concluding the introduction to Chapter 11.

When $\boldsymbol{x}$ is normally distributed, we will see in Exercises 9.19 and 9.20 that $(n-1)\,\boldsymbol{S}$ has the Wishart distribution, which generalizes the χ^2 distribution. To define it, let $\boldsymbol{y}_i \sim \mathrm{IN}_m(\boldsymbol{\mu}_i, \boldsymbol{\Sigma})$ be an independent (but not necessarily identical) normal sequence, where $i = 1, \dots, p$ and $\boldsymbol{\Sigma}$ is nonsingular. Then

$$\boldsymbol{Z} := \sum_{i=1}^{p} \boldsymbol{y}_i \boldsymbol{y}_i' \sim \mathrm{W}_m(p, \boldsymbol{\Sigma}, \boldsymbol{\Delta}),$$

which denotes an m-dimensional *noncentral Wishart distribution* with p degrees of freedom, scale $\boldsymbol{\Sigma}$, and unscaled noncentrality $\boldsymbol{\Delta} := \sum_{i=1}^{p} \boldsymbol{\mu}_i \boldsymbol{\mu}_i'$. When $m = 1$, we get the equivalence of $\mathrm{W}_1(p, \sigma^2, \delta)$ to σ^2 times a $\chi^2(p, \delta/\sigma^2)$ variate. The (central) Wishart distribution occurs when $\boldsymbol{\Delta} = \mathbf{O}$, and is written as $\mathrm{W}_m(p, \boldsymbol{\Sigma})$. Note that, even though we assume that $\boldsymbol{\Sigma}$ is nonsingular, it is *not* assumed that $p \geqslant m$; hence $\boldsymbol{Z}$ is allowed to be singular, as will be shown in Exercise 9.21. Also, even when we have $p = m = 1$ (which we will see corresponds to $n = 2$) and $s^2/\sigma^2 \sim \chi^2(1)$, we have so few data points that the most frequent values of s^2 are very small (there is very little sample variation); see the density of $\chi^2(1)$ in Figure 4.4 corresponding to Exercise 4.14(d).

Two important special statistics can be built out of the previous ones. The *t-ratio* (or t-statistic) is defined as

$$t := \frac{\overline{x} - \mu_0}{s/\sqrt{n}},$$

and its realization is called the *t-value*. The multivariate generalization (in quadratic form) of this statistic is known as *Hotelling's* T^2 and is defined by

$$T^2 := n\,(\overline{\boldsymbol{x}} - \boldsymbol{\mu}_0)'\, \boldsymbol{S}^{-1}\, (\overline{\boldsymbol{x}} - \boldsymbol{\mu}_0),$$

where it is assumed that $\boldsymbol{S}$ is nonsingular with probability 1 (conditions for this are given in Exercise 9.21). In both statistics, μ_0 and $\boldsymbol{\mu}_0$ are constants chosen by the statistician as "maintained" values for μ and $\boldsymbol{\mu}$, respectively. These maintained values may come from some hypothesized theory of economics, or physics, et cetera, and their stipulation will be analyzed in Chapter 14.

In Chapter 7, we introduced another type of statistic, which we repeat here for convenience. Let y_i denote the i-th smallest observation in the sample $x_1, \dots, x_n$, so we have $y_1 \leqslant \dots \leqslant y_n$ where $y_1 = \min_i\{x_i\}$ and $y_n = \max_i\{x_i\}$. These y_i's are the order statistics, and they are the sample counterparts of the i/n quantile; see also the sample median defined earlier in this chapter. As illustrated in Exercise 7.35, the y_i's are not independent (they are defined by being ranked in order) even when the x_i's are drawn from a random sample.

We now introduce the last type of statistic considered in this chapter, which is related to order statistics. It is the *empirical distribution function* (EDF), defined by

$$\widehat{F}_n(u) := \frac{1}{n}(\text{number of } x_i\text{'s less than or equal to } u). \tag{9.1}$$

By counting the number of times $x_i \leqslant u$ in the sample, and dividing by n, we obtain

$$\widehat{F}_n(u) = \frac{1}{n}\sum_{i=1}^{n} 1_{x_i \leqslant u},$$

which is also seen to be the sample average of $1_{x_i \leqslant u}$ (the indicator function of the event $x_i \leqslant u$). In terms of the order statistics y_i,

$$\widehat{F}_n(u) = \begin{cases} 0 & (u < y_1), \\ \frac{i}{n} & (y_i \leqslant u < y_{i+1}), \\ 1 & (u \geqslant y_n), \end{cases}$$

which is a nondecreasing step function as u increases, and is continuous to the right at any point u. It is the sample analogue of the distribution function $F(u)$. The generalization of the definition of an EDF to the multivariate case follows directly from (9.1). Like any pair of order statistics, $\widehat{F}_n(u_1)$ and $\widehat{F}_n(u_2)$ are generally not independent; see, for example, Exercise 9.27. Unlike in the case of moments, we note that the sample's order statistics and EDFs have population analogues that are not parameters.

While population moments can be infinite, their sample counterparts will always be finite when $n < \infty$. This fact has two implications. First, the computed sample means will be spurious if the corresponding population moments do not exist. For example, let x follow the standard Cauchy distribution, $x \sim$ Cau(0,1). Then its population moments do not exist. However, the mean from a sample of one observation, the observation itself, will be finite but is likely to be moderately large. If we add another observation, the sample mean will probably change by another large value. Furthermore, the stable laws of Chapter 4 tell us that $\overline{x}$ is also distributed as Cau(0,1) for any n (see also Exercise 7.3). As a result, for different sampling realizations, the numerical value of $\overline{x}$ may jump from large positive to large negative, and so on. This is a reflection of the fact that the population moments do not exist, so that the sample moments try to estimate a nonexistent quantity. The next chapter will contrast this behavior with that of $\overline{x}$ when calculated for data whose densities have finite mean and variance (such as the normal).

The second implication of the finiteness of sample moments is that it may mislead some into believing that one should disregard densities whose moments do not exist. This is a fallacious argument. For example, the Cauchy distribution does arise in reality as the ratio of two normal variates (see Exercise 4.35). Furthermore, distributions like the Cauchy and the Pareto describe variates whose c.d.f. $F(u)$ approaches 1 at a slow rate as $u \to \infty$, as a power (rather than exponential) function of u; and this feature will be reflected in sample analogues such as $\widehat{F}_n(u)$ when n is moderately large (see Exercise 9.26), despite the fact that the sample moments are never infinite when $n < \infty$.

The exercises in this chapter explore the sample statistics defined above, and derive their distributions. The reader will be able to see how they relate to the distributions introduced earlier, in Part A. We start with sampling and sample moments, then focus on the normal case, and conclude with results relating to EDFs and order statistics.

9.1 Sampling and sample moments

Exercise 9.1 (Harmonic mean) Let $x_1, \ldots, x_n$ be a random sample of a variate $x \in \mathbb{R}_+$. The *harmonic mean* of the sample is defined by

$$\left(\frac{1}{n}\sum_{i=1}^{n}\frac{1}{x_i}\right)^{-1}.$$

Calculate the sample mode, median, mean, geometric mean, and harmonic mean of the sample $1, 1, 2, 100$. What happens when the last observation is replaced by 0.001?

Solution

The sample mode is 1 and the sample median is 1.5. The sample mean is $(104)/4 = 26$, while the geometric mean is $200^{1/4} \approx 3.761 < 26$, as expected from the arithmetic–geometric mean inequality that was proved in Exercise 3.14(c). The harmonic mean is

$$\left(\frac{1+1+\frac{1}{2}+\frac{1}{100}}{4}\right)^{-1} = \frac{400}{251} \approx 1.594.$$

The geometric and harmonic means are less sensitive than the arithmetic mean to extreme large values. Now, if the last observation (100) becomes 0.001, the mode is unchanged, the median becomes 1, the mean $(4.001)/4 \approx 1$, the geometric mean $(0.002)^{1/4} \approx 0.211$, and the harmonic mean

$$\left(\frac{1+1+\frac{1}{2}+100}{4}\right)^{-1} = \frac{8}{205} \approx 0.039.$$

The harmonic mean is therefore sensitive to small values, but it is clearly bounded below by 0. One of its uses in economics is to calculate the average of prices, when one wishes to downplay the influence of large prices. See also Exercise 11.2(c) for a statistical application to variances. Notice that, if all the observations are scaled by a factor $\lambda > 0$, then so is the harmonic mean. It can be written as $(\overline{x^{-1}})^{-1}$, the inverse of the sample mean of x^{-1}.

Exercise 9.2 (Sample mean) Let $x_1, \ldots, x_n$ be a random sample from a distribution with expectation μ and variance σ^2. Show that $\mathrm{E}(\overline{x}) = \mu$ and $\mathrm{var}(\overline{x}) = \sigma^2/n$.

Solution

Using the definition of the sample mean, then exploiting the linearity of expectations, we get

$$\mathrm{E}(\overline{x}) = \mathrm{E}\left(\frac{1}{n}\sum_{i=1}^{n} x_i\right) = \frac{1}{n}\sum_{i=1}^{n} \mathrm{E}(x_i).$$

By the assumption of an identical mean for all i,

$$\mathrm{E}(\overline{x}) = \frac{1}{n}\sum_{i=1}^{n} \mu = \frac{n\mu}{n} = \mu.$$

Independence has played no role in calculating the mean. This is in line with the general principle (noted in the introduction to Chapter 6) for calculating the first moment. Next,

$$\begin{aligned}\operatorname{var}(\overline{x}) &= \operatorname{var}\left(\frac{1}{n}\sum_{i=1}^{n} x_i\right) = \frac{1}{n^2}\operatorname{var}\left(\sum_{i=1}^{n} x_i\right)\\ &= \frac{1}{n^2}\sum_{i=1}^{n}\left(\operatorname{var}(x_i) + 2\sum_{j>i}\operatorname{cov}(x_i, x_j)\right)\\ &= \frac{1}{n^2}\sum_{i=1}^{n}\operatorname{var}(x_i) = \frac{n\sigma^2}{n^2} = \frac{\sigma^2}{n}\end{aligned}$$

since $\operatorname{cov}(x_i, x_j) = 0$ for $i \neq j$. The same result is obtained by defining $\boldsymbol{x} := (x_1, \dots, x_n)'$ and $\overline{x} := \frac{1}{n}\boldsymbol{\imath}'\boldsymbol{x}$, then using Exercise 6.3.

Exercise 9.3 (Sample mean: heteroskedasticity) Let $x_1, \dots, x_n$ be a random sample from a distribution with expectation μ and variance σ^2. Suppose that these observations are gathered into two subsamples of sizes $m > 0$ and $n - m > 0$, respectively, and that we observe only the average of each of the two subsamples, say $\overline{x}_1$ and $\overline{x}_2$. Derive the conditions for $\operatorname{var}(\overline{x}_1) = \operatorname{var}(\overline{x}_2)$.

Solution
From Exercise 9.2, $\mathrm{E}(\overline{x}_1) = \mu = \mathrm{E}(\overline{x}_2)$, but $\operatorname{var}(\overline{x}_1) = \sigma^2/m$ and $\operatorname{var}(\overline{x}_2) = \sigma^2/(n-m)$. Although both sample means are based on i.i.d. drawings from the same distribution of x, their variances are not equal (hence $\overline{x}_1$ and $\overline{x}_2$ are not i.i.d.) if $m \neq n/2$. They are nevertheless independently distributed because $\overline{x}_1$ is based on observations that are independent of those in $\overline{x}_2$.

Exercise 9.4 (Sample variance and de-meaning matrix) Let $x_1, \dots, x_n$ be a random sample from a distribution with expectation μ and variance σ^2.
(a) Prove that $n^{-1}\sum_{i=1}^{n}(x_i - \overline{x})^2 = n^{-1}\sum_{i=1}^{n} x_i^2 - \overline{x}^2 = n^{-1}\sum_{i=1}^{n}(x_i - \mu)^2 - (\overline{x} - \mu)^2$.
(b) Let $\boldsymbol{x} := (x_1, \dots, x_n)'$. Determine the symmetric matrix $\boldsymbol{A}$ such that $\sum_{i=1}^{n}(x_i - \overline{x})^2 = \boldsymbol{x}'\boldsymbol{A}\boldsymbol{x}$. Show that $\boldsymbol{A}$ is idempotent and determine its rank.
(c) Show that $\mathrm{E}(s^2) = \sigma^2$. Does this mean that $\mathrm{E}(s) = \sigma$?

(d) Assume that $\kappa := \mathrm{E}((x_i - \mu)^4/\sigma^4) - 3$ is finite. Show that

$$\mathrm{var}(s^2) = \sigma^4 \left(\frac{2}{n-1} + \frac{\kappa}{n} \right).$$

Solution

(a) The first equality was established in the proof of Exercise 7.16(d). Notice how this result compares with the population's $\mathrm{var}(x) = \mathrm{E}(x^2) - \mu^2$. For the second equality, rearranging and then expanding the quadratic gives

$$\begin{aligned}\sum_{i=1}^{n} (x_i - \overline{x})^2 &= \sum_{i=1}^{n} (x_i - \mu + \mu - \overline{x})^2 \\ &= \sum_{i=1}^{n} \left((x_i - \mu)^2 + (\mu - \overline{x})^2 + 2(x_i - \mu)(\mu - \overline{x}) \right) \\ &= \sum_{i=1}^{n} (x_i - \mu)^2 + n(\mu - \overline{x})^2 + 2(\mu - \overline{x}) \sum_{i=1}^{n} (x_i - \mu) \\ &= \sum_{i=1}^{n} (x_i - \mu)^2 - n(\mu - \overline{x})^2,\end{aligned}$$

because $\sum_{i=1}^{n} (x_i - \mu) = \sum_{i=1}^{n} x_i - \sum_{i=1}^{n} \mu = n\overline{x} - n\mu$. Dividing both sides by n gives the second equality. Compare the results here with the population's counterparts in Exercise 3.17. Notice that we have not used here the fact that $\mu = \mathrm{E}(x)$, so similar relations hold for constants other than μ.

(b) We have a quadratic form in $x_i - \overline{x}$. Consider a vector $\boldsymbol{y}$ with components $y_i := x_i - \overline{x}$, which are the de-meaned x_i. Then

$$\boldsymbol{y} = \boldsymbol{x} - \overline{x}\boldsymbol{\imath} = \boldsymbol{x} - \frac{1}{n}(\boldsymbol{\imath}'\boldsymbol{x})\boldsymbol{\imath} = \boldsymbol{x} - \frac{1}{n}\boldsymbol{\imath}\boldsymbol{\imath}'\boldsymbol{x} = \left(\boldsymbol{I}_n - \frac{1}{n}\boldsymbol{\imath}\boldsymbol{\imath}' \right) \boldsymbol{x}$$

since $\boldsymbol{\imath}'\boldsymbol{x} = n\overline{x}$ is 1×1 and commutes with $\boldsymbol{\imath}$. The $n \times n$ matrix $\boldsymbol{A} := \boldsymbol{I}_n - \frac{1}{n}\boldsymbol{\imath}\boldsymbol{\imath}'$ was already encountered in Exercise 8.34(a). It is symmetric because $\boldsymbol{A} = \boldsymbol{A}'$. It is also idempotent because

$$\begin{aligned}\boldsymbol{A}^2 &= \left(\boldsymbol{I}_n - \frac{1}{n}\boldsymbol{\imath}\boldsymbol{\imath}' \right) \left(\boldsymbol{I}_n - \frac{1}{n}\boldsymbol{\imath}\boldsymbol{\imath}' \right) = \boldsymbol{I}_n - \frac{2}{n}\boldsymbol{\imath}\boldsymbol{\imath}' + \frac{1}{n^2}\boldsymbol{\imath}\boldsymbol{\imath}'\boldsymbol{\imath}\boldsymbol{\imath}' \\ &= \boldsymbol{I}_n - \frac{2}{n}\boldsymbol{\imath}\boldsymbol{\imath}' + \frac{1}{n}\boldsymbol{\imath}\frac{\boldsymbol{\imath}'\boldsymbol{\imath}}{n}\boldsymbol{\imath}' = \boldsymbol{I}_n - \frac{1}{n}\boldsymbol{\imath}\boldsymbol{\imath}' = \boldsymbol{A}.\end{aligned}$$

It is not surprising that $\boldsymbol{A}^2 = \boldsymbol{A}$, because de-meaning x_i more than once has no further effect. Therefore,

$$\sum_{i=1}^{n} (x_i - \overline{x})^2 = \boldsymbol{y}'\boldsymbol{y} = \boldsymbol{x}'\boldsymbol{A}'\boldsymbol{A}\boldsymbol{x} = \boldsymbol{x}'\boldsymbol{A}^2\boldsymbol{x} = \boldsymbol{x}'\boldsymbol{A}\boldsymbol{x},$$

which establishes that the required matrix is $\boldsymbol{A}$. Its rank is

$$\operatorname{rk}(\boldsymbol{A}) = \operatorname{tr}(\boldsymbol{A}) = \operatorname{tr}(\boldsymbol{I}_n) - \frac{1}{n}\operatorname{tr}\left(\boldsymbol{\imath}\boldsymbol{\imath}'\right) = n-1.$$

(c) We prove this in two ways. The direct proof follows by taking expectations in (a):

$$\begin{aligned}\mathrm{E}\left((n-1)s^2\right) &= \sum_{i=1}^{n}\mathrm{E}\left((x_i-\mu)^2\right) - n\,\mathrm{E}\left((\overline{x}-\mu)^2\right)\\ &= \sum_{i=1}^{n}\operatorname{var}(x_i) - n\operatorname{var}(\overline{x}) = n\sigma^2 - n\frac{\sigma^2}{n} = (n-1)\,\sigma^2\end{aligned}$$

by Exercise 9.2. The indirect proof is based on the method first used in Exercise 6.6. Since $\boldsymbol{x}$ has mean $\mu\boldsymbol{\imath}$ and variance $\sigma^2\boldsymbol{I}_n$, we have

$$\begin{aligned}(n-1)\,\mathrm{E}(s^2) &= \mathrm{E}(\boldsymbol{x}'\boldsymbol{A}\boldsymbol{x}) = \operatorname{tr}\left(\boldsymbol{A}\,\mathrm{E}(\boldsymbol{x}\boldsymbol{x}')\right) = \operatorname{tr}\left(\boldsymbol{A}\left(\sigma^2\boldsymbol{I}_n + \mu^2\boldsymbol{\imath}\boldsymbol{\imath}'\right)\right)\\ &= \sigma^2\operatorname{tr}(\boldsymbol{A}) + \mu^2\boldsymbol{\imath}'\boldsymbol{A}\boldsymbol{\imath} = (n-1)\sigma^2\end{aligned}$$

because (b) implies that $\operatorname{tr}(\boldsymbol{A}) = n-1$ and $\boldsymbol{A}\boldsymbol{\imath} = \mathbf{0}$ (the de-meaning of a constant gives zeros). We stress that the normality of $\boldsymbol{x}$ was not assumed; otherwise, we could have stated the stronger result, in Exercise 8.34(b) and earlier, that $(n-1)\,s^2/\sigma^2 \sim \chi^2(n-1)$ with mean $n-1$. Finally,

$$\left(\mathrm{E}\,(s)\right)^2 \leqslant \mathrm{E}(s^2) = \sigma^2$$

by Jensen's inequality, implying that $\mathrm{E}(s) \leqslant \sigma$. The strict inequality will hold whenever $\operatorname{var}(s) > 0$, which is the subject of the next part of the exercise.

(d) This can also be proved directly, but a proof via our knowledge of quadratic functions is easier. We have

$$\operatorname{var}\left(\sigma^{-2}(n-1)s^2\right) = \operatorname{var}\left(\sigma^{-2}\boldsymbol{x}'\boldsymbol{A}\boldsymbol{x}\right) = \operatorname{var}\left(\sigma^{-2}(\boldsymbol{x}-\mu\boldsymbol{\imath})'\boldsymbol{A}(\boldsymbol{x}-\mu\boldsymbol{\imath})\right)$$

since $\boldsymbol{A}\boldsymbol{\imath} = \mathbf{0}$. Now, $\sigma^{-1}(\boldsymbol{x}-\mu\boldsymbol{\imath})$ has mean $\mathbf{0}$ and variance $\boldsymbol{I}_n$, so using Exercise 6.7(a) yields

$$\begin{aligned}\operatorname{var}\left(\sigma^{-2}(n-1)s^2\right) &= 2\operatorname{tr}\left(\boldsymbol{A}^2\right) + \kappa\sum_{i=1}^{n}a_{ii}^2\\ &= 2(n-1) + \kappa n\left(1-\frac{1}{n}\right)^2 = (n-1)^2\left(\frac{2}{n-1}+\frac{\kappa}{n}\right).\end{aligned}$$

The result follows by $\operatorname{var}\left(\sigma^{-2}(n-1)s^2\right) = \sigma^{-4}(n-1)^2\operatorname{var}\left(s^2\right)$.

Exercise 9.5 (Sample mean and variance: multivariate) Let the m-dimensional vector variate $\boldsymbol{x}$ be distributed with expectation $\boldsymbol{\mu}$ and variance $\boldsymbol{\Sigma}$, and let $\boldsymbol{x}_1, \dots, \boldsymbol{x}_n$ be a random sample from it.

(a) Prove that $\mathrm{E}(\overline{\boldsymbol{x}}) = \boldsymbol{\mu}$ and $\operatorname{var}(\overline{\boldsymbol{x}}) = \frac{1}{n}\boldsymbol{\Sigma}$.

(b) Prove that

$$(n-1)\,\boldsymbol{S}=\sum_{i=1}^{n}\boldsymbol{x}_i\boldsymbol{x}_i'-n\overline{\boldsymbol{x}}\,\overline{\boldsymbol{x}}'=\sum_{i=1}^{n}(\boldsymbol{x}_i-\boldsymbol{\mu})(\boldsymbol{x}_i-\boldsymbol{\mu})'-n\,(\overline{\boldsymbol{x}}-\boldsymbol{\mu})\,(\overline{\boldsymbol{x}}-\boldsymbol{\mu})',$$

and hence that $\mathrm{E}(\boldsymbol{S})=\boldsymbol{\Sigma}$.

Solution

(a) We have

$$\mathrm{E}(\overline{\boldsymbol{x}})=\mathrm{E}\left(\frac{1}{n}\sum_{i=1}^{n}\boldsymbol{x}_i\right)=\frac{1}{n}\sum_{i=1}^{n}\mathrm{E}(\boldsymbol{x}_i)=\frac{1}{n}\sum_{i=1}^{n}\boldsymbol{\mu}=\boldsymbol{\mu},$$

and

$$\mathrm{var}\,(\overline{\boldsymbol{x}})=\mathrm{var}\left(\frac{1}{n}\sum_{i=1}^{n}\boldsymbol{x}_i\right)=\frac{1}{n^2}\sum_{i=1}^{n}\mathrm{var}\,(\boldsymbol{x}_i)=\frac{1}{n}\boldsymbol{\Sigma}$$

since $\boldsymbol{x}_i$ and $\boldsymbol{x}_j$ are mutually independent for $i\neq j$.

(b) These results are to be compared with the population's counterparts in Exercise 6.5. We have

$$(n-1)\,\boldsymbol{S}=\sum_{i=1}^{n}(\boldsymbol{x}_i-\overline{\boldsymbol{x}})\,(\boldsymbol{x}_i-\overline{\boldsymbol{x}})'=\sum_{i=1}^{n}\boldsymbol{x}_i\,(\boldsymbol{x}_i-\overline{\boldsymbol{x}})'$$

by $\sum_{i=1}^{n}(\boldsymbol{x}_i-\overline{\boldsymbol{x}})\equiv\boldsymbol{0}$, hence

$$(n-1)\,\boldsymbol{S}=\sum_{i=1}^{n}\boldsymbol{x}_i\boldsymbol{x}_i'-\left(\sum_{i=1}^{n}\boldsymbol{x}_i\right)\overline{\boldsymbol{x}}'=\sum_{i=1}^{n}\boldsymbol{x}_i\boldsymbol{x}_i'-n\overline{\boldsymbol{x}}\,\overline{\boldsymbol{x}}'.$$

Also,

$$\begin{aligned}\sum_{i=1}^{n}(\boldsymbol{x}_i-\boldsymbol{\mu})(\boldsymbol{x}_i-\boldsymbol{\mu})'&=n\boldsymbol{\mu}\boldsymbol{\mu}'-n\overline{\boldsymbol{x}}\boldsymbol{\mu}'-n\boldsymbol{\mu}\overline{\boldsymbol{x}}'+\sum_{i=1}^{n}\boldsymbol{x}_i\boldsymbol{x}_i'\\&=n\boldsymbol{\mu}\boldsymbol{\mu}'-n\overline{\boldsymbol{x}}\boldsymbol{\mu}'-n\boldsymbol{\mu}\overline{\boldsymbol{x}}'+n\overline{\boldsymbol{x}}\,\overline{\boldsymbol{x}}'+\sum_{i=1}^{n}(\boldsymbol{x}_i-\overline{\boldsymbol{x}})\,(\boldsymbol{x}_i-\overline{\boldsymbol{x}})'\\&=n\,(\overline{\boldsymbol{x}}-\boldsymbol{\mu})\,(\overline{\boldsymbol{x}}-\boldsymbol{\mu})'+\sum_{i=1}^{n}(\boldsymbol{x}_i-\overline{\boldsymbol{x}})\,(\boldsymbol{x}_i-\overline{\boldsymbol{x}})'.\end{aligned}$$

Taking expectations in the last equation, and using $\boldsymbol{\mu}=\mathrm{E}(\overline{\boldsymbol{x}})$ from (a),

$$\sum_{i=1}^{n}\mathrm{var}(\boldsymbol{x})=n\,\mathrm{var}(\overline{\boldsymbol{x}})+\mathrm{E}((n-1)\,\boldsymbol{S}).$$

By $\mathrm{var}(\overline{\boldsymbol{x}})=\frac{1}{n}\boldsymbol{\Sigma}$ from (a), we get $n\boldsymbol{\Sigma}=n\left(\frac{1}{n}\boldsymbol{\Sigma}\right)+(n-1)\,\mathrm{E}(\boldsymbol{S})$. Hence, $\mathrm{E}(\boldsymbol{S})=\boldsymbol{\Sigma}$.

Exercise 9.6 (Sample correlation and nonlinear dependence) Calculate the sample correlation for the following data on (x,y):

(a) $(-3, 6), (-1, 2)$;
(b) $(0, 0), (2, 4), (3, 9)$;
(c) the combined data in (a) and (b).

Solution
(a) A straight line will always be able to join two points in (x, y) space, and the line will provide an exact fit of the data:

$$\widehat{\rho}_{y,x} = \frac{\sum_{i=1}^{2} x_i y_i - \frac{1}{2}\left(\sum_{i=1}^{2} x_i\right)\left(\sum_{i=1}^{2} y_i\right)}{\sqrt{\sum_{i=1}^{2} x_i^2 - \frac{1}{2}\left(\sum_{i=1}^{2} x_i\right)^2}\sqrt{\sum_{i=1}^{2} y_i^2 - \frac{1}{2}\left(\sum_{i=1}^{2} y_i\right)^2}}$$

$$= \frac{-18 - 2 - \frac{1}{2}(-4)(8)}{\sqrt{9 + 1 - \frac{1}{2}(-4)^2}\sqrt{36 + 4 - \frac{1}{2}(8)^2}} = -1,$$

where we can see that the perfect linear relation has a negative slope.
(b) For the second sample, we have

$$\widehat{\rho}_{y,x} = \frac{0 + 8 + 27 - \frac{1}{3}(5)(13)}{\sqrt{0 + 4 + 9 - \frac{1}{3}(5)^2}\sqrt{0 + 16 + 81 - \frac{1}{3}(13)^2}} \approx 0.968.$$

Notice how close this is to being a linear relation. For example, had the second point been $(1.5, 4.5)$, all three points would have fallen exactly on the same line and the *sample* correlation would have been 1. Instead, the data given in the question have actually been generated by the *exact* nonlinear relation $y = x^2$, which is being approximated by only a linear fit.
(c) Trying to draw a straight line between a downward sloping line (for $x < 0$) and an upward sloping curve (for $x \geqslant 0$) will necessarily yield a poorer fit than either (a) or (b) separately. Indeed,

$$\widehat{\rho}_{y,x} = \frac{-20 + 35 - \frac{1}{5}(-4 + 5)(8 + 13)}{\sqrt{10 + 13 - \frac{1}{5}(-4 + 5)^2}\sqrt{40 + 97 - \frac{1}{5}(8 + 13)^2}} \approx 0.324,$$

which is much less (in absolute terms) than the correlations in (a) and (b). This is so because correlations measure the extent of linear dependence only, whereas the data have been generated by the exact nonlinear relation

$$y := \begin{cases} -2x & (x < 0), \\ x^2 & (x \geqslant 0). \end{cases}$$

***Exercise 9.7 (Sample multiple correlation and R^2)** The multiple correlation coefficient was introduced in Exercise 6.21. We can define its sample counterpart as follows.

Suppose that the $1 \times (1+m)$ vector $\boldsymbol{x}' := (y, \boldsymbol{z}')$ has a nondegenerate distribution, and let

$$\boldsymbol{S} := \begin{pmatrix} s_{11} & \boldsymbol{s}_{21}' \\ \boldsymbol{s}_{21} & \boldsymbol{S}_{22} \end{pmatrix}$$

be its sample variance matrix based on n observations. Then, $R := (\boldsymbol{s}_{21}' \boldsymbol{S}_{22}^{-1} \boldsymbol{s}_{21}/s_{11})^{1/2}$ is the *sample multiple correlation* (the sample counterpart of $\rho^{\max}$ or $\overline{\rho}$ of Exercise 6.21). Assume that $n > m+1$ and that $\Pr(y = 0) = 0$.

(a) Show that, when y is spherically distributed independently of $\boldsymbol{z}$ (which is allowed to have any distribution), we have

$$\frac{n-m-1}{m} \times \frac{R^2}{1-R^2} \sim \mathrm{F}(m, n-m-1)$$

or, equivalently, $R^2 \sim \mathrm{Beta}(\frac{1}{2}m, \frac{1}{2}(n-m-1))$.

(b) What distribution does (a) imply for $\widehat{\rho}$ when $m = 1$?

(c) Dropping the assumption of the independence of y and $\boldsymbol{z}$, but restricting the setup to normality, assume now that we have a random sample from $\boldsymbol{x} \sim \mathrm{N}(\boldsymbol{0}, \boldsymbol{\Sigma})$, where $\boldsymbol{\Sigma}$ is nonsingular. Show that, conditionally on $\boldsymbol{z}$, we have

$$\frac{n-m-1}{m} \times \frac{R^2}{1-R^2} \sim \mathrm{F}(m, n-m-1, \delta)$$

for some noncentrality parameter δ, yielding the unconditional distribution of R^2 as

$$f_{R^2}(u) = \frac{(n-m-1)\left(1-\overline{\rho}^2\right)^{\frac{n-1}{2}}}{(1-u)^2} \times \sum_{j=0}^{\infty} \binom{\frac{1-n}{2}}{j} \frac{\left(-\overline{\rho}^2\right)^j}{2j+m} f_{\mathrm{F}(2j+m, n-m-1)}\left(\frac{n-m-1}{(2j+m)(u^{-1}-1)}\right).$$

Solution

(a) Define $\boldsymbol{y} := (y_1, \dots, y_n)'$, $\boldsymbol{Z} := (\boldsymbol{z}_1, \dots, \boldsymbol{z}_n)'$, and $\boldsymbol{X} := (\boldsymbol{x}_1, \dots, \boldsymbol{x}_n)' = (\boldsymbol{y}, \boldsymbol{Z})$. Then

$$(n-1)\boldsymbol{S} = \boldsymbol{X}'\boldsymbol{A}\boldsymbol{X} = \begin{pmatrix} \boldsymbol{y}'\boldsymbol{A}\boldsymbol{y} & \boldsymbol{y}'\boldsymbol{A}\boldsymbol{Z} \\ \boldsymbol{Z}'\boldsymbol{A}\boldsymbol{y} & \boldsymbol{Z}'\boldsymbol{A}\boldsymbol{Z} \end{pmatrix},$$

where $\boldsymbol{A} := \boldsymbol{I}_n - \frac{1}{n}\boldsymbol{\imath}\boldsymbol{\imath}'$ is the de-meaning idempotent matrix of rank $n-1$ seen earlier (for example in Exercise 9.4). We can therefore write

$$R^2 = \frac{\boldsymbol{y}'\boldsymbol{A}\boldsymbol{Z}\left(\boldsymbol{Z}'\boldsymbol{A}\boldsymbol{Z}\right)^{-1}\boldsymbol{Z}'\boldsymbol{A}\boldsymbol{y}}{\boldsymbol{y}'\boldsymbol{A}\boldsymbol{y}}$$

and

$$\frac{R^2}{1-R^2} = \frac{\boldsymbol{y}'\boldsymbol{A}\boldsymbol{Z}\left(\boldsymbol{Z}'\boldsymbol{A}\boldsymbol{Z}\right)^{-1}\boldsymbol{Z}'\boldsymbol{A}\boldsymbol{y}}{\boldsymbol{y}'\left(\boldsymbol{A} - \boldsymbol{A}\boldsymbol{Z}\left(\boldsymbol{Z}'\boldsymbol{A}\boldsymbol{Z}\right)^{-1}\boldsymbol{Z}'\boldsymbol{A}\right)\boldsymbol{y}} \equiv \frac{\boldsymbol{y}'\boldsymbol{B}\boldsymbol{y}}{\boldsymbol{y}'\boldsymbol{C}\boldsymbol{y}},$$

where $\boldsymbol{B} := \boldsymbol{AZ}(\boldsymbol{Z}'\boldsymbol{AZ})^{-1}\boldsymbol{Z}'\boldsymbol{A}$ and $\boldsymbol{C} := \boldsymbol{A} - \boldsymbol{B}$. The matrices $\boldsymbol{B}$ and $\boldsymbol{C}$ are both symmetric idempotent and satisfy $\boldsymbol{BC} = \boldsymbol{BA} - \boldsymbol{B}^2 = \mathbf{O}$. Their ranks are given by

$$\operatorname{rk}(\boldsymbol{B}) = \operatorname{tr}\left(\boldsymbol{AZ}(\boldsymbol{Z}'\boldsymbol{AZ})^{-1}\boldsymbol{Z}'\boldsymbol{A}\right) = \operatorname{tr}\left(\boldsymbol{Z}'\boldsymbol{AZ}(\boldsymbol{Z}'\boldsymbol{AZ})^{-1}\right) = \operatorname{tr}(\boldsymbol{I}_m) = m$$

and

$$\operatorname{rk}(\boldsymbol{C}) = \operatorname{tr}(\boldsymbol{C}) = \operatorname{tr}(\boldsymbol{A}) - \operatorname{tr}(\boldsymbol{B}) = n - 1 - m.$$

By the assumption of the independence of $\boldsymbol{y}$ and $\boldsymbol{Z}$, the conditional distribution of $\boldsymbol{y} \mid \boldsymbol{Z}$ is the same as the marginal distribution of $\boldsymbol{y}$, which is spherical as in Exercise 8.37(a); therefore, we can now apply this exercise to get

$$\frac{n-m-1}{m} \times \frac{R^2}{1-R^2} \sim \mathrm{F}(m, n-m-1)$$

given $\boldsymbol{Z}$. This does not depend on $\boldsymbol{Z}$, and is therefore also the unconditional distribution of the ratio as $\boldsymbol{Z}$ varies. This is equivalent, by Exercise 4.31, to the result that R^2 itself is distributed as a $\mathrm{Beta}(\frac{1}{2}m, \frac{1}{2}(n-m-1))$.
(b) When $m = 1$ and $\boldsymbol{z} := (z_1, \dots, z_n)'$,

$$\widehat{\rho} = \frac{\boldsymbol{y}'\boldsymbol{Az}}{\sqrt{\boldsymbol{y}'\boldsymbol{Ay} \times \boldsymbol{z}'\boldsymbol{Az}}}.$$

Since $\widehat{\rho}^2 = R^2 = \boldsymbol{y}'\boldsymbol{By}/\boldsymbol{y}'\boldsymbol{Ay}$ it follows that $\widehat{\rho}\sqrt{n-2}/\sqrt{1-\widehat{\rho}^2} \sim \mathrm{t}(n-2)$, since $\mathrm{F}(1, n-2) = (\mathrm{t}(n-2))^2$ and $\boldsymbol{y}$ being spherically distributed (hence symmetric) means that $\widehat{\rho}$ takes positive and negative values with equal probability. Note that in this last t-distributed ratio, $\widehat{\rho}^2$ and $1-\widehat{\rho}^2$ are definitely not independent (they are complements adding up to 1), even though $\widehat{\rho}^2 s_{11}$ and $(1-\widehat{\rho}^2)s_{11}$ (meaning $\boldsymbol{y}'\boldsymbol{By}$ and $\boldsymbol{y}'\boldsymbol{Cy}$) are independent under normality. This is to say that we should be careful in defining which are the numerator and denominator (obviously not uniquely defined) that are independent in the F and t representations seen in Exercises 4.32 and 4.33.
(c) The conditional part follows from

$$\frac{R^2}{1-R^2} = \frac{\boldsymbol{y}'\boldsymbol{AZ}(\boldsymbol{Z}'\boldsymbol{AZ})^{-1}\boldsymbol{Z}'\boldsymbol{Ay}}{\boldsymbol{y}'\left(\boldsymbol{A} - \boldsymbol{AZ}(\boldsymbol{Z}'\boldsymbol{AZ})^{-1}\boldsymbol{Z}'\boldsymbol{A}\right)\boldsymbol{y}}$$

of (a), but now with the rank-normalized numerator a noncentral $\chi^2(m)$ while the normalized denominator is still a $\chi^2(n-m-1)$, as we will show. To work out the numerator's distribution, Exercise 6.51(a) or Chapter 8 implies $y \mid \boldsymbol{z} \sim \mathrm{N}(c_{1|2}, \sigma_{11|2})$, where

$$c_{1|2} := \boldsymbol{\sigma}_{21}'\boldsymbol{\Sigma}_{22}^{-1}\boldsymbol{z} \quad \text{and} \quad \sigma_{11|2} := \sigma_{11} - \boldsymbol{\sigma}_{21}'\boldsymbol{\Sigma}_{22}^{-1}\boldsymbol{\sigma}_{21} \equiv \sigma_{11}\left(1 - \overline{\rho}^2\right)$$

with $\boldsymbol{\Sigma}$ partitioned in the same way as $\boldsymbol{S}$. The conditional $\sigma_{11|2}$ does not depend on $\boldsymbol{z}$ but the conditional centering $c_{1|2}$ does. The data vector $\boldsymbol{y}'$ has conditional expectation $\boldsymbol{\sigma}_{21}'\boldsymbol{\Sigma}_{22}^{-1}\boldsymbol{Z}'$ and variance $\sigma_{11|2}\boldsymbol{I}_n$; hence Exercise 8.29 gives the required noncentrality parameter as

$$\delta = \frac{\boldsymbol{\sigma}_{21}' \boldsymbol{\Sigma}_{22}^{-1} \boldsymbol{Z}' \left(\boldsymbol{A}\boldsymbol{Z} \left(\boldsymbol{Z}'\boldsymbol{A}\boldsymbol{Z} \right)^{-1} \boldsymbol{Z}'\boldsymbol{A} \right) \boldsymbol{Z} \boldsymbol{\Sigma}_{22}^{-1} \boldsymbol{\sigma}_{21}}{\sigma_{11|2}} = \frac{\boldsymbol{\sigma}_{21}' \boldsymbol{\Sigma}_{22}^{-1} \boldsymbol{Z}'\boldsymbol{A}\boldsymbol{Z} \boldsymbol{\Sigma}_{22}^{-1} \boldsymbol{\sigma}_{21}}{\sigma_{11|2}}.$$

Repeating the same calculation for the denominator, we have the noncentrality

$$\frac{\boldsymbol{\sigma}_{21}' \boldsymbol{\Sigma}_{22}^{-1} \boldsymbol{Z}' \left(\boldsymbol{A} - \boldsymbol{A}\boldsymbol{Z} \left(\boldsymbol{Z}'\boldsymbol{A}\boldsymbol{Z} \right)^{-1} \boldsymbol{Z}'\boldsymbol{A} \right) \boldsymbol{Z} \boldsymbol{\Sigma}_{22}^{-1} \boldsymbol{\sigma}_{21}}{\sigma_{11|2}} = 0$$

by $\boldsymbol{B}\boldsymbol{C} = \mathbf{O}$ as before. This completes the conditional part of the result.

To get the unconditional density of $\xi := R^2 \in (0, 1)$, recall from (6.3) that

$$f_\xi(u) = \mathrm{E}_{\boldsymbol{z}}(f_{\xi|\boldsymbol{z}}(u)),$$

so we first need to write down the conditional density of ξ implied by the previous paragraph's distributional result:

$$\zeta := \frac{n-m-1}{m\left(\xi^{-1} - 1\right)} \equiv \frac{n-m-1}{m\left(R^{-2} - 1\right)} \sim \mathrm{F}(m, n-m-1, \delta).$$

Table 4.2 give the p.d.f. of a noncentral $\mathrm{F}(m, n-m-1, \delta)$ variate as

$$f_{\mathrm{F}(m,n-m-1,\delta)}(w) = \mathrm{e}^{-\delta/2} \sum_{j=0}^{\infty} \frac{(\delta/2)^j}{j!} \frac{m}{2j+m} f_{\mathrm{F}(2j+m,n-m-1)}\left(\frac{mw}{2j+m}\right).$$

Since the Jacobian of the transformation from ζ (or w) to ξ (or u) is

$$\frac{\mathrm{d}\zeta}{\mathrm{d}\xi} = \frac{n-m-1}{m\left(1-\xi\right)^2},$$

we obtain the conditional density of ξ as

$$f_{\xi|\boldsymbol{z}}(u) = \mathrm{e}^{-\delta/2} \sum_{j=0}^{\infty} \frac{(\delta/2)^j}{j!} \frac{n-m-1}{(2j+m)\left(1-u\right)^2} f_{\mathrm{F}(2j+m,n-m-1)}\left(\frac{n-m-1}{(2j+m)\left(u^{-1}-1\right)}\right).$$

To take the expectation of this density with respect to $\boldsymbol{z}$, we see that it appears only in the noncentrality $\delta = \boldsymbol{z}_*'\boldsymbol{z}_*$ with

$$\boldsymbol{z}_* := \frac{1}{\sqrt{\sigma_{11|2}}} \boldsymbol{A}\boldsymbol{Z}\boldsymbol{\Sigma}_{22}^{-1}\boldsymbol{\sigma}_{21}.$$

This $\boldsymbol{z}_*$ is a linear combination of de-meaned normals, hence normal, with $\mathrm{E}(\boldsymbol{z}_*) = \mathbf{0}$ and

$$\begin{aligned}
\mathrm{E}(\boldsymbol{z}_*'\boldsymbol{z}_*) &= \frac{\boldsymbol{\sigma}_{21}' \boldsymbol{\Sigma}_{22}^{-1} \,\mathrm{E}(\boldsymbol{Z}'\boldsymbol{A}\boldsymbol{Z}) \boldsymbol{\Sigma}_{22}^{-1} \boldsymbol{\sigma}_{21}}{\sigma_{11|2}} \\
&= \frac{(n-1)\, \boldsymbol{\sigma}_{21}' \boldsymbol{\Sigma}_{22}^{-1} \,\mathrm{E}(\boldsymbol{S}_{22}) \boldsymbol{\Sigma}_{22}^{-1} \boldsymbol{\sigma}_{21}}{\sigma_{11|2}} \\
&= \frac{(n-1)\, \boldsymbol{\sigma}_{21}' \boldsymbol{\Sigma}_{22}^{-1} \boldsymbol{\sigma}_{21}}{\sigma_{11|2}} = \frac{(n-1)\,\overline{\rho}^2}{1-\overline{\rho}^2} = \frac{n-1}{(\overline{\rho})^{-2} - 1}
\end{aligned}$$

by $\mathrm{E}(\boldsymbol{S}_{22}) = \boldsymbol{\Sigma}_{22}$ and $\overline{\rho}^2 := \boldsymbol{\sigma}_{21}'\boldsymbol{\Sigma}_{22}^{-1}\boldsymbol{\sigma}_{21}/\sigma_{11}$. As a result, $\delta \equiv \boldsymbol{z}_*'\boldsymbol{z}_*$ is a scaled χ^2 by

$$\eta := \left((\overline{\rho})^{-2} - 1\right)\delta \sim \chi^2(n-1)$$

and, to calculate the required $f_\xi(u) = \mathrm{E}_{\boldsymbol{z}}(f_{\xi|\boldsymbol{z}}(u))$, we need

$$\begin{aligned}
\mathrm{E}\left(\delta^j \mathrm{e}^{-\delta/2}\right) &= \left((\overline{\rho})^{-2} - 1\right)^{-j} \mathrm{E}\left(\eta^j \exp\left(-\frac{\eta}{2\left((\overline{\rho})^{-2} - 1\right)}\right)\right) \\
&= \frac{\left((\overline{\rho})^{-2} - 1\right)^{-j}}{2\Gamma\left(\frac{n-1}{2}\right)} \int_0^\infty v^j \exp\left(-\frac{v}{2\left((\overline{\rho})^{-2} - 1\right)} - \frac{v}{2}\right)\left(\frac{v}{2}\right)^{\frac{n-3}{2}} \mathrm{d}v \\
&= \frac{\left((\overline{\rho})^{-2} - 1\right)^{-j} 2^j}{2\Gamma\left(\frac{n-1}{2}\right)} \int_0^\infty \left(\frac{v}{2}\right)^{j+\frac{n-3}{2}} \exp\left(-\frac{v}{2\left(1-\overline{\rho}^2\right)}\right) \mathrm{d}v \\
&= \frac{\left((\overline{\rho})^{-2} - 1\right)^{-j} 2^j}{2\Gamma\left(\frac{n-1}{2}\right)} \left(1-\overline{\rho}^2\right)^{j+\frac{n-1}{2}} \int_0^\infty \left(\frac{w}{2}\right)^{j+\frac{n-3}{2}} \exp\left(-\frac{w}{2}\right) \mathrm{d}w \\
&= \frac{\left((\overline{\rho})^{-2} - 1\right)^{-j} 2^j}{2\Gamma\left(\frac{n-1}{2}\right)} \left(1-\overline{\rho}^2\right)^{j+\frac{n-1}{2}} \left(2\Gamma\left(j + \frac{n-1}{2}\right)\right) \\
&= \left(2\overline{\rho}^2\right)^j \left(1-\overline{\rho}^2\right)^{\frac{n-1}{2}} \frac{\Gamma\left(j + \frac{n-1}{2}\right)}{\Gamma\left(\frac{n-1}{2}\right)},
\end{aligned}$$

where we have substituted the $\chi^2(n-1)$ density and then changed the variable of integration to $w = v/\left(1-\overline{\rho}^2\right)$ before integrating out a $\chi^2(2j+n-1)$ density. Applying

$$\frac{\Gamma\left(j + \frac{n-1}{2}\right)}{j!\,\Gamma\left(\frac{n-1}{2}\right)} = \frac{\left(j - 1 + \frac{n-1}{2}\right)\left(j - 2 + \frac{n-1}{2}\right)\cdots\left(\frac{n-1}{2}\right)}{j!} = (-1)^j \binom{\frac{1-n}{2}}{j}$$

(as in (4.1)) and $f_\xi(u) = \mathrm{E}_{\boldsymbol{z}}(f_{\xi|\boldsymbol{z}}(u))$, we get the required density. The series is absolutely convergent by the formula for the central F density and $\overline{\rho}^2, u \in (0,1)$, with $\overline{\rho}^2 \neq 1$ following from the nonsingularity of $\boldsymbol{\Sigma}$; see Section A.3.2. See the Notes to this chapter for an alternative formulation.

We conclude by noting that, unlike in part (b), we cannot use a symmetry-argument shortcut to get the density of $\widehat{\rho}$ from $R^2 = \widehat{\rho}^2$ when $\rho \neq 0$. The exact density of $\widehat{\rho}$ in the case of general ρ will follow in Exercise 9.25.

Exercise 9.8 (Urn sampled: probabilities) An urn contains m balls, labeled $1, \dots, m$. We draw n balls ($n < m$) from the urn *without* replacement. Let x_1 be the first ball drawn, x_2 the second, and so on. Let $\boldsymbol{x} := (x_1, \dots, x_n)'$ and $\boldsymbol{w} := (w_1, \dots, w_n)'$ where w_i is the label of ball x_i, for $i = 1, \dots, n$.
(a) Show that $f_{\boldsymbol{x}}(\boldsymbol{w}) = 1/(m(m-1)\dots(m-n+1))$.
(b) Show that for each subset of n elements, regardless of the order in which the elements are drawn, the probability of this subset being drawn is equal to $1/\binom{m}{n}$.
(c) Show that $f_{x_i}(w_i) = 1/m$ for any i and $w_i \in \{1, \dots, m\}$.

(d) Is the sampling random?

Solution
(a) We have

$$\Pr(\boldsymbol{x} = \boldsymbol{w}) = \Pr(x_1 = w_1)\Pr(x_2 = w_2 \mid x_1 = w_1)\cdots$$
$$\cdots \Pr(x_n = w_n \mid x_1 = w_1, \dots, x_{n-1} = w_{n-1}),$$

where each $w_i \in \{1, \dots, m\}$ and $w_i \neq w_j$ for $i \neq j$. Hence,

$$\Pr(\boldsymbol{x} = \boldsymbol{w}) = \frac{1}{m} \times \frac{1}{m-1} \times \frac{1}{m-2} \cdots \frac{1}{m-n+1}.$$

(b) There are $\binom{m}{n}$ subsets of n elements.
(c) This follows from (a) by setting $n = 1$.
(d) Sampling without replacement from a finite population ($m < \infty$) cannot lead to an i.i.d. sequence. More specifically, the product of the marginal densities from (c) is not equal to the joint density in (a), so the x_i are not independently distributed. They are, however, identically and uniformly distributed by (c).

Exercise 9.9 (Urn sampled: moments) Now suppose that each ball in the urn has a value v_k ($k = 1, \dots, m$). Define y_i to be the value of ball x_i, and

$$\mu := \frac{1}{m}\sum_{k=1}^{m} v_k \quad \text{and} \quad \sigma^2 := \frac{1}{m}\sum_{k=1}^{m} (v_k - \mu)^2 .$$

(a) Let $\boldsymbol{y} := (y_1, \dots, y_n)'$ and $\boldsymbol{J} := \frac{1}{n}\boldsymbol{\imath}\boldsymbol{\imath}'$. Show that

$$\mathrm{E}(\boldsymbol{y}) = \mu\boldsymbol{\imath} \quad \text{and} \quad \mathrm{var}(\boldsymbol{y}) = \frac{\sigma^2}{m-1}(m\boldsymbol{I}_n - n\boldsymbol{J}).$$

(b) Hence, show that

$$\mathrm{E}(\overline{y}) = \mu \quad \text{and} \quad \mathrm{var}(\overline{y}) = \frac{\sigma^2}{n} \times \frac{m-n}{m-1}.$$

Compare this result with Exercise 9.2.

Solution
(a) Since $\Pr(y_k = v_k) = \Pr(x_k = w_k) = 1/m$,

$$\mathrm{E}(y_i) = \sum_{k=1}^{m} \Pr(y_k = v_k) v_k = \frac{1}{m}\sum_{k=1}^{m} v_k = \mu$$

and

$$\mathrm{E}(y_i^2) = \frac{1}{m}\sum_{k=1}^{m} v_k^2 = \mu^2 + \sigma^2,$$

where we have used the index k (rather than i as in the previous exercise) to stress that the expectation requires the sum over the elements of the population (not the sample). To complete the required variance matrix, we need the covariance terms. From Exercise 9.8(a),

$$\Pr(y_k = v_k, y_l = v_l) = \frac{1}{m\,(m-1)} \qquad (k \neq l);$$

hence, for $i \neq j$,

$$\begin{aligned}\mathrm{E}(y_i y_j) &= \frac{1}{m(m-1)} \sum_{k \neq l} v_k v_l = \frac{1}{m(m-1)} \left(\left(\sum_{k=1}^{m} v_k \right)^2 - \sum_{k=1}^{m} v_k^2 \right) \\ &= \frac{1}{m(m-1)} \left(m^2 \mu^2 - m\left(\mu^2 + \sigma^2\right)\right) = \mu^2 - \frac{\sigma^2}{m-1}.\end{aligned}$$

Then, $\operatorname{var}(y_i) = \sigma^2$ and $\operatorname{cov}(y_i, y_j) = -\sigma^2/(m-1)$ for $i \neq j$, which gives the required result since $n\boldsymbol{J}$ is a matrix of ones. Notice that $\operatorname{cov}(y_i, y_j) < 0$ for $i \neq j$, since drawing a large value of y_i makes the remaining values of y_j likely to be smaller. The sequence of y_i's is not independently distributed.
(b) Using (a) and the fact that $\boldsymbol{J}\boldsymbol{\imath} = \boldsymbol{\imath}$, we obtain

$$\mathrm{E}(\overline{y}) = \frac{1}{n} \mathrm{E}(\boldsymbol{\imath}'\boldsymbol{y}) = \frac{1}{n}\boldsymbol{\imath}' \mathrm{E}(\boldsymbol{y}) = \frac{1}{n}\boldsymbol{\imath}'(\mu\boldsymbol{\imath}) = \mu,$$

and

$$\begin{aligned}\operatorname{var}(\overline{y}) &= \frac{1}{n^2} \operatorname{var}(\boldsymbol{\imath}'\boldsymbol{y}) = \frac{1}{n^2}\boldsymbol{\imath}' \operatorname{var}(\boldsymbol{y})\boldsymbol{\imath} \\ &= \frac{\sigma^2}{n^2\,(m-1)}\boldsymbol{\imath}'\left(m\boldsymbol{I}_n - n\boldsymbol{J}\right)\boldsymbol{\imath} \\ &= \frac{\sigma^2}{n^2\,(m-1)}\boldsymbol{\imath}'\left(m\boldsymbol{\imath} - n\boldsymbol{\imath}\right) = \frac{\sigma^2}{n\,(m-1)}(m-n).\end{aligned}$$

If m is large relative to n, then $\operatorname{var}(\overline{y}) \approx \sigma^2/n$ and $\operatorname{cov}(y_i, y_j) \approx 0$ for $i \neq j$, as in the case of the i.i.d. sampling of Exercise 9.2.

***Exercise 9.10 (Benford's law)** Define the set $A_n := \{1, 2, \dots, n\}$, where $n > 1$. Derive the probability that a natural number is even. Try to derive, by the same method, the probability that a natural number has 1 as its leading (or first) digit. What do you get and why?

Solution
We have $\lim_{n\to\infty} A_n = \mathbb{N}$. Letting $\lfloor \nu \rfloor$ denote the largest integer $\leqslant \nu$, the probability of a natural number being even is $\lim_{n\to\infty}\lfloor \frac{n}{2} \rfloor / n = \frac{1}{2}$.

Now, let p be the frequency with which 1 is the leading digit in A_n. Then, this frequency changes as n increases. It reaches its minimum when $n = 9$, giving $p = 1/9$, and never goes below this value which is again attained when $n = 99, n = 999, \dots$ Clearly, the frequency oscillates up and down as n increases. If its upper bound were to converge to $1/9$, then the frequency would converge to this fraction, which would then be the probability; but this is not true as we now show.

The first maximum for p is reached when $n = 19$, giving $p = 11/19$. The next is reached when $n = 199$, giving $p = 111/199$. Repeating this procedure as $n \to \infty$ gives $p = 111\ldots/199\ldots = 5/9$ as the eventual upper limit for the probability, and this is larger than $1/9$. The sampling scheme is not random, and the frequency does not settle down to the required probability (a single number).

Exercise 9.11 (Sample signs) Consider a random sample of size n from the distribution having p.d.f. $f_x(u) = (u+1)/2$ for $-1 < u < 1$, and 0 elsewhere. Find the probability that exactly $n-1$ elements of the sample exceed zero.

Solution

For each element in the sample, the probability p that it is positive equals

$$\int_0^1 \frac{u+1}{2}\,\mathrm{d}u = \left[\frac{u^2}{4} + \frac{u}{2}\right]_0^1 = \frac{3}{4}.$$

Whether each sample point is positive or not is a repeated Bernoulli trial with probability of success $p = 3/4$. Using the binomial distribution, the desired probability is

$$\binom{n}{n-1} p^{n-1}(1-p) = \frac{n}{4}\left(\frac{3}{4}\right)^{n-1}.$$

This exercise is reminiscent of some derivations seen in Part A, especially in Chapters 4 and 7, and is illustrative of sampling contexts.

***Exercise 9.12 (Poisson arrivals: the prequel)** A function $g(v)$ satisfying $g(v)/v^{\alpha} \to 0$ as $v \to c$ is said to be of *order of magnitude smaller than* v^{α}, as $v \to c$, which is written as $g(v) = o(v^{\alpha})$; see Section A.3.4 for more details.

Customers arrive in a shop according to the following conditions:

(i) the probability of exactly one arrival in a time interval of length δ is $r\delta + o(\delta)$ as $\delta \to 0$, where $r \in \mathbb{R}_+$;

(ii) the probability of more than one arrival in a time interval of length δ is $o(\delta)$ as $\delta \to 0$;

(iii) the numbers of arrivals in nonoverlapping time intervals are all independent.

Let x (where $x \in \mathbb{Z}_{0,+}$) be the number of arrivals in a time interval of finite length τ. Partition τ into n subintervals and let $\delta := \tau/n$. By letting $n \to \infty$, show that:

(a) $\Pr(x = u) = \Pr($at most one arrival in each of the n subintervals, such that the subinterval arrivals add up to $u)$;

(b) $x \sim \text{Poi}(r\tau)$. [Hint: Consider the possibility of an arrival within each subinterval as a Bernoulli trial.]

Solution

(a) To be able to simplify the probability that the joint event involves n subintervals, we will require Boole's inequality from Exercise 1.14,

$$\Pr\left(\bigcup_{i=1}^{n} A_i\right) \leqslant \sum_{i=1}^{n} \Pr(A_i),$$

where we now define A_i ($i = 1, \dots, n$) to be the event of more than one arrival in subinterval i. By Assumption (ii), $\Pr(A_i) = o(\delta)$, where $\delta = \tau/n$, so for fixed τ we have $\Pr(A_i) = o\left(n^{-1}\right)$ and the right-hand side of the displayed inequality sums up to $o(1)$ and tends to zero as $n \to \infty$. Hence, there is probability 0 that more than one arrival occurs in any subinterval, as required.

(b) By Assumption (iii), we can consider this experiment as a sequence of independent Bernoulli trials, with the probability of success (arrival) given by (i) as $r\delta + o(\delta)$. Using the binomial distribution, the required probability is

$$\begin{aligned}
&\binom{n}{u}(r\delta + o(\delta))^u (1 - r\delta - o(\delta))^{n-u} \\
&= \binom{n}{u}\left(\frac{r\tau}{n} + o\left(\frac{1}{n}\right)\right)^u \left(1 - \frac{r\tau}{n} - o\left(\frac{1}{n}\right)\right)^{n-u} \\
&= \frac{n(n-1)\cdots(n-u+1)}{u!}\left(\frac{r\tau}{n} + o\left(\frac{1}{n}\right)\right)^u \left(1 - \frac{r\tau}{n} - o\left(\frac{1}{n}\right)\right)^{n-u}.
\end{aligned}$$

Now,

$$\begin{aligned}
\lim_{n\to\infty} n(n-1)\cdots(n-u+1)\left(\frac{r\tau}{n} + o\left(\frac{1}{n}\right)\right)^u &= \lim_{n\to\infty} n^u \left(\frac{r\tau}{n} + o\left(\frac{1}{n}\right)\right)^u \\
&= \lim_{n\to\infty} (r\tau + o(1))^u = (r\tau)^u
\end{aligned}$$

and, by $\log(1+x) = x + o(x)$ from Section A.3.2,

$$\begin{aligned}
\lim_{n\to\infty}\left(1 - \frac{r\tau}{n} - o\left(\frac{1}{n}\right)\right)^{n-u} &= \lim_{n\to\infty} \exp\left(\log\left(1 - \frac{r\tau}{n} - o\left(\frac{1}{n}\right)\right)^{n-u}\right) \\
&= \lim_{n\to\infty} \exp\left((n-u)\log\left(1 - \frac{r\tau}{n} - o\left(\frac{1}{n}\right)\right)\right) \\
&= \lim_{n\to\infty} \exp\left((n-u)\left(-\frac{r\tau}{n} - o\left(\frac{1}{n}\right)\right)\right) \\
&= \lim_{n\to\infty} \exp(-r\tau - o(1)) = \exp(-r\tau).
\end{aligned}$$

This gives the required probability as

$$\frac{(r\tau)^u}{u!}\exp(-r\tau),$$

which we recognize as the density of a $\text{Poi}(r\tau)$ variate. This justifies the assumption of Poisson arrivals in Exercises 4.8 and 4.16.

9.2 Normal sample's moments, Wishart distribution, and Hotelling's T^2

Exercise 9.13 (Student's t representation) Let $x_1, \dots, x_n$ and $y_1, \dots, y_n$ be two independent random samples from the $\mathrm{N}(\mu, \sigma^2)$ distribution. Define

$$s_1^2 := \frac{1}{n-1} \sum_{i=1}^{n} (x_i - \overline{x})^2 \qquad \text{and} \qquad s_2^2 := \frac{1}{n-1} \sum_{i=1}^{n} (y_i - \overline{y})^2 .$$

(a) What is the distribution of s_1^2/s_2^2?
(b) What is the distribution of $z := \sqrt{n}(\overline{x} - \mu)/s_1$?

Solution
(a) We know that

$$\frac{(n-1)s_1^2}{\sigma^2} \sim \chi^2(n-1), \qquad \frac{(n-1)s_2^2}{\sigma^2} \sim \chi^2(n-1),$$

and that s_1^2 and s_2^2 are independent by the independence of the two samples on which they are based. Hence, by the representation of F distributions in Exercise 4.32,

$$\frac{s_1^2}{s_2^2} = \frac{s_1^2/\sigma^2}{s_2^2/\sigma^2} \sim \mathrm{F}(n-1, n-1).$$

(b) It is possible to write the joint density of $(\overline{x}, s_1)$ by either of Exercises 7.16 or 8.34, then use the transformation theorem to get the p.d.f. of (z, s_1), and finally marginalize with respect to s_1. However, a shortcut is provided by using conditioning and Exercise 2.26 if we let $m := n - 1$ and $p := (n-1)s_1^2/\sigma^2$ there. Conditioning on p (or s_1), we see that $z = \sqrt{n}(\overline{x} - \mu)/s_1$ is just a linear transformation of $\overline{x} \sim \mathrm{N}(\mu, \sigma^2/n)$ into $z \mid p \sim \mathrm{N}(0, m/p)$. We know that $p \sim \chi^2(m)$. Therefore, the unconditional density of z is the mixed normal derived in Exercise 2.26, namely Student's t with m degrees of freedom. For a more general (beyond normality) representation of Student's t, see Exercise 9.7(b).

Exercise 9.14 (Ratio of dependent quadratics) Let x_1, x_2, x_3 be a random sample from an $\mathrm{N}(0, \sigma^2)$ distribution. Show how you would compute

$$\Pr\left(\frac{x_1^2}{x_1^2 + x_2^2 + x_3^2} \leqslant c\right).$$

Solution
Both the numerator and the denominator are χ^2-type variables but they are not independent. However, since $x_1^2/\sigma^2 \sim \chi^2(1)$ and $(x_2^2 + x_3^2)/\sigma^2 \sim \chi^2(2)$ are independent, we can define $z := (x_2^2 + x_3^2)/(2x_1^2)$ and it follows an $\mathrm{F}(2,1)$ distribution. Then,

$$\Pr\left(\frac{x_1^2}{x_1^2 + x_2^2 + x_3^2} \leqslant c\right) = \Pr\left(\frac{1}{1+2z} \leqslant c\right) = 1 - \Pr\left(z \leqslant \frac{1-c}{2c}\right),$$

and we can compute the probability from the c.d.f. of an F variate. Notice the relation of the variate in the question to the beta of Exercise 4.31.

Exercise 9.15 (Independence of the mean from differences) Let $x_1, \dots, x_n$ be a random sample from the $\mathrm{N}(\mu, \sigma^2)$ distribution. Let $y_1 := \sum_{i=1}^n x_i$ and $y_i := x_i - x_1$ for $i \geqslant 2$.
(a) Derive the distribution of $(y_1, \dots, y_n)$.
(b) Show that y_1 and $(y_2, \dots, y_n)$ are independent.

Solution
Let $\boldsymbol{x} := (x_1, \dots, x_n)'$ and $\boldsymbol{y} := (y_1, \dots, y_n)'$. Then $\boldsymbol{x} \sim \mathrm{N}(\mu \boldsymbol{\imath}_n, \sigma^2 \boldsymbol{I}_n)$. Now define the $n \times n$ matrix

$$\boldsymbol{A} := \begin{pmatrix} 1 & \boldsymbol{\imath}_{n-1}' \\ -\boldsymbol{\imath}_{n-1} & \boldsymbol{I}_{n-1} \end{pmatrix}.$$

Then, $\boldsymbol{y} = \boldsymbol{A}\boldsymbol{x}$ and hence $\boldsymbol{y} \sim \mathrm{N}(\mu \boldsymbol{A} \boldsymbol{\imath}_n, \sigma^2 \boldsymbol{A}\boldsymbol{A}')$. Now,

$$\boldsymbol{A}\boldsymbol{A}' = \begin{pmatrix} 1 & \boldsymbol{\imath}_{n-1}' \\ -\boldsymbol{\imath}_{n-1} & \boldsymbol{I}_{n-1} \end{pmatrix} \begin{pmatrix} 1 & -\boldsymbol{\imath}_{n-1}' \\ \boldsymbol{\imath}_{n-1} & \boldsymbol{I}_{n-1} \end{pmatrix} = \begin{pmatrix} n & \boldsymbol{0}_{n-1}' \\ \boldsymbol{0}_{n-1} & \boldsymbol{I}_{n-1} + \boldsymbol{\imath}_{n-1}\boldsymbol{\imath}_{n-1}' \end{pmatrix},$$

and the independence follows from the fact that $\boldsymbol{A}\boldsymbol{A}'$ is block-diagonal.

Note the role of the assumption of a random sample here, which was *not* made in the counterexample of Exercise 8.34(d).

Exercise 9.16 (Normal sample's moments: de-meaning) Let $x_1, \dots, x_n$ be a random sample from the $\mathrm{N}(\mu, \sigma^2)$ distribution. Let $y_1 := \overline{x}$ and $y_i := x_i - \overline{x}$ for $i \geqslant 2$.
(a) Derive the joint distribution of $y_1, \dots, y_n$ and hence prove that y_1 and $(y_2, \dots, y_n)$ are independent.
(b) Prove that s^2 and $\overline{x}$ are independent.
(c) Prove that $(n-1)s^2/\sigma^2 \sim \chi^2(n-1)$.
(d) Prove (b) and (c) by three additional methods, without recourse to the transformation of x_i into y_i.

Solution
(a) A straightforward proof would exploit joint normality and calculate $\mathrm{E}(y_i)$ and $\mathrm{E}(y_i y_j)$ for $i, j = 1, \dots, n$. However, we will take an alternative route that uses matrices and lays the ground for multivariate generalizations later.

Let $\boldsymbol{x} := (x_1, \dots, x_n)'$ and $\boldsymbol{y} := (y_1, \dots, y_n)'$. Then $\boldsymbol{x} \sim \mathrm{N}(\mu \boldsymbol{\imath}_n, \sigma^2 \boldsymbol{I}_n)$. Now define the $n \times n$ matrix

$$\boldsymbol{A} := \begin{pmatrix} \frac{1}{n} & \frac{1}{n}\boldsymbol{\imath}_{n-1}' \\ -\frac{1}{n}\boldsymbol{\imath}_{n-1} & \boldsymbol{B} \end{pmatrix},$$

where

$$\boldsymbol{B} := \boldsymbol{I}_{n-1} - \frac{1}{n}\boldsymbol{\imath}_{n-1}\boldsymbol{\imath}_{n-1}'.$$

Then, $\boldsymbol{y} = \boldsymbol{A}\boldsymbol{x}$ by $\overline{x} = \frac{1}{n}\left(1, \boldsymbol{\imath}_{n-1}'\right)\boldsymbol{x}$ and $\left(-\frac{1}{n}\boldsymbol{\imath}_{n-1}, \boldsymbol{B}\right)$ being the last $n-1$ rows of the de-meaning matrix of Exercise 9.4(b). Hence,

$$\boldsymbol{y} \sim \mathrm{N}(\mu \boldsymbol{A}\boldsymbol{\imath}_n, \sigma^2 \boldsymbol{A}\boldsymbol{A}'),$$

where $\boldsymbol{A}\boldsymbol{\imath}_n = (1, 0, \dots, 0)'$ because the first element is the mean of $\boldsymbol{\imath}_n$ and the remaining elements are the deviation of $\boldsymbol{\imath}_n$ from its mean. We now need to work out the product $\boldsymbol{A}\boldsymbol{A}'$.

The $(n-1) \times (n-1)$ matrix $\boldsymbol{B}$ is *not* idempotent, and

$$n\boldsymbol{B}\boldsymbol{\imath}_{n-1} = n\boldsymbol{\imath}_{n-1} - (n-1)\,\boldsymbol{\imath}_{n-1} = \boldsymbol{\imath}_{n-1}$$

(implying an eigenvalue $1/n$ with eigenvector $\boldsymbol{\imath}_{n-1}$). Defining the idempotent matrix $\boldsymbol{J} := \frac{1}{n-1}\boldsymbol{\imath}_{n-1}\boldsymbol{\imath}_{n-1}'$, we have $\boldsymbol{B} = (\boldsymbol{I}_{n-1} - \boldsymbol{J}) + \frac{1}{n}\boldsymbol{J}$ and

$$\begin{aligned}\boldsymbol{B}^2 &= (\boldsymbol{I}_{n-1} - \boldsymbol{J})^2 + \frac{1}{n^2}\boldsymbol{J}^2 + \frac{2}{n}(\boldsymbol{J} - \boldsymbol{J}^2) = (\boldsymbol{I}_{n-1} - \boldsymbol{J}) + \frac{1}{n^2}\boldsymbol{J} + \mathbf{O}\\ &= \boldsymbol{B} - \frac{1}{n}\boldsymbol{J} + \frac{1}{n^2}\boldsymbol{J} = \boldsymbol{B} - \frac{1}{n^2}\boldsymbol{\imath}_{n-1}\boldsymbol{\imath}_{n-1}'.\end{aligned}$$

The results for $\boldsymbol{B}\boldsymbol{\imath}_{n-1}$ and $\boldsymbol{B}^2$ allow us to work out

$$\boldsymbol{A}\boldsymbol{A}' = \begin{pmatrix} \frac{1}{n} & \frac{1}{n}\boldsymbol{\imath}_{n-1}' \\ -\frac{1}{n}\boldsymbol{\imath}_{n-1} & \boldsymbol{B} \end{pmatrix} \begin{pmatrix} \frac{1}{n} & -\frac{1}{n}\boldsymbol{\imath}_{n-1}' \\ \frac{1}{n}\boldsymbol{\imath}_{n-1} & \boldsymbol{B} \end{pmatrix} = \begin{pmatrix} \frac{1}{n} & \mathbf{0}_{n-1}' \\ \mathbf{0}_{n-1} & \boldsymbol{B} \end{pmatrix}.$$

The independence of y_1 and $(y_2, \dots, y_n)$ now follows from the fact that $\operatorname{var}(\boldsymbol{y})$ is block-diagonal. Notice that the result for $\boldsymbol{A}\boldsymbol{A}'$ implies that the Jacobian of the transformation from $\boldsymbol{x}$ to $\boldsymbol{y}$ is the absolute value of $|\boldsymbol{A}|^{-1}$, namely

$$\begin{aligned}|\boldsymbol{A}\boldsymbol{A}'|^{-1/2} &= n^{1/2}\,|\boldsymbol{B}|^{-1/2}\\ &= n^{1/2}\left|\boldsymbol{I}_{n-1} - \frac{1}{n}\boldsymbol{\imath}_{n-1}\boldsymbol{\imath}_{n-1}'\right|^{-1/2} = n^{1/2}\left(1 - \frac{1}{n}\boldsymbol{\imath}_{n-1}'\boldsymbol{\imath}_{n-1}\right)^{-1/2} = n,\end{aligned}$$

by $|\boldsymbol{I} - \boldsymbol{P}\boldsymbol{Q}| = |\boldsymbol{I} - \boldsymbol{Q}\boldsymbol{P}|$ for conformable $\boldsymbol{P}, \boldsymbol{Q}$.

(b) We have

$$x_1 - \overline{x} = \sum_{i=1}^{n}(x_i - \overline{x}) - \sum_{i=2}^{n}(x_i - \overline{x}) = -\sum_{i=2}^{n}(x_i - \overline{x})$$

since $\sum_{i=1}^{n}(x_i - \overline{x}) = 0$. Hence, $x_1 - \overline{x} = -\sum_{i=2}^{n} y_i$ and

$$\sum_{i=1}^{n}(x_i - \overline{x})^2 = (x_1 - \overline{x})^2 + \sum_{i=2}^{n}(x_i - \overline{x})^2 = \left(\sum_{i=2}^{n} y_i\right)^2 + \sum_{i=2}^{n} y_i^2,$$

which is a function of $(y_2, \dots, y_n)$ only. We see that $\overline{x}$ depends only on y_1, and that s^2 depends only on $(y_2, \dots, y_n)$. This is true regardless of the distribution of $\boldsymbol{x}$ or $\boldsymbol{y}$. In the case of normality, (a) shows that y_1 and $(y_2, \dots, y_n)$ are independent, so we get the required independence of $\overline{x}$ and s^2.

(c) Since

$$(n-1)s^2 = \sum_{i=1}^{n}(x_i - \overline{x})^2 = \sum_{i=2}^{n} y_i^2 + \left(\sum_{i=2}^{n} y_i\right)^2,$$

we have $(n-1)s^2/\sigma^2 = \boldsymbol{y}_*'\boldsymbol{C}\boldsymbol{y}_*$, where $\boldsymbol{C} := \boldsymbol{I}_{n-1} + \boldsymbol{\imath}_{n-1}\boldsymbol{\imath}_{n-1}'$ and $\boldsymbol{y}_* := \frac{1}{\sigma}(y_2, \dots, y_n)' \sim \mathrm{N}(\mathbf{0}_{n-1}, \boldsymbol{B})$. Since $\boldsymbol{B}$ is nonsingular (it was shown in (a) that $|\boldsymbol{B}| \neq 0$), Exercise 8.29 tells us that the quadratic form $\boldsymbol{y}_*'\boldsymbol{C}\boldsymbol{y}_*$ follows a χ^2 distribution if and only if $(\boldsymbol{BC})^2 = \boldsymbol{BC}$. Direct multiplication yields

$$\begin{aligned}\boldsymbol{BC} &= \left(\boldsymbol{I}_{n-1} - \frac{1}{n}\boldsymbol{\imath}_{n-1}\boldsymbol{\imath}_{n-1}'\right)\left(\boldsymbol{I}_{n-1} + \boldsymbol{\imath}_{n-1}\boldsymbol{\imath}_{n-1}'\right) \\ &= \boldsymbol{I}_{n-1} + \frac{n-1}{n}\boldsymbol{\imath}_{n-1}\boldsymbol{\imath}_{n-1}' - \frac{1}{n}\left(\boldsymbol{\imath}_{n-1}\boldsymbol{\imath}_{n-1}'\right)^2 = \boldsymbol{I}_{n-1}\end{aligned}$$

and $\mathrm{rk}(\boldsymbol{C}) = n-1$ since $\boldsymbol{C}$ is nonsingular.

(d) Parts (b) and (c) of this problem have already been solved in Exercise 8.34 and earlier by Helmert's transformation in Exercise 7.16. The third additional proof is just an application of Exercise 8.40 to the decomposition

$$\frac{1}{\sigma^2}\sum_{i=1}^{n}(x_i - \overline{x})^2 = \sum_{i=1}^{n}\left(\frac{x_i - \mu}{\sigma}\right)^2 - \left(\frac{\sqrt{n}(\overline{x} - \mu)}{\sigma}\right)^2$$

obtained from Exercise 9.4(a).

Exercise 9.17 (Joint density of a normal sample) Let $\boldsymbol{x}_1, \dots, \boldsymbol{x}_n$ be a random sample from the $\mathrm{N}_m(\boldsymbol{\mu}, \boldsymbol{\Sigma})$ distribution, where $\boldsymbol{\Sigma}$ is nonsingular. Derive the joint density of the sample.

Solution

The density of $\boldsymbol{x}_i$ $(i = 1, \dots, n)$ is

$$f_{\boldsymbol{x}_i}(\boldsymbol{w}_i) = (2\pi)^{-m/2}|\boldsymbol{\Sigma}|^{-1/2}\exp\left(-\frac{1}{2}(\boldsymbol{w}_i - \boldsymbol{\mu})'\boldsymbol{\Sigma}^{-1}(\boldsymbol{w}_i - \boldsymbol{\mu})\right)$$

and, by independence, the joint density is the product of these:

$$\begin{aligned}f_{\boldsymbol{x}_1,\dots,\boldsymbol{x}_n}(\boldsymbol{w}_1, \dots, \boldsymbol{w}_n) &= (2\pi)^{-mn/2}|\boldsymbol{\Sigma}|^{-n/2}\exp\left(-\frac{1}{2}\sum_{i=1}^{n}(\boldsymbol{w}_i - \boldsymbol{\mu})'\boldsymbol{\Sigma}^{-1}(\boldsymbol{w}_i - \boldsymbol{\mu})\right) \\ &= (2\pi)^{-mn/2}|\boldsymbol{\Sigma}|^{-n/2}\operatorname{etr}\left(-\frac{1}{2}\boldsymbol{\Sigma}^{-1}\sum_{i=1}^{n}(\boldsymbol{w}_i - \boldsymbol{\mu})(\boldsymbol{w}_i - \boldsymbol{\mu})'\right),\end{aligned}$$

where $\operatorname{etr}(\cdot) \equiv \exp(\operatorname{tr}(\cdot))$. Recall that Exercise 9.5(b) showed that

$$\sum_{i=1}^{n}(\boldsymbol{x}_i - \boldsymbol{\mu})(\boldsymbol{x}_i - \boldsymbol{\mu})' = n(\overline{\boldsymbol{x}} - \boldsymbol{\mu})(\overline{\boldsymbol{x}} - \boldsymbol{\mu})' + \sum_{i=1}^{n}(\boldsymbol{x}_i - \overline{\boldsymbol{x}})(\boldsymbol{x}_i - \overline{\boldsymbol{x}})',$$

which we will use later on to rewrite the density. We also make a comment on notation that will be useful. It is often convenient to write the $n \times m$ matrix $(\boldsymbol{x}_1, \dots, \boldsymbol{x}_n)'$ as $\boldsymbol{X}$, with realization $\boldsymbol{W}$ and rows which are mutually independent with $\mathrm{var}(\mathrm{vec}(\boldsymbol{X})) = \boldsymbol{\Sigma} \otimes \boldsymbol{I}_n$ or $\mathrm{var}(\mathrm{vec}(\boldsymbol{X}')) = \boldsymbol{I}_n \otimes \boldsymbol{\Sigma}$. The vec operator stacks the columns of its matrix argument, thus reshaping it into a vector of order mn.

Exercise 9.18 (Independence of $\overline{\boldsymbol{x}}$ and $\boldsymbol{S}$) Let $\boldsymbol{x}_1, \dots, \boldsymbol{x}_n$ be a random sample from the $\mathrm{N}_m(\boldsymbol{\mu}, \boldsymbol{\Sigma})$ distribution, where $\boldsymbol{\Sigma}$ is nonsingular. Derive the density of $\overline{\boldsymbol{x}}$, and show that $\overline{\boldsymbol{x}}$ is distributed independently of the sample variance $\boldsymbol{S}$.

Solution

Recall that $\overline{\boldsymbol{x}} := \frac{1}{n}\sum_{i=1}^n \boldsymbol{x}_i$. Linear combinations of joint normals are also normal, by definition of joint normality, and therefore $\overline{\boldsymbol{x}}$ is normal with mean and variance given by Exercise 9.5(a), namely $\overline{\boldsymbol{x}} \sim \mathrm{N}_m(\boldsymbol{\mu}, \frac{1}{n}\boldsymbol{\Sigma})$ with density

$$\begin{aligned} f_{\overline{\boldsymbol{x}}}(\boldsymbol{w}_{\overline{\boldsymbol{x}}}) &= \left(\frac{n}{2\pi}\right)^{m/2} |\boldsymbol{\Sigma}|^{-1/2} \exp\left(-\frac{n}{2}(\boldsymbol{w}_{\overline{\boldsymbol{x}}} - \boldsymbol{\mu})' \boldsymbol{\Sigma}^{-1} (\boldsymbol{w}_{\overline{\boldsymbol{x}}} - \boldsymbol{\mu})\right) \\ &= \left(\frac{n}{2\pi}\right)^{m/2} |\boldsymbol{\Sigma}|^{-1/2} \operatorname{etr}\left(-\frac{n}{2}\boldsymbol{\Sigma}^{-1} (\boldsymbol{w}_{\overline{\boldsymbol{x}}} - \boldsymbol{\mu})(\boldsymbol{w}_{\overline{\boldsymbol{x}}} - \boldsymbol{\mu})'\right). \end{aligned}$$

Using the density in Exercise 9.17, the joint density of the sample factors into

$$f_{\boldsymbol{X}}(\boldsymbol{W}) = \frac{1}{n^{m/2}} f_{\overline{\boldsymbol{x}}}(\boldsymbol{w}_{\overline{\boldsymbol{x}}}) \times \frac{|\boldsymbol{\Sigma}|^{(1-n)/2}}{(2\pi)^{m(n-1)/2}} \operatorname{etr}\left(-\frac{1}{2}\boldsymbol{\Sigma}^{-1} \sum_{i=1}^n (\boldsymbol{w}_i - \boldsymbol{w}_{\overline{\boldsymbol{x}}})(\boldsymbol{w}_i - \boldsymbol{w}_{\overline{\boldsymbol{x}}})'\right).$$

The sum in the exponent is the realization of the variate

$$(n-1)\boldsymbol{S} := \sum_{i=1}^n (\boldsymbol{x}_i - \overline{\boldsymbol{x}})(\boldsymbol{x}_i - \overline{\boldsymbol{x}})',$$

but it would not be correct to infer from this that the density has been factored into the product of the marginals for $\overline{\boldsymbol{x}}$ and $\boldsymbol{S}$. In fact, the marginal density of $\boldsymbol{S}$ is quite different from $f_{\boldsymbol{X}}/f_{\overline{\boldsymbol{x}}}$, as we will remark on at the end of this exercise.

The joint density of the sample has been factored into the product of independent normal densities for $\overline{\boldsymbol{x}}$ and $n-1$ of the vectors $\boldsymbol{x}_i - \overline{\boldsymbol{x}}$, together with a Jacobian factor $n^{-m/2}$. This is in parallel with Exercise 9.16(a), and independence is obtained in the same way. There are n vectors $\boldsymbol{x}_i - \overline{\boldsymbol{x}}$, but any one of them is linearly dependent on the rest, because $\sum_{i=1}^n (\boldsymbol{x}_i - \overline{\boldsymbol{x}}) \equiv \boldsymbol{0}_m$, and we can therefore rewrite the exponential in the density $f_{\boldsymbol{X}}$ in terms of only $n-1$ of the vectors $\boldsymbol{x}_i - \overline{\boldsymbol{x}}$. Since $\boldsymbol{S}$ is a function of $n-1$ of the vectors $\boldsymbol{x}_i - \overline{\boldsymbol{x}}$, the independence of $\overline{\boldsymbol{x}}$ and $\boldsymbol{S}$ follows from the factorization of the density.

There is a final remark to make about this factorization. Because of its symmetry, the $m \times m$ matrix $\boldsymbol{S}$ cannot depend on more than $m(m+1)/2$ independent variates, and its density is *not* $f_{\boldsymbol{X}}/f_{\overline{\boldsymbol{x}}}$, but is obtainable by transforming and marginalizing when $n > m$; see the Notes to this chapter for the result. This is a case where the following inequality holds: $\boldsymbol{X}$ contains mn elements, $\overline{\boldsymbol{x}}$ has m elements, and the difference is $m(n-1) \geqslant m(m+1)/2$, the latter being the number of distinct elements of $\boldsymbol{S}$. When

$n \leqslant m$, $\boldsymbol{S}$ does not possess a density because, as will be shown in Exercise 9.21, it is a singular variate.

***Exercise 9.19 (Wishart characteristic function)** Let $\boldsymbol{y}_i \sim \mathrm{IN}_m(\boldsymbol{\mu}_i, \boldsymbol{\Sigma})$ be an independent normal sequence, where $i = 1, \ldots, p$ and $\boldsymbol{\Sigma}$ is nonsingular. Derive the c.f. of the noncentral Wishart variate

$$\boldsymbol{Z} := \sum_{i=1}^{p} \boldsymbol{y}_i \boldsymbol{y}_i' \sim \mathrm{W}_m(p, \boldsymbol{\Sigma}, \boldsymbol{\Delta}),$$

where $\boldsymbol{\Delta} := \sum_{i=1}^{p} \boldsymbol{\mu}_i \boldsymbol{\mu}_i'$ and it is not assumed that $p \geqslant m$ (hence $\boldsymbol{Z}$ is allowed to be singular, as will be shown in Exercise 9.21). How does it relate to χ^2 variates?

Solution

There are only $m(m+1)/2$ distinct elements in $\boldsymbol{Z}$. The joint c.f. of these elements is

$$\varphi_{\boldsymbol{Z}}(\boldsymbol{T}) := \mathrm{E}\left(\exp\left(\mathrm{i}\sum_{j=1}^{m}\sum_{k=1}^{j} t_{jk} z_{jk}\right)\right) = \mathrm{E}\left(\operatorname{etr}(\mathrm{i}\boldsymbol{T}\boldsymbol{Z})\right),$$

where $\boldsymbol{T}$ is the lower triangular matrix with typical element t_{jk}, and we define its symmetrized version $\boldsymbol{T}_{\mathrm{s}} := \frac{1}{2}(\boldsymbol{T} + \boldsymbol{T}')$ for later use. Substituting for $\boldsymbol{Z}$ and rearranging,

$$\begin{aligned}\varphi_{\boldsymbol{Z}}(\boldsymbol{T}) &= \mathrm{E}\left(\operatorname{etr}\left(\mathrm{i}\boldsymbol{T}\sum_{i=1}^{p} \boldsymbol{y}_i \boldsymbol{y}_i'\right)\right) = \mathrm{E}\left(\exp\left(\mathrm{i}\sum_{i=1}^{p} \boldsymbol{y}_i' \boldsymbol{T} \boldsymbol{y}_i\right)\right)\\ &= \mathrm{E}\left(\exp\left(\mathrm{i}\sum_{i=1}^{p} \boldsymbol{y}_i' \boldsymbol{T}_{\mathrm{s}} \boldsymbol{y}_i\right)\right)\end{aligned}$$

by Exercise 6.8 or Exercise 6.24(c). Now, the $\boldsymbol{y}_i$'s are from an independent sample, so we can use the known m.g.f. of quadratic forms like $\boldsymbol{y}_i' \boldsymbol{T}_{\mathrm{s}} \boldsymbol{y}_i$ from Exercise 8.25 to write

$$\begin{aligned}\varphi_{\boldsymbol{Z}}(\boldsymbol{T}) &= \prod_{i=1}^{p} \mathrm{E}\left(\exp\left(\mathrm{i}\boldsymbol{y}_i' \boldsymbol{T}_{\mathrm{s}} \boldsymbol{y}_i\right)\right) = \prod_{i=1}^{p} m_{\boldsymbol{y}_i' \boldsymbol{T}_{\mathrm{s}} \boldsymbol{y}_i}(\mathrm{i})\\ &= \prod_{i=1}^{p} \frac{\exp\left(-\frac{1}{2}\boldsymbol{\mu}_i' \boldsymbol{\Sigma}^{-1} \boldsymbol{\mu}_i + \frac{1}{2}\boldsymbol{\mu}_i' \left(\boldsymbol{\Sigma} - 2\mathrm{i}\boldsymbol{\Sigma}\boldsymbol{T}_{\mathrm{s}}\boldsymbol{\Sigma}\right)^{-1} \boldsymbol{\mu}_i\right)}{\left|\boldsymbol{I}_m - 2\mathrm{i}\boldsymbol{T}_{\mathrm{s}}\boldsymbol{\Sigma}\right|^{1/2}}\\ &= \frac{\operatorname{etr}\left(-\frac{1}{2}\boldsymbol{\Sigma}^{-1}\boldsymbol{\Delta} + \frac{1}{2}\left(\boldsymbol{I}_m - 2\mathrm{i}\boldsymbol{T}_{\mathrm{s}}\boldsymbol{\Sigma}\right)^{-1} \boldsymbol{\Sigma}^{-1}\boldsymbol{\Delta}\right)}{\left|\boldsymbol{I}_m - 2\mathrm{i}\boldsymbol{T}_{\mathrm{s}}\boldsymbol{\Sigma}\right|^{p/2}}.\end{aligned}$$

When $m = 1$, we write $\boldsymbol{\Sigma} = (\sigma^2)$ and $\boldsymbol{\Delta} = (\delta) = \sum_{i=1}^{p} \mu_i^2$, obtaining the c.f. (seen in Chapter 4 and in Exercise 7.3) of σ^2 times a $\chi^2(p, \delta/\sigma^2)$ variate. In other words, $\mathrm{W}_1(p, \sigma^2, \delta) = \sigma^2 \cdot \chi^2(p, \delta/\sigma^2)$.

Exercise 9.20 (Sample variance: independence from sample mean (again) and distribution) Recall Helmert's $n \times n$ matrix

$$\boldsymbol{A} := \begin{pmatrix} \frac{1}{\sqrt{n}} & \frac{1}{\sqrt{n}} & \frac{1}{\sqrt{n}} & \cdots & \frac{1}{\sqrt{n}} \\ \frac{1}{\sqrt{2}} & -\frac{1}{\sqrt{2}} & 0 & \cdots & 0 \\ \frac{1}{\sqrt{6}} & \frac{1}{\sqrt{6}} & -\frac{2}{\sqrt{6}} & \cdots & 0 \\ \vdots & \vdots & \vdots & & \vdots \\ \frac{1}{\sqrt{n(n-1)}} & \frac{1}{\sqrt{n(n-1)}} & \frac{1}{\sqrt{n(n-1)}} & \cdots & -\frac{(n-1)}{\sqrt{n(n-1)}} \end{pmatrix}$$

of Exercise 7.16, and define the $n \times m$ matrix $\boldsymbol{X} := (\boldsymbol{x}_1, \dots, \boldsymbol{x}_n)'$ whose rows $\{\boldsymbol{x}_i'\}_{i=1}^n$ are a random sample from $\mathrm{N}_m(\boldsymbol{\mu}', \boldsymbol{\Sigma})$ with nonsingular $\boldsymbol{\Sigma}$. By means of the transformation $\boldsymbol{Y} := \boldsymbol{A}\boldsymbol{X}$, show that

$$(n-1)\,\boldsymbol{S} := \sum_{i=1}^n (\boldsymbol{x}_i - \overline{\boldsymbol{x}})(\boldsymbol{x}_i - \overline{\boldsymbol{x}})' = \sum_{i=2}^n \boldsymbol{y}_i \boldsymbol{y}_i' \sim \mathrm{W}_m(n-1, \boldsymbol{\Sigma}),$$

where $\boldsymbol{y}_i'$ is the i-th row of $\boldsymbol{Y}$.

Solution

The first row of $\boldsymbol{Y}$ is $\boldsymbol{y}_1' = \sqrt{n}\,\overline{\boldsymbol{x}}'$ and

$$(n-1)\,\boldsymbol{S} = \sum_{i=1}^n (\boldsymbol{x}_i - \overline{\boldsymbol{x}})(\boldsymbol{x}_i - \overline{\boldsymbol{x}})' = \sum_{i=1}^n \boldsymbol{x}_i \boldsymbol{x}_i' - \boldsymbol{y}_1 \boldsymbol{y}_1'$$

$$= (\boldsymbol{x}_1, \dots, \boldsymbol{x}_n) \begin{pmatrix} \boldsymbol{x}_1' \\ \vdots \\ \boldsymbol{x}_n' \end{pmatrix} - \boldsymbol{y}_1 \boldsymbol{y}_1' = \boldsymbol{X}'\boldsymbol{X} - \boldsymbol{y}_1 \boldsymbol{y}_1'.$$

By the orthogonality of $\boldsymbol{A}$ (Exercise 7.16), $\boldsymbol{X} = \boldsymbol{A}'\boldsymbol{Y}$ and

$$(n-1)\,\boldsymbol{S} = \boldsymbol{Y}'\boldsymbol{A}\boldsymbol{A}'\boldsymbol{Y} - \boldsymbol{y}_1 \boldsymbol{y}_1' = \boldsymbol{Y}'\boldsymbol{Y} - \boldsymbol{y}_1 \boldsymbol{y}_1' = \sum_{i=2}^n \boldsymbol{y}_i \boldsymbol{y}_i'.$$

Furthermore,

$$\mathrm{vec}\,(\boldsymbol{Y}) = \mathrm{vec}\,(\boldsymbol{A}\boldsymbol{X}) = (\boldsymbol{I}_m \otimes \boldsymbol{A})\,\mathrm{vec}\,(\boldsymbol{X}),$$

so the Jacobian of the transformation from $\mathrm{vec}(\boldsymbol{X})$ to $\mathrm{vec}(\boldsymbol{Y})$ is $|\boldsymbol{I}_m \otimes \boldsymbol{A}|^{-1} = |\boldsymbol{A}|^{-m} = \pm 1$, and the joint p.d.f. of $\boldsymbol{X}$ in Exercise 9.18 translates into a p.d.f. for $\boldsymbol{Y}$ where

$$\boldsymbol{y}_1 = \sqrt{n}\,\overline{\boldsymbol{x}} \sim \mathrm{N}_m(\sqrt{n}\boldsymbol{\mu}, \boldsymbol{\Sigma})$$

independently of the i.i.d. sequence of

$$\boldsymbol{y}_i \sim \mathrm{N}_m(\boldsymbol{0}, \boldsymbol{\Sigma})$$

for $i \geqslant 2$. Note that, alternatively,

$$\begin{aligned}\operatorname{var}(\operatorname{vec}(\boldsymbol{Y})) &= (\boldsymbol{I}_m \otimes \boldsymbol{A}) \operatorname{var}(\operatorname{vec}(\boldsymbol{X})) \left(\boldsymbol{I}_m \otimes \boldsymbol{A}'\right) \\ &= (\boldsymbol{I}_m \otimes \boldsymbol{A}) (\boldsymbol{\Sigma} \otimes \boldsymbol{I}_n) \left(\boldsymbol{I}_m \otimes \boldsymbol{A}'\right) = (\boldsymbol{\Sigma} \otimes \boldsymbol{I}_m),\end{aligned}$$

with the interpretation that $\boldsymbol{A}$ is transforming across the $\boldsymbol{x}_i$'s rather than within any $\boldsymbol{x}_i$ whose variance is $\boldsymbol{\Sigma}$.

The sequence $\boldsymbol{y}_i \sim \mathrm{N}_m(\mathbf{0}, \boldsymbol{\Sigma})$ for $i \geqslant 2$ implies that

$$\sum_{i=2}^{n} \boldsymbol{y}_i \boldsymbol{y}_i' \sim \mathrm{W}_m(n-1, \boldsymbol{\Sigma})$$

by Exercise 9.19, and therefore $(n-1)\,\boldsymbol{S} \sim \mathrm{W}_m(n-1, \boldsymbol{\Sigma})$. The result is a central Wishart distribution, even when $\boldsymbol{\mu} \neq \mathbf{0}$, because $\boldsymbol{S}$ is based on $\boldsymbol{x}_i - \overline{\boldsymbol{x}}$ rather than $\boldsymbol{x}_i$. Notice that the independence of $\boldsymbol{y}_1$ and $\boldsymbol{y}_2, \ldots, \boldsymbol{y}_n$ implies the independence of $\overline{\boldsymbol{x}}$ and $\boldsymbol{S}$; compare with Exercise 9.18.

Exercise 9.21 (Sample variance: nonsingularity) Let $\boldsymbol{x}_1, \ldots, \boldsymbol{x}_n$ be a random sample from the $\mathrm{N}_m(\boldsymbol{\mu}, \boldsymbol{\Sigma})$ distribution, where $\boldsymbol{\Sigma}$ is nonsingular.
(a) Prove that the sample variance $\boldsymbol{S}$ is nonsingular with probability 1 if and only if $n > m$.
(b) Let $\operatorname{vech}(\boldsymbol{S})$ denotes the vector containing s_{ij} for $i \geqslant j$, that is, the vector stacking nonrepeated elements of the columns of the symmetric $\boldsymbol{S}$. (This is known as the "half-vec" operator.) By using a counterexample, show that (a) need not imply the singularity of $\operatorname{var}(\operatorname{vech}(\boldsymbol{S}))$ when $n \leqslant m$, even though $\boldsymbol{S}$ is singular in this case.

Solution
(a) By Exercise 9.20 and a change of index of the variables,

$$(n-1)\,\boldsymbol{S} = \sum_{i=1}^{n-1} \boldsymbol{y}_i \boldsymbol{y}_i',$$

where $\boldsymbol{y}_i \sim \mathrm{IN}_m(\mathbf{0}, \boldsymbol{\Sigma})$ is an independent normal sequence for $i = 1, \ldots, n-1$. For $n \leqslant m$,

$$\operatorname{rk}(\boldsymbol{S}) = \operatorname{rk}\left(\sum_{i=1}^{n-1} \boldsymbol{y}_i \boldsymbol{y}_i'\right) \leqslant \sum_{i=1}^{n-1} \operatorname{rk}\left(\boldsymbol{y}_i \boldsymbol{y}_i'\right) = \sum_{i=1}^{n-1} 1 = n-1 \leqslant m-1,$$

so that $\boldsymbol{S}$ is singular. For $n > m$, the definition of positive definiteness requires all (possibly random) vectors $\boldsymbol{a} \neq \mathbf{0}_m$ to satisfy $\boldsymbol{a}'\boldsymbol{S}\boldsymbol{a} > 0$ with probability 1. Now,

$$(n-1)\,\boldsymbol{a}'\boldsymbol{S}\boldsymbol{a} = \sum_{i=1}^{n-1} \boldsymbol{a}'\boldsymbol{y}_i\boldsymbol{y}_i'\boldsymbol{a} = \sum_{i=1}^{n-1} \left(\boldsymbol{y}_i'\boldsymbol{a}\right)^2.$$

We can always find an m-dimensional vector $\boldsymbol{a}_*$ orthogonal to any realization of $m-1$ independent vectors, say $\boldsymbol{y}_1, \ldots, \boldsymbol{y}_{m-1}$, but we will show that it cannot lead to $\boldsymbol{a}'\boldsymbol{S}\boldsymbol{a} = 0$. We have $\Pr(\boldsymbol{y}_i = \boldsymbol{y}_j) = 0$ for $i \neq j$, and $\Pr(\boldsymbol{y}_i = \mathbf{0}) = 0$, so there is probability 1 that this $\boldsymbol{a}_*$ is *not* orthogonal to the remaining $\boldsymbol{y}_m, \dots, \boldsymbol{y}_{n-1}$. More specifically, conditioning on $\boldsymbol{y}_1, \dots, \boldsymbol{y}_{m-1}$, we have

$$(n-1)\,\boldsymbol{a}_*'\boldsymbol{S}\boldsymbol{a}_* = \sum_{i=m}^{n-1} \left(\boldsymbol{y}_i'\boldsymbol{a}_*\right)^2,$$

where $\boldsymbol{y}_i'\boldsymbol{a}_* \mid (\boldsymbol{y}_1, \dots, \boldsymbol{y}_{m-1}) \sim \text{IN}(0, \boldsymbol{a}_*'\boldsymbol{\Sigma}\boldsymbol{a}_*)$ for $i \geqslant m$, and $\boldsymbol{a}_*'\boldsymbol{\Sigma}\boldsymbol{a}_* > 0$ by the positive definiteness of $\boldsymbol{\Sigma}$. Then

$$(n-1)\,\boldsymbol{a}_*'\boldsymbol{S}\boldsymbol{a}_* \mid (\boldsymbol{y}_1, \dots, \boldsymbol{y}_{m-1}) \sim \boldsymbol{a}_*'\boldsymbol{\Sigma}\boldsymbol{a}_* \cdot \chi^2(n-m),$$

and this is positive with probability 1 since $n > m$. Taking expectations with respect to $\boldsymbol{y}_1, \dots, \boldsymbol{y}_{m-1}$, we see that the unconditional probability is also positive, and this shows that $\Pr(\boldsymbol{a}'\boldsymbol{S}\boldsymbol{a} > 0) = 1$ when $n > m$.

(b) Take $m = n = 2$, and define $\boldsymbol{y} \sim \text{N}(\boldsymbol{0}, \boldsymbol{I}_2)$. We have

$$\boldsymbol{S} = \begin{pmatrix} s_{11} & s_{12} \\ s_{12} & s_{22} \end{pmatrix} = \begin{pmatrix} y_1^2 & y_1 y_2 \\ y_1 y_2 & y_2^2 \end{pmatrix},$$

where $|\boldsymbol{S}| = 0$, so $\boldsymbol{S}$ is singular. Now,

$$\text{var}(\text{vech}(\boldsymbol{S})) = \text{var}\begin{pmatrix} y_1^2 \\ y_1 y_2 \\ y_2^2 \end{pmatrix} = \begin{pmatrix} \text{var}(y_1^2) & \text{cov}(y_1y_2, y_1^2) & \text{cov}(y_1^2, y_2^2) \\ \text{cov}(y_1y_2, y_1^2) & \text{var}(y_1y_2) & \text{cov}(y_1y_2, y_2^2) \\ \text{cov}(y_1^2, y_2^2) & \text{cov}(y_1y_2, y_2^2) & \text{var}(y_2^2) \end{pmatrix}.$$

The independence of y_1 and y_2 gives $\text{cov}(y_1y_2, y_1^2) = 0$, $\text{cov}(y_1^2, y_2^2) = 0$, and

$$\text{var}(y_1y_2) = \text{E}(y_1^2y_2^2) - (\text{E}(y_1y_2))^2 = \text{E}(y_1^2)\,\text{E}(y_2^2) - 0 = 1,$$

while Exercise 8.19 gives $\text{var}(y_1^2) = 2$. Therefore, $\text{var}(\text{vech}(\boldsymbol{S})) = \text{diag}(2, 1, 2)$, which is a nonsingular diagonal matrix. The explanation is simple: there is no *linear* combination of the elements of (y_1^2, y_1y_2, y_2^2) that has zero variance, since these elements are linearly independent when y_1 and y_2 are distinct variates.

***Exercise 9.22 (Wishart reproduction and scaling)** Let $\boldsymbol{\Sigma}$ be positive definite.

(a) For a sequence of independent but not necessarily identical $\boldsymbol{Z}_i \sim \text{W}_m(p_i, \boldsymbol{\Sigma}, \boldsymbol{\Delta}_i)$, $i = 1, \dots, j$, show that

$$\boldsymbol{Z} := \sum_{i=1}^{j} \boldsymbol{Z}_i \sim \text{W}_m(p, \boldsymbol{\Sigma}, \boldsymbol{\Delta}),$$

where $p := \sum_{i=1}^{j} p_i$ and $\boldsymbol{\Delta} := \sum_{i=1}^{j} \boldsymbol{\Delta}_i$.

(b) For $\boldsymbol{Z} \sim \text{W}_m(p, \boldsymbol{\Sigma}, \boldsymbol{\Delta})$ and $\boldsymbol{A}$ a nonrandom $m \times k$ matrix of rank k, prove that $\boldsymbol{A}'\boldsymbol{Z}\boldsymbol{A} \sim \text{W}_k(p, \boldsymbol{A}'\boldsymbol{\Sigma}\boldsymbol{A}, \boldsymbol{A}'\boldsymbol{\Delta}\boldsymbol{A})$.

(c) Prove that the diagonal blocks of a Wishart matrix are also Wishart. When are these blocks mutually independent?

(d) For any m-dimensional vector $\boldsymbol{x}$ satisfying $\Pr(\boldsymbol{x} = \boldsymbol{0}) = 0$ and distributed independently of $\boldsymbol{Z} \sim \text{W}_m(p, \boldsymbol{\Sigma})$, prove that $\boldsymbol{x}'\boldsymbol{Z}\boldsymbol{x}/\boldsymbol{x}'\boldsymbol{\Sigma}\boldsymbol{x} \sim \chi^2(p)$.

Solution

(a) By the independence of the $\boldsymbol{Z}_i$'s and by the Wishart c.f. in Exercise 9.19, we obtain the joint c.f.

$$\begin{aligned}\varphi_{\boldsymbol{Z}}(\boldsymbol{T}) &= \mathrm{E}\left(\operatorname{etr}\left(\mathrm{i}\boldsymbol{T}\sum_{i=1}^{j}\boldsymbol{Z}_i\right)\right) = \prod_{i=1}^{j}\mathrm{E}\left(\operatorname{etr}\left(\mathrm{i}\boldsymbol{T}\boldsymbol{Z}_i\right)\right)\\
&= \prod_{i=1}^{j}\frac{\operatorname{etr}\left(-\frac{1}{2}\boldsymbol{\Sigma}^{-1}\boldsymbol{\Delta}_i+\frac{1}{2}\left(\boldsymbol{I}_m-2\mathrm{i}\boldsymbol{T}_{\mathrm{s}}\boldsymbol{\Sigma}\right)^{-1}\boldsymbol{\Sigma}^{-1}\boldsymbol{\Delta}_i\right)}{\left|\boldsymbol{I}_m-2\mathrm{i}\boldsymbol{T}_{\mathrm{s}}\boldsymbol{\Sigma}\right|^{p_i/2}}\\
&= \frac{\operatorname{etr}\left(-\frac{1}{2}\boldsymbol{\Sigma}^{-1}\sum_{i=1}^{j}\boldsymbol{\Delta}_i+\frac{1}{2}\left(\boldsymbol{I}_m-2\mathrm{i}\boldsymbol{T}_{\mathrm{s}}\boldsymbol{\Sigma}\right)^{-1}\boldsymbol{\Sigma}^{-1}\sum_{i=1}^{j}\boldsymbol{\Delta}_i\right)}{\left|\boldsymbol{I}_m-2\mathrm{i}\boldsymbol{T}_{\mathrm{s}}\boldsymbol{\Sigma}\right|^{\sum_{i=1}^{j}p_i/2}}\\
&= \frac{\operatorname{etr}\left(-\frac{1}{2}\boldsymbol{\Sigma}^{-1}\boldsymbol{\Delta}+\frac{1}{2}\left(\boldsymbol{I}_m-2\mathrm{i}\boldsymbol{T}_{\mathrm{s}}\boldsymbol{\Sigma}\right)^{-1}\boldsymbol{\Sigma}^{-1}\boldsymbol{\Delta}\right)}{\left|\boldsymbol{I}_m-2\mathrm{i}\boldsymbol{T}_{\mathrm{s}}\boldsymbol{\Sigma}\right|^{p/2}},\end{aligned}$$

which identifies the variate as $\boldsymbol{Z} \sim \mathrm{W}_m(p, \boldsymbol{\Sigma}, \boldsymbol{\Delta})$.

(b) The c.f. of the symmetric $\boldsymbol{A}'\boldsymbol{Z}\boldsymbol{A}$ is

$$\varphi_{\boldsymbol{A}'\boldsymbol{Z}\boldsymbol{A}}(\boldsymbol{Q}) = \mathrm{E}\left(\operatorname{etr}\left(\mathrm{i}\boldsymbol{Q}\boldsymbol{A}'\boldsymbol{Z}\boldsymbol{A}\right)\right) = \mathrm{E}\left(\operatorname{etr}\left(\mathrm{i}\left(\boldsymbol{A}\boldsymbol{Q}\boldsymbol{A}'\right)\boldsymbol{Z}\right)\right) = \varphi_{\boldsymbol{Z}}\left(\boldsymbol{A}\boldsymbol{Q}\boldsymbol{A}'\right),$$

where $\boldsymbol{Q}$ is lower triangular. Defining $\boldsymbol{T} := \boldsymbol{A}\boldsymbol{Q}\boldsymbol{A}'$ and its symmetrized version

$$\boldsymbol{T}_{\mathrm{s}} := \frac{1}{2}\left(\boldsymbol{A}\boldsymbol{Q}\boldsymbol{A}'+\boldsymbol{A}\boldsymbol{Q}'\boldsymbol{A}'\right) = \boldsymbol{A}\boldsymbol{Q}_{\mathrm{s}}\boldsymbol{A}',$$

we have

$$\begin{aligned}\varphi_{\boldsymbol{A}'\boldsymbol{Z}\boldsymbol{A}}(\boldsymbol{Q}) = \varphi_{\boldsymbol{Z}}(\boldsymbol{T}) &= \frac{\operatorname{etr}\left(-\frac{1}{2}\boldsymbol{\Sigma}^{-1}\boldsymbol{\Delta}+\frac{1}{2}\left(\boldsymbol{I}_m-2\mathrm{i}\boldsymbol{T}_{\mathrm{s}}\boldsymbol{\Sigma}\right)^{-1}\boldsymbol{\Sigma}^{-1}\boldsymbol{\Delta}\right)}{\left|\boldsymbol{I}_m-2\mathrm{i}\boldsymbol{T}_{\mathrm{s}}\boldsymbol{\Sigma}\right|^{p/2}}\\
&= \frac{\operatorname{etr}\left(-\frac{1}{2}\boldsymbol{\Sigma}^{-1}\boldsymbol{\Delta}+\frac{1}{2}\left(\boldsymbol{I}_m-2\mathrm{i}\boldsymbol{A}\boldsymbol{Q}_{\mathrm{s}}\boldsymbol{A}'\boldsymbol{\Sigma}\right)^{-1}\boldsymbol{\Sigma}^{-1}\boldsymbol{\Delta}\right)}{\left|\boldsymbol{I}_m-2\mathrm{i}\boldsymbol{A}\boldsymbol{Q}_{\mathrm{s}}\boldsymbol{A}'\boldsymbol{\Sigma}\right|^{p/2}}\\
&= \frac{\operatorname{etr}\left(\frac{1}{2}\left(\sum_{i=1}^{\infty}\left(2\mathrm{i}\boldsymbol{A}\boldsymbol{Q}_{\mathrm{s}}\boldsymbol{A}'\boldsymbol{\Sigma}\right)^{i}\right)\boldsymbol{\Sigma}^{-1}\boldsymbol{\Delta}\right)}{\left|\boldsymbol{I}_m-2\mathrm{i}\boldsymbol{A}\boldsymbol{Q}_{\mathrm{s}}\boldsymbol{A}'\boldsymbol{\Sigma}\right|^{p/2}}\end{aligned}$$

by the geometric progression for arbitrarily small $\boldsymbol{Q}_{\mathrm{s}}$ (as in Exercise 8.29). In the denominator, we can use $|\boldsymbol{I}_m - \boldsymbol{A}\boldsymbol{B}| = |\boldsymbol{I}_k - \boldsymbol{B}\boldsymbol{A}|$ for any $k \times m$ matrix $\boldsymbol{B}$, and the result will follow from using $\operatorname{tr}(\boldsymbol{A}\boldsymbol{B}) = \operatorname{tr}(\boldsymbol{B}\boldsymbol{A})$ and collecting the sum in the exponential.

(c) A diagonal block of size k is obtained by substituting into (b) the matrix $\boldsymbol{A}' = (\boldsymbol{I}_k, \mathbf{O})$ or a permutation of these columns. Partitioning accordingly, we obtain

$$\boldsymbol{Z} = \begin{pmatrix}\boldsymbol{Z}_{11} & \boldsymbol{Z}_{12}\\ \boldsymbol{Z}_{21} & \boldsymbol{Z}_{22}\end{pmatrix}, \quad \boldsymbol{\Sigma} = \begin{pmatrix}\boldsymbol{\Sigma}_{11} & \boldsymbol{\Sigma}_{12}\\ \boldsymbol{\Sigma}_{21} & \boldsymbol{\Sigma}_{22}\end{pmatrix}, \quad \boldsymbol{\Delta} = \begin{pmatrix}\boldsymbol{\Delta}_{11} & \boldsymbol{\Delta}_{12}\\ \boldsymbol{\Delta}_{21} & \boldsymbol{\Delta}_{22}\end{pmatrix},$$

and substituting into the c.f. of $\boldsymbol{A}'\boldsymbol{Z}\boldsymbol{A}$ gives $\boldsymbol{Z}_{11} \sim \mathrm{W}_k(p, \boldsymbol{\Sigma}_{11}, \boldsymbol{\Delta}_{11})$. Comparing the

joint c.f. of $\boldsymbol{Z}$ with the product of the marginal c.f.s of $\boldsymbol{Z}_{11}$ and $\boldsymbol{Z}_{22}$, for general $\boldsymbol{T}_{\mathrm{s}}$, independence is obtained when $\boldsymbol{\Sigma}_{12} = \mathbf{O}$.
(d) Let us start by conditioning on $\boldsymbol{x}$ and letting $\boldsymbol{A}$ of (b) be the vector $(\boldsymbol{x}'\boldsymbol{\Sigma}\boldsymbol{x})^{-1/2}\,\boldsymbol{x}$. The distribution of $\boldsymbol{Z} \mid \boldsymbol{x}$ is the same as the distribution of $\boldsymbol{Z}$ (by the assumed independence), thus we can apply the result of (b) where the marginal distribution of $\boldsymbol{Z}$ is used. We get

$$\left(\frac{1}{\sqrt{\boldsymbol{x}'\boldsymbol{\Sigma}\boldsymbol{x}}}\boldsymbol{x}\right)' \boldsymbol{Z} \left(\frac{1}{\sqrt{\boldsymbol{x}'\boldsymbol{\Sigma}\boldsymbol{x}}}\boldsymbol{x}\right) \sim \mathrm{W}_1\left(p, 1, \frac{\boldsymbol{x}'\boldsymbol{\Delta}\boldsymbol{x}}{\boldsymbol{x}'\boldsymbol{\Sigma}\boldsymbol{x}}\right)$$

conditional on $\boldsymbol{x}$. Furthermore, when $\boldsymbol{\Delta} = \mathbf{O}$, this distribution becomes a central $\mathrm{W}_1(p, 1)$ which does not depend on $\boldsymbol{x}$, conditionally and therefore unconditionally too. The result follows because $\mathrm{W}_1(p, 1)$ is the same as a $\chi^2(p)$, by Exercise 9.19.

*__Exercise 9.23 (Wishart conditionals and inversion)__ For $\boldsymbol{Z} \sim \mathrm{W}_m(p, \boldsymbol{\Sigma})$ with a nonsingular $\boldsymbol{\Sigma}$, partition as follows:

$$\boldsymbol{Z} = \begin{pmatrix} \boldsymbol{Z}_{11} & \boldsymbol{Z}_{12} \\ \boldsymbol{Z}_{21} & \boldsymbol{Z}_{22} \end{pmatrix}, \qquad \boldsymbol{\Sigma} = \begin{pmatrix} \boldsymbol{\Sigma}_{11} & \boldsymbol{\Sigma}_{12} \\ \boldsymbol{\Sigma}_{21} & \boldsymbol{\Sigma}_{22} \end{pmatrix},$$

where $\boldsymbol{Z}_{11}$ is $k \times k$ and $p > m - k$. Define $\boldsymbol{Z}_{11|2} := \boldsymbol{Z}_{11} - \boldsymbol{Z}_{12}\boldsymbol{Z}_{22}^{-1}\boldsymbol{Z}_{21}$ and $\boldsymbol{\Sigma}_{11|2} := \boldsymbol{\Sigma}_{11} - \boldsymbol{\Sigma}_{12}\boldsymbol{\Sigma}_{22}^{-1}\boldsymbol{\Sigma}_{21}$. (An alternative notation is $\boldsymbol{Z}_{11\cdot 2}$ and $\boldsymbol{\Sigma}_{11\cdot 2}$, respectively; see the Notes to Chapter 6.)
(a) Prove that $\boldsymbol{Z}_{11|2} \sim \mathrm{W}_k(p+k-m, \boldsymbol{\Sigma}_{11|2})$, independently of $\boldsymbol{Z}_{12}$ and $\boldsymbol{Z}_{22}$. [Hint: Represent the Wishart matrix in terms of normal variates as in Exercise 9.19, then use orthogonal idempotents to represent $\boldsymbol{Z}_{11|2}$ and $\boldsymbol{Z}_{12}$.]
(b) Prove that $\mathrm{vec}(\boldsymbol{Z}_{12}) \sim \mathrm{N}_{(m-k)k}(\mathrm{vec}\left(\boldsymbol{\Sigma}_{12}\boldsymbol{\Sigma}_{22}^{-1}\boldsymbol{Z}_{22}\right), \boldsymbol{Z}_{22} \otimes \boldsymbol{\Sigma}_{11|2})$ when we condition on $\boldsymbol{Z}_{22}$.
(c) For any m-dimensional vector $\boldsymbol{x}$ satisfying $\Pr(\boldsymbol{x} = \mathbf{0}) = 0$ and distributed independently from $\boldsymbol{Z}$, prove that $\boldsymbol{x}'\boldsymbol{\Sigma}^{-1}\boldsymbol{x}/\boldsymbol{x}'\boldsymbol{Z}^{-1}\boldsymbol{x} \sim \chi^2(p+1-m)$. [Hint: Let $\boldsymbol{X}$ be any $m \times m$ matrix that is invertible with probability 1, and distributed independently of $\boldsymbol{Z}$, then condition on $\boldsymbol{X}$ and use Exercise 9.22(b).]

Solution
(a) By the representation of a Wishart matrix (Exercise 9.19), $\boldsymbol{Z} = \boldsymbol{Y}'\boldsymbol{Y}$ where the $p \times m$ matrix $\boldsymbol{Y} := (\boldsymbol{Y}_1, \boldsymbol{Y}_2)$ has rows that are $\boldsymbol{y}_i' \sim \mathrm{IN}_m(\mathbf{0}', \boldsymbol{\Sigma})$ for $i = 1, \dots, p$, and $\boldsymbol{Y}_1$ is $p \times k$. Then

$$\boldsymbol{Z}_{11|2} = \boldsymbol{Y}_1'\boldsymbol{Y}_1 - \boldsymbol{Y}_1'\boldsymbol{Y}_2\left(\boldsymbol{Y}_2'\boldsymbol{Y}_2\right)^{-1}\boldsymbol{Y}_2'\boldsymbol{Y}_1 = (\boldsymbol{P}\boldsymbol{Y}_1)'(\boldsymbol{P}\boldsymbol{Y}_1),$$

where $\boldsymbol{P} := \boldsymbol{I}_p - \boldsymbol{Y}_2\left(\boldsymbol{Y}_2'\boldsymbol{Y}_2\right)^{-1}\boldsymbol{Y}_2'$ is symmetric idempotent. From Chapter 8, the rows of $\boldsymbol{Y}_{1|2} := \boldsymbol{Y}_1 - \boldsymbol{Y}_2\boldsymbol{\Sigma}_{22}^{-1}\boldsymbol{\Sigma}_{21}$ are $\mathrm{IN}_k(\mathbf{0}', \boldsymbol{\Sigma}_{11|2})$ and, by $\boldsymbol{P}\boldsymbol{Y}_2 = \mathbf{O}$, we have $\boldsymbol{P}\boldsymbol{Y}_{1|2} = \boldsymbol{P}\boldsymbol{Y}_1$ and so

$$\boldsymbol{Z}_{11|2} = \left(\boldsymbol{P}\boldsymbol{Y}_{1|2}\right)'\left(\boldsymbol{P}\boldsymbol{Y}_{1|2}\right).$$

Since $\boldsymbol{P}$ is symmetric idempotent of rank $p-(m-k)$, it can be decomposed into

$$\boldsymbol{P}=\boldsymbol{T}\operatorname{diag}\left(\boldsymbol{I}_{p+k-m},\mathbf{O}\right)\boldsymbol{T}'$$

where $\boldsymbol{T}$ is orthogonal and, letting $\boldsymbol{Y}_*:=\operatorname{diag}\left(\boldsymbol{I}_{p+k-m},\mathbf{O}\right)\boldsymbol{T}'\boldsymbol{Y}_{1|2}$, we have $\boldsymbol{Z}_{11|2}=\boldsymbol{Y}_*'\boldsymbol{Y}_*$. Since $\boldsymbol{T}'$ combines the rows of $\boldsymbol{Y}_{1|2}$, which are independent normals (thus invariant to orthogonal transformations), $\boldsymbol{T}'\boldsymbol{Y}_{1|2}$ has rows which are still $\mathrm{IN}_k(\mathbf{0}',\boldsymbol{\Sigma}_{11|2})$ and independent of $\boldsymbol{T}$ (hence independent of $\boldsymbol{Y}_2$ and $\boldsymbol{Z}_{22}$). Now, $\boldsymbol{Y}_*$ is just the selection of the first $p+k-m$ rows of $\boldsymbol{T}'\boldsymbol{Y}_{1|2}$, so $\boldsymbol{Z}_{11|2}=\boldsymbol{Y}_*'\boldsymbol{Y}_*\sim\mathrm{W}_k(p+k-m,\boldsymbol{\Sigma}_{11|2})$ by the representation of Wishart matrices. Finally,

$$\begin{aligned}\boldsymbol{Z}_{12}&=\boldsymbol{Y}_1'\boldsymbol{Y}_2=\left(\boldsymbol{Y}_{1|2}+\boldsymbol{Y}_2\boldsymbol{\Sigma}_{22}^{-1}\boldsymbol{\Sigma}_{21}\right)'\boldsymbol{Y}_2\\&=\boldsymbol{Y}_{1|2}'\left(\boldsymbol{I}_p-\boldsymbol{P}+\boldsymbol{P}\right)\boldsymbol{Y}_2+\boldsymbol{\Sigma}_{12}\boldsymbol{\Sigma}_{22}^{-1}\boldsymbol{Z}_{22}\\&=\boldsymbol{Y}_{1|2}'\left(\boldsymbol{I}_p-\boldsymbol{P}\right)\boldsymbol{Y}_2+\boldsymbol{\Sigma}_{12}\boldsymbol{\Sigma}_{22}^{-1}\boldsymbol{Z}_{22}\end{aligned}$$

by $\boldsymbol{P}\boldsymbol{Y}_2=\mathbf{O}$. Since $\boldsymbol{Z}_{11|2}=\left(\boldsymbol{P}\boldsymbol{Y}_{1|2}\right)'\left(\boldsymbol{P}\boldsymbol{Y}_{1|2}\right)$ is based on $\boldsymbol{P}\boldsymbol{Y}_{1|2}$, while $\boldsymbol{Z}_{12}$ is based on its orthogonal complement $\boldsymbol{Y}_{1|2}'\left(\boldsymbol{I}_p-\boldsymbol{P}\right)$ and on $\boldsymbol{Z}_{22}$ (of which $\boldsymbol{Z}_{11|2}$ is independent), the independence of $\boldsymbol{Z}_{11|2}$ and $\boldsymbol{Z}_{12}$ follows.
(b) The Wishart representation in the proof of part (a) gives

$$\boldsymbol{Z}_{12}=\boldsymbol{Y}_1'\boldsymbol{Y}_2=\left(\boldsymbol{Y}_{1|2}+\boldsymbol{Y}_2\boldsymbol{\Sigma}_{22}^{-1}\boldsymbol{\Sigma}_{21}\right)'\boldsymbol{Y}_2=\boldsymbol{Y}_{1|2}'\boldsymbol{Y}_2+\boldsymbol{\Sigma}_{12}\boldsymbol{\Sigma}_{22}^{-1}\boldsymbol{Z}_{22}.$$

Conditional on $\boldsymbol{Z}_{22}$ (hence on $\boldsymbol{Y}_2$), $\boldsymbol{Z}_{12}$ is a linear transformation of the normally distributed $\boldsymbol{Y}_{1|2}'$ and has

$$\mathrm{E}\left(\boldsymbol{Z}_{12}\right)=\mathrm{E}\left(\boldsymbol{Y}_{1|2}'\right)\boldsymbol{Y}_2+\boldsymbol{\Sigma}_{12}\boldsymbol{\Sigma}_{22}^{-1}\boldsymbol{Z}_{22}=\boldsymbol{\Sigma}_{12}\boldsymbol{\Sigma}_{22}^{-1}\boldsymbol{Z}_{22}$$

by the rows of $\boldsymbol{Y}_{1|2}$ being $\mathrm{IN}_k(\mathbf{0}',\boldsymbol{\Sigma}_{11|2})$, and

$$\begin{aligned}\operatorname{var}\left(\operatorname{vec}\left(\boldsymbol{Z}_{12}\right)\right)&=\mathrm{E}\left(\operatorname{vec}\left(\boldsymbol{Y}_{1|2}'\boldsymbol{Y}_2\right)\operatorname{vec}\left(\boldsymbol{Y}_{1|2}'\boldsymbol{Y}_2\right)'\right)\\&=\left(\boldsymbol{Y}_2'\otimes\boldsymbol{I}_k\right)\mathrm{E}\left(\operatorname{vec}\left(\boldsymbol{Y}_{1|2}'\right)\operatorname{vec}\left(\boldsymbol{Y}_{1|2}'\right)'\right)\left(\boldsymbol{Y}_2\otimes\boldsymbol{I}_k\right)\\&=\left(\boldsymbol{Y}_2'\otimes\boldsymbol{I}_k\right)\left(\boldsymbol{I}_p\otimes\boldsymbol{\Sigma}_{11|2}\right)\left(\boldsymbol{Y}_2\otimes\boldsymbol{I}_k\right)=\boldsymbol{Z}_{22}\otimes\boldsymbol{\Sigma}_{11|2}.\end{aligned}$$

(c) The solution of this part starts from the formula for the partitioned inverse of $\boldsymbol{Z}$ (see Section A.4), which states that $\boldsymbol{Z}_{11|2}^{-1}$ is the first diagonal block of $\boldsymbol{Z}^{-1}$, namely

$$\boldsymbol{Z}_{11|2}=\left(\left(\boldsymbol{I}_k,\mathbf{O}\right)\boldsymbol{Z}^{-1}\begin{pmatrix}\boldsymbol{I}_k\\\mathbf{O}\end{pmatrix}\right)^{-1},$$

and that $\boldsymbol{\Sigma}_{11|2}^{-1}$ is the first block of $\boldsymbol{\Sigma}^{-1}$. Define $\boldsymbol{X}$ to be any $m\times m$ matrix invertible with probability 1, and distributed independently of $\boldsymbol{Z}$. Conditioning on $\boldsymbol{X}$, Exercise 9.22(b) gives

$$\boldsymbol{Z}^{\dagger}:=\boldsymbol{X}^{-1}\boldsymbol{Z}\boldsymbol{X}'^{-1}\sim\mathrm{W}_m(p,\boldsymbol{\Omega})$$

where $\boldsymbol{\Omega} := \boldsymbol{X}^{-1}\boldsymbol{\Sigma}\boldsymbol{X}'^{-1}$ and, by part (a) of the present exercise, we also have $\boldsymbol{Z}^{\dagger}_{11|2} \sim \mathrm{W}_k(p+k-m, \boldsymbol{\Omega}_{11|2})$, where

$$\boldsymbol{Z}^{\dagger}_{11|2} = \left((\boldsymbol{I}_k, \mathrm{O})\left(\boldsymbol{Z}^{\dagger}\right)^{-1}\begin{pmatrix}\boldsymbol{I}_k\\ \mathrm{O}\end{pmatrix}\right)^{-1} = \left((\boldsymbol{I}_k, \mathrm{O})\,\boldsymbol{X}'\boldsymbol{Z}^{-1}\boldsymbol{X}\begin{pmatrix}\boldsymbol{I}_k\\ \mathrm{O}\end{pmatrix}\right)^{-1}$$

and

$$\boldsymbol{\Omega}_{11|2} = \left((\boldsymbol{I}_k, \mathrm{O})\,\boldsymbol{\Omega}^{-1}\begin{pmatrix}\boldsymbol{I}_k\\ \mathrm{O}\end{pmatrix}\right)^{-1} = \left((\boldsymbol{I}_k, \mathrm{O})\,\boldsymbol{X}'\boldsymbol{\Sigma}^{-1}\boldsymbol{X}\begin{pmatrix}\boldsymbol{I}_k\\ \mathrm{O}\end{pmatrix}\right)^{-1}.$$

Setting $k = 1$ and letting $\boldsymbol{x}$ denote the first column of $\boldsymbol{X}$, we get

$$Z^{\dagger}_{11|2} = \frac{1}{\boldsymbol{x}'\boldsymbol{Z}^{-1}\boldsymbol{x}} \sim \mathrm{W}_1\left(p+1-m, \frac{1}{\boldsymbol{x}'\boldsymbol{\Sigma}^{-1}\boldsymbol{x}}\right) = \frac{1}{\boldsymbol{x}'\boldsymbol{\Sigma}^{-1}\boldsymbol{x}}\cdot\chi^2(p+1-m)$$

conditional on $\boldsymbol{x}$. Since $\boldsymbol{x}'\boldsymbol{\Sigma}^{-1}\boldsymbol{x}/\boldsymbol{x}'\boldsymbol{Z}^{-1}\boldsymbol{x} \sim \chi^2(p+1-m)$ independently of $\boldsymbol{x}$, the result holds unconditionally too. Note that, fixing $\boldsymbol{x} = \boldsymbol{a}$, the quadratic form $\boldsymbol{a}'\boldsymbol{Z}^{-1}\boldsymbol{a}$ is distributed as the inverse of a scaled $\chi^2(p+1-m)$ variate.

Exercise 9.24 (Hotelling's T^2) Let $\boldsymbol{x}_1, \ldots, \boldsymbol{x}_n$ be a random sample from the $\mathrm{N}_m(\boldsymbol{\mu}, \boldsymbol{\Sigma})$ distribution, where $n > m$ and $\boldsymbol{\Sigma}$ is nonsingular. Derive the distribution of Hotelling's T^2 statistic,

$$T^2 := n\left(\overline{\boldsymbol{x}} - \boldsymbol{\mu}_0\right)'\boldsymbol{S}^{-1}\left(\overline{\boldsymbol{x}} - \boldsymbol{\mu}_0\right),$$

stating what happens when $\boldsymbol{\mu} \neq \boldsymbol{\mu}_0$.

Solution

The condition $n > m$ guarantees that the sample variance $\boldsymbol{S}$ is nonsingular with probability 1 (by Exercise 9.21), so we can consider $\boldsymbol{S}^{-1}$ as required. By $(n-1)\,\boldsymbol{S} \sim \mathrm{W}_m(n-1, \boldsymbol{\Sigma})$ from Exercise 9.20, and by the independence of $\overline{\boldsymbol{x}}$ from $\boldsymbol{S}$ in Exercises 9.18 or 9.20, we have

$$(n-1)\,\frac{\left(\overline{\boldsymbol{x}} - \boldsymbol{\mu}_0\right)'\boldsymbol{\Sigma}^{-1}\left(\overline{\boldsymbol{x}} - \boldsymbol{\mu}_0\right)}{\left(\overline{\boldsymbol{x}} - \boldsymbol{\mu}_0\right)'\boldsymbol{S}^{-1}\left(\overline{\boldsymbol{x}} - \boldsymbol{\mu}_0\right)} \sim \chi^2(n-m)$$

independently of $\overline{\boldsymbol{x}}$, by Exercise 9.23(c). This is not quite the statistic we want, so we need to investigate the numerator and get rid of it by division.

Since $\sqrt{n}\left(\overline{\boldsymbol{x}} - \boldsymbol{\mu}_0\right) \sim \mathrm{N}_m\left(\sqrt{n}\left(\boldsymbol{\mu} - \boldsymbol{\mu}_0\right), \boldsymbol{\Sigma}\right)$, we have

$$n\left(\overline{\boldsymbol{x}} - \boldsymbol{\mu}_0\right)'\boldsymbol{\Sigma}^{-1}\left(\overline{\boldsymbol{x}} - \boldsymbol{\mu}_0\right) \sim \chi^2(m, \delta)$$

where $\delta = n\left(\boldsymbol{\mu} - \boldsymbol{\mu}_0\right)'\boldsymbol{\Sigma}^{-1}\left(\boldsymbol{\mu} - \boldsymbol{\mu}_0\right)$. The noncentral F representation in Exercise 4.32 gives

$$\frac{n-m}{m} \times \frac{n\left(\overline{\boldsymbol{x}} - \boldsymbol{\mu}_0\right)'\boldsymbol{\Sigma}^{-1}\left(\overline{\boldsymbol{x}} - \boldsymbol{\mu}_0\right)}{\frac{(n-1)(\overline{\boldsymbol{x}}-\boldsymbol{\mu}_0)'\boldsymbol{\Sigma}^{-1}(\overline{\boldsymbol{x}}-\boldsymbol{\mu}_0)}{(\overline{\boldsymbol{x}}-\boldsymbol{\mu}_0)'\boldsymbol{S}^{-1}(\overline{\boldsymbol{x}}-\boldsymbol{\mu}_0)}} \equiv \frac{n-m}{(n-1)\,m}T^2 \sim \mathrm{F}(m, n-m, \delta).$$

When the maintained $\boldsymbol{\mu}_0$ coincides with the unknown $\boldsymbol{\mu}$, we have $\delta = 0$ and the distribution is the central $\mathrm{F}(m, n-m)$. However, when $\boldsymbol{\mu}_0 \neq \boldsymbol{\mu}$, the distribution is noncentral and its density mass is shifted to the right (to large and positive values of T^2); see Chapter 4.

Exercise 9.25 (Sample correlation: general-ρ density) Assume that we have a random sample of size $n > 2$ from $(y, z)' \sim \mathrm{N}(\mathbf{0}, \boldsymbol{\Sigma})$, where $\boldsymbol{\Sigma}$ is nonsingular. By writing the joint density of the three distinct elements of $(n-1)\boldsymbol{S}$, or some transformation thereof, then marginalizing, show that

$$f_{\widehat{\rho}}(u) = \frac{2^{n-3}\left(1-\rho^2\right)^{\frac{n-1}{2}}\left(1-u^2\right)^{\frac{n}{2}-2}}{\pi\,(n-3)!}\sum_{j=0}^{\infty}\frac{\left(\Gamma\left(\frac{j+n-1}{2}\right)\right)^2 (2\rho u)^j}{j!}$$

or, equivalently,

$$f_{\widehat{\rho}}(u) = (n-2)\frac{(n-2)!\left(1-\rho^2\right)^{\frac{n-1}{2}}\left(1-u^2\right)^{\frac{n}{2}-2}}{\sqrt{2\pi}\,\Gamma\left(n-\frac{1}{2}\right)(1-\rho u)^{n-\frac{3}{2}}}$$
$$\times\sum_{j=0}^{\infty}\frac{\left(\Gamma\left(j+\frac{1}{2}\right)/\Gamma\left(\frac{1}{2}\right)\right)^2}{\left(\Gamma\left(j+n-\frac{1}{2}\right)/\Gamma\left(n-\frac{1}{2}\right)\right)j!}\left(\frac{1+\rho u}{2}\right)^j.$$

You may use *Legendre's duplication formula*

$$\sqrt{\pi}\,\Gamma\left(\frac{n}{2}-1\right)\Gamma\left(\frac{n-1}{2}\right) = \frac{\pi}{2^{n-3}}\Gamma(n-2)$$

and, for the second formula of $f_{\widehat{\rho}}$, the integral

$$\int_0^{\infty}\frac{v^{\frac{n-3}{2}}}{\left(1-2\rho u\sqrt{v}+v\right)^{n-1}}\,\mathrm{d}v$$
$$= \frac{(n-2)!\sqrt{\pi}}{2^{n-\frac{5}{2}}\Gamma\left(n-\frac{1}{2}\right)(1-\rho u)^{n-\frac{3}{2}}}\sum_{j=0}^{\infty}\frac{\left(\Gamma\left(j+\frac{1}{2}\right)/\Gamma\left(\frac{1}{2}\right)\right)^2}{\left(\Gamma\left(j+n-\frac{1}{2}\right)/\Gamma\left(n-\frac{1}{2}\right)\right)j!}\left(\frac{1+\rho u}{2}\right)^j.$$

Solution

This exercise completes Exercise 9.7. Write

$$(n-1)\boldsymbol{S} =: \begin{pmatrix}\xi_{11} & \xi_{12}\\ \xi_{12} & \xi_{22}\end{pmatrix}$$

and, because correlations are scale-invariant, we can write

$$\boldsymbol{\Sigma} = \begin{pmatrix}1 & \rho\\ \rho & 1\end{pmatrix},$$

with $\rho^2 \neq 1$ since $\boldsymbol{\Sigma}$ is nonsingular. We have all the ingredients in Exercise 9.23(a), (b) to work out the required density. Conditionally on ξ_{22}, we have the two distributional results:

$$\xi_{11|2} := \xi_{11} - \xi_{12}^2/\xi_{22} \equiv \left(1-\widehat{\rho}^2\right)\xi_{11} \sim \mathrm{W}_1(n-2, \sigma_{11|2}) = \sigma_{11|2}\cdot\chi^2(n-2)$$

(the equality is from Exercise 9.19) with $\sigma_{11|2} := \sigma_{11}\left(1-\rho^2\right)$, independently of

$$\xi_{12} \sim \mathrm{N}\left(\frac{\sigma_{12}}{\sigma_{22}}\xi_{22}, \sigma_{11|2}\xi_{22}\right).$$

Together with $\sigma_{22}^{-1}\xi_{22} \sim \chi^2(n-1)$ and

$$f_{\xi_{11},\xi_{12},\xi_{22}} \equiv f_{\xi_{11},\xi_{12}|\xi_{22}} f_{\xi_{22}} = f_{\xi_{11}|\xi_{22}} f_{\xi_{12}|\xi_{22}} f_{\xi_{22}}$$

by independence, we have (putting $\widehat{\rho} = u$ and $\sigma_{11} = \sigma_{22} = 1$)

$$\begin{aligned}
&f_{\xi_{11},\xi_{12},\xi_{22}}(u_1, u_2, u_3) \\
&= \frac{\left(\frac{1}{2}\left(1-\rho^2\right)^{-1}\left(1-u^2\right)u_1\right)^{\frac{n}{2}-2} \exp\left(-\frac{1}{2}\left(1-\rho^2\right)^{-1}\left(1-u^2\right)u_1\right)}{2\Gamma\left(\frac{n}{2}-1\right)}\left(1-\rho^2\right)^{-1} \\
&\quad \times \frac{1}{\sqrt{2\pi\left(1-\rho^2\right)u_3}} \exp\left(-\frac{\left(u_2-\rho u_3\right)^2}{2\left(1-\rho^2\right)u_3}\right) \times \frac{\left(\frac{1}{2}u_3\right)^{\frac{n-3}{2}} \exp\left(-\frac{1}{2}u_3\right)}{2\Gamma\left(\frac{n-1}{2}\right)} \\
&= \frac{\left(1-\rho^2\right)^{\frac{1-n}{2}}\left(1-u^2\right)^{\frac{n}{2}-2}}{8\sqrt{\pi}\Gamma\left(\frac{n}{2}-1\right)\Gamma\left(\frac{n-1}{2}\right)}\left(\frac{u_1}{2} \times \frac{u_3}{2}\right)^{\frac{n}{2}-2} \\
&\quad \times \exp\left(-\frac{\left(1-u^2\right)u_1}{2\left(1-\rho^2\right)} - \frac{\left(u_2-\rho u_3\right)^2}{2\left(1-\rho^2\right)u_3} - \frac{u_3}{2}\right),
\end{aligned}$$

where the first factor $\left(1-\rho^2\right)^{-1}$ is due to the Jacobian of $\sigma_{11|2} \cdot \chi^2(n-2)$. Note that the first subscript of f is ξ_{11} rather than $\xi_{11|2}$, because the Jacobian from $\xi_{11|2} := \xi_{11} - \xi_{12}^2/\xi_{22}$ to ξ_{11} is 1. By the transformation of the second variate ξ_{12} into $\widehat{\rho}$ as $\xi_{12} = \widehat{\rho}\sqrt{\xi_{11}\xi_{22}}$ (or $u_2 = u\sqrt{u_1 u_3}$) with Jacobian $\sqrt{\xi_{11}\xi_{22}}$ (or $\sqrt{u_1 u_3}$), we have

$$\begin{aligned}
f_{\xi_{11},\widehat{\rho},\xi_{22}}(u_1, u, u_3) &= \frac{\left(1-\rho^2\right)^{\frac{1-n}{2}}\left(1-u^2\right)^{\frac{n}{2}-2}}{4\sqrt{\pi}\Gamma\left(\frac{n}{2}-1\right)\Gamma\left(\frac{n-1}{2}\right)}\left(\frac{u_1}{2} \times \frac{u_3}{2}\right)^{\frac{n-3}{2}} \\
&\quad \times \exp\left(-\frac{\left(1-u^2\right)u_1}{2\left(1-\rho^2\right)} - \frac{\left(u\sqrt{u_1}-\rho\sqrt{u_3}\right)^2}{2\left(1-\rho^2\right)} - \frac{u_3}{2}\right),
\end{aligned}$$

where the argument of the exponential can be simplified as

$$\begin{aligned}
&-\frac{\left(1-u^2\right)u_1}{2\left(1-\rho^2\right)} - \frac{u^2 u_1 - 2\rho u\sqrt{u_1 u_3} + \rho^2 u_3}{2\left(1-\rho^2\right)} - \frac{u_3}{2} \\
&= -\frac{u_1}{2\left(1-\rho^2\right)} + \frac{\rho u\sqrt{u_1 u_3}}{1-\rho^2} - \frac{u_3}{2\left(1-\rho^2\right)}.
\end{aligned}$$

Then $\exp\left(\rho u\sqrt{u_1 u_3}/\left(1-\rho^2\right)\right)$ can be expanded to give

$$f_{\xi_{11},\hat{\rho},\xi_{22}}\left(u_1,u,u_3\right) = \frac{\left(1-\rho^2\right)^{\frac{1-n}{2}}\left(1-u^2\right)^{\frac{n}{2}-2}}{4\sqrt{\pi}\Gamma\left(\frac{n}{2}-1\right)\Gamma\left(\frac{n-1}{2}\right)}\sum_{j=0}^{\infty}\frac{\left(2\rho u/\left(1-\rho^2\right)\right)^j}{j!}$$
$$\times\left(\frac{u_1}{2}\times\frac{u_3}{2}\right)^{\frac{j+n-3}{2}}\exp\left(-\frac{u_1}{2\left(1-\rho^2\right)}-\frac{u_3}{2\left(1-\rho^2\right)}\right).$$

Integrating out $u_1, u_3 \in \mathbb{R}^2_+$ termwise, and noting that the two integrals are identical,

$$f_{\hat{\rho}}(u) = \frac{\left(1-\rho^2\right)^{\frac{1-n}{2}}\left(1-u^2\right)^{\frac{n}{2}-2}}{4\sqrt{\pi}\Gamma\left(\frac{n}{2}-1\right)\Gamma\left(\frac{n-1}{2}\right)}\sum_{j=0}^{\infty}\frac{\left(2\rho u/\left(1-\rho^2\right)\right)^j}{j!}$$
$$\times\left(\int_0^{\infty}\left(\frac{u_1}{2}\right)^{\frac{j+n-3}{2}}\exp\left(-\frac{u_1}{2\left(1-\rho^2\right)}\right)\mathrm{d}u_1\right)^2$$
$$= \frac{\left(1-\rho^2\right)^{\frac{n-1}{2}}\left(1-u^2\right)^{\frac{n}{2}-2}}{\sqrt{\pi}\Gamma\left(\frac{n}{2}-1\right)\Gamma\left(\frac{n-1}{2}\right)}\sum_{j=0}^{\infty}\frac{\left(\Gamma\left(\frac{j+n-1}{2}\right)\right)^2(2\rho u)^j}{j!}$$

using the integral of the $\text{Gam}(\frac{j+n-1}{2}, \frac{1}{2(1-\rho^2)})$ density. The series is absolutely convergent since $\rho^2, u^2 \in (0,1)$; see Section A.3.2. Its statement follows from Legendre's duplication formula and $\Gamma(n-2) = (n-3)!$ since $n-2 \in \mathbb{N}$.

As mentioned in the introduction to Chapter 4, and illustrated for Φ in Exercise 4.21, series expansions of functions are not unique. Here, an alternative expression for $f_{\hat{\rho}}$ can be obtained by not expanding the exponential as before, but instead making the change of variable from u_3 to $v = u_3/u_1 \in \mathbb{R}_+$ and integrating:

$$f_{\hat{\rho}}(u) = \frac{2^{n-3}\left(1-\rho^2\right)^{\frac{1-n}{2}}\left(1-u^2\right)^{\frac{n}{2}-2}}{4\pi(n-3)!}$$
$$\times\int_0^{\infty}\left(\frac{v}{4}\right)^{\frac{n-3}{2}}\int_0^{\infty}u_1^{n-2}\exp\left(-\frac{1-2\rho u\sqrt{v}+v}{2\left(1-\rho^2\right)}u_1\right)\mathrm{d}u_1\,\mathrm{d}v$$
$$= \frac{2^{n-3}\left(1-\rho^2\right)^{\frac{1-n}{2}}\left(1-u^2\right)^{\frac{n}{2}-2}}{4\pi(n-3)!}\int_0^{\infty}\left(\frac{v}{4}\right)^{\frac{n-3}{2}}(n-2)!\left(\frac{1-2\rho u\sqrt{v}+v}{2(1-\rho^2)}\right)^{1-n}\mathrm{d}v$$
$$= \frac{2^{n-3}(n-2)\left(1-\rho^2\right)^{\frac{n-1}{2}}\left(1-u^2\right)^{\frac{n}{2}-2}}{\pi}\int_0^{\infty}\frac{v^{\frac{n-3}{2}}}{\left(1-2\rho u\sqrt{v}+v\right)^{n-1}}\mathrm{d}v$$

using the integral of the $\text{Gam}(n-1, \frac{1-2\rho u\sqrt{v}+v}{2(1-\rho^2)})$ density and $\Gamma(n-1) = (n-2)!$ since $n-2 \in \mathbb{N}$. The result follows by the integral given in the question. Note that the second formula for $f_{\hat{\rho}}(u)$ converges faster than the first when n is large. Actually, as $n \to \infty$, the only nonzero term in the sum becomes the term for $j = 0$. We will cover the limit as $n \to \infty$ in Exercise 10.35.

9.3 Empirical distributions, order statistics, sign and rank correlations

Exercise 9.26 (EDF's pointwise distributions) Let $x_1, \dots, x_n$ be a random sample of a variate x with distribution $F(u)$.
(a) Show that $\Pr(\widehat{F}_n(u) = \frac{k}{n}) = \binom{n}{k}(F(u))^k(1 - F(u))^{n-k}$ for $k = 0, 1, \dots, n$, and 0 otherwise.
(b) Derive $\mathrm{E}(\widehat{F}_n(u))$ and $\mathrm{var}(\widehat{F}_n(u))$.

Solution
(a) Recall that $\widehat{F}_n(u) := n^{-1}\sum_{i=1}^{n} 1_{x_i \leqslant u}$. For a given u, the variates $1_{x_i \leqslant u}$ are i.i.d. with

$$\Pr(1_{x_i \leqslant u} = 1) = \Pr(x_i \leqslant u) = F(u)$$

and $\Pr(1_{x_i \leqslant u} = 0) = 1 - F(u)$. Since $\sum_{i=1}^{n} 1_{x_i \leqslant u}$ is the sum of repeated independent Bernoulli trials, we get $n\widehat{F}_n(u) \sim \mathrm{Bin}(n, F(u))$, as required.
(b) Since $z \sim \mathrm{Bin}(n, p)$ implies that $\mathrm{E}(z) = np$ and $\mathrm{var}(z) = np(1 - p)$, we have

$$\mathrm{E}(\widehat{F}_n(u)) = F(u) \quad \text{and} \quad \mathrm{var}(\widehat{F}_n(u)) = \frac{F(u)(1 - F(u))}{n}.$$

In other words, the statistic $\widehat{F}_n(u)$ is centered around the population value $F(u)$ and, as $n \to \infty$, $\mathrm{var}(\widehat{F}_n(u)) \to 0$ and $\widehat{F}_n(u)$ degenerates to the single value $F(u)$ for any given u.

Exercise 9.27 (EDF's covariance) Let $x_1, \dots, x_n$ be a random sample of a variate x with distribution $F(u)$, and z be the number of x_i's in the interval $(u_1, u_2]$ with $u_2 > u_1$. Show that:
(a) $\Pr(z = w) = \binom{n}{w}(F(u_2) - F(u_1))^w(1 - F(u_2) + F(u_1))^{n-w}$;
(b) $\mathrm{var}(z) = n(F(u_2) - F(u_1))(1 - F(u_2) + F(u_1))$;
(c) $\mathrm{cov}(\widehat{F}_n(u_1), \widehat{F}_n(u_2)) = \frac{1}{n}F(u_1)(1 - F(u_2))$.

Solution
(a) The probability that an observation falls in the interval $(u_1, u_2]$ is $F(u_2) - F(u_1)$. Hence, from the binomial distribution,

$$\Pr(z = w) = \binom{n}{w}(F(u_2) - F(u_1))^w(1 - F(u_2) + F(u_1))^{n-w}.$$

(b) From the binomial's variance, we have

$$\mathrm{var}(z) = n(F(u_2) - F(u_1))(1 - F(u_2) + F(u_1)).$$

(c) Since $\widehat{F}_n(u_2) - \widehat{F}_n(u_1) = \frac{z}{n}$, we have

$$\mathrm{var}(\widehat{F}_n(u_2) - \widehat{F}_n(u_1)) = \frac{1}{n}(F(u_2) - F(u_1))(1 - F(u_2) + F(u_1)).$$

But

$$\begin{aligned}\operatorname{var}(\widehat{F}_n(u_2)-\widehat{F}_n(u_1)) &= \operatorname{var}(\widehat{F}_n(u_2))+\operatorname{var}(\widehat{F}_n(u_1))-2\operatorname{cov}(\widehat{F}_n(u_1),\widehat{F}_n(u_2))\\ &= \frac{F(u_2)(1-F(u_2))+F(u_1)(1-F(u_1))}{n}-2\operatorname{cov}(\widehat{F}_n(u_1),\widehat{F}_n(u_2))\end{aligned}$$

by Exercise 9.26(b), hence

$$\begin{aligned}&\operatorname{cov}(\widehat{F}_n(u_1),\widehat{F}_n(u_2))\\ &= \frac{F(u_2)\left[1-F(u_2)\right]+F(u_1)\left[1-F(u_1)\right]-(F(u_2)-F(u_1))\left[1-F(u_2)+F(u_1)\right]}{2n}\\ &= \frac{F(u_2)\left[-F(u_1)\right]+F(u_1)\left[2-F(u_2)\right]}{2n}=\frac{F(u_1)(1-F(u_2))}{n}.\end{aligned}$$

Exercise 9.28 (Order statistics and quantiles) Let $y_1 \leqslant \cdots \leqslant y_n$ be the order statistics of the random sample $x_1, \dots, x_n$, and let q denote the α quantile satisfying $\Pr(x \leqslant q) = \alpha$, where it is assumed that x has a continuous distribution $F(u)$. Show that, for $i < j$:
(a) $\Pr(y_i \leqslant q \leqslant y_j) = \Pr(F(y_i) \leqslant \alpha) - \Pr(F(y_j) \leqslant \alpha)$;
(b) $\Pr(y_i \leqslant q \leqslant y_j) = \sum_{k=i}^{j-1} \binom{n}{k} \alpha^k (1-\alpha)^{n-k}$.

Solution
(a) Since F is a nondecreasing function,

$$\Pr(y_i \leqslant q \leqslant y_j) = \Pr(F(y_i) \leqslant F(q) \leqslant F(y_j)) = \Pr(F(y_i) \leqslant \alpha \leqslant F(y_j)).$$

By De Morgan's law, $\Pr(F(y_i) \leqslant \alpha$ and $\alpha \leqslant F(y_j)) = 1 - \Pr(F(y_i) > \alpha$ or $F(y_j) < \alpha)$. Now, $F(y_i) > \alpha$ and $F(y_j) < \alpha$ are disjoint events, since $y_i \leqslant y_j$ by the definition of order statistics (the required probability is trivially 0 if $i \geqslant j$). Then

$$\begin{aligned}\Pr(F(y_i) \leqslant \alpha \leqslant F(y_j)) &= 1-\Pr(F(y_i) > \alpha)-\Pr(F(y_j) < \alpha)\\ &= \Pr(F(y_i) \leqslant \alpha)-\Pr(F(y_j) < \alpha).\end{aligned}$$

The stated result follows since $F(y_j)$ has a continuous distribution (see the beta distribution derived in Exercise 7.38). Be careful to distinguish this from the discrete (binomial) distribution of $\widehat{F}_n(u)$ in Exercise 9.26!
(b) We have

$$\begin{aligned}\Pr(y_i \leqslant q) &= \Pr(i\text{-th order statistic} \leqslant q)\\ &= \Pr(\text{at least } i \text{ observations} \leqslant q)\\ &= \sum_{k=i}^{n}\binom{n}{k}(F(q))^k(1-F(q))^{n-k} = \sum_{k=i}^{n}\binom{n}{k}\alpha^k(1-\alpha)^{n-k}.\end{aligned}$$

Using part (a) gives

$$\Pr(y_i \leqslant q \leqslant y_j) = \sum_{k=i}^{n} \binom{n}{k} \alpha^k (1-\alpha)^{n-k} - \sum_{k=j}^{n} \binom{n}{k} \alpha^k (1-\alpha)^{n-k}$$

$$= \sum_{k=i}^{j-1} \binom{n}{k} \alpha^k (1-\alpha)^{n-k}.$$

Exercise 9.29 (Sign and rank correlations) Let $(x_1, y_1), \dots, (x_n, y_n)$ be a bivariate random sample. Assign each pair x_i, x_j a skew-symmetric score ξ_{ij} satisfying $\xi_{ij} = -\xi_{ji}$ (the score takes the opposite sign when the order of x_i and x_j is reversed), hence centered around zero, and a similar score v_{ij} for each pair y_i, y_j. A *tie* is said to occur when an observation is repeated more than once in the sample: $x_i = x_j$ for some $i \neq j$, and similarly for y_i, y_j. Define

$$\widehat{\theta} := \frac{\sum_{i=1}^{n} \sum_{j=1}^{n} \xi_{ij} v_{ij}}{\sqrt{\sum_{i=1}^{n} \sum_{j=1}^{n} \xi_{ij}^2} \sqrt{\sum_{i=1}^{n} \sum_{j=1}^{n} v_{ij}^2}}.$$

(a) If $\xi_{ij} = x_i - x_j$ and $v_{ij} = y_i - y_j$, show that $\widehat{\theta}$ is the sample correlation coefficient, assuming that the population's moments exist.
(b) If $\xi_{ij} = \operatorname{sgn}(x_i - x_j)$ and $v_{ij} = \operatorname{sgn}(y_i - y_j)$, we obtain *Kendall's* τ, which is the correlation of the signs of the differences between the respective elements of any two sample points. Show that it can be rewritten as

$$\widehat{\tau} = \frac{\sum_{i=1}^{n} \sum_{j=1}^{n} \operatorname{sgn}(x_i - x_j) \operatorname{sgn}(y_i - y_j)}{\sqrt{n(n-1) - T_x} \sqrt{n(n-1) - T_y}},$$

where $T_x := \sum_x t_{x_i}(t_{x_i} - 1)$ is the sum over the different x values for which ties occur, and t_{x_i} is the number of tied x_i values (the number of repeated x_i values in the sample).
(c) Let $\mathrm{r}(x_i)$ denote the rank of observation x_i, that is, the position of x_i in the list of order statistics for the sampled x values, or the average such position if x_i is a tied value; for example, if there are three ties for the first place, all three are ranked second. *Spearman's* ρ is a correlation of the ranks of x_i and y_i in their respective sequences, namely

$$\widehat{\rho}_{\mathrm{S}} := \frac{\sum_{i=1}^{n} (\mathrm{r}(x_i) - \bar{\mathrm{r}}(x)) (\mathrm{r}(y_i) - \bar{\mathrm{r}}(y))}{\sqrt{\sum_{i=1}^{n} (\mathrm{r}(x_i) - \bar{\mathrm{r}}(x))^2} \sqrt{\sum_{i=1}^{n} (\mathrm{r}(y_i) - \bar{\mathrm{r}}(y))^2}},$$

where $\bar{\mathrm{r}}(x)$ denotes the sample mean of $\mathrm{r}(x_i)$. Show that Spearman's ρ is $\widehat{\theta}$ with $\xi_{ij} = \mathrm{r}(x_i) - \mathrm{r}(x_j)$ and $v_{ij} = \mathrm{r}(y_i) - \mathrm{r}(y_j)$, and that this $\widehat{\theta}$ can be rewritten as

$$\widehat{\rho}_{\mathrm{S}} = \frac{n(n^2-1) - \frac{1}{2}(T_x + T_y) - 6 \sum_{i=1}^{n} (\mathrm{r}(x_i) - \mathrm{r}(y_i))^2}{\sqrt{n(n^2-1) - T_x} \sqrt{n(n^2-1) - T_y}},$$

where we now define $T_x := \sum_x t_{x_i}(t_{x_i}^2 - 1)$. [Hint: Section A.4.1 gives $\sum_{i=1}^{n} i = n(n+1)/2$ and $\sum_{i=1}^{n} i^2 = n(n+1)(2n+1)/6$.]

Solution

(a) This follows from

$$\sum_{i=1}^{n}\sum_{j=1}^{n}(x_i-x_j)(y_i-y_j)=\sum_{i=1}^{n}\sum_{j=1}^{n}(x_iy_i-x_iy_j-x_jy_i+x_jy_j)$$
$$=2n\sum_{i=1}^{n}x_iy_i-2\sum_{i=1}^{n}x_i\sum_{j=1}^{n}y_j=2n(n-1)s_{xy},$$

where s_{xy} is the sample covariance of x and y. The variances are obtained similarly as s_{xx} and s_{yy}. If one of the first two moments of the joint distribution of (x, y) does not exist, it is still possible to calculate sample moments but they would be spurious. The next two statistics do not presuppose the existence of moments.

(b) The numerator follows directly from the definition. For the denominator, we note that the skew-symmetry of ξ_{ij} implies that $\xi_{ii} = 0$ and we get

$$\sum_{i=1}^{n}\sum_{j=1}^{n}\xi_{ij}^2=\sum_{i=1}^{n}\sum_{j\neq i}(\operatorname{sgn}(x_i-x_j))^2=\sum_{i=1}^{n}\sum_{j\neq i}1_{x_i\neq x_j}$$
$$=\sum_{i=1}^{n}\sum_{j\neq i}\left(1-1_{x_i=x_j}\right)=n(n-1)-\sum_{i=1}^{n}\sum_{j\neq i}1_{x_i=x_j}.$$

If x_i has t_{x_i} ties, then $\sum_{j\neq i}1_{x_i=x_j}=t_{x_i}-1$ and, for that particular tied value (which is repeated for other x's as i varies), the contribution of $\sum_i$ is to add this up t_{x_i} times to give $t_{x_i}(t_{x_i}-1)$. Repeating over distinct values of x gives the stated result for ξ_{ij}^2, and the result for υ_{ij}^2 follows in the same manner.

(c) In the same way as we obtained the result in (a), we get

$$\sum_{i=1}^{n}\sum_{j=1}^{n}(\mathrm{r}(x_i)-\mathrm{r}(x_j))(\mathrm{r}(y_i)-\mathrm{r}(y_j))=2n\sum_{i=1}^{n}(\mathrm{r}(x_i)-\bar{\mathrm{r}}(x))(\mathrm{r}(y_i)-\bar{\mathrm{r}}(y)),$$

hence Spearman's ρ fits the definition of $\widehat{\theta}$ with $\xi_{ij}=\mathrm{r}(x_i)-\mathrm{r}(x_j)$ and $\upsilon_{ij}=\mathrm{r}(y_i)-\mathrm{r}(y_j)$. To derive the second expression in the question from Spearman's ρ, consider the difference of the following two components from the two numerators, one of them scaled such that the cross-product $\sum_{i=1}^{n}\mathrm{r}(x_i)\,\mathrm{r}(y_i)$ will drop out:

$$D:=\sum_{i=1}^{n}(\mathrm{r}(x_i)-\bar{\mathrm{r}}(x))(\mathrm{r}(y_i)-\bar{\mathrm{r}}(y))+\frac{1}{2}\sum_{i=1}^{n}(\mathrm{r}(x_i)-\mathrm{r}(y_i))^2.$$

Now $\bar{\mathrm{r}}(x)=\bar{\mathrm{r}}(y)=n^{-1}\sum_{i=1}^{n}i=(n+1)/2$ whether or not ties exist, allowing us to write all the ranks in D in deviation form $\mathrm{r}_x:=\mathrm{r}(x_i)-\bar{\mathrm{r}}(x)$ and $\mathrm{r}_y:=\mathrm{r}(y_i)-\bar{\mathrm{r}}(y)$ as

$$D=\sum_{i=1}^{n}\left(\mathrm{r}_x\mathrm{r}_y+\frac{1}{2}(\mathrm{r}_x-\mathrm{r}_y)^2\right)=\frac{1}{2}\sum_{i=1}^{n}\mathrm{r}_x^2+\frac{1}{2}\sum_{i=1}^{n}\mathrm{r}_y^2,$$

so what remains for us to show is that

$$\sum_{i=1}^{n} \mathrm{r}_x^2 = \frac{n\left(n^2-1\right)-T_x}{12},$$

and similarly for y.

When there are no ties, the ranks are simply some permutation of $1, \ldots, n$, and

$$\sum_{i=1}^{n} \mathrm{r}_x^2 = \sum_{i=1}^{n} \left(\mathrm{r}\left(x_i\right)-\overline{\mathrm{r}}\left(x\right)\right)^2 = \sum_{i=1}^{n} \mathrm{r}\left(x_i\right)^2 - n\overline{\mathrm{r}}\left(x\right)^2 = \sum_{i=1}^{n} i^2 - n\left(\frac{n+1}{2}\right)^2$$
$$= \frac{n\left(n+1\right)\left(2n+1\right)}{6} - n\left(\frac{n+1}{2}\right)^2 = \frac{n\left(n^2-1\right)}{12}.$$

This is n times the variance of a discrete uniform variate on $i \in \{1, \ldots, n\}$, as seen in Table 4.1 or Exercise 4.1. When a particular x_i is tied t_{x_i} times, the corresponding t_{x_i} ranks should be replaced by their average rank denoted by the shorthand $\bar{\imath}$; for example, if there are $t_{x_i} = 3$ ties for the first place, the ranks $i = 1, 2, 3$ should be replaced by the average rank $\bar{\imath} = 2$. Therefore, to calculate the variance we need the previous sum to contain the contribution $t_{x_i}\left(\bar{\imath}-\overline{\mathrm{r}}\left(x\right)\right)^2$ but to be reduced by $\sum\left(i-\overline{\mathrm{r}}\left(x\right)\right)^2$, where this last sum runs over the set of tied ranks corresponding to x_i. The net addition is then

$$t_{x_i}\left(\bar{\imath}-\overline{\mathrm{r}}\left(x\right)\right)^2 - \sum\left(i-\bar{\imath}+\bar{\imath}-\overline{\mathrm{r}}\left(x\right)\right)^2 = -2\left(\bar{\imath}-\overline{\mathrm{r}}\left(x\right)\right)\sum\left(i-\bar{\imath}\right) - \sum\left(i-\bar{\imath}\right)^2$$
$$= -\sum\left(i-\bar{\imath}\right)^2$$

by $\sum 1 \equiv t_{x_i}$ (the number of x's having the tied value x_i) and $\sum\left(i-\bar{\imath}\right) \equiv 0$, respectively. Since $\sum(i-\bar{\imath})^2$ is unaffected by the level of the average tied rank $\bar{\imath}$ (Exercise 3.15 established the location-invariance of deviations from an average), this sum is affected only by how many contiguous i's are included; for example, $\sum(i-\bar{\imath})^2$ has the same value whether the tied ranks were $i = 1, 2, 3$ or $i = 11, 12, 13$. Therefore, we have

$$\sum\left(i-\bar{\imath}\right)^2 = \frac{t_{x_i}\left(t_{x_i}^2-1\right)}{12}$$

by the same method used to calculate $\sum_{i=1}^{n} \mathrm{r}_x^2$ without ties. Hence,

$$\sum_{i=1}^{n} \mathrm{r}_x^2 = \frac{n\left(n^2-1\right)}{12} - \frac{\sum_x t_{x_i}\left(t_{x_i}^2-1\right)}{12} = \frac{n\left(n^2-1\right)-T_x}{12},$$

and similarly for y.

Exercise 9.30 (Copulas, signs, and ranks) Let (x, y) have a continuous nonsingular distribution $F(u, v)$. Prove that the population's Kendall τ and Spearman ρ are, respectively,

$$\tau = 4\int_0^1\int_0^1 C(p,q)\,\mathrm{d}C(p,q) - 1 \quad \text{and} \quad \rho_{\mathrm{S}} = 12\int_0^1\int_0^1 pq\,\mathrm{d}C(p,q) - 3,$$

where C is the copula function associated with F.

Solution

We first note that there is zero probability of a tie when drawing at random from a population of absolutely continuous variates (see Exercise 5.16) and this will allow us to simplify the definitions of τ and ρ_S. Kendall's τ is the correlation of the signs of the differences. Consider any two pairs (x_1, y_1) and (x_2, y_2) drawn at random from (x, y), hence $\Pr(x_1 = x_2) = 0$ and similarly for y. Since

$$\operatorname{sgn}(x_1 - x_2)\operatorname{sgn}(y_1 - y_2) = 1_{(x_1-x_2)(y_1-y_2)>0} - 1_{(x_1-x_2)(y_1-y_2)<0},$$

Kendall's τ is the difference between the relative frequency (or probability) of the two events in the indicator functions. Therefore,

$$\begin{aligned}\tau &\equiv \Pr((x_1 - x_2)(y_1 - y_2) > 0) - \Pr((x_1 - x_2)(y_1 - y_2) < 0) \\ &= 2\Pr((x_1 - x_2)(y_1 - y_2) > 0) - 1 \\ &= 2(\Pr(x_2 < x_1, y_2 < y_1) + \Pr(x_1 < x_2, y_1 < y_2)) - 1,\end{aligned}$$

since the events in the last two probabilities are disjoint. The first probability is $F(x_1, y_1)$ for any given (x_1, y_1), and is $\mathrm{E}(F(x, y))$ unconditionally, and similarly for the second probability. As a result,

$$\tau = 4\mathrm{E}(F(x, y)) - 1 = 4\int_{-\infty}^{\infty}\int_{-\infty}^{\infty} F(u, v)\,\mathrm{d}F(u, v) - 1.$$

Spearman's ρ is the correlation of ranks or, equivalently, the correlation of marginal c.d.f.s:

$$\rho_S \equiv \frac{\int_{-\infty}^{\infty}\int_{-\infty}^{\infty} F_x(u)\,F_y(v)\,\mathrm{d}F(u, v) - \mathrm{E}(F_x(x))\,\mathrm{E}(F_y(y))}{\sqrt{\operatorname{var}(F_x(x))\operatorname{var}(F_y(y))}}.$$

Because the correlations of signs and of ranks are invariant under increasing transformations of the variates, and the copula is a c.d.f. (see Exercise 5.19) here for continuous variates, we can replace $F(u, v)$ by the corresponding copula $C(p, q)$ and similarly $F_x(u)\,F_y(v)$ by the independence copula pq. By Exercise 7.40, p and q are realizations of standard-uniform variates, and these are known to have mean $\frac{1}{2}$ and variance $\frac{1}{12}$, so that

$$\rho_S = \frac{\int_0^1\int_0^1 pq\,\mathrm{d}C(p, q) - \left(\frac{1}{2}\right)^2}{\frac{1}{12}}$$

and $\tau = 4\int_0^1\int_0^1 C(p, q)\,\mathrm{d}C(p, q) - 1$ as required. It is not surprising to see in ρ_S the expectation of the bilinear function pq (which is linear in p and in q), since Spearman's ρ measures the *linear* correlation of ranks. Other forms of dependence between the ranks (or marginal c.d.f.s) may exist, and τ provides one such example where the nonlinearity appears through the copula function $C(p, q)$ in the integrand.

Note that, under the independence copula $C(p, q) = pq$,

$$\rho_S = 3\tau = 3\left(4\int_0^1 p\,\mathrm{d}p\int_0^1 q\,\mathrm{d}q - 1\right) = 3\left(4\left[\frac{p^2}{2}\right]_0^1\left[\frac{q^2}{2}\right]_0^1 - 1\right) = 0$$

and we get the usual zero "correlation". Note also that the usual correlation coefficient ρ can be rewritten by Exercise 6.29 as

$$\rho \equiv \frac{\int_{-\infty}^{\infty}\int_{-\infty}^{\infty}\left(F\left(u,v\right)-F_x\left(u\right)F_y\left(v\right)\right)\mathrm{d}u\,\mathrm{d}v}{\sqrt{\operatorname{var}\left(x\right)\operatorname{var}\left(y\right)}},$$

with independence, $F\left(u,v\right)=F_x\left(u\right)F_y\left(v\right)$ for all u,v, implying $\rho=0$ as usual.

Notes

In this book, we do not analyze sampling designs and we do not give details on how to design sample surveys. For more on these topics, see Cochran (1977), Kendall and Stuart (1977), and Kendall, Stuart, and Ord (1983). Note that our "random sampling" is short for what is more commonly known in that area as "simple random sampling".

The name of Exercise 9.3 is due to the following: the term *skedasticity* is sometimes used to describe variance. As a result, *heteroskedasticity* refers to the case of unequal variances, while *homoskedasticity* refers to the case of equal variances. In economics, it is often the case that observable averages are not i.i.d., but rather that their variances are different over the sampled groups of individuals (such as households or regions), possibly due to unequal sizes of these groups. Exercise 11.2 will show that the optimal combination of heteroskedastic variates is a weighted average such that each element underlying the sums has the same variance. An extensive treatment of heteroskedasticity can be found in econometric texts; for example, see Paruolo (2019) in this Series.

By substituting for the density of $\mathrm{F}(2j+m,n-m-1)$, the result of Exercise 9.7(c) can be rewritten as

$$\begin{aligned} f_{R^2}(u) &= \frac{\left(1-\overline{\rho}^2\right)^{\frac{n-1}{2}}}{(1-u)^2}\sum_{j=0}^{\infty}\binom{\frac{1-n}{2}}{j}\left(-\overline{\rho}^2\right)^j\frac{\left(\frac{u}{1-u}\right)^{\frac{2j+m}{2}-1}}{B\left(\frac{2j+m}{2},\frac{n-m-1}{2}\right)\left(1+\frac{u}{1-u}\right)^{\frac{2j+n-1}{2}}} \\ &= \frac{\left(1-\overline{\rho}^2\right)^{\frac{n-1}{2}}u^{\frac{m}{2}-1}}{(1-u)^{\frac{m-n+3}{2}}}\sum_{j=0}^{\infty}\binom{\frac{1-n}{2}}{j}\frac{\left(-\overline{\rho}^2u\right)^j}{B\left(\frac{2j+m}{2},\frac{n-m-1}{2}\right)}, \end{aligned}$$

which is a hypergeometric ${}_2F_1$ function of the type introduced in the Notes to Chapter 4. It can be rewritten as

$$\begin{aligned} f_{R^2}(u) &= \frac{\left(1-\overline{\rho}^2\right)^{\frac{n-1}{2}}u^{\frac{m}{2}-1}}{(1-u)^{\frac{m-n+3}{2}}}\sum_{j=0}^{\infty}\frac{\left(\Gamma\left(j+\frac{n-1}{2}\right)\right)^2}{\Gamma\left(\frac{n-1}{2}\right)\Gamma\left(j+\frac{m}{2}\right)\Gamma\left(\frac{n-m-1}{2}\right)}\frac{\left(\overline{\rho}^2u\right)^j}{j!} \\ &= \frac{\left(1-\overline{\rho}^2\right)^{\frac{n-1}{2}}u^{\frac{m}{2}-1}}{B\left(\frac{m}{2},\frac{n-m-1}{2}\right)(1-u)^{\frac{m-n+3}{2}}}\,{}_2F_1\left(\frac{n-1}{2},\frac{n-1}{2};\frac{m}{2};\overline{\rho}^2u\right). \end{aligned}$$

For specific values of m,n (such as when $m=1$ and $R^2=r^2$, or when $n\to\infty$), there are transformations of ${}_2F_1$ that make its expansion converge faster, most of them preprogrammed into the software for calculating such functions. Examples include the symbolic manipulation packages Maple and Mathematica. The same comment applies to the density of $\widehat{\rho}$ in Exercise 9.25, the first formula being the sum of two ${}_2F_1$ functions and the second being

$$f_{\widehat{\rho}}(u) = (n-2)\frac{(n-2)!\left(1-\rho^2\right)^{\frac{n-1}{2}}\left(1-u^2\right)^{\frac{n}{2}-2}}{\sqrt{2\pi}\Gamma\left(n-\frac{1}{2}\right)(1-\rho u)^{n-\frac{3}{2}}}\,{}_2F_1\left(\frac{1}{2},\frac{1}{2};n-\frac{1}{2};\frac{1+\rho u}{2}\right),$$

whose asymptotic analysis we will see in Exercise 10.35. If one does not wish to resort to Exercise 9.23, the proof of Exercise 9.25 can be delayed until Chapter 12: it is possible to use the independence of $\widehat{\beta}$ $(= s_{12}/s_{22})$ and $\widehat{\sigma}^2$ (the estimator of $\sigma_{11|2} := \sigma_{11} - \sigma_{21}^2/\sigma_{22}$) shown there, conditional on the regressor, to get the required joint density of $\boldsymbol{S}$; see Exercise 12.33 for the relation between the two setups. Legendre's duplication formula applies more generally than as stated in Exercise 9.25, for example to $n-2 \in \mathbb{R}_+$.

Various alternatives have been suggested to solve the puzzle of Exercise 9.10, which is known as Benford's law; for example, see Feller (1971, p. 63) and Hill (1995). The required probability is $\log_{10} 2 \approx 0.301$, and this was first obtained empirically from random samples.

We have seen, in Chapters 4 and 7, that sometimes the c.f. of a variate is easier to derive than its density. One such example is the χ^2 distribution. This is also the case with its generalization, the density of $\boldsymbol{Z} \sim \mathrm{W}_m(\nu, \boldsymbol{\Sigma})$. For $\nu \geqslant m$, the density of the nonsingular Wishart matrix $\boldsymbol{Z}$ is

$$f_{\boldsymbol{Z}}(\boldsymbol{W}) = \frac{\left|\frac{1}{2}\boldsymbol{\Sigma}^{-1}\right|^{\nu/2}}{\pi^{m(m-1)/4}\prod_{j=0}^{m-1}\Gamma\left(\frac{1}{2}(\nu-j)\right)}\left|\boldsymbol{W}\right|^{(\nu-m-1)/2}\operatorname{etr}\left(-\frac{1}{2}\boldsymbol{\Sigma}^{-1}\boldsymbol{W}\right)$$

for $\boldsymbol{W}$ positive definite. The Wishart distribution is analyzed extensively in Anderson (1984), Mardia, Kent, and Bibby (1979), Muirhead (1982), and other books on multivariate analysis, to which the reader is referred for more results. We also refer to our companion volume, Abadir and Magnus (2005), for details about the Kronecker product $\otimes$, the vec and vech operators, and properties of the Wishart distribution. In particular, see Chapter 11 there, where the first two moments of the Wishart are derived, and where the reader can find more details on the issue of the nonsingularity of $\operatorname{var}(\operatorname{vech}(\boldsymbol{S}))$ illustrated here in Exercise 9.21(b). See also the same reference for the geometric progression used in Exercise 9.22(b), and for Schur complements (see also Section A.4) which can be used to establish a stronger equivalence result for independence in Exercise 9.22(c).

It is rarely the case that general exact distributional results such as those in Exercise 9.7(a) can be found for samples of finite size n. It is more usual that one needs to make restrictive assumptions such as normality, as in most of Section 9.2. For other finite-sample results that are useful in econometrics, see Ullah (2004). Alternatively, as we will see in the next chapter, we could allow for a wide range of distributions, but let $n \to \infty$ and use limiting densities as an approximation for n "large".

For EDFs $\widehat{F}_n$ and order statistics $y_1, \ldots, y_n$, there exist visual tools to compare these variates with some pattern expected from the c.d.f. F and quantile function Q (see Chapter 2). The *P–P plot* depicts $F(y_i)$ against i/n for $i = 1, \ldots, n$, with the 45° line representing the target of equality of $\widehat{F}_n$ and F. Similarly, the *Q–Q plot* depicts y_i against $Q(i/n)$ for $i = 1, \ldots, n$, with the 45° line representing the target of equality of the order statistic and the corresponding quantile. The former graph is in terms of the c.d.f. range $[0, 1]$, while the latter is in terms of the variate $x \in \mathcal{X}$. If a pattern emerges that differs clearly from the straight equality line, then the presumed c.d.f. F (and hence quantile function Q) is not compatible with the data. Formal decision criteria to assess the difference will be studied in Chapter 14.

Kendall's τ and Spearman's ρ lie in the interval $[-1, 1]$ because of their representation as sample correlations seen in Exercise 9.29. However, if there are too many ties (not likely for continuous variates), these statistics will be erratic because their denominators are too small. A common approximate distribution for $\widehat{\theta}$, when the denominator is large, is given in Exercises 9.7(b) and 10.35. Daniels (1944) also explored the fact that the distribution of Spearman's ρ is obtained from $\widehat{\theta}$ by letting ξ_{ij} and υ_{ij} be permutations of $j - i$, assuming there are no ties. He showed that, in general, $\widehat{\theta}$ is normally distributed in large samples, where $\mathrm{var}(\widehat{\theta})$ becomes

$$\frac{4}{n^3} \frac{\sum_{i,j,k} \xi_{ij}\xi_{ik} \sum_{i,j,k} \upsilon_{ij}\upsilon_{ik}}{\sum_{i,j} \xi_{ij}^2 \sum_{i,j} \upsilon_{ij}^2}$$

and declines at a rate $1/n$ because of the extra sum in k (twice) in the numerator. Under independence, he showed that the correlation between $\widehat{\rho}_S$ and $\widehat{\tau}$ is

$$\frac{2(n+1)}{\sqrt{2n(2n+5)}},$$

which attains its minimum of 0.98 at $n = 5$, a very high correlation indeed, the two statistics becoming proportional as $n \to \infty$. Exercises 14.40(b) and 14.41(c) will show that this proportionality is $\widehat{\rho}_S/\widehat{\tau} \to \frac{3}{2}$ (this seems to contradict the population's counterpart $\rho_S = 3\tau = 0$ from the solution of Exercise 9.30, but the ratio ρ_S/τ is undefined rather than 3). This proportionality means that, under independence, both statistics have the same large-sample properties. A further study of these statistics as a special case of the class of *U-statistics* ("U" for unbiased) is introduced in Hoeffding (1948); this class also includes $\overline{x}$ and s^2.

The notion of ranks is inherently univariate. Its extension to the multivariate setup requires the introduction of the concept of a statistical depth function (the depth of a point within a distribution), first employed by Hotelling in 1929 in economics and Tukey in 1975 in statistics, and more recently developed especially by Liu, Serfling, Zuo, and Hallin; see Hallin, Paindaveine, and Šiman (2010) for this and for an introduction to a contour-based multivariate extension of the notion of quantiles.

10

Asymptotic theory

It should be clear from the previous chapter that sample statistics have distributions depending, in general, on the sample size n. The natural question one may ask is how these distributions are affected as n is varied deterministically and, in particular, as n increases. It turns out that one can get common limiting results, for a variety of settings, by analyzing what happens as $n \to \infty$, the *large-sample asymptotic theory*. Of course n is never infinitely large, but asymptotic results often provide good approximations when samples are "large". Before we can detail such results, we need to introduce some technical machinery which extends, to random setups, the usual concepts of limits, orders of magnitude, and rates of convergence. We will use a, b, c for nonrandom finite real numbers.

Consider a sequence of random variables $x_1, x_2, \dots$ with a corresponding sequence of c.d.f.s $F_1(u), F_2(u), \dots$, where $F_n(u) := \Pr(x_n \leqslant u)$. Now suppose that there exists a random variable x with c.d.f. $F(u)$ and the property that

$$\lim_{n\to\infty} F_n(u) = F(u)$$

for all values u at which the limiting F is continuous.[1] Then, we say that the sequence $\{x_n\}$ *converges in distribution* to x, denoted by $x_n \xrightarrow{d} x$, and we call the distribution of x the *limiting* (or *asymptotic*) *distribution* of x_n. A simple example is obtained by looking at Student's $\mathrm{t}(n)$ distribution, and noting that the standard normal is obtained by letting $n \to \infty$. This was encountered in Exercise 4.36 and in the introduction to Chapter 6. See also Exercises 4.9 and 10.32, which imply further examples of c.d.f. convergence. Multivariate generalizations of $x_n \xrightarrow{d} x$ are obtained by considering the convergence of the *joint* distribution (rather than just the marginal distributions) of the elements of a

[1]The set of discontinuity points of the c.d.f. F is countable (Chapter 2). This and the right-continuity of c.d.f.s imply that the limiting F is unique everywhere.

random vector, or by using the simplifying *Cramér–Wold device* of Exercise 10.15.

A convenient method to determine the limiting c.d.f. $F(u)$ is via the corresponding m.g.f. (if it exists) or c.f., as we will now see. Let each x_n have the c.f. $\varphi_n(\tau)$. Recall from Chapter 3 that this implies, inter alia, that $\varphi_n(\tau)$ is continuous at $\tau = 0$. If

$$\lim_{n\to\infty} \varphi_n(\tau) = \varphi(\tau),$$

where $\varphi(\tau)$ is the c.f. of some random variable x, then $x_n \xrightarrow{d} x$. An alternative formulation is the following: if $\lim_{n\to\infty} \varphi_n(\tau) = h(\tau)$ for all τ, and h is some function (not assumed to be a c.f.) that is continuous at $\tau = 0$, then $h(\tau)$ is the c.f. of some random variable x and $x_n \xrightarrow{d} x$. When formulating this convergence in terms of the m.g.f.s $m_n(t)$ and $m(t)$, rather than c.f.s, we need the further conditions that the m.g.f.s exist for t in an open neighborhood of $t = 0$ and that the convergence occurs in a closed subset of that neighborhood. If they exist, the moments of x are called *asymptotic moments*. Note, however, that they are not necessarily equal to the limit of the moments of x_n; see Exercise 10.8(c) and the end of Exercise 10.38 for counterexamples.

Now that we have described $x_n \xrightarrow{d} x$ in terms of the convergence of c.d.f.s or c.f.s, it is natural to ask whether the third description of random variables, the p.d.f., can be used in a similar way. The answer is unfortunately negative, in general, as will be seen in Exercise 10.2.

If, as $n \to \infty$, the density were to collapse to zero everywhere except at a single value of x, we would get a *degenerate limiting distribution* and we would need stronger modes of convergence to describe more fully what has happened. There are two such modes, which we list in order of increasing strength. The first of these two is

$$\lim_{n\to\infty} \Pr(|x_n - c| < \epsilon) = 1$$

for all $\epsilon > 0$. If this holds we say that x_n *converges in probability* to c as $n \to \infty$, and we write $x_n \xrightarrow{p} c$ or $\operatorname{plim} x_n = c$, usually dropping the subscript $n \to \infty$ from plim because this limit is almost invariably taken with respect to the sample size. The number c is called the *probability limit* of x_n. Clearly, $x_n - c \xrightarrow{p} 0$ and, for $c \neq 0$, we can also write $x_n/c \xrightarrow{p} 1$, using the same manipulations of constants that are allowable in the case of deterministic limits or equality relations.

There are a couple of remarks to make on this definition. First, it is not the same as $\lim_{n\to\infty} \Pr(x_n = c) = 1$; see Exercise 10.5(c). Second, it could be extended to allow for c to be replaced by x, a random variable defined on the same sigma-algebra as x_n but not depending on n, and this would still be a stronger mode of convergence than $x_n \xrightarrow{d} x$ (see Exercise 10.6 for details, as well as for a warning that $x_n \xrightarrow{d} x$ does not imply $x_n - x \xrightarrow{d} 0$). However, we prefer not to do so and, if $\lim_{n\to\infty} \Pr(|x_n - x| < \epsilon) = 1$, we shall write $z_n := x_n - x$ so that $\operatorname{plim} z_n = 0$. We do this to stress that the limit of some variate (in this case z_n) is degenerate.

Next, the strongest mode of stochastic convergence is one which corresponds to uniform convergence in the deterministic case. If the event $\{\lim_{n\to\infty} x_n = c\}$ occurs almost surely, that is,

$$\Pr\left(\lim_{n\to\infty} x_n = c\right) = 1,$$

then we say that x_n *converges almost surely* (or *with probability 1*) to c, and we write $x_n \to c$. Notice how this mode of convergence differs from the previous one. Alternative formulations of $x_n \to c$, which clarify this difference and the link with uniform convergence, include

$$\sup_{m \geqslant n} \{|x_m - c|\} \xrightarrow{p} 0$$

or, equivalently,

$$\lim_{n\to\infty} \Pr(|x_m - c| < \epsilon) = 1$$

for all $\epsilon > 0$ *and* all $m \geqslant n$; see Exercise 10.3(a) for a fourth formulation. The convergence $x_n \xrightarrow{p} c$ allows for subsequences of $\{x_n\}$ that do not converge, as long as the probability of their occurrence goes to 0 as n increases. Furthermore, we have $x_n \to c$ if this probability diminishes at the faster rate of $1/n^{1+\delta}$ with $\delta > 0$, but not necessarily otherwise; see Exercises 10.4 and 10.8(f). Convergence in moments will be introduced and related to the other two modes of convergence in Exercise 10.8. Multivariate generalizations of both modes of convergence considered here are obtained by using norms instead of absolute values.

We started with the mode of convergence that was simplest to formulate, $x_n \xrightarrow{d} x$, then specialized it to the other two: $x_n \xrightarrow{p} c$ and $x_n \to c$, respectively. For pedagogical reasons, we will now reverse the order of treatment when talking about the use of these methods, starting with the simplest applications. The last two modes of convergence have two corresponding important applications, which will be presented here in their simplest form, then generalized in the exercises. Consider a random sample $\{x_n\}$ from some unspecified distribution with mean μ and variance σ^2, both moments assumed to exist, and let $\overline{x}_n := n^{-1}\sum_{i=1}^n x_i$ denote the sample mean based on n observations. The *strong law of large numbers* (SLLN) states that $\overline{x}_n \to \mu$; that is, the sample mean converges almost surely to the population mean as $n \to \infty$. The conditions on the sample (i.i.d. with finite first two moments) can be weakened considerably while retaining the validity of the SLLN. They can be relaxed even further if we are willing to consider a weaker mode of convergence, in which case the result is the *weak law of large numbers* (WLLN) stating that $\overline{x}_n \xrightarrow{p} \mu$.

We saw in the previous chapter (Exercise 9.2) that the sequence of random variables

$$z_n := \frac{\overline{x}_n - \mu}{\sigma/\sqrt{n}} \tag{10.1}$$

is distributed with mean 0 and variance 1 (but is not necessarily $\mathrm{N}(0,1)$), and hence we say that z_n is a *standardized* statistic; see Chapter 4. More fundamentally, the factor $\sqrt{n}$ ensures that the statistic is *normalized* with respect to n: letting $n \to \infty$ will not cause the statistic to degenerate or diverge as a function of n. In addition to the result in (10.1), the *central limit theorem* (CLT) establishes the limiting distribution $z_n \xrightarrow{d} z$, where $z \sim \mathrm{N}(0,1)$. This is written alternatively as $z_n \overset{a}{\sim} \mathrm{N}(0,1)$ or $\sqrt{n}(\overline{x}_n - \mu) \overset{a}{\sim} \mathrm{N}(0,\sigma^2)$, where the symbol $\overset{a}{\sim}$ means *asymptotically distributed*. This alternative notation is more flexible, as it is sometimes used to allow n to be displayed on the right-hand side, for example $\overline{x}_n \overset{a}{\sim} \mathrm{N}(\mu, \sigma^2/n)$, which one should not do when using the convergence notation $\xrightarrow{d}$. We warn again that having a common limiting distribution does not imply that the variates are asymptotically the same: $z_n \overset{a}{\sim} \mathrm{N}(0,1)$ and $-z_n \overset{a}{\sim} \mathrm{N}(0,1)$, but clearly z_n and $-z_n$ are not the same! (It also illustrates the earlier warning that we cannot infer $z_n - z \xrightarrow{d} 0$ from $z_n \xrightarrow{d} z$.) Notice that this limiting distribution arises regardless of the type of distribution followed by x_i (subject to the conditions on x_i given earlier), which is why this type of theorem is also known as an *invariance principle*. Exercise 10.20 shows how to extend such results to continuously differentiable functions of $\overline{x}_n$ by the *delta method*.

We have talked about convergence, but we have not explicitly discussed how fast it occurs as n increases. Just as we have generalized deterministic limits to a stochastic context, we will now extend the definition of deterministic orders of magnitude (which the reader can find in Section A.3.4). We say that a sequence $\{x_n\}$ is *of probabilistic order smaller than* n^α (or *of order smaller than* n^α *in probability*), written as $x_n = o_p(n^\alpha)$, if

$$\frac{x_n}{n^\alpha} \xrightarrow{p} 0,$$

where α is an appropriate constant. This definition gives a strict upper bound on the rate of convergence of x_n as n increases. The next definition gives an upper bound that is weaker, in a similar sense to that in which $|u| \leqslant b$ is a weaker statement than $u = 0$. We say that a sequence $\{x_n\}$ is *of probabilistic order* n^α (or *of order* n^α *in probability*), written as $x_n = O_p(n^\alpha)$, if x_n/n^α is bounded in probability as n increases. More formally, $x_n = O_p(n^\alpha)$ if, for all $0 < \epsilon \leqslant 1$, there exists a finite integer n_ϵ and a finite constant b_ϵ such that

$$\Pr\left(\left|\frac{x_n}{n^\alpha}\right| \leqslant b_\epsilon\right) > 1 - \epsilon \tag{10.2}$$

for all $n > n_\epsilon$.

All the usual relations (for example addition and multiplication) between deterministic orders of magnitude apply here too. It should be borne in mind that orders of magnitude are inequality (not equivalence) relations. For example, if $x_n = o_p(n^\alpha)$, then we also have $x_n = o_p(n^{\alpha+\delta})$ for any $\delta > 0$. There are a few obvious relations between the previous concepts:

- $\operatorname{plim} x_n = c$ implies (but is not implied by) $x_n = O_p(1)$, since the latter can also accommodate $x_n \xrightarrow{d} x$ as is verifiable from (10.2) with $\alpha = 0$;
- $x_n = o_p(n^\alpha)$ implies (but is not implied by) $x_n = O_p(n^\alpha)$.

Notice that a strong mode of convergence will imply a weaker one, just as is the case with inequalities. One has to be careful that $\mathrm{E}\left(O_p\left(n^{\alpha}\right)\right) \neq O\left(n^{\alpha}\right)$ in general; see Exercise 10.8(c) for a counterexample.

Applying these new tools to the CLT seen earlier, we have $\overline{x}_n = O_p(1)$ since it converges to μ and, furthermore, $\overline{x}_n - \mu = O_p\left(1/\sqrt{n}\right)$. But can we derive any sharper bounds for the variate $\overline{x}_n - \mu$ or its standardized counterpart z_n of (10.1)? There is a *law of the iterated logarithm* (LIL) which states that

$$\Pr\left(\liminf_{n\to\infty}\frac{z_n}{\sqrt{2\log\left(\log\left(n\right)\right)}} = -1\right) = \Pr\left(\limsup_{n\to\infty}\frac{z_n}{\sqrt{2\log\left(\log\left(n\right)\right)}} = +1\right) = 1.$$

This is a very strong result, since these bounds hold almost surely. It also tells us that the tails of the limiting normal fill up at the very slow rate of $\sqrt{2\log\left(\log\left(n\right)\right)}$; for example,

$$\frac{\sqrt{2\log\left(\log\left(10^9\right)\right)}}{\sqrt{2\log\left(\log\left(10^3\right)\right)}} \approx 1.252,$$

where increasing n from one thousand to one billion will only increase the bound by about 25.2%.

It may be that convergence does not occur, in which case we would like to know what happens to $\overline{x}_n$. We have alluded to this situation in the introduction to Chapter 9, when talking about the average of Cauchy variates. The Cauchy distribution is one where moments do not exist, and it violates the CLT (and LLN) since its sample mean does not settle down to any single value as $n \to \infty$. For example, the distribution of insurance claims may be such that very large values can occur with substantial probability, so what happens to the insurance firm's average claim $\overline{x}_n$? In the CLT case, we assumed that the variance was finite. Here, instead, we consider the rate of decay of the c.d.f.'s tail. We give a simple version of the theorem. Assume that $\{x_n\}$ is a random sample from a distribution symmetric around 0 and satisfying

$$\lim_{u\to\infty} u^p \Pr\left(|x| > u\right) = 2c, \tag{10.3}$$

where c is a positive finite constant and $p \in (0,2)$, implying that the p.d.f. decays at a rate of $1/u^{p+1}$ (these tails are also called Pareto-like: see Table 4.2). Then, we have the *stable limit theorem* (SLT) that $n^{1-1/p}\,\overline{x}_n \overset{a}{\sim} \mathrm{S}^p(0,\lambda,0)$, where S^p is the stable law with index p and scale parameter

$$\lambda = \begin{cases} \left(2c\Gamma\left(1-p\right)\cos\left(p\pi/2\right)\right)^{1/p} & (p \neq 1), \\ \pi c & (p = 1), \end{cases}$$

and we say that the distribution in (10.3) is *in the domain of attraction* of S^p; see the introduction to Chapter 4 for the definition of S^p. Recall that the stable distribution with $p = 2$ is the normal c.d.f. whose tails decay exponentially (see Exercise 10.40 for further details), unlike those of (10.3). It is covered in the CLT, but not in the SLT where we focus on $p \in (0,2)$. As implied by the derivations in Exercises 3.9 and 3.24, the tails of our distribution in (10.3) lead to the variance of x being infinite. To continue the discussion of the previous chapter, $p = 1$ is a case where the sample mean, $\overline{x}_n$, is of the same order of magnitude as the individual observations, x_i. The SLT says that its limit is a centered Cauchy with scale πc; equivalently, $\overline{x}_n / (\pi c) \overset{a}{\sim} \text{Cau}(0, 1)$. To verify this scale, recall that the standard Cauchy c.d.f. tends to 0 or 1 at the rate of $1/|\pi u|$, so (10.3) for $x_i \sim \text{Cau}(0, 1)$ has $p = 1$ and $c = 1/\pi$ (since symmetry around 0 implies $\Pr(|x| \geqslant u) = 2F_x(-u)$ for $u > 0$), and the SLT implies a scale of $\pi c = 1$ also for $\overline{x}_n \overset{a}{\sim} \text{Cau}(0, 1)$, something we already know exactly (not just asymptotically) from Exercise 7.3(a). For $p < 1$, the mean $\overline{x}_n$ needs to be *divided* by an increasing function of n to make it stable! Contrast this with the CLT, where $\overline{x}_n$ is multiplied by $\sqrt{n}$ to normalize it. The reader is encouraged to revisit the details of stable laws given in Chapter 4.

Our example of an insurance firm motivates the last limit theorem of this chapter. Such a firm would be interested not only in the behavior of the average claim, but also that of the largest one. After all, the firm's survival may depend on it! This is the subject matter of *extreme value theory* (EVT), and we touched on it in Exercise 7.37. It turns out that we can find another invariance principle, this time for extreme observations (instead of the mean) of a random sample $\{x_n\}$ drawn from the common distribution $F_1(u)$. We will focus on the maximum only, since the minimum of a variate is the maximum of its negative. Let $y_n := \max_{i \leqslant n} \{x_i\}$ be the largest order statistic, and assume that we can find deterministic sequences $\{a_n\}$ and $\{b_n\}$ such that $b_n > 0$ and $z_n := (y_n - a_n)/b_n$ has a nondegenerate limiting distribution. Then, this limiting distribution is the generalized extreme value (GEV) c.d.f. $\exp(-(1 + \lambda w/p)^{-p})$; see the introduction to Chapter 4 and Exercise 4.28 (we have changed the sign of p here so that it corresponds to the rest of the discussion). There are only three possible types of limit. Type I (the Gumbel case of $p^{-1} \to 0$) is obtained if and only if $1 - F_1(u)$ decays exponentially fast as u increases. Type II (the Fréchet case of $p > 0$) is obtained if and only if the upper tail $1 - F_1(u)$ decays when $u \to \infty$ as

$$cl(u)/u^p \qquad (p > 0), \tag{10.4}$$

where $c > 0$ is a constant and l is a *slowly varying function* as $u \to \infty$: l is positive and

$$\lim_{u \to \infty} \frac{l(tu)}{l(u)} = 1 \qquad (\text{for all } t > 0).$$

In addition to the simplest example where l is a constant, a famous special case of l is that of logarithmic functions, including the iterated logarithm seen earlier. Comparing this tail of $1 - F_1(u)$ with (10.3), we see that it decays in a Pareto-like manner, apart from the slowly varying function, hence the importance of this distribution for extreme events. Finally, Type III (the Weibull case of $p < 0$) is obtained if and only if $1 - F_1(u)$ decays as

$$cl(u_{\max} - u) \times (u_{\max} - u)^{-p} \qquad (p < 0) \tag{10.5}$$

when $u \to u_{\max}$ and the variate x is bounded above by a finite constant $u_{\max}$, namely one at which $F_1(u_{\max}) = 1$ but $F_1(u_{\max} - \epsilon) < 1$ for all $\epsilon > 0$, and here we define $l(w)$ to be slowly varying as $w \to 0^+$ instead:

$$\lim_{w \to 0^+} \frac{l(tw)}{l(w)} = 1 \qquad (\text{for all } t > 0).$$

Such a $u_{\max}$ is known as a finite *upper-terminal* value. For $0 < -p < 1$, the c.d.f. F_1 is not S-shaped as usual: as $u \to u_{\max}$, the c.d.f. becomes a convex function whose increase accelerates until it reaches $F_1(u_{\max}) = 1$, unlike in all the remaining cases where deceleration happens. As before, we say that a distribution satisfying one of the tail conditions (such as (10.5)) is in the domain of attraction of the corresponding limit law (such as Type III or Weibull).

The exercises in this chapter follow roughly the same sequence of topics introduced above, split into three sections: convergence modes (univariate then more general), central limits, and other limits. The mathematical expression $g(n) = O(n^{\alpha})$ is sometimes not sufficiently precise for the required purposes, since it is an inequality relation. We therefore occasionally use the mathematical (not statistical) symbol $\sim$ to denote the asymptotic equivalence of the two sides: $a_n \sim b_n$ means that $a_n/b_n \to 1$. The first term of a series expansion arranged by declining orders of magnitude is called its *leading term*. For example, $g(n) := 3n^2 + n \sim 3n^2$, where $3n^2$ is the leading term as $n \to \infty$. This could have been written as $g(n) = O(n^2)$ without indicating the constant 3, or even as $g(n) = O(n^4)$ since $g(n)/n^4$ is also bounded as $n \to \infty$. Both these examples show that the order notation may not be sufficiently informative for some purposes, which is why the leading-term symbol $\sim$ is useful. In this chapter, we resort to the latter mainly in Exercises 10.41, 10.43, and 10.48. More about this symbol can be found in Section A.3.4.

10.1 Modes of convergence of variates

Exercise 10.1 (Discrete to continuous uniform) Consider the sequence of random variables $\{x_n\}$ with $\Pr(x_n = i/n) = 1/n$ for all $i = 1, \dots, n$. Show that $x_n \xrightarrow{d} x$, where x has a continuous standard uniform distribution.

Solution

We provide two solutions. The first solution uses the c.d.f. where, for $j = 1, \dots, n-1$,

$$F_n(u) := \Pr(x_n \leqslant u) = \begin{cases} 0 & (u < 1/n), \\ j/n & (j/n \leqslant u < (j+1)/n), \\ 1 & (u \geqslant 1), \end{cases} \to \begin{cases} 0 & (u < 0), \\ u & (0 \leqslant u < 1), \\ 1 & (u \geqslant 1), \end{cases}$$

since $u \in [j/n, (j+1)/n)$ becomes the point $u = \lim_{n\to\infty} j/n$. (Rationals are dense in the set of real numbers, so any real u can be written as the limit of a rational sequence; see Section A.3.1.) The displayed limiting c.d.f. is that of a $\mathrm{U}_{(0,1)}$ variate.

The second solution is based on the m.g.f.:

$$m_{x_n}(t) = \mathrm{E}(\mathrm{e}^{tx_n}) = \frac{1}{n}\sum_{j=1}^{n} \mathrm{e}^{tj/n} = \frac{\mathrm{e}^{t/n}}{n}\sum_{i=0}^{n-1}\left(\mathrm{e}^{t/n}\right)^i$$

$$= \frac{\mathrm{e}^{t/n}(1-\mathrm{e}^t)}{n(1-\mathrm{e}^{t/n})} = \frac{1-\mathrm{e}^t}{t} \times \frac{(t/n)\mathrm{e}^{t/n}}{1-\mathrm{e}^{t/n}}.$$

Since, by l'Hôpital's rule,

$$\lim_{\tau\to 0}\frac{\tau \mathrm{e}^\tau}{1-\mathrm{e}^\tau} = \lim_{\tau\to 0}\frac{\mathrm{e}^\tau + \tau\mathrm{e}^\tau}{-\mathrm{e}^\tau} = -1,$$

we obtain

$$\lim_{n\to\infty} m_{x_n}(t) = \frac{\mathrm{e}^t - 1}{t},$$

which we recognize as the m.g.f. of the $\mathrm{U}_{(0,1)}$ distribution; see, for example, Table 4.2.

Exercise 10.2 (Continuity point of limiting c.d.f.) For $n = 1, 2, \dots$, let x_n be a random variable such that

$$\Pr\left(x_n = 1 + \frac{1}{n}\right) = \Pr\left(x_n = 2 + \frac{1}{n}\right) = \frac{1}{2},$$

and denote the c.d.f. of x_n by F_n. Similarly, let F be the c.d.f. of x that has p.d.f.

$$\Pr(x = 1) = \Pr(x = 2) = \frac{1}{2}.$$

Show that $F_n(u) \to F(u)$ as $n \to \infty$, where u is a continuity point of F.

Solution

We have

$$\Pr(x_n \leqslant u) = \begin{cases} 0 & (u < 1 + \frac{1}{n}), \\ \frac{1}{2} & (1 + \frac{1}{n} \leqslant u < 2 + \frac{1}{n}), \\ 1 & (u \geqslant 2 + \frac{1}{n}), \end{cases} \to \begin{cases} 0 & (u < 1), \\ \frac{1}{2} & (1 \leqslant u < 2), \\ 1 & (u \geqslant 2). \end{cases}$$

Now F_n tends to F, except at the two points $u = 1$ and $u = 2$. For all finite n, we have $F_n(1) = 0$ but $F(1) = \frac{1}{2}$, and $F_n(2) = \frac{1}{2}$ but $F(2) = 1$. However, $u = 1, 2$ are not continuity points of F. This explains the requirement that u is a continuity point in the definition of convergence in distribution: x is a well-defined random variable to which x_n converges, and points like $u = 1, 2$ must be ruled out of the comparison of $\lim_n F_n$ and F. Note that the corresponding p.d.f.s $\{f_n(u)\}$ do *not* converge to $f(u)$ as $n \to \infty$, neither at the continuity points of F nor elsewhere. We have $f(u) = 0$ at continuity points of F, but $f_n(u) = \frac{1}{2}$ at two of these points ($1 + 1/n$ and $2 + 1/n$). At $u = 1, 2$, we have $f_n(u) = 0$ but $f(u) = \frac{1}{2}$.

***Exercise 10.3 (Borel–Cantelli lemmas)** Let $\{A_n\}$ be a sequence of events belonging to some sigma-field of an experiment. Define the set

$$\{A_n \text{ i.o.}\} := \lim_{m\to\infty} \bigcup_{n\geqslant m} A_n,$$

which is shorthand for the event that is called "A_n occurs *infinitely often* (i.o.)"; to understand the i.o. terminology, let $D_m := \bigcup_{n=m}^{\infty} A_n$ in the relation obtained in Exercise 1.7(b).
(a) Prove that if $\sum_{n=1}^{\infty} \Pr(A_n) < \infty$, then $\Pr(A_n \text{ i.o.}) = 0$. Use this to obtain an alternative definition of almost-sure convergence by defining A_n of $\Pr(A_n \text{ i.o.})$ and $\Pr(A_n^c \text{ i.o.})$.
(b) Prove that if the sequence of events $\{A_n\}$ is independent and $\sum_{n=1}^{\infty} \Pr(A_n) = \infty$, then $\Pr(A_n \text{ i.o.}) = 1$. [Hint: Use the inequality in Exercise 1.20.]

Solution

(a) In this part, we do not assume that $\{A_n\}$ is an independent sequence. By Exercise 1.7,

$$\Pr(A_n \text{ i.o.}) \equiv \Pr\left(\lim_{m\to\infty} \bigcup_{n=m}^{\infty} A_n\right) = \lim_{m\to\infty} \Pr\left(\bigcup_{n=m}^{\infty} A_n\right)$$

since $\bigcup_{n=m}^{\infty} A_n \subseteq \bigcup_{n=m-1}^{\infty} A_n$ (or $D_m \subseteq D_{m-1}$). Then

$$\Pr(A_n \text{ i.o.}) \leqslant \lim_{m\to\infty} \sum_{n=m}^{\infty} \Pr(A_n).$$

But the question states that $\{\Pr(A_n)\}_{n=1}^{\infty}$ is an absolutely convergent series, so its terms must decline at a rate $n^{-1-\delta}$ for some $\delta > 0$ (see Section A.3.2), hence $\sum_{n=m}^{\infty} \Pr(A_n) = O(m^{-\delta})$ and tends to zero as $m \to \infty$.

This lemma clarifies the relation between the alternative definitions of almost-sure convergence, $x_n \to c$, given in the introduction. It also suggests a further alternative definition: for all $\epsilon > 0$,

$$\Pr(|x_n - c| \geqslant \epsilon \text{ i.o.}) = 0$$

or, equivalently, $\Pr(|x_n - c| < \epsilon \text{ i.o.}) = 1$. We need to sound a note of caution in connection with this last equivalence. In general, $\{A_n \text{ i.o.}\}^c \neq \{A_n^c \text{ i.o.}\}$. The complement of $\{A_n \text{ i.o.}\}$ is

$$\{A_n \text{ occurs for finitely many } n\},$$

that is, $\{A_n^c$ occurs for all but finitely many $n\}$, and is denoted by $\lim_{m\to\infty} \bigcap_{n\geqslant m} A_n^c$ (the complement of $\lim_{m\to\infty} \bigcup_{n\geqslant m} A_n$). It is a subset of $\lim_{m\to\infty} \bigcup_{n\geqslant m} A_n^c$ or $\{A_n^c \text{ i.o.}\}$, and may or may not be equal to it in the limit. In the special case of $\Pr(A_n^c \text{ i.o.}) = 0$, its subset $\{A_n \text{ i.o.}\}^c$ will also have zero probability and hence $\Pr(A_n \text{ i.o.}) = 1$, as we have done in redefining almost-sure convergence. However, in general,

$$\Pr(A_n \text{ i.o.}) = 1 - \Pr(\{A_n \text{ i.o.}\}^c) \geqslant 1 - \Pr(A_n^c \text{ i.o.}).$$

(b) By the independence of $\{A_n\}$, we can use the inequality in Exercise 1.20 as

$$\Pr\left(\bigcap_{n=m}^{\infty} A_n^c\right) \leqslant \exp\left(-\sum_{n=m}^{\infty} \Pr(A_n)\right) = \exp(-\infty) = 0$$

for any m, hence $\Pr(\bigcap_{n=m}^{\infty} A_n^c) = 0$ and De Morgan's law implies that

$$\Pr\left(\bigcup_{n=m}^{\infty} A_n\right) = 1 - \Pr\left(\bigcap_{n=m}^{\infty} A_n^c\right) = 1.$$

Exercise 10.4 (Divergent subsequence) Let $\{x_n\}$ be an independent sequence, where each x_n has only two possible values,

$$\Pr(x_n = c) = 1 - \frac{1}{n} \quad \text{and} \quad \Pr(x_n = n) = \frac{1}{n}.$$

Show that x_n converges to c in probability, but not almost surely. Can we still say that $x_n = O_p(1)$?

Solution

We have $\lim_{n\to\infty} \Pr(x_n = c) = 1$; hence

$$\lim_{n\to\infty} \Pr(|x_n - c| < \epsilon) = 1$$

for all $\epsilon > 0$, as required for convergence in probability to c. We can see that convergence in probability allows for divergent subsequences whenever their probability tends to 0. However, for $\epsilon > 0$,

$$\sum_{n=1}^{\infty} \Pr(|x_n - c| > \epsilon) = \sum_{n=1}^{\infty} \Pr(x_n = n) = \sum_{n=1}^{\infty} \frac{1}{n} = -\log(0^+) = \infty$$

by the logarithmic expansion in Section A.3.2. Therefore,

$$\Pr(|x_n - c| > \epsilon \quad \text{i.o.}) = 1$$

by the second Borel–Cantelli lemma in Exercise 10.3(b), and almost-sure convergence does not take place. There is a divergent subsequence of $\{x_n\}$ having $x_n = n$ which causes this phenomenon, but a divergent subsequence, per se, is not enough to violate almost-sure convergence, as we shall see in Exercises 10.5(d) and 10.8(f). In fact, the first Borel–Cantelli lemma shows that a.s. convergence obtains (regardless of whether the sequence is independent) whenever $\Pr(|x_n - c| > \epsilon) = O(1/n^{1+\delta})$ and $\delta > 0$, by the criteria for the convergence of infinite series in Section A.3.2.

The answer is yes, $x_n = O_p(1)$ in spite of the divergent subsequence. We will need to show that x_n satisfies the definition of $O_p(1)$ as stated in the introduction. Taking $b_\epsilon = |c|$ in (10.2),

$$\Pr(|x_n| \leqslant b_\epsilon) \geqslant \Pr(x_n = c) = 1 - \frac{1}{n} > 1 - \frac{1}{n_\epsilon}$$

for all $n > n_\epsilon$, and the result follows by choosing some $n_\epsilon \geqslant 1/\epsilon$. A similar derivation can be used to show that any variate converging in probability will also be $O_p(1)$.

***Exercise 10.5 (Convergence a.s. and in p)** Consider a sequence $\{x_n\}$ of random variables. Show that:
(a) $x_n \to c$ implies that $x_n \xrightarrow{p} c$;
(b) $x_n \xrightarrow{p} c$ implies that there is a subsequence of $\{x_n\}$ which converges a.s. to c. [Hint: Choose a subsequence of $\{x_n\}$ such that Exercise 10.3(a) applies.]
(c) $\lim_{n\to\infty} \Pr(x_n = c) = 1$ is stronger than $x_n \xrightarrow{p} c$;
(d) $\lim_{n\to\infty} \Pr(x_n = c) = 1$ is neither stronger nor weaker than $x_n \to c$.

Solution
(a) If $\sup_{m\geqslant n}\{|x_m - c|\} \xrightarrow{p} 0$, then $|x_n - c| \xrightarrow{p} 0$ as required.
(b) We need to prove that there exists a nonrandom subsequence of the index $\{n\}_{n=1}^{\infty}$, say $\{n_i\}_{i=1}^{\infty}$, such that $x_{n_i} \to c$. Now, $x_n \xrightarrow{p} c$ means that the deterministic sequence of $\Pr(|x_n - c| \geqslant \epsilon) \in [0,1]$ has

$$\lim_{n\to\infty} \Pr(|x_n - c| \geqslant \epsilon) = 0$$

for all $\epsilon > 0$, so there are infinitely many n_i's that we can choose from this sequence such that

$$\Pr(|x_{n_i} - c| > 1/i) \leqslant 1/i^{1+\delta},$$

where $\delta > 0$. Then, for $\epsilon > 1/i$, we have $\Pr(|x_{n_i} - c| > \epsilon) \leqslant \Pr(|x_{n_i} - c| > 1/i)$ and

$$\sum_{i>1/\epsilon} \Pr(|x_{n_i} - c| > \epsilon) \leqslant \sum_{i>1/\epsilon} \Pr(|x_{n_i} - c| > 1/i) \leqslant \sum_{i>1/\epsilon} 1/i^{1+\delta} < \infty$$

by the criteria for the convergence of infinite series in Section A.3.2. This holds for each $\epsilon > 0$, so the first Borel–Cantelli lemma of Exercise 10.3(a) implies that $\Pr(|x_{n_i} - c| > \epsilon \text{ i.o.}) = 0$.
(c) If $\lim_{n\to\infty} \Pr(x_n = c) = 1$, then

$$\lim_{n\to\infty} \Pr(|x_n - c| < \epsilon) = 1$$

for all $\epsilon > 0$, hence $x_n \xrightarrow{p} c$. However, if

$$\Pr(x_n = 0) = \frac{1}{n} \quad \text{and} \quad \Pr\left(x_n = \frac{1}{n}\right) = 1 - \frac{1}{n},$$

then $\lim_{n\to\infty} \Pr(x_n = 0) \neq 1$ in spite of $x_n \xrightarrow{p} 0$.
(d) Define a sequence $\{x_n\}$ such that

$$\Pr(x_n = 0) = \frac{1}{n} \quad \text{and} \quad \Pr\left(x_n = \frac{1}{n}\right) = 1 - \frac{1}{n},$$

where we see that $\lim_{n\to\infty} \Pr(x_n = 0) = 0 \neq 1$. However, as in the proof of (b),

$$\sum_{n>1/\epsilon} \Pr(x_n > \epsilon) \leqslant \sum_{n>1/\epsilon} \Pr(x_n > 1/n) = 0,$$

so $\Pr(x_n > \epsilon \text{ i.o.}) = 0$ and $x_n \to 0$.

To show that the reverse implication does not hold either, define an independent sequence $\{x_n\}$ such that

$$\Pr(x_n = 0) = 1 - \frac{1}{n} \quad \text{and} \quad \Pr(x_n = 1) = \frac{1}{n},$$

then $\lim_{n\to\infty} \Pr(x_n = 0) = 1$, but applying the second Borel–Cantelli lemma as in Exercise 10.4 shows that x_n does not converge almost surely to zero. Note that the concept $\lim_{n\to\infty} \Pr(x_n = c) = 1$ is not as practical as $x_n \to c$, since it considers only one value of the variate.

Exercise 10.6 (Convergence in p and in d) Consider a sequence $\{x_n\}$ of random variables. Show that:
(a) $x_n \xrightarrow{d} c$ is equivalent to $x_n \xrightarrow{p} c$ (where we stress that c is a constant);
(b) $x_n \xrightarrow{d} x$ does not necessarily imply that $x_n - x \xrightarrow{p} 0$ (or $x_n \xrightarrow{p} x$);
(c) $x_n \xrightarrow{d} x$ does not necessarily imply that $x_n - x \xrightarrow{d} 0$.

Solution
(a) First, assume that $x_n \xrightarrow{d} c$; hence $F_n(u) \to 0$ for every $u < c$ and $F_n(u) \to 1$ for every $u > c$ (note that c is not a continuity point of F, which is why we have excluded $u = c$ from consideration here). Then, for $\epsilon > 0$,

$$\begin{aligned}\Pr(|x_n - c| \geqslant \epsilon) &= \Pr(x_n - c \leqslant -\epsilon) + \Pr(x_n - c \geqslant \epsilon)\\ &= \Pr(x_n \leqslant c - \epsilon) + \Pr(x_n \geqslant c + \epsilon)\\ &= F_n(c - \epsilon) + \Pr(x_n = c + \epsilon) + 1 - F_n(c + \epsilon).\end{aligned}$$

As $n \to \infty$, we have $F(c - \epsilon) = 0$ and $\Pr(x = c + \epsilon) = 0$, while $F(c + \epsilon) = 1$, hence

$$x_n \xrightarrow{d} c \implies x_n \xrightarrow{p} c.$$

The same decomposition,

$$\Pr(|x_n - c| \geqslant \epsilon) = \Pr(x_n \leqslant c - \epsilon) + \Pr(x_n \geqslant c + \epsilon),$$

also shows the reverse implication. As the left-hand side goes to zero when $n \to \infty$, so does each term on the right-hand side because probabilities cannot be negative. Since this holds for all $\epsilon > 0$, we get $\Pr(x_n = c) = 1$ in the limit, hence establishing $x_n \xrightarrow{d} c$.
(b) Consider a random sample $\{x_n\}$ from a distribution with mean 0 and variance 1. Then $x_n \xrightarrow{d} x_1$, but $\Pr(|x_n - x_1| > \epsilon) = \Pr(|y| > \epsilon)$, where y has mean 0 and variance 2, and hence does not depend on n. This probability is strictly positive for some $\epsilon > 0$, so the sequence does not converge in probability.

(c) The counterexample in (b) also illustrates that $x_n \xrightarrow{d} x$ does not necessarily imply that $x_n - x \xrightarrow{d} 0$. In fact, if the implication held, then (a) would further imply $x_n - x \xrightarrow{p} 0$, in contradiction of (b)! This highlights the fact that two variates (such as x and x_n) can have the same asymptotic distribution without being identical variates in the limit. We noted a similar idea as far back as in Chapter 2. It cautions us not to regard $x_n \xrightarrow{d} x$ as an equality where x can be subtracted from both sides. This is in contrast with the definition of $\operatorname{plim} x_n$. It also explains why the proof of the next exercise is nontrivial, even though $x_n \xrightarrow{p} c \Longrightarrow x_n \xrightarrow{d} c$ is easy to show as in (a).

Exercise 10.7 (Convergence in p and in d, continued) Consider a sequence of variates $\{x_n\}$ with c.d.f.s $\{F_n\}$, and a variate x with c.d.f. F. Show that:
(a) $\Pr(x_n \leqslant u) \leqslant F(u+\epsilon) + \psi_n(\epsilon)$, where $\epsilon > 0$ is arbitrary and

$$\psi_n(\epsilon) := \Pr(|x_n - x| > \epsilon);$$

(b) $x_n - x \xrightarrow{p} 0$ (or $x_n \xrightarrow{p} x$) implies that $x_n \xrightarrow{d} x$.

Solution
(a) Intuitively, this decomposition provides a separation of the limiting F from the deviations $x_n - x$. We shall use shorthand such as $\{x_n \leqslant u\}$ for the set $\{x_n : x_n \leqslant u\}$. We may partition the set (see Exercise 1.6)

$$\{x_n \leqslant u\} = \{x_n \leqslant u, x \leqslant u+\epsilon\} \cup \{x_n \leqslant u, x > u+\epsilon\},$$

such that

$$\Pr(x_n \leqslant u) = \Pr(x \leqslant u+\epsilon, x_n \leqslant u) + \Pr(x > u+\epsilon, u \geqslant x_n).$$

Since $\{x \leqslant u+\epsilon, x_n \leqslant u\} \subseteq \{x \leqslant u+\epsilon\}$ and

$$x > u+\epsilon \quad \text{and} \quad u \geqslant x_n \quad \Longrightarrow \quad x > x_n + \epsilon,$$

Exercise 1.5(c) gives

$$\Pr(x_n \leqslant u) \leqslant \Pr(x \leqslant u+\epsilon) + \Pr(x - x_n > \epsilon) \leqslant F(u+\epsilon) + \psi_n(\epsilon),$$

the last inequality following from $\{x - x_n > \epsilon\} \subseteq \{|x - x_n| > \epsilon\}$.
(b) As before,

$$\{x \leqslant u-\epsilon\} = \{x \leqslant u-\epsilon, x_n \leqslant u\} \cup \{x \leqslant u-\epsilon, x_n > u\}$$

implies that

$$F(u-\epsilon) \leqslant \Pr(x_n \leqslant u) + \psi_n(\epsilon).$$

Hence,

$$F(u-\epsilon) - \psi_n(\epsilon) \leqslant \Pr(x_n \leqslant u) \leqslant F(u+\epsilon) + \psi_n(\epsilon).$$

Now choose u to be a continuity point of F, then take limits as $n \to \infty$. Since $x_n - x \xrightarrow{p} 0$, we have $\psi_n(\epsilon) \to 0$. Furthermore, since F is continuous at u, we have $F(u-\epsilon) \to F(u)$ and $F(u+\epsilon) \to F(u)$ as $\epsilon \to 0$, and the result follows. Note that this result also means that $x_n - x \xrightarrow{d} 0$ implies $x_n \xrightarrow{d} x$, because of the equivalence in Exercise 10.6(a).

Exercise 10.8 (Convergence in moments, in p, and a.s.) Consider a sequence of random variables $\{x_n\}$. Suppose that $\lim_{n\to\infty} \mathrm{E}\left(|x_n - c|^\alpha\right) = 0$ for some $\alpha > 0$. This is known as *convergence in the α-th moment* (or *convergence in L_α*), with the special cases of *convergence in mean* when $\alpha = 1$ and *convergence in mean-square* when $\alpha = 2$.
(a) Show that convergence in L_α implies that $x_n \xrightarrow{p} c$.
(b) Hence, show that if $\mathrm{E}(x_n) \to \mu$ and $\mathrm{var}(x_n) \to 0$ as $n \to \infty$, then $x_n \xrightarrow{p} \mu$. (We stress that $\mathrm{E}(x_n) \to \mu$ is a weaker condition than $\mathrm{E}(|x_n - \mu|) \to 0$.)
(c) Show that the converse of (b) is not true.
(d) Show that the converse of (a) is not true.
(e) Show that convergence in L_α need not imply almost-sure convergence.
(f) Show that almost-sure convergence need not imply convergence in L_α.

Solution
(a) To link expectations with probabilities, we use Markov's inequality (Exercise 3.12) to find that

$$\Pr(|x_n - c| \geqslant \epsilon) = \Pr(|x_n - c|^\alpha \geqslant \epsilon^\alpha) \leqslant \frac{\mathrm{E}\left(|x_n - c|^\alpha\right)}{\epsilon^\alpha}$$

for $\epsilon > 0$. As $n \to \infty$, convergence in L_α gives $\mathrm{E}\left(|x_n - c|^\alpha\right) \to 0$, and the inequality implies that $\Pr\left(|x_n - c| \geqslant \epsilon\right) \to 0$.
(b) Let $c = \mu$ and $\alpha = 2$. Exercise 3.17 implies that

$$\mathrm{E}\left[(x_n - \mu)^2\right] = \mathrm{var}(x_n) + \left(\mathrm{E}(x_n) - \mu\right)^2,$$

where $\mathrm{var}(x_n) := \mathrm{E}\left[(x_n - \mathrm{E}(x_n))^2\right]$. If $\mathrm{E}(x_n) \to \mu$ and $\mathrm{var}(x_n) \to 0$ as $n \to \infty$, then $\mathrm{E}\left[(x_n - \mu)^2\right] \to 0$. By part (a), this implies that $x_n \xrightarrow{p} \mu$.
(c) In the example of Exercise 10.4, we have $\operatorname{plim} x_n = c$, but

$$\mathrm{E}(x_n) = \left(1 - \frac{1}{n}\right)c + \left(\frac{1}{n}\right)n \to c + 1 \neq c = \mathrm{E}(x_\infty).$$

Furthermore,

$$\mathrm{E}\left(x_n^2\right) = \left(1 - \frac{1}{n}\right)c^2 + \left(\frac{1}{n}\right)n^2 = O(n)$$

and $\mathrm{var}(x_n) \to \infty$. Clearly, convergence in probability does not require the existence of moments.

Notice that this shows that $x_n^2 = O_p(1)$ but $\mathrm{E}\left(x_n^2\right) \neq O(1)$, so it does not necessarily hold that $\mathrm{E}\left(O_p(1)\right) = O(1)$. Notice also that $\mathrm{E}\left(|x_n|\right) \to |c| + 1 < \infty$, so the mean exists even asymptotically. However, we did *not* have convergence in mean in this example, as we shall now see.

(d) We can alter the counterexample in (c) slightly to show that the converse of (a) is not generally true. Suppose that

$$\Pr(x_n = c) = 1 - \frac{1}{n} \quad \text{and} \quad \Pr\left(x_n = n^{1/\alpha}\right) = \frac{1}{n}.$$

We still have convergence in probability, but there exists no b such that $\mathrm{E}(|x_n - b|^\alpha) \to 0$, because

$$\mathrm{E}(|x_n - b|^\alpha) = \left(1 - \frac{1}{n}\right)|c - b|^\alpha + \left(\frac{1}{n}\right)\left|n^{1/\alpha} - b\right|^\alpha$$

has a strictly positive limit for all b, c.

(e) We can alter the counterexample in (c) again to obtain this result. Suppose that

$$\Pr(x_n = c) = 1 - \frac{1}{n} \quad \text{and} \quad \Pr\left(x_n = n^{1/(2\alpha)}\right) = \frac{1}{n}.$$

We now have convergence in L_α, since

$$\mathrm{E}(|x_n - c|^\alpha) = \left(1 - \frac{1}{n}\right)|c - c|^\alpha + \left(\frac{1}{n}\right)\left|n^{1/(2\alpha)} - c\right|^\alpha \to 0$$

at a rate $1/\sqrt{n}$, but we still have no almost-sure convergence because the divergent subsequence has probability $1/n$, and the same proof as in Exercise 10.4 applies here.

(f) Suppose that

$$\Pr(x_n = c) = 1 - \frac{1}{n^2} \quad \text{and} \quad \Pr\left(x_n = n^{2/\alpha}\right) = \frac{1}{n^2}.$$

We do not have convergence in L_α, because

$$\mathrm{E}(|x_n - b|^\alpha) = \left(1 - \frac{1}{n^2}\right)|c - b|^\alpha + \left(\frac{1}{n^2}\right)\left|n^{2/\alpha} - b\right|^\alpha$$

has a strictly positive limit for all b, c. However, we have almost sure convergence. The reason is that, by the criteria for the convergence of series in Section A.3.2,

$$\sum_{n=1}^{\infty} \frac{1}{n^2} < \infty$$

(actually $\sum_{n=1}^{\infty} 1/n^2 = \pi^2/6$) and the first Borel–Cantelli lemma (Exercise 10.3(a)) gives $\Pr(x_n \neq c \text{ i.o.}) = 0$. Note that the subsequence having $x_n = n^{2/\alpha}$ is divergent, but sufficiently improbable (by the Borel–Cantelli lemma) that we get almost-sure convergence.

Exercise 10.9 (Helly–Bray theorem) Let F_n, F be the c.d.f.s of x_n, x. Prove that, if $F_n \to F$ at the continuity points of F, then $\mathrm{E}(g(x_n)) \to \mathrm{E}(g(x))$ for every bounded continuous function g. [Hint: Use the interval-splitting and convergence properties of Stieltjes integrals, given in Section A.4.3.]

Solution

Since g is a bounded function, its expectations exist. Taking two continuity points $u_1 < u_2$

of F, we obtain

$$\mathrm{E}\left(g(x_n)\right) - \mathrm{E}\left(g(x)\right) = \left(\int_{-\infty}^{u_1} + \int_{u_1}^{u_2} + \int_{u_2}^{\infty}\right) g\left(u\right) \mathrm{d}(F_n\left(u\right) - F\left(u\right))$$

by applying (twice) the interval-splitting property of Stieltjes integrals. Since g is continuous, we can apply the convergence property of Stieltjes integrals to the middle integral. We get

$$\int_{u_1}^{u_2} g\left(u\right) \mathrm{d}(F_n\left(u\right) - F\left(u\right)) \to 0$$

as $F_n\left(u\right) \to F\left(u\right)$ at any continuity point u and as the domains of definition of F_n and F coincide. It remains to show that the two integrals over the tails of the distribution also converge to zero. Since g is bounded, we write $|g\left(u\right)| < c$ for some $c < \infty$ and

$$\begin{aligned}\left|\int_{-\infty}^{u_1} g\left(u\right) \mathrm{d}(F_n\left(u\right) - F\left(u\right))\right| &\leqslant \left|\int_{-\infty}^{u_1} g\left(u\right) \mathrm{d}F_n\left(u\right)\right| + \left|\int_{-\infty}^{u_1} g\left(u\right) \mathrm{d}F\left(u\right)\right| \\ &\leqslant \int_{-\infty}^{u_1} |g\left(u\right)| \,\mathrm{d}F_n\left(u\right) + \int_{-\infty}^{u_1} |g\left(u\right)| \,\mathrm{d}F\left(u\right) \\ &< c\int_{-\infty}^{u_1} \mathrm{d}F_n\left(u\right) + c\int_{-\infty}^{u_1} \mathrm{d}F\left(u\right) \\ &= c\left(F_n\left(u_1\right) + F\left(u_1\right)\right).\end{aligned}$$

Choosing u_1 arbitrarily large negative makes both $F_n\left(u_1\right)$ and $F\left(u_1\right)$ sufficiently small, and hence the limit of $\int_{-\infty}^{u_1} g\left(u\right) \mathrm{d}(F_n\left(u\right) - F\left(u\right))$ is zero for any continuity point u_1 of F. Similarly, we obtain the convergence $\int_{u_2}^{\infty} g\left(u\right) \mathrm{d}(F_n\left(u\right) - F\left(u\right)) \to 0$ by choosing u_2 arbitrarily large positive. Thus, we get $\mathrm{E}\left(g(x_n)\right) - \mathrm{E}\left(g(x)\right) \to 0$.

***Exercise 10.10 (Helly's selection lemma)** Let $\{F_n\left(u\right)\}$ be a sequence of distribution functions. Prove that there exists a subsequence which tends to a bounded nondecreasing right-continuous function $G\left(u\right)$ (but not necessarily a c.d.f.) at all continuity points u of G. [Hint: Start with some $u = q_1 \in \mathbb{Q}$, then select a succession of nested convergent subsequences such that eventually $\{F_{n_i}\left(q\right)\}_{i=1}^{\infty} \to G_{\mathbb{Q}}\left(q\right)$ for all $q \in \mathbb{Q}$. Afterwards, consider the properties of $G\left(u\right) := \sup_{q_j<u} G_{\mathbb{Q}}\left(q_j\right)$, then use the fact (in Section A.3.1) that the rationals are dense in the reals.]

Solution

Choose some $u = q_1 \in \mathbb{Q}$. The sequence of c.d.f.s is bounded in $[0, 1]$, so the Bolzano–Weierstrass theorem (see Section A.3.1) implies that there exists a subsequence of $\{F_n\left(q_1\right)\}$ that converges to (say) $G_{\mathbb{Q}}\left(q_1\right)$. Now consider a further subsequence of this subsequence, such that it converges for another $q_2 \in \mathbb{Q}$, hence converging for both q_1 and q_2. The set of rational numbers is countable (nonzero rationals are expressible as a signed ratio of naturals), so we can continue selecting further subsequences in this way until we achieve $\{F_{n_i}\left(q\right)\}_{i=1}^{\infty} \to G_{\mathbb{Q}}\left(q\right)$ for each and every $q \in \mathbb{Q}$.

Consider a sequence of rationals $q_1 < q_2 < \dots$ that is bounded by some $u \in \mathbb{R}$, and define

$$G(u) := \sup_{q_j < u} G_{\mathbb{Q}}(q_j)$$

for $j = 1, 2, \dots$. The sequence of $G_{\mathbb{Q}}(q_j)$ is nondecreasing and bounded, so the limit $G(u)$ exists. This limit is therefore also nondecreasing and bounded as u increases. That it is right-continuous follows from

$$G(u^+) \equiv \sup_{q_j < u^+} G_{\mathbb{Q}}(q_j) \equiv \sup_{q_j^- < u} G_{\mathbb{Q}}(q_j) \equiv \sup_{q_j < u} G_{\mathbb{Q}}(q_j^+) = \sup_{q_j < u} G_{\mathbb{Q}}(q_j) \equiv G(u),$$

where the only equality follows from the right-continuity of each c.d.f. in $\{F_{n_i}(q_j)\}$ and hence also of their limit $G_{\mathbb{Q}}(q_j)$. Note that, although G is bounded between 0 and 1, it may not be a proper c.d.f.: further conditions will be required, as we shall see in Exercise 10.11(c).

As the final step of the proof, we need to show that $\{F_{n_i}(u)\}_{i=1}^{\infty} \to G(u)$ when $u \in \mathbb{R}$ is a continuity point of G. Taking $q_j < u < q_k$, we have

$$F_{n_i}(u) \in [F_{n_i}(q_j), F_{n_i}(q_k)].$$

We have seen that, as $n_i \to \infty$, the limit of this interval is $[G_{\mathbb{Q}}(q_j), G_{\mathbb{Q}}(q_k)]$. Since the rationals are dense in the reals, every real u can be written as the limit of a sequence of rationals, so we can choose sequences $\{q_j\}$ and $\{q_k\}$ converging to u from below and above, respectively. Since u is a continuity point of G, we can make $G_{\mathbb{Q}}(q_k) - G_{\mathbb{Q}}(q_j)$ arbitrarily small. Therefore, the limit of $F_{n_i}(u)$ exists and is given by $\sup_{q_j < u} G_{\mathbb{Q}}(q_j) = G(u)$.

*__Exercise 10.11 (Continuity theorem)__ Let φ_n, φ be the c.f.s of x_n, x, respectively, and F_n, F the c.d.f.s of x_n, x. Prove that:
(a) if $F_n \to F$ at the continuity points of F, then $\varphi_n(\tau) \to \varphi(\tau)$ for all $\tau \in \mathbb{R}$;
(b) if $\varphi_n(\tau) \to \varphi(\tau)$ for all $\tau \in \mathbb{R}$, then $F_n \to F$ at the continuity points of F;
(c) if $\varphi_n(\tau) \to h(\tau)$ for all $\tau \in \mathbb{R}$, and h is some function (not assumed to be a c.f.) that is continuous at $\tau = 0$, then $h(\tau) = \varphi(\tau)$ and $F_n \to F$ at the continuity points of F.
[Hint: Define $c_{n,t} := t^{-1} \int_0^t \varphi_n(\tau)\, d\tau$ and show that $\lim_{t \to 0} \lim_{n \to \infty} c_{n,t} = 1$. Next, use Helly's lemma (Exercise 10.10) to select a subsequence $\{n_i\}_{i=1}^{\infty}$ such that $F_{n_i} \to G$ at the continuity points of G, and show that it implies $\lim_{t \to 0} \lim_{n_i \to \infty} c_{n_i,t} = G(\infty) - G(-\infty)$.]

Solution
(a) Take $g(x) = \exp(i\tau x)$ in the Helly–Bray theorem (Exercise 10.9). The result follows by the fact that $|\exp(i\tau x)| = 1$ (and hence is bounded) for τx real, and that

$$\exp(i\tau x) = \cos(\tau x) + i \sin(\tau x)$$

is a continuous function of x.
(b) Since $\varphi(\tau)$ is continuous at $\tau = 0$, by one of the defining properties of c.f.s, it is sufficient to prove (c) and then (b) follows.

(c) Define $c_{n,t} := t^{-1}\int_0^t \varphi_n(\tau)\,\mathrm{d}\tau$, and first consider its limit as $n \to \infty$. By the dominated convergence theorem (see Section A.4.3), $\lim_n$ and $\int_0^t$ can be interchanged because $|\varphi_n(\tau)| \leqslant 1$ (see Chapter 3); hence

$$\lim_{t\to 0}\lim_{n\to\infty} c_{n,t} = \lim_{t\to 0}\frac{\int_0^t \lim_{n\to\infty}\varphi_n(\tau)\,\mathrm{d}\tau}{t} = \lim_{t\to 0}\frac{\int_0^t h(\tau)\,\mathrm{d}\tau}{t}.$$

By applying the rules of l'Hôpital (for the ratio) and then Leibniz (for differentiating the numerator), we obtain

$$\lim_{t\to 0}\lim_{n\to\infty} c_{n,t} = \lim_{t\to 0}\frac{h(t)}{1} = h(0)$$

by the continuity of h. We know that $h(0) = \lim_{n\to\infty}\varphi_n(0) = \lim_{n\to\infty} 1 = 1$, so we have $\lim_{t\to 0}\lim_{n\to\infty} c_{n,t} = 1$. Notice that, if h were not continuous at $\tau = 0$, the convergence of $c_{n,t}$ would not be uniform: taking limits first with respect to t and then n would give different results from taking them in the reverse order.

Now consider the definition of $c_{n,t}$ again. Denoting the c.d.f. of x_n by F_n,

$$\begin{aligned} c_{n,t} &= t^{-1}\int_0^t\int_{-\infty}^{\infty} \mathrm{e}^{\mathrm{i}\tau u}\,\mathrm{d}F_n(u)\,\mathrm{d}\tau = \int_{-\infty}^{\infty} t^{-1}\int_0^t \mathrm{e}^{\mathrm{i}\tau u}\,\mathrm{d}\tau\,\mathrm{d}F_n(u) \\ &= \int_{-\infty}^{\infty}\frac{\mathrm{e}^{\mathrm{i}tu}-1}{\mathrm{i}tu}\,\mathrm{d}F_n(u), \end{aligned}$$

where we are allowed to exchange the integral and expectation since the former is over a finite interval and the latter exists (see Section A.3.5). We know that $\lim_{t\to 0}\lim_{n\to\infty} c_{n,t} = 1$ and this holds for all subsequences $\{n_i\}_{i=1}^{\infty}$ of $\{n\}_{n=1}^{\infty}$ satisfying $n_i \to \infty$. By Helly's selection lemma (Exercise 10.10), there is a subsequence $\{F_{n_i}(u)\}$ such that $F_{n_i}(u) \to G(u)$ where G is a nondecreasing right-continuous function, and u is a continuity point of G. We also know that G is bounded between 0 and 1, but we now need to show that $\lim_{t\to 0}\lim_{n_i\to\infty} c_{n_i,t} = 1$ implies that G also satisfies the last remaining property of a c.d.f., namely that $G(-\infty) = 0$ and $G(\infty) = 1$.

The integrand in the last expression for $c_{n,t}$ is continuous everywhere, even for $u \to 0$, because

$$\frac{\mathrm{e}^{\mathrm{i}tu}-1}{\mathrm{i}tu} = \frac{\mathrm{i}tu + \sum_{j=2}^{\infty}(\mathrm{i}tu)^j/j!}{\mathrm{i}tu} = 1 + \sum_{j=2}^{\infty}\frac{(\mathrm{i}tu)^{j-1}}{j!}$$

for finite u. Therefore, the convergence property of Stieltjes integrals gives

$$\int_{u_1}^{u_2}\frac{\mathrm{e}^{\mathrm{i}tu}-1}{\mathrm{i}tu}\,\mathrm{d}(F_{n_i}(u) - G(u)) \to 0$$

for arbitrarily large but (here) finite u_1 and u_2 that are continuity points of G. To show that the remainder integrals $\int_{-\infty}^{u_1}$ and $\int_{u_2}^{\infty}$ tend to zero, we use the same derivation as in Exercise 10.9 but here with $\lim_{|u|\to\infty} g(u) \to 0$ for the integrand, since we have

$\lim_{|u|\to\infty}(\mathrm{e}^{itu}-1)/u=0$. Therefore,

$$\lim_{n_i\to\infty} c_{n_i,t} = \int_{-\infty}^{\infty} \frac{\mathrm{e}^{itu}-1}{itu}\,\mathrm{d}G(u).$$

Using $1=\lim_{t\to 0}\lim_{n_i\to\infty} c_{n_i,t}$, we have

$$1 = \lim_{t\to 0}\int_{-\infty}^{\infty} \frac{\mathrm{e}^{itu}-1}{itu}\,\mathrm{d}G(u) = \int_{-\infty}^{\infty} \lim_{t\to 0}\frac{\mathrm{e}^{itu}-1}{itu}\,\mathrm{d}G(u)$$
$$= \int_{-\infty}^{\infty} \mathrm{d}G(u) = G(\infty)-G(-\infty),$$

where the interchange of limit and integral is allowed by the dominated convergence theorem, since the integrand is bounded (it is continuous everywhere and tends to zero as $|u|\to\infty$). Since G is bounded between 0 and 1, the result $G(\infty)-G(-\infty)=1$ implies that $G(\infty)=1$ and $G(-\infty)=0$, so G is a proper c.d.f. and therefore convergence in distribution to F occurs for the subsequences $\{F_{n_i}(u)\}$. This convergence also occurs for $\{F_n(u)\}$, because otherwise there would be an infinite subsequence $\{n_j\}_{j=1}^{\infty}$ for which no subsequence of $\{F_{n_j}(u)\}$ would converge, which would lead to a contradiction. Finally, by (a), the limiting $h(\tau)$ is the c.f. of x.

Exercise 10.12 (Equivalence of convergence by c.d.f., c.f., and expectations) Using the notation of Exercise 10.11, prove that the following three modes of convergence are equivalent:
(i) $F_n \to F$ at the continuity points of F;
(ii) $\varphi_n(\tau)\to\varphi(\tau)$ for all τ;
(iii) $\mathrm{E}(g(x_n))\to\mathrm{E}(g(x))$ for every bounded continuous function g.

Solution
The equivalence of (i) and (ii) follows from Exercise 10.11, while Exercise 10.9 proves that (i) implies (iii). Now we need to show that (iii) implies (i). Taking $g(x_n)=\exp(\mathrm{i}\tau x_n)$ in (iii) implies (ii), and the equivalence of (ii) and (i) does the rest.

Exercise 10.13 (Convergence of continuous functions: CMT)
(a) Prove the *continuous mapping theorem* (CMT), that $x_n \xrightarrow{d} x$ implies $g(x_n)\xrightarrow{d} g(x)$ for any real-valued continuous function g.
(b) What if the continuity of g is dropped?

Solution
(a) Denote the c.f.s of $g(x_n)$ and $g(x)$ by $\varphi_{g(x_n)}(\tau)$ and $\varphi_{g(x)}(\tau)$, respectively. Writing

$$\varphi_{g(x)}(\tau) := \mathrm{E}\left(\exp\left(\mathrm{i}\tau g(x)\right)\right),$$

we have $|\exp(\mathrm{i}\tau g(x))|=1$ for $\tau, g(x)$ real. Furthermore, g and the exponential functions are both continuous, so their composition is a continuous function. Therefore, the Helly–

Bray theorem (Exercise 10.9) gives $\varphi_{g(x_n)}(\tau) \to \varphi_{g(x)}(\tau)$. The result follows by Exercise 10.11(b).
(b) Convergence need not hold if the continuity of the function is dropped. A simple counterexample is obtained by taking a variate $x_n := 1/n$ that converges almost surely to $x = 0$. The function $z_n := 1/x_n$ is discontinuous at the origin, and $z_n \to +\infty$ almost surely, but $z = 1/x = \pm\infty$ (undefined).

Exercise 10.14 (Convergence of c.f.s: tightness) A sequence of c.d.f.s $\{F_n\}$ is said to be *tight* if, for all small $\epsilon > 0$ and all n, there exist finite u_1 and u_2 such that $F_n(u_1) < \epsilon$ and $F_n(u_2) > 1 - \epsilon$. Let $x_n \sim \text{Cau}(0, n)$. By analyzing the convergence of the c.f.s of x_n,

$$\varphi_n(\tau) = \mathrm{e}^{-n|\tau|},$$

prove that $\lim_{n\to\infty} \varphi_n(\tau)$ is not a c.f. and explain what happens to the limiting c.d.f. in terms of tightness.

Solution
Clearly, $h(\tau) := \lim_{n\to\infty} \varphi_n(\tau) = 0$ for $\tau \neq 0$, and

$$h(0) = \lim_{n\to\infty} \varphi_n(0) = \lim_{n\to\infty} 1 = 1.$$

Since $h(\tau)$ is not a continuous function of τ, it cannot be a c.f. (see Chapter 3), and so the condition for convergence in distribution (by c.f.s) is violated. The convergence of $\varphi_n(\tau)$ is not uniform, and there is a loss of continuity at $\tau = 0$. To see what is happening to the sequence of variates $\{x_n\}$, defining $z := x_n/n \sim \text{Cau}(0, 1)$ we get

$$F_n(u) = \Pr(nz \leqslant u) = \Pr\left(z \leqslant \frac{u}{n}\right).$$

As $n \to \infty$,

$$F(u) \equiv \lim_{n\to\infty} F_n(u) = \Pr(z \leqslant 0) = \frac{1}{2}$$

for all finite u, and this is not a proper c.d.f.: the sequence $\{F_n\}$ does not converge to the c.d.f. of a variate $x \in (-\infty, \infty)$, hence violating the condition for convergence in distribution (by c.d.f.s). Expressing this in another way, there exist no finite u_1 and u_2 satisfying the definition of tightness as $n \to \infty$. Note that the assumption of continuity of h in Exercise 10.11(c) ensured tightness and prevented the current situation from arising there. It is worth pointing out that $\pm\infty$ are not continuity "points" of F here.

Exercise 10.15 (Cramér–Wold device) Let $\{\boldsymbol{x}_n\}$ be a random sample of $m \times 1$ vectors. Show that, if we have $\boldsymbol{a}'\boldsymbol{x}_n \xrightarrow{d} \boldsymbol{a}'\boldsymbol{x}$ for every real nonrandom vector $\boldsymbol{a}$, then $\boldsymbol{x}_n \xrightarrow{d} \boldsymbol{x}$.

Solution
Since $\boldsymbol{a}'\boldsymbol{x}_n \xrightarrow{d} \boldsymbol{a}'\boldsymbol{x}$, we have the convergence of the c.f.s $\varphi_{\boldsymbol{a}'\boldsymbol{x}_n}(\tau) \to \varphi_{\boldsymbol{a}'\boldsymbol{x}}(\tau)$ for all $\boldsymbol{a}, \tau$

as $n \to \infty$. Hence, for all $\boldsymbol{t} := \tau \boldsymbol{a}$,

$$\begin{aligned} \varphi_{\boldsymbol{x}_n}(\boldsymbol{t}) &= \mathrm{E}(\mathrm{e}^{\mathrm{i}(\tau \boldsymbol{a})'\boldsymbol{x}_n}) = \mathrm{E}(\mathrm{e}^{\mathrm{i}\tau(\boldsymbol{a}'\boldsymbol{x}_n)}) \\ &= \varphi_{\boldsymbol{a}'\boldsymbol{x}_n}(\tau) \to \varphi_{\boldsymbol{a}'\boldsymbol{x}}(\tau) = \mathrm{E}(\mathrm{e}^{\mathrm{i}\tau(\boldsymbol{a}'\boldsymbol{x})}) = \mathrm{E}(\mathrm{e}^{\mathrm{i}(\tau \boldsymbol{a})'\boldsymbol{x}}) = \varphi_{\boldsymbol{x}}(\boldsymbol{t}). \end{aligned}$$

This implies that $\boldsymbol{x}_n \xrightarrow{d} \boldsymbol{x}$.

***Exercise 10.16 (Convergence in p of sums and products)** Let $\{x_n\}$ and $\{y_n\}$ be two sequences of random variables with $x_n \xrightarrow{p} a$ and $y_n \xrightarrow{p} b$.
(a) Prove that $x_n + y_n \xrightarrow{p} a + b$. [Hint: Use the triangle inequality $|c_1 + c_2| \leqslant |c_1| + |c_2|$, and the fact that $|c_1| + |c_2| \geqslant |c_3|$ implies that $|c_1| \geqslant |c_3|/2$ or $|c_2| \geqslant |c_3|/2$.]
(b) Prove that $x_n y_n \xrightarrow{p} ab$.
(c) If $x_n > 0$ a.s., then show that $\operatorname{plim}(y_n/x_n) = \operatorname{plim} y_n / \operatorname{plim} x_n$. Does this imply that $\mathrm{E}(y_n/x_n) - \mathrm{E}(y_n)/\mathrm{E}(x_n) \to 0$, and what does this mean for Jensen's inequality when the variates are degenerate?

Solution
(a) Letting $\epsilon > 0$, we obtain

$$\Pr\left(|x_n + y_n - a - b| \geqslant \epsilon\right) \leqslant \Pr\left(|x_n - a| + |y_n - b| \geqslant \epsilon\right)$$

by the triangle inequality. Since $|x_n - a| + |y_n - b| \geqslant \epsilon$ implies that $|x_n - a| \geqslant \epsilon/2$ or $|y_n - b| \geqslant \epsilon/2$, Exercise 1.5(c) gives

$$\begin{aligned} \Pr\left(|x_n - a| + |y_n - b| \geqslant \epsilon\right) &\leqslant \Pr\left(|x_n - a| \geqslant \frac{\epsilon}{2} \text{ or } |y_n - b| \geqslant \frac{\epsilon}{2}\right) \\ &\leqslant \Pr\left(|x_n - a| \geqslant \frac{\epsilon}{2}\right) + \Pr\left(|y_n - b| \geqslant \frac{\epsilon}{2}\right) \end{aligned}$$

and both probabilities approach 0 as $n \to \infty$ since $x_n \xrightarrow{p} a$ and $y_n \xrightarrow{p} b$. This implies that $\Pr\left(|x_n + y_n - a - b| \geqslant \epsilon\right) \to 0$. Notice how the hint given in the question is used to separate x from y.
(b) First consider the case where $a = b = 0$. A product version of the second hint in (a) yields the following for use here: $|\gamma_1 \gamma_2| \geqslant |\gamma_3|$ implies that $|\gamma_1| \geqslant \sqrt{|\gamma_3|}$ or $|\gamma_2| \geqslant \sqrt{|\gamma_3|}$. Then

$$\Pr(|x_n y_n| \geqslant \epsilon) \leqslant \Pr(|x_n| \geqslant \sqrt{\epsilon}) + \Pr(|y_n| \geqslant \sqrt{\epsilon}) \to 0$$

as $n \to \infty$. In the general case, we find

$$\begin{aligned} \Pr\left(|x_n y_n - ab| \geqslant \epsilon\right) &= \Pr\left(|(x_n - a)(y_n - b) + a(y_n - b) + b(x_n - a)| \geqslant \epsilon\right) \\ &\leqslant \Pr\left(|x_n - a||y_n - b| + |a||y_n - b| + |b||x_n - a| \geqslant \epsilon\right). \end{aligned}$$

Then the second part of the hint in (a), generalized to three components instead of two, implies this time that

$$\begin{aligned}\Pr\left(|x_n y_n - ab| \geqslant \epsilon\right) &\leqslant \Pr\left(|x_n - a||y_n - b| \geqslant \frac{\epsilon}{3}\right)\\ &\quad + \Pr\left(|a||y_n - b| \geqslant \frac{\epsilon}{3}\right) + \Pr\left(|b||x_n - a| \geqslant \frac{\epsilon}{3}\right)\\ &\leqslant \Pr\left(|x_n - a| \geqslant \sqrt{\frac{\epsilon}{3}}\right) + \Pr\left(|y_n - b| \geqslant \sqrt{\frac{\epsilon}{3}}\right)\\ &\quad + \Pr\left(|a||y_n - b| \geqslant \frac{\epsilon}{3}\right) + \Pr\left(|b||x_n - a| \geqslant \frac{\epsilon}{3}\right).\end{aligned}$$

Since each of the four terms approaches 0 as $n \to \infty$, the result follows.
(c) It follows directly from (b) that $\operatorname{plim}(y_n/x_n) = b/a \equiv \operatorname{plim} y_n / \operatorname{plim} x_n$. For a counterexample on the expectations, assume they exist and that x_n and y_n are independent, so that $\mathrm{E}(y_n/x_n) = \mathrm{E}(y_n)\,\mathrm{E}(1/x_n) \geqslant \mathrm{E}(y_n)/\mathrm{E}(x_n)$ by Jensen's inequality when $\mathrm{E}(y_n) \geqslant 0$. In the specific example of Exercise 10.8(c) with $c > 0$, we have

$$\lim \mathrm{E}\left(\frac{1}{x_n}\right) = \frac{1}{c} > \frac{1}{c+1} = \lim \frac{1}{\mathrm{E}(x_n)},$$

and we do not get $\mathrm{E}(y_n/x_n) - \mathrm{E}(y_n)/\mathrm{E}(x_n) \to 0$. This indicates that, when extending Jensen's inequality to degenerate sequences, we should rule out divergent subsequences if we wish to retain the result of Chapter 3 that $\mathrm{E}(g(x)) = g(\mathrm{E}(x))$ for degenerate x, or we should consider the stronger (than plim) convergence in moments (Exercise 10.8). In general, it is *not* enough that the variance goes to zero, because this may not rule out divergent subsequences. For example,

$$\Pr\left(x_n = 0\right) = 1 - \frac{1}{n} \quad \text{and} \quad \Pr\left(x_n = n^{1/4}\right) = \frac{1}{n}$$

has $\mathrm{E}(x^\nu) \to 0$ for $0 < \nu < 4$ but not for $\nu \geqslant 4$, so $g(x) = x^4$ is again a case where $\lim \mathrm{E}(g(x)) > \lim g(\mathrm{E}(x))$ even though $\operatorname{var}(x) \to 0$. The additional operation of taking limits requires extra care in comparison to the setup of earlier chapters.

Exercise 10.17 (Convergence in d of independent sums and products) Let $\{x_n\}$ be a sequence of random variables independently distributed from the sequence $\{y_n\}$, with $x_n \xrightarrow{d} x$ and $y_n \xrightarrow{d} y$. Prove that:
(a) $x_n + y_n \xrightarrow{d} x + y$;
(b) $x_n y_n \xrightarrow{d} xy$.

Solution
(a) The joint c.f. of $x_n + y_n$ is

$$\varphi_{x_n+y_n}(\tau) \equiv \mathrm{E}\left(\mathrm{e}^{\mathrm{i}\tau(x_n+y_n)}\right) = \mathrm{E}\left(\mathrm{e}^{\mathrm{i}\tau x_n}\right)\mathrm{E}\left(\mathrm{e}^{\mathrm{i}\tau y_n}\right) \equiv \varphi_{x_n}(\tau)\,\varphi_{y_n}(\tau)$$

by independence. Since $x_n \xrightarrow{d} x$ and $y_n \xrightarrow{d} y$, we have

$$\lim_{n\to\infty} \varphi_{x_n+y_n}(\tau) = \lim_{n\to\infty} \left(\varphi_{x_n}(\tau)\,\varphi_{y_n}(\tau)\right) = \varphi_x(\tau)\,\varphi_y(\tau) = \mathrm{E}\left(\mathrm{e}^{\mathrm{i}\tau(x+y)}\right),$$

which establishes the result.
(b) By the law of iterated expectations, the joint c.f. of $x_n y_n$ is

$$\varphi_{x_n y_n}(\tau) \equiv \mathrm{E}\left(\mathrm{e}^{\mathrm{i}\tau x_n y_n}\right) = \mathrm{E}_{y_n}\left(\varphi_{x_n}(\tau y_n)\right),$$

where the conditioning has been dropped because of the independence of the variates. Their independence also allows us to take limits for x_n and y_n separately, and we have

$$\begin{aligned}\lim_{n\to\infty} \mathrm{E}_{y_n}\left(\varphi_{x_n}(\tau y_n)\right) &= \lim_{n\to\infty} \mathrm{E}_{y_n}\left(\varphi_x(\tau y_n)\right) = \lim_{n\to\infty} \mathrm{E}\left(\mathrm{e}^{\mathrm{i}\tau x y_n}\right)\\ &= \mathrm{E}_x\left(\lim_{n\to\infty}\varphi_{y_n}(\tau x)\right) = \mathrm{E}_x\left(\varphi_y(\tau x)\right) = \varphi_{xy}(\tau),\end{aligned}$$

which establishes the result. The interchange of the expectation and the limit is allowed by the dominated convergence theorem, since $|\varphi_{x_n}|, |\varphi_{y_n}| \leqslant 1$. Note that the independence of $\{x_n\}$ and $\{y_n\}$ is essential for this proof.

***Exercise 10.18 (Slutsky's lemma)** Consider the sequences $\{x_n\}$ and $\{y_n\}$ of random variables. Assume that $x_n \xrightarrow{d} x$. Prove that:
(a) $y_n \xrightarrow{p} 0$ implies $x_n y_n \xrightarrow{p} 0$;
(b) $x_n - y_n \xrightarrow{p} 0$ implies $y_n \xrightarrow{d} x$;
(c) $y_n \xrightarrow{p} c$ implies $x_n + y_n \xrightarrow{d} x + c$ and $x_n y_n \xrightarrow{d} cx$.

Solution
(a) Let $\epsilon > 0$. For any choice of constant $a > 0$, we have

$$\Pr(|x_n y_n| \geqslant \epsilon) = \Pr(|x_n y_n| \geqslant \epsilon, |y_n| > \epsilon/a) + \Pr(|x_n y_n| \geqslant \epsilon, |y_n| \leqslant \epsilon/a).$$

Since $\Pr(A \cap B) \leqslant \Pr(A)$ for any events A, B, and since $|x_n y_n| \geqslant \epsilon$ and $|y_n| \leqslant \epsilon/a$ together imply that $|x_n| \geqslant a$, we get

$$\Pr(|x_n y_n| \geqslant \epsilon) \leqslant \Pr(|y_n| > \epsilon/a) + \Pr(|x_n| \geqslant a).$$

Choosing $a \to \infty$ gives $\Pr(|x_n| \geqslant a) \to 0$, and the result follows because $y_n \xrightarrow{p} 0$ implies that $\Pr(|y_n| > \epsilon/a) \to 0$ as $n \to \infty$.
(b) Let F be the c.d.f. of x and let u be a continuity point of F. Define $z_n := x_n - y_n$. Then

$$\begin{aligned}F_{y_n}(u) &:= \Pr(y_n \leqslant u) = \Pr(x_n - z_n \leqslant u)\\ &= \Pr(x_n - z_n \leqslant u, z_n \leqslant \epsilon) + \Pr(x_n - z_n \leqslant u, z_n > \epsilon)\\ &\leqslant \Pr(x_n \leqslant u + \epsilon) + \Pr(z_n > \epsilon).\end{aligned}$$

But $z_n \xrightarrow{p} 0$ implies $\Pr(z_n > \epsilon) \to 0$ for $\epsilon > 0$, hence $\lim_{n\to\infty} F_{y_n}(u) \leqslant F(u + \epsilon)$. In a similar way, we find

$$\begin{aligned}1 - F_{y_n}(u) &= \Pr(y_n > u) = \Pr(x_n - z_n > u)\\ &= \Pr(x_n - z_n > u, z_n > -\epsilon) + \Pr(x_n - z_n > u, z_n \leqslant -\epsilon)\\ &\leqslant \Pr(x_n > u - \epsilon) + \Pr(z_n \leqslant -\epsilon) \to 1 - F(u - \epsilon)\end{aligned}$$

for $\epsilon > 0$. Hence

$$F(u - \epsilon) \leqslant \lim_{n\to\infty} F_{y_n}(u) \leqslant F(u + \epsilon).$$

Since $\epsilon > 0$ is arbitrary and F is continuous at u, we have $F(u^-) = F(u^+)$ and the result follows.
(c) We are given that $(x_n + y_n) - (x_n + c) = y_n - c \xrightarrow{p} 0$ and $x_n + c \xrightarrow{d} x + c$. Hence, $x_n + y_n \xrightarrow{d} x + c$ by (b). Also, since $cx_n \xrightarrow{d} cx$, (a) gives $x_n y_n - cx_n = x_n(y_n - c) \xrightarrow{p} 0$. Then $x_n y_n \xrightarrow{d} cx$ follows from (b).

***Exercise 10.19 (Expansion of expectations of functions)** Let g be a function that is continuously differentiable k times at a fixed point θ that is finite, $\left|g^{(j)}(\theta)\right| < \infty$ for $j = 1, \dots, k$. Assume that $x_n - \theta = O_p(1/n^p)$ for some $p > 0$ and define $z_n := n^p(x_n - \theta)$. Assume further that $\mathrm{E}\left(z_n^k\right)$ and $\mathrm{E}\left(g\left(x_n\right)\right)$ exist for all n, and that $g^{(k)}\left(x_n\right)$ converges in mean (see Exercise 10.8) to $g^{(k)}\left(\theta\right)$. Show that

$$\mathrm{E}\left(g\left(x_n\right)\right) = \sum_{j=0}^{k-1} \frac{g^{(j)}\left(\theta\right)}{j!} \mathrm{E}\left(\left(x_n - \theta\right)^j\right) + O\left(\frac{1}{n^{pk}}\right).$$

Solution
By the continuity of the k-th derivative, Taylor's theorem gives

$$g\left(x_n\right) = \sum_{j=0}^{k-1} \frac{g^{(j)}\left(\theta\right)}{j!}\left(x_n - \theta\right)^j + \frac{g^{(k)}\left(\overline{\theta}_n\right)}{k!}\left(x_n - \theta\right)^k = \sum_{j=0}^{k-1} \frac{g^{(j)}\left(\theta\right)}{j! n^{pj}} z_n^j + \frac{g^{(k)}\left(\overline{\theta}_n\right)}{k! n^{pk}} z_n^k$$

for some $\overline{\theta}_n := \alpha_n x_n + (1 - \alpha_n)\theta = \theta + \alpha_n z_n / n^p$ and $\alpha_n \in (0, 1)$ random (as a function of x_n). The existence of the k-th moment of z_n implies the existence of lower-order moments by Exercise 3.25. Coupled with $\left|g^{(j)}(\theta)\right| < \infty$ and the existence of $\mathrm{E}\left(g\left(x_n\right)\right)$, this implies that the expectation of the expansion's remainder,

$$\mathrm{E}\left(\frac{g^{(k)}\left(\overline{\theta}_n\right) z_n^k}{k! n^{pk}}\right) = \mathrm{E}\left(g\left(x_n\right)\right) - \sum_{j=0}^{k-1} \frac{g^{(j)}\left(\theta\right)}{j! n^{pj}} \mathrm{E}\left(z_n^j\right),$$

exists. It remains for us to determine its order of magnitude. Consider

$$h(z_n) := g^{(k)}\left(\overline{\theta}_n\right) z_n^k = g^{(k)}\left(\theta + \alpha_n z_n / n^p\right) z_n^k.$$

Note that $\operatorname{plim} \overline{\theta}_n = \theta$ (by $x_n \xrightarrow{p} \theta$) and $g^{(k)}$ is a continuous function, so the CMT of Exercise 10.13 gives $\operatorname{plim} g^{(k)}(\overline{\theta}_n) = g^{(k)}(\theta)$, hence $h(z_n) = O_p(1)$. However, this is not enough to guarantee that $\mathrm{E}(h(z_n)) = O(1)$; see Exercise 10.8(c) for a counterexample. The final condition in the statement of the exercise rules out such exceptions. It states that

$$\int_{-\infty}^{\infty} \left| g^{(k)}\left(\theta + w/n^p\right) - g^{(k)}(\theta) \right| \mathrm{d}F_{z_n}(w) \to 0 \quad \text{as } n \to \infty,$$

and hence is a fortiori true for $g^{(k)}\left(\theta + \alpha_n w/n^p\right)$ where w is dampened by a factor α_n numerically smaller than 1 (a similar effect to that of a larger n) and α_n is now a deterministic function of w by the mean-value theorem; see Section A.3.4. Therefore, we have $g^{(k)}\left(\theta + \alpha_n w/n^p\right) = g^{(k)}(\theta) + o(1)$ on intervals where F_{z_n} is an increasing function of w. By $|o(1)| < c$ for some finite c and for all n exceeding some constant n_0, the triangle inequality $|a + b| \leqslant |a| + |b|$ gives

$$\left| g^{(k)}\left(\theta + \alpha_n w/n^p\right) \right| \leqslant \left| g^{(k)}(\theta) \right| + c,$$

hence

$$\begin{aligned} \mathrm{E}\left(|h(z_n)|\right) &= \int_{-\infty}^{\infty} \left| g^{(k)}\left(\theta + \alpha_n w/n^p\right) w^k \right| \mathrm{d}F_{z_n}(w) \\ &\leqslant \left| g^{(k)}(\theta) \right| \int_{-\infty}^{\infty} \left| w^k \right| \mathrm{d}F_{z_n}(w) + c \int_{-\infty}^{\infty} \left| w^k \right| \mathrm{d}F_{z_n}(w) \end{aligned}$$

for all $n > n_0$. Using $\int_{-\infty}^{\infty} |w^k| \, \mathrm{d}F_{z_n}(w) = \mathrm{E}(|z_n^k|) < \infty$ and $\left| g^{(k)}(\theta) \right| < \infty$, we have $\mathrm{E}(h(z_n)) = O(1)$ and hence $\mathrm{E}\left(h(z_n)/(k! n^{pk})\right) = O\left(1/n^{pk}\right)$, as required. Note that the result generalizes Exercise 3.29 and that the order of the remainder is also more precise here, but at the cost of strong assumptions on $g^{(k)}$.

Exercise 10.20 (Delta method) Let $\{\boldsymbol{x}_n\}$ be a sequence of $m \times 1$ random vectors.
(a) For $m = 1$, assume that $n^p(x_n - \theta) \overset{a}{\sim} \mathrm{N}(0, \sigma^2)$, where $p > 0$ and $\sigma \geqslant 0$ do not depend on n. Let g be continuously differentiable at θ. Show that

$$n^p\left(g(x_n) - g(\theta)\right) \overset{a}{\sim} \mathrm{N}\left(0, (g'(\theta))^2 \sigma^2\right),$$

where $g'(\theta)$ denotes the derivative of $g(x)$ evaluated at $x = \theta$. How do you reconcile this result with inequalities relating $\mathrm{E}(g(x_n))$ to $g(\mathrm{E}(x_n))$?
(b) For $m \geqslant 1$, assume that $\boldsymbol{A}_n(\boldsymbol{x}_n - \boldsymbol{\theta}) \overset{a}{\sim} \mathrm{N}(\boldsymbol{0}_m, \boldsymbol{\Sigma})$ where $\boldsymbol{A}_n := \operatorname{diag}(a_1, \dots, a_m)$ is nonrandom, with $a_i \to \infty$ (for $i = 1, \dots, m$) as $n \to \infty$, and $\boldsymbol{\Sigma}$ is positive semidefinite and does not depend on n. Let $\boldsymbol{g} : \mathbb{R}^m \mapsto \mathbb{R}^k$ be continuously differentiable at $\boldsymbol{\theta}$. Show that

$$\boldsymbol{B}_n\left(\boldsymbol{g}(\boldsymbol{x}_n) - \boldsymbol{g}(\boldsymbol{\theta})\right) \overset{a}{\sim} \mathrm{N}\left(\boldsymbol{0}_k, \boldsymbol{C}\boldsymbol{\Sigma}\boldsymbol{C}'\right),$$

where $\boldsymbol{B}_n := \operatorname{diag}(b_1, \dots, b_k)$ is chosen such that

$$\boldsymbol{C} := \lim_{n \to \infty} \boldsymbol{B}_n \frac{\partial \boldsymbol{g}(\boldsymbol{\theta})}{\partial \boldsymbol{\theta}'} \boldsymbol{A}_n^{-1}$$

is finite and the principal submatrices of $\boldsymbol{C}\boldsymbol{\Sigma}\boldsymbol{C}'$ are nonzero; $\partial \boldsymbol{g}(\boldsymbol{\theta})/\partial \boldsymbol{\theta}'$ denotes the $k \times m$ matrix of the partial derivatives of $\boldsymbol{g}(\boldsymbol{x})$ evaluated at $\boldsymbol{x} = \boldsymbol{\theta}$.

(c) Let $\boldsymbol{z}_n \sim \mathrm{N}(\mathbf{0}_2, \boldsymbol{D}_n)$, where $\boldsymbol{D}_n := \mathrm{diag}(1/n, 1/n^2)$, and define $\boldsymbol{x}_n := (z_1, z_1 + z_2)'$. Derive the limiting distributions of the normalized $\boldsymbol{x}_n$ and $\boldsymbol{z}_n$. Which of the two limits is more informative, and what does this imply for the choice of $\boldsymbol{A}_n$ in part (b)?

Solution

(a) There is no loss of generality in assuming that θ does not depend on n, since one could redefine x_n (and p if necessary) to achieve this. Expanding $g(x_n)$ around $x_n = \theta$,

$$n^p \left(g(x_n) - g(\theta)\right) = g'(\overline{\theta}_n) \times n^p \left(x_n - \theta\right)$$

for some $\overline{\theta}_n := \alpha_n x_n + (1 - \alpha_n)\theta$ and $\alpha_n \in (0, 1)$. Therefore,

$$\operatorname{plim} \overline{\theta}_n = \theta + \operatorname{plim} \alpha_n \left(x_n - \theta\right) = \theta$$

by the fact that α_n is bounded and by Slutsky's lemma (Exercise 10.18); hence, $\operatorname{plim} g'(\overline{\theta}_n) = g'(\theta)$ by the CMT of Exercise 10.13. It then follows from Slutsky's lemma that

$$n^p \left(g(x_n) - g(\theta)\right) \overset{a}{\sim} g'(\theta)\mathrm{N}(0, \sigma^2) = \mathrm{N}\left(0, (g'(\theta))^2\sigma^2\right).$$

Note that normality was used only in the last equality and that the relation between the asymptotic moments of x_n and $g(x_n)$ holds regardless. Finally, Jensen's inequality shows that $\mathrm{E}(g(x_n))$ is not necessarily equal to $g(\mathrm{E}(x_n))$ for a nonlinear function g, but that equality holds if the variate is degenerate and has no divergent subsequences; see Exercise 10.16(c). This is the case here, whether or not g is convex, and we have $\mathrm{E}(g(x_n)) \to g(\theta)$.

(b) Write $\boldsymbol{x}_n \overset{a}{\sim} \mathrm{N}(\boldsymbol{\theta}, \boldsymbol{\Omega})$ where $\boldsymbol{\Omega} := \boldsymbol{A}_n^{-1}\boldsymbol{\Sigma}\boldsymbol{A}_n^{-1}$. Since $\boldsymbol{\Omega} \to \mathbf{O}$, we have that $\operatorname{plim} \boldsymbol{x}_n = \boldsymbol{\theta}$ and

$$g_j(\boldsymbol{x}_n) - g_j(\boldsymbol{\theta}) = \left.\frac{\partial g_j(\boldsymbol{x})}{\partial \boldsymbol{x}'}\right|_{\boldsymbol{x}=\overline{\boldsymbol{\theta}}_{j,n}} (\boldsymbol{x}_n - \boldsymbol{\theta}) \qquad (j = 1, \dots, k),$$

where $\overline{\boldsymbol{\theta}}_{j,n} := \alpha_{j,n}\boldsymbol{x}_n + (1 - \alpha_{j,n})\,\boldsymbol{\theta}$ and $\alpha_{j,n} \in (0, 1)$, so $\overline{\boldsymbol{\theta}}_{j,n} = \boldsymbol{\theta} + o_p(1)$. Notice that, unlike in (a), we cannot write $\overline{\boldsymbol{\theta}}_n = \alpha_n\boldsymbol{x}_n + (1 - \alpha_n)\boldsymbol{\theta}$ for a single α_n, although we can do this expansion for each element of $\boldsymbol{g}$ separately; see Section A.4. Stacking the k expansions and normalizing both sides by $\boldsymbol{B}_n$,

$$\boldsymbol{B}_n \left(\boldsymbol{g}(\boldsymbol{x}_n) - \boldsymbol{g}(\boldsymbol{\theta})\right) = \boldsymbol{B}_n \frac{\partial \boldsymbol{g}(\boldsymbol{\theta})}{\partial \boldsymbol{\theta}'} \boldsymbol{A}_n^{-1}\boldsymbol{A}_n \left(\boldsymbol{x}_n - \boldsymbol{\theta}\right) + o_p(1) = \boldsymbol{C}\boldsymbol{y} + o_p(1),$$

where $\boldsymbol{y} \sim \mathrm{N}(\mathbf{0}_m, \boldsymbol{\Sigma})$. The required result is obtained from $\boldsymbol{C}\boldsymbol{y}$ because linear combinations of joint normals are normal. Notice that if $\boldsymbol{A}_n$ were a scalar matrix such as $\boldsymbol{A}_n = n^p\boldsymbol{I}_m$, then $\boldsymbol{B}_n$ would be of order $n^p\boldsymbol{I}_k$. Otherwise, b_i^{-1} is of the order of magnitude of the maximal element in row i of $(\partial \boldsymbol{g}(\boldsymbol{\theta})/\partial \boldsymbol{\theta}')\boldsymbol{A}_n^{-1}$. Note that the principal submatrices of $\boldsymbol{C}\boldsymbol{\Sigma}\boldsymbol{C}'$ are required to be nonzero, so that no marginal distribution has a zero variance matrix owing to an inappropriate choice of normalization $\boldsymbol{B}_n$. This, however, does not prevent the submatrices from being singular, as the next part will show.

(c) Normalizing, we have $\boldsymbol{D}_n^{-1/2}\boldsymbol{z}_n \sim \mathrm{N}(\boldsymbol{0}, \boldsymbol{I}_2)$ and

$$\sqrt{n}\boldsymbol{x}_n := \begin{pmatrix} 1 & 0 \\ 1 & 1 \end{pmatrix} \sqrt{n}\boldsymbol{z}_n \overset{a}{\sim} \mathrm{N}\left(\begin{pmatrix} 0 \\ 0 \end{pmatrix}, \begin{pmatrix} 1 & 1 \\ 1 & 1 \end{pmatrix}\right)$$

since $\operatorname{var}(\sqrt{n}\boldsymbol{z}_n) \to \operatorname{diag}(1, 0)$ and

$$\operatorname{var}(\sqrt{n}\boldsymbol{x}_n) \to \begin{pmatrix} 1 & 0 \\ 1 & 1 \end{pmatrix}\begin{pmatrix} 1 & 0 \\ 0 & 0 \end{pmatrix}\begin{pmatrix} 1 & 0 \\ 1 & 1 \end{pmatrix}' = \begin{pmatrix} 1 & 0 \\ 1 & 0 \end{pmatrix}\begin{pmatrix} 1 & 1 \\ 0 & 1 \end{pmatrix} = \begin{pmatrix} 1 & 1 \\ 1 & 1 \end{pmatrix}.$$

This variance matrix is singular and the linear combination in $x_2 := z_1 + z_2$ is eventually dominated by z_1, so that both components of $\sqrt{n}\boldsymbol{x}_n$ converge to the same variate: all information on z_2 is lost asymptotically. Therefore, when the limiting $\boldsymbol{\Sigma}$ of part (b) is singular, it is more informative to work with $\boldsymbol{z}_n$ (if such a variate can be found) than $\boldsymbol{x}_n$. The derivations of (b) do not require that $\boldsymbol{A}_n$ be diagonal, but rather that it be invertible, and part (c) is saying that it can be useful to separate the different-rate components of $\boldsymbol{x}_n$ (transform $\boldsymbol{x}_n$ into $\boldsymbol{z}_n$) prior to applying the delta method and taking limits. In other words, instead of the diagonal $\boldsymbol{A}_n = \sqrt{n}\boldsymbol{I}_2$ used for normalizing $\boldsymbol{x}_n$ above, use

$$\sqrt{n}\begin{pmatrix} 1 & 0 \\ 1 & 1 \end{pmatrix}^{-1} = \sqrt{n}\begin{pmatrix} 1 & 0 \\ -1 & 1 \end{pmatrix}$$

as $\boldsymbol{A}_n$, hence transforming $\boldsymbol{x}_n$ into $\boldsymbol{z}_n$.

***Exercise 10.21 (Convergence of sequences having finite mean: truncation)** Let $x_1, x_2, \dots$ be a sequence of random variables whose elements all have the same distribution, and $\mathrm{E}(|x_1|) < \infty$. Define the truncated sequence

$$y_n := \begin{cases} x_n & (|x_n| < n), \\ 0 & (|x_n| \geqslant n). \end{cases}$$

(a) Show that $\Pr(|x_1| \geqslant n) \leqslant \int_{n-1}^{n} \Pr(|x_1| \geqslant u)\, \mathrm{d}u$.
(b) Prove that $\lim_{n\to\infty} \Pr(x_n \neq y_n) = 0$.
(c) Prove that the sequences $\{x_n\}$ and $\{y_n\}$ are almost surely identical.
(d) Suppose that the elements of the sequence $\{x_n\}$ are pairwise independent, and let $b_n := \lfloor a^n \rfloor$ where $a > 1$ is a constant ($\lfloor a^n \rfloor$ is the integer part of a^n). Show that

$$\sum_{n=1}^{\infty} \operatorname{var}\left(\overline{y}_{b_n}\right) < \infty,$$

where $\overline{y}_{b_n} := b_n^{-1} \sum_{i=1}^{b_n} y_i$. [Hint: Show that $\operatorname{var}\left(\overline{y}_{b_n}\right) \leqslant b_n^{-1} \mathrm{E}\left(x_1^2 1_{|x_1|<b_n}\right)$, then consider a bound in terms of x_1 for $\sum_{n=1}^{\infty} b_n^{-1} 1_{|x_1|<b_n}$.]

Solution

(a) This follows from the facts that $\Pr(|x_1| \geqslant u)$ is a nonincreasing function of u and the interval of integration has unit length:

$$\int_{n-1}^{n} \Pr(|x_1| \geqslant u)\,du \geqslant \int_{n-1}^{n} \Pr(|x_1| \geqslant n)\,du$$
$$= \Pr(|x_1| \geqslant n)\int_{n-1}^{n} du = \Pr(|x_1| \geqslant n).$$

This result holds regardless of whether $\mathrm{E}(|x_1|) < \infty$.
(b) This essentially implies that $x_n - y_n \xrightarrow{p} 0$, by Exercise 10.5(c). Because of the truncation, $\Pr(x_n \neq y_n) = \Pr(|x_n| \geqslant n)$. This is the same as $\Pr(|x_1| \geqslant n)$, since x_1 and x_n have identical distributions. But Markov's inequality gives $\Pr(|x_1| \geqslant n) \leqslant \mathrm{E}(|x_1|)/n$, which tends to zero since $\mathrm{E}(|x_1|) < \infty$.
(c) The previous parts have shown that

$$\Pr(x_n \neq y_n) = \Pr(|x_1| \geqslant n) \leqslant \int_{n-1}^{n} \Pr(|x_1| \geqslant u)\,du,$$

hence

$$\Pr\left(\bigcup_{m=n}^{\infty}\{x_m \neq y_m\}\right) \leqslant \sum_{m=n}^{\infty} \Pr(x_m \neq y_m)$$
$$\leqslant \sum_{m=n}^{\infty}\int_{m-1}^{m} \Pr(|x_1| \geqslant u)\,du = \int_{n-1}^{\infty} \Pr(|x_1| \geqslant u)\,du.$$

Since $|x_1| \geqslant 0$, Exercise 3.9 yields

$$\mathrm{E}(|x_1|) = \int_0^{\infty} (1 - F_{|x_1|}(u))\,du = \int_0^{\infty} \Pr(|x_1| > u)\,du,$$

and our premise that $\mathrm{E}(|x_1|) < \infty$ therefore implies that $\lim_{n\to\infty}\int_{n-1}^{\infty}\Pr(|x_1| \geqslant u)\,du = 0$, as required. The sequences $\{x_n\}$ and $\{y_n\}$ are therefore almost surely identical as $n \to \infty$.
(d) The independence of $\{x_n\}$ carries over to $\{y_n\}$, implying $\operatorname{cov}(y_i, y_j) = 0$ for all $i \neq j$ (the covariances exist since the y's are truncated), and $\operatorname{var}(\overline{y}_{b_n}) = b_n^{-2}\sum_{i=1}^{b_n}\operatorname{var}(y_i)$. Hence

$$\operatorname{var}(\overline{y}_{b_n}) \leqslant \frac{1}{b_n^2}\sum_{i=1}^{b_n}\mathrm{E}(y_i^2) = \frac{1}{b_n^2}\sum_{i=1}^{b_n}\mathrm{E}\left(x_i^2 1_{|x_i|<i}\right) = \frac{1}{b_n^2}\sum_{i=1}^{b_n}\mathrm{E}\left(x_1^2 1_{|x_1|<i}\right)$$

since the x's all have the same marginal distribution. By $i \leqslant b_n$ in the sum over i, we have $\mathrm{E}\left(x_1^2 1_{|x_1|<i}\right) \leqslant \mathrm{E}\left(x_1^2 1_{|x_1|<b_n}\right)$, where the latter does not depend on the index i, and

$$\operatorname{var}(\overline{y}_{b_n}) \leqslant \frac{1}{b_n^2}\sum_{i=1}^{b_n}\mathrm{E}\left(x_1^2 1_{|x_1|<b_n}\right) = \frac{1}{b_n}\mathrm{E}\left(x_1^2 1_{|x_1|<b_n}\right);$$

hence

$$\sum_{n=1}^{\infty} \operatorname{var}\left(\overline{y}_{b_n}\right) \leqslant \sum_{n=1}^{\infty} \frac{1}{b_n} \operatorname{E}\left(x_1^2 1_{|x_1|<b_n}\right).$$

It is tempting to interchange the expectation (an integral) and the sum. This is allowed if absolute convergence occurs (see Section A.3.5). Since p.d.f.s are nonnegative and $x_1^2, b_n^{-1}, 1_{|x_1|<b_n} \geqslant 0$, the interchange will be justified if we can show that

$$\operatorname{E}\left(x_1^2 \sum_{n=1}^{\infty} \frac{1}{b_n} 1_{|x_1|<b_n}\right) < \infty,$$

in which case the desired result has been established. Now, for any given x_1,

$$\sum_{n=1}^{\infty} \frac{1}{b_n} 1_{|x_1|<b_n} = \sum_{b_n>|x_1|} \frac{1}{b_n}.$$

Since $b_n = \lfloor a^n \rfloor$ and $a > 1$, the terms of the series decay at an exponential rate. The sum is therefore convergent (see Section A.3.2) and its leading term implies that

$$\sum_{b_n>|x_1|} \frac{1}{b_n} \leqslant \frac{c}{|x_1|}$$

for some finite c. Hence

$$\operatorname{E}\left(x_1^2 \sum_{n=1}^{\infty} \frac{1}{b_n} 1_{|x_1|<b_n}\right) \leqslant c \operatorname{E}\left(|x_1|\right),$$

and we get the required result by the assumption that $\operatorname{E}(|x_1|) < \infty$. Notice that all the moments of $\{y_n\}$ exist, when $n < \infty$, even though we have not assumed that the second moment of x_1 exists. Furthermore, the limit of the variance of $\{y_n\}$ can exist, even if the variance of x_1 (or y_∞) does not exist: we will illustrate in Exercise 10.38 that the limit of truncated moments can exist even if the corresponding limiting moment does not.

10.2 Laws of large numbers and central limit theorems

Exercise 10.22 (Weak law of large numbers: Khinchine) Let $\{x_n\}$ be a random sample from a distribution whose mean exists and is given by μ. Prove that $\overline{x}_n \xrightarrow{p} \mu$.

Solution

The c.f. of $\overline{x}_n$ is

$$\varphi_{\overline{x}_n}(\tau) = \operatorname{E}\left(e^{i\tau\overline{x}_n}\right) = \operatorname{E}\left(e^{i\tau x_1/n+\cdots+i\tau x_n/n}\right).$$

The assumptions that $x_1, \ldots, x_n$ are independent and identically distributed give, respectively,

$$\varphi_{\overline{x}_n}(\tau) = \mathrm{E}\left(\mathrm{e}^{\mathrm{i}\tau x_1/n}\right)\cdots\mathrm{E}\left(\mathrm{e}^{\mathrm{i}\tau x_n/n}\right) = \left(\varphi_1\left(\frac{\tau}{n}\right)\right)^n,$$

where φ_1 is the c.f. of x_1. The existence of the mean implies that

$$\varphi_1(\tau/n) = 1 + \mathrm{i}\mu\tau/n + o(1/n)$$

by Exercise 3.29 with c.f. argument τ/n instead of τ. Hence,

$$\varphi_{\overline{x}_n}(\tau) = \left(1 + \mathrm{i}\mu\frac{\tau}{n} + o\left(\frac{1}{n}\right)\right)^n = \mathrm{e}^{n\log(1+\mathrm{i}\mu\tau/n+o(1/n))} = \mathrm{e}^{\mathrm{i}\mu\tau+o(1)}$$

by $\log(1+a) = a + o(a)$ for $a \to 0$. We know that $\mathrm{e}^{\mathrm{i}\mu\tau}$ is the c.f. of a degenerate variate which is equal to μ with probability 1. Hence, $\overline{x}_n \xrightarrow{d} \mu$ and, by Exercise 10.6, $\overline{x}_n \xrightarrow{p} \mu$.

Exercise 10.23 (Weak law of large numbers: Chebyshev) Consider a sequence $\{x_n\}$ of uncorrelated random variables. Assume that the mean and variance of x_n exist for all n.
(a) Prove that

$$\lim_{n\to\infty} \mathrm{var}(\overline{x}_n) = 0 \quad \Longrightarrow \quad \overline{x}_n - \mathrm{E}(\overline{x}_n) \xrightarrow{p} 0.$$

(b) Comment on the difference between Khinchine's and Chebyshev's law. Why are they called "weak" laws?

Solution
(a) To link expectations with probabilities, we use Chebyshev's inequality (Exercise 3.12):

$$\Pr(|\overline{x}_n - \mathrm{E}(\overline{x}_n)| \geqslant \epsilon) \leqslant \frac{\mathrm{var}(\overline{x}_n)}{\epsilon^2}.$$

Since $\mathrm{var}(\overline{x}_n) \to 0$, we get $\Pr(|\overline{x}_n - \mathrm{E}(\overline{x}_n)| \geqslant \epsilon) \to 0$ as required.
(b) If we assume that the sample is random, we have a special case of (a) where $\mathrm{E}(\overline{x}_n) = \mu$ and $\mathrm{var}(\overline{x}_n) = \sigma^2/n$. Compared with Khinchine's law, Chebyshev's allows some dependence and heterogeneity (at the expense of assuming finite variances), so that the sequence is not necessarily independently and identically distributed. Recall from Chapter 6 (see, for example, Exercise 6.13) that lack of correlation implies lack of linear dependence only. Both laws are called "weak" because they are concerned with convergence in probability rather than the stronger mode of almost-sure convergence.

Exercise 10.24 (Nonlinear transformation and randomness: dependent sequence) Let $\{x_n\}$ be a sequence (possibly correlated) that takes the values -1 or $+1$. Obtain the distribution of the sequence $\{y_n\}$ defined by $y_n := x_n^2$.

Solution
Clearly, $y_n = 1$ with probability 1 for all n. It is a degenerate variate and we have

$$\mathrm{cov}(y_i, y_j) = \mathrm{E}(y_i y_j) - \mathrm{E}(y_i)\,\mathrm{E}(y_j) = 1 - 1 = 0$$

for all i, j (including the case $i = j$, that is, the variance). The dependence in the sequence has been altered by the nonlinear transformation. In general, nonlinear transformations alter correlation, unless the original $\{x_n\}$ was an independent sequence (in which case element-by-element transformations like $y_n = g(x_n)$ cannot introduce dependence).

Exercise 10.25 (Next time lucky?) You observe a fair coin being tossed repeatedly. Heads (H) has come up 10 consecutive times, and you now decide to gamble on the 11-th toss. Should you bet on tails (T) because "the law of averages tells us that H and T should eventually come up equally often", or on H because "it has come up so many times that it will probably come up again"?

Solution

The sequence of tosses is i.i.d., so what happens on the next toss is independent of the previous tosses. You also know that the coin is fair, so there is no reason to believe that H is more probable than T, or vice versa. Therefore, it makes no difference which one you choose, and you may gamble on either (toss a coin to decide)!

***Exercise 10.26 (Strong law of large numbers: Kolmogorov–Etemadi)** Let $\{x_n\}$ be a sequence of i.i.d. random variables. Prove that $\overline{x}_n \to c$ if and only if $\mathrm{E}(|x_1|) < \infty$ and $c = \mathrm{E}(x_1)$. [Hint: For the "only if" part, use Exercise 3.13 and then Exercise 10.3(b). For the "if" part, use Exercise 10.21 and then Exercise 10.3(a).]

Solution

There are two parts to prove. First, suppose that $\overline{x}_n \to c$. Exercise 3.13 gives

$$\mathrm{E}(|x_1|) \leqslant 1 + \sum_{n=2}^{\infty} \Pr(|x_1| \geqslant n-1) = 1 + \sum_{n=2}^{\infty} \Pr(|x_{n-1}| \geqslant n-1),$$

the equality following as x_1 and x_{n-1} are identically distributed for all $n > 1$. We will show that this sum is finite. Define the event A_n as the occurrence of $|x_n/n| \geqslant 1$. We know that $\overline{x}_n \to c$, so

$$\frac{x_n}{n} = \overline{x}_n - \frac{n-1}{n}\overline{x}_{n-1} \to c - c = 0.$$

Since x_n/n converges almost surely to 0, we have $\Pr(A_n \text{ i.o.}) = 0$. Restating the contrapositive of the second Borel–Cantelli lemma of Exercise 10.3(b): if $\Pr(A_n \text{ i.o.}) \neq 1$, then either $\{A_n\}$ is not an independent sequence or $\sum_{n=1}^{\infty} \Pr(A_n) < \infty$. However, we know that $\{x_n\}$ is an independent sequence, so $\{A_n\}$ is independent too. Therefore, $\Pr(A_n \text{ i.o.}) = 0 \neq 1$ implies that $\sum_{n=1}^{\infty} \Pr(A_n) < \infty$, and hence

$$\mathrm{E}(|x_1|) \leqslant 1 + \sum_{n=2}^{\infty} \Pr(A_{n-1}) < \infty.$$

Now, recall that we have assumed that $\overline{x}_n \to c$ and hence, by Exercise 10.5(a), $\overline{x}_n \xrightarrow{p} c$.

Since we have shown that $\mathrm{E}(x_1)$ exists, Khinchine's WLLN can be applied to find that $c = \mathrm{E}(x_1)$.

In the second part, suppose that $\mathrm{E}(x_1)$ exists and is equal to c. We may assume that $\{x_n\}$ is a positive sequence, because

$$\overline{x}_n \equiv \frac{1}{n}\sum_{i=1}^{n} \max\{0, x_i\} - \frac{1}{n}\sum_{i=1}^{n} |\min\{0, x_i\}|,$$

so proving convergence for positive sequences implies that each sum converges separately to its expectation (their sum is finite by $\mathrm{E}(|x_1|) < \infty$), and

$$\overline{x}_n \to \mathrm{E}(\max\{0, x_1\}) - \mathrm{E}(|\min\{0, x_1\}|) \equiv \mathrm{E}(x_1).$$

Now, define the truncated sequence

$$y_n := \begin{cases} x_n & (x_n < n), \\ 0 & (x_n \geqslant n). \end{cases}$$

From Exercise 10.21(c), $\{x_n\}$ and $\{y_n\}$ are almost surely identical as $n \to \infty$, so it is enough to establish that $\overline{y}_n \to c$ to complete the proof. By Chebyshev's inequality (Exercise 3.12),

$$\Pr(|\overline{y}_n - \mathrm{E}(\overline{y}_n)| \geqslant \epsilon) \leqslant \mathrm{var}(\overline{y}_n)/\epsilon^2$$

for all $\epsilon > 0$. Exercise 10.21(d) shows that, for $b_n := \lfloor a^n \rfloor$ where $a > 1$ is a constant, $\sum_{n=1}^{\infty} \mathrm{var}(\overline{y}_{b_n}) < \infty$, so that

$$\sum_{n=1}^{\infty} \Pr\left(\left|\overline{y}_{b_n} - \mathrm{E}\left(\overline{y}_{b_n}\right)\right| \geqslant \epsilon\right) \leqslant \frac{1}{\epsilon^2}\sum_{n=1}^{\infty} \mathrm{var}\left(\overline{y}_{b_n}\right) < \infty.$$

Note the subscript b_n (not n) for $\overline{y}$. The first Borel–Cantelli lemma (Exercise 10.3(a)) implies that we have just shown that $\overline{y}_{b_n} - \mathrm{E}\left(\overline{y}_{b_n}\right) \to 0$. By the dominated convergence theorem, the convergence of the sample mean of x implies the convergence of its truncated counterpart y as $\mathrm{E}\left(\overline{y}_{b_n}\right) \to \mathrm{E}(x_1) = c$, so $\overline{y}_{b_n} \to c$ and it remains for us to show that $\overline{y}_{b_n} - \overline{y}_n \to 0$. For any $m \in \mathbb{N}$ satisfying $b_n \leqslant m \leqslant b_{n+1}$ (hence $1/b_{n+1} \leqslant 1/m \leqslant 1/b_n$), the fact that the sum $\sum_{i=1}^{b_n} y_i$ is nondecreasing in n (since $y_n \geqslant 0$ for all n) implies that

$$\frac{1}{b_{n+1}}\sum_{i=1}^{b_n} y_i \leqslant \frac{1}{m}\sum_{i=1}^{m} y_i \leqslant \frac{1}{b_n}\sum_{i=1}^{b_{n+1}} y_i$$

or, equivalently,

$$\frac{b_n}{b_{n+1}}\overline{y}_{b_n} \leqslant \overline{y}_m \leqslant \frac{b_{n+1}}{b_n}\overline{y}_{b_{n+1}}.$$

As $n \to \infty$, we have $b_{n+1}/b_n = \lfloor a^{n+1} \rfloor / \lfloor a^n \rfloor \to a$ since the fractional part is finite (allowing us to drop the integer-value operator in the limit), and therefore $\overline{y}_m \in \left[a^{-1}\overline{y}_{b_n}, a\overline{y}_{b_{n+1}}\right]$ almost surely. Letting $a \to 1^+$ and using $\overline{y}_{b_n} \to c$ gives the result as $m \to \infty$. Notice that, in this second part, we required only the pairwise independence of the elements of the sequence, as required by Exercise 10.21(d).

Exercise 10.27 (Central limit theorem: Lindeberg–Lévy) Let $\{x_n\}$ be a random sample from a distribution whose mean μ and variance $\sigma^2 > 0$ both exist. Show that

$$z_n := \frac{\overline{x}_n - \mu}{\sigma/\sqrt{n}} \overset{a}{\sim} \mathrm{N}(0,1).$$

Solution

Writing

$$z_n = \frac{1}{\sigma\sqrt{n}} \sum_{i=1}^{n} (x_i - \mu),$$

the c.f. of z_n is

$$\varphi_{z_n}(\tau) = \mathrm{E}\left(\exp\left(\mathrm{i}\tau z_n\right)\right) = \mathrm{E}\left(\prod_{i=1}^{n} \exp\left(\mathrm{i}\tau\frac{x_i - \mu}{\sigma\sqrt{n}}\right)\right) = \prod_{i=1}^{n} \mathrm{E}\left(\exp\left(\mathrm{i}\tau\frac{x_i - \mu}{\sigma\sqrt{n}}\right)\right),$$

where the last step is due to the independence of $\{x_n\}$. Since they are identically distributed,

$$\varphi_{z_n}(\tau) = \left[\mathrm{E}\left(\exp\left(\mathrm{i}\tau\frac{x_1 - \mu}{\sigma\sqrt{n}}\right)\right)\right]^n.$$

Then, by Exercise 3.29 and the existence of the first two moments of x_1,

$$\begin{aligned}\mathrm{E}\left(\exp\left(\mathrm{i}\tau\frac{x_1 - \mu}{\sigma\sqrt{n}}\right)\right) &= 1 + \mathrm{i}\tau\frac{\mathrm{E}\left(x_1 - \mu\right)}{\sigma\sqrt{n}} - \tau^2\frac{\mathrm{E}\left((x_1 - \mu)^2\right)}{2\sigma^2 n} + o\left(\frac{1}{n}\right) \\ &= 1 - \frac{\tau^2}{2n} + o\left(\frac{1}{n}\right);\end{aligned}$$

hence

$$\varphi_{z_n}(\tau) = \exp\left(n\log\left(1 - \frac{\tau^2}{2n} + o\left(\frac{1}{n}\right)\right)\right) = \exp\left(-\frac{\tau^2}{2} + o\left(1\right)\right) \to \exp\left(-\frac{\tau^2}{2}\right)$$

as $n \to \infty$. We have used $\log\left(1 + a\right) = a + o(a)$ for $a \to 0$. The limiting c.f. is that of a $\mathrm{N}(0, 1)$ variate, which establishes the required result for z_n. Note that, if the third moment of x_1 exists, then $\varphi_{z_n}(\tau) = \left(1 + O\left(1/\sqrt{n}\right)\right)\exp\left(-\tau^2/2\right)$ and $z_n = z + O_p\left(1/\sqrt{n}\right)$ with $z \sim \mathrm{N}(0, 1)$. We shall explore this further in Exercise 13.37.

Exercise 10.28 (Binomial difference: asymptotics) Let $x_n \sim \mathrm{Bin}(n, p_1)$ and $z_n \sim \mathrm{Bin}(n, p_2)$, and assume that x_n and z_n are independently distributed. Derive the limiting distribution of $x_n - z_n$.

Solution

We use the representation of binomials, seen as early as in Exercise 4.3. Let $\{\xi_n\}$ be a random sample from the $\mathrm{Bin}(1, p_1)$ distribution and let $x_n := \sum_{i=1}^{n} \xi_i$. Independently, let

$\{\zeta_n\}$ be a random sample from the Bin$(1, p_2)$ distribution and let $z_n := \sum_{i=1}^n \zeta_i$. Define $y_i := \xi_i - \zeta_i$. Then

$$\mu := \mathrm{E}(y_i) = p_1 - p_2 \quad \text{and} \quad \sigma^2 := \mathrm{var}(y_i) = p_1(1-p_1) + p_2(1-p_2).$$

From the CLT, we obtain $\sqrt{n}(\overline{y}_n - \mu) \overset{a}{\sim} \mathrm{N}(0, \sigma^2)$. Therefore, since $x_n - z_n = n\overline{y}_n$,

$$n^{-1/2}(x_n - z_n - n\mu) \overset{a}{\sim} \mathrm{N}(0, \sigma^2).$$

Exercise 10.29 (Central limit theorem: multivariate) Let $\{\boldsymbol{x}_n\}$ be a random sample of $m \times 1$ vectors from a distribution whose mean $\boldsymbol{\mu}$ and positive definite variance $\boldsymbol{\Sigma}$ both exist. Show that

$$\boldsymbol{z}_n := \sqrt{n}\,(\overline{\boldsymbol{x}}_n - \boldsymbol{\mu}) \overset{d}{\longrightarrow} \boldsymbol{z} \sim \mathrm{N}(\mathbf{0}_m, \boldsymbol{\Sigma}).$$

Solution

Recall the definition of joint normality in Chapter 8, namely that any arbitrary linear combination $\boldsymbol{a}'\boldsymbol{z} \sim \mathrm{N}(0, \boldsymbol{a}'\boldsymbol{\Sigma}\boldsymbol{a})$ for $\boldsymbol{a} \in \mathbb{R}^m$ nonrandom. The variate

$$y_n := \boldsymbol{a}'\boldsymbol{z}_n = \frac{1}{\sqrt{n}} \sum_{i=1}^n \boldsymbol{a}'\,(\boldsymbol{x}_i - \boldsymbol{\mu})$$

satisfies

$$\mathrm{E}(y_n) = \frac{1}{\sqrt{n}} \boldsymbol{a}' \sum_{i=1}^n \mathrm{E}(\boldsymbol{x}_i - \boldsymbol{\mu}) = \frac{1}{\sqrt{n}} \boldsymbol{a}'\mathbf{0} = 0$$

and

$$\mathrm{var}(y_n) = \boldsymbol{a}'\,\mathrm{var}(\boldsymbol{z}_n)\,\boldsymbol{a} = \boldsymbol{a}'\boldsymbol{\Sigma}\boldsymbol{a}$$

for all n. But $y_n/\sqrt{n}$ is the sample average of the i.i.d. sequence $\{\boldsymbol{a}'(\boldsymbol{x}_n - \boldsymbol{\mu})\}$ and is therefore asymptotically normal, by the Lindeberg–Lévy CLT, and we have

$$y_n = \boldsymbol{a}'\boldsymbol{z}_n \overset{a}{\sim} \mathrm{N}(0, \boldsymbol{a}'\boldsymbol{\Sigma}\boldsymbol{a}).$$

Since this holds for all $\boldsymbol{a} \in \mathbb{R}^m$, the Cramér–Wold device implies that $\boldsymbol{z}_n \overset{d}{\longrightarrow} \boldsymbol{z}$.

Exercise 10.30 (Convergence of EDF and order statistics) Let $\{x_n\}$ be a random sample from a variate with c.d.f. $F(u)$, and denote its EDF by $\widehat{F}_n(u)$. Let the set C be the collection of the continuity points of F.

(a) Prove that the EDF converges almost surely to $F(u)$ for every $u \in C$.

(b) Prove that $\sqrt{n}(\widehat{F}_n(u) - F(u)) \overset{d}{\longrightarrow} z(u) \sim \mathrm{N}(0, F(u)(1 - F(u)))$ for every $u \in C$.

(c) Prove that any two elements of the sequence $\{z(u)\}_{u \in C}$ are bivariate normal with means zero and covariance $F(u_1)(1 - F(u_2))$, for $u_2 \geqslant u_1$.

(d) Suppose that this variate having c.d.f. F is continuous, and write its density as f. Show that the i-th order statistic is asymptotically distributed as

$$y_i \overset{a}{\sim} \mathrm{N}\left(q_\alpha, \frac{F(q_\alpha)(1-F(q_\alpha))}{n\left(f\left(q_\alpha\right)\right)^2}\right),$$

where q_α is the α quantile (hence $F\left(q_\alpha\right) = \alpha$), with $i/n \to \alpha \in (0,1)$ (or $i = \lfloor \alpha n \rfloor$). It is assumed that $0 < f(q_\alpha) < \infty$ and that f is continuous at q_α.

(e) Continuing with the setup of (d), let $y_i < y_j$ be two order statistics. Show that their asymptotic distribution is bivariate normal with covariance

$$\frac{F(q_\alpha)(1-F(q_\beta))}{nf\left(q_\alpha\right)f\left(q_\beta\right)},$$

where $q_\alpha < q_\beta$ are the α and β quantiles, respectively, with $i/n \to \alpha \in (0,1)$ and $j/n \to \beta \in (0,1)$. It is assumed that $0 < f(q_\alpha), f\left(q_\beta\right) < \infty$ and that f is continuous at q_α, q_β.

Solution

(a) We refer the reader back to Chapter 7, whose introduction defines the EDF as

$$\widehat{F}_n(u) := \frac{1}{n}\sum_{i=1}^{n} 1_{x_i \leqslant u}.$$

Because this is the average of the i.i.d. variates $1_{x_i \leqslant u}$, the SLLN implies that $\widehat{F}_n(u)$ converges almost surely to $\mathrm{E}(\widehat{F}_n(u)) = F(u)$, the latter equality being the result of Exercise 9.26(b).

(b) By applying the CLT, the pointwise (that is, for any given point u) distribution of $\widehat{F}_n(u)$ can be obtained from its definition as the average of an i.i.d. sequence, and Exercise 9.26(b) gives us the required mean and variance.

(c) Part (a) shows that the mean of each element of the sequence $\{z(u)\}_{u \in C}$ is zero, and Exercise 9.27(c) tells us that

$$\mathrm{cov}(\sqrt{n}\widehat{F}_n(u_1), \sqrt{n}\widehat{F}_n(u_2)) = F(u_1)(1-F(u_2)) \qquad (u_2 \geqslant u_1)$$

for all n. (The case $u_2 = u_1$ follows from Exercise 9.26(b).) Joint normality follows from the multivariate CLT, for any finite-dimensional selection of $\boldsymbol{u} := (u_1, \ldots, u_k)'$ where $k < \infty$.

(d) Since the density is continuous and positive at q_α, the c.d.f is increasing and we have $q_\alpha = F^{-1}(\alpha)$ uniquely for $\alpha \in (0,1)$. (We will tackle the extreme cases $\alpha = 0, 1$ in the last exercise of this chapter.) This quantile function is also continuously differentiable by the assumptions on $f(q_\alpha)$. To apply the delta method of Exercise 10.20, we need to work out $\mathrm{d}F^{-1}(\alpha)/\mathrm{d}\alpha$. We obtain this from differentiating both sides of $\alpha = F\left(q_\alpha\right)$:

$$1 = \frac{\mathrm{d}F\left(q_\alpha\right)}{\mathrm{d}\alpha} = f\left(q_\alpha\right)\frac{\mathrm{d}q_\alpha}{\mathrm{d}\alpha} = f\left(q_\alpha\right)\frac{\mathrm{d}F^{-1}(\alpha)}{\mathrm{d}\alpha},$$

where we use the assumption that $f\left(q_\alpha\right)$ is finite. Since we also assumed that $f\left(q_\alpha\right) > 0$, dividing both sides of (b) by $\sqrt{n}f(q_\alpha)$ gives the result. Notice that this is equivalent to

$$y_i \overset{a}{\sim} \mathrm{N}\left(q_\alpha, \frac{\alpha(1-\alpha)}{n\left(f\left(q_\alpha\right)\right)^2}\right).$$

As an application, the sample median is asymptotically normal, with mean equal to the population median and variance $1/(2\sqrt{n}f(q_{1/2}))^2$.
(e) This follows from (c) and (d), by transforming $(\widehat{F}_n(u_1), \widehat{F}_n(u_2))'$, then making a change of variable by premultiplying the resulting vector by $n^{-1/2}\operatorname{diag}(f(q_\alpha)^{-1}, f(q_\beta)^{-1})$. The asymptotic means and variances of y_i, y_j are given in (d), and the asymptotic covariance is

$$\frac{\alpha(1-\beta)}{nf\left(q_\alpha\right)f\left(q_\beta\right)}.$$

Exercise 10.31 (t-ratio: asymptotics) Let $\{x_n\}$ be a random sample from a distribution with mean μ and variance $\sigma^2 > 0$, both finite. Let $s_n^2 := \sum_{i=1}^n (x_i - \overline{x}_n)^2/(n-1)$. Show that:
(a) $\operatorname{plim} s_n^2 = \sigma^2$;
(b) $z_n := \sqrt{n}(\overline{x}_n - \mu)/s_n \overset{d}{\longrightarrow} z \sim \mathrm{N}(0,1)$.

Solution
(a) By Exercise 9.4,

$$s_n^2 = \frac{n}{n-1}\left(\frac{1}{n}\sum_{i=1}^n (x_i-\mu)^2 - (\overline{x}_n-\mu)^2\right);$$

hence

$$\operatorname{plim} s_n^2 = \operatorname{plim}\frac{1}{n}\sum_{i=1}^n (x_i-\mu)^2 - \operatorname{plim}\left(\overline{x}_n-\mu\right)^2.$$

By Khinchine's WLLN for $\left\{(x_n-\mu)^2\right\}$,

$$\operatorname{plim}\frac{1}{n}\sum_{i=1}^n (x_i-\mu)^2 = \mathrm{E}\left((x-\mu)^2\right) = \sigma^2 < \infty.$$

Then, applying Exercise 10.6(a) and the CMT, $\operatorname{plim}\overline{x}_n = \mu$ gives $\operatorname{plim}\left(\overline{x}_n-\mu\right)^2 = 0$ and the result follows.
(b) We know from the CLT that $\sqrt{n}(\overline{x}_n-\mu)/\sigma \overset{d}{\longrightarrow} z$, and from (a) that $\operatorname{plim} s_n^2 = \sigma^2$. The result now follows from Slutsky's lemma; see Exercise 10.18(c). Notice that z_n is not necessarily distributed as Student's t, which would require further assumptions on the distribution of $\{x_n\}$; see Exercises 9.7(b) and 9.13.

Exercise 10.32 (Approximations and convergence)
(a) Suppose that $x_n \sim \chi^2(n)$. Approximate $\Pr(x_n < n)$.

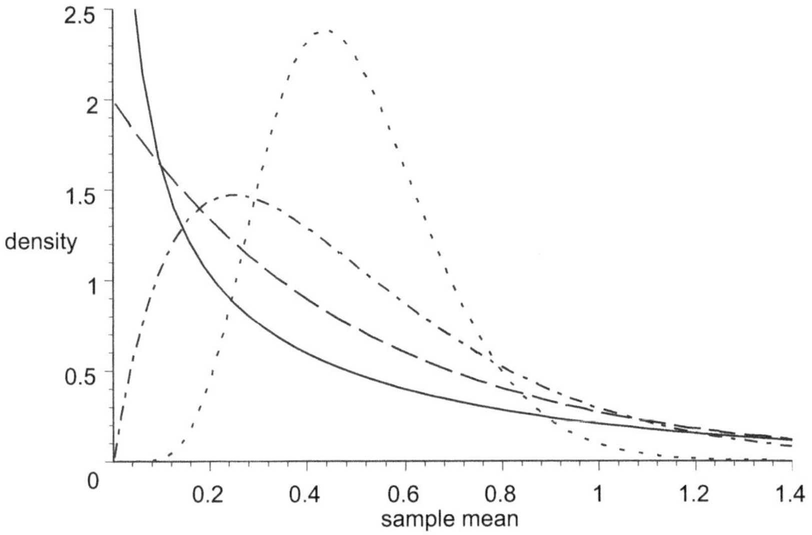

Figure 10.1. Exact densities of the mean of a random sample from $x \sim \mathrm{Gam}\left(\frac{1}{2}, 1\right)$, for $n = 1$ (solid line), 2 (dashes), 4 (dashes-dots), 16 (dots).

(b) Derive the exact and limiting distributions of $\overline{x}_n$ based on a random sample from $x \sim \mathrm{Gam}(\nu, \lambda)$. Plot the exact densities for $x \sim \mathrm{Gam}\left(\frac{1}{2}, 1\right)$ and $n = 1, 2, 4, 16$, commenting on their relation to the asymptotic result.
(c) Suppose that $x_n \sim \mathrm{t}(n)$. Approximate the value of c_n defined by $\Pr(|x_n| \leqslant c_n) = 0.95$, given that $\Phi(1.960) \approx 0.975$.
(d) Suppose that $x_n \sim \mathrm{F}(n, m)$. Prove that $\Pr(x_n > c) \to \Pr(\chi^2(m) < m/c)$ as $n \to \infty$.
(e) Let $\{x_n\}$ be a random sample from the uniform distribution $\mathrm{U}_{(0,\sqrt{12})}$, and take $n = 30$. Approximate $\Pr(|\overline{x}_n - \sqrt{3}| \leqslant 0.5)$, given that $\Phi(-2.74) \approx 0.003$.

Solution
(a) As seen in earlier chapters, x_n can be represented as the sum of squares of n independent $\mathrm{N}(0, 1)$ variates, which allows us to use the CLT to assess the limiting distribution of this sum. From the moments of a $\chi^2(n)$, we have $\mathrm{E}(x_n) = n$ and $\mathrm{var}(x_n) = 2n$. Then $z_n := (x_n - n)/\sqrt{2n}$ converges in distribution to $z \sim \mathrm{N}(0, 1)$ by the CLT, and

$$\Pr(x_n < n) = \Pr(z_n < 0) \approx \Pr(z < 0) = 0.5.$$

The exact results can be obtained from Exercise 4.20, where the c.d.f. can be expressed as a finite series expansion since $n \in \mathbb{N}$. To illustrate, we have $\Pr(\chi^2(10) < 10) \approx 0.560$, $\Pr(\chi^2(30) < 30) \approx 0.534$, and $\Pr(\chi^2(60) < 60) \approx 0.524$, exact to three decimal places, converging monotonically to 0.5 as $n \to \infty$.
(b) Using Exercises 7.18 and 7.19, $n\overline{x}_n \sim \mathrm{Gam}(n\nu, \lambda)$ or equivalently $2\lambda n\overline{x}_n \sim \chi^2(2n\nu)$. This gives $\mathrm{E}(\overline{x}_n) = \nu/\lambda$ and $\mathrm{var}(\overline{x}_n) = \nu/(\lambda^2 n)$, so that $\overline{x}_n \to \nu/\lambda$ which is the population mean of $x \sim \mathrm{Gam}(\nu, \lambda)$. By the CLT, $(\lambda\overline{x}_n - \nu)\sqrt{n/\nu}$ tends to a standard normal.

This is seen in Figure 10.1 where the density of $\overline{x}_n$ looks increasingly like a normal, even though $\text{Gam}\left(\frac{1}{2}, 1\right)$ is infinite at the origin. The density becomes more concentrated around $\frac{1}{2}$ until it eventually collapses to this single value with probability 1. We could have plotted the density of the normalized $(\overline{x}_n - \frac{1}{2})\sqrt{2n}$ instead of $\overline{x}_n$, in which case the p.d.f. would not have piled up near the asymptotic mean (the point $\frac{1}{2}$) but its shape would still have tended to the normal density.

(c) As seen in earlier chapters, Student's $\text{t}(n)$ has the representation $x_n \equiv z/\sqrt{y_n/n}$ where $z \sim \text{N}(0, 1)$ is independent of $y_n \sim \chi^2(n)$. Exercise 10.31 showed in a more general setup that $\text{plim}_{n\to\infty} y_n/n = 1$, and hence $x_n \xrightarrow{d} z$. Alternatively, Exercise 4.36 showed that the limit of the c.d.f. of $\text{t}(n)$, as $n \to \infty$, is the standard normal distribution. Hence,

$$\begin{aligned} 0.95 &= \Pr(|x_n| \leqslant c_n) \approx \Pr(|z| \leqslant c_n) = \Phi(c_n) - \Phi(-c_n) \\ &= \Phi(c_n) - (1 - \Phi(c_n)) = 2\Phi(c_n) - 1, \end{aligned}$$

implying that $c_n \approx 1.960$. The sequence $\{c_n\}$ decreases monotonically and converges to 1.960 as $n \to \infty$. For example, standard tables or the c.d.f. in Exercise 4.11 give $c_{10} \approx 2.228$, $c_{30} \approx 2.042$, and $c_{60} \approx 2.000$.

(d) Since $1/x_n \sim \text{F}(m, n)$ and $\chi^2(n)/n \to 1$ independently of the $\chi^2(m)/m$ numerator of $\text{F}(m, n)$, we have $m/x_n \overset{a}{\sim} \chi^2(m)$ and

$$\Pr(x_n > c) = \Pr(m/x_n < m/c) \to \Pr(\chi^2(m) < m/c).$$

Notice that, in general, the lower tail quantiles of $\text{F}(m, n)$ are obtained from the upper tail quantiles of $\text{F}(n, m)$, which is why statistical tables only have the latter. Notice also that this limiting result explains the asymptotic relation between χ^2 and F, seen also in Exercise 8.37(b).

(e) Since $\text{E}(x_i) = \sqrt{3}$ and

$$\text{var}(x_i) = \frac{1}{\sqrt{12}} \int_0^{\sqrt{12}} u^2 \, du - \left(\sqrt{3}\right)^2 = 1,$$

we see that $z_n := \sqrt{n}(\overline{x}_n - \sqrt{3}) \xrightarrow{d} z \sim \text{N}(0, 1)$. Hence,

$$\begin{aligned} \Pr(|\overline{x}_n - \sqrt{3}| \leqslant 0.5) &= \Pr(|z_n| \leqslant 0.5\sqrt{n}) \\ &\approx \Pr(|z| \leqslant 0.5\sqrt{n}) \approx \Pr(|z| \leqslant 2.74) \approx 0.994. \end{aligned}$$

Recall Exercise 7.13, where the sum of two independent uniforms had a triangular p.d.f., which is already (at $n = 2$) much closer to the normal's bell shape than to the uniform's flat density.

Exercise 10.33 (Sample variance: asymptotics) Let $\{x_n\}$ be a random sample from a distribution with mean μ, variance $\sigma^2 > 0$, and excess kurtosis $\kappa := \text{E}((x - \mu)^4/\sigma^4) - 3$, all finite. Prove that the sample variance s_n^2 satisfies $\sqrt{n}(s_n^2 - \sigma^2) \overset{a}{\sim} \text{N}\left(0, (2 + \kappa)\sigma^4\right)$.

Solution

We first observe that $\sum_{i=1}^n (x_i-\mu)^2 = \sum_{i=1}^n (x_i-\overline{x}_n)^2 + n(\overline{x}_n-\mu)^2$, so that

$$s_n^2 = \frac{1}{n-1}\sum_{i=1}^n (x_i-\overline{x}_n)^2 = \frac{n}{n-1}\left(\frac{1}{n}\sum_{i=1}^n (x_i-\mu)^2 - (\overline{x}_n-\mu)^2\right).$$

Letting $y_i := (x_i-\mu)^2$,

$$s_n^2 - \sigma^2 = \frac{n}{n-1}\left(\overline{y}_n - \sigma^2 + \frac{\sigma^2}{n} - (\overline{x}_n-\mu)^2\right).$$

By definition, we also have that $\mathrm{E}(y_i)=\sigma^2$ and

$$\mathrm{var}(y_i) = \mathrm{E}((x_i-\mu)^4) - \left[\mathrm{E}((x_i-\mu)^2)\right]^2 = (3+\kappa)\sigma^4 - \sigma^4 = (2+\kappa)\sigma^4,$$

so the CLT gives

$$\sqrt{n}(\overline{y}_n-\sigma^2) \overset{a}{\sim} \mathrm{N}(0,(2+\kappa)\sigma^4).$$

Therefore,

$$\sqrt{n}(s_n^2-\sigma^2) = \frac{n}{n-1}\left(\sqrt{n}(\overline{y}_n-\sigma^2) + \frac{\sigma^2 - \left(\sqrt{n}(\overline{x}_n-\mu)\right)^2}{\sqrt{n}}\right) \overset{a}{\sim} \mathrm{N}(0,(2+\kappa)\sigma^4)$$

since $\sqrt{n}(\overline{x}_n-\mu) = O_p(1)$ by the CLT. Note that $s_n^2 \to \sigma^2$ almost surely, because the SLLN applies to $\overline{y}_n$ and to $\overline{x}_n$.

Exercise 10.34 (Sample variance: multivariate asymptotics) Let the $m\times 1$ variate $\boldsymbol{x}$ have mean $\boldsymbol{\mu}$ and variance matrix $\boldsymbol{\Sigma}$, both assumed finite. Assume also that $\mathrm{E}(x_i x_j x_k x_l)$ exists for all $i,j,k,l=1,\dots,m$.

(a) Let $\{\boldsymbol{x}_n\}$ be a random sample from $\boldsymbol{x}$. Show that $\boldsymbol{S} := (n-1)^{-1}\sum_{i=1}^n (\boldsymbol{x}_i-\overline{\boldsymbol{x}})(\boldsymbol{x}_i-\overline{\boldsymbol{x}})'$ satisfies

$$\sqrt{n}\,\mathrm{vech}\,(\boldsymbol{S}-\boldsymbol{\Sigma}) \overset{a}{\sim} \mathrm{N}(\mathbf{0}_{(m+1)m/2},\boldsymbol{\Omega}),$$

where $\boldsymbol{\Omega} := \mathrm{var}(\mathrm{vech}\,((\boldsymbol{x}-\boldsymbol{\mu})(\boldsymbol{x}-\boldsymbol{\mu})'))$ and $\mathrm{vech}\,(\boldsymbol{A})$ denotes the vector containing a_{ij} for $i \geqslant j$ (that is, the vector obtained by stacking nonrepeated elements of the columns of the symmetric $\boldsymbol{A}$).

(b) Assuming $\boldsymbol{x} = (x_1,x_2)'$ is elliptically distributed with variance

$$\boldsymbol{\Sigma} = \begin{pmatrix} 1 & \rho \\ \rho & 1 \end{pmatrix}$$

and $\kappa := \mathrm{E}((x_1-\mu_1)^4)-3$, show by means of Exercise 8.20 that

$$\boldsymbol{\Omega} = \begin{pmatrix} 2+\kappa & (2+\kappa)\rho & (1+2\rho^2)(1+\kappa/3)-1 \\ (2+\kappa)\rho & (1+2\rho^2)(1+\kappa/3)-\rho^2 & (2+\kappa)\rho \\ (1+2\rho^2)(1+\kappa/3)-1 & (2+\kappa)\rho & 2+\kappa \end{pmatrix}.$$

Solution

(a) Exercise 9.5(b) established $\mathrm{E}(\boldsymbol{S}) = \boldsymbol{\Sigma}$ and the identity

$$\boldsymbol{S} = -\frac{n}{n-1}(\overline{\boldsymbol{x}} - \boldsymbol{\mu})(\overline{\boldsymbol{x}} - \boldsymbol{\mu})' + \frac{1}{n-1}\sum_{i=1}^{n}(\boldsymbol{x}_i - \boldsymbol{\mu})(\boldsymbol{x}_i - \boldsymbol{\mu})'.$$

By the multivariate CLT, the first term on the right-hand side tends to zero at a rate $O_p(1/n)$, and the second is asymptotically normal around its expectation $\boldsymbol{\Sigma} \equiv \mathrm{E}((\boldsymbol{x} - \boldsymbol{\mu})(\boldsymbol{x} - \boldsymbol{\mu})')$. Therefore, multiplying both sides by $\sqrt{n}$ and subtracting $\sqrt{n}\boldsymbol{\Sigma}$ gives

$$\begin{aligned}\sqrt{n}(\boldsymbol{S} - \boldsymbol{\Sigma}) &= \sqrt{n}\frac{1}{n-1}\sum_{i=1}^{n}(\boldsymbol{x}_i - \boldsymbol{\mu})(\boldsymbol{x}_i - \boldsymbol{\mu})' - \sqrt{n}\boldsymbol{\Sigma} + o_p(1)\\ &= \sqrt{n}\frac{1}{n-1}\sum_{i=1}^{n}\left((\boldsymbol{x}_i - \boldsymbol{\mu})(\boldsymbol{x}_i - \boldsymbol{\mu})' - \boldsymbol{\Sigma}\right) + o_p(1)\end{aligned}$$

since $(n-1)^{-1}\sum_{i=1}^{n}\boldsymbol{\Sigma} = \boldsymbol{\Sigma}(1 + O(1/n))$. The summands are random matrices minus their common expectation and, given the assumed existence of the fourth-order moments of $\boldsymbol{x}$, the multivariate CLT applies to $\mathrm{vech}(\sqrt{n}(\boldsymbol{S} - \boldsymbol{\Sigma}))$ and we get the required result. Note that vech is a linear operator, since it just reshapes the matrix into a vector.

(b) When $m = 2$, we have

$$\mathrm{vech}(\boldsymbol{S} - \boldsymbol{\Sigma}) = \begin{pmatrix} s_{11} - \sigma_{11} \\ s_{21} - \sigma_{21} \\ s_{22} - \sigma_{22} \end{pmatrix} \quad \text{and} \quad \boldsymbol{\Omega} = \mathrm{var}\begin{pmatrix} (x_1 - \mu_1)^2 \\ (x_1 - \mu_1)(x_2 - \mu_2) \\ (x_2 - \mu_2)^2 \end{pmatrix}.$$

Substituting from Exercise 8.20 (where x_1 and x_2 are already de-meaned) into

$$\boldsymbol{\Omega} = \begin{pmatrix} \mathrm{var}(x_1^2) & \mathrm{cov}(x_1x_2, x_1^2) & \mathrm{cov}(x_1^2, x_2^2) \\ \mathrm{cov}(x_1x_2, x_1^2) & \mathrm{var}(x_1x_2) & \mathrm{cov}(x_1x_2, x_2^2) \\ \mathrm{cov}(x_1^2, x_2^2) & \mathrm{cov}(x_1x_2, x_2^2) & \mathrm{var}(x_2^2) \end{pmatrix},$$

we get the stated result. See also (8.2) in the Notes to Chapter 8 (on Exercise 8.20) for an alternative formulation of $\boldsymbol{\Omega}$.

Exercise 10.35 (Transformation of correlations by Fisher's z) Let $\boldsymbol{x}$ be a 2×1 elliptically distributed vector whose correlation coefficient ρ and excess kurtosis κ exist. Define $\widehat{\rho}$ to be the correlation calculated from a random sample of size n from this distribution. Prove that:

(a) $\sqrt{n}(\widehat{\rho} - \rho) \overset{a}{\sim} \mathrm{N}(0, (1-\rho^2)^2(1+\kappa/3))$, comparing this result with Exercises 9.7(b) and 9.25 [use $n^{b-a}\Gamma(n+a)/\Gamma(n+b) \to 1$ from Section A.3.4];

(b) $\sqrt{n}(\tanh^{-1}(\widehat{\rho}) - \tanh^{-1}(\rho)) \overset{a}{\sim} \mathrm{N}(0, 1+\kappa/3)$, comparing it with part (a).

Solution

(a) Since correlations are scale-invariant, by construction, we can set the variance matrix as $\boldsymbol{\Sigma}$ of Exercise 10.34(b). Note however that the *sample* variances (s_{11} and s_{22} below) are random and therefore are *not* set to 1 by this simplification. The sample correlation can be written in terms of the elements of the sample variance matrix $\boldsymbol{S}$ as

$$\widehat{\rho}=\frac{s_{12}}{\sqrt{s_{11}s_{22}}}=\frac{\rho+(s_{12}-\rho)}{\sqrt{1+(s_{11}-1)}\sqrt{1+(s_{22}-1)}}.$$

From Exercise 10.34, we know that the three terms in parentheses are $O_p(1/\sqrt{n})$; thus we define

$$y_{11}:=\sqrt{n}\,(s_{11}-1)\,,\quad y_{12}:=\sqrt{n}\,(s_{12}-\rho)\,,\quad y_{22}:=\sqrt{n}\,(s_{22}-1)\,.$$

The binomial expansion implies that $(1+n^{-1/2}z)^{-1/2}=1-n^{-1/2}z/2+O_p(n^{-1})$ for any $z=O_p(1)$; hence

$$\begin{aligned}\widehat{\rho}&=\left(\rho+\frac{y_{12}}{\sqrt{n}}\right)\left(1-\frac{y_{11}}{2\sqrt{n}}+O_p\left(\frac{1}{n}\right)\right)\left(1-\frac{y_{22}}{2\sqrt{n}}+O_p\left(\frac{1}{n}\right)\right)\\&=\left(\rho+\frac{y_{12}}{\sqrt{n}}\right)\left(1-\frac{y_{11}}{2\sqrt{n}}-\frac{y_{22}}{2\sqrt{n}}+O_p\left(\frac{1}{n}\right)\right)\\&=\rho\left(1-\frac{y_{11}}{2\sqrt{n}}-\frac{y_{22}}{2\sqrt{n}}\right)+\frac{y_{12}}{\sqrt{n}}+O_p\left(\frac{1}{n}\right).\end{aligned}$$

Rearranging,

$$\sqrt{n}\,(\widehat{\rho}-\rho)=-\frac{\rho}{2}y_{11}+y_{12}-\frac{\rho}{2}y_{22}+O_p\left(\frac{1}{\sqrt{n}}\right)\equiv\boldsymbol{a}'\sqrt{n}\,\mathrm{vech}\,(\boldsymbol{S}-\boldsymbol{\Sigma})+O_p\left(\frac{1}{\sqrt{n}}\right),$$

where $\boldsymbol{a}':=\left(-\rho/2,\,1,\,-\rho/2\right)$. Using Exercise 10.34,

$$\sqrt{n}\,(\widehat{\rho}-\rho)\overset{a}{\sim}\mathrm{N}\left(\boldsymbol{a}'\mathbf{0}_{(m+1)m/2},\boldsymbol{a}'\boldsymbol{\Omega}\boldsymbol{a}\right)=\mathrm{N}\left(0,\left(1-\rho^2\right)^2\left(1+\frac{\kappa}{3}\right)\right),$$

as required.

Now, Exercise 9.7(b) gave $z:=\widehat{\rho}\sqrt{n-2}/\sqrt{1-\widehat{\rho}^2}\sim\mathrm{t}(n-2)$ exactly (that is, for any n) and allowed one of the two variates to have any distribution, but it required their independence (implying that $\rho=0$). As $n\to\infty$, we have $\mathrm{t}(n-2)\to\mathrm{N}(0,1)$ so that z converges a.s. to a standard normal. But, letting $\rho=0$ in the current exercise, we get $\widehat{\rho}\sqrt{n-2}\overset{a}{\sim}\mathrm{N}(0,1+\kappa/3)$ and $\sqrt{1-\widehat{\rho}^2}\overset{p}{\longrightarrow}1$, so that $z\overset{a}{\sim}\mathrm{N}(0,1+\kappa/3)$. The apparent contradiction between the two limiting distributions of z is resolved by noting that κ must be zero here: the only bivariate elliptical where $\rho=0$ *and* the components are independent is the normal (see Exercise 8.10).

As in Exercise 9.25, we will show only that the limiting density is $\mathrm{N}(0,(1-\rho^2)^2)$; see Exercise 4.36 for an example of a more formal treatment. Applying the transformation theorem to the second formula of Exercise 9.25 gives the density of $z_n:=\sqrt{n}(\widehat{\rho}-\rho)$ under the normality of $\boldsymbol{x}$, with limit

$$f_{z_\infty}(w)=\lim_{n\to\infty}\frac{(n-2)\,\Gamma\,(n-1)\left(1-\rho^2\right)^{\frac{n-1}{2}}\left(1-\left(\rho+w/\sqrt{n}\right)^2\right)^{\frac{n}{2}-2}}{\sqrt{n}\sqrt{2\pi}\Gamma\left(n-\frac{1}{2}\right)\left(1-\rho\left(\rho+w/\sqrt{n}\right)\right)^{n-\frac{3}{2}}}$$

since the sum collapses to 1 (the only nonzero term is the one for $j = 0$) as $n \to \infty$. By

$$\frac{(n-2)\,\Gamma(n-1)}{\sqrt{n}\Gamma\left(n-\frac{1}{2}\right)} \to 1,$$

we can write $\sqrt{2\pi}\left(1-\rho^2\right) f_{z_\infty}(w)$ as

$$\sqrt{2\pi}\left(1-\rho^2\right)\lim_{n\to\infty}\frac{\left(1-\rho^2\right)^{\frac{n-1}{2}}\left(1-\left(\rho+w/\sqrt{n}\right)^2\right)^{\frac{n}{2}-2}}{\sqrt{2\pi}\left(1-\rho\left(\rho+w/\sqrt{n}\right)\right)^{n-\frac{3}{2}}}$$

$$= \lim_{n\to\infty}\frac{\left(1-\frac{2\rho w/\sqrt{n}+w^2/n}{1-\rho^2}\right)^{\frac{n}{2}-2}}{\left(1-\frac{\rho w/\sqrt{n}}{1-\rho^2}\right)^{n-\frac{3}{2}}}$$

$$= \lim_{n\to\infty}\frac{\exp\left(\left(\frac{n}{2}-2\right)\log\left(1-\frac{2\rho w/\sqrt{n}+w^2/n}{1-\rho^2}\right)\right)}{\exp\left(\left(n-\frac{3}{2}\right)\log\left(1-\frac{\rho w/\sqrt{n}}{1-\rho^2}\right)\right)}$$

$$= \lim_{n\to\infty}\frac{\exp\left(\left(\frac{n}{2}-2\right)\left(-\frac{2\rho w/\sqrt{n}+w^2/n}{1-\rho^2}-\frac{\left(2\rho w/\sqrt{n}+w^2/n\right)^2}{2(1-\rho^2)^2}+O\left(n^{-\frac{3}{2}}\right)\right)\right)}{\exp\left(\left(n-\frac{3}{2}\right)\left(-\frac{\rho w/\sqrt{n}}{1-\rho^2}-\frac{\rho^2 w^2/n}{2(1-\rho^2)^2}+O\left(n^{-\frac{3}{2}}\right)\right)\right)}$$

$$= \lim_{n\to\infty}\frac{\exp\left(-\frac{2\rho w\sqrt{n}+w^2}{2(1-\rho^2)}-\frac{(2\rho w)^2}{4(1-\rho^2)^2}\right)}{\exp\left(-\frac{\rho w\sqrt{n}}{1-\rho^2}-\frac{\rho^2 w^2}{2(1-\rho^2)^2}\right)}$$

$$= \exp\left(-\frac{w^2}{2\left(1-\rho^2\right)}-\frac{\rho^2 w^2}{2\left(1-\rho^2\right)^2}\right) = \exp\left(-\frac{w^2}{2\left(1-\rho^2\right)^2}\right),$$

which implies a normal density with mean zero and variance $(1-\rho^2)^2$.

(b) Part (a) can be translated, by the delta method, into the required result by means of $\mathrm{d}\tanh^{-1}(\rho)/\mathrm{d}\rho = 1/(1-\rho^2)$, which is obtained by differentiating the expansion of $\tanh^{-1}$ in Section A.3.3. Notice that the limiting distribution is now unaffected by the value of ρ, an effect known as *variance stabilization*. (Another variance stabilization that is common in economics is provided by use of logarithms, for the reason indicated at the end of Exercise 4.23.) In fact, the $\tanh^{-1}$ transformation could have been obtained (from the delta method) as the solution for the function g in the differential equation

$$\mathrm{var}(\widehat{\rho})(g'(\rho))^2 = \text{constant not depending on } \rho,$$

namely

$$g(\rho) \propto \int \frac{1}{\sqrt{\mathrm{var}(\widehat{\rho})}}\,\mathrm{d}\rho \propto \int \frac{1}{1-\rho^2}\,\mathrm{d}\rho = \tanh^{-1}(\rho).$$

The function

$$z_a := \tanh^{-1}(a) \equiv \frac{1}{2}\log\left(\frac{1+a}{1-a}\right)$$

is called *Fisher's z transformation*. It maps $\widehat{\rho} \in (-1, 1)$ into $\tanh^{-1}(\widehat{\rho}) \in \mathbb{R}$, the latter support being more appropriate for a normal variate. To see what it does, let $\rho > 0$ (we would get the mirror image for $\rho < 0$). The bulk of the density is concentrated around $\widehat{\rho} > 0$ but it has an upper bound at $\rho = +1$. The density of $\widehat{\rho}$ is typically asymmetric (unless $\rho = 0$) until n becomes very large: $\widehat{\rho}$ approaches ρ and the whole density piles up around that point, almost looking like a normal (see Figure 10.1 for a pictorial illustration of this type of behavior in a different setup). The $\tanh^{-1}$ mapping stretches the smaller upper tail of the density of $\widehat{\rho}$, translating into an improved shape for the density approximation when n is finite, especially if ρ is close to ± 1. We will revisit such issues in Exercise 11.21.

Exercise 10.36 (Expectation of ratios: asymptotic approximation) Define $z := x_1/\sqrt{x_2 x_3}$, where x_2 and x_3 are positive with probability 1, and assume that the vector (x_1, x_2, x_3) has finite moments up to order 3. Defining $\mu_i := \mathrm{E}(x_i)$, assume further that $x_i - \mu_i = O_p(1/\sqrt{n})$ as $n \to \infty$.
(a) Prove that, if $\mathrm{E}(z)$ exists, then

$$\mathrm{E}(z) = \frac{1}{\sqrt{\mu_2 \mu_3}} \left[\mu_1 - \frac{1}{2} \operatorname{cov}\left(x_1, \frac{x_2}{\mu_2} \right) - \frac{1}{2} \operatorname{cov}\left(x_1, \frac{x_3}{\mu_3} \right) + \frac{\mu_1}{4} \operatorname{cov}\left(\frac{x_2}{\mu_2}, \frac{x_3}{\mu_3} \right) \right.$$
$$\left. + \frac{3\mu_1}{8} \operatorname{var}\left(\frac{x_2}{\mu_2} \right) + \frac{3\mu_1}{8} \operatorname{var}\left(\frac{x_3}{\mu_3} \right) \right] + O\left(\frac{1}{n^{3/2}} \right).$$

(b) Hence prove that

$$\mathrm{E}\left(\frac{x_1}{x_2} \right) = \frac{1}{\mu_2} \left[\mu_1 \left(1 + \operatorname{var}\left(\frac{x_2}{\mu_2} \right) \right) - \operatorname{cov}\left(x_1, \frac{x_2}{\mu_2} \right) \right] + O\left(\frac{1}{n^{3/2}} \right).$$

(c) If x_1/x_2 and x_2 are uncorrelated, prove that $\mathrm{E}(x_1/x_2) = \mu_1/\mu_2$ exactly. Compare this result with (b), showing that it is not true that $\mu_1 \operatorname{var}(x_2/\mu_2) = \operatorname{cov}(x_1, x_2/\mu_2)$. What additional conditions are needed for this equality to hold?

Solution

(a) We employ binomial expansions similar to those in Exercise 10.35(a), but around the expectation of x_i and to higher order (that is, taking more terms). Let $y_i := \sqrt{n}(x_i - \mu_i) = O_p(1)$ for $i = 1, 2, 3$. Then, for $i = 2$ and $i = 3$, we have

$$x_i^{-1/2} = \left(\mu_i + \frac{y_i}{\sqrt{n}} \right)^{-1/2}$$
$$= \mu_i^{-1/2} \left(1 + \frac{y_i}{\mu_i \sqrt{n}} \right)^{-1/2}$$
$$= \mu_i^{-1/2} \left(1 - \frac{y_i}{2\mu_i \sqrt{n}} + \frac{3y_i^2}{8\mu_i^2 n} + O_p\left(\frac{1}{n^{3/2}} \right) \right),$$

and hence

$$z = \frac{\mu_1 + n^{-1/2} y_1}{\sqrt{\mu_2 + n^{-1/2} y_2}\sqrt{\mu_3 + n^{-1/2} y_3}}$$
$$= \frac{\mu_1 + n^{-1/2} y_1}{\sqrt{\mu_2 \mu_3}} \left(1 - \frac{y_2}{2\mu_2\sqrt{n}} + \frac{3y_2^2}{8\mu_2^2 n} + O_p\left(\frac{1}{n^{3/2}}\right)\right)$$
$$\times \left(1 - \frac{y_3}{2\mu_3\sqrt{n}} + \frac{3y_3^2}{8\mu_3^2 n} + O_p\left(\frac{1}{n^{3/2}}\right)\right).$$

Multiplying out the terms,

$$z = \frac{\mu_1 + n^{-1/2} y_1}{\sqrt{\mu_2 \mu_3}}$$
$$\times \left(1 - \frac{1}{\sqrt{n}}\left(\frac{y_2}{2\mu_2} + \frac{y_3}{2\mu_3}\right) + \frac{1}{n}\left(\frac{y_2}{2\mu_2}\frac{y_3}{2\mu_3} + \frac{3y_2^2}{8\mu_2^2} + \frac{3y_3^2}{8\mu_3^2}\right) + O_p\left(\frac{1}{n^{3/2}}\right)\right)$$
$$= \frac{\mu_1}{\sqrt{\mu_2 \mu_3}}\left(1 - \frac{1}{\sqrt{n}}\left(\frac{y_2}{2\mu_2} + \frac{y_3}{2\mu_3}\right) + \frac{1}{n}\left(\frac{y_2}{2\mu_2}\frac{y_3}{2\mu_3} + \frac{3y_2^2}{8\mu_2^2} + \frac{3y_3^2}{8\mu_3^2}\right)\right)$$
$$+ \frac{y_1}{\sqrt{\mu_2\mu_3}\sqrt{n}}\left(1 - \frac{1}{\sqrt{n}}\left(\frac{y_2}{2\mu_2} + \frac{y_3}{2\mu_3}\right)\right) + O_p\left(\frac{1}{n^{3/2}}\right).$$

Taking expectations, the terms containing $n^{-1/2}$ vanish because $\mathrm{E}(y_i) = 0$, and we obtain the required expression by substituting $\mathrm{E}(y_i y_j) = n \operatorname{cov}(x_i, x_j)$. If $\mu_1 \neq 0$, we can rewrite the result in the normalized version

$$\mathrm{E}(z) = \frac{\mu_1}{\sqrt{\mu_2\mu_3}}\left[1 - \frac{1}{2}\operatorname{cov}\left(\frac{x_1}{\mu_1}, \frac{x_2}{\mu_2}\right) - \frac{1}{2}\operatorname{cov}\left(\frac{x_1}{\mu_1}, \frac{x_3}{\mu_3}\right) + \frac{1}{4}\operatorname{cov}\left(\frac{x_2}{\mu_2}, \frac{x_3}{\mu_3}\right)\right.$$
$$\left. + \frac{3}{8}\operatorname{var}\left(\frac{x_2}{\mu_2}\right) + \frac{3}{8}\operatorname{var}\left(\frac{x_3}{\mu_3}\right)\right] + O\left(\frac{1}{n^{3/2}}\right),$$

where we note that $\mathrm{E}(x_i/\mu_i) = 1$ and the remainder term is bounded by third-order moments (see the details of Exercise 10.40) which exist by assumption. Note that the order notation is an inequality relation. Therefore, as we have seen the terms containing $n^{-1/2}$ vanish when taking expectations, the $O\left(n^{-3/2}\right)$ remainder term may or may not contain a nonzero term in $n^{-3/2}$. This will depend on the value of the higher-order moments of (x_1, x_2, x_3).

(b) The formula for the special case of $z = x_1/x_2$ is obtained by setting $x_2 = x_3$.

(c) Defining $z := x_1/x_2$, we have the exact relation

$$\mathrm{E}(x_1) = \mathrm{E}(z x_2) = \mathrm{E}(z)\,\mathrm{E}(x_2)$$

as z and x_2 are uncorrelated (but not necessarily independent). The required result follows by using $\mu_i := \mathrm{E}(x_i)$ and dividing throughout by μ_2.

Compared with (b), we do not need the existence of third-order moments here. More importantly, we have an exact relation that translates into

$$\mathrm{E}\left(\frac{x_1}{x_2}\right) = \frac{1}{\mu_2}\left[\mu_1\left(1+\mathrm{var}\left(\frac{x_2}{\mu_2}\right)\right) - \mathrm{cov}\left(x_1, \frac{x_2}{\mu_2}\right)\right] + O\left(\frac{1}{n^{3/2}}\right),$$

but *not* into

$$\mathrm{E}\left(\frac{x_1}{x_2}\right) = \frac{1}{\mu_2}\left[\mu_1\left(1+\mathrm{var}\left(\frac{x_2}{\mu_2}\right)\right) - \mathrm{cov}\left(x_1, \frac{x_2}{\mu_2}\right)\right]$$

unless we make further assumptions. This seemingly unusual result is obtained because, although $\mu_1 \,\mathrm{var}(x_2/\mu_2)$ and $\mathrm{cov}(x_1, x_2/\mu_2)$ are individually $O(1/n)$, their difference is a smaller-order term that cancels with the $O\left(1/n^{3/2}\right)$ term. To see why, consider

$$\mathrm{cov}\left(x_1, \frac{x_2}{\mu_2}\right) = \mathrm{E}\left(zx_2\frac{x_2}{\mu_2}\right) - \mathrm{E}(zx_2)\,\mathrm{E}\left(\frac{x_2}{\mu_2}\right) = \mu_2\,\mathrm{E}\left(z\frac{x_2^2}{\mu_2^2}\right) - \mu_1.$$

The last expectation gives a covariance term that explains the puzzle, and the strength of the (nonlinear) relation between z and x_2 is crucial.

If we assume that z is also uncorrelated with x_2^2 (in addition to being uncorrelated with x_2), then

$$\mathrm{cov}\left(x_1, \frac{x_2}{\mu_2}\right) = \mu_1\,\mathrm{var}\left(\frac{x_2}{\mu_2}\right)$$

and

$$\mathrm{E}\left(\frac{x_1}{x_2}\right) = \frac{1}{\mu_2}\left[\mu_1\left(1+\mathrm{var}\left(\frac{x_2}{\mu_2}\right)\right) - \mathrm{cov}\left(x_1, \frac{x_2}{\mu_2}\right)\right]$$

exactly. See the Notes to Chapter 3 for an earlier discussion of such exact results.

***Exercise 10.37 (Central limit theorem: Lindeberg–Feller)** Let $\{x_n\}$ be an independent sequence, with means $\{\mu_n\}$ and nonzero variances $\{\sigma_n^2\}$, both existing, and c.d.f.s $\{F_n\}$. Defining $\lambda_n > 0$ by

$$\lambda_n^2 := \sum_{i=1}^{n} \sigma_i^2,$$

prove that *Lindeberg's condition*

$$\lim_{n\to\infty} \sum_{i=1}^{n} \int_{|u-\mu_i|\geqslant\lambda_n\epsilon} \left(\frac{u-\mu_i}{\lambda_n}\right)^2 \mathrm{d}F_i(u) = 0 \quad \text{for all } \epsilon > 0$$

is equivalent to

$$z_n := \frac{\sum_{i=1}^{n}(x_i - \mu_i)}{\lambda_n} \overset{a}{\sim} \mathrm{N}(0,1) \quad \text{and} \quad \lim_{n\to\infty} \max_{i\leqslant n}\left\{\Pr\left(\frac{|x_i-\mu_i|}{\lambda_n} \gtrsim \epsilon\right)\right\} = 0,$$

where the latter limit is called the *uniform asymptotic negligibility* (u.a.n.) *condition*. (One can usually interpret λ_n^2 as the variance of the numerator of z_n, but see Exercise 10.38.) [Hint: To derive Lindeberg's condition from the other two, write the logarithm of the c.f. of z_n in terms of c.f.s of x_i, expand the logarithmic function, and then use the inequality (compare Exercise 3.29) $t^2/2 + \operatorname{Re}(e^{it}) - 1 \geqslant 0$ for any $t \in \mathbb{R}$.]

Solution

In the statement of the theorem, all the expressions are in terms of the centered sequence $\{x_n - \mu_n\}$, so there is no loss of generality in setting $\mu_n = 0$ in our derivations.

First, we assume that Lindeberg's condition holds, and show that it implies u.a.n. and asymptotic standard-normality. In Lindeberg's condition, the summands (integrals) are nonnegative, hence each of them tends to zero. But

$$\sigma_i^2 := \int_{|u|\geqslant 0} u^2 \, dF_i(u) = \int_{|u|>0} u^2 \, dF_i(u)$$

since the integrand is zero at $u = 0$, so we can choose $\epsilon \to 0^+$ in Lindeberg's condition to get

$$\lim_{n\to\infty} \frac{\max_{i\leqslant n}\{\sigma_i^2\}}{\lambda_n^2} = 0,$$

which is known as *Feller's condition*, to be used below. We started from a truncated expectation (Lindeberg's condition), and we want to infer something about a probability, so Exercise 3.12 is again the place to look! In proving Chebyshev's inequality, we have made use of $\Pr(|x_i| \geqslant \lambda_n\epsilon) \leqslant \int_{|u|\geqslant\lambda_n\epsilon} (u/(\lambda_n\epsilon))^2 \, dF_i(u)$. Therefore,

$$\sum_{i=1}^{n} \Pr(|x_i| \geqslant \lambda_n\epsilon) \leqslant \sum_{i=1}^{n} \int_{|u|\geqslant\lambda_n\epsilon} \left(\frac{u}{\lambda_n\epsilon}\right)^2 dF_i(u)$$

and Lindeberg's condition implies u.a.n., as required. We also want to show that it implies the convergence of z_n to a standard normal. The c.f. of z_n is

$$\varphi_{z_n}(\tau) = \mathrm{E}(\exp(i\tau z_n)) = \mathrm{E}\left(\exp\left(\frac{i\tau}{\lambda_n}\sum_{i=1}^{n} x_i\right)\right) = \prod_{i=1}^{n} \varphi_i\left(\frac{\tau}{\lambda_n}\right)$$

by the independence of the sequence $\{x_n\}$ which has c.f.s $\{\varphi_n\}$. Using the values of the first two moments of x_i, we obtain

$$\varphi_{z_n}(\tau) = \prod_{i=1}^{n}\left(1 - \frac{\tau^2\sigma_i^2}{2\lambda_n^2} + o\left(\frac{\sigma_i^2}{\lambda_n^2}\right)\right),$$

where the remainder is bounded by Feller's condition (similarly to Exercise 3.29 where $\tau \to 0$ instead). Taking logarithms on both sides and expanding the right-hand side gives

$$\begin{aligned}\log(\varphi_{z_n}(\tau)) &= \sum_{i=1}^{n} \log\left(1 - \frac{\tau^2\sigma_i^2}{2\lambda_n^2} + o\left(\frac{\sigma_i^2}{\lambda_n^2}\right)\right) \\ &= -\sum_{i=1}^{n}\left(\frac{\tau^2\sigma_i^2}{2\lambda_n^2} + o\left(\frac{\sigma_i^2}{\lambda_n^2}\right)\right) = -\frac{\tau^2}{2} + o(1)\end{aligned}$$

by the definition of λ_n^2 in terms of σ_n^2. This is the required asymptotic standard-normality.

For the second part, we start with the premise that

$$\lim_{n\to\infty}\sum_{i=1}^{n}\log\left(\varphi_i\left(\frac{\tau}{\lambda_n}\right)\right)=-\frac{\tau^2}{2}\quad\text{and}\quad\lim_{n\to\infty}\max_{i\leqslant n}\left\{\Pr\left(\frac{|x_i|}{\lambda_n}\geqslant\epsilon\right)\right\}=0$$

for all $\epsilon>0$. The latter implies a degenerate x_i/λ_n in the limit and hence

$$\lim_{n\to\infty}\max_{i\leqslant n}\{|\varphi_i(\tau/\lambda_n)-1|\}=0,$$

while expansion of the logarithm in the former gives

$$-\frac{\tau^2}{2}=\lim_{n\to\infty}\sum_{i=1}^{n}\left(\varphi_i\left(\frac{\tau}{\lambda_n}\right)-1+o\left(\varphi_i\left(\frac{\tau}{\lambda_n}\right)-1\right)\right)=\lim_{n\to\infty}\sum_{i=1}^{n}\left(\varphi_i\left(\frac{\tau}{\lambda_n}\right)-1\right).$$

The left-hand side, $-\tau^2/2$, is real and it implies that the imaginary part of $\varphi_i(\tau/\lambda_n)$ (in the right-hand side) will vanish in the limit. Furthermore, $\lambda_n^2=\sum_{i=1}^{n}\mathrm{E}\left(x_i^2\right)$, so we can rewrite the last equation as

$$\begin{aligned}0&=\lim_{n\to\infty}\sum_{i=1}^{n}\left(\frac{\tau^2\,\mathrm{E}\left(x_i^2\right)}{2\lambda_n^2}+\mathrm{Re}\left(\mathrm{E}\left(\mathrm{e}^{\mathrm{i}\tau x_i/\lambda_n}-1\right)\right)\right)\\&=\lim_{n\to\infty}\sum_{i=1}^{n}\int_{-\infty}^{\infty}\left(\frac{\tau^2u^2}{2\lambda_n^2}+\mathrm{Re}\left(\mathrm{e}^{\mathrm{i}\tau u/\lambda_n}\right)-1\right)\mathrm{d}F_i(u),\end{aligned}$$

where we can use $\mathrm{Re}\left(\mathrm{e}^{\mathrm{i}t}\right)=\cos(t)$ for $t\in\mathbb{R}$. For any $\tau\in\mathbb{R}$, the integrand is nonnegative everywhere since $\frac{1}{2}t^2+\cos(t)-1\geqslant 0$, as in the hint to the question, and so the last displayed equation implies that for all $\epsilon>0$

$$\begin{aligned}0&=\lim_{n\to\infty}\sum_{i=1}^{n}\int_{|u|\geqslant\lambda_n\epsilon}\left(\frac{\tau^2u^2}{2\lambda_n^2}+\cos\left(\frac{\tau u}{\lambda_n}\right)-1\right)\mathrm{d}F_i(u)\\&\geqslant\lim_{n\to\infty}\sum_{i=1}^{n}\int_{|u|\geqslant\lambda_n\epsilon}\left(\frac{\tau^2u^2}{2\lambda_n^2}-2\right)\mathrm{d}F_i(u)\qquad(\text{since }\cos(t)\geqslant-1)\\&=\lim_{n\to\infty}\sum_{i=1}^{n}\left(\int_{|u|\geqslant\lambda_n\epsilon}\frac{\tau^2u^2}{2\lambda_n^2}\mathrm{d}F_i(u)-2\Pr(|x_i|\geqslant\lambda_n\epsilon)\right).\end{aligned}$$

As in the first part of the proof, using $\Pr(|x_i|\geqslant\lambda_n\epsilon)\leqslant\int_{|u|\geqslant\lambda_n\epsilon}(u/(\lambda_n\epsilon))^2\,\mathrm{d}F_i(u)$, we get

$$0\geqslant\left(\frac{\tau^2}{2}-\frac{2}{\epsilon^2}\right)\lim_{n\to\infty}\sum_{i=1}^{n}\int_{|u|\geqslant\lambda_n\epsilon}\frac{u^2}{\lambda_n^2}\mathrm{d}F_i(u).$$

Since this holds for any $\tau\in\mathbb{R}$, including those satisfying $\tau^2>4/\epsilon^2$, and the integral is not negative, it follows that the limit is zero.

***Exercise 10.38 (CLT: normal despite conditions)** Give two examples where asymptotic normality holds in spite of the violation of some conditions in Exercise 10.37.

Solution

First, Exercise 10.37 established an elaborate equivalence, which needs to be interpreted carefully as we will now show. To start, the proof of Exercise 10.37 implies the following relation between the various conditions:

$$\text{Lindeberg's} \implies \text{Feller's} \implies \text{u.a.n.},$$

the latter implication following by Chebyshev's inequality; compare with Exercise 10.8(a). Violation of one of the latter two conditions has the consequence that Lindeberg's is also violated, by contrapositive. The limiting distribution of z_n may be a normal, even if Lindeberg's condition fails. For example, one may take the sequence $\{x_n\}$ to be normal, so that any arbitrary linear combination of $\{x_n\}$ is normal. If we choose σ_n^2 (the variance of the last x_n) as any positive proportion of λ_n^2, then u.a.n. is violated. One such choice is $\sigma_n^2 = \exp(-1 + 1/n)\,\lambda_n^2$, with $\sigma_1^2 = \lambda_1^2$ and $\lim_{n\to\infty} \sigma_n^2/\lambda_n^2 = 1/\mathrm{e} \neq 0$.

Second, and perhaps more striking, asymptotic normality can hold even if the $\{x_n\}$ have infinite variances, but we will require the truncated second moments to satisfy Lindeberg's condition. For simplicity, take the sequence $\{x_n\}$ to be i.i.d. and assume λ_n^2 is some scaling factor (rather than a variance) satisfying $\lambda_n \to \infty$ as $n \to \infty$, such that the u.a.n. condition $\lim_{n\to\infty} \max_{i\leqslant n}\{\Pr(|x_i|/\lambda_n \geqslant \epsilon)\} = 0$ holds. Therefore, $\log(\varphi_i(\tau/\lambda_n))$ is asymptotically equivalent to $\varphi_i(\tau/\lambda_n) - 1$, and the required asymptotic normality of the sample mean reduces to finding x_i and λ_n such that

$$-\frac{\tau^2}{2} = \lim_{n\to\infty} \sum_{i=1}^{n} \left(\mathrm{E}\left(\mathrm{e}^{\mathrm{i}x_i\tau/\lambda_n}\right) - 1\right).$$

Expanding the exponential for large λ_n and assuming x_i is symmetric around zero (see Exercise 3.23), we obtain

$$-\frac{\tau^2}{2} = -\frac{\tau^2}{2} \lim_{n\to\infty} \sum_{i=1}^{n} \int_{|u|<\lambda_n\epsilon} \frac{u^2}{\lambda_n^2}\, \mathrm{d}F(u), \quad \lambda_n \to \infty,$$

where the integral is the truncated (when $n < \infty$) and scaled second moment. We need to find the appropriate $F(u)$ and λ_n^2 which make the latter limit equal to 1 for all $\epsilon > 0$. Notice that this limit is the complement of Lindeberg's condition. From the stable limit theorem in the introduction to this chapter, we know that the limiting distribution cannot be normal if the tails of the p.d.f. decay at a rate $1/u^{p+1}$ where $p < 2$, so we need a density whose tails decay faster (hence also implying that $\mathrm{E}(x_i)$ exists). Looking at Table 4.2, we can choose Student's t(2), which is symmetric and which possesses no moments of order $\geqslant 2$ since its density decays at the rate $1/u^3$ and has the truncated variance

$$\int_{-c\sqrt{2}}^{c\sqrt{2}} \frac{u^2}{\sqrt{8}\,(1+u^2/2)^{3/2}}\, \mathrm{d}u = 2\log\left(\sqrt{1+c^2} + c\right) - \frac{2c}{\sqrt{1+c^2}}$$
$$= 2\sinh^{-1}(c) - \frac{2c}{\sqrt{1+c^2}};$$

see Section A.3.3 for the expression of inverse hyperbolic functions in terms of logarithms. This is precisely the integral required for Lindeberg's condition where, since we have chosen $\{x_n\}$ to be i.i.d., $\sum_{i=1}^{n}$ is replaced by n. Therefore, we only need to solve

$$1 = \lim_{n\to\infty} \frac{n}{\lambda_n^2} \int_{|u|<\lambda_n \epsilon} u^2 \, \mathrm{d}F(u) = \lim_{n\to\infty} \frac{2n \sinh^{-1}\left(\lambda_n \epsilon/\sqrt{2}\right)}{\lambda_n^2},$$

where we have dropped $2c/\sqrt{1+c^2} \to 2$ because it is dominated by $\sinh^{-1}(c) \to \infty$. As $\sinh^{-1}(c) = \log(\sqrt{1+c^2}+c)$, the condition which we need to solve simplifies (in the limit) to

$$1 = \lim_{n\to\infty} \frac{2n \log(\lambda_n)}{\lambda_n^2}$$

by $\log\left(\lambda_n \epsilon \sqrt{2}\right) = \log(\lambda_n) + \log\left(\epsilon\sqrt{2}\right) \sim \log(\lambda_n)$ as $n \to \infty$. Therefore, $\lambda_n = \sqrt{n \log(n)}$ or any asymptotically equivalent function such as $\sqrt{n\log(n)} + \sqrt{n}$. To sum up, a random sample from Student's $\mathrm{t}(2)$ will have the asymptotically normal mean

$$\overline{x}\sqrt{\frac{n}{\log(n)}} \overset{a}{\sim} \mathrm{N}(0,1),$$

even though $\mathrm{var}(x_i) = \infty$. Contrast this with $\mathrm{t}(\nu)$ for $\nu > 2$, where the standard conditions of the CLT apply to give $\overline{x}\sqrt{n} \overset{a}{\sim} \mathrm{N}(0,1)$. It is enough to dampen the usual $\overline{x}\sqrt{n}$ by $\sqrt{\log(n)}$ to get asymptotic normality for $\mathrm{t}(2)$. To get a feel for how slowly $\log(n)$ grows as $n \to \infty$, take n equal to one billion: $\log 10^9 \approx 20.7$. This should also be kept in mind later, when we are interpreting the law of the iterated logarithm. Notice also that

$$\mathrm{var}\left(\overline{x}\sqrt{n/\log(n)}\right) = \infty$$

for any $n < \infty$, since $\mathrm{var}(x_i) = \infty$, but that the limiting variance is finite and equal to 1 because of the $\mathrm{N}(0,1)$ asymptotic distribution. The limiting variance is *not* the limit of the finite-sample variances as $n \to \infty$. See also Exercise 10.8(c).

10.3 Law of iterated log, stable limit theorem, distribution of extremes

Exercise 10.39 (Gamma asymptotics: Stirling and Poisson) Let $\{x_n\}$ be a random sample from the $\mathrm{Poi}(1)$ distribution.
(a) Derive $\Pr(-1/n < \overline{x}_n - 1 \leqslant 0)$.
(b) By applying the CLT to the probability in (a), prove *Stirling's approximation* for $n!$, which can be stated as

$$\lim_{n\to\infty} \frac{n!}{\sqrt{2\pi} n^{n+1/2} \mathrm{e}^{-n}} = 1$$

Solution

(a) The variate $n\overline{x}_n = x_1 + \cdots + x_n$ is Poi(n) by Exercise 4.8, and

$$\begin{aligned}\Pr\left(-\frac{1}{n} < \overline{x}_n - 1 \leqslant 0\right) &= \Pr\left(-1 < x_1 + \cdots + x_n - n \leqslant 0\right) \\ &= \Pr(n - 1 < x_1 + \cdots + x_n \leqslant n) \\ &= \Pr(x_1 + \cdots + x_n = n) = \mathrm{e}^{-n} n^n / n!.\end{aligned}$$

(b) Since $n\overline{x}_n \sim$ Poi(n) with both mean and variance equal to n, the CLT implies that $\sqrt{n}\,(\overline{x}_n - 1) \overset{a}{\sim} \mathrm{N}(0,1)$. Hence, for any $p > 0$,

$$\begin{aligned}\lim_{n\to\infty} n^p \Pr\left(-\frac{1}{n^p} < \sqrt{n}\,(\overline{x}_n - 1) \leqslant 0\right) &= \lim_{n\to\infty} n^p \int_{-1/n^p}^{0} \frac{\mathrm{e}^{-u^2/2}}{\sqrt{2\pi}}\,\mathrm{d}u \\ &= \frac{1}{\sqrt{2\pi}} \lim_{n\to\infty} n^p \int_{-1/n^p}^{0} \left(1 - \frac{u^2}{2} + \cdots\right) \mathrm{d}u \\ &= \frac{1}{\sqrt{2\pi}} \lim_{n\to\infty} n^p \left(\frac{1}{n^p} - \frac{1}{6n^{3p}} + \cdots\right) = \frac{1}{\sqrt{2\pi}}.\end{aligned}$$

The expansion and termwise integration are allowed because of the finite interval for u. Taking $p = \frac{1}{2}$, we have

$$\lim_{n\to\infty} \sqrt{n} \Pr\left(-\frac{1}{n} < \overline{x}_n - 1 \leqslant 0\right) = \frac{1}{\sqrt{2\pi}},$$

where substituting from part (a) gives

$$\lim_{n\to\infty} \sqrt{n}\,\frac{\mathrm{e}^{-n} n^n}{n!} = \frac{1}{\sqrt{2\pi}},$$

as required.

***Exercise 10.40 (Incomplete-gamma asymptotics)** Let $\Gamma(\nu, w) := \int_w^\infty \tau^{\nu-1}\mathrm{e}^{-\tau}\,\mathrm{d}\tau$ be the incomplete gamma function of Exercises 4.20 and 4.21 (needed to express the c.d.f.s of gamma and normal variates), where $\nu, w > 0$.

(a) Prove that, as $w \to \infty$ (given a fixed ν),

$$\Gamma(\nu, w) = w^{\nu-1}\mathrm{e}^{-w} \sum_{k=0}^{m-1} \mathrm{P}_k^{\nu-1} w^{-k} + O\left(w^{\nu-1-m}\mathrm{e}^{-w}\right),$$

where $\mathrm{P}_k^{\nu-1} := \prod_{i=1}^{k} (\nu - i)$ is the permutation symbol from Chapter 1. [Hint: In the integrand, expand $\tau^{\nu-1}$ in the neighborhood of $\tau = w$.]

(b) Show that this implies that, for $|u| \to \infty$,

$$\Phi(u) = 1_{u>0} - \frac{\phi(u)}{u}\left(1 - \frac{1}{u^2} + \frac{3}{u^4} - \frac{15}{u^6} + \cdots\right).$$

The function $(1-\Phi(u))/\phi(u)$, or equivalently $\Phi(-u)/\phi(u)$, is Mills' ratio seen in Exercise 6.42. It is the reciprocal of the hazard rate (Exercise 2.18) of the normal distribution.

Solution

(a) By the change of variable $\vartheta = \tau - w$, we have

$$\Gamma(\nu, w) = w^{\nu-1}\mathrm{e}^{-w}\int_0^\infty \left(1+\frac{\vartheta}{w}\right)^{\nu-1}\mathrm{e}^{-\vartheta}\,\mathrm{d}\vartheta.$$

Now

$$\left(1+\frac{\vartheta}{w}\right)^{\nu-1} = \sum_{k=0}^{m-1}\binom{\nu-1}{k}\left(\frac{\vartheta}{w}\right)^k + (\nu-m)\binom{\nu-1}{m-1}\left(1+\frac{\vartheta}{w}\right)^{\nu-1}\int_0^{\vartheta/w}\frac{s^{m-1}}{(1+s)^\nu}\,\mathrm{d}s,$$

from the complement of the incomplete beta function in Exercise 4.11. (To compare with that result, divide both sides here by $(1+\vartheta/w)^{\nu-1}$ and use the relation of F to beta,

$$\int_0^c \frac{s^{m-1}}{(1+s)^\nu}\,\mathrm{d}s = \int_0^{c/(1+c)}(1-\tau)^{\nu-m-1}\tau^{m-1}\,\mathrm{d}\tau = \int_{1/(1+c)}^1 t^{\nu-m-1}(1-t)^{m-1}\,\mathrm{d}t,$$

analyzed in Exercise 4.31.) Since $\nu > 0$ and $\vartheta/w \geqslant 0$, the integral over s is positive and bounded as follows:

$$\int_0^{\vartheta/w}\frac{s^{m-1}}{(1+s)^\nu}\,\mathrm{d}s < \int_0^{\vartheta/w} s^{m-1}\,\mathrm{d}s = \frac{(\vartheta/w)^m}{m},$$

where m is the number of terms in the expansion (hence $m > 0$). Letting $w \to \infty$,

$$\Gamma(\nu, w) = w^{\nu-1}\mathrm{e}^{-w}\int_0^\infty\left(\sum_{k=0}^{m-1}\binom{\nu-1}{k}\left(\frac{\vartheta}{w}\right)^k + O\left(\left(\frac{\vartheta}{w}\right)^m\right)\right)\mathrm{e}^{-\vartheta}\,\mathrm{d}\vartheta$$

since $(1+\vartheta/w)^{\nu-1} = O(1)$ as $w \to \infty$. As the integral is convergent for any finite m, we can rewrite it as

$$\begin{aligned}\Gamma(\nu, w) &= w^{\nu-1}\mathrm{e}^{-w}\sum_{k=0}^{m-1}\binom{\nu-1}{k}w^{-k}\int_0^\infty \vartheta^k\mathrm{e}^{-\vartheta}\,\mathrm{d}\vartheta + O\left(w^{\nu-1-m}\mathrm{e}^{-w}\right)\\ &= w^{\nu-1}\mathrm{e}^{-w}\sum_{k=0}^{m-1}\mathrm{P}_k^{\nu-1}w^{-k} + O\left(w^{\nu-1-m}\mathrm{e}^{-w}\right)\end{aligned}$$

using the integral representation of the gamma function. Note that the series is divergent (see Sections A.3.2 and A.3.4), as is usually the case with asymptotic series. However, it is a very useful representation, as we shall see for example in Exercise 10.43.

(b) The representation follows from

$$\Phi(u) = \frac{1+\operatorname{sgn}(u)}{2} - \frac{\operatorname{sgn}(u)}{2\sqrt{\pi}}\Gamma\left(\frac{1}{2}, \frac{u^2}{2}\right)$$

derived in Exercise 4.21. Note that, as $u \to -\infty$, this expansion implies a sharper inequality than $\Phi(u) \leqslant \exp(-u^2/2)$, which holds for any $u < 0$, from Exercise 3.12(e).

***Exercise 10.41 (Large deviations)** Let $\{x_n\}$ be an i.i.d. sequence with mean μ and variance $0 < \sigma^2 < \infty$. There is a class of results called *large-deviation* theorems, one of which states that

$$\Pr\left(\sqrt{n}(\overline{x}_n - \mu)/\sigma > w_n\right) \sim \Phi(-w_n)$$

for any $w_n \to \infty$ such that $w_n = o\left(n^{1/6}\right)$. To prove this result, establish the following:
(a) Let $\varphi(\tau)$ be the c.f. of

$$\xi_i := \frac{x_i - \mu}{\sigma} \quad (i = 1, \dots, n).$$

Show that the relation of interest, $\varphi'(\tau)/\mathrm{i} \sim w_n/\sqrt{n}$, implies that $\tau \sim -\mathrm{i}w_n/\sqrt{n}$.
(b) Show that (a) implies that the corresponding c.g.f. $\varkappa(t)$ exists as $t \to 0$, that $\varkappa(t) \sim t^2/2$, and that $t \sim w_n/\sqrt{n}$.
(c) Let $y_i(t)$ be the exponential tilting (see Exercises 3.36(d) and 7.34) of ξ_i, such that $\varkappa_y(s) = \varkappa(s+t) - \varkappa(t)$ with $s = O(t)$. Defining $z_n \sim \mathrm{N}(\sqrt{n}\varkappa'(t), \varkappa''(t))$, show that the c.f.s of $z_n\sqrt{n}$ and $\zeta_n(t) := \sum_{i=1}^n y_i(t)$ are asymptotically equal. [Hint: Expand $\varkappa(s+t)$ in the neighborhood of $s = 0$.]
(d) By formulating $\Pr(n^{-1/2}\sum_{i=1}^n \xi_i > w_n)$ in terms of $\zeta_n(t)$ and then z_n, show that the stated large-deviation result holds.

Solution
The CLTs tell us what happens to $\Pr(z_n > w)$ when $w = O(1)$, and that the limiting distribution of z_n is $\mathrm{N}(0,1)$. They do not tell us what happens as we go further into the tails of z_n by taking w to be an increasing function of n. Our large-deviation result therefore extends the applicability of CLTs to w_n when it increases with n, subject to $w_n = o\left(n^{1/6}\right)$.
(a) Since $(x_i - \mu)/\sigma$ has mean 0 and variance 1, both existing, we have

$$\varphi(\tau) = 1 - \tau^2/2 + o\left(\tau^2\right) \sim 1 - \tau^2/2$$

as $\tau \to 0$; see Exercise 3.29. Then $\varphi'(\tau)/\mathrm{i} \sim w_n/\sqrt{n}$ is equivalent to $-\tau/\mathrm{i} \sim w_n/\sqrt{n}$, that is, $\tau \sim -\mathrm{i}w_n/\sqrt{n}$. Recall that $w_n/\sqrt{n} \to 0$ since $w_n = o\left(n^{1/6}\right)$.
(b) As $\tau \to 0$, the c.f. $\varphi(\tau)$ in (a) is that of a variate that becomes degenerate around its mean 0. Therefore, $\varkappa(t)$ exists in the limit and is given by

$$\varkappa(t) = \log(\varphi(t/\mathrm{i})) \sim \log\left(1 + t^2/2\right) \sim t^2/2$$

by the logarithmic expansion and $t \sim w_n/\sqrt{n} \to 0$ (implied by replacing τ by t/i in (a)).

Recall from Exercise 3.38(d) or Table 4.2 that $t^2/2$ (the leading term of $\varkappa(t)$) is the c.g.f. of $\mathrm{N}(0,1)$. Here, $\varkappa'(t) \sim t \sim w_n/\sqrt{n}$ implies that $w_n\sqrt{n}$ is close to $n\varkappa'(t)$, a quantity that we shall encounter shortly for centering a normal approximation.

(c) By the independence of $\{y_n(t)\}$, and by the definition $z_n\sqrt{n} \sim \mathrm{N}(n\varkappa'(t), n\varkappa''(t))$,

$$\begin{aligned}\varphi_{\zeta_n(t)}(v)/\varphi_{z_n\sqrt{n}}(v) &= (\exp(\varkappa_y(\mathrm{i}v)))^n / \exp\left(\mathrm{i}vn\varkappa'(t) - v^2 n\varkappa''(t)/2\right)\\ &= \exp\left[n\left(\varkappa(\mathrm{i}v+t) - \varkappa(t) - \mathrm{i}v\varkappa'(t) + v^2\varkappa''(t)/2\right)\right].\end{aligned}$$

By $\varkappa(\mathrm{i}v+t) = \varkappa(t) + \mathrm{i}v\varkappa'(t) - v^2\varkappa''(t)/2 + O(v^3)$, $\mathrm{i}v \equiv s = O(t) = O(w_n/\sqrt{n})$, and

$$O(v^3) = O\left(w_n^3/n^{3/2}\right) = o\left(n^{3/6}/n^{3/2}\right) = o(1/n),$$

we get $\varphi_{\zeta_n(t)}(v)/\varphi_{z_n\sqrt{n}}(v) = \exp(o(1)) \to \exp(0) = 1$.

We have gone further than the usual CLT, in that both $z_n\sqrt{n}$ and $\zeta_n(t)$ are diverging, rather than being $O_p(1)$ as in the Lindeberg–Lévy CLT (Exercise 10.27), and yet their distributions are asymptotically indistinguishable. The exponential tilting has improved the accuracy of the normal approximation, and less tilting is needed as $n \to \infty$, since $t \to 0$ gives $y_i(t) \to \xi_i$ with probability 1. Notice that, in accordance with Exercise 3.36(d), $\mathrm{E}(y_1(t)) = \varkappa'(t) = \mathrm{E}(z_n/\sqrt{n})$ and $\mathrm{var}(y_1(t)) = \varkappa''(t) = \mathrm{var}(z_n)$.

(d) We have shown that $\zeta_n(t)$ can be approximated by the continuous variate $z_n\sqrt{n}$, so we can assume without loss of generality that $y_i(t)$ and ξ_i are continuous for the purpose of our derivations and apply Exercise 7.34. Therefore, the density $f_{\zeta_n(t)}(v)$ of $\zeta_n(t) := \sum_{i=1}^n y_i(t)$ is $\exp(tv - n\varkappa(t))$ times the density of $\sum_{i=1}^n \xi_i$ and

$$\Pr\left(\sum_{i=1}^n \xi_i > w_n\sqrt{n}\right) = \mathrm{e}^{n\varkappa(t)}\int_{w_n\sqrt{n}}^{\infty} \mathrm{e}^{-tv} f_{\zeta_n(t)}(v)\,\mathrm{d}v.$$

Part (c) gives this probability, up to a multiplicative factor of $1 + o(1)$, as

$$\begin{aligned}p &:= \mathrm{e}^{n\varkappa(t)}\int_{w_n\sqrt{n}}^{\infty} \mathrm{e}^{-tv}\frac{\exp\left(-(v-n\varkappa'(t))^2/(2n\varkappa''(t))\right)}{\sqrt{2\pi n\varkappa''(t)}}\,\mathrm{d}v\\ &= \frac{\exp\left(n\varkappa(t) - n\varkappa'(t)^2/(2\varkappa''(t))\right)}{\sqrt{2\pi n\varkappa''(t)}}\int_{w_n\sqrt{n}}^{\infty}\exp\left(\frac{vn(\varkappa'(t) - t\varkappa''(t)) - v^2/2}{n\varkappa''(t)}\right)\mathrm{d}v.\end{aligned}$$

Completing the square in the integrand's exponent by the change of variable

$$u = v/\sqrt{n\varkappa''(t)} - (\varkappa'(t) - t\varkappa''(t))\sqrt{n/\varkappa''(t)},$$

and defining $c_n := \left[w_n - (\varkappa'(t) - t\varkappa''(t))\sqrt{n}\right]/\sqrt{\varkappa''(t)}$, we get

$$\begin{aligned}p &= \frac{\exp\left(n\varkappa(t) - n\varkappa'(t)^2/(2\varkappa''(t))\right)}{\sqrt{2\pi}}\int_{c_n}^{\infty}\exp\left(\frac{n(\varkappa'(t) - t\varkappa''(t))^2}{2\varkappa''(t)} - \frac{u^2}{2}\right)\mathrm{d}u\\ &= \exp\left(n\varkappa(t) - nt\varkappa'(t) + nt^2\varkappa''(t)/2\right)\Phi(-c_n),\end{aligned}$$

by $\Phi(-c_n) = 1 - \Phi(c_n)$. Since (b) implies that

$$n\varkappa(t) - nt\varkappa'(t) + nt^2\varkappa''(t)/2 \sim nt^2/2 - nt^2 + nt^2/2 = 0,$$

with a remainder of order $nt^3 \sim w_n^3/\sqrt{n} = o(1)$, and $c_n \sim w_n - (t-t)\sqrt{n} = w_n$ (where $t\sqrt{n} \sim w_n$), we get the required result.

Exercise 10.42 (Random walk: maximum versus last observation) For $\{x_n\}$ an i.i.d. sequence with mean 0 and variance $\sigma^2 < \infty$, define the sequence of *partial sums* $\{y_n\}$ as

$$y_1 := x_1, \quad y_2 := x_1 + x_2, \quad \dots, \quad y_n := x_1 + \dots + x_n,$$

or equivalently $y_n = y_{n-1} + x_n$ with $y_0 := 0$. The process $\{y_n\}$ or any deterministic linear transformation thereof is known as a *random walk* (the definition is also valid for any $\sigma^2 > 0$); see also the Notes to Exercises 1.10 and 4.23. Suppose that x_n is a continuous variate which is symmetrically distributed around 0. Let the first time that the partial sum y_i exceeds v_n be defined as event A_i. Show that:
(a) $\Pr(\max_{i\leqslant n}\{y_i\} > v_n) = \sum_{i=1}^n (\Pr(A_i \text{ and } y_n > y_i) + \Pr(A_i \text{ and } y_n < y_i))$;
(b) $\Pr(\max_{i\leqslant n}\{y_i\} > v_n) \leqslant 2\Pr(y_n > v_n)$.

Solution
(a) We shall use again shorthand such as $\{y_n < y_i\}$ for the set $\{y_i : y_n < y_i\}$. The sets $A_1, A_2, \dots$ are mutually disjoint and

$$\Pr\left(\max_{i\leqslant n}\{y_i\} > v_n\right) = \sum_{i=1}^n \Pr(A_i)$$

$$= \sum_{i=1}^n (\Pr(A_i \cap \{y_n > y_i\}) + \Pr(A_i \cap \{y_n < y_i\}) + \Pr(A_i \cap \{y_n = y_i\}))$$

$$= \sum_{i=1}^n (\Pr(A_i \cap \{y_n > y_i\}) + \Pr(A_i \cap \{y_n < y_i\}))$$

by continuity of the variate x_n (hence y_n).
(b) Since $\{x_n\}$ is i.i.d. and each component is symmetrically distributed around 0, we see that the variate

$$y_n - y_i \equiv \sum_{j=i+1}^n x_j$$

is also symmetric around 0 (and has variance $(n-i)\sigma^2$). Two implications follow: that $\Pr(y_n > y_i) = \Pr(y_n < y_i)$, and that $y_n - y_i$ is independent of $x_1, \dots, x_i$ (and hence y_i). With y_i the only random quantity in A_i,

$$\Pr(A_i \cap \{y_n > y_i\}) + \Pr(A_i \cap \{y_n < y_i\}) = 2\Pr(A_i \cap \{y_n > y_i\}).$$

The event A_i implies that $y_i > v_n$, an inequality which yields

$$2\Pr(A_i \cap \{y_n > y_i\}) \leqslant 2\Pr(A_i \cap \{y_n > v_n\})$$

and therefore

$$\Pr\left(\max_{i\leqslant n}\{y_i\} > v_n\right) \leqslant 2\sum_{i=1}^{n}\Pr\left(A_i \cap \{y_n > v_n\}\right) \leqslant 2\Pr\left(y_n > v_n\right),$$

where the last inequality follows from $\Pr(\bigcup_{i=1}^{n} A_i) \leqslant 1$ (see Exercise 1.6).

*__Exercise 10.43 (Law of the iterated logarithm)__ For $\{x_n\}$ an i.i.d. sequence with mean μ and variance $0 < \sigma^2 < \infty$, consider the law of the iterated logarithm stating that

$$\limsup_{n\to\infty}\frac{z_n}{c_n} = 1 \quad \text{and} \quad \liminf_{n\to\infty}\frac{z_n}{c_n} = -1$$

almost surely, where $z_n := \sqrt{n}(\overline{x}_n - \mu)/\sigma$ and $c_n := \sqrt{2\log\left(\log\left(n\right)\right)}$. Prove this LIL by establishing the following:
(a) Show that the CLT and the large deviations result that $\Pr\left(z_n > \alpha c_n\right) \sim \Phi\left(-\alpha c_n\right)$ for any fixed $\alpha > 0$ (see Exercise 10.41) allow us to assume that $\{x_n\} \sim \text{IN}(0,1)$ for the rest of this exercise.
(b) Show that $\limsup_n z_n/c_n = 1$ if and only if $\liminf_n z_n/c_n = -1$.
(c) Show that $\Pr(\limsup_n z_n/c_n = 1) = 1$ if and only if, for all $\epsilon > 0$,

$$\Pr\left(z_n \geqslant \left(1+\epsilon\right)c_n \text{ i.o.}\right) = 0 \quad \text{and} \quad \Pr\left(z_n \geqslant \left(1-\epsilon\right)c_n \text{ i.o.}\right) = 1.$$

(d) Define the partial sums by $y_n := n\overline{x}_n = \sqrt{n}z_n$, and let $v_n := \left(1+\epsilon\right)c_n\sqrt{n} = \left(1+\epsilon\right)\sqrt{2n\log\left(\log\left(n\right)\right)}$. Consider the nonrandom subsequence of the index $\{n\}_{n=1}^{\infty}$, written as $\{n_i\}_{i=1}^{m}$ and defined by $n_i = \lfloor a^i \rfloor$ where $a > 1$ is a constant. By choosing an appropriate a, show that

$$\Pr\left(z_n \geqslant \left(1+\epsilon\right)c_n \text{ i.o.}\right) \leqslant \Pr\left(\max_{i\leqslant m}\{y_{n_i}\} \geqslant v_{n_{m-1}} \text{ i.o.}\right) \to 0$$

as $m \to \infty$. [Hint: Use Exercise 10.42 to analyze the maximum of this subsequence $\{y_{n_m}\}$, then choose a to satisfy Exercise 10.3(a).]
(e) Define the increments of the partial sums by $\xi_{n_m} := y_{n_m} - y_{n_{m-1}}$. By choosing appropriate constants a and b, show that $\Pr\left(\xi_{n_m} \geqslant bc_{n_m}\sqrt{n_m} \text{ i.o.}\right) = 1$ and that, together with (d), this implies that $\Pr\left(z_n \geqslant \left(1-\epsilon\right)c_n \text{ i.o.}\right) = 1$. [Hint: Use Exercise 10.3(b) on $\{\xi_{n_m}\}$.]

Solution
(a) We need a large-deviation theorem here, because we will be considering $z_n > \alpha c_n$ for $\alpha > 0$ and $c_n \to \infty$, albeit at a rate $o\left(n^{\delta}\right)$ for any $\delta > 0$. The theorem of Exercise 10.41 is then applicable. It says that, when z_n exceeds αc_n, it does so according to the limiting normal and another amount that is of smaller order and hence negligible. If so, then any nonnormal behavior can be ruled out when establishing the limiting results of this exercise. Furthermore, by the CLT, the invariance of the limiting distribution of z_n implies that there is no loss of generality in assuming that $\{x_n\} \sim \text{IN}(0,1)$ henceforth. In addition to normality, this means that we let $\mu = 0$ and $\sigma = 1$.

(b) The result follows by the symmetry of the limiting distribution of z_n.
(c) This follows directly from the definition of the i.o. device of Exercise 10.3.
(d) We choose m such that $n_{m-1} < n \leqslant n_m$, because we may not be able to find an m such that $n = n_m$ exactly. Therefore, since $y_n = \sqrt{n} z_n$ and $v_{n_{m-1}} < v_{n_m}$ by definition,

$$\begin{aligned}\Pr\left(y_n \geqslant v_n \text{ i.o.}\right) &= \Pr\left(y_{n_m} \geqslant v_{n_m} \text{ i.o.}\right)\\ &\leqslant \Pr\left(y_{n_m} \geqslant v_{n_{m-1}} \text{ i.o.}\right) \leqslant \Pr\left(\max_{i \leqslant m}\{y_{n_i}\} \geqslant v_{n_{m-1}} \text{ i.o.}\right).\end{aligned}$$

Consider the event in the last probability. As $m \to \infty$, the fractional part of $\lfloor a^m \rfloor$ is finite and

$$\frac{v_{n_{m-1}}}{v_{n_m}} = \sqrt{\frac{n_{m-1}\log(\log(n_{m-1}))}{n_m \log(\log(n_m))}} \sim \sqrt{\frac{\log((m-1)\log(a))}{a\log(m\log(a))}} \sim \frac{1}{\sqrt{a}},$$

so the event is asymptotically equivalent to $\{\max_{i \leqslant m}\{y_{n_i}\} \geqslant v_{n_m}/\sqrt{a}\}$, to be denoted by A_{n_m}. Using Exercise 10.42, we find

$$\Pr\left(A_{n_m}\right) \leqslant 2\Pr\left(y_{n_m} \geqslant v_{n_m}/\sqrt{a}\right) = 2\Pr\left(z_{n_m} \geqslant v_{n_m}/\sqrt{n_m a}\right) = 2\Phi\left(-v_{n_m}/\sqrt{n_m a}\right)$$

since $\Phi(-w_m) = \Pr(z_{n_m} \geqslant w_m)$ for $w_m > 0$. Letting $n_m \to \infty$ and using the asymptotic expansion $\Phi(-w_m) \sim \phi(w_m)/w_m$ from Exercise 10.40(b), we have the asymptotic relation

$$\Pr\left(A_{n_m}\right) \leqslant \exp\left(-\frac{v_{n_m}^2}{2n_m a}\right)\frac{\sqrt{2n_m a}}{v_{n_m}\sqrt{\pi}} \equiv \frac{1}{\eta\sqrt{\pi}\log(\eta)} < \frac{1}{\eta\sqrt{\pi}},$$

where

$$\begin{aligned}\eta &:= \exp\left(\frac{v_{n_m}^2}{2n_m a}\right) = \exp\left(\frac{(1+\epsilon)^2\log(\log(n_m))}{a}\right)\\ &= \left(\log(n_m)\right)^{(1+\epsilon)^2/a} = \left(\log\lfloor a^m \rfloor\right)^{(1+\epsilon)^2/a} \sim \left(m\log(a)\right)^{(1+\epsilon)^2/a}.\end{aligned}$$

Choosing a such that $(1+\epsilon)^2/a > 1$ ensures that $\Pr(A_{n_m})$ decreases faster than $1/m$, so that $\sum_{i=1}^{\infty}\Pr(A_{n_i}) < \infty$ and the first Borel–Cantelli lemma (Exercise 10.3(a)) implies that $\Pr(A_{n_i} \text{ i.o.}) = 0$.
(e) To exploit the second Borel–Cantelli lemma (Exercise 10.3(b)), we need an independent subsequence of events. This is not true of the partial sums y_{n_m}, but it is true of their increments $\xi_{n_m} := y_{n_m} - y_{n_{m-1}}$ (see Exercise 10.42) which are independent $\mathrm{N}(0, n_m - n_{m-1})$. Choosing $a > 1$ to be an integer, we have $n_m - n_{m-1} = a^{m-1}(a-1) \to \infty$ as $m \to \infty$, and the asymptotic expansion of the normal's c.d.f. gives

$$\Pr\left(\frac{\xi_{n_m}}{\sqrt{n_m - n_{m-1}}} \geqslant w_m\right) \sim \frac{\exp\left(-w_m^2/2\right)}{\sqrt{2\pi w_m^2}}$$

for any $w_m \to \infty$. The second Borel–Cantelli lemma is applicable if this probability decays at a rate $1/m$ or slower. To this end, take

$$w_m^2 := \frac{b^2 c_{n_m}^2 n_m}{n_m - n_{m-1}} = \frac{2b^2 (\log(m) + \log(\log(a)))\, a^m}{a^{m-1}(a-1)} \sim \frac{2b^2 \log(m)}{1 - 1/a}$$

for some constant $b > 0$ to be chosen later to achieve the required rate. Substituting into the asymptotic expansion of the normal's c.d.f.,

$$\Pr\left(\xi_{n_m} \geqslant w_m \sqrt{n_m - n_{m-1}}\right) \sim \frac{\exp\left(-w_m^2/2\right)}{\sqrt{2\pi w_m^2}} \sim \frac{\sqrt{1-1/a}}{2bm^{b^2/(1-1/a)}\sqrt{\pi \log(m)}},$$

which achieves the required rate for some $b < \sqrt{1-1/a}$ since $\log(m) = o\left(m^\delta\right)$ for all $\delta > 0$. This gives $\Pr\left(\xi_{n_m} \geqslant bc_{n_m}\sqrt{n_m} \text{ i.o.}\right) = 1$.

We need to find out what happens to the left-hand side of $y_{n_m} = y_{n_{m-1}} + \xi_{n_m}$. We have just shown what happens to ξ_{n_m}, and part (d) has done the same for $y_{n_{m-1}}$: since y_n is symmetrically distributed around 0, part (d) has also proved that $\Pr(y_n \leqslant -v_n \text{ i.o.}) = 0$, that is, $\Pr(y_n > -v_n \text{ i.o.}) = 1$, where $v_n = (1+\epsilon)\, c_n\sqrt{n}$. Adding up the inequalities for each of $y_{n_{m-1}}$ and ξ_{n_m}, we obtain

$$y_{n_m} > c_{n_m}\sqrt{n_m}\left(b - (1+\epsilon)\frac{v_{n_{m-1}}}{v_{n_m}}\right) \sim c_{n_m}\sqrt{n_m}\left(b - \frac{1+\epsilon}{\sqrt{a}}\right)$$

infinitely often, with probability 1. Choosing a such that $b - (1+\epsilon)/\sqrt{a} \geqslant 1 - \epsilon$ gives $\Pr\left(y_{n_m} > c_{n_m}\sqrt{n_m}\,(1-\epsilon) \text{ i.o.}\right) = 1$, and the required probability follows from $y_n = \sqrt{n} z_n$. Since it is sufficient to choose $a > \max\{1, (1+\epsilon)^2 / (b + \epsilon - 1)^2\}$, we can take a as an arbitrarily large integer and $b \in \left(\max\{0, 1-\epsilon\}, \sqrt{1-1/a}\right)$.

*__Exercise 10.44 (Stable limit theorem: symmetric continuous)__ Let $\{x_n\}$ be a random sample from a continuous variate x, which is symmetric around 0 and has a density satisfying $\lim_{u\to\infty} u^{p+1} f_x(u) = pc$, where $0 < c < \infty$ and $0 < p < 2$.
(a) Derive the c.f. $\varphi_z(\tau)$ of $z_n := n^{-1/p}(x_1 + \cdots + x_n)$ in terms of the c.f. $\varphi_x(t)$ of x.
(b) Show that $\lim_{n\to\infty} \log(\varphi_z(\tau)) = \lim_{n\to\infty} n \operatorname{Re}\left(\varphi_x\left(n^{-1/p}\tau\right) - 1\right)$.
(c) Hence prove that $n^{1-1/p}\,\overline{x}_n \overset{a}{\sim} \mathrm{S}^p(0, \lambda, 0)$, where it is given that

$$\lambda^p := cp\int_{-\infty}^{\infty} \frac{1-\cos(v)}{|v|^{p+1}}\,\mathrm{d}v = \begin{cases} 2c\Gamma(1-p)\cos(p\pi/2) & (p \neq 1), \\ \pi c & (p = 1). \end{cases}$$

Solution

(a) We have that $\{x_n\}$ is i.i.d. with c.f. $\varphi_x(t)$. By the definition of z_n in terms of a sum of these, z_n is infinitely divisible. More specifically, the c.f. of z_n can be decomposed as follows:

$$\varphi_z(\tau) = \mathrm{E}\left(\mathrm{e}^{\mathrm{i}\tau z_n}\right) = \mathrm{E}\left(\mathrm{e}^{\mathrm{i}\tau n^{-1/p}(x_1+\cdots+x_n)}\right) = \prod_{i=1}^{n}\mathrm{E}\left(\mathrm{e}^{\mathrm{i}\tau n^{-1/p}x_i}\right) = \left(\varphi_x\left(\frac{\tau}{n^{1/p}}\right)\right)^n.$$

The rest of this exercise will prove that z_n is more than just infinitely divisible: it is asymp-

totically stable because its c.f. will be shown to satisfy $\log(\varphi_z(\tau)) \to -\lambda^p|\tau|^p$ (see the introduction to Chapter 4 for the c.f. of stable variates).
(b) Since x is symmetric around 0, Exercise 3.23 gives us two results. First, the expansion of $\varphi_x(\tau/n^{1/p})$ does not contain a linear term and is $\varphi_x(\tau/n^{1/p}) = 1 + o(1/n^{1/p})$ (see Exercise 3.29 for the remainder term); hence

$$\lim_{n\to\infty} \log(\varphi_z(\tau)) = \lim_{n\to\infty} n \log\left(\varphi_x\left(\frac{\tau}{n^{1/p}}\right)\right) = \lim_{n\to\infty} n\left(\varphi_x\left(\frac{\tau}{n^{1/p}}\right) - 1\right),$$

as the logarithmic expansion implies that the next term is $o(n^{1-2/p})$ with $1 - 2/p < 0$ and is therefore vanishing. Second, $\varphi_x(\tau/n^{1/p})$ is a real-valued function for $\tau \in \mathbb{R}$. The result follows.
(c) By definition,

$$\varphi_x\left(\frac{\tau}{n^{1/p}}\right) - 1 = \int_{-\infty}^{\infty} \left(\exp\left(\frac{\mathrm{i}\tau u}{n^{1/p}}\right) - 1\right) f_x(u)\, \mathrm{d}u.$$

Since $\mathrm{Re}\left(\exp\left(\mathrm{i}\tau u/n^{1/p}\right)\right) = \cos\left(\tau u/n^{1/p}\right)$ for $\tau \in \mathbb{R}$, the change of variable $v = \tau u/n^{1/p}$ (for $\tau < 0$ or $\tau > 0$) gives

$$\lim_{n\to\infty} \log(\varphi_z(\tau)) = |\tau|^{-1} \int_{-\infty}^{\infty} (\cos(v) - 1) \lim_{n\to\infty} n^{1+1/p} f_x\left(n^{1/p} v/\tau\right) \mathrm{d}v$$
$$= cp\,|\tau|^p \int_{-\infty}^{\infty} \frac{\cos(v) - 1}{|v|^{p+1}}\, \mathrm{d}v = -\lambda^p\,|\tau|^p\,.$$

The limit and integral have been interchanged by the dominated convergence theorem, since $\cos(v) - 1 \in [-2, 0]$ and the integral of a density is a c.d.f. (and hence bounded).

Exercise 10.45 (Portfolio underdiversification and SLT) The SLT has some implications for portfolio allocation too. Assume that x is a stock return whose distribution is symmetric around 0 (alternatively x can represent the excess return), and that we have n independent shares following this distribution. Any portfolio $y \equiv \sum_{i=1}^n w_i x_i$ (with the $w_i \geqslant 0$ adding up to 1) will have a median return of 0, so minimizing a measure of risk such as $\Pr(y < q)$ (with $q < 0$) yields an "optimal" portfolio. Obtain this portfolio's weights when n is large.

Solution
By the i.i.d. assumption, the weights will be

$$\left(\frac{1}{n}, \frac{1}{n}, \dots, \frac{1}{n}\right) \quad \text{or} \quad \left(\frac{1}{m}, \dots, \frac{1}{m}, 0, \dots, 0\right),$$

where the latter can be viewed as a case of excluding any $n - m > 0$ shares and including any $m > 0$.

The case $p = 1$ includes the situation where the averages of standard Cauchy variates are also standard Cauchy: the resulting distribution is unaffected by the choice of weights and we are indifferent between the two possible set of weights or linear combinations thereof.

This holds more generally for $p = 1$ when n is large; compare the tails of x and $\overline{x}$ in the statement of the SLT.

The case $p > 1$ gives $1 - 1/p > 0$ and the normalization of the stable $m^{1-1/p}\overline{x}_m$ indicates that $\overline{x}_m$ has a distribution that is more concentrated as m increases. It is therefore better to maximize the number of included shares and to diversify as $(\frac{1}{n}, \frac{1}{n}, \dots, \frac{1}{n})$; see also the case $p = 2$ in Exercise 7.4.

The case $p < 1$ leads to $(1, 0, \dots, 0)$, because the distribution of $\overline{x}_m$ explodes with m, so it is better to minimize m.

***Exercise 10.46 (Infinitely divisible as a limit of compound Poissons)** Let $\varphi_z(\tau)$ be the c.f. of a variate z. Prove that z is infinitely divisible if and only if $\lim_{n\to\infty}(\varphi_y(\tau))^n = \varphi_z(\tau)$ where $\varphi_y(\tau)$ is the c.f. of some compound Poisson variate y.

Solution

The "if" part is easy to establish. A compound Poisson is infinitely divisible, by definition (see Chapter 4). Therefore, any power of its c.f., such as $(\varphi_y(\tau))^n$ with $n \in \mathbb{N}$, also represents an infinitely divisible variate and the limit follows. To establish the "only if" part, the fact that z is infinitely divisible indicates that there exists a variate x_n such that $\varphi_z(\tau) = (\varphi_{x_n}(\tau))^n$. Letting $n \to \infty$, convergence to $\varphi_z(\tau)$ occurs if and only if $\varphi_{x_n}(\tau) = 1 + O(1/n)$. Therefore,

$$\log(\varphi_z(\tau)) = n\log(\varphi_{x_n}(\tau)) = n(\varphi_{x_n}(\tau) - 1) + o(1);$$

hence

$$\varphi_z(\tau) = \lim_{n\to\infty} \mathrm{e}^{n(\varphi_{x_n}(\tau)-1)} = \lim_{n\to\infty}\left(\mathrm{e}^{\varphi_{x_n}(\tau)-1}\right)^n \equiv \lim_{n\to\infty}(\varphi_y(\tau))^n,$$

by the definition of compound Poisson c.f.s.

Exercise 10.47 (Max uniform is Weibull) Consider a random sample of size n from a uniform distribution $\mathrm{U}_{(0,\alpha)}$. Let y_n denote the largest observation. Prove that:

(a) $\operatorname{plim} n^p(y_n - \alpha) = 0$ for every $p < 1$;

(b) $n(\alpha - y_n) \xrightarrow{d} z$, where z has p.d.f. $f(w) = \alpha^{-1}\exp(-w/\alpha)$ for $w > 0$ and 0 elsewhere.

Solution

(a) We first remark that the result will mean that $\sqrt{n}(y_n - \alpha)$ is degenerate, unlike the normalizations seen in connection with CLTs. We provide two solutions. The first is based on Markov's inequality:

$$\Pr(n^p|y_n - \alpha| \geqslant \epsilon) \leqslant \frac{\mathrm{E}(n^p|y_n - \alpha|)}{\epsilon} = \frac{n^p}{\epsilon}(\alpha - \mathrm{E}(y_n))$$

since $y_n < \alpha$. From Exercise 7.35, we know that the p.d.f. of y_n is given by $f_{y_n}(v) = n\alpha^{-n}v^{n-1}$ for $0 < v < \alpha$ and 0 elsewhere. This implies that $\mathrm{E}(y_n) = n\alpha^{-n}\int_0^\alpha v^n \, \mathrm{d}v =$

$n\alpha/(n+1)$. Hence,

$$\Pr(n^p|y_n - \alpha| \geqslant \epsilon) \leqslant \frac{n^p\alpha}{\epsilon}\left(1 - \frac{n}{n+1}\right) = \frac{n^p\alpha}{(n+1)\,\epsilon} \to 0 \text{ as } n \to \infty \text{ for } p < 1.$$

The second proof uses only standard calculus. Letting $\psi_n := \alpha - n^{-p}\epsilon$, we have for $0 \leqslant p < 1$ and $n^p > \epsilon/\alpha$ (hence $\psi_n > 0$),

$$\Pr(n^p|y_n - \alpha| \geqslant \epsilon) = \Pr(y_n \leqslant \psi_n) = \int_0^{\psi_n} \frac{nv^{n-1}}{\alpha^n}\,\mathrm{d}v$$

$$= \left(\frac{\psi_n}{\alpha}\right)^n = \left(1 - \frac{\epsilon}{\alpha n^p}\right)^n \to \exp\left(-\lim_{n\to\infty}\frac{n\epsilon}{\alpha n^p}\right) = 0.$$

For $\psi_n \leqslant 0$, we have $\Pr(y_n \leqslant \psi_n) = 0$.
(b) We have

$$\Pr(n(\alpha - y_n) \leqslant w) = \Pr\left(y_n \geqslant \alpha - \frac{w}{n}\right) = \frac{n}{\alpha^n}\int_{\alpha - w/n}^{\alpha} v^{n-1}\,\mathrm{d}v$$

$$= 1 - \left(\frac{\alpha - w/n}{\alpha}\right)^n \to 1 - \mathrm{e}^{-w/\alpha},$$

where we recognize the exponential c.d.f., a special case of the Weibull distribution, not surprisingly since $\mathrm{U}_{(0,\alpha)}$ has an upper-terminal value of α. The maximum is not expressible as a sum to which a CLT applies directly (such as the sample mean) or indirectly (such as the non-extreme order statistics in Exercise 10.30(d)), so the CLT does not apply here.

***Exercise 10.48 (Extreme-value asymptotics: Gnedenko's theorem)** Let $\{x_n\}$ be a random sample from a distribution $F_1(u)$. Let $y_n := \max_{i \leqslant n}\{x_i\}$ be the largest order statistic, and assume that we can find deterministic sequences $\{a_n\}$ and $\{b_n\}$ such that $b_n > 0$ and $z_n := (y_n - a_n)/b_n \xrightarrow{d} z$, where z has c.d.f. $F_z(w)$ and is nondegenerate. By first showing that

$$F_z(a_{jk} + b_{jk}w) = (F_z(a_j + b_jw))^k = F_z(a_k + b_k(a_j + b_jw)), \quad \text{for } j, k \in \mathbb{N},$$

prove that this limiting distribution can only be one of the following:
(a) GEV Type I (Gumbel) if and only if $1 - F_1(u)$ decays exponentially as u increases;
(b) GEV Type II (Fréchet) if and only if $F_1(u) \sim 1 - cl(u)/u^p$, where l is a slowly varying function at ∞, $c > 0, p > 0$, and $u \to \infty$;
(c) GEV Type III (Weibull) if and only if $F_1(u) \sim 1 - cl(u_{\max} - u)(u_{\max} - u)^{-p}$, where l is a slowly varying function at 0, $c > 0, p < 0$, and $u \to u_{\max}$, the latter being the upper terminal of x.
[Hint: For (a), take $b_j = 1$ for all j, then work out the implied a_r for any $r \in \mathbb{R}_+$ and use it to relate $F_z(w)$ to $F_z(0)$. You will need to use two results from Appendix A: first, the rationals are dense in the reals; second, the only continuous solution for $a_{\bullet}$ (as a function of its subscript) in $a_{rs} = a_r + a_s$ $(r, s \in \mathbb{R}_+)$ is $a_r = c\log(r)$, where $c \in \mathbb{R}$ is a constant.]

Solution

By means of the same idea that was used as early as in Exercises 1.18(b) and 2.11(a),

$$F_{z_n}(w) \equiv \Pr(y_n \leqslant a_n + b_n w) = \prod_{i=1}^{n} \Pr(x_i \leqslant a_n + b_n w) \equiv (F_1(a_n + b_n w))^n, \tag{10.6}$$

and this exercise will find the three types of upper tail of $F_1(u)$ that will allow z to have a nondegenerate c.d.f. given by $F_z(w) := \lim_{n\to\infty}(F_1(a_n + b_n w))^n$ at the continuity points of F_z. Assume that this limiting c.d.f. exists and consider only the continuity points of F_z. Now let $j \in \mathbb{N}$ and take the maximum from nj observations as $n \to \infty$. Its limiting distribution is the same as that found when taking the largest from j groups, each of size n, and the argument used in (10.6) leads to $F_z(a_j + b_j w) = (F_z(w))^j$. (The deterministic a_j and b_j are not the same as would be needed for the normalization of y_j, but we use the same symbols for economy of notation.) Repeating the process for $j \times k$ groups,

$$F_z(a_{jk} + b_{jk}w) = \left((F_z(w))^j\right)^k = (F_z(a_j + b_j w))^k = F_z(a_k + b_k(a_j + b_j w)),$$

which gives $a_{jk} = a_k + b_k a_j$ and $b_{jk} = b_j b_k$ that we will now solve.

(a) Let $b_j = 1$ for all j. Then $a_{jk} = a_j + a_k$ for all $j, k \in \mathbb{N}$. One solution to this additivity is given by $a_j = c\log(j)$ (compare with Exercise 6.2 or Hamel's equation in Section A.2), and we will show that this additivity is required over a continuum of j values rather than just $j \in \mathbb{N}$, hence confirming $a_r = c\log(r)$ as the unique continuous solution for $r \in \mathbb{R}_+$. Since $(F_z(a_k + w))^{1/k} = F_z(w)$ can be written as $(F_z(u))^{1/k} = F_z(u - a_k)$, we also have

$$(F_z(u))^{j/k} = F_z(u + a_j - a_k),$$

so that $a_{j/k} = a_j - a_k$; again $a_q = c\log(q)$ solves this for $q \in \mathbb{Q}_+$. Now $\mathbb{Q}_+$ is dense in $\mathbb{R}_+$, so every $r \in \mathbb{R}_+$ can be represented as the supremum (or alternatively infimum) of some sequence of $q \in \mathbb{Q}_+$. Therefore, the relation

$$(F_z(w))^r = F_z(w + a_r)$$

applies again with $a_r = c\log(r)$, thus establishing a_r as a continuous function over the positive real line. We can use this to relate $F_z(w)$ to $F_z(0)$ by taking $a_r = -w$ and using $r = \exp(a_r/c) = 1/\exp(w/c)$, hence

$$F_z(w) = (F_z(0))^{\exp(w/c)} = \exp\left(\log(F_z(0))\exp\left(\frac{w}{c}\right)\right).$$

As seen in Chapter 4 after (4.3), this is the c.d.f. of a Gum$(0, -1/c)$, with $c < 0$; hence $F_z(w) = \exp(-\exp(w/c))$. We now need to show that this entails the exponential decay of $1 - F_1(u)$ as u increases. By (10.6) at the start of the solution, $F_z(w) = \exp(-\exp(w/c))$ is the limit as $n \to \infty$ of

$$(F_1(a_n + w))^n = (1 - (1 - F_1(a_n + w)))^n,$$

thus identifying F_1 as $n(1 - F_1(a_n + w)) \sim \exp(w/c)$. Also, since $a_n = c\log(n)$, we have $n = \exp(a_n/c)$, so this convergence occurs if and only if the tail's decay is given by $1 - F_1(a_n + w) \sim \exp(w/c - a_n/c)$ for large and negative w/c, given any n. Since $c < 0$,

this means large and positive w; hence $1 - F_1(u)$ decays exponentially as u increases.
(b) Assume that there is no finite upper terminal and that $1 - F_1(u)$ decays as follows:

$$F_1(u) \sim 1 - \frac{cl(u)}{u^p} \qquad (p > 0).$$

We can substitute this into (10.6) to get

$$F_{z_n}(w) = (F_1(a_n + b_n w))^n \sim (1 - cl(a_n + b_n w)/ (a_n + b_n w)^p)^n .$$

Since a_n is chosen by its definition to adjust the location of the limiting distribution of z_n, we can drop it from the limit (or consider $F_{z_n}(u)$ where $u = w - a_n/b_n$) although $a_n/b_n \to 0$ is required for a distribution that does not shift asymptotically. Consider

$$\begin{aligned}\left(1 - c\frac{l(b_n w)}{(b_n w)^p}\right)^n &= \exp\left(n \log\left(1 - c\frac{l(b_n w)}{(b_n w)^p}\right)\right)\\ &= \exp\left(-\frac{c}{w^p}\frac{nl(b_n w)}{b_n^p} + O\left(\frac{n\left(l(b_n w)\right)^2}{b_n^{2p}}\right)\right)\end{aligned}$$

as $n \to \infty$. For the right-hand side to be nondegenerate, we need $b_n \to \infty$ (since $p > 0$), in which case

$$\frac{l(b_n w)}{l(b_n)} \to 1 \qquad (w > 0)$$

by slow variation. We need also

$$\frac{nl(b_n)}{b_n^p} \to r$$

for some finite $r > 0$; hence $b_n^p \sim nl_1(n)/r \to \infty$ for l_1 some slowly varying function, and we get $F_{z_n}(w) \to \exp(-cr/w^p) = F_z(w)$ identifying a Fréchet c.d.f. since $p > 0$. The final part of the proof of equivalence will be given in the last paragraph of the solution, after the answer to part (c).
(c) Assume that there is a finite upper terminal $u_{\max}$ and that $1 - F_1(u)$ decays as follows:

$$F_1(u) \sim 1 - cl(u_{\max} - u)\,(u_{\max} - u)^{-p} \qquad (p < 0).$$

We can substitute this into (10.6) to get

$$F_{z_n}(w) = (F_1(b_n w))^n \sim \left(1 - cl(b_n\,(w_{\max} - w))\, b_n^{-p}\,(w_{\max} - w)^{-p}\right)^n$$

as in part (b). For the right-hand side to be nondegenerate as $n \to \infty$, we need $b_n^{-p} \to 0$, in which case

$$\frac{l(b_n\,(w_{\max} - w))}{l(b_n)} \to 1 \qquad (w < w_{\max})$$

since $-p > 0$. We need also

$$nl(b_n)b_n^{-p} \to r$$

for some finite $r > 0$, hence $b_n^{-p} \sim rl_1(n)/n \to 0$ for l_1 a slowly varying function at ∞ (not 0), and we get $F_{z_n}(w) \to \exp(-cr(w_{\max} - w)^{-p}) = F_z(w)$ identifying a Weibull c.d.f. (for the variate $w_{\max} - z > 0$) since $-p > 0$.

Finally, it remains for us to show that we have exhausted all the possibilities with (a)–(c), meaning that $1 - F_1(u)$ must decay as a power function when it does not decay exponentially. This is established by noting that the conditions obtained at the beginning of this exercise simplify to $b_{jk} = b_j b_k$ in the nonexponential case, and this is solved by the same method as that used in (a) showing that b_j is a power function of j when j is finite. The asymptotic solution (as $j \to \infty$) results in the slowly varying component used in (b) and (c).

Notes

In addition to the general references of Chapter 1, we recommend Breiman (1992), Chung (1974), Grimmett and Stirzaker (2001), Hoffmann-Jørgensen (1994), and Loève (1977). The "infinitely often" device which we have used is detailed in Chapter 4 of Chung (1974). Quite a bit of complex analysis has been swept under the rug in our treatment (for example, logarithms of complex-valued c.f.s), and we refer the reader to these books and to our Appendix A for a fuller discussion. A useful collection of counterexamples can be found in Romano and Siegel (1986), Wise and Hall (1993), and Stoyanov (1997). For example, the result of Exercise 10.17 need not necessarily hold if the independence of the sequences is dropped, but it will hold (by using the CMT) if the *joint* distribution of (x_n, y_n) converges.

The convergence criterion for m.g.f.s, given in the introduction, was proved by Curtiss (1942). *Slutsky's theorem* (not the same as Slutsky's lemma of Exercise 10.18) is the CMT of Exercise 10.13 with $\xrightarrow{p}$ instead of $\xrightarrow{d}$, and it follows from the application of Exercise 10.6(a) to Exercise 10.13(a). The CMT of Mann and Wald allows the function g to be discontinuous at a set of points having probability 0 under the limiting F, and is therefore more general than Exercise 10.13. Their result can be proved more concisely by means of the following theorem. Denote the quantile functions of $\{x_n\}$ and x by $\{Q_n\}$ and Q, respectively. The *Skorokhod representation theorem* shows that, if $x_n \xrightarrow{d} x$, then the quantile functions with random arguments will have the same c.d.f.s as $\{x_n\}$ and x, but will converge almost surely (rather than in distribution).

We have covered extensions of the WLLN and CLT to *heterogeneous* sequences, those that have nonidentically distributed elements. However, we have not relaxed the independence assumption in CLTs, this being more of a time-series issue that is left for future volumes of this Series. When heterogeneity is allowed, we can obtain the convergence of a sample moment of order j by requiring the boundedness of $\mathrm{E}(\max_i\{|x_i|^j\})$ or of $\mathrm{E}(|x_i|^{j+\delta})$ for some small $\delta > 0$. Examples include Markov's SLLN and martingale limit theorems, not covered here. The example of Exercise 10.38, the CLT for Student's $\mathrm{t}(2)$ where variances are infinite, was given by Abadir and Magnus (2004b).

A sequence $\{x_n\}$ is *uniformly integrable* when

$$\sup_n \mathrm{E}(|x_n| \, 1_{|x_n|>c}) \to 0 \quad \text{as } c \to \infty.$$

When $x_n \xrightarrow{p} x$, this condition is equivalent to L_1 convergence with $\mathrm{E}(|x_n|) < \infty$ for all n (including the limiting x). Exercise 10.19 could have used uniform integrability instead of L_1 convergence. Such a condition fails, for example, in the case of the variances for t(2) in Exercise 10.38. See also the Notes to Chapter 12 for the discussion of further counterexamples.

In Exercises 10.41 and 10.44, we found that there is a relation between the tail of the density and the corresponding c.f. near its origin. This relation applies more generally, and the decay of $1 - F(u)$ (as $u \to \infty$) at a power rate is equivalent to the decay of $\varphi(\tau)$ at the same rate (up to scale) as $\tau \to 0$. More details can be found in Feller (1971, Chapter 13). See also Exercise 4.29 for an illustration with the Cauchy and Laplace densities, though the focus there was on the tails of both functions.

The SLT that we gave in this chapter's introduction and proved in Exercise 10.44 is simplified. It can be extended to allow for slowly varying functions in the normalization of $\overline{x}_n$, and for asymmetry in the underlying distributions. The SLT gives the nondegenerate limiting distribution when the partial sum $y_n := n\overline{x}_n$ is to be divided further by $n^{1/p}$, where $1/p \in (1/2, \infty)$. The *Poisson limit theorem* arises when the partial sums require no further normalization by powers of n (hence $y_n \xrightarrow{d} y$ where y is nondegenerate) and y turns out to be Poisson. This is the case only if each component of the sum becomes negligible as $n \to \infty$. As an illustration, recall the representation in Exercise 7.1 and the limit in Exercise 4.9. As stated in Chapter 4, one should remember that the Poisson distribution is infinitely divisible but not stable; for example, its support excludes nonintegers.

Exercise 10.45 touched on the issue of portfolio optimization under the SLT, as opposed to the CLT. For further implications of SLTs in economics and finance, see Ibragimov, Ibragimov, and Walden (2015).

There are other invariance principles, where convergence to more complicated infinite-dimensional distributions occurs. Functional CLTs (FCLTs) arise in dealing with nonstationary time series (such as will be seen in Exercise 12.43(b) with $\alpha = 1$), and they can lead to convergence to the Brownian motion (the limit of random walks) mentioned in the Notes to earlier chapters. For example, Exercise 10.30(c) can be strengthened when the variate is continuous, so that we get the *joint* convergence of $\widehat{F}_n(u)$ for *all* $u \in \mathbb{R}$; hence the qualifier "functional". To do this, one would need to establish the tightness of the sequence by bounding $\sup_{u \in C} z(u)$. The limit distribution of the EDF is a standard *Brownian bridge* (or *tied-down Brownian motion*) $B(u)$, that is, one starting at 0 but also forced to end at 0 (see the variance term in Exercise 10.30(c) when $u_1 = u_2 \to \infty$) by a linear tilting of the Brownian motion's path. In addition to the earlier references, a specialized introduction can be found in Billingsley (1999). There, one can also find a related result on uniform convergence for all $u \in \mathbb{R}$, the *Glivenko–Cantelli theorem* which states that $z_n := \sup_{u \in \mathbb{R}} |\widehat{F}_n(u) - F(u)| \to 0$ almost surely. Note that, by the PIT of Chapter 7, the distribution of z_n is the same for *any* continuous F. This distribution is, however, not normal: the *Kolmogorov–Smirnov statistic* standardizes this distance as $\sqrt{n} z_n$, which is shown to converge in distribution to the supremum (over the standardized $u \in (0, 1)$) of $|B(u)|$.

We will revisit such measures of distance at the end of Chapter 14.

There are refinements to limit theorems in the form of bounds and/or expansions for the finite-sample c.d.f.s around the limiting c.d.f. (for example, normal), such as Berry–Esséen bounds, Edgeworth expansions, and more generally asymptotic expansions whose j-th term is of order $1/n^{j\delta}$ for some $\delta > 0$ (typically $\delta = \frac{1}{2}$). The latter are usually divergent, as Exercise 10.40 illustrates. Divergent series are useful analytically, but they can also be used numerically before the explosive part of the expansion kicks in. See the Notes to Chapter 4 (the expansions in Exercise 10.40 can be written in terms of ${}_2F_0$) and Appendix A for references on such series.

There are also some refinements to approximating discrete distributions by corresponding continuous ones. The *continuity correction* for approximating $F_x(u)$, where $u \in \mathbb{Z}$, by some continuous c.d.f. G requires the latter to be evaluated at $u + \frac{1}{2}$ instead of u. For further analysis, see Cox (1970).

The result given in Exercise 10.39 is found in Hu (1988), Billingsley (1995, p. 370), and Grimmett and Stirzaker (2001, pp. 357–358). For further results on the probabilistic interpretation of the gamma function, see Gordon (1994). See also Section A.3.4 for a refinement of Stirling's formula, in the form of the asymptotic expansion of the gamma function.

Finally, our proof of part (a) in Exercise 10.48 was closer to that of Billingsley (1995) than to the more conventional derivation, for example the one in Kendall and Stuart (1977), and we did not fully characterize all the distributions that give rise to Type I (the statement of the exercise does not ask for it). The GEV arises for y_n; however, for large thresholds, above which more than one order statistic will typically lie, we need the *generalized Pareto* distribution

$$F(w) = 1 - (1 + \lambda w/p)^{-p},$$

where $\lambda \in \mathbb{R}_+$ and $p^{-1} \in \mathbb{R}$, with $w \in \mathbb{R}_+$ if $p^{-1} \geqslant 0$ and $w \in (0, -p/\lambda)$ if $p < 0$. It arises as the limiting distribution of scaled excesses over large thresholds; see Embrechts, Klüppelberg, and Mikosch (1997).

11

Principles of point estimation

Suppose we have a $k \times 1$ variate $\boldsymbol{x}$ whose density is determined by the $m \times 1$ vector of unknown parameters $\boldsymbol{\theta}$. As mentioned in the introduction to Chapter 9, we may have a sample of n values of $\boldsymbol{x}$ which conveys to us some idea about $\boldsymbol{\theta}$. For example, the sample mean $\overline{\boldsymbol{x}}$ can be used to approximate the unknown mean $\boldsymbol{\mu}$ of a population; we explored aspects of such approximations in the last two chapters. A statistic that provides a formula for approximating $\boldsymbol{\theta}$ from the data is called an *estimator* of $\boldsymbol{\theta}$, and will usually be denoted by a hat or a tilde, $\widehat{\boldsymbol{\theta}}$ or $\widetilde{\boldsymbol{\theta}}$, a notation that was used implicitly in Chapter 9. An estimator (such as the sample mean) must be computable from the data only, and must not be formulated in terms of unknowns. In general, the estimator is itself a random variable, and an *estimate* of $\boldsymbol{\theta}$ is a specific numerical value for the estimator, usually arising from a sample of realized values in the data. The estimate is therefore the realization of the estimator. The vector $\boldsymbol{\theta}$ can be regarded as a point in the set of allowable values, say $\boldsymbol{\theta} \in \Theta$, hence the title *point estimation*.

The chapter starts by considering some desirable properties of point estimators, a sort of "the good, the bad, and the ugly" classification! We then introduce methods of summarizing the data via statistics that retain the relevant sample information about $\boldsymbol{\theta}$, and we see how they achieve the desirable properties of estimators. We conclude by introducing the most common model in statistics, the linear model, which will be used for illustrations in this chapter and covered more extensively in the following chapters.

On the most optimistic of accounts, $\boldsymbol{\theta}$ and $\widehat{\boldsymbol{\theta}}$ will hardly ever coincide exactly. We do, however, require that they are not too far apart, and we now discuss the main desirable properties of estimators.

1. Unbiasedness. An estimator is said to be *unbiased* if and only if $\mathrm{E}(\widehat{\boldsymbol{\theta}}) = \boldsymbol{\theta}$ for all $\boldsymbol{\theta} \in \Theta$. Hence, on average as the sampling is repeated, the estimator $\widehat{\boldsymbol{\theta}}$ (which is random) gets it right: there is no systematic tendency away from the true value $\boldsymbol{\theta}$. Otherwise, the *bias* of $\widehat{\boldsymbol{\theta}}$ is the difference:

$$\text{bias}(\widehat{\boldsymbol{\theta}}) := \mathrm{E}(\widehat{\boldsymbol{\theta}}) - \boldsymbol{\theta}.$$

If the mean of the distribution of $\widehat{\boldsymbol{\theta}}$ does not exist (as, for example, in the Cauchy case), then *median unbiasedness* is an alternative criterion to be considered, whereby the mean is replaced by the median.

2. Minimum variance. An estimator that is too erratic (volatile) is not reliable, even if it is unbiased. For example, in a random sample $\{x_i\}_{i=1}^n \sim \mathrm{IN}(\mu, 1)$ of size $n \geqslant 2$, the mean μ can be estimated by the usual sample mean, $\overline{x}$, or by $\widetilde{\mu} := (x_1 + x_2)/2$. Then $\overline{x} \sim \mathrm{N}(\mu, 1/n)$ while $\widetilde{\mu} \sim \mathrm{N}(\mu, 1/2)$. Both are unbiased, but the latter is less efficient as soon as $n > 2$ because it disregards the information in all the observations from $i = 3, \dots, n$. The concept of efficiency is inversely related to volatility, and the *efficiency of $\overline{x}$ relative to $\widetilde{\mu}$* is defined as

$$\mathrm{eff}_n(\overline{x}, \widetilde{\mu}) := \frac{\mathrm{var}\,(\widetilde{\mu})}{\mathrm{var}\,(\overline{x})} = \frac{1/2}{1/n} = \frac{n}{2}.$$

Their *asymptotic relative efficiency* (ARE) is $\mathrm{eff}_\infty(\overline{x}, \widetilde{\mu}) = \infty$. In other words, $\overline{x}$ becomes infinitely more efficient than $\widetilde{\mu}$ as $n \to \infty$. In general, one should be careful that the relative efficiency of asymptotic distributions is not necessarily the limit of the finite-sample relative efficiencies, $\mathrm{eff}_\infty \neq \lim_{n\to\infty} \mathrm{eff}_n$; see Exercise 10.38 for a counterexample and the Notes to Chapter 12 for further discussion.

The square root of $\mathrm{var}(\widehat{\theta})$ is known as the *standard error* of the estimator $\widehat{\theta}$; contrast this with the standard deviation of a distribution, defined in Chapter 3. In the vector case, we define the variance matrix of an estimator $\widehat{\boldsymbol{\theta}}$ as

$$\mathrm{var}(\widehat{\boldsymbol{\theta}}) = \mathrm{E}\left[\left(\widehat{\boldsymbol{\theta}} - \mathrm{E}(\widehat{\boldsymbol{\theta}})\right)\left(\widehat{\boldsymbol{\theta}} - \mathrm{E}(\widehat{\boldsymbol{\theta}})\right)'\right].$$

We wish to find an estimator $\widehat{\boldsymbol{\theta}}$ that is a *best* (or *uniformly minimum variance*) *estimator*: any other estimator $\widetilde{\boldsymbol{\theta}}$ would imply that

$$\boldsymbol{\Delta} := \mathrm{var}(\widetilde{\boldsymbol{\theta}}) - \mathrm{var}(\widehat{\boldsymbol{\theta}})$$

is positive semidefinite or, equivalently, $\boldsymbol{a}'\boldsymbol{\Delta}\boldsymbol{a} \geqslant 0$ for any arbitrary real $m \times 1$ vector of constants $\boldsymbol{a}$. This inequality has to hold regardless of the true value of $\boldsymbol{\theta}$, that is, for all $\boldsymbol{\theta} \in \Theta$.

3. BUE (or UMVUE). An estimator that combines Properties 1 and 2 is a *best* (or *uniformly minimum variance*) *unbiased estimator*, abbreviated BUE (or UMVUE).

4. Minimum MSE. The estimation error is $\widehat{\boldsymbol{\theta}} - \boldsymbol{\theta}$. In choosing a good estimator $\widehat{\boldsymbol{\theta}}$, an alternative criterion to minimize is again a quadratic form, as in Property 2, but is now the *mean squared error* (MSE):

$$\mathrm{MSE}(\widehat{\boldsymbol{\theta}}) := \mathrm{E}\left(\left(\widehat{\boldsymbol{\theta}} - \boldsymbol{\theta}\right)\left(\widehat{\boldsymbol{\theta}} - \boldsymbol{\theta}\right)'\right)$$

rather than the variance. The MSE is a quadratic measure of the distance between the elements of $\widehat{\boldsymbol{\theta}}$ and $\boldsymbol{\theta}$. It relates to the previous measures by

$$\mathrm{MSE}(\widehat{\boldsymbol{\theta}}) = \mathrm{var}(\widehat{\boldsymbol{\theta}}) + \mathrm{bias}(\widehat{\boldsymbol{\theta}})\,\mathrm{bias}(\widehat{\boldsymbol{\theta}})';$$

see Exercise 11.4. To minimize the MSE, we may thus tolerate a small nonzero bias if it helps us to achieve a much lower $\mathrm{var}(\widehat{\boldsymbol{\theta}})$. Notice, however, that expectations are linear operators, and thus Properties 1–4 are not necessarily invariant to nonlinear transformations of the parameters; see, for example, Exercise 11.5(a).

5. Consistency. If one were able to obtain a sample covering the whole population of x (that is, a sample where every possible outcome for the random variable is represented as in the population),[1] a good estimator $\widehat{\boldsymbol{\theta}}$ should be "consistent" with the true value $\boldsymbol{\theta}$ in the sense of coinciding with it. This is known as the *Fisher-consistency* of the estimator. More generally, the *consistency* of $\widehat{\boldsymbol{\theta}}$ requires that

$$\mathrm{plim}\,\widehat{\boldsymbol{\theta}} = \boldsymbol{\theta}$$

as the sample size increases towards infinity or, equivalently, $\widehat{\boldsymbol{\theta}} \xrightarrow{p} \boldsymbol{\theta}$. (Sometimes we write $\widehat{\boldsymbol{\theta}}_n$ or $\overline{x}_n$ to stress that the random $\widehat{\boldsymbol{\theta}}$ or $\overline{x}$ depends on n.) One could also consider *strong consistency* by requiring almost-sure convergence instead of convergence in probability. The largest $\delta > 0$ for which $n^{\delta}(\widehat{\boldsymbol{\theta}} - \boldsymbol{\theta})$ is $O_p(1)$ (and hence bounded in probability) leads us to the *consistency rate* n^{δ} of $\widehat{\boldsymbol{\theta}}$, and $\widehat{\boldsymbol{\theta}}$ is said to be n^{δ}*-consistent*. Relating consistency to previous concepts, if $\mathrm{bias}(\widehat{\boldsymbol{\theta}}) \to \mathbf{0}_m$ and $\mathrm{var}(\widehat{\boldsymbol{\theta}}) \to \mathbf{O}_{m,m}$ as $n \to \infty$, then $\widehat{\boldsymbol{\theta}} \xrightarrow{p} \boldsymbol{\theta}$. The reverse implication is not necessarily true, as we saw in Exercises 10.8 and 10.38. Consistency does not require the existence of moments. As seen in connection with Property 2, a random sample from the $\mathrm{N}(\mu, 1)$ distribution gives $\overline{x} \sim \mathrm{N}(\mu, 1/n)$, implying that $\overline{x}$ is a $\sqrt{n}$-consistent estimator of μ in this example. As n increases, the distribution of $\overline{x}$ concentrates more and more around the true unknown value μ, and eventually the distribution becomes degenerate around this single point: the convergence of $\overline{x}$ to μ has occurred. The same cannot be said about the inconsistent $\widetilde{\mu}$ whose variance remains strictly positive as $n \to \infty$: the density of $\widetilde{\mu}$ does not become more closely concentrated around the correct mean μ as n increases.

6. Robustness. Uncharacteristic occasional extremes in the data, so-called *outliers*, can affect some estimators more than others, and we would like our estimators to be relatively insensitive to them. For example, the sample median is completely unaffected if we increase the size of *any* observation exceeding it (that's almost 50% of the lot!). The sample mode is quite robust too, but not the sample mean; we saw an example of this earlier, in Exercise 9.1. Let us give an illustration. Typing data can be pretty boring. Someone has a large dataset to type in, loses concentration, and presses the button 8 for too long, inadvertently turning it into 88. The mean will jump immediately, but the other two estimators of central location (the mode and median) may not change at all. To illustrate this more dramatically, ask our typist to replace the 8 by ∞ (or rotate by 90° the piece of paper from

[1] A sample like this is not possible for a continuous random variable because the set of outcomes is uncountable, as seen in the introduction to Chapter 2.

which he or she was copying the number 8) and see which of the three estimators changes and by how much!

7. Invariance. There are many types of invariance argument. Here, we focus on only one. Suppose the quantity of interest is the function $\boldsymbol{\lambda} := \boldsymbol{g}(\boldsymbol{\theta})$; for example, $\lambda := 1/\theta$ in the case of $m = 1$. We could estimate this directly and obtain $\widehat{\lambda}$, or we could estimate θ by $\widehat{\theta}$ then compute $1/\widehat{\theta}$ as an estimator of λ. The latter estimator may differ from $\widehat{\lambda}$ (for example, in the case of least-squares estimators to be studied in Chapter 13) or they may be equal (for example, the maximum-likelihood estimators to be considered in Chapter 12). Ideally, we would like to have $\widehat{\theta}\widehat{\lambda} = 1$, just as $\theta\lambda \equiv 1$ by definition. If $\widehat{\boldsymbol{\lambda}} = \boldsymbol{g}(\widehat{\boldsymbol{\theta}})$, or equivalently $\widehat{\boldsymbol{g}(\boldsymbol{\theta})} = \boldsymbol{g}(\widehat{\boldsymbol{\theta}})$, the estimator is said to be *invariant to transformations of the parameters* or *invariant to reparameterizations*.

8. Decision-theoretic criteria. Finally, we introduce a framework for deciding which estimators to choose, based on the implications of such a choice on a prespecified criterion. Define a *loss* (or *cost*) *function* $C(\widehat{\boldsymbol{\theta}})$ as a real-valued function quantifying the loss arising from $\widehat{\boldsymbol{\theta}} \neq \boldsymbol{\theta}$. As the random $\widehat{\boldsymbol{\theta}}$ varies with the data, the expected loss is known as the *risk* of the estimator $\widehat{\boldsymbol{\theta}}$ and is written as $\text{risk}(\widehat{\boldsymbol{\theta}}) := \mathrm{E}(C(\widehat{\boldsymbol{\theta}}))$. Examples include the familiar quadratic criterion

$$C(\widehat{\boldsymbol{\theta}}) = \left(\widehat{\boldsymbol{\theta}} - \boldsymbol{\theta}\right)' \boldsymbol{A} \left(\widehat{\boldsymbol{\theta}} - \boldsymbol{\theta}\right)$$

for some chosen matrix of fixed weights $\boldsymbol{A}$ that do not depend on $\boldsymbol{\theta}$, and where $\boldsymbol{A}$ is usually positive definite. Instead of quadratic functions, criteria that are asymmetric in $\widehat{\boldsymbol{\theta}} - \boldsymbol{\theta}$ may also be of interest in economic applications, where losses and gains may not have the same consequences. Note that when $m = 1$, minimizing $\mathrm{E}(a(\widehat{\theta} - \theta)^2)$, where $a > 0$, leads to a minimum-MSE estimator. However, in general, the MSE is $m \times m$, and we considered arbitrary quadratic forms thereof in Property 4, not just combinations with prespecified weights. An estimator $\widehat{\boldsymbol{\theta}}$ is *admissible* if there are no other estimators $\widetilde{\boldsymbol{\theta}}$ such that

$$\begin{aligned} &\text{risk}(\widetilde{\boldsymbol{\theta}}) \leqslant \text{risk}(\widehat{\boldsymbol{\theta}}) \quad \text{for all } \boldsymbol{\theta} \in \Theta\text{; and} \\ &\text{risk}(\widetilde{\boldsymbol{\theta}}) < \text{risk}(\widehat{\boldsymbol{\theta}}) \quad \text{for some } \boldsymbol{\theta} \in \Theta. \end{aligned}$$

If there exists another estimator $\widetilde{\boldsymbol{\theta}}$ which does better (in terms of risk) than $\widehat{\boldsymbol{\theta}}$ at some point in the parameter space, while doing no worse elsewhere, then $\widehat{\boldsymbol{\theta}}$ is *inadmissible*. Finally, suppose that some specific value of $\boldsymbol{\theta}$ has dreadful implications for the expected loss, so much so that one may prefer to choose instead an estimator that minimizes the risk function in this worst-case scenario, namely opting to choose $\widehat{\boldsymbol{\theta}}$ to minimize

$$\sup_{\boldsymbol{\theta} \in \Theta} \text{risk}(\widehat{\boldsymbol{\theta}}).$$

Then this $\widehat{\boldsymbol{\theta}}$ is called a *minimax* estimator. Incidentally, the notations $\text{bias}(\widehat{\boldsymbol{\theta}})$ and $\text{risk}(\widehat{\boldsymbol{\theta}})$ have been designed in the same way as for $\mathrm{E}(\widehat{\boldsymbol{\theta}})$ and $\text{var}(\widehat{\boldsymbol{\theta}})$, and this should not conceal the dependence of these expectations on the nonrandom $\boldsymbol{\theta}$; they are all functions of $\boldsymbol{\theta}$.

Now that we have specified criteria that depend on the sampling distribution of $\widehat{\boldsymbol{\theta}}$, we need to be more explicit about the sampling setup itself. Suppose that we have a random sample $\{\boldsymbol{x}_i\}_{i=1}^n$, which we henceforth collate in an $n \times k$ data matrix $\boldsymbol{X} := (\boldsymbol{x}_1, \dots, \boldsymbol{x}_n)'$ (as in Chapter 9) having the joint density $f_{\boldsymbol{X}}(\boldsymbol{W}) = \prod_{i=1}^n f_{\boldsymbol{x}}(\boldsymbol{w}_i)$ with $\boldsymbol{w}_i$ the realization of $\boldsymbol{x}_i$. The i.i.d. assumption is made to simplify the exposition and it is not necessary for the factorization of the density of $\boldsymbol{X}$, to which we now turn.

If we can find a statistic $\boldsymbol{z}$ such that the conditional distribution of $\boldsymbol{X} \mid \boldsymbol{z}$ does not depend on $\boldsymbol{\theta}$, then the vector $\boldsymbol{z}$ is called a *sufficient statistic* because it contains all that the data's density can tell us about $\boldsymbol{\theta}$. Note that because $\boldsymbol{z}$ is a statistic, it contains no unobservables and can be computed from the data alone. The sufficiency of $\boldsymbol{z}$ also implies that, given $\boldsymbol{z}$, the distribution of *any* other statistic will not depend on $\boldsymbol{\theta}$. *Neyman's factorization theorem* shows that this sufficiency is equivalent to $f_{\boldsymbol{X}}$ factoring into the product of two nonnegative functions,

$$f_{\boldsymbol{X}}(\boldsymbol{W}; \boldsymbol{\theta}) = h_1(\boldsymbol{w}_{\boldsymbol{z}}; \boldsymbol{\theta}) \times h_2(\boldsymbol{W}), \tag{11.1}$$

one depending on the realization of $\boldsymbol{z}$ and the unknown $\boldsymbol{\theta}$, and the other depending on the data values $\boldsymbol{W}$ but not on $\boldsymbol{\theta}$. For example, as seen in Exercises 9.17 and 9.18 where θ is μ, $\{x_i\}_{i=1}^n \sim \mathrm{IN}(\mu, 1)$ has a joint density that factors into the realization of

$$\frac{\exp\left(-\frac{n}{2}(\overline{x} - \mu)^2\right)}{\sqrt{2\pi}} \times \frac{\exp\left(-\frac{n-1}{2}s^2\right)}{(2\pi)^{\frac{n-1}{2}}}, \tag{11.2}$$

where $s^2 := \sum_{i=1}^n (x_i - \overline{x})^2/(n-1)$ and the second factor does not depend on μ. We therefore say that here $\overline{x}$ is a sufficient statistic for μ. In other words, knowing $\overline{x}$ reveals all that the sample's density can tell us about calculating a value for μ: for estimating μ, it is "sufficient" to know $\overline{x}$ here. The reader may have noticed that the realization of the first factor in (11.2), when multiplied by $\sqrt{n}$, is the density of $\overline{x} \sim \mathrm{N}(\mu, 1/n)$. This is no coincidence. It is for this reason that Neyman's factorization theorem is often restated as follows:

$$\boldsymbol{z} \text{ is sufficient} \iff f_{\boldsymbol{X}}/f_{\boldsymbol{z}} \text{ does not depend on } \boldsymbol{\theta} \text{ at the points where } f_{\boldsymbol{z}} \neq 0. \tag{11.3}$$

Note, however, that the second factor of (11.2) is not the density of $\{x_i\}_{i=1}^n \mid \overline{x}$, which is singular because $\sum_{i=1}^n (x_i - \overline{x}) \equiv 0$ by definition. This factor relates to the conditional density of only $n-1$ of the observations, such as $\{x_i\}_{i=1}^{n-1} \mid \overline{x}$ (or the joint density of $\{x_i - \overline{x}\}_{i=1}^{n-1}$ as seen in Exercise 9.16); see, for example, the discussion in Exercise 9.18. We therefore have to be careful not to confuse $f_{\boldsymbol{X}}/f_{\boldsymbol{z}}$ with $f_{\boldsymbol{X}|\boldsymbol{z}}$ when $\boldsymbol{X}$ is a continuous variate.[2] Also, (11.2) is not the joint density of $(\overline{x}, s^2)$! To obtain this would require calculating the Jacobian of the transformation from $\boldsymbol{X}$ and then marginalizing, leading to a multiplicative factor involving s^{n-3} from the $\chi^2(n-1)$ density; see Exercise 7.16(e)

[2]The definition of sufficiency in terms of distribution rather than density avoids this problem. Illustrating by means of the last example, with $n = 2$, the conditional c.d.f. $\Pr(x_1 \leqslant u_1, x_2 \leqslant u_2 \mid \overline{x} = v)$ is still well defined, though care is required in specifying the domain of definition (the probability is zero for $u_1 + u_2 < 2v$, hence is trivially independent of μ for these values).

earlier and the elaboration of this point in Exercise 11.10.

Later on, it will be useful to partition the parameter vector as $\boldsymbol{\theta}' := (\boldsymbol{\theta}_1', \boldsymbol{\theta}_2')$, where we wish to focus on the *parameters of interest* $\boldsymbol{\theta}_1$, and the remainder $\boldsymbol{\theta}_2$ are *nuisance parameters* that need to be accounted for (to avoid misspecification) while not being of immediate interest. Effectively, what we did in the example of the random sample from $\mathrm{N}(\mu, \sigma^2)$ was to focus on μ and treat σ^2 as a nuisance parameter; see Exercise 11.10.

A motivating idea behind sufficiency is to summarize the data as much as possible, insofar as we are interested in estimating $\boldsymbol{\theta}$. But, by definition, the whole dataset $\boldsymbol{X}$ itself is sufficient! For the concept to be meaningful, we are really interested in the *minimal sufficiency*, defined as a maximal reduction in the dimension of the sufficient statistic $\boldsymbol{z}$. Minimal sufficiency is trivially the case if $\boldsymbol{z}$ is of dimension 1, such as in our example in (11.2), but the general method of checking for minimality is given in Exercise 11.17. Some of our exercises will illustrate this reduction, but it has to be borne in mind that there are cases (for example, sampling from a Cauchy distribution) where no reduction is possible beyond $\boldsymbol{X}$. The dimensions of $\boldsymbol{z}$ and $\boldsymbol{\theta}$ need not be equal, and $\boldsymbol{z}$ is unique only up to one-to-one transformations.

An *ancillary statistic* is one whose marginal distribution does not depend on $\boldsymbol{\theta}$. (Contrast this with the case of sufficiency of $\boldsymbol{z}$, where the *conditional* distribution of $\boldsymbol{X} \mid \boldsymbol{z}$ is the one that did not depend on $\boldsymbol{\theta}$, the marginal $f_{\boldsymbol{z}}$ being the source of information on $\boldsymbol{\theta}$.) Suppose that $\boldsymbol{z}' := (\boldsymbol{z}_1', \boldsymbol{z}_2')$ is minimal sufficient, but $\boldsymbol{z}_2$ is ancillary. The conditional distribution of $\boldsymbol{z}_1 \mid \boldsymbol{z}_2$ is therefore the only part of the joint distribution that depends on $\boldsymbol{\theta}$, and we call $\boldsymbol{z}_1$ a *conditionally sufficient statistic*. For example, letting $(x, y)' \sim \mathrm{N}(\mathbf{0}, \boldsymbol{\Sigma})$ with

$$\boldsymbol{\Sigma} = \begin{pmatrix} 1 & \rho \\ \rho & 1 \end{pmatrix} \qquad (|\rho| < 1) \tag{11.4}$$

and $n = 1$, we have that (x, y) is minimal sufficient for ρ, while x or y are individually ancillary $\mathrm{N}(0, 1)$ that do not depend on ρ! Neither, alone, carries *any* information about ρ: all the information is in either $y \mid x \sim \mathrm{N}(\rho x, 1 - \rho^2)$ or $x \mid y \sim \mathrm{N}(\rho y, 1 - \rho^2)$. In general, one should not take the finding that $\boldsymbol{z}_2$ is ancillary to mean that it is not informative about $\boldsymbol{\theta}$, since $\boldsymbol{z}_2$ appears in the conditional density $f_{\boldsymbol{z}_1|\boldsymbol{z}_2}$. Furthermore, the minimal sufficiency of $\boldsymbol{z}$ means that $\boldsymbol{z}_2$ is an essential component of the sufficient statistic: the distribution of $\boldsymbol{X} \mid \boldsymbol{z}$ does not depend on $\boldsymbol{\theta}$ but that of $\boldsymbol{X} \mid \boldsymbol{z}_1$ does, so that $\boldsymbol{z}_1$ on its own is not sufficient for $\boldsymbol{\theta}$. As seen in the example in (11.4) and as will be seen in Exercise 11.13(c), unlike in the case of minimal sufficiency, the choice of $\boldsymbol{z}_1$ and $\boldsymbol{z}_2$ is not unique, not even if we disregard one-to-one transformations within each of $\boldsymbol{z}_1$ and $\boldsymbol{z}_2$.

We have seen that the law of iterated expectations (Exercise 6.28) implies that

$$\mathrm{var}(h(x)) = \mathrm{var}_z(\mathrm{E}_{x|z}(h(x))) + \mathrm{E}_z(\mathrm{var}_{x|z}(h(x))) \geqslant \mathrm{var}_z(\mathrm{E}_{x|z}(h(x))), \tag{11.5}$$

the expressions being equal when $\mathrm{var}_{x|z}(h(x)) = 0$ almost surely. In the current context, let z be a sufficient statistic and $h(x)$ be an unbiased estimator of some function $\eta(\boldsymbol{\theta})$. The function $h(x)$ does not contain $\boldsymbol{\theta}$ (because $h(x)$ is an estimator) and $F_{x|z}$ does not depend on $\boldsymbol{\theta}$ (by sufficiency), so

$$g(z) := \mathrm{E}_{x|z}(h(x)) \equiv \int h(u)\, \mathrm{d}F_{x|z}(u)$$

does not depend on the unknown $\boldsymbol{\theta}$ and therefore it too is an estimator of $\eta(\boldsymbol{\theta})$. It is unbiased because

$$\mathrm{E}(g(z)) \equiv \mathrm{E}\left(\mathrm{E}_{x|z}(h(x))\right) = \mathrm{E}_z\left(\mathrm{E}_{x|z}(h(x))\right) = \mathrm{E}(h(x)),$$

but it has a better variance than $h(x)$ by virtue of the inequality in (11.5). This result for g is known as the *Rao–Blackwell theorem*. It applies to the case of multivariate $\boldsymbol{X}$ and $\boldsymbol{z}$ and, when $\boldsymbol{h}(\boldsymbol{x})$ is a vector-valued function, the difference $\mathrm{var}(\boldsymbol{h}(\boldsymbol{X})) - \mathrm{var}_{\boldsymbol{z}}(\mathrm{E}_{\boldsymbol{X}|\boldsymbol{z}}(\boldsymbol{h}(\boldsymbol{X})))$ is positive semidefinite. The theorem tells us that conditioning on the sufficient statistic z always improves the efficiency of unbiased estimators, unless z is the only variate affecting $h(x)$ in the first place (that is, $\mathrm{var}_{x|z}(h(x)) = 0$). Conditioning, to obtain the unbiased estimator g, is referred to as *Rao–Blackwellization*.

We have now gone full circle back to the start of this chapter. We are talking again about the efficiency of unbiased estimators, but how can we find an unbiased estimator that will achieve maximal efficiency, and will it be unique? To answer these two questions, we need to introduce the concept of completeness. The sufficient statistic $\boldsymbol{z}$ is said to be *complete* if

$$\mathrm{E}(\psi(\boldsymbol{z})) = 0 \qquad \Longrightarrow \qquad \psi(\boldsymbol{z}) = 0 \text{ with probability } 1$$

for any $\boldsymbol{\theta} \in \Theta$ and any function ψ not depending on $\boldsymbol{\theta}$ and having a finite expectation. In connection with the example of (11.2), where $\overline{x} \sim \mathrm{N}(\mu, 1/n)$ is nondegenerate for $n < \infty$, the only function of $\overline{x}$ alone (not of $\overline{x}$ and μ) that has zero expectation for any arbitrary $\mu \in \mathbb{R}$ must be a degenerate function, more specifically one that is zero almost surely. As a result, $\overline{x}$ is a complete sufficient statistic for μ.

If, in addition, we restrict ψ to being a bounded function, completeness (in this special case called *bounded completeness*) guarantees minimal sufficiency because it rules out the existence of combinations of $\boldsymbol{z}$ which are uninformative about $\boldsymbol{\theta}$. Bounded completeness being a weaker condition than completeness, we get

$$\text{completeness} \implies \text{bounded completeness} \implies \text{minimal sufficiency.}$$

The contrapositive of this implication is illustrated in Exercise 11.10(b), while a counterexample of the reverse implication is found in Exercise 11.13(c). Importantly, completeness allows us to formulate some influential theorems, of which we give two here.

Continuing with the setup introduced after (11.5), the *Lehmann–Scheffé theorem* states that if $\boldsymbol{z}$ is a complete sufficient statistic and $g(\boldsymbol{z})$ is an unbiased estimator of $\eta(\boldsymbol{\theta})$, then $g(\boldsymbol{z})$ is *the* BUE of $\eta(\boldsymbol{\theta})$ with probability 1. The estimator $g(\boldsymbol{z})$ is unique almost surely, and the exercises will illustrate how to derive it for samples drawn from various distributions, including in Exercise 11.15 for the large exponential family seen in Chapter 4. Our earlier example on the sample mean is a simple illustration of this family.

From Neyman's factorization (11.1), it follows that if a statistic $\boldsymbol{h}(\boldsymbol{X})$ is independent of the sufficient statistic $\boldsymbol{z}$, then $\boldsymbol{h}(\boldsymbol{X})$ is ancillary. When, furthermore, $\boldsymbol{z}$ is boundedly complete, D. Basu gave a striking converse to this result. *Basu's theorem* states that if $\boldsymbol{z}$ is a boundedly-complete sufficient statistic and $\boldsymbol{h}(\boldsymbol{X})$ is ancillary, then $\boldsymbol{h}(\boldsymbol{X})$ is independent of $\boldsymbol{z}$. Applied to (11.2), it tells us immediately that s^2 is independent of $\overline{x}$, a result that took us quite some effort to derive earlier in some of the exercises of Chapters 7–9 (such as Exercise 7.16). The theorem is also applicable to the regular exponential family, by virtue of Exercise 11.15(c).

When introducing estimation, we should mention the most common of all setups, the linear model. We have already seen the case of a random (i.i.d.) sample $\{y_i\}_{i=1}^n \sim \text{IID}(\mu, \sigma^2)$, where the mean and variance are given by μ and σ^2, respectively, but the distribution D is otherwise unspecified. It can be rewritten as $y_i := \mu + \varepsilon_i$, where $\{\varepsilon_i\}_{i=1}^n \sim \text{IID}(0, \sigma^2)$. This is known as a *location and scale model* (μ and σ, respectively), where we observe y_i but μ (hence ε_i) and σ are unknown. It is a special case of the famous *linear model* (or *linear regression model*)

$$y_i := x_{i1}\beta_1 + \cdots + x_{ik}\beta_k + \varepsilon_i = (x_{i1}, \ldots, x_{ik}) \begin{pmatrix} \beta_1 \\ \vdots \\ \beta_k \end{pmatrix} + \varepsilon_i \tag{11.6}$$

for $i = 1, \ldots, n$ observations ($n > k$) and where $\{\varepsilon_i\}_{i=1}^n \sim \text{IID}(0, \sigma^2)$ are the *disturbances* (or *errors*). The special case $\varepsilon_i \sim \text{N}(0, \sigma^2)$ gives rise to the *normal linear model*. In general, the ε's are typically assumed to be centered around zero, because one can absorb any nonzero value into the other terms on the right-hand side, for example by defining the artificial variable $x_{i1} := 1$ for all i. This x_{i1} is a special case of an indicator function (see the definition in Chapter 2) and is called a *dummy variable* in this context. The k variables labeled by x are called *explanatory variables* (or *regressors*), while y is the *dependent variable* (or *regressand*). For example, one may attempt to explain the level of a river, y, by k factors including variables such as the amount of daily rainfall over the previous week. By stacking the n equations, they can be written in a convenient matrix form:

$$\begin{pmatrix} y_1 \\ \vdots \\ y_n \end{pmatrix} = \begin{pmatrix} x_{11} & \ldots & x_{1k} \\ \vdots & & \vdots \\ x_{n1} & \ldots & x_{nk} \end{pmatrix} \begin{pmatrix} \beta_1 \\ \vdots \\ \beta_k \end{pmatrix} + \begin{pmatrix} \varepsilon_1 \\ \vdots \\ \varepsilon_n \end{pmatrix} \tag{11.7}$$

abbreviated as $\boldsymbol{y} = \boldsymbol{X\beta} + \boldsymbol{\varepsilon}$. It is assumed that $\boldsymbol{X}$ is of full column rank k: the columns of $\boldsymbol{X}$ must be linearly independent, otherwise some explanatory variables would be redundant. If the variance of the ε's exists, then it is given by σ^2 and the i.i.d. assumption implies that $\text{var}(\boldsymbol{\varepsilon}) = \sigma^2 \boldsymbol{I}_n$. The model is often expressed as $\boldsymbol{y} \mid \boldsymbol{X} \sim \text{D}(\boldsymbol{X\beta}, \sigma^2 \boldsymbol{I}_n)$, with conditional mean and variance listed respectively. This allows us to apply many results from earlier chapters, especially starting with the definition and properties of error terms in Exercise 6.43. In fact, one justification for the choice of a linear relation between y_i and $(x_{i1}, \ldots, x_{ik})$ was encountered in Exercise 6.51; that is, if the variates are jointly elliptical and thus have a linear conditional mean. This is something that we will revisit in Exercise 12.33(c) and in Chapter 13. There are also linear models generalizing $\text{var}(\boldsymbol{\varepsilon}) = \sigma^2 \boldsymbol{I}_n$ to the *nonspherical* case of unrestricted positive definite matrices. Furthermore, the *generalized linear model* (GLM) allows $\boldsymbol{X}\boldsymbol{\beta}$ to be related to $\text{E}(\boldsymbol{y})$ by means of a possibly nonlinear *link function* of $\text{E}(\boldsymbol{y})$. For example, this is useful when a logarithmic transformation is required, such as was discussed at the end of Exercise 4.23(b). We will encounter another example in Exercise 12.1(e).

In the linear model with $\text{var}(\boldsymbol{\varepsilon}) = \sigma^2 \boldsymbol{I}_n$, the parameter vector is $\boldsymbol{\theta}' := (\boldsymbol{\beta}', \sigma^2)$ if σ^2 is unknown, and we saw earlier in this chapter what constitutes a good estimator of $\boldsymbol{\theta}$ if we treat $\boldsymbol{X}$ as given. For example, when $k = 2$ and $x_{i1} := 1$ for all i, we would be trying to fit a *regression line* linking y to x (shorthand for the only nonconstant regressor), which requires estimating $\boldsymbol{\beta} = (\beta_1, \beta_2)'$ where β_1 is the intercept and β_2 is the slope. The graph of the n data points (x_i, y_i) in (x, y) space is called the *scatter plot* (an illustration will be seen in Figure 13.2), and estimators of $\boldsymbol{\beta}$ try to locate the ideal place for a line to fit between these data points. Note that there are n data points which, in general, will not all be exactly located on a single hyperplane in the $(k+1)$-dimensional space of $(x_{i1}, \dots, x_{ik}, y_i)$; hence, we have the problem of finding the ideal line. Furthermore, the vector $\boldsymbol{\varepsilon}$ is not observed and the $\boldsymbol{X}$ matrix is not square and cannot be inverted to estimate $\boldsymbol{\beta}$ from $\boldsymbol{y} = \boldsymbol{X}\boldsymbol{\beta} + \boldsymbol{\varepsilon}$. A *fitted regression line* is defined by $\widehat{\boldsymbol{y}} = \boldsymbol{X}\widehat{\boldsymbol{\beta}}$, where $\widehat{\boldsymbol{\beta}}$ is an estimator of $\boldsymbol{\beta}$, and the realization of $\boldsymbol{\varepsilon}$ is $\widehat{\boldsymbol{\varepsilon}} := \boldsymbol{y} - \widehat{\boldsymbol{y}}$, the *residual* of the relation.

Before embarking on the exercises in this chapter, we need to comment on two underlying structures. First, we have assumed that we know the correct type of distribution for the data, and that our problem is simply to estimate the parameter vector. Things may be more complicated in practice, however, and models may be misspecified. The data may have been generated by an alternative mechanism or *data-generating process* (DGP). Most of this book focuses on the simpler case of no misspecification. Second, we have assumed that the models are *parametric*, being fully described by a vector of parameters $\boldsymbol{\theta}$ and the functional form of the distribution, and that estimation amounts to finding a good approximation for $\boldsymbol{\theta}$. *Nonparametric* (NP) *models* will be considered in Chapter 13, and they do not specify a functional form or parameters to estimate. They can be *nonparametric density estimates* (see Exercise 2.23), possibly multivariate, or simply the conditional expectation of one variate in terms of the others, which is known as *nonparametric regression*. Implicitly, we saw a parametric counterpart of the latter in most of the exercises in Section 6.4. We will analyze both types of regression in the next two chapters, where various methods of estimation will be considered explicitly, whereas this chapter focuses on the principles of estimation. The exercises start with bias, efficiency, and consistency. We then move on to cover sufficiency, completeness, best-unbiasedness, and admissibility. We conclude with the ancillarity and independence of statistics.

11.1 Estimators' bias, efficiency, and consistency

Exercise 11.1 (Coverage probabilities of normal intervals) Consider two estimators $\widehat{\mu}_1$ and $\widehat{\mu}_2$ of μ.

(a) Assume that $\widehat{\mu}_i \sim \mathrm{N}(\mu, \sigma_i^2)$ for $i = 1, 2$. Show that if $0 < \sigma_1 \leqslant \sigma_2$, we have

$$\Pr(|\widehat{\mu}_1 - \mu| < \delta) \geqslant \Pr(|\widehat{\mu}_2 - \mu| < \delta)$$

for all $\delta > 0$.

(b) What if $\Pr(\widehat{\mu}_i \leqslant \mu + \sigma_i w) = H(w)$ for some nondecreasing function H instead of Φ, and $0 < \sigma_1 \leqslant \sigma_2$?

Solution

(a) Let $\Phi(u)$ denote the standard normal distribution function. Then

$$\begin{aligned}\Pr(|\widehat{\mu}_1 - \mu| < \delta) &= \Pr(-\delta < \widehat{\mu}_1 - \mu < \delta)\\ &= \Pr\left(-\frac{\delta}{\sigma_1} < \frac{\widehat{\mu}_1 - \mu}{\sigma_1} < \frac{\delta}{\sigma_1}\right)\\ &= \Phi\left(\frac{\delta}{\sigma_1}\right) - \Phi\left(\frac{-\delta}{\sigma_1}\right) = 2\Phi\left(\frac{\delta}{\sigma_1}\right) - 1,\end{aligned}$$

where we have used the fact that the standard normal density is symmetric around 0. In the case of $\widehat{\mu}_2$, we have $\Pr(|\widehat{\mu}_2 - \mu| < \delta) = 2\Phi(\delta/\sigma_2) - 1$. If $\sigma_2 \geqslant \sigma_1$, then $\Phi(\delta/\sigma_2) \leqslant \Phi(\delta/\sigma_1)$, and the result follows. The first estimator is at least as efficient as the second, since $\sigma_1 \leqslant \sigma_2$, and this is reflected in the dispersion of the possible values of $\widehat{\mu}_1$ relative to $\widehat{\mu}_2$.

(b) This is a location-scale formulation of c.d.f.s, seen in Exercise 3.16. We have

$$\begin{aligned}\Pr(|\widehat{\mu}_1 - \mu| < \delta) &= \Pr\left(-\frac{\delta}{\sigma_1} < \frac{\widehat{\mu}_1 - \mu}{\sigma_1} < \frac{\delta}{\sigma_1}\right)\\ &= \Pr\left(\frac{\widehat{\mu}_1 - \mu}{\sigma_1} < \frac{\delta}{\sigma_1}\right) - \Pr\left(\frac{\widehat{\mu}_1 - \mu}{\sigma_1} \leqslant -\frac{\delta}{\sigma_1}\right)\\ &= H\left(\frac{\delta^-}{\sigma_1}\right) - H\left(-\frac{\delta}{\sigma_1}\right),\end{aligned}$$

and similarly for $\widehat{\mu}_2$, giving

$$\begin{aligned}&\Pr(|\widehat{\mu}_1 - \mu| < \delta) - \Pr(|\widehat{\mu}_2 - \mu| < \delta)\\ &\quad = \left(H\left(\frac{\delta^-}{\sigma_1}\right) - H\left(\frac{\delta^-}{\sigma_2}\right)\right) + \left(H\left(-\frac{\delta}{\sigma_2}\right) - H\left(-\frac{\delta}{\sigma_1}\right)\right).\end{aligned}$$

Since H is a nondecreasing function of its argument, and since

$$\frac{\delta^-}{\sigma_1} \geqslant \frac{\delta^-}{\sigma_2} \quad \text{and} \quad -\frac{\delta}{\sigma_2} \geqslant -\frac{\delta}{\sigma_1},$$

we have $\Pr(|\widehat{\mu}_1 - \mu| < \delta) \geqslant \Pr(|\widehat{\mu}_2 - \mu| < \delta)$ again. Therefore, the result applies to *any* distribution that is common to both standardized variates $(\widehat{\mu}_1 - \mu)/\sigma_1$ and $(\widehat{\mu}_2 - \mu)/\sigma_2$. Notice that we have not made use of the existence of moments here: μ and σ_1, σ_2 could be regarded as centering and scaling, respectively.

Exercise 11.2 (Weighted averages and pooled estimators) Let $x_1, \dots, x_n$ be a random sample of a variate x having $\mu := \mathrm{E}(x)$ and a finite second moment, and define $\widetilde{\mu} := \sum_{i=1}^n \alpha_i x_i$, which is linear in $\{x_n\}$. We say that $\widetilde{\mu}$ is a *weighted average* of the $\{x_n\}$, and the $\{a_n\}$ are the *weights*; compare with the population counterpart in the introduction to Chapter 3.
(a) Show that $\widetilde{\mu}$ is an unbiased estimator of μ (for arbitrary μ) if and only if $\sum_{i=1}^n \alpha_i = 1$.
(b) Let $\widetilde{\mu}$ be unbiased. Show that the variance of $\widetilde{\mu}$ is minimized when $\alpha_i = 1/n$, that is, $\widetilde{\mu} = \overline{x}$ is the *best linear unbiased estimator* (BLUE) of μ. The term "linear" is used because $\widetilde{\mu}$ is a linear function of the x's.
(c) Now suppose that $y_1, \dots, y_n$ are independent with common mean μ, but known variances σ_i^2 which differ with i. Minimize the variance of $\widehat{\mu} := \sum_{i=1}^n a_i y_i$ when $\widehat{\mu}$ is an unbiased estimator of μ.
(d) Apply the result in (c) to combining $\overline{x}_1$ and $\overline{x}_2$ of Exercise 9.3 into a single estimator (called a *pooled* estimator) of the mean μ.

Solution

(a) We know that

$$\mathrm{E}\left(\sum_{i=1}^n \alpha_i x_i\right) = \sum_{i=1}^n \alpha_i \mathrm{E}(x_i) = \mu \sum_{i=1}^n \alpha_i;$$

hence $\widetilde{\mu}$ is unbiased for *any* μ if and only if $\sum_{i=1}^n \alpha_i = 1$. However, not all such estimators are efficient, as we shall now see.
(b) As in many previous exercises (especially in Chapters 7 and 9), the i.i.d. assumption implies that

$$\mathrm{var}\left(\sum_{i=1}^n \alpha_i x_i\right) = \sum_{i=1}^n \alpha_i^2 \mathrm{var}(x_i) = \mathrm{var}(x_1) \sum_{i=1}^n \alpha_i^2.$$

Write $\alpha_i = 1/n + \beta_i$. Then, part (a) gives $\sum_{i=1}^n \alpha_i = 1$; hence $\sum_{i=1}^n \beta_i = 0$ and we get

$$\begin{aligned}\mathrm{var}\left(\sum_{i=1}^n \alpha_i x_i\right) &= \mathrm{var}(x_1) \sum_{i=1}^n \alpha_i^2 = \mathrm{var}(x_1)\left(\sum_{i=1}^n \frac{1}{n^2} + \frac{2}{n}\sum_{i=1}^n \beta_i + \sum_{i=1}^n \beta_i^2\right)\\ &= \frac{\mathrm{var}(x_1)}{n} + \mathrm{var}(x_1)\sum_{i=1}^n \beta_i^2.\end{aligned}$$

Since $\beta_i^2 \geqslant 0$, the variance of $\widetilde{\mu}$ is minimized when $\beta_i = 0$ hence $\alpha_i = 1/n$ for $i = 1, \dots, n$.
(c) As in (a), $\mathrm{E}(\widehat{\mu}) = \mu$ if and only if $\sum_{i=1}^n a_i = 1$. Writing $\widehat{\mu} = \boldsymbol{a}'\boldsymbol{y}$, we get $\mathrm{var}(\widehat{\mu}) = \boldsymbol{a}' \mathrm{diag}(\sigma_1^2, \dots, \sigma_n^2)\, \boldsymbol{a}$. We could minimize this, subject to $\boldsymbol{a}'\boldsymbol{\imath} = 1$, by means of a La-

grangian function. Alternatively, define $\lambda^2 := (\sum_{i=1}^n \sigma_i^{-2})^{-1}$, which is n^{-1} times the harmonic mean of $\{\sigma_n^2\}$, introduced in Exercise 9.1. Then write $a_i = \lambda^2/\sigma_i^2 + b_i$. Since $\sum_{i=1}^n a_i = 1$, we have $\sum_{i=1}^n b_i = 0$ and the same method as that used in (b) gives

$$\operatorname{var}\left(\sum_{i=1}^n a_i y_i\right) = \sum_{i=1}^n a_i^2\sigma_i^2 = \sum_{i=1}^n \left(\frac{\lambda^4}{\sigma_i^4} + 2\lambda^2\frac{b_i}{\sigma_i^2} + b_i^2\right)\sigma_i^2 = \lambda^2 + \sum_{i=1}^n b_i^2\sigma_i^2,$$

which is minimized by choosing $b_i = 0$ for $i = 1, \dots, n$. Hence, the optimal weights are given by $a_i = \lambda^2/\sigma_i^2$. Notice the important result that, when observations have different variances, one should downplay (give less weight to) less reliable components that have a high variance. This result will be generalized in Section 13.2.

(d) To find the optimal weight for combining $\overline{x}_1$ and $\overline{x}_2$ of Exercise 9.3, recall that var $(\overline{x}_1) = \sigma^2/m$ and var $(\overline{x}_2) = \sigma^2/(n-m)$, giving

$$\lambda^2 = \left(\frac{m}{\sigma^2} + \frac{n-m}{\sigma^2}\right)^{-1} = \frac{\sigma^2}{n}.$$

Then (c) gives the optimal weights as $a_1 = m/n$ and $a_2 = 1 - m/n$. Note that, if we could observe the x_i directly, then

$$\widehat{\mu} = \frac{m}{n}\overline{x}_1 + \frac{n-m}{n}\overline{x}_2 = \frac{1}{n}\left(\sum_{i=1}^m x_i + \sum_{i=m+1}^n x_i\right) = \frac{1}{n}\sum_{i=1}^n x_i = \overline{x}.$$

Exercise 11.3 (Relative efficiency: LS versus LAD again) Suppose that we have a random sample of size n for a continuous variate x with density $f_x(u)$. Assume further that the density is symmetric, that the mean μ and variance σ^2 exist, that $0 < f_x(\mu) < \infty$, and that f_x is continuous at μ. Consider the sample mean $\overline{x}$ and median $\widetilde{x}$ (or $\widehat{q}_{1/2}$), respectively.

(a) Using the limiting distributions in Chapter 10, prove that the asymptotic efficiency of $\widetilde{x}$ relative to $\overline{x}$ (their ARE) is $(2\sigma f_x(\mu))^2$.

(b) Calculate this ARE for Student's t(ν) distribution, where $\nu > 2$. What if $0 < \nu \leqslant 2$?

Solution

(a) Exercise 3.19 tells us that the population's mean and median coincide for symmetric continuous variates having $f_x(\mu) > 0$. Now, we have from Chapter 10 the asymptotic distributions $\overline{x} \overset{a}{\sim} \mathrm{N}(\mu, \sigma^2/n)$ and $\widetilde{x} \overset{a}{\sim} \mathrm{N}(\mu, 1/(2f_x(\mu)\sqrt{n})^2)$, the latter being in Exercise 10.30(d). Then, the required ARE is

$$\operatorname{eff}_\infty(\widetilde{x}, \overline{x}) = \left.\frac{\sigma^2/n}{1/(2f_x(\mu)\sqrt{n})^2}\right|_{n=\infty} = (2\sigma f_x(\mu))^2.$$

This is invariant to σ, as can be seen from either the proof of Exercise 3.16(b) or the transformation theorem.

(b) For Student's t(ν), where $\nu > 2$, we have $\mu = 0$ and $z := x^2 \sim \mathrm{F}(1, \nu)$ gives

$\mathrm{E}\left(x^2\right) = \nu/\left(\nu-2\right)$ from Table 4.2. Hence,

$$\sigma^2 = \frac{\nu}{\nu-2} \quad \text{and} \quad f_x(0) = \frac{\Gamma\left((\nu+1)/2\right)}{\sqrt{\pi\nu}\,\Gamma\left(\nu/2\right)},$$

implying that

$$\operatorname{eff}_\infty(\widetilde{x}, \overline{x}) = \frac{4}{\pi\left(\nu-2\right)}\left(\frac{\Gamma\left((\nu+1)/2\right)}{\Gamma\left(\nu/2\right)}\right)^2$$

which is less than 1 for $\nu \geqslant 4.68$ (to two decimal places) and larger than 1 for $2 < \nu \leqslant 4.67$. Stirling's formula (or the formula for the ratio of gamma functions given in Section A.3.4) implies that the relative efficiency of the median falls to only $2/\pi \approx 0.637$ as $\nu \to \infty$.

Taking ν in the opposite direction, $\nu = 2$ gives $\overline{x} \overset{a}{\sim} \mathrm{N}(0, \log(n)/n)$, as seen in Exercise 10.38, which implies that the ARE is $\log(\infty) = \infty$. Furthermore, $\operatorname{var}\left(\overline{x}\right) = \infty$ for $0 < \nu < 2$, while $\operatorname{var}\left(\widetilde{x}\right)$ is finite, and the sample median is infinitely more efficient than the sample mean as an estimator of central location in these cases. As discussed in the introduction to this chapter, the median is more robust than the mean in general.

Exercise 11.4 (MSE) Prove that $\operatorname{MSE}(\widehat{\boldsymbol{\theta}}) = \operatorname{var}(\widehat{\boldsymbol{\theta}}) + \boldsymbol{b}\boldsymbol{b}'$, where $\boldsymbol{b} := \operatorname{bias}(\widehat{\boldsymbol{\theta}})$.

Solution

We saw a related method of solution in Exercise 6.5. Rewriting the definition of the MSE by means of $\boldsymbol{b} := \mathrm{E}(\widehat{\boldsymbol{\theta}}) - \boldsymbol{\theta}$, we have

$$\begin{aligned}\operatorname{MSE}(\widehat{\boldsymbol{\theta}}) &= \mathrm{E}\left[\left(\widehat{\boldsymbol{\theta}} - \mathrm{E}(\widehat{\boldsymbol{\theta}}) + \boldsymbol{b}\right)\left(\widehat{\boldsymbol{\theta}} - \mathrm{E}(\widehat{\boldsymbol{\theta}}) + \boldsymbol{b}\right)'\right] \\ &= \mathrm{E}\left[\left(\widehat{\boldsymbol{\theta}} - \mathrm{E}(\widehat{\boldsymbol{\theta}})\right)\left(\widehat{\boldsymbol{\theta}} - \mathrm{E}(\widehat{\boldsymbol{\theta}})\right)'\right] + \mathrm{E}\left[\left(\widehat{\boldsymbol{\theta}} - \mathrm{E}(\widehat{\boldsymbol{\theta}})\right)\boldsymbol{b}'\right] \\ &\quad + \mathrm{E}\left[\boldsymbol{b}\left(\widehat{\boldsymbol{\theta}} - \mathrm{E}(\widehat{\boldsymbol{\theta}})\right)'\right] + \mathrm{E}\left(\boldsymbol{b}\boldsymbol{b}'\right).\end{aligned}$$

By the definition of $\operatorname{var}(\widehat{\boldsymbol{\theta}})$, and by the nonrandomness of $\mathrm{E}(\widehat{\boldsymbol{\theta}})$ and $\boldsymbol{b}$,

$$\begin{aligned}\operatorname{MSE}(\widehat{\boldsymbol{\theta}}) &= \operatorname{var}(\widehat{\boldsymbol{\theta}}) + \mathrm{E}\left(\widehat{\boldsymbol{\theta}} - \mathrm{E}(\widehat{\boldsymbol{\theta}})\right)\boldsymbol{b}' + \boldsymbol{b}\,\mathrm{E}\left(\widehat{\boldsymbol{\theta}} - \mathrm{E}(\widehat{\boldsymbol{\theta}})\right)' + \boldsymbol{b}\boldsymbol{b}' \\ &= \operatorname{var}(\widehat{\boldsymbol{\theta}}) + \left(\mathrm{E}(\widehat{\boldsymbol{\theta}}) - \mathrm{E}(\widehat{\boldsymbol{\theta}})\right)\boldsymbol{b}' + \boldsymbol{b}\left(\mathrm{E}(\widehat{\boldsymbol{\theta}}) - \mathrm{E}(\widehat{\boldsymbol{\theta}})\right)' + \boldsymbol{b}\boldsymbol{b}' \\ &= \operatorname{var}(\widehat{\boldsymbol{\theta}}) + \boldsymbol{b}\boldsymbol{b}'.\end{aligned}$$

Exercise 11.5 (MSE of sample variance) Let $x_1, \dots, x_n$ be a random sample of $x \sim \mathrm{N}(\mu, \sigma^2)$, where $\sigma > 0$. Denote the sample variance by s^2.

(a) Why is s a biased estimator of σ when $n < \infty$?

(b) Calculate the bias of s.
(c) Find the a for which as^2 has the smallest MSE as an estimator of σ^2, and find $\text{bias}(as^2)$.
(d) Assume that x is not necessarily normal, but that $\kappa := \mathrm{E}((x-\mu)^4/\sigma^4) - 3$ is finite; then answer (c) again.

Solution

(a) We have already encountered this result; for example, see Exercise 9.4(c). However, we now recast it in terms of the bias of an estimator. We know that $\mathrm{E}(s^2) = \sigma^2$, hence s^2 is unbiased for σ^2. Therefore, Jensen's inequality implies that

$$(\mathrm{E}(s))^2 < \mathrm{E}\left(s^2\right) = \sigma^2$$

for $\sigma > 0$ and $n < \infty$, so that s a negatively biased estimator of σ.
(b) We know that $z := (n-1)\,s^2/\sigma^2 \sim \chi^2(n-1)$; see, for example, Exercise 9.16. We can either use the transformation theorem to find the density of $\sqrt{z}$, or we can work out directly the fractional moment $\mathrm{E}(\sqrt{z})$ from the density of z. Taking the latter route,

$$\begin{aligned}\mathrm{E}\left(\sqrt{z}\right) &= \int_0^\infty \sqrt{w}\frac{(w/2)^{(n-1)/2-1}}{2\Gamma\left((n-1)/2\right)}\exp\left(-w/2\right)\mathrm{d}w \\ &= \frac{\sqrt{2}\Gamma\left(n/2\right)}{\Gamma\left((n-1)/2\right)}\int_0^\infty \frac{(w/2)^{n/2-1}}{2\Gamma\left(n/2\right)}\exp\left(-w/2\right)\mathrm{d}w = \frac{\sqrt{2}\Gamma\left(n/2\right)}{\Gamma\left((n-1)/2\right)},\end{aligned}$$

where the last integrand is the density of a $\chi^2(n)$ which integrates to 1. Since $s = \sigma\sqrt{z/(n-1)}$, we get

$$\mathrm{E}(s) - \sigma = \left(\frac{\sqrt{2}\Gamma\left(n/2\right)}{\sqrt{n-1}\Gamma\left((n-1)/2\right)} - 1\right)\sigma.$$

Note that the asymptotic expansion of the gamma function (Section A.3.4) implies that this ratio tends to 1 from below, with the bias vanishing asymptotically as $n \to \infty$.
(c) We know that the MSE decomposition (Exercise 11.4) gives

$$\mathrm{E}\left((as^2-\sigma^2)^2\right) = \mathrm{var}(as^2) + \left(\mathrm{E}\left(as^2\right) - \sigma^2\right)^2 = a^2\,\mathrm{var}(s^2) + \left(a\,\mathrm{E}\left(s^2\right) - \sigma^2\right)^2.$$

We also know that $(n-1)s^2/\sigma^2 \sim \chi^2(n-1)$; hence $\mathrm{E}(s^2) = \sigma^2$ and

$$\mathrm{var}(s^2) = \frac{\sigma^4}{(n-1)^2}\,\mathrm{var}\left(\frac{(n-1)s^2}{\sigma^2}\right) = \frac{2(n-1)\sigma^4}{(n-1)^2} = \frac{2\sigma^4}{n-1}.$$

As a result,

$$\begin{aligned}\mathrm{E}\left((as^2-\sigma^2)^2\right) &= \frac{2a^2\sigma^4}{n-1} + \sigma^4(a-1)^2 \\ &= \sigma^4\left(\frac{2a^2}{n-1} + a^2 - 2a + 1\right) = \sigma^4\left(\frac{n+1}{n-1}a^2 - 2a + 1\right).\end{aligned}$$

Minimizing this expression with respect to a gives $a = (n-1)/(n+1)$, and therefore $(n+1)^{-1}\sum_{i=1}^n (x_i - \overline{x})^2$ has the smallest MSE, but has $\text{bias}(as^2) = \sigma^2(a-1) < 0$.

Notice that since a is smaller than 1 when $n < \infty$, it shrinks (or dampens) s^2. An equivalent derivation of a is obtained by differentiating the MSE itself, $\mathrm{E}\left((as^2 - \sigma^2)^2\right)$, with respect to a, obtaining the MSE-optimal a as $\sigma^2\,\mathrm{E}(s^2)/\mathrm{E}(s^4)$, then working out the first two moments of s^2. We will see a generalization of this result in Exercise 13.11.
(d) From Exercise 9.4(d), we have

$$\operatorname{var}(s^2) = \sigma^4\left(\frac{2}{n-1} + \frac{\kappa}{n}\right).$$

Exercise 9.4(c) shows that $\mathrm{E}(s^2) = \sigma^2$ regardless of normality, so

$$\mathrm{E}\left((as^2 - \sigma^2)^2\right) = a^2\sigma^4\left(\frac{2}{n-1} + \frac{\kappa}{n}\right) + \sigma^4(a-1)^2.$$

Minimizing with respect to a gives the optimal

$$a = \frac{n-1}{n+1+(1-1/n)\,\kappa}.$$

The larger the kurtosis (hence the thicker the tails), the more we need to shrink s^2.

Exercise 11.6 (Gamma's estimator) Let $x_1, \dots, x_n$ be a random sample of $x \sim \mathrm{Gam}(2, \lambda)$, where $\lambda > 0$. Assume that $n > 1$ and consider $1/\overline{x}$ as an estimator of λ.
(a) Show that $1/\overline{x}$ is a biased estimator of λ.
(b) Calculate the MSE of $1/\overline{x}$.
(c) Does there exist an a such that $a/\overline{x}$ is an unbiased estimator of λ?
(d) Show that $\sqrt{n}(\lambda - 2/\overline{x}) \overset{a}{\sim} \mathrm{N}(0, \lambda^2/2)$.
(e) Show that $2/\overline{x}$ is a consistent estimator of λ.

Solution
(a) Remember that $x \sim \mathrm{Gam}(2, \lambda)$ implies, by Exercise 7.18, that $z := \sum_{i=1}^n x_i \sim \mathrm{Gam}(2n, \lambda)$ with density $f_z(w) = \lambda^{2n} w^{2n-1} \exp(-\lambda w)/(2n-1)!$ for $w > 0$. Then

$$\mathrm{E}\left(\frac{1}{\overline{x}}\right) = \mathrm{E}\left(\frac{n}{z}\right) = n\int_0^\infty \frac{\lambda^{2n} w^{2n-2}\exp(-\lambda w)}{(2n-1)!}\,\mathrm{d}w$$
$$= \frac{n\lambda}{2n-1}\int_0^\infty \frac{\lambda^{2n-1} w^{2n-2}\exp(-\lambda w)}{(2n-2)!}\,\mathrm{d}w = \frac{n\lambda}{2n-1} \neq \lambda.$$

(b) By the definition of z in (a) and the MSE decomposition, we have

$$\mathrm{MSE}\left(\frac{1}{\overline{x}}\right) = \mathrm{MSE}\left(\frac{n}{z}\right) = \mathrm{E}\left(\left(\frac{n}{z} - \lambda\right)^2\right) = \operatorname{var}\left(\frac{n}{z}\right) + \left(\mathrm{E}\left(\frac{n}{z}\right) - \lambda\right)^2.$$

In addition to $\mathrm{E}(n/z)$ from (a), we need

$$\mathrm{E}\left(\frac{n^2}{z^2}\right) = n^2\int_0^\infty \frac{\lambda^{2n} w^{2n-3}\exp(-\lambda w)}{(2n-1)!}\,\mathrm{d}w = \frac{n^2\lambda^2}{(2n-1)(2n-2)},$$

where the condition $n > 1$ is required to ensure that the integral is convergent. Hence,

$$\begin{aligned}\operatorname{MSE}\left(\frac{n}{z}\right) &= \frac{n^2\lambda^2}{(2n-1)(2n-2)} - \frac{n^2\lambda^2}{(2n-1)^2} + \lambda^2\left(\frac{n}{2n-1} - 1\right)^2 \\ &= \lambda^2\left(\frac{n^2(2n-1) - n^2(2n-2) + (n-1)^2(2n-2)}{(2n-1)^2(2n-2)}\right) \\ &= \lambda^2\frac{n^2-2n+2}{(2n-1)(2n-2)}.\end{aligned}$$

(c) From (a), it follows that $a = (2n-1)/n = 2 - 1/n$.
(d) From Table 4.2, the mean of Gam$(2, \lambda)$ is $2/\lambda$ and its variance is $2/\lambda^2$. Then, the CLT implies that $\sqrt{n}(\overline{x} - \theta) \overset{a}{\sim} \mathrm{N}(0, \theta^2/2)$, where $\theta := 2/\lambda$. Letting $g(x) := 2/x$, we have

$$\sqrt{n}\left(\lambda - 2/\overline{x}\right) = -\sqrt{n}(g(\overline{x}) - g(\theta)) \overset{a}{\sim} \mathrm{N}\left(0, (g'(\theta))^2\theta^2/2\right)$$

by the delta method of Exercise 10.20. Then, $g'(\theta) = -2/\theta^2$ gives the required result.
(e) This follows directly from (d). Alternatively, we know that, a.s., $\overline{x} \to \mathrm{E}(x) = 2/\lambda > 0$; hence $2/\overline{x} \to \lambda > 0$ by the continuous mapping theorem.

Exercise 11.7 (Max uniform's estimator) Let $x_1, \dots, x_n$ be a random sample of $x \sim \mathrm{U}_{(-\alpha,\alpha)}$, and consider $y_n := \max_i \{|x_i|\}$.
(a) Derive the bias and MSE of y_n as an estimator of α.
(b) Construct an unbiased estimator of α based on y_n.
(c) Show, by more than one method, that y_n is a consistent estimator of α.
(d) Obtain the asymptotic distribution of $n(y_n - \alpha)$.

Solution
First, define $z_i := |x_i|$. It follows that $f_{z_i}(w) = 1/\alpha$ for $0 < w < \alpha$ and 0 otherwise. Then, for $0 < v < \alpha$, the density of $y_n = \max_i \{z_i\}$ is

$$f_{y_n}(v) = nf_z(v)\left(F_z(v)\right)^{n-1} = \frac{n}{\alpha}\left(\frac{v}{\alpha}\right)^{n-1} = \frac{nv^{n-1}}{\alpha^n}$$

by Exercise 7.35, and the corresponding c.d.f. is

$$F_{y_n}(v) = \int_0^v \frac{nu^{n-1}}{\alpha^n}\,\mathrm{d}u = \left(\frac{v}{\alpha}\right)^n.$$

Hence, for $j > 0$,

$$\mathrm{E}(y_n^j) = \int_0^\alpha \frac{n}{\alpha^n}v^{n+j-1}\,\mathrm{d}v = \left[\frac{n}{(n+j)\alpha^n}v^{n+j}\right]_0^\alpha = \frac{n}{n+j}\alpha^j.$$

(a) Using the results above, we have

$$\operatorname{bias}(y_n) = \mathrm{E}(y_n) - \alpha = \frac{n}{n+1}\alpha - \alpha = -\frac{1}{n+1}\alpha$$

and

$$\operatorname{var}(y_n) = \frac{n}{n+2}\alpha^2 - \frac{n^2}{(n+1)^2}\alpha^2$$
$$= \frac{n^2+2n+1-n^2-2n}{(n+2)(n+1)^2}n\alpha^2 = \frac{n\alpha^2}{(n+2)(n+1)^2};$$

hence

$$\operatorname{MSE}(y_n) = \frac{n\alpha^2}{(n+2)(n+1)^2} + \frac{\alpha^2}{(n+1)^2} = \frac{2\alpha^2}{(n+2)(n+1)}.$$

(b) Since the bias of y_n is linear in α, consider the estimator ay_n and find the a that will make it unbiased, that is, $\mathrm{E}(ay_n) = \alpha$. From

$$\mathrm{E}(ay_n) = a\frac{n}{n+1}\alpha,$$

it follows that $a = 1 + 1/n$ and that $y_n + y_n/n$ is the required unbiased estimator. The MSE of this estimator will be derived and compared with others in Exercises 12.8 and 13.3.
(c) From part (a), $\operatorname{MSE}(y_n) \to 0$ as $n \to \infty$, hence $y_n \xrightarrow{p} \alpha$; see Exercise 10.8(a). A second (but related) solution is obtained by using Markov's inequality: for $\epsilon > 0$,

$$\Pr(|y_n - \alpha| > \epsilon) \leqslant \frac{\mathrm{E}(|y_n-\alpha|)}{\epsilon} = \frac{\mathrm{E}(\alpha - y_n)}{\epsilon} = \frac{\alpha}{\epsilon} - \frac{n\alpha}{(n+1)\,\epsilon} \to 0$$

as $n \to \infty$. Notice that, exceptionally here, we need only to show that the bias of y_n as an estimator of α tends to 0, and we get consistency as a result. To see why, recall that α is the upper terminal of the distribution, and so $y_n - \alpha$ cannot be positive. Thus, $\mathrm{E}(y_n - \alpha) \to 0$ implies that, with probability 1, $y_n - \alpha$ will not be negative either, and that y_n becomes degenerate. Finally, as a third solution, taking $0 < \epsilon \leqslant \alpha$,

$$\Pr(|y_n - \alpha| < \epsilon) = \Pr(\alpha - y_n < \epsilon) = \Pr(y_n > \alpha - \epsilon)$$
$$= 1 - \Pr(y_n \leqslant \alpha - \epsilon) = 1 - \left(\frac{\alpha-\epsilon}{\alpha}\right)^n \to 1$$

as $n \to \infty$. (A larger ϵ would have made $\Pr(|y_n - \alpha| < \epsilon) = 1$ trivially.)
(d) For $u < 0$, we have

$$\Pr(n(y_n - \alpha) \leqslant u) = \Pr(y_n \leqslant \alpha + u/n) = \left(\frac{\alpha + u/n}{\alpha}\right)^n \to \exp(u/\alpha)$$

as $n \to \infty$. Notice the following. There is an upper terminal, and this distribution is therefore a GEV of Type III (Weibull) as seen in the introduction to Chapter 10; see also Exercise 10.47. The consistency rate is n (not the usual $\sqrt{n}$ of sample means and CLTs), and the MSE in (a) is of order $1/n^2$ rather than the usual $1/n$.

Exercise 11.8 (Jackknife for reduction of asymptotic bias) Assume that the bias of an estimator based on a random sample of size n has the asymptotic expansion

$$\operatorname{bias}(\widehat{\theta}_n) = \frac{h_1(\theta)}{n} + \frac{h_2(\theta)}{n^2} + o\left(\frac{1}{n^2}\right)$$

for some nonrandom functions h_1 and h_2 not depending on n. Suppose that we eliminate one observation at a time from the sample, say the j-th observation, and recalculate the estimator now labeled as $\widehat{\theta}_{-j}$.

(a) Show that there are n values of $\widehat{\theta}_{-j}$.

(b) Denoting the average of these values by $\overline{\widehat{\theta}}_{n-1} := n^{-1}\sum_{j=1}^{n}\widehat{\theta}_{-j}$ (called a *cross-validation estimator*, to be used again in Exercise 13.17), prove that

$$\mathrm{E}(\overline{\widehat{\theta}}_{n-1}) = \theta + \frac{h_1(\theta)}{n-1} + \frac{h_2(\theta)}{(n-1)^2} + o\left(\frac{1}{n^2}\right).$$

(c) Let the Quenouille–Tukey *jackknife estimator* be defined by

$$\widetilde{\theta}_{n,1} := n\widehat{\theta}_n - (n-1)\,\overline{\widehat{\theta}}_{n-1} = n\widehat{\theta}_n - \frac{n-1}{n}\sum_{j=1}^{n}\widehat{\theta}_{-j}.$$

Show that the $O(1/n)$ term that was in the bias of $\widehat{\theta}_n$ has now disappeared from the bias of $\widetilde{\theta}_{n,1}$, and that $\mathrm{E}(\widetilde{\theta}_{n,1}) = \theta + o(1/n)$. The procedure leading to $\widetilde{\theta}$ is called the *jackknifing* of $\widehat{\theta}$, and it effectively infers the leading term of the bias of $\widehat{\theta}_n$ by comparing the estimation procedures based on n and on $n-1$ observations.

(d) Using the setup of Exercise 11.5, show by a counterexample that $\widetilde{\theta}_{n,1}$ does not necessarily have a lower MSE than $\widehat{\theta}_n$.

(e) Continuing with the setup of Exercise 11.5, show that jackknifing

$$\breve{\sigma}^2 := \frac{1}{n+1}\sum_{i=1}^{n}(x_i - \overline{x})^2 \quad \text{and} \quad \widehat{\sigma}^2 := \frac{1}{n}\sum_{i=1}^{n}(x_i - \overline{x})^2$$

does not give the same $\widetilde{\theta}_{n,1}$, although both jackknife estimators are unbiased to $O(1/n)$.

Solution

(a) For leaving out one observation from a sample of size n, there are $\binom{n}{1} = n$ possible combinations of the observations (the sample is i.i.d. and therefore the order of the observations does not matter).

(b) From the definition of $\overline{\widehat{\theta}}_{n-1}$ and the given expansion of $\operatorname{bias}(\widehat{\theta}_n)$,

$$\mathrm{E}(\overline{\widehat{\theta}}_{n-1}) = \frac{1}{n}\sum_{j=1}^{n}\mathrm{E}(\widehat{\theta}_{-j}) = \frac{1}{n}\sum_{j=1}^{n}\left(\theta + \frac{h_1(\theta)}{n-1} + \frac{h_2(\theta)}{(n-1)^2} + o\left(\frac{1}{n^2}\right)\right)$$

since each $\widehat{\theta}_{-j}$ is based on $n-1$ observations, rather than n, and $o(1/(n-1)^2) = o(1/n^2)$. We get the required result by noting that none of the summands depends on j.

(c) From the definition of $\widetilde{\theta}_{n,1}$,

$$\begin{aligned}
\mathrm{E}(\widetilde{\theta}_{n,1}) &= n\,\mathrm{E}(\widehat{\theta}_n) - (n-1)\,\mathrm{E}(\overline{\widehat{\theta}}_{n-1}) \\
&= \left(n\theta + h_1(\theta) + \frac{h_2(\theta)}{n} + o\left(\frac{1}{n}\right)\right) - \left((n-1)\,\theta + h_1(\theta) + \frac{h_2(\theta)}{n-1} + o\left(\frac{1}{n}\right)\right) \\
&= \theta + h_2(\theta)\left(\frac{1}{n} - \frac{1}{n-1}\right) + o\left(\frac{1}{n}\right) = \theta - \frac{h_2(\theta)}{n(n-1)} + o\left(\frac{1}{n}\right) = \theta + o\left(\frac{1}{n}\right).
\end{aligned}$$

One should interpret this carefully: it is the *order* of the bias that is reduced (bias reduction in "large" samples) but nothing is said about what happens to the bias when n is small.

(d) The jackknife is a tool that can be applied numerically, without having to work out analytically the bias for a specific model, apart from knowing that its leading term has the form given here. However, to provide an example where bias reduction is not desirable from the MSE perspective, we take the simple model of Exercise 11.5, where the estimator

$$\breve{\sigma}^2 := \frac{1}{n+1}\sum_{i=1}^{n}(x_i - \overline{x})^2 = \frac{\sum_{i=1}^n x_i^2 - \frac{1}{n}\left(\sum_{i=1}^n x_i\right)^2}{n+1}$$

was shown to be minimum-MSE for σ^2. If there is a $O(1/n)$ term in its bias, and we were to remove it, then this new estimator would no longer be minimum-MSE. This is unfortunately the case, as Exercise 11.5(c) implies that

$$\operatorname{bias}\left(\breve{\sigma}^2\right) = -\frac{2\sigma^2}{n+1} = -\frac{2\sigma^2}{n(1+1/n)} = -\frac{2\sigma^2}{n}\left(1 - \frac{1}{n} + \frac{1}{n^2} - \cdots\right).$$

(e) Let $s^2 := (n-1)^{-1}\sum_{i=1}^n (x_i - \overline{x})^2$, which we have shown earlier to be an unbiased estimator of σ^2, and recall that $\sum_{i=1}^n x_i^2 = (n-1)s^2 + n\overline{x}^2$. Jackknifing $\breve{\sigma}^2$ gives

$$\begin{aligned}
&n\frac{n-1}{n+1}s^2 - \frac{n-1}{n}\sum_{j=1}^{n}\frac{\sum_{i\neq j} x_i^2 - \frac{1}{n-1}\left(\sum_{i\neq j} x_i\right)^2}{n} \\
&= n\frac{n-1}{n+1}s^2 - \sum_{j=1}^{n}\frac{(n-1)\left(-x_j^2 + (n-1)\,s^2 + n\overline{x}^2\right) - (n\overline{x} - x_j)^2}{n^2} \\
&= n\frac{n-1}{n+1}s^2 \\
&\quad - \frac{n(n-1)^2 s^2 + (n-1)\,n^2\overline{x}^2 - (n-1)\sum_{j=1}^n x_j^2 - \sum_{j=1}^n\left(x_j^2 + n^2\overline{x}^2 - 2n\overline{x}x_j\right)}{n^2} \\
&= n\frac{n-1}{n+1}s^2 - \frac{n(n-1)^2 s^2 - n\sum_{j=1}^n x_j^2 + n^2\overline{x}^2}{n^2} \\
&= n\frac{n-1}{n+1}s^2 - \frac{(n-1)^2 s^2 - (n-1)\,s^2}{n} = \frac{(n-1)(n+2)}{n(n+1)}s^2.
\end{aligned}$$

It is unbiased to $O(1/n)$ because s^2 is unbiased and

$$\frac{n-1}{n}\frac{n+2}{n+1} = \left(1-\frac{1}{n}\right)\left(1+\frac{1}{n+1}\right) = \left(1-\frac{1}{n}\right)\left(1+\frac{1}{n(1+1/n)}\right)$$
$$= \left(1-\frac{1}{n}\right)\left(1+\frac{1}{n}\left(1-\frac{1}{n}+\frac{1}{n^2}-\cdots\right)\right) = 1+O\left(\frac{1}{n^2}\right).$$

This is different from jackknifing $\widehat{\sigma}^2$, since using the same method gives

$$n\frac{n-1}{n}s^2 - \frac{n-1}{n}\sum_{j=1}^{n}\frac{\sum_{i\neq j}x_i^2 - \frac{1}{n-1}\left(\sum_{i\neq j}x_i\right)^2}{n-1}$$
$$= (n-1)s^2 - \frac{(n-1)^2 s^2 - (n-1)s^2}{n} \times \frac{n}{n-1}$$
$$= (n-1)s^2 - \left((n-1)s^2 - s^2\right) = s^2,$$

which is unbiased to any order.

Exercise 11.9 (Bootstrap for variance estimation) In the previous exercise, we considered a method of resampling without replacement from a set of observations. Now consider the following method of resampling with replacement. Let $\{x_i\}_{i=1}^n$ be a random sample drawn from a density f. The *bootstrap* treats this sample as if it were itself the population and generates m samples, now each of size n and drawn with replacement from $\{x_i\}_{i=1}^n$.

Suppose that we are interested in estimating the variance of the sample median $\widetilde{x}$ of a continuous variate satisfying the conditions in Exercise 10.30(d). The bootstrap generates m samples and m corresponding medians, $\{\widetilde{x}_{\mathrm{b},j}\}_{j=1}^m$, and we can now estimate the variance of $\widetilde{x}$ as follows:

$$\widehat{\operatorname{var}}(\widetilde{x}) := \frac{1}{m}\sum_{j=1}^{m}(\widetilde{x}_{\mathrm{b},j} - \overline{\widetilde{x}}_{\mathrm{b}})^2,$$

where $\overline{\widetilde{x}}_{\mathrm{b}}$ is the average of the bootstrap samples' m medians. Denoting the population median by $q_{1/2}$, show that $\widehat{\operatorname{var}}(\widetilde{x})$ is a consistent estimator of the variance of $\widetilde{x}$ in

$$\widetilde{x} \overset{a}{\sim} \mathrm{N}\left(q_{1/2}, \frac{1}{\left(2f\left(q_{1/2}\right)\right)^2 n}\right)$$

as $n, m \to \infty$. [Hint: Consider the distribution of $z_j := \widetilde{x}_{\mathrm{b},j} - \widetilde{x}$ given $\widetilde{x}$, then the unconditional distribution.]

Solution

"Pulling yourself up by your bootstraps" is an expression used for an individual lifting herself off the ground by simply pulling up the straps of her boots; in other words, a trick for getting something out of nothing! Here, the "statistical" bootstrap provides us with an estimate of the variance of a median from a single sample, something that we could not have obtained directly from the original sample itself. (In practice, we do not know f in the asymptotic distribution of $\widetilde{x}$: we have encountered a method of estimating it in Exercise 2.23, to be investigated in Chapter 13, but the bootstrap will provide a simple solution here.)

For any j, the asymptotic distribution of $z_j := \widetilde{x}_{\mathrm{b},j} - \widetilde{x}$ given $\widetilde{x}$ is obtained from Exercise 10.30(d) as

$$z_j \mid \widetilde{x} \overset{a}{\sim} \mathrm{N}\left(q_{1/2} - \widetilde{x}, \frac{1}{\left(2f\left(q_{1/2}\right)\right)^2 n} \right)$$

since the resampled data are drawn from asymptotically the same density f (by the convergence of the EDF $\widehat{F}_n$ to F as in Exercise 10.30). The variance of this conditional distribution equals the one given in the statement of the exercise in the asymptotic distribution of $\widetilde{x}$. This is the moment that we are required to estimate. The $j = 1, \dots, m$ bootstrap samples are drawn randomly, so a WLLN such as Khinchine's implies that the sample variance of $z_j \mid \widetilde{x}$ provides a consistent estimator as $m \to \infty$ of the asymptotic (as $n \to \infty$) $\mathrm{var}(z_j \mid \widetilde{x})$.

Notice that the unconditional distribution of z_j, which is the expectation of the conditional distribution as $\widetilde{x}$ varies, is asymptotically centered around zero (regardless of the value of $q_{1/2}$) since the asymptotic mean of $\widetilde{x}$ is $q_{1/2}$. The exact finite-sample distribution of $z_j \mid \boldsymbol{x}$ can be obtained from Exercise 9.28(b). Notice also that $\widehat{\mathrm{var}}(\widetilde{x}) = m^{-1} \sum_{j=1}^{m} (z_j - \overline{z})^2$ differs somewhat from the alternative estimator $m^{-1} \sum_{j=1}^{m} z_j^2$.

11.2 Sufficiency, completeness, best-unbiasedness, and admissibility

Exercise 11.10 (Normal density: joint sufficiency) Let $\{x_i\}_{i=1}^n \sim \mathrm{IN}(\mu, \sigma^2)$ and denote the sample mean and variance by $\overline{x}$ and s^2, respectively.
(a) Prove that the vector $(\overline{x}, s^2)'$ is sufficient for $\boldsymbol{\theta} := (\mu, \sigma^2)'$.
(b) Is $(\overline{x}/s, s^2)'$ sufficient for $\boldsymbol{\theta}$? What about $(\sum_{i=1}^n x_i, \sum_{i=1}^n x_i^2)'$?
(c) If σ^2 is known, is $\overline{x}$ sufficient for μ? If μ is known, is s^2 sufficient for σ^2?

Solution
(a) As in the chapter's introduction (see also Exercise 9.18), the data have a joint density that factors into

$$\frac{\sqrt{n} \exp\left(-\frac{n}{2\sigma^2}(w-\mu)^2\right)}{\sqrt{2\pi\sigma^2}} \times \frac{\exp\left(-\frac{n-1}{2\sigma^2} v\right)}{\left(2\pi\sigma^2\right)^{\frac{n-1}{2}} \sqrt{n}},$$

where w and v are the realizations of $\overline{x}$ and s^2, respectively. We know that $(n-1)\,s^2/\sigma^2 \sim$

$\chi^2(n-1)$, hence

$$f_{s^2}(v) = \frac{n-1}{\sigma^2} \frac{\left(\frac{n-1}{2\sigma^2}v\right)^{\frac{n-3}{2}} \exp\left(-\frac{n-1}{2\sigma^2}v\right)}{2\Gamma\left(\frac{n-1}{2}\right)}$$

by the transformation theorem. We also know that s^2 is distributed independently from $\overline{x}$. Therefore, we can rewrite the factorization of the joint density of the data as

$$f_{\overline{x},s^2}(w,v) \times \frac{\Gamma\left(\frac{n-1}{2}\right)}{\left((n-1)\pi\right)^{\frac{n-1}{2}} \sqrt{n} v^{\frac{n-3}{2}}},$$

where the first factor is now the joint density of $(\overline{x}, s^2)$, and the second factor does not depend on μ or σ^2. Then Neyman's factorization implies the stated result.

(b) Yes, to both questions, as follows directly from using the transformation theorem on $f_{\overline{x},s^2}$. Any one-to-one transformation of $(\overline{x}, s^2)$ will be sufficient. The first transformation is invertible because $s > 0$ with probability 1, for $n > 1$, as seen in Exercise 9.21. For the second transformation, recall that $(n-1)s^2 = \sum_{i=1}^n x_i^2 - n\overline{x}^2$. Notice the role of the assumption $n > 1$, implicit here but made explicit in the introduction to Chapter 9 when s^2 was defined. To illustrate this, if $n = 1$, then $\overline{x} = x_1$ is minimal sufficient since the information in x_1^2 is already contained in $\overline{x}$: there is no need for the second component of the sufficient $(z_1, z_2) := (\sum_{i=1}^n x_i, \sum_{i=1}^n x_i^2)$, which is therefore not minimal and so cannot be complete either (completeness fails clearly since the nonnull function $z_1^2 - z_2$ is always zero). This is an unusual case where the dimension of $\boldsymbol{\theta}$ is larger than the dimension of the sufficient $\overline{x}$.

(c) First, suppose that σ^2 is known. From (a), the joint density of the data factors into

$$f_{\overline{x}}(w) \times \frac{\exp\left(-\frac{n-1}{2\sigma^2}v\right)}{\left(2\pi\sigma^2\right)^{\frac{n-1}{2}} \sqrt{n}},$$

where μ enters the first factor only (via the density of $\overline{x}$) and hence $\overline{x}$ is sufficient for μ. Second, for known μ, the situation is different. The joint density of the data factors into

$$f_{s^2}(v) \times \frac{\exp\left(-\frac{n}{2\sigma^2}(w-\mu)^2\right)\Gamma\left(\frac{n-1}{2}\right)}{\sqrt{2\pi\sigma^2}\left((n-1)\pi\right)^{\frac{n-1}{2}} v^{\frac{n-3}{2}}}.$$

Clearly, σ^2 does not disappear from the second factor, and s^2 is not sufficient for σ^2. Nevertheless, the same factorization as used in (a) shows that $\overline{x}$ and s^2 are *jointly* sufficient for σ^2. However, $(\overline{x}, s^2)$ is not *minimal* sufficient for σ^2 because, with μ known, $\sum_{i=1}^n (x_i - \mu)^2$ becomes a statistic (no unknowns in it) and is sufficient for σ^2.

Exercise 11.11 (Normal linear model: joint sufficiency) Consider the normal linear model

$$\boldsymbol{y} = \boldsymbol{X}\boldsymbol{\beta} + \boldsymbol{\varepsilon}, \qquad \boldsymbol{\varepsilon} \sim \mathrm{N}(\mathbf{0}, \sigma^2 \boldsymbol{I}_n),$$

where n is the sample size, $\boldsymbol{y}$ and $\boldsymbol{\varepsilon}$ are $n \times 1$ random vectors, $\boldsymbol{X}$ is an $n \times k$ matrix of k

regressors, $n > k$ and $\sigma^2 > 0$. Suppose that the rank of $\boldsymbol{X}$ is k, so that $\boldsymbol{X}'\boldsymbol{X}$ is positive definite. Suppose also that the density of $\boldsymbol{X}$ does not depend on unknown parameters, so that the $m = k + 1$ parameters of this model are $\boldsymbol{\theta}' := (\boldsymbol{\beta}', \sigma^2)$.
(a) Obtain the joint density of the data.
(b) Defining

$$\widehat{\boldsymbol{\beta}} := \left(\boldsymbol{X}'\boldsymbol{X}\right)^{-1} \boldsymbol{X}'\boldsymbol{y}, \quad \widehat{\boldsymbol{\varepsilon}} := \boldsymbol{y} - \boldsymbol{X}\widehat{\boldsymbol{\beta}}, \quad \widehat{\sigma}^2 := \frac{1}{n}\widehat{\boldsymbol{\varepsilon}}'\widehat{\boldsymbol{\varepsilon}},$$

prove that $\widehat{\boldsymbol{\beta}}, \widehat{\sigma}^2$, and $\boldsymbol{X}'\boldsymbol{X}$ are jointly sufficient for the parameters.
(c) Are the statistics in (b) minimal sufficient? Do they contain an ancillary? What if σ^2 is known?
(d) How does this model relate to that in Exercise 11.10?

Solution
(a) We have $\boldsymbol{y} \mid \boldsymbol{X} \sim \mathrm{N}\left(\boldsymbol{X}\boldsymbol{\beta}, \sigma^2 \boldsymbol{I}_n\right)$ by the linear relation linking $\boldsymbol{y}$ to $\boldsymbol{\varepsilon}$. Then, the joint density of the data factors into the product of the densities of $\boldsymbol{X}$ and $\boldsymbol{y} \mid (\boldsymbol{X} = \boldsymbol{W}) \sim \mathrm{N}\left(\boldsymbol{W}\boldsymbol{\beta}, \sigma^2 \boldsymbol{I}_n\right)$. Therefore, by the formula for the multivariate normal density, the joint density of the data is

$$\begin{aligned} f_{\boldsymbol{X},\boldsymbol{y}}\left(\boldsymbol{W}, \boldsymbol{w}_{\boldsymbol{y}}\right) &= f_{\boldsymbol{X}}\left(\boldsymbol{W}\right) \times \frac{\exp\left(-\frac{1}{2}\left(\boldsymbol{w}_{\boldsymbol{y}} - \boldsymbol{W}\boldsymbol{\beta}\right)'\left(\sigma^2 \boldsymbol{I}_n\right)^{-1}\left(\boldsymbol{w}_{\boldsymbol{y}} - \boldsymbol{W}\boldsymbol{\beta}\right)\right)}{(2\pi)^{n/2}\left|\sigma^2 \boldsymbol{I}_n\right|^{1/2}} \\ &= f_{\boldsymbol{X}}\left(\boldsymbol{W}\right) \times \frac{\exp\left(-\frac{1}{2\sigma^2}\left(\boldsymbol{w}_{\boldsymbol{y}} - \boldsymbol{W}\boldsymbol{\beta}\right)'\left(\boldsymbol{w}_{\boldsymbol{y}} - \boldsymbol{W}\boldsymbol{\beta}\right)\right)}{(2\pi\sigma^2)^{n/2}}. \end{aligned}$$

(b) Only the second factor in the density in (a) depends on the parameters. The quadratic form in the exponential is the realization of

$$\begin{aligned} z &:= (\boldsymbol{y} - \boldsymbol{X}\boldsymbol{\beta})'(\boldsymbol{y} - \boldsymbol{X}\boldsymbol{\beta}) \\ &= \left(\widehat{\boldsymbol{\varepsilon}} + \boldsymbol{X}\widehat{\boldsymbol{\beta}} - \boldsymbol{X}\boldsymbol{\beta}\right)'\left(\widehat{\boldsymbol{\varepsilon}} + \boldsymbol{X}\widehat{\boldsymbol{\beta}} - \boldsymbol{X}\boldsymbol{\beta}\right) \\ &= \widehat{\boldsymbol{\varepsilon}}'\widehat{\boldsymbol{\varepsilon}} + 2\left(\widehat{\boldsymbol{\beta}} - \boldsymbol{\beta}\right)'\boldsymbol{X}'\widehat{\boldsymbol{\varepsilon}} + \left(\widehat{\boldsymbol{\beta}} - \boldsymbol{\beta}\right)'\boldsymbol{X}'\boldsymbol{X}\left(\widehat{\boldsymbol{\beta}} - \boldsymbol{\beta}\right), \end{aligned}$$

since $(\widehat{\boldsymbol{\beta}} - \boldsymbol{\beta})'\boldsymbol{X}'\widehat{\boldsymbol{\varepsilon}} = \widehat{\boldsymbol{\varepsilon}}'\boldsymbol{X}(\widehat{\boldsymbol{\beta}} - \boldsymbol{\beta})$ as they are both 1×1. Now, by the definitions of $\widehat{\boldsymbol{\varepsilon}}$ and $\widehat{\boldsymbol{\beta}}$, respectively,

$$\boldsymbol{X}'\widehat{\boldsymbol{\varepsilon}} = \boldsymbol{X}'\boldsymbol{y} - \boldsymbol{X}'\boldsymbol{X}\widehat{\boldsymbol{\beta}} = \boldsymbol{X}'\boldsymbol{y} - \boldsymbol{X}'\boldsymbol{y} = \mathbf{0}_k.$$

Thus,

$$z = n\widehat{\sigma}^2 + \left(\widehat{\boldsymbol{\beta}} - \boldsymbol{\beta}\right)'\boldsymbol{X}'\boldsymbol{X}\left(\widehat{\boldsymbol{\beta}} - \boldsymbol{\beta}\right),$$

and the result follows. Notice that $\boldsymbol{X}'\boldsymbol{X}$ is $k \times k$, whereas $\boldsymbol{X}$ is $n \times k$ and hence larger (usually n is *much* larger than k).
(c) These statistics are not minimal sufficient, since the $k \times k$ matrix $\boldsymbol{X}'\boldsymbol{X}$ is symmet-

ric and thus contains $k(k-1)/2$ duplicated elements. This can be overcome by using $\operatorname{vech}(\boldsymbol{X}'\boldsymbol{X})$ instead of $\boldsymbol{X}'\boldsymbol{X}$ in the statement of sufficiency. We can also say that $\boldsymbol{X}'\boldsymbol{X}$ is ancillary, since the density of $\boldsymbol{X}$ does not depend on $\boldsymbol{\theta}$. Furthermore, if σ^2 is known, then the factorization of z in (b) shows that $\widehat{\boldsymbol{\beta}}$ is sufficient for $\boldsymbol{\beta}$, since $\boldsymbol{\beta}$ appears only through the quadratic form in $\widehat{\boldsymbol{\beta}}-\boldsymbol{\beta}$.
(d) By letting $k=1$ and $\boldsymbol{X}=\boldsymbol{\imath}$ (a vector of ones), we get $y_i=\beta+\varepsilon_i$ with $\{\varepsilon_n\}\sim \mathrm{IN}(0,\sigma^2)$. We can write this as $\{y_n\}\sim \mathrm{IN}(\beta,\sigma^2)$, which is identical to the model of Exercise 11.10. Compare the results of the two exercises.

Exercise 11.12 (Uniform's complete) Consider a random sample $x_1,\dots,x_n$ of $x\sim \mathrm{U}_{(0,\alpha)}$.
(a) Obtain a sufficient statistic. Is it complete?
(b) Construct the BUE of α.

Solution
(a) The joint density of the sample is

$$f_{x_1,\dots,x_n}(u_1,\dots,u_n)=\begin{cases}\frac{1}{\alpha^n} & (0<u_i<\alpha,\ i=1,\dots,n),\\ 0 & (\text{elsewhere}).\end{cases}$$

Using the indicator function introduced in Chapter 2, we have

$$f_{x_1,\dots,x_n}(u_1,\dots,u_n)=\frac{1}{\alpha^n}\prod_{i=1}^n 1_{u_i\in(0,\alpha)}=\left(\frac{1}{\alpha^n}1_{\max_i\{u_i\}<\alpha}\right)\left(1_{\min_i\{u_i\}>0}\right),$$

and hence $y_n:=\max_i\{x_i\}$ is a sufficient statistic. Notice that *all* the u's satisfy $u\in(0,\alpha)$, so α is an upper bound for $\max_i\{u_i\}$. Note also that, for *any* density, the whole sample is sufficient and accordingly the order statistics (which are just a reordering of the sample) are sufficient. For the density in this exercise, it is the last order statistic that is *minimal* sufficient. For it to be complete, $\mathrm{E}(\psi(y_n))=0$ has to imply $\Pr(\psi(y_n)=0)=1$. By the density in Exercise 11.7 (or Exercise 7.35),

$$\mathrm{E}(\psi(y_n))\equiv\int_0^\alpha \psi(v)\frac{n}{\alpha^n}v^{n-1}\,\mathrm{d}v=0 \quad\iff\quad \int_0^\alpha \psi(v)v^{n-1}\,\mathrm{d}v=0.$$

As a general rule, when the support of the density depends on α, the integral equation can be simplified. Differentiating with respect to α yields $\psi(\alpha)\alpha^{n-1}=0$ and hence $\psi(\alpha)=0$ for all $\alpha>0$, and so y_n is complete.
(b) We have $\mathrm{E}(y_n)=\alpha n/(n+1)$ from Exercise 11.7 and thus, by the Lehmann–Scheffé theorem, $(1+1/n)y_n$ is the BUE of α.

***Exercise 11.13 (General uniform's complete and ancillary)** Let $x_1,\dots,x_n$ be a random sample of $x\sim \mathrm{U}_{(\alpha_1,\alpha_2)}$, where $n>1$. Define $y_1:=\min_i\{x_i\}$ and $y_n:=\max_i\{x_i\}$.
(a) Show that the pair (y_1,y_n) is sufficient and complete for (α_1,α_2).
(b) Obtain the BUE of $\alpha_1+\alpha_2$ and $\alpha_2-\alpha_1$.
(c) Let $\alpha_1=\alpha>0$ and $\alpha_2=2\alpha$ henceforth. Show that the completeness in (a) is no

longer true, and interpret this result in terms of ancillarity. [Hint: Find a nonzero function of y_1, y_n that has a zero expectation. For the ancillarity, derive the density of y_n/y_1.]
(d) Show that $y_1, y_n/2$, and $y_n - y_1$ are all consistent estimators of α.

Solution
(a) We have

$$f_{x_1,\dots,x_n}(u_1,\dots,u_n) = \frac{1}{(\alpha_2-\alpha_1)^n} 1_{\min_i\{u_i\}>\alpha_1} 1_{\max_i\{u_i\}<\alpha_2}$$

and so the pair (y_1, y_n) is jointly sufficient for (α_1, α_2). Next, Exercise 7.35 gives

$$\begin{aligned} f_{y_1,y_n}(v_1,v_n) &= n(n-1)f_x(v_1)f_x(v_n)\left(F_x(v_n)-F_x(v_1)\right)^{n-2} \\ &= \frac{n(n-1)}{(\alpha_2-\alpha_1)^2}\left(\frac{v_n-v_1}{\alpha_2-\alpha_1}\right)^{n-2} \end{aligned}$$

for $\alpha_1 < v_1 < v_n < \alpha_2$, and 0 otherwise. To establish completeness, consider solving for the function ψ in

$$\mathrm{E}(\psi(y_1,y_n)) \equiv \frac{n(n-1)}{(\alpha_2-\alpha_1)^n}\int_{\alpha_1}^{\alpha_2}\int_{\alpha_1}^{v_n}(v_n-v_1)^{n-2}\psi(v_1,v_n)\,\mathrm{d}v_1\,\mathrm{d}v_n = 0.$$

Define $h(v_n) := \int_{\alpha_1}^{v_n}(v_n-v_1)^{n-2}\psi(v_1,v_n)\,\mathrm{d}v_1$, so that we need to solve $\int_{\alpha_1}^{\alpha_2} h(v_n)\,\mathrm{d}v_n = 0$. Differentiating the latter with respect to α_2 yields that $h(\alpha_2) = 0$ needs to be solved, that is,

$$\int_{\alpha_1}^{\alpha_2}(\alpha_2-v_1)^{n-2}\psi(v_1,\alpha_2)\,\mathrm{d}v_1 = 0.$$

Differentiating once again, but now with respect to α_1, yields $-(\alpha_2-\alpha_1)^{n-2}\psi(\alpha_1,\alpha_2) = 0$. Hence, $\psi(y_1,y_n) = 0$ with probability 1 and (y_1, y_n) is complete for (α_1, α_2).
(b) We need to construct an unbiased estimator based on (y_1, y_n). The marginal densities of y_1 and y_n are given in Exercise 7.35, yielding

$$\begin{aligned} \mathrm{E}(y_n) &= \int_{\alpha_1}^{\alpha_2} v\frac{n}{\alpha_2-\alpha_1}\left(\frac{v-\alpha_1}{\alpha_2-\alpha_1}\right)^{n-1}\mathrm{d}v \\ &= \left[v\left(\frac{v-\alpha_1}{\alpha_2-\alpha_1}\right)^n\right]_{\alpha_1}^{\alpha_2} - \int_{\alpha_1}^{\alpha_2}\left(\frac{v-\alpha_1}{\alpha_2-\alpha_1}\right)^n\mathrm{d}v = \alpha_2 - \frac{\alpha_2-\alpha_1}{n+1} \end{aligned}$$

upon integration by parts, and

$$\begin{aligned} \mathrm{E}(y_1) &= \int_{\alpha_1}^{\alpha_2} v\frac{n}{\alpha_2-\alpha_1}\left(\frac{\alpha_2-v}{\alpha_2-\alpha_1}\right)^{n-1}\mathrm{d}v \\ &= \left[-v\left(\frac{\alpha_2-v}{\alpha_2-\alpha_1}\right)^n\right]_{\alpha_1}^{\alpha_2} + \int_{\alpha_1}^{\alpha_2}\left(\frac{\alpha_2-v}{\alpha_2-\alpha_1}\right)^n\mathrm{d}u = \alpha_1 + \frac{\alpha_2-\alpha_1}{n+1}. \end{aligned}$$

Notice from the marginals that $\alpha_2 - y_n$ and $y_1 - \alpha_1$ have the same density function. This could have been inferred at the start, by the symmetry of x, so we could have obtained directly (without working out the integrals) that $\mathrm{E}(y_1 - \alpha_1 + y_n - \alpha_2) = 0$ and hence that $y_1 + y_n$ is the BUE of $\alpha_1 + \alpha_2$. Unsurprisingly, this BUE is twice the sample midrange $\frac{1}{2}(y_1 + y_n)$. Now, for $\alpha_2 - \alpha_1$, we have

$$\mathrm{E}(y_n - y_1) = (\alpha_2 - \alpha_1) - 2\frac{\alpha_2 - \alpha_1}{n+1} = \frac{n-1}{n+1}(\alpha_2 - \alpha_1)$$

and hence $(y_n - y_1)(n+1)/(n-1)$ is the BUE of $\alpha_2 - \alpha_1$. Again unsurprisingly, this BUE is proportional to the sample range $y_n - y_1$, with the proportionality factor tending to 1 as $n \to \infty$.

(c) Sufficiency, the first half of (a), remains true because the factorization of the sample's density is unaltered. For the other half, the expectations in (b) give

$$\mathrm{E}(y_n) = 2\alpha - \frac{2\alpha - \alpha}{n+1} = \frac{2n+1}{n+1}\alpha \quad \text{and} \quad \mathrm{E}(y_1) = \alpha + \frac{2\alpha - \alpha}{n+1} = \frac{n+2}{n+1}\alpha.$$

Hence, $\mathrm{E}\left(y_n/(2n+1) - y_1/(n+2)\right) = 0$ in spite of $\Pr(y_n/(2n+1) = y_1/(n+2)) = 0$ (the variate is continuous), so (y_1, y_n) is not complete for α: we have found a function of (y_1, y_n) that is nonzero but has zero expectation. In fact, looking at the new density $f_x(u) = 1/\alpha$ for $\alpha < u < 2\alpha$, we realize that all the "information" on α is in the scale of x, and that x_i/x_j is scale-invariant for all i, j. Consider the transformation of (y_1, y_n) whose density is

$$f_{y_1,y_n}(v_1, v_n) = \frac{n(n-1)}{\alpha^n}(v_n - v_1)^{n-2} \qquad (\alpha < v_1 < v_n < 2\alpha),$$

into $(z_1, z_2) := (y_1, y_n/y_1)$ with p.d.f.

$$f_{z_1,z_2}(w_1, w_2) = w_1\frac{n(n-1)}{\alpha^n}(w_1 w_2 - w_1)^{n-2} = \frac{n(n-1)}{\alpha^n}w_1^{n-1}(w_2 - 1)^{n-2}$$

for $\alpha < w_1 < w_1 w_2 < 2\alpha$. We have

$$\begin{aligned} f_{z_2}(w_2) &= (n-1)(w_2 - 1)^{n-2} \int_{\alpha}^{2\alpha/w_2} \frac{n}{\alpha^n} w_1^{n-1}\,\mathrm{d}w_1 \\ &= (n-1)(w_2 - 1)^{n-2}\left[\left(\frac{w_1}{\alpha}\right)^n\right]_{\alpha}^{2\alpha/w_2} = (n-1)(w_2 - 1)^{n-2}\left(\left(\frac{2}{w_2}\right)^n - 1\right) \end{aligned}$$

for $1 < w_2 < 2$, and 0 otherwise. This shows that f_{z_2} does not depend on α, and that z_2 is therefore ancillary. In other words, y_1 is conditionally sufficient for α. Notice the nonuniqueness of this choice. We could have equally well chosen $z_1 := y_n$ or $z_1 := y_n - y_1$ to show that it is conditionally (on z_2) sufficient for α. Once the ratio $z_2 := y_n/y_1$ is fixed, any of the three choices of z_1 carries all there is to know about α from the sample's density. But without fixing this ratio here, both components of the minimal sufficient statistic convey information for the estimation of α.

(d) Using Markov's inequality, we have

$$\Pr(|y_1 - \alpha| > \epsilon) \leqslant \frac{\mathrm{E}(|y_1 - \alpha|)}{\epsilon} = \frac{\mathrm{E}(y_1 - \alpha)}{\epsilon} = \frac{\alpha}{(n+1)\epsilon} \to 0$$

as $n \to \infty$, hence $y_1 \xrightarrow{p} \alpha$. Similarly,

$$\Pr(|y_n - 2\alpha| > \epsilon) \leqslant \frac{\mathrm{E}(|y_n - 2\alpha|)}{\epsilon} = \frac{\mathrm{E}(2\alpha - y_n)}{\epsilon} = \frac{\alpha}{(n+1)\epsilon} \to 0,$$

hence $y_n/2 \xrightarrow{p} \alpha$. Combining the two, $y_n - y_1 \xrightarrow{p} \alpha$ as well.

***Exercise 11.14 (Neyman's factorization theorem)** Suppose that a sample is arranged into the data matrix $\boldsymbol{X}$ with density $f_{\boldsymbol{X}}$ depending on a parameter vector $\boldsymbol{\theta}$. Prove that $f_{\boldsymbol{X}}/f_{\boldsymbol{z}}$ (when $f_{\boldsymbol{z}} \neq 0$) does not depend on $\boldsymbol{\theta}$ if and only if $\boldsymbol{z}$ is a sufficient statistic. (You may treat the cases of discrete $\boldsymbol{X}$ and continuous $\boldsymbol{X}$ separately.)

Solution

We start by pointing out the fact that the joint density $f_{\boldsymbol{X},\boldsymbol{z}}$ is singular for continuous variates, see the discussion following (11.2) in the introduction to this chapter. Therefore, we will resort to the transformation from $\mathrm{vec}(\boldsymbol{X})$ to $(\boldsymbol{z}', \boldsymbol{\xi}')'$, where $\boldsymbol{\xi}$ is the identity mapping of a subset of $\mathrm{vec}(\boldsymbol{X})$ of a dimension appropriate to complement $\boldsymbol{z}$, and such that the distribution of $(\boldsymbol{z}', \boldsymbol{\xi}')$ is nonsingular. For an illustration, see the example in the introduction to Chapter 7.

We prove the "only if" part first. Suppose that $f_{\boldsymbol{X}}/f_{\boldsymbol{z}}$ does not depend on $\boldsymbol{\theta}$. We can write

$$f_{\boldsymbol{X}}(\boldsymbol{W};\boldsymbol{\theta}) = f_{\boldsymbol{z}}(\boldsymbol{w}_{\boldsymbol{z}};\boldsymbol{\theta})\, h(\boldsymbol{W})$$

for some function $h(\boldsymbol{W}) \geqslant 0$ that does not depend on $\boldsymbol{\theta}$, while stressing the dependence of the functions $f_{\boldsymbol{X}}$ and $f_{\boldsymbol{z}}$ on $\boldsymbol{\theta}$. We will need to prove that $\boldsymbol{z}$ is a sufficient statistic by showing that the distribution of $\boldsymbol{X} \mid \boldsymbol{z}$ does not depend on $\boldsymbol{\theta}$. Transforming by means of the general formulae given in the introduction to Chapter 7,

$$\begin{aligned} f_{\boldsymbol{\xi}|\boldsymbol{z}=\boldsymbol{w}_{\boldsymbol{z}}}(\boldsymbol{w}_{\boldsymbol{\xi}};\boldsymbol{\theta}) &\equiv \frac{f_{\boldsymbol{\xi},\boldsymbol{z}}(\boldsymbol{w}_{\boldsymbol{\xi}},\boldsymbol{w}_{\boldsymbol{z}};\boldsymbol{\theta})}{f_{\boldsymbol{z}}(\boldsymbol{w}_{\boldsymbol{z}};\boldsymbol{\theta})} \\ &= \begin{cases} \dfrac{\sum_{\boldsymbol{W}\in A} f_{\boldsymbol{X}}(\boldsymbol{W};\boldsymbol{\theta})}{f_{\boldsymbol{z}}(\boldsymbol{w}_{\boldsymbol{z}};\boldsymbol{\theta})} & \text{(discrete case)}, \\ \dfrac{\sum_{\boldsymbol{W}\in A} |\det \boldsymbol{J}_A|\, f_{\boldsymbol{X}}(\boldsymbol{W};\boldsymbol{\theta})}{f_{\boldsymbol{z}}(\boldsymbol{w}_{\boldsymbol{z}};\boldsymbol{\theta})} & \text{(continuous case)}, \end{cases} \end{aligned}$$

where the summations are over the set A of distinct values of $\boldsymbol{X}$ implied by $\boldsymbol{z} = \boldsymbol{w}_{\boldsymbol{z}}$ (since $\boldsymbol{\xi}$ is an identity mapping and so does not imply a partition of the $\boldsymbol{X}$ values). Note that the second summation (the continuous case) contains the Jacobian factors $|\det \boldsymbol{J}_A|$ applicable within each partition where the function $\boldsymbol{z}$ of the data is piecewise invertible. Substituting for $f_{\boldsymbol{X}}$ from the assumed factorization, these ratios simplify to

$$f_{\boldsymbol{\xi}|\boldsymbol{z}=\boldsymbol{w}_{\boldsymbol{z}}}(\boldsymbol{w}_{\boldsymbol{\xi}};\boldsymbol{\theta}) = \begin{cases} \sum_{\boldsymbol{W}\in A} h(\boldsymbol{W}) & \text{(discrete case)}, \\ \sum_{\boldsymbol{W}\in A} |\det \boldsymbol{J}_A|\, h(\boldsymbol{W}) & \text{(continuous case)}. \end{cases}$$

Now the transformation of the data from $\mathrm{vec}(\boldsymbol{X})$ to $(\boldsymbol{z}', \boldsymbol{\xi}')'$ does not involve any unknown parameters, which implies that A and the Jacobians do not contain $\boldsymbol{\theta}$. Also, $h(\boldsymbol{W})$ does not depend on $\boldsymbol{\theta}$, by assumption. Therefore, the distribution of $\boldsymbol{\xi} \mid \boldsymbol{z}$ is not affected by $\boldsymbol{\theta}$, and similarly for the augmented $(\boldsymbol{\xi}', \boldsymbol{z}') \mid \boldsymbol{z}$ (since we are conditioning on $\boldsymbol{z}$) and hence for $\boldsymbol{X} \mid \boldsymbol{z}$ (since the transformation from $(\boldsymbol{\xi}', \boldsymbol{z}')$ to $\boldsymbol{X}$ does not involve the unknown $\boldsymbol{\theta}$). As a result, $\boldsymbol{z}$ is sufficient for $\boldsymbol{\theta}$.

We will now prove the "if" part. If $\boldsymbol{z}$ is a sufficient statistic then, by definition, $F_{\boldsymbol{X}|\boldsymbol{z}}$ does not depend on $\boldsymbol{\theta}$. Therefore, the distribution of the subset $\boldsymbol{\xi} \mid \boldsymbol{z}$ also does not depend on $\boldsymbol{\theta}$. By the relation $f_{\boldsymbol{\xi}|\boldsymbol{z}=\boldsymbol{w}_{\boldsymbol{z}}} = f_{\boldsymbol{\xi},\boldsymbol{z}}/f_{\boldsymbol{z}}$, the right-hand side is also free from $\boldsymbol{\theta}$, and the same follows for the ratio $f_{\boldsymbol{X}}/f_{\boldsymbol{z}}$ since the transformation from $(\boldsymbol{\xi}', \boldsymbol{z}')$ to $\boldsymbol{X}$ does not involve the unknown $\boldsymbol{\theta}$.

***Exercise 11.15 (Exponential family's complete, almost)** Suppose that we have a random sample $x_1, \dots, x_n$ from the exponential family with natural parameterization

$$f_x(u) = m_0(\boldsymbol{\nu}) h_0(u) \exp\left(\boldsymbol{\nu}' \boldsymbol{h}(u)\right),$$

where $\boldsymbol{\nu} := (\nu_1, \dots, \nu_j)'$ is a function of the m-dimensional $\boldsymbol{\theta}$ and the support does not depend on $\boldsymbol{\theta}$. Define $H_l(x) := \sum_{i=1}^{n} h_l(x_i)$ for $l = 1, \dots, j$ and $\boldsymbol{z} := (H_1(x), \dots, H_j(x))'$, with realization $\boldsymbol{w}_{\boldsymbol{z}} := (H_1(u), \dots, H_j(u))'$. Prove that:
(a) $\boldsymbol{z}$ is sufficient for $\boldsymbol{\theta}$;
(b) if $n \geqslant j$, then $\boldsymbol{z}$ is a member of the *multivariate exponential family* defined by the p.d.f.

$$f_{\boldsymbol{z}}(\boldsymbol{w}_{\boldsymbol{z}}) = (m_0(\boldsymbol{\nu}))^n \exp\left(\boldsymbol{\nu}' \boldsymbol{w}_{\boldsymbol{z}}\right) \eta(\boldsymbol{w}_{\boldsymbol{z}})$$

for some function η, and its c.g.f. is

$$\varkappa_{\boldsymbol{z}}(\boldsymbol{s}) = \varkappa(\boldsymbol{s} + \boldsymbol{\nu}) - \varkappa(\boldsymbol{\nu}),$$

where $\varkappa(\boldsymbol{t}) := -n \log(m_0(\boldsymbol{t}))$;
(c) if $n \geqslant j$ and the family is regular (see the definition in Chapter 4), then $\boldsymbol{z}$ is complete.
[Hint: Use the uniqueness of the Fourier transform pairs, discussed in Chapters 3 and 6.]

Solution
(a) Define $\boldsymbol{x} := (x_1, \dots, x_n)'$. The joint density of the sample is

$$\begin{aligned} f_{\boldsymbol{x}}(u_1, \dots, u_n) &= \prod_{i=1}^{n} \left(m_0(\boldsymbol{\nu}) h_0(u_i) \exp\left(\boldsymbol{\nu}' \boldsymbol{h}(u_i)\right)\right) \\ &= (m_0(\boldsymbol{\nu}))^n \exp\left(\boldsymbol{\nu}' \left(\sum_{i=1}^{n} \boldsymbol{h}(u_i)\right)\right) \prod_{i=1}^{n} h_0(u_i) \\ &= (m_0(\boldsymbol{\nu}))^n \exp\left(\boldsymbol{\nu}' \boldsymbol{w}_{\boldsymbol{z}}\right) \prod_{i=1}^{n} h_0(u_i). \end{aligned}$$

Sufficiency follows from the factorization theorem, because $\prod_{i=1}^{n} h_0(u_i)$ is not a function of $\boldsymbol{\theta}$, while the preceding factors depend exclusively on $\boldsymbol{\theta}$ and $\boldsymbol{z}$. As an illustration, see Exercise 11.10(b), where $\sum_{i=1}^{n} (x_i, x_i^2)$ are jointly sufficient in the case of the normal dis-

tribution. Note that, if the support depended on $\boldsymbol{\theta}$, then we would have extra terms in the density, as we have seen in earlier exercises. See also Exercise 11.30.
(b) Recall Exercise 11.14. The condition $n \geqslant j$ ensures that the transformation from the $n \times 1$ data vector $\boldsymbol{x}$ to the $j \times 1$ sufficient $\boldsymbol{z}$ is not degenerate; we now need to marginalize the joint density

$$f_{\boldsymbol{\xi},\boldsymbol{z}}\left(\boldsymbol{w}_{\boldsymbol{\xi}}, \boldsymbol{w}_{\boldsymbol{z}}\right) = \begin{cases} \sum_{(u_1,\dots,u_n)\in A} f_{\boldsymbol{x}}\left(u_1, \dots, u_n\right) & \text{(discrete case)}, \\ \sum_{(u_1,\dots,u_n)\in A} \left|\det \boldsymbol{J}_A\right| f_{\boldsymbol{x}}\left(u_1, \dots, u_n\right) & \text{(continuous case)}, \end{cases}$$

with respect to $\boldsymbol{\xi}$. For any given $\boldsymbol{w}_{\boldsymbol{z}}$, part (a) has just shown that $\boldsymbol{z} = \boldsymbol{w}_{\boldsymbol{z}}$ is constant in A and hence over the sum, and that $f_{\boldsymbol{x}}$ factors in such a way that only the term $\prod_{i=1}^n h_0(u_i)$ varies with $\boldsymbol{w}_{\boldsymbol{\xi}}$:

$$f_{\boldsymbol{\xi},\boldsymbol{z}}\left(\boldsymbol{w}_{\boldsymbol{\xi}}, \boldsymbol{w}_{\boldsymbol{z}}\right) = \left(m_0(\boldsymbol{\nu})\right)^n \exp\left(\boldsymbol{\nu}'\boldsymbol{w}_{\boldsymbol{z}}\right) \times \begin{cases} \sum_{(u_1,\dots,u_n)\in A} \prod_{i=1}^n h_0(u_i) & \text{(discrete case)}, \\ \sum_{(u_1,\dots,u_n)\in A} \left|\det \boldsymbol{J}_A\right| \prod_{i=1}^n h_0(u_i) & \text{(continuous case)}, \end{cases}$$

Marginalizing this factor with respect to $\boldsymbol{w}_{\boldsymbol{\xi}}$ gives the required result for $f_{\boldsymbol{z}}$.
The m.g.f. of $\boldsymbol{z}$ is obtained from its density as

$$m_{\boldsymbol{z}}(\boldsymbol{s}) = \mathrm{E}\left(\exp\left(\boldsymbol{s}'\boldsymbol{z}\right)\right) = \left(m_0(\boldsymbol{\nu})\right)^n \int_{\boldsymbol{w}_{\boldsymbol{z}}\in\mathbb{R}^j} \eta\left(\boldsymbol{w}_{\boldsymbol{z}}\right) \exp\left(\boldsymbol{\nu}'\boldsymbol{w}_{\boldsymbol{z}} + \boldsymbol{s}'\boldsymbol{w}_{\boldsymbol{z}}\right) \mathrm{d}\boldsymbol{w}_{\boldsymbol{z}}$$

$$= \left(m_0(\boldsymbol{\nu})\right)^n \int_{\boldsymbol{w}_{\boldsymbol{z}}\in\mathbb{R}^j} \eta\left(\boldsymbol{w}_{\boldsymbol{z}}\right) \exp\left(\left(\boldsymbol{\nu}+\boldsymbol{s}\right)'\boldsymbol{w}_{\boldsymbol{z}}\right) \mathrm{d}\boldsymbol{w}_{\boldsymbol{z}} = \frac{\left(m_0(\boldsymbol{\nu})\right)^n}{\left(m_0(\boldsymbol{\nu}+\boldsymbol{s})\right)^n}$$

in the continuous case, and similarly but with a sum for the discrete case. Taking logs gives the required result, one which we have seen in Exercises 3.36(d) and 7.34 in the one-dimensional case.
(c) We need to prove that

$$\mathrm{E}(\psi(\boldsymbol{z})) = 0 \quad \Longrightarrow \quad \psi(\boldsymbol{z}) = 0 \text{ a.s.}$$

for any $\boldsymbol{\theta} \in \Theta$ and any function ψ not depending on $\boldsymbol{\theta}$, assuming that the expectation exists. Consider the condition $\mathrm{E}(\psi(\boldsymbol{z})) = 0$. Because regularity implies that $m_0(\boldsymbol{\nu}) > 0$, we can divide both sides of $0 = \mathrm{E}(\psi(\boldsymbol{z}))$ by $(m_0(\boldsymbol{\nu}))^n$, and we get

$$0 = \int_{\boldsymbol{w}_{\boldsymbol{z}}\in\mathbb{R}^j} \psi\left(\boldsymbol{w}_{\boldsymbol{z}}\right) \eta\left(\boldsymbol{w}_{\boldsymbol{z}}\right) \exp\left(\boldsymbol{\nu}'\boldsymbol{w}_{\boldsymbol{z}}\right) \mathrm{d}\boldsymbol{w}_{\boldsymbol{z}} \equiv \mathcal{F}_{\mathrm{i}^{-1}\boldsymbol{\nu}}\left\{\psi\left(\boldsymbol{w}_{\boldsymbol{z}}\right)\eta\left(\boldsymbol{w}_{\boldsymbol{z}}\right)\right\}$$

in the case of continuous $\boldsymbol{z}$. (The discrete case requires a sum instead; see (3.10) and (6.4).) The expectation is assumed to exist, which is why we are allowed to have a real-valued exponent in the Fourier transform. The uniqueness of the inverse of a Fourier transform, and the fact that $\eta(\boldsymbol{w}_{\boldsymbol{z}})$ is not identically zero, ensure that $\psi(\boldsymbol{w}_{\boldsymbol{z}}) = 0$ as required. Note that, had $\nu_1, \dots, \nu_j$ not been linearly independent, there would have existed a nontrivial function of $\boldsymbol{z}$ with zero expectation. The regularity of the family rules this out. Recall that completeness implies minimal sufficiency, which will be discussed further at the end of Exercise 11.17.

Finally, it is worth pointing out that a similar proof extend the properties in this exercise to the case where the data are themselves drawn from a multivariate exponential family.

Exercise 11.16 (Conditioning implies partitioning the sample space) Suppose that a sample is arranged into the data matrix $\boldsymbol{X} \in \mathcal{X}$, with density $f(\boldsymbol{W})$. Let $\boldsymbol{z} \in \mathcal{Z}$ be some statistic. Write the set implied for $\boldsymbol{W}$ by the condition $\boldsymbol{z} = \boldsymbol{w}$, and show that it yields a partition (see Chapter 1) of the sample space $\mathcal{X}$ as $\boldsymbol{w}$ takes values in $\mathcal{Z}$.

Solution
The set is

$$A_{\boldsymbol{w}} := \{\boldsymbol{W} : \boldsymbol{z} = \boldsymbol{w}\}.$$

To prove that it yields a partition of the sample space $\boldsymbol{W}$, we need to show that the sets implied by different values of $\boldsymbol{w} \in \mathcal{Z}$ are all mutually disjoint and that their union (not necessarily countable) gives $\cup_{\boldsymbol{w} \in \mathcal{Z}} A_{\boldsymbol{w}} = \mathcal{X}$. The latter property follows directly from the definition of the statistic $\boldsymbol{z}$ as some function $\boldsymbol{h}$ of the data: $\boldsymbol{z} = \boldsymbol{h}(\boldsymbol{X})$ implies that, for all $\boldsymbol{X} \in \mathcal{X}$, we get $\boldsymbol{z} \in \mathcal{Z}$. The former property follows likewise, since $\boldsymbol{w}_1 \neq \boldsymbol{w}_2$ gives

$$A_{\boldsymbol{w}_1} \cap A_{\boldsymbol{w}_2} \equiv \{\boldsymbol{W} : \boldsymbol{z} = \boldsymbol{w}_1 \text{ and } \boldsymbol{z} = \boldsymbol{w}_2\} = \varnothing.$$

***Exercise 11.17 (Minimal sufficiency and partitioning)** Suppose that a sample is arranged into the data matrix $\boldsymbol{X} \in \mathcal{X}$ with density $f(\boldsymbol{W}; \boldsymbol{\theta})$, where we stress the dependence on the parameter vector $\boldsymbol{\theta}$. Define the set

$$B_{\boldsymbol{W}_0} := \left\{ \boldsymbol{W} : \frac{f(\boldsymbol{W}; \boldsymbol{\theta})}{f(\boldsymbol{W}_0; \boldsymbol{\theta})} \text{ does not depend on } \boldsymbol{\theta}, \text{ for all } \boldsymbol{\theta} \in \Theta \right\},$$

where $\boldsymbol{W}_0$ is any given constant matrix satisfying $f(\boldsymbol{W}_0; \boldsymbol{\theta}) \neq 0$ for all $\boldsymbol{\theta} \in \Theta$. Suppose that there exists a statistic $\boldsymbol{z}$ whose partitioning of the sample space (see Exercise 11.16) is identical to that obtained from $B_{\boldsymbol{W}_0}$. Prove that $\boldsymbol{z}$ is minimal sufficient. [Hint: The statistic $\boldsymbol{z}$ is *minimal* sufficient if it is a function of any other sufficient statistic.]

Solution
We have two parts to prove: that $\boldsymbol{z}$ is sufficient, and that it is also minimal. First, we compare the sets $A_{\boldsymbol{w}} := \{\boldsymbol{W} : \boldsymbol{z} = \boldsymbol{w}\}$ and $B_{\boldsymbol{W}_0}$. Notice that $B_{\boldsymbol{W}_0}$ also partitions the sample space, because one could write the condition given in set $B_{\boldsymbol{W}_0}$ as

$$\frac{f(\boldsymbol{W}; \boldsymbol{\theta})}{f(\boldsymbol{W}_0; \boldsymbol{\theta})} = h(\boldsymbol{W}, \boldsymbol{W}_0)$$

for some function h that does not depend on $\boldsymbol{\theta}$, and h is therefore a statistic (it depends on the data alone). We are told that there exists a statistic $\boldsymbol{z}$ that makes the two partitionings identical, that is, the value of $\boldsymbol{z}$ is unchanged when $\boldsymbol{W}$ varies within any given set $B_{\boldsymbol{W}_0}$. Therefore, the distribution of $\boldsymbol{X}$ given $\boldsymbol{z} = \boldsymbol{w}$ does not vary with $\boldsymbol{\theta}$ (see $h(\boldsymbol{W}, \boldsymbol{W}_0)$) and

$\boldsymbol{z}$ is therefore sufficient. It is worth mentioning that the ratio of densities will be revisited in Chapter 14 in the context of inferences about different values of $\boldsymbol{\theta}$.

Second, suppose that there is another sufficient statistic $\boldsymbol{y}$. By the factorization theorem, there exist two functions h_1 and h_2 such that

$$f(\boldsymbol{W};\boldsymbol{\theta}) = h_1(\boldsymbol{w_y};\boldsymbol{\theta})\, h_2(\boldsymbol{W}).$$

For any given $\boldsymbol{w_y}$, we have

$$\frac{f(\boldsymbol{W};\boldsymbol{\theta})}{f(\boldsymbol{W}_0;\boldsymbol{\theta})} = \frac{h_1(\boldsymbol{w_y};\boldsymbol{\theta})\, h_2(\boldsymbol{W})}{h_1(\boldsymbol{w_y};\boldsymbol{\theta})\, h_2(\boldsymbol{W}_0)} = \frac{h_2(\boldsymbol{W})}{h_2(\boldsymbol{W}_0)},$$

which does not depend on $\boldsymbol{\theta}$ and hence satisfies the condition in $B_{\boldsymbol{W}_0}$. This, together with the equivalence of the partitionings by $B_{\boldsymbol{W}_0}$ and $A_{\boldsymbol{w}} = \{\boldsymbol{W} : \boldsymbol{z} = \boldsymbol{w}\}$, implies that $\boldsymbol{z} = \boldsymbol{w}$ for that given $\boldsymbol{w_y}$. Therefore, for any given $\boldsymbol{y} = \boldsymbol{w_y}$, we get a corresponding $\boldsymbol{z} = \boldsymbol{w}$; that is, $\boldsymbol{z}$ is a function of $\boldsymbol{y}$.

Notice that the proof indicates the following alternative characterization of the minimal sufficiency of $\boldsymbol{z}$. The ratio $f(\boldsymbol{W};\boldsymbol{\theta})/f(\boldsymbol{W}_0;\boldsymbol{\theta})$ is a constant function of $\boldsymbol{\theta}$ if and only if the value of the sufficient statistic $\boldsymbol{z}$ (which is a function of the data) is unchanged when the data takes the values $\boldsymbol{W}$ instead of $\boldsymbol{W}_0$. The sufficient statistic $\boldsymbol{z}$ is minimal sufficient for $\boldsymbol{\theta}$ when this equivalence holds. This characterization avoids explicit mention of the partitioning of the sample space, although the concept is required for the proof. Notice also that it implies that, in a regular exponential family, $\boldsymbol{z}$ is minimal sufficient for $\boldsymbol{\theta}$; see also Exercise 11.15. A simple illustration obtained from the $\mathrm{N}(\mu,\sigma^2)$ of Exercise 11.10(a) (with a more detailed notation for the realization of $\overline{x}$ as $w_{\overline{x}}$) is

$$\frac{f(\boldsymbol{W};\mu,\sigma^2)}{f(\boldsymbol{W}_0;\mu,\sigma^2)} = \exp\left(-\frac{n}{2\sigma^2}\left((w_{\overline{x}}-\mu)^2 - (w_{\overline{x}_0}-\mu)^2\right)\right)\exp\left(-\frac{n-1}{2\sigma^2}(v-v_0)\right),$$

where μ and σ^2 disappear if and only if $w_{\overline{x}} = w_{\overline{x}_0}$ and $v = v_0$, hence making $(\overline{x}, s^2)$ (whose realization is $(w_{\overline{x}}, v)$) minimal sufficient for (μ, σ^2). This holds for any combination of data values $\boldsymbol{W}$ leading to a fixed $\boldsymbol{z} := (\overline{x}, s^2)'$, as the next exercise illustrates.

Exercise 11.18 (Minimal sufficiency and partitioning, example) Suppose that a random sample of size $n = 2$ is drawn from $x \sim \mathrm{N}(\mu, 1)$. Use $z = \overline{x}$ to illustrate the previous exercise.

Solution

For any given value $\overline{x} = w_{\overline{x}}$, we have the restriction on the data that $x_2 = 2w_{\overline{x}} - x_1$; in other words,

$$A_{w_{\overline{x}}} = \{(w_1, 2w_{\overline{x}} - w_1) : w_1 \in \mathbb{R}\},$$

where w_1 is the realization of x_1. Clearly, different choices of $w_{\overline{x}}$ lead to different values of x_2 in $A_{w_{\overline{x}}}$, and therefore to a disjoint collection of $A_{w_{\overline{x}}}$ sets. Also,

$$\bigcup_{w_1 \in \mathbb{R}, w_{\overline{x}} \in \mathbb{R}} (w_1, 2w_{\overline{x}} - w_1) = \mathbb{R}^2 = \mathcal{X};$$

recall that we have not required the union to be countable (see the derivations in Exercise 11.16).

As for the densities required for the set B, we start by recalling the sufficiency factorization given in (11.2) of the introduction,

$$\exp\left(-(\overline{x} - \mu)^2\right) \times \frac{\exp\left(-\frac{1}{2}\sum_{i=1}^{2}(x_i - \overline{x})^2\right)}{2\pi}$$

for $n = 2$ here. The only ratio of densities that would not depend on μ, for any $\mu \in \mathbb{R}$, is one where $(\overline{x} - \mu)^2$ is the same for both densities in the ratio defining set B; in other words, the case where the same value of $\overline{x}$ (namely $\overline{x} = w_{\overline{x}}$) applies to both densities, leading to the same $\overline{x}$-based partition of the sample space as with $A_{w_{\overline{x}}}$. This confirms, by the new route of Exercise 11.17, the minimal sufficiency of $\overline{x}$ for μ. Using the notation of Exercise 11.17, for any chosen values $\boldsymbol{w}_0$ for $(x_1, x_2)'$, their mean value of $w_{\overline{x}}$ dictates the restriction $\boldsymbol{w} = (w_1, 2w_{\overline{x}} - w_1)'$ (with $w_1 \in \mathbb{R}$) as the set $B_{\boldsymbol{w}_0}$.

Exercise 11.19 (Lehmann–Scheffé theorem) Suppose that a sample is arranged into the data matrix $\boldsymbol{X}$ with density depending on a parameter vector $\boldsymbol{\theta}$. Prove that if $\boldsymbol{z}$ is a complete sufficient statistic and $g(\boldsymbol{z})$ is an unbiased estimator of $\eta(\boldsymbol{\theta})$, then $g(\boldsymbol{z})$ is almost surely the unique BUE of $\eta(\boldsymbol{\theta})$.

Solution

There are two requirements for demonstrating that $g(\boldsymbol{z})$ is the BUE. First, assume there is another estimator, $h_1(\boldsymbol{z})$ which is also unbiased. Then

$$\mathrm{E}\left(g(\boldsymbol{z}) - h_1(\boldsymbol{z})\right) = 0$$

for all $\boldsymbol{\theta} \in \Theta$. However, the completeness of $\boldsymbol{z}$ implies that $g(\boldsymbol{z}) - h_1(\boldsymbol{z}) = 0$ almost surely, because both the functions g and h_1 are estimators and hence depend on $\boldsymbol{z}$ only. Therefore, $g(\boldsymbol{z})$ is the unique unbiased estimator that depends only on $\boldsymbol{z}$. We now turn to the second requirement, the optimality of the variance of $g(\boldsymbol{z})$. Assume that there is another estimator which is unbiased but may depend on $\boldsymbol{X}$ rather than just $\boldsymbol{z}$, say $h_2(\boldsymbol{X})$. By the Rao–Blackwell theorem, the variance of the latter is improved by considering $\mathrm{E}_{\boldsymbol{X}|\boldsymbol{z}}(h_2(\boldsymbol{X}))$ instead. But this conditional expectation is a function of $\boldsymbol{z}$ alone, and therefore coincides with $g(\boldsymbol{z})$ with probability 1, as seen in the first part of the proof.

***Exercise 11.20 (BUE of product)** Consider a random sample of size $n > 1$ from $x \sim \mathrm{N}(\mu, \sigma^2)$.

(a) Derive the BUE of $\exp(2\mu + \sigma^2)$ when both μ and σ^2 are unknown. [Hint: Use the independence of $\overline{x}$ and s^2.]

(b) Is this BUE consistent? [Hint: Use $\Gamma(n+a)/\Gamma(n+b) = n^{a-b}(1+O(1/n))$ from Section A.3.4.]

Solution

(a) The distribution $\mathrm{N}(\mu, \sigma^2)$ is a member of the regular exponential family when μ and σ^2 are functionally independent. Now, Exercises 11.10 and 11.15 showed that $(\overline{x}, s^2)$ is a two-dimensional complete sufficient statistic, and we shall use the fact that $\overline{x}$ and s^2 are independent. First, the m.g.f. of $\overline{x} \sim \mathrm{N}(\mu, \sigma^2/n)$ yields

$$\mathrm{E}(\exp(2\overline{x})) = \exp(2\mu + (1/2)2^2\sigma^2/n) = \exp(2\mu + 2\sigma^2/n).$$

If we can construct a unbiased estimator of $\exp(\sigma^2(1-2/n))$ based on s^2 alone, then the product of this estimator and $\exp(2\overline{x})$ has the required expectation $\exp(2\mu+\sigma^2)$. Let $z := \sum_{i=1}^n (x_i - \overline{x})^2$, so that $z/\sigma^2 \sim \chi^2(n-1)$ and

$$\mathrm{E}\left(\left(z/\sigma^2\right)^j\right) = \int_0^\infty \frac{t^{(n-1)/2-1+j}\exp(-t/2)}{2^{(n-1)/2}\Gamma((n-1)/2)}\,\mathrm{d}t$$

$$= \frac{2^{(n+2j-1)/2}\Gamma((n+2j-1)/2)}{2^{(n-1)/2}\Gamma((n-1)/2)} = 2^j\frac{\Gamma((n+2j-1)/2)}{\Gamma((n-1)/2)}.$$

We now have an expression for $\mathrm{E}(z^j)$ which we will use for estimating (unbiasedly)

$$\exp((1-2/n)\sigma^2) \equiv \sum_{j=0}^\infty \frac{\left((1-2/n)\,\sigma^2\right)^j}{j!}$$

by

$$\sum_{j=0}^\infty \frac{\left((1-2/n)\,z\right)^j}{j!}\frac{\Gamma((n-1)/2)}{2^j\Gamma((n+2j-1)/2)}.$$

Since $\overline{x}$ and z are independent,

$$\exp(2\overline{x}) \times \sum_{j=0}^\infty \frac{\Gamma((n-1)/2)((1-2/n)z/2)^j}{\Gamma((n+2j-1)/2)j!}$$

is unbiased for $\exp(2\mu+\sigma^2)$. The random part of our estimator is based only on the complete sufficient statistic $(\overline{x}, s^2)$, since $s^2 = z/(n-1)$, and our estimator is therefore the BUE. Notice that the series is absolutely convergent (see Section A.3.2) because the terms decline exponentially in j; see also ${}_0F_1$ in (4.13) of the Notes to Chapter 4. Notice also that this series is related to the p.d.f.s of $\chi^2(n-1)$ and the noncentral $\chi^2(n-1, 2-4/n)$, given in Table 4.2, as follows:

$$\exp\left(1-\frac{2}{n}\right)\exp(2\overline{x})\,\frac{f_{\chi^2(n-1,2-4/n)}(z)}{f_{\chi^2(n-1)}(z)},$$

where the argument of the p.d.f.s is the random z.

(b) As $n \to \infty$,

$$\frac{\Gamma((n-1)/2)}{\Gamma((n+2j-1)/2)} = \left(\frac{n}{2}\right)^{-j}\left(1+O\left(\frac{1}{n}\right)\right),$$

so that the BUE in (a) is asymptotically

$$\exp(2\overline{x})\sum_{j=0}^{\infty}\frac{((1-2/n)z/n)^j}{j!}\left(1+O\left(\frac{1}{n}\right)\right) = \exp\left(2\overline{x}+\left(1-\frac{2}{n}\right)\frac{z}{n}\right)+O_p\left(\frac{1}{n}\right).$$

Since $\overline{x} \to \mu$ a.s. and $z/n \to \sigma^2$ a.s. (see Chapter 10), the CMT of Exercise 10.13 implies that the estimator converges to $\exp\left(2\mu+\sigma^2\right)$, as required.

Exercise 11.21 (Bias of ellipticals' correlation) Let $\boldsymbol{x}_1, \dots, \boldsymbol{x}_n$ be a random sample from a bivariate elliptical distribution with nonsingular variance $\boldsymbol{\Sigma}$, correlation ρ, and excess kurtosis κ. Define $\boldsymbol{S} := (n-1)^{-1}\sum_{i=1}^{n}(\boldsymbol{x}_i-\overline{\boldsymbol{x}})(\boldsymbol{x}_i-\overline{\boldsymbol{x}})'$ and $\widehat{\rho} := s_{12}/\sqrt{s_{11}s_{22}}$.
(a) Prove that $\operatorname{bias}(\widehat{\rho}) = -(3+\kappa)\left(1-\rho^2\right)\rho/(6n)+o(1/n)$, using the results in Exercises 10.36 and 10.34(b), respectively.
(b) Prove that $\operatorname{bias}\left(\tanh^{-1}(\widehat{\rho})\right) = (3+\kappa)\rho/(6n)+o(1/n)$, using the fact that

$$\tanh^{-1}(a) := \frac{1}{2}\log\left(\frac{1+a}{1-a}\right) = \frac{1}{2}\log\left(\frac{1+b}{1-b}\right)+\frac{a-b}{1-b^2}+\frac{b(a-b)^2}{(1-b^2)^2}+O\left((a-b)^3\right)$$

for a in the neighborhood of b.
(c) For the case of a normal distribution, prove that $\widehat{\rho}+\left(1-\widehat{\rho}^2\right)\widehat{\rho}/(2n)$ and $\tanh^{-1}(\widehat{\rho})-\widehat{\rho}/(2n)$ are unbiased up to $O(1/n)$ as estimators of ρ and of $\tanh^{-1}(\rho)$, respectively. Are they the BUEs?

Solution

(a) Since correlations are scale-invariant, by construction, we can set $\sigma_{11}=\sigma_{22}=1$. The sample is i.i.d., so $\boldsymbol{S}$ satisfies the CLT of Exercise 10.34 and the existence of the moments required for Exercise 10.36 to give

$$\begin{aligned}\mathrm{E}\left(\frac{s_{12}}{\sqrt{s_{11}s_{22}}}\right) &= \rho-\frac{1}{2}\operatorname{cov}(s_{12},s_{11})-\frac{1}{2}\operatorname{cov}(s_{12},s_{22})+\frac{\rho}{4}\operatorname{cov}(s_{11},s_{22})\\ &\quad+\frac{3\rho}{8}\operatorname{var}(s_{11})+\frac{3\rho}{8}\operatorname{var}(s_{22})+o\left(\frac{1}{n}\right)\\ &= \rho-\operatorname{cov}(s_{12},s_{11})+\frac{\rho}{4}\operatorname{cov}(s_{11},s_{22})+\frac{3\rho}{4}\operatorname{var}(s_{11})+o\left(\frac{1}{n}\right).\end{aligned}$$

The covariances and variances were worked out in Exercise 10.34(b), giving

$$\begin{aligned}\mathrm{E}(\widehat{\rho})-\rho &= -\frac{\rho}{n}(2+\kappa)+\frac{\rho}{4n}\left(\left(1+2\rho^2\right)\left(1+\frac{\kappa}{3}\right)-1\right)+\frac{3\rho(2+\kappa)}{4n}+o\left(\frac{1}{n}\right)\\ &= -\frac{(3+\kappa)\left(1-\rho^2\right)\rho}{6n}+o\left(\frac{1}{n}\right).\end{aligned}$$

Notice that the bias is of the opposite sign to ρ. Thus, on average, $\widehat{\rho}$ underestimates ρ when positive and overestimates it when negative. Nevertheless, the bias vanishes asymptotically, as we would expect from the asymptotic centering of $\widehat{\rho}$ in Exercise 10.35.

(b) From the expansion given in the question,

$$\begin{aligned}\mathrm{E}\left(\tanh^{-1}(\widehat{\rho})\right)-\tanh^{-1}(\rho) &= \mathrm{E}\left(\frac{\widehat{\rho}-\rho}{1-\rho^2}+\frac{\rho\,(\widehat{\rho}-\rho)^2}{(1-\rho^2)^2}+O_p\left((\widehat{\rho}-\rho)^3\right)\right)\\ &= \frac{\operatorname{bias}(\widehat{\rho})}{1-\rho^2}+\frac{\rho\operatorname{MSE}(\widehat{\rho})}{(1-\rho^2)^2}+o\left(\frac{1}{n}\right)\end{aligned}$$

and $\operatorname{MSE}(\widehat{\rho}) = \operatorname{var}(\widehat{\rho}) + (\operatorname{bias}(\widehat{\rho}))^2 = \operatorname{var}(\widehat{\rho}) + o(1/n)$ here. Notice that we have implicitly assumed that the expectation of the remainder term is finite, which is true since $|\widehat{\rho}| \leqslant 1$ allows us to use dominated convergence. The variance of $\widehat{\rho}$ is of order $1/n$, and the leading term was derived in Exercise 10.35. Hence

$$\begin{aligned}\operatorname{bias}\left(\tanh^{-1}(\widehat{\rho})\right) &= -\frac{(3+\kappa)\rho}{6n}+\rho\frac{\left(1-\rho^2\right)^2(1+\kappa/3)/n}{(1-\rho^2)^2}+o\left(\frac{1}{n}\right)\\ &= \frac{(3+\kappa)\rho}{6n}+o\left(\frac{1}{n}\right).\end{aligned}$$

Notice the change of sign for the bias of Fisher's z, relative to (a): the bias is now of the same sign as ρ. Also, the asymptotic bias of $\widehat{\rho}$ is numerically smaller than that for $\tanh^{-1}(\widehat{\rho})$, by a factor $1-\rho^2$. This is not surprising, since the transformation stretches $\rho \in [-1,1]$ into $\tanh^{-1}(\rho) \in \mathbb{R}$.

(c) For the normal distribution, $\kappa = 0$. From the previous parts of the exercise, we have

$$\begin{aligned}\mathrm{E}\left(\widehat{\rho}+\frac{\left(1-\widehat{\rho}^2\right)\widehat{\rho}}{2n}\right)-\rho &= \operatorname{bias}(\widehat{\rho})+\frac{\mathrm{E}(\widehat{\rho})}{2n}-\frac{\mathrm{E}\left(\widehat{\rho}^3\right)}{2n}\\ &= -\frac{\left(1-\rho^2\right)\rho}{2n}+\frac{\rho+o(1)}{2n}-\frac{\rho^3+o(1)}{2n}=o\left(\frac{1}{n}\right),\end{aligned}$$

where $\mathrm{E}(\widehat{\rho}^3) = \rho^3 + o(1)$ is obtained by applying the delta method to the distribution of $\widehat{\rho}$ in Exercise 10.35(a), and

$$\mathrm{E}\left(\tanh^{-1}(\widehat{\rho})-\frac{\widehat{\rho}}{2n}\right)-\tanh^{-1}(\rho)=\left(\frac{\rho}{2n}+o\left(\frac{1}{n}\right)\right)-\frac{\rho+o(1)}{2n}=o\left(\frac{1}{n}\right),$$

as required. Now, the bivariate normal is a five-parameter member of the regular exponential family (for example, compare the density in Exercise 6.1 with the general exponential form in Exercise 11.15(b)) and so $(\overline{x}_1, \overline{x}_2, s_{11}, s_{22}, s_{12})$ is sufficient and complete when $(\mu_1, \mu_2, \sigma_{11}, \sigma_{22}, \sigma_{12})$ are all unknown. Therefore, the adjusted estimators of ρ and $\tanh^{-1}(\rho)$ are the BUEs, but to $O(1/n)$ rather than exactly.

***Exercise 11.22 (Rao–Blackwellization for BUE: Expo)** Let $x_1, \dots, x_n$ be a random sample from $x \sim \operatorname{Expo}(\lambda)$, with $n > 1$ and $\lambda > 0$.

(a) Obtain the BUEs for λ^{-1} and λ. Why are they not reciprocals of one another?
(b) Obtain the BUE of $\Pr(x > c)$ where c is known. [Hint: Consider the estimator $h(x_1) := 1_{x_1>c}$.]
(c) Show that the BUE obtained in (b) is consistent.

Solution

(a) We are dealing with a simple member of the regular exponential family (the exponential itself!), and $z := \sum_{i=1}^{n} x_i$ is a complete and sufficient statistic by Exercise 11.15. Its density can be obtained from first principles (for example, Exercise 7.18) or from the factorization theorem. Taking the latter route, Exercise 11.15(b) tells us that we need to find the factor that will make $\lambda^n \exp(-\lambda w)$ a proper density function, namely

$$f_z(w) = \frac{\lambda^n w^{n-1} \exp(-\lambda w)}{(n-1)!} \qquad (w > 0),$$

from Table 4.2. We have $\mathrm{E}(z) = n/\lambda$, and the Lehmann–Scheffé theorem implies that $z/n \equiv \overline{x}$ is the BUE of $1/\lambda$. However, for the BUE of λ, we have

$$\mathrm{E}\left(\frac{1}{z}\right) = \int_0^\infty \frac{\lambda^n w^{n-2} \exp(-\lambda w)}{(n-1)!} \mathrm{d}w = \frac{\lambda}{n-1} \qquad (n > 1);$$

hence $(n-1)/z \equiv (1 - 1/n)/\overline{x}$ is the BUE of λ. It is only as $n \to \infty$ that the two BUEs become reciprocals of one another. Moments (hence unbiasedness and minimum-variance) are *not* invariant to nonlinear transformations: Jensen's inequality ensures that $\mathrm{E}(\overline{x})\,\mathrm{E}(1/\overline{x}) > 1$ in finite samples. Asymptotically, we have

$$\mathrm{E}(\overline{x})\,\mathrm{E}(1/\overline{x}) = \frac{\lambda n}{\lambda(n-1)} \to 1.$$

(b) Consider $h(x_1) := 1_{x_1>c}$, which has $\mathrm{E}(h(x_1)) = \Pr(x_1 > c) = \Pr(x > c)$ and is therefore an unbiased estimator of this probability. The Rao–Blackwell theorem tells us that $\mathrm{E}_{x_1|z}(h(x_1))$ is a function of z that is a better unbiased estimator of $\Pr(x > c)$. Furthermore, since z is sufficient and complete, the Lehmann–Scheffé theorem says that $\mathrm{E}_{x_1|z}(h(x_1))$ is also the unique BUE. Now, we need to work out an expectation with respect to $x_1 \mid z$. Define $z_2 := \sum_{i=2}^{n} x_i$, so we have $f_{x_1,z_2}(u, w_2) = f_{x_1}(u) f_{z_2}(w_2)$. The transformation from (x_1, z_2) to (x_1, z) has Jacobian factor 1, hence $f_{x_1,z}(u, w) = f_{x_1}(u) f_{z_2}(w - u)$ and $f_{x_1|z}(u) = f_{x_1}(u) f_{z_2}(w - u)/f_z(w)$ for $u > 0$ and $w - u > 0$. Notice that this conditional p.d.f. is valid more generally than for this problem. Then

$$\begin{aligned}
\mathrm{E}_{x_1|z=w}(h(x_1)) = \Pr(x_1 > c \mid z = w) &= \int_c^w \frac{f_{x_1}(u) f_{z_2}(w-u)}{f_z(w)} \mathrm{d}u \\
&= \int_c^w \frac{\lambda \exp(-\lambda u) \times \lambda^{n-1}(w-u)^{n-2} \exp(-\lambda(w-u))/(n-2)!}{\lambda^n w^{n-1} \exp(-\lambda w)/(n-1)!} \mathrm{d}u \\
&= \frac{n-1}{w^{n-1}} \int_c^w (w-u)^{n-2} \mathrm{d}u = \left[\frac{-(w-u)^{n-1}}{w^{n-1}}\right]_c^w = \left(\frac{w-c}{w}\right)^{n-1}.
\end{aligned}$$

Hence, the required BUE is $(1 - c/z)^{n-1}$ for $z > c$, and 0 otherwise. Notice that this estimator, which is based on the sample mean z/n, differs from the unbiased estimator

$$\frac{1}{n}\sum_{i=1}^{n} 1_{x_i > c},$$

which is based on the EDF's complement (see Section 9.3 and Exercise 10.30), the latter therefore having a higher variance when data are drawn specifically from an exponential distribution.

(c) Since $z/n = \overline{x} \to 1/\lambda$ a.s., the BUE in (b) tends a.s. to

$$\lim_{n\to\infty}\left(1 - \frac{\lambda c}{n}\right)^{n-1} = \exp(-\lambda c),$$

by the CMT of Exercise 10.13. This then proves the consistency, because of the fact that $\Pr(x > c) = \int_c^\infty \lambda \exp(-\lambda u)\, du = \exp(-\lambda c)$.

Exercise 11.23 (Rao–Blackwellization for BUE: Ber) Let $x_1, \dots, x_n$ be a random sample from a Bernoulli distribution with parameter $p \in (0, 1)$, and assume that $n > 2$.

(a) Obtain the BUE of $p(1 - p)$, which is the variance of the distribution.

(b) Obtain the BUE of p^2.

Solution

This is a member of the one-parameter regular exponential family, as can be seen by rewriting the density in the form

$$f_x(u) = p^u (1-p)^{1-u} = (1-p)\left(\frac{1-p}{p}\right)^{-u} = (1-p)\exp\left(-u\log\left(\frac{1}{p} - 1\right)\right)$$

for $u = 0, 1$. Hence, $z := n\overline{x} = \sum_{i=1}^n x_i \sim \text{Bin}(n, p)$ is a complete and sufficient statistic by Exercise 11.15. Notice that z is the number of successes in n Bernoulli trials; see, for example, Exercise 7.1.

(a) Define the estimator $h(\boldsymbol{x}) := 1_{x_1=1}1_{x_2=0}$, where $\boldsymbol{x} := (x_1, \dots, x_n)'$. It is unbiased for $p(1-p)$ because $\text{E}(h(\boldsymbol{x})) = \Pr(x_1 = 1, x_2 = 0) = p(1-p)$, by the independence of x_1 and x_2. Then,

$$\begin{aligned}
\text{E}_{\boldsymbol{x}|z=w}(h(\boldsymbol{x})) &= \Pr(x_1 = 1, x_2 = 0 \mid z = w) \\
&= \frac{\Pr\left(x_1 = 1, x_2 = 0, \sum_{i=3}^n x_i = w - 1\right)}{\Pr\left(\sum_{i=1}^n x_i = w\right)} \\
&= \frac{p(1-p) \times \binom{n-2}{w-1} p^{w-1}(1-p)^{n-1-w}}{\binom{n}{w} p^w (1-p)^{n-w}} = \frac{\binom{n-2}{w-1}}{\binom{n}{w}} = \frac{(n-w)\,w}{n(n-1)},
\end{aligned}$$

which gives $(1 - \overline{x})\overline{x}n/(n-1)$ as the BUE.

Another way to derive it is by working out

$$\begin{aligned}\mathrm{E}(z(n-z)) &= \mathrm{E}(nz) - \mathrm{E}(z^2) = \mathrm{E}(nz) - \mathrm{var}(z) - (\mathrm{E}(z))^2 \\ &= n^2p - np\,(1-p) - n^2p^2 = p\,(1-p)\left(n^2-n\right)\end{aligned}$$

from the moments of the binomial in Table 4.1, so that $z(n-z)/(n^2-n)$ is the BUE. The latter approach requires some guesswork in choosing a function of z whose expectation is proportional to the required $p\,(1-p)$, but it is directly valid for $n > 1$.
(b) From (a), $n^2p^2 = \mathrm{E}(z^2) - np(1-p) = \mathrm{E}(z^2) - \mathrm{E}(z(n-z)/(n-1))$, so

$$\frac{1}{n^2}\left(z^2 - \frac{z(n-z)}{n-1}\right) = \frac{z\,(z-1)}{n\,(n-1)}$$

is the BUE of p^2. Notice that $\mathrm{E}\left(z(z-1)\right) = n\,(n-1)\,p^2$ is the second factorial moment of z.

Alternatively, define $h\left(\boldsymbol{x}\right) := 1_{x_1=1}1_{x_2=1}$ which is an unbiased estimator of p^2. Then

$$\begin{aligned}\mathrm{E}_{\boldsymbol{x}|z=w}\left(h\left(\boldsymbol{x}\right)\right) &= \frac{\Pr\left(x_1=1, x_2=1, \sum_{i=3}^{n} x_i = w-2\right)}{\Pr\left(\sum_{i=1}^{n} x_i = w\right)} \\ &= \frac{p^2 \times \binom{n-2}{w-2}p^{w-2}\left(1-p\right)^{n-w}}{\binom{n}{w}p^w\left(1-p\right)^{n-w}} = \frac{\binom{n-2}{w-2}}{\binom{n}{w}} = \frac{w(w-1)}{n(n-1)}\end{aligned}$$

implies the required result.

Exercise 11.24 (BUE can be strange) Let $x \sim \mathrm{Poi}(\lambda)$ with $\lambda > 0$.
(a) Show that $(-1)^x$ is the BUE of $\mathrm{e}^{-2\lambda}$ from a single observation x. What is wrong with this estimator of $\mathrm{e}^{-2\lambda} \in (0,1)$?
(b) If we had a random sample of size $n > 2$, what would be the BUE of $\mathrm{e}^{-2\lambda}$?
(c) Show that the BUE from part (b) is consistent.

Solution
(a) The Poisson is a one-parameter member of the regular exponential family, and x is the complete and sufficient statistic from a sample of one observation (see Exercise 11.15). We have

$$\mathrm{E}((-1)^x) = \sum_{u=0}^{\infty}(-1)^u\frac{\lambda^u\mathrm{e}^{-\lambda}}{u!} = \mathrm{e}^{-2\lambda},$$

and thus $(-1)^x$ is the BUE. Now, $0 < \mathrm{e}^{-2\lambda} < 1$ but the estimator $(-1)^x$ is either 1 or -1, neither of which is a value taken by $\mathrm{e}^{-2\lambda}$.
(b) Consider the estimator $h\left(\boldsymbol{x}\right) := 1_{x_1=0}1_{x_2=0}$, where $\boldsymbol{x} := (x_1, \dots, x_n)'$. We know that

$$\mathrm{E}\left(h\left(\boldsymbol{x}\right)\right) = \Pr\left(x_1=0, x_2=0\right) = \Pr\left(x_1=0\right)\Pr\left(x_2=0\right) = \mathrm{e}^{-\lambda}\mathrm{e}^{-\lambda} = \mathrm{e}^{-2\lambda}$$

by the independence of x_1, x_2. Also, $z := \sum_{i=1}^{n} x_i \sim \mathrm{Poi}(n\lambda)$ by Exercise 4.8, and z is the complete and sufficient statistic by Exercise 11.15. Thus,

$$\begin{aligned}
\mathrm{E}_{\boldsymbol{x}|z=w}\left(h\left(\boldsymbol{x}\right)\right) &= \Pr\left(x_1 = 0, x_2 = 0 \mid z = w\right) \\
&= \frac{\Pr\left(x_1 = 0, x_2 = 0, \sum_{i=3}^{n} x_i = w\right)}{\Pr(z = w)} \\
&= \frac{\mathrm{e}^{-2\lambda} \times \mathrm{e}^{-(n-2)\lambda}((n-2)\lambda)^w/w!}{\mathrm{e}^{-n\lambda}(n\lambda)^w/w!} = \left(\frac{n-2}{n}\right)^w,
\end{aligned}$$

and $(1-2/n)^z$ is the BUE of $\mathrm{e}^{-2\lambda}$.
(c) Writing $\overline{x} = z/n \to \lambda$ a.s., the BUE in (b) tends a.s. to $\lim_{n\to\infty}(1-2/n)^{n\lambda} = \mathrm{e}^{-2\lambda}$. We can see that the strange property in (a) does not persist. After all, $n = 1$ is a very small sample indeed!

***Exercise 11.25 (Best ain't admissible)** Let $\boldsymbol{x}_1, \ldots, \boldsymbol{x}_n$ be a random sample from $\boldsymbol{x} \sim \mathrm{N}(\boldsymbol{\mu}, \boldsymbol{I}_m)$, and define the quadratic loss function $C(\widehat{\boldsymbol{\mu}}) = \|\widehat{\boldsymbol{\mu}} - \boldsymbol{\mu}\|^2$.
(a) Show that the risk of using the sample mean $\overline{\boldsymbol{x}}$ as an estimator of $\boldsymbol{\mu}$ does not depend on $\boldsymbol{\mu}$.
(b) For $m > 1$, we define the *James–Stein* shrinkage estimator as

$$\widetilde{\boldsymbol{\mu}} := \left(1 - \frac{m-2}{n\left\|\overline{\boldsymbol{x}}\right\|^2}\right)\overline{\boldsymbol{x}}.$$

Show that $\mathrm{risk}(\widetilde{\boldsymbol{\mu}}) = \mathrm{risk}(\overline{\boldsymbol{x}}) - ((m-2)/n)^2\,\mathrm{E}(\|\overline{\boldsymbol{x}}\|^{-2})$. [Hint: Use Exercise 6.15.]
(c) Show that $\mathrm{risk}(\widetilde{\boldsymbol{\mu}}) < \mathrm{risk}(\overline{\boldsymbol{x}})$ for $m > 2$.

Solution
(a) Since $\overline{\boldsymbol{x}} \sim \mathrm{N}(\boldsymbol{\mu}, \frac{1}{n}\boldsymbol{I}_m)$, we have $\mathrm{E}\left((\overline{x}_j - \mu_j)^2\right) = 1/n$ for $j = 1, \ldots, m$ and

$$\mathrm{risk}(\overline{\boldsymbol{x}}) = \mathrm{E}\left(\sum_{j=1}^{m}(\overline{x}_j - \mu_j)^2\right) = \sum_{j=1}^{m}\mathrm{E}\left((\overline{x}_j - \mu_j)^2\right) = \frac{m}{n}.$$

(b) For $\widetilde{\boldsymbol{\mu}}$, we have

$$\begin{aligned}
\mathrm{risk}(\widetilde{\boldsymbol{\mu}}) &= \mathrm{E}\left(\sum_{j=1}^{m}\left(\left(1 - \frac{m-2}{n\left\|\overline{\boldsymbol{x}}\right\|^2}\right)\overline{x}_j - \mu_j\right)^2\right) \\
&= \mathrm{E}\left(\sum_{j=1}^{m}\left((\overline{x}_j - \mu_j) - \frac{m-2}{n\left\|\overline{\boldsymbol{x}}\right\|^2}\overline{x}_j\right)^2\right) \\
&= \mathrm{risk}(\overline{\boldsymbol{x}}) + \left(\frac{m-2}{n}\right)^2\mathrm{E}\left(\frac{\sum_{j=1}^{m}\overline{x}_j^2}{\left\|\overline{\boldsymbol{x}}\right\|^4}\right) - 2\frac{m-2}{n}\mathrm{E}\left(\sum_{j=1}^{m}\frac{(\overline{x}_j - \mu_j)\,\overline{x}_j}{\left\|\overline{\boldsymbol{x}}\right\|^2}\right) \\
&= \mathrm{risk}(\overline{\boldsymbol{x}}) + \left(\frac{m-2}{n}\right)^2\mathrm{E}\left(\frac{1}{\left\|\overline{\boldsymbol{x}}\right\|^2}\right) - 2\frac{m-2}{n}\mathrm{E}\left(\sum_{j=1}^{m}\frac{(\overline{x}_j - \mu_j)\,\overline{x}_j}{\left\|\overline{\boldsymbol{x}}\right\|^2}\right)
\end{aligned}$$

by $\sum_{j=1}^m \overline{x}_j^2 \equiv \|\overline{\boldsymbol{x}}\|^2$. Exercise 6.15 implies that $\mathrm{E}\left((\overline{x}_j-\mu_j)\,h(\overline{x}_j)\right)=\frac{1}{n}\,\mathrm{E}\left(h'(\overline{x}_j)\right)$, so

$$\begin{aligned}\mathrm{E}\left(\sum_{j=1}^m \frac{(\overline{x}_j-\mu_j)\,\overline{x}_j}{\|\overline{\boldsymbol{x}}\|^2}\right) &= \sum_{j=1}^m \mathrm{E}\left((\overline{x}_j-\mu_j)\frac{\overline{x}_j}{\|\overline{\boldsymbol{x}}\|^2}\right)\\ &= \frac{1}{n}\sum_{j=1}^m \mathrm{E}\left(\frac{\partial\left(\overline{x}_j/\|\overline{\boldsymbol{x}}\|^2\right)}{\partial \overline{x}_j}\right) \qquad (m\neq 1)\\ &= \frac{1}{n}\sum_{j=1}^m \mathrm{E}\left(\frac{1}{\|\overline{\boldsymbol{x}}\|^2}-\frac{2\overline{x}_j^2}{\|\overline{\boldsymbol{x}}\|^4}\right)=\frac{1}{n}\,\mathrm{E}\left(\frac{m}{\|\overline{\boldsymbol{x}}\|^2}-\frac{2}{\|\overline{\boldsymbol{x}}\|^2}\right),\end{aligned}$$

and collecting terms gives the required result. Note the condition $m \neq 1$ in applying Exercise 6.15, since $\mathrm{E}(1/\overline{x}^2)=\infty$ does not exist (this expectation is an integral that diverges as $\overline{x}$ approaches 0).

(c) For $m=2$, we get $\widetilde{\boldsymbol{\mu}}=\overline{\boldsymbol{x}}$. For $m>2$, we get the striking result that $\mathrm{risk}(\widetilde{\boldsymbol{\mu}})<\mathrm{risk}(\overline{\boldsymbol{x}})$, which makes the sample mean inadmissible for quadratic loss functions. When $m>2$, reducing the *joint* risk over all $j=1,\dots,m$ causes this result, even though each $\overline{x}_j$ is individually admissible for μ_j. The reason for the term "shrinkage estimator" is that $\widetilde{\boldsymbol{\mu}}$ dampens the magnitude of the elements of the vector $\overline{\boldsymbol{x}}$, pulling them towards the origin $\mathbf{0}_m$. The result is surprising, to say the least. First and foremost, the components of $\overline{\boldsymbol{x}}$ are all independent of one another, and yet some adjustment of each component of $\overline{\boldsymbol{x}}$ by the others is needed. Some interpretation of this is given in the Notes at the end of this chapter. Second, with $\mathrm{var}(\boldsymbol{x})$ known, $\overline{\boldsymbol{x}}$ is a complete sufficient statistic and, since it is unbiased, it is also the BUE. However, some bias may be allowed if the *sum* of the MSEs of $\overline{x}_j$ can be reduced, and (b) shows this to be feasible when $m>2$. We encountered this idea in a different context in Exercise 11.5(c).

11.3 Ancillarity and independence of statistics

Exercise 11.26 (Basu's theorem) Suppose that a sample is arranged into the data matrix $\boldsymbol{X}$ with density depending on a parameter vector $\boldsymbol{\theta}$. Prove that if $\boldsymbol{z}$ is a boundedly-complete sufficient statistic and $\boldsymbol{h}(\boldsymbol{X})$ is an ancillary statistic, then $\boldsymbol{h}(\boldsymbol{X})$ is independent of $\boldsymbol{z}$.

Solution

By the definition of conditional probability,

$$\Pr\left(\boldsymbol{h}(\boldsymbol{X})\in A\right)=\mathrm{E}_{\boldsymbol{z}}\left(\Pr\left(\boldsymbol{h}(\boldsymbol{X})\in A \mid \boldsymbol{z}\right)\right)$$

for any given set A. We can rewrite this as

$$\mathrm{E}_{\boldsymbol{z}}\left[\Pr\left(\boldsymbol{h}(\boldsymbol{X})\in A\mid \boldsymbol{z}\right)-\Pr\left(\boldsymbol{h}(\boldsymbol{X})\in A\right)\right]=0,$$

where the probability is a bounded function. First, this conditional probability is a function that does not depend on $\boldsymbol{\theta}$, by the sufficiency of $\boldsymbol{z}$. Second, $\Pr(\boldsymbol{h}(\boldsymbol{X}) \in A)$ is free from $\boldsymbol{\theta}$, by the ancillarity of $\boldsymbol{h}(\boldsymbol{X})$. Therefore, the argument of the expectation is a function of $\boldsymbol{z}$ that does not depend on $\boldsymbol{\theta}$, and hence the completeness of $\boldsymbol{z}$ implies that, with probability 1, $\Pr(\boldsymbol{h}(\boldsymbol{X}) \in A \mid \boldsymbol{z}) - \Pr(\boldsymbol{h}(\boldsymbol{X}) \in A) = 0$.

Exercise 11.27 (Gamma's statistics: independence) Let $x_1, \ldots, x_n$ be a random sample from $x \sim \text{Gam}(2, \lambda)$, where $\lambda > 0$.
(a) Show that $x_1 / \sum_{i=1}^n x_i$ and $\sum_{i=1}^n x_i$ are independent.
(b) For $n > 2$, show that $(x_1 + x_2)/(x_3 + x_n)$ and $\sum_{i=1}^n x_i$ are independent.

Solution
(a) We are dealing with a one-parameter member of the regular exponential family, in which $z := \sum_{i=1}^n x_i$ is a complete and sufficient statistic for λ. Looking at the scale-invariant $y := \lambda x \in \mathbb{R}_+$, we have $f_y(v) = v \exp(-v)$, which does not depend on λ. By $x_1 / \sum_{i=1}^n x_i = \lambda x_1 / \sum_{i=1}^n \lambda x_i$, whose distribution does not depend on λ, Basu's theorem yields the required result.
(b) The result follows directly from using $(x_1 + x_2)/(x_3 + x_n) = (\lambda x_1 + \lambda x_2)/(\lambda x_3 + \lambda x_n)$ and the same approach as in (a). (If $n < 3$, then some of the variables in the ratio are not defined.) Contrast the ease of this approach with Exercise 7.18!

Exercise 11.28 (Pareto's statistics: independence in regular case) Let $x_1, \ldots, x_n$ be a random sample from x, with p.d.f. $f_x(u) = p(1 + u)^{-(1+p)}$ for $u \in \mathbb{R}_+$ and 0 otherwise, where $p > 0$.
(a) Find a complete and sufficient statistic for p.
(b) Show that the BUE of $1/p$ is $n^{-1} \sum_{i=1}^n \log(1 + x_i)$.
(c) For $n > 1$, show that $\log(1 + x_1)/\log(1 + x_2)$ and $\prod_{i=1}^n (1 + x_i)$ are independent.

Solution
(a) This is a shifted Pareto variate whose support does not depend on unknown parameters. Writing it in the canonical form of a regular exponential family, the density is

$$p \exp(-(1 + p) \log(1 + u));$$

hence $z := \sum_{i=1}^n \log(1 + x_i)$ is complete and sufficient.
(b) Let $y_i := \log(1 + x_i)$. Then y_i has the p.d.f. $f_{y_i}(v) = p \exp(-pv)$ for $v \in \mathbb{R}_+$, namely $y_i \sim \text{Expo}(p)$. Therefore $z = \sum_{i=1}^n y_i \sim \text{Gam}(n, p)$ and $\text{E}(z) = n/p$, giving z/n as the BUE of $1/p$. Notice that this estimator is the logarithm of the geometric mean of $1 + x_n$.
(c) Since $py_i \sim \text{Expo}(1)$ is free from p, so is

$$\frac{\log(1 + x_1)}{\log(1 + x_2)} = \frac{py_1}{py_2}.$$

Then Basu's theorem implies that this ratio is distributed independently of $z = \sum_{i=1}^n \log(1+$

x_i), and hence also of $\exp(z) = \prod_{i=1}^{n}(1 + x_i)$.

Exercise 11.29 (Pareto's statistics: independence in nonregular case) Let $x_1, \dots, x_n$ be a random sample from x with p.d.f.

$$f_x(u) = \begin{cases} \frac{3\alpha^3}{u^4} & (\alpha < u < \infty), \\ 0 & \text{(elsewhere)}, \end{cases}$$

where $\alpha > 0$.

(a) Show that $y_1 := \min_i \{x_i\}$ is a complete and sufficient statistic for α.
(b) Show that it is a consistent estimator of α.
(c) Derive the asymptotic distribution of this statistic.
(d) Construct the BUE of α.
(e) Show that $\sum_{i=1}^{n} x_i/x_1$ and y_1 are independent.
(f) Show that $\mathrm{E}\left(\sum_{i=1}^{n} x_i/y_1\right) = \mathrm{E}\left(\sum_{i=1}^{n} x_i\right)/\mathrm{E}\left(y_1\right)$.

Solution

(a) The joint density of the sample is

$$f_{x_1,\dots,x_n}(u_1, \dots, u_n) = \frac{3^n \alpha^{3n}}{\prod_{i=1}^{n} u_i^4} \prod_{i=1}^{n} 1_{u_i > \alpha} = \left(3^n \alpha^{3n} 1_{\min_i\{u_i\} > \alpha}\right) \prod_{i=1}^{n} u_i^{-4},$$

and the factorization theorem implies that $y_1 := \min_i \{x_i\}$ is sufficient. To establish completeness, the density of the first order statistic is in Exercise 7.35 and, for $\alpha < v < \infty$,

$$f_{y_1}(v) = n f_x(v)(1 - F_x(v))^{n-1} = \frac{3n\alpha^3}{v^4}\left(\frac{\alpha^3}{v^3}\right)^{n-1} = \frac{3n\alpha^{3n}}{v^{3n+1}}$$

since $1 - F_x(v) = 3\alpha^3 \int_v^\infty u^{-4}\, \mathrm{d}u = (\alpha/v)^3$. Now,

$$\mathrm{E}(\psi(y_1)) \equiv \int_\alpha^\infty \frac{3n\alpha^{3n}}{v^{3n+1}} \psi(v)\, \mathrm{d}v = 0 \quad \iff \quad \int_\alpha^\infty \frac{1}{v^{3n+1}} \psi(v)\, \mathrm{d}v = 0.$$

Differentiating the last integral with respect to α yields $-\alpha^{-3n-1}\psi(\alpha) = 0$, implying that $\psi(\alpha) = 0$ for all $\alpha > 0$. Thus, y_1 is also complete.

(b) Applying Markov's inequality yields

$$\Pr(|y_1 - \alpha| > \epsilon) \leqslant \frac{\mathrm{E}\left(|y_1 - \alpha|\right)}{\epsilon} = \frac{\mathrm{E}(y_1 - \alpha)}{\epsilon},$$

so that it is sufficient to show that $\mathrm{bias}(y_1) \to 0$, as in Exercise 11.7(c). We have

$$\mathrm{E}(y_1) = \int_\alpha^\infty \frac{3n\alpha^{3n}}{v^{3n}}\, \mathrm{d}v = \frac{3n}{-3n+1}\left[\frac{\alpha^{3n}}{v^{3n-1}}\right]_\alpha^\infty = \frac{3n}{3n-1}\alpha,$$

so that $\mathrm{E}(y_1 - \alpha)/\epsilon \to 0$ as $n \to \infty$.

(c) We derived the density of y_1 in (a); hence

$$1 - F_{y_1}(v) = 3n\alpha^{3n} \int_v^\infty u^{-3n-1}\, \mathrm{d}u = (\alpha/v)^{3n}$$

and

$$\Pr(n(y_1 - \alpha) \leqslant u) = \Pr\left(y_1 \leqslant \alpha + \frac{u}{n}\right) = 1 - \left(\frac{\alpha}{\alpha + u/n}\right)^{3n}$$
$$= 1 - (1 + u/(\alpha n))^{-3n} \to 1 - \exp(-3u/\alpha)$$

as $n \to \infty$. It may come as a surprise that this is again (compare with Exercise 11.7) Weibull, although there is no *apparent* upper-terminal value here. However, this is resolved immediately once one realizes that $\alpha - y_1$ does indeed have an upper-terminal value of 0. Notice that the consistency rate is n, not the usual $\sqrt{n}$ for sample means.

(d) The idea is to construct an unbiased estimator based on the sufficient y_1. From (b), we have $\mathrm{E}(y_1) = 3n\alpha/(3n-1)$ and hence $y_1(3n-1)/(3n)$ is the BUE of α by the Lehmann–Scheffé theorem.

(e) Let $\xi_i := x_i/\alpha$, with p.d.f. $f_{\xi_i}(u) = 3/u^4$ for $u > 1$ and 0 elsewhere. This distribution does not depend on α. Hence, $\sum_{i=1}^n x_i/x_1 = \sum_{i=1}^n x_i\alpha^{-1}/(x_1\alpha^{-1}) = \sum_{i=1}^n \xi_i/\xi_1$ has a distribution independent of α and thus is independent of y_1, by Basu's theorem.

(f) By the same method as in part (e), $\sum_{i=1}^n x_i/y_1$ and y_1 are independent. Hence,

$$\mathrm{E}\left(\frac{\sum_{i=1}^n x_i}{y_1} y_1\right) = \mathrm{E}\left(\frac{\sum_{i=1}^n x_i}{y_1}\right) \mathrm{E}(y_1),$$

which implies the required result. Notice that $\sum_{i=1}^n x_i$ and y_1 are *not* independent, so that $\mathrm{E}\left(\sum_{i=1}^n x_i/y_1\right) \neq \mathrm{E}\left(\sum_{i=1}^n x_i\right)\mathrm{E}(1/y_1)$; see also the discussion in Exercise 10.36(c).

Exercise 11.30 (Exponential's statistics: independence in nonregular case) Let $x_1, \dots, x_n$ be a random sample from x, with p.d.f. $f_x(u) = \lambda\exp(-\lambda(u-\alpha))$ for $u > \alpha$ and 0 otherwise, where $\lambda > 0$. Let $y_1, \dots, y_n$ be the corresponding order statistics, and assume that $n > 1$.

(a) Assume that $\lambda = 1$. Show that y_1 is sufficient for α.

(b) Assume that $\lambda > 0$ and is unknown. Obtain a sufficient statistic, and compare it with the results in (a) and in Exercise 11.22(a).

(c) Show, by more than one method, that $y_n - y_1$ (the range) and y_1 (the minimum) are independent.

Solution

(a) The joint density of the sample is

$$f_{x_1,\dots,x_n}(u_1, \dots, u_n) = \exp\left(-\sum_{i=1}^n (u_i - \alpha)\right) \prod_{i=1}^n 1_{u_i > \alpha}$$
$$= \left(\exp(n\alpha)\, 1_{\min_i\{u_i\} > \alpha}\right) \exp\left(-\sum_{i=1}^n u_i\right),$$

hence $y_1 := \min_i\{x_i\}$ is sufficient for α.

(b) The joint density becomes

$$f_{x_1,\dots,x_n}(u_1,\dots,u_n) = \lambda^n \exp(n\lambda\alpha)\, 1_{\min_i\{u_i\}>\alpha} \exp\left(-\lambda\sum_{i=1}^n u_i\right),$$

and we get the joint sufficiency of y_1 and $n\overline{x}$. The former was expected from (a), and the latter from Exercises 11.15(a) or 11.22(a). The reason for the extra component y_1, compared with these other exercises, is that the support here depends on α. Note that, if $n = 1$, we have only one sufficient $y_1 = n\overline{x}$ (the sample itself).
(c) The p.d.f. of y_1 was given in Exercise 7.35, and

$$f_{y_1}(v) = n f_x(v)(1 - F_x(v))^{n-1} = n\lambda \exp(-n\lambda(v-\alpha))$$

for $v > \alpha$. We have

$$\mathrm{E}(\psi(y_1)) \equiv \int_\alpha^\infty \psi(v) n\lambda \exp(-n\lambda(v-\alpha))\, \mathrm{d}v = 0 \iff \int_\alpha^\infty \psi(v)\exp(-n\lambda v)\, \mathrm{d}v = 0.$$

Differentiating with respect to α, we have $-\psi(\alpha)\exp(-n\lambda\alpha) = 0$, hence $\Pr(\psi(y_1) = 0) = 1$ and y_1 is complete. Define $z := \lambda(x-\alpha) \in \mathbb{R}_+$, which has a standard Expo(1) distribution which is free from α, λ. Therefore, $\lambda(y_n - y_1) = \max_i\{z_i\} - \min_i\{z_i\}$ is invariant to both location and scale, hence ancillary. Basu's theorem implies that $\lambda(y_n - y_1)$ and y_1 are independent, hence the stated result.

To confirm this independence, Exercise 7.35(b) implies that (through the transformation theorem)

$$\begin{aligned} f_{y_1, y_n - y_1}(v_1, v_n) &= n(n-1) f_x(v_1) f_x(v_n + v_1)\left(F_x(v_n+v_1) - F_x(v_1)\right)^{n-2} \\ &= n(n-1)\lambda^2 \exp\left(-\lambda(v_1-\alpha)\right)\exp\left(-\lambda(v_n+v_1-\alpha)\right) \\ &\quad \times \left(\exp\left(-\lambda(v_1-\alpha)\right) - \exp\left(-\lambda(v_n+v_1-\alpha)\right)\right)^{n-2} \\ &= n\lambda\exp\left(-n\lambda(v_1-\alpha)\right) \\ &\quad \times (n-1)\lambda\exp(-\lambda v_n)\left(1-\exp(-\lambda v_n)\right)^{n-2}. \end{aligned}$$

Since $f_{y_1}(v_1) = n\lambda\exp(-n\lambda(v_1-\alpha))$ and the conditional $f_{y_1,y_n-y_1}(v_1,v_n)/f_{y_1}(v_1)$ does not depend on v_1, we get the required independence and

$$f_{y_n-y_1}(v_n) = (n-1)\lambda\exp(-\lambda v_n)\left(1-\exp(-\lambda v_n)\right)^{n-2}.$$

Notice, however, that Basu's theorem provides a shortcut when compared with this second route which requires the derivations in Exercise 7.35(b).

Notes

General references for this chapter are the same as the statistics references for Chapter 2. Additionally, we recommend Cox and Hinkley (1974), Gouriéroux and Monfort (1995, vol. 1), Lehmann and Casella (1998), and Peracchi (2001).

Robust estimation is a large discipline in statistics; see Huber (1981) and Hampel, Ronchetti, Rousseeuw, and Stahel (1986). See also Cook and Weisberg (1982) for the analysis of residuals and influential data points. In our introduction and in Exercise 11.3, the median is a simple illustration of a robust estimator. In the introductory example, we described implicitly the *breakdown point* of an estimator, that is, the smallest fraction of contamination of the true distribution by another distribution, such that we get an arbitrarily large deviation from the true parameter value. The mixture of distributions $F(u) := (1 - \epsilon) F_1(u) + \epsilon F_2(u)$ is known as an *ϵ-contamination of* F_1. The median has a much higher breakdown point than the mean.

The relation between sufficiency, ancillarity, and information will be revisited and quantified in Exercises 12.25 and 12.26. In defining the ancillarity of a statistic, Cox and Hinkley (1974, pp. 24, 34) have a stricter definition, first requiring its minimal sufficiency in order to minimize the instances of nonuniqueness of an ancillary. However, even their definition would lead to the nonuniqueness illustrated in the introduction after (11.4) and in Exercise 11.13(c). They also pointed out the following, previously remarked by Fisher. For $\boldsymbol{z}$ sufficient, the distribution of $\boldsymbol{X} \mid \boldsymbol{z}$ does not depend on $\boldsymbol{\theta}$. However, even though $\boldsymbol{X} \mid \boldsymbol{z}$ contains no information about $\boldsymbol{\theta}$, it is not useless. For example, it can be used to check the model's specification, since it is not affected by the particular value taken by $\boldsymbol{\theta}$. We can illustrate this with the example of a random sample from $\mathrm{N}(\mu, \sigma^2)$: even though $\overline{x}$ is sufficient for the *estimation* of μ from the normal density, we can use s^2 to check for the accuracy of this simple linear model. A lower realization of s^2 gives a higher density in (11.2), and we will analyze this more fully in the next chapter. Furthermore, as we shall see in the final chapter, s^2 may not be employed in estimating μ but it is directly useful in inference on μ and testing hypotheses about it through the t-ratio. From $f_{\overline{x},s^2} = f_{\overline{x}} f_{s^2}$, where the latter can be thought of as $f_{s^2|\overline{x}}$, we find that $\overline{x}$ is sufficient for μ but $\overline{x} \sim \mathrm{N}(\mu, \sigma^2/n)$ means that its density depends on both μ and the unknown σ^2; see Reid (1995, pp. 144–145) for further discussion of this issue. Finally, for another use of ancillaries see Brown (1990), where it is shown that discarding them can lead to the inadmissibility of estimators. This is done in the context of shrinkage estimation, even in the case of estimating a single parameter of interest (contrast with Exercise 11.25(c) where $m > 2$).

We have not considered the problem of nuisance parameters in detail here. This will be covered to some extent in Chapters 12 and 14. Omitting them from the analysis is *not* the answer, as the model is then misspecified. See, for example, the omitted-variables bias in Exercise 12.39(e).

Completeness can be defined for families of densities, instead of statistics. In this case, one would use the family of densities of $\boldsymbol{z}$ in formulating the expectation $\mathrm{E}(\psi(\boldsymbol{z})) = 0$ in the condition for completeness, with the densities' parameters given by $\boldsymbol{\theta}$. For example, see Hogg and Craig (1989), and Lehmann and Casella (1998).

In re-expressing the linear model as $\boldsymbol{y} \mid \boldsymbol{X} \sim \mathrm{D}(\boldsymbol{X\beta}, \sigma^2 \boldsymbol{I}_n)$, we assumed that this conditioning is meaningful. It may not be the case in some models of time series, where the process generating $\boldsymbol{X}$ is the same as that of $\boldsymbol{y}$. An example is the *stochastic difference equation* $y_i = \alpha y_{i-1} + \varepsilon_i$, for $i = 1, \dots, n$ and y_0 fixed. This model is also known as an *auto-regressive* model of order 1, an AR(1), which is an example of a first-order Markov process. We saw a special case of it in Exercise 10.42. It is possible to condition on $\sum_{i=1}^{n} y_{i-1}^2$, which we will see in Exercises 12.31 and 12.43 to be related to the information. However, it is *not* meaningful to condition on the right-hand side of the AR, namely the sequence $\{y_{i-1}\}_{i=1}^{n}$, because then only the last observation y_n becomes random.

The multivariate extension of Exercise 11.2 underlies that the generalized least squares (GLS) estimator is the BLUE. This is to be covered mainly in Chapter 13 (see also Chapter 12). We also refer to volumes 1 and 3 in this Series, by Abadir and Magnus (2005, Chapter 12) and Paruolo (2019).

In Exercise 11.8 on the jackknife, we removed one observation at a time. The method is in fact more general: it allows for the removal of more than one observation at a time. For an introduction, see Cox and Hinkley (1974). Also, the method was used for analyzing the first moment of an estimator, but it could be used further to estimate its variance; see also the related cross-validation procedure that will be used in Exercise 13.17. For some intuition on this, consider the simple example of a sample of three values $(3, 1, 11)$ whose mean is $\overline{x} = 5$, with subsamples and corresponding means given as follows:

$$\text{the mean of } (3,1) \text{ is } 2,$$

$$\text{the mean of } (3,11) \text{ is } 7,$$

$$\text{the mean of } (1,11) \text{ is } 6;$$

and the variance of these means can be used to approximate $\operatorname{var}(\overline{x})/n$ where $n = 3$; see Efron and Stein (1981) for some properties. However, for estimating variances and the more elaborate features of estimators' distributions, the method is dominated by the bootstrap of Exercise 11.9, as was shown by Efron (1979). The bootstrap often produces accurate finite-sample distributions, not just the asymptotics that we tackled in Exercise 11.9; see, for example, Hall (1994). Notice in that exercise that the statistic $z_j/(m^{-1}\sum_{j=1}^{m} z_j^2)^{1/2}$ is asymptotically unaffected by the value of the population median $q_{1/2}$. This is no coincidence, and the choice of z_j to imply such a required property will be explored further in Chapter 13 when we define pivotal quantities. However, sufficiency is not required for such an application. Finally, the bootstrap can also be used to estimate the bias, as we have done with the jackknife. The bootstrap estimator of the bias of $\widehat{\theta}$ is $\widehat{\text{bias}}_{\text{b}}(\widehat{\theta}) := \overline{\widehat{\theta}}_{\text{b}} - \widehat{\theta}$, since $\widehat{\theta}$ is treated as if it were the population value and $\overline{\widehat{\theta}}_{\text{b}}$ is the bootstrap mean of the estimator of $\widehat{\theta}$ from the m generated samples' $\{\widehat{\theta}_{\text{b},j}\}_{j=1}^{m}$. The bias-corrected bootstrap estimator is therefore $\widehat{\theta} - \widehat{\text{bias}}_{\text{b}}(\widehat{\theta}) = 2\widehat{\theta} - \overline{\widehat{\theta}}_{\text{b}}$.

It is clear from Exercise 11.15 that, in a random sample of size n, the dimension j of the sufficient statistic is fixed as n varies. There is a converse to this result, but in a more general setup, known as Dynkin's (1951) theorem; see also Denny (1969, 1972). Excluding the case of the order statistics being minimal sufficient (in which case j would vary equally with n), the existence of a sufficient statistic of dimension $j < n$ implies an exponential family when we restrict our attention to discrete or continuously differentiable densities.

This means that, for most practical purposes, nonexponential p.d.f.s will not allow data reductions by sufficiency. This can be verified in our exercises in this chapter.

Still in connection with Exercise 11.15, it can be shown (for example by twice differentiation) that $\varkappa(\boldsymbol{\nu}) := -n \log(m_0(\boldsymbol{\nu}))$ is a convex function on the space Υ of $\boldsymbol{\nu}$, a space that is itself convex. This applies for all $n \in \mathbb{N}$ (not just $n \geqslant j$). Compare this with the earlier special case in Exercise 8.6. It can also be illustrated with the factorization of $m_0(\cdot)$ in (4.6).

In Exercise 11.21, $\rho = 0$ implied a zero bias for $\widehat{\rho}$. This need not be the case when the setup is altered. In estimating the correlation of a sequence $\{y_i\}_{i=1}^n$ with its past $\{y_{i-1}\}_{i=1}^n$, known as *serial correlation* or *auto-correlation* in time series, the usual estimators $\widehat{\rho}$ of ρ are negatively biased even if the series is i.i.d. (hence $\rho = 0$)! For example, see Kendall (1954), corrected for a typo in Kendall, Stuart, and Ord (1983, pp. 550–551). As an application, if we allow for the estimation of a mean (as we do when calculating the usual correlation), the AR(1) model, mentioned a few paragraphs ago, becomes the more general $y_i = \delta + \alpha y_{i-1} + \varepsilon_i$ and Kendall's result on the bias is applicable. For the bias in the case $\delta = 0$ where we do not estimate a mean (and the bias is an odd function of α or ρ), see White (1961) and Shenton and Johnson (1965).

The idea behind Exercise 11.24 is well known; see Hogg and Craig (1989, pp. 363–364) or Bain and Engelhardt (1992, p. 355). Notice that, as mentioned in the introduction to this chapter, Properties 1–4 are not necessarily invariant to nonlinear transformations of the parameters. Therefore, one is able to find a case such as Exercise 11.24 where applying these properties gives peculiar results. Compare this with the maximum-likelihood estimator in Exercise 12.5.

Cox and Hinkley (1974) defined the opposite of a loss function, calling it a *utility function*. See also the Notes to Chapter 3. Cox and Hinkley (1974, p. 449) and Stigler (1990) provided an interesting interpretation of the shrinkage in Exercise 11.25, in terms of a regression linking $\overline{\boldsymbol{x}}$ to values of $\boldsymbol{\mu}$; see also the regression fallacy in Exercise 13.8. The James–Stein estimator is itself inadmissible, and has undergone various generalizations. Meng (2005) gives a new constructive method of obtaining these estimators, by differentiating the risk function directly and then using the method of Exercise 7.24(e). Berger (1982) showed that, although $\overline{\boldsymbol{x}}$ is inadmissible, it is almost minimax. Efron (2006) gives a related lower bound. It is possible to shrink estimators towards a point other than the origin, which was chosen in Exercise 11.25(b), but Perlman and Chaudhuri (2012) warned that doing so will be detrimental if this point is not based on prior information about the parameter in question.

Many exercises in the second and third sections of this chapter highlighted a simple yet general fact. Differences between pairs of order statistics are location-invariant and hence ancillary for the location parameter, and similarly for differences between any pair of i.i.d. data. Likewise, ratios (when the denominator is nonzero a.s.) are scale-invariant and hence ancillary for the scale parameter.

12

Likelihood, information, and maximum likelihood estimation

Suppose that one has a set of data that arises from a specific distribution with unknown parameter vector $\boldsymbol{\theta}$. A natural question to ask is the following: what value of $\boldsymbol{\theta}$ is most likely to have generated these data? The answer to this question is given by the *maximum-likelihood estimator* (MLE). Likelihood and related functions are the subject of this chapter. It will turn out that we have already seen some examples of MLEs in the previous chapters.

Let $\boldsymbol{x}$ be a $k \times 1$ variate whose density is determined by the $m \times 1$ vector of unknown parameters $\boldsymbol{\theta}$. We wish to estimate $\boldsymbol{\theta}$ from a sample $\{\boldsymbol{x}_i\}_{i=1}^n$, which we collate in the $n \times k$ matrix $\boldsymbol{X} := (\boldsymbol{x}_1, \dots, \boldsymbol{x}_n)'$. We assume that k and m are fixed and do not vary with n. Once we have sampled $\boldsymbol{x}$, the only remaining unknown in the sample's density is $\boldsymbol{\theta}$. To stress this state, we will change the notation and consider the joint density as a function of $\boldsymbol{\theta}$, writing $L(\boldsymbol{\theta}) := f_{\boldsymbol{X}}(\boldsymbol{X}; \boldsymbol{\theta})$ as the *likelihood function* of $\boldsymbol{\theta}$, where the random data $\boldsymbol{X}$ have replaced $\boldsymbol{W}$ in the argument of the usual density $f_{\boldsymbol{X}}(\boldsymbol{W}; \boldsymbol{\theta})$ or $f_{\boldsymbol{X}}(\boldsymbol{W})$. Alternative notation includes $L(\boldsymbol{\theta} \mid \boldsymbol{X})$ and $L(\boldsymbol{\theta}; \boldsymbol{X})$, typically used when one wishes to stress the conditioning on $\boldsymbol{X}$ in the likelihood. If the sample is random, then $f_{\boldsymbol{X}}(\boldsymbol{X}) = \prod_{i=1}^n f_{\boldsymbol{x}}(\boldsymbol{x}_i)$. We will not assume this, unless stated.

The MLE of the parameters is the vector $\widehat{\boldsymbol{\theta}}$ that maximizes $L(\boldsymbol{\theta})$, and its existence will be established in Exercise 12.19 under the following sufficient conditions:

Condition 1(i). The sample is drawn from a specific density (one that has a known functional form) that is continuous in $\boldsymbol{\theta} \in \Theta$; and

Condition 1(ii). Θ is a compact set.

When investigating asymptotics ($n \to \infty$), as in Exercises 12.27–12.29, we replace Condition 1(ii) with:

Condition 1(ii$'$). The *true* $\boldsymbol{\theta}$ (meaning the $\boldsymbol{\theta}$ that generated the data) belongs to the interior of the parameter space Θ.

This allows Θ to be unbounded and/or open, but places some further restriction on $\boldsymbol{\theta}$. For example, $\Theta = [0, \infty)$ is allowed but the point $\theta = 0$ is ruled out.

We now highlight two differences between likelihoods and densities. First, as Condition 1(ii) implies, and as is illustrated in Exercises 12.5 and 12.8, the MLE may not exist if we define Θ to be an open set. Therefore, unlike the convention for p.d.f.s introduced in Chapter 2, where the support $\mathcal{X}$ excludes endpoints, we define $L(\boldsymbol{\theta})$ for $\boldsymbol{\theta}$ in a closed set (the closure of Θ) whenever feasible; see the exceptions in Exercises 12.3 and 12.5, for example. Second, for $L(\boldsymbol{\theta})$ to integrate to 1, it should be divided by $\int_{\boldsymbol{\theta}\in\Theta} L(\boldsymbol{\theta})\,\mathrm{d}\boldsymbol{\theta}$, assuming the integral is finite. However, this integral is free from $\boldsymbol{\theta}$ and does not affect the choice of $\widehat{\boldsymbol{\theta}}$ and the subsequent properties we study. It is therefore conventionally omitted from the definition of $L(\boldsymbol{\theta})$. Notice a slight abuse of notation: $\boldsymbol{\theta}$ always denotes the single value of the true but unknown parameter vector, except when it appears in $L(\boldsymbol{\theta})$ as the argument of a function to be optimized over all values of $\boldsymbol{\theta} \in \Theta$. Thus, the $\boldsymbol{\theta}$ in $L(\boldsymbol{\theta})$ is not necessarily the true $\boldsymbol{\theta}$. If there is potential for ambiguity, which is rarely the case, we shall make the distinction explicit.

To illustrate these ideas, consider the sample $\{x_i\}_{i=1}^n \sim \mathrm{IN}(\mu, 1)$. Here, there is only one unknown parameter, $\theta \equiv \mu$, with likelihood

$$L(\mu) = \frac{\exp\left(-\frac{1}{2}\sum_{i=1}^n (x_i - \mu)^2\right)}{(2\pi)^{n/2}}.$$

The value of μ that maximize this function is the MLE, and is denoted by $\widehat{\mu}$. The function $L(\mu)$ being differentiable, we can obtain $\widehat{\mu}$ by solving for the derivative being zero, as we can see in Figure 12.1. We have

$$\frac{\mathrm{d}L(\mu)}{\mathrm{d}\mu} = \frac{\exp\left(-\frac{1}{2}\sum_{i=1}^n (x_i - \mu)^2\right)}{(2\pi)^{n/2}} \sum_{i=1}^n (x_i - \mu),$$

implying that $\sum_{i=1}^n (x_i - \widehat{\mu}) = 0$ and hence $n\overline{x} = n\widehat{\mu}$; the MLE of μ in this example is the usual sample mean. Of course, we should also check that this is a maximum, rather than a minimum, typically by considering the sign of the second derivative of $L(\mu)$ evaluated at $\widehat{\mu}$. Actually, all these derivations could have been simplified by the sufficiency factorization encountered earlier (for example, in the previous chapter and/or Exercise 9.17)

$$L(\mu) = c \exp\left(-\frac{n}{2}(\overline{x} - \mu)^2\right),$$

where $c := \exp\left(-\frac{1}{2}\sum_{i=1}^n (x_i - \overline{x})^2\right) / (2\pi)^{n/2}$ is constant as the parameter μ varies (given any data $\{x_n\}$) and the remaining exponential is $\leqslant 1$, with equality to 1 (hence the maximum) achieved at $\widehat{\mu} = \overline{x}$. In connection with a remark made in the previous paragraph, the factor that makes $\int_{-\infty}^{\infty} L(\mu)\,\mathrm{d}\mu = 1$ is not c, but rather $\sqrt{n/(2\pi)}$.

The sufficiency factorization of $L(\mu)$ is important and holds more generally, well beyond

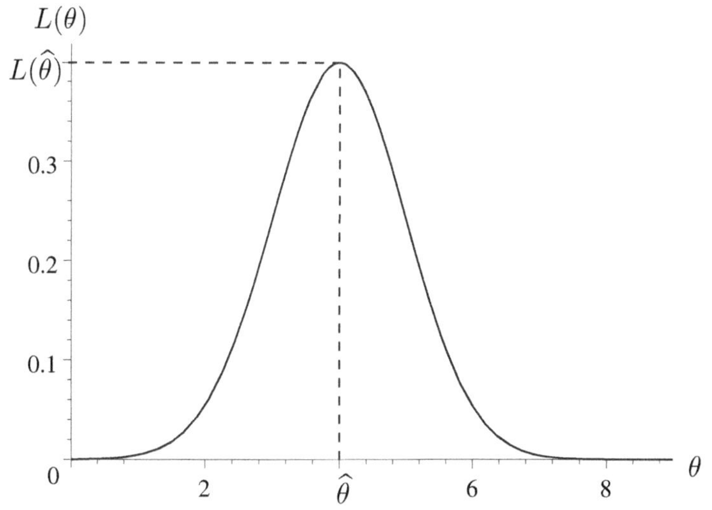

Figure 12.1. Likelihood function for the mean ($\theta \equiv \mu$) of a normal random sample having $\overline{x} = 4$.

this simple example. Recall Chapter 11. Neyman's factorization implies directly that the MLE is *fully* determined by the sufficient-statistic vector. If the latter is complete and the MLE is unbiased, then the MLE will be the BUE with probability 1. Furthermore, as mentioned in the introduction to Chapter 11, the MLE is invariant to parameter transformations; see Exercise 12.20 for a proof.

The above example highlights another possible simplification. The maxima of $L(\mu)$ and $\ell(\mu) := \log(L(\mu))$ are achieved at the same $\widehat{\mu}$, since the logarithm is a one-to-one transformation. Differentiating $\ell(\mu)$ is easier than $L(\mu)$ when dealing with members of the exponential family. More fundamentally,

$$\frac{\mathrm{d}\ell(\mu)}{\mathrm{d}\mu} = \frac{\mathrm{d}L(\mu)/\mathrm{d}\mu}{L(\mu)}$$

is the percentage change in the likelihood, and is known as the *score*. For our example,

$$\ell(\mu) = -\frac{n}{2}\log(2\pi) - \frac{1}{2}\sum_{i=1}^{n}(x_i - \mu)^2 \tag{12.1}$$

gives

$$\frac{\mathrm{d}\ell(\mu)}{\mathrm{d}\mu} = \sum_{i=1}^{n}(x_i - \mu) \quad \Longrightarrow \quad \sum_{i=1}^{n}(x_i - \widehat{\mu}) = 0, \tag{12.2}$$

hence $\widehat{\mu} = \overline{x}$. The second derivative is now easily obtained as

$$\frac{\mathrm{d}^2\ell(\mu)}{\mathrm{d}\mu^2} = \sum_{i=1}^{n}(-1) = -n < 0, \tag{12.3}$$

which confirms a maximum at $\widehat{\mu}$.

Generalizing these notions, if the likelihood is twice differentiable, then we have the *score vector*

$$q(\boldsymbol{\theta}) := \frac{\partial \ell(\boldsymbol{\theta})}{\partial \boldsymbol{\theta}} \equiv \begin{pmatrix} \partial \ell(\boldsymbol{\theta}) / \partial \theta_1 \\ \vdots \\ \partial \ell(\boldsymbol{\theta}) / \partial \theta_m \end{pmatrix}$$

and the *Hessian matrix*

$$\mathcal{H}(\boldsymbol{\theta}) := \frac{\partial^2 \ell(\boldsymbol{\theta})}{\partial \boldsymbol{\theta} \partial \boldsymbol{\theta}'} \equiv \begin{pmatrix} \partial^2 \ell(\boldsymbol{\theta}) / \partial \theta_1^2 & \dots & \partial^2 \ell(\boldsymbol{\theta}) / \partial \theta_1 \partial \theta_m \\ \vdots & & \vdots \\ \partial^2 \ell(\boldsymbol{\theta}) / \partial \theta_m \partial \theta_1 & \dots & \partial^2 \ell(\boldsymbol{\theta}) / \partial \theta_m^2 \end{pmatrix}.$$

See Section A.4 for the derivatives of some common functions with respect to vectors. Now assume that:

Condition 2. The log-likelihood $\ell(\boldsymbol{\theta}) := \log(L(\boldsymbol{\theta}))$ is continuously differentiable twice, and the expectations of $\ell(\boldsymbol{\theta})$ and its first two derivatives exist.

Notice that, when requiring the likelihood to be a continuously differentiable function of $\boldsymbol{\theta}$, the support $\mathcal{X}$ of $\boldsymbol{X}$ cannot depend on $\boldsymbol{\theta}$. For example, this condition rules out the type of indicator functions $1_{\min_i\{x_i\}>\theta}$ that come out of densities like the nonregular exponential of Exercise 11.30. Without Condition 2, we may also have a case such as $L(\theta) = 1/|\theta|$ where L is unbounded at the origin, achieving a maximum there but not satisfying $q(0) = 0$ since the likelihood is not differentiable at $\widehat{\theta} = 0$. We now turn to additional requirements such that we get $q(\widehat{\boldsymbol{\theta}}) = \mathbf{0}_m$.

When Condition 1 is satisfied, the MLE $\widehat{\boldsymbol{\theta}}$ exists. If $n < \infty$, we will occasionally assume the following additional condition:

Condition A. With probability 1, $\widehat{\boldsymbol{\theta}}$ belongs to the interior of Θ.

Then, with this additional assumption, Conditions 1 and 2 imply that $q(\widehat{\boldsymbol{\theta}}) = \mathbf{0}_m$ with probability 1. Without the additional assumption, we may get $q(\widehat{\boldsymbol{\theta}}) \neq \mathbf{0}_m$, since the maximum may not be the point where the derivatives vanish; see the corner solution of Exercise 12.2. When the MLE is strongly consistent, Condition A is implied by Condition 1(ii′) as $n \to \infty$.

If the maximum is not unique, for example because of a bimodal likelihood, then there will be more than one solution to the MLE, and we need to select the solution(s) with the highest likelihood. We shall denote such a global maximum value of the likelihood by $L(\widehat{\boldsymbol{\theta}})$ or $\widehat{L}$. It can be regarded as a special case of the *profile* (or *concentrated*) *likelihood*

$$L_{\mathrm{p}}(\boldsymbol{\theta}_1) := L\left(\boldsymbol{\theta}_1, \widehat{\boldsymbol{\theta}}_2(\boldsymbol{\theta}_1)\right) \equiv \sup_{\boldsymbol{\theta}_2} L(\boldsymbol{\theta}),$$

where the parameter vector has been partitioned as $\boldsymbol{\theta}' := (\boldsymbol{\theta}_1', \boldsymbol{\theta}_2')$ and optimization is carried out only with respect to the subset $\boldsymbol{\theta}_2$. The resulting $\widehat{\boldsymbol{\theta}}_2(\boldsymbol{\theta}_1)$ is a function of $\boldsymbol{\theta}_1$

and is known as the *partial MLE*, but we sometimes use the shorthand $\widehat{\boldsymbol{\theta}}_2$ when there is no potential mixup with the full MLE of $\boldsymbol{\theta}_2$ (which is $\widehat{\boldsymbol{\theta}}_2 \equiv \widehat{\boldsymbol{\theta}}_2(\widehat{\boldsymbol{\theta}}_1)$, as Exercise 12.18 will show). Profile likelihoods are a useful device for finding the partial MLE of $\boldsymbol{\theta}_2$ and then that of $\boldsymbol{\theta}_1$, or vice versa, thereby reducing the dimension of the problem; see, for example, Exercises 12.12–12.14 and 12.17 for illustrations, and Exercise 12.18 for a proof. They will also be useful when $\boldsymbol{\theta}_1$ are the parameters of interest that one wishes to focus on. However, profile likelihoods need to be treated with caution, as Exercises 12.40–12.42 will illustrate.

Notice that $\boldsymbol{q}(\widehat{\boldsymbol{\theta}}) \equiv \mathbf{0}_m$ means that the randomness of the estimator $\widehat{\boldsymbol{\theta}}$ is cancelled by the randomness of the function $\boldsymbol{q}$. However, the same function but with nonrandom argument $\boldsymbol{\theta}$, namely $\boldsymbol{q}(\boldsymbol{\theta})$, is random. For example, the score in (12.2) is $q(\mu) = n\overline{x} - n\mu$, which is random because of the sample's $\overline{x}$. We need to be able to describe the general properties of the random vector $\boldsymbol{q}(\boldsymbol{\theta})$, without assuming Condition A. We start with properties that hold for any sample size n. Assuming Condition 2, Exercise 12.21 will demonstrate the *information-matrix equivalence* (or the first two of *Bartlett's identities*):

$$\mathrm{E}(\boldsymbol{q}(\boldsymbol{\theta})) = \mathbf{0}_m \quad \text{and} \quad \mathrm{var}(\boldsymbol{q}(\boldsymbol{\theta})) = \boldsymbol{\mathcal{I}}(\boldsymbol{\theta}),$$

where $\boldsymbol{\mathcal{I}}(\boldsymbol{\theta}) := \mathrm{E}(-\boldsymbol{\mathcal{H}}(\boldsymbol{\theta}))$ is *Fisher's information matrix*. It is so called because it summarizes the information contained in the data, as we shall see. We will also see, in Exercise 12.25, that it is related to the Kullback–Leibler information studied in Part A. Notice that, by $\mathrm{E}(\boldsymbol{q}(\boldsymbol{\theta})) = \mathbf{0}_m$,

$$\mathrm{var}(\boldsymbol{q}(\boldsymbol{\theta})) = \mathrm{E}\left(\boldsymbol{q}(\boldsymbol{\theta})\,\boldsymbol{q}(\boldsymbol{\theta})'\right) \equiv \mathrm{E}\left(\frac{\partial \ell(\boldsymbol{\theta})}{\partial \boldsymbol{\theta}}\frac{\partial \ell(\boldsymbol{\theta})}{\partial \boldsymbol{\theta}'}\right),$$

and the second part of the information-matrix equivalence can be restated as

$$\mathrm{E}\left(-\frac{\partial^2 \ell(\boldsymbol{\theta})}{\partial \boldsymbol{\theta}\,\partial \boldsymbol{\theta}'}\right) = \mathrm{E}\left(\frac{\partial \ell(\boldsymbol{\theta})}{\partial \boldsymbol{\theta}}\frac{\partial \ell(\boldsymbol{\theta})}{\partial \boldsymbol{\theta}'}\right),$$

which links the second derivatives to the first derivatives. Continuing with our discussion of partitioning from the previous paragraph, when we have the block-diagonality $\boldsymbol{\mathcal{I}} = \mathrm{diag}(\boldsymbol{\mathcal{I}}_{11}, \boldsymbol{\mathcal{I}}_{22})$, the parameterization is said to be *orthogonal* for the corresponding partitioned $\boldsymbol{\theta}' := (\boldsymbol{\theta}_1', \boldsymbol{\theta}_2')$. In this case, the method of Exercise 12.25 can be used to show that the expansion of the joint log-likelihood $\ell(\boldsymbol{\theta})$ factors into the sum of separate expansions for $\ell(\boldsymbol{\theta}_1)$ and $\ell(\boldsymbol{\theta}_2)$, up to the second derivatives, when $\boldsymbol{\mathcal{H}}$ satisfies a WLLN that is essentially $-\boldsymbol{\mathcal{H}}(\boldsymbol{\theta}) = (1 + o_p(1))\,\boldsymbol{\mathcal{I}}(\boldsymbol{\theta})$.

Variance matrices are positive semidefinite, as seen in Exercise 6.3. However, if $\boldsymbol{\mathcal{I}}$ is singular, some components of $\boldsymbol{\theta}$ are redundant and the parameters are said to be *unidentified* or *not identified*. The parameters of a density $f_{\boldsymbol{X}}(\boldsymbol{W}; \boldsymbol{\theta})$ are *identified* if and only if, for every $\boldsymbol{\theta}_i, \boldsymbol{\theta}_j \in \Theta$ and $\boldsymbol{\theta}_i \neq \boldsymbol{\theta}_j$, the functions $f_{\boldsymbol{X}}(\boldsymbol{X}; \boldsymbol{\theta}_i)$ and $f_{\boldsymbol{X}}(\boldsymbol{X}; \boldsymbol{\theta}_j)$ are different with probability 1 (here, $\boldsymbol{\theta}_i$ and $\boldsymbol{\theta}_j$ denote different values of $\boldsymbol{\theta}$, not a partitioning of the latter). See Exercise 12.25(c) which shows that identification implies a positive definite $\boldsymbol{\mathcal{I}}$. Unless stated otherwise, we will assume that:

Condition 3. The information matrix, $\mathcal{I}$, is positive definite, and it is an increasing function of n.

The assumptions listed so far are collectively known as *regularity conditions*. The latter part of Condition 3 is trivially satisfied for i.i.d. samples, where enlarging the sample increases the information at the same rate as n. This is so because i.i.d. leads to

$$\ell(\boldsymbol{\theta}) = \sum_{i=1}^{n} \log\left(f_{\boldsymbol{x}}(\boldsymbol{x}_i)\right),$$

$$\boldsymbol{q}(\boldsymbol{\theta}) = \sum_{i=1}^{n} \frac{\partial \log\left(f_{\boldsymbol{x}}(\boldsymbol{x}_i)\right)}{\partial \boldsymbol{\theta}},$$

$$\mathcal{H}(\boldsymbol{\theta}) = \sum_{i=1}^{n} \frac{\partial^2 \log\left(f_{\boldsymbol{x}}(\boldsymbol{x}_i)\right)}{\partial \boldsymbol{\theta} \partial \boldsymbol{\theta}'},$$

where the components of the sums are also i.i.d., yielding

$$\operatorname{var}\left(\boldsymbol{q}(\boldsymbol{\theta})\right) = \sum_{i=1}^{n} \operatorname{var}\left(\frac{\partial \log\left(f_{\boldsymbol{x}}(\boldsymbol{x}_i)\right)}{\partial \boldsymbol{\theta}}\right) = n \operatorname{var}\left(\frac{\partial \log\left(f_{\boldsymbol{x}}(\boldsymbol{x}_i)\right)}{\partial \boldsymbol{\theta}}\right). \tag{12.4}$$

For example, in the case of our earlier normal random sample, (12.3) gives $\mathcal{I} = n$. In the i.i.d. setup, the *information per observation* is $\operatorname{var}(\partial \log(f_{\boldsymbol{x}}(\boldsymbol{x}_i))/\partial \boldsymbol{\theta})$, which is an intrinsic property of the density $f_{\boldsymbol{x}}$, just as the entropy and KLIC were in earlier chapters. Also in this setup, $-n^{-1}\ell(\boldsymbol{\theta})$ is the *sample* (or *empirical*) *entropy*, and we saw how to optimize this quantity at the end of Chapter 4.

In addition to containing the information about $\operatorname{var}(\boldsymbol{q}(\boldsymbol{\theta}))$, the matrix $\mathcal{I}$ contains another piece of valuable information regarding *any* estimator of $\boldsymbol{\theta}$, when the regularity conditions are satisfied. The *Cramér–Rao lower bound* (CRLB) *theorem* states that, for any unbiased estimator of $\boldsymbol{\theta}$ denoted by $\widetilde{\boldsymbol{\theta}}$, the matrix

$$\operatorname{var}(\widetilde{\boldsymbol{\theta}}) - \mathcal{I}^{-1}$$

is positive semidefinite; that is, $\mathcal{I}^{-1}$ provides the lower bound for the variance of *any* unbiased estimator. This best outcome will be achieved if and only if the score is linearly related to $\widetilde{\boldsymbol{\theta}}$, with probability 1. In our example of the mean of a normal sample, the lower bound was simply $1/\mathcal{I} = 1/n$, which coincides with $\operatorname{var}(\overline{x})$, unsurprisingly because the score $q(\mu) = n\overline{x} - n\mu$ is linearly related to the unbiased estimator $\overline{x}$. In fact, for the i.i.d. case, the CRLB is achieved for unbiased estimators *if and only if* the density $f_{\boldsymbol{x}}$ belongs to the regular exponential family. This follows directly because the family's $\log(f_{\boldsymbol{X}})$ (the logarithm of the *joint* density) is linear in the sufficient-statistic vector; see Exercise 11.15 and the illustration in Exercise 12.10(c). Regularity of the family is needed to satisfy the conditions given earlier in this chapter.

The CRLB theorem provides us with an *explicit* (unlike in Chapter 11) benchmark for maximal efficiency. However, two complications can arise. First, as will be seen in some exercises in Section 12.1 and in Exercise 12.31, BUEs can exist even when the lower bound is not attainable by any unbiased estimator. Second, the theorem can be extended to the case of possibly biased estimators, where the lower bound becomes

$$\frac{\partial \operatorname{E}(\widetilde{\boldsymbol{\theta}})}{\partial \boldsymbol{\theta}'} \boldsymbol{\mathcal{I}}^{-1} \frac{\partial \operatorname{E}(\widetilde{\boldsymbol{\theta}})'}{\partial \boldsymbol{\theta}}$$

instead of $\boldsymbol{\mathcal{I}}^{-1}$. If the estimator is unbiased, we have $\operatorname{E}(\widetilde{\boldsymbol{\theta}}) = \boldsymbol{\theta}$ and the CRLB is obtained. See Exercises 12.23 and 12.24.

In the case of samples that are not necessarily i.i.d., the joint log-likelihood factors into

$$\begin{aligned}\ell(\boldsymbol{\theta}) &= \log\left(f_{\boldsymbol{X}}(\boldsymbol{X})\right) = \log\left(f_{\boldsymbol{x}}(\boldsymbol{x}_n \mid \boldsymbol{x}_{n-1}, \dots, \boldsymbol{x}_1) \cdots f_{\boldsymbol{x}}(\boldsymbol{x}_2 \mid \boldsymbol{x}_1) f_{\boldsymbol{x}}(\boldsymbol{x}_1)\right) \\ &= \sum_{i=1}^{n} \log\left(f_{\boldsymbol{x}}(\boldsymbol{x}_i \mid \boldsymbol{x}_{i-1}, \dots, \boldsymbol{x}_1)\right), \qquad (12.5)\end{aligned}$$

where the term for $i = 1$ is understood to contain no conditioning variate ($\boldsymbol{x}_{i-1}, \dots, \boldsymbol{x}_1$ is an empty sequence of descending indices when $i = 1$). The information-matrix equivalence tells us that the score has mean $\mathbf{0}$ and variance $\boldsymbol{\mathcal{I}}$. If, in addition to the regularity conditions seen in this chapter, the conditions for one of the CLTs in Chapter 10 applies to the sequence $\{\partial \log(f_{\boldsymbol{x}}(\boldsymbol{x}_i \mid \boldsymbol{x}_{i-1}, \dots, \boldsymbol{x}_1))/\partial \boldsymbol{\theta}\}_{i=1}^{n}$, then

$$\boldsymbol{q}(\boldsymbol{\theta}) = \sum_{i=1}^{n} \frac{\partial \log(f_{\boldsymbol{x}}(\boldsymbol{x}_i \mid \boldsymbol{x}_{i-1}, \dots, \boldsymbol{x}_1))}{\partial \boldsymbol{\theta}} \overset{a}{\sim} \operatorname{N}(\mathbf{0}, \boldsymbol{\mathcal{I}}) \qquad (12.6)$$

as $n \to \infty$. This is true even when the underlying data are not normally distributed and/or when some non-i.i.d. behavior is allowed for the $\boldsymbol{x}_i$'s. Something is possibly hidden by the notation here, in the sense that $\boldsymbol{\mathcal{I}}$ is an increasing function of n. In the i.i.d. case which gives (12.4), we could rewrite (12.6) as

$$\frac{1}{\sqrt{n}} \boldsymbol{q}(\boldsymbol{\theta}) = \frac{1}{\sqrt{n}} \sum_{i=1}^{n} \frac{\partial \log(f_{\boldsymbol{x}}(\boldsymbol{x}_i))}{\partial \boldsymbol{\theta}} \overset{a}{\sim} \operatorname{N}\left(\mathbf{0}, \frac{1}{n} \boldsymbol{\mathcal{I}}\right),$$

where $n^{-1}\boldsymbol{\mathcal{I}} = \operatorname{var}(\partial \log(f_{\boldsymbol{x}}(\boldsymbol{x}_i))/\partial \boldsymbol{\theta})$ is the information per observation, which is independent of n. For a general normalization for use in (12.6), one can follow the approach used in Exercise 10.20(b), which is avoided here for expository purposes. Because a normal distribution is fully characterized by its first two moments, the only nontrivial moment here, $\boldsymbol{\mathcal{I}}$, conveys all the information about this distribution. This is another reason to use the name "information matrix".

In some sense, we are really interested in $\widehat{\boldsymbol{\theta}}$, rather than the random function $\boldsymbol{q}$. Under the conditions that lead to (12.6), and assuming that the sum

$$\boldsymbol{\mathcal{H}}(\boldsymbol{\theta}) = \sum_{i=1}^{n} \frac{\partial^2 \log(f_{\boldsymbol{x}}(\boldsymbol{x}_i \mid \boldsymbol{x}_{i-1}, \dots, \boldsymbol{x}_1))}{\partial \boldsymbol{\theta} \partial \boldsymbol{\theta}'}$$

(but with a random argument for $\boldsymbol{\mathcal{H}}$) satisfies some WLLN as in Exercises 12.28 and 12.29, we have

$$\widehat{\boldsymbol{\theta}} \overset{a}{\sim} \operatorname{N}(\boldsymbol{\theta}, \boldsymbol{\mathcal{I}}^{-1}), \qquad (12.7)$$

where $\boldsymbol{\theta}$ is the true value of the parameter vector and $\mathcal{I}$ is evaluated at $\boldsymbol{\theta}$. Some of these conditions (like Conditions 2 and 3) can be weakened to hold only in an open neighborhood of the true $\boldsymbol{\theta}$, as the CLT is a local approximation (but others cannot be weakened, as Exercises 12.8 and 12.12 illustrate). However, the consistency of $\widehat{\boldsymbol{\theta}}$ is needed for all $\boldsymbol{\theta} \in \Theta$, although the conditions used in Exercise 12.27 to establish strong consistency can be weakened.

Clearly, the MLE in (12.7) is asymptotically a BUE: as $n \to \infty$, it is unbiased and achieves the CRLB. Furthermore, it is normally distributed as $n \to \infty$. It is therefore said to be *best asymptotically normal* (BAN). Any consistent estimator whose limiting distribution achieves this variance is said to be *asymptotically efficient*. There are two important remarks to make about this. First, any asymptotically efficient estimator of $\boldsymbol{g}(\boldsymbol{\theta})$, for some continuously differentiable function $\boldsymbol{g}$, has a variance that follows directly as in the delta method of Exercise 10.20. Second, as seen in Exercise 10.38, the limiting moments may exist even when the finite-sample moments do not. Therefore, asymptotic efficiency is a weaker criterion than requiring the estimator's finite-sample bias to tend to zero and its variance to tend to the CRLB. See also the one-way implication in the introduction to the concept of consistency in Chapter 11.

One feature that is striking in comparing (12.7) with (12.6) is that the asymptotic variances of the MLE and the score are inversely related. As $n \to \infty$, more information accrues and $\mathcal{I}$ increases. As a result, the precision of $\widehat{\boldsymbol{\theta}}$ increases since it becomes more concentrated around the true value, while the reverse happens for the distribution of the score around the origin. One variate can therefore be thought of as the asymptotic *dual* of the other; see Exercise 12.28(b) for the relation between them. A visual interpretation follows from our earlier example on the sample mean and from Figure 12.1. As n increases, the log-likelihood becomes more tightly concentrated around the true value of μ (or θ), which means that its derivative q swings more violently from very positive to very negative as we move along the horizontal axis. The volatility of q increases with n, concurrently with a fall in the variance of $\widehat{\mu}$ (or $\widehat{\theta}$). Note that, at the MLE point $\widehat{\theta}$, the curvature[1] of the log-likelihood equals the Hessian (second derivative) and it becomes more negative as n increases.

The exercises in this chapter start with some examples of MLEs. Once the reader gains familiarity with some simple special cases, we move on to general properties of the MLE, score, and information. We then look at the case of the linear model in some detail, where maximum-likelihood estimation tries to find the most likely place for a plane (or line if in two dimensions) to fit the scatter plot of the data. We conclude with some properties of MLEs in nonstandard setups.

[1] In general, the (signed) *curvature* of a function ℓ of a scalar is $\ell''/(1+\ell'^2)^{3/2}$. Here, we have $\ell' = 0$ at the MLE.

12.1 Examples of MLEs and efficiency bounds

Exercise 12.1 (Bernoulli: MLE) Let $x_1, \dots, x_n$ be a random sample from a $\text{Ber}(p)$ distribution, $p \in [0, 1]$.
(a) Derive the MLE of p, and apply it to Exercise 4.3.
(b) Derive the MLE of the *odds ratio*, defined by $p/(1-p)$, then the MLE of $p(1-p)$.
(c) Are the three estimators in (a) and (b) unbiased?
(d) Derive the asymptotic distribution of the MLEs in (b).
(e) Suppose you are told that p (hence x_i) depends on some factors, including for example the general health of the patients in Exercise 4.3. Why is it inappropriate to consider a linear relation of p to these factors?

Solution
(a) The likelihood function is given by

$$L(p) = \prod_{i=1}^{n} \left(p^{x_i} (1-p)^{1-x_i} \right) = p^{\sum_{i=1}^n x_i} (1-p)^{n - \sum_{i=1}^n x_i} = p^{n\overline{x}} (1-p)^{n(1-\overline{x})}$$

for $p \in [0, 1]$, and 0 otherwise. This function of p is proportional to a beta density, which was plotted in Exercise 4.14(a). Clearly, it is continuous, even though the density of x is discrete. There are two cases where we get a corner solution and we cannot optimize the function by differentiation. If $\sum_{i=1}^n x_i = 0$ (hence $\overline{x} = 0$), then $L(p) = (1-p)^n$ is maximized at $\widehat{p} = 0$; hence $\widehat{p} = \overline{x}$. If $\sum_{i=1}^n x_i = n$ (hence $\overline{x} = 1$), then $L(p) = p^n$ is maximized at $\widehat{p} = 1$; hence $\widehat{p} = \overline{x}$ again. For other values of $\sum_{i=1}^n x_i$, we write

$$\frac{\mathrm{d}\ell(p)}{\mathrm{d}p} = \frac{\mathrm{d}}{\mathrm{d}p} \left(n\overline{x} \log(p) + n(1-\overline{x}) \log(1-p) \right) = n\frac{\overline{x}}{p} - n\frac{1-\overline{x}}{1-p} = n\frac{\overline{x}-p}{p(1-p)},$$

and equating this score to 0 gives the MLE $\widehat{p} = \overline{x}$, the sample mean again. In this third case, we have $L(0) = 0 = L(1)$ with $L(p) > 0$ in between. Therefore, $L(p)$ has at least one maximum in $(0, 1)$, and it is the one we have derived: we do not have to check further the sign of the second-order derivative of $L(p)$ at $\widehat{p}$. For an application, Exercise 4.3 gives us 85% as the most likely success rate of the new drug.
(b) We could write the likelihood in terms of $\theta := p/(1-p)$, or replace p by $\theta/(1+\theta)$, then solve for $\widehat{\theta}$. Alternatively, using the invariance property of MLEs, we obtain directly

$$\widehat{\left(\frac{p}{1-p}\right)} = \frac{\widehat{p}}{1-\widehat{p}}.$$

Similarly, $\widehat{p(1-p)} = \widehat{p}(1-\widehat{p})$.
(c) Since the sample is random, $\mathrm{E}(\overline{x}) = \mathrm{E}(x_i)$ and $\mathrm{var}(\overline{x}) = \mathrm{var}(x_i)/n$; see, for example, Exercise 9.2. These moments are available from Table 4.1 for $\text{Ber}(p)$ as p and $p(1-p)$, respectively. Therefore, $\mathrm{E}(\overline{x}) = p$ and $\widehat{p}$ is unbiased for p. However, $p/(1-p) = (p^{-1} - 1)^{-1} \in (0, \infty)$ is a strictly convex function of $p \in (0, 1)$, and Jensen's inequality implies

that

$$\mathrm{E}\left(\frac{\widehat{p}}{1-\widehat{p}}\right) > \frac{\mathrm{E}(\widehat{p})}{1-\mathrm{E}(\widehat{p})} = \frac{p}{1-p},$$

so the MLE of $p/(1-p)$ is biased. Finally,

$$\begin{aligned}\mathrm{E}\left(\widehat{p}(1-\widehat{p})\right) &= \mathrm{E}(\widehat{p}) - \mathrm{E}(\widehat{p}^2) = p - \mathrm{E}(\overline{x}^2) = p - \mathrm{var}(\overline{x}) - (\mathrm{E}(\overline{x}))^2 \\ &= p - \frac{p(1-p)}{n} - p^2 = p(1-p)\left(1-\frac{1}{n}\right),\end{aligned}$$

so the bias vanishes only asymptotically.

(d) The CLT gives us $\sqrt{n}(\overline{x}-p) \overset{a}{\sim} \mathrm{N}\left(0, p(1-p)\right)$. Using the delta method (Exercise 10.20),

$$\sqrt{n}\left(\frac{\overline{x}}{1-\overline{x}} - \frac{p}{1-p}\right) \overset{a}{\sim} \mathrm{N}\left(0, \left(\frac{\mathrm{d}}{\mathrm{d}p}\frac{p}{1-p}\right)^2 p\left(1-p\right)\right) = \mathrm{N}\left(0, \frac{p}{\left(1-p\right)^3}\right)$$

since $\mathrm{d}\left(p^{-1}-1\right)^{-1}/\,\mathrm{d}p = (1-p)^{-2}$. Similarly, since $\mathrm{d}(p\left(1-p\right))\,/\,\mathrm{d}p = 1-2p$,

$$\sqrt{n}\left(\overline{x}(1-\overline{x}) - p(1-p)\right) \overset{a}{\sim} \mathrm{N}\left(0, (1-2p)^2 p\left(1-p\right)\right).$$

(e) Clearly, p is a probability that lies between 0 and 1. A straight line linking it to other variables will not be appropriate, because a line is not restricted to $[0,1]$. However, the logit transformation $\log\left(p/\left(1-p\right)\right) \in \mathbb{R}$ suggested by Exercise 4.30(b) can be linearly related to these factors. For example, suppose that we have the relation

$$\log\left(\frac{p}{1-p}\right) = \beta z.$$

Then,

$$\exp\left(-\beta z\right) = \frac{1-p}{p} = \frac{1}{p} - 1$$

and

$$p = \frac{1}{1+\exp\left(-\beta z\right)}.$$

This function (the logistic c.d.f.) maps $z \in \mathbb{R}$ to $p \in [0,1]$, and values of p outside this interval do not arise.

The logit transformation can also be seen in the likelihood obtained in (a),

$$L(p) = (1-p)^n \exp\left(n\overline{x}\log\left(\frac{p}{1-p}\right)\right),$$

where the logit of p is the natural parameter associated with the sufficient statistic $n\overline{x}$; see the exponential-family density in Exercise 11.15(b). Alternatively,

$$\ell(p) = n\log\left(1-p\right) + n\overline{x}\log\left(\frac{p}{1-p}\right),$$

where the second term is the only one where the data $\overline{x}$ and the parameter p interact. Generally, the natural parameter yields the link function of the generalized linear model introduced in Chapter 11 (here, p is the expectation of the Bernoulli dependent variate). The logit is also the link function for the binomial, as well as for the Bernoulli of this exercise.

Exercise 12.2 (Bernoulli: constrained MLE) Suppose that you have a single observation from a Ber(p) distribution, and it is known that $p \in [1/5, 4/5]$. Find the MLE of p.

Solution
The likelihood function is given by $L(p) = p^x (1-p)^{1-x}$, that is,

$$L(p) = \begin{cases} 1-p & (x=0), \\ p & (x=1). \end{cases}$$

If the observation is $x = 0$, then $L(p)$ is maximized by $\widehat{p} = 1/5$. If it is $x = 1$, then $L(p)$ is maximized by $\widehat{p} = 4/5$. Notice that the derivative of $\ell(p)$,

$$\frac{\mathrm{d}\ell(p)}{\mathrm{d}p} = \frac{\mathrm{d}}{\mathrm{d}p}\left(x \log(p) + (1-x)\log(1-p)\right) = \frac{x}{p} - \frac{1-x}{1-p},$$

is *not* zero at $\widehat{p}$, and that $\widehat{p}$ is at the edge of the parameter space (it is a corner solution).

Exercise 12.3 (Geometric: MLE) Suppose that $x_1, \dots, x_n$ is a random sample from a Geo(p) distribution, $p \in (0, 1]$.
(a) What is the MLE of p?
(b) Show that the MLE is a consistent estimator of p.
(c) Derive the asymptotic distribution of the MLE.

Solution
(a) The likelihood function is given by

$$L(p) = \prod_{i=1}^{n} \left(p(1-p)^{x_i}\right) = p^n (1-p)^{\sum_{i=1}^n x_i} = p^n (1-p)^{n\overline{x}}$$

for $p \in (0, 1]$, and 0 otherwise. Notice that the parameter space is not compact, but that the MLE exists, as we shall see. This is so because Condition 1 from the introduction to this chapter is sufficient but not necessary. If $\overline{x} = 0$, then $L(p) = p^n$ is maximized at $\widehat{p} = 1$. Otherwise,

$$\frac{\mathrm{d}\ell(p)}{\mathrm{d}p} = \frac{\mathrm{d}}{\mathrm{d}p}\left(n\log(p) + n\overline{x}\log(1-p)\right) = \frac{n}{p} - \frac{n\overline{x}}{1-p}$$

implies that the MLE of p is given by

$$\widehat{p} = \frac{1}{1+\overline{x}}$$

and, since $L(0) = 0 = L(1)$ with $L(p) > 0$ in between, we have that $L(\widehat{p})$ is a maximum. Both cases therefore lead to $\widehat{p} = 1/(1+\overline{x})$. Note that there are two ways to describe the geometric distribution. One can count the number of failures before the first success and

have $x \in \{0, 1, \dots\}$, as we have done here, or one can count the number of trials until the first success and have $x \in \{1, 2, \dots\}$. In the latter case, $\widehat{p} = 1/\overline{x}$, the reciprocal of the sample mean.
(b) As $\mathrm{E}(x_i) = (1-p)/p$, we have that $\overline{x} \to (1-p)/p$ almost surely and

$$\widehat{p} = \frac{1}{1+\overline{x}} \to \frac{1}{1+\frac{1-p}{p}} = p$$

by the CMT of Exercise 10.13 (applicable since the function is continuous for $p \in (0, 1]$).
(c) Define $\mu := (1-p)/p$. Then $\mathrm{var}(x_i) = (1-p)/p^2 = \mu(\mu+1)$, and the CLT shows that

$$\sqrt{n}\,(\overline{x} - \mu) \overset{a}{\sim} \mathrm{N}(0, \mu(\mu+1)).$$

Taking $g(x) := 1/(1+x)$, the delta method yields

$$\sqrt{n}\,(\widehat{p} - p) \overset{a}{\sim} \mathrm{N}\left(0, \frac{\mu}{(\mu+1)^3}\right),$$

where the variance can be written as $(1-p)p^2$.

Exercise 12.4 (Recaptured again!) Shahira now knows about maximum likelihood, and she decides to revisit Exercise 4.7. She wants to find the MLE of the number of sharks in the lake, denoted by m. What will she get for $\widehat{m}$, and how does it relate to her earlier calculations?

Solution
The likelihood follows from Exercise 4.7(a) as

$$L(m) = \frac{\binom{k}{x}\binom{m-k}{n-x}}{\binom{m}{n}},$$

where x is the number of recaptured tagged sharks. Its maximization with respect to x (but not the required m) was solved in Exercise 4.7(c). There are nevertheless some similarities with the method of solution, because m has to be an integer (unlike other exercises in this chapter) satisfying $m \geqslant \max\{k, n\}$. Consider the ratio

$$R := \frac{L(m)}{L(m-1)} = \frac{\binom{m-k}{n-x}\binom{m-1}{n}}{\binom{m-k-1}{n-x}\binom{m}{n}} = \frac{(m-k)(m-n)}{(m-k-n+x)\,m}.$$

As we go from $m-1$ to m, the likelihood increases if $R > 1$ or, equivalently, $m < kn/x$; it decreases if $m > kn/x$. Therefore, if $kn/x \notin \mathbb{N}$, then the MLE is the integer part of kn/x. If $kn/x \in \mathbb{N}$, then kn/x and $kn/x - 1$ are both MLEs. Comparing with Exercise 4.7(b), the MLE is not far off the seemingly naïve estimator obtained by replacing x by $\mathrm{E}(x)$. More on the latter will follow in the next chapter, in connection with method-of-moments estimation; see Exercise 13.2.

Exercise 12.5 (Poisson: MLE or BUE?) Let $x_1, \dots, x_n$ denote a random sample from the Poi(λ) distribution, $\lambda > 0$.
(a) Show that there are cases where there exists no MLE of λ.
(b) If the MLE exists, derive its bias and variance.
(c) What is the MLE of $\mathrm{e}^{-2\lambda}$? How does its MSE compare with that of the BUE $(-1)^{x_1}$ of Exercise 11.24(a) when $n = 1$?

Solution
(a) The likelihood function is given by

$$L(\lambda) = \frac{\mathrm{e}^{-n\lambda}\lambda^{\sum_{i=1}^n x_i}}{\prod_{i=1}^n x_i!}.$$

If $x_i = 0$ for all i, then $L(\lambda) = \mathrm{e}^{-n\lambda}$ does not have a global maximum, because $\lambda \to 0^+$ increases the likelihood but $\lambda = 0$ is not part of the parameter space. We can take any tiny λ, and $\lambda/2$ will have a higher likelihood! The event $\sum_{i=1}^n x_i = 0$ can happen with positive probability, x being a discrete variate with support over $\mathbb{Z}_{0,+}$. However, if $\sum_{i=1}^n x_i \neq 0$, then

$$\frac{\mathrm{d}\ell(\lambda)}{\mathrm{d}\lambda} = -n + \frac{\sum_{i=1}^n x_i}{\lambda}$$

gives $\widehat{\lambda} = \overline{x}$. Since $L(0) = 0 = L(\infty)$, we have a maximum at $\widehat{\lambda} = \overline{x}$.
(b) We know that $\mathrm{E}(x_i) = \mathrm{var}(x_i) = \lambda$. Therefore, as the sample is random, $\mathrm{E}(\overline{x}) = \lambda$ (hence the bias is zero) and the variance is λ/n.
(c) By the invariance of the MLE to parameter transformations, the required estimator is $\mathrm{e}^{-2\overline{x}}$. This is a strictly convex function of $\overline{x}$, so Jensen's inequality applies and the MLE of $\mathrm{e}^{-2\lambda}$ is biased. However, unlike the BUE of Exercise 11.24(a), the MLE satisfies $0 < \mathrm{e}^{-2\overline{x}} \leqslant 1$. Furthermore, for $n = 1$, we have $\overline{x} = x_1$ and the MSE of the MLE is

$$\begin{aligned}
\mathrm{E}\left(\left(\mathrm{e}^{-2x_1} - \mathrm{e}^{-2\lambda}\right)^2\right) &= \mathrm{E}(\mathrm{e}^{-4x_1}) - 2\mathrm{e}^{-2\lambda}\,\mathrm{E}(\mathrm{e}^{-2x_1}) + \mathrm{e}^{-4\lambda} \\
&= \sum_{u=0}^{\infty} \mathrm{e}^{-4u}\frac{\mathrm{e}^{-\lambda}\lambda^u}{u!} - 2\mathrm{e}^{-2\lambda}\sum_{u=0}^{\infty} \mathrm{e}^{-2u}\frac{\mathrm{e}^{-\lambda}\lambda^u}{u!} + \mathrm{e}^{-4\lambda} \\
&= \exp\left(-\lambda + \lambda\mathrm{e}^{-4}\right) - 2\exp\left(-3\lambda + \lambda\mathrm{e}^{-2}\right) + \exp\left(-4\lambda\right),
\end{aligned}$$

while the unbiasedness of $(-1)^{x_1}$ implies that $\mathrm{MSE}\left((-1)^{x_1}\right) = \mathrm{var}\left((-1)^{x_1}\right)$ with

$$\begin{aligned}
\mathrm{var}\left((-1)^{x_1}\right) &= \mathrm{E}\left((-1)^{2x_1}\right) - (\mathrm{E}((-1)^{x_1}))^2 = \mathrm{E}(1) - \left(\sum_{u=0}^{\infty}(-1)^u\frac{\mathrm{e}^{-\lambda}\lambda^u}{u!}\right)^2 \\
&= 1 - \exp\left(-4\lambda\right),
\end{aligned}$$

since x_1 is an integer and $(-1)^{2x_1} = 1^{x_1} = 1$. The difference is

$$\begin{aligned}&\operatorname{MSE}\left((-1)^{x_1}\right) - \operatorname{MSE}\left(\mathrm{e}^{-2x_1}\right)\\ &\quad = 1 + 2\exp\left(-3\lambda + \lambda \mathrm{e}^{-2}\right) - \exp\left(-\lambda + \lambda \mathrm{e}^{-4}\right) - 2\exp\left(-4\lambda\right).\end{aligned}$$

It is positive if and only if

$$\exp(\lambda) + 2\exp\left(-2\lambda + \lambda \mathrm{e}^{-2}\right) > \exp\left(\lambda \mathrm{e}^{-4}\right) + 2\exp(-3\lambda),$$

which is the case since $\exp(\lambda) > \exp\left(\lambda \mathrm{e}^{-4}\right)$ and $\exp\left(-2\lambda + \lambda \mathrm{e}^{-2}\right) > \exp(-3\lambda)$. In other words, the MSE of the MLE is lower than that of the BUE. Furthermore, as λ increases, so does the difference in MSEs, reaching a maximum of 1 as $\lambda \to \infty$.

Exercise 12.6 (Weibull: no explicit MLE) Let $x_1, \dots, x_n$ be a random sample from $x \in \mathbb{R}_+$ with p.d.f.

$$f_x(u) = \lambda p u^{p-1} \exp\left(-\lambda u^p\right),$$

where $p, \lambda > 0$.
(a) Suppose that p is known. Derive the MLE of λ.
(b) Suppose that λ is known. Derive the score for p. Is the MLE unique?

Solution
(a) From

$$L(\lambda) = \lambda^n p^n \left(\prod_{i=1}^n x_i\right)^{p-1} \exp\left(-\lambda \sum_{i=1}^n x_i^p\right),$$

we have

$$\ell(\lambda) = n\log(\lambda) + n\log(p) + (p-1)\sum_{i=1}^n \log(x_i) - \lambda \sum_{i=1}^n x_i^p.$$

Hence,

$$\frac{\mathrm{d}\ell(\lambda)}{\mathrm{d}\lambda} = \frac{n}{\lambda} - \sum_{i=1}^n x_i^p \quad \text{and} \quad \frac{\mathrm{d}^2\ell(\lambda)}{\mathrm{d}\lambda^2} = -\frac{n}{\lambda^2} < 0,$$

and there is a maximum at

$$\widehat{\lambda}^{-1} = \frac{1}{n}\sum_{i=1}^n x_i^p.$$

(b) By considering the likelihood in (a), but as a function of p,

$$\frac{\mathrm{d}\ell(p)}{\mathrm{d}p} = \frac{n}{p} + \sum_{i=1}^n \log(x_i) - \lambda \sum_{i=1}^n x_i^p \log(x_i).$$

As $p \to 0^+$ the score goes to $+\infty$, while $p \to \infty$ makes it go to $-\infty$ if $\exists x_i > 1$ or to $\sum_{i=1}^n \log(x_i) < 0$ almost surely if $\nexists x_i > 1$, so we clearly have at least one solution to

$\mathrm{d}\ell(p)/\mathrm{d}p = 0$. In general, this equation has no simple explicit solution for p. However, the MLE is unique. The easiest way to show this is by demonstrating the strict concavity of the log-likelihood. One possibility is to differentiate the score once more, and show that the result is negative for all p. Alternatively, since $x_i > 0$ with probability 1, using $x_i = \exp(\log(x_i))$ gives

$$\ell(p) = n\log(\lambda) + n\log(p) + (p-1)\sum_{i=1}^{n}\log(x_i) - \lambda\sum_{i=1}^{n} \mathrm{e}^{p\log(x_i)}.$$

The result follows by observing that $\log(p)$ and $-\exp(p\log(x_i))$ are strictly concave functions of p, and that the linear function $(p-1)$ is also concave.

Exercise 12.7 (Uniform: nonuniqueness of MLE) Let $x_1, \ldots, x_n$ be a random sample from $x \sim \mathrm{U}_{(\alpha,\alpha+1)}$.
(a) Derive the MLE of α, and show that it is not unique.
(b) Derive the MSE of this estimator for $n > 1$.
(c) Assuming $1 < n < \infty$, is the MSE lower when the MLE is unbiased?

Solution
(a) Let $y_1 := \min_i\{x_i\}$ and $y_n := \max_i\{x_i\}$. Then

$$L(\alpha) = \prod_{i=1}^{n} 1_{x_i \in [\alpha,\alpha+1]} = 1_{y_1 \geqslant \alpha} 1_{y_n \leqslant \alpha+1}$$

since *all* the x's satisfy $x_i \in [\alpha, \alpha+1]$; hence α cannot be bigger than $\min_i\{x_i\}$ and $\alpha+1$ cannot be smaller than $\max_i\{x_i\}$. The pair (y_1, y_n) is a sufficient statistic for α, as seen in Exercise 11.13. We have the maximum $L(\alpha) = 1$ for all $\alpha \leqslant y_1 \leqslant y_n \leqslant \alpha+1$, that is, $y_n - 1 \leqslant \alpha \leqslant y_1$. Therefore, the MLE of α is *any* point in the interval $[y_n - 1, y_1]$, and $\widehat{\alpha} = \lambda(y_n - 1) + (1-\lambda)y_1$ for *any* constant $\lambda \in [0,1]$. Notice that the likelihood is not continuously differentiable in α, because the support of x depends on α: the regularity requirement given by Condition 2 is violated.
(b) Recall that $y_1 - \alpha$ and $\alpha + 1 - y_n$ have the same distribution; see, for example, Exercise 11.13, which also gives

$$\mathrm{E}(y_1) = \alpha + \frac{1}{n+1} \quad \text{and} \quad \mathrm{E}(y_n) = \alpha + 1 - \frac{1}{n+1}.$$

Hence,

$$\mathrm{E}(\widehat{\alpha}) = \lambda\left(\alpha - \frac{1}{n+1}\right) + (1-\lambda)\left(\alpha + \frac{1}{n+1}\right) = \alpha + \frac{1-2\lambda}{n+1},$$

which is unbiased for $\lambda = \frac{1}{2}$. Now, $\mathrm{MSE}(\widehat{\alpha}) = \mathrm{var}(\widehat{\alpha}) + (1-2\lambda)^2/(n+1)^2$, where

$$\begin{aligned}\mathrm{var}(\lambda(y_n - 1) + (1-\lambda)y_1) &= \lambda^2\,\mathrm{var}(y_n) + (1-\lambda)^2\,\mathrm{var}(y_1) + 2\lambda(1-\lambda)\,\mathrm{cov}(y_n, y_1) \\ &= \left(\lambda^2 + (1-\lambda)^2\right)\mathrm{var}(y_n) + 2\lambda(1-\lambda)\,\mathrm{cov}(y_n, y_1)\end{aligned}$$

since $\mathrm{var}(y_1 - \alpha) = \mathrm{var}(\alpha + 1 - y_n) = \mathrm{var}(y_n)$. Variances are location-invariant, and so we have already worked out the required

$$\mathrm{var}(y_n) = \frac{n}{(n+1)^2(n+2)}$$

in Exercise 11.7(a) for uniform variates defined on intervals of unit length. For the covariance, when $n > 1$, the joint density seen earlier (such as in Exercise 11.13) gives

$$\begin{aligned}
\mathrm{E}(y_1 y_n) &= n(n-1)\int_{\alpha}^{\alpha+1} v_n \int_{\alpha}^{v_n} v_1 (v_n - v_1)^{n-2}\,\mathrm{d}v_1\,\mathrm{d}v_n \\
&= \int_{\alpha}^{\alpha+1} v_n \left(-n\left[v_1(v_n - v_1)^{n-1}\right]_{\alpha}^{v_n} + n\int_{\alpha}^{v_n}(v_n - v_1)^{n-1}\,\mathrm{d}v_1\right)\mathrm{d}v_n \\
&= \int_{\alpha}^{\alpha+1} v_n \left(n\alpha(v_n-\alpha)^{n-1} + (v_n-\alpha)^n\right)\mathrm{d}v_n \\
&= \left[v_n\left(\alpha(v_n-\alpha)^n + \frac{(v_n-\alpha)^{n+1}}{n+1}\right)\right]_{\alpha}^{\alpha+1} - \left[\frac{\alpha(v_n-\alpha)^{n+1}}{n+1} + \frac{(v_n-\alpha)^{n+2}}{(n+1)(n+2)}\right]_{\alpha}^{\alpha+1} \\
&= (\alpha+1)\left(\alpha + \frac{1}{n+1}\right) - \left(\frac{\alpha}{n+1} + \frac{1}{(n+1)(n+2)}\right),
\end{aligned}$$

hence

$$\begin{aligned}
\mathrm{cov}(y_n, y_1) &= (\alpha+1)\left(\alpha + \frac{1}{n+1}\right) - \frac{\alpha}{n+1} - \frac{1}{(n+1)(n+2)} \\
&\quad - \left(\alpha + 1 - \frac{1}{n+1}\right)\left(\alpha + \frac{1}{n+1}\right) \\
&= -\frac{\alpha}{n+1} - \frac{1}{(n+1)(n+2)} + \frac{1}{n+1}\left(\alpha + \frac{1}{n+1}\right) \\
&= -\frac{1}{(n+1)(n+2)} + \frac{1}{(n+1)^2} = \frac{1}{(n+1)^2(n+2)}.
\end{aligned}$$

The MSE of $\widehat{\alpha}$ is

$$\begin{aligned}
\mathrm{MSE}(\widehat{\alpha}) &= \frac{n\left(\lambda^2 + (1-\lambda)^2\right)}{(n+1)^2(n+2)} + \frac{2\lambda(1-\lambda)}{(n+1)^2(n+2)} + \left(\frac{(1-\lambda)-\lambda}{n+1}\right)^2 \\
&= \frac{n\left(\lambda^2 + (1-\lambda)^2\right) + 2\lambda(1-\lambda) + (n+2)\left(\lambda^2 + (1-\lambda)^2\right) - (n+2)\left(2\lambda(1-\lambda)\right)}{(n+1)^2(n+2)} \\
&= \frac{(2n+2)\left(\lambda^2 + (1-\lambda)^2\right) - (n+1)\left(2\lambda(1-\lambda)\right)}{(n+1)^2(n+2)} \\
&= \frac{2\left(\lambda^2 + (1-\lambda)^2\right) - 2\lambda(1-\lambda)}{(n+1)(n+2)} = \frac{6\lambda^2 - 6\lambda + 2}{(n+1)(n+2)}.
\end{aligned}$$

(c) The answer is yes: the MSE in (b) is minimized for $\lambda = \frac{1}{2}$, the unique unbiased MLE when n is finite.

Exercise 12.8 (Max uniform: MLE or BUE?) Let $x_1, \dots, x_n$ be a random sample from $x \sim \mathrm{U}_{(-\alpha,\alpha)}$.
(a) Derive the MLE of α.
(b) Derive the BUE of α.
(c) Compare the MSEs of the MLE and the BUE of α.
(d) Derive the limiting distribution of the MLE, and obtain its consistency rate.

Solution
(a) We have

$$L(\alpha) = \frac{1}{(2\alpha)^n} 1_{\min_i\{x_i\} \geqslant -\alpha} 1_{\max_i\{x_i\} \leqslant \alpha} = \frac{1}{(2\alpha)^n} 1_{\max_i\{|x_i|\} \leqslant \alpha}.$$

The likelihood is zero for $\alpha < \max_i \{|x_i|\}$, then jumps at the point $\alpha = \max_i \{|x_i|\}$, and declines as α increases further. The MLE is therefore $\widehat{\alpha} = \max_i \{|x_i|\}$. This makes sense: the observation that is the largest, in absolute value, indicates the most likely value of the unknown upper bound α of the distribution of $|x|$. (The sample mean would be an estimator of the mean of the distribution of x, which is zero!) Notice that the likelihood is not continuously differentiable in α, the cause being that the support of x depends on α: the regularity requirement given by Condition 2 is violated. Notice also that the likelihood is defined on the closed interval $[-\alpha, \alpha]$; otherwise, the parameter space would not be compact and there would be no solution to the MLE (for example, take $\widehat{\alpha}$ arbitrarily close to $\max_i \{|x_i|\}$).
(b) From the factorization in (a), $y_n := \max_i \{|x_i|\}$ is sufficient for α. Exercise 11.7 gave the density of y_n, and Exercise 11.12 showed that this y_n is complete. Now, the MLE $\widehat{\alpha} = y_n$ is biased, because Exercise 11.7 showed that

$$\mathrm{E}(y_n) = \frac{n}{n+1}\alpha,$$

and the BUE of α is given by $\widetilde{\alpha} := \widehat{\alpha}(1 + 1/n)$.
(c) The MSE of the BUE is

$$\begin{aligned}
\mathrm{MSE}(\widetilde{\alpha}) &= \mathrm{E}\left((\widetilde{\alpha} - \alpha)^2\right) = \mathrm{E}\left[\left(\left(1 + \frac{1}{n}\right)(\widehat{\alpha} - \alpha) + \frac{\alpha}{n}\right)^2\right] \\
&= \left(1 + \frac{1}{n}\right)^2 \mathrm{MSE}(\widehat{\alpha}) + \frac{2\alpha}{n}\left(1 + \frac{1}{n}\right)\mathrm{E}(\widehat{\alpha} - \alpha) + \frac{\alpha^2}{n^2} \\
&= \mathrm{MSE}(\widehat{\alpha}) + \left(\frac{2}{n} + \frac{1}{n^2}\right)\mathrm{MSE}(\widehat{\alpha}) + \frac{2\alpha^2}{n}\left(1 + \frac{1}{n}\right)\left(\frac{n}{n+1} - 1\right) + \frac{\alpha^2}{n^2} \\
&= \mathrm{MSE}(\widehat{\alpha}) + \left(\frac{2}{n} + \frac{1}{n^2}\right)\mathrm{MSE}(\widehat{\alpha}) - \frac{\alpha^2}{n^2},
\end{aligned}$$

where $\operatorname{MSE}(\widehat{\alpha})$ is given in Exercise 11.7(a). Hence,

$$\begin{aligned}\operatorname{MSE}(\widetilde{\alpha}) &= \operatorname{MSE}(\widehat{\alpha}) + \left(2+\frac{1}{n}\right)\frac{2\alpha^2}{n(n+1)(n+2)} - \frac{\alpha^2}{n^2}\\ &= \operatorname{MSE}(\widehat{\alpha}) + \frac{(4n+2)-(n+1)(n+2)}{n^2(n+1)(n+2)}\alpha^2\\ &= \operatorname{MSE}(\widehat{\alpha}) - \frac{n-1}{n(n+1)(n+2)}\alpha^2 < \operatorname{MSE}(\widehat{\alpha}).\end{aligned}$$

The difference vanishes asymptotically, at a rate $1/n^2$. We will continue with such comparisons in Exercise 13.3.
(d) Exercise 11.7(d) yielded $\Pr(n(y_n-\alpha)\leqslant u)\to\exp(u/\alpha)$ for $u<0$, so that $n(\alpha - y_n) \overset{a}{\sim} \operatorname{Expo}(1/\alpha)$. The limiting distribution of the MLE is not normal, and the consistency rate is n rather than $\sqrt{n}$. Notice also that the MSE is of order $1/n^2$, and not $1/n$. This is so because, rather than the usual CLT, it is a special case of the extreme-value Weibull limiting distribution that applies here. The maximum is not expressible as a sum to which a CLT applies directly (like the sample mean) or indirectly (like non-extreme order statistics, as in Exercise 10.30(d)), so the CLT does not apply to the MLE of this problem. See Chapter 10.

Exercise 12.9 (Pareto's MLE and CRLB: regular case) Let $x_1,\dots,x_n$ be a random sample from the p.d.f.

$$f_x(u) = \begin{cases} pu^{-p-1} & (u>1),\\ 0 & (\text{elsewhere}),\end{cases}$$

where $p>0$.
(a) Derive the MLE of p.
(b) Is the MLE unbiased, and does it coincide with the BUE?
(c) Derive the lower bound for biased estimators of p, and show how it relates to the variances of the MLE and BUE.
(d) Redo the previous parts of the exercise to find the MLE of $1/p$.

Solution
(a) We have

$$L(p) = p^n\left(\prod_{i=1}^n x_i\right)^{-p-1},$$

where $L(p)$ has the same functional form as a gamma density, apart from a constant of proportionality. Solving for the MLE,

$$\frac{\mathrm{d}\ell(p)}{\mathrm{d}p} = \frac{n}{p} - \sum_{i=1}^n \log(x_i)$$

and $\mathrm{d}^2\ell(p)/\mathrm{d}p^2 = -n/p^2 < 0$ imply that $\widehat{p} = n/\sum_{i=1}^n \log(x_i)$. In other words, $\exp(1/\widehat{p})$ is the geometric mean of the sample values of x.
(b) Let $y_i := \log(x_i) > 0$. The p.d.f. of y_i is given by $f_{y_i}(v) = p\mathrm{e}^v \mathrm{e}^{-v(p+1)} = p\mathrm{e}^{-vp}$, which is an Expo$(p)$. Hence, $z := \sum_{i=1}^n y_i \sim \mathrm{Gam}(n, p)$ by Exercise 7.18, and

$$\mathrm{E}(\widehat{p}) = \mathrm{E}\left(\frac{n}{z}\right) = \frac{np}{n-1}\int_0^\infty \frac{p^{n-1}w^{n-2}\mathrm{e}^{-pw}}{(n-2)!}\,\mathrm{d}w = \frac{np}{n-1}$$

for $n > 1$. For $n = 1$, the integral is divergent (infinite). The bias of this estimator is $p/(n-1) > 0$ but vanishes as $n \to \infty$. Because the regular Pareto belongs to the exponential family, the BUE is simply $(1 - 1/n)\,\widehat{p}$ and dominates the MLE in terms of having a smaller variance by a factor $(1 - 1/n)^2$, as well as being unbiased. Notice the existence of $\mathrm{E}(\widehat{p})$ regardless of whether the mean of the Pareto exists, that is, whether $p > 1$. All that is required for $\mathrm{E}(\widehat{p})$ and $\mathrm{var}(\widehat{p})$ to exist is that $n > 1$ and $n > 2$, respectively. This is so because the density for x is Pareto, but $1/z$ is an inverse gamma (see the generalized gamma of Chapter 4).
(c) We get $\mathrm{E}(-\mathrm{d}^2\ell(p)/\mathrm{d}p^2) = n/p^2$ from (a), so the CRLB for the BUE is p^2/n. For the MLE of (b), we get the bound

$$\frac{(\mathrm{dE}(\widehat{p})/\mathrm{d}p)^2}{n/p^2} = \frac{np^2}{(n-1)^2}.$$

The actual variances of the estimators can be obtained from

$$\mathrm{E}(\widehat{p}^2) = \mathrm{E}\left(\frac{n^2}{z^2}\right) = \frac{n^2p^2}{(n-1)(n-2)}\int_0^\infty \frac{p^{n-2}w^{n-3}\mathrm{e}^{-pw}}{(n-3)!}\,\mathrm{d}w = \frac{n^2p^2}{(n-1)(n-2)}$$

for $n > 2$. Hence,

$$\mathrm{var}(\widehat{p}) = \frac{n^2p^2}{(n-1)(n-2)} - \frac{n^2p^2}{(n-1)^2} = \frac{n^2p^2}{(n-1)^2(n-2)} > \frac{np^2}{(n-1)^2},$$

and the BUE's variance is

$$\left(1 - \frac{1}{n}\right)^2 \mathrm{var}(\widehat{p}) = \frac{p^2}{n-2} > \frac{p^2}{n}.$$

Neither variance attains its respective lower bound when $n < \infty$.
(d) The MLE of p^{-1} is $\widehat{p}^{-1}$, by the invariance property. It is unbiased because

$$\mathrm{E}(\widehat{p}^{-1}) = \mathrm{E}\left(\frac{z}{n}\right) = \frac{1}{p}\int_0^\infty \frac{p^{n+1}w^n\mathrm{e}^{-pw}}{n!}\,\mathrm{d}w = \frac{1}{p},$$

and is therefore also the BUE. From

$$\mathrm{E}(\widehat{p}^{-2}) = \mathrm{E}\left(\frac{z^2}{n^2}\right) = \frac{n+1}{np^2}\int_0^\infty \frac{p^{n+2}w^{n+1}\mathrm{e}^{-pw}}{(n+1)!}\,\mathrm{d}w = \left(1 + \frac{1}{n}\right)\frac{1}{p^2},$$

we obtain the variance as $1/(np^2)$. This is actually the CRLB. To see this, define $\theta := p^{-1}$.

Then

$$\ell(\theta) = -n\log(\theta) - \left(\frac{1}{\theta}+1\right)\sum_{i=1}^{n}\log(x_i) = -n\log(\theta) - \left(\frac{1}{\theta}+1\right)n\widehat{\theta}$$

gives

$$\frac{\mathrm{d}\ell(\theta)}{\mathrm{d}\theta} = -\frac{n}{\theta} + \frac{n\widehat{\theta}}{\theta^2},$$

$$\frac{\mathrm{d}^2\ell(\theta)}{\mathrm{d}\theta^2} = \frac{n}{\theta^2} - \frac{2n\widehat{\theta}}{\theta^3},$$

$$\mathrm{E}\left(-\frac{\mathrm{d}^2\ell(\theta)}{\mathrm{d}\theta^2}\right) = -\frac{n}{\theta^2} + \frac{2n\,\mathrm{E}(\widehat{\theta})}{\theta^3} = -\frac{n}{\theta^2} + \frac{2n}{\theta^2} = \frac{n}{\theta^2}$$

and the CRLB is $\theta^2/n = 1/(np^2)$. We could have guessed this since the score is linear in $\widehat{\theta}$.

Exercise 12.10 (GG's MLE and CRLB) Let $x_1, \dots, x_n$ be a random sample from $x \in \mathbb{R}_+$ with p.d.f.

$$f_x(u) = p\lambda^{\nu} u^{\nu p-1}\exp(-\lambda u^p)/\Gamma(\nu),$$

where ν and p are known positive constants.
(a) Derive the MLE of λ.
(b) Is the MLE unbiased and consistent?
(c) For which function of λ does there exist an unbiased estimator attaining the CRLB?

Solution
(a) We have the log-likelihood

$$\ell(\lambda) = n\log(p/\Gamma(\nu)) + (\nu p-1)\sum_{i=1}^{n}\log(x_i) + n\nu\log(\lambda) - \lambda\sum_{i=1}^{n}x_i^p;$$

hence

$$\frac{\mathrm{d}\ell(\lambda)}{\mathrm{d}\lambda} = \frac{n\nu}{\lambda} - \sum_{i=1}^{n}x_i^p$$

and $\mathrm{d}^2\ell(\lambda)/\mathrm{d}\lambda^2 = -n\nu/\lambda^2 < 0$. Therefore, $\widehat{\lambda} = n\nu/\sum_{i=1}^{n}x_i^p = \nu/\overline{x^p}$, where $\overline{x^p}$ denotes the sample mean of x^p.
(b) Because $x^p \sim \mathrm{Gam}(\nu,\lambda)$ and $z := \sum_{i=1}^{n}x_i^p \sim \mathrm{Gam}(n\nu,\lambda)$, we have

$$\mathrm{E}\left(\frac{n\nu}{z}\right) = \frac{n\nu\lambda}{n\nu-1}\int_0^{\infty}\frac{\lambda^{n\nu-1}w^{n\nu-2}\mathrm{e}^{-\lambda w}}{\Gamma(n\nu-1)}\,\mathrm{d}w = \frac{n\nu\lambda}{n\nu-1}$$

for $n\nu > 1$. Otherwise, the integral is divergent. Therefore, the MLE is positively biased in finite samples, but asymptotically unbiased. It is consistent because $\overline{x^p} \to \mathrm{E}(x^p) = \nu/\lambda$ a.s. and hence $\widehat{\lambda} \to \lambda$ by the CMT (this is applicable since $\lambda = 0$ is ruled out).

(c) The MLE is invariant to reparameterizations, and we need to find a transformation of λ, say $g(\lambda)$, such that the score is linear in $g(\widehat{\lambda})$. Rewriting the score as

$$\frac{\mathrm{d}\ell(\lambda)}{\mathrm{d}\lambda} = n\nu\left(\frac{1}{\lambda} - \frac{1}{\widehat{\lambda}}\right),$$

we see that the function is $g(\lambda) = 1/\lambda$ and the required estimator is $1/\widehat{\lambda} = \overline{x^p}/\nu$.

Exercise 12.11 (Curved normal: MLE) Let $x_1, \dots, x_n$ be a random sample from a random variable x with mean $\mu > 0$.
(a) If $x \sim \mathrm{N}(\mu, \mu)$, obtain the MLE of μ.
(b) What if $x \sim \mathrm{N}(\mu, \mu^2)$?

Solution

In both cases, we are dealing with a curved normal density, a special case of the curved (hence nonregular) exponential family; see the introduction to Chapter 4.
(a) The log-likelihood is

$$\ell(\mu) = -\frac{n}{2}\log(2\pi) - \frac{n}{2}\log\left(\sigma^2\right) - \frac{\sum_{i=1}^n (x_i - \mu)^2}{2\sigma^2}$$

where $\sigma^2 = \mu$. As $\mu \to 0$, the function $\log\left(1/\sigma^2\right)$ goes to ∞ slower than $\left(1/\sigma^2\right)^p$ for any power $p > 0$. Since $-\sum_{i=1}^n x_i^2 < 0$ with probability 1, we have $\lim_{\mu\to 0} \ell(\mu) = -\infty$. As for the other points, we have

$$\begin{aligned}\frac{\mathrm{d}\ell(\mu)}{\mathrm{d}\mu} &= -\frac{n}{2\mu} + \frac{\sum_{i=1}^n (x_i - \mu)^2}{2\mu^2} + \frac{\sum_{i=1}^n (x_i - \mu)}{\mu} \\ &= -\frac{n}{2\mu} + \frac{\sum_{i=1}^n x_i^2 - 2\mu n\overline{x} + n\mu^2}{2\mu^2} + \frac{n\overline{x} - n\mu}{\mu} = -\frac{n}{2\mu} + \frac{\sum_{i=1}^n x_i^2}{2\mu^2} - \frac{n}{2}.\end{aligned}$$

Equating this to 0 and solving for $\widehat{\mu}$ gives the quadratic equation $\widehat{\mu}^2 + \widehat{\mu} - \overline{x^2} = 0$, where $\overline{x^2}$ is the sample mean of x_i^2. It has only one positive solution,

$$\widehat{\mu} = -\frac{1}{2} + \sqrt{\frac{1}{4} + \overline{x^2}}.$$

We have

$$\frac{\mathrm{d}^2\ell(\mu)}{\mathrm{d}\mu^2} = \frac{n}{2\mu^2} - \frac{n\overline{x^2}}{\mu^3} = \frac{n}{\mu^3}\left(\frac{\mu}{2} - \left(\widehat{\mu} + \frac{1}{2}\right)^2 + \frac{1}{4}\right) = \frac{n}{\mu^3}\left(\frac{\mu}{2} - \widehat{\mu} - \widehat{\mu}^2\right)$$

which is negative at $\mu = \widehat{\mu} > 0$, hence confirming $\widehat{\mu}$ as the MLE. Notice that $\widehat{\mu}$ is close to zero for $\overline{x^2} \approx 0$ and increases at the same rate as $\sqrt{\overline{x^2}}$.
(b) If $x \sim \mathrm{N}(\mu, \mu^2)$, then $\sigma^2 = \mu^2$ and the first equation of (a) becomes

$$\ell(\mu) = -\frac{n}{2}\log(2\pi) - n\log(\mu) - \frac{\sum_{i=1}^n (x_i - \mu)^2}{2\mu^2}.$$

Hence

$$\frac{\mathrm{d}\ell(\mu)}{\mathrm{d}\mu} = -\frac{n}{\mu} + \frac{\sum_{i=1}^{n}(x_i-\mu)^2}{\mu^3} + \frac{\sum_{i=1}^{n}(x_i-\mu)}{\mu^2}$$

$$= -\frac{n}{\mu} + \frac{n\overline{x^2} - 2\mu n\overline{x} + n\mu^2}{\mu^3} + \frac{n\overline{x} - n\mu}{\mu^2} = -\frac{n}{\mu} + \frac{n\overline{x^2}}{\mu^3} - \frac{n\overline{x}}{\mu^2},$$

and there is a unique positive solution to the MLE from $\widehat{\mu}^2 + \overline{x}\widehat{\mu} - \overline{x^2} = 0$, given by

$$\widehat{\mu} = -\frac{\overline{x}}{2} + \sqrt{\frac{\overline{x}^2}{4} + \overline{x^2}}.$$

It is a maximum, because

$$\frac{\mathrm{d}^2\ell(\mu)}{\mathrm{d}\mu^2} = \frac{n}{\mu^2} - \frac{3n\overline{x^2}}{\mu^4} + \frac{2n\overline{x}}{\mu^3}$$

$$= \frac{n}{\mu^4}\left(\mu^2 - 3\left(\left(\widehat{\mu} + \frac{\overline{x}}{2}\right)^2 - \frac{\overline{x}^2}{4}\right) + 2\overline{x}\mu\right)$$

$$= \frac{n}{\mu^4}\left(\mu^2 - 3\widehat{\mu}^2 - 3\overline{x}\widehat{\mu} + 2\overline{x}\mu\right)$$

is negative at $\mu = \widehat{\mu} > 0$. Notice that $\widehat{\mu}$ now depends on $\overline{x}$ too, and that the coefficient of variation is fixed at $\sigma/\mu = 1$.

Exercise 12.12 (Exponential's profile likelihood: nonregular case) Let $x_1, \ldots, x_n$ be a random sample from the p.d.f.

$$f_x(u) = \begin{cases} \lambda \exp(-\lambda(u-\alpha)) & (u > \alpha), \\ 0 & (\text{elsewhere}), \end{cases}$$

where $\lambda > 0$.

(a) Derive the MLE of λ, when it is known that $\alpha = 0$.

(b) Using the profile likelihood of λ, derive the MLEs for α and λ.

(c) What is the value of the score vector at the MLE?

(d) Is $\widehat{\alpha}$ unbiased?

(e) What does (d) imply for the expectation of the score from the profile likelihood of λ? Is this property shared by $\mathrm{E}\left(\partial\ell(\alpha,\lambda)/\partial\lambda\right)$?

Solution

(a) In the special case $\alpha = 0$, we have a regular exponential density. The likelihood is

$$L(\lambda) = \lambda^n \exp\left(-\lambda \sum_{i=1}^{n} x_i\right) = \lambda^n \exp\left(-n\lambda\overline{x}\right)$$

for $\lambda > 0$ and 0 elsewhere, so

$$\frac{\mathrm{d}\ell(\lambda)}{\mathrm{d}\lambda} = \frac{n}{\lambda} - n\overline{x} \quad \text{and} \quad \frac{\mathrm{d}^2\ell(\lambda)}{\mathrm{d}\lambda^2} = -\frac{n}{\lambda^2} < 0$$

imply that $\widehat{\lambda} = 1/\overline{x}$. Compare this with Exercise 12.10(a).

(b) We will follow a two-step procedure. We start by keeping λ fixed and maximizing $L(\alpha, \lambda)$ with respect to α, then we maximize this profile likelihood $L(\widehat{\alpha}, \lambda)$ with respect to λ. Defining the first order statistic $y_1 := \min_i \{x_i\}$,

$$L(\alpha, \lambda) = \lambda^n \exp\left(-\lambda \sum_{i=1}^{n} (x_i - \alpha)\right) 1_{y_1 \geqslant \alpha} = \lambda^n \exp(-\lambda n\overline{x} + \lambda n\alpha)\, 1_{y_1 \geqslant \alpha}.$$

This expression is maximized if α attains the largest possible value, hence $\widehat{\alpha} = y_1$ and the lower bound of the variate is estimated by the smallest observation. Now, maximizing $L(\widehat{\alpha}, \lambda)$, we calculate

$$\frac{\mathrm{d}\ell(\widehat{\alpha}, \lambda)}{\mathrm{d}\lambda} = \frac{n}{\lambda} - n\overline{x} + ny_1,$$

hence $\widehat{\lambda}^{-1} = \overline{x} - \min_i \{x_i\}$. The second derivative being $-n/\lambda^2 < 0$, this is a maximum. Notice that $\widehat{\lambda}$, the estimator of the scale, is location-invariant since we can write

$$\widehat{\lambda}^{-1} = \frac{1}{n} \sum_{j=1}^{n} \left(x_j - \min_i \{x_i\}\right) = \frac{1}{n} \sum_{j=1}^{n} \left((x_j - c) - \min_i \{(x_i - c)\}\right)$$

for any c.

(c) We have

$$\frac{\partial \ell(\alpha, \lambda)}{\partial \lambda} = \frac{n}{\lambda} - n\overline{x} + n\alpha,$$

which, evaluated at the MLE, gives $n(\overline{x} - y_1) - n\overline{x} + ny_1 = 0$. However, the likelihood is not differentiable with respect to α, because of the discontinuity of the indicator function. Condition 2 has been violated.

(d) The MLE of α is y_1, which cannot be unbiased since the observations are all larger than α. Using the p.d.f. of y_1 from Exercise 7.35,

$$\begin{aligned}
\mathrm{E}(y_1) &= \int_{\alpha}^{\infty} v n f_x(v)(1 - F_x(v))^{n-1}\, \mathrm{d}v \\
&= \int_{\alpha}^{\infty} v n\lambda \exp(-n\lambda(v - \alpha))\, \mathrm{d}v \\
&= \left[-v \exp(-n\lambda(v - \alpha))\right]_{\alpha}^{\infty} + \int_{\alpha}^{\infty} \exp(-n\lambda(v - \alpha))\, \mathrm{d}v = \alpha + \frac{1}{n\lambda},
\end{aligned}$$

where the bias is $1/(n\lambda) > 0$. Notice that, as in Exercise 12.8(d), the MLE y_1 is not asymptotically normal (it is a special case of the extreme-value distributions of Chapter 10).

(e) As a result of (d) and $\mathrm{E}(x_i - \alpha) = 1/\lambda$,

$$\mathrm{E}\left(\frac{\mathrm{d}\ell(\widehat{\alpha}, \lambda)}{\mathrm{d}\lambda}\right) = \frac{n}{\lambda} - n\,\mathrm{E}(\overline{x} - \alpha) + n\,\mathrm{E}(y_1 - \alpha)$$
$$= \frac{n}{\lambda} - \frac{n}{\lambda} + \frac{1}{\lambda} = \frac{1}{\lambda} > 0,$$

and the profile likelihood has a score which does *not* have mean zero. However,

$$\mathrm{E}\left(\frac{\partial \ell(\alpha, \lambda)}{\partial \lambda}\right) = \mathrm{E}\left(\frac{n}{\lambda} - n\overline{x} + n\alpha\right) = \frac{n}{\lambda} - n\,\mathrm{E}(\overline{x} - \alpha) = \frac{n}{\lambda} - \frac{n}{\lambda} = 0.$$

Exercise 12.13 (Neyman–Scott problem: inconsistent MLE) Consider the sample $\{\{y_{ij}\}_{i=1}^{n_1}\}_{j=1}^{n_2} \sim \mathrm{IN}(\mu_i, \sigma^2)$ where, although the data are independent, they are not identically distributed since the mean varies with i. We assume that $n_2 > 1$, and we suppose that σ^2 is the parameter of interest.
(a) Obtain the MLE of σ^2.
(b) Show that this MLE is inconsistent as $n_1 \to \infty$.
(c) What is the expectation of the score from the profile likelihood of σ^2?

Solution
(a) The likelihood is

$$L\left(\sigma^2, \mu_1, \ldots, \mu_{n_1}\right) = \prod_{i=1}^{n_1}\prod_{j=1}^{n_2} \frac{\exp\left(-\frac{1}{2\sigma^2}\left(y_{ij} - \mu_i\right)^2\right)}{\sqrt{2\pi\sigma^2}}$$
$$= \frac{\prod_{i=1}^{n_1} \exp\left(-\frac{1}{2\sigma^2}\sum_{j=1}^{n_2}\left(y_{ij} - \mu_i\right)^2\right)}{\left(2\pi\sigma^2\right)^{n_1 n_2/2}}$$
$$= \frac{\prod_{i=1}^{n_1}\left(\exp\left(-\frac{1}{2\sigma^2}\sum_{j=1}^{n_2}\left(y_{ij} - \overline{y}_i\right)^2\right)\exp\left(-\frac{1}{2\sigma^2}n_2\left(\overline{y}_i - \mu_i\right)^2\right)\right)}{\left(2\pi\sigma^2\right)^{n_1 n_2/2}},$$

where $\overline{y}_i := n_2^{-1}\sum_{j=1}^{n_2} y_{ij}$. This is the sufficiency factorization seen earlier. The likelihood is maximized with respect to μ_i by choosing $\widehat{\mu}_i = \overline{y}_i$. The profile likelihood is therefore

$$L_{\mathrm{p}}\left(\sigma^2\right) = \frac{\prod_{i=1}^{n_1}\exp\left(-\frac{1}{2\sigma^2}\sum_{j=1}^{n_2}\left(y_{ij} - \overline{y}_i\right)^2\right)}{\left(2\pi\sigma^2\right)^{n_1 n_2/2}} = \frac{\exp\left(-\frac{1}{2\sigma^2}\sum_{i=1}^{n_1}\sum_{j=1}^{n_2}\left(y_{ij} - \overline{y}_i\right)^2\right)}{\left(2\pi\sigma^2\right)^{n_1 n_2/2}},$$

and has the corresponding profile log-likelihood

$$\ell_{\mathrm{p}}\left(\sigma^2\right) = -\frac{n_1 n_2}{2}\log\left(2\pi\right) - \frac{n_1 n_2}{2}\log\left(\sigma^2\right) - \frac{1}{2\sigma^2}\sum_{i=1}^{n_1}\sum_{j=1}^{n_2}\left(y_{ij} - \overline{y}_i\right)^2.$$

Differentiating with respect to the parameter $\theta_1 := \sigma^2$ (the differentiation is done here with respect to the parameter σ^2 rather than its square root σ),

$$\frac{\mathrm{d}\ell_{\mathrm{p}}\left(\sigma^2\right)}{\mathrm{d}\sigma^2} = -\frac{n_1 n_2}{2\sigma^2} + \frac{1}{2\left(\sigma^2\right)^2} \sum_{i=1}^{n_1} \sum_{j=1}^{n_2} \left(y_{ij} - \overline{y}_i\right)^2$$

$$\frac{\mathrm{d}^2\ell_{\mathrm{p}}\left(\sigma^2\right)}{\left(\mathrm{d}\sigma^2\right)^2} = \frac{n_1 n_2}{2\sigma^4} - \frac{1}{\sigma^6} \sum_{i=1}^{n_1} \sum_{j=1}^{n_2} \left(y_{ij} - \overline{y}_i\right)^2$$

Hence

$$\widehat{\sigma}^2 = \frac{1}{n_1 n_2} \sum_{i=1}^{n_1} \sum_{j=1}^{n_2} \left(y_{ij} - \overline{y}_i\right)^2,$$

with corresponding second derivative at $\widehat{\sigma}^2$

$$\frac{n_1 n_2}{2\widehat{\sigma}^4} - \frac{n_1 n_2}{\widehat{\sigma}^4} = -\frac{n_1 n_2}{2\widehat{\sigma}^4} < 0$$

confirming a maximum at $\widehat{\sigma}^2$. We could have solved this part of the question by using matrices, following the route to be seen in Exercises 12.42 and 12.17, respectively.
(b) For any given i, we have $z_i := \sum_{j=1}^{n_2} \left(y_{ij} - \overline{y}_i\right)^2 / \sigma^2 \sim \chi^2\left(n_2 - 1\right)$ when $n_2 > 1$, as seen in Chapter 7. Furthermore, since $\{z_i\}_{i=1}^{n_1}$ is an independent sequence, we have

$$\frac{1}{\sigma^2} \sum_{i=1}^{n_1} \sum_{j=1}^{n_2} \left(y_{ij} - \overline{y}_i\right)^2 \sim \chi^2\left(n_1\left(n_2 - 1\right)\right)$$

by the reproductive property of the χ^2 distribution. From applying the SLLN to the decomposition in Exercise 10.32(a), as $n_1 \to \infty$ we get

$$\widehat{\sigma}^2 \to \lim_{n_1 \to \infty} \frac{\mathrm{E}\left(\chi^2\left(n_1\left(n_2 - 1\right)\right)\right)}{n_1 n_2} \sigma^2 = \left(1 - \frac{1}{n_2}\right) \sigma^2$$

with probability 1. Therefore, $\widehat{\sigma}^2$ will almost surely not converge to σ^2 when n_2 is finite. In fact, for small n_2, the inconsistency can be quite bad. This is a case where the parameter vector is not fixed as n_1 increases, which violates the assumption employed in the definition of $\boldsymbol{\theta}$ in the introduction. The number of nuisance parameters increases with n_1. This is called the *incidental-parameters problem*.
(c) Taking the expectation of the profile score from (a),

$$\mathrm{E}\left(\frac{\mathrm{d}\ell_{\mathrm{p}}\left(\sigma^2\right)}{\mathrm{d}\sigma^2}\right) = -\frac{n_1 n_2}{2\sigma^2} + \frac{1}{2\sigma^4} \mathrm{E}\left(\sum_{i=1}^{n_1} \sum_{j=1}^{n_2} \left(y_{ij} - \overline{y}_i\right)^2\right)$$

$$= -\frac{n_1 n_2}{2\sigma^2} + \frac{n_1\left(n_2 - 1\right)}{2\sigma^2} = -\frac{n_1}{2\sigma^2} \neq 0.$$

Exercise 12.14 (Laplace: MLE) Let $x_1, \dots, x_n$ be a random sample from the p.d.f.

$$f_x(u) = \frac{\lambda}{2} \exp(-\lambda|u - \alpha|),$$

where $\lambda > 0$.
(a) Find the MLE of α, when $\lambda = 1$.
(b) Find the MLE of α and λ, when both are unknown.

Solution
(a) In general, the likelihood is

$$L(\alpha, \lambda) = \frac{\lambda^n}{2^n} \exp\left(-\lambda \sum_{i=1}^{n} |x_i - \alpha|\right).$$

If λ is a known constant (1 or otherwise), maximizing the likelihood is tantamount to minimizing $\sum_{i=1}^{n} |x_i - \alpha|$ with respect to α. Whatever the distribution of x_i, the *empirical density* (the density implied by the EDF) for each x_i is $1/n$, or k/n if there are k ties for any value x_i, and $n^{-1} \sum_{i=1}^{n} |x_i - \alpha|$ is the expectation of $|x - \alpha|$ with respect to this EDF. We have already solved an analogous optimization problem in Exercise 3.18(b), and the solution is the empirical (or sample) median.
(b) As in Exercise 12.12, we use the profile likelihood. The first step is to maximize $L(\alpha, \lambda)$ with respect to α, getting $\widehat{\alpha}$ as the sample median. The second step is to maximize $L(\widehat{\alpha}, \lambda)$ with respect to λ. This yields $\widehat{\lambda}^{-1} = n^{-1} \sum_{i=1}^{n} |x_i - \widehat{\alpha}|$, the average of the absolute deviations from the sample median. Compare these with the usual sample mean and sample standard deviation that arise from the normal distribution, for example in Exercise 12.17.

Exercise 12.15 (EDF is the nonparametric MLE of the c.d.f.) Let $\{x_i\}_{i=1}^{n}$ be a random sample from a variate x with distribution F. Prove that the empirical distribution function, $\widehat{F}_n$, maximizes the *nonparametric likelihood*, defined by

$$L(F) := \prod_{i=1}^{n} \left(F(x_i) - F\left(x_i^-\right)\right).$$

Solution
Let y_i $(i = 1, \dots, k \leqslant n)$ represent the k distinct values of x in the sample. Let n_i be the number of tied (repeated) y_i values in the sample, such that $n_i \geqslant 1$ and $\sum_{i=1}^{k} n_i = n$. Then $L(F) = \prod_{i=1}^{k} p_i^{n_i}$, where $p_i := F(y_i) - F\left(y_i^-\right)$. Hence

$$\ell(F) := \log(L(F)) = \sum_{i=1}^{k} n_i \log(p_i) \equiv n \sum_{i=1}^{k} \widehat{p}_i \log(p_i),$$

where $\widehat{p}_i := n_i/n$ is the empirical density. The quantity $-\sum_{i=1}^{k} \widehat{p}_i \log(p_i)$ is the cross-entropy of p_i with respect to the EDF, and Exercise 4.42(b) showed that it is minimized with respect to p_i by taking $p_i = \widehat{p}_i$.

***Exercise 12.16 (Product-limit estimator of Kaplan and Meier)** Suppose that a journal receives a random sample of submitted academic papers in weekly batches at the start of every week. Its editor wishes to estimate the distribution $F_z(w)$ of the time z that an author waits for a decision on the suitability of his/her new submission. Suppose that submissions and decisions do not depend on the time of the year, and that data are available for $w = 1, 2, \dots, n$, where n is the maximum waiting time (in weeks). Denote the number of papers that remain awaiting a decision w weeks after submission by c_w, and denote the number of new decisions taken during week w of submission by d_w. By definition, $c_w > d_w$ for $w < n$, and $c_n = d_n > 0$.
(a) Is the stock of all papers awaiting decisions a random sample?
(b) Let $p_w := \Pr(z = w \mid z \geqslant w)$ be the hazard rate of $F_z(w)$, introduced in Exercise 2.18. Show that the nonparametric likelihood is

$$L(F) = \prod_{w=1}^{n} \left(p_w^{d_w} (1 - p_w)^{c_w - d_w} \right),$$

when profiled with respect to whether F is discrete or continuous. [Hint: Use sequential conditioning as in (12.5).]
(c) Find the nonparametric MLE (NP MLE) of F, known as the *Kaplan–Meier product-limit estimator*.

Solution

(a) This part of the question is about clarifying the sampling setup. One should distinguish submission (or calendar) time from the weeks waited. Although the weekly submitted batches are assumed to be a random sample, the complete stock of papers does not constitute a random sample. For example, the probability of accepting or rejecting papers submitted one week ago need not be the same as for papers that have survived in the stock for ten weeks, unless the distribution satisfies the no-memory property. This tells us that, as a first step, we should consider the hazard rate: the probability of a decision w weeks after submission, given that a paper has survived without a decision for w weeks.
(b) Because the NP MLE will be a discrete distribution, as in Exercise 12.15, we can restrict attention to discrete F when maximizing $L(F)$. The hazard rate $p_w := \Pr(z = w \mid z \geqslant w)$ is common to all submitted papers, because it is a property of the common F. It is the probability that a decision will be taken on any paper in week w of the submission. (Decisions are independent of the time of the year: editors don't go on holidays!) In such a week w, there are d_w decisions while $c_w - d_w$ are still awaiting decisions. These decisions are all independent, since the papers were submitted together in the same random batch w weeks ago, and since decisions on them are taken independently of one another. Thus, the joint probability that d_w decisions will be made in any given week w is the binomial

$$\binom{c_w}{d_w} p_w^{d_w} (1 - p_w)^{c_w - d_w},$$

conditionally on these papers having waited for a decision until week w. Sequential conditioning gives the required joint probability over the n weeks. The binomial coefficients are omitted from it, since they are multiplicative factors that are given (fixed) by the sample values and do not affect the optimization of L with respect to the p_w's.
(c) Because

$$\frac{\partial \log(L(F))}{\partial p_w} = \frac{d_w}{p_w} - \frac{c_w - d_w}{1 - p_w} \qquad (w = 1, 2, \dots, n),$$

with

$$\frac{\partial^2 \log(L(F))}{\partial p_w^2} = -\frac{d_w}{p_w^2} - \frac{c_w - d_w}{(1 - p_w)^2} < 0 \quad \text{and} \quad \frac{\partial^2 \log(L(F))}{\partial p_w \partial p_v} = 0 \quad (v \neq w),$$

we have $\widehat{p}_w = d_w / c_w$. This derivation is similar to that in Exercise 4.40, except that we have not treated explicitly p_n or $F_z(n) = 1$, for a reason that will become apparent at the end of this exercise. Now recall that $\widehat{p}_w$ is an estimator of the hazard rate p_w, which needs to be translated into an estimator of $F_z(w)$. By the invariance of the MLE to transformations, we can infer $\widehat{F}$ once we have a relation between F and p. By definition, the survival function is

$$1 - F_z(w) = \Pr(z > w) = \Pr(z > w, z > w - 1, \dots, z > 0),$$

since the composite event in the last probability is equivalent to $z > w$. By sequential conditioning, starting with $\Pr(z > 0) = 1$,

$$\begin{aligned} 1 - F_z(w) &= \Pr(z > w \mid z > w - 1) \Pr(z > w - 1 \mid z > w - 2) \cdots \Pr(z > 1 \mid z > 0) \\ &= \prod_{v=1}^{w} \Pr(z > v \mid z > v - 1) = \prod_{v=1}^{w} \Pr(z > v \mid z \geqslant v) = \prod_{v=1}^{w} (1 - p_v), \end{aligned}$$

so that

$$\widehat{F}_z(w) = 1 - \prod_{v=1}^{w} (1 - \widehat{p}_v) = 1 - \prod_{v=1}^{w} \left(1 - \frac{d_v}{c_v}\right).$$

We have $\widehat{F}_z(n) = 1$ since $c_n = d_n$.

Exercise 12.17 (Multivariate normal: MLE and its distribution) Let $\boldsymbol{x}_1, \dots, \boldsymbol{x}_n$ be a random sample from $\boldsymbol{x} \sim \mathrm{N}_k(\boldsymbol{\mu}, \boldsymbol{\Sigma})$, where $\boldsymbol{\Sigma}$ is nonsingular.
(a) Derive the MLEs for $\boldsymbol{\mu}$ and $\boldsymbol{\Sigma}$. [Hint: Use $\mathrm{d} \log |\boldsymbol{\Sigma}| = \operatorname{tr}(\boldsymbol{\Sigma}^{-1} \mathrm{d}\boldsymbol{\Sigma})$ and $\mathrm{d}\boldsymbol{\Sigma}^{-1} = -\boldsymbol{\Sigma}^{-1} (\mathrm{d}\boldsymbol{\Sigma}) \boldsymbol{\Sigma}^{-1}$.]
(b) Obtain the finite-sample distribution of the MLEs and their asymptotic distribution.

Solution
(a) We will use the sufficiency factorization in Exercise 9.17, which gives

$$L(\boldsymbol{\mu}, \boldsymbol{\Sigma}) = (2\pi)^{-kn/2} |\boldsymbol{\Sigma}|^{-n/2} \operatorname{etr}\left(-\frac{n}{2} \boldsymbol{\Sigma}^{-1} (\overline{\boldsymbol{x}} - \boldsymbol{\mu}) (\overline{\boldsymbol{x}} - \boldsymbol{\mu})' - \frac{n-1}{2} \boldsymbol{\Sigma}^{-1} \boldsymbol{S}\right),$$

where $\boldsymbol{S} := (n-1)^{-1}\sum_{i=1}^{n}(\boldsymbol{x}_i-\overline{\boldsymbol{x}})(\boldsymbol{x}_i-\overline{\boldsymbol{x}})'$ and $\operatorname{etr}(\cdot) \equiv \exp(\operatorname{tr}(\cdot))$. Note that $(\overline{\boldsymbol{x}}, \boldsymbol{S})$ is sufficient, but not minimal since $\boldsymbol{S}$ is symmetric (and hence contains $k(k-1)/2$ repeated elements). For any given positive definite $\boldsymbol{\Sigma}$, this likelihood is maximized by $\widehat{\boldsymbol{\mu}} = \overline{\boldsymbol{x}}$, which gives rise to the profile log-likelihood

$$\ell(\widehat{\boldsymbol{\mu}}, \boldsymbol{\Sigma}) = -\frac{kn}{2}\log(2\pi) - \frac{n}{2}\log|\boldsymbol{\Sigma}| - \frac{n-1}{2}\operatorname{tr}\left(\boldsymbol{\Sigma}^{-1}\boldsymbol{S}\right).$$

To find the $\widehat{\boldsymbol{\Sigma}}$ that minimizes $\ell(\widehat{\boldsymbol{\mu}}, \boldsymbol{\Sigma})$, consider the first differential:

$$\begin{aligned}
\mathrm{d}\ell(\widehat{\boldsymbol{\mu}}, \boldsymbol{\Sigma}) &= -\frac{n}{2}\,\mathrm{d}\log|\boldsymbol{\Sigma}| - \frac{n-1}{2}\operatorname{tr}\left(\left(\mathrm{d}\boldsymbol{\Sigma}^{-1}\right)\boldsymbol{S}\right)\\
&= -\frac{n}{2}\operatorname{tr}\left(\boldsymbol{\Sigma}^{-1}\,\mathrm{d}\boldsymbol{\Sigma}\right) + \frac{n-1}{2}\operatorname{tr}\left(\boldsymbol{\Sigma}^{-1}(\mathrm{d}\boldsymbol{\Sigma})\,\boldsymbol{\Sigma}^{-1}\boldsymbol{S}\right)\\
&= -\frac{n}{2}\operatorname{tr}\left(\boldsymbol{\Sigma}^{-1}\left(\boldsymbol{\Sigma} - \frac{n-1}{n}\boldsymbol{S}\right)\boldsymbol{\Sigma}^{-1}\,\mathrm{d}\boldsymbol{\Sigma}\right),
\end{aligned}$$

since $\operatorname{tr}(\boldsymbol{AB}) = \operatorname{tr}(\boldsymbol{BA})$. This yields

$$\widehat{\boldsymbol{\Sigma}} = \frac{1}{n}(n-1)\,\boldsymbol{S} = \frac{1}{n}\sum_{i=1}^{n}(\boldsymbol{x}_i-\overline{\boldsymbol{x}})(\boldsymbol{x}_i-\overline{\boldsymbol{x}})'.$$

It is a maximum because

$$\begin{aligned}
\mathrm{d}^2\ell(\widehat{\boldsymbol{\mu}}, \boldsymbol{\Sigma}) = &-\frac{n}{2}\operatorname{tr}\left(-\boldsymbol{\Sigma}^{-1}(\mathrm{d}\boldsymbol{\Sigma})\,\boldsymbol{\Sigma}^{-1}\left(\boldsymbol{I}_k - \frac{n-1}{n}\boldsymbol{S}\boldsymbol{\Sigma}^{-1}\right)\mathrm{d}\boldsymbol{\Sigma}\right)\\
&-\frac{n}{2}\operatorname{tr}\left(\boldsymbol{\Sigma}^{-1}\left(\frac{n-1}{n}\boldsymbol{S}\boldsymbol{\Sigma}^{-1}(\mathrm{d}\boldsymbol{\Sigma})\,\boldsymbol{\Sigma}^{-1}\right)\mathrm{d}\boldsymbol{\Sigma}\right)
\end{aligned}$$

and, writing $\boldsymbol{Z} := \widehat{\boldsymbol{\Sigma}}^{-1}\,\mathrm{d}\boldsymbol{\Sigma}$, we have

$$\mathrm{d}^2\ell(\widehat{\boldsymbol{\mu}}, \widehat{\boldsymbol{\Sigma}}) = 0 - \frac{n}{2}\operatorname{tr}\left(\boldsymbol{Z}^2\right) < 0$$

with probability 1.

Notice from Exercise 6.23 that $\operatorname{tr}\left(\boldsymbol{\Sigma}^{-1}\boldsymbol{S}\right)$ itself is also minimized by taking $\boldsymbol{\Sigma} \propto \boldsymbol{S}$. Notice also that the formula for the MLE of $\boldsymbol{\Sigma}$ is different if $\boldsymbol{\mu}$ is known and does not need to be estimated by $\overline{\boldsymbol{x}}$, in which case similar derivations (actually identical except for the sufficiency factorization) yield the MLE $\frac{1}{n}\sum_{i=1}^{n}(\boldsymbol{x}_i-\boldsymbol{\mu})(\boldsymbol{x}_i-\boldsymbol{\mu})'$.

(b) Exercises 9.18 and 9.20 give the finite-sample distribution of the MLEs: $\overline{\boldsymbol{x}} \sim \mathrm{N}_k(\boldsymbol{\mu}, \frac{1}{n}\boldsymbol{\Sigma})$ independently from $n\widehat{\boldsymbol{\Sigma}} \sim \mathrm{W}_k(n-1, \boldsymbol{\Sigma})$. Exercise 10.34 gives the asymptotic-normal formulation of the distribution of $\widehat{\boldsymbol{\Sigma}}$ as

$$\sqrt{n}\operatorname{vech}(\widehat{\boldsymbol{\Sigma}} - \boldsymbol{\Sigma}) \overset{a}{\sim} \mathrm{N}(\mathbf{0}_{(k+1)k/2}, \boldsymbol{\Omega}),$$

where $\boldsymbol{\Omega} := \operatorname{var}(\operatorname{vech}((\boldsymbol{x}-\boldsymbol{\mu})(\boldsymbol{x}-\boldsymbol{\mu})'))$, because $(n-1)/n \to 1$ and $\widehat{\boldsymbol{\Sigma}}$ is asymptotically equal to $\boldsymbol{S}$.

12.2 General properties of MLE, score, and information

Exercise 12.18 (MLE via profile) Assume that MLEs of $\boldsymbol{\theta}' := (\boldsymbol{\theta}_1', \boldsymbol{\theta}_2')$ exist. Prove that maximizing $L(\boldsymbol{\theta})$ by maximizing the profile likelihood gives rise to ML estimators.

Solution

For any given $\boldsymbol{\theta}_1$, we have

$$\widehat{\boldsymbol{\theta}}_2(\boldsymbol{\theta}_1) = \operatorname*{argsup}_{\boldsymbol{\theta}_2} L(\boldsymbol{\theta}_1, \boldsymbol{\theta}_2),$$

where the partial MLE usually depends on $\boldsymbol{\theta}_1$, hence the notation $\widehat{\boldsymbol{\theta}}_2(\boldsymbol{\theta}_1)$. Now, maximizing the profile likelihood $L(\boldsymbol{\theta}_1, \widehat{\boldsymbol{\theta}}_2(\boldsymbol{\theta}_1))$, we get

$$L(\widetilde{\boldsymbol{\theta}}_1, \widehat{\boldsymbol{\theta}}_2(\widetilde{\boldsymbol{\theta}}_1)) = \sup_{\boldsymbol{\theta}_1} L(\boldsymbol{\theta}_1, \widehat{\boldsymbol{\theta}}_2(\boldsymbol{\theta}_1))$$

and we need to show that $(\widetilde{\boldsymbol{\theta}}_1, \widehat{\boldsymbol{\theta}}_2(\widetilde{\boldsymbol{\theta}}_1))$ is a maximum-likelihood solution. This follows from

$$L(\widetilde{\boldsymbol{\theta}}_1, \widehat{\boldsymbol{\theta}}_2(\widetilde{\boldsymbol{\theta}}_1)) \geqslant L(\boldsymbol{\theta}_1, \widehat{\boldsymbol{\theta}}_2(\boldsymbol{\theta}_1)) \geqslant L(\boldsymbol{\theta}_1, \boldsymbol{\theta}_2),$$

the inequalities holding for all $\boldsymbol{\theta}_1$ and $\boldsymbol{\theta}_2$. But this is the definition of the maximization of the likelihood. Therefore, $(\widetilde{\boldsymbol{\theta}}_1, \widehat{\boldsymbol{\theta}}_2(\widetilde{\boldsymbol{\theta}}_1))$ are the required MLEs $(\widehat{\boldsymbol{\theta}}_1, \widehat{\boldsymbol{\theta}}_2)$.

Exercise 12.19 (Existence of MLE) Let $L(\boldsymbol{\theta})$ be a likelihood which is a continuous function of the parameter vector $\boldsymbol{\theta} \in \Theta$, and assume that Θ is a compact subset of $\mathbb{R}^m$. Prove that a maximum-likelihood estimator $\widehat{\boldsymbol{\theta}}$ exists with probability 1.

Solution

We start by remarking that we need to prove the existence of one or more MLEs, and that we are not concerned here about conditions for uniqueness, such as the strict concavity of $L(\boldsymbol{\theta})$. We also note that we need to prove this result only for the first parameter of the m-dimensional vector $\boldsymbol{\theta}$, and that the existence of a maximum with respect to the remaining components follows by applying the same proof recursively to the profile likelihood. We know from Exercise 12.18 that the maximum thus obtained is the MLE, and we therefore take $m = 1$ here without loss of generality.

Take any arbitrary sequence $\theta_1, \dots, \theta_j \in \Theta$, where j is possibly infinite, and define

$$\widehat{\theta}_1 := \operatorname*{argsup}_{i=1,\dots,j} \{L(\theta_i)\}.$$

By the continuity of the likelihood function, $\widehat{\theta}_1$ belongs to the closure of the set $\{\theta_i\}_{i=1}^j$. Since the parameter space Θ is compact, the closure of the set $\{\theta_i\}_{i=1}^j$ is a subset of Θ. Therefore, there exist local MLEs $\widehat{\theta}_1 \in \Theta$. Repeating the process for all arbitrary sequences in Θ, the global MLEs follow by taking $\widehat{\theta} := \sup\{\widehat{\theta}_1, \widehat{\theta}_2, \dots\}$. The compactness of Θ ensures that $\widehat{\theta} \in \Theta$.

Exercise 12.20 (Invariance of MLE) Let $L(\boldsymbol{\theta})$ be a likelihood that is maximized by $\widehat{\boldsymbol{\theta}}$. Suppose that $\boldsymbol{g}(\boldsymbol{\theta})$ is a function which is not necessarily of the same dimension as $\boldsymbol{\theta}$ (hence not necessarily invertible). Prove that the MLE of $\boldsymbol{g}(\boldsymbol{\theta})$ is $\boldsymbol{g}(\widehat{\boldsymbol{\theta}})$, if the latter is defined.

Solution

The equality $\boldsymbol{g}(\boldsymbol{\theta}) = \boldsymbol{c}$ defines a set of values $\Theta_{\boldsymbol{c}} := \{\boldsymbol{\theta} : \boldsymbol{g}(\boldsymbol{\theta}) = \boldsymbol{c}\} \subseteq \Theta$. Therefore, for any $\boldsymbol{c}$,

$$\sup_{\boldsymbol{\theta}\in\Theta_{\boldsymbol{c}}} L(\boldsymbol{\theta}) \leqslant \sup_{\boldsymbol{\theta}\in\Theta} L(\boldsymbol{\theta}) = L(\widehat{\boldsymbol{\theta}}) = \sup_{\boldsymbol{\theta}\in\Theta_{\boldsymbol{g}(\widehat{\boldsymbol{\theta}})}} L(\boldsymbol{\theta}),$$

where the last equality follows because $\widehat{\boldsymbol{\theta}}$ belongs to the set $\{\boldsymbol{\theta} : \boldsymbol{g}(\boldsymbol{\theta}) = \boldsymbol{g}(\widehat{\boldsymbol{\theta}})\}$. Since this inequality holds for all $\boldsymbol{c}$, we have that $\boldsymbol{c} = \boldsymbol{g}(\widehat{\boldsymbol{\theta}})$ is a value that maximizes the likelihood.

Exercise 12.21 (Information-matrix equivalence) Assume that the log-likelihood $\ell(\boldsymbol{\theta})$ of the $m \times 1$ parameter vector $\boldsymbol{\theta}$ is continuously differentiable twice, and that the expectations of $\ell(\boldsymbol{\theta})$ and its first two derivatives exist. This is Condition 2 of the introduction. Prove that:

(a) $\mathrm{E}(\boldsymbol{q}(\boldsymbol{\theta})) = \mathbf{0}_m$, where $\boldsymbol{q}(\boldsymbol{\theta}) := \partial\ell(\boldsymbol{\theta})/\partial\boldsymbol{\theta}$ is the score vector;

(b) $\mathrm{var}(\boldsymbol{q}(\boldsymbol{\theta})) = \boldsymbol{\mathcal{I}}(\boldsymbol{\theta})$, where $\boldsymbol{\mathcal{I}}(\boldsymbol{\theta})$ is Fisher's information about $\boldsymbol{\theta}$.

Solution

(a) We start by assuming that $\boldsymbol{X}$ is a continuous variate. Then,

$$\begin{aligned}\mathrm{E}(\boldsymbol{q}(\boldsymbol{\theta})) &= \int_{\boldsymbol{W}\in\mathcal{X}} \frac{\partial \log(f_{\boldsymbol{X}}(\boldsymbol{W}))}{\partial\boldsymbol{\theta}} f_{\boldsymbol{X}}(\boldsymbol{W})\,\mathrm{d}\boldsymbol{W} \\ &= \int_{\boldsymbol{W}\in\mathcal{X}} \frac{\partial f_{\boldsymbol{X}}(\boldsymbol{W})}{\partial\boldsymbol{\theta}}\,\mathrm{d}\boldsymbol{W} \\ &= \frac{\partial\left(\int_{\boldsymbol{W}\in\mathcal{X}} f_{\boldsymbol{X}}(\boldsymbol{W})\,\mathrm{d}\boldsymbol{W}\right)}{\partial\boldsymbol{\theta}} = \frac{\partial(1)}{\partial\boldsymbol{\theta}} = \mathbf{0}_m,\end{aligned}$$

where interchange of differentiation and integration is allowed since the likelihood is a continuously differentiable function of $\boldsymbol{\theta}$ (hence the support $\mathcal{X}$ of $\boldsymbol{X}$ does not depend on $\boldsymbol{\theta}$). The same result is obtained when $\boldsymbol{X}$ is discrete (but having a p.d.f. which is a continuously differentiable function of $\boldsymbol{\theta}$, as assumed), upon replacing the integral by a sum.

(b) Differentiating both sides of

$$\int_{\boldsymbol{W}\in\mathcal{X}} \frac{\partial \log(f_{\boldsymbol{X}}(\boldsymbol{W}))}{\partial\boldsymbol{\theta}} f_{\boldsymbol{X}}(\boldsymbol{W})\,\mathrm{d}\boldsymbol{W} = \mathbf{0}_m$$

(both column vectors) with respect to the row vector $\boldsymbol{\theta}'$ gives

$$\int_{\boldsymbol{W}\in\mathcal{X}} \frac{\partial^2 \log(f_{\boldsymbol{X}}(\boldsymbol{W}))}{\partial\boldsymbol{\theta}\partial\boldsymbol{\theta}'} f_{\boldsymbol{X}}(\boldsymbol{W})\,\mathrm{d}\boldsymbol{W} + \int_{\boldsymbol{W}\in\mathcal{X}} \frac{\partial \log(f_{\boldsymbol{X}}(\boldsymbol{W}))}{\partial\boldsymbol{\theta}} \frac{\partial f_{\boldsymbol{X}}(\boldsymbol{W})}{\partial\boldsymbol{\theta}'}\,\mathrm{d}\boldsymbol{W} = \mathbf{O}_{m,m},$$

where we are again allowed to interchange the differentiation and integration. The matrix of second partial derivatives is the Hessian $\boldsymbol{\mathcal{H}}$, and the corresponding integral is its expectation, so this becomes

$$\begin{aligned}\mathrm{E}(-\mathcal{H}) &= \int_{\boldsymbol{W}\in\mathcal{X}} \frac{\partial \log(f_{\boldsymbol{X}}(\boldsymbol{W}))}{\partial \boldsymbol{\theta}} \frac{\partial \log(f_{\boldsymbol{X}}(\boldsymbol{W}))}{\partial \boldsymbol{\theta}'} f_{\boldsymbol{X}}(\boldsymbol{W})\,\mathrm{d}\boldsymbol{W} \\ &= \mathrm{E}\left(\frac{\partial \log(f_{\boldsymbol{X}}(\boldsymbol{X}))}{\partial \boldsymbol{\theta}} \frac{\partial \log(f_{\boldsymbol{X}}(\boldsymbol{X}))}{\partial \boldsymbol{\theta}'}\right) = \mathrm{E}\left(\boldsymbol{q}(\boldsymbol{\theta})\,\boldsymbol{q}(\boldsymbol{\theta})'\right) = \mathrm{var}(\boldsymbol{q}(\boldsymbol{\theta}))\end{aligned}$$

since $\mathrm{E}(\boldsymbol{q}(\boldsymbol{\theta})) = \mathbf{0}_m$ from (a). The stated result follows from the definition of Fisher's information as $\boldsymbol{\mathcal{I}} := \mathrm{E}(-\boldsymbol{\mathcal{H}})$. Again, the same outcome is obtained when replacing integrals by sums, for $\boldsymbol{X}$ discrete.

Exercise 12.22 (Martingale representation of the score) Assume that the log-likelihood $\ell(\boldsymbol{\theta})$ of the $m \times 1$ parameter vector $\boldsymbol{\theta}$ is continuously differentiable and that the expectations of $\ell(\boldsymbol{\theta})$ and its derivative exist. Using the general decomposition of log-likelihoods

$$\ell(\boldsymbol{\theta}) = \sum_{i=1}^{n} \log\left(f_{\boldsymbol{x}}(\boldsymbol{x}_i \mid \boldsymbol{x}_{i-1}, \dots, \boldsymbol{x}_1)\right)$$

which was given in (12.5), prove that

$$\mathrm{E}(\boldsymbol{q}_n(\boldsymbol{\theta}) \mid \boldsymbol{x}_{n-1}, \dots, \boldsymbol{x}_1) = \boldsymbol{q}_{n-1}(\boldsymbol{\theta}),$$

where $\boldsymbol{q}_i(\boldsymbol{\theta})$ is the score based on the first i observations.

Solution

Differentiating the log-likelihood decomposition, we get

$$\boldsymbol{q}_n(\boldsymbol{\theta}) = \sum_{i=1}^{n} \boldsymbol{\delta}_i(\boldsymbol{\theta}),$$

where $\boldsymbol{\delta}_i(\boldsymbol{\theta}) := \partial \log\left(f_{\boldsymbol{x}}(\boldsymbol{x}_i \mid \boldsymbol{x}_{i-1}, \dots, \boldsymbol{x}_1)\right)/\partial \boldsymbol{\theta}$; hence

$$\mathrm{E}(\boldsymbol{q}_n(\boldsymbol{\theta}) \mid \boldsymbol{x}_{n-1}, \dots, \boldsymbol{x}_1) = \sum_{i=1}^{n-1} \boldsymbol{\delta}_i(\boldsymbol{\theta}) + \mathrm{E}(\boldsymbol{\delta}_n(\boldsymbol{\theta}) \mid \boldsymbol{x}_{n-1}, \dots, \boldsymbol{x}_1).$$

The last conditional expectation is zero by the same method as in Exercise 12.21(a); hence

$$\mathrm{E}(\boldsymbol{q}_n(\boldsymbol{\theta}) \mid \boldsymbol{x}_{n-1}, \dots, \boldsymbol{x}_1) = \sum_{i=1}^{n-1} \boldsymbol{\delta}_i(\boldsymbol{\theta}) = \boldsymbol{q}_{n-1}(\boldsymbol{\theta}).$$

An alternative way of writing this representation of the score is

$$\boldsymbol{q}_j(\boldsymbol{\theta}) = \boldsymbol{q}_{j-1}(\boldsymbol{\theta}) + \boldsymbol{\delta}_j(\boldsymbol{\theta}), \qquad j = 1, \dots, n.$$

This representation is known as a *martingale* when $\mathrm{E}(\boldsymbol{q})$ exists, as is assumed. Comparing it with the random walk in Exercise 10.42, here the sequence $\{\boldsymbol{\delta}_n(\boldsymbol{\theta})\}$ is not necessarily i.i.d.

Exercise 12.23 (Lower bound for estimators' variance: one parameter) Let $\widetilde{\theta}$ be

an estimator of the scalar parameter θ of a model which satisfies the regularity conditions given in the introduction, and let $\mathcal{I}$ be Fisher's information about the parameter θ. Assume that the first two moments of $\widetilde{\theta}$ exist.
(a) Prove that $\mathrm{dE}(\widetilde{\theta})/\,\mathrm{d}\theta = \operatorname{cov}(\widetilde{\theta}, q(\theta))$.
(b) Prove that $\operatorname{var}(\widetilde{\theta}) \geqslant (\mathrm{dE}(\widetilde{\theta})/\,\mathrm{d}\theta)^2/\mathcal{I}$. When does equality hold?
(c) What happens when $\widetilde{\theta}$ is unbiased?

Solution
(a) As in Exercise 12.21, assume that $\boldsymbol{X}$ is continuous (the proof follows the same steps for $\boldsymbol{X}$ discrete). Differentiating $\mathrm{E}(\widetilde{\theta})$ with respect to θ, we get

$$\frac{\mathrm{dE}(\widetilde{\theta})}{\mathrm{d}\theta} = \frac{\mathrm{d}}{\mathrm{d}\theta}\int_{\boldsymbol{W}\in\mathcal{X}} \widetilde{\theta} f_{\boldsymbol{X}}(\boldsymbol{W})\,\mathrm{d}\boldsymbol{W} = \int_{\boldsymbol{W}\in\mathcal{X}} \widetilde{\theta}\,\frac{\mathrm{d}f_{\boldsymbol{X}}(\boldsymbol{W})}{\mathrm{d}\theta}\,\mathrm{d}\boldsymbol{W},$$

where we have interchanged the derivative and integral by using the regularity conditions, and where we have used the fact that $\widetilde{\theta}$ is an estimator and hence a function of the data alone (and not of the unknown θ). Using the definition of the score in terms of the log-likelihood,

$$\begin{aligned}\frac{\mathrm{dE}(\widetilde{\theta})}{\mathrm{d}\theta} &= \int_{\boldsymbol{W}\in\mathcal{X}} \widetilde{\theta}\,\frac{\mathrm{d}\log\left(f_{\boldsymbol{X}}(\boldsymbol{W})\right)}{\mathrm{d}\theta} f_{\boldsymbol{X}}(\boldsymbol{W})\,\mathrm{d}\boldsymbol{W} \\ &= \int_{\boldsymbol{W}\in\mathcal{X}} \widetilde{\theta} q(\theta) f_{\boldsymbol{X}}(\boldsymbol{W})\,\mathrm{d}\boldsymbol{W} = \mathrm{E}(\widetilde{\theta} q(\theta)).\end{aligned}$$

We know from the information-matrix equivalence that $\mathrm{E}(q(\theta)) = 0$, so that $\mathrm{E}(\widetilde{\theta} q(\theta)) = \operatorname{cov}(\widetilde{\theta}, q(\theta))$.
(b) We are required to link this covariance to the variances of $q(\theta)$ (which is $\mathcal{I}$) and $\widetilde{\theta}$. This is done by means of their correlation

$$\rho^2_{\widetilde{\theta},q(\theta)} \equiv \frac{\left(\operatorname{cov}(\widetilde{\theta}, q(\theta))\right)^2}{\operatorname{var}(\widetilde{\theta})\operatorname{var}(q(\theta))} \leqslant 1,$$

where the Cauchy–Schwarz inequality has been used, and it becomes an equality if and only if the two variates are linearly related with probability 1. The result follows by substituting for $\operatorname{cov}(\widetilde{\theta}, q(\theta))$ and $\operatorname{var}(q(\theta))$, then multiplying both sides of the inequality by $\operatorname{var}(\widetilde{\theta})$.
(c) When $\widetilde{\theta}$ is unbiased, $\mathrm{E}(\widetilde{\theta}) = \theta$. Hence, $\mathrm{dE}(\widetilde{\theta})/\,\mathrm{d}\theta = 1$ and $\operatorname{var}(\widetilde{\theta}) \geqslant 1/\mathcal{I}$. This is the Cramér–Rao lower bound for one parameter.

***Exercise 12.24 (Cramér–Rao lower bound)** Let $\widetilde{\boldsymbol{\theta}}$ be an unbiased estimator of the m-dimensional parameter vector $\boldsymbol{\theta}$ of a model which satisfies the regularity conditions given in the introduction to this chapter, and let $\boldsymbol{\mathcal{I}}$ be Fisher's information about $\boldsymbol{\theta}$. Prove that $\operatorname{var}(\widetilde{\boldsymbol{\theta}}) - \boldsymbol{\mathcal{I}}^{-1}$ is positive semidefinite, and that $\operatorname{var}(\widetilde{\boldsymbol{\theta}}) = \boldsymbol{\mathcal{I}}^{-1}$ if and only if the score is linearly related to $\widetilde{\boldsymbol{\theta}}$ with probability 1. [Hint: Use linear combinations as in Exercise 6.21.]

Solution

Again, we prove this for $\boldsymbol{X}$ continuous, and the same steps then follow for $\boldsymbol{X}$ discrete. We are told that $\boldsymbol{\theta} = \mathrm{E}(\widetilde{\boldsymbol{\theta}})$, so differentiating both sides (both are column vectors) with respect to the row vector $\boldsymbol{\theta}'$ gives

$$\boldsymbol{I}_m = \frac{\partial}{\partial \boldsymbol{\theta}'} \int_{\boldsymbol{W}\in\mathcal{X}} \widetilde{\boldsymbol{\theta}} f_{\boldsymbol{X}}(\boldsymbol{W})\,\mathrm{d}\boldsymbol{W} = \int_{\boldsymbol{W}\in\mathcal{X}} \widetilde{\boldsymbol{\theta}} \frac{\partial f_{\boldsymbol{X}}(\boldsymbol{W})}{\partial \boldsymbol{\theta}'}\,\mathrm{d}\boldsymbol{W}$$

$$= \int_{\boldsymbol{W}\in\mathcal{X}} \widetilde{\boldsymbol{\theta}} \frac{\partial \log(f_{\boldsymbol{X}}(\boldsymbol{W}))}{\partial \boldsymbol{\theta}'} f_{\boldsymbol{X}}(\boldsymbol{W})\,\mathrm{d}\boldsymbol{W} = \mathrm{E}(\widetilde{\boldsymbol{\theta}}\boldsymbol{q}(\boldsymbol{\theta})') = \mathrm{cov}(\widetilde{\boldsymbol{\theta}}, \boldsymbol{q}(\boldsymbol{\theta}))$$

by the regularity conditions and by $\mathrm{E}(\boldsymbol{q}(\boldsymbol{\theta})) = \mathbf{0}_m$. In order to follow the steps of Exercise 12.23 and to be able to use the Cauchy–Schwarz inequality, we need to consider the correlation of arbitrary nonrandom linear combinations of $\widetilde{\boldsymbol{\theta}}$ and $\boldsymbol{q}(\boldsymbol{\theta})$; compare with Exercise 6.21. Remember that we need to show that

$$\boldsymbol{a}'\left(\mathrm{var}(\widetilde{\boldsymbol{\theta}}) - (\mathrm{var}(\boldsymbol{q}(\boldsymbol{\theta})))^{-1}\right)\boldsymbol{a} \geqslant 0$$

for any arbitrary nonrandom vector $\boldsymbol{a}$. Define $\boldsymbol{a}$ and $\boldsymbol{c}$ to be any nonrandom and nonzero $m \times 1$ vectors. Then, by the same method as that of Exercise 6.3,

$$\mathrm{var}(\boldsymbol{a}'\widetilde{\boldsymbol{\theta}}) = \boldsymbol{a}'\,\mathrm{var}(\widetilde{\boldsymbol{\theta}})\boldsymbol{a},$$

$$\mathrm{var}(\boldsymbol{c}'\boldsymbol{q}(\boldsymbol{\theta})) = \boldsymbol{c}'\,\mathrm{var}(\boldsymbol{q}(\boldsymbol{\theta}))\boldsymbol{c} = \boldsymbol{c}'\boldsymbol{\mathcal{I}}\boldsymbol{c},$$

$$\mathrm{cov}(\boldsymbol{a}'\widetilde{\boldsymbol{\theta}}, \boldsymbol{c}'\boldsymbol{q}(\boldsymbol{\theta})) = \boldsymbol{a}'\,\mathrm{cov}(\widetilde{\boldsymbol{\theta}}, \boldsymbol{q}(\boldsymbol{\theta}))\boldsymbol{c} = \boldsymbol{a}'\boldsymbol{I}_m\boldsymbol{c} = \boldsymbol{a}'\boldsymbol{c}.$$

These are all 1×1 quantities, so the Cauchy–Schwarz inequality gives

$$\rho^2_{\boldsymbol{a}'\widetilde{\boldsymbol{\theta}},\boldsymbol{c}'\boldsymbol{q}(\boldsymbol{\theta})} \equiv \frac{(\boldsymbol{a}'\boldsymbol{c})^2}{\boldsymbol{a}'\,\mathrm{var}(\widetilde{\boldsymbol{\theta}})\boldsymbol{a} \times \boldsymbol{c}'\boldsymbol{\mathcal{I}}\boldsymbol{c}} \leqslant 1.$$

Choosing $\boldsymbol{c} = \boldsymbol{\mathcal{I}}^{-1}\boldsymbol{a}$ and then rearranging the inequality gives the required result. The equality holds if and only if $\boldsymbol{a}'\widetilde{\boldsymbol{\theta}}$ and $\boldsymbol{c}'\boldsymbol{q}(\boldsymbol{\theta})$ can be written as linear transformations of one another, a.s.; that is, if and only if they are linearly related with probability 1.

Exercise 12.25 (KLIC, $\boldsymbol{\mathcal{I}}$, sufficiency, and identification) Assume that the following holds in an open neighborhood of a point $\boldsymbol{\theta}_1 \in \Theta$. The log-likelihood $\ell(\boldsymbol{\theta}) := \log(L(\boldsymbol{\theta}))$ is almost-surely continuously differentiable twice, and the expectations of $\ell(\boldsymbol{\theta})$ and its first two derivatives exist. This is weaker than Condition 2 of the introduction. Assume further that in this neighborhood of $\boldsymbol{\theta}_1$, the third derivatives of $\ell(\boldsymbol{\theta})$ exist almost surely and are bounded by a function of $\boldsymbol{X}$ (the data) having finite expectations. Finally, assume that the parameter space Θ is convex.

(a) Define $\mathrm{KL}(L(\boldsymbol{\theta}_1), L(\boldsymbol{\theta}_2)) := \mathrm{E}_1(\ell(\boldsymbol{\theta}_1) - \ell(\boldsymbol{\theta}_2))$, where $\boldsymbol{\theta}_1$ and $\boldsymbol{\theta}_2$ are two points in Θ and the expectation is taken with respect to the density implied by $\ell(\boldsymbol{\theta}_1)$. Prove that, for

$\boldsymbol{\theta}_1, \boldsymbol{\theta}_2$ in an arbitrarily small neighborhood,

$$\mathrm{KL}\left(L\left(\boldsymbol{\theta}_1\right), L\left(\boldsymbol{\theta}_2\right)\right)=\frac{1}{2}\left(\boldsymbol{\theta}_2-\boldsymbol{\theta}_1\right)' \boldsymbol{\mathcal{I}}\left(\boldsymbol{\theta}_1\right)\left(\boldsymbol{\theta}_2-\boldsymbol{\theta}_1\right)+o\left(\left\|\boldsymbol{\theta}_2-\boldsymbol{\theta}_1\right\|^2\right).$$

(b) Let $\boldsymbol{z}$ be a statistic which is a function of the data $\boldsymbol{X}$; then define $L_{\boldsymbol{z}}(\boldsymbol{\theta}):=f_{\boldsymbol{z}}(\boldsymbol{z})$ and $\ell_{\boldsymbol{z}}(\boldsymbol{\theta}):=\log \left(L_{\boldsymbol{z}}(\boldsymbol{\theta})\right)$. Assume that

$$\boldsymbol{\mathcal{I}}_{\boldsymbol{z}}(\boldsymbol{\theta}):=\mathrm{E}_{\boldsymbol{X}}\left(-\frac{\partial^2 \ell_{\boldsymbol{z}}(\boldsymbol{\theta})}{\partial \boldsymbol{\theta} \partial \boldsymbol{\theta}'}\right)$$

exists. Prove that: (i) $\boldsymbol{\mathcal{I}}-\boldsymbol{\mathcal{I}}_{\boldsymbol{z}}$ is positive semidefinite, (ii) $\boldsymbol{\mathcal{I}}_{\boldsymbol{z}}=\boldsymbol{\mathcal{I}}$ if and only if $\boldsymbol{z}$ is sufficient, and (iii) $\boldsymbol{\mathcal{I}}_{\boldsymbol{z}}=\mathbf{O}$ if and only if $\boldsymbol{z}$ ancillary. [Hint: Apply (a) to Exercise 6.30(b).]
(c) Prove that if the parameter vector $\boldsymbol{\theta}$ is identified, then $\boldsymbol{\mathcal{I}}$ is nonsingular.

Solution
(a) Using Taylor's theorem (see Section A.4) to expand $\ell(\boldsymbol{\theta}_2)$ locally around the point $\boldsymbol{\theta}_1$, we have

$$\begin{aligned}\ell\left(\boldsymbol{\theta}_2\right)= & \ell\left(\boldsymbol{\theta}_1\right)+\left(\boldsymbol{\theta}_2-\boldsymbol{\theta}_1\right)' \boldsymbol{q}\left(\boldsymbol{\theta}_1\right) \\ & +\frac{1}{2}\left(\boldsymbol{\theta}_2-\boldsymbol{\theta}_1\right)' \boldsymbol{\mathcal{H}}\left(\boldsymbol{\theta}_1\right)\left(\boldsymbol{\theta}_2-\boldsymbol{\theta}_1\right)+o_p\left(\left\|\boldsymbol{\theta}_2-\boldsymbol{\theta}_1\right\|^2\right),\end{aligned}$$

where we use the shorthand o_p to indicate a function of $\boldsymbol{X}$ containing the third derivatives of ℓ. Rearranging and taking expectations gives

$$\begin{aligned}\mathrm{E}_1\left(\ell\left(\boldsymbol{\theta}_1\right)-\ell\left(\boldsymbol{\theta}_2\right)\right)= & -\left(\boldsymbol{\theta}_2-\boldsymbol{\theta}_1\right)' \mathrm{E}_1\left(\boldsymbol{q}\left(\boldsymbol{\theta}_1\right)\right) \\ & -\frac{1}{2}\left(\boldsymbol{\theta}_2-\boldsymbol{\theta}_1\right)' \mathrm{E}_1\left(\boldsymbol{\mathcal{H}}\left(\boldsymbol{\theta}_1\right)\right)\left(\boldsymbol{\theta}_2-\boldsymbol{\theta}_1\right)+o\left(\left\|\boldsymbol{\theta}_2-\boldsymbol{\theta}_1\right\|^2\right),\end{aligned}$$

where the order of the remainder follows by the existence of a bounding function of $\boldsymbol{X}$ with finite expectations. The convexity of Θ is needed so that we can find a hyperrectangle, bounded by $\boldsymbol{\theta}_1$ and $\boldsymbol{\theta}_2$, at which we can evaluate the elements of these derivatives in the remainder. Then, the required result follows by the information-matrix equivalence.

Notice the resemblance of the resulting KL formula to that in Exercise 8.12, even though we have not assumed normality here. Notice also that

$$\left.\frac{\partial^2 \mathrm{KL}\left(L\left(\boldsymbol{\theta}_1\right), L\left(\boldsymbol{\theta}_2\right)\right)}{\partial \boldsymbol{\theta}_2 \partial \boldsymbol{\theta}_2'}\right|_{\boldsymbol{\theta}_2=\boldsymbol{\theta}_1}=\boldsymbol{\mathcal{I}}\left(\boldsymbol{\theta}_1\right),$$

so that we are able to obtain Fisher's information matrix from differentiating the definition of KLIC twice and evaluating at $\boldsymbol{\theta}_2=\boldsymbol{\theta}_1$, without requiring the additional assumptions (further than the weakened Condition 2) used for the expansion in part (a).
(b) We know from Exercise 6.30(b) that the marginal and joint KLICs satisfy

$$\mathrm{KL}\left(L_{\boldsymbol{z}}\left(\boldsymbol{\theta}_1\right), L_{\boldsymbol{z}}\left(\boldsymbol{\theta}_2\right)\right) \leqslant \mathrm{KL}\left(L\left(\boldsymbol{\theta}_1\right), L\left(\boldsymbol{\theta}_2\right)\right),$$

so part (a) here implies that

$$\left(\boldsymbol{\theta}_2-\boldsymbol{\theta}_1\right)' \boldsymbol{\mathcal{I}}_{\boldsymbol{z}}\left(\boldsymbol{\theta}_1\right)\left(\boldsymbol{\theta}_2-\boldsymbol{\theta}_1\right) \leqslant\left(\boldsymbol{\theta}_2-\boldsymbol{\theta}_1\right)' \boldsymbol{\mathcal{I}}\left(\boldsymbol{\theta}_1\right)\left(\boldsymbol{\theta}_2-\boldsymbol{\theta}_1\right)$$

for any arbitrary sequence of $\boldsymbol{\theta}_2$ in a shrinking neighborhood of any $\boldsymbol{\theta}_1 \in \Theta$; that is, $\mathcal{I} - \mathcal{I}_{\boldsymbol{z}}$ is positive semidefinite as required in (i). Furthermore, Exercise 6.30(b) implies that the marginal and joint KLICs are equal if and only if the distribution of $\boldsymbol{X}$ conditional on $\boldsymbol{z}$ is the same almost surely for both $\boldsymbol{\theta}_1$ and $\boldsymbol{\theta}_2$, namely when $\boldsymbol{z}$ is a sufficient statistic, thus yielding (ii). Finally, the marginal $\mathrm{KL}(L_{\boldsymbol{z}}(\boldsymbol{\theta}_1), L_{\boldsymbol{z}}(\boldsymbol{\theta}_2)) = 0$ if and only if the marginal distribution of $\boldsymbol{z}$ is the same whether the density has parameters $\boldsymbol{\theta}_1$ or $\boldsymbol{\theta}_2$, in other words, when $\boldsymbol{z}$ does not depend on $\boldsymbol{\theta}$ and is therefore ancillary as required in (iii). As in the discussion at the end of Exercise 6.30, note that $\mathcal{I}_{\boldsymbol{z}} = \mathbf{O}$ does not mean that $\boldsymbol{z}$ contains no information about $\boldsymbol{\theta}$. It can contribute information but only insofar as it affects the distribution of $\boldsymbol{X} \mid \boldsymbol{z}$.

(c) The parameter vector is identified if and only if $f_{\boldsymbol{X}}(\boldsymbol{X};\boldsymbol{\theta}_1) = f_{\boldsymbol{X}}(\boldsymbol{X};\boldsymbol{\theta}_2)$ with probability 0 for all $\boldsymbol{\theta}_1 \neq \boldsymbol{\theta}_2$, which means that $\mathrm{KL}(L(\boldsymbol{\theta}_1), L(\boldsymbol{\theta}_2))$ is strictly positive for all distinct $\boldsymbol{\theta}_1, \boldsymbol{\theta}_2 \in \Theta$. Taking any $\boldsymbol{\theta}_2$ in an arbitrarily small neighborhood of $\boldsymbol{\theta}_1$ (but excluding the point $\boldsymbol{\theta}_1$ itself) and using part (a) implies that $\mathcal{I}(\boldsymbol{\theta}_1)$ is positive definite for all $\boldsymbol{\theta}_1 \in \Theta$. Notice that there is some analogy with the idea of the completeness of a *statistic*: identification of the *parameter* vector implies that there is no combination of its elements that gives zero information, apart from the null combination itself.

Exercise 12.26 (Local sufficiency of the score) Assume that the log-likelihood $\ell(\boldsymbol{\theta}) := \log(L(\boldsymbol{\theta}))$ is almost-surely continuously differentiable twice for any $\boldsymbol{\theta}_1, \boldsymbol{\theta}_2$ in a small neighborhood belonging to a convex parameter space Θ. Prove the local sufficiency of the score.

Solution

For any two such vectors $\boldsymbol{\theta}_1$ and $\boldsymbol{\theta}_2$, we can expand $\log(L(\boldsymbol{\theta}_1)/L(\boldsymbol{\theta}_2))$ to first order, as in Exercise 12.25(a). We get

$$\ell(\boldsymbol{\theta}_1) - \ell(\boldsymbol{\theta}_2) = -(\boldsymbol{\theta}_2 - \boldsymbol{\theta}_1)' \boldsymbol{q}(\boldsymbol{\theta}_1) + O_p\left(\|\boldsymbol{\theta}_2 - \boldsymbol{\theta}_1\|^2\right),$$

and the ratio of likelihoods depends on the data only through $\boldsymbol{q}(\boldsymbol{\theta}_1)$, to first order. But Neyman's factorization theorem implies that the ratio of likelihoods depends only on the sufficient statistic and on $\boldsymbol{\theta}_1, \boldsymbol{\theta}_2$, so this reveals the score as the locally sufficient statistic. We will revisit this in Chapter 14, and Exercise 14.23 will consider the factorization again.

Exercise 12.27 (Consistency of MLE) Let $\boldsymbol{x}$ be a $k \times 1$ variate whose density $f_{\boldsymbol{x}}$ is determined by the $m \times 1$ vector of unknown parameters $\boldsymbol{\theta}$. Assume that $\mathrm{E}(\log(f_{\boldsymbol{x}}(\boldsymbol{x})))$ exists and is a continuous function of $\boldsymbol{\theta}$. Suppose that we have a random sample $\{\boldsymbol{x}_i\}_{i=1}^n$, and that Conditions 1 and 3 given in the chapter introduction are satisfied.

(a) Prove that $n^{-1}\sum_{i=1}^n \log(f_{\boldsymbol{x}}(\boldsymbol{x}_i))$ converges a.s. to $\mathrm{E}(\log(f_{\boldsymbol{x}}(\boldsymbol{x})))$.

(b) Prove that the MLE $\widehat{\boldsymbol{\theta}}$ is strongly consistent.

(c) Can Condition 1(ii) be relaxed, while retaining the result in (b)? What about Condition 3?

Solution

(a) We start by remarking that the MLE may not be unique when $n < \infty$, but that this exercise will establish that all MLEs converge to the single true value $\boldsymbol{\theta}$ as $n \to \infty$. First, at each sample point $\boldsymbol{x}_i$, define a transformation from $f_{\boldsymbol{x}}(\boldsymbol{x}_i)$ to $y_i := -\log(f_{\boldsymbol{x}}(\boldsymbol{x}_i))$. The sequence $\{\boldsymbol{x}_i\}_{i=1}^n$ is i.i.d., and so is the transformed $\{y_i\}_{i=1}^n$. Furthermore, $\mathrm{E}(y)$ exists by assumption, so the SLLN (for example, Exercise 10.26) implies that $\overline{y} \to \mathrm{E}(y)$ almost surely; that is, the sample entropy converges a.s. to the true entropy:

$$\Pr\left(\lim_{n\to\infty} -\frac{1}{n}\sum_{i=1}^{n}\log\left(f_{\boldsymbol{x}}(\boldsymbol{x}_i)\right) = -\mathrm{E}\left(\log\left(f_{\boldsymbol{x}}(\boldsymbol{x})\right)\right)\right) = 1.$$

(b) We saw in Exercise 4.42(b) that the population entropy is minimized by taking expectations with respect to the true density $f_{\boldsymbol{x}}$ and its true parameters $\boldsymbol{\theta}$, since the cross-entropy exceeds the entropy. This value $\boldsymbol{\theta}$ is unique because the parameter vector is identified (which follows from Condition 3). Now, the sample entropy equals $-n^{-1}\ell(\boldsymbol{\theta})$ and, by the definition of the MLE, it is minimized by $\widehat{\boldsymbol{\theta}}$ for any given n. Since we have assumed that the log-likelihood (hence the sample entropy) and its limit are both continuous in the parameters, the minimizers of the sample entropy converge to the unique minimizer of $-\mathrm{E}\left(\log(f_{\boldsymbol{x}}(\boldsymbol{x}))\right)$ a.s., that is, $\widehat{\boldsymbol{\theta}} \to \boldsymbol{\theta}$ with probability 1. Note that this continuity is required to achieve the uniformity (in n) inherent in a.s. convergence.

(c) Yes. We needed Condition 1(ii) to establish the existence of the MLE for any fixed $n < \infty$; see Exercise 12.19. When dealing with asymptotics, we can replace Condition 1(ii) with Condition 1(ii′): $\boldsymbol{\theta}$ belongs to the interior of the parameter space Θ. In the context of the current exercise, the latter condition is weaker because it allows Θ to be unbounded (for example $\mathbb{R}^m$) and/or open. For any finite n, this may not be sufficient to guarantee the existence of the MLE, as we saw in Exercise 12.5. However, the new condition is sufficient for (a) and (b) when $n \to \infty$, since convergence will occur within a compact subset of Θ that includes the true $\boldsymbol{\theta}$.

Yes, Condition 3 can also be relaxed, to apply only in an open neighborhood of the true $\boldsymbol{\theta}$; see Exercise 12.25(c).

Exercise 12.28 (Asymptotic sufficiency of the MLE, and its linearity in the score) Assume that Conditions 1(i), 1(ii′), 2, and 3 of the chapter introduction are satisfied, the last two in an open neighborhood of the true $\boldsymbol{\theta}$. Assume further that the MLE is weakly consistent ($\widehat{\boldsymbol{\theta}} \xrightarrow{p} \boldsymbol{\theta}$) and that the following WLLN holds for $\boldsymbol{\mathcal{H}}$: for every $\epsilon > 0$, there exists a neighborhood $B_\epsilon(\boldsymbol{\theta})$ of the true $\boldsymbol{\theta}$ such that

$$\lim_{n\to\infty}\Pr\left(\sup_{\boldsymbol{\theta}_1\in B_\epsilon(\boldsymbol{\theta})}\left\|\boldsymbol{\mathcal{I}}(\boldsymbol{\theta})^{-1}\boldsymbol{\mathcal{H}}(\boldsymbol{\theta}_1) + \boldsymbol{I}_m\right\| \geqslant \epsilon\right) = 0.$$

Notice that a random (i.i.d.) sample has not been assumed here. Prove that:

(a) the MLE is asymptotically sufficient for $\boldsymbol{\theta}$;

(b) the MLE is asymptotically linear in the score vector.

Solution

(a) This property may seem to follow intuitively from Exercise 12.25: given the conditions here, the MLE exists (hence we can take $\boldsymbol{\theta}_1 = \widehat{\boldsymbol{\theta}}$ in Exercise 12.25) and satisfies $\boldsymbol{q}(\widehat{\boldsymbol{\theta}}) = \mathbf{0}$ asymptotically for the derivations in Exercise 12.25(a). However, we need additional conditions. Analyzing the second-order remainder term more closely,

$$\ell(\widehat{\boldsymbol{\theta}}) - \ell(\boldsymbol{\theta}) = -(\boldsymbol{\theta} - \widehat{\boldsymbol{\theta}})'\boldsymbol{q}(\widehat{\boldsymbol{\theta}}) - \frac{1}{2}(\boldsymbol{\theta} - \widehat{\boldsymbol{\theta}})'\boldsymbol{\mathcal{H}}(\overline{\boldsymbol{\theta}})(\boldsymbol{\theta} - \widehat{\boldsymbol{\theta}}),$$

where the linear term containing $\boldsymbol{q}(\widehat{\boldsymbol{\theta}})$ drops out asymptotically (or $\boldsymbol{q}(\widehat{\boldsymbol{\theta}}) = \mathbf{0}$ exactly if we assume Condition A from the introduction) and $\overline{\boldsymbol{\theta}}$ is some point in a hyperrectangle bounded by $\boldsymbol{\theta}$ and $\widehat{\boldsymbol{\theta}}$. We have $\overline{\boldsymbol{\theta}} \xrightarrow{p} \boldsymbol{\theta}$ by the consistency of the MLE, but we need to show that our assumptions allow us to replace $\boldsymbol{\mathcal{H}}(\overline{\boldsymbol{\theta}})$ asymptotically by $\mathrm{E}(\boldsymbol{\mathcal{H}}(\boldsymbol{\theta}))$ or equivalently $-\boldsymbol{\mathcal{I}}(\boldsymbol{\theta})$. The main difficulty is that $\boldsymbol{\mathcal{H}}(\cdot)$ is a random function *and* its argument $\overline{\boldsymbol{\theta}}$ is also random. Defining

$$\boldsymbol{Y} := \boldsymbol{\mathcal{I}}(\boldsymbol{\theta})^{-1}\boldsymbol{\mathcal{H}}(\overline{\boldsymbol{\theta}}) + \boldsymbol{I}_m,$$

we need to show that $\operatorname{plim} \boldsymbol{Y} = \mathbf{O}$. (We avoid writing $\operatorname{plim} \boldsymbol{\mathcal{H}}(\overline{\boldsymbol{\theta}}) = -\boldsymbol{\mathcal{I}}(\boldsymbol{\theta})$ because the latter tends to $-\infty$ as n increases.) For all $\epsilon > 0$,

$$\begin{aligned}\Pr\left(\|\boldsymbol{Y}\| \geqslant \epsilon\right) &= \Pr\left(\|\boldsymbol{Y}\| \geqslant \epsilon \text{ and } \overline{\boldsymbol{\theta}} \in B_\epsilon(\boldsymbol{\theta})\right) + \Pr\left(\|\boldsymbol{Y}\| \geqslant \epsilon \text{ and } \overline{\boldsymbol{\theta}} \notin B_\epsilon(\boldsymbol{\theta})\right) \\ &\leqslant \Pr\left(\|\boldsymbol{Y}\| \geqslant \epsilon \text{ and } \overline{\boldsymbol{\theta}} \in B_\epsilon(\boldsymbol{\theta})\right) + \Pr\left(\overline{\boldsymbol{\theta}} \notin B_\epsilon(\boldsymbol{\theta})\right) \\ &\leqslant \Pr\left(\sup_{\boldsymbol{\theta}_1 \in B_\epsilon(\boldsymbol{\theta})} \left\|\boldsymbol{\mathcal{I}}(\boldsymbol{\theta})^{-1}\boldsymbol{\mathcal{H}}(\boldsymbol{\theta}_1) + \boldsymbol{I}_m\right\| \geqslant \epsilon\right) + \Pr\left(\overline{\boldsymbol{\theta}} \notin B_\epsilon(\boldsymbol{\theta})\right),\end{aligned}$$

where the last two probabilities tend to zero by our WLLN for $\boldsymbol{\mathcal{H}}$ and by the consistency of the MLE, respectively. Hence, $\operatorname{plim} \boldsymbol{Y} = \mathbf{O}$ and

$$\ell(\widehat{\boldsymbol{\theta}}) - \ell(\boldsymbol{\theta}) - \frac{1}{2}(\boldsymbol{\theta} - \widehat{\boldsymbol{\theta}})'\boldsymbol{\mathcal{I}}(\boldsymbol{\theta})(\boldsymbol{\theta} - \widehat{\boldsymbol{\theta}}) \xrightarrow{p} 0$$

by Slutsky's lemma (Exercise 10.18). Therefore, asymptotically, the ratio of likelihoods depends on the data only through $\widehat{\boldsymbol{\theta}}$, and Neyman's factorization implies the sufficiency of $\widehat{\boldsymbol{\theta}}$.

The reader is referred to Exercise 12.9(d) for an illustration of a Hessian satisfying our WLLN, and to Exercise 12.43(b) for a Hessian whose limiting distribution is not degenerate (hence satisfying no LLNs). The statement of our WLLN can be simplified if we are willing to assume the existence and boundedness of third-order derivatives and to use Taylor's theorem with an extra term as a remainder. Note that our WLLN is weaker than the uniform weak convergence that holds if $B_\epsilon(\boldsymbol{\theta})$ is the same for all ϵ.

(b) In a way, we have already derived this result in (a). The two results are essentially equivalent. Consider the following alternative derivation. Expand each component (see Section A.4 for the expansion of vector-valued functions) of the score in the neighborhood of the MLE:

$$q_j(\boldsymbol{\theta}) = q_j(\widehat{\boldsymbol{\theta}}) + \left.\frac{\partial q_j(\boldsymbol{\theta})}{\partial \boldsymbol{\theta}'}\right|_{\boldsymbol{\theta}=\overline{\boldsymbol{\theta}}_j} (\boldsymbol{\theta} - \widehat{\boldsymbol{\theta}}) \equiv \boldsymbol{e}_j' \boldsymbol{\mathcal{H}}(\overline{\boldsymbol{\theta}}_j)(\boldsymbol{\theta} - \widehat{\boldsymbol{\theta}})$$

for $j = 1, \dots, m$ and $\boldsymbol{e}_j$ the elementary vector with 1 in its j-th row and zeros elsewhere. By the same arguments as in (a), $\boldsymbol{\mathcal{H}}(\overline{\boldsymbol{\theta}}_j)$ and $-\boldsymbol{\mathcal{I}}(\boldsymbol{\theta})$ are asymptotically interchangeable with probability tending to 1, giving

$$\boldsymbol{q}(\boldsymbol{\theta}) = \boldsymbol{\mathcal{I}}(\boldsymbol{\theta})(\widehat{\boldsymbol{\theta}} - \boldsymbol{\theta})\left(1 + o_p(1)\right).$$

Because $\boldsymbol{\mathcal{I}}(\boldsymbol{\theta})$ is nonrandom, the required linearity has been established. An immediate implication of this linear relation is that the CRLB is achieved whenever $\widehat{\boldsymbol{\theta}}$ is asymptotically unbiased.

Exercise 12.29 (BAN, the MLE!) Assume that the conditions of Exercise 12.28 hold. Additionally, assume that the sample of $m \times 1$ vectors $\{\boldsymbol{x}_n\}$ is random. Prove that $\widehat{\boldsymbol{\theta}} \overset{a}{\sim} \mathrm{N}(\boldsymbol{\theta}, \boldsymbol{\mathcal{I}}^{-1})$, that is, the MLE is best asymptotically normal.

Solution

Exercise 12.28(b) linked the MLE to the score by

$$\boldsymbol{\mathcal{I}}^{-1/2}\boldsymbol{q}(\boldsymbol{\theta}) = \boldsymbol{\mathcal{I}}^{1/2}(\widehat{\boldsymbol{\theta}} - \boldsymbol{\theta})\left(1 + o_p(1)\right).$$

Linear combinations of normals are also normal, so we need only to establish that

$$\boldsymbol{\mathcal{I}}^{-1/2}\boldsymbol{q}(\boldsymbol{\theta}) \overset{a}{\sim} \mathrm{N}(\boldsymbol{0}, \boldsymbol{I}_m)$$

for $\boldsymbol{q}$ evaluated at the true $\boldsymbol{\theta}$, and the required result follows.

First, the i.i.d. assumption on the $\{\boldsymbol{x}_n\}$ implies that the $\{\partial \log(f_{\boldsymbol{x}}(\boldsymbol{x}_n))/\partial\boldsymbol{\theta}\}$ are also i.i.d., and we can apply the multivariate CLT of Exercise 10.29 to their sample average,

$$\frac{1}{n}\boldsymbol{q}(\boldsymbol{\theta}) = \frac{1}{n}\sum_{i=1}^{n} \frac{\partial \log\left(f_{\boldsymbol{x}}(\boldsymbol{x}_i)\right)}{\partial \boldsymbol{\theta}},$$

if their first two moments exist. Condition 2 implies the information-matrix equivalence, hence the existence of the mean and variance per observation as $\mathrm{E}(\partial \log(f_{\boldsymbol{x}}(\boldsymbol{x}_i))/\partial\boldsymbol{\theta}) = \boldsymbol{0}$ and $\mathrm{var}(\partial \log(f_{\boldsymbol{x}}(\boldsymbol{x}_i))/\partial\boldsymbol{\theta}) = n^{-1}\boldsymbol{\mathcal{I}}$, respectively. Since, by assumption, this condition holds in the neighborhood of the true $\boldsymbol{\theta}$, we have

$$\frac{1}{\sqrt{n}}\boldsymbol{q}(\boldsymbol{\theta}) \overset{a}{\sim} \mathrm{N}\left(\boldsymbol{0}, \frac{1}{n}\boldsymbol{\mathcal{I}}\right),$$

as required.

12.3 Likelihood for normal linear model

Exercise 12.30 (Likelihood and MLE) Consider the normal linear model

$$\boldsymbol{y} = \boldsymbol{X}\boldsymbol{\beta} + \boldsymbol{\varepsilon}, \qquad \boldsymbol{\varepsilon} \sim \mathrm{N}(\mathbf{0}, \sigma^2 \boldsymbol{I}_n),$$

where n is the sample size, $\boldsymbol{y}$ and $\boldsymbol{\varepsilon}$ are $n \times 1$ random vectors, $\boldsymbol{X}$ is an $n \times k$ matrix of k nonrandom regressors (for example, as a result of conditioning on $\boldsymbol{X}$ as in Exercise 11.11(a)), $n > k$, and $\sigma^2 > 0$. Suppose that the rank of $\boldsymbol{X}$ is k, so that $\boldsymbol{X}'\boldsymbol{X}$ is positive definite.

(a) Derive the log-likelihood, score vector, and Hessian matrix for the $m = k + 1$ parameters $\boldsymbol{\theta}' := (\boldsymbol{\beta}', \sigma^2)$ of this model.

(b) Derive the MLEs $\widehat{\boldsymbol{\beta}}$ and $\widehat{\sigma}^2$ of the parameters.

(c) Calculate $\ell(\widehat{\boldsymbol{\beta}}, \widehat{\sigma}^2)$.

Solution

(a) To set up the likelihood, we can use either $\boldsymbol{\varepsilon} \sim \mathrm{N}(\mathbf{0}, \sigma^2 \boldsymbol{I}_n)$ or $\{\varepsilon_i\}_{i=1}^n \sim \mathrm{IN}(0, \sigma^2)$. The former route was taken in Exercise 11.11(a), so taking the latter route gives

$$L\left(\boldsymbol{\beta}, \sigma^2\right) = \prod_{i=1}^{n} \left(\frac{\exp\left(-\frac{1}{2\sigma^2}\varepsilon_i^2\right)}{\sigma\sqrt{2\pi}} \right) = \frac{\exp\left(-\frac{1}{2\sigma^2}\boldsymbol{\varepsilon}'\boldsymbol{\varepsilon}\right)}{(2\pi\sigma^2)^{n/2}}.$$

The expression is in terms of the unobservable $\boldsymbol{\varepsilon}$. Let us reformulate it in terms of the data ($\boldsymbol{y}$ and $\boldsymbol{X}$) that we can observe, and the parameters to be estimated, by using the defining equation of the linear model $\boldsymbol{y} - \boldsymbol{X}\boldsymbol{\beta} = \boldsymbol{\varepsilon}$. The log-likelihood is therefore

$$\begin{aligned}
\ell\left(\boldsymbol{\beta}, \sigma^2\right) &= \log\left(\frac{\exp\left(-\frac{1}{2\sigma^2}\left(\boldsymbol{y} - \boldsymbol{X}\boldsymbol{\beta}\right)'\left(\boldsymbol{y} - \boldsymbol{X}\boldsymbol{\beta}\right)\right)}{(2\pi\sigma^2)^{n/2}} \right) \\
&= -\frac{n}{2}\log\left(2\pi\right) - \frac{n}{2}\log\left(\sigma^2\right) - \frac{1}{2\sigma^2}\left(\boldsymbol{y} - \boldsymbol{X}\boldsymbol{\beta}\right)'\left(\boldsymbol{y} - \boldsymbol{X}\boldsymbol{\beta}\right).
\end{aligned}$$

Differentiating this quadratic function of $\boldsymbol{\beta}$ (see Section A.4), we have

$$\frac{\partial \ell\left(\boldsymbol{\beta}, \sigma^2\right)}{\partial \boldsymbol{\beta}} = \frac{1}{\sigma^2}\boldsymbol{X}'\left(\boldsymbol{y} - \boldsymbol{X}\boldsymbol{\beta}\right),$$

and the score is obtained by stacking this $k \times 1$ vector and the 1×1 derivative

$$\frac{\partial \ell\left(\boldsymbol{\beta}, \sigma^2\right)}{\partial \sigma^2} = -\frac{n}{2\sigma^2} + \frac{1}{2\sigma^4}\left(\boldsymbol{y} - \boldsymbol{X}\boldsymbol{\beta}\right)'\left(\boldsymbol{y} - \boldsymbol{X}\boldsymbol{\beta}\right).$$

Notice that the latter derivative is with respect to the parameter $\theta_{k+1} := \sigma^2$ rather than σ. To obtain the Hessian, we need to find the components of the $(k + 1) \times (k + 1)$ partitioned matrix

$$\mathcal{H} = \begin{pmatrix} \dfrac{\partial^2 \ell\left(\boldsymbol{\beta}, \sigma^2\right)}{\partial \boldsymbol{\beta}\partial \boldsymbol{\beta}'} & \dfrac{\partial^2 \ell\left(\boldsymbol{\beta}, \sigma^2\right)}{\partial \boldsymbol{\beta}\partial \sigma^2} \\ \dfrac{\partial^2 \ell\left(\boldsymbol{\beta}, \sigma^2\right)}{\partial \sigma^2\partial \boldsymbol{\beta}'} & \dfrac{\partial^2 \ell\left(\boldsymbol{\beta}, \sigma^2\right)}{(\partial \sigma^2)^2} \end{pmatrix}.$$

By differentiating the score vector again, we have the diagonal blocks

$$\mathcal{H}_{11} = -\frac{1}{\sigma^2}\boldsymbol{X}'\boldsymbol{X} \qquad \text{and} \qquad \mathcal{H}_{22} = \frac{n}{2\sigma^4} - \frac{1}{\sigma^6}(\boldsymbol{y} - \boldsymbol{X\beta})'(\boldsymbol{y} - \boldsymbol{X\beta});$$

and the off-diagonal column vector $\mathcal{H}_{12} = -\sigma^{-4}\boldsymbol{X}'(\boldsymbol{y} - \boldsymbol{X\beta}) = \mathcal{H}_{21}'$.
(b) The MLEs follow by solving for the score equal to a vector of zeros, then checking the second-order condition. Solving

$$\begin{pmatrix} \frac{1}{\widehat{\sigma}^2}\boldsymbol{X}'(\boldsymbol{y} - \boldsymbol{X}\widehat{\boldsymbol{\beta}}) \\ -\frac{n}{2\widehat{\sigma}^2} + \frac{1}{2\widehat{\sigma}^4}(\boldsymbol{y} - \boldsymbol{X}\widehat{\boldsymbol{\beta}})'(\boldsymbol{y} - \boldsymbol{X}\widehat{\boldsymbol{\beta}}) \end{pmatrix} = \begin{pmatrix} \mathbf{0}_k \\ 0 \end{pmatrix},$$

we get $\boldsymbol{X}'\boldsymbol{y} = \boldsymbol{X}'\boldsymbol{X}\widehat{\boldsymbol{\beta}}$ and $\widehat{\sigma}^2 = n^{-1}\widehat{\boldsymbol{\varepsilon}}'\widehat{\boldsymbol{\varepsilon}}$, where

$$\widehat{\boldsymbol{\varepsilon}} := \boldsymbol{y} - \boldsymbol{X}\widehat{\boldsymbol{\beta}}.$$

Note that $\widehat{\sigma}^2$ is the sample average of the squared residuals $\widehat{\varepsilon}_i^2$ $(i = 1, \dots, n)$. Note also that the matrix $\boldsymbol{X}$ is $n \times k$ and cannot be inverted. However, it is of full rank, so the $k \times k$ square matrix $\boldsymbol{X}'\boldsymbol{X}$ is invertible, and we can write $\widehat{\boldsymbol{\beta}}$ explicitly as $\widehat{\boldsymbol{\beta}} = (\boldsymbol{X}'\boldsymbol{X})^{-1}\boldsymbol{X}'\boldsymbol{y}$. (In terms of the *Moore–Penrose generalized inverse* of $\boldsymbol{X}$, denoted by $\boldsymbol{X}^+$, we have $\widehat{\boldsymbol{\beta}} = \boldsymbol{X}^+\boldsymbol{y}$.) The result on $\widehat{\boldsymbol{\beta}}$ helps us to expand $\widehat{\boldsymbol{\varepsilon}}'\widehat{\boldsymbol{\varepsilon}}$. To see this, write

$$\widehat{\boldsymbol{\varepsilon}}'\widehat{\boldsymbol{\varepsilon}} = (\boldsymbol{y} - \boldsymbol{X}\widehat{\boldsymbol{\beta}})'(\boldsymbol{y} - \boldsymbol{X}\widehat{\boldsymbol{\beta}}) = \boldsymbol{y}'\boldsymbol{y} - \boldsymbol{y}'\boldsymbol{X}\widehat{\boldsymbol{\beta}} - \widehat{\boldsymbol{\beta}}'\boldsymbol{X}'\boldsymbol{y} + \widehat{\boldsymbol{\beta}}'\boldsymbol{X}'\boldsymbol{X}\widehat{\boldsymbol{\beta}},$$

where $\boldsymbol{y}'\boldsymbol{X}\widehat{\boldsymbol{\beta}} = \widehat{\boldsymbol{\beta}}'\boldsymbol{X}'\boldsymbol{y}$ (by transposing this 1×1 quantity) and $\widehat{\boldsymbol{\beta}}'\boldsymbol{X}'\boldsymbol{X}\widehat{\boldsymbol{\beta}} = \widehat{\boldsymbol{\beta}}'\boldsymbol{X}'\boldsymbol{y}$ by the formula for $\widehat{\boldsymbol{\beta}}$, yielding

$$\widehat{\boldsymbol{\varepsilon}}'\widehat{\boldsymbol{\varepsilon}} = \boldsymbol{y}'\boldsymbol{y} - \widehat{\boldsymbol{\beta}}'\boldsymbol{X}'\boldsymbol{X}\widehat{\boldsymbol{\beta}}.$$

Finally, $\widehat{\mathcal{H}}$ is negative definite, because

$$\widehat{\mathcal{H}} = \begin{pmatrix} -\frac{1}{\widehat{\sigma}^2}\boldsymbol{X}'\boldsymbol{X} & -\frac{1}{\widehat{\sigma}^4}\boldsymbol{X}'\widehat{\boldsymbol{\varepsilon}} \\ -\frac{1}{\widehat{\sigma}^4}\widehat{\boldsymbol{\varepsilon}}'\boldsymbol{X} & \frac{n}{2\widehat{\sigma}^4} - \frac{1}{\widehat{\sigma}^6}\widehat{\boldsymbol{\varepsilon}}'\widehat{\boldsymbol{\varepsilon}} \end{pmatrix} = \begin{pmatrix} -\frac{1}{\widehat{\sigma}^2}\boldsymbol{X}'\boldsymbol{X} & \mathbf{0}_k \\ \mathbf{0}_k' & -\frac{n}{2\widehat{\sigma}^4} \end{pmatrix}$$

since the formula for the MLEs implies that $\widehat{\boldsymbol{\varepsilon}}'\widehat{\boldsymbol{\varepsilon}} = n\widehat{\sigma}^2$ and $\boldsymbol{X}'\widehat{\boldsymbol{\varepsilon}} = \boldsymbol{X}'\boldsymbol{y} - \boldsymbol{X}'\boldsymbol{X}\widehat{\boldsymbol{\beta}} = \mathbf{0}_k$.
(c) The maximized log-likelihood is

$$\ell(\widehat{\boldsymbol{\beta}}, \widehat{\sigma}^2) = -\frac{n}{2}\log(2\pi) - \frac{n}{2}\log(\widehat{\sigma}^2) - \frac{1}{2\widehat{\sigma}^2}\widehat{\boldsymbol{\varepsilon}}'\widehat{\boldsymbol{\varepsilon}} = -\frac{n}{2}(\log(2\pi) + 1) - \frac{n}{2}\log(\widehat{\sigma}^2),$$

where only the last term is random.

Exercise 12.31 (MLE properties) Consider the normal linear model of Exercise 12.30.
(a) Calculate the Cramér–Rao lower bound for the MLEs in this model.
(b) Derive the distribution of $\widehat{\boldsymbol{\beta}}$ for any $n > k$.
(c) Is $\widehat{\boldsymbol{\beta}}$ a BUE of $\boldsymbol{\beta}$?
(d) Prove that $\widehat{\boldsymbol{\beta}}$ is a consistent estimator of $\boldsymbol{\beta}$. Comment on the case $k = 1$.
(e) Derive an unbiased estimator of σ^2. Is it a BUE of σ^2? How does its MSE compare with $\mathrm{MSE}(\widehat{\sigma}^2)$ in terms of n and k?
(f) Show that $\widehat{\boldsymbol{\beta}}$ and $\widehat{\sigma}^2$ are independent.

(g) Calculate $\mathcal{I}(\boldsymbol{\theta})^{-1}\mathcal{H}(\widehat{\boldsymbol{\theta}})$, then show that $\mathcal{I}(\widehat{\boldsymbol{\theta}})^{-1}\mathcal{H}(\widehat{\boldsymbol{\theta}})$ is ancillary. Is $\mathcal{I}(\boldsymbol{\theta})^{-1}\mathcal{H}(\widehat{\boldsymbol{\theta}})$ ancillary?
(h) Verify that the score is asymptotically $\mathrm{N}(\mathbf{0}, \mathcal{I})$.

Solution

(a) To obtain the CRLB, we need to find $\mathcal{I} = \mathrm{E}(-\mathcal{H})$. Since $\boldsymbol{X}$ is a nonrandom matrix,

$$\mathrm{E}\left(-\mathcal{H}_{11}\right) = \mathrm{E}\left(\frac{1}{\sigma^2}\boldsymbol{X}'\boldsymbol{X}\right) = \frac{1}{\sigma^2}\boldsymbol{X}'\boldsymbol{X},$$

$$\mathrm{E}\left(-\mathcal{H}_{12}\right) = \mathrm{E}\left(-\mathcal{H}_{21}'\right) = \frac{1}{\sigma^4}\boldsymbol{X}'\,\mathrm{E}\left(\boldsymbol{\varepsilon}\right) = \mathbf{0}_k,$$

$$\mathrm{E}\left(-\mathcal{H}_{22}\right) = -\frac{n}{2\sigma^4} + \frac{\mathrm{E}\left(\boldsymbol{\varepsilon}'\boldsymbol{\varepsilon}\right)}{\sigma^6} = -\frac{n}{2\sigma^4} + \frac{\mathrm{E}\left(\sum_{i=1}^n \varepsilon_i^2\right)}{\sigma^6} = -\frac{n}{2\sigma^4} + \frac{n\sigma^2}{\sigma^6} = \frac{n}{2\sigma^4},$$

since $\mathrm{E}\left(\varepsilon_i^2\right) = \sigma^2$ for all i. Notice the difference between the expectations of the inner product $\mathrm{E}\left(\boldsymbol{\varepsilon}'\boldsymbol{\varepsilon}\right) = n\sigma^2$ and the outer product $\mathrm{E}\left(\boldsymbol{\varepsilon}\boldsymbol{\varepsilon}'\right) = \mathrm{var}(\boldsymbol{\varepsilon}) = \sigma^2\boldsymbol{I}_n$, related in matrix terms by

$$\mathrm{E}\left(\boldsymbol{\varepsilon}'\boldsymbol{\varepsilon}\right) = \mathrm{E}\left(\mathrm{tr}\left(\boldsymbol{\varepsilon}\boldsymbol{\varepsilon}'\right)\right) = \mathrm{tr}\left(\mathrm{E}\left(\boldsymbol{\varepsilon}\boldsymbol{\varepsilon}'\right)\right) = \mathrm{tr}\left(\sigma^2\boldsymbol{I}_n\right) = n\sigma^2.$$

Because $\mathcal{I}$ is a block-diagonal matrix, its inverse (the CRLB) is

$$\mathcal{I}^{-1} = \mathrm{diag}\left(\sigma^2\left(\boldsymbol{X}'\boldsymbol{X}\right)^{-1}, \frac{2\sigma^4}{n}\right),$$

and we note that $\boldsymbol{\beta}$ and σ^2 have an orthogonal parameterization.
(b) From Exercise 12.30(b), $\widehat{\boldsymbol{\beta}} = \left(\boldsymbol{X}'\boldsymbol{X}\right)^{-1}\boldsymbol{X}'\boldsymbol{y}$. Since $\boldsymbol{X}$ is fixed, the only random variable here is $\boldsymbol{y}$, which inherits its randomness from $\boldsymbol{\varepsilon}$ in $\boldsymbol{y} = \boldsymbol{X}\boldsymbol{\beta} + \boldsymbol{\varepsilon}$. Therefore

$$\widehat{\boldsymbol{\beta}} = \left(\boldsymbol{X}'\boldsymbol{X}\right)^{-1}\boldsymbol{X}'\left(\boldsymbol{X}\boldsymbol{\beta} + \boldsymbol{\varepsilon}\right) = \boldsymbol{\beta} + \left(\boldsymbol{X}'\boldsymbol{X}\right)^{-1}\boldsymbol{X}'\boldsymbol{\varepsilon}.$$

Even though it expresses $\widehat{\boldsymbol{\beta}}$ in terms of the unknown $\boldsymbol{\beta}$ and $\boldsymbol{\varepsilon}$, this decomposition is very useful for investigating the distributional properties of $\widehat{\boldsymbol{\beta}}$. Because $\boldsymbol{X}$ is fixed, $\widehat{\boldsymbol{\beta}}$ is just a linear transformation of the normally distributed vector $\boldsymbol{\varepsilon}$, so $\widehat{\boldsymbol{\beta}}$ is normal too. It has

$$\mathrm{E}\left(\widehat{\boldsymbol{\beta}}\right) = \mathrm{E}\left(\boldsymbol{\beta}\right) + \mathrm{E}\left(\left(\boldsymbol{X}'\boldsymbol{X}\right)^{-1}\boldsymbol{X}'\boldsymbol{\varepsilon}\right) = \boldsymbol{\beta} + \left(\boldsymbol{X}'\boldsymbol{X}\right)^{-1}\boldsymbol{X}'\,\mathrm{E}\left(\boldsymbol{\varepsilon}\right) = \boldsymbol{\beta},$$

showing that it is unbiased, and

$$\begin{aligned}
\mathrm{var}(\widehat{\boldsymbol{\beta}}) &= \mathrm{E}\left[\left(\widehat{\boldsymbol{\beta}} - \mathrm{E}(\widehat{\boldsymbol{\beta}})\right)\left(\widehat{\boldsymbol{\beta}} - \mathrm{E}(\widehat{\boldsymbol{\beta}})\right)'\right] = \mathrm{E}\left[\left(\widehat{\boldsymbol{\beta}} - \boldsymbol{\beta}\right)\left(\widehat{\boldsymbol{\beta}} - \boldsymbol{\beta}\right)'\right] \\
&= \mathrm{E}\left[\left(\left(\boldsymbol{X}'\boldsymbol{X}\right)^{-1}\boldsymbol{X}'\boldsymbol{\varepsilon}\right)\left(\boldsymbol{\varepsilon}'\boldsymbol{X}\left(\boldsymbol{X}'\boldsymbol{X}\right)^{-1}\right)\right] \\
&= \left(\boldsymbol{X}'\boldsymbol{X}\right)^{-1}\boldsymbol{X}'\,\mathrm{E}\left(\boldsymbol{\varepsilon}\boldsymbol{\varepsilon}'\right)\boldsymbol{X}\left(\boldsymbol{X}'\boldsymbol{X}\right)^{-1} \\
&= \left(\boldsymbol{X}'\boldsymbol{X}\right)^{-1}\boldsymbol{X}'\sigma^2\boldsymbol{I}_n\boldsymbol{X}\left(\boldsymbol{X}'\boldsymbol{X}\right)^{-1} = \sigma^2\left(\boldsymbol{X}'\boldsymbol{X}\right)^{-1}.
\end{aligned}$$

So $\widehat{\boldsymbol{\beta}} \sim \mathrm{N}(\boldsymbol{\beta}, \sigma^2(\boldsymbol{X}'\boldsymbol{X})^{-1})$ for any sample size $n > k$, not just asymptotically. Note

that if $\boldsymbol{X}$ were random and if it were feasible to condition on it without fixing $\boldsymbol{\varepsilon}$ (see Exercise 12.43(b) for a violation of this condition), then using the LIE would give $\operatorname{var}(\widehat{\boldsymbol{\beta}}) = \sigma^2 \operatorname{E}((\boldsymbol{X}'\boldsymbol{X})^{-1})$ which differs from the CRLB $\sigma^2(\operatorname{E}(\boldsymbol{X}'\boldsymbol{X}))^{-1}$; recall Jensen's inequality.
(c) There are two ways to show that $\widehat{\boldsymbol{\beta}}$ is a BUE of $\boldsymbol{\beta}$. First, we have just seen in (b) that the unbiased $\widehat{\boldsymbol{\beta}}$ achieves the CRLB given in (a), so $\widehat{\boldsymbol{\beta}}$ is a BUE of $\boldsymbol{\beta}$. This is no surprise, given that the score was linear in $\widehat{\boldsymbol{\beta}}$:

$$\frac{\partial \ell\left(\boldsymbol{\beta}, \sigma^2\right)}{\partial \boldsymbol{\beta}} = \frac{1}{\sigma^2}\boldsymbol{X}'\left(\boldsymbol{y} - \boldsymbol{X}\boldsymbol{\beta}\right) = \frac{1}{\sigma^2}\boldsymbol{X}'\boldsymbol{X}(\widehat{\boldsymbol{\beta}} - \boldsymbol{\beta}),$$

since $\boldsymbol{X}'\boldsymbol{y} = \boldsymbol{X}'\boldsymbol{X}\widehat{\boldsymbol{\beta}}$. Second, Exercises 11.11 and 11.15 can be used here. Since we are dealing with a member of the exponential family, where $\widehat{\boldsymbol{\beta}}, \widehat{\sigma}^2$ form a complete sufficient statistic ($\boldsymbol{X}$ is fixed here), it follows by the Lehmann–Scheffé theorem that $\widehat{\boldsymbol{\beta}}$ is *the* BUE of $\boldsymbol{\beta}$ with probability 1.
(d) To establish consistency, recall from Exercise 12.30(a) that the sample is i.i.d., so that Condition 3 of the introduction is satisfied and the information grows with n. Hence, $\operatorname{var}(\widehat{\boldsymbol{\beta}})$ tends to zero and, given that the bias is also zero, $\operatorname{plim}\widehat{\boldsymbol{\beta}} = \boldsymbol{\beta}$. When $k = 1$,

$$\operatorname{var}(\widehat{\beta}) = \frac{\sigma^2}{\sum_{i=1}^n x_i^2} = \frac{\sigma^2}{n\,\overline{x^2}},$$

where $\overline{x^2} > 0$ denotes the sample average of x_i^2 values. As $n \to \infty$, we have $\operatorname{var}(\widehat{\beta}) \to 0$ at least at a rate $1/n$ (assuming that x_n does not tend to 0, which we will illustrate in the solution of Exercise 14.16(c)).
(e) Define the symmetric idempotent $\boldsymbol{P} := \boldsymbol{X}(\boldsymbol{X}'\boldsymbol{X})^{-1}\boldsymbol{X}'$ (sometimes called the *hat matrix* because it transforms $\boldsymbol{y}$ into $\widehat{\boldsymbol{y}} = \boldsymbol{P}\boldsymbol{y}$) and its complement $\boldsymbol{M} := \boldsymbol{I}_n - \boldsymbol{P}$. The estimated residual is

$$\widehat{\boldsymbol{\varepsilon}} = \boldsymbol{y} - \widehat{\boldsymbol{y}} = \boldsymbol{\varepsilon} + \boldsymbol{X}(\boldsymbol{\beta} - \widehat{\boldsymbol{\beta}}) = \boldsymbol{\varepsilon} - \boldsymbol{X}\left(\boldsymbol{X}'\boldsymbol{X}\right)^{-1}\boldsymbol{X}'\boldsymbol{\varepsilon} = \boldsymbol{M}\boldsymbol{\varepsilon},$$

since $\widehat{\boldsymbol{\beta}} - \boldsymbol{\beta} = \left(\boldsymbol{X}'\boldsymbol{X}\right)^{-1}\boldsymbol{X}'\boldsymbol{\varepsilon}$ from (b). As we did in (b) for $\widehat{\boldsymbol{\beta}}$, we have formulated $\widehat{\boldsymbol{\varepsilon}}$ here in terms of the source of randomness in the model: $\boldsymbol{\varepsilon}$. Notice that $\boldsymbol{M}$ is not invertible, otherwise we would know the unknown $\boldsymbol{\varepsilon}$! Notice also that the estimated residuals are not i.i.d., since $\widehat{\boldsymbol{\varepsilon}} = \boldsymbol{M}\boldsymbol{\varepsilon} \sim \operatorname{N}\left(\boldsymbol{0}, \sigma^2\boldsymbol{M}\right)$ by $\boldsymbol{M}^2 = \boldsymbol{M}$. Now, Exercise 8.38 implies that $\sigma^{-2}\widehat{\boldsymbol{\varepsilon}}'\widehat{\boldsymbol{\varepsilon}} = \sigma^{-2}\boldsymbol{\varepsilon}'\boldsymbol{M}\boldsymbol{\varepsilon} \sim \chi^2(n-k)$. By $\sigma^{-2}\widehat{\boldsymbol{\varepsilon}}'\widehat{\boldsymbol{\varepsilon}} = n\sigma^{-2}\widehat{\sigma}^2$, and by the mean and variance of the χ^2 distribution,

$$\operatorname{E}\left(\widehat{\sigma}^2\right) = \frac{n-k}{n}\sigma^2 = \sigma^2 - \frac{k}{n}\sigma^2 < \sigma^2$$

and

$$\operatorname{var}(\widehat{\sigma}^2) = 2\frac{n-k}{n^2}\sigma^4.$$

Clearly, the bias and the variance both tend to zero as $n \to \infty$, so that $\widehat{\sigma}^2$ is consistent. The unbiased estimator of σ^2 is $s^2 := (n-k)^{-1}\widehat{\boldsymbol{\varepsilon}}'\widehat{\boldsymbol{\varepsilon}}$, and is a generalization of the usual sample variance of the simpler location model (for example, the normal case in Exercise 11.10), where we had $k = 1$ and $\boldsymbol{X} = \boldsymbol{\imath}$ (an $n \times 1$ column of ones). Since the denominator of s^2

comes from $\chi^2(n-k)$, the use of k to adjust the denominator n of $\widehat{\sigma}^2$ is often referred to as a *degrees-of-freedom correction*. As discussed in (c) for $\widehat{\boldsymbol{\beta}}$, Exercises 11.11 and 11.15 imply that s^2 is the BUE of σ^2. However, the CRLB for unbiased estimators of σ^2 is not reachable for $n < \infty$, since

$$\mathrm{MSE}\left(s^2\right) = \mathrm{var}\left(s^2\right) = \mathrm{var}\left(\frac{n\widehat{\sigma}^2}{n-k}\right) = \frac{2\sigma^4}{n-k} > \frac{2\sigma^4}{n}.$$

Comparing the MSE of s^2 to that for the MLE,

$$\mathrm{MSE}\left(\widehat{\sigma}^2\right) - \mathrm{MSE}\left(s^2\right) = \frac{k^2}{n^2}\sigma^4 + 2\frac{n-k}{n^2}\sigma^4 - \frac{2}{n-k}\sigma^4 = \frac{(k-4)(n-k)-2k}{n^2(n-k)}k\sigma^4.$$

If $k \leqslant 4$, the MLE has a lower MSE. Otherwise, n would need to be smaller than $k(k-2)/(k-4)$ for this to happen. Notice that s^2 is the BUE, being an unbiased function of the complete sufficient statistic, but it is not minimum-MSE; see Exercise 11.5 for example.

(f) This independence can be established in many ways; also recall the stronger *equivalence* result in Exercise 8.34. One solution uses Basu's theorem. For any given σ^2, the estimator $\widehat{\boldsymbol{\beta}}$ is a complete sufficient statistic and $\widehat{\sigma}^2 = n^{-1}\boldsymbol{\varepsilon}'\boldsymbol{M}\boldsymbol{\varepsilon}$ is ancillary for $\boldsymbol{\beta}$, so Basu's theorem implies that $\widehat{\sigma}^2$ is independent of $\widehat{\boldsymbol{\beta}}$. Another solution exploits the fact that the linear form (in $\boldsymbol{\varepsilon}$) defined by $\widehat{\boldsymbol{\beta}} \equiv \boldsymbol{\beta} + (\boldsymbol{X}'\boldsymbol{X})^{-1}\boldsymbol{X}'\boldsymbol{\varepsilon}$ from (b) is independent of the quadratic form $\widehat{\sigma}^2 \equiv n^{-1}\boldsymbol{\varepsilon}'\boldsymbol{M}\boldsymbol{\varepsilon}$ from (e), since $(\boldsymbol{X}'\boldsymbol{X})^{-1}\boldsymbol{X}'\boldsymbol{M} = \mathbf{O}$; see Exercise 8.31(b). Notice that the information matrix of the parameter vector $\boldsymbol{\theta}' = (\boldsymbol{\beta}', \sigma^2)$ is block diagonal.

(g) We have

$$-\boldsymbol{\mathcal{I}}^{-1}\widehat{\boldsymbol{\mathcal{H}}} = \mathrm{diag}\left(\sigma^2(\boldsymbol{X}'\boldsymbol{X})^{-1}, \frac{2\sigma^4}{n}\right)\mathrm{diag}\left(\frac{1}{\widehat{\sigma}^2}\boldsymbol{X}'\boldsymbol{X}, \frac{n}{2\widehat{\sigma}^4}\right) = \mathrm{diag}\left(\frac{\sigma^2}{\widehat{\sigma}^2}\boldsymbol{I}_k, \frac{\sigma^4}{\widehat{\sigma}^4}\right),$$

and it follows that

$$\widehat{\boldsymbol{\mathcal{I}}}^{-1}\widehat{\boldsymbol{\mathcal{H}}} = -\mathrm{diag}(\boldsymbol{I}_k, 1) = -\boldsymbol{I}_{k+1}$$

is ancillary. Now for $\boldsymbol{\mathcal{I}}^{-1}\widehat{\boldsymbol{\mathcal{H}}}$. We know from (e) that $n(\widehat{\sigma}/\sigma)^2 \sim \chi^2(n-k)$, a distribution which does not depend on $\boldsymbol{\beta}$ or σ^2. In fact, this is asymptotically true of any setup where $\widehat{\boldsymbol{\mathcal{H}}}$ satisfies some WLLN, such as in Exercise 12.28. However, $\boldsymbol{\mathcal{I}}^{-1}\widehat{\boldsymbol{\mathcal{H}}}$ is not ancillary because it is not a statistic: it depends on the unknown σ.

(h) Recall that

$$\frac{\partial \ell(\boldsymbol{\beta}, \sigma^2)}{\partial \boldsymbol{\beta}} = \frac{1}{\sigma^2}\boldsymbol{X}'\boldsymbol{\varepsilon} \quad \text{and} \quad \frac{\partial \ell(\boldsymbol{\beta}, \sigma^2)}{\partial \sigma^2} = -\frac{n}{2\sigma^2} + \frac{1}{2\sigma^4}\boldsymbol{\varepsilon}'\boldsymbol{\varepsilon},$$

with $\boldsymbol{\varepsilon} \sim \mathrm{N}(\mathbf{0}, \sigma^2\boldsymbol{I}_n)$. Partitioning the score as $\boldsymbol{q}' \equiv (\boldsymbol{q}_1', q_2)$, we get

$$\boldsymbol{q}_1 = \frac{1}{\sigma^2}\boldsymbol{X}'\boldsymbol{\varepsilon} \sim \mathrm{N}\left(\mathbf{0}, \frac{1}{\sigma^2}\boldsymbol{X}'\boldsymbol{X}\right)$$

by the same method as in (b). As for q_2, we write

$$\frac{1}{n}\boldsymbol{\varepsilon}'\boldsymbol{\varepsilon} = \frac{1}{n}\sum_{i=1}^{n}\varepsilon_i^2.$$

Since $\mathrm{E}(\varepsilon_i^2) = \sigma^2$ and $\mathrm{var}(\varepsilon_i^2) = \mathrm{E}(\varepsilon_i^4) - (\sigma^2)^2 = 2\sigma^4$, the CLT for i.i.d. sequences implies that

$$\frac{1}{n}\boldsymbol{\varepsilon}'\boldsymbol{\varepsilon} \overset{a}{\sim} \mathrm{N}\left(\sigma^2, \frac{2\sigma^4}{n}\right) \quad \text{or} \quad \frac{1}{2\sigma^4}\boldsymbol{\varepsilon}'\boldsymbol{\varepsilon} \overset{a}{\sim} \mathrm{N}\left(\frac{n}{2\sigma^2}, \frac{n}{2\sigma^4}\right),$$

as required. The zero off-diagonal block of $\boldsymbol{\mathcal{I}}$ is verified, in a simple way, by the zero covariance of quadratic and linear forms; for example, see Exercise 6.14. Since q_2 is asymptotically normal, this zero covariance implies the independence of $\boldsymbol{q}_1$ and q_2, and hence their *joint* normality. Note that we cannot use Basu's theorem, as in (f), since $\boldsymbol{\varepsilon}'\boldsymbol{\varepsilon}$ is not a statistic (it is not computable from the data $\boldsymbol{X}$ and $\boldsymbol{y}$ alone), and that the independence established here is asymptotic only ($\boldsymbol{\varepsilon}'\boldsymbol{\varepsilon}$ is a quadratic function of $\boldsymbol{\varepsilon}$ hence dependent on it for any finite n).

Exercise 12.32 (Equivalent MLEs) Consider the normal linear model of Exercise 12.30 and define $\widehat{\boldsymbol{\beta}} := (\boldsymbol{X}'\boldsymbol{X})^{-1}\boldsymbol{X}'\boldsymbol{y}$. Show that

$$\operatorname*{argmin}_{\boldsymbol{\beta}} \boldsymbol{\varepsilon}'\boldsymbol{\varepsilon} = \operatorname*{argmin}_{\boldsymbol{\beta}} (\widehat{\boldsymbol{\beta}} - \boldsymbol{\beta})'\boldsymbol{X}'\boldsymbol{X}(\widehat{\boldsymbol{\beta}} - \boldsymbol{\beta})$$

and that the solution is $\widehat{\boldsymbol{\beta}}$. In other words, for known $\boldsymbol{X}$, show that the normal linear model $\boldsymbol{y} \sim \mathrm{N}_n(\boldsymbol{X}\boldsymbol{\beta}, \sigma^2\boldsymbol{I}_n)$ and the model $\widehat{\boldsymbol{\beta}} \sim \mathrm{N}_k(\boldsymbol{\beta}, \sigma^2(\boldsymbol{X}'\boldsymbol{X})^{-1})$ have likelihoods maximized by the same solution for $\boldsymbol{\beta}$.

Solution

Define the symmetric idempotents $\boldsymbol{P} := \boldsymbol{X}(\boldsymbol{X}'\boldsymbol{X})^{-1}\boldsymbol{X}'$ and $\boldsymbol{M} := \boldsymbol{I}_n - \boldsymbol{P}$. We have

$$\boldsymbol{\varepsilon}'\boldsymbol{\varepsilon} = (\boldsymbol{P}\boldsymbol{\varepsilon} + \boldsymbol{M}\boldsymbol{\varepsilon})'(\boldsymbol{P}\boldsymbol{\varepsilon} + \boldsymbol{M}\boldsymbol{\varepsilon}) = \boldsymbol{\varepsilon}'\boldsymbol{P}\boldsymbol{\varepsilon} + \boldsymbol{\varepsilon}'\boldsymbol{M}\boldsymbol{\varepsilon},$$

by the repeated projection $\boldsymbol{P}^2 = \boldsymbol{P}$ and by the orthogonality of the projections $\boldsymbol{P}\boldsymbol{M} = \mathbf{O}$. Since $\boldsymbol{\varepsilon} = \boldsymbol{y} - \boldsymbol{X}\boldsymbol{\beta}$,

$$\boldsymbol{\varepsilon}'\boldsymbol{\varepsilon} = (\boldsymbol{P}\boldsymbol{y} - \boldsymbol{P}\boldsymbol{X}\boldsymbol{\beta})'(\boldsymbol{P}\boldsymbol{y} - \boldsymbol{P}\boldsymbol{X}\boldsymbol{\beta}) + (\boldsymbol{M}\boldsymbol{y} - \boldsymbol{M}\boldsymbol{X}\boldsymbol{\beta})'(\boldsymbol{M}\boldsymbol{y} - \boldsymbol{M}\boldsymbol{X}\boldsymbol{\beta}).$$

By $\boldsymbol{P}\boldsymbol{y} = \boldsymbol{X}\widehat{\boldsymbol{\beta}}$ (see the hat matrix of Exercise 12.31(e)), $\boldsymbol{P}\boldsymbol{X} = \boldsymbol{X}(\boldsymbol{X}'\boldsymbol{X})^{-1}\boldsymbol{X}'\boldsymbol{X} = \boldsymbol{X}$ (projecting $\boldsymbol{X}$ onto the space spanned by $\boldsymbol{X}$ does not alter $\boldsymbol{X}$), and $\boldsymbol{M}\boldsymbol{X} = \mathbf{O}$, we get

$$\boldsymbol{\varepsilon}'\boldsymbol{\varepsilon} = (\widehat{\boldsymbol{\beta}} - \boldsymbol{\beta})'\boldsymbol{X}'\boldsymbol{X}(\widehat{\boldsymbol{\beta}} - \boldsymbol{\beta}) + \boldsymbol{y}'\boldsymbol{M}\boldsymbol{y}.$$

The latter quadratic (which is also equal to $\widehat{\boldsymbol{\varepsilon}}'\widehat{\boldsymbol{\varepsilon}}$ by $\widehat{\boldsymbol{\varepsilon}} = \boldsymbol{M}\boldsymbol{\varepsilon}$) is a function of the data, and therefore this part of the objective function will not vary as we optimize with respect to $\boldsymbol{\beta}$, hence the stated result. By the positive definiteness of $\boldsymbol{X}'\boldsymbol{X}$,

$$\min_{\boldsymbol{\beta}} (\widehat{\boldsymbol{\beta}} - \boldsymbol{\beta})'\boldsymbol{X}'\boldsymbol{X}(\widehat{\boldsymbol{\beta}} - \boldsymbol{\beta}) = 0$$

and the minimum of this quadratic form is achieved by taking $\boldsymbol{\beta} = \widehat{\boldsymbol{\beta}}$. Compare this with the sufficiency factorization seen earlier in this chapter and in Exercise 11.11(b), and notice the difference in dimensions between $\widehat{\boldsymbol{\beta}}$ and $\boldsymbol{y}$, with k typically much smaller than n; hence, it is a simpler statistical model.

Exercise 12.33 (Relation of MLE to the mean of conditional normals) Consider the normal linear model of Exercise 12.30. Suppose that $k \geqslant 2$ and $\boldsymbol{X} = (\boldsymbol{\imath}, \boldsymbol{Z})$, where $\boldsymbol{\imath}$ is an $n \times 1$ column of ones and $\boldsymbol{Z}$ is an $n \times (k-1)$ matrix of fixed regressors. Define the de-meaning matrix $\boldsymbol{A} := \boldsymbol{I}_n - \frac{1}{n}\boldsymbol{\imath\imath}'$, first used in Exercise 8.34(a) and then in Chapter 9.
(a) Show that

$$\widehat{\boldsymbol{\beta}} = \begin{pmatrix} \frac{1}{n}\boldsymbol{\imath}'(\boldsymbol{y} - \boldsymbol{Z}\widehat{\boldsymbol{\beta}}_2) \\ \widehat{\boldsymbol{\beta}}_2 \end{pmatrix},$$

where $\widehat{\boldsymbol{\beta}}_2 := (\boldsymbol{Z}'\boldsymbol{A}\boldsymbol{Z})^{-1}\boldsymbol{Z}'\boldsymbol{A}\boldsymbol{y}$.
(b) The model can be rewritten in terms of the variables $y = \beta_1 + \boldsymbol{z}'\boldsymbol{\beta}_2 + \varepsilon$, where $\boldsymbol{z}$ denotes the vector of $k-1$ explanatory variables excluding the constant. Reformulate the computation of $\widehat{\boldsymbol{\beta}}_2$ and its variance in terms of this model when $i = 1, \dots, n$ observations are available.
(c) How does $\widehat{\boldsymbol{\beta}}_2$ relate to the mean of the distribution of $y \mid \boldsymbol{z}$?
(d) Interpret $\widehat{\beta}_1$, the first 1×1 component of $\widehat{\boldsymbol{\beta}}$. What is the value of $\boldsymbol{\imath}'\widehat{\boldsymbol{\varepsilon}}$? Show that it implies that the sample means of $\boldsymbol{y}$ and $\widehat{\boldsymbol{y}}$ coincide.

Solution
(a) Using the formula for partitioned inverses (see Section A.4),

$$(\boldsymbol{X}'\boldsymbol{X})^{-1} = \begin{pmatrix} n & \boldsymbol{\imath}'\boldsymbol{Z} \\ \boldsymbol{Z}'\boldsymbol{\imath} & \boldsymbol{Z}'\boldsymbol{Z} \end{pmatrix}^{-1} = \begin{pmatrix} \frac{1}{n} + \frac{1}{n^2}\boldsymbol{\imath}'\boldsymbol{Z}(\boldsymbol{Z}'\boldsymbol{A}\boldsymbol{Z})^{-1}\boldsymbol{Z}'\boldsymbol{\imath} & -\frac{1}{n}\boldsymbol{\imath}'\boldsymbol{Z}(\boldsymbol{Z}'\boldsymbol{A}\boldsymbol{Z})^{-1} \\ -\frac{1}{n}(\boldsymbol{Z}'\boldsymbol{A}\boldsymbol{Z})^{-1}\boldsymbol{Z}'\boldsymbol{\imath} & (\boldsymbol{Z}'\boldsymbol{A}\boldsymbol{Z})^{-1} \end{pmatrix},$$

which specializes to

$$(\boldsymbol{X}'\boldsymbol{X})^{-1} = \begin{pmatrix} n & n\overline{z} \\ n\overline{z} & \sum_{i=1}^n z_i^2 \end{pmatrix}^{-1} = \frac{1}{\sum_i (z_i - \overline{z})^2} \begin{pmatrix} \frac{1}{n}\sum_i z_i^2 & -\overline{z} \\ -\overline{z} & 1 \end{pmatrix}$$

when $k = 2$. Then,

$$\begin{aligned}(\boldsymbol{X}'\boldsymbol{X})^{-1}\boldsymbol{X}'\boldsymbol{y} &= \begin{pmatrix} \frac{1}{n} + \frac{1}{n^2}\boldsymbol{\imath}'\boldsymbol{Z}(\boldsymbol{Z}'\boldsymbol{A}\boldsymbol{Z})^{-1}\boldsymbol{Z}'\boldsymbol{\imath} & -\frac{1}{n}\boldsymbol{\imath}'\boldsymbol{Z}(\boldsymbol{Z}'\boldsymbol{A}\boldsymbol{Z})^{-1} \\ -\frac{1}{n}(\boldsymbol{Z}'\boldsymbol{A}\boldsymbol{Z})^{-1}\boldsymbol{Z}'\boldsymbol{\imath} & (\boldsymbol{Z}'\boldsymbol{A}\boldsymbol{Z})^{-1} \end{pmatrix} \begin{pmatrix} \boldsymbol{\imath}'\boldsymbol{y} \\ \boldsymbol{Z}'\boldsymbol{y} \end{pmatrix} \\ &= \begin{pmatrix} \frac{1}{n}\boldsymbol{\imath}'\boldsymbol{y} - \frac{1}{n}\boldsymbol{\imath}'\boldsymbol{Z}(\boldsymbol{Z}'\boldsymbol{A}\boldsymbol{Z})^{-1}\boldsymbol{Z}'\left(\boldsymbol{I}_n - \frac{1}{n}\boldsymbol{\imath\imath}'\right)\boldsymbol{y} \\ (\boldsymbol{Z}'\boldsymbol{A}\boldsymbol{Z})^{-1}\boldsymbol{Z}'\left(\boldsymbol{I}_n - \frac{1}{n}\boldsymbol{\imath\imath}'\right)\boldsymbol{y} \end{pmatrix} \\ &= \begin{pmatrix} \frac{1}{n}\boldsymbol{\imath}'(\boldsymbol{y} - \boldsymbol{Z}\widehat{\boldsymbol{\beta}}_2) \\ \widehat{\boldsymbol{\beta}}_2 \end{pmatrix}.\end{aligned}$$

An alternative (and more general) proof will be given in Exercise 12.39(b).
(b) De-meaning the data transforms $\boldsymbol{y}$ into $\boldsymbol{A}\boldsymbol{y}$ and $\boldsymbol{Z}$ into $\boldsymbol{A}\boldsymbol{Z}$. Recalling that $\boldsymbol{A}$ is symmetric idempotent, we have

$$\widehat{\boldsymbol{\beta}}_2 = \left((\boldsymbol{A}\boldsymbol{Z})'\boldsymbol{A}\boldsymbol{Z}\right)^{-1}(\boldsymbol{A}\boldsymbol{Z})'\boldsymbol{A}\boldsymbol{y},$$

that is, $\widehat{\boldsymbol{\beta}}_2$ is the $(k-1)\times 1$ vector obtained from applying the usual formula for the MLE of $\boldsymbol{\beta}_2$ to $\boldsymbol{Ay}$ (instead of $\boldsymbol{y}$) and $\boldsymbol{AZ}$ (rather than the full $\boldsymbol{AX}$ whose first column is $\mathbf{0}_n$). Since $\mathrm{E}(y) = \beta_1 + \mathrm{E}(\boldsymbol{z})'\boldsymbol{\beta}_2$ leads to

$$y - \mathrm{E}(y) = (\boldsymbol{z} - \mathrm{E}(\boldsymbol{z}))'\boldsymbol{\beta}_2 + \varepsilon,$$

we have just shown that $\widehat{\boldsymbol{\beta}}_2$ is the MLE of $\boldsymbol{\beta}_2$ in this reformulated model. Notice that this also implies that $\widehat{\boldsymbol{\beta}}_2 \sim \mathrm{N}(\boldsymbol{\beta}_2, \sigma^2 (\boldsymbol{Z}'\boldsymbol{AZ})^{-1})$, by Exercise 12.31(b).
(c) The expectation of $y \mid \boldsymbol{z}$, given in Exercise 6.51 for elliptical distributions and in Chapter 8 for the special case of the normal, is

$$\mathrm{E}(y \mid \boldsymbol{z}) = \mathrm{E}(y) + (\boldsymbol{z} - \mathrm{E}(\boldsymbol{z}))'\boldsymbol{\gamma} = \mathrm{E}(y - \boldsymbol{z}'\boldsymbol{\gamma}) + \boldsymbol{z}'\boldsymbol{\gamma},$$

where $\boldsymbol{\gamma} := (\mathrm{var}(\boldsymbol{z}))^{-1}\mathrm{cov}(\boldsymbol{z}, y)$. We can rewrite $\widehat{\boldsymbol{\beta}}_2$ of (b) in terms of the sample variances and covariances (which are based on de-meaned observations) as

$$\widehat{\boldsymbol{\beta}}_2 = (n\,\widehat{\mathrm{var}}(\boldsymbol{z}))^{-1} n\,\widehat{\mathrm{cov}}(\boldsymbol{z}, y) = (\widehat{\mathrm{var}}(\boldsymbol{z}))^{-1}\widehat{\mathrm{cov}}(\boldsymbol{z}, y),$$

which is the same as $\boldsymbol{\gamma}$ but with sample counterparts used instead of the population variance and covariance. Note that this formula is also the sample counterpart of the "best linear predictors" $\boldsymbol{b}$ of Exercise 6.21 and b of Exercise 6.46. We shall explore this point further in Chapter 13, in connection with least-squares estimation.

As for the variance, we immediately get $\mathrm{var}(\widehat{\boldsymbol{\beta}}_2) = \sigma^2(n\,\widehat{\mathrm{var}}(\boldsymbol{z}))^{-1}$, implying that more variation in the regressors allows us to estimate $\boldsymbol{\beta}_2$ with more precision. In terms of scatter plots, the slope of a fitted line is more reliably determined if the points span a larger portion of the horizontal axis than if they are all concentrated around a single point.
(d) The formula for $\widehat{\boldsymbol{\beta}}$ indicates that, once $\widehat{\boldsymbol{\beta}}_2$ is computed, we can obtain $\widehat{\beta}_1$ as the average of the elements in the column vector $\boldsymbol{y} - \boldsymbol{Z}\widehat{\boldsymbol{\beta}}_2$. This is also obvious from the term $\mathrm{E}(y - \boldsymbol{z}'\boldsymbol{\gamma})$ in the conditional expectation in (c). Therefore

$$\boldsymbol{\imath}'\widehat{\boldsymbol{\varepsilon}} = \boldsymbol{\imath}'(\boldsymbol{y} - \boldsymbol{Z}\widehat{\boldsymbol{\beta}}_2 - \boldsymbol{\imath}\widehat{\beta}_1) = n\widehat{\beta}_1 - \boldsymbol{\imath}'\boldsymbol{\imath}\widehat{\beta}_1 = 0,$$

showing that the estimated residuals $\widehat{\boldsymbol{\varepsilon}}$ have a sample mean of 0. Then the definition $\widehat{\boldsymbol{\varepsilon}} := \boldsymbol{y} - \widehat{\boldsymbol{y}}$ implies that the sample means of the fitted values $\widehat{\boldsymbol{y}}$ and of the observed values $\boldsymbol{y}$ coincide. Contrast this with $\boldsymbol{\varepsilon}$: although $\mathrm{E}(\boldsymbol{\varepsilon}) = \mathbf{0}$, we have almost surely $\boldsymbol{\imath}'\boldsymbol{\varepsilon} \neq 0$ since the components of $\boldsymbol{\varepsilon}$ are independent continuous variates.

Exercise 12.34 (Partitioned inverse of the data's quadratic matrix) Consider the normal linear model of Exercise 12.30. Writing $\boldsymbol{Z} := (\boldsymbol{y}, \boldsymbol{X})$, show that

$$(\boldsymbol{Z}'\boldsymbol{Z})^{-1} = (n\widehat{\sigma}^2)^{-1}\begin{pmatrix} 1 & -\widehat{\boldsymbol{\beta}}' \\ -\widehat{\boldsymbol{\beta}} & n\widehat{\sigma}^2(\boldsymbol{X}'\boldsymbol{X})^{-1} + \widehat{\boldsymbol{\beta}}\widehat{\boldsymbol{\beta}}' \end{pmatrix},$$

where it is easy to extract all the components of the MLE and their variances (see Exercises 12.30 and 12.31).

Solution

This follows directly from the application of the formula for a partitioned inverse to

$$Z'Z = \begin{pmatrix} y'y & y'X \\ X'y & X'X \end{pmatrix},$$

and using $y'My = \hat{\varepsilon}'\hat{\varepsilon} = n\hat{\sigma}^2$, where $M := I_n - X(X'X)^{-1}X'$. This is unsurprising given the close connection between conditioning and normal linear regression, highlighted in Exercise 12.33(c). One should think of the normal linear model as arising from conditioning in a joint normal distribution, as was first discussed in the introduction to Chapter 11 and in Exercise 11.11. See also Exercise 9.23(a) for independence results concerning functions of the sample variance matrix, such as $\hat{\beta}$ and $\hat{\sigma}^2$. Finally, notice the close connection with projections, where the Schur complement (see Section A.4) of the sum of squares $X'X$ is just the residual sum of squares $y'My = \hat{\varepsilon}'\hat{\varepsilon}$.

Exercise 12.35 (Variance decompositions) Consider the normal linear model of Exercise 12.30 and define the de-meaning matrix $A := I_n - \frac{1}{n}\imath\imath'$.

(a) Prove that $y'y = \hat{y}'\hat{y} + \hat{\varepsilon}'\hat{\varepsilon}$, where $\hat{y}'\hat{y}$ is the sum of squares explained by the model while $\hat{\varepsilon}'\hat{\varepsilon}$ is the unexplained (or residual) sum of squares.

(b) How does (a) imply that $\hat{y}$ is independent of $\hat{\varepsilon}$?

(c) Prove that

$$\frac{\sum_{i=1}^n \hat{y}_i^2}{\sum_{i=1}^n y_i^2} = 1 - \frac{\sum_{i=1}^n (y_i - \hat{y}_i)^2}{\sum_{i=1}^n y_i^2} \in [0,1].$$

(d) When $k \geqslant 2$ and $X = (\imath, Z)$, prove that

$$\frac{\sum_{i=1}^n (\hat{y}_i - \overline{y})^2}{\sum_{i=1}^n (y_i - \overline{y})^2} = 1 - \frac{\sum_{i=1}^n (y_i - \hat{y}_i)^2}{\sum_{i=1}^n (y_i - \overline{y})^2}.$$

The left-hand side is the ratio of the explained and the total sum of squared deviations from $\overline{y}$. This ratio is known as the *coefficient of determination* and is denoted by R^2.

(e) For the conditions in (d), show that $R^2 \in [0,1]$ and $R^2 = \hat{\rho}_{y,\hat{y}}^2$, the square of the sample correlation between y and $\hat{y}$.

(f) Let $k \geqslant 2$ and $X = (\imath, Z)$, and partition the true (unknown) $\beta' := (\beta_1, \beta_2')$ accordingly. First, for $\beta_2 = 0_{k-1}$, show that

$$\frac{\sum_{i=1}^n (\hat{y}_i - \overline{y})^2/(k-1)}{\sum_{i=1}^n (y_i - \hat{y}_i)^2/(n-k)} = \frac{n-k}{k-1} \times \frac{R^2}{1-R^2} \sim \mathrm{F}(k-1, n-k).$$

Second, for any $\beta_2 \in \mathbb{R}^{k-1}$, show that

$$\frac{n-k}{k-1} \times \frac{(\hat{\beta}_2 - \beta_2)'Z'AZ(\hat{\beta}_2 - \beta_2)}{\hat{\varepsilon}'\hat{\varepsilon}} \sim \mathrm{F}(k-1, n-k).$$

(g) Suppose that $\{y_i\}_{i=1}^n \sim \mathrm{IN}(0, \sigma^2)$, $\sigma > 0$, where it is known that $\mathrm{E}(y_i) = 0$ and that y does not depend on X. Show that $1 - \sum_{i=1}^n (y_i - \hat{y}_i)^2 / \sum_{i=1}^n y_i^2 = 0$, but that $1 - \sum_{i=1}^n (y_i - \hat{y}_i)^2 / \sum_{i=1}^n (y_i - \overline{y})^2 < 0$ a.s. Discuss this result in the contexts of (c)–(d).

Solution

(a) Define the symmetric idempotent $\boldsymbol{P} := \boldsymbol{X}(\boldsymbol{X}'\boldsymbol{X})^{-1}\boldsymbol{X}'$ and its complement $\boldsymbol{M} := \boldsymbol{I}_n - \boldsymbol{P}$, satisfying $\boldsymbol{PM} = \mathbf{O}$. Now, $\boldsymbol{y} = \widehat{\boldsymbol{y}} + \widehat{\boldsymbol{\varepsilon}}$ with

$$\widehat{\boldsymbol{y}} = \boldsymbol{X}\widehat{\boldsymbol{\beta}} = \boldsymbol{P}\boldsymbol{y} \qquad \text{and} \qquad \widehat{\boldsymbol{\varepsilon}} = (\boldsymbol{I}_n - \boldsymbol{P})\,\boldsymbol{y} = \boldsymbol{M}\boldsymbol{y}.$$

Therefore,

$$\boldsymbol{y}'\boldsymbol{y} = (\widehat{\boldsymbol{y}} + \widehat{\boldsymbol{\varepsilon}})'\,(\widehat{\boldsymbol{y}} + \widehat{\boldsymbol{\varepsilon}}) = \widehat{\boldsymbol{y}}'\widehat{\boldsymbol{y}} + \widehat{\boldsymbol{\varepsilon}}'\widehat{\boldsymbol{\varepsilon}} + 2\widehat{\boldsymbol{y}}'\widehat{\boldsymbol{\varepsilon}} = \widehat{\boldsymbol{y}}'\widehat{\boldsymbol{y}} + \widehat{\boldsymbol{\varepsilon}}'\widehat{\boldsymbol{\varepsilon}} + 2\boldsymbol{y}'\boldsymbol{PM}\boldsymbol{y} = \widehat{\boldsymbol{y}}'\widehat{\boldsymbol{y}} + \widehat{\boldsymbol{\varepsilon}}'\widehat{\boldsymbol{\varepsilon}},$$

and $\boldsymbol{y}$ can be decomposed into the mutually orthogonal components $\widehat{\boldsymbol{y}}$ and $\widehat{\boldsymbol{\varepsilon}}$. Notice the analogy with Pythagoras' theorem on orthogonal projections: the result can be restated as $\|\boldsymbol{y}\|^2 = \|\widehat{\boldsymbol{y}}\|^2 + \|\widehat{\boldsymbol{\varepsilon}}\|^2$.

(b) We have $\boldsymbol{y} \sim \mathrm{N}\left(\boldsymbol{X\beta}, \sigma^2\boldsymbol{I}_n\right)$. Then,

$$\mathrm{cov}(\widehat{\boldsymbol{y}}, \widehat{\boldsymbol{\varepsilon}}) = \mathrm{cov}(\boldsymbol{P}\boldsymbol{y}, \boldsymbol{M}\boldsymbol{y}) = \boldsymbol{P}\,\mathrm{cov}(\boldsymbol{y}, \boldsymbol{y})\boldsymbol{M} = \boldsymbol{P}\left(\sigma^2\boldsymbol{I}_n\right)\boldsymbol{M} = \mathbf{O}.$$

Furthermore, the normality of $\boldsymbol{y}$ is transmitted to $\widehat{\boldsymbol{y}} = \boldsymbol{P}\boldsymbol{y}$ and $\widehat{\boldsymbol{\varepsilon}} = \boldsymbol{M}\boldsymbol{y}$, ensuring that the absence of a linear relation is equivalent to independence (see Chapter 8). Note that

$$\mathrm{E}(\widehat{\boldsymbol{\varepsilon}}) = \mathrm{E}\,(\boldsymbol{M}\boldsymbol{y}) = \boldsymbol{M}\,\mathrm{E}\,(\boldsymbol{y}) = \boldsymbol{MX\beta} = \mathbf{0}$$

since $\boldsymbol{PX} = \boldsymbol{X}$, and similarly $\mathrm{E}(\widehat{\boldsymbol{y}}) = \boldsymbol{X\beta} = \mathrm{E}(\boldsymbol{y})$, which is the population counterpart of the result about sample means in Exercise 12.33(d).

(c) This follows directly by dividing both sides of the result in (a) by $\boldsymbol{y}'\boldsymbol{y}$, which is allowed since $\sigma > 0$ implies $\sum_{i=1}^n y_i^2 > 0$ with probability 1. The range $[0,1]$ follows from $\sum_{i=1}^n \widehat{y}_i^2 \geqslant 0$ and $\sum_{i=1}^n (y_i - \widehat{y}_i)^2 \geqslant 0$, respectively.

(d) Exercise 12.33(d) showed that the sample means of $\boldsymbol{y}$ and $\widehat{\boldsymbol{y}}$ coincide in this setup, and that $\widehat{\boldsymbol{\varepsilon}}$ has a sample mean of zero. Therefore,

$$\boldsymbol{y}'\boldsymbol{A}\boldsymbol{y} = \widehat{\boldsymbol{y}}'\boldsymbol{A}\widehat{\boldsymbol{y}} + \widehat{\boldsymbol{\varepsilon}}'\boldsymbol{A}\widehat{\boldsymbol{\varepsilon}} + 2\widehat{\boldsymbol{y}}'\boldsymbol{A}\widehat{\boldsymbol{\varepsilon}} = \widehat{\boldsymbol{y}}'\boldsymbol{A}\widehat{\boldsymbol{y}} + \widehat{\boldsymbol{\varepsilon}}'\widehat{\boldsymbol{\varepsilon}} + 2\widehat{\boldsymbol{y}}'\widehat{\boldsymbol{\varepsilon}}$$

since de-meaning has no effect on $\widehat{\boldsymbol{\varepsilon}}$ (hence $\boldsymbol{A}\widehat{\boldsymbol{\varepsilon}} = \widehat{\boldsymbol{\varepsilon}}$). The required decomposition follows by the orthogonality $\widehat{\boldsymbol{y}}'\widehat{\boldsymbol{\varepsilon}} = 0$ proved in general in (a), and by dividing both sides by $\boldsymbol{y}'\boldsymbol{A}\boldsymbol{y}$. The latter division is allowed, since $n > k$ implies that $\sum_{i=1}^n (y_i - \overline{y})^2 > 0$ a.s.; see Exercise 9.21. Notice that the stated equality need not hold if $\boldsymbol{X}$ does not contain a column of ones, in which case $\boldsymbol{A}\widehat{\boldsymbol{\varepsilon}} \neq \widehat{\boldsymbol{\varepsilon}}$ in general and the relevant relation is (a) or (c). Notice also that, in the trivial case $y_i = \mu + \varepsilon_i$, we have $\widehat{y}_i = \overline{y}$ and $R^2 = 0$.

(e) We have

$$\widehat{\rho}^{\,2}_{\boldsymbol{y},\widehat{\boldsymbol{y}}} = \frac{(\boldsymbol{y}'\boldsymbol{A}\widehat{\boldsymbol{y}})^2}{\boldsymbol{y}'\boldsymbol{A}\boldsymbol{y} \times \widehat{\boldsymbol{y}}'\boldsymbol{A}\widehat{\boldsymbol{y}}} = \frac{((\widehat{\boldsymbol{y}} + \widehat{\boldsymbol{\varepsilon}})'\boldsymbol{A}\widehat{\boldsymbol{y}})^2}{\boldsymbol{y}'\boldsymbol{A}\boldsymbol{y} \times \widehat{\boldsymbol{y}}'\boldsymbol{A}\widehat{\boldsymbol{y}}} = \frac{(\widehat{\boldsymbol{y}}'\boldsymbol{A}\widehat{\boldsymbol{y}})^2}{\boldsymbol{y}'\boldsymbol{A}\boldsymbol{y} \times \widehat{\boldsymbol{y}}'\boldsymbol{A}\widehat{\boldsymbol{y}}} = \frac{\widehat{\boldsymbol{y}}'\boldsymbol{A}\widehat{\boldsymbol{y}}}{\boldsymbol{y}'\boldsymbol{A}\boldsymbol{y}} = R^2,$$

and the range of R^2 follows from $\widehat{\rho}^{\,2}_{\boldsymbol{y},\widehat{\boldsymbol{y}}} \in [0,1]$. Therefore, R^2 measures the strength of the linear relation between $\boldsymbol{y}$ and its prediction by means of $\boldsymbol{X}$.

(f) First, (b) defines R^2 as $\widehat{\boldsymbol{y}}'\boldsymbol{A}\widehat{\boldsymbol{y}}/\boldsymbol{y}'\boldsymbol{A}\boldsymbol{y}$, so

$$\frac{R^2}{1 - R^2} = \frac{\widehat{\boldsymbol{y}}'\boldsymbol{A}\widehat{\boldsymbol{y}}}{\boldsymbol{y}'\boldsymbol{A}\boldsymbol{y} - \widehat{\boldsymbol{y}}'\boldsymbol{A}\widehat{\boldsymbol{y}}} = \frac{\widehat{\boldsymbol{y}}'\boldsymbol{A}\widehat{\boldsymbol{y}}}{\widehat{\boldsymbol{\varepsilon}}'\widehat{\boldsymbol{\varepsilon}}},$$

as required. It is the ratio of explained to unexplained (or residual) sum of squares. We can use Exercise 12.33(a) to write

$$\boldsymbol{A}\widehat{\boldsymbol{y}} = \boldsymbol{A}\boldsymbol{Z}\widehat{\boldsymbol{\beta}}_2 = \boldsymbol{B}\boldsymbol{y},$$

where $\boldsymbol{B} := \boldsymbol{A}\boldsymbol{Z}\left(\boldsymbol{Z}'\boldsymbol{A}\boldsymbol{Z}\right)^{-1}\boldsymbol{Z}'\boldsymbol{A}$ is symmetric idempotent. As a result, we can rewrite $R^2/\left(1-R^2\right)$ as we did in the proof of Exercise 9.7(a); the notation R^2 was already hinted at there. The first required distributional result follows from that exercise, since $\boldsymbol{\beta}_2 = \mathbf{0}_{k-1}$ yields $\boldsymbol{A}\boldsymbol{y} = \boldsymbol{A}\boldsymbol{\varepsilon}$ and

$$\frac{R^2}{1-R^2} = \frac{\boldsymbol{y}'\boldsymbol{B}\boldsymbol{y}}{\boldsymbol{y}'\boldsymbol{A}\boldsymbol{y} - \boldsymbol{y}'\boldsymbol{B}\boldsymbol{y}} = \frac{\boldsymbol{\varepsilon}'\boldsymbol{B}\boldsymbol{\varepsilon}}{\boldsymbol{\varepsilon}'\boldsymbol{C}\boldsymbol{\varepsilon}},$$

where $\boldsymbol{C} := \boldsymbol{A} - \boldsymbol{B}$ is symmetric idempotent and orthogonal to $\boldsymbol{B}$, with $\boldsymbol{\varepsilon}$ normal (hence spherical) and independent of the constant $\boldsymbol{Z}$ here. Notice that the estimator $\widehat{\boldsymbol{\beta}}_2$ is nonzero, with probability 1, even when the true $\boldsymbol{\beta}_2$ is zero. They will only coincide as $n \to \infty$.

Second, for any $\boldsymbol{\beta}_2$ not necessarily equal to zero, the numerator's quadratic form needs to be properly centered before we can apply standard distributional results. Instead of $\boldsymbol{A}\widehat{\boldsymbol{y}}$, we will use the more general

$$\boldsymbol{A}\widehat{\boldsymbol{y}} - \boldsymbol{A}\boldsymbol{Z}\boldsymbol{\beta}_2 = \boldsymbol{A}\boldsymbol{Z}(\widehat{\boldsymbol{\beta}}_2 - \boldsymbol{\beta}_2) = \boldsymbol{B}\boldsymbol{\varepsilon},$$

the last equality following from

$$\widehat{\boldsymbol{\beta}}_2 = \left(\boldsymbol{Z}'\boldsymbol{A}\boldsymbol{Z}\right)^{-1}\boldsymbol{Z}'\boldsymbol{A}\left(\beta_1\boldsymbol{\imath} + \boldsymbol{Z}\boldsymbol{\beta}_2 + \boldsymbol{\varepsilon}\right) = \boldsymbol{\beta}_2 + \left(\boldsymbol{Z}'\boldsymbol{A}\boldsymbol{Z}\right)^{-1}\boldsymbol{Z}'\boldsymbol{A}\boldsymbol{\varepsilon}.$$

This $\boldsymbol{B}\boldsymbol{\varepsilon}$ has zero expectation, which is required for the application of Exercise 9.7 to give

$$\frac{n-k}{k-1} \times \frac{(\widehat{\boldsymbol{\beta}}_2 - \boldsymbol{\beta}_2)'\boldsymbol{Z}'\boldsymbol{A}\boldsymbol{Z}(\widehat{\boldsymbol{\beta}}_2 - \boldsymbol{\beta}_2)}{\widehat{\boldsymbol{\varepsilon}}'\widehat{\boldsymbol{\varepsilon}}} \sim \mathrm{F}(k-1, n-k)$$

and, for $k = 2$,

$$\frac{\widehat{\beta}_2 - \beta_2}{\sqrt{\frac{1}{n-2}\sum_{i=1}^n \widehat{\varepsilon}_i^2} \Big/ \sqrt{\sum_{i=1}^n (z_i - \overline{z})^2}} \sim \mathrm{t}(n-2);$$

both results will be analyzed further in Chapter 14. As shown in Exercise 9.7, the distributions of these statistics are robust and extend to cases beyond normal data, although $\widehat{\boldsymbol{\beta}} = (\boldsymbol{X}'\boldsymbol{X})^{-1}\boldsymbol{X}'\boldsymbol{y}$ may not be the MLE for a nonnormal likelihood. It is instead the least-squares estimator, to be seen in more detail Chapter 13.

(g) As pointed out at the end of the solution to (d), when there is no constant term in the model, the relevant equality is (a) or (c), and we cannot claim the results in (d) and (e) any longer. More specifically, we will show that

$$R^2 \neq 1 - \frac{\sum_{i=1}^n (y_i - \widehat{y}_i)^2}{\sum_{i=1}^n (y_i - \overline{y})^2} \notin [0, 1],$$

with the result that one can get "negative" values for R^2 if erroneously using the right-hand side of the last equation. This part of the question is intended to illustrate this problem with an extremely special case of the model, taking $k = 0$. In this case, $\widehat{\boldsymbol{y}} = \mathbf{0}_n$ because

$\mathrm{E}(\boldsymbol{y}) = \mathbf{0}_n$ is known and, from (a),

$$\boldsymbol{y}'\boldsymbol{y} = \widehat{\boldsymbol{y}}'\widehat{\boldsymbol{y}} + \widehat{\boldsymbol{\varepsilon}}'\widehat{\boldsymbol{\varepsilon}} = \widehat{\boldsymbol{\varepsilon}}'\widehat{\boldsymbol{\varepsilon}}.$$

Dividing by $\boldsymbol{y}'\boldsymbol{y}$ gives the first required result. The second follows by recalling that

$$\sum_{i=1}^{n} (y_i - \overline{y})^2 - \sum_{i=1}^{n} y_i^2 = -n\overline{y}^2,$$

which is negative with probability 1. In general, when the model does not contain a constant and $k > 0$, this result can occur, but not necessarily with probability 1.

Exercise 12.36 (R^2 can be manipulated) Show that R^2 is not invariant to reparameterization.

Solution

Let $y_i = \delta + \beta z_i + \varepsilon_i$ for $i = 1, \dots, n$, and denote the R^2 of this model by

$$R_0^2 := 1 - \frac{\sum_{i=1}^{n} (y_i - \widehat{y}_i)^2}{\sum_{i=1}^{n} (y_i - \overline{y})^2}.$$

Now consider the equivalent model obtained by adding cz_i to both sides of the equation, with c a known constant (a known quantity is added to both sides). Then, $\zeta_i = \delta + \gamma z_i + \eta_i$, where η_i is the same as ε_i but $\zeta_i := y_i + cz_i$ and $\gamma := \beta + c$. The R^2 of this new model is

$$R_1^2 := 1 - \frac{\sum_{i=1}^{n} (\zeta_i - \widehat{\zeta}_i)^2}{\sum_{i=1}^{n} (\zeta_i - \overline{\zeta})^2}.$$

We will show that the numerator is identical to that of R_0^2, but the denominator is not and can be manipulated to be larger, hence making R_1^2 larger than R_0^2.

Using the notation of the previous exercise, $\widehat{\boldsymbol{\varepsilon}} = \boldsymbol{M}\boldsymbol{y}$ while $\widehat{\boldsymbol{\eta}} = \boldsymbol{M}\boldsymbol{\zeta}$ since the z_i regressors (and hence $\boldsymbol{M}$) are the same for both models. Substituting for $\boldsymbol{\zeta} = \boldsymbol{y} + c\boldsymbol{z}$,

$$\widehat{\boldsymbol{\eta}} = \widehat{\boldsymbol{\varepsilon}} + c\boldsymbol{M}\boldsymbol{z} = \widehat{\boldsymbol{\varepsilon}} + c\boldsymbol{M}\boldsymbol{X}\begin{pmatrix} 0 \\ 1 \end{pmatrix} = \widehat{\boldsymbol{\varepsilon}},$$

since $\boldsymbol{M}\boldsymbol{X} = \mathbf{O}$. Hence, $y_i - \widehat{y}_i$ and $\zeta_i - \widehat{\zeta}_i$ coincide for all i, and so do the numerators of $1 - R_0^2$ and $1 - R_1^2$. As for the denominators, they are related by

$$\begin{aligned}\sum_{i=1}^{n} (\zeta_i - \overline{\zeta})^2 &= \sum_{i=1}^{n} ((y_i - \overline{y}) + c(z_i - \overline{z}))^2 \\ &= \sum_{i=1}^{n} (y_i - \overline{y})^2 + c^2 \sum_{i=1}^{n} (z_i - \overline{z})^2 + 2c \sum_{i=1}^{n} (y_i - \overline{y})(z_i - \overline{z}),\end{aligned}$$

and we can choose c arbitrarily large (positive if $\widehat{\rho}_{y,z} \geqslant 0$ or negative if $\widehat{\rho}_{y,z} \leqslant 0$) to inflate this quantity in any given sample, which is equivalent to making the sample variation in ζ

larger. Notice that, however,

$$\frac{\widehat{\beta}-\beta}{\sqrt{\frac{1}{n-2}\sum_{i=1}^{n}\widehat{\varepsilon}_i^2}\Big/\sqrt{\sum_{i=1}^{n}(z_i-\overline{z})^2}}=\frac{\widehat{\gamma}-\gamma}{\sqrt{\frac{1}{n-2}\sum_{i=1}^{n}\widehat{\eta}_i^2}\Big/\sqrt{\sum_{i=1}^{n}(z_i-\overline{z})^2}}\sim \mathrm{t}(n-2)$$

is unaffected by this manipulation, because $\widehat{\varepsilon}_i = \widehat{\eta}_i$ and the general formula $\widehat{\boldsymbol{\beta}}-\boldsymbol{\beta} = (\boldsymbol{X}'\boldsymbol{X})^{-1}\boldsymbol{X}'\boldsymbol{\varepsilon}$ depends on the unchanged $\boldsymbol{X}, \boldsymbol{\varepsilon}$ but not on $\boldsymbol{y}$ which has been manipulated.

We could visualize this phenomenon graphically with a picture like Figure 6.4, though that picture focused on correlations ρ in the population. Redefining the left-hand side variable as we have done has increased the correlation by rotating (and stretching) the ellipse from being vertical if $\beta = 0$ to having a 45° inclination as a result of making the two variables ζ and cz almost identical for large $|c|$, hence highly correlated (recall that the previous exercise implies that $R^2 = \widehat{\rho}^2_{\zeta,\widehat{\zeta}}$). We will discuss this figure further in Section 13.2.

Exercise 12.37 (R^2 on subsamples) Suppose that you have four observations on two variates, x and y, and that you calculate the R^2 for $y_i = \alpha + \beta x_i + \varepsilon_i$, $i = 1, \dots, 4$. Now split this into two subsets of the data, two observations each, and redo the calculations. Which R^2 is larger, and why?

Solution

Regardless of which two points are chosen in each subsample, the regression line can be fitted exactly to the two data points and so the residual is zero (see Exercise 9.6(a) for an illustration); hence $R^2 = 1$ and this cannot be less than R^2 for the full sample. This applies also to $|\widehat{\rho}|$ ($\widehat{\rho}$ is the sample correlation between x and y) because $R^2 = \widehat{\rho}^2$ in the bivariate case.

Exercise 12.38 (Predictions) Consider the normal linear model of Exercise 12.30. Suppose that $k = 2$ and $\boldsymbol{X} = (\boldsymbol{\imath}, \boldsymbol{z})$, where $\boldsymbol{\imath}$ is an $n \times 1$ column of ones and $\boldsymbol{z}$ is an $n \times 1$ vector of fixed regressors.

(a) Derive $\mathrm{var}(\widehat{\varepsilon}_i)$, where $i = 1, \dots, n$.

(b) Suppose we want to predict y_0 when $z = z_0$ (not necessarily a value in the sample). Derive $\mathrm{var}(\widehat{y}_0)$.

(c) Now suppose that $z = z_0$ is a value that does not occur in the sample, that is, $z_0 \neq z_i$ for all $i = 1, \dots, n$. Derive $\mathrm{var}(\widehat{\varepsilon}_0)$ and compare it with $\mathrm{var}(\widehat{\varepsilon}_i)$ of (a).

Solution

(a) Exercise 12.31(e) showed that $\widehat{\boldsymbol{\varepsilon}} = \boldsymbol{M}\boldsymbol{\varepsilon}$, where $\boldsymbol{M} := \boldsymbol{I}_n - \boldsymbol{X}(\boldsymbol{X}'\boldsymbol{X})^{-1}\boldsymbol{X}'$. If $\boldsymbol{e}_i$ is the i-th elementary vector, with a one in the i-th position and zeros elsewhere, then

$$\begin{aligned}\mathrm{var}(\widehat{\varepsilon}_i) &= \mathrm{var}(\boldsymbol{e}_i'\widehat{\boldsymbol{\varepsilon}}) = \sigma^2\boldsymbol{e}_i'\left(\boldsymbol{I}_n - \boldsymbol{X}(\boldsymbol{X}'\boldsymbol{X})^{-1}\boldsymbol{X}'\right)\boldsymbol{e}_i \\ &= \sigma^2\left(1 - \boldsymbol{e}_i'\boldsymbol{X}(\boldsymbol{X}'\boldsymbol{X})^{-1}\boldsymbol{X}'\boldsymbol{e}_i\right),\end{aligned}$$

which is valid for any k. Using the explicit formula for $(\boldsymbol{X}'\boldsymbol{X})^{-1}$ for $k = 2$ from Exercise 12.33(a), we obtain

$$\begin{aligned}\operatorname{var}(\widehat{\varepsilon}_i) &= \sigma^2 - \frac{\sigma^2}{\sum_j (z_j - \overline{z})^2} (1,\, z_i) \begin{pmatrix} \frac{1}{n}\sum_j z_j^2 & -\overline{z} \\ -\overline{z} & 1 \end{pmatrix} \begin{pmatrix} 1 \\ z_i \end{pmatrix} \\ &= \sigma^2 - \frac{\sigma^2 \left(\frac{1}{n}\sum_j z_j^2 + z_i^2 - 2\overline{z}z_i\right)}{\sum_j (z_j - \overline{z})^2} = \sigma^2 - \frac{\sigma^2 \left(\frac{1}{n}\sum_j (z_j - \overline{z})^2 + \overline{z}^2 + z_i^2 - 2\overline{z}z_i\right)}{\sum_j (z_j - \overline{z})^2} \\ &= \sigma^2 \left(1 - \frac{1}{n} - \frac{(z_i - \overline{z})^2}{\sum_j (z_j - \overline{z})^2}\right),\end{aligned}$$

and we can use it to check that $\sum_{i=1}^n \operatorname{var}(\widehat{\varepsilon}_i)/\sigma^2 = n-2 = \operatorname{tr}(\boldsymbol{M})$ as expected. Notice that $\operatorname{var}(\widehat{\varepsilon}_i) < \operatorname{var}(\varepsilon_i)$. Notice also that, in general, the variances are not constant as i varies: the further z_i is from its mean $\overline{z}$, the smaller the variance of $\widehat{\varepsilon}_i$.

(b) Since, for any vector $\boldsymbol{x}_0 := (1, z_0)'$, the corresponding predicted value of y is $\widehat{y}_0 = \boldsymbol{x}_0'\widehat{\boldsymbol{\beta}}$, we get

$$\begin{aligned}\operatorname{var}(\widehat{y}_0) = \boldsymbol{x}_0' \operatorname{var}(\widehat{\boldsymbol{\beta}})\boldsymbol{x}_0 &= \frac{\sigma^2}{\sum_j (z_j - \overline{z})^2} (1,\, z_0) \begin{pmatrix} \frac{1}{n}\sum_j z_j^2 & -\overline{z} \\ -\overline{z} & 1 \end{pmatrix} \begin{pmatrix} 1 \\ z_0 \end{pmatrix} \\ &= \sigma^2 \left(\frac{1}{n} + \frac{(z_0 - \overline{z})^2}{\sum_j (z_j - \overline{z})^2}\right)\end{aligned}$$

by the same derivations as in (a). The reverse picture occurs, compared with what we had in (a): the further z_0 is from the center of the scatter plot (meaning $\overline{z}$), the less reliable the estimator of y_0 becomes. To understand this, remember the decomposition of the variances in Exercise 12.35: $\operatorname{var}(y_i) = \operatorname{var}(\widehat{y}_i) + \operatorname{var}(\widehat{\varepsilon}_i) = \sigma^2$ for $i = 1, \dots, n$.

(c) We have

$$\operatorname{var}(\widehat{\varepsilon}_0) = \operatorname{var}(y_0 - \widehat{y}_0) = \operatorname{var}(y_0 - \boldsymbol{x}_0'\widehat{\boldsymbol{\beta}}) = \operatorname{var}(y_0) + \operatorname{var}(\boldsymbol{x}_0'\widehat{\boldsymbol{\beta}}),$$

since $\widehat{\boldsymbol{\beta}}$ depends only on the sample values of the random $y_1, \dots, y_n$ (hence $\varepsilon_1, \dots, \varepsilon_n$), and is thus independent of y_0. Adding $\operatorname{var}(y_0) = \operatorname{var}(\varepsilon_0) = \sigma^2$ to the result in (b) gives

$$\operatorname{var}(\widehat{\varepsilon}_0) = \sigma^2 \left(1 + \frac{1}{n} + \frac{(z_0 - \overline{z})^2}{\sum_j (z_j - \overline{z})^2}\right) > \operatorname{var}(\varepsilon_i) > \operatorname{var}(\widehat{\varepsilon}_i).$$

The difference between $\operatorname{var}(\widehat{\varepsilon}_0)$ and $\operatorname{var}(\varepsilon_i)$ increases as the distance between z_0 and $\overline{z}$ increases: predicting far from the sample average increases the uncertainty.

Exercise 12.39 (Projection decompositions) Consider the normal linear model of Exercise 12.30. Suppose that $\boldsymbol{X} := (\boldsymbol{X}_1, \boldsymbol{X}_2)$, a special case of which is to be found in Exercise 12.33. Define the symmetric idempotent matrices

$$\boldsymbol{P} := \boldsymbol{X}\left(\boldsymbol{X}'\boldsymbol{X}\right)^{-1}\boldsymbol{X}', \quad \boldsymbol{P}_1 := \boldsymbol{X}_1\left(\boldsymbol{X}_1'\boldsymbol{X}_1\right)^{-1}\boldsymbol{X}_1', \quad \boldsymbol{P}_2 := \boldsymbol{X}_2\left(\boldsymbol{X}_2'\boldsymbol{X}_2\right)^{-1}\boldsymbol{X}_2',$$

and their complements $\boldsymbol{M} := \boldsymbol{I}_n - \boldsymbol{P}$, $\boldsymbol{M}_1 := \boldsymbol{I}_n - \boldsymbol{P}_1$, and $\boldsymbol{M}_2 := \boldsymbol{I}_n - \boldsymbol{P}_2$.
(a) Show that $\boldsymbol{P}_2\boldsymbol{P} = \boldsymbol{P}\boldsymbol{P}_2 = \boldsymbol{P}_2$ and interpret this result in terms of projections. What does it imply for $\boldsymbol{M}_2\boldsymbol{M}$?
(b) Show that

$$\widehat{\boldsymbol{\beta}} := \begin{pmatrix} \widehat{\boldsymbol{\beta}}_1 \\ \widehat{\boldsymbol{\beta}}_2 \end{pmatrix} = \begin{pmatrix} (\boldsymbol{X}_1'\boldsymbol{M}_2\boldsymbol{X}_1)^{-1}\boldsymbol{X}_1'\boldsymbol{M}_2\boldsymbol{y} \\ (\boldsymbol{X}_2'\boldsymbol{M}_1\boldsymbol{X}_2)^{-1}\boldsymbol{X}_2'\boldsymbol{M}_1\boldsymbol{y} \end{pmatrix}.$$

(c) Derive the mean and variance of $\widehat{\boldsymbol{\beta}}_1$, and show that $\widehat{\boldsymbol{\beta}}_1$ is also the MLE of $\boldsymbol{\beta}_1$ in the model $\boldsymbol{M}_2\boldsymbol{y} = \boldsymbol{M}_2\boldsymbol{X}_1\boldsymbol{\beta}_1 + \boldsymbol{\eta}$, where $\boldsymbol{\eta} \sim \mathrm{N}(\boldsymbol{0}, \sigma^2\boldsymbol{I}_n)$.
(d) Show that $\widehat{\boldsymbol{\eta}} = \widehat{\boldsymbol{\varepsilon}}$. Does this mean that $\boldsymbol{\eta} = \boldsymbol{\varepsilon}$?
(e) Let $\widetilde{\boldsymbol{\beta}}_1 := (\boldsymbol{X}_1'\boldsymbol{X}_1)^{-1}\boldsymbol{X}_1'\boldsymbol{y}$. Derive the mean of $\widetilde{\boldsymbol{\beta}}_1$. When is it an unbiased estimator of $\boldsymbol{\beta}_1$? Notice that $\widetilde{\boldsymbol{\beta}}_1$ is the MLE obtained by regressing $\boldsymbol{y}$ on $\boldsymbol{X}_1$ only, omitting $\boldsymbol{X}_2$ erroneously from the estimated model.
(f) Suppose that $\boldsymbol{X}_1$ contains a constant term (a column of ones), and that β_2 is a scalar so that $\boldsymbol{X}_2 = \boldsymbol{x}_2$ is a column vector. Show that $R^2 = R_1^2 + \left(1 - R_1^2\right) r^2_{\boldsymbol{y},\boldsymbol{x}_2|\boldsymbol{X}_1}$, where R^2 is the coefficient of determination from the regression of $\boldsymbol{y}$ on $\boldsymbol{X}$, and R_1^2 that from the regression of $\boldsymbol{y}$ on $\boldsymbol{X}_1$ only; $r_{\boldsymbol{y},\boldsymbol{x}_2|\boldsymbol{X}_1}$ is the correlation between $\boldsymbol{y}$ and $\boldsymbol{x}_2$ conditional on $\boldsymbol{X}_1$. (See Chapter 6 for the population counterpart of $r_{\boldsymbol{y},\boldsymbol{x}_2|\boldsymbol{X}_1}$.)

Solution

(a) By postmultiplying both sides of $\boldsymbol{P}\boldsymbol{X} = \boldsymbol{X}$ by $(\mathbf{O}, \boldsymbol{I})'$, we obtain $\boldsymbol{P}\boldsymbol{X}_2 = \boldsymbol{X}_2$. Postmultiplying this by $(\boldsymbol{X}_2'\boldsymbol{X}_2)^{-1}\boldsymbol{X}_2'$, we have $\boldsymbol{P}\boldsymbol{P}_2 = \boldsymbol{P}_2$. By the symmetry of $\boldsymbol{P}_2$, transposing both sides gives $\boldsymbol{P}_2\boldsymbol{P} = \boldsymbol{P}_2 = \boldsymbol{P}\boldsymbol{P}_2$. This is an intuitive property: projecting onto a space spanned by $\boldsymbol{X} = (\boldsymbol{X}_1, \boldsymbol{X}_2)$ then onto the subspace spanned by $\boldsymbol{X}_2$ would be the same as projecting directly onto the latter. In fact, we have already encountered this tower property in Chapter 6 (the nested LIE in Exercise 6.28 and the Note on it at the end of that chapter). This stresses the relation between conditioning and orthogonal projection in the normal linear model; see also Exercises 12.33 and 12.34. The result and its interpretation both imply that the complement projections satisfy

$$\boldsymbol{M}_2\boldsymbol{M} = (\boldsymbol{I}_n - \boldsymbol{P}_2)\,\boldsymbol{M} = \boldsymbol{M} - \boldsymbol{P}_2\,(\boldsymbol{I}_n - \boldsymbol{P}) = \boldsymbol{M} - (\boldsymbol{P}_2 - \boldsymbol{P}_2\boldsymbol{P}) = \boldsymbol{M}.$$

(b) By the partitioned inverse of $\boldsymbol{X}'\boldsymbol{X}$, using both Schur complements,

$$(\boldsymbol{X}'\boldsymbol{X})^{-1} = \begin{pmatrix} (\boldsymbol{X}_1'\boldsymbol{M}_2\boldsymbol{X}_1)^{-1} & -(\boldsymbol{X}_1'\boldsymbol{M}_2\boldsymbol{X}_1)^{-1}\boldsymbol{X}_1'\boldsymbol{X}_2\,(\boldsymbol{X}_2'\boldsymbol{X}_2)^{-1} \\ -(\boldsymbol{X}_2'\boldsymbol{M}_1\boldsymbol{X}_2)^{-1}\boldsymbol{X}_2'\boldsymbol{X}_1\,(\boldsymbol{X}_1'\boldsymbol{X}_1)^{-1} & (\boldsymbol{X}_2'\boldsymbol{M}_1\boldsymbol{X}_2)^{-1} \end{pmatrix},$$

and we obtain

$$\widehat{\boldsymbol{\beta}} = (\boldsymbol{X}'\boldsymbol{X})^{-1}\begin{pmatrix} \boldsymbol{X}_1'\boldsymbol{y} \\ \boldsymbol{X}_2'\boldsymbol{y} \end{pmatrix} = \begin{pmatrix} (\boldsymbol{X}_1'\boldsymbol{M}_2\boldsymbol{X}_1)^{-1}\boldsymbol{X}_1'\boldsymbol{M}_2\boldsymbol{y} \\ (\boldsymbol{X}_2'\boldsymbol{M}_1\boldsymbol{X}_2)^{-1}\boldsymbol{X}_2'\boldsymbol{M}_1\boldsymbol{y} \end{pmatrix}.$$

(c) The mean and variance of $\widehat{\boldsymbol{\beta}}_1$ are the first block of the mean and variance of $\widehat{\boldsymbol{\beta}}$, which were derived in Exercise 12.31(b) as β and $\sigma^2 \left(\boldsymbol{X}'\boldsymbol{X}\right)^{-1}$, respectively. Therefore, $\widehat{\beta}_1$ is unbiased for β_1 and has $\operatorname{var}(\widehat{\beta}_1) = \sigma^2(\boldsymbol{X}_1'\boldsymbol{M}_2\boldsymbol{X}_1)^{-1}$. By Exercise 12.30(b), the MLE of β_1 in $\boldsymbol{M}_2\boldsymbol{y} = \boldsymbol{M}_2\boldsymbol{X}_1\beta_1 + \boldsymbol{\eta}$ is $(\boldsymbol{X}_1\boldsymbol{M}_2^2\boldsymbol{X}_1)^{-1}\boldsymbol{X}_1'\boldsymbol{M}_2^2\boldsymbol{y}$, which coincides with our estimator from $\boldsymbol{y} = \boldsymbol{X}\beta + \boldsymbol{\varepsilon}$ because $\boldsymbol{M}_2^2 = \boldsymbol{M}_2$. Note that $\boldsymbol{M}_2\boldsymbol{y}$ are the residuals from the regression of $\boldsymbol{y}$ on $\boldsymbol{X}_2$, since

$$\boldsymbol{M}_2\boldsymbol{y} = \boldsymbol{y} - \boldsymbol{X}_2\left(\left(\boldsymbol{X}_2'\boldsymbol{X}_2\right)^{-1}\boldsymbol{X}_2'\boldsymbol{y}\right),$$

while $\boldsymbol{M}_2\boldsymbol{X}_1$ are the residuals from the regression of the columns of $\boldsymbol{X}_1$ on $\boldsymbol{X}_2$. We have thus shown that this two-step procedure (regressing the residuals $\boldsymbol{M}_2\boldsymbol{y}$ on the residuals $\boldsymbol{M}_2\boldsymbol{X}_1$) is an equivalent way to obtain $\widehat{\beta}_1$ from the full regression of $\boldsymbol{y}$ on $(\boldsymbol{X}_1, \boldsymbol{X}_2)$.

(d) First, the defining equation of $\boldsymbol{y}$ in the original model gives

$$\boldsymbol{M}_2\boldsymbol{y} = \boldsymbol{M}_2\left(\boldsymbol{X}\beta + \boldsymbol{\varepsilon}\right) = \boldsymbol{M}_2\boldsymbol{X}_1\beta_1 + \boldsymbol{M}_2\boldsymbol{\varepsilon}$$

since $\boldsymbol{M}_2\boldsymbol{X}_2 = \mathbf{O}$. Comparing this with the alternative model $\boldsymbol{M}_2\boldsymbol{y} = \boldsymbol{M}_2\boldsymbol{X}_1\beta_1 + \boldsymbol{\eta}$, we see that $\boldsymbol{\varepsilon}$ and $\boldsymbol{\eta}$ are not the same variate. In fact, the two models (the one having error $\boldsymbol{\varepsilon}$ and the other having error $\boldsymbol{\eta}$) *cannot* be the same, since $\boldsymbol{M}_2\boldsymbol{\varepsilon} \sim \mathrm{N}(\mathbf{0}, \sigma^2\boldsymbol{M}_2)$ is not the distribution of $\boldsymbol{\eta}$. However, the models have the same MLE solution for β_1. Moreover,

$$\boldsymbol{M}_2\boldsymbol{y} = \boldsymbol{M}_2(\boldsymbol{X}\widehat{\beta} + \widehat{\boldsymbol{\varepsilon}}) = \boldsymbol{M}_2(\boldsymbol{X}\widehat{\beta} + \boldsymbol{M}\boldsymbol{y}) = \boldsymbol{M}_2\boldsymbol{X}_1\widehat{\beta}_1 + \boldsymbol{M}\boldsymbol{y} = \boldsymbol{M}_2\boldsymbol{X}_1\widehat{\beta}_1 + \widehat{\boldsymbol{\varepsilon}},$$

and $\widehat{\boldsymbol{\eta}} = \boldsymbol{M}_2\boldsymbol{y} - \boldsymbol{M}_2\boldsymbol{X}_1\widehat{\beta}_1$ implies that $\widehat{\boldsymbol{\eta}} = \widehat{\boldsymbol{\varepsilon}}$ and the two models have the same maximum value of the likelihood function, by Exercise 12.30(c).

(e) We have

$$\begin{aligned}
\mathrm{E}(\widetilde{\beta}_1) &= \mathrm{E}\left(\left(\boldsymbol{X}_1'\boldsymbol{X}_1\right)^{-1}\boldsymbol{X}_1'\left(\boldsymbol{X}_1\beta_1 + \boldsymbol{X}_2\beta_2 + \boldsymbol{\varepsilon}\right)\right) \\
&= \beta_1 + \left(\boldsymbol{X}_1'\boldsymbol{X}_1\right)^{-1}\boldsymbol{X}_1'\boldsymbol{X}_2\beta_2 + \left(\boldsymbol{X}_1'\boldsymbol{X}_1\right)^{-1}\boldsymbol{X}_1'\,\mathrm{E}\left(\boldsymbol{\varepsilon}\right) \\
&= \beta_1 + \left(\boldsymbol{X}_1'\boldsymbol{X}_1\right)^{-1}\boldsymbol{X}_1'\boldsymbol{X}_2\beta_2.
\end{aligned}$$

For general $\boldsymbol{X}_2$, the estimator $\widetilde{\beta}_1$ is unbiased when $\beta_2 = \mathbf{0}$ (hence $\boldsymbol{X}_2$ is absent from all the models anyway) or when $\boldsymbol{X}_1'\boldsymbol{X}_2 = \mathbf{O}$ (and so $\boldsymbol{X}_1$ and $\boldsymbol{X}_2$ are orthogonal to one another). Otherwise, we have an *omitted-variables bias*. Contrast this with (c), where regressing $\boldsymbol{y}$ on $\boldsymbol{X}_1$ is only part of the first step towards obtaining the unbiased MLE $\widehat{\beta}_1$.

(f) Recall the relation of conditioning to regression in the normal linear model, from Exercise 12.33. The sample mean of $\boldsymbol{y}$ given $\boldsymbol{X}_1$ is the fitted part of the regression of $\boldsymbol{y}$ on $\boldsymbol{X}_1$, namely

$$\boldsymbol{X}_1\widetilde{\beta}_1 = \boldsymbol{X}_1\left(\left(\boldsymbol{X}_1'\boldsymbol{X}_1\right)^{-1}\boldsymbol{X}_1'\boldsymbol{y}\right) = \boldsymbol{P}_1\boldsymbol{y},$$

while $\boldsymbol{P}_1\boldsymbol{x}_2$ is the sample mean of $\boldsymbol{x}_2$ given $\boldsymbol{X}_1$. Therefore, the correlation $r_{y,x_2|\boldsymbol{X}_1}$ is given by

$$\frac{\left(\boldsymbol{y} - \boldsymbol{P}_1\boldsymbol{y}\right)'\left(\boldsymbol{x}_2 - \boldsymbol{P}_1\boldsymbol{x}_2\right)}{\sqrt{\left(\boldsymbol{y} - \boldsymbol{P}_1\boldsymbol{y}\right)'\left(\boldsymbol{y} - \boldsymbol{P}_1\boldsymbol{y}\right)}\sqrt{\left(\boldsymbol{x}_2 - \boldsymbol{P}_1\boldsymbol{x}_2\right)'\left(\boldsymbol{x}_2 - \boldsymbol{P}_1\boldsymbol{x}_2\right)}} = \frac{\boldsymbol{y}'\boldsymbol{M}_1\boldsymbol{x}_2}{\sqrt{\boldsymbol{y}'\boldsymbol{M}_1\boldsymbol{y}}\sqrt{\boldsymbol{x}_2'\boldsymbol{M}_1\boldsymbol{x}_2}},$$

where no further de-meaning of $\boldsymbol{y}$ or $\boldsymbol{x}_2$ is needed because $\boldsymbol{X}_1$ includes the constant term. Letting $\boldsymbol{A} := \boldsymbol{I}_n - \frac{1}{n}\boldsymbol{\imath}\boldsymbol{\imath}'$, we have

$$1 - R^2 = \frac{\boldsymbol{y}'\boldsymbol{M}\boldsymbol{y}}{\boldsymbol{y}'\boldsymbol{A}\boldsymbol{y}} \quad \text{and} \quad 1 - R_1^2 = \frac{\boldsymbol{y}'\boldsymbol{M}_1\boldsymbol{y}}{\boldsymbol{y}'\boldsymbol{A}\boldsymbol{y}};$$

hence

$$1 - R_1^2 - \left(1 - R_1^2\right) r^2_{\boldsymbol{y},\boldsymbol{x}_2|\boldsymbol{X}_1} = \frac{\boldsymbol{y}'\boldsymbol{M}_1\boldsymbol{y}}{\boldsymbol{y}'\boldsymbol{A}\boldsymbol{y}} - \frac{\boldsymbol{y}'\boldsymbol{M}_1\boldsymbol{y}}{\boldsymbol{y}'\boldsymbol{A}\boldsymbol{y}} \frac{\left(\boldsymbol{y}'\boldsymbol{M}_1\boldsymbol{x}_2\right)^2}{\boldsymbol{y}'\boldsymbol{M}_1\boldsymbol{y}\boldsymbol{x}_2'\boldsymbol{M}_1\boldsymbol{x}_2}$$

$$= \frac{\boldsymbol{y}'\boldsymbol{M}_1\boldsymbol{y}}{\boldsymbol{y}'\boldsymbol{A}\boldsymbol{y}} - \frac{\boldsymbol{x}_2'\boldsymbol{M}_1\boldsymbol{x}_2}{\boldsymbol{y}'\boldsymbol{A}\boldsymbol{y}} \left(\frac{\boldsymbol{y}'\boldsymbol{M}_1\boldsymbol{x}_2}{\boldsymbol{x}_2'\boldsymbol{M}_1\boldsymbol{x}_2}\right)^2 = \frac{\boldsymbol{y}'\boldsymbol{M}_1\boldsymbol{y} - \widehat{\beta}_2^2\boldsymbol{x}_2'\boldsymbol{M}_1\boldsymbol{x}_2}{\boldsymbol{y}'\boldsymbol{A}\boldsymbol{y}},$$

where $\widehat{\beta}_2$ is obtained from (b). If we can show that $\boldsymbol{y}'\boldsymbol{M}_1\boldsymbol{y} - \widehat{\beta}_2^2\boldsymbol{x}_2'\boldsymbol{M}_1\boldsymbol{x}_2 = \boldsymbol{y}'\boldsymbol{M}\boldsymbol{y}$, then we are done. From (c) and (d), we know that the residuals $\boldsymbol{M}_1\boldsymbol{y} - \widehat{\beta}_2\boldsymbol{M}_1\boldsymbol{x}_2$ are equal to $\widehat{\boldsymbol{\varepsilon}}$ (that is, $\boldsymbol{M}\boldsymbol{y}$). Therefore,

$$\begin{aligned} \boldsymbol{y}'\boldsymbol{M}\boldsymbol{y} &= (\boldsymbol{M}_1\boldsymbol{y} - \widehat{\beta}_2\boldsymbol{M}_1\boldsymbol{x}_2)'(\boldsymbol{M}_1\boldsymbol{y} - \widehat{\beta}_2\boldsymbol{M}_1\boldsymbol{x}_2) \\ &= \boldsymbol{y}'\boldsymbol{M}_1\boldsymbol{y} + \widehat{\beta}_2^2\boldsymbol{x}_2'\boldsymbol{M}_1\boldsymbol{x}_2 - 2\widehat{\beta}_2\boldsymbol{y}'\boldsymbol{M}_1\boldsymbol{x}_2 \\ &= \boldsymbol{y}'\boldsymbol{M}_1\boldsymbol{y} + \widehat{\beta}_2^2\boldsymbol{x}_2'\boldsymbol{M}_1\boldsymbol{x}_2 - 2\widehat{\beta}_2^2\boldsymbol{x}_2'\boldsymbol{M}_1\boldsymbol{x}_2 \end{aligned}$$

as required. Notice that, dividing the last equation by $\boldsymbol{y}'\boldsymbol{A}\boldsymbol{y}$, we get $1 - R^2 = 1 - R_1^2 - \left(1 - R_1^2\right) r^2_{\boldsymbol{y},\boldsymbol{x}_2|\boldsymbol{X}_1}$, hence

$$1 - R^2 = \left(1 - R_1^2\right)\left(1 - r^2_{\boldsymbol{y},\boldsymbol{x}_2|\boldsymbol{X}_1}\right);$$

that is, the percentage of unexplained sum of squares decomposes into the product of the marginal and the conditional percentages.

Our result implies that $R^2 \geqslant R_1^2$ when $\boldsymbol{X}_1$ contains a constant term, regardless of whether $\beta_2 = 0$. Adding a variable to a regression cannot decrease R^2, even if the variable is irrelevant ($\beta_2 = 0$); see the distribution of R^2 in Exercise 12.35(f), which implies strictly positive realizations. We will start addressing the detection of irrelevant variables in Chapter 13 and more fully in Chapter 14.

12.4 Further properties of likelihoods: nonstandard aspects

Exercise 12.40 (MLE via profile, continued) We saw in Exercise 12.18 that optimizing profile likelihoods leads to MLEs. However, this exercise will show that profile likelihoods do not have all the properties of standard likelihood functions (such as the information-matrix equivalence).

Assume the MLEs of $\boldsymbol{\theta}' := (\boldsymbol{\theta}_1', \boldsymbol{\theta}_2')$ exist and are denoted by $(\widehat{\boldsymbol{\theta}}_1', \widehat{\boldsymbol{\theta}}_2')$ of dimensions m_1 and m_2, respectively, where $m_1 + m_2 = m$. Assume further that Condition 2 of the introduction holds: the log-likelihood $\ell(\boldsymbol{\theta})$ is continuously differentiable twice, and the

expectations of $\ell(\boldsymbol{\theta})$ and its first two derivatives exist.
(a) Assume that Condition A of the introduction holds: $\widehat{\boldsymbol{\theta}}$ belongs to the interior of Θ, with probability 1. Denoting the profile log-likelihood of $\boldsymbol{\theta}_1$ by $\ell_{\mathrm{p}}(\boldsymbol{\theta}_1) := \sup_{\boldsymbol{\theta}_2} \ell(\boldsymbol{\theta})$, show that

$$q_{\mathrm{p}}(\widehat{\boldsymbol{\theta}}_1) := \left.\frac{\partial \ell_{\mathrm{p}}(\boldsymbol{\theta}_1)}{\partial \boldsymbol{\theta}_1}\right|_{\boldsymbol{\theta}_1=\widehat{\boldsymbol{\theta}}_1} = \mathbf{0}_{m_1}.$$

(b) Assume that Condition A holds. Assume further that $\mathcal{H}(\widehat{\boldsymbol{\theta}})$ is negative definite with probability 1. Show that

$$\mathcal{H}_{\mathrm{p}}(\widehat{\boldsymbol{\theta}}_1) := \left.\frac{\partial^2 \ell_{\mathrm{p}}(\boldsymbol{\theta}_1)}{\partial \boldsymbol{\theta}_1 \partial \boldsymbol{\theta}_1'}\right|_{\boldsymbol{\theta}_1=\widehat{\boldsymbol{\theta}}_1} = \mathcal{H}_{11|2}(\widehat{\boldsymbol{\theta}}),$$

where $\mathcal{H}_{11|2} := \mathcal{H}_{11} - \mathcal{H}_{12}\mathcal{H}_{22}^{-1}\mathcal{H}_{21}$.
(c) Show that the profile's score does not satisfy $\mathrm{E}(q_{\mathrm{p}}(\boldsymbol{\theta}_1)) = \mathbf{0}_{m_1}$ in general. What if $\mathcal{H}_{12} = \mathbf{O}$?

Solution
(a) This follows from Exercise 12.18, where we have seen that the MLE $\widehat{\boldsymbol{\theta}}_1$ maximizes the profile likelihood. Here, we present an alternative proof of $q_{\mathrm{p}}(\widehat{\boldsymbol{\theta}}_1) = \mathbf{0}_{m_1}$ which exploits the differentiability of the likelihood, and which will be required for the rest of the exercise. Partitioning, we obtain

$$q(\boldsymbol{\theta}) := \begin{pmatrix} q_1(\boldsymbol{\theta}) \\ q_2(\boldsymbol{\theta}) \end{pmatrix} = \begin{pmatrix} \partial \ell(\boldsymbol{\theta})/\partial \boldsymbol{\theta}_1 \\ \partial \ell(\boldsymbol{\theta})/\partial \boldsymbol{\theta}_2 \end{pmatrix},$$

the MLE is obtained by solving $q_1(\boldsymbol{\theta}) = \mathbf{0}_{m_1}$ and $q_2(\boldsymbol{\theta}) = \mathbf{0}_{m_2}$, by Condition A. Solving the latter equation gives rise to the function $\widehat{\boldsymbol{\theta}}_2(\boldsymbol{\theta}_1)$ and, solving both equations, we note for later use that, at $\widehat{\boldsymbol{\theta}}_1$ and $\widehat{\boldsymbol{\theta}}_2(\widehat{\boldsymbol{\theta}}_1)$, we have $q_1(\boldsymbol{\theta}) = \mathbf{0}_{m_1}$. Now,

$$\ell_{\mathrm{p}}(\boldsymbol{\theta}_1) = \ell\left(\boldsymbol{\theta}_1, \widehat{\boldsymbol{\theta}}_2(\boldsymbol{\theta}_1)\right).$$

Differentiating with respect to $\boldsymbol{\theta}_1$,

$$q_{\mathrm{p}}(\boldsymbol{\theta}_1) = \frac{\partial \ell\left(\boldsymbol{\theta}_1, \widehat{\boldsymbol{\theta}}_2(\boldsymbol{\theta}_1)\right)}{\partial \boldsymbol{\theta}_1} = \left.\left(\frac{\partial \ell(\boldsymbol{\theta}_1, \boldsymbol{\theta}_2)}{\partial \boldsymbol{\theta}_1} + \frac{\partial \widehat{\boldsymbol{\theta}}_2(\boldsymbol{\theta}_1)'}{\partial \boldsymbol{\theta}_1} \frac{\partial \ell(\boldsymbol{\theta}_1, \boldsymbol{\theta}_2)}{\partial \boldsymbol{\theta}_2}\right)\right|_{\boldsymbol{\theta}_2=\widehat{\boldsymbol{\theta}}_2(\boldsymbol{\theta}_1)}$$

$$= \left.\left(q_1(\boldsymbol{\theta}) + \frac{\partial \widehat{\boldsymbol{\theta}}_2(\boldsymbol{\theta}_1)'}{\partial \boldsymbol{\theta}_1} q_2(\boldsymbol{\theta})\right)\right|_{\boldsymbol{\theta}_2=\widehat{\boldsymbol{\theta}}_2(\boldsymbol{\theta}_1)} = q_1(\boldsymbol{\theta})\big|_{\boldsymbol{\theta}_2=\widehat{\boldsymbol{\theta}}_2(\boldsymbol{\theta}_1)}$$

since we have seen that $\widehat{\boldsymbol{\theta}}_2(\boldsymbol{\theta}_1)$ solves $q_2(\boldsymbol{\theta}) = \mathbf{0}_{m_2}$. The result follows by evaluating the displayed equation at $\boldsymbol{\theta}_1 = \widehat{\boldsymbol{\theta}}_1$.
(b) This part will show that the inverse of the Hessian for $\boldsymbol{\theta}_1$ is the same (at $\widehat{\boldsymbol{\theta}}_1$) whether one uses the full or profile likelihood, that is,

$$\left(\mathcal{H}_{\mathrm{p}}(\widehat{\boldsymbol{\theta}}_1)\right)^{-1} = \mathcal{H}^{11}(\widehat{\boldsymbol{\theta}}),$$

where $\mathcal{H}^{11} := \left(\mathcal{H}_{11} - \mathcal{H}_{12}\mathcal{H}_{22}^{-1}\mathcal{H}_{21}\right)^{-1}$ is the first block (corresponding to $\boldsymbol{\theta}_1$) in the inverse of the partitioned $\mathcal{H}$. This matrix is particularly important for the linear model, because the partitioning in Exercise 12.31 shows that it is the negative of the variance of $\widehat{\boldsymbol{\beta}}$, conditional on $\boldsymbol{X}$. Differentiating both sides of $\boldsymbol{q}_\mathrm{p}(\boldsymbol{\theta}_1) = \boldsymbol{q}_1(\boldsymbol{\theta})|_{\boldsymbol{\theta}_2=\widehat{\boldsymbol{\theta}}_2(\boldsymbol{\theta}_1)}$ with respect to $\boldsymbol{\theta}_1'$, we obtain

$$\mathcal{H}_\mathrm{p}(\boldsymbol{\theta}_1) = \frac{\partial \boldsymbol{q}_1\left(\boldsymbol{\theta}_1, \widehat{\boldsymbol{\theta}}_2(\boldsymbol{\theta}_1)\right)}{\partial \boldsymbol{\theta}_1'} = \left(\mathcal{H}_{11}(\boldsymbol{\theta}) + \mathcal{H}_{12}(\boldsymbol{\theta}) \frac{\partial \widehat{\boldsymbol{\theta}}_2(\boldsymbol{\theta}_1)}{\partial \boldsymbol{\theta}_1'}\right)\Bigg|_{\boldsymbol{\theta}_2=\widehat{\boldsymbol{\theta}}_2(\boldsymbol{\theta}_1)}.$$

To obtain the required result, we need to express the derivative of $\widehat{\boldsymbol{\theta}}_2(\boldsymbol{\theta}_1)$ in terms of the Hessian. From (a), $\mathbf{0}_{m_2} = \boldsymbol{q}_2(\boldsymbol{\theta})|_{\boldsymbol{\theta}_2=\widehat{\boldsymbol{\theta}}_2(\boldsymbol{\theta}_1)}$ for all $\boldsymbol{\theta}_1$. Differentiating both sides gives

$$\mathrm{O} = \frac{\partial \boldsymbol{q}_2(\boldsymbol{\theta})}{\partial \boldsymbol{\theta}_1'} = \mathcal{H}_{21}(\boldsymbol{\theta}) + \mathcal{H}_{22}(\boldsymbol{\theta}) \frac{\partial \boldsymbol{\theta}_2}{\partial \boldsymbol{\theta}_1'}$$

at $\boldsymbol{\theta}_2 = \widehat{\boldsymbol{\theta}}_2(\boldsymbol{\theta}_1)$, hence $\partial\widehat{\boldsymbol{\theta}}_2(\boldsymbol{\theta}_1)/\partial\boldsymbol{\theta}_1' = -\mathcal{H}_{22}(\boldsymbol{\theta})^{-1}\mathcal{H}_{21}(\boldsymbol{\theta})$ as required.
(c) As before, we can show that

$$\begin{aligned}\boldsymbol{q}_\mathrm{p}(\boldsymbol{\theta}_1) &= \left(\boldsymbol{q}_1(\boldsymbol{\theta}) + \frac{\partial \widehat{\boldsymbol{\theta}}_2(\boldsymbol{\theta}_1)'}{\partial \boldsymbol{\theta}_1} \boldsymbol{q}_2(\boldsymbol{\theta})\right)\Bigg|_{\boldsymbol{\theta}_2=\widehat{\boldsymbol{\theta}}_2(\boldsymbol{\theta}_1)} \\ &= \left(\boldsymbol{q}_1(\boldsymbol{\theta}) - \mathcal{H}_{12}(\boldsymbol{\theta})\mathcal{H}_{22}(\boldsymbol{\theta})^{-1}\boldsymbol{q}_2(\boldsymbol{\theta})\right)\Big|_{\boldsymbol{\theta}_2=\widehat{\boldsymbol{\theta}}_2(\boldsymbol{\theta}_1)},\end{aligned}$$

where we have not assumed Condition A, so we should not substitute $\boldsymbol{q}_2(\boldsymbol{\theta}) = \mathbf{0}_{m_2}$ at the partial MLE. On the other hand, for all $\boldsymbol{\theta}_1$ (hence also for all partial MLEs $\widehat{\boldsymbol{\theta}}_2(\boldsymbol{\theta}_1)$), we have $\mathrm{E}(\boldsymbol{q}_1(\boldsymbol{\theta})) = \mathbf{0}_{m_1}$ and $\mathrm{E}(\boldsymbol{q}_2(\boldsymbol{\theta})) = \mathbf{0}_{m_2}$ by the information-matrix equivalence. Now, $\mathcal{H}_{12}$ and $\mathcal{H}_{22}$ are random and

$$\mathrm{E}\left(\boldsymbol{q}_\mathrm{p}(\boldsymbol{\theta}_1)\right) = -\mathrm{E}\left(\mathcal{H}_{12}(\boldsymbol{\theta})\mathcal{H}_{22}(\boldsymbol{\theta})^{-1}\boldsymbol{q}_2(\boldsymbol{\theta})\Big|_{\boldsymbol{\theta}_2=\widehat{\boldsymbol{\theta}}_2(\boldsymbol{\theta}_1)}\right)$$

need not be zero, even though the regularity conditions are met (unlike in Exercise 12.12(e)). Therefore, $\ell_\mathrm{p}(\boldsymbol{\theta}_1)$ is not really a log-likelihood function, and we have seen here that it violates the information-matrix equivalence. If it happens that $\mathcal{H}_{12} = \mathrm{O}$, a very strong condition indeed (to second order, the likelihood separates into the marginal likelihoods of $\boldsymbol{\theta}_1$ and $\boldsymbol{\theta}_2$), then $\mathrm{E}\left(\boldsymbol{q}_\mathrm{p}(\boldsymbol{\theta}_1)\right) = \mathbf{0}_{m_1}$. The condition $\mathcal{H}_{12} = \mathrm{O}$ is sufficient (but not necessary) for the information matrix to become block-diagonal and for the parameterization to be orthogonal.

Exercise 12.41 (Modify that profile!) For the general setup of Exercise 12.40, the Barndorff-Nielsen's *modified profile log-likelihood* is defined as

$$\ell_\mathrm{m}(\boldsymbol{\theta}_1) := \ell_\mathrm{p}(\boldsymbol{\theta}_1) - \frac{1}{2}\log\left|-\mathcal{H}_{22}(\boldsymbol{\theta})|_{\boldsymbol{\theta}_2=\widehat{\boldsymbol{\theta}}_2(\boldsymbol{\theta}_1)}\right| - \log\left|\frac{\partial \widehat{\boldsymbol{\theta}}_2(\boldsymbol{\theta}_1)}{\partial \widehat{\boldsymbol{\theta}}_2'}\right|.$$

Now, consider the normal linear model of Exercise 12.30 and suppose further that we have

$\boldsymbol{\theta}' := (\theta_1, \boldsymbol{\theta}_2') = (\sigma^2, \widehat{\boldsymbol{\beta}}')$, that is, the parameter of interest is σ^2. Show that:
(a) $\mathrm{E}\left(\mathrm{d}\ell_{\mathrm{p}}\left(\sigma^2\right)/\mathrm{d}\sigma^2\right) = -k/(2\sigma^2) \neq 0$;
(b) $\mathrm{E}\left(\mathrm{d}\ell_{\mathrm{m}}\left(\sigma^2\right)/\mathrm{d}\sigma^2\right) = 0$.

Solution

(a) From Exercise 12.30, we have $\widehat{\boldsymbol{\theta}}_2(\theta_1) = \widehat{\boldsymbol{\beta}}$, which does not depend on σ^2. The profile log-likelihood is obtained by substituting $\boldsymbol{\beta} = \widehat{\boldsymbol{\beta}}$ in the log-likelihood, and we have

$$\ell_{\mathrm{p}}\left(\sigma^2\right) = -\frac{n}{2}\log(2\pi) - \frac{n}{2}\log\left(\sigma^2\right) - \frac{1}{2\sigma^2}(\boldsymbol{y} - \boldsymbol{X}\widehat{\boldsymbol{\beta}})'(\boldsymbol{y} - \boldsymbol{X}\widehat{\boldsymbol{\beta}}).$$

Differentiating with respect to σ^2,

$$\frac{\mathrm{d}\ell_{\mathrm{p}}\left(\sigma^2\right)}{\mathrm{d}\sigma^2} = -\frac{n}{2\sigma^2} + \frac{1}{2\sigma^4}(\boldsymbol{y} - \boldsymbol{X}\widehat{\boldsymbol{\beta}})'(\boldsymbol{y} - \boldsymbol{X}\widehat{\boldsymbol{\beta}}).$$

Now, $\boldsymbol{y} - \boldsymbol{X}\widehat{\boldsymbol{\beta}} \equiv \widehat{\boldsymbol{\varepsilon}} = \boldsymbol{M}\boldsymbol{\varepsilon}$ by Exercise 12.31(e), with $\boldsymbol{M} := \boldsymbol{I}_n - \boldsymbol{X}\left(\boldsymbol{X}'\boldsymbol{X}\right)^{-1}\boldsymbol{X}'$. Therefore,

$$\mathrm{E}\left(\boldsymbol{\varepsilon}'\boldsymbol{M}\boldsymbol{\varepsilon}\right) = \operatorname{tr}\left(\boldsymbol{M}\,\mathrm{E}\left(\boldsymbol{\varepsilon}\boldsymbol{\varepsilon}'\right)\right) = \operatorname{tr}\left(\boldsymbol{M}\left(\sigma^2\boldsymbol{I}_n\right)\right) = (n-k)\,\sigma^2,$$

and the result follows.
(b) Since $\widehat{\boldsymbol{\theta}}_2(\theta_1) = \widehat{\boldsymbol{\beta}}$ does not depend on σ^2, we have

$$\log\left|\frac{\partial\widehat{\boldsymbol{\theta}}_2(\theta_1)}{\partial\widehat{\boldsymbol{\theta}}_2'}\right| = \log|\boldsymbol{I}_k| = \log 1 = 0,$$

so the last term of $\ell_{\mathrm{m}}(\theta_1)$ drops out. From Exercise 12.30(a), after the change of index of the Hessian there, we have

$$\begin{aligned}\ell_{\mathrm{m}}\left(\sigma^2\right) &= \ell_{\mathrm{p}}\left(\sigma^2\right) - \frac{1}{2}\log\left|\frac{1}{\sigma^2}\boldsymbol{X}'\boldsymbol{X}\right| = \ell_{\mathrm{p}}\left(\sigma^2\right) - \frac{1}{2}\log\left(\frac{1}{\sigma^{2k}}\left|\boldsymbol{X}'\boldsymbol{X}\right|\right)\\ &= \ell_{\mathrm{p}}\left(\sigma^2\right) + \frac{k}{2}\log\left(\sigma^2\right) - \frac{1}{2}\log\left|\boldsymbol{X}'\boldsymbol{X}\right|.\end{aligned}$$

Differentiating with respect to σ^2 gives a correction factor of $k/(2\sigma^2)$ for the expectation in (a), as required. Notice that the estimator of σ^2 obtained from maximizing $\ell_{\mathrm{m}}\left(\sigma^2\right)$ is $(n-k)^{-1}\,\widehat{\boldsymbol{\varepsilon}}'\widehat{\boldsymbol{\varepsilon}}$, which is the BUE s^2 discussed in Exercise 12.31(e).

Exercise 12.42 (Neyman–Scott problem, solved) Consider the setup of Exercise 12.13. Show that applying the modified profile likelihood introduced in Exercise 12.41 to that setup yields $\mathrm{E}\left(\mathrm{d}\ell_{\mathrm{m}}\left(\sigma^2\right)/\mathrm{d}\sigma^2\right) = 0$.

Solution

This follows by writing the model of Exercise 12.13 in terms of matrices, as a normal linear model, then applying the result in Exercise 12.41(b). The model $\{\{y_{ij}\}_{i=1}^{n_1}\}_{j=1}^{n_2} \sim$

$\text{IN}(\mu_i, \sigma^2)$ is equivalent to $\boldsymbol{y} = \boldsymbol{X\beta} + \boldsymbol{\varepsilon}$, where $n = n_1 n_2$ and $k = n_1$, with

$$\boldsymbol{X} = \boldsymbol{I}_{n_1} \otimes \boldsymbol{\imath}_{n_2}, \quad \boldsymbol{\beta} = \begin{pmatrix} \mu_1 \\ \vdots \\ \mu_{n_1} \end{pmatrix},$$

and the vector $\boldsymbol{y}$ is obtained from the matrix $\boldsymbol{Y} := (y_{ij})$ as $\boldsymbol{y} = \text{vec}(\boldsymbol{Y}')$. The estimator resulting from the maximization of $\ell_{\text{m}}(\sigma^2)$ is the BUE $(n-k)^{-1}\widehat{\boldsymbol{\varepsilon}}'\widehat{\boldsymbol{\varepsilon}} = n_1^{-1}(n_2-1)^{-1}\widehat{\boldsymbol{\varepsilon}}'\widehat{\boldsymbol{\varepsilon}}$.

***Exercise 12.43 (Time-series examples)** The following are two examples where the observations $\{y_i\}_{i=1}^n$ are arranged chronologically (a *time series*) over $i = 1, \dots, n$, where $n > 2$.
(a) Let $y_i = \beta i + \varepsilon_i$, where $\{\varepsilon_n\} \sim \text{IN}(0, \sigma^2)$. Show that $n^{3/2}(\widehat{\beta} - \beta) \overset{a}{\sim} \text{N}(0, 3\sigma^2)$, where $\widehat{\beta}$ is the MLE of β.
(b) Let $y_i = \alpha y_{i-1} + \varepsilon_i$, for $i = 1, \dots, n$, where $\{\varepsilon_n\} \sim \text{IN}(0, \sigma^2)$ and y_0 is a fixed constant. This is the AR(1) process defined in the Notes to Chapter 11. Writing $\boldsymbol{\theta} := (\alpha, \sigma^2)'$, derive the MLE $\widehat{\alpha}$ and the corresponding $\mathcal{H}_{11}, \mathcal{I}_{11}$, showing that WLLNs fail for $\mathcal{H}_{11}$ when $|\alpha| \geqslant 1$ and $y_0 = 0$. [Hint: Consider the variance of $\mathcal{H}_{11}/\text{E}(\mathcal{H}_{11})$ as $n \to \infty$.]

Solution

(a) Because the explanatory variable i is nonrandom (it is actually called a *linear time trend*), this follows directly from Exercise 12.31(b), where we replace $\boldsymbol{X}'\boldsymbol{X}$ by

$$\sum_{i=1}^n i^2 = \frac{n^3}{3} + O\left(n^2\right)$$

of Section A.4.1. Notice that, unlike in the case of i.i.d. observations mentioned in the introduction, $\mathcal{I} = O\left(n^3\right)$ instead of $O(n)$. This is so because the sequence $\{y_n\}$ is independently but *not* identically distributed, since $y_i \sim \text{N}\left(\beta i, \sigma^2\right)$. Notice the effect of this on the normalization of $\widehat{\beta} - \beta$ by $n^{3/2}$ instead of $\sqrt{n}$.
(b) The explanatory variable here is y_{i-1}, which is random unlike in the previous exercises of this chapter. Nevertheless, the results of Exercise 12.30 go through since y_0 is not random (so the likelihood is based on the only origin of randomness, $\{\varepsilon_n\}$), but the results in Exercise 12.31 no longer apply since $\boldsymbol{X}$ is now random and is generated from $\boldsymbol{\varepsilon}$: we cannot condition on $\boldsymbol{X}$ without fixing $\boldsymbol{\varepsilon}$. Exercise 12.30 gives $\widehat{\alpha} = \sum_{i=1}^n y_i y_{i-1} / \sum_{i=1}^n y_{i-1}^2$, with corresponding $\mathcal{H}_{11} = -\sigma^{-2}\sum_{i=1}^n y_{i-1}^2$. To take the expectation of the latter sum, we need to work out $\{y_n\}$ in terms of $\{\varepsilon_n\}$. By recursive substitution,

$$y_i = \alpha y_{i-1} + \varepsilon_i = \alpha\left(\alpha y_{i-2} + \varepsilon_{i-1}\right) + \varepsilon_i = \dots = \alpha^i y_0 + \sum_{j=0}^{i-1} \alpha^j \varepsilon_{i-j},$$

so $\boldsymbol{y} := (y_1, \dots, y_{n-1})'$ is normally distributed with $\text{E}(y_i) = \alpha^i y_0$ (notice that αy_{i-1} is the mean of y_i *conditional* on the past) and variance matrix $\boldsymbol{\Sigma}$ whose elements are, for

$k = 0, 1, \dots, n - i,$

$$\begin{aligned}\sigma_{i,i+k} &:= \operatorname{cov}(y_i, y_{i+k}) \\ &= \mathrm{E}\left(\left(\alpha^{i-1}\varepsilon_1 + \cdots + \varepsilon_i\right)\left(\alpha^{i+k-1}\varepsilon_1 + \cdots + \varepsilon_{i+k}\right)\right) \\ &= \sigma^2\alpha^k \sum_{j=0}^{i-1} \alpha^{2j} = \begin{cases} \sigma^2\alpha^k \dfrac{1-\alpha^{2i}}{1-\alpha^2} & (|\alpha| \neq 1), \\ \sigma^2\alpha^k i & (|\alpha| = 1), \end{cases}\end{aligned}$$

since $\mathrm{E}(\varepsilon_i\varepsilon_j) = 0$ for $i \neq j$ by the independence of the sequence $\{\varepsilon_n\}$, and $\mathrm{E}(\varepsilon_i^2) = \sigma^2$ for all i. This covariance is known as the *auto-covariance* of $\{y_n\}$, that is, the covariance of y_i with its future values (or y_{i+k} with its past values). Notice that $\lim_{k\to\infty} \operatorname{cov}(y_i, y_{i+k}) = 0$ for $|\alpha| < 1$ but not otherwise, the case $|\alpha| > 1$ being called an *explosive model* because $\lim_{k\to\infty} \operatorname{cov}(y_i, y_{i+k}) = \pm\infty$ (depending on the sign of α^k). Defining $c := y_0/\sigma$, we have

$$\begin{aligned}\frac{1}{\sigma^2}\mathrm{E}\left(y_{i-1}^2\right) &= \frac{1}{\sigma^2}\mathrm{E}\left(\left(\alpha^{i-1}y_0 + \sum_{j=0}^{i-2}\alpha^j\varepsilon_{i-j-1}\right)^2\right) \\ &= \alpha^{2i-2}c^2 + \sum_{j=0}^{i-2}\alpha^{2j} \\ &= \begin{cases} \alpha^{2i-2}\left(c^2 + \dfrac{1}{\alpha^2-1}\right) + \dfrac{1}{1-\alpha^2} & (|\alpha| \neq 1), \\ c^2 + i - 1 & (|\alpha| = 1), \end{cases}\end{aligned}$$

hence

$$\mathcal{I}_{11} = \frac{1}{\sigma^2}\sum_{i=1}^{n}\mathrm{E}\left(y_{i-1}^2\right) = \begin{cases} \dfrac{\alpha^{2n}-1}{\alpha^2-1}\left(c^2 + \dfrac{1}{\alpha^2-1}\right) + \dfrac{n}{1-\alpha^2} & (|\alpha| \neq 1), \\ nc^2 + \dfrac{n(n-1)}{2} & (|\alpha| = 1). \end{cases}$$

If $\mathcal{H}_{11}$ satisfies a WLLN, then $\mathcal{H}_{11}/\mathrm{E}(\mathcal{H}_{11}) \xrightarrow{p} 1$. Using a contrapositive argument, to demonstrate that WLLNs fail for $\mathcal{H}_{11}$ when $|\alpha| \geqslant 1$, we will show that $\mathcal{H}_{11}/\mathrm{E}(\mathcal{H}_{11})$ or $\mathcal{H}_{11}/\mathcal{I}_{11}$ is a nondegenerate variate as $n \to \infty$. Note that we need to divide by $\mathrm{E}(\mathcal{H}_{11})$ because $-\mathcal{H}_{11} > 0$ increases with n for all α, and we first have to neutralize this effect before we check the limit of the variance of $\mathcal{H}_{11}$. For $y_0 = 0$, we know from the introduction to Chapter 8 that $\operatorname{var}(\boldsymbol{y}'\boldsymbol{y}) = 2\operatorname{tr}\left(\boldsymbol{\Sigma}^2\right)$. Also, as $n \to \infty$,

$$\mathcal{I}_{11}^2 = \begin{cases} O\left(n^2\right) & (|\alpha| < 1), \\ O\left(n^4\right) & (|\alpha| = 1), \\ O\left(\alpha^{4n}\right) & (|\alpha| > 1), \end{cases}$$

which we will compare to the orders of magnitude of

$$\operatorname{var}\left(\boldsymbol{y}'\boldsymbol{y}\right) = 2\operatorname{tr}\left(\boldsymbol{\Sigma}^2\right) = 2\sum_{i=1}^{n-1}\sum_{j=1}^{n-1}\sigma_{ij}^2 = 2\sum_{i=1}^{n-1}\left(\sigma_{ii}^2 + 2\sum_{k=1}^{n-1-i}\sigma_{i,i+k}^2\right),$$

the last step following from the symmetry of $\boldsymbol{\Sigma}$. For $|\alpha| = 1$,

$$\begin{aligned}
\operatorname{var}\left(\frac{\boldsymbol{y}'\boldsymbol{y}}{n^2}\right) &= \frac{2}{n^4}\sum_{i=1}^{n-1}\left(\sigma^4 i^2 + 2\sum_{k=1}^{n-1-i}\sigma^4 i^2\right) \\
&= \frac{2\sigma^4}{n^4}\sum_{i=1}^{n-1} i^2\left(1 + 2\left(n-1-i\right)\right) \\
&= O\left(\frac{1}{n}\right) + \frac{4\sigma^4\left(n-1\right)}{n^4}\sum_{i=1}^{n-1} i^2 - \frac{4\sigma^4}{n^4}\sum_{i=1}^{n-1} i^3 \\
&= O\left(\frac{1}{n}\right) + \frac{4\sigma^4\left(n-1\right)}{n^4}\frac{n^3}{3}\left(1 + O\left(\frac{1}{n}\right)\right) - \frac{4\sigma^4}{n^4}\frac{n^4}{4}\left(1 + O\left(\frac{1}{n}\right)\right) \\
&= \frac{4\sigma^4}{3} - \sigma^4 + O\left(\frac{1}{n}\right) = \frac{\sigma^4}{3} + O\left(\frac{1}{n}\right) \to \frac{\sigma^4}{3} > 0,
\end{aligned}$$

so the variance of $\mathcal{H}_{11}/\mathcal{I}_{11}$ does not tend to zero. For $|\alpha| > 1$,

$$\begin{aligned}
\operatorname{var}\left(\frac{\boldsymbol{y}'\boldsymbol{y}}{\alpha^{2n}}\right) &= \frac{2}{\alpha^{4n}}\sum_{i=1}^{n-1}\sigma^4\left(\frac{\alpha^{2i}-1}{\alpha^2-1}\right)^2\left(1 + 2\sum_{k=1}^{n-1-i}\alpha^{2k}\right) \\
&= \frac{2}{\alpha^{4n}}\sum_{i=1}^{n-1}\sigma^4\left(\frac{\alpha^{2i}-1}{\alpha^2-1}\right)^2\left(1 + 2\frac{\alpha^{2n-2i}-\alpha^2}{\alpha^2-1}\right) \\
&= \frac{2\sigma^4}{\left(\alpha^2-1\right)^3\alpha^{4n}}\sum_{i=1}^{n-1}\left(\alpha^{2i}-1\right)^2\left(2\alpha^{2n-2i}-\alpha^2-1\right).
\end{aligned}$$

By $\left(\alpha^{2i}-1\right)^2 = \alpha^{4i} - 2\alpha^{2i} + 1$ and

$$\frac{1}{\alpha^{4n}}\sum_{i=1}^{n-1}\left(2\alpha^{2n-2i} - \left(\alpha^2+1\right)\right) = 2\frac{\alpha^{2n}-\alpha^2}{\alpha^{4n}\left(\alpha^2-1\right)} - \left(\alpha^2+1\right)\frac{n-1}{\alpha^{4n}} = O\left(\frac{1}{\alpha^{2n}}\right),$$

$$\frac{1}{\alpha^{4n}}\sum_{i=1}^{n-1}\alpha^{2i}\left(2\alpha^{2n-2i} - \left(\alpha^2+1\right)\right) = 2\frac{n-1}{\alpha^{2n}} - \left(\alpha^2+1\right)\frac{\alpha^{2n}-\alpha^2}{\alpha^{4n}\left(\alpha^2-1\right)} = O\left(\frac{n}{\alpha^{2n}}\right),$$

$$\begin{aligned}
\frac{1}{\alpha^{4n}}\sum_{i=1}^{n-1}\alpha^{4i}\left(2\alpha^{2n-2i} - \left(\alpha^2+1\right)\right) &= 2\frac{\alpha^{2n}-\alpha^2}{\alpha^{2n}\left(\alpha^2-1\right)} - \left(\alpha^2+1\right)\frac{\alpha^{4n}-\alpha^4}{\alpha^{4n}\left(\alpha^4-1\right)} \\
&= \frac{2}{\alpha^2-1} - \frac{\alpha^2+1}{\alpha^4-1} + O\left(\frac{1}{\alpha^{2n}}\right) = \frac{1}{\alpha^2-1} + O\left(\frac{1}{\alpha^{2n}}\right),
\end{aligned}$$

we get

$$\operatorname{var}\left(\frac{\boldsymbol{y}'\boldsymbol{y}}{\alpha^{2n}}\right) = \frac{2\sigma^4}{\left(\alpha^2-1\right)^4} + O\left(\frac{n}{\alpha^{2n}}\right) \to \frac{2\sigma^4}{\left(\alpha^2-1\right)^4} > 0.$$

Note that this violation of WLLNs for $\mathcal{H}_{11}$ takes place in spite of $\{\varepsilon_n\}$ being i.i.d.

Notes

General references for this chapter are the same as for Chapter 11. See also Spanos (1986) and Paruolo (2019) for econometrics texts where the emphasis is on likelihood.

The term *observed information* can be found in the literature, usually referring to $-\mathcal{H}$ and occasionally to $-\widehat{\mathcal{H}}$. The term *expected information* is then used for $\mathcal{I}$. We prefer to use the terms Hessian and information for $\mathcal{H}$ and $\mathcal{I}$, respectively, to avoid potential misunderstandings.

In the introduction to this chapter, we defined *global* identification. *Local identification* can be defined by weakening the condition of the uniqueness of $f(\boldsymbol{X};\boldsymbol{\theta}_1)$, instead of being over all $\boldsymbol{\theta}_2 \neq \boldsymbol{\theta}_1$, to simply being able to find a neighborhood of $\boldsymbol{\theta}_1$ where $f(\boldsymbol{X};\boldsymbol{\theta}_1)$ is unique. More details are given in Rothenberg (1971) and Catchpole and Morgan (1997).

There is more than one definition of asymptotic efficiency. Some authors include normality in addition to our conditions. On the subject of efficiency, we have not considered Hodges' *points of superefficiency*, that is, points in the parameter space where an asymptotically efficient estimator can breach the CRLB. For example, in Exercise 11.2, consider the point $\mu = 0$. We could have chosen

$$\alpha_1 = \frac{1}{n^p}, \qquad \alpha_2 = -\frac{1}{n^p}, \qquad \alpha_i = 0 \text{ for } i > 2,$$

for some $p \geqslant 1$, leading to an unbiased estimator in the case $\mu = 0$, with variance

$$\operatorname{var}(\widetilde{\mu}) = \frac{2\operatorname{var}(x_1)}{n^{2p}}$$

which is less than $\operatorname{var}(\overline{x})$ if $n > 2$ ($\widetilde{\mu}$ is also superefficient at $\mu = 0$ when $n = 2$ and $p > 1$). A more traditional example is obtained by shrinking the sample mean $\overline{x}$ from a normal population, when $|\overline{x}|$ is below some threshold, giving a superefficient estimator when $\mu = 0$ (the point of superefficiency). Points of superefficiency are countable, as shown by Le Cam (1952, 1953). Furthermore, if exploited to adjust the MLE as in our second example, they increase substantially the adjusted estimator's risk. Examples based on the usual quadratic loss can be found in Lehmann and Casella (1998) and Cox and Hinkley (1974). See also the topic of pretest estimation in, for example, Magnus (1999).

As seen in Chapter 10, when $x_n \xrightarrow{d} x$, the definition of asymptotic moments is in terms of expectations of x, not the limit of the expectations of x_n. The asymptotic variance is not necessarily equal to the limit of the variances. The counterexample based on Student's t(2) in Exercise 10.38 demonstrates this. Another counterexample is found in Cox and Hinkley (1974): the MLE of $1/\mu$ in a sample from the Poisson distribution is $1/\overline{x}$, which has infinite variance for all finite n because $\Pr(\overline{x} = 0) > 0$. However, the normalized limiting distribution has variance $1/\mu^3$, as can be seen by applying the delta method to Exercise 12.5(b). A similar warning applies in the Poisson case to the limit of the bias, compared with the asymptotic bias, as mentioned more generally in the introduction to this chapter.

Recall the nonparametric likelihood $L(F)$ of Exercise 12.15, which is maximized by $\widehat{F}_n$. The *empirical likelihood* (EL) is defined as the profile likelihood $L(\widehat{F}_n)$ when F is made to depend on some parameters $\boldsymbol{\theta}$ such as the population mean (if it is assumed to exist). The EL can then be optimized numerically with respect to $\boldsymbol{\theta}$, without having to assume a functional form for F. See Owen (2001) for uses of EL and applications, including generalizations of Exercise 12.16. The product-limit estimator of Kaplan and Meier (1958) was derived initially without reference to the EL.

For an alternative derivation of Exercise 12.17, see Section 13.12 in Abadir and Magnus (2005), where the information matrix and its inverse are also derived. Their proof does not rely on the statistical concept of sufficiency.

The entropy-based proof of Exercise 12.27(b) is also at the heart of demonstrating the monotone convergence of an iterative procedure for ML estimation when some data are missing. It is called the *EM algorithm*: starting with an estimate $\widehat{\boldsymbol{\theta}}$ of $\boldsymbol{\theta}$ from the available data, the algorithm alternates between the two steps of calculating the expectation (E) of the log-likelihood given $\boldsymbol{\theta} = \widehat{\boldsymbol{\theta}}$, and the maximization (M) of this expectation yielding a new $\widehat{\boldsymbol{\theta}}$; see Dempster, Laird, and Rubin (1977).

Exercises 12.27 and 12.29, on (strong) consistency and asymptotic normality, were proved for the i.i.d. setup here. For the non-i.i.d. cases, see Heijmans and Magnus (1986a, b), respectively. There have been refinements of the asymptotic sufficiency of Exercise 12.28, yielding approximations of the density of the MLE to $O(1/n)$ rather than $O(1/\sqrt{n})$. The p^* or *magic formula* for the density of the MLE for exponential families, due to Durbin (1980) and Barndorff-Nielsen (1980), is a constant multiple of

$$\left|-\boldsymbol{\mathcal{H}}(\widehat{\boldsymbol{\theta}})\right|^{1/2} \exp(\ell(\boldsymbol{\theta}) - \ell(\widehat{\boldsymbol{\theta}})).$$

This formula has led to a number of subsequent results, one of which we encountered in Exercise 12.41. To see how, start by considering conditional and marginal "likelihoods"; for example, compare Exercises 11.11(a) and 12.30(a). In the former case, the conditioning is with respect to a statistic such that the conditional density (of $\boldsymbol{y} \mid \boldsymbol{X}$) does not depend on the nuisance parameter $\boldsymbol{\theta}_2$ (parameters of the density of $\boldsymbol{X}$ in this instance). In the latter case, the marginal density (of $\boldsymbol{y}$) is the one that does not depend on $\boldsymbol{\theta}_2$. When such a conditioning statistic can be found, the marginal and conditional likelihoods satisfy the usual properties of likelihoods, unlike $\ell_{\mathrm{p}}(\boldsymbol{\theta}_1)$; conditionals are easier to compute than marginals which require integration. Barndorff-Nielsen's formula for the modified profile likelihood can then be obtained by applying the p^* asymptotic expansion to the joint log-likelihood and either the marginal or the conditional log-likelihood. The formula is valid more generally, without requiring the existence of the aforementioned conditioning statistic and the resulting factorization of likelihoods. Note that the correction factor for ℓ_{p} in Exercise 12.41 satisfies an invariance that can be established by the same method that will be used in Exercise 13.23(c).

When the partial MLE $\widehat{\boldsymbol{\theta}}_2(\boldsymbol{\theta}_1)$ does not vary with $\boldsymbol{\theta}_1$, we get $\partial\widehat{\boldsymbol{\theta}}_2(\boldsymbol{\theta}_1)/\partial\widehat{\boldsymbol{\theta}}_2' = \boldsymbol{I}_{m_2}$ and $\ell_{\mathrm{m}}(\boldsymbol{\theta}_1)$ of Exercise 12.41 reduces to the *adjusted profile likelihood* of Cox and Reid (1987), denoted by $\ell_a(\boldsymbol{\theta}_1)$. (If the parameterization is orthogonal, then this holds asymptotically.) Note, however, that $\ell_a(\boldsymbol{\theta}_1)$ is not invariant to reparameterizations, because it is missing the factor $|\partial\widehat{\boldsymbol{\theta}}_2(\boldsymbol{\theta}_1)/\partial\widehat{\boldsymbol{\theta}}_2'|$ relative to $\ell_m(\boldsymbol{\theta}_1)$. Another approach, due to McCullagh and Tibshirani (1990), is to modify directly the score of the profile log-likelihood in such a way that it satisfies the first few Bartlett's identities (including the information-matrix equivalence). On this topic, see Severini (2000). There is also a large relevant literature on the interpretation of likelihood and related quantities (such as gradients and tangents) in terms of differential geometry and tensors. For example, see McCullagh (1987), Kass (1989), and Barndorff-Nielsen and Cox (1989).

Exercise 12.39(c) and (d) implies the *Frisch–Waugh decomposition*. The context of Frisch and Waugh (1933) is one where $\boldsymbol{X}_2$ represents a linear time trend, and they showed that estimating the complete model gives the same $\widehat{\boldsymbol{\beta}}$ as detrending first and then estimating the smaller model. See also Davidson and MacKinnon (2004) for a geometrical approach to this and related problems.

The result of Exercise 12.40(b) has sometimes been used to show that the Hessian of the profile log-likelihood can be used to estimate the variance of subsets of $\widehat{\boldsymbol{\theta}}$. A couple of warnings apply here. First, the appropriate variance is based on $\mathcal{H}^{11} := (\mathcal{H}_{11} - \mathcal{H}_{12}\mathcal{H}_{22}^{-1}\mathcal{H}_{21})^{-1}$ and not on $\mathcal{H}_{11}^{-1}$, the latter being the Hessian from the marginal likelihood. See also Pierce (1982) for the asymptotic effect (on the variance) of substituting estimates for nuisance parameters. Second, one should be aware that

$$\begin{aligned}\mathrm{E}(-\widehat{\mathcal{H}}^{-1}) &\equiv \mathrm{E}(\mathrm{diag}(\widehat{\sigma}^2(\boldsymbol{X}'\boldsymbol{X})^{-1}, 2\widehat{\sigma}^4/n)) \\ &\neq \mathrm{diag}(\sigma^2(\boldsymbol{X}'\boldsymbol{X})^{-1}, 2\sigma^4/n) \equiv (\mathrm{E}(-\mathcal{H}))^{-1} \equiv \mathcal{I}^{-1}\end{aligned}$$

in the linear model. Also recall that, by Jensen's inequality, $\mathrm{E}(\widehat{\sigma}^{-2}) \neq 1/\mathrm{E}(\widehat{\sigma}^2)$ except as the variate $\widehat{\sigma}$ degenerates asymptotically; see Exercise 10.16(c).

The problem of Neyman and Scott (1948) introduced in Exercise 12.13 was tackled in Exercise 12.42 using the modified profile likelihood, and was solved in this case. Hahn and Newey (2004) attenuated this problem, in a more general model, by using the jackknife introduced in the previous chapter.

In Exercise 12.43, we obtained a classification of the cases of failure ($|\alpha| \geqslant 1$) or otherwise ($|\alpha| < 1$) of WLLNs for $\mathcal{H}$. This classification holds also for $y_0 \neq 0$. It is a manifestation of a more general problem, with nonnormal limiting distributions of $\widehat{\alpha}$ arising for $|\alpha| = 1$ and $|\alpha| > 1$; see White (1958, 1959), Dickey and Fuller (1979), Evans and Savin (1981), Chan and Wei (1987), Phillips (1987), Perron (1991), Abadir (1993a, 1995), and Larsson (1995). This problem occurs in spite of the consistency of $\widehat{\alpha}$ for all α:

$$\widehat{\alpha} - \alpha = \frac{\sum_{i=1}^n \varepsilon_i y_{i-1}}{\sum_{i=1}^n y_{i-1}^2} = O_p\left(\mathcal{I}_{11}^{-1/2}\right) = \begin{cases} O_p(1/\sqrt{n}) & (|\alpha| < 1), \\ O_p(1/n) & (|\alpha| = 1), \\ O_p(1/|\alpha|^n) & (|\alpha| > 1). \end{cases}$$

Magdalinos (2007) showed that $\mathcal{I}_{11}(\widehat{\alpha})$ is an inconsistent estimator of $\mathcal{I}_{11}(\alpha)$ when $\alpha = 1$, even though $\widehat{\alpha}$ is consistent; see also the warning in the solution of Exercise 12.28(a). This inconsistency arises because of the following result. When $\alpha = 1$, we have $\widehat{\alpha} - 1 = O_p(1/n)$ and, substituting this into our exercise's expressions for $\mathcal{I}_{11}(\widehat{\alpha})$, we have a term

$$\widehat{\alpha}^n = \left(1 + \frac{n(\widehat{\alpha} - 1)}{n}\right)^n = \mathrm{e}^{n(\widehat{\alpha}-1)} + o_p(1)$$

containing $n(\widehat{\alpha} - 1)$ which is nondegenerate and so $\widehat{\alpha}^n$ does not converge to $1^n = 1$ as $n \to \infty$; hence $\mathcal{I}_{11}(\widehat{\alpha})$ does not tend to $\mathcal{I}_{11}(1)$. Finally, when $\alpha = 1$, Lai and Siegmund (1983) showed that the normality of $\widehat{\alpha}$ can be restored by using the sequential *fixed-accuracy* approach: this involves conditioning on the observed information (or $\sum_{i=1}^n y_{i-1}^2$) to reach some preassigned level, and stopping sampling when this level is reached. Note that n becomes a random variable in this case, but this prevents the WLLN failure seen earlier. Note also that we are dealing in this exercise with a curved exponential case, where the sufficient statistic is three-dimensional while we have only two parameters.

13

Other methods of estimation

There is a proliferation of methods of point estimation other than ML, which are used for various reasons that can be grouped as follows (apart from the fact that some methods preceded the introduction of ML). First, MLEs may not have an explicit formula, in many cases, and may thus be computationally more demanding than alternative methods. Second, MLEs typically require the specification of a distribution before the estimation of its parameters can begin. Third, the optimization of criteria other than the likelihood may have some justification. The first argument has become less relevant with the advent of cheap and fast computers, and the alternative estimators based on it usually entail a loss of optimality properties. The second can be countered to some extent with large-sample invariance arguments that are typically based on asymptotic normality, or with the nonparametric MLE seen, for example, in Exercises 12.15 and 12.16; see also the empirical likelihood in the Notes to Chapter 12. However, the third reason can be more fundamental.

This chapter presents a selection of four common methods of point estimation, addressing the reasons outlined above to varying degrees. In addition to these reasons for alternative estimators, point estimation itself may not be the most informative way to summarize what the data indicate about the parameters, but this is not a criticism of MLEs per se. Therefore, this chapter also introduces interval estimation and its multivariate generalization, a topic that leads quite naturally to the subject matter of Chapter 14.

Suppose that a random sample $x_1, \dots, x_n$ is drawn from a density with m parameters, and that m of the moments from this density are in one-to-one relation with these parameters. The *method of moments* (MM or MOM) equates these m moments (say $\mathrm{E}(g_j(x))$ with $j = 1, \dots, m$) to their sample counterparts (say $n^{-1}\sum_{i=1}^n g_j(x_i)$), then solves for the implied parameter estimates. For example, if $\{x_i\}_{i=1}^n \sim \mathrm{IN}(\mu, \sigma^2)$, then the *MM estimators* (MMEs) are $\widetilde{\mu} = n^{-1}\sum_{i=1}^n x_i$ (which is the same as $\overline{x}$ here) and, by using $\sigma^2 \equiv \mathrm{E}(x^2) - \mu^2$, we find that

$$\widetilde{\sigma}^2 = \frac{1}{n}\sum_{i=1}^{n} x_i^2 - \widetilde{\mu}^2 \equiv \frac{1}{n}\sum_{i=1}^{n}(x_i - \overline{x})^2.$$

This example is very simple and uncontroversial, illustrating the appeal of the method. However, it does not reflect the difficulties that the MM can run into. First, moments may not exist, for example when we are dealing with some Pareto or Student-t variates, in which case the method is inapplicable; see Exercise 13.5. Second, we can get different estimates depending on which moments are selected. What if we use raw moments instead of central moments? What if we select moments other than the first m moments? The latter question is related to "what if we transformed the variate before applying the method?". All the resulting estimators qualify as MMEs but, in general, the results of estimation will be altered by these choices; see Exercise 13.4. As we will see, the method tends to do well when it is a close approximation of ML anyway.

Least squares (LS) is arguably the method of estimation closest to ML. As we shall see, almost all the results derived for MLEs under normality will apply to LS estimators (LSEs), with a few exceptions to be highlighted in the exercises and Notes to this chapter. Suppose that we have a sample $y_1, \dots, y_n$ (not necessarily i.i.d.) from *any* distribution with finite first two moments. Then, the LS procedure requires finding the values $\widehat{y}_1, \dots, \widehat{y}_n$ such that the sum of squared residuals $\sum_{i=1}^{n}(y_i - \widehat{y}_i)^2 \equiv (\boldsymbol{y} - \widehat{\boldsymbol{y}})'(\boldsymbol{y} - \widehat{\boldsymbol{y}})$ is minimized, hence the name *least squares*. This is an idea that we have already seen, in particular in Exercises 3.18(a) and 6.46. For the linear model $\boldsymbol{y} = \boldsymbol{X\beta} + \boldsymbol{\varepsilon}$ with its earlier assumptions except for the normality of $\boldsymbol{\varepsilon}$ (see Section 12.3), minimizing

$$\sum_{i=1}^{n}(y_i - \widehat{y}_i)^2 \equiv (\boldsymbol{y} - \boldsymbol{X}\widehat{\boldsymbol{\beta}})'(\boldsymbol{y} - \boldsymbol{X}\widehat{\boldsymbol{\beta}})$$

with respect to $\widehat{\boldsymbol{\beta}}$ is equivalent to solving

$$\operatorname*{argmin}_{\boldsymbol{\beta}} (\boldsymbol{y} - \boldsymbol{X\beta})'(\boldsymbol{y} - \boldsymbol{X\beta}),$$

that is, $\operatorname{argmin}_{\boldsymbol{\beta}} \boldsymbol{\varepsilon}'\boldsymbol{\varepsilon}$. This has already been found in Exercises 12.30(b) and 12.32, giving $\widehat{\boldsymbol{\beta}} = (\boldsymbol{X}'\boldsymbol{X})^{-1}\boldsymbol{X}\boldsymbol{y}$ when we assume $\boldsymbol{X}'\boldsymbol{X}$ to be invertible, just like the MLE of the *normal* linear model. Little wonder that this is the case, since normality implies that the conditional (on $\boldsymbol{X}$) log-likelihood for $\boldsymbol{\beta}$ is just a scaled version of the LS criterion; see Exercise 12.30. However, LS does not presuppose normality, so $(\boldsymbol{X}'\boldsymbol{X})^{-1}\boldsymbol{X}\boldsymbol{y}$ is the LSE in the linear model even when $\boldsymbol{\varepsilon}$ is nonnormal. For given $\boldsymbol{X}$, this LSE is called a *linear estimator* because it is a linear function of the random $\boldsymbol{y}$. We will show that LS provides the unique *best linear unbiased estimator* (BLUE) in the linear model, a result known as the *Gauss–Markov theorem*.

Suppose that a random sample $x_1, \dots, x_n$ is drawn from a density $f_x(u)$, or simply

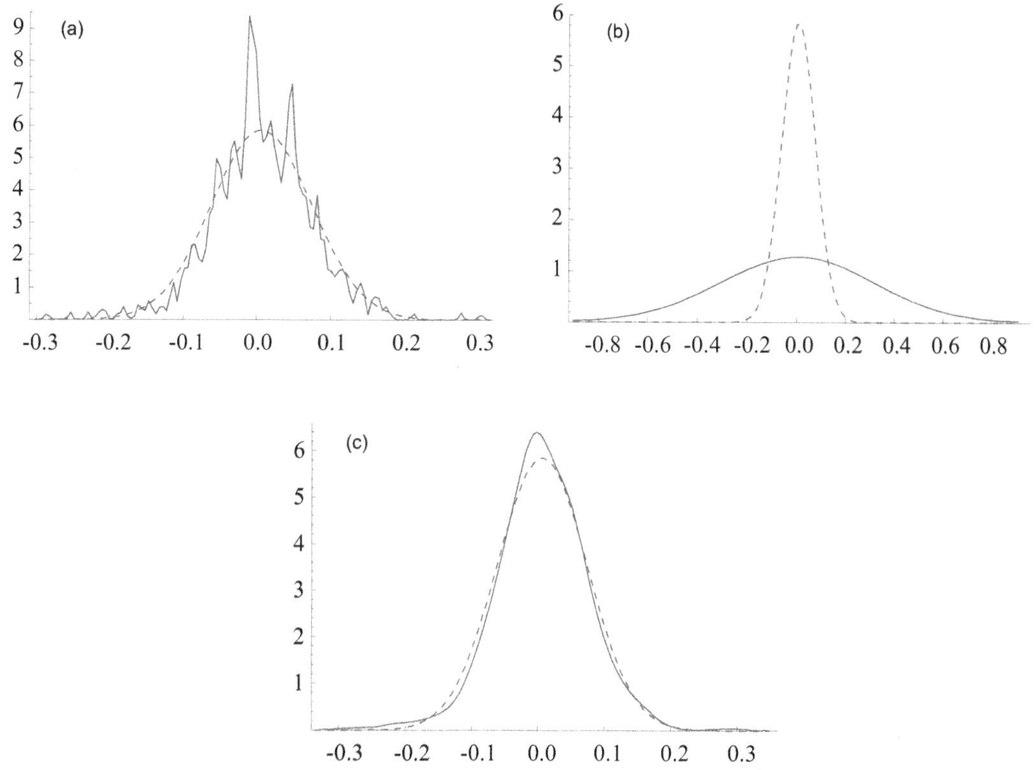

Figure 13.1. Each of the three graphs contains the NP density estimate (solid line) and the N(0.6%,(7%)^2) (dotted line), both fitted to the monthly returns on IBM shares from January 1962 to September 2017. They differ in the chosen bandwidths λ: (a) small, (b) large, (c) intermediate.

$f(u)$, which is assumed to be a continuous function. If we know that the data come from a normal distribution, we can estimate its parameters (the mean and variance). But, in general, we do not know what distribution generated the data. So how do we estimate the density without any parametric assumptions, that is, how can we obtain a *nonparametric* (NP) *density estimator*? The EDF introduced in Chapter 9 can be viewed as an NP estimator of the c.d.f., but it does not imply an estimator of the density that is continuous as assumed. We address this issue here. Also, how do we generalize this NP density estimator to more than one variate, and find out what it tells us about the NP relation between the variates?

An answer to the first question was given in Exercise 2.23. A smooth approximation of $f(u)$, say $\widehat{f}(u)$, may be obtained from the data by using a weighting function K called a *kernel* and satisfying $\int_{-\infty}^{\infty} K(t)\,\mathrm{d}t = 1$: the *kernel density estimator* is

$$\widehat{f}(u) := \frac{1}{n\lambda}\sum_{i=1}^{n} K\left(\frac{u-x_i}{\lambda}\right), \tag{13.1}$$

where $\lambda > 0$ is the *bandwidth* (or *smoothing parameter* or *window width*). We allow some of the weights to be negative here, unlike in Exercise 2.23 where $K(t) \geqslant 0$ everywhere.

To illustrate the formula, if we choose $K_{\rm n}(t) := \phi(t) \equiv \exp(-\frac{1}{2}t^2)/\sqrt{2\pi}$, we can rewrite $\widehat{f}$ as the sum of rescaled kernels each centered around one of the n data points:

$$\widehat{f}(u) = \frac{1}{n\lambda\sqrt{2\pi}} \exp\left(-\frac{1}{2}\left(\frac{u-x_1}{\lambda}\right)^2\right) + \cdots + \frac{1}{n\lambda\sqrt{2\pi}} \exp\left(-\frac{1}{2}\left(\frac{u-x_n}{\lambda}\right)^2\right); \tag{13.2}$$

for example, the sample $\{x_1, x_2, x_3\} = \{1.2, 2.0, 1.1\}$ gives the following function of u:

$$\widehat{f}(u) = \frac{\exp(-(u-1.2)^2/2\lambda^2)}{3\lambda\sqrt{2\pi}} + \frac{\exp(-(u-2)^2/2\lambda^2)}{3\lambda\sqrt{2\pi}} + \frac{\exp(-(u-1.1)^2/2\lambda^2)}{3\lambda\sqrt{2\pi}}, \tag{13.3}$$

where the scale λ is yet to be chosen. We now turn to optimality considerations for the choice of K and λ.

Exercise 13.14(a) will show that optimality considerations require further that the mean of K be zero, $\int_{-\infty}^{\infty} tK(t)\,\mathrm{d}t = 0$, when additional conditions on the differentiability of f are satisfied. From the point of view of minimizing the *integrated mean squared error* (IMSE), defined by $\int_{-\infty}^{\infty} \mathrm{E}\left((\widehat{f}(u) - f(u))^2\right) \mathrm{d}u$ and assumed to exist, Exercise 13.16 will show that the asymptotically optimal standardized kernel is the *Epanechnikov* (or *quadratic*) kernel

$$K_{\rm e}(t) := \begin{cases} \frac{3}{4\sqrt{5}}\left(1 - \frac{1}{5}t^2\right) & (|t| < \sqrt{5}), \\ 0 & \text{(elsewhere)}. \end{cases} \tag{13.4}$$

Nevertheless, the increase in the asymptotic IMSE (AIMSE) is not substantial if one uses other kernels instead, such as the normal $K_{\rm n}(t)$; see Exercise 13.16. More crucial for the AIMSE is the choice of λ, which determines how smooth the resulting density estimate is. We illustrate this in Figure 13.1 with the monthly returns on IBM shares over the period January 1962 to September 2017, downloaded from Yahoo. The returns are not quite i.i.d., but they are almost uncorrelated; see Exercise 4.23 and the Notes to it for a related discussion. (You may also wish to try out the three probabilities at the end of the solution to Exercise 7.37(d): they are quite accurate for this series.) Each of the three graphs in the figure contains the NP density estimate and an N(0.006,0.005), the latter being obtained from the sample's mean return of 0.6% (monthly) with a standard deviation of 7%. The graphs differ in the chosen bandwidths λ: (a) small (notice how erratic the estimate is, especially in the tails, with "gaps" between the estimated modes), (b) large (notice how the scale of the horizontal axis changes due to oversmoothing, assigning too much probability to points far away from the data, such as an 80% monthly crash in the IBM share price!), then (c) intermediate. Recall that Exercise 2.23 implies that we can interpret $\widehat{f}(u)$ of (13.1) as an average of n scaled kernels $\lambda^{-1}K\left(\lambda^{-1}(u - x_i)\right)$, each centered around the corresponding x_i, and that a higher λ increases the spread of K, hence there is more smoothing; see also the example in (13.2)–(13.3). Exercise 13.15(b) will show that the optimal λ is $O(n^{-1/5})$, so less smoothing is needed as the sample size increases because there are more observations to fill the data gaps along the horizontal axis. Exercise 13.17 and the Notes to it

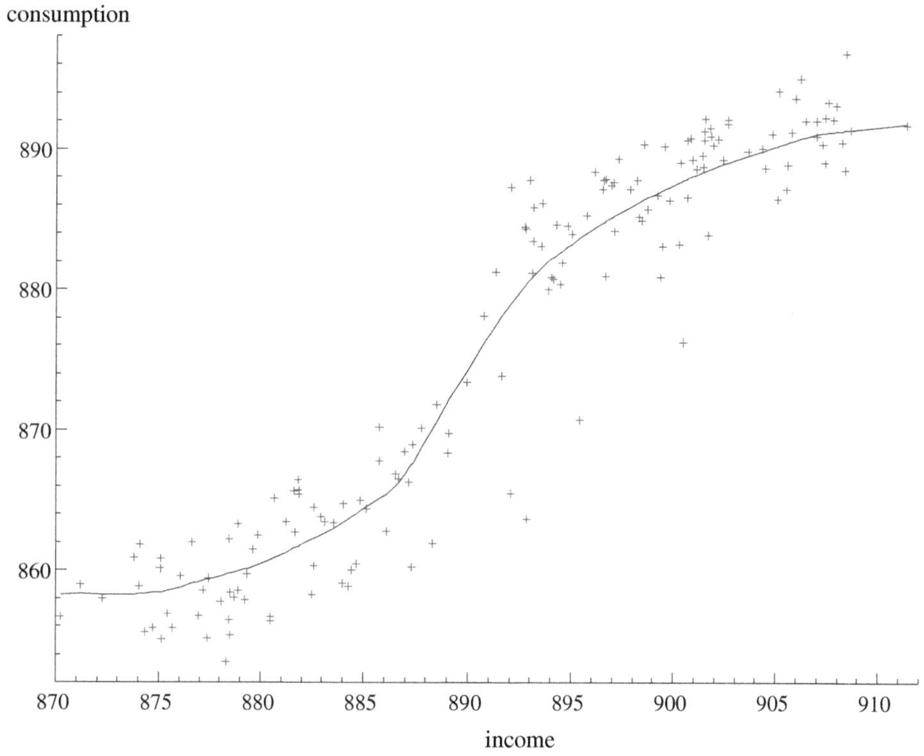

Figure 13.2. The scatter plot and NP regression of quarterly consumption on income.

discuss how to choose the optimal λ in practice. Notice that the sum in (13.1) gives rise to a plot of $\widehat{f}$ that need not be normal, even if the kernels used are the normal $K_{\rm n}$ as in (13.2); see also Exercise 7.5.

We saw in the previous two chapters and in Exercises 6.43–6.51 (see also Exercise 13.8) that regression analysis can be formulated as

$$\boldsymbol{y} = \mathrm{E}\left(\boldsymbol{y} \mid \boldsymbol{X}\right) + \boldsymbol{\varepsilon} \equiv \boldsymbol{g}(\boldsymbol{X}) + \boldsymbol{\varepsilon},$$

decomposing $\boldsymbol{y}$ into expected and unexpected parts, and we write $\widehat{\boldsymbol{y}} = \widehat{\boldsymbol{g}}(\boldsymbol{X})$ for the estimated (or fitted) regression curve. For elliptical distributions, the conditional expectation is a linear function. For other distributions, other specific functional forms emerge. *Nonparametric regression* does not presuppose a functional form. One possibility is to estimate the conditional expectation from the nonparametric estimate of the joint density of the variates. Exercise 13.18 will show how this gives rise in the bivariate case to the *Nadaraya–Watson estimator* of $\mathrm{E}\left(y \mid x = u\right)$, namely

$$\widehat{y}(u) = \sum_{i=1}^{n} w_i(u) \times y_i, \qquad w_i(u) := \frac{K\left(\lambda^{-1}(u - x_i)\right)}{\sum_{j=1}^{n} K\left(\lambda^{-1}(u - x_j)\right)}, \tag{13.5}$$

where $\widehat{y}$ can be regarded as a weighted average of the y_i's, with weights w_i's that add up to 100%. Each weight w_i depends on λ and on the whole sequence $\{x_n\}$ (to varying extents, as we shall see), evaluated at the point $x = u$ along the horizontal axis. Another way to view this averaging is through a scatter plot such as in Figure 13.2, where we also plot the NP regression of quarterly consumption on income, a dataset in OxMetrics. (Notice the S-shaped – rather than linear – relation, which could be consistent with an economic model where interest rates on borrowing and saving differ; see Flemming (1973).) Roughly speaking, for any value u on the horizontal axis, a small "window" around this u will contain x_i's whose corresponding y_i's are averaged to give the NP regression estimate for that point u. More formally, (13.5) says that, for each u along the horizontal axis, the x_i's in a small neighborhood of it provide the largest weight in calculating the weighted average of the corresponding y_i's, a *local averaging* of y_i. This is so because a large value of $|u - x_i|$ corresponds to the tail of the kernel, which has a small value (low probability); for example, let $|t|$ be large in (13.4). Tracing the sequence of such averages as u changes, we get the NP regression curve.

Bayesian methods start from the idea that we have some prior beliefs about the values of the parameter vector $\boldsymbol{\theta}$ of the model, quantified by a *prior distribution* for $\boldsymbol{\theta}$, so these priors must be incorporated into the estimation procedure. As data become available, the priors about $\boldsymbol{\theta}$ are updated by Bayes' formula (see Chapter 1) into a *posterior distribution* for $\boldsymbol{\theta}$. The parameters are therefore not treated as fixed. Also, the estimates of $\boldsymbol{\theta}$ are in general not fully determined by the likelihood (or the data), but are also affected by the prior. A main difference from the non-Bayesian approaches seen earlier, called *frequentist* or *classical*, is the choice of a prior distribution function for $\boldsymbol{\theta}$.

We will use the notation introduced for the notion of mixing in Chapter 2, writing $\boldsymbol{\theta}$ for the realization of the random $\boldsymbol{\vartheta} \in \Theta$. Let $f_{\boldsymbol{\vartheta}}(\boldsymbol{\theta})$ denote the prior density and $L(\boldsymbol{\theta}) := f_{\boldsymbol{X}|\boldsymbol{\theta}}(\boldsymbol{X})$ be the likelihood. Then, Bayes' law implies that the posterior density $f_{\boldsymbol{\vartheta}|\boldsymbol{X}}(\boldsymbol{\theta})$ is given by

$$f_{\boldsymbol{\vartheta}|\boldsymbol{X}}(\boldsymbol{\theta}) = \frac{f_{\boldsymbol{\vartheta}}(\boldsymbol{\theta})\, f_{\boldsymbol{X}|\boldsymbol{\theta}}(\boldsymbol{X})}{\int_{\boldsymbol{\theta}\in\Theta} f_{\boldsymbol{\vartheta}}(\boldsymbol{\theta})\, f_{\boldsymbol{X}|\boldsymbol{\theta}}(\boldsymbol{X})\,\mathrm{d}\boldsymbol{\theta}} \propto f_{\boldsymbol{\vartheta}}(\boldsymbol{\theta})\, L(\boldsymbol{\theta}). \tag{13.6}$$

The denominator is the marginal density of $\boldsymbol{X}$ obtained from integrating $\boldsymbol{\theta}$ out of the joint density of $\boldsymbol{X}$ and $\boldsymbol{\vartheta}$; it is understood that when the prior is discrete, the integral is replaced by a sum. This density is free from $\boldsymbol{\theta}$, hence the proportionality of the posterior to the product of the prior and the likelihood, the latter representing the way in which the data are used to update the prior. Using Neyman's factorization (Chapter 11), the likelihood can be factored further so that the posterior is proportional to the prior times the density of the sufficient statistic, since the rest does not depend on $\boldsymbol{\theta}$.

Bayesian estimators are obtained from the posterior density, and they can be classified as either point or interval estimators, the latter being more representative of the Bayesian philosophy. The former are chosen to optimize a criterion related to the idea of loss functions that we introduced in Chapter 11, but the loss is now regarded primarily as a function of the varying $\boldsymbol{\vartheta}$; for example, the quadratic loss $C(\boldsymbol{\vartheta}, \widehat{\boldsymbol{\theta}}) = (\boldsymbol{\vartheta} - \widehat{\boldsymbol{\theta}})'(\boldsymbol{\vartheta} - \widehat{\boldsymbol{\theta}})$, with $\widehat{\boldsymbol{\theta}}$ an estimator to be chosen, as a function of the given data. *Bayes estimators* choose $\widehat{\boldsymbol{\theta}}_b$ such that it minimizes the *posterior risk*

$$\text{risk}_{\text{p}}(\widehat{\boldsymbol{\theta}}) := \text{E}_{\boldsymbol{\vartheta}|\boldsymbol{X}}(C(\boldsymbol{\vartheta}, \widehat{\boldsymbol{\theta}})),$$

where the expectation is taken with respect to the posterior density that we get for $\boldsymbol{\vartheta}$ after having conditioned on the data $\boldsymbol{X}$. It is assumed that the expectation exists. Notice that we now condition on $\boldsymbol{X}$, hence making any estimator $\widehat{\boldsymbol{\theta}}$ nonrandom in $C(\boldsymbol{\vartheta}, \widehat{\boldsymbol{\theta}})$. Exercise 13.25 will show that Bayes estimators can be equivalently obtained by minimizing the *Bayes risk*

$$\text{risk}_{\text{b}}(\widehat{\boldsymbol{\theta}}) := \text{E}_{\boldsymbol{\vartheta}}(\text{risk}(\widehat{\boldsymbol{\theta}})),$$

where the expectation is taken with respect to the prior (rather than the posterior) density of $\boldsymbol{\vartheta}$, and $\text{risk}(\widehat{\boldsymbol{\theta}}) := \text{E}_{\boldsymbol{X}|\boldsymbol{\vartheta}}(C(\boldsymbol{\vartheta}, \widehat{\boldsymbol{\theta}}))$ is the frequentist risk defined in Chapter 11. Exercise 13.26 will show further that Bayes estimators are admissible, but biased in a frequentist sense. (Recall that Exercise 11.25 illustrated that efficient unbiased estimators can be nevertheless inadmissible.) Exercise 13.27 (see also Exercises 13.20 and 13.21) will show that, as the sample size n tends to infinity, Bayes estimators tend to resemble the MLE. If the prior does not rule out parameter values implied by the data, the effect of the prior in (13.6) diminishes relative to the likelihood as $n \to \infty$, hence the relation to the MLE. The posterior density becomes a normal that is centered around the MLE, and has variance $\mathcal{I}^{-1}$ or conditional variance $-\mathcal{H}^{-1}$ evaluated at the MLE. As we shall see, because we are conditioning on the data $\boldsymbol{X}$, this normal approximation holds for assumptions (on the likelihood) that are weaker than those required for the MLE to satisfy a CLT as in Chapter 12. Notice that it is legitimate in the Bayesian context to consider probability limits of estimators that converge to nonrandom parameter values. However, frequentists and Bayesians differ in that the latter do not consider repeated drawings from the data density: $\boldsymbol{X}$ is conditioned upon, rather than expectations being taken with respect to all the possible realizations of $\boldsymbol{X}$. This can be another point of debate with some frequentist practices, if they involve taking expectations.

Frequentist and Bayesian methods give rise to distributions relating to estimators and parameters, respectively. These distributions can be used to construct statements about the probability that the parameter vector lies in some region, known as a *confidence region*, although the frequentist and Bayesian formulations differ. In the former case, the boundaries of the region are based on the estimator $\widehat{\boldsymbol{\theta}}$ and hence are random, in contrast with the latter case where the boundaries are based on the posterior density and are therefore not random. *Confidence intervals* (CIs) arise as a special case when there is a single parameter of interest. Unlike in point estimation, confidence regions enable us to conduct *inference* on the parameters of interest, that is, draw probabilistic conclusions about them.

We start with frequentist regions. Confidence intervals can be written as

$$\Pr\left(h_1\left(\boldsymbol{X}\right) \leqslant \theta \leqslant h_2\left(\boldsymbol{X}\right)\right) = 1 - \alpha, \quad \forall \theta \in \Theta, \tag{13.7}$$

where h_1 and h_2 are both functions of the data $\boldsymbol{X}$, hence the *coverage* (or *confidence level*) is $1 - \alpha \in [0,1]$ and does not depend on θ. Clearly, h_1 and h_2 depend on α too, since α affects the length of the interval, but α is nonrandom and is therefore omitted from the arguments of the functions h_1 and h_2. A typical example from elementary statistics is the following. For $\{x_i\}_{i=1}^n \sim \text{IN}(\mu, 1)$, the sample mean $\overline{x} \sim \text{N}(\mu, 1/n)$ gives

$$\Pr\left(\overline{x} - \frac{1.96}{\sqrt{n}} \leqslant \mu \leqslant \overline{x} + \frac{1.96}{\sqrt{n}}\right) \approx 95\%, \tag{13.8}$$

from the quantiles of the normal distribution $\int_{-1.96}^{1.96} \phi(u)\, du \approx 0.95$, denoted by $\text{N}_{0.975} = -\text{N}_{0.025} \approx 1.96$ (see Chapter 4 for this notation). The length of the confidence interval in (13.8) tends to 0 as $n \to \infty$, for any α, and one can use this to visualize the almost-sure convergence $\overline{x} \to \mu$ (from the SLLN) with an interval shrinking around μ as $n \to \infty$. The interval could have been written alternatively as

$$\Pr\left(-1.96 \leqslant \sqrt{n}\,(\overline{x} - \mu) \leqslant 1.96\right) \approx 95\%. \tag{13.9}$$

The idea of CIs is not limited to parameters, although this is the main focus of our analysis. They can also be provided, inter alia, for predictions (for example, using the variance of predictions from Exercise 12.38), estimates of densities (Exercise 13.14(c)), or functionals of densities (Exercise 13.36).

The confidence interval of the example in (13.9) is *two-sided* because neither of ± 1.96 is a bound for the variate $\sqrt{n}\,(\overline{x} - \mu)$, and it is *central* because the two tails that are excluded from the CI have equal probability. If h_1 is the smallest value in Θ, then the general (13.7) implies the *one-sided* CI in $\Pr(\theta \leqslant h_2(\boldsymbol{X})) = 1 - \alpha$; and if h_2 is the largest value in Θ, then we get the *one-sided* CI in $\Pr(h_1(\boldsymbol{X}) \leqslant \theta) = 1 - \alpha$. When we have more than one parameter, the $1 - \alpha$ confidence region for $\boldsymbol{\theta}$ is written as

$$\Pr(\boldsymbol{\theta} \in A) = 1 - \alpha, \quad \forall \boldsymbol{\theta} \in \Theta, \tag{13.10}$$

where the set A depends on the data $\boldsymbol{X}$. The region A may contain disjoint intervals, for example if the underlying density is multimodal. But, once α is fixed at some chosen level, how should we determine the best region? One approach is to minimize the length of these intervals or the volume of the region, but a more complete frequentist answer will be based on likelihood, and will follow in Chapter 14. For now, we outline some elementary principles in the next paragraph, focusing on intervals. The same ideas extend readily to confidence regions.

In our definition of CIs, we have assumed that the inequalities given by the interval hold for all $\theta \in \Theta$, in which case the variate that is used to construct the CI is called a *pivot* (or *pivotal quantity*) for θ and its distribution does not vary with θ. In our example, (13.9) shows that this condition is satisfied, with pivot $z := \sqrt{n}\,(\overline{x} - \mu) \sim \text{N}(0,1)$ since the distribution of z does not depend on μ. (If the pivot did not contain the unknown parameter, then it would actually be the ancillary statistic seen in Chapter 11.) A pivot is the first ingredient in constructing a reliable confidence interval. For example, if the length of the 95% interval varied with μ, then we would not be able to construct a reliable CI since we do not know μ. As a second ingredient, we wish to reduce the extent of the dependence of the functions h_1 and h_2 on $\boldsymbol{X}$, and we will often consider instead sufficient statistics because these summarize what the sample's density tells us about θ. In our simple example, $\overline{x}$ is sufficient for μ, hence the traditional choice of using $\overline{x}$ to construct confidence intervals for μ. Taking the idea of sufficiency further, *conditional* confidence intervals can be constructed by conditioning on the ancillaries because their densities do not depend on θ. We now turn to Bayesian intervals, where we condition on the whole of $\boldsymbol{X}$ in constructing the posterior density.

The posterior density of $\boldsymbol{\vartheta}$ provides a tool to calculate Bayesian confidence regions,

$$\Pr(\boldsymbol{\vartheta} \in A \mid \boldsymbol{X}) = 1 - \alpha,$$

by means of $\Pr(\boldsymbol{\vartheta} \in A \mid \boldsymbol{X}) = \int_{\boldsymbol{\theta} \in A} f_{\boldsymbol{\vartheta}|\boldsymbol{X}}(\boldsymbol{\theta}) \,\mathrm{d}\boldsymbol{\theta}$. Compared with (13.10), the region A here is not random, because we are now conditioning on the data $\boldsymbol{X}$, but the parameter $\boldsymbol{\vartheta}$ itself is random. The *highest posterior density* (HPD) region A is chosen such that, for all $\boldsymbol{\theta}_1 \in A$ and $\boldsymbol{\theta}_2 \notin A$, we have

$$f_{\boldsymbol{\vartheta}|\boldsymbol{X}}(\boldsymbol{\theta}_1) \geqslant f_{\boldsymbol{\vartheta}|\boldsymbol{X}}(\boldsymbol{\theta}_2),$$

and $\Pr(\boldsymbol{\vartheta} \in A \mid \boldsymbol{X}) = 1 - \alpha$; in other words, we choose a value c such that

$$f_{\boldsymbol{\vartheta}|\boldsymbol{X}}(\boldsymbol{\theta}_1) \geqslant c \quad \text{while} \quad f_{\boldsymbol{\vartheta}|\boldsymbol{X}}(\boldsymbol{\theta}_2) \leqslant c.$$

Exercise 13.42 will show that HPD regions are equivalent to regions having the smallest volume, for any given α and any given posterior density. As $n \to \infty$, under some regularity conditions, if the prior does not rule out parameter regions having positive probability in the data, then the HPD region is asymptotically equivalent to one based on the likelihood.

The exercises are grouped into five sections. The first four sections tackle point estimation by MM, LS, NP, and Bayesian techniques, respectively. Note that NP provides point estimation, but for a continuum of points in the data space rather than a single point in the parameter space. The final section is mainly concerned with interval estimation, from the frequentist then from the Bayesian viewpoint.

13.1 Method of moments

Exercise 13.1 (Laplace: MM) Let $x_1, \dots, x_n$ be a random sample from the p.d.f.

$$f_x(u) = \frac{\lambda}{2} \exp(-\lambda |u|),$$

where $\lambda > 0$. Find the MME of λ.

Solution

By symmetry, $\mathrm{E}(x) = \mathrm{E}(-x) = 0$ and

$$\mathrm{E}(x^2) = \frac{\lambda}{2} \int_{-\infty}^{\infty} u^2 \exp(-\lambda |u|) \,\mathrm{d}u = \lambda \int_0^{\infty} u^2 \exp(-\lambda u) \,\mathrm{d}u = \frac{2}{\lambda^2}$$

since the Gam(3, λ) density integrates to 1 (or one could directly read off the variance of the Laplace distribution from Table 4.2). Hence, the MME based on the second moment satisfies

$$\frac{1}{n}\sum_{i=1}^{n} x_i^2 = \frac{2}{\widetilde{\lambda}^2},$$

that is,

$$\widetilde{\lambda} = \left(\frac{1}{2n}\sum_{i=1}^{n} x_i^2\right)^{-1/2}.$$

Compare this with Exercise 12.14(b).

Exercise 13.2 (Recaptured by MOM!) Shahira now knows about the method of moments, and she decides to revisit Exercises 4.7 and 12.4. She wants to find the MME of the number of sharks in the lake, which she had denoted by m. What should she get for $\widetilde{m}$, and how does it relate to her earlier calculations?

Solution

Exercise 4.7(b) gives the expected proportion of tagged sharks as $\mathrm{E}(x/n) = k/m$. Equating $k/\widetilde{m}$ to the sample proportion x/n gives

$$\widetilde{m} = \frac{k}{x/n},$$

which is the simple estimator mentioned in Exercise 12.4 as an approximate MLE. Forcing $\widetilde{m} \in \mathbb{N}$, we can choose to round kn/x to the nearest integer, getting either $\lfloor kn/x \rfloor$ or $\lfloor kn/x \rfloor + 1$; compare with Exercise 12.4.

Exercise 13.3 (Max uniform: MM and ML) Consider a random sample $x_1, \ldots, x_n$ of $x \sim \mathrm{U}_{(0,\alpha)}$.

(a) Derive the MME of α.

(b) Derive the MLE of α.

(c) Are both estimators unbiased?

(d) Which of the two estimators has the smaller MSE?

(e) Show that the two estimators are consistent.

Solution

(a) Calculating the first moment, $\mathrm{E}(x) = \alpha^{-1}\int_0^\alpha u\,\mathrm{d}u = \alpha/2$ yields the MME $\widetilde{\alpha} = 2\overline{x}$.

(b) Let $y_1 := \min_i \{x_i\}$ and $y_n := \max_i \{x_i\}$. Then

$$L(\alpha) = \prod_{i=1}^{n}\left(\frac{1}{\alpha}1_{x_i\in[0,\alpha]}\right) = \frac{1}{\alpha^n}1_{y_1\geqslant 0}1_{y_n\leqslant\alpha} = \frac{1}{\alpha^n}1_{y_n\leqslant\alpha},$$

since $\Pr(y_1 \geqslant 0) = 1$ regardless of α. Hence, the MLE is $\widehat{\alpha} = y_n$; see also Exercise 12.8.

(c) $\mathrm{E}(\widetilde{\alpha}) = 2\,\mathrm{E}(\overline{x}) = 2\,\mathrm{E}(x_1) = 2(\alpha/2) = \alpha$ and, from Exercises 11.7 or 12.8,

$$\mathrm{E}(\widehat{\alpha}) = \frac{n}{n+1}\alpha.$$

(d) For the MME,

$$\mathrm{MSE}(\widetilde{\alpha}) = \mathrm{var}(\widetilde{\alpha}) = 4\,\mathrm{var}(\overline{x}) = \frac{4}{n}\,\mathrm{var}(x_1) = \frac{4\alpha^2}{12n} = \frac{\alpha^2}{3n},$$

where $\mathrm{var}(x_1)$ is obtained from Table 4.2. From Exercises 11.7 or 12.8,

$$\mathrm{MSE}(\widehat{\alpha}) = \frac{2\alpha^2}{(n+2)(n+1)}.$$

Now $\mathrm{MSE}(\widetilde{\alpha}) > \mathrm{MSE}(\widehat{\alpha})$ if $(n+2)(n+1) > 6n$, that is, if

$$n^2 - 3n + 2 = (n-2)(n-1)$$

is positive. The two estimators have the same MSE when $n = 1$ or $n = 2$. Otherwise, the MLE has a lower MSE than the MME. Tolerating a small bias in the MLE has made it much more efficient than the MME, and the latter's MSE is never smaller than the former's when $n > 2$. There are two implications of this result when $n > 2$. First, the MME is inadmissible when a quadratic loss function is used. Second, the MME that is based on the sample mean is not as good an estimator as the largest order statistic (the MLE) in this problem. It is not a good idea to automatically base estimators of the population moment on its sample counterpart. The largest observation is a much more efficient estimator of this parameter, which is related to the upper bound of the distribution, and the result is a lower MSE as well as a smaller variance. Think of x as the grade that some teacher gives to his/her students. His/her marking is such that all grades are equally probable, but he/she is stingy and does not give 100% even if the answers are all correct! You can collect grades from this teacher's courses, and discover the upper bound α more efficiently from the maximum grade than from the mean (quite literally!) grade.

(e) This follows as both MSEs tend to zero as $n \to \infty$. Note, however, that $\mathrm{MSE}(\widehat{\alpha}) = O(1/n^2)$ and tends to zero much faster than $\mathrm{MSE}(\widetilde{\alpha}) = O(1/n)$.

Exercise 13.4 (Uniform's MM: too many moments?) Let $x_1, \dots, x_n$ be a random sample of $x \sim \mathrm{U}_{(-\alpha,\alpha)}$. Derive the MME of α implied by two different moments.

Solution

We have $\mathrm{E}(x) = 0$, which tells us nothing about α. Now,

$$\mathrm{E}(x^2) = \int_{-\alpha}^{\alpha} \frac{u^2}{2\alpha}\,\mathrm{d}u = \frac{\alpha^2}{3},$$

hence

$$\widetilde{\alpha}_1 = \sqrt{\frac{3}{n}\sum_{i=1}^{n} x_i^2}.$$

The next nonzero moment is

$$\mathrm{E}(x^4) = \int_{-\alpha}^{\alpha} \frac{u^4}{2\alpha}\, \mathrm{d}u = \frac{\alpha^4}{5},$$

giving the alternative estimator

$$\widetilde{\alpha}_2 = \left(\frac{5}{n}\sum_{i=1}^{n} x_i^4\right)^{1/4}.$$

One could continue finding many more MMEs for α.

Exercise 13.5 (Pareto's MM: to be or not to be?) Let $x_1, \dots, x_n$ be a random sample from the p.d.f.

$$f_x(u) = \begin{cases} pu^{-p-1} & (u > 1), \\ 0 & \text{(elsewhere)}, \end{cases}$$

where $p > 0$. Derive the MME of p.

Solution

We have $\mathrm{E}(x) = \int_1^\infty upu^{-p-1}\, \mathrm{d}u$. For $p \in (0, 1]$, the mean does not exist and there is no MME. For $p > 1$,

$$\mathrm{E}(x) = \left[\frac{pu^{1-p}}{1-p}\right]_1^\infty = \frac{p}{p-1},$$

and $\overline{x} = 1/(1 - 1/\widetilde{p})$ implies that $\widetilde{p} = 1/(1 - 1/\overline{x})$. However, we do not know p, as this was the whole purpose of the estimation exercise! Therefore, we cannot predict whether the MME formula is usable. If we were to ignore this problem and use the formula, we would always end up with $\widetilde{p} > 1$ (since $x_i > 1$, hence $\overline{x} > 1$) regardless of whether this is the case (recall that the parameter space allows $p > 0$).

13.2 Least squares

Exercise 13.6 (Linear model: orthogonal parameterization) Consider the model $y_i = \beta_1 + \beta_2 x_i + \varepsilon_i$, where the $\{x_i\}_{i=1}^n$ are fixed and the $\{\varepsilon_i\}_{i=1}^n$ are i.i.d. with mean 0 and variance σ^2. The model is reparameterized as $y_i = \gamma_1 + \gamma_2(x_i - \overline{x}) + \varepsilon_i$ and then estimated by LS. Show that:
(a) $\widehat{\gamma}_2 = \widehat{\beta}_2$, but that $\widehat{\gamma}_1 \neq \widehat{\beta}_1$;
(b) $\widehat{\gamma}_1$ is uncorrelated with $\widehat{\gamma}_2$;
(c) $\mathrm{cov}(\widehat{\beta}_1, \widehat{\beta}_2) = -\sigma^2 \overline{x} / \sum_{j=1}^n (x_j - \overline{x})^2 \neq 0$, by three methods.

Solution

(a) From Exercise 12.33, we get

$$\widehat{\beta}_2 = \frac{\sum_{i=1}^n (x_i - \overline{x})(y_i - \overline{y})}{\sum_{i=1}^n (x_i - \overline{x})^2} \quad \text{and} \quad \widehat{\beta}_1 = \overline{y} - \widehat{\beta}_2 \overline{x}.$$

Similarly, defining $z_i := x_i - \overline{x}$, we have

$$\widehat{\gamma}_2 = \frac{\sum_{i=1}^n z_i (y_i - \overline{y})}{\sum_{i=1}^n z_i^2} = \frac{\sum_{i=1}^n z_i y_i}{\sum_{i=1}^n z_i^2} \quad \text{and} \quad \widehat{\gamma}_1 = \overline{y},$$

because the sample average of the z's is zero. Clearly, $\widehat{\gamma}_2 = \widehat{\beta}_2$, an invariance that follows from the Frisch–Waugh decomposition (see the Notes to Chapter 12). However, $\widehat{\gamma}_1 \neq \widehat{\beta}_1$ in general.

(b) Let $\boldsymbol{X} := (\boldsymbol{\imath}, \boldsymbol{z})$. We know that the variance matrix of $(\widehat{\gamma}_1, \widehat{\gamma}_2)$ is

$$\sigma^2 \left(\boldsymbol{X}'\boldsymbol{X}\right)^{-1} = \sigma^2 \begin{pmatrix} n & n\overline{z} \\ n\overline{z} & \sum_{i=1}^n z_i^2 \end{pmatrix}^{-1} = \sigma^2 \begin{pmatrix} n & 0 \\ 0 & \sum_{i=1}^n z_i^2 \end{pmatrix}^{-1} = \sigma^2 \begin{pmatrix} 1/n & 0 \\ 0 & 1/\sum_{i=1}^n z_i^2 \end{pmatrix},$$

hence that $\widehat{\gamma}_1$ and $\widehat{\gamma}_2$ are uncorrelated.

(c) The partitioned inverse of $\boldsymbol{X}'\boldsymbol{X}$ from Exercise 12.33 gives the required result. Alternatively, write

$$\widehat{\beta}_2 = \frac{\sum_{i=1}^n (x_i - \overline{x})(y_i - \overline{y})}{\sum_{i=1}^n (x_i - \overline{x})^2} = \frac{\sum_{i=1}^n (x_i - \overline{x}) y_i}{\sum_{i=1}^n (x_i - \overline{x})^2} = \frac{\boldsymbol{z}'\boldsymbol{y}}{\boldsymbol{z}'\boldsymbol{z}} = \boldsymbol{y}' \left(\frac{1}{\boldsymbol{z}'\boldsymbol{z}} \boldsymbol{z}\right),$$

where the second equality follows as in Chapter 9 (see its introduction and Section 9.1), and

$$\begin{aligned}
\widehat{\beta}_1 &= \frac{1}{n} \sum_{i=1}^n y_i - \overline{x} \sum_{i=1}^n \frac{x_i - \overline{x}}{\sum_{j=1}^n (x_j - \overline{x})^2} y_i \\
&= \sum_{i=1}^n \left(\frac{1}{n} - \overline{x} \frac{x_i - \overline{x}}{\sum_{j=1}^n (x_j - \overline{x})^2}\right) y_i \\
&= \left(\frac{1}{n}\boldsymbol{\imath} - \frac{\overline{x}}{\boldsymbol{z}'\boldsymbol{z}} \boldsymbol{z}\right)' \boldsymbol{y}.
\end{aligned}$$

Since the $\{x_n\}$ are fixed,

$$\begin{aligned}
\operatorname{cov}(\widehat{\beta}_1, \widehat{\beta}_2) &= \left(\frac{1}{n}\boldsymbol{\imath} - \frac{\overline{x}}{\boldsymbol{z}'\boldsymbol{z}} \boldsymbol{z}\right)' \operatorname{var}(\boldsymbol{y}) \left(\frac{1}{\boldsymbol{z}'\boldsymbol{z}} \boldsymbol{z}\right) = \left(\frac{1}{n}\boldsymbol{\imath} - \frac{\overline{x}}{\boldsymbol{z}'\boldsymbol{z}} \boldsymbol{z}\right)' (\sigma^2 \boldsymbol{I}_n) \left(\frac{1}{\boldsymbol{z}'\boldsymbol{z}} \boldsymbol{z}\right) \\
&= \frac{\sigma^2}{\boldsymbol{z}'\boldsymbol{z}} \left(\frac{1}{n}\boldsymbol{\imath}'\boldsymbol{z} - \overline{x}\right) = -\frac{\sigma^2 \overline{x}}{\boldsymbol{z}'\boldsymbol{z}} = -\frac{\sigma^2 \overline{x}}{\sum_{j=1}^n (x_j - \overline{x})^2}
\end{aligned}$$

by $\frac{1}{n}\boldsymbol{\imath}'\boldsymbol{z} = \overline{z} = 0$. Finally, this can also be obtained by

$$\begin{aligned}
\operatorname{cov}(\widehat{\beta}_1, \widehat{\beta}_2) &= \operatorname{cov}(\overline{y} - \widehat{\beta}_2 \overline{x}, \widehat{\beta}_2) = \operatorname{cov}(\overline{y}, \widehat{\beta}_2) - \overline{x} \operatorname{cov}(\widehat{\beta}_2, \widehat{\beta}_2) \\
&= \operatorname{cov}(\widehat{\gamma}_1, \widehat{\gamma}_2) - \overline{x} \operatorname{var}(\widehat{\beta}_2) = -\overline{x} \operatorname{var}(\widehat{\beta}_2).
\end{aligned}$$

Exercise 13.7 (LS is not invariant to the choice of LHS) Consider the linear model

$$y_i = \beta_1 + \beta_2 x_i + \varepsilon_i,$$

where $\beta_2 \neq 0$ and $\{\varepsilon_i\}_{i=1}^n$ are i.i.d. with mean zero. The equation may be rewritten as

$$x_i = \gamma_1 + \gamma_2 y_i + \eta_i,$$

with $\eta_i := -\varepsilon_i/\beta_2$. Show that, although $\beta_2\gamma_2 \equiv 1$, the LSEs satisfy $\widehat{\beta}_2\widehat{\gamma}_2 = \widehat{\rho}_{y,x}^2 \leqslant 1$, where $\widehat{\rho}_{y,x}$ is the sample correlation between y and x.

Solution
By applying the usual formula for the LSE,

$$\widehat{\beta}_2 = \frac{\sum_{i=1}^n (x_i - \overline{x})(y_i - \overline{y})}{\sum_{i=1}^n (x_i - \overline{x})^2} \quad \text{and} \quad \widehat{\gamma}_2 = \frac{\sum_{i=1}^n (y_i - \overline{y})(x_i - \overline{x})}{\sum_{i=1}^n (y_i - \overline{y})^2}.$$

Therefore,

$$\widehat{\beta}_2\widehat{\gamma}_2 = \left(\frac{\frac{1}{n}\sum_{i=1}^n (x_i - \overline{x})(y_i - \overline{y})}{\sqrt{\frac{1}{n}\sum_{i=1}^n (x_i - \overline{x})^2}\sqrt{\frac{1}{n}\sum_{i=1}^n (y_i - \overline{y})^2}} \right)^2 = \widehat{\rho}_{y,x}^2.$$

In other words, even though the identity $\beta_2 \equiv 1/\gamma_2$ holds for the parameters, this relation does not hold for the corresponding LSEs. In terms of the properties seen in the introduction to Chapter 11, LS is not invariant to reparameterizations. This is so because LS ignores the presence of β_2 in $\eta_i \equiv -\varepsilon_i/\beta_2$, whereas ML takes it into account. In terms of the scatter plot of (x_i, y_i), if we were to swap the axes, then the LS regression line would *not* be reflected across a 45° line; see also the figure in the next exercise.

***Exercise 13.8 (Galton's fallacy, regression, and conditioning)** Let $(x, y)' \sim \mathrm{N}(\boldsymbol{\mu}, \boldsymbol{\Sigma})$, with $\boldsymbol{\mu} := (\mu_1, \mu_2)'$ and

$$\boldsymbol{\Sigma} := \sigma^2 \begin{pmatrix} 1 & \rho \\ \rho & 1 \end{pmatrix} \qquad (|\rho| < 1 \text{ and } \sigma > 0).$$

(a) Show that, given x, the function $h(x)$ that minimizes $\mathrm{E}\left[(y - h(x))^2\right]$ is

$$h(x) = \mathrm{E}_{y|x}(y) = (\mu_2 - \rho\mu_1) + \rho x.$$

(b) Show that, given x, we have the regression model

$$y = \beta_1 + \beta_2 x + \varepsilon,$$

where $\beta_1 = \mu_2 - \rho\mu_1$, $\beta_2 = \rho$, $\varepsilon \sim \mathrm{N}(0, \sigma_{22|1})$, and $\sigma_{22|1} := \left(1 - \rho^2\right)\sigma^2 \leqslant \sigma^2$.
(c) Show that, given y, we have the regression model

$$x = \gamma_1 + \gamma_2 y + \eta,$$

where $\gamma_1 = \mu_1 - \rho\mu_2$, $\gamma_2 = \rho = \beta_2$, $\eta \sim \mathrm{N}(0, \sigma_{11|2})$, and $\sigma_{11|2} := \left(1 - \rho^2\right)\sigma^2 = \sigma_{22|1}$.
(d) Compare results (b) and (c), interpreting them in the light of Figure 6.4 of Exercise 6.1.

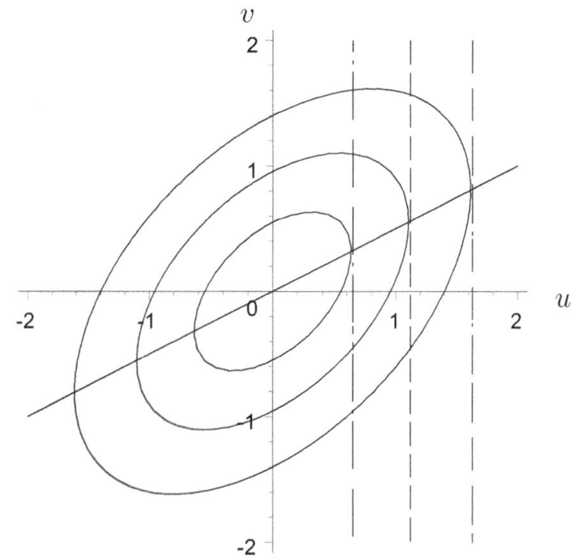

Figure 13.3. Ellipses from the bivariate normal of Figure 6.4, centered around $\mathbf{0}_2$ with unit variances and $\rho = \frac{1}{2}$. In addition, this graph contains the regression line obtained as the locus of the tangency points of the vertical lines with the ellipses.

Solution

(a) Exercise 6.46 on "best predictors" shows that LS on the population (not sample) moment $\mathrm{E}\left[(y - h(x))^2\right]$ leads to $h(x) = \mathrm{E}_{y|x}(y)$. Then, Chapter 8 yields $\mathrm{E}_{y|x}(y) = \mu_2 + \rho(x - \mu_1)$.

(b) This follows from writing $\varepsilon = y - \beta_1 - \beta_2 x$ and using the distribution of $y \mid x$ derived in Chapter 8. Comparing with (a), we see that $y = \mathrm{E}_{y|x}(y) + \varepsilon$.

(c) This follows from reversing the roles of x and y in (b).

(d) There is a certain amount of "shrinkage" (hence the name "regression") inherent in the slope of an LS regression; see the Notes to Chapter 11. This is reflected here in that both slopes are numerically smaller than 1: $|\beta_2| = |\rho| < 1$ and $|\gamma_2| = |\rho| < 1$. For the sample counterparts, see Exercise 13.7. However, unlike in that exercise, neither (b) nor (c) is the "true" model (or generating process): they are both obtained by applying LS to the population.

The conditional mean is the peak of the conditional density in the case of the bivariate normal (see Exercise 6.1), and (a) shows that the sequence of such peaks is the LS (based on population expectations) regression line. On the basis of Figure 6.4, where $\boldsymbol{\mu} = \mathbf{0}_2$, the regression line is calculated in Figure 13.3 as follows: for every given x value (depicted by a vertical dashed line at a given number for u), we choose the maximum of the conditional density (depicted by the tangency point because the inner ellipses define a higher value of the p.d.f.). Since x and y have equal variances, the slope is ρ and never exceeds 1 in absolute value. In the figure, the slope is $\rho = \frac{1}{2}$: the regression line is less steep than the 45° line around which the ellipses are centered.

This exercise illustrates that it would be fallacious to equate causality (for example, if x increases by 1 unit then y increases by β_2 on average) to regression, since (b) and (c) give opposite conclusions about the slope of the linear relation linking y and x. Rather, regression is about correlation or association: given x, the "best" estimate of y is $\beta_1 + \beta_2 x$. We should keep in mind that it is the parameters of the joint distribution of x, y (such as the correlation) that are being obtained from regression analysis.

Exercise 13.9 (Conditional and marginal effects) Suppose that we have a random sample of size n for three variates, y, x_1, x_2, and that the de-meaned observations are stacked into the three vectors $\boldsymbol{y}, \boldsymbol{x}_1, \boldsymbol{x}_2$, respectively. Define the projection matrix

$$\boldsymbol{M}_1 := \boldsymbol{I}_n - \frac{1}{\boldsymbol{x}_1'\boldsymbol{x}_1}\boldsymbol{x}_1\boldsymbol{x}_1',$$

and similarly for $\boldsymbol{M}_2$.
(a) Show that

$$\frac{\boldsymbol{x}_1'\boldsymbol{y}}{\boldsymbol{x}_1'\boldsymbol{x}_1} - \frac{\boldsymbol{x}_1'\boldsymbol{M}_2\boldsymbol{y}}{\boldsymbol{x}_1'\boldsymbol{M}_2\boldsymbol{x}_1} = \frac{\boldsymbol{x}_2'\boldsymbol{M}_1\boldsymbol{y}}{\boldsymbol{x}_2'\boldsymbol{M}_1\boldsymbol{x}_2}\frac{\boldsymbol{x}_1'\boldsymbol{x}_2}{\boldsymbol{x}_1'\boldsymbol{x}_1}.$$

(b) Interpret (a) in terms of regression.

Solution
(a) We start by noting that inner products such as $\boldsymbol{x}_1'\boldsymbol{x}_2$ are 1×1 quantities that commute with the rest, and that $\boldsymbol{x}_1'\boldsymbol{x}_2 = \boldsymbol{x}_2'\boldsymbol{x}_1$. We can rewrite the left-hand side of the equation as

$$\begin{aligned}
&\boldsymbol{x}_1'\frac{\boldsymbol{M}_2\boldsymbol{x}_1\boldsymbol{x}_1' - \boldsymbol{x}_1\boldsymbol{x}_1'\boldsymbol{M}_2}{\boldsymbol{x}_1'\boldsymbol{x}_1\boldsymbol{x}_1'\boldsymbol{M}_2\boldsymbol{x}_1}\boldsymbol{y} \\
&= \boldsymbol{x}_1'\frac{\boldsymbol{x}_1\boldsymbol{x}_1' - \frac{1}{\boldsymbol{x}_2'\boldsymbol{x}_2}\boldsymbol{x}_2\boldsymbol{x}_2'\boldsymbol{x}_1\boldsymbol{x}_1' - \boldsymbol{x}_1\boldsymbol{x}_1' + \frac{1}{\boldsymbol{x}_2'\boldsymbol{x}_2}\boldsymbol{x}_1\boldsymbol{x}_1'\boldsymbol{x}_2\boldsymbol{x}_2'}{\boldsymbol{x}_1'\boldsymbol{x}_1\boldsymbol{x}_1'\boldsymbol{M}_2\boldsymbol{x}_1}\boldsymbol{y} \\
&= \frac{\boldsymbol{x}_2'\boldsymbol{x}_1}{\boldsymbol{x}_2'\boldsymbol{x}_2}\boldsymbol{x}_1'\frac{\boldsymbol{x}_1\boldsymbol{x}_2' - \boldsymbol{x}_2\boldsymbol{x}_1'}{\boldsymbol{x}_1'\boldsymbol{x}_1\boldsymbol{x}_1'\boldsymbol{M}_2\boldsymbol{x}_1}\boldsymbol{y} = \frac{\boldsymbol{x}_2'\boldsymbol{x}_1}{\boldsymbol{x}_2'\boldsymbol{x}_2}\frac{\boldsymbol{x}_2'\boldsymbol{M}_1\boldsymbol{y}}{\boldsymbol{x}_1'\boldsymbol{M}_2\boldsymbol{x}_1}.
\end{aligned}$$

The result follows since the denominator is

$$\boldsymbol{x}_2'\boldsymbol{x}_2\boldsymbol{x}_1'\boldsymbol{M}_2\boldsymbol{x}_1 = \boldsymbol{x}_2'\boldsymbol{x}_2\boldsymbol{x}_1'\boldsymbol{x}_1 - \left(\boldsymbol{x}_2'\boldsymbol{x}_1\right)^2 = \boldsymbol{x}_1'\boldsymbol{x}_1\boldsymbol{x}_2'\boldsymbol{M}_1\boldsymbol{x}_2.$$

Note that dividing the last equation by $\boldsymbol{x}_1'\boldsymbol{x}_1\boldsymbol{x}_2'\boldsymbol{x}_2$ leads to a reformulation of Exercise 13.7, because $\boldsymbol{x}_1'\boldsymbol{M}_2\boldsymbol{x}_1$ is the sum of squares of the residuals from regressing $\boldsymbol{x}_1$ on $\boldsymbol{x}_2$, and

$$\frac{\boldsymbol{x}_1'\boldsymbol{M}_2\boldsymbol{x}_1}{\boldsymbol{x}_1'\boldsymbol{x}_1} = 1 - \widehat{\rho}^{\,2}_{x_1,x_2}.$$

(b) In terms of regression analysis, (a) shows that

$$\widehat{\beta}_{yx_1} - \widehat{\beta}_{yx_1|x_2} = \widehat{\beta}_{yx_2|x_1}\widehat{\beta}_{x_2x_1},$$

where $\widehat{\beta}_{yx_1}$ is the estimator obtained from regressing y on x_1, and $\widehat{\beta}_{yx_1|x_2}$ is the estimator obtained after taking into account the effect of x_2 (that is, the coefficient of x_1 in the regression of y on x_1 and x_2); see, for example, Exercise 12.39. The difference between $\widehat{\beta}_{yx_1}$ and $\widehat{\beta}_{yx_1|x_2}$ explains the Yule–Simpson paradox, which is illustrated in the Notes to Chapter 6, on conditioning and sign-reversal.

***Exercise 13.10 (Gauss–Markov theorem)** Let $\boldsymbol{y} = \boldsymbol{X\beta} + \boldsymbol{\varepsilon}$, where $\boldsymbol{X}$ is nonrandom and of rank k, and $\boldsymbol{\varepsilon}$ has mean $\mathbf{0}_n$ and positive definite variance $\sigma^2 \boldsymbol{I}_n$. Show that $\widehat{\boldsymbol{\beta}} := (\boldsymbol{X}'\boldsymbol{X})^{-1} \boldsymbol{X}'\boldsymbol{y}$ is the best linear unbiased estimator of $\boldsymbol{\beta}$. [Hint: Write the linear estimators as $\widetilde{\boldsymbol{\beta}} := \boldsymbol{C}\boldsymbol{y}$, where $\boldsymbol{C}$ is nonrandom, and work out the restriction implied on $\boldsymbol{C}$ by unbiasedness. Then, compare the variances of $\widehat{\boldsymbol{\beta}}$ and $\widetilde{\boldsymbol{\beta}}$.]

Solution

Write the linear estimators as $\widetilde{\boldsymbol{\beta}} := \boldsymbol{C}\boldsymbol{y}$, where $\boldsymbol{C} := (\boldsymbol{X}'\boldsymbol{X})^{-1} \boldsymbol{X}' + \boldsymbol{B}$ and $\boldsymbol{B}$ is nonrandom. Therefore, $\widetilde{\boldsymbol{\beta}} = \widehat{\boldsymbol{\beta}} + \boldsymbol{B}\boldsymbol{y}$. We need to show that the BLUE property implies that $\boldsymbol{B} = \mathbf{O}$. First, since $\mathrm{E}(\widehat{\boldsymbol{\beta}}) = \boldsymbol{\beta}$, the unbiasedness of $\widetilde{\boldsymbol{\beta}}$ requires that $\mathrm{E}(\boldsymbol{B}\boldsymbol{y}) = \mathbf{0}$. Substituting for $\boldsymbol{y}$ from the definition of the model,

$$\mathrm{E}(\boldsymbol{B}\boldsymbol{y}) = \mathrm{E}(\boldsymbol{BX\beta} + \boldsymbol{B\varepsilon}) = \boldsymbol{BX\beta} + \boldsymbol{B}\,\mathrm{E}(\boldsymbol{\varepsilon}) = \boldsymbol{BX\beta}$$

and, for this to be equal to $\mathbf{0}$ for any $\boldsymbol{\beta}$, we require $\boldsymbol{BX} = \mathbf{O}$. Second,

$$\begin{aligned}
\operatorname{var}(\widetilde{\boldsymbol{\beta}}) &= \operatorname{var}(\boldsymbol{C}\boldsymbol{y}) = \boldsymbol{C}\operatorname{var}(\boldsymbol{y})\,\boldsymbol{C}' = \boldsymbol{C}\left(\sigma^2 \boldsymbol{I}_n\right)\boldsymbol{C}' \\
&= \sigma^2 \left((\boldsymbol{X}'\boldsymbol{X})^{-1} \boldsymbol{X}' + \boldsymbol{B} \right) \left(\boldsymbol{X} (\boldsymbol{X}'\boldsymbol{X})^{-1} + \boldsymbol{B}' \right) \\
&= \sigma^2 (\boldsymbol{X}'\boldsymbol{X})^{-1} + \sigma^2 (\boldsymbol{X}'\boldsymbol{X})^{-1} \boldsymbol{X}'\boldsymbol{B}' + \sigma^2 \boldsymbol{BX} (\boldsymbol{X}'\boldsymbol{X})^{-1} + \sigma^2 \boldsymbol{BB}' \\
&= \sigma^2 (\boldsymbol{X}'\boldsymbol{X})^{-1} + \sigma^2 \boldsymbol{BB}' = \operatorname{var}(\widehat{\boldsymbol{\beta}}) + \sigma^2 \boldsymbol{BB}'.
\end{aligned}$$

The matrix $\boldsymbol{BB}'$ is positive semidefinite: for any arbitrary real $k \times 1$ vector of constants $\boldsymbol{a}$, we have

$$\boldsymbol{a}' \left(\operatorname{var}(\widetilde{\boldsymbol{\beta}}) - \operatorname{var}(\widehat{\boldsymbol{\beta}}) \right) \boldsymbol{a} = \sigma^2 \boldsymbol{a}'\boldsymbol{BB}'\boldsymbol{a} \equiv \boldsymbol{\alpha}'\boldsymbol{\alpha} \geqslant 0,$$

where $\boldsymbol{\alpha} := \sigma \boldsymbol{B}'\boldsymbol{a}$. Equality to zero is achieved if and only if $\boldsymbol{B} = \mathbf{O}$. Note that if $k = 1$ and $\boldsymbol{X} = \boldsymbol{\imath}$, we get the result in Exercise 11.2(b).

Exercise 13.11 (Sample variance: efficiency, again) Let $\boldsymbol{y} = \boldsymbol{X\beta} + \boldsymbol{\varepsilon}$, where $\boldsymbol{X}$ is $n \times k$ nonrandom and of rank $r \leqslant k$, and the components of the continuous variate $\boldsymbol{\varepsilon}$ are i.i.d. with mean 0, variance $\sigma^2 > 0$, and kurtosis 3.

(a) If we restrict the BUE of σ^2 further to be positive and a quadratic function $\boldsymbol{y}'\boldsymbol{B}\boldsymbol{y}$ with $\boldsymbol{B}$ deterministic, show that it is given by

$$\widetilde{\sigma^2} := \frac{1}{n-r}\, \boldsymbol{y}' \left(\boldsymbol{I}_n - \boldsymbol{X}\boldsymbol{X}^+ \right) \boldsymbol{y},$$

where $\boldsymbol{X}^+$ is the Moore–Penrose inverse of $\boldsymbol{X}$. You may assume the following result, derived in Exercise 13.60 of Abadir and Magnus (2005): for $\boldsymbol{B}$ positive semidefinite, minimizing $\operatorname{tr}(\boldsymbol{B}^2)$ subject to $\boldsymbol{BX} = \mathbf{O}$ and $\operatorname{tr}(\boldsymbol{B}) = 1$ yields the optimum

$$\widetilde{\boldsymbol{B}} = \frac{1}{n-r}\left(\boldsymbol{I}_n - \boldsymbol{X}\boldsymbol{X}^+\right).$$

(b) Suppose that we wish to derive the minimum-MSE estimator of σ^2, and that we also wish to restrict attention to the class of estimators that are positive and invariant to $\boldsymbol{\beta}$ in the sense that

$$(\boldsymbol{y} - \boldsymbol{X}\boldsymbol{\beta}_0)'\,\boldsymbol{B}\,(\boldsymbol{y} - \boldsymbol{X}\boldsymbol{\beta}_0) = \boldsymbol{y}'\boldsymbol{B}\boldsymbol{y} \qquad \text{for all } \boldsymbol{\beta}_0.$$

Show that this estimator is given by

$$\widetilde{\sigma^2} := \frac{1}{n-r+2}\,\boldsymbol{y}'\left(\boldsymbol{I}_n - \boldsymbol{X}\boldsymbol{X}^+\right)\boldsymbol{y}.$$

You may assume the following result: for $\boldsymbol{B}$ positive semidefinite, minimizing $2\operatorname{tr}(\boldsymbol{B}^2) + (\operatorname{tr}(\boldsymbol{B}) - 1)^2$ subject to $\boldsymbol{BX} = \mathbf{O}$ yields the optimum

$$\widetilde{\boldsymbol{B}} = \frac{1}{n-r+2}\left(\boldsymbol{I}_n - \boldsymbol{X}\boldsymbol{X}^+\right).$$

Solution

(a) We start by noting that $\widetilde{\sigma^2} \neq \tilde{\sigma}^2$, as discussed in Exercise 11.5(a), and this is more generally the case when estimators are based on moment restrictions, in contrast with the MLE which is invariant to transformations of the parameters (Exercise 12.20). Note also that, since $\boldsymbol{X}\boldsymbol{\beta}$ is deterministic, $\boldsymbol{y}$ and $\boldsymbol{\varepsilon}$ must have the same distribution apart from the mean $\operatorname{E}(\boldsymbol{y}) = \boldsymbol{X}\boldsymbol{\beta}$. Consider

$$\widetilde{\sigma^2} = \boldsymbol{y}'\boldsymbol{B}\boldsymbol{y},$$

where $\boldsymbol{B} \neq \mathbf{O}$ is taken to be a positive semidefinite matrix that we can decompose as $\boldsymbol{B} = \boldsymbol{C}'\boldsymbol{C}$. This ensures the positivity of $\widetilde{\sigma^2}$ because, defining $\boldsymbol{z} := \boldsymbol{C}\boldsymbol{y} \sim \operatorname{D}(\boldsymbol{C}\boldsymbol{X}\boldsymbol{\beta}, \sigma^2\boldsymbol{C}\boldsymbol{C}')$, we have

$$\Pr\left(\widetilde{\sigma^2} = 0\right) = \Pr\left(\boldsymbol{y}'\boldsymbol{C}'\boldsymbol{C}\boldsymbol{y} = 0\right) = \Pr\left(\boldsymbol{z}'\boldsymbol{z} = 0\right) = \Pr\left(\boldsymbol{z} = \mathbf{0}\right) = 0$$

since $\boldsymbol{z}$ is a continuous variate (even if it is degenerate in the case where $\boldsymbol{C}\boldsymbol{C}'$ is singular).

For unbiasedness of $\widetilde{\sigma^2}$, we need

$$\operatorname{E}\left(\boldsymbol{y}'\boldsymbol{C}'\boldsymbol{C}\boldsymbol{y}\right) = \sigma^2$$

for all $\boldsymbol{\beta}$ and σ. Using the definition of the linear model,

$$\begin{aligned}\operatorname{E}\left(\boldsymbol{y}'\boldsymbol{C}'\boldsymbol{C}\boldsymbol{y}\right) &= \operatorname{E}\left(\left(\boldsymbol{\beta}'\boldsymbol{X}' + \boldsymbol{\varepsilon}'\right)\boldsymbol{C}'\boldsymbol{C}\left(\boldsymbol{X}\boldsymbol{\beta} + \boldsymbol{\varepsilon}\right)\right)\\ &= \boldsymbol{\beta}'\boldsymbol{X}'\boldsymbol{C}'\boldsymbol{C}\boldsymbol{X}\boldsymbol{\beta} + \operatorname{E}\left(\boldsymbol{\varepsilon}'\boldsymbol{C}'\boldsymbol{C}\boldsymbol{\varepsilon}\right) + 2\boldsymbol{\beta}'\boldsymbol{X}'\boldsymbol{C}'\boldsymbol{C}\operatorname{E}\left(\boldsymbol{\varepsilon}\right)\\ &= \boldsymbol{\beta}'\boldsymbol{X}'\boldsymbol{C}'\boldsymbol{C}\boldsymbol{X}\boldsymbol{\beta} + \operatorname{tr}\left(\operatorname{E}\left(\boldsymbol{\varepsilon}\boldsymbol{\varepsilon}'\right)\boldsymbol{C}'\boldsymbol{C}\right) + 0\\ &= \boldsymbol{\beta}'\boldsymbol{X}'\boldsymbol{C}'\boldsymbol{C}\boldsymbol{X}\boldsymbol{\beta} + \sigma^2\operatorname{tr}\left(\boldsymbol{C}'\boldsymbol{C}\right)\end{aligned}$$

and the condition for unbiasedness becomes $\boldsymbol{CX} = \mathbf{O}$ (since $\boldsymbol{A'A} = \mathbf{O}$ if and only if $\boldsymbol{A} = \mathbf{O}$) and $\operatorname{tr}(\boldsymbol{C'C}) = 1$. The first requirement implies that

$$\boldsymbol{y'C'Cy} = \boldsymbol{\varepsilon'C'C\varepsilon};$$

hence $\widetilde{\sigma^2} = \boldsymbol{\varepsilon'C'C\varepsilon}$, and minimizing the variance of $\widetilde{\sigma^2}$ is the same as minimizing

$$\operatorname{var}\left(\boldsymbol{\varepsilon'C'C\varepsilon}\right) = \sigma^4 \operatorname{var}\left(\left(\sigma^{-1}\boldsymbol{\varepsilon}\right)' \boldsymbol{C'C}\left(\sigma^{-1}\boldsymbol{\varepsilon}\right)\right) = 2\sigma^4 \operatorname{tr}\left(\left(\boldsymbol{C'C}\right)^2\right),$$

which is obtained from Exercise 6.7(a). The matrix optimization result stated in the exercise gives the required result.

There are a few properties to note. First, the skewness is not necessarily zero, but this has no impact on the solution. Second, when $\boldsymbol{X} = \boldsymbol{\imath}$, we get

$$\boldsymbol{X}^+ = \left(\boldsymbol{\imath'\imath}\right)^{-1}\boldsymbol{\imath}' = \frac{1}{n}\boldsymbol{\imath}'$$

(see the solution of Exercise 12.30(b) for the definition of $\boldsymbol{X}^+$ when $r = k$) and

$$\widetilde{\boldsymbol{B}} = \frac{1}{n-1}\left(\boldsymbol{I}_n - \frac{1}{n}\boldsymbol{\imath\imath}'\right),$$

where the matrix in parentheses is the usual idempotent de-meaning matrix. In this case, our solution is $\widetilde{\sigma^2} = s^2$, which is the usual sample variance matrix. We now see that this relation between BUE and σ^2 is more generally the case when $r = k$; see Exercise 12.31(e), though we do not assume normality here.

(b) This part generalizes Exercise 11.5(c). Positivity follows as in (a) by letting $\boldsymbol{B} = \boldsymbol{C'C}$. Invariance requires $\boldsymbol{CX} = \mathbf{O}$ or equivalently $\boldsymbol{BX} = \mathbf{O}$, giving the same variance of the estimator as in (a):

$$\operatorname{var}\left(\widetilde{\sigma^2}\right) = 2\sigma^4 \operatorname{tr}\left(\boldsymbol{B}^2\right).$$

Its bias is

$$\mathrm{E}\left(\boldsymbol{\varepsilon'B\varepsilon}\right) - \sigma^2 = \operatorname{tr}\left(\mathrm{E}\left(\boldsymbol{\varepsilon\varepsilon}'\right)\boldsymbol{B}\right) - \sigma^2 = \operatorname{tr}\left(\sigma^2\boldsymbol{I}_n\boldsymbol{B}\right) - \sigma^2 = \sigma^2\left(\operatorname{tr}(\boldsymbol{B}) - 1\right),$$

which gives the MSE as $2\sigma^4 \operatorname{tr}\left(\boldsymbol{B}^2\right) + \sigma^4\left(\operatorname{tr}(\boldsymbol{B}) - 1\right)^2$, whose minimization subject to $\boldsymbol{BX} = \mathbf{O}$ gives

$$\widetilde{\boldsymbol{B}} = \frac{1}{n-r+2}\left(\boldsymbol{I}_n - \boldsymbol{XX}^+\right),$$

as stated in the question.

Exercise 13.12 (GLS) Let $\boldsymbol{y} = \boldsymbol{X\beta} + \boldsymbol{u}$, where $\boldsymbol{X}$ is of rank k, and $\boldsymbol{u}$ has mean $\mathbf{0}_n$ and a positive definite variance $\boldsymbol{\Sigma}$ that is known.

(a) Show that the LSE of $\boldsymbol{\beta}$, based on a spherical $\boldsymbol{\varepsilon}$, is $\left(\boldsymbol{X'\Sigma}^{-1}\boldsymbol{X}\right)^{-1}\boldsymbol{X'\Sigma}^{-1}\boldsymbol{y}$. This is known as the *generalized LS* (GLS) estimator of $\boldsymbol{\beta}$, whereas $\left(\boldsymbol{X'X}\right)^{-1}\boldsymbol{X'y}$ is the *ordinary LS* (OLS) estimator.

(b) Assuming $\boldsymbol{X}$ is nonrandom, derive the mean and variance of the OLS and GLS estimators in this model.

Solution

(a) Since $\boldsymbol{\Sigma}$ is positive definite, there exists a decomposition of the form $\boldsymbol{\Sigma} = \boldsymbol{A}\boldsymbol{A}'$, where $\boldsymbol{A}$ is nonsingular. Premultiplying the model by $\boldsymbol{A}^{-1}$ gives

$$\boldsymbol{A}^{-1}\boldsymbol{y} = \boldsymbol{A}^{-1}\boldsymbol{X}\boldsymbol{\beta} + \boldsymbol{\varepsilon},$$

where $\boldsymbol{\varepsilon} := \boldsymbol{A}^{-1}\boldsymbol{u}$ has $\mathrm{E}(\boldsymbol{\varepsilon}) = \boldsymbol{A}^{-1}\mathrm{E}(\boldsymbol{u}) = \boldsymbol{0}$, since $\boldsymbol{A}$ is a nonrandom matrix, and

$$\mathrm{var}(\boldsymbol{\varepsilon}) = \mathrm{var}\left(\boldsymbol{A}^{-1}\boldsymbol{u}\right) = \boldsymbol{A}^{-1}\mathrm{var}(\boldsymbol{u})\,\boldsymbol{A}'^{-1} = \boldsymbol{A}^{-1}\boldsymbol{\Sigma}\boldsymbol{A}'^{-1} = \boldsymbol{A}^{-1}\boldsymbol{A}\boldsymbol{A}'\boldsymbol{A}'^{-1} = \boldsymbol{I}_n.$$

We are therefore back to the standard linear model, but the variables are now $\boldsymbol{A}^{-1}\boldsymbol{y}$ and $\boldsymbol{A}^{-1}\boldsymbol{X}$ (both known since $\boldsymbol{\Sigma}$ is known) instead of $\boldsymbol{y}$ and $\boldsymbol{X}$, and the LS estimator in the transformed model follows as before:

$$\left(\left(\boldsymbol{A}^{-1}\boldsymbol{X}\right)'\left(\boldsymbol{A}^{-1}\boldsymbol{X}\right)\right)^{-1}\left(\boldsymbol{A}^{-1}\boldsymbol{X}\right)'\boldsymbol{A}^{-1}\boldsymbol{y} = \left(\boldsymbol{X}'\boldsymbol{\Sigma}^{-1}\boldsymbol{X}\right)^{-1}\boldsymbol{X}'\boldsymbol{\Sigma}^{-1}\boldsymbol{y},$$

since $\boldsymbol{\Sigma}^{-1} = \boldsymbol{A}'^{-1}\boldsymbol{A}^{-1}$. Exercise 13.13(a) will follow the alternative route of minimizing explicitly the LS criterion $\boldsymbol{\varepsilon}'\boldsymbol{\varepsilon} \equiv \boldsymbol{u}'\boldsymbol{\Sigma}^{-1}\boldsymbol{u}$. Notice that the formula for GLS generalizes Exercise 11.2(c). Notice also that GLS reduces to OLS when $\boldsymbol{\Sigma}$ is a scalar matrix and the disturbances are uncorrelated. Recall that the lack of correlation is a much weaker requirement than independence, when the normality assumption is dropped.

(b) Denoting the OLS and GLS estimators by $\widehat{\boldsymbol{\beta}}_{\mathrm{OLS}}$ and $\widehat{\boldsymbol{\beta}}_{\mathrm{GLS}}$, respectively, we have

$$\widehat{\boldsymbol{\beta}}_{\mathrm{OLS}} = \left(\boldsymbol{X}'\boldsymbol{X}\right)^{-1}\boldsymbol{X}'\left(\boldsymbol{X}\boldsymbol{\beta} + \boldsymbol{u}\right) = \boldsymbol{\beta} + \left(\boldsymbol{X}'\boldsymbol{X}\right)^{-1}\boldsymbol{X}'\boldsymbol{u}$$

and

$$\widehat{\boldsymbol{\beta}}_{\mathrm{GLS}} = \left(\boldsymbol{X}'\boldsymbol{\Sigma}^{-1}\boldsymbol{X}\right)^{-1}\boldsymbol{X}'\boldsymbol{\Sigma}^{-1}\left(\boldsymbol{X}\boldsymbol{\beta} + \boldsymbol{u}\right) = \boldsymbol{\beta} + \left(\boldsymbol{X}'\boldsymbol{\Sigma}^{-1}\boldsymbol{X}\right)^{-1}\boldsymbol{X}'\boldsymbol{\Sigma}^{-1}\boldsymbol{u}.$$

Taking expectations and using $\mathrm{E}(\boldsymbol{u}) = \boldsymbol{0}$, both estimators are unbiased when $\boldsymbol{X}$ is nonrandom (needed for OLS and GLS) and $\boldsymbol{\Sigma}$ is known (needed for GLS). Since the estimators are unbiased, $\mathrm{var}(\widehat{\boldsymbol{\beta}}) = \mathrm{E}((\widehat{\boldsymbol{\beta}} - \boldsymbol{\beta})(\widehat{\boldsymbol{\beta}} - \boldsymbol{\beta})')$ for both, giving

$$\mathrm{var}(\widehat{\boldsymbol{\beta}}_{\mathrm{OLS}}) = \left(\boldsymbol{X}'\boldsymbol{X}\right)^{-1}\boldsymbol{X}'\mathrm{E}(\boldsymbol{u}\boldsymbol{u}')\boldsymbol{X}\left(\boldsymbol{X}'\boldsymbol{X}\right)^{-1} = \left(\boldsymbol{X}'\boldsymbol{X}\right)^{-1}\boldsymbol{X}'\boldsymbol{\Sigma}\boldsymbol{X}\left(\boldsymbol{X}'\boldsymbol{X}\right)^{-1}$$

and

$$\mathrm{var}(\widehat{\boldsymbol{\beta}}_{\mathrm{GLS}}) = \left(\boldsymbol{X}'\boldsymbol{\Sigma}^{-1}\boldsymbol{X}\right)^{-1}\boldsymbol{X}'\boldsymbol{\Sigma}^{-1}\mathrm{E}(\boldsymbol{u}\boldsymbol{u}')\boldsymbol{\Sigma}^{-1}\boldsymbol{X}\left(\boldsymbol{X}'\boldsymbol{\Sigma}^{-1}\boldsymbol{X}\right)^{-1} = \left(\boldsymbol{X}'\boldsymbol{\Sigma}^{-1}\boldsymbol{X}\right)^{-1}.$$

Note that (a) implies that now the BLUE is not the OLS, but rather the GLS estimator, and Exercise 13.10 showed indirectly that the difference between their variances is positive semidefinite. The intuitive explanation is that there is a loss of efficiency if we ignore the information given by the correlation between the components of $\boldsymbol{u}$. GLS minimizes $\boldsymbol{u}'\boldsymbol{\Sigma}^{-1}\boldsymbol{u} \equiv \boldsymbol{\varepsilon}'\boldsymbol{\varepsilon}$ (as required for the BLUE in terms of the spherical errors $\boldsymbol{\varepsilon}$), whereas OLS now minimizes $\boldsymbol{u}'\boldsymbol{u}$.

Exercise 13.13 (CLS) Let $\boldsymbol{y} = \boldsymbol{X}\boldsymbol{\beta} + \boldsymbol{u}$, where $\boldsymbol{X}$ is of rank k, and $\boldsymbol{u}$ has mean $\boldsymbol{0}_n$ and a positive definite variance $\boldsymbol{\Sigma}$ that is known. We saw in Exercise 13.12 that the GLS estimator is $\widehat{\boldsymbol{\beta}} := \left(\boldsymbol{X}'\boldsymbol{\Sigma}^{-1}\boldsymbol{X}\right)^{-1}\boldsymbol{X}'\boldsymbol{\Sigma}^{-1}\boldsymbol{y}$ with $\boldsymbol{\Omega} := \mathrm{var}(\widehat{\boldsymbol{\beta}}) = \left(\boldsymbol{X}'\boldsymbol{\Sigma}^{-1}\boldsymbol{X}\right)^{-1}$.

Suppose we know that $\boldsymbol{R}'\boldsymbol{\beta} = \boldsymbol{c}$, where $\boldsymbol{R}$ is a nonrandom $k \times r$ matrix of rank $r < k$ and $\boldsymbol{c}$ is a nonrandom vector.
(a) Obtain the *constrained LS* (CLS) estimator $\widetilde{\boldsymbol{\beta}} := \widehat{\boldsymbol{\beta}} - \boldsymbol{\Omega}\boldsymbol{R}(\boldsymbol{R}'\boldsymbol{\Omega}\boldsymbol{R})^{-1}(\boldsymbol{R}'\widehat{\boldsymbol{\beta}} - \boldsymbol{c})$ by minimizing $\frac{1}{2}\boldsymbol{u}'\boldsymbol{\Sigma}^{-1}\boldsymbol{u}$ subject to $\boldsymbol{R}'\boldsymbol{\beta} = \boldsymbol{c}$.
(b) Assuming $\boldsymbol{X}$ is nonrandom, derive the mean and variance of $\widetilde{\boldsymbol{\beta}}$ in this model.
(c) Show that $\operatorname{var}(\widehat{\boldsymbol{\beta}}) - \operatorname{var}(\widetilde{\boldsymbol{\beta}})$ is positive semidefinite.
(d) Show that

$$\widetilde{\boldsymbol{u}}'\boldsymbol{\Sigma}^{-1}\widetilde{\boldsymbol{u}} - \widehat{\boldsymbol{u}}'\boldsymbol{\Sigma}^{-1}\widehat{\boldsymbol{u}} = (\widetilde{\boldsymbol{\beta}} - \widehat{\boldsymbol{\beta}})'\boldsymbol{\Omega}^{-1}(\widetilde{\boldsymbol{\beta}} - \widehat{\boldsymbol{\beta}}) = (\boldsymbol{R}'\widehat{\boldsymbol{\beta}} - \boldsymbol{c})'(\boldsymbol{R}'\boldsymbol{\Omega}\boldsymbol{R})^{-1}(\boldsymbol{R}'\widehat{\boldsymbol{\beta}} - \boldsymbol{c}),$$

where $\widetilde{\boldsymbol{u}}$ and $\widehat{\boldsymbol{u}}$ are the CLS and GLS residuals, respectively. How do you reconcile the first equality with (c) when $\boldsymbol{\Sigma} = \sigma^2 \boldsymbol{I}_n$?
(e) Suppose that $\boldsymbol{u}$ is spherically distributed (hence $\boldsymbol{\Sigma} = \sigma^2 \boldsymbol{I}_n$), independently of $\boldsymbol{X}$. Prove that

$$\frac{n-k}{r} \times \frac{\widetilde{\boldsymbol{u}}'\widetilde{\boldsymbol{u}} - \widehat{\boldsymbol{u}}'\widehat{\boldsymbol{u}}}{\widehat{\boldsymbol{u}}'\widehat{\boldsymbol{u}}} \sim \mathrm{F}(r, n-k).$$

Solution
(a) We start by remarking that if we had $r = k$, then $\boldsymbol{\beta} = \boldsymbol{R}'^{-1}\boldsymbol{c}$ and there would be no need to go any further. Now, for $r < k$, we set up the Lagrangian (see Section A.4.5)

$$\begin{aligned} S(\boldsymbol{\beta}) &:= \frac{1}{2}(\boldsymbol{y} - \boldsymbol{X}\boldsymbol{\beta})'\boldsymbol{\Sigma}^{-1}(\boldsymbol{y} - \boldsymbol{X}\boldsymbol{\beta}) + \boldsymbol{\lambda}'(\boldsymbol{c} - \boldsymbol{R}'\boldsymbol{\beta}) \\ &= \frac{1}{2}(\boldsymbol{y} - \boldsymbol{X}\boldsymbol{\beta})'\boldsymbol{\Sigma}^{-1}(\boldsymbol{y} - \boldsymbol{X}\boldsymbol{\beta}) + (\boldsymbol{c} - \boldsymbol{R}'\boldsymbol{\beta})'\boldsymbol{\lambda}, \end{aligned}$$

which contains quadratic and linear forms in $\boldsymbol{\beta}$, and $\boldsymbol{\lambda}$ which is an r-dimensional vector of Lagrange multipliers. Differentiating,

$$\frac{\partial S(\boldsymbol{\beta})}{\partial \boldsymbol{\beta}} = -\boldsymbol{X}'\boldsymbol{\Sigma}^{-1}(\boldsymbol{y} - \boldsymbol{X}\boldsymbol{\beta}) - \boldsymbol{R}\boldsymbol{\lambda},$$

and the first-order conditions are $\boldsymbol{X}'\boldsymbol{\Sigma}^{-1}\boldsymbol{X}\widetilde{\boldsymbol{\beta}} - \boldsymbol{R}\widetilde{\boldsymbol{\lambda}} = \boldsymbol{X}'\boldsymbol{\Sigma}^{-1}\boldsymbol{y}$ and $\boldsymbol{R}'\widetilde{\boldsymbol{\beta}} = \boldsymbol{c}$. These k and r equations can be stacked as

$$\begin{pmatrix} \boldsymbol{X}'\boldsymbol{\Sigma}^{-1}\boldsymbol{X} & \boldsymbol{R} \\ \boldsymbol{R}' & \mathrm{O} \end{pmatrix} \begin{pmatrix} \widetilde{\boldsymbol{\beta}} \\ -\widetilde{\boldsymbol{\lambda}} \end{pmatrix} = \begin{pmatrix} \boldsymbol{X}'\boldsymbol{\Sigma}^{-1}\boldsymbol{y} \\ \boldsymbol{c} \end{pmatrix},$$

where the first matrix is symmetric. We will write henceforth $\boldsymbol{\Omega} := \left(\boldsymbol{X}'\boldsymbol{\Sigma}^{-1}\boldsymbol{X}\right)^{-1}$ for the variance of the GLS estimator $\widehat{\boldsymbol{\beta}} = \boldsymbol{\Omega}\boldsymbol{X}'\boldsymbol{\Sigma}^{-1}\boldsymbol{y}$, seen in Exercise 13.12(b). By the formula for a partitioned inverse (see Section A.4),

$$\begin{pmatrix} \boldsymbol{\Omega}^{-1} & \boldsymbol{R} \\ \boldsymbol{R}' & \mathrm{O} \end{pmatrix}^{-1} = \begin{pmatrix} \boldsymbol{\Omega}^{1/2}(\boldsymbol{I}_k - \boldsymbol{P})\boldsymbol{\Omega}^{1/2} & \boldsymbol{\Omega}\boldsymbol{R}(\boldsymbol{R}'\boldsymbol{\Omega}\boldsymbol{R})^{-1} \\ (\boldsymbol{R}'\boldsymbol{\Omega}\boldsymbol{R})^{-1}\boldsymbol{R}'\boldsymbol{\Omega} & -(\boldsymbol{R}'\boldsymbol{\Omega}\boldsymbol{R})^{-1} \end{pmatrix},$$

where the $r \times r$ matrix $\boldsymbol{R}'\boldsymbol{\Omega}\boldsymbol{R}$ is of full rank and we have the symmetric idempotent

$$\boldsymbol{P} := \boldsymbol{\Omega}^{1/2}\boldsymbol{R}\left(\boldsymbol{R}'\boldsymbol{\Omega}\boldsymbol{R}\right)^{-1}\boldsymbol{R}'\boldsymbol{\Omega}^{1/2}$$

satisfying $\operatorname{tr}(\boldsymbol{P}) = r$. Then, we get

$$\begin{pmatrix} \widetilde{\boldsymbol{\beta}} \\ -\widetilde{\boldsymbol{\lambda}} \end{pmatrix} = \begin{pmatrix} \widehat{\boldsymbol{\beta}} - \boldsymbol{\Omega}\boldsymbol{R}\left(\boldsymbol{R}'\boldsymbol{\Omega}\boldsymbol{R}\right)^{-1}\left(\boldsymbol{R}'\widehat{\boldsymbol{\beta}} - \boldsymbol{c}\right) \\ \left(\boldsymbol{R}'\boldsymbol{\Omega}\boldsymbol{R}\right)^{-1}\left(\boldsymbol{R}'\widehat{\boldsymbol{\beta}} - \boldsymbol{c}\right) \end{pmatrix}.$$

This is a minimum, since the objective function is convex and the constraint is linear.
(b) Since $\mathrm{E}(\widehat{\boldsymbol{\beta}}) = \boldsymbol{\beta}$, we have

$$\mathrm{E}(\widetilde{\boldsymbol{\beta}}) = \boldsymbol{\beta} - \boldsymbol{\Omega}\boldsymbol{R}\left(\boldsymbol{R}'\boldsymbol{\Omega}\boldsymbol{R}\right)^{-1}\left(\boldsymbol{R}'\boldsymbol{\beta} - \boldsymbol{c}\right) = \boldsymbol{\beta}$$

by $\boldsymbol{R}'\boldsymbol{\beta} = \boldsymbol{c}$. For the variance, we collect the terms in $\widehat{\boldsymbol{\beta}}$ and

$$\widetilde{\boldsymbol{\beta}} = \boldsymbol{\Omega}^{1/2}\left(\boldsymbol{I}_k - \boldsymbol{P}\right)\boldsymbol{\Omega}^{-1/2}\widehat{\boldsymbol{\beta}} + \boldsymbol{b}$$

where $\boldsymbol{b} := \boldsymbol{\Omega}\boldsymbol{R}\left(\boldsymbol{R}'\boldsymbol{\Omega}\boldsymbol{R}\right)^{-1}\boldsymbol{c}$ is nonrandom. Then, using $\operatorname{var}(\widehat{\boldsymbol{\beta}}) = \boldsymbol{\Omega}$, we obtain

$$\begin{aligned} \operatorname{var}(\widetilde{\boldsymbol{\beta}}) &= \boldsymbol{\Omega}^{1/2}\left(\boldsymbol{I}_k - \boldsymbol{P}\right)\boldsymbol{\Omega}^{-1/2}\operatorname{var}(\widehat{\boldsymbol{\beta}})\boldsymbol{\Omega}^{-1/2}\left(\boldsymbol{I}_k - \boldsymbol{P}\right)\boldsymbol{\Omega}^{1/2} \\ &= \boldsymbol{\Omega}^{1/2}\left(\boldsymbol{I}_k - \boldsymbol{P}\right)\left(\boldsymbol{I}_k - \boldsymbol{P}\right)\boldsymbol{\Omega}^{1/2} \\ &= \boldsymbol{\Omega}^{1/2}\left(\boldsymbol{I}_k - \boldsymbol{P}\right)\boldsymbol{\Omega}^{1/2} = \boldsymbol{\Omega} - \boldsymbol{\Omega}\boldsymbol{R}\left(\boldsymbol{R}'\boldsymbol{\Omega}\boldsymbol{R}\right)^{-1}\boldsymbol{R}'\boldsymbol{\Omega} \end{aligned}$$

since $\boldsymbol{I}_k - \boldsymbol{P}$ is idempotent. Notice that this is exactly the first block of the partitioned inverse in (a). We will revisit this phenomenon in Chapter 14, where the context will be extended to nonlinear restrictions and general ML estimation; see Exercise 14.18(b).
(c) For any vector $\boldsymbol{a}$,

$$\boldsymbol{a}'\left(\operatorname{var}(\widehat{\boldsymbol{\beta}}) - \operatorname{var}(\widetilde{\boldsymbol{\beta}})\right)\boldsymbol{a} = \boldsymbol{a}'\boldsymbol{\Omega}^{1/2}\boldsymbol{P}\boldsymbol{\Omega}^{1/2}\boldsymbol{a} = \boldsymbol{\alpha}'\boldsymbol{\alpha},$$

where $\boldsymbol{\alpha} := \boldsymbol{P}\boldsymbol{\Omega}^{1/2}\boldsymbol{a}$ and we use $\boldsymbol{P} = \boldsymbol{P}^2$ (idempotent $\boldsymbol{P}$). Therefore, this quadratic form is nonnegative and the difference of variances is positive semidefinite. In other words, incorporating the restriction $\boldsymbol{R}'\boldsymbol{\beta} = \boldsymbol{c}$ into the estimation of $\boldsymbol{\beta}$ has improved the efficiency (precision) of our estimator. As a special case, we get the implication that including irrelevant variables (those whose true parameter value is zero) in the regression reduces the precision of the estimates; compare with R^2 at the end of the solution of Exercise 12.39.
(d) Expressing $\widetilde{\boldsymbol{u}}$ in terms of $\widehat{\boldsymbol{u}}$, we have

$$\widetilde{\boldsymbol{u}} = \boldsymbol{y} - \boldsymbol{X}\widetilde{\boldsymbol{\beta}} = \boldsymbol{y} - \boldsymbol{X}\widehat{\boldsymbol{\beta}} + (\boldsymbol{X}\widehat{\boldsymbol{\beta}} - \boldsymbol{X}\widetilde{\boldsymbol{\beta}}) = \widehat{\boldsymbol{u}} + \boldsymbol{X}(\widehat{\boldsymbol{\beta}} - \widetilde{\boldsymbol{\beta}});$$

hence

$$\begin{aligned} \widetilde{\boldsymbol{u}}'\boldsymbol{\Sigma}^{-1}\widetilde{\boldsymbol{u}} &= \left(\widehat{\boldsymbol{u}} + \boldsymbol{X}(\widehat{\boldsymbol{\beta}} - \widetilde{\boldsymbol{\beta}})\right)'\boldsymbol{\Sigma}^{-1}\left(\widehat{\boldsymbol{u}} + \boldsymbol{X}(\widehat{\boldsymbol{\beta}} - \widetilde{\boldsymbol{\beta}})\right) \\ &= \widehat{\boldsymbol{u}}'\boldsymbol{\Sigma}^{-1}\widehat{\boldsymbol{u}} + 2(\widehat{\boldsymbol{\beta}} - \widetilde{\boldsymbol{\beta}})'\boldsymbol{X}'\boldsymbol{\Sigma}^{-1}\widehat{\boldsymbol{u}} + (\widehat{\boldsymbol{\beta}} - \widetilde{\boldsymbol{\beta}})'\boldsymbol{X}'\boldsymbol{\Sigma}^{-1}\boldsymbol{X}(\widehat{\boldsymbol{\beta}} - \widetilde{\boldsymbol{\beta}}) \\ &= \widehat{\boldsymbol{u}}'\boldsymbol{\Sigma}^{-1}\widehat{\boldsymbol{u}} + (\widehat{\boldsymbol{\beta}} - \widetilde{\boldsymbol{\beta}})'\boldsymbol{\Omega}^{-1}(\widehat{\boldsymbol{\beta}} - \widetilde{\boldsymbol{\beta}}), \end{aligned}$$

since $\boldsymbol{X}'\boldsymbol{\Sigma}^{-1}\widehat{\boldsymbol{u}} = \boldsymbol{X}'\boldsymbol{\Sigma}^{-1}(\boldsymbol{y} - \boldsymbol{X}\widehat{\boldsymbol{\beta}}) = \mathbf{0}$ from the definition of $\widehat{\boldsymbol{\beta}}$. From (a),

$$\widetilde{\boldsymbol{\beta}} - \widehat{\boldsymbol{\beta}} = -\boldsymbol{\Omega}\boldsymbol{R}\left(\boldsymbol{R}'\boldsymbol{\Omega}\boldsymbol{R}\right)^{-1}\left(\boldsymbol{R}'\widehat{\boldsymbol{\beta}} - \boldsymbol{c}\right),$$

so

$$\begin{aligned}\widetilde{\boldsymbol{u}}'\boldsymbol{\Sigma}^{-1}\widetilde{\boldsymbol{u}} - \widehat{\boldsymbol{u}}'\boldsymbol{\Sigma}^{-1}\widehat{\boldsymbol{u}} &= \left(\boldsymbol{R}'\widehat{\boldsymbol{\beta}} - \boldsymbol{c}\right)'\left(\boldsymbol{R}'\boldsymbol{\Omega}\boldsymbol{R}\right)^{-1}\boldsymbol{R}'\boldsymbol{\Omega}\boldsymbol{\Omega}^{-1}\boldsymbol{\Omega}\boldsymbol{R}\left(\boldsymbol{R}'\boldsymbol{\Omega}\boldsymbol{R}\right)^{-1}\left(\boldsymbol{R}'\widehat{\boldsymbol{\beta}} - \boldsymbol{c}\right)\\ &= \left(\boldsymbol{R}'\widehat{\boldsymbol{\beta}} - \boldsymbol{c}\right)'\left(\boldsymbol{R}'\boldsymbol{\Omega}\boldsymbol{R}\right)^{-1}\left(\boldsymbol{R}'\widehat{\boldsymbol{\beta}} - \boldsymbol{c}\right).\end{aligned}$$

To reconcile this with (c) when $\boldsymbol{\Sigma} = \sigma^2\boldsymbol{I}_n$, we write

$$\widetilde{\boldsymbol{u}}'\widetilde{\boldsymbol{u}} - \widehat{\boldsymbol{u}}'\widehat{\boldsymbol{u}} = (\widehat{\boldsymbol{\beta}} - \widetilde{\boldsymbol{\beta}})'\boldsymbol{X}'\boldsymbol{X}(\widehat{\boldsymbol{\beta}} - \widetilde{\boldsymbol{\beta}}) \geqslant 0.$$

In estimating the model $\boldsymbol{y} = \boldsymbol{X}\boldsymbol{\beta} + \boldsymbol{u}$, imposing the constraint on $\widetilde{\boldsymbol{\beta}}$ reduces the variability of the estimator (the result in (c)) at the cost of a larger sum of squared residuals $\widetilde{\boldsymbol{u}}'\widetilde{\boldsymbol{u}}$ (the result here in (d)). Given $\boldsymbol{X}$, the difference in the sums of squared residuals is small whenever $\widetilde{\boldsymbol{\beta}}$ is close to the unconstrained $\widehat{\boldsymbol{\beta}}$, that is, when $\boldsymbol{R}'\widehat{\boldsymbol{\beta}}$ is close to $\boldsymbol{c}$.

(e) We start by stressing the generality of this result, which holds even when $\boldsymbol{u}$ is not normally distributed. Some precedents can be found in Exercises 8.37(a), 9.7(a), and 12.35(f). Defining the idempotent $\boldsymbol{C} := \boldsymbol{I}_n - \boldsymbol{X}(\boldsymbol{X}'\boldsymbol{X})^{-1}\boldsymbol{X}'$, where $\operatorname{tr}(\boldsymbol{C}) = n - k$, we have

$$\widehat{\boldsymbol{u}} = \boldsymbol{y} - \widehat{\boldsymbol{y}} = \boldsymbol{u} + \boldsymbol{X}\left(\boldsymbol{\beta} - \widehat{\boldsymbol{\beta}}\right) = \boldsymbol{u} - \boldsymbol{X}\left(\boldsymbol{X}'\boldsymbol{X}\right)^{-1}\boldsymbol{X}'\boldsymbol{u} = \boldsymbol{C}\boldsymbol{u}.$$

Now, $\boldsymbol{\Omega} = \sigma^2\left(\boldsymbol{X}'\boldsymbol{X}\right)^{-1}$ and

$$\begin{aligned}\widehat{\boldsymbol{\beta}} - \widetilde{\boldsymbol{\beta}} &= \left(\boldsymbol{X}'\boldsymbol{X}\right)^{-1}\boldsymbol{R}\left(\boldsymbol{R}'\left(\boldsymbol{X}'\boldsymbol{X}\right)^{-1}\boldsymbol{R}\right)^{-1}\left(\boldsymbol{R}'\widehat{\boldsymbol{\beta}} - \boldsymbol{c}\right)\\ &= \left(\boldsymbol{X}'\boldsymbol{X}\right)^{-1}\boldsymbol{R}\left(\boldsymbol{R}'\left(\boldsymbol{X}'\boldsymbol{X}\right)^{-1}\boldsymbol{R}\right)^{-1}\left(\boldsymbol{R}'\left(\boldsymbol{X}'\boldsymbol{X}\right)^{-1}\boldsymbol{X}'\boldsymbol{u} + \boldsymbol{R}'\boldsymbol{\beta} - \boldsymbol{c}\right)\\ &= \left(\boldsymbol{X}'\boldsymbol{X}\right)^{-1}\boldsymbol{R}\left(\boldsymbol{R}'\left(\boldsymbol{X}'\boldsymbol{X}\right)^{-1}\boldsymbol{R}\right)^{-1}\boldsymbol{R}'\left(\boldsymbol{X}'\boldsymbol{X}\right)^{-1}\boldsymbol{X}'\boldsymbol{u},\end{aligned}$$

since $\boldsymbol{R}'\boldsymbol{\beta} = \boldsymbol{c}$. We can rewrite this as $\widehat{\boldsymbol{\beta}} - \widetilde{\boldsymbol{\beta}} = \left(\boldsymbol{X}'\boldsymbol{X}\right)^{-1/2}\boldsymbol{P}\left(\boldsymbol{X}'\boldsymbol{X}\right)^{-1/2}\boldsymbol{X}'\boldsymbol{u}$, using the idempotent $\boldsymbol{P}$ defined in (a). Consider the ratio

$$\begin{aligned}\frac{\widetilde{\boldsymbol{u}}'\widetilde{\boldsymbol{u}} - \widehat{\boldsymbol{u}}'\widehat{\boldsymbol{u}}}{\widehat{\boldsymbol{u}}'\widehat{\boldsymbol{u}}} &= \frac{(\widetilde{\boldsymbol{\beta}} - \widehat{\boldsymbol{\beta}})'\boldsymbol{X}'\boldsymbol{X}(\widetilde{\boldsymbol{\beta}} - \widehat{\boldsymbol{\beta}})}{\widehat{\boldsymbol{u}}'\widehat{\boldsymbol{u}}}\\ &= \frac{\boldsymbol{u}'\boldsymbol{X}\left(\boldsymbol{X}'\boldsymbol{X}\right)^{-1/2}\boldsymbol{P}\left(\boldsymbol{X}'\boldsymbol{X}\right)^{-1/2}\boldsymbol{X}'\boldsymbol{X}\left(\boldsymbol{X}'\boldsymbol{X}\right)^{-1/2}\boldsymbol{P}\left(\boldsymbol{X}'\boldsymbol{X}\right)^{-1/2}\boldsymbol{X}'\boldsymbol{u}}{\boldsymbol{u}'\boldsymbol{C}\boldsymbol{u}}\\ &= \frac{\boldsymbol{u}'\boldsymbol{B}\boldsymbol{u}}{\boldsymbol{u}'\boldsymbol{C}\boldsymbol{u}},\end{aligned}$$

where $\boldsymbol{B} := \boldsymbol{X}\left(\boldsymbol{X}'\boldsymbol{X}\right)^{-1/2}\boldsymbol{P}\left(\boldsymbol{X}'\boldsymbol{X}\right)^{-1/2}\boldsymbol{X}'$ is idempotent, since

$$\begin{aligned}&\boldsymbol{X}\left(\boldsymbol{X}'\boldsymbol{X}\right)^{-1/2}\boldsymbol{P}\left(\boldsymbol{X}'\boldsymbol{X}\right)^{-1/2}\boldsymbol{X}'\boldsymbol{X}\left(\boldsymbol{X}'\boldsymbol{X}\right)^{-1/2}\boldsymbol{P}\left(\boldsymbol{X}'\boldsymbol{X}\right)^{-1/2}\boldsymbol{X}'\\ &\qquad = \boldsymbol{X}\left(\boldsymbol{X}'\boldsymbol{X}\right)^{-1/2}\boldsymbol{P}\left(\boldsymbol{X}'\boldsymbol{X}\right)^{-1/2}\boldsymbol{X}',\end{aligned}$$

and satisfies $\text{tr}(\boldsymbol{B}) = \text{tr}(\boldsymbol{P}) = r$. Now, since $\boldsymbol{X}'\boldsymbol{C} = \mathbf{O}$ and $\sigma^2 > 0$ (hence $\Pr(\boldsymbol{u} = \mathbf{0}) = 0$), we can apply Exercise 8.37(a) to get the required result, conditionally on $\boldsymbol{X}$. Since $\boldsymbol{X}$ does not affect the conditional distribution, the result holds unconditionally too. Note that Exercise 8.37(a) did not require the existence of the moments of $\boldsymbol{u}$, although we have made this simplifying assumption for the mean and variance here.

13.3 Nonparametric estimation

Exercise 13.14 (Kernel density estimator: pointwise distributions) Suppose that we have a random sample $x_1, \dots, x_n$ from a density $f(u)$, whose first three derivatives exist and are bounded for all $u \in \mathcal{X}$. The kernel density estimator is

$$\widehat{f}(u) := \frac{1}{n\lambda} \sum_{i=1}^{n} K\left(\frac{u - x_i}{\lambda}\right),$$

where $\lambda > 0$ is the bandwidth. The kernel K can be chosen as any function such that $c_{jk} := \int_{-\infty}^{\infty} t^j K(t)^k \, \mathrm{d}t$ satisfies

$$c_{01} = 1, \quad c_{11} = 0, \quad c_{21} \neq 0,$$

and c_{21}, c_{31}, c_{12} are all finite. Let $n \to \infty$ faster than $\lambda \to 0$, such that $n\lambda \to \infty$.
(a) Show that the asymptotic expansion of the bias is $\mathrm{E}(\widehat{f}(u) - f(u)) = \frac{1}{2}\lambda^2 c_{21} f''(u) + o(\lambda^2)$.
(b) Show that $\text{var}(\widehat{f}(u)) = \frac{1}{n\lambda} c_{02} f(u) + o(\frac{1}{n\lambda})$.
(c) Obtain the limiting distribution of $\widehat{f}(u)$.
(d) Is $\widehat{f}(u)$ a consistent estimator of $f(u)$?

Solution
(a) As seen in the introduction to this chapter, $\widehat{f}(u) = n^{-1} \sum_{i=1}^{n} \psi_i$ where we define $\psi_i := \lambda^{-1} K\left(\lambda^{-1}(u - x_i)\right)$. Since $\{x_n\}$ are i.i.d., then so are $\{\psi_n\}$ and we get (as in Section 9.1)

$$\mathrm{E}(\widehat{f}(u)) = \mathrm{E}(\psi_1) \quad \text{and} \quad \text{var}(\widehat{f}(u)) = \frac{1}{n} \text{var}(\psi_1),$$

where the sample size affects the latter but not the former. Now, the random variable in ψ_1 is x_1 and, taking expectations with respect to it, we have

$$\mathrm{E}(\widehat{f}(u)) = \mathrm{E}\left(\frac{1}{\lambda} K\left(\frac{u - x_1}{\lambda}\right)\right) = \frac{1}{\lambda} \int_{-\infty}^{\infty} K\left(\frac{u - w}{\lambda}\right) f(w) \, \mathrm{d}w.$$

By the change of variable $t = (u - w)/\lambda$,

$$\mathrm{E}(\widehat{f}(u)) = \frac{1}{\lambda} \int_{\infty}^{-\infty} K(t) f(u - \lambda t) \, \mathrm{d}(-\lambda t) = \int_{-\infty}^{\infty} K(t) f(u - \lambda t) \, \mathrm{d}t,$$

where we note the changes in the limits of integration. Since $\lambda \to 0$ and f is differentiable three times, Taylor's theorem gives

$$\mathrm{E}(\widehat{f}(u)) = \int_{-\infty}^{\infty} K(t) \left(f(u) - \lambda t f'(u) + \frac{\lambda^2 t^2}{2} f''(u) + O(\lambda^3) \right) \mathrm{d}t,$$

Since the $O(\lambda^3)$ term contains a bounded f''', a finite $\int_{-\infty}^{\infty} t^3 K(t)\,\mathrm{d}t$ guarantees that the integral of the $O(\lambda^3)$ term is finite. Hence,

$$\begin{aligned}
&\mathrm{E}(\widehat{f}(u)) \\
&= f(u) \int_{-\infty}^{\infty} K(t)\,\mathrm{d}t - \lambda f'(u) \int_{-\infty}^{\infty} tK(t)\,\mathrm{d}t + \frac{\lambda^2}{2} f''(u) \int_{-\infty}^{\infty} t^2 K(t)\,\mathrm{d}t + O(\lambda^3) \\
&= f(u) + \frac{\lambda^2 c_{21}}{2} f''(u) + O(\lambda^3)
\end{aligned}$$

by the assumptions on K. Notice four features. First, if K is nonnegative everywhere, then it is a proper density and c_{21} is its variance. Second, the formula shows that the bias is a direct function of λ but not n. Third, the bias increases with the bandwidth λ. Fourth, assuming that K has zero mean ($c_{11} = 0$) makes the $O(\lambda)$ term vanish, thereby reducing the bias asymptotically.

(b) For the variance,

$$\operatorname{var}(\widehat{f}(u)) = \frac{1}{n} \operatorname{var}(\psi_1) = \frac{1}{n} \mathrm{E}(\psi_1^2) - \frac{1}{n} (\mathrm{E}(\psi_1))^2 .$$

We have worked out $\mathrm{E}(\psi_1) = f(u) + O(\lambda^2)$ in (a), and we now derive

$$\begin{aligned}
\mathrm{E}(\psi_1^2) &= \frac{1}{\lambda^2} \int_{-\infty}^{\infty} K\left(\frac{u-w}{\lambda}\right)^2 f(w)\,\mathrm{d}w = \frac{1}{\lambda} \int_{-\infty}^{\infty} K(t)^2 f(u - \lambda t)\,\mathrm{d}t \\
&= \frac{1}{\lambda} \int_{-\infty}^{\infty} K(t)^2 (f(u) + O(\lambda))\,\mathrm{d}t = \frac{c_{02}}{\lambda} f(u) + O(1),
\end{aligned}$$

where a bounded f' and a finite $\int_{-\infty}^{\infty} tK(t)^2\,\mathrm{d}t$ justify the last step, as in (a). Therefore,

$$\operatorname{var}(\widehat{f}(u)) = \frac{1}{n} \left(\frac{c_{02}}{\lambda} f(u) + O(1) \right) - \frac{1}{n} \left(f(u) + O(\lambda^2) \right)^2 = \frac{c_{02}}{n\lambda} f(u) + O\left(\frac{1}{n}\right)$$

and since $n \to \infty$ faster than $n\lambda \to \infty$, the order of magnitude is as stated in the question. Unlike the bias, the variance depends directly on both λ and n. Also, in contrast with the bias, the variance *decreases* as the bandwidth increases. We saw this visually in Figure 13.1, where a wider window made the estimate $\widehat{f}$ less erratic (there was less vertical volatility of this estimate) while assigning a higher probability to points far from the data (hence causing a bias in $\widehat{f}$). We will see in Exercise 13.15(b) that the IMSE-optimal λ balances the bias and variance terms.

(c) Since $\widehat{f}(u) = n^{-1} \sum_{i=1}^{n} \psi_i$ where the $\{\psi_n\}$ are i.i.d., the limiting distribution is normal (by the CLT) with mean and variance derived in (a) and (b), respectively. Therefore,

$$\sqrt{n\lambda}\left(\widehat{f}(u) - f(u)\right) \overset{a}{\sim} \mathrm{N}\left(\frac{c_{21}\delta}{2} f''(u), c_{02} f(u)\right),$$

where $\delta := \lambda^2\sqrt{n\lambda}$. Such distributional results can be used to construct pointwise (for each $u \in \mathcal{X}$) asymptotic CIs for $\widehat{f}(u)$.
(d) With $\sup_u |f''(u)| < \infty$ and $\sup_u f(u) < \infty$, the consistency of $\widehat{f}(u)$ is implied by choosing $\lambda \to 0$ and $n\lambda \to \infty$ in order to squash the bias and variance, respectively. We will see in Exercise 13.15 that the optimal δ is $O(1)$ as $n \to \infty$. Note that the convergence in (c) occurs at a slower rate than in parametric models, namely it is $\sqrt{n\lambda}$ rather than $\sqrt{n}$. A consistent estimator of the density is intrinsically useful, but it could also be helpful in Exercises 10.30(d) and 11.3 when the density is unknown (see Exercise 11.9 for an alternative approach). It is certainly useful in the context of the NP estimation of hazard rates; see Exercise 2.18(d).

***Exercise 13.15 (Kernel density estimator: IMSE)** Continuing with the setup of Exercise 13.14, let $\gamma := \int_{-\infty}^{\infty} f''(u)^2 \, \mathrm{d}u < \infty$.
(a) Obtain the leading term of the asymptotic expansions of the MSE of $\widehat{f}(u)$ and the IMSE of $\widehat{f}$.
(b) Show that the bandwidth that minimizes this AIMSE is

$$\widehat{\lambda} = \left(\frac{c_{02}}{\gamma c_{21}^2 n}\right)^{1/5},$$

where c_{21} and c_{02} are defined in Exercise 13.14, and calculate the corresponding value of the AIMSE.
(c) Is the value of this minimum AIMSE affected by the choice of c_{21}? What does your answer imply for $\widehat{\lambda}$?
(d) Use these results to factorize the AIMSE of (a) into the product of a factor containing c_{02} and c_{21} but not λ, and another for λ only. Discuss the implications.

Solution
(a) We know that the MSE is the sum of the squared bias and the variance. Therefore, the leading term of the MSE of $\widehat{f}(u)$ is

$$\frac{\lambda^4 c_{21}^2}{4} f''(u)^2 + \frac{c_{02}}{n\lambda} f(u),$$

and the corresponding AIMSE is

$$C := \frac{\lambda^4 c_{21}^2}{4} \int_{-\infty}^{\infty} f''(u)^2 \, \mathrm{d}u + \frac{c_{02}}{n\lambda} \int_{-\infty}^{\infty} f(u) \, \mathrm{d}u = \frac{\lambda^4 c_{21}^2 \gamma}{4} + \frac{c_{02}}{n\lambda}.$$

(b) Minimizing C with respect to λ,

$$\frac{\partial C}{\partial \lambda} = \lambda^3 c_{21}^2 \gamma - \frac{c_{02}}{n\lambda^2} = 0$$

is solved uniquely by $\widehat{\lambda}^5 = c_{02}/\left(\gamma c_{21}^2 n\right)$, and we have

$$\frac{\partial^2 C}{\partial \lambda^2} = 3\lambda^2 c_{21}^2 \gamma + \frac{2c_{02}}{n\lambda^3} > 0.$$

The optimal value is therefore

$$\widehat{C} = \frac{c_{02}^{4/5} c_{21}^2 \gamma}{4\left(\gamma c_{21}^2 n\right)^{4/5}} + \frac{c_{02}\left(\gamma c_{21}^2 n\right)^{1/5}}{n c_{02}^{1/5}} = \frac{1}{4}\left(\frac{c_{21}^2 c_{02}^4 \gamma}{n^4}\right)^{1/5} + \left(\frac{c_{21}^2 c_{02}^4 \gamma}{n^4}\right)^{1/5}$$

$$= \frac{5}{4}\left(\frac{c_{21}^2 c_{02}^4 \gamma}{n^4}\right)^{1/5},$$

where we see that the optimal squared bias is of the same order of magnitude as the optimal variance. There is a balancing tradeoff between bias and variance, for the sake of minimizing C. See also the discussion at the end of Exercise 13.14(b).

(c) We will show that $\widehat{C}$ is unaffected by the choice of c_{21} (the kernel's variance if $K \geqslant 0$ everywhere), because it depends on c_{21} through $c_{21}^2 c_{02}^4$, which will turn out to be invariant to changes in the kernels' scale. Consider

$$\sqrt{|c_{21}|}c_{02} = \int_{-\infty}^{\infty}\left(\sqrt{|c_{21}|}K(t)\right)^2 \mathrm{d}\left(t/\sqrt{|c_{21}|}\right) = \int_{-\infty}^{\infty}\left(\sqrt{|c_{21}|}K\left(w\sqrt{|c_{21}|}\right)\right)^2 \mathrm{d}w,$$

using the change of variable $w = t/\sqrt{|c_{21}|}$. The function $K_z(w) := \sqrt{|c_{21}|}K(w\sqrt{|c_{21}|})$ is a standardized kernel satisfying the definition in Exercise 13.14:

$$\int_{-\infty}^{\infty} K_z(w)\,\mathrm{d}w = \int_{-\infty}^{\infty} K\left(w\sqrt{|c_{21}|}\right)\mathrm{d}(w\sqrt{|c_{21}|}) = \int_{-\infty}^{\infty} K(t)\,\mathrm{d}t = 1,$$

$$\int_{-\infty}^{\infty} wK_z(w)\,\mathrm{d}w = \frac{1}{\sqrt{|c_{21}|}}\int_{-\infty}^{\infty} w\sqrt{|c_{21}|}K\left(w\sqrt{|c_{21}|}\right)\mathrm{d}(w\sqrt{|c_{21}|}) = 0,$$

$$\int_{-\infty}^{\infty} w^2 K_z(w)\,\mathrm{d}w = \frac{1}{|c_{21}|}\int_{-\infty}^{\infty} w^2\,|c_{21}|\,K\left(w\sqrt{|c_{21}|}\right)\mathrm{d}(w\sqrt{|c_{21}|}) = \frac{c_{21}}{|c_{21}|} \neq 0,$$

since $c_{21}/|c_{21}| = \operatorname{sgn}(c_{21}) \neq 0$. We say that $K_z(w)$ is standardized because the integral $\int_{-\infty}^{\infty} w^2 K_z(w)\,\mathrm{d}w$ takes only the values ± 1, whatever the (nonzero) value of c_{21} of $K(t)$. In the case of $K(t) \geqslant 0$ everywhere, $K_z(w) := \sqrt{|c_{21}|}K(w\sqrt{|c_{21}|})$ defines a density by the transformation theorem, and z is the corresponding variate having mean zero and variance 1. In general, given a kernel $K_z(w)$, we can generate a kernel $K(t)$ having any chosen value of $c_{21} \neq 0$, while $\int_{-\infty}^{\infty} K_z(w)^2\,\mathrm{d}w = \sqrt{|c_{21}|}c_{02}$ remains the same whatever the value of c_{21}.

This invariance has an implication for $\widehat{\lambda}$ too. Define $c := \sqrt{|c_{21}|}c_{02}$, which is invariant to c_{21}. Then

$$\widehat{\lambda} = \left(\frac{c}{\gamma\,|c_{21}|^{5/2}\,n}\right)^{1/5} = |c_{21}|^{-1/2}\left(\frac{c}{\gamma n}\right)^{1/5}.$$

Therefore, when K is a proper density and c_{21} is its variance, $\widehat{\lambda}^2$ is *inversely* proportional to this variance. Investigating in more detail,

$$\widehat{f}(u) := \frac{1}{n}\sum_{i=1}^{n}\frac{1}{\lambda}K\left(\frac{u-x_i}{\lambda}\right)$$

shows that λ scales at the same rate as the kernel's $\sqrt{c_{21}}$. For example, for

$$K(t) = \frac{1}{\sqrt{2\pi c_{21}}}\exp\left(-\frac{t^2}{2c_{21}}\right),$$

we have

$$\frac{1}{\lambda}K\left(\frac{u-x_i}{\lambda}\right) = \frac{1}{\left(\lambda\sqrt{c_{21}}\right)\sqrt{2\pi}}\exp\left(-\frac{(u-x_i)^2}{2\left(\lambda^2 c_{21}\right)}\right)$$

and the product $\lambda^2 c_{21}$ is the variance of the scaled kernel. If a chosen kernel has a high c_{21}, we should adjust λ^2 down accordingly to compensate for this in the calculation of $\widehat{f}$.
(d) Recall the factor $\left(c_{21}^2 c_{02}^4\right)^{1/5}$ in $\widehat{C}$ of (b). It suggests rewriting the AIMSE C of (a) as

$$C = \left(c_{21}^2 c_{02}^4\right)^{1/5}\left(\frac{\gamma}{4}\lambda^4\frac{c_{21}^{8/5}}{c_{02}^{4/5}} + \frac{c_{02}^{1/5}}{n\lambda c_{21}^{2/5}}\right) \equiv \left(c_{21}^2 c_{02}^4\right)^{1/5}\left(\frac{\gamma}{4}(\lambda/b)^4 + \frac{1}{n(\lambda/b)}\right),$$

with $b := \left(c_{02}/c_{21}^2\right)^{1/5}$. Rescaling the kernel using the transformation from λ/b to λ (or by $b^{-1}K(t/b)$) achieves the required separation. The new standardized optimal window is then $(\gamma n)^{-1/5}$, or b times this in terms of the old kernel. The new optimal $(\gamma n)^{-1/5}$ is common to different kernels if they are rescaled by b, which one may use to translate asymptotically optimal windows across various kernels, such as the two in the next exercise.

Exercise 13.16 (Optimal kernel: Epanechnikov) Let K be a kernel satisfying $K(t) \geqslant 0$ for all $t \in \mathbb{R}$.
(a) Show that minimizing $S(K) := \int_{-\infty}^{\infty} K(t)^2\,\mathrm{d}t$ subject to

$$\int_{-\infty}^{\infty} K(t)\,\mathrm{d}t = 1, \quad \int_{-\infty}^{\infty} tK(t)\,\mathrm{d}t = 0, \quad \int_{-\infty}^{\infty} t^2K(t)\,\mathrm{d}t = 1$$

gives rise to the Epanechnikov kernel

$$K_{\mathrm{e}}(t) := \begin{cases} \frac{3}{4\sqrt{5}}\left(1-\frac{1}{5}t^2\right) & (|t| < \sqrt{5}), \\ 0 & (\text{elsewhere}). \end{cases}$$

Show that $S(K_{\mathrm{e}}) = 3/\left(5\sqrt{5}\right)$, as compared with $S(K_{\mathrm{n}}) = 1/\left(2\sqrt{\pi}\right)$ for $K_{\mathrm{n}}(t) := \phi(t)$.
(b) Show that minimizing $\widehat{C}$ of Exercise 13.15(b) with respect to $K \geqslant 0$ gives rise to $K_{\mathrm{e}}(t)$ or scaled versions thereof.
(c) What is the minimized $\widehat{C}$ and the corresponding $\widehat{\lambda}$? Comment on this result, comparing the optimal $\widehat{C}$ and $\widehat{\lambda}$ for K_{e} with those for K_{n}.

Solution

(a) This follows directly from Exercise 4.41(b). Replacing $-f\log(f)$ there by K^2, we get the first-order condition

$$\frac{\partial S(K)}{\partial K} \equiv 2K(t) - l_0 - l_1 t - l_2 t^2 = 0,$$

where l_0, l_1, l_2 are Lagrange multipliers. The above equation shows that the optimal kernel is the quadratic $\left(l_0 + l_1 t + l_2 t^2\right)/2$. The second constraint implies that this quadratic is centered around 0, hence $l_1 = 0$. Since K is nonnegative, $l_0 \geqslant -l_2 t^2$ and the support of the kernel is $t^2 < a^2$ where $a := \sqrt{-l_0/l_2}$ and $l_2 < 0$. We can rewrite the optimal kernel, over its support, as

$$K(t) = \frac{l_0}{2}\left(1 - \frac{1}{a^2}t^2\right),$$

and use the other two constraints to solve for a and l_0 from

$$1 = \frac{l_0}{2}\int_{-a}^{a}\left(1 - \frac{1}{a^2}t^2\right)\mathrm{d}t = \frac{2}{3}l_0 a$$

$$1 = \frac{l_0}{2}\int_{-a}^{a}\left(t^2 - \frac{1}{a^2}t^4\right)\mathrm{d}t = \frac{2}{15}l_0 a^3.$$

Comparing the two equations, $a^2/5 = 1$ and the result for l_0 follows from the first of the two equations. This gives the stated K_e.

By the symmetry of K_e, the minimum value of the objective function is

$$S(K_\mathrm{e}) = 2\int_0^{\sqrt{5}} K_\mathrm{e}(t)^2\,\mathrm{d}t = \frac{9}{40}\int_0^{\sqrt{5}}\left(1 - \frac{1}{5}t^2\right)^2\mathrm{d}t = \frac{9}{16\sqrt{5}}\int_0^1 \frac{(1-w)^2}{\sqrt{w}}\,\mathrm{d}w$$

where we have made the change of variable $w = t^2/5$. From the $\mathrm{Beta}_{(0,1)}(\frac{1}{2},3)$ density (Table 4.2), we get

$$S(K_\mathrm{e}) = \frac{9B\left(\frac{1}{2},3\right)}{16\sqrt{5}} = \frac{9\Gamma\left(\frac{1}{2}\right)\Gamma(3)}{16\sqrt{5}\Gamma\left(\frac{7}{2}\right)} = \frac{9\Gamma\left(\frac{1}{2}\right)2!}{16\sqrt{5}\left(\frac{5}{2}\times\frac{3}{2}\times\frac{1}{2}\Gamma\left(\frac{1}{2}\right)\right)} = \frac{3}{5\sqrt{5}} \approx 0.268.$$

For a standard normal kernel,

$$S(K_\mathrm{n}) = \int_{-\infty}^{\infty}\frac{\exp\left(-t^2\right)}{2\pi}\,\mathrm{d}t = \frac{1}{2\sqrt{\pi}}\int_{-\infty}^{\infty}\frac{\exp\left(-t^2/\left(2\times\frac{1}{2}\right)\right)}{\sqrt{2\pi\times\frac{1}{2}}}\,\mathrm{d}t = \frac{1}{2\sqrt{\pi}} \approx 0.282,$$

from the integral of the $\mathrm{N}(0,\frac{1}{2})$ density.

(b) From Exercise 13.15(b),

$$\widehat{C} = \frac{5}{4}\left(\frac{c_{21}^2 c_{02}^4 \gamma}{n^4}\right)^{1/5},$$

with $c_{jk} := \int_{-\infty}^{\infty} t^j K(t)^k\,\mathrm{d}t$; hence $c_{02} = S(K)$. Since $\gamma := \int_{-\infty}^{\infty} f''(u)^2\,\mathrm{d}u$ is fixed by the true unknown density, $\widehat{C}$ is optimized by minimizing $c_{21}^2 c_{02}^4$. We saw in Exercise 13.15(c) that $\widehat{C}$ is invariant to c_{21}. Therefore, since $c_{02} > 0$, minimizing c_{02} for any

given variance c_{21} solves our problem. We did so in (a) for $c_{21} = 1$ and the result was the Epanechnikov kernel. For any given c_{21}, rescaling this kernel and its support by $\sqrt{c_{21}}$ gives the required solution. Alternatively, minimizing C itself by using the factorization in Exercise 13.15(d) and also the invariance in Exercise 13.15(c) of $c_{21}^2 c_{02}^4$ to the scale of K, we get K_{e} as the solution again.
(c) From (a), the minimized $\widehat{C}$ is

$$\frac{5}{4}\left(\frac{S(K_{\mathrm{e}})^4 \gamma}{n^4}\right)^{1/5} = \frac{1}{4}\left(\frac{81\gamma}{5n^4}\right)^{1/5} \approx 0.436\left(\frac{\gamma}{n^4}\right)^{1/5}.$$

The corresponding $\widehat{\lambda}$ (with $c_{21} = 1$) is

$$\left(\frac{S(K_{\mathrm{e}})}{\gamma n}\right)^{1/5} = \left(\frac{3/5^{3/2}}{\gamma n}\right)^{1/5} \approx \frac{0.769}{(\gamma n)^{1/5}}.$$

Now to the comparison. Using the normal kernel instead of the Epanechnikov, the minimized AIMSE $\widehat{C}$ would be higher by a factor of

$$\left(\frac{5\sqrt{5}}{6\sqrt{\pi}}\right)^{4/5} \approx 1.041,$$

implying a *relative* loss of only 4.1% and an absolute loss that vanishes at the rate of $n^{-4/5}$. The results on $S(K)$ (or c_{02}) here, taken together with Exercise 13.15(b) and (c), imply that the calculation of the asymptotically optimal $\widehat{\lambda}$ is not much affected by these two choices of standardized kernels (K_z in the terminology of Exercise 13.15): in large samples, more or less the same size of optimal window applies to both standardized kernels. Furthermore, b of Exercise 13.15(d) is $S(K)^{1/5}$ here, so

$$\frac{b_{\mathrm{e}}}{b_{\mathrm{n}}} = \left(\frac{3}{5\sqrt{5}} 2\sqrt{\pi}\right)^{1/5} \approx 0.990,$$

meaning that there is only a 1% difference in the scale required for the bandwidth. The only remaining unknown in the optimal $\widehat{\lambda}$ is γ.

***Exercise 13.17 (CV and the band)** Now that we know the optimal kernel from Exercise 13.16, the remaining obstacle to the implementation of the estimation of f is the undetermined bandwidth. Since the optimal $\widehat{\lambda}$ of Exercise 13.16(c) contains the unknown $\gamma := \int_{-\infty}^{\infty} f''(u)^2 \,\mathrm{d}u < \infty$, one possibility is the *plug-in* method, whereby a preliminary estimate of f (or some hypothesized f) is substituted into γ. In this exercise, we will analyze another method which does not require such choices. It is called *LS cross validation* (CV) and exploits a resampling procedure introduced in Exercise 11.8 and in the corresponding Note to Chapter 11.

The first step of the procedure is to delete one observation at a time, say x_j ($j = 1, \dots, n$), then calculate the usual kernel estimator based on the remaining $n - 1$ data points

$$\widehat{f}_{-j}(u) := \frac{1}{(n-1)\lambda} \sum_{i \neq j} K\left(\frac{u - x_i}{\lambda}\right), \quad j = 1, \dots, n.$$

Defining $\overline{\widehat{f}}_{n-1}(\boldsymbol{x}) := \frac{1}{n}\sum_{j=1}^{n} \widehat{f}_{-j}(x_j)$, where $\boldsymbol{x} := (x_1, \dots, x_n)'$, the procedure minimizes with respect to λ the objective function $S := S_1 + S_2 + S_3$, with

$$S_1 := \int_{-\infty}^{\infty} f(u)^2 \, du, \qquad S_2 := \int_{-\infty}^{\infty} \widehat{f}(u)^2 \, du, \qquad S_3 := -2\overline{\widehat{f}}_{n-1}(\boldsymbol{x}).$$

Assuming that S_1 is finite and that the expectations of S_2 and S_3 exist, show that the LSCV procedure is justified by proving that $\mathrm{E}(S)$ is the IMSE.

Solution

We note that S_1 does not depend on λ, so that minimizing S is equivalent to minimizing $S_2 + S_3$ which contains no unknowns. We also note that the finiteness condition on S_1 rules out densities that are unbounded at a point $u = a$ at the rate $|u - a|^{-\delta - 1/2}$ with $\delta \geqslant 0$. This is the case for densities such as $\chi^2(1)$, some GG (and its two-sided extension), and some beta; see Chapter 4.

Taking expectations,

$$\mathrm{E}(S) = \int_{-\infty}^{\infty} f(u)^2 \, du + \int_{-\infty}^{\infty} \mathrm{E}(\widehat{f}(u)^2) \, du - 2\,\mathrm{E}(\overline{\widehat{f}}_{n-1}(\boldsymbol{x})),$$

where the existence of $\mathrm{E}(S_2)$ allows the interchange of the expectation and integration. If we can show that $\mathrm{E}(\overline{\widehat{f}}_{n-1}(\boldsymbol{x})) = \int_{-\infty}^{\infty} \mathrm{E}((\widehat{f}(u)) f(u) \, du$, then we are done. Intuitively, this should be the case since $\overline{\widehat{f}}_{n-1}(\boldsymbol{x})$ is an average which estimates the "expectation" of $\widehat{f}(x_i)$ that is represented by $\int_{-\infty}^{\infty} \widehat{f}(u) f(u) \, du$. To show this, $\{x_n\}$ being i.i.d. implies that

$$\mathrm{E}(\overline{\widehat{f}}_{n-1}(\boldsymbol{x})) = \frac{1}{n} \sum_{j=1}^{n} \mathrm{E}(\widehat{f}_{-j}(x_j)) = \mathrm{E}(\widehat{f}_{-1}(x_1)),$$

where we stress that the argument of $\overline{\widehat{f}}$ is random. The derivations of Exercise 13.14(a) show that the last expectation does not depend on the sample size ($n - 1$ here) because of the i.i.d. assumption. Therefore, $\mathrm{E}(\widehat{f}_{-1}(x_1)) = \mathrm{E}(\widehat{f}(\xi))$, where

$$\widehat{f}(\xi) = \frac{1}{n\lambda} \sum_{i=1}^{n} K\left(\frac{\xi - x_i}{\lambda}\right)$$

and the random argument ξ is independent of $\{x_n\}$ but is drawn from the same distribution. There are $n + 1$ independent variates in $\widehat{f}(\xi)$, namely ξ and the random sample $\boldsymbol{x}$. Using the law of iterated expectations,

$$\mathrm{E}(\widehat{f}(\xi)) = \mathrm{E}_{\boldsymbol{x}}\left(\mathrm{E}_{\xi}(\widehat{f}(\xi))\right) = \mathrm{E}_{\boldsymbol{x}}\left(\int_{-\infty}^{\infty} \widehat{f}(u) f(u) \, du\right) = \int_{-\infty}^{\infty} \mathrm{E}_{\boldsymbol{x}}(\widehat{f}(u)) f(u) \, du.$$

Exercise 13.18 (Estimator of Nadaraya and Watson) Suppose that we have a random sample $\{(x_i, y_i)\}_{i=1}^n$ from a bivariate density $f_{x,y}(u, v)$, or simply $f(u, v)$, assumed to be a continuous function. Define

$$\widehat{f}(u, v) := \frac{1}{n} \sum_{i=1}^{n} \psi (u - x_i, v - y_i),$$

where ψ is a scaled bivariate kernel such that

$$\psi_x(u) := \int_{-\infty}^{\infty} \psi(u, v) \, dv, \quad \psi_y(v) := \int_{-\infty}^{\infty} \psi(u, v) \, du, \quad \int_{-\infty}^{\infty} v\psi(u, v) \, dv = 0,$$

with ψ_x and ψ_y univariate kernels (such as $\psi_x(u) = \lambda^{-1} K(\lambda^{-1} u)$ where K is as seen earlier). Show that the estimator of $\mathrm{E}(y \mid x = u)$ implied by $\widehat{f}(u, v)$ is

$$\sum_{i=1}^{n} \frac{\psi_x(u - x_i)}{\sum_{j=1}^{n} \psi_x(u - x_j)} y_i.$$

Solution

We first need an estimator of the conditional density of $y \mid x$, then we can calculate the implied mean. We are given an estimator of the joint density, from which we can obtain the estimator of the marginal density,

$$\begin{aligned}
\widehat{f}_x(u) &= \int_{-\infty}^{\infty} \widehat{f}(u, v) \, dv = \frac{1}{n} \sum_{i=1}^{n} \int_{-\infty}^{\infty} \psi(u - x_i, v - y_i) \, dv \\
&= \frac{1}{n} \sum_{i=1}^{n} \int_{-\infty}^{\infty} \psi(u - x_i, t) \, dt = \frac{1}{n} \sum_{i=1}^{n} \psi_x(u - x_i)
\end{aligned}$$

using the change of variable $t = v - y_i$. This is the same univariate estimator $\widehat{f}_x(u)$ as before. For $\widehat{f}_x(u) > 0$, the estimator of $\mathrm{E}(y \mid x = u)$ is therefore

$$\begin{aligned}
\int_{-\infty}^{\infty} v \widehat{f}_{y|x=u}(v) \, dv &= \frac{\int_{-\infty}^{\infty} v \widehat{f}_{x,y}(u, v) \, dv}{\widehat{f}_x(u)} = \frac{\int_{-\infty}^{\infty} v \sum_{i=1}^{n} \psi(u - x_i, v - y_i) \, dv}{\sum_{i=1}^{n} \psi_x(u - x_i)} \\
&= \sum_{i=1}^{n} \frac{\int_{-\infty}^{\infty} (t + y_i) \psi(u - x_i, t) \, dt}{\sum_{j=1}^{n} \psi_x(u - x_j)}.
\end{aligned}$$

The result follows from $\int_{-\infty}^{\infty} t\psi(u - x_i, t) \, dt = 0$ and $\int_{-\infty}^{\infty} \psi(u - x_i, t) \, dt = \psi_x(u - x_i)$. Notice that the resulting estimator requires only one marginal kernel ψ_x, with only one smoothing parameter; this was not imposed at the outset.

Exercise 13.19 (Estimator of Nadaraya and Watson: bandwidth) Suppose that we use

$$\sum_{i=1}^{n} \frac{K\left(\lambda^{-1}(u-x_i)\right)}{\sum_{j=1}^{n} K\left(\lambda^{-1}(u-x_j)\right)} y_i$$

as the estimator of $\mathrm{E}(y \mid x = u)$. Describe how it is affected if we let $\lambda \to 0$ or $\lambda \to \infty$.

Solution

When $\lambda \to \infty$, a very large window width means that the regression curve is just a horizontal line given by the average of y_i. This is because

$$K\left(\frac{u - x_i}{\lambda}\right) \to K(0)$$

for all u, and

$$\lim_{\lambda\to\infty} \sum_{i=1}^{n} \frac{K\left(\lambda^{-1}(u-x_i)\right)}{\sum_{j=1}^{n} K\left(\lambda^{-1}(u-x_j)\right)} y_i = \sum_{i=1}^{n} \frac{K(0)}{nK(0)} y_i = \frac{1}{n}\sum_{i=1}^{n} y_i = \overline{y}.$$

At the other extreme, when $\lambda \to 0$,

$$K\left(\frac{u - x_i}{\lambda}\right) \to \begin{cases} K(0) & (u = x_i), \\ K(\pm\infty) & (\text{otherwise}), \end{cases}$$

where $K(\pm\infty) = 0$, and the value of the function at u becomes

$$\sum_{i=1}^{n} \frac{1_{x_i=u} K(0)}{\sum_{j=1}^{n} 1_{x_j=u} K(0)} y_i = \sum_{i=1}^{n} \frac{1_{x_i=u}}{\sum_{j=1}^{n} 1_{x_j=u}} y_i.$$

This is an average of the points whose coordinates are of the form (u, y_i). If there are no ties in the x's, the regression function at $u = x_i$ is simply y_i: the window width is shrinking around each point in the dataset, and the NP regression is just the sequence of points.

The optimal bandwidth λ is somewhere in between. LSCV (see Exercise 13.17) can be used here too for selecting the bandwidth, but the objective function becomes a weighted quadratic function of the regression error ε. (The estimates at the edges of the curve are based on few points, and these should be downweighted in the objective criterion.)

13.4 Bayesian estimation

Exercise 13.20 (Normal conjugates) Suppose that $x \sim \mathrm{N}(\vartheta, \sigma_x^2)$, where it is believed that $\vartheta \sim \mathrm{N}(\mu_0, \sigma_0^2)$ and $\mu_0, \sigma_0^2, \sigma_x^2$ are known constants. Calculate the posterior distribution of ϑ if:

(a) we have a sample of one observation, x_1;
(b) we have a random sample $x_1, \dots, x_n$.

Solution

(a) From the introduction, we know that $f_{\vartheta|x_1}(\theta) \propto f_\vartheta(\theta)\, f_{x_1|\theta}(x_1)$; hence

$$f_{\vartheta|x_1}(\theta) \propto \frac{\exp\left(-(\theta-\mu_0)^2/(2\sigma_0^2)\right)}{\sigma_0\sqrt{2\pi}} \frac{\exp\left(-(x_1-\theta)^2/(2\sigma_x^2)\right)}{\sigma_x\sqrt{2\pi}}$$
$$\propto \exp\left(-\frac{\theta^2-2\mu_0\theta}{2\sigma_0^2} - \frac{\theta^2-2x_1\theta}{2\sigma_x^2}\right)$$

since multiplicative terms such as $\exp\left(-\mu_0^2/(2\sigma_0^2)\right)$ do not contain θ. Defining the precision parameter $\sigma_1^{-2} := \sigma_0^{-2} + \sigma_x^{-2}$ (compare with the harmonic mean in Exercises 9.1 and 11.2(c)), and $\mu_1/\sigma_1^2 := \mu_0/\sigma_0^2 + x_1/\sigma_x^2$, we get

$$f_{\vartheta|x_1}(\theta) \propto \exp\left(-\frac{\theta^2-2\mu_1\theta}{2\sigma_1^2}\right),$$

which we recognize as the density of $\mathrm{N}(\mu_1, \sigma_1^2)$. Whenever the prior and posterior densities are of the same form, they are said to be *conjugate*. In this instance, they are both normal densities.

(b) Similarly, for $\boldsymbol{x} := (x_1, \dots, x_n)'$,

$$f_{\vartheta|\boldsymbol{x}}(\theta) \propto \frac{\exp\left(-(\theta-\mu_0)^2/(2\sigma_0^2)\right)}{\sigma_0\sqrt{2\pi}} \prod_{i=1}^{n} \frac{\exp\left(-(x_i-\theta)^2/(2\sigma_x^2)\right)}{\sigma_x\sqrt{2\pi}}$$
$$= \frac{1}{(2\pi)^{(n+1)/2}\sigma_0\sigma_x^n} \exp\left(-\frac{(\theta-\mu_0)^2}{2\sigma_0^2} - \frac{\sum_{i=1}^{n}(\theta-x_i)^2}{2\sigma_x^2}\right)$$
$$\propto \exp\left(-\frac{\theta^2-2\mu_0\theta}{2\sigma_0^2} - \frac{\theta^2-2\overline{x}\theta}{2\sigma_x^2/n}\right).$$

Defining $\sigma_n^{-2} := \sigma_0^{-2} + n\sigma_x^{-2}$ and $\mu_n/\sigma_n^2 := \mu_0/\sigma_0^2 + n\overline{x}/\sigma_x^2$ gives $\mathrm{N}(\mu_n, \sigma_n^2)$ as the posterior of ϑ. Notice that the role of the prior diminishes as the sample size n increases, and the data (through the likelihood) play a larger role in determining μ_n and σ_n^2. As $n \to \infty$, the posterior distribution of ϑ (the population mean of x) becomes concentrated around the sample mean, since $(\vartheta \mid \boldsymbol{x}) \overset{a}{\sim} \mathrm{N}(\overline{x}, \sigma_x^2/n)$. Notice also that the role of the prior would diminish if we let its variance increase by taking $\sigma_0^2 \to \infty$, in which case the prior is said to become *diffuse*.

Exercise 13.21 (Parameter values that are "impossible") Let $x \sim \mathrm{N}(\vartheta, 1)$, where it is believed that $\vartheta \sim \mathrm{Expo}(1)$. Suppose that we have a random sample $x_1, \dots, x_n$. Calculate the posterior distribution of ϑ, comparing it with the distribution in Exercise 13.20.

Solution

We have

$$f_{\vartheta|\boldsymbol{x}}(\theta) \propto 1_{\theta>0} \exp(-\theta) \prod_{i=1}^{n} \frac{\exp\left(-(x_i-\theta)^2/2\right)}{\sqrt{2\pi}}$$

$$= 1_{\theta>0} \frac{\exp\left(-\theta - \sum_{i=1}^{n} (\theta - x_i)^2/2\right)}{(2\pi)^{n/2}}$$

$$\propto 1_{\theta>0} \exp\left(-\frac{n}{2}\theta^2 + (n\overline{x} - 1)\theta\right).$$

The posterior is therefore a truncated normal density (see Exercises 2.18 and 6.42). It differs from the posterior in Exercise 13.20 because the new prior imposes that ϑ cannot be negative. Therefore, such values are assigned zero density in the posterior, even if the data give a large negative $\overline{x}$. This feature may remain even as $n \to \infty$, and asymptotic normality need not hold, in contrast with Exercise 13.20(b).

Exercise 13.22 (Noninvariance of priors) There are uninformative priors other than diffuse priors (which were introduced at the end of Exercise 13.20). For example, for a parameter that is defined on the interval $(0, 1)$, we can use the uniform prior $f_\vartheta(\theta) = 1_{\theta\in(0,1)}$, which assigns an equal density to all values in $(0, 1)$. Derive the corresponding prior for $\varrho := \vartheta^2 \in (0, 1)$, showing that it is not a uniform prior.

Solution

This follows from the transformation theorem as

$$f_\varrho(\rho) = \frac{\mathrm{d}\theta}{\mathrm{d}\rho} 1_{\rho\in(0,1)} = \frac{1}{2\sqrt{\rho}} 1_{\rho\in(0,1)}.$$

According to this latter prior, small values of ϱ are presumed to be more probable than large values.

Exercise 13.23 (Data-driven prior of Jeffreys) Let $\boldsymbol{\mathcal{I}}(\boldsymbol{\theta})$ be the information matrix for the parameter vector $\boldsymbol{\theta}$ of a model. Jeffreys proposed that the prior for $\boldsymbol{\vartheta}$ be proportional to $\sqrt{\det \boldsymbol{\mathcal{I}}(\boldsymbol{\theta})}$ in general.

(a) Apply this to Exercise 13.20, obtaining the prior and posterior. You may use the formula for the required $\boldsymbol{\mathcal{I}}$ that was derived for a more general model in Exercise 12.31(a).

(b) Apply this to the scale parameter $\theta := \lambda$ of the generalized gamma in Exercise 12.10, obtaining the prior and posterior.

(c) Let $\boldsymbol{\phi} := \boldsymbol{g}(\boldsymbol{\theta})$ be a one-to-one continuously differentiable function of $\boldsymbol{\theta}$, and assume that the likelihood is a continuous function of $\boldsymbol{\theta}$. Prove that transforming Jeffreys' prior for $\boldsymbol{\vartheta}$ gives rise to a prior for $\boldsymbol{\varphi}$ that satisfies Jeffreys' rule.

Solution

(a) From Exercise 12.31(a) but with the current notation, we have $\mathcal{I} = n/\sigma_x^2$, since $\boldsymbol{X}'\boldsymbol{X} = \boldsymbol{\imath}'\boldsymbol{\imath} = n$ here. The prior is constant with respect to ϑ and, if ϑ is defined on an interval of infinite length, it will be an *improper prior*, that is, $\int_{\theta \in \Theta} f_\vartheta(\theta)\,\mathrm{d}\theta = \infty$ for any $f_\vartheta(\theta) =$ constant. However, the posterior remains proper and it is the solution obtained earlier but with a diffuse prior (let $\sigma_0^2 \to \infty$ in Exercise 13.20(b)).

(b) Exercise 12.10(a) gives $\mathcal{I} = n\nu/\theta^2$, so the prior is proportional to $1/\theta$ (notice how n disappears; see condition (i) in Exercise 13.27 below). The prior is still improper because $\int_0^\infty (1/\theta)\,\mathrm{d}\theta = \infty$. However,

$$f_{\vartheta|\boldsymbol{x}}(\theta) \propto \frac{1}{\theta}\theta^{n\nu} \exp\left(-n\overline{x^p}\theta\right),$$

which is a $\mathrm{Gam}(n\nu, n\overline{x^p})$. This posterior distribution is centered around its mean, which is given by $(n\nu)/(n\overline{x^p}) = \nu/\overline{x^p}$; this is also the MLE derived in Exercise 12.10(a).

(c) By the transformation theorem, the prior of φ that arises from $f_{\boldsymbol{\vartheta}}(\boldsymbol{\theta}) \propto \sqrt{\det \boldsymbol{\mathcal{I}}(\boldsymbol{\theta})}$ is

$$f_{\varphi}(\boldsymbol{\phi}) \propto \left|\det\left(\frac{\partial \boldsymbol{\theta}}{\partial \boldsymbol{\phi}'}\right)\right| \sqrt{\det \boldsymbol{\mathcal{I}}(\boldsymbol{\theta})},$$

where $\boldsymbol{\theta} = \boldsymbol{g}^{-1}(\boldsymbol{\phi})$. We now need to show that the right-hand side is equal to $\sqrt{\det \boldsymbol{\mathcal{I}}(\boldsymbol{\phi})}$. Since the information matrix is the variance of the score vector (see the information-matrix equivalence in Chapter 12), we have

$$\boldsymbol{\mathcal{I}}(\boldsymbol{\phi}) \equiv \mathrm{E}\left(\frac{\partial \ell}{\partial \boldsymbol{\phi}}\frac{\partial \ell}{\partial \boldsymbol{\phi}'}\right) = \mathrm{E}\left(\frac{\partial \boldsymbol{\theta}'}{\partial \boldsymbol{\phi}}\frac{\partial \ell}{\partial \boldsymbol{\theta}}\frac{\partial \ell}{\partial \boldsymbol{\theta}'}\frac{\partial \boldsymbol{\theta}}{\partial \boldsymbol{\phi}'}\right)$$

by the chain rule. Since the Jacobian is nonrandom,

$$\boldsymbol{\mathcal{I}}(\boldsymbol{\phi}) = \frac{\partial \boldsymbol{\theta}'}{\partial \boldsymbol{\phi}} \mathrm{E}\left(\frac{\partial \ell}{\partial \boldsymbol{\theta}}\frac{\partial \ell}{\partial \boldsymbol{\theta}'}\right)\frac{\partial \boldsymbol{\theta}}{\partial \boldsymbol{\phi}'} = \frac{\partial \boldsymbol{\theta}'}{\partial \boldsymbol{\phi}}\boldsymbol{\mathcal{I}}(\boldsymbol{\theta})\frac{\partial \boldsymbol{\theta}}{\partial \boldsymbol{\phi}'}.$$

Taking determinants gives

$$\det \boldsymbol{\mathcal{I}}(\boldsymbol{\phi}) = \left(\det\left(\frac{\partial \boldsymbol{\theta}}{\partial \boldsymbol{\phi}'}\right)\right)^2 \det \boldsymbol{\mathcal{I}}(\boldsymbol{\theta}),$$

so $f_{\varphi}(\boldsymbol{\phi}) \propto \sqrt{\det \boldsymbol{\mathcal{I}}(\boldsymbol{\phi})}$. This invariance result is of independent interest, and the derivations are applicable to non-Bayesian problems as well; for example, see its implication for the factor correcting ℓ_{p} in Exercise 12.41.

Exercise 13.24 (Bayes estimator, with quadratic loss) Show that minimizing the following posterior risk

$$\mathrm{risk}_{\mathrm{p}}(\widehat{\boldsymbol{\theta}}) = \mathrm{E}_{\boldsymbol{\vartheta}|\boldsymbol{X}}((\widehat{\boldsymbol{\theta}} - \boldsymbol{\vartheta})'(\widehat{\boldsymbol{\theta}} - \boldsymbol{\vartheta}))$$

gives rise to $\widehat{\boldsymbol{\theta}}_{\mathrm{b}} = \mathrm{E}_{\boldsymbol{\vartheta}|\boldsymbol{X}}(\boldsymbol{\vartheta})$ as the Bayes estimator.

Solution

Differentiation of the quadratic with respect to $\widehat{\boldsymbol{\theta}}$ shows that the minimum is achieved at

$$\mathrm{E}_{\boldsymbol{\vartheta}|\boldsymbol{X}}(2(\widehat{\boldsymbol{\theta}}_{\mathrm{b}} - \boldsymbol{\vartheta})) = \mathbf{0}.$$

Since $\widehat{\boldsymbol{\theta}}_{\mathrm{b}}$ is a function of $\boldsymbol{X}$ alone, and we have conditioned on $\boldsymbol{X}$, we can use $\mathrm{E}_{\boldsymbol{\vartheta}|\boldsymbol{X}}(\widehat{\boldsymbol{\theta}}_{\mathrm{b}}) = \widehat{\boldsymbol{\theta}}_{\mathrm{b}}$ and obtain the solution $\widehat{\boldsymbol{\theta}}_{\mathrm{b}} = \mathrm{E}_{\boldsymbol{\vartheta}|\boldsymbol{X}}(\boldsymbol{\vartheta})$. Notice that this is the standard solution of a least-squares problem, seen as early as in Exercise 3.18. We are assuming that this expectation exists, which may not be true for some posterior densities. For an illustration of a Bayes estimator, see the mean of the posterior in Exercise 13.23(b), a case where this estimator equals the MLE.

Exercise 13.25 (Posterior and Bayes risks deliver twins!) Show that, under appropriate conditions, Bayes estimators minimize the Bayes risk.

Solution

By the law of iterated expectations,

$$\begin{aligned}\mathrm{risk}_{\mathrm{b}}(\widehat{\boldsymbol{\theta}}) &= \mathrm{E}_{\boldsymbol{\vartheta}}[\mathrm{E}_{\boldsymbol{X}|\boldsymbol{\vartheta}}(C(\boldsymbol{\vartheta}, \widehat{\boldsymbol{\theta}}))] = \mathrm{E}_{\boldsymbol{X},\boldsymbol{\vartheta}}(C(\boldsymbol{\vartheta}, \widehat{\boldsymbol{\theta}})) \\ &= \mathrm{E}_{\boldsymbol{X}}[\mathrm{E}_{\boldsymbol{\vartheta}|\boldsymbol{X}}(C(\boldsymbol{\vartheta}, \widehat{\boldsymbol{\theta}}))] = \mathrm{E}_{\boldsymbol{X}}(\mathrm{risk}_{\mathrm{p}}(\widehat{\boldsymbol{\theta}}))\end{aligned}$$

if the expectations exist. Bayes estimators minimize $\mathrm{risk}_{\mathrm{p}}(\widehat{\boldsymbol{\theta}})$, by definition. Minimizing $\mathrm{risk}_{\mathrm{p}}(\widehat{\boldsymbol{\theta}})$ for each given $\boldsymbol{X}$ leads to a minimum $\mathrm{risk}_{\mathrm{b}}(\widehat{\boldsymbol{\theta}})$ for any $\boldsymbol{X}$. Therefore, Bayes estimators also minimize $\mathrm{risk}_{\mathrm{b}}(\widehat{\boldsymbol{\theta}})$.

***Exercise 13.26 (Frequentist properties of Bayes estimators)** Stating the appropriate conditions, show that Bayes estimators are:

(a) admissible; but

(b) in a frequentist sense, either degenerate ($\mathrm{var}_{\boldsymbol{X}|\boldsymbol{\vartheta}}(\widehat{\boldsymbol{\theta}}_{\mathrm{b}}) = \mathbf{O}$) or biased ($\mathrm{E}_{\boldsymbol{X}|\boldsymbol{\vartheta}}(\widehat{\boldsymbol{\theta}}_{\mathrm{b}}) \neq \boldsymbol{\vartheta}$).

[Hint: Use Exercise 6.28(d) twice, and the equivalence $\boldsymbol{A} + \boldsymbol{B} = \mathbf{O} \iff \boldsymbol{A} = \boldsymbol{B} = \mathbf{O}$ for $\boldsymbol{A}$ and $\boldsymbol{B}$ positive semidefinite (the "only if" part of this equivalence follows by taking $\mathrm{tr}(\boldsymbol{A} + \boldsymbol{B}) = 0$).]

Solution

(a) We start by assuming that the expectations in the solution to Exercise 13.25 exist, so that we can write $\mathrm{risk}_{\mathrm{b}}(\widehat{\boldsymbol{\theta}}) = \mathrm{E}_{\boldsymbol{\vartheta}}(\mathrm{risk}(\widehat{\boldsymbol{\theta}}))$ for any estimator, where $\mathrm{risk}(\widehat{\boldsymbol{\theta}})$ is the frequentist risk from Chapter 11. We need to show that, if $\widehat{\boldsymbol{\theta}}_{\mathrm{b}}$ is a Bayes estimator and $\widetilde{\boldsymbol{\theta}}$ is not, then we cannot have

$$\begin{aligned}&\mathrm{risk}(\widetilde{\boldsymbol{\theta}}) \leqslant \mathrm{risk}(\widehat{\boldsymbol{\theta}}_{\mathrm{b}}) \quad \text{for all } \boldsymbol{\theta} \in \Theta\text{; and} \\ &\mathrm{risk}(\widetilde{\boldsymbol{\theta}}) < \mathrm{risk}(\widehat{\boldsymbol{\theta}}_{\mathrm{b}}) \quad \text{for some } \boldsymbol{\theta} \in \Theta.\end{aligned}$$

We use proof by contradiction. Suppose that the inequalities are satisfied. Then

$$\operatorname{risk}_{\mathrm{b}}(\widetilde{\boldsymbol{\theta}}) = \int_{\boldsymbol{\theta}\in\Theta} \operatorname{risk}(\widetilde{\boldsymbol{\theta}}) f_{\boldsymbol{\vartheta}}(\boldsymbol{\theta})\,\mathrm{d}\boldsymbol{\theta} \leqslant \int_{\boldsymbol{\theta}\in\Theta} \operatorname{risk}(\widehat{\boldsymbol{\theta}}_{\mathrm{b}}) f_{\boldsymbol{\vartheta}}(\boldsymbol{\theta})\,\mathrm{d}\boldsymbol{\theta} = \operatorname{risk}_{\mathrm{b}}(\widehat{\boldsymbol{\theta}}_{\mathrm{b}}),$$

where it is assumed that the prior $f_{\boldsymbol{\vartheta}}$ is proper (otherwise the displayed integral inequality need not hold). However, Exercise 13.25 showed that Bayes estimators minimize Bayes risk, that is, $\operatorname{risk}_{\mathrm{b}}(\widetilde{\boldsymbol{\theta}}) \geqslant \operatorname{risk}_{\mathrm{b}}(\widehat{\boldsymbol{\theta}}_{\mathrm{b}})$. Therefore, $\operatorname{risk}_{\mathrm{b}}(\widetilde{\boldsymbol{\theta}}) = \operatorname{risk}_{\mathrm{b}}(\widehat{\boldsymbol{\theta}}_{\mathrm{b}})$, which contradicts the premise that "$\widehat{\boldsymbol{\theta}}_{\mathrm{b}}$ is a Bayes estimator and $\widetilde{\boldsymbol{\theta}}$ is not".
(b) There are two possibilities. First, if $\mathrm{E}_{\boldsymbol{X}|\boldsymbol{\vartheta}}(\widehat{\boldsymbol{\theta}}_{\mathrm{b}}) \neq \boldsymbol{\vartheta}$, then the Bayes estimator $\widehat{\boldsymbol{\theta}}_{\mathrm{b}}$ is biased in a frequentist sense (as $\boldsymbol{X}$ varies, given $\boldsymbol{\vartheta}$). Second, if $\mathrm{E}_{\boldsymbol{X}|\boldsymbol{\vartheta}}(\widehat{\boldsymbol{\theta}}_{\mathrm{b}}) = \boldsymbol{\vartheta}$, then we can substitute this into the law of iterated expectations to get

$$\operatorname{var}(\widehat{\boldsymbol{\theta}}_{\mathrm{b}}) = \operatorname{var}_{\boldsymbol{\vartheta}}(\mathrm{E}_{\boldsymbol{X}|\boldsymbol{\vartheta}}(\widehat{\boldsymbol{\theta}}_{\mathrm{b}})) + \mathrm{E}_{\boldsymbol{\vartheta}}(\operatorname{var}_{\boldsymbol{X}|\boldsymbol{\vartheta}}(\widehat{\boldsymbol{\theta}}_{\mathrm{b}})) = \operatorname{var}(\boldsymbol{\vartheta}) + \mathrm{E}_{\boldsymbol{\vartheta}}(\operatorname{var}_{\boldsymbol{X}|\boldsymbol{\vartheta}}(\widehat{\boldsymbol{\theta}}_{\mathrm{b}})),$$

where it is again assumed that the expectations exist. Applying the same law to $\operatorname{var}(\boldsymbol{\vartheta})$,

$$\operatorname{var}(\boldsymbol{\vartheta}) = \operatorname{var}_{\boldsymbol{X}}(\mathrm{E}_{\boldsymbol{\vartheta}|\boldsymbol{X}}(\boldsymbol{\vartheta})) + \mathrm{E}_{\boldsymbol{X}}(\operatorname{var}_{\boldsymbol{\vartheta}|\boldsymbol{X}}(\boldsymbol{\vartheta})).$$

Now $\mathrm{E}_{\boldsymbol{\vartheta}|\boldsymbol{X}}(\boldsymbol{\vartheta})$ is the posterior mean of $\boldsymbol{\vartheta}$, and this is the Bayes estimator $\widehat{\boldsymbol{\theta}}_{\mathrm{b}}$ which depends on $\boldsymbol{X}$ only. Therefore,

$$\operatorname{var}(\boldsymbol{\vartheta}) = \operatorname{var}(\widehat{\boldsymbol{\theta}}_{\mathrm{b}}) + \mathrm{E}_{\boldsymbol{X}}(\operatorname{var}_{\boldsymbol{\vartheta}|\boldsymbol{X}}(\boldsymbol{\vartheta})).$$

Substituting this into the equation for $\operatorname{var}(\widehat{\boldsymbol{\theta}}_{\mathrm{b}})$ gives

$$\operatorname{var}(\widehat{\boldsymbol{\theta}}_{\mathrm{b}}) = \left(\operatorname{var}(\widehat{\boldsymbol{\theta}}_{\mathrm{b}}) + \mathrm{E}_{\boldsymbol{X}}(\operatorname{var}_{\boldsymbol{\vartheta}|\boldsymbol{X}}(\boldsymbol{\vartheta}))\right) + \mathrm{E}_{\boldsymbol{\vartheta}}(\operatorname{var}_{\boldsymbol{X}|\boldsymbol{\vartheta}}(\widehat{\boldsymbol{\theta}}_{\mathrm{b}})),$$

hence $\mathrm{E}_{\boldsymbol{X}}(\operatorname{var}_{\boldsymbol{\vartheta}|\boldsymbol{X}}(\boldsymbol{\vartheta})) + \mathrm{E}_{\boldsymbol{\vartheta}}(\operatorname{var}_{\boldsymbol{X}|\boldsymbol{\vartheta}}(\widehat{\boldsymbol{\theta}}_{\mathrm{b}})) = \mathbf{O}$. Any conditional variance matrix is positive semidefinite, and so is its expectation (a weighted average with nonnegative weights). Therefore, the equivalence in the hint to the question gives $\mathrm{E}_{\boldsymbol{\vartheta}}(\operatorname{var}_{\boldsymbol{X}|\boldsymbol{\vartheta}}(\widehat{\boldsymbol{\theta}}_{\mathrm{b}})) = \mathbf{O}$. Applying the same hint again to the latter expectation (a nonnegative-weighted average of values of $\operatorname{var}_{\boldsymbol{X}|\boldsymbol{\vartheta}}(\widehat{\boldsymbol{\theta}}_{\mathrm{b}})$), we get $\operatorname{var}_{\boldsymbol{X}|\boldsymbol{\vartheta}}(\widehat{\boldsymbol{\theta}}_{\mathrm{b}}) = \mathbf{O}$ a.s. with respect to $\boldsymbol{\vartheta}$.

Exercise 13.27 (Asymptotics for Bayes estimators) Assume that the conditions of Exercise 12.28 are satisfied. Assume further that the prior: (i) is not a function of n; (ii) is nonzero in an open neighborhood of the MLE $\widehat{\boldsymbol{\theta}}$; (iii) is a continuous function of $\boldsymbol{\theta}$ in that neighborhood. (The prior need not be proper.) Show that $\boldsymbol{\vartheta} \mid \boldsymbol{X}$ is asymptotically normal with mean $\widehat{\boldsymbol{\theta}}$ and variance $-\boldsymbol{\mathcal{H}}(\widehat{\boldsymbol{\theta}})^{-1}$.

Solution
Define $\ell(\boldsymbol{\theta}) := \log(L(\boldsymbol{\theta}))$ and let $n \to \infty$. Exercise 12.28(a) implies that

$$\ell(\boldsymbol{\theta}) - \left(\ell(\widehat{\boldsymbol{\theta}}) + \frac{1}{2}\left(\boldsymbol{\theta} - \widehat{\boldsymbol{\theta}}\right)' \boldsymbol{\mathcal{H}}(\widehat{\boldsymbol{\theta}}) \left(\boldsymbol{\theta} - \widehat{\boldsymbol{\theta}}\right)\right) \xrightarrow{p} 0$$

since $\overline{\boldsymbol{\theta}} - \widehat{\boldsymbol{\theta}} \xrightarrow{p} \mathbf{0}$ and $\boldsymbol{\mathcal{H}}(\boldsymbol{\theta})$ is a continuous function of $\boldsymbol{\theta}$ in this neighborhood. Two implications arise. First, the likelihood $L(\boldsymbol{\theta})$ becomes zero for values outside a shrinking neighborhood of $\widehat{\boldsymbol{\theta}}$, so

$$f_{\boldsymbol{\vartheta}|\boldsymbol{X}}(\boldsymbol{\theta}) \propto f_{\boldsymbol{\vartheta}}(\boldsymbol{\theta})L(\boldsymbol{\theta})$$

implies that the posterior also becomes zero outside this neighborhood. Second, within this shrinking neighborhood, we get the asymptotic proportionality

$$\begin{aligned} f_{\boldsymbol{\vartheta}|\boldsymbol{X}}(\boldsymbol{\theta}) &\propto f_{\boldsymbol{\vartheta}}(\widehat{\boldsymbol{\theta}}) \exp\left(\ell(\widehat{\boldsymbol{\theta}}) + \frac{1}{2}\left(\boldsymbol{\theta}-\widehat{\boldsymbol{\theta}}\right)' \mathcal{H}(\widehat{\boldsymbol{\theta}}) \left(\boldsymbol{\theta}-\widehat{\boldsymbol{\theta}}\right)\right) \\ &\propto \exp\left(\frac{1}{2}\left(\boldsymbol{\theta}-\widehat{\boldsymbol{\theta}}\right)' \mathcal{H}(\widehat{\boldsymbol{\theta}}) \left(\boldsymbol{\theta}-\widehat{\boldsymbol{\theta}}\right)\right), \end{aligned}$$

hence the stated results. Note that, because we condition on the data $\boldsymbol{X}$, asymptotic normality is easily achieved even if $\boldsymbol{X}$ does not arise from a random sample; compare Exercise 12.29.

13.5 Parametric confidence regions

Exercise 13.28 (Gamma: CI) Let $x_1, \dots, x_n$ be a random sample of $x \in \mathbb{R}_+$ from

$$f_x(u) = \frac{\lambda^4 u^3}{6} \exp(-\lambda u),$$

where $\lambda > 0$. Construct a level $1-\alpha$ central CI for λ, and another that is one-sided and of the form $\lambda \leqslant y$.

Solution

This is a Gam(4, λ) density, a special case of the exponential family for which we know that $z := n\overline{x} = \sum_{i=1}^{n} x_i$ is a sufficient statistic. We also know from Exercises 7.18(a) and 7.19(a) that $2\lambda z \sim \chi^2(8n)$, which is therefore pivotal. Hence,

$$1-\alpha = \Pr\left(\chi^2_{\alpha/2}(8n) \leqslant 2\lambda z \leqslant \chi^2_{1-\alpha/2}(8n)\right) = \Pr\left(\frac{\chi^2_{\alpha/2}(8n)}{2n\overline{x}} \leqslant \lambda \leqslant \frac{\chi^2_{1-\alpha/2}(8n)}{2n\overline{x}}\right)$$

since $z > 0$ with probability 1.

The required one-sided interval is

$$1-\alpha = \Pr\left(\lambda \leqslant \frac{\chi^2_{1-\alpha}(8n)}{2n\overline{x}}\right),$$

where one should remember that $0 < \lambda$ by definition. Notice that $\chi^2_{1-\alpha} < \chi^2_{1-\alpha/2}$ for any finite degree of freedom and any $\alpha \neq 0$.

Exercise 13.29 (Laplace: CI) Let $x_1, \dots, x_n$ be a random sample of $x \in \mathbb{R}_+$ from

$$f_x(u) = \frac{\lambda}{2} \exp(-\lambda|u|),$$

where $\lambda > 0$. Construct a level $1-\alpha$ central CI for $1/\lambda$.

Solution

As $z := \sum_{i=1}^{n} |x_i|$ is sufficient, we shall try to construct a pivotal quantity with it. Now, $f_{|x|}(v) = \lambda \exp(-\lambda v)$; hence $2\lambda z \sim \chi^2(2n)$ and

$$1-\alpha = \Pr\left(\frac{\chi^2_{\alpha/2}(2n)}{2z} \leqslant \lambda \leqslant \frac{\chi^2_{1-\alpha/2}(2n)}{2z}\right) = \Pr\left(\frac{2z}{\chi^2_{1-\alpha/2}(2n)} \leqslant \frac{1}{\lambda} \leqslant \frac{2z}{\chi^2_{\alpha/2}(2n)}\right),$$

since $z > 0$ with probability 1 and the quantiles of $\chi^2(2n)$ are positive.

Exercise 13.30 (Two samples: mean difference) Let $x_1, \dots, x_m$ be a random sample from $\mathrm{N}(\mu_1, \sigma^2)$, that is independent of the random sample $y_1, \dots, y_n$ from $\mathrm{N}(\mu_2, \lambda\sigma^2)$, where $\lambda > 0$ is known but $\sigma > 0$ is not. Obtain a pivot for $\mu_1 - \mu_2$ that does not depend on the nuisance parameter σ.

Solution

By the independence of the two normal samples, $\overline{x} - \overline{y} \sim \mathrm{N}(\mu_1 - \mu_2, \sigma^2(1/m + \lambda/n))$. Hence,

$$\sqrt{\frac{mn}{n+\lambda m}}\,\frac{\overline{x} - \overline{y} - (\mu_1 - \mu_2)}{\sigma} \sim \mathrm{N}(0,1)$$

and, again by the independence of the samples of x and y,

$$\frac{(m-1)s_x^2}{\sigma^2} + \frac{(n-1)s_y^2}{\lambda\sigma^2} \sim \chi^2(m+n-2),$$

where s_x^2 and s_y^2 are the sample variances of x and y, respectively. This implies (for example by Exercise 9.13) that

$$\sqrt{\frac{mn}{n+\lambda m}}\sqrt{\lambda(m+n-2)}\,\frac{\overline{x} - \overline{y} - (\mu_1 - \mu_2)}{\sqrt{\lambda(m-1)s_x^2 + (n-1)s_y^2}} \sim \mathrm{t}(m+n-2),$$

which is pivotal for $\mu_1 - \mu_2$. Notice that the pooled estimator (see Exercise 11.2(d)) of the variance σ^2 is

$$s^2 := \frac{(m-1)s_x^2 + (n-1)s_y^2/\lambda}{m+n-2},$$

where λ is known.

Exercise 13.31 (Two samples: variance ratio) Let $x_1, \dots, x_m$ and $y_1, \dots, y_n$ be two independent random samples from $\mathrm{N}(\mu_1, \sigma_1^2)$ and $\mathrm{N}(\mu_2, \sigma_2^2)$, respectively. Obtain a central CI for σ_1^2/σ_2^2.

Solution

We start by looking for a suitable pivotal quantity. We know that $(m-1)s_x^2/\sigma_1^2 \sim \chi^2(m-1)$

and $(n-1)s_y^2/\sigma_2^2 \sim \chi^2(n-1)$. These two quantities are independent, so we have $(\sigma_1^2/\sigma_2^2)(s_y^2/s_x^2) \sim \mathrm{F}(n-1, m-1)$. Therefore,

$$\Pr\left(\frac{s_x^2}{s_y^2}\mathrm{F}_{\alpha/2}(n-1,m-1) \leqslant \frac{\sigma_1^2}{\sigma_2^2} \leqslant \frac{s_x^2}{s_y^2}\mathrm{F}_{1-\alpha/2}(n-1,m-1)\right) = 1-\alpha$$

as required.

Exercise 13.32 (Curved normal: CI) Let $x_1, \dots, x_n$ be a random sample from $\mathrm{N}(\mu, \mu^2)$ with $\mu > 0$. Use two different pivots to construct level $1-\alpha$ confidence regions for μ, basing these on central intervals from each pivot's distribution. You may assume that α and n are such that $\sqrt{n} > -\mathrm{N}_{\alpha/2}$.

Solution

Since $\mu > 0$ and here its square is the variance, we start with $(n-1)s^2/\mu^2 \sim \chi^2(n-1)$. Hence,

$$1-\alpha = \Pr\left(\frac{(n-1)s^2}{\chi^2_{1-\alpha/2}(n-1)} \leqslant \mu^2 \leqslant \frac{(n-1)s^2}{\chi^2_{\alpha/2}(n-1)}\right)$$

$$= \Pr\left(s\sqrt{\frac{n-1}{\chi^2_{1-\alpha/2}(n-1)}} \leqslant \mu \leqslant s\sqrt{\frac{n-1}{\chi^2_{\alpha/2}(n-1)}}\right),$$

since $\mu > 0$. Alternatively, we could use $\sqrt{n}(\overline{x}-\mu)/\mu \sim \mathrm{N}(0,1)$ to get

$$1-\alpha = \Pr\left(\mathrm{N}_{\alpha/2} \leqslant \sqrt{n}\left(\frac{\overline{x}}{\mu}-1\right) \leqslant \mathrm{N}_{1-\alpha/2}\right) = \Pr\left(1+\frac{\mathrm{N}_{\alpha/2}}{\sqrt{n}} \leqslant \frac{\overline{x}}{\mu} \leqslant 1+\frac{\mathrm{N}_{1-\alpha/2}}{\sqrt{n}}\right)$$

$$= \Pr\left(\left(1+\frac{\mathrm{N}_{\alpha/2}}{\sqrt{n}}\right)\mu \leqslant \overline{x} \leqslant \left(1+\frac{\mathrm{N}_{1-\alpha/2}}{\sqrt{n}}\right)\mu\right),$$

since $\mu > 0$. This CI represents a region that requires cautious interpretation because $\overline{x} \in \mathbb{R}$. If one wishes to invert it to get a CI for μ, then there are two inequalities to consider. The latter is $\overline{x}/\left(1+\mathrm{N}_{1-\alpha/2}/\sqrt{n}\right) \leqslant \mu$ and the former is $\mu \leqslant \overline{x}/\left(1+\mathrm{N}_{\alpha/2}/\sqrt{n}\right)$ because $\sqrt{n}+\mathrm{N}_{\alpha/2} > 0$. Note that $\overline{x}$ can be nonpositive, although $\mu > 0$, in which case the region would be empty. Therefore, the random CI that is implied for μ is nonempty only in cases where $\overline{x} > 0$. Such considerations do not arise for the CI based on s^2 (the first CI above).

***Exercise 13.33 (Shortest CI and highest coverage for unimodal symmetric densities)** Let $x_1, \dots, x_n$ be a random sample from $\mathrm{N}(\mu, \sigma^2)$ with σ^2 known.
(a) Use x to construct the shortest CI for μ, for any given coverage $\gamma \in (0,1)$. (For the definition of coverage, see after (13.7).)
(b) Maximize γ, for any given length of the CI, and compare your result with that in (a).

Solution

(a) We have $\sqrt{n}(\overline{x}-\mu)/\sigma \sim \mathrm{N}(0,1)$. Hence

$$\Pr\left(a \leqslant \sqrt{n}\,\frac{\overline{x}-\mu}{\sigma} \leqslant b\right) = \Pr\left(\overline{x} - \frac{\sigma b}{\sqrt{n}} \leqslant \mu \leqslant \overline{x} - \frac{\sigma a}{\sqrt{n}}\right) = \gamma$$

for every $a < b$ satisfying $\Phi(b) - \Phi(a) = \gamma$. We stress the following: for any given γ, this last equation determines b, once a is chosen (or vice versa) by $b = \Phi^{-1}(\Phi(a)+\gamma)$. Therefore, the length of the CI, $(b-a)\sigma/\sqrt{n}$, is a function of a only. Differentiating it with respect to a,

$$\frac{\mathrm{d}}{\mathrm{d}a}\frac{\sigma}{\sqrt{n}}(b-a) = \frac{\sigma}{\sqrt{n}}\left(\frac{\mathrm{d}b}{\mathrm{d}a} - 1\right),$$

so the first-order condition is $\mathrm{d}b/\mathrm{d}a = 1$. Now, we know that $\Phi(b) = \Phi(a) + \gamma$, so $\mathrm{d}\Phi(b)/\mathrm{d}a = \mathrm{d}\Phi(a)/\mathrm{d}a$, or equivalently,

$$\phi(b)\frac{\mathrm{d}b}{\mathrm{d}a} = \phi(a)$$

by the chain rule. Substituting into the first-order condition gives $\phi(\widehat{a})/\phi(\widehat{b}) = 1$, which holds if $\widehat{a} = -\widehat{b}$ (the solution $\widehat{a} = \widehat{b}$ gives zero coverage hence violating $\Phi(\widehat{b}) - \Phi(\widehat{a}) = \gamma$ when $\gamma \neq 0$). Together with $\widehat{a} < \widehat{b}$, this implies that $\widehat{a} < 0 < \widehat{b}$. Using that $\mathrm{d}\phi(u)/\mathrm{d}u = -u\phi(u)$ for all $u \in \mathbb{R}$ (which says that the density has a single mode located at the origin), we have

$$\begin{aligned}\frac{\mathrm{d}^2}{\mathrm{d}a^2}\frac{\sigma}{\sqrt{n}}(b-a) &= \frac{\mathrm{d}}{\mathrm{d}a}\frac{\sigma}{\sqrt{n}}\left(\frac{\phi(a)}{\phi(b)} - 1\right) = \frac{\sigma}{\sqrt{n}}\left(-a\frac{\phi(a)}{\phi(b)} - \frac{\phi(a)}{(\phi(b))^2}\frac{\mathrm{d}\phi(b)}{\mathrm{d}b}\frac{\mathrm{d}b}{\mathrm{d}a}\right)\\ &= \frac{\sigma}{\sqrt{n}}\left(-a\frac{\phi(a)}{\phi(b)} + \frac{\phi(a)}{(\phi(b))^2}b\phi(b)\frac{\phi(a)}{\phi(b)}\right)\\ &= \frac{\sigma}{\sqrt{n}}\left(-a\frac{\phi(a)}{\phi(b)} + b\left(\frac{\phi(a)}{\phi(b)}\right)^2\right).\end{aligned}$$

By $\widehat{a} < 0 < \widehat{b}$, the second derivative is positive at the optimum, and we have a minimum. Hence, the shortest interval for μ is the one where the lower and upper limits are equidistant from $\overline{x}$, as in the example given in the introduction to this chapter. Notice two features. First, it is a result of the derivations that the interval should be two-sided and central, rather than by assumption. Second, identical derivations apply to the density of *any* statistic that is unimodal and symmetric around the origin, as is the case with $\sqrt{n}(\overline{x}-\mu)/s \sim \mathrm{t}(n-1)$ when σ is unknown.

(b) Maximizing the coverage $\Phi(b) - \Phi(a)$, we need to solve

$$\phi(b)\frac{\mathrm{d}b}{\mathrm{d}a} - \phi(a) = 0,$$

which gives $\mathrm{d}b/\mathrm{d}a|_{a=\widehat{a}} = \phi(\widehat{a})/\phi(\widehat{b})$. We have the restriction of a preassigned length l given by $(b-a)\sigma/\sqrt{n} = l$, so $\mathrm{d}b/\mathrm{d}a = 1$, and substituting into the first-order condition gives $1 = \phi(\widehat{a})/\phi(\widehat{b})$ whose solution is $\widehat{a} = -\widehat{b}$ as before. The second derivative of the coverage is $-b\phi(b) + a\phi(a)$ since $\mathrm{d}b/\mathrm{d}a = 1$. Substituting $\widehat{a} = -\widehat{b} < 0$ confirms a maximum.

Exercise 13.34 (Shortest CI, monotone beta) Let $x_1, \dots, x_n$ be a random sample from the p.d.f. $f_x(u) = 2u/\beta^2$ for $u \in (0, \beta)$.
(a) Using the sufficient statistic, construct a CI for β and then minimize its length for a given coverage $\gamma \in (0, 1)$.
(b) What is the expected length of the interval in (a)?

Solution
(a) The sufficient statistic is the last order statistic, $y_n = \max_i \{x_i\}$. Exercise 7.35(a) implies that

$$f_{y_n}(v) = \frac{2nv}{\beta^2}\left(\frac{v^2}{\beta^2}\right)^{n-1} = \frac{2n\,(v/\beta)^{2n-1}}{\beta}.$$

Letting $z := y_n/\beta$, we have $f_z(w) = 2nw^{2n-1}$ for $w \in (0, 1)$, hence z is a pivotal quantity. Therefore

$$\gamma = \Pr\left(w_1 \leqslant \frac{y_n}{\beta} \leqslant w_2\right) = \Pr\left(\frac{y_n}{w_2} \leqslant \beta \leqslant \frac{y_n}{w_1}\right),$$

where $\int_{w_1}^{w_2} f_z(w)\,\mathrm{d}w = \gamma$, that is, $w_2^{2n} - w_1^{2n} = \gamma$.

We need to minimize $1/w_1 - 1/w_2$ subject to $w_2 = (\gamma + w_1^{2n})^{1/(2n)}$. Now,

$$\begin{aligned}\frac{\mathrm{d}}{\mathrm{d}w_1}\left(\frac{1}{w_1} - \frac{1}{(\gamma + w_1^{2n})^{1/(2n)}}\right) &= -\frac{1}{w_1^2} + \frac{w_1^{2n-1}}{(\gamma + w_1^{2n})^{(2n+1)/(2n)}}\\ &= \frac{-(\gamma + w_1^{2n})^{(2n+1)/(2n)} + w_1^{2n+1}}{w_1^2(\gamma + w_1^{2n})^{(2n+1)/(2n)}}\\ &= \frac{w_1^{2n+1}\left(1 - (\gamma w_1^{-2n} + 1)^{(2n+1)/(2n)}\right)}{w_1^2(\gamma + w_1^{2n})^{(2n+1)/(2n)}} < 0,\end{aligned}$$

since $(\gamma w_1^{-2n} + 1) > 1$. The length diminishes as w_1 increases, so we choose w_1 as large as possible while preserving the required coverage $w_2^{2n} - w_1^{2n} = \gamma$. Hence, $w_2 = 1$ (the upper limit of z) and $w_1 = \alpha^{1/(2n)}$, where $\alpha := 1 - \gamma$. It turns out in this case that the shortest CI is one sided, since the density of the pivot z increases with z, and it is best to exclude the lower tail in order to maximize the coverage of the CI.
(b) The expected length is

$$\begin{aligned}\mathrm{E}\left(\frac{y_n}{w_1} - \frac{y_n}{w_2}\right) &= \left(\frac{1}{w_1} - \frac{1}{w_2}\right)\mathrm{E}(y_n) = \left(\frac{1}{\alpha^{1/(2n)}} - 1\right)\int_0^\beta 2n\,(v/\beta)^{2n}\,\mathrm{d}v\\ &= \left(\frac{1}{\alpha^{1/(2n)}} - 1\right)\frac{2n\beta}{2n+1}.\end{aligned}$$

Since $\alpha \neq 0, 1$, the expected length increases with β (the upper limit of the variate) and with the coverage $\gamma \equiv 1-\alpha$. As $n \to \infty$, we have $\alpha^{1/(2n)} \to 1$ since $\alpha \in (0,1)$, and the expected length goes to zero.

Exercise 13.35 (Prespecified precision for the mean) Let $\{x_i\}_{i=1}^n \sim \text{IN}(\mu,1)$. Find n such that the 95% central CI for μ is of length at most 0.4.

Solution
The sample mean $\overline{x} \sim \text{N}(\mu, 1/n)$ gives

$$\Pr\left(\overline{x} - \frac{1.96}{\sqrt{n}} \leqslant \mu \leqslant \overline{x} + \frac{1.96}{\sqrt{n}}\right) \approx 95\%,$$

and the length is $3.92/\sqrt{n}$. Equating this to 0.4 and solving gives $n \approx 96.04$. Since n must be an integer, and we want the interval to be no longer than 0.4, the solution is $n = 97$.

Exercise 13.36 (CI for a quantile, and tolerance for distributions) Let $x_1, \dots, x_n$ be a random sample from a continuous variate x with density function f, and let $y_1, \dots, y_n$ be the order statistics.
(a) Suppose that q is the β quantile, satisfying $\Pr(x \leqslant q) = \beta$. Calculate the coverage of $y_i \leqslant q \leqslant y_j$ as a confidence interval for q for some $y_i, y_j \in \{y_1, \dots, y_n\}$.
(b) Suppose that q is the median and that $j = i+1$, so the CI is $y_i \leqslant q \leqslant y_{i+1}$. What is the value of i that maximizes the coverage?
(c) Let h_1 and h_2 be two functions of the data such that

$$\Pr\left(\int_{h_1}^{h_2} f(u)\,\mathrm{d}u \geqslant \gamma_1\right) = \gamma_2$$

for prespecified γ_1 and γ_2; that is, a fraction of at least γ_1 of the population falls in the stochastic interval $[h_1, h_2]$, with probability γ_2. Since we do not make any assumption about f beyond the continuity of x, the functions h_1 and h_2 are called *distribution-free tolerance limits*. Now consider $h_1 := y_i$ and $h_2 := y_j$ $(i < j)$, and let $z := \int_{h_1}^{h_2} f(u)\,\mathrm{d}u$. Show that $z \sim \text{Beta}(j-i, n-j+i+1)$ and obtain the implied formula for γ_2.

Solution
(a) This part is Exercise 9.28 in a different guise, and the answer is

$$\Pr(y_i \leqslant q \leqslant y_j) = \sum_{k=i}^{j-1} \binom{n}{k} \beta^k (1-\beta)^{n-k},$$

where $i < j$.
(b) Since q is the median and x is continuous, we have $\beta = \frac{1}{2}$. Together with $j = i+1$, this yields

$$\Pr(y_i \leqslant q \leqslant y_{i+1}) = \binom{n}{i}\left(\frac{1}{2}\right)^i \left(1-\frac{1}{2}\right)^{n-i} = 2^{-n}\binom{n}{i}.$$

For any given n, this is maximized by choosing $i = \lfloor n/2 \rfloor$, from Pascal's triangle and more specifically from $\binom{n}{i} = \binom{n}{n-i}$ and Exercise 1.33(a). As a result, the highest coverage of the CI for the population median q is achieved by basing the interval on the sample median, if one decides to use two contiguous (immediately neighboring) order statistics.
(c) We write $z = F(y_j) - F(y_i)$, where F is the c.d.f. of x. Exercise 7.35(c) gave the joint density of y_i, y_j, for $i < j$ and $v_i < v_j$, as

$$f_{y_i,y_j}(v_i, v_j) = \frac{n! f(v_i) f(v_j) (F(v_i))^{i-1} (F(v_j) - F(v_i))^{j-i-1} (1 - F(v_j))^{n-j}}{(i-1)!\,(j-i-1)!\,(n-j)!}.$$

The transformation to $y := F(y_i)$ and $z = F(y_j) - F(y_i)$ has Jacobian

$$\begin{vmatrix} \mathrm{d}F(y_i)/\,\mathrm{d}y_i & 0 \\ -\,\mathrm{d}F(y_i)/\,\mathrm{d}y_i & \mathrm{d}F(y_j)/\,\mathrm{d}y_j \end{vmatrix}^{-1} = \begin{vmatrix} f(y_i) & 0 \\ -f(y_i) & f(y_j) \end{vmatrix}^{-1} = \frac{1}{f(y_i) f(y_j)}.$$

Hence

$$f_{y,z}(v, w) = \frac{n! v^{i-1} w^{j-i-1} (1 - w - v)^{n-j}}{(i-1)!\,(j-i-1)!\,(n-j)!} \qquad (0 < v < 1 - w,\ 0 < w < 1),$$

implying that

$$\begin{aligned} f_z(w) &= \frac{n! w^{j-i-1}}{(i-1)!\,(j-i-1)!\,(n-j)!} \int_0^{1-w} v^{i-1} (1 - w - v)^{n-j}\,\mathrm{d}v \\ &= \frac{n! w^{j-i-1}}{(i-1)!\,(j-i-1)!\,(n-j)!} (1-w)^{n-j+i}\, B(i, n-j+1) \end{aligned}$$

as the density of $\text{Beta}_{(0,1-w)}(i, n-j+1)$ integrates to 1. Then

$$\frac{B(i, n-j+1)}{(i-1)!\,(n-j)!} = \frac{1}{(n-j+i)!}$$

gives the required result. Exercise 7.38 gave us $F(y_i) \sim \text{Beta}(i, n-i+1)$ and $F(y_j) \sim \text{Beta}(j, n-j+1)$, but the two variates are dependent. The present exercise has demonstrated that their difference is also a beta, namely $z \sim \text{Beta}(j-i, n-j+i+1)$.

The implied formula for γ_2 is

$$\gamma_2 = \Pr(z \geqslant \gamma_1) = \int_{\gamma_1}^{1} \frac{n! w^{j-i-1} (1-w)^{n-j+i}}{(j-i-1)!\,(n-j+i)!}\,\mathrm{d}w;$$

see Exercise 4.11 for the various series formulations of this incomplete-beta integral. Note that γ_1 and γ_2 are predetermined, and that it is customary to specify $j = n - i + 1$ for symmetry reasons, which leaves i or n to be determined by the user.

***Exercise 13.37 (Coverage of asymptotic CIs)** Let $x_1, \dots, x_n$ be a random sample from a distribution whose first four moments exist and whose mean and variance are denoted by μ and σ^2, respectively. Let $\overline{x}_n := \sum_{i=1}^n x_i/n$ and $s_n^2 := \sum_{i=1}^n (x_i - \overline{x}_n)^2/(n-1)$.
(a) Prove that $\Pr\left(-\mathrm{N}_{1-\alpha/2} \leqslant \sqrt{n}(\overline{x}_n - \mu)/\sigma \leqslant \mathrm{N}_{1-\alpha/2}\right) = 1 - \alpha + O(1/n)$. [Hint: Use derivations along the lines of Exercise 10.27, then use the inversion theorem of Chapter 3.]

(b) Prove that $\Pr\left(-N_{1-\alpha/2} \leqslant \sqrt{n}(\overline{x}_n - \mu)/s_n \leqslant N_{1-\alpha/2}\right) = 1-\alpha+O\left(1/n\right)$. [Hint: Use Exercise 10.33 to approximate s_n by σ, then expand the probability integral in (a) by the method of Exercise 4.21.]

Solution

(a) Let $z_n := \sqrt{n}\left(\overline{x}_n - \mu\right)/\sigma$ and denote the third central moment of x_1 by $\sigma^{(3)}$. By following the steps of the Lindeberg–Lévy CLT of Exercise 10.27, we have

$$\varphi_{z_n}(\tau) = \left(\mathrm{E}\left(\exp\left(\frac{\mathrm{i}\tau\left(x_1-\mu\right)}{\sigma\sqrt{n}}\right)\right)\right)^n = \left(1 - \frac{\tau^2}{2n} - \frac{\mathrm{i}\tau^3\sigma^{(3)}}{6\sigma^3 n^{3/2}} + O\left(\frac{1}{n^2}\right)\right)^n,$$

where we have used the existence of moments up to the fourth to do this expansion; see Exercise 3.29 and use the existence of the fourth moment to ascertain that the remainder is $O(1/n^2)$. As $a^n = \exp\left(n\log\left(a\right)\right)$ and $\log\left(1+b\right) = b + O\left(b^2\right)$, we have

$$\begin{aligned}
\varphi_{z_n}(\tau) &= \exp\left(n\log\left(1 - \frac{\tau^2}{2n} - \frac{\mathrm{i}\tau^3\sigma^{(3)}}{6\sigma^3 n^{3/2}} + O\left(\frac{1}{n^2}\right)\right)\right)\\
&= \exp\left(-\frac{\tau^2}{2} - \frac{\mathrm{i}\tau^3\sigma^{(3)}}{6\sigma^3 n^{1/2}} + O\left(\frac{1}{n}\right)\right) = \exp\left(-\frac{\tau^2}{2}\right)\exp\left(-\frac{\mathrm{i}\tau^3\sigma^{(3)}}{6\sigma^3 n^{1/2}} + O\left(\frac{1}{n}\right)\right)\\
&= \mathrm{e}^{-\tau^2/2} - \frac{\mathrm{i}\tau^3\sigma^{(3)}}{6\sigma^3 n^{1/2}}\mathrm{e}^{-\tau^2/2} + O\left(\frac{1}{n}\right)
\end{aligned}$$

using the exponential expansion. The inversion theorem states that

$$F_{z_n}(w) = \frac{1}{2} + \frac{1}{2\pi}\int_0^\infty \frac{\mathrm{e}^{\mathrm{i}w\tau}\varphi_{z_n}(-\tau) - \mathrm{e}^{-\mathrm{i}w\tau}\varphi_{z_n}(\tau)}{\mathrm{i}\tau}\,\mathrm{d}\tau,$$

so a symmetric central interval will have coverage

$$\begin{aligned}
F_{z_n}(w) - F_{z_n}(-w) &= \frac{1}{2\pi}\int_0^\infty \frac{\mathrm{e}^{\mathrm{i}w\tau} - \mathrm{e}^{-\mathrm{i}w\tau}}{\mathrm{i}\tau}\left(\varphi_{z_n}(-\tau) + \varphi_{z_n}(\tau)\right)\mathrm{d}\tau\\
&= \frac{1}{\pi}\int_0^\infty \frac{\sin\left(w\tau\right)}{\tau}\left(\varphi_{z_n}(-\tau) + \varphi_{z_n}(\tau)\right)\mathrm{d}\tau.
\end{aligned}$$

The components of $\varphi_{z_n}(\tau)$ that are odd functions of τ will make no contribution to the integral, since $\varphi_{z_n}(-\tau) + \varphi_{z_n}(\tau)$ produces 0 for these components, and we end up with

$$\begin{aligned}
F_{z_n}(w) - F_{z_n}(-w) &= \frac{1}{\pi}\int_0^\infty \frac{\sin\left(w\tau\right)}{\tau}\left(2\mathrm{e}^{-\tau^2/2} + O\left(\frac{1}{n}\right)\right)\mathrm{d}\tau\\
&= \frac{1}{\pi}\int_0^\infty \frac{\sin\left(w\tau\right)}{\tau}\left(2\mathrm{e}^{-\tau^2/2}\right)\mathrm{d}\tau + O\left(\frac{1}{n}\right),
\end{aligned}$$

the last step following because the c.d.f. is finite. The integrand represents the limiting $\mathrm{N}(0,1)$ c.f., so using the inversion theorem again implies that

$$F_{z_n}(w) - F_{z_n}(-w) = \Phi\left(w\right) - \Phi\left(-w\right) + O\left(1/n\right).$$

(b) Since the fourth moment of x_1 exists, Exercise 10.33 (the CLT for s_n^2) implies the binomial expansion

$$\left(\frac{s_n}{\sigma}\right)^c = \left(1 + O_p\left(\frac{1}{\sqrt{n}}\right)\right)^c = 1 + O_p\left(\frac{1}{\sqrt{n}}\right)$$

for any finite constant c. Defining $\tilde{z}_n := \sqrt{n}\left(\overline{x}_n - \mu\right)/s_n$, we have $z_n = \tilde{z}_n + y/\sqrt{n}$, where $y = O_p(1)$ and has finite first two moments. It is possible to condition on y without z_n becoming deterministic, because s_n^2 is not a deterministic function of $\overline{x}_n$. Therefore

$$\begin{aligned}\Pr\left(-w \leqslant \tilde{z}_n \leqslant w \mid y\right) &= \Pr\left(-w + y/\sqrt{n} \leqslant z_n \leqslant w + y/\sqrt{n} \mid y\right)\\ &= \Phi\left(w + y/\sqrt{n}\right) - \Phi\left(-w + y/\sqrt{n}\right) + O(1/n)\end{aligned}$$

from (a). Using the integral representation of Φ,

$$\begin{aligned}\Phi\left(w + y/\sqrt{n}\right) - \Phi\left(-w + y/\sqrt{n}\right) &= \frac{1}{\sqrt{2\pi}}\int_{-w+y/\sqrt{n}}^{w+y/\sqrt{n}} \mathrm{e}^{-t^2/2}\,\mathrm{d}t\\ &= \frac{1}{\sqrt{2\pi}}\int_{-w}^{w} \mathrm{e}^{-\left(u+y/\sqrt{n}\right)^2/2}\,\mathrm{d}u\end{aligned}$$

by a change of variable. Expanding the exponential, we obtain

$$\begin{aligned}\Phi\left(w + y/\sqrt{n}\right) - \Phi\left(-w + y/\sqrt{n}\right) &= \frac{1}{\sqrt{2\pi}}\int_{-w}^{w} \mathrm{e}^{-u^2/2 - uy/\sqrt{n}}\,\mathrm{d}u + O\left(\frac{1}{n}\right)\\ &= \frac{1}{\sqrt{2\pi}}\int_{-w}^{w}\left(1 - \frac{y}{\sqrt{n}}u + O\left(\frac{1}{n}\right)\right)\mathrm{e}^{-u^2/2}\,\mathrm{d}u + O\left(\frac{1}{n}\right)\\ &= \Phi(w) - \Phi(-w) - \frac{y/\sqrt{n}}{\sqrt{2\pi}}\int_{-w}^{w} u\mathrm{e}^{-u^2/2}\,\mathrm{d}u + O\left(\frac{1}{n}\right)\end{aligned}$$

and, because $\int_{-w}^{w} u\mathrm{e}^{-u^2/2}\,\mathrm{d}u = 0$, this gives us

$$\Pr\left(-w \leqslant \tilde{z}_n \leqslant w \mid y\right) = \Phi(w) - \Phi(-w) + O(1/n).$$

Taking expectations with respect to y, it follows that the coverage is also unconditionally correct to $O(1/n)$.

Exercise 13.38 (Binomial drug, revisited) A new drug will cure a proportion p of patients suffering from a disease, but p is not yet known. The drug is tested in a large trial and turns out to cure a proportion $\widehat{p}$ of patients. Construct an approximate 95% central CI for p.

Solution

We know from Exercise 4.3 that $z := n\widehat{p} \sim \mathrm{Bin}(n, p)$, where n is the number of subjects in the trial. Since the trial is large, the CLT and the first two moments of the binomial give

$$\sqrt{n}\,\frac{n\widehat{p} - np}{\sqrt{n\widehat{p}\left(1 - \widehat{p}\right)}} \overset{a}{\sim} \mathrm{N}(0, 1).$$

Hence, the approximate CI is

$$95\% \approx \Pr\left(-1.96 \leqslant n\frac{\widehat{p}-p}{\sqrt{\widehat{p}(1-\widehat{p})}} \leqslant 1.96\right)$$

$$= \Pr\left(\widehat{p} - \frac{1.96}{n}\sqrt{\widehat{p}(1-\widehat{p})} \leqslant p \leqslant \widehat{p} + \frac{1.96}{n}\sqrt{\widehat{p}(1-\widehat{p})}\right).$$

To get an idea of the orders of magnitude involved for the numbers in Exercise 4.3,

$$\pm\frac{1.96}{n}\sqrt{\widehat{p}(1-\widehat{p})} = \pm\frac{1.96}{100}\sqrt{0.85\,(1-0.85)} \approx \pm 0.007$$

so the CI extends to less than $\pm 1\%$ around $\widehat{p}$, quite a long way from the 5% difference that the old drug represented. We are now very confident that the new drug is an improvement.

Exercise 13.39 (Bonferroni–Boole CI is conservative) Suppose that h_1 and h_2 are random variables such that $h_1 < h_2$ a.s., $\Pr(h_1 \leqslant \theta) = 1-\alpha_1$, and $\Pr(h_2 \geqslant \theta) = 1-\alpha_2$, where $\alpha := \alpha_1 + \alpha_2 < 1$ and θ is the parameter of interest. Show that $[h_1, h_2]$ is a *conservative confidence interval* for θ, that is, $\Pr(h_1 \leqslant \theta \leqslant h_2) \geqslant 1-\alpha$.

Solution

This follows directly from Exercise 1.14 on Bonferroni and Boole inequalities, more specifically $\Pr(A_1 \cup A_2) \leqslant \Pr(A_1) + \Pr(A_2)$. To see how, write

$$\begin{aligned}
\Pr(h_1 \leqslant \theta \leqslant h_2) &= \Pr(\{h_1 \leqslant \theta\} \cap \{\theta \leqslant h_2\}) \\
&= 1 - \Pr(\{\{h_1 \leqslant \theta\} \cap \{\theta \leqslant h_2\}\}^c) \\
&= 1 - \Pr(\{h_1 \leqslant \theta\}^c \cup \{\theta \leqslant h_2\}^c) \\
&\geqslant 1 - \Pr(\{h_1 \leqslant \theta\}^c) - \Pr(\{\theta \leqslant h_2\}^c) \\
&= 1 - \alpha_1 - \alpha_2 = 1 - \alpha.
\end{aligned}$$

Exercise 13.40 (Elliptical confidence regions) Let $\widehat{\boldsymbol{\theta}} \sim \mathrm{N}_m(\boldsymbol{\theta}, \boldsymbol{\Sigma})$, where $\boldsymbol{\Sigma}$ is known and is nonsingular.

(a) For $m = 1$, construct a level $1-\alpha$ central CI for θ.

(b) Construct a level $1-\alpha$ confidence region for $\boldsymbol{\theta}$.

Solution

(a) Using the convention that $\boldsymbol{\Sigma}$ reduces to σ^2 when $k = 1$ (see Chapter 6), we have

$$1-\alpha = \Pr\left(-\mathrm{N}_{1-\alpha/2} \leqslant \frac{\widehat{\theta}-\theta}{\sigma} \leqslant \mathrm{N}_{1-\alpha/2}\right) = \Pr\left(\left|\widehat{\theta}-\theta\right| \leqslant \mathrm{N}_{1-\alpha/2}\sigma\right),$$

where the interval can be rewritten as $\left[\widehat{\theta} - \mathrm{N}_{1-\alpha/2}\sigma,\, \widehat{\theta} + \mathrm{N}_{1-\alpha/2}\sigma\right]$. Notice that the CI is equivalent to

$$1-\alpha=\Pr\left(\left(\frac{\widehat{\theta}-\theta}{\sigma}\right)^2\leqslant\chi^2_{1-\alpha}(1)\right),$$

since $z\sim\mathrm{N}(0,1)$ implies that $z^2\sim\chi^2(1)$ and $\Pr(|z|\leqslant c)=\Pr(z^2\leqslant c^2)$ for all $c>0$.
(b) We know from Exercise 8.28(a) that $\widehat{\boldsymbol{\theta}}\sim\mathrm{N}_m(\boldsymbol{\theta},\boldsymbol{\Sigma})$ implies that

$$z:=(\widehat{\boldsymbol{\theta}}-\boldsymbol{\theta})'\boldsymbol{\Sigma}^{-1}(\widehat{\boldsymbol{\theta}}-\boldsymbol{\theta})\sim\chi^2(m).$$

The distribution does not depend on $\boldsymbol{\theta}$, so z is a pivot. Therefore, $1-\alpha=\Pr(z\leqslant\chi^2_{1-\alpha}(m))$ gives the required confidence region, which is the interior of an ellipsoid (or ellipse for $m=2$) defined by

$$(\boldsymbol{\theta}-\widehat{\boldsymbol{\theta}})'\boldsymbol{\Sigma}^{-1}(\boldsymbol{\theta}-\widehat{\boldsymbol{\theta}})=\chi^2_{1-\alpha}(m)$$

and centered around $\widehat{\boldsymbol{\theta}}$. This was discussed in Exercise 8.28(a) and, for $m=2$, it was illustrated in Figure 6.4 of Exercise 6.1. This ellipsoid bounds the confidence region, generalizing (a) where the region (an interval) is bounded by only two points.

Exercise 13.41 (Normal conjugates: CI) Construct a 95% highest posterior density region for ϑ of Exercise 13.20(b).

Solution

The posterior of ϑ is given by $(\vartheta\mid\boldsymbol{x})\sim\mathrm{N}(\mu_n,\sigma_n^2)$, where μ_n and σ_n are known and given in Exercise 13.20(b). Since the normal density is symmetric around the mean μ_n, and monotonically declining as we move away from μ_n, the HPD interval is

$$\Pr(\mu_n-1.96\sigma_n\leqslant\vartheta\leqslant\mu_n+1.96\sigma_n\mid\boldsymbol{x})\approx 95\%.$$

It also follows from Exercise 13.33(a) that this interval has minimum length, for a given coverage.

Exercise 13.42 (HPD minimizes volume) Prove that a region A of coverage $1-\alpha$ has minimum volume if and only if A is a HPD region.

Solution

We start by rephrasing the question, using the dual formulation of the optimization problem: minimizing the volume subject to a fixed coverage is equivalent to maximizing the coverage subject to a fixed volume. (This can be verified from the Lagrangian function; it is known as the *saddlepoint* of the Lagrangian.) The "if" part is easy to prove, as it follows directly from the definition of the HPD. Since the density is never smaller for any point inside A than outside it, the coverage is maximized for any given volume. We now prove the "only if" part by contradiction.

Suppose that A has maximum coverage, but is not HPD. If A is not HPD, then there exists $\boldsymbol{\theta}_1$ in the interior of A and $\boldsymbol{\theta}_2 \notin A$, such that

$$f_{\vartheta|\mathbf{X}}(\boldsymbol{\theta}_1) < f_{\vartheta|\mathbf{X}}(\boldsymbol{\theta}_2).$$

This implies that, for $\epsilon > \mathbf{0}$ but arbitrarily small,

$$\int_{\boldsymbol{\theta}_1}^{\boldsymbol{\theta}_1+\epsilon} \mathrm{d}F_{\vartheta|\mathbf{X}}(\boldsymbol{\theta}) < \int_{\boldsymbol{\theta}_2}^{\boldsymbol{\theta}_2+\epsilon} \mathrm{d}F_{\vartheta|\mathbf{X}}(\boldsymbol{\theta})$$

since c.d.f.s are right-continuous. This means that we can remove the region between $\boldsymbol{\theta}_1$ and $\boldsymbol{\theta}_1 + \epsilon$ (a hyperrectangle) from A, and replace it with a region of the same volume between $\boldsymbol{\theta}_2$ and $\boldsymbol{\theta}_2 + \epsilon$ but with higher coverage. This contradicts the statement that A has maximum coverage, thus completing the proof. Note that we have not shown here that the HPD region is unique. For this, we would need to impose additional conditions on the posterior $f_{\vartheta|\mathbf{X}}$.

Notes

General references for this chapter are the same as for Chapter 11. We will not go into detailed refinements and extensions of the methods of estimation introduced here. They will be analyzed more fully in subsequent volumes of this Series.

When there is more than one parameter to estimate, and the equations for the sample moments are correlated, it is more efficient to use Hansen's (1982) generalized method of moments (GMM) than just MM. The GMM also uses asymptotics to circumvent the necessity with MM to specify the underlying distribution. Alternatives to GMM, based on optimizing KLIC, were proposed by Kitamura and Stutzer (1997). In relation to the latter reference and KLIC, see the pseudo or quasi MLEs in White (1982), Gouriéroux, Monfort, and Trognon (1984), and Nishii (1988). See also Le Cam (1953). The efficient method of moments (EMM) of Gallant and Tauchen (1996) modifies the GMM criterion so that it mimics the score of an auxiliary model. For optimal estimating equations and their relation to the score, see the literature started by Durbin (1960), Godambe (1960), and Hendry (1976). See also M estimators and their robustified versions, in Huber (1981) and Hampel, Ronchetti, Rousseeuw, and Stahel (1986).

Galton's name is associated with the introduction of the term "regression"; see Stigler (1986) or Hald (1998). Galton studied the relation between the heights of children (y) and their parents (x), reaching the conclusion that there was a "regression" (initially termed "reversion") towards the mean height. We can see from the illustration of Exercise 13.8 how this could be an artifact of $|\rho| < 1$.

Least squares is a special case of an l_p *estimator*, which is the solution to minimizing $\sum_{i=1}^{n} |y_i - \widehat{y}_i|^p$ for some $p > 0$, typically $p \geqslant 1$ for convexity. In the case $p = 1$, we have the *least absolute deviations* (LAD) estimator encountered earlier; see, for example, Exercise 12.14. It too can be viewed as an MLE, in the context of a Laplace (rather than normal) distribution; see also the GED in Chapter 4 and Exercise 12.10 for general p.

The robustness of LAD was illustrated in the introduction to Chapter 11 and in Exercise 11.3. LAD estimators are one way to remedy the sensitivity of LS (the case $p = 2$ in l_p) to outliers, as there is no squaring of large residuals. See Chapter 13 of Abadir and Magnus (2005) for the sensitivity analysis of LSEs. Notice that we take the absolute value of the residuals in the l_p criterion, where positive and negative errors are equally penalized. Unfortunately, l_p estimators do not have an explicit solution in general, but these can be calculated numerically. Furthermore, because the l_p criterion is defined in terms of sample moments, which are not invariant to transformations, these estimators do not share the invariance property of MLEs; see also the illustration in Exercise 13.7.

A generalization of LAD, in Koenker and Bassett (1978), is the *quantile regression* that solves

$$\min_{\widehat{y}_i} \left(\lambda \sum\nolimits_{y_i \geqslant \widehat{y}_i} (y_i - \widehat{y}_i) + (1 - \lambda) \sum\nolimits_{y_i < \widehat{y}_i} (\widehat{y}_i - y_i) \right),$$

where $\lambda \in (0, 1)$ and, for example, $\widehat{\boldsymbol{y}} = \boldsymbol{X}\widehat{\boldsymbol{\beta}}$. When $\lambda = \frac{1}{2}$, the solution is the LAD estimator since the criterion becomes $\frac{1}{2} \sum_i |\widehat{y}_i - y_i|$. Another special case is obtained when $\widehat{y}_i = \beta$: rewriting the criterion as

$$\lambda \sum\nolimits_{i=1}^{n} (y_i - \beta) + \sum\nolimits_{y_i < \beta} (\beta - y_i)$$

and differentiating with respect to β yields $\lambda n = \sum_{y_i < \widehat{\beta}} 1$, a solution between the $\lfloor \lambda n \rfloor$-th and $\lfloor \lambda n + 1 \rfloor$-th order statistic for continuous y. A zero mean for $y_i - \widehat{y}_i$ then ensures that the λ term drops out from the objective function, and the lower of these two values is selected. While on the topic of quantiles, there is a different approach explained by Gilchrist (2000). It revolves around fitting the whole quantile function to data. Approaches based on a linear combination of order statistics are called *L estimators*. If optimizing a function of the ranks instead (hence achieving further robustness to extremes), the result is known as *R estimators*. Ranks were encountered in Section 9.3 (see also the final Note to Chapter 9 for an extension) and will be seen again in Section 14.4.

When the number of regressors is large, LS does not produce a parsimonious model. To remedy this, Tibshirani (1996) minimized the LS criterion subject to $\sum_{i=1}^{k} |\beta_i| \leqslant c$, calling it the *least absolute shrinkage and selection operator* (LASSO). This produces the required parsimony which another shrinkage estimator, *ridge regression* which uses $\sum_{i=1}^{k} \beta_i^2 \leqslant c$ instead, cannot produce. The intuition for this, in two dimensions ($k = 2$), is that optimization over domains delimited by lozenges will produce corner solutions much more often than over ellipses which produce tangencies pretty much anywhere instead.

An alternative but longer proof of the Gauss–Markov theorem of Exercise 13.10 can be obtained by differentiating $\operatorname{var}(\boldsymbol{a}'\widetilde{\boldsymbol{\beta}})$ subject to $\operatorname{E}(\boldsymbol{a}'\widetilde{\boldsymbol{\beta}}) = \boldsymbol{a}'\boldsymbol{\beta}$, for any nonrandom $\boldsymbol{a} \neq \boldsymbol{0}$, and checking the second-order condition for a minimum. This, and an alternative approach to the estimation part (a) of Exercises 13.12 and 13.13, can be found in Chapters 12 and 13 of Abadir and Magnus (2005). They also showed, by direct methods, how the difference between the variances is positive semidefinite. There are two further important comments in connection with Exercise 13.10. First, the shrinkage estimator of Exercise 11.25 illustrates (in the simplest linear model, $y_i = \mu + \varepsilon_i$) that the BLUE does not necessarily achieve minimum risk. In fact, the shrinkage estimator is not linear in the left-hand side variable of the linear model, so it is not covered by the class of estimators considered in Exercise 13.10. Second, the MLE estimator in the AR model of Exercise 12.43(b) is not linear in the left-hand side variable either. That estimator is biased in finite samples (see the references in the Notes to Chapter 11), as follows from $x_i \equiv y_{i-1}$ and

$$\mathrm{E}\left((\boldsymbol{X}'\boldsymbol{X})^{-1}\boldsymbol{X}'\boldsymbol{\varepsilon}\right) \neq \mathrm{E}\left((\boldsymbol{X}'\boldsymbol{X})^{-1}\boldsymbol{X}'\right)\mathrm{E}\left(\boldsymbol{\varepsilon}\right)$$

since $\boldsymbol{X}$ is random and correlated with $\boldsymbol{\varepsilon}$. Alternatively,

$$\widehat{\alpha} - \alpha = \sum_{i=1}^{n} \frac{y_{i-1}}{\sum_{j=1}^{n} y_{j-1}^2} \varepsilon_i,$$

where $\sum_{j=1}^{n} y_{j-1}^2$ depends on $\varepsilon_1, \dots, \varepsilon_{n-1}$ and is therefore correlated with all ε_i except the last, ε_n. The estimator is, nonetheless, consistent; see the final Note to Chapter 12.

In the normal linear model, ML and LS estimators of $\boldsymbol{\beta}$ share the same functional form $(\boldsymbol{X}'\widehat{\boldsymbol{\Sigma}}^{-1}\boldsymbol{X})^{-1}\boldsymbol{X}'\widehat{\boldsymbol{\Sigma}}^{-1}\boldsymbol{y}$ when $\boldsymbol{\Sigma}$ is unknown, as a result of optimization with respect to $\boldsymbol{\beta}$ for any given $\boldsymbol{\Sigma}$ (the same as the procedure for the partial MLE). They are numerically equal when the ML and LS estimators $\widehat{\boldsymbol{\Sigma}}$ of $\boldsymbol{\Sigma}$ differ only by a scale factor. Such is the case when $\boldsymbol{\Sigma} = \sigma^2\boldsymbol{A}$, where $\boldsymbol{A}$ is known and σ is functionally independent of $\boldsymbol{\beta}$. (It is traditional in this case to use the unbiased estimator $s^2 := (n-k)^{-1}\,\widehat{\boldsymbol{\varepsilon}}'\widehat{\boldsymbol{\varepsilon}}$ for LS, obtained in Exercises 12.31(e) and 13.11(a) with $r = k$.) Otherwise, if the unknown $\boldsymbol{\Sigma}$ depends on fewer parameters than the sample size ($\boldsymbol{\Sigma}$ could contain as many as $n\,(n+1)\,/2$ unknown elements), it may be feasible to estimate $\boldsymbol{\Sigma}$ but ML and LS will differ in general because the log-likelihood, having the additional term $-\frac{1}{2}\log|\boldsymbol{\Sigma}|$, produces an estimator of $\boldsymbol{\Sigma}$ that differs from LS by more than a scale factor.

In NP estimation, the term "window width" should be treated with caution. The "window", on which each $\lambda^{-1}K\left(\lambda^{-1}(u - x_i)\right)$ is defined, can be infinitely large if K is chosen to have support on $\mathbb{R}$, such as when K is the normal $K_{\mathrm{n}} = \phi$. The quantity λ actually measures scaling rather than length. Note also that the kernel's zero mean does not necessarily imply that it is symmetric (see Chapter 3). However, Cline (1988) showed that, if there are no reasons to believe that the density is asymmetric in a particular way, then asymmetric kernels are inadmissible in large samples (though not by an order of magnitude). But, if qualitative information on the skewness is available, it is more efficient to incorporate it into the estimation procedure, since density estimates tend to inherit the salient properties of their kernels in moderately sized samples. Abadir and Lawford (2004) extended the result of Exercise 13.16 to asymmetric kernels, also studying the conversion of optimal bandwidths implied by Exercise 13.15(d) and introduced by Marron and Nolan (1989). Hansen (2005) showed that the choice of kernels becomes important when considering the exact (finite-sample) IMSE rather than the AIMSE.

Stone (1984) showed that the bandwidth selected by the LSCV method in Exercise 13.17 is asymptotically optimal, in terms of the integrated squared error (ISE) criterion $\int_{-\infty}^{\infty}(\widehat{f}\,(u) - f\,(u))^2\,\mathrm{d}u$ whose expectation is the IMSE. See Jones (1991) for a comparison of ISE and IMSE criteria. LSCV is not the only popular bandwidth selection method, not even within the class of CV methods. See Jones, Marron, and Park (1991) for a list of these methods, as well as a study of their optimality, and see Fan and Marron (1992) for a CRLB-type result for bandwidths. Explicit formulae for asymptotically optimal bandwidths in CV problems are given in Abadir and Lubrano (2016). In the case of possibly dependent data, Hart and Vieu (1990) proposed a simple modification of the CV criteria, deleting a block of contiguous observations at a time. For this type of context, Hall, Lahiri, and Truong (1995) expanded the AIMSE further. They then derived the optimal bandwidth and showed that it is not very different from the formula for random samples. However, they also showed that CV does less well than a plug-in method that they proposed.

When parts of f are thin (as can be in the tail of a density), more smoothing of $\widehat{f}$ is needed locally in the thin part; see the first graph in Figure 13.1. It is then recommended in practice to use adaptive bandwidths, such as implied by the *nearest neighborhood method* that takes λ to be proportional to the distance between the points; see, for example, Mack and Rosenblatt (1979) for the multivariate case. For the application of kernels to quantile estimation, see Sheather and Marron (1990), whose conclusion is generally not favorable to the use of kernels in this case.

The extension of NP regression to higher dimensions is not as a straightforward as with parametric models, because of the curse of dimensionality (rates of convergence slower than in Exercises 13.14 and 13.15 occur), and because there are many ways in which the right-hand side variates could be combined. Some prominent existing methods take additive NP functions (Hastie and Tibshirani, 1986) or dimension-reducing linear combinations of these variates (projection pursuit analyzed by Huber, 1985; average derivatives introduced by Stoker, 1986) possibly by first considering $\mathrm{E}(\boldsymbol{x} \mid y)$ instead of $\mathrm{E}(y \mid \boldsymbol{x})$ (the sliced inverse regression of Li, 1991). Alternatively, functions can be represented in terms of orthogonal series, smoothing splines (see Härdle and Linton, 1994), wavelets (see Härdle, Kerkyacharian, Picard, and Tsybakov, 1998), or neural networks (see Kuan and White, 1994). See also the local polynomial regression of Cleveland (1979). The method of sieves provides a general asymptotic approach, whereby m (the dimension of $\boldsymbol{\theta}$) increases with n but at a slower rate. For a summary text in NP econometrics, see Li and Racine (2006).

Nonparametric estimation is robust to most misspecifications of functional forms, except discontinuities (or nondifferentiabilities) in the density or the regression. For example, the product of two normals has a discontinuity at the origin; see Exercise 7.22(c) and the corresponding Note at the end of Chapter 7. Estimating a kernel density for such a product can be misleading. We have presented NP methods as a tool for data exploration. However, more formal testing for various parametric (and nonparametric) hypotheses can be carried out. These are beyond the scope of this volume.

For Bayesian estimation and inference, additional references include Bernardo and Smith (2000) and Lee (2004). See Zaman (1996) for an econometric perspective or, in this Series, Koop, Poirier, and Tobias (2007) and its forthcoming revised edition covering the numerous developments in numerical methods. There exist random-parameter models in frequentist analysis too, so the difference from the Bayesian approach does not concern random parameters. The posterior depends on the prior, which involves a subjective element. For this reason, *empirical Bayes estimators* are those where the parameters of the prior are also estimated, by means of the marginal density of $\boldsymbol{X}$. Unlike standard Bayes estimators, the resulting estimators may no longer be admissible.

The conjugacy of the priors in Exercise 13.20 extends to exponential families, subject to the provisions given in Diaconis and Ylvisaker (1979). Jeffreys' prior is data-driven, thus reducing an element of arbitrariness in the choice of priors. It also satisfies the transformation invariance in Exercise 13.23. It has evolved into Bernardo–Berger reference priors, which satisfy further desirable properties. See also the ML prior in Hartigan (1998).

In a sense, point estimation can be regarded legitimately as inference, and some authors have done so. However, we prefer adding the requirement that probability statements be made when using the word "inference". Crucial to this is the *distribution* of estimators and that it is used to make probability statements such as CIs.

One should be careful with the terminology when substituting estimates (realizations of estimators) into frequentist confidence regions, which then become nonrandom. The coverage is then assigned a frequency interpretation of probability, that is, it represents the frequency with which the region covers the true parameter over repeated samples. This explains our cautious terminology in Exercise 13.38, when we talked about orders of magnitude. It is also clear that a difficulty will arise in the second CI of Exercise 13.32 when the realization of $\overline{x}$ is not positive and cannot be substituted into the CI. Decision rules based on comparing estimates to hypothesized values of the parameter will follow in Chapter 14.

There are refinements that are less conservative than Bonferroni-type CIs (Exercise 13.39). They can be found in Holm (1979), Hommel (1988), Hochberg (1988), and Benjamini and Hochberg (1995). They will be discussed further in the Notes to Chapter 14.

There are a few general remarks to be made on pivots for CIs. First, suppose that x is a continuous variate with known c.d.f. F, and that we have a random sample $\{x_i\}_{i=1}^n$. Recalling Exercise 7.38 on the PIT, we have immediately that $F(x_i) \sim \mathrm{U}_{(0,1)}$, where we stress that x_i is random. This standard-uniform distribution is invariant to the parameters $\boldsymbol{\theta}$ of F, and therefore $F(x_i)$ is pivotal for $\boldsymbol{\theta}$. Furthermore, when F is not necessarily known, Exercise 10.30(a) shows that the EDF F_n converges almost surely to the true F, so the EDF is asymptotically pivotal. Second, note that the exercises have highlighted two common features. If θ is a location parameter, then $x_i - \theta$ is location-invariant; if θ is the scale of the variate (such that x_i/θ has scale not depending on θ), then x_i/θ is scale-invariant. For a related point, see the last paragraph in the Notes to Chapter 11.

Finally, continuing with the discussion of shrinkage estimators of Chapter 11, such ideas have been extended to confidence sets. See Hwang and Ullah (1994) and the survey of Casella and Hwang (2012).

14

Tests of hypotheses

We concluded the previous chapter (Sections 13.4 and 13.5) by introducing two methods of *inference* concerning the parameter vector $\boldsymbol{\theta}$. It is fair to say that this is the most contentious topic in statistics: there is no single answer to the question of how to use an estimator $\widehat{\boldsymbol{\theta}}$ and its distribution to conduct inference on $\boldsymbol{\theta}$. The debate goes beyond the choice of optimality criteria (necessary for estimation too) to deeper philosophical questions. The Bayesian approach was introduced in the previous chapter, so here we focus on the competing frequentist or classical approach and how it attempts to draw conclusions about the value of $\boldsymbol{\theta}$.

In a parametric setup, two types of hypotheses about $\boldsymbol{\theta}$ are specified. We start with a hypothesis of interest, a *null hypothesis*, stipulating that

$$\mathrm{H}_0 : \boldsymbol{\theta} \in \Theta_0, \tag{14.1}$$

which is to say that this hypothesis specifies that $\boldsymbol{\theta}$ belongs to some parameter space Θ_0, with an implied joint p.d.f. f_0 for the data. For example, supposing that $\{x_n\} \sim \mathrm{IN}(\mu, 1)$ and $\mathrm{H}_0 : \mu = 1$, the implied joint density f_0 for $x_1, \ldots, x_n$ is the product of the n marginal $\mathrm{N}(1, 1)$ densities, namely

$$f_0(u_1, \ldots, u_n) = \prod_{i=1}^{n} \phi(u_i - 1) = \frac{\exp\left(-\frac{1}{2}\sum_{i=1}^{n}(u_i - 1)^2\right)}{(2\pi)^{n/2}}. \tag{14.2}$$

The hypothesis H_0 may be competing with another potential representation of $\boldsymbol{\theta}$, an *alternative hypothesis*, denoted by

$$\mathrm{H}_1 : \boldsymbol{\theta} \in \Theta_1, \tag{14.3}$$

where $\Theta_0 \cap \Theta_1 = \varnothing$ and Θ_1 implies the p.d.f. f_1. Also, $\Theta_0 \cup \Theta_1 \subseteq \Theta$ where Θ is the parameter space of $\boldsymbol{\theta}$. A hypothesis is said to be *simple* if it fully determines the corresponding density f, which then contains no unknown parameters; otherwise, it is said to be *composite*. In the previous example, $\mathrm{H}_0 : \mu = 1$ was simple since (14.2) can be computed numerically for any $(u_1, \ldots, u_n)$, but (say) $H_1 : \mu \neq 1$ would be composite because f_1 would then depend on the true value of μ which may be any unspecified number in $\mathbb{R}$ except $\mu = 1$. We also call a hypothesis like $H_1 : \mu \neq 1$ *two-sided*, just as we did with CIs in Chapter 13, since it allows either $\mu < 1$ or $\mu > 1$, whereas $H_1 : \mu > 1$ would be called *one-sided*.

In *hypothesis testing*, we decide which of the competing hypotheses holds by asking which is supported by the data. To do this, we need a decision rule. A *test statistic* τ is a data-based (meaning that it contains no unknown quantities) decision rule that tells us whether it is reasonable to reject H_0 as a result of observing some data. It takes the form "reject H_0 if $\tau \in C$", where C is the *critical region* of the test. Taking the simple example $\{x_n\} \sim \mathrm{IN}(\mu, \sigma^2)$, a familiar illustration of τ from elementary statistics is the test based on the t-ratio (or t-statistic) for $H_0 : \mu = \mu_0$ (which is a simpler way of stating the hypothesis (14.1) for this example):

$$t := \frac{\overline{x} - \mu_0}{s/\sqrt{n}}, \tag{14.4}$$

encountered in Chapter 9. This is a case where the hypothesis focuses only on a subset of the parameter vector $\boldsymbol{\theta} := (\mu, \sigma^2)'$, namely the first component μ, which is then called the parameter of interest while σ^2 is called a nuisance parameter; see Chapter 11 for the general definitions of such a classification of parameters. We can also view this as a case where the same values of σ^2 are allowed by both H_0 and H_1, and the two hypotheses can be written in terms of the full vector $\boldsymbol{\theta}$, although it is simpler to adopt the approach of just focusing on the parameter of interest in specifying the hypotheses. Note that $\Theta_0 \cap \Theta_1 = \varnothing$ even though σ^2 is allowed the same value under both H_0 and H_1, because μ differs under the two hypotheses and thus $\boldsymbol{\theta}_0 \neq \boldsymbol{\theta}_1$. In this chapter, the subscripts of $\boldsymbol{\theta}$ denote the values implied by H_0 or H_1, such as $\boldsymbol{\theta}_0$ or $\boldsymbol{\theta}_1$, unless specified otherwise.

If we specify $H_1 : \mu \neq \mu_0$ and we get a "large" value of $|t|$ in (14.4), it indicates that $\overline{x}$ is too far from μ_0 for the hypothesis H_0 to be correct. We then reject H_0 and say that $\overline{x}$ (the estimator, not the parameter μ) is *significantly different* from μ_0. If $\mu_0 = 0$, we can also say "$\overline{x}$ is statistically significant", a terminology that applies more generally to the case of testing for any parameter to be zero. This simple example illustrates the important fact that the hypothesis H_0 is the one that usually takes center stage in classical testing: t is based on μ_0 rather than a value under H_1, and H_1 typically indicates suspected directions for violations of H_0. The two hypotheses are usually not treated symmetrically, and rejecting $H_0 : \boldsymbol{\theta} \in \Theta_0$ is not necessarily equivalent to "accepting" $H_1 : \boldsymbol{\theta} \in \Theta_1$.

Any decision can entail errors. There are two possible types of error here:

I. rejecting H_0 incorrectly, with probability $\alpha := \Pr_{H_0}(\tau \in C)$; or
II. not rejecting H_0 although H_0 is incorrect, with probability

$$\beta := \Pr_{H_1}(\tau \notin C) = 1 - \Pr_{H_1}(\tau \in C).$$

The subscript of Pr indicates which state of affairs (meaning which hypothesis and p.d.f.) holds. The first type of error of inference is called the *size* of the test or the *Type I error*, sometimes also the *significance level* because of its connection with testing for significance (see the previous paragraph). The *power* of a test is

$$\Pi := \Pr_{H_1}(\tau \in C) = 1 - \beta, \tag{14.5}$$

which measures the ability of a test to reject H_0 when H_1 holds instead. It is negatively related to the second type of error of inference, β, the *Type II error*. The standard classical approach is to fix the Type I error to an "acceptable" level, and proceed to find a τ that minimizes the Type II error (equivalently, maximizes the power). This is so because of the principal role played by H_0, making it more serious to reject H_0 incorrectly (the Type I error). An analogy can be made with an individual being presumed innocent (the stated H_0) until proven guilty, and it is a more serious error to convict an innocent person (reject H_0 incorrectly).

Before proceeding further, let us illustrate these concepts with the simple example of $\{x_n\} \sim \mathrm{IN}(\mu, 1)$. We know (for example, from Exercise 7.16 or Chapter 8) that $\overline{x} \sim \mathrm{N}(\mu, 1/n)$. Suppose that we are interested in testing

$$H_0 : \mu = \mu_0 \qquad \text{against} \qquad H_1 : \mu > \mu_0. \tag{14.6}$$

We cannot base our decision rule τ on $\overline{x} - \mu \sim \mathrm{N}(0, 1/n)$ directly, since it contains the unknown μ. We therefore use the value of μ maintained under H_0 and define

$$\tau := \frac{\overline{x} - \mu_0}{\sqrt{\mathrm{var}(\overline{x})}} = \sqrt{n}\,(\overline{x} - \mu_0); \tag{14.7}$$

compare with (14.4), where we did not know the value of σ^2 and needed to estimate it by s^2. Then, applying $\overline{x} \sim \mathrm{N}(\mu, 1/n)$ to $\tau = \sqrt{n}\,(\overline{x} - \mu_0)$, we have that τ is also normal (because it is a linear transformation of $\overline{x}$), with mean

$$\mathrm{E}\left(\sqrt{n}\,(\overline{x} - \mu_0)\right) = \sqrt{n}\,(\mu - \mu_0)$$

and variance

$$n\,\mathrm{var}\,(\overline{x} - \mu_0) = n\,\mathrm{var}\,(\overline{x}) = \frac{n}{n} = 1.$$

Hence

$$\tau \sim \begin{cases} \mathrm{N}(0,1) & \text{under } H_0 : \mu = \mu_0, \\ \mathrm{N}(\delta,1) & \text{under } H_1 : \mu > \mu_0, \end{cases} \tag{14.8}$$

where $\delta := \sqrt{n}\,(\mu - \mu_0)$. Suppose that we take $\alpha = 2.5\%$; then the upper-tail quantile $\mathrm{N}_{0.975} \approx 1.96$ (last seen in Chapter 13) is the *critical value* of τ for the one-sided test of (14.6), such that $\tau > 1.96$ defines the critical region C. Figure 14.1 provides an illustration: here we plot the two densities of τ given in (14.8), that obtained when H_0 holds (the left-hand curve) and that obtained when H_1 holds with $\delta = 3$ (the right-hand curve). The critical region C is what lies to the right of the vertical dashed line at $\tau = 1.96$, with the horizontally striped area given by

$$\alpha = \Pr_{H_0}(\tau > 1.96) = \int_{1.96}^{\infty} \phi(u)\,\mathrm{d}u = 1 - \Phi(1.96) = \Phi(-1.96) \approx 0.025$$

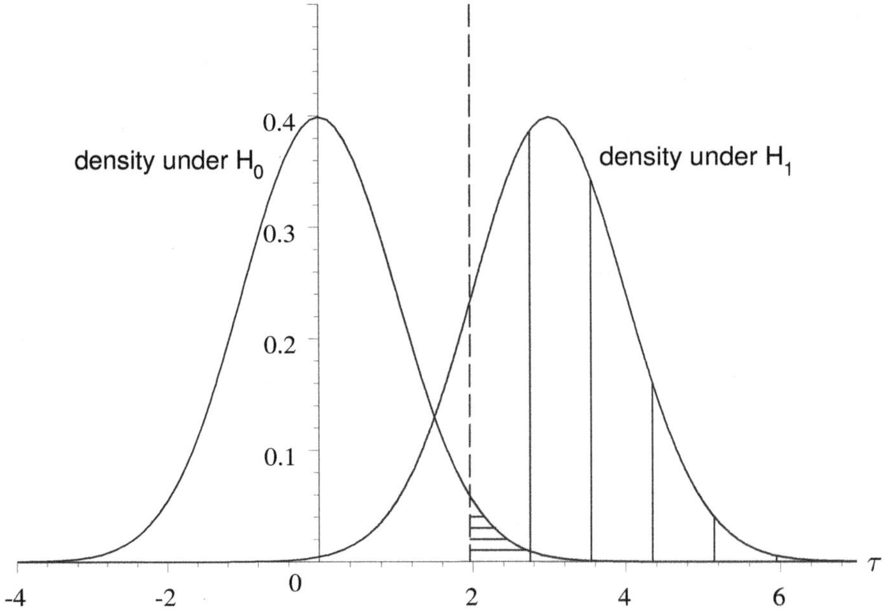

Figure 14.1. Densities of τ under H_0 (left-hand curve) and under H_1 (right-hand curve). The critical region C is to the right of the vertical dashed line at $\tau = 1.96$, with the small horizontally striped area denoting the size α and the large vertically striped area the power Π of τ.

and the vertically striped area is the power of the test when $\delta = 3$

$$\Pi = \Pr_{\mathrm{H}_1}(\tau > 1.96) = \int_{1.96}^{\infty} \phi(u-3)\,\mathrm{d}u = \int_{-1.04}^{\infty} \phi(v)\,\mathrm{d}v$$
$$= 1 - \Phi(-1.04) = \Phi(1.04)$$
$$\approx \frac{1}{2} + \frac{1.04}{\sqrt{2\pi}} - \frac{1.04}{\sqrt{2\pi}}\frac{(1.04)^2/2}{3} + \frac{1.04}{\sqrt{2\pi}}\frac{((1.04)^2/2)^2}{10} - \frac{1.04}{\sqrt{2\pi}}\frac{((1.04)^2/2)^3}{42} \approx 0.851$$

calculated (exactly to three decimal places) by Exercise 4.21. The power of a test is its ability to disentangle (or tell apart) competing hypotheses. Here, the densities $\mathrm{N}(0,1)$ and $\mathrm{N}(\delta,1)$ become further apart as δ increases and the latter density shifts to the right in the graph, implying that Π (the vertically striped area) increases. Recalling that $\delta := \sqrt{n}\,(\mu - \mu_0)$, this happens when either n increases or when μ is further from μ_0. This is intuitive: it is easier to distinguish the two competing hypotheses if we have more data, or if the values of μ under H_0 and H_1 are further apart.

As we shall see later in the next graph, it is customary to plot Π as a function of μ (for any given n). The result will be the usual S-shaped curve that we get from c.d.f.s such as Φ, but this time starting at $\mu = \mu_0$ with corresponding value $\Pi = \alpha = \Phi(-1.96) \approx 0.025$ then, as μ increases, the curve ends up at the value $\Pi = \lim_{\delta\to\infty} \Phi(\delta - 1.96) = 1$. A larger sample size n would shift this power curve up everywhere, except at its extremities, which would still start at 0.025 and end at 1.

The choice of τ in the last example may seem arbitrary. Why did we use this test as opposed to another? As we did in Chapter 11 for estimation, we need to introduce some criteria for the goodness of a test. We have already started this discussion by mentioning the power of a test before the last example. We now formalize this. Many names describing desirable properties for estimating parameters and testing hypotheses are the same, though carrying different meanings that depend on the context (estimation or testing).

1. Unbiasedness. A test is *unbiased* if and only if

$$\Pi \geqslant \alpha$$

for *all* values of the parameter vector $\boldsymbol{\theta} \in \Theta_1$. Otherwise, for *some* $\boldsymbol{\theta} \in \Theta_1$ we would have $\Pi < \alpha$, which would mean (by the definitions of Π, α) that

$$\Pr(\text{rejecting } H_0 \text{ when false}) < \Pr(\text{rejecting } H_0 \text{ when true})$$

and this would contradict the concept of a test: you would be more likely to reject H_0 when true than when false! An alternative way of writing $\Pi \geqslant \alpha$ makes use of (14.5), and unbiasedness becomes the requirement that

$$1 \geqslant \alpha + \beta$$

for all $\boldsymbol{\theta} \in \Theta_1$; in other words, an unbiased test is one where potential errors occur with a total probability of $\alpha + \beta$ which is nowhere greater than 100%. (A test would definitely be useless – worse than just biased – if errors occurred with probability 100% for *all* $\boldsymbol{\theta}$!)

2. UMP. In order to stress that the power is a function of the parameter vector $\boldsymbol{\theta}$, and that it differs from one test τ to another, we shall write here $\Pi_\tau(\boldsymbol{\theta}) := \Pr_{\boldsymbol{\theta}}(\tau \in C)$, where we also extend the notation of the function Π to any $\boldsymbol{\theta} \in \Theta$ rather than just $\boldsymbol{\theta} \in \Theta_1$. Then, for a test based on τ to be a *uniformly most powerful* (UMP) *test of size* α, it needs to satisfy

$$\sup_{\boldsymbol{\theta} \in \Theta_0} \Pi_\tau(\boldsymbol{\theta}) = \alpha$$

and

$$\Pi_\tau(\boldsymbol{\theta}) \geqslant \Pi_{\tau^\dagger}(\boldsymbol{\theta}), \qquad \forall \boldsymbol{\theta} \in \Theta_1 \text{ and } \forall \tau^\dagger \text{ of size} \leqslant \alpha.$$

The first condition ensures that the size of τ is no larger than α, whenever $H_0 : \boldsymbol{\theta} \in \Theta_0$ holds. The second condition shows that, whenever $H_1 : \boldsymbol{\theta} \in \Theta_1$ holds, any other test $\tau^\dagger$ of size no larger than α can do no better (in terms of power) than τ.[1] The adjective "uniform" is required when dealing with composite hypotheses, such as when $\forall \boldsymbol{\theta} \in \Theta_1$ refers to more than one value of $\boldsymbol{\theta}$ in the second condition above, and we need to establish this inequality of powers for all these values of $\boldsymbol{\theta}$. The corresponding critical region C_α for this UMP τ is a *most powerful region* (MPR) *of size* α. The terminology "best" (seen in connection with

[1]Of course, one can make Π artificially larger by increasing α, for any given test; see Figure 14.1 where we could illustrate this by shifting the dashed vertical line to the left. There is always a tradeoff between Type I (α) and Type II ($\beta = 1 - \Pi$) errors: you cannot lower both, for any given test. This explains why the definition of UMP requires $\tau^\dagger$ to have size no larger than α, so that it remains comparable with τ.

estimators in Chapter 11) is sometimes also used here to describe such a test τ and/or its corresponding critical region C_α.

Recalling the definitions of admissibility and inadmissibility in Chapter 11 (Property 8 in the introduction to that chapter), we can adapt them to the current context. In the UMP definition if, in addition, $\tau^\dagger$ has power strictly less than τ at some value $\boldsymbol{\theta} \in \Theta_1$, we say that $\tau^\dagger$ is *inadmissible*. A similar adaptation applies to admissibility. Note that a UMP test need not necessarily exist, as we shall show shortly.

3. UMPU. A test that combines Properties 1 and 2 above is a *uniformly most powerful unbiased* (UMPU) *test*. By definition, a UMPU test is admissible since it does better than UMP tests where the latter are biased for some value of $\boldsymbol{\theta}$, even if it does worse for other values of $\boldsymbol{\theta}$.

At this point, it is useful to illustrate these new concepts with (again) the simple example of $\{x_n\} \sim \mathrm{IN}(\mu, 1)$, but now with

$$\mathrm{H}_0 : \mu = \mu_0 \qquad \text{against} \qquad \mathrm{H}_1 : \mu \neq \mu_0 \tag{14.9}$$

instead of the one-sided H_1 in (14.6). Consider two tests, one based on "reject H_0 if $\tau > 1.65$" (the same τ as before) and one based on "reject H_0 if $\tau^\dagger > 1.96$" with $\tau^\dagger := |\tau|$, both tests having the same $\alpha = 5\%$:

$$\Pr{}_{\mathrm{H}_0}(\tau > 1.65) = \Pr{}_{\mathrm{H}_0}(|\tau| > 1.96) \approx 0.05$$

from $\mathrm{N}_{0.95} \approx 1.65$ (see Chapter 4) and $\mathrm{N}_{0.975} = -\mathrm{N}_{0.025} \approx 1.96$. The second test is the one usually employed in elementary statistics for this two-sided context, and the reason is that the first test is biased in the setup of (14.9): if $\mu < \mu_0$, we have $\Pi_\tau < \alpha$ (this can be seen by comparing the striped areas of Figure 14.1 by shifting the H_1 density to the *left* of the H_0 density) and the test is biased. However, for $\mu > \mu_0$, we have $\Pi_\tau > \Pi_{\tau^\dagger}$ for all finite $\delta := \sqrt{n}\,(\mu - \mu_0)$ and τ has superior power there. The power functions are given by

$$\begin{aligned}\Pi_\tau &= \Pr{}_{\mathrm{H}_1}(\tau > 1.65) = \int_{1.65}^{\infty} \phi(u-\delta)\,\mathrm{d}u = \int_{1.65-\delta}^{\infty} \phi(v)\,\mathrm{d}v \\ &= 1 - \Phi(1.65-\delta) = \Phi(-1.65+\delta)\end{aligned} \tag{14.10}$$

and

$$\begin{aligned}\Pi_{\tau^\dagger} &= \Pr{}_{\mathrm{H}_1}(|\tau| > 1.96) = \left(\int_{-\infty}^{-1.96} + \int_{1.96}^{\infty}\right) \phi(u-\delta)\,\mathrm{d}u \\ &= \left(\int_{-\infty}^{-1.96-\delta} + \int_{1.96-\delta}^{\infty}\right) \phi(v)\,\mathrm{d}v = \Phi(-1.96-\delta) + 1 - \Phi(1.96-\delta) \\ &= \Phi(-1.96-\delta) + \Phi(-1.96+\delta).\end{aligned} \tag{14.11}$$

To illustrate, we plot these two power functions for $n = 9$ (hence $\delta = 3\,(\mu - \mu_0)$) in Figure 14.2, using a dashed line for Π_τ and a solid line for $\Pi_{\tau^\dagger}$. Both functions are equal to $\alpha = 5\%$ when $\delta = 0$, but neither power function dominates the other everywhere, if we allow the comparison of biased and unbiased tests: no UMP test exists in this two-sided

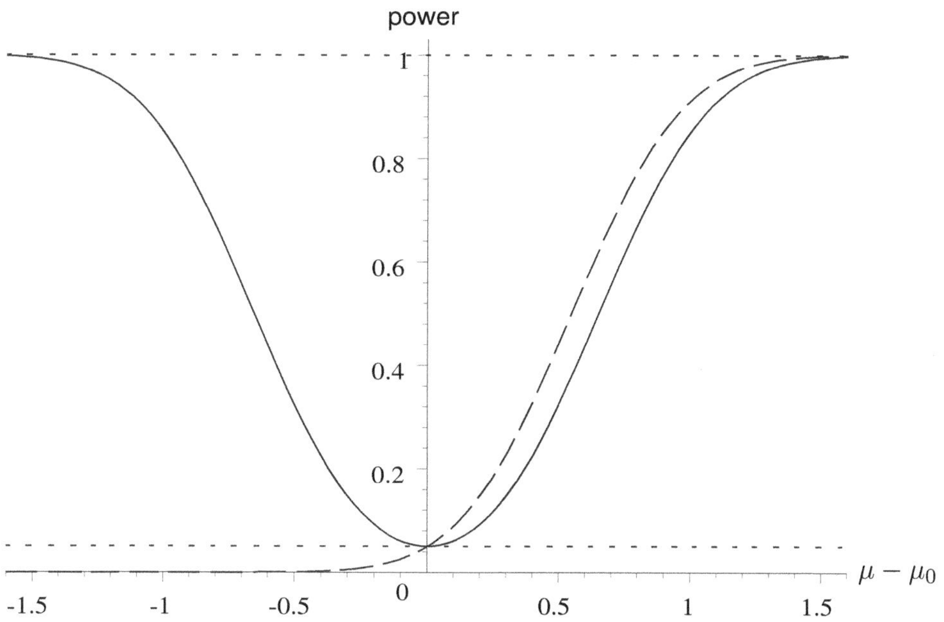

Figure 14.2. Power functions of τ (dashed) and $\tau^\dagger$ (solid). The test size $\alpha = 0.05$ is represented by a horizontal dotted line, and so is the maximum power of 1.

case. However, excluding biased tests, we can find a UMPU test and it is the one given here by $\tau^\dagger$, as we shall show in Exercise 14.29 for any test (we have compared only τ and $\tau^\dagger$ here). Note that the power function of the unbiased test has derivative zero at $\mu = \mu_0$, the function $\Pi_{\tau^\dagger}$ achieving its minimum at this point, a remark that will be useful in Exercises 14.29(b) and 14.32(b).

4. Consistency. As $n \to \infty$, a *consistent test* will have $\Pi \to 1$. The distributions of τ implied by each of H_0 and H_1 then become clearly distinguishable and have no area in common. Our earlier examples of τ for (14.6) and $\tau^\dagger$ for (14.9) illustrated this feature,[2] because $n \to \infty$ implied that $\delta \to \infty$ and $|\delta| \to \infty$, respectively. This can be seen in Figure 14.1, for example, by noting that a larger δ means an increase in the distance between the densities under H_0 and H_1, until they eventually separate as $\delta \to \infty$.

5. Invariance. There are many types of invariance argument. Here, we focus on only one, which is nevertheless different from that introduced in Chapter 11. We may require that the test (and the corresponding hypotheses) be *invariant to some group of transformations of the data*. This concept and its motivation are best illustrated by a series of examples. **(a)** The sample correlation coefficient is invariant to the group of increasing linear transformations of the data, and tests based on it will also be invariant to these transformations. For example, the strength of the linear relation between the temperatures in two places should not be affected by whether they are measured in degrees Fahrenheit or Celsius. This is a

[2] Note that τ of (14.7) is consistent for $H_1 : \mu \neq \mu_0$ of (14.9) in only one of the two directions of this H_1.

case of invariance to changes of location or (positive) scale.
(b) Another example is obtained by returning to Part A, in particular Chapters 6 and 8. Let the $n \times 1$ random vector $\boldsymbol{x}$ be distributed as $\boldsymbol{x} \sim \mathrm{N}(\mathbf{0}, \boldsymbol{I}_n)$, and take $\boldsymbol{T}$ to be any $n \times n$ orthogonal matrix. Then $\boldsymbol{z} := \boldsymbol{T}\boldsymbol{x} \neq \boldsymbol{x}$ in general, but fortunately the statistic (which measures the quadratic distance or squared length $\|\boldsymbol{x}\|^2$)

$$\tau := \boldsymbol{x}'\boldsymbol{x} = \boldsymbol{z}'\boldsymbol{T}\boldsymbol{T}'\boldsymbol{z} = \boldsymbol{z}'\boldsymbol{z} \sim \chi^2(n)$$

is invariant to orthogonal transformations of the data since τ based on $\boldsymbol{x}$ is the same as τ based on $\boldsymbol{z}$ (since $\boldsymbol{x}'\boldsymbol{x} = \boldsymbol{z}'\boldsymbol{z}$), and this invariance carries over to any test based on τ. This is an example of requiring invariance to changes of coordinates, by rotation and/or permutation, of the spherically distributed data vector $\boldsymbol{x}$. Otherwise, just reordering the elements of $\boldsymbol{x}$ would affect the outcome of the test!
(c) Let $\varepsilon_1, \dots, \varepsilon_n$ be an i.i.d. sequence. The joint density of the sequence is invariant to any permutation of its elements $\varepsilon_1, \dots, \varepsilon_n$, because they are independently and identically distributed. Premultiplying the $n \times 1$ vector $\boldsymbol{\varepsilon} := (\varepsilon_1, \dots, \varepsilon_n)'$ by a permutation matrix (which is a special case of an orthogonal matrix) leaves the likelihood function unchanged, and any test based on this likelihood (to be introduced below) will be invariant to the group of permutations of the data.

A test that is *uniformly most powerful invariant* (UMPI) to some class of data transformations is a test that is UMP within a class of tests sharing the same invariance property. Note, however, that UMPI tests are not necessarily admissible because invariance restricts the class of tests under consideration in the following way: there may exist a noninvariant UMP test that dominates a UMPI for all $\boldsymbol{\theta}$. Finally, regarding unbiasedness and invariance, one of these two properties sometimes does not help in finding a restricted UMP, while the other one does; for example, compare Exercises 14.36 and 14.37. But when UMPU and UMPI tests exist for the same problem, they often coincide; for example, compare Exercises 14.34 and 14.37 (for $k = 1$), or Exercises 14.35 and 14.38.

6. Similarity. We start with two examples that clarify the need for this property. First, as discussed after (14.4), there are many cases where the parameters of interest for H_0 are a subset of $\boldsymbol{\theta}$. The value taken by the nuisance parameters should not be relevant to the hypothesis, and the distribution of a "good" τ should not be affected by them when H_0 holds. Imagine if a distribution under H_0, like that on the left-hand side in Figure 14.1, kept shifting around as the nuisance parameters changed value (which was not the case in the nuisance-free example there): we would have difficulty controlling the Type I error α because the value of the nuisance parameters is unknown. Second, H_0 may not necessarily fix a unique value for the parameters of interest, such as in $\mathrm{H}_0 : \theta_1 + \theta_2 = 1$, and a good τ should not be affected by whether $(\theta_1, \theta_2) = (\frac{1}{2}, \frac{1}{2})$ or $(\theta_1, \theta_2) = (1, 0)$, since both are compatible with H_0 in this case.

In general, a good τ should not be affected by the values of $\boldsymbol{\theta}$ when H_0 holds (at least not on the boundary between Θ_0 and Θ_1, as will be discussed in the text around (14.15)). A test statistic whose distribution under H_0 is unaffected by $\boldsymbol{\theta}$ is *similar*, and the resulting critical regions are *similar regions*. We have already shown implicitly that the t-ratio (14.4), for the parameter of interest μ, satisfies this property of similarity with respect to the nuisance parameter σ; for example, replace μ by μ_0 in Exercise 9.13(b) to get the t-ratio (14.4). The same holds for its multivariate generalization into Hotelling's T^2; see Exercise 9.24. Notice that pivotality (see Chapter 13) is different from similarity: the latter requires a statistic (it contains no unknown parameters) and focuses on the distribution under H_0 only. For example, in spite of being similar, Hotelling's T^2 (and hence the t-ratio) has a distribution in Exercise 9.24 that depends on $\boldsymbol{\theta}$ through a noncentrality parameter arising under H_1.

Having listed some desirable properties, many of which revolve around power, the first question that arises is how to construct a UMP test, or more simply a most powerful test in the case of only two competing parameter values. The Neyman–Pearson lemma will give the answer in the easiest setting, that of the simple hypotheses $\text{H}_0 : \boldsymbol{\theta} = \boldsymbol{\theta}_0$ and $\text{H}_1 : \boldsymbol{\theta} = \boldsymbol{\theta}_1$, where $\boldsymbol{\theta}_0$ and $\boldsymbol{\theta}_1$ are vectors of known constant numbers. Informally, the lemma says that a most powerful test is given by the ratio of likelihoods $\wp := L(\boldsymbol{\theta}_0)/L(\boldsymbol{\theta}_1)$ or monotone transformations thereof (such as $\log(\wp)$), with a low $\wp$ (low likelihood of $\boldsymbol{\theta}_0$) leading to a rejection of H_0. Denoting the data matrix by $\boldsymbol{X}$, as in the earlier chapters of Part B, we can state the following.

Lemma (Neyman–Pearson). Let $\text{H}_0 : \boldsymbol{\theta} = \boldsymbol{\theta}_0$ and $\text{H}_1 : \boldsymbol{\theta} = \boldsymbol{\theta}_1$ both be simple hypotheses, with $L_0 := f_{\boldsymbol{X}}(\boldsymbol{X}; \boldsymbol{\theta}_0)$ and $L_1 := f_{\boldsymbol{X}}(\boldsymbol{X}; \boldsymbol{\theta}_1)$, respectively. If

$$\Pr{}_{\text{H}_0}(\boldsymbol{X} \in C_\alpha) = \alpha \in (0,1) \qquad \text{and} \qquad \wp := L_0/L_1 \begin{cases} < \gamma & (\boldsymbol{X} \in C_\alpha), \\ \geqslant \gamma & (\boldsymbol{X} \notin C_\alpha), \end{cases}$$

for some $\gamma > 0$, then $\wp$ (or any one-to-one transformation of it) is a most powerful test of size α, and the corresponding critical region C_α is an MPR of size α.

Consider the case $\boldsymbol{X} \notin C_\alpha$: the data do not fall in some critical region C_α and we do not reject H_0. In the lemma, this is a case where the data lead to a large L_0 relative to L_1, and the hypothesis H_0 (which gives rise to the former) is more likely than its competitor H_1. The hypotheses are simple, specifying the constants $\boldsymbol{\theta}_0, \boldsymbol{\theta}_1$, so L_0, L_1 are determined by the sample values of $\boldsymbol{X}$ and the decision is in terms of whether $\boldsymbol{X} \in C_\alpha$ or not (and the sample space partitioned accordingly, as seen in Exercises 11.16–11.18). Note that C_α is the critical region for $\boldsymbol{X}$, and $[0, \gamma)$ is the one for $\wp$. To illustrate, let $\{x_n\} \sim \text{IN}(\mu, 1)$ and take the simple hypotheses $\text{H}_0 : \mu = \mu_0$ and $\text{H}_1 : \mu = \mu_1$, where $\mu_1 > \mu_0$. Then

$$\begin{aligned} \wp &= \frac{\exp\left(\frac{1}{2}\sum_{i=1}^n (x_i - \mu_1)^2\right)}{\exp\left(\frac{1}{2}\sum_{i=1}^n (x_i - \mu_0)^2\right)} = \frac{\exp\left(\frac{1}{2}\sum_{i=1}^n ((x_i - \mu_0) + (\mu_0 - \mu_1))^2\right)}{\exp\left(\frac{1}{2}\sum_{i=1}^n (x_i - \mu_0)^2\right)} \\ &= \exp\left(\frac{1}{2}\sum_{i=1}^n (\mu_0 - \mu_1)^2 + (\mu_0 - \mu_1)\sum_{i=1}^n (x_i - \mu_0)\right) \\ &= \exp\left(\frac{n}{2}(\mu_0 - \mu_1)^2\right)\exp\left(n(\mu_0 - \mu_1)(\overline{x} - \mu_0)\right). \end{aligned} \tag{14.12}$$

Recalling that μ_0 and μ_1 are known constants, any decision rule based on rejecting H_0 if $\wp < \gamma$ (where γ is a known critical value of the test) is equivalent to a critical region based on $\overline{x}$ satisfying

$$\exp\left(n\left(\mu_0 - \mu_1\right)\left(\overline{x} - \mu_0\right)\right) < \gamma \exp\left(-\frac{n}{2}\left(\mu_0 - \mu_1\right)^2\right)$$

or, since $\mu_0 - \mu_1 < 0$,

$$\sqrt{n}\left(\overline{x} - \mu_0\right) > \frac{\log\left(\gamma\right) - \frac{n}{2}\left(\mu_0 - \mu_1\right)^2}{\sqrt{n}\left(\mu_0 - \mu_1\right)}, \tag{14.13}$$

which is exactly what we did in (14.7), albeit for the case of a composite H_1 there. From what we saw there, the critical region is determined by $\mathrm{N}(0,1)$, which does not change with μ_0 or μ_1, so the right-hand side of (14.13) is actually independent of these: γ is a combination of μ_0 and μ_1 that make the right-hand side of (14.13) free of these parameters; see Exercises 14.4 and 14.5 for further examples.

It turns out that extending the Neyman–Pearson lemma to more elaborate hypotheses is not necessarily feasible, except in some single-parameter cases or with some further restrictions on the multiparameter setup, as we shall see later in this introduction and in the exercises. For now, we focus on extending the use of the likelihood function in devising three widespread classical testing principles. Define

$$\mathrm{H}_0 : \boldsymbol{h}\left(\boldsymbol{\theta}\right) = \mathbf{0}_r \qquad (r \leqslant m), \tag{14.14}$$

where $\boldsymbol{h}\left(\cdot\right)$ is a continuously differentiable and deterministic function of the $m \times 1$ parameter vector $\boldsymbol{\theta}$. We also assume that the $r \times m$ matrix of partial derivatives $\partial \boldsymbol{h}\left(\boldsymbol{\theta}\right) / \partial \boldsymbol{\theta}'$ has rank r in the neighborhood of the true $\boldsymbol{\theta}$. Note that there are r hypotheses to be tested *jointly*, and they involve the m parameters in $\boldsymbol{\theta} := \left(\theta_1, \dots, \theta_m\right)'$; for example, we could be testing

$$\mathrm{H}_0 : \begin{pmatrix} \theta_1\theta_2 - \theta_3^2 \\ \theta_1 - \theta_3 - 1 \end{pmatrix} = \begin{pmatrix} 0 \\ 0 \end{pmatrix},$$

which is made up of the two hypotheses $\theta_1\theta_2 = \theta_3^2$ and $\theta_1 = \theta_3 + 1$; the rejection of H_0 would mean that *at least* one of the two does not hold (the negation of "A and B" is "not A or not B"). The alternative hypotheses that we consider initially are of the form $\mathrm{H}_1 : \boldsymbol{h}\left(\boldsymbol{\theta}\right) \neq \mathbf{0}_r$. One special case of the class of hypotheses in (14.14) is $\mathrm{H}_0 : \boldsymbol{\theta} = \boldsymbol{\theta}_0$, with $\mathrm{H}_1 : \boldsymbol{\theta} \neq \boldsymbol{\theta}_0$, and these are called *linear invertible* because they are linear in $\boldsymbol{\theta}$ and imply an invertible function $\boldsymbol{h}\left(\cdot\right)$. There are three main measures of the closeness of $\boldsymbol{\theta}_0$ to the parameter values implied by the data, and they give rise to the three main classical testing principles:

1. *Wald tests*: how far is $\boldsymbol{\theta}_0$ from some estimator $\widehat{\boldsymbol{\theta}}$, typically the MLE?
2. *Likelihood-ratio tests*: how large is the maximum value of the likelihood when H_0 holds, relative to its maximum unrestricted value when either H_0 or H_1 holds?
3. *Score tests*: how far is $\boldsymbol{q}(\boldsymbol{\theta}_0)$ from $\mathbf{0}$, where $\mathbf{0}$ is the value of the score at the MLE $\boldsymbol{q}(\widehat{\boldsymbol{\theta}}_{\mathrm{ML}})$ when regularity conditions are met?

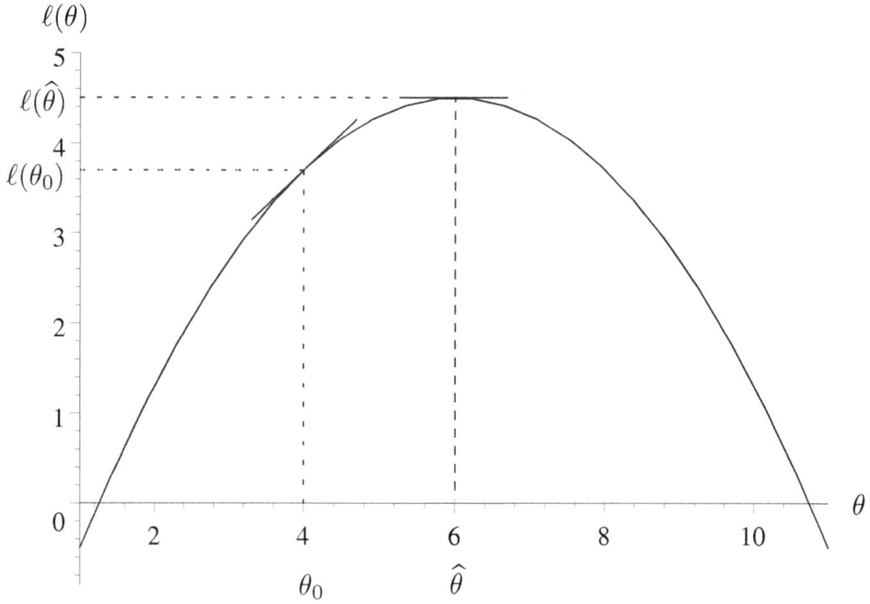

Figure 14.3. The log-likelihood of θ, denoted by $\ell(\theta)$, has a maximum at $\widehat{\theta}$. The value θ_0 is hypothesized by $\mathrm{H}_0 : \theta = \theta_0$. The two tangents illustrate the log-likelihood's slope (which is the score $q(\theta)$) at the points $\widehat{\theta}$ and θ_0, with $q(\widehat{\theta}) \equiv 0$.

These are illustrated graphically in the case $m = 1$ in Figure 14.3, where the log-likelihood $\ell(\theta)$ is on the vertical axis as a function of θ. As listed above, there are three ways to measure the distance between H_0 and H_1. The first is based on the horizontal distance between θ_0 and $\widehat{\theta}$ (the MLE in this case), while the second is based on the vertical distance between $\ell(\theta_0)$ and $\ell(\widehat{\theta})$. The first two ways measure distances along the axes, but the third one goes along the curve itself by comparing the slope of the log-likelihood at θ_0 (which is $q(\theta_0)$) to the value 0 that arises at the maximum of the log-likelihood at $\widehat{\theta}$. We now illustrate each of these three testing principles for the pair $\mathrm{H}_0 : \boldsymbol{\theta} = \boldsymbol{\theta}_0$ and $\mathrm{H}_1 : \boldsymbol{\theta} \neq \boldsymbol{\theta}_0$.

Suppose that a consistent estimator $\widehat{\boldsymbol{\theta}}$ has the distribution $\widehat{\boldsymbol{\theta}} \sim \mathrm{N}(\boldsymbol{\theta}, \boldsymbol{\Omega})$, where $\boldsymbol{\Omega}$ is nonsingular. Then, the *Wald statistic* (W) is the quadratic form that is based on standardizing, by $\mathrm{var}(\widehat{\boldsymbol{\theta}})$, the quadratic distance between $\widehat{\boldsymbol{\theta}}$ and $\boldsymbol{\theta}_0$ (see the Mahalanobis distance in Chapter 6):

$$W := \left(\widehat{\boldsymbol{\theta}} - \boldsymbol{\theta}_0\right)' \boldsymbol{\Omega}^{-1} \left(\widehat{\boldsymbol{\theta}} - \boldsymbol{\theta}_0\right) \sim \chi^2(m, \delta),$$

with noncentrality parameter $\delta := (\boldsymbol{\theta} - \boldsymbol{\theta}_0)' \boldsymbol{\Omega}^{-1} (\boldsymbol{\theta} - \boldsymbol{\theta}_0)$ as in Exercise 8.28, and we get a large value of δ if the true $\boldsymbol{\theta}$ is far from the hypothesized $\boldsymbol{\theta}_0$. This is the quadratic (and multivariate) version of tests of the form

$$\frac{\widehat{\theta} - \theta_0}{\sqrt{\mathrm{var}(\widehat{\theta})}}$$

seen earlier in this chapter. As in the univariate case, if $\mathrm{var}(\widehat{\boldsymbol{\theta}})$ contains unknown parameters, then it is replaced by a consistent estimator and we resort to Slutsky's lemma (Exercise 10.18) for the limiting distribution. For example, if the usual regularity conditions of Chapter 12 are fulfilled, $\widehat{\boldsymbol{\theta}}_{\mathrm{ML}} \overset{a}{\sim} \mathrm{N}(\boldsymbol{\theta}, \boldsymbol{\mathcal{I}}^{-1})$ and one needs to replace $\boldsymbol{\Omega}^{-1}$ in W by a consistent estimator of $\boldsymbol{\mathcal{I}}$, usually[3] $\widehat{\boldsymbol{\mathcal{I}}} := \boldsymbol{\mathcal{I}}(\widehat{\boldsymbol{\theta}})$, which is the information matrix evaluated at $\boldsymbol{\theta} = \widehat{\boldsymbol{\theta}}$. However, the resulting exact distribution of W is affected, as we shall see in the exercises and as we have already seen in the univariate examples given earlier (the normal distribution arose when σ was known, as opposed to Student's t when σ was unknown and we used s to estimate it). Even in the context of the general $\mathrm{H}_0 : \boldsymbol{h}(\boldsymbol{\theta}) = \mathbf{0}_r$ of (14.14), which we shall encounter in Exercise 14.18, to compute W we need only to estimate $\widehat{\boldsymbol{\theta}}$ without imposing the restrictions that H_0 implies on the estimator of $\boldsymbol{\theta}$. This is by design, and it is usually not the case for the next test which typically requires both restricted and unrestricted estimation of the likelihoods. Notice also that W is obtainable through likelihood-based approximations, as was hinted by the expansions in Exercises 12.25(a) and 12.28(a).

Define the *generalized likelihood ratio* (GLR) *statistic*

$$\wp := \frac{\sup_{\boldsymbol{\theta} \in \Theta_0} L(\boldsymbol{\theta})}{\sup_{\boldsymbol{\theta} \in \Theta_0 \cup \Theta_1} L(\boldsymbol{\theta})},$$

and the corresponding $LR := -2\log(\wp)$. In the case of our hypotheses $\mathrm{H}_0 : \boldsymbol{\theta} = \boldsymbol{\theta}_0$ and $\mathrm{H}_1 : \boldsymbol{\theta} \neq \boldsymbol{\theta}_0$ (hence $\Theta_0 \cup \Theta_1 = \Theta$), it specializes to

$$LR = -2\log\left(\frac{L(\boldsymbol{\theta}_0)}{L(\widehat{\boldsymbol{\theta}}_{\mathrm{ML}})}\right) = 2\left(\ell(\widehat{\boldsymbol{\theta}}_{\mathrm{ML}}) - \ell(\boldsymbol{\theta}_0)\right).$$

This generalized $\wp$ is essentially a generalized (for composite H_1) version of the $\wp$ of the Neyman–Pearson lemma, and thus is possibly a "good" test in spite of the different setting; the adjective "generalized" is often dropped when obviated by the context of composite hypotheses. Since the H_0-restricted maximum of $L(\boldsymbol{\theta})$ cannot exceed the unrestricted maximum, now $\wp \in [0, 1]$.

Finally, we know from Chapter 12 that $\boldsymbol{q}(\boldsymbol{\theta}) \overset{a}{\sim} \mathrm{N}(\mathbf{0}, \boldsymbol{\mathcal{I}})$ when regularity conditions hold, so $\boldsymbol{q}(\boldsymbol{\theta}_0) \overset{a}{\sim} \mathrm{N}(\mathbf{0}, \boldsymbol{\mathcal{I}})$ if the null hypothesis is correct. The standardized quadratic distance between $\boldsymbol{q}(\widehat{\boldsymbol{\theta}}_{\mathrm{ML}}) \equiv \mathbf{0}$ (by definition) and $\boldsymbol{q}(\boldsymbol{\theta}_0)$ is the *score* (or *Lagrange multiplier*) *statistic*

$$LM := \boldsymbol{q}(\boldsymbol{\theta}_0)' \boldsymbol{\mathcal{I}}(\boldsymbol{\theta}_0)^{-1} \boldsymbol{q}(\boldsymbol{\theta}_0),$$

where we denote H_0-restricted estimators by a tilde while using hats for unrestricted estimators; for example, $\widetilde{\boldsymbol{\mathcal{I}}} := \boldsymbol{\mathcal{I}}(\boldsymbol{\theta}_0)$. Note that it is sufficient to compute H_0-restricted quantities in order to calculate LM; compare with the two earlier statistics. The reason for the name LM is that the statistic arises equivalently (in this context) from a Lagrangian

[3]See the Notes to Chapter 12 for a counterexample.

optimization problem. This will be detailed in the exercises, where it will also be shown that the score test is equivalent to the other two procedures asymptotically (but not necessarily in finite samples) under H_0, where they all share a common $\chi^2(m)$ distribution. In the exercises, we will also investigate the properties of the three classical tests for the more general hypotheses in (14.14), as well as for alternatives H_1 that contain multivariate inequalities.

We now turn to some further optimality analysis. Let us start with the Neyman–Pearson lemma again and consider $\wp := L(\boldsymbol{\theta}_0)/L(\boldsymbol{\theta}_1)$. Neyman's factorization theorem (Chapter 11) implies directly that the ratio of densities $\wp$ will depend only on $\boldsymbol{\theta}$ and the sufficient statistic, hence basing UMP tests on the latter; this is shown in Exercise 14.23. This allows us to consider an extension of the Neyman–Pearson lemma to single-parameter one-sided composite hypotheses. But first, we need the following definition. A class of densities $f_z(w;\theta)$ is said to have a *monotone likelihood ratio* (MLR) if, for every $\theta_2 > \theta_1$, the ratio $f_z(z;\theta_2)/f_z(z;\theta_1)$ is a monotone function of z over the set where numerator and denominator are not both zero. (There is zero probability that z takes values from a set where $f = 0$ for both θ_1 and θ_2.) To simplify this paragraph and the next, we will take monotone to mean nondecreasing, as nonincreasing would yield the same results but with the inequalities reversed. The MLR property can therefore be rewritten as follows:

$$\log \frac{f_z(z;\theta_2)}{f_z(z;\theta_1)} = \log f_z(z;\theta_2) - \log f_z(z;\theta_1)$$

is nondecreasing in z for every $\theta_2 - \theta_1 > 0$. It is satisfied if $\partial \log f_z(z;\theta)/\partial\theta$ is nondecreasing in z for all θ, or if $\partial^2 \log f_z(z;\theta)/\partial\theta\partial z \geqslant 0$ for all θ, z with probability 1.

Now suppose that our sample $\boldsymbol{X}$ has density f depending on a parameter θ. Let z be a sufficient statistic for θ and assume that $f_z(w;\theta)$ has an MLR. Then the *Karlin–Rubin theorem* (Exercise 14.25) states that a test rejecting H_0 when $z > w_0$ is UMP of size $\alpha = \Pr_{\theta_c}(z > w_0)$ for testing $H_0 : \theta \leqslant \theta_c$ against $H_1 : \theta > \theta_c$, where we note that the probability $\Pr_{\theta_c}$ is evaluated at $\theta = \theta_c$ and not at any other point in Θ_0. Similarly, for testing $H_0 : \theta \geqslant \theta_c$ against $H_1 : \theta < \theta_c$, a test rejecting H_0 when $z < w_0$ is UMP.

This optimality result also holds for testing $H_0 : \theta = \theta_0$ against $H_1 : \theta > \theta_0$. However, it does not apply to testing the harder problem of $H_0 : \theta = \theta_0$ against $H_1 : \theta \neq \theta_0$: there is no UMP test, as seen earlier in connection with the example in Figure 14.2 and its discussion in Property 3. We need to restrict our attention to the class of unbiased tests if we are to make progress. The following approach suggests a way to obtain UMPU tests, when they exist, by making use of the more easily verifiable property of similarity.

Suppose that a sufficient statistic $\boldsymbol{z}$ exists when $\boldsymbol{\theta}$ is on the boundary between Θ_0 and Θ_1, denoted by Θ_{01}. A test τ is said to possess a *Neyman structure* with respect to $\boldsymbol{z}$ if

$$\Pi_\tau(\boldsymbol{\theta}; \boldsymbol{z}) := \Pr_{\boldsymbol{\theta}}(\boldsymbol{X} \in C_\alpha \mid \boldsymbol{z}) \tag{14.15}$$

is constant almost surely (recall that $\boldsymbol{z}$ is random and that this conditional probability is a function of it in general) when $\boldsymbol{\theta} \in \Theta_{01}$. Taking expectations with respect to $\boldsymbol{z}$, this property implies that the unconditional $\Pi_{\tau}(\boldsymbol{\theta})$ takes the same constant value for all $\boldsymbol{\theta} \in \Theta_{01}$. The Neyman structure therefore implies the similarity of τ for $\boldsymbol{\theta} \in \Theta_{01}$. In fact, subject to the additional assumption that $\boldsymbol{z}$ is boundedly complete (a weaker requirement than completeness) in Θ_{01}, this implication becomes an equivalence, as shown in Exercise 14.30. It remains for us to link this property with UMPU tests.

If τ is size-α unbiased (hence $\Pi \geqslant \alpha$ in Θ_1) and $\Pi(\boldsymbol{\theta})$ is a continuous function of $\boldsymbol{\theta}$ then, as $\boldsymbol{\theta}$ approaches the boundary between Θ_0 and Θ_1, we must obtain the value $\Pi = \alpha$ (the size of τ) on Θ_{01}; so all these unbiased τ tests are size-α similar on this boundary Θ_{01} where

$$\{\text{unbiased } \tau\} \subseteq \{\text{similar tests}\}.$$

Hence, finding a UMP among the more easily verifiable class of similar tests of size α on Θ_{01}, uniformity means that this UMP test cannot have a lower power than τ somewhere (as would be the case with a biased test): the outcome will be a UMPU test of size α. Furthermore, finding UMP tests within those possessing the Neyman structure simplifies the task because of the conditioning on $\boldsymbol{z}$ in (14.15): it can reduce composite to simple hypotheses and/or reduce the dimension of a multiparameter problem that contains nuisance parameters to a smaller dimension. For an illustration of these reductions, see Exercises 14.31 and 14.32 (with subsequent applications). To illustrate, in particular, the former reduction of hypotheses, consider testing the composite $\mathrm{H}_0 : p_1 = p_2$ for the multinomials of Exercise 6.32, where conditioning on $x_1 + x_2 = t$ simplifies the density under H_0 to

$$\Pr(x_1 = s \mid x_1 + x_2 = t) = \binom{t}{s}\left(\frac{1}{2}\right)^t \qquad (s = 0, 1, \dots, t),$$

hence reducing it to a test of the simple hypothesis $\mathrm{H}_0' : p = \frac{1}{2}$ in a binomial density. Note that $x_1 + x_2$ is not a sufficient statistic in general, but it *is* sufficient on the boundary $p_1 = p_2$ where conditioning on it gets rid of $\boldsymbol{\theta} := (p_1, p_2)'$ from the density of the data.

The final part of this chapter is about *distribution-free methods*: they do not presuppose that the data are drawn from a particular distribution. They are therefore robust to violations of parametric assumptions, but this comes at the cost of some loss of efficiency relative to tests where the distribution is known (correctly) to belong to a specific family. (The relative efficiency of tests will be defined in Exercise 14.39.) In many cases to be seen in Section 14.4, it turns out that the maximum loss of efficiency is actually quite small, even in relative terms, while the gains can be unlimited if one of the parametric assumptions is wrong. (Precursors to the results in Section 14.4 have been studied in Section 9.3 and in Exercises 10.30 and 13.36.) Such *nonparametric tests* are therefore quite attractive, and we present tests relating to hypotheses of: (i) the independence of variates x and y; and (ii) the equality of distributions F_x and F_y. We also present a class of tests relating to how close a variate's distribution F is to a prespecified function F_0, known as *goodness-of-fit tests*. Such tests rely on estimating F by the EDF $\widehat{F}_n$ and calculating the weighted average of the squared deviations

$$D_n := \int_{-\infty}^{\infty} \left(\widehat{F}_n(u) - F_0(u)\right)^2 w(u)\,\mathrm{d}F_0(u), \tag{14.16}$$

where $w(u)$ is a chosen nonrandom weight function (this is in addition to the probability-determined weights implied by $\mathrm{d}F_0(u)$, specializing to $f_0(u)\,\mathrm{d}u$ in the continuous case), of which two examples are the statistics of *Cramér and von Mises* for $w(u) = 1$ or of *Anderson and Darling* for

$$w(u) = \frac{1}{F_0(u)\,(1 - F_0(u))},$$

the latter giving more weight to tails where either F_0 or $1 - F_0$ are small. Unlike the Kolmogorov–Smirnov statistic seen in the Notes to Chapter 10, the statistic D_n takes the weighted average over all points $u \in \mathbb{R}$, rather than a maximal deviation, and D_n is therefore better behaved and has a rate of convergence n instead of $\sqrt{n}$; see Exercise 14.45 for these rates and for the invariance of the distribution of D_n with respect to F_0 in the continuous case.

The exercises in this chapter are classified into four sections, starting with basic results, then studying the various tests that have been introduced here, before going on to a more challenging investigation of some aspects of optimality, and concluding with distribution-free methods. In this chapter, we introduce an additional notation for the asymptotic equality of two statistics τ_1 and τ_2, namely $\tau_1 \overset{a}{=} \tau_2$ as a shorthand for $\tau_1 = \tau_2\,(1 + o_p\,(1))$.

14.1 Basic results

Exercise 14.1 (Binomial drug, tested!) A standard drug is known to cure 80% of patients suffering from a disease. A new drug cures 85 patients out of 100 in a trial. Use a large-sample test of the hypothesis that the new drug is better, taking $\alpha = 5\%$ as the probability of a Type I error. Are your conclusions altered if you take $\alpha = 2.5\%$ instead?

Solution

This is a setup we have seen before in Exercises 4.3 and 13.38. The latter exercise showed that, in large samples,

$$n\frac{\widehat{p} - p}{\sqrt{\widehat{p}\,(1 - \widehat{p})}} \overset{a}{\sim} \mathrm{N}(0,1).$$

Now, $n = 100, \widehat{p} = 85\%$, and we have $\mathrm{H}_0 : p = 80\%$ against $\mathrm{H}_1 : p > 80\%$. Our test is therefore based on comparing

$$\tau := n\frac{\widehat{p} - p_0}{\sqrt{\widehat{p}\,(1 - \widehat{p})}} = 100\frac{0.85 - 0.8}{\sqrt{(0.85)\,(0.15)}} \approx 14.00$$

with the critical value $\mathrm{N}_{0.95} \approx 1.65$. Clearly, τ is much larger than 1.65 and falls in the critical region, so we reject the null hypothesis at the 5% level and conclude that the new drug is significantly better.

Using $\alpha = 2.5\%$ instead does not alter our conclusions in this case, since $\mathrm{N}_{0.975} \approx 1.96$ still implies that $\tau = 14$ falls in the critical region. In general, it is harder to reject H_0 if α is smaller, although in the present case there was no difference in the conclusion of the tests.

Another way to approach the question about α and significance is to use "p-values" (notice that this p is not in italics, unlike the previous ones which are unrelated to this p). The p-value is defined as the size (or area) of the critical region delimited by the actual value of τ. It can be viewed as the value of α that would take H_0 to a borderline rejection. Here, the region is the interval $(14, \infty)$ and the p-value is the probability (under H_0) of having values in this interval, namely

$$\Pr_{\mathrm{H}_0}(\tau > 14) = 1 - \Phi(14) \approx 8 \times 10^{-45}$$

by Exercise 10.40(b), so we know that even an α value as low as 1% would have led to a rejection of H_0!

Exercise 14.2 (Testing the mean: multivariate) Suppose that we have a sequence of $m \times 1$ vectors $\{\boldsymbol{x}_n\} \sim \mathrm{IN}(\boldsymbol{\mu}, \boldsymbol{\Sigma})$, where $\boldsymbol{\Sigma}$ is nonsingular and known, but $\boldsymbol{\mu}$ is unknown. This generalizes to m dimensions the typical example used in the introduction to this chapter. Using the sample mean $\overline{\boldsymbol{x}}$, design a Wald-type test of

$$\mathrm{H}_0 : \boldsymbol{\mu} = \boldsymbol{\mu}_0 \qquad \text{against} \qquad \mathrm{H}_1 : \boldsymbol{\mu} \neq \boldsymbol{\mu}_0,$$

where $\boldsymbol{\mu}_0$ is a vector of constants.

Solution

Using the same derivations as in the introduction, but this time with vectors, we get

$$\overline{\boldsymbol{x}} := \frac{1}{n}\sum_{i=1}^{n} \boldsymbol{x}_i \sim \mathrm{N}\left(\boldsymbol{\mu}, \frac{1}{n}\boldsymbol{\Sigma}\right).$$

Defining

$$W := (\overline{\boldsymbol{x}} - \boldsymbol{\mu}_0)' \left(\mathrm{var}\left(\overline{\boldsymbol{x}}\right)\right)^{-1} (\overline{\boldsymbol{x}} - \boldsymbol{\mu}_0) = n\left(\overline{\boldsymbol{x}} - \boldsymbol{\mu}_0\right)' \boldsymbol{\Sigma}^{-1} (\overline{\boldsymbol{x}} - \boldsymbol{\mu}_0),$$

Exercise 8.28 gives $W \sim \chi^2(m, \delta)$, where $\delta := n\left(\boldsymbol{\mu} - \boldsymbol{\mu}_0\right)' \boldsymbol{\Sigma}^{-1} (\boldsymbol{\mu} - \boldsymbol{\mu}_0)$. We notice that δ/n is the Mahalanobis distance between $\boldsymbol{\mu}_1$ and $\boldsymbol{\mu}_2$, which can also be formulated as twice the Kullback–Leibler distance $\mathrm{KL}(f_0, f_1)$ in the normal setup; see Exercise 8.12. When $\mathrm{H}_0 : \boldsymbol{\mu} = \boldsymbol{\mu}_0$ is correct, $\delta = 0$ and we get the central $\chi^2(m)$ distribution for W. However, when $\mathrm{H}_1 : \boldsymbol{\mu} \neq \boldsymbol{\mu}_0$ holds, $W \sim \chi^2(m, \delta)$ with $\delta > 0$. Note that the value of δ changes with n, $\boldsymbol{\mu} - \boldsymbol{\mu}_0$, and $\boldsymbol{\Sigma}$. Furthermore, for given values of $\boldsymbol{\mu}_0, \boldsymbol{\mu}$ $(\boldsymbol{\mu} \neq \boldsymbol{\mu}_0)$, and $\boldsymbol{\Sigma}$, we have $\delta \to \infty$ as $n \to \infty$ and the test is consistent, a property that we will see in a more general setup in the next exercise. Recall that, as δ increases, the distribution is centered further to the right; see Figure 4.5 of Exercise 4.14(e).

Notice the resemblance of this W to Hotelling's T^2 (studied in Chapter 9):

$$T^2 := n\left(\overline{\boldsymbol{x}} - \boldsymbol{\mu}_0\right)' \boldsymbol{S}^{-1}\left(\overline{\boldsymbol{x}} - \boldsymbol{\mu}_0\right),$$

where the sample variance matrix $\boldsymbol{S}$ is used when $\boldsymbol{\Sigma}$ is unknown; compare with the univariate cases of σ^2 known or unknown, given in the introduction. As in the univariate case (normal versus Student's t), the finite-sample distributions are different for W and T^2. For the equality of their asymptotic distributions, compare the results here with Exercise 9.24, by means of Exercise 10.32(d). We shall return to T^2 in Exercises 14.13, 14.28, and 14.37.

Exercise 14.3 (Unbiasedness, power monotonicity, and consistency of χ^2-based tests) Consider the power function

$$\Pi(\delta) := \Pr\left(z > \chi^2_{1-\alpha}(m)\right),$$

where $z \sim \chi^2(m, \delta)$, $m \in \mathbb{N}$, $\alpha \in (0, 1)$, and $\chi^2_{1-\alpha}(m)$ is the $1 - \alpha$ quantile of the $\chi^2(m)$ distribution. Show that $\Pi(\delta)$ is increasing in δ, with $\Pi(0) = \alpha$ and $\Pi(\delta) \to 1$ as $\delta \to \infty$. [Hint: Decompose z by Exercise 7.3(a) into the sum of independent $y := \chi^2(1, \delta)$ and $x := \chi^2(m-1)$ for $m > 1$, write

$$\Pi(\delta) = \mathrm{E}_x\left(\Pr\left(y > \chi^2_{1-\alpha}(m) - x \mid x\right)\right) = 1 - \mathrm{E}_x\left(F_{y|x}\left(\chi^2_{1-\alpha}(m) - x\right)\right)$$

by the representation of joint c.d.f.s seen in Chapter 6, then consider the derivative of F (which is in Exercise 4.25) as δ changes.]

Solution

For $m > 1$, using the hint in the question and $v := \chi^2_{1-\alpha}(m) - x$ gives

$$\Pi(\delta) = 1 - \mathrm{E}_x\left(F_{y|x}(v)\right) = 1 - \mathrm{E}_x\left(\Phi\left(-\sqrt{\delta} + \sqrt{v}\right) - \Phi\left(-\sqrt{\delta} - \sqrt{v}\right)\right),$$

where $F_{y|x}$ is obtained from Exercise 4.25. By the chain rule,

$$\frac{\mathrm{d}\Pi(\delta)}{\mathrm{d}\delta} = \frac{1}{2\sqrt{\delta}} \mathrm{E}_x\left(\phi\left(-\sqrt{\delta} + \sqrt{v}\right) - \phi\left(-\sqrt{\delta} - \sqrt{v}\right)\right),$$

where we can interchange expectation and derivative because the density of x does not depend on δ. Now $\phi(u)$ is decreasing in $|u|$, so $\phi(-\sqrt{\delta} + \sqrt{v}) > \phi(-\sqrt{\delta} - \sqrt{v})$ when δ is positive and finite, implying that $\mathrm{d}\Pi(\delta)/\mathrm{d}\delta > 0$ since the expectation of a positive variate is positive. For $m = 1$, simpler derivations apply, along the same lines, since we have

$$\Pi(\delta) = 1 - F_y(v)$$

with $v = \chi^2_{1-\alpha}(1)$ and $y = z$.

Now, we complete the question by working out the values of $\Pi(0)$ and $\Pi(\infty)$. First, $\delta = 0$ gives $z \sim \chi^2(m, 0) \sim \chi^2(m)$; hence $\Pi(0) = \Pr\left(z > \chi^2_{1-\alpha}(m)\right) = \alpha$, by definition of the $\chi^2(m)$ quantile. Second,

$$\lim_{\delta\to\infty} \Pi(\delta) = 1 - \lim_{\delta\to\infty} \mathrm{E}_x\left(\Phi\left(-\sqrt{\delta} + \sqrt{v}\right) - \Phi\left(-\sqrt{\delta} - \sqrt{v}\right)\right) = 1,$$

by $\Phi(-\infty) = 0$, as required.

Exercise 14.4 (Neyman–Pearson: normal) Let $x_1, \dots, x_n$ be a random sample from $\mathrm{N}(0, \sigma^2)$. Derive a most powerful test of size α for $\mathrm{H}_0 : \sigma^2 = \sigma_0^2$ against $\mathrm{H}_1 : \sigma^2 = \sigma_1^2$, where $0 < \sigma_1^2 < \sigma_0^2$.

Solution
Applying the Neyman–Pearson lemma, the ratio of likelihoods is

$$\wp = \frac{\left(\sigma_0\sqrt{2\pi}\right)^{-n} \exp\left(-\frac{1}{2\sigma_0^2}\sum_{i=1}^n x_i^2\right)}{\left(\sigma_1\sqrt{2\pi}\right)^{-n} \exp\left(-\frac{1}{2\sigma_1^2}\sum_{i=1}^n x_i^2\right)} = \left(\frac{\sigma_1}{\sigma_0}\right)^n \exp\left(\frac{1}{2}\left(\frac{1}{\sigma_1^2} - \frac{1}{\sigma_0^2}\right)\sum_{i=1}^n x_i^2\right).$$

Rejecting H_0 if $\wp < \gamma$ is equivalent to rejecting it if

$$\sum_{i=1}^n x_i^2 < \frac{2\log\left(\left(\sigma_1/\sigma_0\right)^{-n}\gamma\right)}{\sigma_1^{-2} - \sigma_0^{-2}}$$

since $\sigma_1^{-2} - \sigma_0^{-2} > 0$. Note that $n^{-1}\sum_{i=1}^n x_i^2$ is an estimator of the variance (because the mean is known to be zero), and we reject H_0 in favor of H_1 if this estimator is small, hence focusing on the lower tail of the distribution of $\sum_{i=1}^n x_i^2$. We know that $\sum_{i=1}^n x_i^2/\sigma_0^2 \sim \chi^2(n)$ under H_0, so γ is obtained from the α quantile $\chi^2_\alpha(n)$ by the relation

$$\chi^2_\alpha(n) = \frac{2\log\left(\left(\sigma_1/\sigma_0\right)^{-n}\gamma\right)}{\sigma_0^2\left(\sigma_1^{-2} - \sigma_0^{-2}\right)}$$

or

$$\gamma = \left(\frac{\sigma_1}{\sigma_0}\right)^n \exp\left(\frac{1}{2}\left(\frac{1}{\sigma_1^2} - \frac{1}{\sigma_0^2}\right)\sigma_0^2\chi^2_\alpha(n)\right),$$

where $\chi^2_\alpha(n), \sigma_0, \sigma_1$ are all known constants.

Exercise 14.5 (Neyman–Pearson: gamma) Let $x_1, \dots, x_n$ be a random sample from

$$f_x(u) = \theta^2 u \mathrm{e}^{-\theta u}$$

for $u \in \mathbb{R}_+$. Derive a most powerful test of size α for $\mathrm{H}_0 : \theta = \theta_0$ against $\mathrm{H}_1 : \theta = \theta_1$, where $\theta_1 > \theta_0 > 0$.

Solution
This is the density $x \sim \mathrm{Gam}(2, \theta)$. The ratio of likelihoods is

$$\wp = \frac{\theta_0^{2n}\left(\prod_{i=1}^n x_i\right)\exp\left(-\theta_0\sum_{i=1}^n x_i\right)}{\theta_1^{2n}\left(\prod_{i=1}^n x_i\right)\exp\left(-\theta_1\sum_{i=1}^n x_i\right)} = \left(\frac{\theta_0}{\theta_1}\right)^{2n} \exp\left(\left(\theta_1 - \theta_0\right)\sum_{i=1}^n x_i\right),$$

where $\sum_{i=1}^n x_i = n\overline{x} \sim \mathrm{Gam}(2n, \theta_0)$ and $z := 2\theta_0\sum_{i=1}^n x_i \sim \chi^2(4n)$ under H_0; see Exercises 7.18(a) and 7.19(a), respectively. Rejecting H_0 if $\wp < \gamma$ is equivalent to rejecting it if

$$z < \frac{2\theta_0\log\left(\left(\theta_0/\theta_1\right)^{-2n}\gamma\right)}{\theta_1 - \theta_0}$$

since $\theta_1 - \theta_0 > 0$. Rejecting when z is small means that we focus on the lower tail of the χ^2, and we have the correspondence

$$\chi^2_\alpha(4n) = \frac{2\theta_0 \log\left((\theta_0/\theta_1)^{-2n}\gamma\right)}{\theta_1 - \theta_0}$$

or

$$\gamma = \left(\frac{\theta_0}{\theta_1}\right)^{2n} \exp\left(\left(\frac{\theta_1}{\theta_0} - 1\right)\frac{\chi^2_\alpha(4n)}{2}\right).$$

Exercise 14.6 (Neyman–Pearson: two normals) Let $x_1 \sim \mathrm{N}(\mu, \sigma^2)$ independently of $x_2 \sim \mathrm{N}(2\mu, \sigma^2)$, with $\sigma^2 > 0$ and known. Derive a most powerful test of size α for $\mathrm{H}_0 : \mu = \mu_0$ against $\mathrm{H}_1 : \mu = \mu_1$, where $\mu_1 < \mu_0$.

Solution

Applying the Neyman–Pearson lemma, the ratio of likelihoods is

$$\begin{aligned}
\wp &= \frac{\frac{1}{\sigma\sqrt{2\pi}} \exp\left(-\frac{(x_1-\mu_0)^2}{2\sigma^2}\right) \frac{1}{\sigma\sqrt{2\pi}} \exp\left(-\frac{(x_2-2\mu_0)^2}{2\sigma^2}\right)}{\frac{1}{\sigma\sqrt{2\pi}} \exp\left(-\frac{(x_1-\mu_1)^2}{2\sigma^2}\right) \frac{1}{\sigma\sqrt{2\pi}} \exp\left(-\frac{(x_2-2\mu_1)^2}{2\sigma^2}\right)} \\
&= \exp\left(-\frac{(x_1-\mu_0)^2 - (x_1-\mu_1)^2 + (x_2-2\mu_0)^2 - (x_2-2\mu_1)^2}{2\sigma^2}\right) \\
&= \exp\left(\frac{x_1\mu_0 - x_1\mu_1 + 2x_2\mu_0 - 2x_2\mu_1}{\sigma^2} - \frac{\mu_0^2 - \mu_1^2 + 4\mu_0^2 - 4\mu_1^2}{2\sigma^2}\right) \\
&= \exp\left(\frac{\mu_0 - \mu_1}{\sigma}\left(\frac{x_1 + 2x_2}{\sigma} - 5\frac{\mu_0 + \mu_1}{2\sigma}\right)\right).
\end{aligned}$$

Since $x_1 + 2x_2 \sim \mathrm{N}(5\mu, 5\sigma^2)$, we have that under H_0

$$z := \frac{x_1 + 2x_2 - 5\mu_0}{\sigma\sqrt{5}} \sim \mathrm{N}(0,1).$$

Hence, rejecting H_0 if $\wp < \gamma$ is equivalent to rejecting it if

$$\exp\left(\frac{\mu_0 - \mu_1}{\sigma}\sqrt{5}\left(\left(z + \sqrt{5}\frac{\mu_0}{\sigma}\right) - \sqrt{5}\frac{\mu_0 + \mu_1}{2\sigma}\right)\right) < \gamma$$

or, since $\mu_0 - \mu_1 > 0$,

$$z < \sqrt{5}\frac{\mu_1 - \mu_0}{2\sigma} + \frac{\sigma \log(\gamma)}{(\mu_0 - \mu_1)\sqrt{5}}$$

and we can use the N_α quantile for this purpose.

***Exercise 14.7 (Neyman–Pearson lemma)** Let $\mathrm{H}_0 : \boldsymbol{\theta} = \boldsymbol{\theta}_0$ and $\mathrm{H}_1 : \boldsymbol{\theta} = \boldsymbol{\theta}_1$ both be simple hypotheses, with $L_0 := f_{\boldsymbol{X}}(\boldsymbol{X}; \boldsymbol{\theta}_0)$ and $L_1 := f_{\boldsymbol{X}}(\boldsymbol{X}; \boldsymbol{\theta}_1)$, respectively. Suppose that

$$\Pr_{H_0}(\boldsymbol{X} \in C_\alpha) = \alpha \in (0,1) \qquad \text{and} \qquad \wp := L_0/L_1 \begin{cases} < \gamma & (\boldsymbol{X} \in C_\alpha), \\ \geqslant \gamma & (\boldsymbol{X} \notin C_\alpha), \end{cases}$$

for some $\gamma > 0$. Show that $\wp$ is a most powerful test of size α and that the corresponding critical region C_α (with complement C_α^c) is an MPR of size α. [Hint: From the general definition of a UMP test, consider the difference between its power and the power of another test of size $\alpha^\dagger \leqslant \alpha$, writing this difference as an integral under H_1, then use the displayed inequalities to go from L_1 to $\gamma^{-1}L_0$.]

Solution

Recall the definition of a most powerful test from the introduction. Suppose there exists another region (associated with another test) denoted by $C_{\alpha^\dagger}$ such that

$$\Pr_{H_0}(\boldsymbol{X} \in C_{\alpha^\dagger}) = \alpha^\dagger \leqslant \alpha.$$

Then, defining $\Pi - \Pi^\dagger := \Pr_{H_1}(\boldsymbol{X} \in C_\alpha) - \Pr_{H_1}(\boldsymbol{X} \in C_{\alpha^\dagger})$, we must show that $\Pi - \Pi^\dagger \geqslant 0$, that is, any such $C_{\alpha^\dagger}$ must lead to a power that is no better than before: a most powerful critical region must therefore be defined in terms of the ratio of likelihoods $\wp$.

By the definition of the power,

$$\Pi - \Pi^\dagger = \int_{C_\alpha} f_1 - \int_{C_{\alpha^\dagger}} f_1,$$

using $\int_{C_\alpha} f_1$ as a shorthand for $\int_{\boldsymbol{W} \in C_\alpha} \mathrm{d}F_{\boldsymbol{X}}(\boldsymbol{W}; \boldsymbol{\theta}_1)$. The two integrals contain a common region of integration, namely

$$A := C_{\alpha^\dagger} \cap C_\alpha,$$

where the integrands are also equal; hence we can cancel out to simplify:

$$\Pi - \Pi^\dagger = \int_{C_\alpha \backslash A} f_1 - \int_{C_{\alpha^\dagger} \backslash A} f_1. \tag{14.17}$$

The inequality that is displayed in the lemma links f_1 to f_0, the realizations of L_1 and L_0, respectively. It is stated in terms of C_α and its complement C_α^c, and here we have

$$C_\alpha \backslash A \subseteq C_\alpha \qquad \text{and} \qquad C_{\alpha^\dagger} \backslash A = C_{\alpha^\dagger} \cap C_\alpha^c \subseteq C_\alpha^c.$$

Therefore, since $\gamma > 0$,

$$L_1 \begin{cases} > \gamma^{-1} L_0 & (\boldsymbol{X} \in C_\alpha \backslash A), \\ \leqslant \gamma^{-1} L_0 & (\boldsymbol{X} \in C_{\alpha^\dagger} \backslash A), \end{cases}$$

implying that

$$\int_{C_\alpha \backslash A} f_1 \geqslant \frac{1}{\gamma} \int_{C_\alpha \backslash A} f_0 \qquad \text{and} \qquad -\int_{C_{\alpha^\dagger} \backslash A} f_1 \geqslant -\frac{1}{\gamma} \int_{C_{\alpha^\dagger} \backslash A} f_0,$$

where the switch from $>$ to $\geqslant$ makes the first inequality valid even when $C_\alpha \backslash A$ is empty.

Hence

$$\Pi - \Pi^{\dagger} \geqslant \frac{1}{\gamma}\left(\int_{C_\alpha \backslash A} f_0 - \int_{C_{\alpha^\dagger} \backslash A} f_0\right) = \frac{1}{\gamma}\left(\int_{C_\alpha} f_0 - \int_{C_{\alpha^\dagger}} f_0\right),$$

where the equality arises by adding the same quantity, $\int_A f_0$, to each of the two integrals. This last step effectively reverses the earlier cancellation in (14.17), which was necessary for the use of the lemma's inequality which is stated in terms of regions inside and outside C_α (hence requiring the decomposition of $C_{\alpha^\dagger}$ as is, for example, illustrated in Figure 1.2 in Exercise 1.5). Finally, from the definition at the start of the solution, we have

$$\int_{C_{\alpha^\dagger}} f_0 \equiv \alpha^\dagger \leqslant \alpha,$$

implying $\Pi - \Pi^\dagger \geqslant \gamma^{-1}\left(\alpha - \alpha^\dagger\right) \geqslant 0$ as required.

14.2 GLR $\wp$, LR, W, and LM tests

Exercise 14.8 (GLR: gamma) Let $x_1, \dots, x_n$ be a random sample from $x \sim \text{Gam}(2, \theta)$, where $\theta > 0$. Derive the GLR test statistic for $\text{H}_0 : \theta \leqslant \theta_c$ against $\text{H}_1 : \theta > \theta_c$. You may use the result (from Exercise 12.10) that the MLE of θ is $2/\overline{x}$.

Solution

The density $f_x(u) = \theta^2 u e^{-\theta u}$, for $u \in \mathbb{R}_+$, implies that the (generalized) ratio of likelihoods is

$$\wp = \frac{\sup_{\theta \leqslant \theta_c} \theta^{2n}(\prod_{i=1}^n x_i)\exp(-\theta\sum_{i=1}^n x_i)}{\sup_\theta \theta^{2n}(\prod_{i=1}^n x_i)\exp(-\theta\sum_{i=1}^n x_i)} = \frac{\max_{\theta \leqslant \theta_c} \theta^{2n}\exp(-\theta n\overline{x})}{\max_\theta \theta^{2n}\exp(-\theta n\overline{x})};$$

compare with Exercise 14.5. Writing $\wp$ in terms of the unconstrained MLE $\widehat{\theta} := 2/\overline{x}$ and rearranging (because n does not depend on θ), we obtain

$$\wp = \frac{\max_{\theta \leqslant \theta_c} \theta^{2n}\exp(-2\theta n/\widehat{\theta})}{\max_\theta \theta^{2n}\exp(-2\theta n/\widehat{\theta})} = \left(\frac{\max_{\theta \leqslant \theta_c} \theta\exp(-\theta/\widehat{\theta})}{\max_\theta \theta\exp(-\theta/\widehat{\theta})}\right)^{2n}.$$

Since the function $\theta\exp(-\theta/\widehat{\theta})$ has its maximum at $\widehat{\theta}$, we get $\wp = 1$ when $\widehat{\theta} \leqslant \theta_c$ (the unrestricted MLE is in Θ_0) and

$$\wp = \left(\frac{\theta_c\exp(-\theta_c/\widehat{\theta})}{\widehat{\theta}\exp(-1)}\right)^{2n} = \left(\frac{\theta_c/\widehat{\theta}}{\exp(\theta_c/\widehat{\theta} - 1)}\right)^{2n}$$

otherwise. Note that a function like $a/\exp(a)$ has a unique maximum at $a = 1$ for $a > 0$, so the latter formula for $\wp$ is decreasing in $\widehat{\theta}$ when $\theta_c/\widehat{\theta} < 1$; this is logical because a higher $\widehat{\theta}$ makes $\text{H}_0 : \theta \leqslant \theta_c$ less likely than $\text{H}_1 : \theta > \theta_c$.

***Exercise 14.9 (GLR: two exponentials)** Consider two independent random samples, of sizes m and n, from $x \sim \text{Expo}(\theta_1^{-1})$ and $y \sim \text{Expo}(\theta_2^{-1})$, respectively, with $0 < \theta_1, \theta_2 < \infty$ and $m, n \geqslant 1$. Derive the size-α GLR test for $\text{H}_0 : \theta_1 = \theta_2$ against $\text{H}_1 : \theta_1 \neq \theta_2$. [Hint: To calculate the size α of a test based on the GLR $\wp$, work out the c.d.f. of $\wp$.]

Solution

In general, $\widehat{\theta}_1 = \overline{x}$ and $\widehat{\theta}_2 = \overline{y}$, by applying the MLE's invariance property to Exercises 12.10 or 12.12. Under H_0, we have a restricted $\theta = \theta_1 = \theta_2$; hence the MLE is

$$\widehat{\theta} = \frac{1}{m+n}\left(\sum_{i=1}^{m} x_i + \sum_{i=1}^{n} y_i\right) = \frac{m\overline{x} + n\overline{y}}{m+n},$$

a weighted average of the two means. As the $x \sim \text{Expo}(\theta^{-1})$ density is $f_x(u) = \theta^{-1}\text{e}^{-u/\theta}$ for $u > 0$, we get the ratio of likelihoods

$$\wp = \frac{L(\widehat{\theta})}{L(\widehat{\theta}_1)L(\widehat{\theta}_2)} = \frac{\prod_{i=1}^{m}\left(\widehat{\theta}^{-1}\text{e}^{-x_i/\widehat{\theta}}\right)\prod_{i=1}^{n}\left(\widehat{\theta}^{-1}\text{e}^{-y_i/\widehat{\theta}}\right)}{\prod_{i=1}^{m}\left(\widehat{\theta}_1^{-1}\text{e}^{-x_i/\widehat{\theta}_1}\right)\prod_{i=1}^{n}\left(\widehat{\theta}_2^{-1}\text{e}^{-y_i/\widehat{\theta}_2}\right)}$$

$$= \left(\frac{\widehat{\theta}_1}{\widehat{\theta}}\right)^m \left(\frac{\widehat{\theta}_2}{\widehat{\theta}}\right)^n \frac{\text{e}^{-(m\overline{x}+n\overline{y})/\widehat{\theta}}}{\text{e}^{-m\overline{x}/\widehat{\theta}_1}\text{e}^{-n\overline{y}/\widehat{\theta}_2}},$$

where we note that $L(\widehat{\theta}_1)L(\widehat{\theta}_2)$ is the unrestricted *joint* likelihood of the two samples. By expressing the MLEs in terms of the sample means, we find that

$$\wp = (m+n)^{m+n}\left(\frac{\overline{x}}{m\overline{x}+n\overline{y}}\right)^m \left(\frac{\overline{y}}{m\overline{x}+n\overline{y}}\right)^n \frac{\text{e}^{-m-n}}{\text{e}^{-m}\text{e}^{-n}}$$

$$= \frac{(m+n)^{m+n}}{m^m n^n}\left(\frac{m\overline{x}}{m\overline{x}+n\overline{y}}\right)^m \left(\frac{n\overline{y}}{m\overline{x}+n\overline{y}}\right)^n = \frac{(m+n)^{m+n}}{m^m n^n}\zeta^m (1-\zeta)^n,$$

where

$$\zeta := \frac{m\overline{x}}{m\overline{x}+n\overline{y}} \in (0,1).$$

Notice that $\wp$ is minimized when $\zeta \to 0$ or $\zeta \to 1$, which would lead to a rejection of H_0.

Before we can determine the critical values of a test based on $\wp$, we need to work out the distribution of ζ (and hence $\wp$) under $\text{H}_0 : \theta_1 = \theta_2 = \theta$. This was done in Exercise 7.19(b) by letting $\nu = 1$ and $\lambda = \theta^{-1}$ there. We have $2m\overline{x}/\theta \sim \chi^2(2m)$ and $2n\overline{y}/\theta \sim \chi^2(2n)$; hence $z := \overline{x}/\overline{y} \sim \text{F}(2m, 2n)$ and Exercise 4.31 implies that $\zeta \sim \text{Beta}(m, n)$, whose c.d.f. F_ζ was obtained in Exercise 4.11(b) in terms of the incomplete beta function.

Now, we need to obtain a γ such that $\alpha = \Pr(\wp < \gamma)$, which we will translate into a probability involving ζ whose c.d.f. is the known F_ζ. Consider $\wp$ as a function of ζ:

$$\wp = \frac{(m+n)^{m+n}}{m^m n^n}\zeta^m (1-\zeta)^n,$$

which resembles the dashed curve of Figure 4.1 in Exercise 4.14 when $m, n \geqslant 1$ as assumed here. It has a unique maximum at $\zeta_{\mathrm{M}} = m/(m+n)$, with $\wp$ a monotone function of ζ on either side of ζ_{M}. Therefore,

$$\alpha = \Pr(\wp < \gamma) = \Pr(\zeta < q_1) + \Pr(\zeta > q_2)$$
$$= F_{\zeta}(q_1) + 1 - F_{\zeta}(q_2),$$

which is solved numerically for some $q_1 < q_2$ satisfying

$$q_1^m (1-q_1)^n = q_2^m (1-q_2)^n ,$$

and hence

$$\gamma = \frac{(m+n)^{m+n}}{m^m n^n} q_1^m (1-q_1)^n = \frac{(m+n)^{m+n}}{m^m n^n} q_2^m (1-q_2)^n .$$

(You can use Figure 4.1 to illustrate this last equation: draw a horizontal line $\wp = \gamma$ intersecting the concave curve $\wp$ as a function of ζ, at the two points corresponding to $\zeta = q_1, q_2$.)

Exercise 14.10 (GLR: two normals) Let $\{x_i\}_{i=1}^m$ and $\{y_i\}_{i=1}^n$ be independent random samples from $\mathrm{N}(\mu_1, \sigma_1^2)$ and $\mathrm{N}(\mu_2, \sigma_2^2)$, respectively, and suppose that $m, n > 1$.
(a) Derive the GLR test of size α for $\mathrm{H}_0 : \mu_1 = \mu_2$ against $\mathrm{H}_1 : \mu_1 \neq \mu_2$, assuming that $\sigma_1^2 = \sigma_2^2$.
(b) Derive the GLR test of size α for $\mathrm{H}_0 : \sigma_1^2 = \sigma_2^2$ against $\mathrm{H}_1 : \sigma_1^2 \neq \sigma_2^2$, assuming that μ_1 and μ_2 are known.
(c) Rework part (b) assuming that μ_1 and μ_2 are unknown.

Solution
(a) Any $z \sim \mathrm{N}(\mu, \sigma^2)$ can be rewritten as a special case of the normal linear model as $z = \mu + \varepsilon$ with $\varepsilon \sim \mathrm{N}(0, \sigma^2)$, so we can use Exercise 12.30(c) to write the profile (or concentrated) likelihood as

$$\exp\left(-\frac{n}{2}\left(\log\left(2\pi\right)+1\right)\right)\left(\widehat{\sigma}^2\right)^{-(m+n)/2}$$

for a sample of size $m+n$; hence

$$\wp = \frac{\max_{\mu_1=\mu_2,\sigma^2}\left(\frac{1}{\sigma\sqrt{2\pi}}\right)^{m+n} \exp\left(-\frac{1}{2\sigma^2}\left(\sum_{i=1}^m (x_i-\mu_1)^2 + \sum_{i=1}^n (y_i-\mu_2)^2\right)\right)}{\max_{\mu_1,\mu_2,\sigma^2}\left(\frac{1}{\sigma\sqrt{2\pi}}\right)^{m+n} \exp\left(-\frac{1}{2\sigma^2}\left(\sum_{i=1}^m (x_i-\mu_1)^2 + \sum_{i=1}^n (y_i-\mu_2)^2\right)\right)}$$
$$= \left(\frac{\widetilde{\sigma}^2}{\widehat{\sigma}^2}\right)^{-(m+n)/2},$$

where we denote by $\widehat{\sigma}^2$ the unrestricted MLE and by $\widetilde{\sigma}^2$ the MLE under H_0. Under H_0 we have $\widetilde{\mu} = (m\overline{x} + n\overline{y})/(m+n)$ and

$$\widetilde{\sigma}^2 = \frac{1}{m+n}\left(\sum_{i=1}^m (x_i - \widetilde{\mu})^2 + \sum_{i=1}^n (y_i - \widetilde{\mu})^2\right),$$

while the unrestricted estimators are $\widehat{\mu}_1 = \overline{x}$, $\widehat{\mu}_2 = \overline{y}$, and

$$\widehat{\sigma}^2 = \frac{1}{m+n}\left(\sum_{i=1}^{m}(x_i-\overline{x})^2 + \sum_{i=1}^{n}(y_i-\overline{y})^2\right).$$

Rejecting H_0 if $\wp < \gamma$ is equivalent to rejecting it if

$$\frac{\sum_{i=1}^m (x_i-\overline{x})^2 + \sum_{i=1}^n (y_i-\overline{y})^2}{\sum_{i=1}^m (x_i-\widetilde{\mu})^2 + \sum_{i=1}^n (y_i-\widetilde{\mu})^2} < \gamma^{2/(m+n)}.$$

We know that

$$\begin{aligned}\sum_{i=1}^{m}(x_i-\widetilde{\mu})^2 = \sum_{i=1}^{m}(x_i-\overline{x}+\overline{x}-\widetilde{\mu})^2 &= \sum_{i=1}^{m}(x_i-\overline{x})^2 + m(\overline{x}-\widetilde{\mu})^2\\ &\equiv \sum_{i=1}^{m}(x_i-\overline{x})^2 + m\left(\overline{x}-\frac{m\overline{x}+n\overline{y}}{m+n}\right)^2\\ &= \sum_{i=1}^{m}(x_i-\overline{x})^2 + \frac{m}{(m+n)^2}\left(n\left(\overline{x}-\overline{y}\right)\right)^2,\end{aligned}$$

and we get a similar result for the sum in y by swapping x with y and m with n, so the procedure is now to reject H_0 if

$$\begin{aligned}\gamma^{2/(m+n)} &> \frac{\sum_{i=1}^m (x_i-\overline{x})^2 + \sum_{i=1}^n (y_i-\overline{y})^2}{\sum_{i=1}^m (x_i-\overline{x})^2 + \sum_{i=1}^n (y_i-\overline{y})^2 + \frac{mn^2(\overline{x}-\overline{y})^2}{(m+n)^2} + \frac{nm^2(\overline{x}-\overline{y})^2}{(m+n)^2}}\\ &= \left(1 + \frac{mn(\overline{x}-\overline{y})^2}{(m+n)\left(\sum_{i=1}^m (x_i-\overline{x})^2 + \sum_{i=1}^n (y_i-\overline{y})^2\right)}\right)^{-1}.\end{aligned}$$

Under H_0,

$$\frac{\sum_{i=1}^m (x_i-\overline{x})^2 + \sum_{i=1}^n (y_i-\overline{y})^2}{\sigma^2} \sim \chi^2(m+n-2)$$

by the independence of x_i, y_i and the reproductive property of χ^2 variates, and $\overline{x}-\overline{y} \sim \mathrm{N}(0, \sigma^2/m + \sigma^2/n)$ implies that

$$\frac{(\overline{x}-\overline{y})^2}{\sigma^2/m+\sigma^2/n} = \frac{mn\left(\overline{x}-\overline{y}\right)^2}{\sigma^2(m+n)} \sim \chi^2(1)$$

independently of $\sum_{i=1}^m (x_i-\overline{x})^2$ and $\sum_{i=1}^n (y_i-\overline{y})^2$ (as seen in Exercise 8.34 and elsewhere). Hence, we reject H_0 if

$$\gamma^{-2/(m+n)} < 1 + \frac{mn(\overline{x}-\overline{y})^2}{(m+n)\left(\sum_{i=1}^m (x_i-\overline{x})^2 + \sum_{i=1}^n (y_i-\overline{y})^2\right)}$$

or, equivalently,

$$\left(\gamma^{-2/(m+n)}-1\right)(m+n-2) < \frac{mn\left(\overline{x}-\overline{y}\right)^2/(m+n)}{\left(\sum_{i=1}^m (x_i-\overline{x})^2 + \sum_{i=1}^n (y_i-\overline{y})^2\right)/(m+n-2)},$$

where the right-hand side of the latter inequality is distributed as $\mathrm{F}(1, m+n-2)$. Notice

that the signed square-root of the right-hand side is a t-ratio that has a Student's t distribution with $m+n-2$ degrees of freedom arising from combining the two samples (after estimating one mean for each) in estimating σ^2; see also Exercise 13.30.
(b) Under $\mathrm{H}_0 : \sigma_1^2 = \sigma_2^2 = \sigma^2$, with μ_1 and μ_2 known, we have

$$\widetilde{\sigma}^2 = \frac{1}{m+n}\left(\sum_{i=1}^{m}(x_i-\mu_1)^2 + \sum_{i=1}^{n}(y_i-\mu_2)^2\right).$$

In general, the separate samples of x, y give

$$\widehat{\sigma}_1^2 = \frac{1}{m}\sum_{i=1}^{m}(x_i-\mu_1)^2 \qquad \text{and} \qquad \widehat{\sigma}_2^2 = \frac{1}{n}\sum_{i=1}^{n}(y_i-\mu_2)^2.$$

Therefore,

$$\wp = \left(\frac{\widehat{\sigma}_1^2}{\widetilde{\sigma}^2}\right)^{m/2}\left(\frac{\widehat{\sigma}_2^2}{\widetilde{\sigma}^2}\right)^{n/2}.$$

But

$$\widetilde{\sigma}^2 = \frac{m\widehat{\sigma}_1^2 + n\widehat{\sigma}_2^2}{m+n}$$

implies that

$$\begin{aligned}\wp &= (m+n)^{(m+n)/2}\left(\frac{\widehat{\sigma}_1^2}{m\widehat{\sigma}_1^2+n\widehat{\sigma}_2^2}\right)^{m/2}\left(\frac{\widehat{\sigma}_2^2}{m\widehat{\sigma}_1^2+n\widehat{\sigma}_2^2}\right)^{n/2}\\ &= \left(\frac{m+n}{m}\right)^{m/2}\left(\frac{m+n}{n}\right)^{n/2}\left(\frac{m\widehat{\sigma}_1^2}{m\widehat{\sigma}_1^2+n\widehat{\sigma}_2^2}\right)^{m/2}\left(\frac{n\widehat{\sigma}_2^2}{m\widehat{\sigma}_1^2+n\widehat{\sigma}_2^2}\right)^{n/2}\\ &= \left(\frac{m+n}{m}\right)^{m/2}\left(\frac{m+n}{n}\right)^{n/2}\zeta^{m/2}(1-\zeta)^{n/2},\end{aligned}$$

where

$$\zeta := \frac{m\widehat{\sigma}_1^2}{m\widehat{\sigma}_1^2+n\widehat{\sigma}_2^2} \in (0,1).$$

Under $\mathrm{H}_0 : \sigma_1^2 = \sigma_2^2 = \sigma^2$, we have $m\widehat{\sigma}_1^2/\sigma^2 \sim \chi^2(m)$ and $n\widehat{\sigma}_2^2/\sigma^2 \sim \chi^2(n)$ since μ_1 and μ_2 are known; hence $z := \widehat{\sigma}_1^2/\widehat{\sigma}_2^2 \sim \mathrm{F}(m,n)$ and Exercise 4.31 implies that $\zeta \sim \mathrm{Beta}(\frac{1}{2}m, \frac{1}{2}n)$ whose c.d.f. F_ζ is in Exercise 4.11(b) in terms of the incomplete beta function. The required γ for $\Pr(\wp < \gamma) = \alpha$ can then be worked out as in the previous exercise.
(c) Now we have

$$\widetilde{\sigma}^2 = \frac{1}{m+n}\left(\sum_{i=1}^{m}(x_i-\overline{x})^2 + \sum_{i=1}^{n}(y_i-\overline{y})^2\right)$$

while

$$\widehat{\sigma}_1^2 = \frac{1}{m}\sum_{i=1}^{m}(x_i-\overline{x})^2 \qquad \text{and} \qquad \widehat{\sigma}_2^2 = \frac{1}{n}\sum_{i-1}^{n}(y_i-\overline{y})^2.$$

The formula for $\wp$ in terms of ζ is the same, but the relevant null distributions differ. We have $m\widehat{\sigma}_1^2/\sigma^2 \sim \chi^2(m-1)$ and $n\widehat{\sigma}_2^2/\sigma^2 \sim \chi^2(n-1)$ with one degree of freedom less than in (b) because now we have to estimate the means; hence

$$z := \frac{m\,(n-1)\,\widehat{\sigma}_1^2}{n\,(m-1)\,\widehat{\sigma}_2^2} \sim \mathrm{F}(m-1, n-1).$$

The distribution of

$$\zeta := \frac{m\widehat{\sigma}_1^2}{m\widehat{\sigma}_1^2 + n\widehat{\sigma}_2^2} \in (0,1)$$

is no longer a beta, but we can use

$$\begin{aligned}\Pr(\zeta \leqslant q) &= \Pr\left(\frac{z\,(m-1)\,/\,(n-1)}{1+z\,(m-1)\,/\,(n-1)} \leqslant q\right) = \Pr\left(\frac{1}{z\,(m-1)\,/\,(n-1)} + 1 \geqslant \frac{1}{q}\right)\\ &= \Pr\left(\frac{1}{z} \geqslant \frac{m-1}{n-1} \times \frac{1-q}{q}\right) = \Pr\left(z \leqslant \frac{n-1}{m-1} \times \frac{q}{1-q}\right),\end{aligned}$$

where we remark that $1/z \sim \mathrm{F}(n-1, m-1)$ could be used as an alternative to the last equality. The required γ for $\Pr(\wp < \gamma) = \alpha$ can then be worked out as in the previous exercise in terms of the new F_ζ.

Exercise 14.11 (GLR: linear model) Consider the linear model $y_i = \beta_1 + \beta_2 x_i + \varepsilon_i$, ($i = 1, \dots, n > 2$), where $\varepsilon_i \sim \mathrm{IN}(0, \sigma^2)$ and the x_i are nonrandom regressors (for example, as a result of conditioning as in Section 12.3). Derive the GLR test statistic for $\mathrm{H}_0 : \beta_1 = \beta_2$ against $\mathrm{H}_1 : \beta_1 \neq \beta_2$.

Solution

Under H_0, we have the log-likelihood

$$\ell(\beta_2, \sigma^2) = -\frac{n}{2}\log(2\pi) - \frac{n}{2}\log\left(\sigma^2\right) - \frac{1}{2\sigma^2}\sum_{i=1}^{n}\left(y_i - \beta_2(1+x_i)\right)^2;$$

hence

$$\frac{\partial \ell(\beta_2, \sigma^2)}{\partial \beta_2} = \frac{1}{\sigma^2}\sum_{i=1}^{n}(1+x_i)\left(y_i - \beta_2(1+x_i)\right)$$

and

$$\frac{\partial \ell(\beta_2, \sigma^2)}{\partial \sigma^2} = -\frac{n}{2\sigma^2} + \frac{1}{2\sigma^4}\sum_{i=1}^{n}\left(y_i - \beta_2(1+x_i)\right)^2$$

lead to the H_0-constrained MLEs

$$\widetilde{\beta}_2 := \frac{\sum_{i=1}^{n}(1+x_i)y_i}{\sum_{i=1}^{n}(1+x_i)^2} \qquad \text{and} \qquad \widetilde{\sigma}^2 := \frac{1}{n}\sum_{i=1}^{n}\left(y_i - \widetilde{\beta}_2(1+x_i)\right)^2,$$

the second-order conditions being easy to verify as in Section 12.3. Since the profile (or concentrated) likelihood is

$$L(\widetilde{\beta}_2, \widetilde{\sigma}^2) = \exp\left(-\frac{n}{2}\left(\log(2\pi) + 1\right)\right)\left(\widetilde{\sigma}^2\right)^{-n/2},$$

we get

$$\wp = \left(\frac{\sum_{i=1}^n \left(y_i - \widehat{\beta}_1 - \widehat{\beta}_2 x_i\right)^2}{\sum_{i=1}^n \left(y_i - \widetilde{\beta}_2(1 + x_i)\right)^2}\right)^{n/2},$$

where $\widehat{\beta}_1, \widehat{\beta}_2$ are the unconstrained MLEs.

Exercise 14.12 (GLR: two linear models) Consider the linear models $y_i = \beta_2 z_{2,i} + \varepsilon_i$ and $x_i = \beta_1 z_{1,i} + \eta_i$ ($i = 1, \dots, n > 1$), where the regressors are nonrandom and $\varepsilon_i \sim \text{IN}(0, \sigma^2)$ independently of $\eta_i \sim \text{IN}(0, \sigma^2)$. Derive the size-$\alpha$ GLR test for $\text{H}_0 : \beta_1 = \beta_2$ against $\text{H}_1 : \beta_1 \neq \beta_2$.

Solution

Exercise 14.10 was a precursor to this exercise, with $z_{1,i} = z_{2,i} = 1$ for all i. Write the restriction in H_0 as $\beta_1 = \beta_2 = \beta$, where this common parameter β is not to be confused with the notation for the Type II error, which is not used in this exercise. Under H_0, we have the MLEs

$$\widetilde{\beta} = \frac{\sum_{i=1}^n z_{2,i} y_i + \sum_{i=1}^n z_{1,i} x_i}{\sum_{i=1}^n z_{2,i}^2 + \sum_{i=1}^n z_{1,i}^2}$$

and

$$\widetilde{\sigma}^2 = \frac{1}{2n}\left(\sum_{i=1}^n (y_i - \widetilde{\beta} z_{2,i})^2 + \sum_{i=1}^n (x_i - \widetilde{\beta} z_{1,i})^2\right).$$

In general, the unrestricted MLEs are

$$\widehat{\beta}_2 = \frac{\sum_{i=1}^n z_{2,i} y_i}{\sum_{i=1}^n z_{2,i}^2}, \qquad \widehat{\beta}_1 = \frac{\sum_{i=1}^n z_{1,i} x_i}{\sum_{i=1}^n z_{1,i}^2},$$

and

$$\widehat{\sigma}^2 = \frac{1}{2n}\left(\sum_{i=1}^n (y_i - \widehat{\beta}_2 z_{2,i})^2 + \sum_{i=1}^n (x_i - \widehat{\beta}_1 z_{1,i})^2\right).$$

Hence,

$$\wp = \left(\frac{\sum_{i=1}^n (y_i - \widehat{\beta}_2 z_{2,i})^2 + \sum_{i=1}^n (x_i - \widehat{\beta}_1 z_{1,i})^2}{\sum_{i=1}^n (y_i - \widetilde{\beta} z_{2,i})^2 + \sum_{i=1}^n (x_i - \widetilde{\beta} z_{1,i})^2}\right)^n.$$

In order to find its distribution, we now need to reformulate $\wp$ as we did in the simpler case of Exercise 14.10(a). First, write

$$\sum_{i=1}^{n}(y_i - \widetilde{\beta} z_{2,i})^2 = \sum_{i=1}^{n}(y_i - \widehat{\beta}_2 z_{2,i} + (\widehat{\beta}_2 - \widetilde{\beta}) z_{2,i})^2$$
$$= \sum_{i=1}^{n}(y_i - \widehat{\beta}_2 z_{2,i})^2 + (\widehat{\beta}_2 - \widetilde{\beta})^2 \sum_{i=1}^{n} z_{2,i}^2$$

since

$$\sum_{i=1}^{n}(y_i - \widehat{\beta}_2 z_{2,i}) z_{2,i} = \sum_{i=1}^{n} y_i z_{2,i} - \widehat{\beta}_2 \sum_{i=1}^{n} z_{2,i}^2 = 0$$

by the definition of $\widehat{\beta}_2$; similarly,

$$\sum_{i=1}^{n}(x_i - \widetilde{\beta} z_{1,i})^2 = \sum_{i=1}^{n}(x_i - \widehat{\beta}_1 z_{1,i})^2 + (\widehat{\beta}_1 - \widetilde{\beta})^2 \sum_{i=1}^{n} z_{1,i}^2.$$

Second, we also have, by the definitions of $\widetilde{\beta}$, $\widehat{\beta}_1$, and $\widehat{\beta}_2$,

$$\widetilde{\beta} = \frac{\sum_{i=1}^{n} z_{2,i}^2 \widehat{\beta}_2 + \sum_{i=1}^{n} z_{1,i}^2 \widehat{\beta}_1}{\sum_{i=1}^{n} z_{2,i}^2 + \sum_{i=1}^{n} z_{1,i}^2}$$
$$= \widehat{\beta}_2 - \frac{\sum_{i=1}^{n} z_{1,i}^2 \widehat{\beta}_2}{\sum_{i=1}^{n} z_{2,i}^2 + \sum_{i=1}^{n} z_{1,i}^2} + \frac{\sum_{i=1}^{n} z_{1,i}^2 \widehat{\beta}_1}{\sum_{i=1}^{n} z_{2,i}^2 + \sum_{i=1}^{n} z_{1,i}^2};$$

hence

$$\widehat{\beta}_2 - \widetilde{\beta} = \frac{\sum_{i=1}^{n} z_{1,i}^2}{\sum_{i=1}^{n} z_{2,i}^2 + \sum_{i=1}^{n} z_{1,i}^2} (\widehat{\beta}_2 - \widehat{\beta}_1)$$

and similarly

$$\widehat{\beta}_1 - \widetilde{\beta} = \frac{\sum_{i=1}^{n} z_{2,i}^2}{\sum_{i=1}^{n} z_{2,i}^2 + \sum_{i=1}^{n} z_{1,i}^2} (\widehat{\beta}_1 - \widehat{\beta}_2).$$

Using these two sets of results to rewrite $\wp$, we get

$$\wp = \left(\frac{\sum_{i=1}^{n}(y_i - \widehat{\beta}_2 z_{2,i})^2 + \sum_{i=1}^{n}(x_i - \widehat{\beta}_1 z_{1,i})^2}{\sum_{i=1}^{n}(y_i - \widehat{\beta}_2 z_{2,i})^2 + \sum_{i=1}^{n}(x_i - \widehat{\beta}_1 z_{1,i})^2 + \xi} \right)^n,$$

where

$$\xi := (\widehat{\beta}_2 - \widehat{\beta}_1)^2 \frac{\left(\sum_{i=1}^{n} z_{1,i}^2\right)^2 \sum_{i=1}^{n} z_{2,i}^2 + \left(\sum_{i=1}^{n} z_{2,i}^2\right)^2 \sum_{i=1}^{n} z_{1,i}^2}{\left(\sum_{i=1}^{n} z_{1,i}^2 + \sum_{i=1}^{n} z_{2,i}^2\right)^2}$$
$$= (\widehat{\beta}_2 - \widehat{\beta}_1)^2 \frac{\sum_{i=1}^{n} z_{1,i}^2 \sum_{i=1}^{n} z_{2,i}^2}{\sum_{i=1}^{n} z_{1,i}^2 + \sum_{i=1}^{n} z_{2,i}^2}.$$

Recall that the question assumes that the z's are nonrandom, thus allowing us to use a result of Section 12.3 that $\widehat{\beta}_1 \sim \mathrm{N}(\beta_1, \sigma^2/\sum_{i=1}^n z_{1,i}^2)$ and $\widehat{\beta}_2 \sim \mathrm{N}(\beta_2, \sigma^2/\sum_{i=1}^n z_{2,i}^2)$, independently of one another since ε_i and η_i are independent. Under $\mathrm{H}_0 : \beta_1 = \beta_2 = \beta$,

$$\widehat{\beta}_1 - \widehat{\beta}_2 \sim \mathrm{N}\left(0, \sigma^2 \left(\frac{1}{\sum_{i=1}^n z_{1,i}^2} + \frac{1}{\sum_{i=1}^n z_{2,i}^2}\right)\right) = \mathrm{N}\left(0, \sigma^2 \frac{\sum_{i=1}^n z_{1,i}^2 + \sum_{i=1}^n z_{2,i}^2}{\sum_{i=1}^n z_{1,i}^2 \sum_{i=1}^n z_{2,i}^2}\right);$$

hence $\xi/\sigma^2 \sim \chi^2(1)$. Furthermore,

$$\frac{\sum_{i=1}^n (y_i - \widehat{\beta}_2 z_{2,i})^2 + \sum_{i=1}^n (x_i - \widehat{\beta}_1 z_{1,i})^2}{\sigma^2} \sim \chi^2(2n-2)$$

independently of $\widehat{\beta}_1$ and $\widehat{\beta}_2$ (see Exercise 12.31(f)), so $\wp^{1/n} \sim \mathrm{Beta}\left(n-1, \frac{1}{2}\right)$ and we can determine γ for $\Pr(\wp < \gamma) = \alpha$ as before.

Exercise 14.13 (GLR: normal's mean vector) Let $\boldsymbol{x}_1, \dots, \boldsymbol{x}_n$ be a random sample from $\boldsymbol{x} \sim \mathrm{N}_k(\boldsymbol{\mu}, \boldsymbol{\Sigma})$, where $\boldsymbol{\Sigma}$ is nonsingular and $n > k$. Derive the GLR test statistic for $\mathrm{H}_0 : \boldsymbol{\mu} = \mathbf{0}$ against $\mathrm{H}_1 : \boldsymbol{\mu} \neq \mathbf{0}$. What if we had instead $\mathrm{H}_0 : \boldsymbol{\mu} = \boldsymbol{\mu}_0$ against $\mathrm{H}_1 : \boldsymbol{\mu} \neq \boldsymbol{\mu}_0$?

Solution

Using the setup of Exercise 12.17, we need to solve

$$\wp = \frac{\sup_{\boldsymbol{\Sigma}} L(\mathbf{0}, \boldsymbol{\Sigma})}{\sup_{\boldsymbol{\mu}, \boldsymbol{\Sigma}} L(\boldsymbol{\mu}, \boldsymbol{\Sigma})},$$

where

$$L(\boldsymbol{\mu}, \boldsymbol{\Sigma}) = (2\pi)^{-kn/2} |\boldsymbol{\Sigma}|^{-n/2} \operatorname{etr}\left(-\frac{n}{2}\boldsymbol{\Sigma}^{-1}(\overline{\boldsymbol{x}} - \boldsymbol{\mu})(\overline{\boldsymbol{x}} - \boldsymbol{\mu})' - \frac{n-1}{2}\boldsymbol{\Sigma}^{-1}\boldsymbol{S}\right)$$

and $\boldsymbol{S} := \frac{1}{n-1}\sum_{i=1}^n (\boldsymbol{x}_i - \overline{\boldsymbol{x}})(\boldsymbol{x}_i - \overline{\boldsymbol{x}})'$, by the sufficiency factorization given there. The denominator has already been worked out there, with $\widehat{\boldsymbol{\mu}} = \overline{\boldsymbol{x}}$ and $\widehat{\boldsymbol{\Sigma}} = \frac{n-1}{n}\boldsymbol{S}$. For the numerator,

$$L(\mathbf{0}, \boldsymbol{\Sigma}) = (2\pi)^{-kn/2} |\boldsymbol{\Sigma}|^{-n/2} \operatorname{etr}\left(-\frac{1}{2}\boldsymbol{\Sigma}^{-1}\left(n\overline{\boldsymbol{x}}\,\overline{\boldsymbol{x}}' + (n-1)\boldsymbol{S}\right)\right)$$

and the same derivations as done there lead us to the H_0-restricted optimum

$$\widetilde{\boldsymbol{\Sigma}} := \overline{\boldsymbol{x}}\,\overline{\boldsymbol{x}}' + \frac{n-1}{n}\boldsymbol{S} = \frac{1}{n}\sum_{i=1}^n \boldsymbol{x}_i \boldsymbol{x}_i',$$

the equality following from the introduction to Chapter 9 (or Exercise 9.5(b)). As a result,

$$\wp = \frac{\left|\overline{\boldsymbol{x}}\,\overline{\boldsymbol{x}}' + \frac{n-1}{n}\boldsymbol{S}\right|^{-n/2} \operatorname{etr}\left(-\frac{n}{2}\boldsymbol{I}_k\right)}{\left|\frac{n-1}{n}\boldsymbol{S}\right|^{-n/2} \operatorname{etr}\left(-\frac{n}{2}\boldsymbol{I}_k\right)} = \left|\frac{n}{n-1}\overline{\boldsymbol{x}}\,\overline{\boldsymbol{x}}'\boldsymbol{S}^{-1} + \boldsymbol{I}_k\right|^{-n/2}$$

$$= \left(\frac{n}{n-1}\overline{\boldsymbol{x}}'\boldsymbol{S}^{-1}\overline{\boldsymbol{x}} + 1\right)^{-n/2},$$

where the last step is valid as $n > k$ implies that $\boldsymbol{S}$ is nonsingular a.s.; see Exercise 9.21(a). Recalling the definition of Hotelling's T^2 from Chapter 9,

$$T^2 := n\left(\overline{\boldsymbol{x}} - \boldsymbol{\mu}_0\right)' \boldsymbol{S}^{-1}\left(\overline{\boldsymbol{x}} - \boldsymbol{\mu}_0\right),$$

we have (with $\boldsymbol{\mu}_0 = \mathbf{0}$ in this paragraph)

$$\wp = \left(\frac{T^2}{n-1} + 1\right)^{-n/2}$$

and we reject $\mathrm{H}_0 : \boldsymbol{\mu} = \mathbf{0}$ when $\wp$ is small or T^2 is large, as we have done before for both of these statistics. See also Exercise 14.2.

In the general setup of $\mathrm{H}_0 : \boldsymbol{\mu} = \boldsymbol{\mu}_0$ for $\boldsymbol{x} \sim \mathrm{N}_k(\boldsymbol{\mu}, \boldsymbol{\Sigma})$, we can rewrite the problem as that of testing for a zero mean of $\boldsymbol{y} := \boldsymbol{x} - \boldsymbol{\mu}_0 \sim \mathrm{N}_k(\boldsymbol{\mu} - \boldsymbol{\mu}_0, \boldsymbol{\Sigma})$, and the relation between $\wp$ and T^2 is unchanged.

Exercise 14.14 (GLR: normal's scalar variance matrix) Let $\boldsymbol{x}_1, \dots, \boldsymbol{x}_n$ be a random sample from $\boldsymbol{x} \sim \mathrm{N}_k(\boldsymbol{\mu}, \boldsymbol{\Sigma})$, where $\boldsymbol{\Sigma}$ is nonsingular and $n > k$. Derive the GLR test statistic for $\mathrm{H}_0 : \boldsymbol{\Sigma} = \sigma^2 \boldsymbol{I}_k$ against $\mathrm{H}_1 : \boldsymbol{\Sigma} \neq \sigma^2 \boldsymbol{I}_k$.

Solution

We use the setup of Exercise 12.17 again. We need to solve

$$\wp = \frac{\sup_{\boldsymbol{\mu},\sigma} L\left(\boldsymbol{\mu}, \sigma^2 \boldsymbol{I}_k\right)}{\sup_{\boldsymbol{\mu},\boldsymbol{\Sigma}} L\left(\boldsymbol{\mu}, \boldsymbol{\Sigma}\right)},$$

where

$$L\left(\boldsymbol{\mu}, \boldsymbol{\Sigma}\right) = (2\pi)^{-kn/2} \left|\boldsymbol{\Sigma}\right|^{-n/2} \operatorname{etr}\left(-\frac{n}{2}\boldsymbol{\Sigma}^{-1}\left(\overline{\boldsymbol{x}} - \boldsymbol{\mu}\right)\left(\overline{\boldsymbol{x}} - \boldsymbol{\mu}\right)' - \frac{n-1}{2}\boldsymbol{\Sigma}^{-1}\boldsymbol{S}\right)$$

and $\boldsymbol{S} := \frac{1}{n-1}\sum_{i=1}^n \left(\boldsymbol{x}_i - \overline{\boldsymbol{x}}\right)\left(\boldsymbol{x}_i - \overline{\boldsymbol{x}}\right)'$, by the sufficiency factorization given there, where it is also shown that the optimization problem can be rewritten in terms of the profile likelihood as

$$\wp = \frac{\sup_{\sigma} L\left(\overline{\boldsymbol{x}}, \sigma^2 \boldsymbol{I}_k\right)}{\sup_{\boldsymbol{\Sigma}} L\left(\overline{\boldsymbol{x}}, \boldsymbol{\Sigma}\right)}$$

with

$$L\left(\overline{\boldsymbol{x}}, \boldsymbol{\Sigma}\right) = (2\pi)^{-kn/2} \left|\boldsymbol{\Sigma}\right|^{-n/2} \operatorname{etr}\left(-\frac{n-1}{2}\boldsymbol{\Sigma}^{-1}\boldsymbol{S}\right).$$

The differential obtained in Exercise 12.17(a) gave $\widehat{\boldsymbol{\Sigma}} = \frac{n-1}{n}\boldsymbol{S}$ for the unrestricted optimization and, similarly for optimization subject to $\mathrm{H}_0 : \boldsymbol{\Sigma} = \sigma^2 \boldsymbol{I}_k$, it would give

$$\operatorname{tr}\left(\widetilde{\sigma}^2 \boldsymbol{I}_k - \frac{n-1}{n}\boldsymbol{S}\right) = 0$$

(this can also be obtained by direct optimization of $L\left(\overline{\boldsymbol{x}}, \sigma^2 \boldsymbol{I}_k\right)$ here); hence $\widetilde{\sigma}^2 = \frac{n-1}{nk}\operatorname{tr}(\boldsymbol{S})$.

The result is

$$\wp = \frac{\left|\frac{n-1}{nk}\operatorname{tr}(\boldsymbol{S})\boldsymbol{I}_k\right|^{-n/2}\operatorname{etr}\left(-\frac{nk}{2\operatorname{tr}(\boldsymbol{S})}\boldsymbol{S}\right)}{\left|\frac{n-1}{n}\boldsymbol{S}\right|^{-n/2}\operatorname{etr}\left(-\frac{n}{2}\boldsymbol{I}_k\right)} = \left(\frac{(\operatorname{tr}(\boldsymbol{S})/k)^k}{|\boldsymbol{S}|}\right)^{-n/2}.$$

This is a ratio whose constituents we have already encountered in Exercise 6.23 (but as population counterparts): the generalized sample variance $|\boldsymbol{S}|$ and the total sample variance $\operatorname{tr}(\boldsymbol{S})$. We saw that this ratio is 1 if and only if $\boldsymbol{S} = \widetilde{\sigma}^2\boldsymbol{I}_k$, but $|\boldsymbol{S}| < (\operatorname{tr}(\boldsymbol{S})/k)^k$ and $\wp < 1$ otherwise. Thus, values of $\wp$ close to 1 tend to be associated with H_0, as one would expect from a GLR. Notice that $1 < n \leqslant k$ would have given $|\boldsymbol{S}| = 0$ (see the proof of Exercise 9.21(a)) and hence $\wp = 0$ regardless of which hypothesis holds.

Exercise 14.15 (GLR: normal's correlation) Suppose we have a random sample of size $n > 2$ for $\boldsymbol{x} \sim \mathrm{N}_2(\boldsymbol{\mu}, \boldsymbol{\Sigma})$, where

$$\boldsymbol{\Sigma} := \begin{pmatrix} \sigma_1^2 & \rho\sigma_1\sigma_2 \\ \rho\sigma_1\sigma_2 & \sigma_2^2 \end{pmatrix} \qquad (|\rho| < 1 \text{ and } \sigma_1, \sigma_2 > 0).$$

Derive the GLR test statistic for $\mathrm{H}_0 : \rho = \rho_0$ against $\mathrm{H}_1 : \rho \neq \rho_0$.

Solution

We require $n > 2$ to exclude the case $\widehat{\rho}^2 \equiv 1$ when $n = 2$; see Exercises 9.6(a) or 12.37 for illustrations, and the derivations of Exercise 9.21(a) for a proof. Using the notation $\boldsymbol{\Sigma}_0 := \boldsymbol{\Sigma}|_{\rho=\rho_0}$, the sufficiency factorization seen earlier allows us to write

$$\wp = \frac{\sup_{\boldsymbol{\Sigma}_0} L(\overline{\boldsymbol{x}}, \boldsymbol{\Sigma}_0)}{\sup_{\boldsymbol{\Sigma}} L(\overline{\boldsymbol{x}}, \boldsymbol{\Sigma})}$$

with

$$L(\overline{\boldsymbol{x}}, \boldsymbol{\Sigma}) = (2\pi)^{-kn/2}|\boldsymbol{\Sigma}|^{-n/2}\operatorname{etr}\left(-\frac{n-1}{2}\boldsymbol{\Sigma}^{-1}\boldsymbol{S}\right).$$

In the denominator of $\wp$, the supremum is obtained for $\widehat{\boldsymbol{\Sigma}} = \frac{n-1}{n}\boldsymbol{S}$ as before. For $k = 2$, this gives

$$\begin{aligned} L(\overline{\boldsymbol{x}}, \widehat{\boldsymbol{\Sigma}}) &= (2\pi)^{-n}\left|\frac{n-1}{n}\boldsymbol{S}\right|^{-n/2}\operatorname{etr}\left(-\frac{n-1}{2}\left(\frac{n-1}{n}\boldsymbol{S}\right)^{-1}\boldsymbol{S}\right) \\ &= \left(\frac{2(n-1)\pi}{n}\right)^{-n}|\boldsymbol{S}|^{-n/2}\operatorname{etr}\left(-\frac{n}{2}\boldsymbol{I}_2\right) \\ &= \left(\frac{2(n-1)\pi\mathrm{e}}{n}\right)^{-n}\left(s_{11}s_{22} - s_{12}^2\right)^{-n/2} \\ &\equiv \left(\frac{2(n-1)\pi\mathrm{e}}{n}\sqrt{s_{11}s_{22}}\right)^{-n}\left(1 - \widehat{\rho}^2\right)^{-n/2}, \end{aligned}$$

where $\widehat{\rho} := s_{12}/\sqrt{s_{11}s_{22}}$.

To obtain the numerator of $\wp$, it will be convenient to define

$$\omega_1 := \sigma_1\sigma_2, \qquad \omega_2 := \sigma_1/\sigma_2.$$

Then, $\sigma_1^2 = \omega_1\omega_2$ and $\sigma_2^2 = \omega_1/\omega_2$; hence $\boldsymbol{\Sigma}_0 = \omega_1 \boldsymbol{V}$ with

$$\boldsymbol{V} := \begin{pmatrix} \omega_2 & \rho_0 \\ \rho_0 & \omega_2^{-1} \end{pmatrix} \quad \text{and} \quad \boldsymbol{V}^{-1} = \frac{1}{1-\rho_0^2}\begin{pmatrix} \omega_2^{-1} & -\rho_0 \\ -\rho_0 & \omega_2 \end{pmatrix}.$$

For $k = 2$, we obtain

$$L(\overline{\boldsymbol{x}}, \boldsymbol{\Sigma}_0) = (2\pi)^{-n} \left|\omega_1 \boldsymbol{V}\right|^{-n/2} \operatorname{etr}\left(-\frac{n-1}{2}\omega_1^{-1}\boldsymbol{V}^{-1}\boldsymbol{S}\right)$$

$$= (2\pi\omega_1)^{-n}\left(1-\rho_0^2\right)^{-n/2} \exp\left(-\frac{n-1}{2\omega_1}\frac{\omega_2^{-1}s_{11} - 2\rho_0 s_{12} + \omega_2 s_{22}}{1-\rho_0^2}\right).$$

By the invariance property of MLEs, we now maximize the log of this likelihood with respect to the scalars ω_1 and ω_2 (instead of $\boldsymbol{\Sigma}_0$), to get

$$\frac{\partial \ell}{\partial \omega_1} = -\frac{n}{\omega_1} + \frac{(n-1)\left(\omega_2^{-1}s_{11} - 2\rho_0 s_{12} + \omega_2 s_{22}\right)}{2\omega_1^2\left(1-\rho_0^2\right)}$$

and

$$\frac{\partial \ell}{\partial \omega_2} = -\frac{n-1}{2\omega_1\left(1-\rho_0^2\right)}\left(-\omega_2^{-2}s_{11} + s_{22}\right).$$

Setting the two partial derivatives equal to zero leads to $\widetilde{\omega}_2 = \sqrt{s_{11}/s_{22}}$ (meaning that the ratio $\omega_2 \equiv \sigma_1/\sigma_2$ is estimated by its sample counterpart) and

$$\widetilde{\omega}_1 = \frac{n-1}{2n}\frac{\widetilde{\omega}_2^{-1}s_{11} - 2\rho_0 s_{12} + \widetilde{\omega}_2 s_{22}}{1-\rho_0^2} = \frac{n-1}{n}\frac{\sqrt{s_{11}s_{22}} - \rho_0 s_{12}}{1-\rho_0^2}$$

$$= \frac{n-1}{n}\sqrt{s_{11}s_{22}}\,\frac{1-\rho_0\widehat{\rho}}{1-\rho_0^2}$$

(meaning that the product $\omega_1 \equiv \sigma_1\sigma_2$ is estimated by its unrestricted MLE counterpart $\frac{n-1}{n}\sqrt{s_{11}s_{22}}$ *only* asymptotically under H_0 where $\widehat{\rho} \xrightarrow{p} \rho_0$). To confirm a maximum, we need to consider the second-order conditions. These lead to

$$\mathcal{H} = \begin{pmatrix} \dfrac{n}{\omega_1^2} - \dfrac{(n-1)\left(\omega_2^{-1}s_{11} - 2\rho_0 s_{12} + \omega_2 s_{22}\right)}{\omega_1^3\left(1-\rho_0^2\right)} & \dfrac{n-1}{2\omega_1^2\left(1-\rho_0^2\right)}\left(-\omega_2^{-2}s_{11} + s_{22}\right) \\ \dfrac{n-1}{2\omega_1^2\left(1-\rho_0^2\right)}\left(-\omega_2^{-2}s_{11} + s_{22}\right) & -\dfrac{n-1}{\omega_1\omega_2^3\left(1-\rho_0^2\right)}s_{11} \end{pmatrix}$$

being diagonal at $\widetilde{\omega}_1, \widetilde{\omega}_2$ with negative diagonal elements, since

$$\frac{n}{\widetilde{\omega}_1^2} - \frac{2n}{\widetilde{\omega}_1^3}\frac{(n-1)\left(\widetilde{\omega}_2^{-1}s_{11} - 2\rho_0 s_{12} + \widetilde{\omega}_2 s_{22}\right)}{2n\left(1-\rho_0^2\right)} = \frac{n}{\widetilde{\omega}_1^2} - \frac{2n}{\widetilde{\omega}_1^3}\widetilde{\omega}_1 = -\frac{n}{\widetilde{\omega}_1^2}.$$

The profile likelihood under H_0 is therefore

$$L(\overline{\boldsymbol{x}}, \widetilde{\boldsymbol{\Sigma}}) = (2\pi\widetilde{\omega}_1)^{-n}\left(1-\rho_0^2\right)^{-n/2}\exp(-n)$$
$$= \left(\frac{2(n-1)\pi\mathrm{e}}{n}\sqrt{s_{11}s_{22}}\right)^{-n}\left(\frac{(1-\rho_0\widehat{\rho})^2}{1-\rho_0^2}\right)^{-n/2},$$

which will allow us to obtain $\wp$ explicitly.

We are now in a position to write

$$\wp = \left(\frac{(1-\rho_0\widehat{\rho})^2}{\left(1-\rho_0^2\right)\left(1-\widehat{\rho}^2\right)}\right)^{-n/2},$$

rejecting H_0 when $\wp < \gamma$ or

$$(1-\rho_0\widehat{\rho})^2 > \gamma^{-2/n}\left(1-\rho_0^2\right)\left(1-\widehat{\rho}^2\right).$$

This quadratic function of $\widehat{\rho}$ can be rewritten as

$$\left(\left(\gamma^{2/n}-1\right)\rho_0^2+1\right)\widehat{\rho}^2 - 2\gamma^{2/n}\rho_0\widehat{\rho} + \left(\gamma^{2/n}-1+\rho_0^2\right) > 0$$

and the roots of the left-hand side imply a rejection when

$$\widehat{\rho} \notin \left[\frac{\rho_0\gamma^{2/n}-\left(1-\rho_0^2\right)\sqrt{1-\gamma^{2/n}}}{1+\left(\gamma^{2/n}-1\right)\rho_0^2}, \frac{\rho_0\gamma^{2/n}+\left(1-\rho_0^2\right)\sqrt{1-\gamma^{2/n}}}{1+\left(\gamma^{2/n}-1\right)\rho_0^2}\right].$$

Note that γ is determined by making $\wp < \gamma$ with probability α under H_0, the distribution of $\widehat{\rho}$ following from Exercise 9.25. Unless $\rho_0 = 0$, the interval for $\widehat{\rho}$ is neither symmetric around ρ_0 nor central (it does not have equal-probability critical tails; see the introduction to Chapter 13) for $n < \infty$.

Exercise 14.16 (LR, W, LM: linear invertible restrictions in linear model) Consider the normal linear model

$$\boldsymbol{y} = \boldsymbol{X}\boldsymbol{\beta} + \boldsymbol{\varepsilon}, \qquad \boldsymbol{\varepsilon} \sim \mathrm{N}(\mathbf{0}, \sigma^2\boldsymbol{I}_n),$$

where n is the sample size, $n > k$, $\sigma^2 > 0$, $\boldsymbol{y}$ and $\boldsymbol{\varepsilon}$ are $n \times 1$ random vectors, and $\boldsymbol{X}$ is an $n \times k$ matrix of k nonrandom regressors (for example, as a result of conditioning as in Exercises 12.30 and 12.31, whose results you may use here). Suppose that the rank of $\boldsymbol{X}$ is k, so that $\boldsymbol{X}'\boldsymbol{X}$ is positive definite.

(a) Apply the general definitions of W, LM, and LR (found in the introduction to this chapter) to testing $\mathrm{H}_0 : \boldsymbol{\beta} = \boldsymbol{\beta}_0$ against $\mathrm{H}_1 : \boldsymbol{\beta} \neq \boldsymbol{\beta}_0$ in this model.

(b) Express LM and LR in terms of W, hence showing that $W \geqslant LR \geqslant LM$.

(c) Obtain the asymptotic distributions of W, LM, and LR, assuming that $\boldsymbol{X}'\boldsymbol{X} = O(n)$.

(d) Now consider instead the *sequence of local alternatives*

$$\mathrm{H}_1 : \boldsymbol{\beta} = \boldsymbol{\beta}_0 + \frac{1}{\sqrt{n}}\boldsymbol{c} \qquad (\boldsymbol{c} \neq \mathbf{0}_k)$$

with $\boldsymbol{c}$ a nonrandom vector, assumed here to be fixed as n varies. (The alternatives are called "local" because β is in the vicinity of β_0 for n large.) Answer part (c) again, assuming further that $\frac{1}{n}X'X$ tends to a finite positive definite matrix.

Solution

(a) To apply the definitions of W, LM, and LR to this model, we need some results from Section 12.3, namely

$$\begin{aligned}\widehat{\beta} &= \left(X'X\right)^{-1}Xy \sim \mathrm{N}(\beta, \sigma^2(X'X)^{-1}),\\ \ell(\widehat{\beta}, \widehat{\sigma}^2) &= -\frac{n}{2}\left(\log\left(2\pi\right)+1\right) - \frac{n}{2}\log\left(\widehat{\sigma}^2\right),\\ \frac{\partial \ell(\beta, \sigma^2)}{\partial \beta} &= \frac{1}{\sigma^2}X'\left(y - X\beta\right),\\ \mathcal{I}^{-1} &= \mathrm{diag}\left(\sigma^2\left(X'X\right)^{-1}, \frac{2\sigma^4}{n}\right),\\ \widehat{\sigma}^2 &= \frac{1}{n}(y - X\widehat{\beta})'(y - X\widehat{\beta}).\end{aligned}$$

Then, letting $\theta' = \left(\beta', \sigma^2\right)$, we obtain

$$\begin{aligned}W &= \left(\widehat{\beta} - \beta_0\right)'\left(\sigma^2\left(X'X\right)^{-1}\right)^{-1}\Big|_{\theta=\widehat{\theta}}\left(\widehat{\beta} - \beta_0\right)\\ &= \widehat{\sigma}^{-2}\left(\widehat{\beta} - \beta_0\right)'X'X\left(\widehat{\beta} - \beta_0\right).\end{aligned}$$

Next, $\mathcal{I}$ is block-diagonal for the parameter vector (β', σ^2) and, as the score vector is asymptotically $\mathrm{N}(\mathbf{0}, \mathcal{I})$, its two components become independent and we can focus on the first (the score for β, or $\partial\ell/\partial\beta$) when defining LM for $\mathrm{H}_0 : \beta = \beta_0$. (This issue will be revisited in Exercise 14.18.) For the formula, we need the H_0-restricted MLE $\widetilde{\sigma}^2 := n^{-1}(y - X\beta_0)'(y - X\beta_0)$, which we note as being random (hence the notation $\widetilde{\sigma}$ and not σ_0) even though $\mathrm{H}_0 : \beta = \beta_0$ implies a fixed known value for β. Then

$$\begin{aligned}LM &= \left(\frac{(X'\left(y - X\beta\right))'}{\sigma^2}\sigma^2\left(X'X\right)^{-1}\frac{X'\left(y - X\beta\right)}{\sigma^2}\right)\Bigg|_{\theta=\theta_0}\\ &= \widetilde{\sigma}^{-2}\left(yX' - \beta_0'X'X\right)\left(X'X\right)^{-1}\left(X'y - X'X\beta_0\right)\\ &= \widetilde{\sigma}^{-2}\left(\widehat{\beta} - \beta_0\right)'X'X\left(\widehat{\beta} - \beta_0\right),\end{aligned}$$

since $\widehat{\beta} = (X'X)^{-1}Xy$. Finally,

$$LR = 2\left(\frac{n}{2}\log\left(\widetilde{\sigma}^2\right) - \frac{n}{2}\log\left(\widehat{\sigma}^2\right)\right) = n\log\left(\frac{\widetilde{\sigma}^2}{\widehat{\sigma}^2}\right).$$

(b) Clearly,

$$LM = \frac{\widehat{\sigma}^2}{\widetilde{\sigma}^2}W,$$

where the ratio $\tilde{\sigma}^2/\hat{\sigma}^2$ is found in the definition of LR also. To study it, write

$$\begin{aligned}\tilde{\sigma}^2 &= \frac{1}{n}(\boldsymbol{y} - \boldsymbol{X}\boldsymbol{\beta}_0)'(\boldsymbol{y} - \boldsymbol{X}\boldsymbol{\beta}_0)\\ &= \frac{1}{n}\left(\boldsymbol{y} - \boldsymbol{X}\widehat{\boldsymbol{\beta}} + \boldsymbol{X}\left(\widehat{\boldsymbol{\beta}} - \boldsymbol{\beta}_0\right)\right)'\left(\boldsymbol{y} - \boldsymbol{X}\widehat{\boldsymbol{\beta}} + \boldsymbol{X}\left(\widehat{\boldsymbol{\beta}} - \boldsymbol{\beta}_0\right)\right)\\ &= \frac{1}{n}\left(\boldsymbol{y} - \boldsymbol{X}\widehat{\boldsymbol{\beta}}\right)'\left(\boldsymbol{y} - \boldsymbol{X}\widehat{\boldsymbol{\beta}}\right) + \frac{1}{n}\left(\widehat{\boldsymbol{\beta}} - \boldsymbol{\beta}_0\right)'\boldsymbol{X}'\boldsymbol{X}\left(\widehat{\boldsymbol{\beta}} - \boldsymbol{\beta}_0\right)\\ &\quad + \frac{2}{n}\left(\widehat{\boldsymbol{\beta}} - \boldsymbol{\beta}_0\right)'\boldsymbol{X}'\left(\boldsymbol{y} - \boldsymbol{X}\widehat{\boldsymbol{\beta}}\right)\\ &= \hat{\sigma}^2 + \frac{\hat{\sigma}^2}{n}W + 0,\end{aligned}$$

since $\boldsymbol{X}'\boldsymbol{y} - \boldsymbol{X}'\boldsymbol{X}\widehat{\boldsymbol{\beta}} = \mathbf{0}_k$ from the definition of $\widehat{\boldsymbol{\beta}}$. Note that $\tilde{\sigma}^2 \geqslant \hat{\sigma}^2$, in line with the explanation given at the end of the solution of Exercise 13.13(d). Now,

$$\frac{\tilde{\sigma}^2}{\hat{\sigma}^2} = 1 + \frac{1}{n}W;$$

hence

$$LM = \frac{W}{1 + W/n} \leqslant W$$

and

$$\frac{1}{n}LR = \log\left(1 + \frac{1}{n}W\right) \leqslant \frac{1}{n}W$$

since $\exp(z) = 1 + z + z^2/2! + \cdots \geqslant 1 + z$ for $z := W/n \geqslant 0$. Finally, $LM \leqslant LR$ is implied by

$$\frac{z}{1+z} \leqslant \log(1+z),$$

by the same method as that used to establish the hint of Exercise 1.20 (the function $z/(1+z) - \log(1+z)$ has a unique maximum of zero at $z = 0$ when $z > -1$).

(c) By the consistency of the MLE, $\hat{\sigma}^2 \xrightarrow{p} \sigma^2$ and we get that W has the same asymptotic distribution as

$$W_\infty := \left(\widehat{\boldsymbol{\beta}} - \boldsymbol{\beta}_0\right)'\frac{\boldsymbol{X}'\boldsymbol{X}}{\sigma^2}\left(\widehat{\boldsymbol{\beta}} - \boldsymbol{\beta}_0\right).$$

The distribution of W_∞ is obtained from

$$\widehat{\boldsymbol{\beta}} - \boldsymbol{\beta}_0 \sim \mathrm{N}\left(\boldsymbol{\beta} - \boldsymbol{\beta}_0, \sigma^2\left(\boldsymbol{X}'\boldsymbol{X}\right)^{-1}\right)$$

and Exercise 8.28 as $W_\infty \sim \chi^2(k, \delta)$ with $\delta := \sigma^{-2}(\boldsymbol{\beta} - \boldsymbol{\beta}_0)'\boldsymbol{X}'\boldsymbol{X}(\boldsymbol{\beta} - \boldsymbol{\beta}_0)$. When $\mathrm{H}_0 : \boldsymbol{\beta} = \boldsymbol{\beta}_0$ holds, we get $\delta = 0$ and $W \overset{a}{\sim} \chi^2(k)$; otherwise, we get $W \overset{a}{\sim} \chi^2(k, \delta)$ with $\delta > 0$ and the test is consistent, as shown in Exercise 14.3, since $\delta \to \infty$ as $n \to \infty$ when $\boldsymbol{\beta} \neq \boldsymbol{\beta}_0$ and $\boldsymbol{X}'\boldsymbol{X}$ diverges. Note the use of the term "asymptotic" distribution, unlike in previous exercises where the *exact* finite-sample distribution was obtained; for example, here we would have

$$\frac{n-k}{nk}W = \frac{n-k}{k}\frac{(\widehat{\boldsymbol{\beta}}-\boldsymbol{\beta}_0)'\boldsymbol{X}'\boldsymbol{X}(\widehat{\boldsymbol{\beta}}-\boldsymbol{\beta}_0)}{n\widehat{\sigma}^2} \sim \mathrm{F}(k, n-k),$$

since $n\widehat{\sigma}^2/\sigma^2 \sim \chi^2(n-k)$ independently of the $\chi^2(k)$ in the numerator. Notice the important fact that, as a result, the exact finite-sample distribution of W is robust, in that it applies more generally to linear models that allow for nonnormal residuals such as spherically distributed ones; see the solution of Exercise 12.35(f). Also, for the asymptotic relation between χ^2 and F, see Exercises 8.37(b) and 10.32(d).

For LM, consider the limiting behavior of the variate $z := W/n$ and recall that $LM = W/(1+z)$. If $\mathrm{H}_0 : \boldsymbol{\beta} = \boldsymbol{\beta}_0$ holds, then $W \overset{a}{\sim} \chi^2(k)$; hence $W = O_p(1)$ and $z \xrightarrow{p} 0$, implying $LM \overset{a}{\sim} \chi^2(k)$. Otherwise, $W \overset{a}{\sim} \chi^2(k, \delta)$ and we would get

$$\mathrm{E}\left(\frac{W_\infty}{n}\right) = \frac{\mathrm{E}(\chi^2(k,\delta))}{n} = \frac{k+\delta}{n}, \qquad \mathrm{var}\left(\frac{W_\infty}{n}\right) = \frac{\mathrm{var}(\chi^2(k,\delta))}{n^2} = \frac{2k+4\delta}{n^2}$$

from Table 4.2. Since $\boldsymbol{X}'\boldsymbol{X} = o(n^2)$, as is implied by the assumption that $\boldsymbol{X}'\boldsymbol{X} = O(n)$ in the question, then $\delta/n^2 \to 0$ gives $\mathrm{var}(z) \to 0$ and z is asymptotically degenerate and centered around δ/n (since k is fixed as n increases); hence

$$LM \overset{a}{\sim} \frac{1}{1+\delta/n} \cdot \chi^2(k,\delta),$$

where we recall the dependence of δ on n on the right-hand side (LM and $\chi^2(k,\delta)$ can be normalized here if we assume an exact rate of divergence of $\boldsymbol{X}'\boldsymbol{X}$ and hence δ). To illustrate the condition $\boldsymbol{X}'\boldsymbol{X} = o(n^2)$, letting $k = 1$ (an illustration used earlier in Exercise 12.31(d)), we get

$$\sum_{i=1}^n x_i^2 = n\,\overline{x^2},$$

where $\overline{x^2} > 0$ denotes the sample average of x_i^2 values. This condition can be violated if the data have a deterministic trend such as that in Exercise 12.43(a); for example, $x_i = i^p$ (with $p > 0$) gives

$$\sum_{i=1}^n x_i^2 = \sum_{i=1}^n i^{2p} = \frac{n^{2p+1}}{2p+1}\left(1 + o(1)\right),$$

where $p \geqslant \frac{1}{2}$ implies that $\boldsymbol{X}'\boldsymbol{X} = o(n^2)$ is not satisfied.

For $LR = n\log\left(1 + \frac{1}{n}W\right)$, it follows from $\mathrm{H}_0 : \boldsymbol{\beta} = \boldsymbol{\beta}_0$ that $W \overset{a}{\sim} \chi^2(k)$; hence $W = O_p(1)$, and

$$LR = n\log\left(1 + \frac{1}{n}W\right) = n\left(\frac{W}{n} - \frac{W^2}{2n^2} + \cdots\right) = W + o_p(1)$$

(by the logarithmic expansion) gives $LR \overset{a}{\sim} \chi^2(k)$. In general, we can use the transformation theorem to get the asymptotic density of LR from W_∞. We have

$$W = n\left(\exp\left(\frac{LR}{n}\right) - 1\right);$$

hence the asymptotic density of LR is

$$f_{LR}(u) = \exp\left(\frac{u}{n}\right) f_{\chi^2(k,\delta)}\left(n\left(\exp\left(\frac{u}{n}\right) - 1\right)\right), \qquad u \in \mathbb{R}_+;$$

see Table 4.2 for the formula of $f_{\chi^2(k,\delta)}$.

(d) The distributions under H_0 are unchanged. At the start of this exercise, we had assumed that $\boldsymbol{X}'\boldsymbol{X}$ has full rank. Now, assume further that $\frac{1}{n}\boldsymbol{X}'\boldsymbol{X}$ tends to a finite positive definite matrix $\boldsymbol{V}$. Under

$$\mathrm{H}_1 : \boldsymbol{\beta} = \boldsymbol{\beta}_0 + \frac{1}{\sqrt{n}}\boldsymbol{c},$$

we get $\delta = \sigma^{-2}(\boldsymbol{\beta} - \boldsymbol{\beta}_0)'\boldsymbol{X}'\boldsymbol{X}(\boldsymbol{\beta} - \boldsymbol{\beta}_0) \to \sigma^{-2}\boldsymbol{c}'\boldsymbol{V}\boldsymbol{c} > 0$. As in (c), $W \overset{a}{\sim} \chi^2(k,\delta)$, but now δ is finite under H_1 when $\boldsymbol{c}$ is fixed. However, the property in Exercise 14.3 that $\Pi(\delta)$ is increasing in δ means that $\Pi(\delta) > \alpha$ under H_1.

The advantage of considering such local alternatives is that the three tests become asymptotically equivalent under *both* H_0 and H_1, not just the former. This follows directly from

$$LM = \frac{W}{1 + \frac{1}{n}W} = W\left(1 - \frac{W}{n} + \cdots\right)$$

(by the geometric progression) and

$$LR = n\log\left(1 + \frac{1}{n}W\right) = n\left(\frac{W}{n} - \frac{W^2}{2n^2} + \cdots\right) = W\left(1 - \frac{W}{2n} + \cdots\right)$$

(by the logarithmic expansion), but with $W = O_p(1)$ now under H_1 as well. Hence W, LR, and LM are all asymptotically equivalent to $W_\infty \sim \chi^2(k,\delta)$. Note that the choice of the $\sqrt{n}$ rate of convergence of $\boldsymbol{\beta}_0$ to $\boldsymbol{\beta}$ in the specification of the local alternatives is to ensure that W_∞ is properly normalized in this setup. Other rates may be required in nonstandard setups.

Exercise 14.17 (LR, W, LM: linear invertible restrictions) Suppose that we have a model where the MLE is consistent and satisfies $\widehat{\boldsymbol{\theta}} \overset{a}{\sim} \mathrm{N}(\boldsymbol{\theta}, \boldsymbol{\mathcal{I}}^{-1})$. Suppose further that $\widehat{\boldsymbol{\mathcal{I}}} := \boldsymbol{\mathcal{I}}(\widehat{\boldsymbol{\theta}})$ is a consistent estimator of $\boldsymbol{\mathcal{I}}$, in the sense that $\widehat{\boldsymbol{\mathcal{I}}}\boldsymbol{\mathcal{I}}^{-1} \xrightarrow{p} \boldsymbol{I}_m$, and that the conditions of Exercise 12.28 hold, with m and n denoting the dimension of $\boldsymbol{\theta}$ and the sample size, respectively. Consider testing $\mathrm{H}_0 : \boldsymbol{\theta} = \boldsymbol{\theta}_0$ against $\mathrm{H}_1 : \boldsymbol{\theta} \neq \boldsymbol{\theta}_0$.

(a) Using the definitions of W, LR, and LM in the introduction to the chapter, obtain their asymptotic distributions under H_0.

(b) Solve the constrained optimization $\sup_{\boldsymbol{\theta}} \ell(\boldsymbol{\theta})$ subject to $\boldsymbol{\theta} = \boldsymbol{\theta}_0$, and base a test (of H_0 against H_1) on the resulting Lagrange multiplier.

Solution

(a) From the introduction,

$$W = \left(\widehat{\boldsymbol{\theta}} - \boldsymbol{\theta}_0\right)' \widehat{\mathcal{I}} \left(\widehat{\boldsymbol{\theta}} - \boldsymbol{\theta}_0\right),$$

$$LR = 2\left(\ell(\widehat{\boldsymbol{\theta}}) - \ell(\boldsymbol{\theta}_0)\right),$$

$$LM = \boldsymbol{q}(\boldsymbol{\theta}_0)' \widetilde{\mathcal{I}}^{-1} \boldsymbol{q}(\boldsymbol{\theta}_0).$$

The consistency of $\widehat{\mathcal{I}}$ implies that W has the same asymptotic distribution as

$$W_\infty := \left(\widehat{\boldsymbol{\theta}} - \boldsymbol{\theta}_0\right)' \mathcal{I} \left(\widehat{\boldsymbol{\theta}} - \boldsymbol{\theta}_0\right) \sim \chi^2(m, \delta),$$

where $\delta := (\boldsymbol{\theta} - \boldsymbol{\theta}_0)' \mathcal{I} (\boldsymbol{\theta} - \boldsymbol{\theta}_0)$ in general and $\delta = 0$ when H_0 holds.

For the distribution of LR, we use the same expansion as in Exercise 12.28(a), but this time with $\boldsymbol{\theta} = \boldsymbol{\theta}_0$, which occurs when H_0 holds. Hence, under H_0,

$$\ell(\widehat{\boldsymbol{\theta}}) - \ell(\boldsymbol{\theta}_0) - \frac{1}{2}\left(\boldsymbol{\theta}_0 - \widehat{\boldsymbol{\theta}}\right)' \mathcal{I} \left(\boldsymbol{\theta}_0 - \widehat{\boldsymbol{\theta}}\right) \xrightarrow{p} 0$$

and we therefore have that $\ell(\widehat{\boldsymbol{\theta}}) - \ell(\boldsymbol{\theta}_0)$ is asymptotically equivalent to $\frac{1}{2}W_\infty$, hence establishing that $LR \overset{a}{\sim} \chi^2(m)$. Notice that actually we have established the stronger result, that the two statistics LR and W coincide asymptotically under H_0, which is more than just sharing the same limiting distribution. Recall that two variates may have the same distribution but be different variates, a simple example being $z \sim N(0,1)$ and $-z \sim N(0,1)$.

For LM, Exercise 12.28(b) with $\boldsymbol{\theta} = \boldsymbol{\theta}_0$ implies that

$$\boldsymbol{q}(\boldsymbol{\theta}_0) = \mathcal{I}(\boldsymbol{\theta}_0)\left(\widehat{\boldsymbol{\theta}} - \boldsymbol{\theta}_0\right)(1 + o_p(1)),$$

where $\widetilde{\mathcal{I}} \equiv \mathcal{I}(\boldsymbol{\theta}_0) = \mathcal{I}(\boldsymbol{\theta}) \equiv \mathcal{I}$; hence $LM = W_\infty + o_p(1)$ under H_0 and we obtain the same asymptotic $\chi^2(m)$. Note that the displayed relation between the score and the MLE implies that our assumption of $\widehat{\boldsymbol{\theta}} \overset{a}{\sim} N(\boldsymbol{\theta}, \mathcal{I}^{-1})$ is equivalent to $\boldsymbol{q}(\boldsymbol{\theta}_0) \overset{a}{\sim} N(\mathbf{0}_m, \mathcal{I})$ under H_0.

(b) We set up the Lagrangian (see Section A.4.5)

$$S(\boldsymbol{\theta}) := \ell(\boldsymbol{\theta}) + (\boldsymbol{\theta}_0 - \boldsymbol{\theta})' \boldsymbol{\lambda},$$

where $\boldsymbol{\lambda}$ is an m-dimensional vector of Lagrange multipliers. Differentiating,

$$\frac{\partial S(\boldsymbol{\theta})}{\partial \boldsymbol{\theta}} = \boldsymbol{q}(\boldsymbol{\theta}) - \boldsymbol{\lambda}$$

and the first-order conditions are $\boldsymbol{q}(\widetilde{\boldsymbol{\theta}}) = \widetilde{\boldsymbol{\lambda}}$ and $\boldsymbol{\theta}_0 = \widetilde{\boldsymbol{\theta}}$, where $\widetilde{\boldsymbol{\theta}}$ denotes the restricted MLE. In the case of the straightforward H_0 in this exercise, the restricted MLE is simply the vector of constants $\boldsymbol{\theta}_0$, but this Lagrangian approach will be useful for subsequent exercises. Furthermore, we get $\widetilde{\boldsymbol{\lambda}} = \boldsymbol{q}(\boldsymbol{\theta}_0)$, where the latter's distribution was obtained in part (a) as $\boldsymbol{q}(\boldsymbol{\theta}_0) \overset{a}{\sim} N(\mathbf{0}_m, \mathcal{I})$ under H_0; hence we can build a quadratic form in $\widetilde{\boldsymbol{\lambda}}$ as follows:

$$LM_\lambda := \widetilde{\boldsymbol{\lambda}}'\boldsymbol{\mathcal{I}}(\boldsymbol{\lambda}_0)^{-1}\widetilde{\boldsymbol{\lambda}},$$

which is $\chi^2(m)$ under H_0 because it is equal to the earlier formula

$$LM_q := \boldsymbol{q}(\boldsymbol{\theta}_0)'\widetilde{\boldsymbol{\mathcal{I}}}^{-1}\boldsymbol{q}(\boldsymbol{\theta}_0)$$

whose new subscript q is to stress that this is the statistic based on the score $\boldsymbol{q}$. The statistics LM_q and LM_λ are known as *Rao's score* and *Silvey's Lagrange multiplier* test statistics, respectively. They need not have identical expressions in more complicated setups, as we shall see in the following exercises for different hypotheses. Note that the second-order conditions for a maximum are satisfied since $\partial^2 S(\boldsymbol{\theta})/\partial\boldsymbol{\theta}\partial\boldsymbol{\theta}'$ is simply the Hessian of the log-likelihood.

The interpretation of $\widetilde{\boldsymbol{\lambda}}$ is the usual one; see the end of Appendix A. The magnitude of $\widetilde{\boldsymbol{\lambda}}$ reflects the marginal cost (in terms of log-likelihood) of imposing the m constraints in $\text{H}_0 : \boldsymbol{\theta} = \boldsymbol{\theta}_0$, and LM_λ quantifies this cost in a one-dimensional measure through a quadratic form in $\widetilde{\boldsymbol{\lambda}}$ where $\text{var}(\widetilde{\boldsymbol{\lambda}})$ is used for normalization (standardization). If this cost is large, then the constraints imposed by H_0 are not supported by the data.

***Exercise 14.18 (LR, W, LM: nonlinear restrictions)** Assume the same setup as in Exercise 14.17, except that we now have $\text{H}_0 : \boldsymbol{h}(\boldsymbol{\theta}) = \mathbf{0}_r$ against $\text{H}_1 : \boldsymbol{h}(\boldsymbol{\theta}) \neq \mathbf{0}_r$ with $r \leqslant m$ and $\boldsymbol{h}(\cdot)$ a continuously differentiable and deterministic function of $\boldsymbol{\theta}$ that does not depend on n and for which $\boldsymbol{R}(\boldsymbol{\theta})' := \partial\boldsymbol{h}(\boldsymbol{\theta})/\partial\boldsymbol{\theta}'$ has rank r in the neighborhood of the true $\boldsymbol{\theta}$. Henceforth, we write $\boldsymbol{R}$ for $\boldsymbol{R}(\boldsymbol{\theta})$ and express the asymptotic equality of two statistics as $\tau_1 \overset{a}{=} \tau_2$.

(a) Using the Wald testing principle, devise a test of H_0 against H_1 and obtain the limiting distribution of this W.

(b) Solve the constrained optimization $\sup_{\boldsymbol{\theta}} \ell(\boldsymbol{\theta})$ subject to $\boldsymbol{h}(\boldsymbol{\theta}) = \mathbf{0}_r$, and base a test (of H_0 against H_1) on the resulting Lagrange multiplier. Show that $LM_q = LM_\lambda$, and explain this relation. [Hint: Expand $\boldsymbol{q}(\widetilde{\boldsymbol{\theta}})$ and $\boldsymbol{h}(\widetilde{\boldsymbol{\theta}})$ in the neighborhood of the true $\boldsymbol{\theta}$ in the first-order conditions, then obtain the joint distribution of $\widetilde{\boldsymbol{\theta}}$ and $\widetilde{\boldsymbol{\lambda}}$.]

(c) Establish that $W \overset{a}{=} LM_\lambda$ under H_0. [Hint: Expand $\boldsymbol{h}(\widehat{\boldsymbol{\theta}})$ from W around $\widetilde{\boldsymbol{\theta}}$, and expand $\boldsymbol{q}(\widetilde{\boldsymbol{\theta}})$ from LM_q around $\widehat{\boldsymbol{\theta}}$.]

(d) Establish that $W \overset{a}{=} LR$ under H_0.

Solution

(a) Since $\widehat{\boldsymbol{\theta}} \overset{a}{\sim} \text{N}\left(\boldsymbol{\theta}, \boldsymbol{\mathcal{I}}^{-1}\right)$ and $\boldsymbol{\mathcal{I}}^{-1} \to \mathbf{O}$ as $n \to \infty$, the delta method of Exercise 10.20 gives

$$\boldsymbol{h}(\widehat{\boldsymbol{\theta}}) \overset{a}{\sim} \text{N}\left(\boldsymbol{h}(\boldsymbol{\theta}), \boldsymbol{\varOmega}\right),$$

where $\boldsymbol{\varOmega} := \boldsymbol{R}'\boldsymbol{\mathcal{I}}^{-1}\boldsymbol{R}$ is a full-rank $r \times r$ matrix. Under $\text{H}_0 : \boldsymbol{h}(\boldsymbol{\theta}) = \mathbf{0}_r$, we have $\text{E}(\boldsymbol{h}(\widehat{\boldsymbol{\theta}})) = \mathbf{0}_r$ and we can build the usual quadratic form W from $\boldsymbol{h}(\widehat{\boldsymbol{\theta}})$ as follows:

$$W := \boldsymbol{h}(\widehat{\boldsymbol{\theta}})'\widehat{\boldsymbol{\varOmega}}^{-1}\boldsymbol{h}(\widehat{\boldsymbol{\theta}}),$$

where $\widehat{\boldsymbol{\Omega}} := \boldsymbol{\Omega}|_{\boldsymbol{\theta}=\widehat{\boldsymbol{\theta}}}$. The estimator $\widehat{\boldsymbol{\Omega}}$ is consistent because the function $\partial \boldsymbol{h}(\boldsymbol{\theta})/\partial \boldsymbol{\theta}'$ does not depend on n (implying the consistency of $\partial \boldsymbol{h}(\boldsymbol{\theta})/\partial \boldsymbol{\theta}'|_{\boldsymbol{\theta}=\widehat{\boldsymbol{\theta}}}$) and because $\widehat{\boldsymbol{\mathcal{I}}}$ is consistent; see Exercise 10.16(b). As a result, $W \overset{a}{\sim} \chi^2(r, \delta)$ with $\delta := \boldsymbol{h}(\boldsymbol{\theta})'\boldsymbol{\Omega}^{-1}\boldsymbol{h}(\boldsymbol{\theta})$.
(b) As before, we set up the Lagrangian

$$S(\boldsymbol{\theta}) := \ell(\boldsymbol{\theta}) + (\mathbf{0}_r - \boldsymbol{h}(\boldsymbol{\theta}))' \boldsymbol{\lambda};$$

hence

$$\frac{\partial S(\boldsymbol{\theta})}{\partial \boldsymbol{\theta}} = \boldsymbol{q}(\boldsymbol{\theta}) - \boldsymbol{R}\boldsymbol{\lambda}$$

and the first-order conditions are

$$\boldsymbol{q}(\widetilde{\boldsymbol{\theta}}) = \boldsymbol{R}|_{\boldsymbol{\theta}=\widetilde{\boldsymbol{\theta}}} \widetilde{\boldsymbol{\lambda}} \qquad \text{and} \qquad \boldsymbol{h}(\widetilde{\boldsymbol{\theta}}) = \mathbf{0}_r,$$

where we see that $\widetilde{\boldsymbol{\theta}}$ is now random in general (as was the case for $\widetilde{\sigma}^2$ in Exercise 14.16). As a result, any quadratic form based on $\boldsymbol{q}(\widetilde{\boldsymbol{\theta}})$ will be identical to the corresponding form based on $\boldsymbol{R}|_{\boldsymbol{\theta}=\widetilde{\boldsymbol{\theta}}} \widetilde{\boldsymbol{\lambda}}$, as we will see later when defining LM_q and LM_λ.

Since $\widetilde{\boldsymbol{\theta}}$ is consistent for $\boldsymbol{\theta}$ when H_0 holds, and since the function $\partial \boldsymbol{h}(\boldsymbol{\theta})/\partial \boldsymbol{\theta}'$ does not depend on n, we can replace $\boldsymbol{R}|_{\boldsymbol{\theta}=\widetilde{\boldsymbol{\theta}}}$ by $\boldsymbol{R}$ in the above first-order conditions and rewrite them as

$$\boldsymbol{q}(\widetilde{\boldsymbol{\theta}}) \overset{a}{=} \boldsymbol{R}\widetilde{\boldsymbol{\lambda}} \qquad \text{and} \qquad \boldsymbol{h}(\widetilde{\boldsymbol{\theta}}) = \mathbf{0}_r.$$

Furthermore, under H_0, we can expand both left-hand sides, $\boldsymbol{q}(\widetilde{\boldsymbol{\theta}})$ and $\boldsymbol{h}(\widetilde{\boldsymbol{\theta}})$, in the neighborhood of $\boldsymbol{\theta}$ (to which $\widetilde{\boldsymbol{\theta}}$ tends under H_0) as

$$\boldsymbol{q}(\boldsymbol{\theta}) - \boldsymbol{\mathcal{I}}\left(\widetilde{\boldsymbol{\theta}} - \boldsymbol{\theta}\right) \overset{a}{=} \boldsymbol{R}\widetilde{\boldsymbol{\lambda}}$$

by using Exercise 12.28(b) and

$$\mathbf{0}_r + \boldsymbol{R}'\left(\widetilde{\boldsymbol{\theta}} - \boldsymbol{\theta}\right) \overset{a}{=} \mathbf{0}_r$$

by $\boldsymbol{h}(\boldsymbol{\theta}) = \mathbf{0}_r$ and $\boldsymbol{R}' \equiv \partial \boldsymbol{h}(\boldsymbol{\theta})/\partial \boldsymbol{\theta}'$ evaluated in a hyperrectangle bounded by $\widetilde{\boldsymbol{\theta}}$ and $\boldsymbol{\theta}$ that shrinks to $\boldsymbol{\theta}$ as $\widetilde{\boldsymbol{\theta}} \overset{p}{\longrightarrow} \boldsymbol{\theta}$ under H_0. (Note that the constraint function $\boldsymbol{h}(\widetilde{\boldsymbol{\theta}})$ is asymptotically linear in the neighborhood of $\boldsymbol{\theta}$, which means that the second-order conditions follow as in the previous exercise.) Stacking these two equations to obtain the joint distribution of $\widetilde{\boldsymbol{\theta}} - \boldsymbol{\theta}$ and $\widetilde{\boldsymbol{\lambda}}$ in terms of the known distribution of $\boldsymbol{q}(\boldsymbol{\theta}) \overset{a}{\sim} \mathrm{N}(\mathbf{0}_m, \boldsymbol{\mathcal{I}})$, we get

$$\begin{pmatrix} \boldsymbol{\mathcal{I}} & \boldsymbol{R} \\ \boldsymbol{R}' & \mathbf{O}_{r,r} \end{pmatrix} \begin{pmatrix} \widetilde{\boldsymbol{\theta}} - \boldsymbol{\theta} \\ \widetilde{\boldsymbol{\lambda}} \end{pmatrix} \overset{a}{=} \begin{pmatrix} \boldsymbol{q}(\boldsymbol{\theta}) \\ \mathbf{0}_r \end{pmatrix} \overset{a}{\sim} \mathrm{N}(\mathbf{0}_{m+r}, \mathrm{diag}\,(\boldsymbol{\mathcal{I}}, \mathbf{O})).$$

Recall that we encountered a similar equation in Exercise 13.13(a). The formula for the partitioned inverse (see Section A.4) gives

$$\boldsymbol{Q} := \begin{pmatrix} \boldsymbol{\mathcal{I}} & \boldsymbol{R} \\ \boldsymbol{R}' & \mathbf{O}_{r,r} \end{pmatrix}^{-1} = \begin{pmatrix} \boldsymbol{\mathcal{I}}^{-1/2}(\boldsymbol{I}_m - \boldsymbol{P})\boldsymbol{\mathcal{I}}^{-1/2} & \boldsymbol{\mathcal{I}}^{-1}\boldsymbol{R}\left(\boldsymbol{R}'\boldsymbol{\mathcal{I}}^{-1}\boldsymbol{R}\right)^{-1} \\ \left(\boldsymbol{R}'\boldsymbol{\mathcal{I}}^{-1}\boldsymbol{R}\right)^{-1}\boldsymbol{R}'\boldsymbol{\mathcal{I}}^{-1} & -\left(\boldsymbol{R}'\boldsymbol{\mathcal{I}}^{-1}\boldsymbol{R}\right)^{-1} \end{pmatrix},$$

where we have the symmetric idempotent

$$P := \mathcal{I}^{-1/2} R \left(R'\mathcal{I}^{-1}R\right)^{-1} R'\mathcal{I}^{-1/2}$$

satisfying $\operatorname{tr}(P) = r$. Therefore,

$$\begin{pmatrix} \widetilde{\theta} - \theta \\ \widetilde{\lambda} \end{pmatrix} \overset{a}{=} Q \begin{pmatrix} q(\theta) \\ 0_r \end{pmatrix} \overset{a}{\sim} \mathrm{N}(0_{m+r}, Q \operatorname{diag}(\mathcal{I}, \mathrm{O})\, Q),$$

where

$$Q \operatorname{diag}\left(\mathcal{I}^{1/2}, \mathrm{O}\right) \operatorname{diag}\left(\mathcal{I}^{1/2}, \mathrm{O}\right) Q$$

$$= \begin{pmatrix} \mathcal{I}^{-1/2}(I_m - P) & \mathrm{O} \\ \left(R'\mathcal{I}^{-1}R\right)^{-1} R'\mathcal{I}^{-1/2} & \mathrm{O} \end{pmatrix} \begin{pmatrix} (I_m - P)\mathcal{I}^{-1/2} & \mathcal{I}^{-1/2} R \left(R'\mathcal{I}^{-1}R\right)^{-1} \\ \mathrm{O} & \mathrm{O} \end{pmatrix}$$

implies $\widetilde{\lambda} \overset{a}{\sim} \mathrm{N}(0_r, \Omega^{-1})$ by the definition from (a) of $\Omega = R'\mathcal{I}^{-1}R$. (Note that the asymptotic variance of $\widetilde{\theta}$ is $\mathcal{I}^{-1/2}(I_m - P)\mathcal{I}^{-1/2} < \mathcal{I}^{-1}$, the latter being the asymptotic variance of the unrestricted MLE $\widehat{\theta}$; compare Exercise 13.13(b), (c).) From the distribution of $\widetilde{\lambda}$, and defining $\widetilde{\Omega} := \Omega|_{\theta=\widetilde{\theta}}$, we have under H_0 that

$$LM_\lambda := \widetilde{\lambda}'\widetilde{\Omega}\widetilde{\lambda} \overset{a}{\sim} \chi^2(r),$$

with $\widetilde{\Omega}$ a consistent estimator of Ω in this case.

Returning to the first-order condition (which holds for both H_0 and H_1) obtained in the previous paragraph, namely

$$q(\widetilde{\theta}) = R|_{\theta=\widetilde{\theta}}\, \widetilde{\lambda},$$

we can write

$$LM_\lambda = \widetilde{\lambda}'\widetilde{\Omega}\widetilde{\lambda} = \widetilde{\lambda}'\left(R'\mathcal{I}^{-1}R\right)\big|_{\theta=\widetilde{\theta}}\, \widetilde{\lambda} = q(\widetilde{\theta})'\widetilde{\mathcal{I}}^{-1} q(\widetilde{\theta}) =: LM_q,$$

where we see that the expression for LM_q is unchanged from that found in previous exercises. However, one should be aware this time that LM_q is a quadratic form in the m-dimensional score and yet it has a distribution with r (not m) degrees of freedom. There is an $(m - r)$-dimensional nullspace (singularity) in the distribution of the m-dimensional $q(\widetilde{\theta})$, which is inherited from the smaller r-dimensional $\widetilde{\lambda}$ through

$$q(\widetilde{\theta}) \overset{a}{=} R\widetilde{\lambda} \overset{a}{\sim} \mathrm{N}(0_r, R\Omega^{-1}R')$$

under H_0, that is, $q(\widetilde{\theta})$ can be seen to be normalized in LM_q with $\mathcal{I}^{-1}$ as the *generalized* inverse of its variance $R\Omega^{-1}R'$ (a generalized inverse A^- of A satisfies $AA^-A = A$). This is so because H_0 imposes r restrictions on $\widetilde{\theta}$: the extreme cases are zero restrictions, leading to a completely degenerate $q(\widehat{\theta}) \equiv 0_m$ at the unrestricted MLE, and m restrictions, leading to $q(\theta_0) \overset{a}{\sim} \mathrm{N}(0_m, \mathcal{I})$ as in the previous exercise.

(c) Assume that $\mathrm{H}_0 : h(\theta) = 0_r$ holds. Expanding $h(\widehat{\theta})$ from W around $\widetilde{\theta}$, we have

$$h(\widehat{\theta}) \overset{a}{=} 0_r + R'\left(\widehat{\theta} - \widetilde{\theta}\right)$$

by $\boldsymbol{h}(\widetilde{\boldsymbol{\theta}}) = \mathbf{0}_r$ and using the same argument for the evaluation of $\boldsymbol{R}$ at $\boldsymbol{\theta}$ as in (b). Therefore,

$$W \overset{a}{=} \left(\widehat{\boldsymbol{\theta}} - \widetilde{\boldsymbol{\theta}}\right)' \boldsymbol{R}\boldsymbol{\Omega}^{-1}\boldsymbol{R}' \left(\widehat{\boldsymbol{\theta}} - \widetilde{\boldsymbol{\theta}}\right)$$

by the consistency of $\widehat{\boldsymbol{\Omega}}$. Expanding $\boldsymbol{q}(\widetilde{\boldsymbol{\theta}})$ from LM_q around $\widehat{\boldsymbol{\theta}}$, we get

$$\boldsymbol{q}(\widetilde{\boldsymbol{\theta}}) \overset{a}{=} \mathbf{0}_m - \boldsymbol{\mathcal{I}}\left(\widetilde{\boldsymbol{\theta}} - \widehat{\boldsymbol{\theta}}\right)$$

by $\boldsymbol{q}(\widehat{\boldsymbol{\theta}}) = \mathbf{0}_m$ and using similar derivations to those in Exercise 12.28(b); hence

$$\left(\widehat{\boldsymbol{\theta}} - \widetilde{\boldsymbol{\theta}}\right) \overset{a}{=} \boldsymbol{\mathcal{I}}^{-1}\boldsymbol{q}(\widetilde{\boldsymbol{\theta}}) \overset{a}{=} \boldsymbol{\mathcal{I}}^{-1}\boldsymbol{R}\widetilde{\boldsymbol{\lambda}}$$

by the first-order condition in (b). Substituting into W, we obtain

$$W \overset{a}{=} \widetilde{\boldsymbol{\lambda}}'\boldsymbol{R}'\boldsymbol{\mathcal{I}}^{-1}\boldsymbol{R}\boldsymbol{\Omega}^{-1}\boldsymbol{R}'\boldsymbol{\mathcal{I}}^{-1}\boldsymbol{R}\widetilde{\boldsymbol{\lambda}}$$

and $\boldsymbol{\Omega} = \boldsymbol{R}'\boldsymbol{\mathcal{I}}^{-1}\boldsymbol{R}$ gives

$$W \overset{a}{=} \widetilde{\boldsymbol{\lambda}}'\boldsymbol{\Omega}\widetilde{\boldsymbol{\lambda}} \overset{a}{=} LM_\lambda$$

by the consistency of $\widetilde{\boldsymbol{\Omega}}$.

(d) As with LM_q, the expression for LR is unchanged; this is true more generally of likelihood-based tests. It is obtained from the general definition as

$$LR = 2\left(\ell(\widehat{\boldsymbol{\theta}}) - \ell(\widetilde{\boldsymbol{\theta}})\right).$$

Assume that $\mathrm{H}_0 : \boldsymbol{h}(\boldsymbol{\theta}) = \mathbf{0}_r$ holds. Expanding $\ell(\widetilde{\boldsymbol{\theta}})$ around $\widehat{\boldsymbol{\theta}}$ as in Exercise 14.17(a), we get

$$\ell(\widehat{\boldsymbol{\theta}}) - \ell(\widetilde{\boldsymbol{\theta}}) \overset{a}{=} \frac{1}{2}\left(\widetilde{\boldsymbol{\theta}} - \widehat{\boldsymbol{\theta}}\right)' \boldsymbol{\mathcal{I}}\left(\widetilde{\boldsymbol{\theta}} - \widehat{\boldsymbol{\theta}}\right).$$

From (c), we have $\widehat{\boldsymbol{\theta}} - \widetilde{\boldsymbol{\theta}} \overset{a}{=} \boldsymbol{\mathcal{I}}^{-1}\boldsymbol{q}(\widetilde{\boldsymbol{\theta}})$; hence

$$LR \overset{a}{=} \boldsymbol{q}(\widetilde{\boldsymbol{\theta}})'\boldsymbol{\mathcal{I}}^{-1}\boldsymbol{q}(\widetilde{\boldsymbol{\theta}}) \overset{a}{=} LM_q$$

since $\widetilde{\boldsymbol{\mathcal{I}}}$ is consistent under H_0.

Exercise 14.19 (Examples of W for nonlinear restrictions) Suppose that the conditions of Exercise 14.18 hold. Using the formulae

$$W := \boldsymbol{h}(\widehat{\boldsymbol{\theta}})'\widehat{\boldsymbol{\Omega}}^{-1}\boldsymbol{h}(\widehat{\boldsymbol{\theta}}),$$

$$\boldsymbol{\Omega} := \frac{\partial \boldsymbol{h}(\boldsymbol{\theta})}{\partial \boldsymbol{\theta}'}\boldsymbol{\mathcal{I}}^{-1}\left(\frac{\partial \boldsymbol{h}(\boldsymbol{\theta})}{\partial \boldsymbol{\theta}'}\right)',$$

given there, specialize W to the case of testing the following:

(a) $\mathrm{H}_0 : \boldsymbol{h}(\boldsymbol{\theta}) = \mathbf{0}_r$ against $\mathrm{H}_1 : \boldsymbol{h}(\boldsymbol{\theta}) \neq \mathbf{0}_r$, where $\boldsymbol{h}(\boldsymbol{\theta}) := \boldsymbol{R}'\boldsymbol{\theta} - \boldsymbol{c}$, here with $\boldsymbol{R}$ an invertible matrix of constants and $\boldsymbol{c}$ a vector of constants.

(b) $\mathrm{H}_0 : \boldsymbol{\beta} = \boldsymbol{\beta}_0$ against $\mathrm{H}_1 : \boldsymbol{\beta} \neq \boldsymbol{\beta}_0$ in the normal linear model of Exercise 14.16, with $\boldsymbol{\theta}' := (\boldsymbol{\beta}', \sigma^2)$.

(c) $\mathrm{H}_0 : \beta_1 + \beta_2 = 1$ against $\mathrm{H}_1 : \beta_1 + \beta_2 \neq 1$ in $y_i = \beta_1 x_{i1} + \beta_2 x_{i2} + \varepsilon_i$, with $\varepsilon_i \sim \mathrm{IN}(0, \sigma^2)$.
(d) Model $y_i = \theta_1 y_{i-1} + \theta_2 x_i + \theta_3 x_{i-1} + \varepsilon_i$ against the model

$$y_i = \beta x_i + e_i,$$
$$e_i = \rho e_{i-1} + \varepsilon_i \qquad (|\rho| < 1);$$

for both models $\varepsilon_i \sim \mathrm{IN}(0, \sigma^2)$. [Hint: Combine the two equations of the latter model to write it as a special case of the former.]

Solution

(a) This is the special case of linear invertible restrictions, since $\boldsymbol{h}(\boldsymbol{\theta}) = \mathbf{0}_r$ is simply $\boldsymbol{R}'\boldsymbol{\theta} = \boldsymbol{c}$ or

$$\boldsymbol{\theta} = \boldsymbol{R}'^{-1}\boldsymbol{c} =: \boldsymbol{\theta}_0,$$

which we analyzed in Exercise 14.17. Casting this in the general formulation of Exercise 14.18, we have

$$W := \boldsymbol{h}(\widehat{\boldsymbol{\theta}})'\widehat{\boldsymbol{\Omega}}^{-1}\boldsymbol{h}(\widehat{\boldsymbol{\theta}}) = \left(\boldsymbol{R}'\widehat{\boldsymbol{\theta}} - \boldsymbol{c}\right)' \widehat{\boldsymbol{\Omega}}^{-1} \left(\boldsymbol{R}'\widehat{\boldsymbol{\theta}} - \boldsymbol{c}\right)$$

with $\boldsymbol{\Omega} := \boldsymbol{R}'\boldsymbol{\mathcal{I}}^{-1}\boldsymbol{R}$. Substituting the latter into W, then using the invertibility of $\boldsymbol{R}$ in this case,

$$\begin{aligned} W &= \left(\boldsymbol{R}'\widehat{\boldsymbol{\theta}} - \boldsymbol{c}\right)' \left(\boldsymbol{R}'\widehat{\boldsymbol{\mathcal{I}}}^{-1}\boldsymbol{R}\right)^{-1} \left(\boldsymbol{R}'\widehat{\boldsymbol{\theta}} - \boldsymbol{c}\right) = \left(\boldsymbol{R}'\widehat{\boldsymbol{\theta}} - \boldsymbol{c}\right)' \boldsymbol{R}^{-1}\widehat{\boldsymbol{\mathcal{I}}}\boldsymbol{R}'^{-1} \left(\boldsymbol{R}'\widehat{\boldsymbol{\theta}} - \boldsymbol{c}\right) \\ &= \left(\widehat{\boldsymbol{\theta}} - \boldsymbol{R}'^{-1}\boldsymbol{c}\right)' \widehat{\boldsymbol{\mathcal{I}}} \left(\widehat{\boldsymbol{\theta}} - \boldsymbol{R}'^{-1}\boldsymbol{c}\right) = \left(\widehat{\boldsymbol{\theta}} - \boldsymbol{\theta}_0\right)' \widehat{\boldsymbol{\mathcal{I}}} \left(\widehat{\boldsymbol{\theta}} - \boldsymbol{\theta}_0\right). \end{aligned}$$

(b) This is a case where $m = k + 1$, with $r = k$, and the function $\boldsymbol{h}$ is

$$\boldsymbol{h}(\boldsymbol{\theta}) = (\boldsymbol{I}_k, \mathbf{0}_k)\,\boldsymbol{\theta} - \boldsymbol{\beta}_0 = (\boldsymbol{I}_k, \mathbf{0}_k) \begin{pmatrix} \boldsymbol{\beta} \\ \sigma^2 \end{pmatrix} - \boldsymbol{\beta}_0 = \boldsymbol{\beta} - \boldsymbol{\beta}_0,$$

where $(\boldsymbol{I}_k, \mathbf{0}_k)$ is rectangular and hence not invertible, so the first displayed equality means that $\boldsymbol{h}(\boldsymbol{\theta})$ is not invertible in $\boldsymbol{\theta}$. Substituting into the general definition,

$$\boldsymbol{\Omega} := \frac{\partial \boldsymbol{h}(\boldsymbol{\theta})}{\partial \boldsymbol{\theta}'} \boldsymbol{\mathcal{I}}^{-1} \left(\frac{\partial \boldsymbol{h}(\boldsymbol{\theta})}{\partial \boldsymbol{\theta}'}\right)',$$

we obtain

$$\boldsymbol{\Omega} = (\boldsymbol{I}_k, \mathbf{0}_k)\,\mathrm{diag}\left(\sigma^2 \left(\boldsymbol{X}'\boldsymbol{X}\right)^{-1}, \frac{2\sigma^4}{n}\right) (\boldsymbol{I}_k, \mathbf{0}_k)' = \sigma^2 \left(\boldsymbol{X}'\boldsymbol{X}\right)^{-1}$$

and hence

$$\begin{aligned} W &:= \boldsymbol{h}(\widehat{\boldsymbol{\theta}})'\widehat{\boldsymbol{\Omega}}^{-1}\boldsymbol{h}(\widehat{\boldsymbol{\theta}}) = \left(\widehat{\boldsymbol{\beta}} - \boldsymbol{\beta}_0\right)' \left(\widehat{\sigma}^2 \left(\boldsymbol{X}'\boldsymbol{X}\right)^{-1}\right)^{-1} \left(\widehat{\boldsymbol{\beta}} - \boldsymbol{\beta}_0\right) \\ &= \frac{1}{\widehat{\sigma}^2} \left(\widehat{\boldsymbol{\beta}} - \boldsymbol{\beta}_0\right)' \boldsymbol{X}'\boldsymbol{X} \left(\widehat{\boldsymbol{\beta}} - \boldsymbol{\beta}_0\right). \end{aligned}$$

(c) We have here a linear model with a linear restriction that is nevertheless not invertible. The function $\boldsymbol{h}$ becomes one-dimensional:

$$h(\boldsymbol{\theta}) = (1, 1, 0) \begin{pmatrix} \beta_1 \\ \beta_2 \\ \sigma^2 \end{pmatrix} - 1.$$

Hence, using $\operatorname{var}(\widehat{\boldsymbol{\beta}}) = \sigma^2 (\boldsymbol{X}'\boldsymbol{X})^{-1}$,

$$\begin{aligned} \omega^2 :=& \frac{\partial h(\boldsymbol{\theta})}{\partial \boldsymbol{\theta}'} \boldsymbol{\mathcal{I}}^{-1} \left(\frac{\partial h(\boldsymbol{\theta})}{\partial \boldsymbol{\theta}'} \right)' \\ &= (1, 1, 0) \operatorname{diag} \left(\operatorname{var}(\widehat{\boldsymbol{\beta}}), \frac{2\sigma^4}{n} \right) \begin{pmatrix} 1 \\ 1 \\ 0 \end{pmatrix} = (1, 1) \operatorname{var}(\widehat{\boldsymbol{\beta}}) \begin{pmatrix} 1 \\ 1 \end{pmatrix} \\ &= \operatorname{var}(\widehat{\beta}_1) + \operatorname{var}(\widehat{\beta}_2) + 2 \operatorname{cov}(\widehat{\beta}_1, \widehat{\beta}_2), \end{aligned}$$

unsurprisingly because

$$\operatorname{var}(h(\widehat{\boldsymbol{\theta}})) = \operatorname{var}(\widehat{\beta}_1 + \widehat{\beta}_2 - 1) = \operatorname{var}(\widehat{\beta}_1 + \widehat{\beta}_2) = \operatorname{var}(\widehat{\beta}_1) + \operatorname{var}(\widehat{\beta}_2) + 2 \operatorname{cov}(\widehat{\beta}_1, \widehat{\beta}_2).$$

(We follow the same notational convention for variances as that introduced in Chapter 6: $\boldsymbol{\Sigma}$ is the multivariate version of σ^2, and similarly for $\boldsymbol{\Omega}$ and ω^2.) Therefore,

$$W = \frac{(\widehat{\beta}_1 + \widehat{\beta}_2 - 1)^2}{\widehat{\omega}^2},$$

which is the square of the familiar t-ratio, except that $\widehat{\omega}^2$ contains $\widehat{\sigma}^2 = n^{-1} \sum_{i=1}^n \widehat{\varepsilon}_i^2$ whose normalization is by n, not $n - k$ with $k = 2$.

(d) These are models for time series data (a term defined in Exercise 12.43). The first is called an *auto-regressive distributed lag* model of orders 1 and 1, respectively, abbreviated to ADL$(1, 1)$. The second is a linear model with auto-correlated errors. The two models are *nested*, meaning that one is a special case of the other. (We will tackle nonnested models in Exercise 14.22.) In the second model, $e_i = y_i - \beta x_i$; hence $e_i = \rho e_{i-1} + \varepsilon_i$ becomes

$$(y_i - \beta x_i) = \rho\,(y_{i-1} - \beta x_{i-1}) + \varepsilon_i.$$

Rearranging gives

$$y_i = \rho y_{i-1} + \beta x_i - \beta \rho x_{i-1} + \varepsilon_i,$$

which is the same as the first model with

$$(\theta_1, \theta_2, \theta_3) = (\rho, \beta, -\beta\rho).$$

In other words, the second model equals the first plus the one-dimensional nonlinear restriction $h(\boldsymbol{\theta}) := \theta_1 \theta_2 + \theta_3 = 0$. We can estimate the first model as a linear model and test this restriction as our H_0 to decide whether the special case (the second model) holds.

Hence,

$$\omega^2 := \frac{\partial h(\boldsymbol{\theta})}{\partial(\theta_1, \theta_2, \theta_3)} \mathcal{I}^{-1} \frac{\partial h(\boldsymbol{\theta})}{\partial(\theta_1, \theta_2, \theta_3)'} = (\theta_2, \theta_1, 1)\,\mathcal{I}^{-1} \begin{pmatrix} \theta_2 \\ \theta_1 \\ 1 \end{pmatrix}$$

and

$$W = \frac{(\widehat{\theta}_1 \widehat{\theta}_2 + \widehat{\theta}_3)^2}{\widehat{\omega}^2}$$

such that $(\widehat{\theta}_2, \widehat{\theta}_1, 1)$ and $\widehat{\mathcal{I}}$ are used in $\widehat{\omega}^2$. We warn that, as in Exercise 12.43, $\mathcal{I} = -\operatorname{E}(\boldsymbol{\mathcal{H}}) = \sigma^{-2}\operatorname{E}(\boldsymbol{X}'\boldsymbol{X})$, where the latter expectation needs to be taken since $\boldsymbol{X}$ is usually random in time series. Sometimes just the Hessian is used instead, which leads to a different test in small samples (and also in large samples, in some setups).

Exercise 14.20 (W is not invariant to nonlinear transformations) Suppose that we have a model where a consistent estimator (not necessarily the MLE) satisfies $\widehat{\boldsymbol{\theta}} \overset{a}{\sim} \mathrm{N}\left(\boldsymbol{\theta}, \mathcal{I}^{-1}\right)$, and that $\widehat{\mathcal{I}} := \mathcal{I}(\widehat{\boldsymbol{\theta}})$ is a consistent estimator of $\mathcal{I}$ in the sense that $\widehat{\mathcal{I}}\mathcal{I}^{-1} \overset{p}{\longrightarrow} \boldsymbol{I}_m$.
(a) Show that testing $\mathrm{H}_0 : \boldsymbol{h}(\boldsymbol{\theta}) = \mathbf{0}_r$ against $\mathrm{H}_1 : \boldsymbol{h}(\boldsymbol{\theta}) \neq \mathbf{0}_r$ gives a different W from that obtained for testing $\mathrm{H}_0 : \boldsymbol{g}(\boldsymbol{h}(\boldsymbol{\theta})) = \boldsymbol{g}(\mathbf{0}_r)$ against $\mathrm{H}_1 : \boldsymbol{g}(\boldsymbol{h}(\boldsymbol{\theta})) \neq \boldsymbol{g}(\mathbf{0}_r)$ when $\boldsymbol{g}$ is an invertible but nonlinear function.
(b) Illustrate (a) with $\mathrm{H}_0 : \theta - \theta_0 = 0$ and the transformed $\mathrm{H}_0 : \mathrm{e}^{a(\theta-\theta_0)} = 1$ for some known fixed $a \neq 0$.
(c) Reconcile this result with the asymptotic equivalence of W to the LR and LM statistics given in the previous exercises.

Solution
(a) Since $\boldsymbol{g}$ is an invertible function, the pair

$$\mathrm{H}_0 : \boldsymbol{g}(\boldsymbol{h}(\boldsymbol{\theta})) = \boldsymbol{g}(\mathbf{0}_r) \qquad \text{and} \qquad \mathrm{H}_1 : \boldsymbol{g}(\boldsymbol{h}(\boldsymbol{\theta})) \neq \boldsymbol{g}(\mathbf{0}_r)$$

is identical to the pair

$$\mathrm{H}_0 : \boldsymbol{h}(\boldsymbol{\theta}) = \mathbf{0}_r \qquad \text{and} \qquad \mathrm{H}_1 : \boldsymbol{h}(\boldsymbol{\theta}) \neq \mathbf{0}_r;$$

yet we will now show that the W statistics obtained for each pair of hypotheses are different unless $\boldsymbol{g}$ is a linear function. Define

$$\boldsymbol{r}(\boldsymbol{\theta}) := \boldsymbol{g}(\boldsymbol{h}(\boldsymbol{\theta})) - \boldsymbol{g}(\mathbf{0}_r);$$

hence W for the transformed hypotheses is

$$W_2 := \boldsymbol{r}(\widehat{\boldsymbol{\theta}})' \widehat{\boldsymbol{\Omega}}_2^{-1} \boldsymbol{r}(\widehat{\boldsymbol{\theta}}),$$

where the chain rule gives

$$\boldsymbol{\Omega}_2 := \frac{\partial \boldsymbol{r}(\boldsymbol{\theta})}{\partial \boldsymbol{\theta}'} \mathcal{I}^{-1} \left(\frac{\partial \boldsymbol{r}(\boldsymbol{\theta})}{\partial \boldsymbol{\theta}'}\right)' = \frac{\partial \boldsymbol{g}(\boldsymbol{h}(\boldsymbol{\theta}))}{\partial \boldsymbol{h}(\boldsymbol{\theta})'} \frac{\partial \boldsymbol{h}(\boldsymbol{\theta})}{\partial \boldsymbol{\theta}'} \mathcal{I}^{-1} \left(\frac{\partial \boldsymbol{g}(\boldsymbol{h}(\boldsymbol{\theta}))}{\partial \boldsymbol{h}(\boldsymbol{\theta})'} \frac{\partial \boldsymbol{h}(\boldsymbol{\theta})}{\partial \boldsymbol{\theta}'}\right)'.$$

Letting $\boldsymbol{G}' := \partial \boldsymbol{g}(\boldsymbol{h}(\boldsymbol{\theta}))/\partial \boldsymbol{h}(\boldsymbol{\theta})'$ be an invertible matrix, we have

$$\boldsymbol{\Omega}_2^{-1} = \boldsymbol{G}^{-1}\boldsymbol{\Omega}_1^{-1}\boldsymbol{G}'^{-1},$$

where

$$\boldsymbol{\Omega}_1^{-1} := \left(\frac{\partial \boldsymbol{h}(\boldsymbol{\theta})}{\partial \boldsymbol{\theta}'}\boldsymbol{\mathcal{I}}^{-1}\left(\frac{\partial \boldsymbol{h}(\boldsymbol{\theta})}{\partial \boldsymbol{\theta}'}\right)'\right)^{-1}$$

is the matrix needed for the original W statistic (the statistic for the untransformed hypotheses):

$$W_1 := \boldsymbol{h}(\widehat{\boldsymbol{\theta}})'\widehat{\boldsymbol{\Omega}}_1^{-1}\boldsymbol{h}(\widehat{\boldsymbol{\theta}}).$$

The equivalence of W_1 with

$$W_2 = \boldsymbol{r}(\widehat{\boldsymbol{\theta}})'\widehat{\boldsymbol{G}}^{-1}\widehat{\boldsymbol{\Omega}}_1^{-1}\widehat{\boldsymbol{G}}'^{-1}\boldsymbol{r}(\widehat{\boldsymbol{\theta}}) \qquad (\widehat{\boldsymbol{G}} := \boldsymbol{G}|_{\boldsymbol{\theta}=\widehat{\boldsymbol{\theta}}})$$

holds in general if and only if

$$\widehat{\boldsymbol{G}}'^{-1}\boldsymbol{r}(\widehat{\boldsymbol{\theta}}) = \boldsymbol{h}(\widehat{\boldsymbol{\theta}}),$$

which, using the definition $\boldsymbol{r}(\boldsymbol{\theta}) := \boldsymbol{g}(\boldsymbol{h}(\boldsymbol{\theta})) - \boldsymbol{g}(\mathbf{0}_r)$, gives

$$\boldsymbol{g}(\boldsymbol{h}(\widehat{\boldsymbol{\theta}})) = \boldsymbol{g}(\mathbf{0}_r) + \widehat{\boldsymbol{G}}'\boldsymbol{h}(\widehat{\boldsymbol{\theta}});$$

hence $\boldsymbol{g}$ is a linear function of $\boldsymbol{h}$.

(b) For $\mathrm{H}_0 : \theta = \theta_0$ and $\mathrm{H}_1 : \theta \neq \theta_0$, we have

$$W_1 = (\widehat{\theta} - \theta_0)^2\widehat{\mathcal{I}}$$

and, for the transformed $\mathrm{H}_0 : \mathrm{e}^{a(\theta-\theta_0)} = 1$ and $\mathrm{H}_1 : \mathrm{e}^{a(\theta-\theta_0)} \neq 1$ for some known fixed $a \neq 0$, we have

$$W_2 = \frac{(\mathrm{e}^{a(\widehat{\theta}-\theta_0)} - 1)^2\widehat{\mathcal{I}}}{a^2\mathrm{e}^{2a(\widehat{\theta}-\theta_0)}}.$$

Clearly, $W_1 \neq W_2$ unless $a \to 0$, in which case the stochastic limit of W_2 is

$$(\widehat{\theta} - \theta_0)^2\widehat{\mathcal{I}} = W_1$$

by the linear expansion $\mathrm{e}^c = 1 + c + o(c)$. For general $a > 0$, a similar expansion may be made when $\widehat{\theta} \xrightarrow{p} \theta_0$ under H_0, but it would not apply under H_1.

(c) The formulation of W requires only unrestricted estimators, while LM requires only restricted estimators. When these restrictions simplify the model (such as $\boldsymbol{\theta}_0 = \mathbf{0}_m$), LM can be easier to calculate than W but, when the restrictions are complicated, W may be preferred on computational grounds. We showed in Exercise 14.18(c) that they provide the same asymptotic answer under H_0. However, we have shown here (and before) that this equivalence does not hold otherwise and, more specifically here, that a simple reformulation of the hypotheses makes W change further under H_1. It is straightforward to establish that LM_λ is invariant to the reformulation of the hypotheses because the two pairs of hypotheses imply identical constraints on the objective function (the log-likelihood) in the constrained optimization, and similarly for LM_q and LR because the restriction on the space of MLE solutions is the same before and after the transformation of the hypotheses.

Exercise 14.21 (**LR, W, LM: multiple one-sided restrictions**) Assume the same setup as in Exercise 14.18 except that, instead of $\mathrm{H}_1 : \boldsymbol{h}(\boldsymbol{\theta}) \neq \mathbf{0}_r$, we have $\mathrm{H}_1 : \boldsymbol{h}(\boldsymbol{\theta}) \geqslant \mathbf{0}_r$ and $\boldsymbol{\imath}'\boldsymbol{h}(\boldsymbol{\theta}) > 0$, the latter inequality meaning that at least one of the r components of $\boldsymbol{h}(\boldsymbol{\theta})$ is strictly positive (so that $\mathrm{H}_0 : \boldsymbol{h}(\boldsymbol{\theta}) = \mathbf{0}_r$ cannot occur under H_1).
(a) We have seen how to solve the H_0-constrained optimization $\sup_{\boldsymbol{\theta}} \ell(\boldsymbol{\theta})$ subject to $\boldsymbol{h}(\boldsymbol{\theta}) = \mathbf{0}_r$. Now, solve the optimization under either H_0 or H_1, namely $\sup_{\boldsymbol{\theta}} \ell(\boldsymbol{\theta})$ subject to $\boldsymbol{h}(\boldsymbol{\theta}) \geqslant \mathbf{0}_r$, by using the Kuhn–Tucker approach given at the end of Section A.4.5.
(b) Using the testing principles seen earlier, devise W, LR, LM_λ, and LM_q tests of H_0 against H_1.
(c) Establish that $LM_\lambda \overset{a}{=} LM_q$ under H_0.
(d) Establish that $W \overset{a}{=} LM_\lambda$ under H_0, stating any additional assumptions you may need.
(e) Establish that $W \overset{a}{=} LR$ under H_0, stating any additional assumptions you may need.

Solution
(a) First, we need to define some notation. We write

$$\widetilde{\boldsymbol{\theta}} := \underset{\boldsymbol{\theta} \in \Theta_0}{\operatorname{argsup}} L(\boldsymbol{\theta}) \qquad \text{and} \qquad \breve{\boldsymbol{\theta}} := \underset{\boldsymbol{\theta} \in \Theta_0 \cup \Theta_1}{\operatorname{argsup}} L(\boldsymbol{\theta}),$$

reserving $\widehat{\boldsymbol{\theta}}$ for the optimization over $\boldsymbol{\theta} \in \Theta \supseteq \Theta_0 \cup \Theta_1$ and using $\breve{\boldsymbol{\theta}}$ for the estimator under the constraints $\boldsymbol{h}(\boldsymbol{\theta}) \geqslant \mathbf{0}_r$ arising from $\Theta_0 \cup \Theta_1$. Using the results in the Appendix, we get

$$S(\boldsymbol{\theta}) := \ell(\boldsymbol{\theta}) + (\mathbf{0}_r - \boldsymbol{h}(\boldsymbol{\theta}))' \boldsymbol{\lambda}$$

and the Kuhn–Tucker conditions

$$\left. \frac{\partial S(\boldsymbol{\theta})}{\partial \boldsymbol{\theta}} \right|_{\boldsymbol{\theta} = \breve{\boldsymbol{\theta}}} \equiv \breve{\boldsymbol{q}} - \breve{\boldsymbol{R}} \breve{\boldsymbol{\lambda}} = \mathbf{0}_m,$$

$$\breve{\boldsymbol{h}} \geqslant \mathbf{0}_r \quad \text{and} \quad \breve{\boldsymbol{\lambda}} \leqslant \mathbf{0}_r,$$

$$\breve{h}_i \breve{\lambda}_i = 0 \quad \text{for all } i = 1, \dots, r,$$

where $\boldsymbol{R}' := \partial \boldsymbol{h}(\boldsymbol{\theta}) / \partial \boldsymbol{\theta}'$ with $\breve{\boldsymbol{R}} := \left. \boldsymbol{R} \right|_{\boldsymbol{\theta} = \breve{\boldsymbol{\theta}}}$ and similarly for $\breve{\boldsymbol{h}}, \breve{\boldsymbol{q}}, \breve{\boldsymbol{\mathcal{I}}}$, and

$$\breve{\boldsymbol{\Omega}} := \left. \left(\boldsymbol{R}' \boldsymbol{\mathcal{I}}^{-1} \boldsymbol{R} \right) \right|_{\boldsymbol{\theta} = \breve{\boldsymbol{\theta}}}.$$

Using a tilde instead for $\boldsymbol{h}, \boldsymbol{q}, \boldsymbol{\mathcal{I}}, \boldsymbol{\Omega}, \boldsymbol{R}$ refers to quantities in which $\boldsymbol{\theta} = \widetilde{\boldsymbol{\theta}}$ has been substituted. Note that $\breve{\boldsymbol{\lambda}}$ is the result of the Kuhn–Tucker optimization; it differs from the vector obtained earlier under equality restrictions in Exercise 14.18, which is denoted by $\widetilde{\boldsymbol{\lambda}}$.
(b) As before,

$$W := \breve{\boldsymbol{h}}' \breve{\boldsymbol{\Omega}}^{-1} \breve{\boldsymbol{h}}$$

measures how close $\breve{\boldsymbol{h}}$ is to the H_0-presumed value of $\mathbf{0}_r$. However, unlike before, the distributions are not χ^2 because the quadratic form is based on a truncated (hence nonnormal) variate $\breve{h} \geqslant \mathbf{0}_r$. As for LR, the same GLR principle applies as before to give

$$LR := 2\left(\ell(\breve{\theta}) - \ell(\widetilde{\theta})\right).$$

Finally, *both* $\widetilde{\lambda}$ and $\breve{\lambda}$ are now random (the latter is nonzero because it is not necessarily the case that $\Theta_0 \cup \Theta_1 = \Theta$) and the quadratic distance between them leads to

$$LM_\lambda := \left(\breve{\lambda} - \widetilde{\lambda}\right)' \widetilde{\Omega} \left(\breve{\lambda} - \widetilde{\lambda}\right)$$

and similarly

$$LM_q := (\breve{q} - \widetilde{q})' \widetilde{\mathcal{I}}^{-1} (\breve{q} - \widetilde{q}),$$

where the same remark applies about $\breve{q}$ being random and nonzero.

(c) Since LM_λ and LM_q are no longer exactly equal, we will now show that they are asymptotically equal under H_0. Recalling the first-order conditions here and in Exercise 14.18(b), we have

$$\widetilde{q} = \widetilde{R}\widetilde{\lambda} \qquad \text{and} \qquad \breve{q} = \breve{R}\breve{\lambda}$$

and the result will follow if $\breve{R} \stackrel{a}{=} \widetilde{R}$ under H_0 because of the definition $\widetilde{\Omega} := \widetilde{R}'\widetilde{\mathcal{I}}^{-1}\widetilde{R}$. This is the case since $\widetilde{\theta} - \breve{\theta} \stackrel{p}{\longrightarrow} \mathbf{0}_m$ when H_0 holds.

(d) The statistic W contains $\breve{h} \equiv h(\breve{\theta}) \geqslant \mathbf{0}_r$. Expanding this function (the constraints) around the point $\widetilde{\theta}$ where $\widetilde{h} = \mathbf{0}_r$, we get

$$\breve{h} = \mathbf{0}_r + \widetilde{R}'\left(\breve{\theta} - \widetilde{\theta}\right) + z,$$

where z is of smaller order than the leading term when H_0 holds because $\widetilde{\theta} - \breve{\theta} \stackrel{p}{\longrightarrow} \mathbf{0}_m$. Furthermore, H_0 implies that $\widetilde{R}, \breve{R}$ are consistent for R, hence

$$W \stackrel{a}{=} \left(\breve{\theta} - \widetilde{\theta}\right)' R\left(R'\breve{\mathcal{I}}^{-1}R\right)^{-1} R'\left(\breve{\theta} - \widetilde{\theta}\right).$$

In previous exercises we assumed that $\widehat{\mathcal{I}}$ was a consistent estimator of $\mathcal{I}$, and we now need to assume this for $\breve{\mathcal{I}}$, in which case we get

$$W \stackrel{a}{=} Q_1 := \left(\breve{\theta} - \widetilde{\theta}\right)' R\left(R'\mathcal{I}^{-1}R\right)^{-1} R'\left(\breve{\theta} - \widetilde{\theta}\right).$$

We now need to relate these θ's to the λ's of LM_λ. Both $\widetilde{\theta}$ and $\breve{\theta}$ are random and satisfy their respective optimization problem's first-order conditions, where expanding the score around the true θ gives

$$\widetilde{R}\widetilde{\lambda} = \widetilde{q} \stackrel{a}{=} q + \mathcal{H}\left(\widetilde{\theta} - \theta\right),$$

$$\breve{R}\breve{\lambda} = \breve{q} \stackrel{a}{=} q + \mathcal{H}\left(\breve{\theta} - \theta\right),$$

under H_0. We have seen earlier that $\widetilde{R}$ and $\breve{R}$ are asymptotically the same, so subtraction of the equations gives

$$\boldsymbol{R}\left(\breve{\boldsymbol{\lambda}}-\widetilde{\boldsymbol{\lambda}}\right) \stackrel{a}{=} \boldsymbol{\mathcal{H}}\left(\breve{\boldsymbol{\theta}}-\widetilde{\boldsymbol{\theta}}\right)$$

and, as in Exercise 14.17(a), $\boldsymbol{R}(\breve{\boldsymbol{\lambda}}-\widetilde{\boldsymbol{\lambda}}) \stackrel{a}{=} -\boldsymbol{\mathcal{I}}(\breve{\boldsymbol{\theta}}-\widetilde{\boldsymbol{\theta}})$; hence

$$\left(\breve{\boldsymbol{\theta}}-\widetilde{\boldsymbol{\theta}}\right) \stackrel{a}{=} -\boldsymbol{\mathcal{I}}^{-1}\boldsymbol{R}\left(\breve{\boldsymbol{\lambda}}-\widetilde{\boldsymbol{\lambda}}\right),$$

leading to

$$Q_1 \stackrel{a}{=} \left(\breve{\boldsymbol{\lambda}}-\widetilde{\boldsymbol{\lambda}}\right)'\boldsymbol{R}'\boldsymbol{\mathcal{I}}^{-1}\boldsymbol{R}\left(\breve{\boldsymbol{\lambda}}-\widetilde{\boldsymbol{\lambda}}\right).$$

As seen in (c), this is asymptotically the same as LM_λ if $\widetilde{\boldsymbol{\mathcal{I}}}$ and $\boldsymbol{\mathcal{I}}$ coincide asymptotically, which is the case when H_0 is correct because of the assumption of consistency of the estimator of $\boldsymbol{\mathcal{I}}$. Hence, $W \stackrel{a}{=} LM_\lambda$.

The relation linking $\breve{\boldsymbol{\theta}}-\widetilde{\boldsymbol{\theta}}$ to $\breve{\boldsymbol{\lambda}}-\widetilde{\boldsymbol{\lambda}}$ is important. For example, it leads to

$$\left(\breve{\boldsymbol{\lambda}}-\widetilde{\boldsymbol{\lambda}}\right)'\boldsymbol{R}'\boldsymbol{\mathcal{I}}^{-1/2}\boldsymbol{\mathcal{I}}^{-1/2}\boldsymbol{R}\left(\breve{\boldsymbol{\lambda}}-\widetilde{\boldsymbol{\lambda}}\right) \stackrel{a}{=} \left(\breve{\boldsymbol{\theta}}-\widetilde{\boldsymbol{\theta}}\right)'\boldsymbol{\mathcal{I}}^{1/2}\boldsymbol{\mathcal{I}}^{1/2}\left(\breve{\boldsymbol{\theta}}-\widetilde{\boldsymbol{\theta}}\right) =: Q_2$$

under H_0. The left-hand side is the quadratic form we have just finished analyzing, while the right-hand side is known as a *Durbin–Wu–Hausman* test statistic if we replace $\boldsymbol{\mathcal{I}}$ by a consistent estimator. In Q_2, the estimators $\widetilde{\boldsymbol{\theta}}$ and $\breve{\boldsymbol{\theta}}$ are both consistent under H_0, but $\widetilde{\boldsymbol{\theta}}$ is inconsistent under H_1, so that $Q_2 \to \infty$ and the test based on it is consistent (has power tending to 1).

(e) For LR, we expand $\ell(\widetilde{\boldsymbol{\theta}})$ as before in the neighborhood of $\breve{\boldsymbol{\theta}}$ but, this time, we will need to use the first-order conditions for $\breve{\boldsymbol{\theta}}$ to simplify the resulting expression (as opposed to resorting to $\boldsymbol{q}(\widehat{\boldsymbol{\theta}}) \equiv \mathbf{0}_m$ as earlier). We get

$$\ell(\widetilde{\boldsymbol{\theta}}) = \ell(\breve{\boldsymbol{\theta}}) + \breve{\boldsymbol{q}}'\left(\widetilde{\boldsymbol{\theta}}-\breve{\boldsymbol{\theta}}\right) + \frac{1}{2}\left(\widetilde{\boldsymbol{\theta}}-\breve{\boldsymbol{\theta}}\right)'\breve{\boldsymbol{\mathcal{H}}}\left(\widetilde{\boldsymbol{\theta}}-\breve{\boldsymbol{\theta}}\right) + \xi,$$

where ξ represents the smaller-order terms under H_0. Assuming that $\breve{\boldsymbol{\mathcal{H}}}$ is a consistent estimator of $-\boldsymbol{\mathcal{I}}$, the last quadratic form is asymptotically equivalent to $-Q_2/2$, defined at the end of part (d). To establish $W \stackrel{a}{=} LR$, all that remains to be shown is that the term containing $\breve{\boldsymbol{q}}$ vanishes asymptotically under H_0. For this, recalling the first-order conditions obtained in (a), we use two of them, namely

$$\breve{\boldsymbol{q}} = \breve{\boldsymbol{R}}\breve{\boldsymbol{\lambda}} \equiv \sum_{i=1}^{r}\breve{\lambda}_i \left.\frac{\partial h_i(\boldsymbol{\theta})}{\partial\boldsymbol{\theta}}\right|_{\boldsymbol{\theta}=\breve{\boldsymbol{\theta}}}$$

and $\breve{\lambda}_i\breve{h}_i = 0$. Expanding $\breve{h}_i$ under H_0 as in (d), we obtain

$$\breve{h}_i \stackrel{a}{=} \left.\frac{\partial h_i(\boldsymbol{\theta})}{\partial\boldsymbol{\theta}'}\right|_{\boldsymbol{\theta}=\widetilde{\boldsymbol{\theta}}}\left(\breve{\boldsymbol{\theta}}-\widetilde{\boldsymbol{\theta}}\right) \stackrel{a}{=} \left.\frac{\partial h_i(\boldsymbol{\theta})}{\partial\boldsymbol{\theta}'}\right|_{\boldsymbol{\theta}=\breve{\boldsymbol{\theta}}}\left(\breve{\boldsymbol{\theta}}-\widetilde{\boldsymbol{\theta}}\right)$$

and the two first-order conditions combine to give

$$0 = \sum_{i=1}^{r}\breve{\lambda}_i\breve{h}_i \stackrel{a}{=} \sum_{i=1}^{r}\breve{\lambda}_i \left.\frac{\partial h_i(\boldsymbol{\theta})}{\partial\boldsymbol{\theta}'}\right|_{\boldsymbol{\theta}=\breve{\boldsymbol{\theta}}}\left(\breve{\boldsymbol{\theta}}-\widetilde{\boldsymbol{\theta}}\right) = \breve{\boldsymbol{q}}'\left(\breve{\boldsymbol{\theta}}-\widetilde{\boldsymbol{\theta}}\right),$$

as required. Hence

$$\ell(\widetilde{\theta}) - \ell(\breve{\theta}) \overset{a}{=} \frac{1}{2}\left(\widetilde{\theta} - \breve{\theta}\right)' \breve{\mathcal{H}} \left(\widetilde{\theta} - \breve{\theta}\right)$$

and $LR \overset{a}{=} W$. Notice that $\breve{q}$ itself is nonzero (unlike $q(\widehat{\theta}) \equiv \mathbf{0}_m$); instead, it is $\breve{q}'(\widetilde{\theta} - \breve{\theta})$ that is zero; recall the discussion of nullspaces of constrained scores at the end of the solution of Exercise 14.18(b), and the discussion of the duality of q and θ at the end of the introduction to Chapter 12.

***Exercise 14.22** (**LR for nonnested models: Cox test**) Suppose that we have a random sample $x_1, \dots, x_n$ and that there are two distinct competing models to explain the data. The models need not be nested; see Exercise 14.19(d) for the definition and an example. Denote their postulated densities and log-likelihoods by, respectively,

$$\begin{array}{lll} g(u;\alpha) & \text{and} & \ell_g(\alpha) = \sum_{i=1}^n \log g(x_i;\alpha), \\ h(u;\beta) & \text{and} & \ell_h(\beta) = \sum_{i=1}^n \log h(x_i;\beta), \end{array}$$

where the dimensions of the parameter vectors α and β need not be the same. Let H_g be the hypothesis that the first model is correct, and let the alternative hypothesis H_h be that it is the second model instead. Define the LR statistic for H_g against H_h as

$$LR := 2\left(\ell_h(\widehat{\beta}) - \ell_g(\widehat{\alpha})\right),$$

where the hats denote the estimators that maximize the respective likelihoods, and let f refer to the true density of the variate x. Assuming some regularity conditions,
(a) establish the almost-sure divergence $LR \to -\infty$ under H_g and $LR \to +\infty$ under H_h;
(b) by recentering and scaling LR, modify it into a test statistic that does not diverge under H_g but does so under H_h, working out its limiting distribution under H_g.
[Hint: For (a), consider LR as a difference of entropies, and express it in terms of the KLIC under each hypothesis. To work out the distribution in (b), rewrite LR as a sample mean and apply a CLT.]

Solution
(a) If the SLLN applies as in Exercise 12.27(a), we have

$$\frac{1}{n}\ell_g(\widehat{\alpha}) - \mathrm{E}(\log g(x;\widehat{\alpha})) \to 0 \quad \text{and} \quad \frac{1}{n}\ell_h(\widehat{\beta}) - \mathrm{E}(\log h(x;\widehat{\beta})) \to 0,$$

where the expectations are taken with respect to the true density f from which the sampling occurs. Under $\mathrm{H}_g : f = g$, we can state further that

$$\frac{1}{n}\ell_g(\widehat{\alpha}) \to \mathrm{E}(\log g(x;\alpha)) \quad \text{and} \quad \frac{1}{n}\ell_h(\widehat{\beta}) \to \mathrm{E}(\log h(x;\beta_\alpha)),$$

where β_α is the value of β implied by α; for example, if h is normal, then β_α would be the mean and variance implied by the density g. Define the following general function, which can be calculated whatever the true f:

$$K(\alpha_c) := \mathrm{E}_g(\log h(x;\beta_{\alpha_c}) - \log g(x;\alpha_c)) \equiv -\mathrm{KL}(g,h) < 0$$

for any given vector $\boldsymbol{\alpha}_c$ (which we drop from $\mathrm{KL}(g,h)$ for notational convenience), with equality $\mathrm{KL} = 0$ holding trivially when $g = h$ (ruled out by assumption). Then, under H_g,

$$\frac{1}{n}LR \to -2\mathrm{KL}(g,h)$$

with $\boldsymbol{\alpha}_c = \boldsymbol{\alpha}$, hence the stated $LR \to -\infty$. Under the alternative H_h, the roles would be reversed and we would get $LR \to \infty$, with $\mathrm{KL}(h,g)$ replacing $-\mathrm{KL}(g,h)$ in the normalized limit. In this $\mathrm{KL}(h,g)$, we would have the $\boldsymbol{\alpha}$ implied by $\boldsymbol{\beta}$, as under H_h we have a true $\boldsymbol{\beta}$ but no $\boldsymbol{\alpha}$.

(b) It is clear that we need to consider $n^{-1}LR$ for a normalized statistic, but it would need to be centered asymptotically around $2K(\boldsymbol{\alpha})$ under the null H_g. Since $\boldsymbol{\alpha}$ is unknown and statistics should contain no unknowns, we use $K(\widehat{\boldsymbol{\alpha}})$ for centering as follows:

$$C := \frac{1}{n}\left(\ell_h(\widehat{\boldsymbol{\beta}}) - \ell_g(\widehat{\boldsymbol{\alpha}})\right) - K(\widehat{\boldsymbol{\alpha}}).$$

This converges almost surely to 0 under the null H_g if regularity conditions on g, h are satisfied such that $K(\widehat{\boldsymbol{\alpha}}) \to K(\boldsymbol{\alpha})$ when $\widehat{\boldsymbol{\alpha}} \to \boldsymbol{\alpha}$. Under the alternative H_h, the same conditions would lead to $C \to \mathrm{KL}(h,g) + \mathrm{KL}(g,h) > 0$, which is Jeffreys' divergence; see Exercise 4.42.

To normalize C further, so that it is not degenerate under H_g but diverges to $+\infty$ under H_h (hence providing a consistent one-sided test), consider $\sqrt{n}C$. This normalization is used because an SLLN applies to $n^{-1}LR$, which is a sample mean that we have recentered in C, and we will show further that this sample mean can satisfy a standard $\sqrt{n}$-CLT under appropriate conditions. We shall work henceforth under $\mathrm{H}_g : f = g$.

We have seen in previous exercises on LR for nested hypotheses that $\ell_g(\widehat{\boldsymbol{\alpha}}) - \ell_g(\boldsymbol{\alpha}) = O_p(1)$, since it has a nondegenerate distribution under the null, and similarly for the implied $\boldsymbol{\beta}_{\boldsymbol{\alpha}}$. Hence,

$$C = \frac{1}{n}\left(\ell_h(\boldsymbol{\beta}_{\boldsymbol{\beta}}) - \ell_g(\boldsymbol{\alpha}) + O_p(1)\right) - K(\widehat{\boldsymbol{\alpha}}).$$

Assume that the conditions of Exercise 12.29 hold and that the regularity conditions apply to $f = g$. Then,

$$\widehat{\boldsymbol{\alpha}} - \boldsymbol{\alpha} \overset{a}{=} \boldsymbol{\mathcal{I}}^{-1}\boldsymbol{q}(\boldsymbol{\alpha}) \overset{a}{\sim} \mathrm{N}(\mathbf{0}, \boldsymbol{\mathcal{I}}^{-1}),$$

where

$$\boldsymbol{\mathcal{I}} = n \operatorname{var}\left(\frac{\partial \log g(x;\boldsymbol{\alpha})}{\partial \boldsymbol{\alpha}}\right) \quad \text{and} \quad \boldsymbol{q}(\boldsymbol{\alpha}) = \sum_{i=1}^{n} \frac{\partial \log g(x_i;\boldsymbol{\alpha})}{\partial \boldsymbol{\alpha}}.$$

Expanding the term $K(\widehat{\boldsymbol{\alpha}})$ in C around $\widehat{\boldsymbol{\alpha}} = \boldsymbol{\alpha}$, with $\widehat{\boldsymbol{\alpha}} - \boldsymbol{\alpha} = O_p(1/\sqrt{n})$, gives

$$\begin{aligned} K(\widehat{\boldsymbol{\alpha}}) &= K(\boldsymbol{\alpha}) + \frac{\partial K(\boldsymbol{\alpha})}{\partial \boldsymbol{\alpha}'}(\widehat{\boldsymbol{\alpha}} - \boldsymbol{\alpha}) + o_p(\|\widehat{\boldsymbol{\alpha}} - \boldsymbol{\alpha}\|) \\ &\overset{a}{=} K(\boldsymbol{\alpha}) + \frac{\partial K(\boldsymbol{\alpha})}{\partial \boldsymbol{\alpha}'}\boldsymbol{\mathcal{I}}^{-1}\boldsymbol{q}(\boldsymbol{\alpha}). \end{aligned}$$

Hence, $C \overset{a}{=} n^{-1}\sum_{i=1}^{n} C_i$ with

$$C_i = \log \frac{h(x_i; \boldsymbol{\beta}_{\boldsymbol{\alpha}})}{g(x_i; \boldsymbol{\alpha})} - K(\boldsymbol{\alpha}) - \frac{\partial K(\boldsymbol{\alpha})}{\partial \boldsymbol{\alpha}'} \left(\operatorname{var}\left(\frac{\partial \log g(x; \boldsymbol{\alpha})}{\partial \boldsymbol{\alpha}} \right) \right)^{-1} \frac{\partial \log g(x_i; \boldsymbol{\alpha})}{\partial \boldsymbol{\alpha}},$$

where the second term is the expectation of the first, and the third sum being $O_p(1/\sqrt{n})$ dominates the omitted terms. Now, the definition of K leads to

$$\frac{\partial K(\boldsymbol{\alpha})}{\partial \boldsymbol{\alpha}} \equiv \frac{\partial}{\partial \boldsymbol{\alpha}} \int_{u \in \mathcal{X}} (\log h(u; \boldsymbol{\beta}_{\boldsymbol{\alpha}}) - \log g(u; \boldsymbol{\alpha}))\, g(u; \boldsymbol{\alpha})\, \mathrm{d}u,$$

where we can interchange the derivative and integral because of the regularity conditions on g, giving

$$\begin{aligned}
\frac{\partial K(\boldsymbol{\alpha})}{\partial \boldsymbol{\alpha}} &= \int_{u \in \mathcal{X}} \left(\frac{\partial \boldsymbol{\beta}_{\boldsymbol{\alpha}}}{\partial \boldsymbol{\alpha}'} \right)' \frac{\partial \log h(u; \boldsymbol{\beta}_{\boldsymbol{\alpha}})}{\partial \boldsymbol{\beta}_{\boldsymbol{\alpha}}} g(u; \boldsymbol{\alpha})\, \mathrm{d}u - \int_{u \in \mathcal{X}} \frac{\partial \log g(u; \boldsymbol{\alpha})}{\partial \boldsymbol{\alpha}} g(u; \boldsymbol{\alpha})\, \mathrm{d}u \\
&\quad + \int_{u \in \mathcal{X}} (\log h(u; \boldsymbol{\beta}_{\boldsymbol{\alpha}}) - \log g(u; \boldsymbol{\alpha})) \frac{\partial \log g(u; \boldsymbol{\alpha})}{\partial \boldsymbol{\alpha}} g(u; \boldsymbol{\alpha})\, \mathrm{d}u \\
&\equiv \left(\frac{\partial \boldsymbol{\beta}_{\boldsymbol{\alpha}}}{\partial \boldsymbol{\alpha}'} \right)' \mathrm{E}\left(\frac{\partial \log h(x; \boldsymbol{\beta}_{\boldsymbol{\alpha}})}{\partial \boldsymbol{\beta}_{\boldsymbol{\alpha}}} \right) - \mathrm{E}\left(\frac{\partial \log g(x; \boldsymbol{\alpha})}{\partial \boldsymbol{\alpha}} \right) \\
&\quad + \mathrm{E}\left(\log \frac{h(x; \boldsymbol{\beta}_{\boldsymbol{\alpha}})}{g(x; \boldsymbol{\alpha})} \frac{\partial \log g(x; \boldsymbol{\alpha})}{\partial \boldsymbol{\alpha}} \right),
\end{aligned}$$

where we needed to assume the differentiability of $\boldsymbol{\beta}_{\boldsymbol{\alpha}}$ in using the chain rule. The score per observation has zero mean (by the more general derivations in Exercise 12.21(a)), so the second expectation drops out and the third becomes a covariance, while the first expectation is asymptotically zero since $\boldsymbol{\beta}_{\boldsymbol{\alpha}}$ is the g-implied value to which the MLE $\widehat{\boldsymbol{\beta}}$ converges (see part (a)). We can substitute this into C as $C \overset{a}{=} n^{-1}\sum_{i=1}^{n} \xi_i$ with

$$\xi_i := \log \frac{h}{g} - K(\boldsymbol{\alpha}) - \operatorname{cov}\left(\log \frac{h}{g}, \frac{\partial \log g}{\partial \boldsymbol{\alpha}} \right) \left(\operatorname{var}\left(\frac{\partial \log g}{\partial \boldsymbol{\alpha}} \right) \right)^{-1} \frac{\partial \log g}{\partial \boldsymbol{\alpha}},$$

where we have dropped the arguments of the functions in ξ_i to focus the exposition on the following: the ξ_i are the mean-zero residuals from the least squares regression of $\log(h/g)$ on a constant (its mean) and the mean-zero $\partial \log g / \partial \boldsymbol{\alpha}$ (see Exercise 12.33(c) and Chapter 13), and Exercise 6.51 gives the variance as

$$\begin{aligned}
\operatorname{var}(\xi_i) &= \operatorname{var}\left(\log \frac{h}{g} \right) - \operatorname{cov}\left(\log \frac{h}{g}, \frac{\partial \log g}{\partial \boldsymbol{\alpha}} \right) \\
&\quad \times \left(\operatorname{var}\left(\frac{\partial \log g}{\partial \boldsymbol{\alpha}} \right) \right)^{-1} \operatorname{cov}\left(\frac{\partial \log g}{\partial \boldsymbol{\alpha}}, \log \frac{h}{g} \right);
\end{aligned}$$

recall from the introduction to Chapter 6 that $(\operatorname{cov}(\boldsymbol{y}, \boldsymbol{z}))' = \operatorname{cov}(\boldsymbol{z}, \boldsymbol{y})$. The CLT for the i.i.d. $\{\xi_n\}$ implies that $C \overset{a}{\sim} \mathrm{N}(0, \operatorname{var}(\xi_i)/n)$.

14.3 Further analysis of test optimality

Exercise 14.23 (UMP test depends on data through sufficient statistic) Suppose that a sample (not necessarily i.i.d.) is arranged into the data matrix $\boldsymbol{X}$ with density f depending on a parameter vector $\boldsymbol{\theta}$, a setup often encountered in Chapter 11. Let $\boldsymbol{z}$ be a sufficient statistic for $\boldsymbol{\theta}$. Show that most powerful tests of $\mathrm{H}_0 : \boldsymbol{\theta} = \boldsymbol{\theta}_0$ against $\mathrm{H}_1 : \boldsymbol{\theta} = \boldsymbol{\theta}_1$ can be expressed as a function of $\boldsymbol{z}$ alone.

Solution

Neyman's factorization theorem (Exercise 11.14) implies that

$$\frac{L(\boldsymbol{\theta}_0)}{L(\boldsymbol{\theta}_1)} = \frac{f(\boldsymbol{X};\boldsymbol{\theta}_0)}{f(\boldsymbol{X};\boldsymbol{\theta}_1)} = \frac{f_{\boldsymbol{z}}(\boldsymbol{z};\boldsymbol{\theta}_0)h(\boldsymbol{X})}{f_{\boldsymbol{z}}(\boldsymbol{z};\boldsymbol{\theta}_1)h(\boldsymbol{X})} = \frac{f_{\boldsymbol{z}}(\boldsymbol{z};\boldsymbol{\theta}_0)}{f_{\boldsymbol{z}}(\boldsymbol{z};\boldsymbol{\theta}_1)}.$$

Therefore, by the Neyman–Pearson lemma, most powerful tests of H_0 against H_1 can be expressed as a function of $\boldsymbol{z}$ alone. See Section 14.1 for examples illustrating this result.

Exercise 14.24 (Monotone LR depends on data through sufficient statistic) Suppose that a sample (not necessarily i.i.d.) is arranged into the data matrix $\boldsymbol{X}$ with density f depending on a single parameter θ, and let z be a sufficient statistic for θ. Assuming that there exists an MLR, show that this MLR can be expressed as a function of z only.

Solution

Neyman's factorization theorem implies that

$$\frac{L(\theta_2)}{L(\theta_1)} = \frac{f_z(z;\theta_2)}{f_z(z;\theta_1)}.$$

Therefore, if an MLR exists, it can be expressed as a function of z only.

***Exercise 14.25 (Karlin–Rubin theorem)** Continuing with the setup of Exercise 14.24, taking monotone to mean nondecreasing, suppose that we wish to test $\mathrm{H}_0 : \theta \leqslant \theta_c$ against $\mathrm{H}_1 : \theta > \theta_c$. Show that a test rejecting H_0 when $z > w_0$ is UMP of size $\alpha = \Pr_{\theta_c}(z > w_0)$. [Hint: Use the definition of a UMP test of size α to fix α, then apply the Neyman–Pearson lemma pointwise in Θ_1.]

Solution

In order to apply the definition of a UMP test (Property 2 in the introduction to this chapter), we start by considering its size,

$$\alpha = \sup_{\theta \in \Theta_0} \Pi(\theta) = \sup_{\theta \leqslant \theta_c} \Pi(\theta),$$

where $\Pi(\theta) := \Pr_\theta(z > w_0) = \int_{w_0}^{\infty} \mathrm{d}F_z(w;\theta)$. By the MLR property, $f_z(z;\theta_0)/f_z(z;\theta_0')$ is a nondecreasing function of z on the subset $\mathcal{Z}_1$ of (w_0,∞) in which the numerator and denominator are not both zero, for every pair $\theta_0' < \theta_0$. As a result, maximizing the integral $\Pi(\theta)$ within $\mathrm{H}_0 : \theta \leqslant \theta_c$ gives the corner solution $\theta = \theta_c$. Note that the critical region is determined under $\theta = \theta_c$ and therefore does not depend on any $\theta \in \Theta_1$.

Now consider testing $\mathrm{H}_0' : \theta = \theta_c$ against $\mathrm{H}_1' : \theta = \theta_1$, with $\theta_1 > \theta_c$, both simple hypotheses. The Neyman–Pearson lemma, as formulated in terms of the sufficient statistic (Exercise 14.23), implies that z is most powerful and satisfies $f_z(z;\theta_1)/f_z(z;\theta_c) > \gamma^{-1}$ for $z \in \mathcal{Z}_1$, where

$$\gamma^{-1} = \inf_{z \in \mathcal{Z}_1} \frac{f_z(z;\theta_1)}{f_z(z;\theta_c)}$$

follows from the MLR property. Since $\mathcal{Z}_1$ does not vary with θ_1, as pointed out in the last paragraph, this test is UMP of size α for all θ in $\mathrm{H}_1 : \theta > \theta_c$. Note that it follows, by integration, that the power function of z is strictly increasing in θ until it reaches 1.

We have also implicitly shown that the same optimality result holds for testing $\mathrm{H}_0 : \theta = \theta_c$ against $\mathrm{H}_1 : \theta > \theta_c$, in which case the first step of the proof (about α) is not needed and can be skipped. As for $\mathrm{H}_0 : \theta \geqslant \theta_c$ against $\mathrm{H}_1 : \theta < \theta_c$, a test rejecting H_0 when $z < w_0$ is UMP by the same logic used in this proof, with the inequalities reversed.

Exercise 14.26 (UMP for composite hypotheses: exponential's MLR) Let $x_1, \dots, x_n$ be a random sample from $x \sim \mathrm{Expo}(\theta)$, where $\theta > 0$.
(a) Show that this family of densities has an MLR in $z := \sum_{i=1}^n x_i$.
(b) Derive a uniformly most powerful test of size α for $\mathrm{H}_0 : \theta \geqslant \theta_c$ against $\mathrm{H}_1 : \theta < \theta_c$.

Solution
(a) Consider

$$\frac{L(\theta_2)}{L(\theta_1)} = \frac{\theta_2^n \exp\left(-\theta_2 \sum_{i=1}^n x_i\right)}{\theta_1^n \exp\left(-\theta_1 \sum_{i=1}^n x_i\right)} = \left(\frac{\theta_2}{\theta_1}\right)^n \exp\left((\theta_1 - \theta_2)\, z\right).$$

For $\theta_1 < \theta_2$, this is a decreasing function of z (increasing in $-z$).
(b) The last paragraph of the proof of Exercise 14.25 deals with the hypotheses we have here, but here it is $-z$ that we need to use in the inequality in order to reject H_0 (that is, $-z < -w_0$), because of the result in (a) of an increasing LR in $-z$. Thus, by the Karlin–Rubin theorem, we use

$$\alpha = \Pr{}_{\theta_c}(z > w_0) = \Pr{}_{\theta_c}(2\theta_c z > 2\theta_c w_0) = \Pr{}_{\theta_c}(\chi^2(2n) > 2\theta_c w_0),$$

where the last equality follows from Exercises 7.18 and 7.19. Hence, we have $w_0 = (2\theta_c)^{-1} \chi^2_{1-\alpha}(2n)$. Recall that the sample mean z/n is estimating θ^{-1}, and that we are rejecting H_0 in favor of $\mathrm{H}_1 : \theta < \theta_c$ when z is large.

Exercise 14.27 (UMP for composite hypotheses: uniform's MLR) Let $x_1, \dots, x_n$ be a random sample from $x \sim \mathrm{U}_{(0,\theta)}$, where $\theta > 0$.
(a) Show that this family of densities has an MLR in $y_n := \max_i \{x_i\}$.
(b) Derive a uniformly most powerful test of size α for $\mathrm{H}_0 : \theta \leqslant \theta_c$ against $\mathrm{H}_1 : \theta > \theta_c$.

Solution
(a) For $\theta_2 > \theta_1$,

$$\frac{L(\theta_2)}{L(\theta_1)} = \left(\frac{1/\theta_2}{1/\theta_1}\right)^n \frac{1_{y_n \in [0,\theta_2]}}{1_{y_n \in [0,\theta_1]}} = \left(\frac{\theta_1}{\theta_2}\right)^n \times \begin{cases} 1 & (0 \leqslant y_n \leqslant \theta_1), \\ \infty & (\theta_1 < y_n \leqslant \theta_2), \end{cases}$$

which is a monotone nondecreasing function of y_n.
(b) For $0 < v < \theta$, the density of y_n is

$$f_{y_n}(v) = n f_z(v) \left(F_z(v)\right)^{n-1} = \frac{n}{\theta}\left(\frac{v}{\theta}\right)^{n-1} = \frac{n v^{n-1}}{\theta^n},$$

by Exercise 7.35. From the Karlin–Rubin theorem, it follows from (a) that we have to reject H_0 when y_n is large. Hence

$$\Pr{}_{\theta_c}(y_n > v_0) = \frac{1}{\theta_c^n} \int_{v_0}^{\theta_c} n v^{n-1}\, \mathrm{d}v = \left[\frac{v^n}{\theta_c^n}\right]_{v_0}^{\theta_c} = 1 - \left(\frac{v_0}{\theta_c}\right)^n,$$

and equating this to α gives the size-α critical value $v_0 = \theta_c(1-\alpha)^{1/n}$.

***Exercise 14.28 (Power monotonicity w.r.t. ν_1, ν_2 for tests based on $\mathrm{F}(\nu_1, \nu_2)$, via MLR property)** Let $0 < \nu_1, \nu_2 < \infty$ and $\delta \geqslant 0$, then define

$$\tau := \tau(\nu_1, \nu_2, \delta) \sim \mathrm{F}^\dagger(\nu_1, \nu_2, \delta) := \frac{\nu_1}{\nu_2} \times \mathrm{F}(\nu_1, \nu_2, \delta)$$

with $\tau(\nu_1, \nu_2) := \tau(\nu_1, \nu_2, 0)$. Take $\alpha \in (0,1)$.
(a) Show that $\mathrm{F}^\dagger(\nu_1, \nu_2)$ satisfies the MLR property with respect to ν_1.
(b) Show that

$$\Pr\left(\tau(\nu_1 + \theta, \nu_2 + c) > \mathrm{F}_\alpha^\dagger(\nu_1, \nu_2 + c)\right) > \Pr\left(\tau(\nu_1 + \theta, \nu_2) > \mathrm{F}_\alpha^\dagger(\nu_1, \nu_2)\right)$$

for all finite $\theta, c > 0$, hence that $\Pi_\tau := \Pr(\tau > \mathrm{F}_\alpha^\dagger(\nu_1, \nu_2))$ is monotone increasing in ν_2 for any $0 < \delta < \infty$. [Hint: To get the inequality above, define the independent variates

$$z_1 \sim \chi^2(\nu_1 + \theta), \quad z_2 \sim \chi^2(\nu_2), \quad z_3 \sim \chi^2(c),$$

then base on $x_1 := z_1/(z_2 + z_3)$ and $x_2 := z_2/(z_2 + z_3)$ a UMP test for $\theta = 0$ against $\theta > 0$ and a suboptimal test, both of size α. To get the result for Π_τ, use the formula for the density of $\mathrm{F}(\nu_1, \nu_2, \delta)$ from Table 4.2.]
(c) Show that

$$\Pr\left(\tau(\nu_1 + \theta + c, \nu_2) > \mathrm{F}_\alpha^\dagger(\nu_1 + c, \nu_2)\right) < \Pr\left(\tau(\nu_1 + \theta, \nu_2) > \mathrm{F}_\alpha^\dagger(\nu_1, \nu_2)\right)$$

for all finite $\theta, c > 0$, hence that Π_τ is monotone decreasing in ν_1 for any $0 < \delta < \infty$. [Hint: Define $x_1 := z_1/z_2$ and $x_2 := z_3/(z_1 + z_2)|_{\theta=0}$ to obtain a suboptimal $y' := x_1 + (1 + x_1)x_2$ for testing $\theta = 0$ again, this time as an intermediate variate that dominates $y := (z_1 + z_3)/z_2 \sim \mathrm{F}^\dagger(\nu_1 + \theta + c, \nu_2)$.]
(d) For a random sample of size n from $\boldsymbol{x} \sim \mathrm{N}_k(\boldsymbol{\mu}, \boldsymbol{\Sigma})$ with $n > k$ and $\boldsymbol{\Sigma}$ nonsingular,

Exercise 9.24 implies that Hotelling's T^2 satisfies

$$\frac{1}{n-1}T^2 \sim \mathrm{F}^{\dagger}(k, n-k, \delta),$$

with $\delta := n(\boldsymbol{\mu}-\boldsymbol{\mu}_0)' \boldsymbol{\Sigma}^{-1}(\boldsymbol{\mu}-\boldsymbol{\mu}_0)$. Show that the power of Hotelling's T^2 for testing $\mathrm{H}_0 : \boldsymbol{\mu} = \boldsymbol{\mu}_0$ against $\mathrm{H}_1 : \boldsymbol{\mu} \neq \boldsymbol{\mu}_0$ is monotone decreasing in k, and interpret the result in the context of adding variables to a regression.

Solution

(a) Table 4.2 (with the transformation theorem) implies that the density of an $\mathrm{F}^{\dagger}(\nu_1, \nu_2)$ variate is

$$f_{\mathrm{F}^{\dagger}(\nu_1,\nu_2)}(u) = \frac{u^{\frac{\nu_1}{2}-1}}{B(\frac{\nu_1}{2}, \frac{\nu_2}{2})(1+u)^{\frac{\nu_1+\nu_2}{2}}}.$$

For $\nu_1' > \nu_1$, the ratio of $\mathrm{F}^{\dagger}(\nu_1', \nu_2)$ to $\mathrm{F}^{\dagger}(\nu_1, \nu_2)$ densities is

$$\frac{B(\frac{\nu_1}{2}, \frac{\nu_2}{2})}{B(\frac{\nu_1'}{2}, \frac{\nu_2}{2})}\left(\frac{u}{1+u}\right)^{\frac{\nu_1'-\nu_1}{2}} = \frac{B(\frac{\nu_1}{2}, \frac{\nu_2}{2})}{B(\frac{\nu_1'}{2}, \frac{\nu_2}{2})}\left(1+u^{-1}\right)^{-\frac{\nu_1'-\nu_1}{2}},$$

which is increasing in u for all $u \in \mathbb{R}_+$. Notice that the same property applies to $\mathrm{F}(\nu_1, \nu_2)$ densities as well.

(b) Using the z-variates in the hint, we have

$$x_1 := \frac{z_1}{z_2+z_3} \sim \mathrm{F}^{\dagger}(\nu_1+\theta, \nu_2+c)$$

by Exercise 4.32 which, together with Exercise 4.31, implies also that

$$x_2 := \frac{z_2}{z_2+z_3} = \frac{z_2/z_3}{1+z_2/z_3} \sim \mathrm{Beta}\left(\frac{\nu_2}{2}, \frac{c}{2}\right).$$

Exercise 7.18(c) shows that x_2 is independent of z_2+z_3, hence also independent of x_1 (whose z_1 is independent of the rest). In the sample $\{x_1, x_2\}$, the joint density factors as $f_{x_1}f_{x_2}$ implying that x_1 is a sufficient statistic for θ, so (a) and the Karlin–Rubin theorem give a size-α UMP test of $\theta = 0$ against $\theta > 0$ as one based on the critical region

$$x_1 > \mathrm{F}^{\dagger}_{\alpha}(\nu_1, \nu_2+c).$$

Comparing this test's power with that of the suboptimal test

$$y := \frac{x_1}{x_2} = \frac{z_1}{z_2} \sim \mathrm{F}^{\dagger}(\nu_1+\theta, \nu_2),$$

we get $\Pi_{x_1} > \Pi_y$ for all finite $\theta, c > 0$ and $\alpha \in (0,1)$, that is,

$$\Pr\left(\tau(\nu_1+\theta, \nu_2+c) > \mathrm{F}^{\dagger}_{\alpha}(\nu_1, \nu_2+c)\right) > \Pr\left(\tau(\nu_1+\theta, \nu_2) > \mathrm{F}^{\dagger}_{\alpha}(\nu_1, \nu_2)\right).$$

Notice that y is numerically larger than x_1 (since $x_2 < 1$), but so is its quantile: a larger test statistic does not alone guarantee a higher H_0-rejection rate (i.e., power).

To get the required result for the power function, Table 4.2 gives the density of the noncentral $\mathrm{F}(\nu_1, \nu_2 + c, \delta)$ as

$$f_{\mathrm{F}(\nu_1,\nu_2+c,\delta)}(u) = \mathrm{e}^{-\delta/2} \sum_{j=0}^{\infty} \frac{(\delta/2)^j}{j!} f_{\mathrm{F}^\dagger(\nu_1+2j,\nu_2+c)}(u),$$

where it is assumed that δ is finite. By integrating termwise, the power function is

$$\Pi_{\tau(\nu_1,\nu_2+c,\delta)} = \mathrm{e}^{-\delta/2} \sum_{j=0}^{\infty} \frac{(\delta/2)^j}{j!} \Pr\left(\tau\left(\nu_1 + 2j, \nu_2 + c\right) > \mathrm{F}_\alpha^\dagger(\nu_1, \nu_2 + c)\right)$$

$$> \mathrm{e}^{-\delta/2} \sum_{j=0}^{\infty} \frac{(\delta/2)^j}{j!} \Pr\left(\tau\left(\nu_1 + 2j, \nu_2\right) > \mathrm{F}_\alpha^\dagger(\nu_1, \nu_2)\right) = \Pi_{\tau(\nu_1,\nu_2,\delta)},$$

where the inequality follows by taking $\theta = 2j > 0$ in the result of the previous paragraph. Strict inequality holds for $0 < \delta < \infty$, and equality of the Π's holds in the case where $\delta = 0$ implies that $j = 0$ is the only nonzero term and $\Pr\left(\tau\left(\nu_1, \nu_2\right) > \mathrm{F}_\alpha^\dagger(\nu_1, \nu_2)\right) = \alpha$. Since $\Pi_{\tau(\nu_1,\nu_2+c,\delta)} > \Pi_{\tau(\nu_1,\nu_2,\delta)}$ for $c > 0$, the power is increased by increasing ν_2.
(c) This time, define

$$x_1 := \frac{z_1}{z_2} \sim \mathrm{F}^\dagger(\nu_1 + \theta, \nu_2)$$

for constructing a UMP test (about θ again) to use for the right-hand side of the required inequality, by the Karlin–Rubin theorem as in (b). We also need to combine x_1 with a variate to produce one distributed as $\mathrm{F}^\dagger(\nu_1 + \theta + c, \nu_2)$ on the left-hand side of the inequality, which we now do.

Introduce

$$x_2 := \left.\frac{z_3}{z_1 + z_2}\right|_{\theta=0} \sim \mathrm{F}^\dagger(c, \nu_1 + \nu_2)$$

which does not depend on θ. It is independent of x_1, because $1 + x_1 = (z_1 + z_2)/z_2$ is independent of $z_1 + z_2$, by Exercise 7.18(c), and z_3 is independent of the rest. Combining x_1, x_2 into a suboptimal variate

$$y' := x_1 + (1 + x_1)\, x_2 = \frac{z_1 + (z_1 + z_2)\, x_2}{z_2},$$

we see that the following hold:

$$(z_1 + z_2) \sim \chi^2(\nu_1 + \nu_2 + \theta), \qquad x_2 \sim \frac{\chi^2(c)}{\chi^2(\nu_1 + \nu_2)},$$

and $\theta = 0$ gives $(z_1 + z_2)\, x_2 = z_3 \sim \chi^2(c)$ hence $y' \sim \mathrm{F}^\dagger(\nu_1 + c, \nu_2)$, while $\theta > 0$ yields

$$x_2 > \frac{z_3}{z_1 + z_2}$$

hence y' larger than

$$y := \frac{z_1 + z_3}{z_2} \sim \mathrm{F}^\dagger(\nu_1 + \theta + c, \nu_2).$$

Thus, for a size α,

$$\Pr\left(\tau\left(\nu_1+\theta+c,\nu_2\right) > \mathrm{F}^{\dagger}_{\alpha}(\nu_1+c,\nu_2)\right) < \Pr\left(y' > \mathrm{F}^{\dagger}_{\alpha}(\nu_1+c,\nu_2)\right),$$

and both are dominated by the corresponding probability for the UMP $x_1 \sim \mathrm{F}^{\dagger}(\nu_1+\theta,\nu_2)$; whence the required

$$\Pr\left(\tau\left(\nu_1+\theta+c,\nu_2\right) > \mathrm{F}^{\dagger}_{\alpha}(\nu_1+c,\nu_2)\right) < \Pr\left(\tau\left(\nu_1+\theta,\nu_2\right) > \mathrm{F}^{\dagger}_{\alpha}(\nu_1,\nu_2)\right).$$

The consequent proof that $\Pi_{\tau(\nu_1+c,\nu_2,\delta)} < \Pi_{\tau(\nu_1,\nu_2,\delta)}$ is as in (b).

(d) The result on power follows directly from (b) and (c). Now, to the interpretation. In Section 12.3, we analyzed the correspondence between linear regression and the conditional mean in normal distributions, on which T^2 is based. Furthermore, Exercises 12.35–12.39 introduced precursors to testing for the significance of estimates in regressions and, in particular, gave a discussion of adding variables to a model in Exercise 12.39(f); see also the solution of Exercise 13.13(c). The implication of the results in the present exercise on the question of adding variables is that, unless they contribute to a sufficiently increased δ, the power of T^2 will decrease owing to the increase of k in $\mathrm{F}^{\dagger}(k, n-k, \delta)$. We will revisit the question of the power of T^2 in Exercise 14.37.

Exercise 14.29 (UMPU for composite hypotheses: normal with known variance) Let $x_1, \dots, x_n$ be a random sample from $x \sim \mathrm{N}(\mu, \sigma_0^2)$, where σ_0^2 is a known positive constant.

(a) Derive a size-α UMP test for $\mathrm{H}_0 : \mu \leqslant \mu_c$ against $\mathrm{H}_1 : \mu > \mu_c$.

(b) Derive a size-α UMPU test for $\mathrm{H}_0 : \mu = \mu_c$ against $\mathrm{H}_1 : \mu \neq \mu_c$.

Solution

(a) Let us use the Neyman–Pearson lemma instead of the MLR property. Consider testing $\mathrm{H}_0' : \mu = \mu_0$ $(\mu_0 \leqslant \mu_c)$ against $\mathrm{H}_1' : \mu = \mu_1$ $(\mu_1 > \mu_c)$, both simple hypotheses. Now,

$$\begin{aligned}\wp &= \exp\left(\frac{1}{2\sigma_0^2}\sum_{i=1}^{n}\left((x_i-\mu_1)^2-(x_i-\mu_0)^2\right)\right)\\ &= \exp\left(\frac{n(\mu_1^2-\mu_0^2)}{2\sigma_0^2}\right)\exp\left(\frac{\mu_0-\mu_1}{\sigma_0^2}\sum_{i=1}^{n}x_i\right).\end{aligned}$$

Since $\mu_0 - \mu_1 < 0$, a UMP test would reject H_0' if $z := \sum_{i=1}^n x_i \sim \mathrm{N}(n\mu, n\sigma_0^2)$ is large for given n. This is the test τ appearing in (14.7) and discussed subsequently in the introduction. It is most-powerful pointwise, for H_1', hence UMP for H_1 since the critical region is determined by H_0 and does not vary with μ_1. Now, $\sup_{\mu_0 \leqslant \mu_c} \Pr_{\mu_0}(z > w_0) = \alpha$ delivers a critical value w_0 not depending on μ_1, and we have

$$\begin{aligned}\sup_{\mu_0\leqslant\mu_c}\Pr{}_{\mu_0}(z>w_0) &= \sup_{\mu_0\leqslant\mu_c}\Pr{}_{\mu_0}\left(\frac{z-n\mu_0}{\sigma_0\sqrt{n}} > \frac{w_0-n\mu_0}{\sigma_0\sqrt{n}}\right)\\ &= \sup_{\mu_0\leqslant\mu_c}\Phi\left(-\frac{w_0-n\mu_0}{\sigma_0\sqrt{n}}\right) = \Phi\left(\frac{n\mu_c-w_0}{\sigma_0\sqrt{n}}\right),\end{aligned}$$

which does not depend on μ_0 either. Note that we have used $\Pr(y > v) = \Pr(y < -v) = \Phi(-v)$ for $y \sim \mathrm{N}(0,1)$. Equating this probability to α, we get

$$w_0 = n\mu_c - \sigma_0\sqrt{n}\Phi^{-1}(\alpha).$$

(b) The one-sided test z given in (a) is biased when we allow $\mathrm{H}_1' : \mu = \mu_1 < \mu_c$ as well as $\mu_1 > \mu_c$, as seen in the introduction to this chapter. The sufficiency of z allows us to restrict our attention to tests, denoted by $g(z)$, that are functions of z and not of the rest of the data. We will now derive this function g.

Unbiasedness requires that the power function $\Pi_{g(z)}(\mu) := \Pr_\mu(z \in C_\alpha)$ achieves a minimum at $\mu = \mu_c$ and that the minimum value is α; see, for example, the horizontal dotted tangency line at $\Pi = \alpha$ in Figure 14.2 indicating that $\mathrm{d}\Pi/\mathrm{d}\mu = 0$. Therefore, for any critical region C_α, the minimum point $\mathrm{H}_0 : \mu = \mu_c$ should lead to

$$\frac{\mathrm{d}}{\mathrm{d}\mu_c}\int_{C_\alpha} \exp\left(-\frac{(w-n\mu_c)^2}{2n\sigma_0^2}\right)\mathrm{d}w = 0,$$

where the integrand comes from the density of $z \sim \mathrm{N}(n\mu_c, n\sigma_0^2)$. Since C_α will depend on the centered $z - n\mu_c \sim \mathrm{N}(0, n\sigma_0^2)$, whose density does not contain μ_c, we can differentiate the integrand (with respect to μ_c) and renormalize to get

$$0 = \frac{1}{\sqrt{2\pi n\sigma_0^2}}\int_{C_\alpha}(w-n\mu_c)\exp\left(-\frac{(w-n\mu_c)^2}{2n\sigma_0^2}\right)\mathrm{d}w = \mathrm{E}((z-n\mu_c)\,1_{z\in C_\alpha}),$$

where the expectation is taken under $\mu = \mu_c$. The condition requires the covariance of z (which is centered around $n\mu_c$ under $\mu = \mu_c$) with $1_{z\in C_\alpha}$ to be zero, and Exercise 6.14 shows that this can be achieved by taking $1_{z\in C_\alpha}$ to be an even function of the symmetric variate $z - n\mu_c$. Applying the Neyman–Pearson lemma pointwise, as in (a), and subject to the new additional restriction, a UMPU test statistic can take the form $g(z) := |z - n\mu_c|$ or $\tau^\dagger := g(z)/\sqrt{n} = \sqrt{n}\,|\overline{x} - \mu_c|$ seen in the introduction after (14.9). See also Exercise 14.3 for a proof of the unbiasedness of a test based on a related quadratic function, although the proof there does not establish the UMPU property.

Exercise 14.30 (Relation between similarity and Neyman structure) As seen in the introduction, the Neyman structure of a test τ relative to the sufficient $\boldsymbol{z}$ for $\boldsymbol{\theta} \in \Theta_{01}$ implies the similarity of τ in Θ_{01}. Assuming $\boldsymbol{z}$ to be boundedly complete, prove the reverse implication.

Solution

By the definition of conditional probability,

$$\Pr_{\boldsymbol{\theta}}(\boldsymbol{X} \in C_\alpha) = \mathrm{E}_{\boldsymbol{z}}\left(\Pr_{\boldsymbol{\theta}}(\boldsymbol{X} \in C_\alpha \mid \boldsymbol{z})\right),$$

and similarity implies that we can equate the left-hand side to α for $\boldsymbol{\theta} \in \Theta_0$ and hence for

$\boldsymbol{\theta} \in \Theta_{01}$, giving

$$\mathrm{E}_{\boldsymbol{z}}\left(\Pr_{\boldsymbol{\theta}}(\boldsymbol{X} \in C_\alpha \mid \boldsymbol{z}) - \alpha\right) = 0.$$

First, this conditional probability is a function of $\boldsymbol{z}$ that does not depend on $\boldsymbol{\theta}$, by the sufficiency of $\boldsymbol{z}$. Second, probability being a bounded function, the bounded completeness of $\boldsymbol{z}$ implies that there are no functions of $\boldsymbol{z}$ having zero expectation apart from the null function

$$\Pr_{\boldsymbol{\theta}}(\boldsymbol{X} \in C_\alpha \mid \boldsymbol{z}) - \alpha = 0,$$

with probability 1. As a result, for $\boldsymbol{\theta} \in \Theta_{01}$ we get $\Pr_{\boldsymbol{\theta}}(\boldsymbol{X} \in C_\alpha \mid \boldsymbol{z}) = \alpha$ almost surely, which defines a Neyman structure for τ (with its C_α) with respect to $\boldsymbol{z}$.

***Exercise 14.31 (t-ratio is UMP similar (w.r.t. σ) test for the normal's mean)** Taking a random sample of size n from $x \sim \mathrm{N}(\mu, \sigma^2)$, with the positive σ^2 unknown, show that the t-ratio is UMP similar (with respect to σ) for testing $\mathrm{H}_0 : \mu = \mu_0$ against $\mathrm{H}_1 : \mu = \mu_1$. What if $\mathrm{H}_1 : \mu > \mu_0$ or $\mathrm{H}_1 : \mu \neq \mu_0$ instead? [Hint: Condition on a complete sufficient statistic for σ^2 (say the H_0-restricted MLE $\widetilde{\sigma}^2$) in order to reduce H_0 to a simple hypothesis, then use the Neyman–Pearson lemma and show what its MPR implies for t under a fixed and then a varying $\widetilde{\sigma}^2$.]

Solution
Since σ is unknown, $\mathrm{H}_0 : \mu = \mu_0$ and $\mathrm{H}_1 : \mu = \mu_1$ are both composite. Under H_0, which specifies $\mu = \mu_0$,

$$\widetilde{\sigma}^2 := \frac{1}{n} \sum_{i=1}^{n} (x_i - \mu_0)^2$$

is a complete sufficient statistic for the remaining unknown parameter σ^2 (see Chapter 11). Therefore, Exercise 14.30 shows that the critical region for a similar test of H_0 will have

$$\Pr_{\mu_0}\left(\boldsymbol{x} \in C_\alpha \mid \widetilde{\sigma}^2\right) = \alpha,$$

with probability 1. In search of such a test, conditioning on $\widetilde{\sigma}^2$ now gives a simple H_0' and we consider another simple hypothesis

$$\mathrm{H}_1' : \mu = \mu_1, \sigma^2 = \sigma_1^2,$$

in order to use the Neyman–Pearson lemma, giving

$$\wp = \frac{\widetilde{\sigma}^{-n} \exp\left(-\frac{1}{2\widetilde{\sigma}^2} \sum_{i=1}^{n} (x_i - \mu_0)^2\right)}{\sigma_1^{-n} \exp\left(-\frac{1}{2\sigma_1^2} \sum_{i=1}^{n} (x_i - \mu_1)^2\right)} = \left(\frac{\sigma_1}{\widetilde{\sigma}}\right)^n \exp\left(-\frac{n}{2}\right) \exp\left(\frac{1}{2\sigma_1^2} \sum_{i=1}^{n} (x_i - \mu_1)^2\right)$$

by the definition of $\widetilde{\sigma}^2$. As in (14.12) in the introduction, we have

$$\begin{aligned}\frac{1}{n} \sum_{i=1}^{n} (x_i - \mu_1)^2 &= \frac{1}{n} \sum_{i=1}^{n} \left((x_i - \mu_0) + (\mu_0 - \mu_1)\right)^2 \\ &= \widetilde{\sigma}^2 + (\mu_0 - \mu_1)^2 + 2(\mu_0 - \mu_1)(\overline{x} - \mu_0)\end{aligned}$$

and $\wp < \gamma$ gives rise to an MPR C_α rejecting H_0' when $(\mu_0 - \mu_1)(\overline{x} - \mu_0)$ is smaller than some constant: for $\mu_1 < \mu_0$, rejection occurs when $\overline{x}$ is significantly lower than μ_0 (closer to H_1'), while $\mu_0 < \mu_1$ requires $\overline{x}$ to be significantly larger than μ_0 for a rejection. Before extending our result from the simple $\mathrm{H}_0', \mathrm{H}_1'$ to the composite $\mathrm{H}_0, \mathrm{H}_1$, we need to consider further implications of fixing $\widetilde{\sigma}$.

As in the introduction to Chapter 9 or in Exercise 9.4(a), we can rewrite $\widetilde{\sigma}^2$ as

$$\widetilde{\sigma}^2 = \widehat{\sigma}^2 + (\overline{x} - \mu_0)^2 \equiv \widehat{\sigma}^2 \left(1 + \frac{t^2}{n-1}\right),$$

the last equivalence following from the definition of the t-ratio in the introduction as $t := \sqrt{n}\,(\overline{x} - \mu_0)/s$ in (14.4), with $n\widehat{\sigma}^2 \equiv (n-1)\,s^2$. We saw in the previous paragraph that an MPR rejecting H_0' is obtained when $(\overline{x} - \mu_0)^2$ is large and, with $\widetilde{\sigma}^2$ fixed, this means a small $\widehat{\sigma}^2 = \widetilde{\sigma}^2 - (\overline{x} - \mu_0)^2$: a violation of H_0' is therefore associated with a large numerical value of the t-ratio, the direction of the violation depending on whether μ_1 is greater or less than μ_0 (a one-sided MPR).

Since t has a Student's $\mathrm{t}(n-1)$ distribution (see Section 9.2) that is independent of σ under the composite H_0, Basu's theorem (see Chapter 11) tells us that it is independent of the complete sufficient $\widetilde{\sigma}$ and therefore satisfies the required Neyman structure. This means that t is most-powerful similar for H_0 against H_1', but also against H_1 since the result applies pointwise for σ_1. Therefore, the result applies uniformly, as we needed: t is UMP similar for the composite pair $\mathrm{H}_0 : \mu = \mu_0$ and $\mathrm{H}_1 : \mu = \mu_1$. The same reasoning as for $\mathrm{H}_1 : \mu = \mu_1$ applies to $\mathrm{H}_1 : \mu > \mu_0$, and also for $\mathrm{H}_1 : \mu \neq \mu_0$ but the latter is rejected when t^2 is large (a two-sided MPR).

***Exercise 14.32 (Exponential family's UMPU)** Suppose that we have a random sample $\boldsymbol{x} := (x_1, \dots, x_n)'$ from the exponential family with density

$$f_x(u) = m_0(\boldsymbol{\theta}) h_0(u) \exp\left(\sum_{l=1}^{m} \theta_l h_l(u)\right),$$

where we use the natural-parameter formulation but write $\boldsymbol{\theta}$ instead of $\boldsymbol{\nu}$ to conform with the notation for the testing setup; see (4.5). Assume that the family is regular and that $n \geqslant m$. Defining $H_l(x) := \sum_{i=1}^{n} h_l(x_i)$ and $\boldsymbol{z} := (H_1(x), \dots, H_j(x))'$, Exercise 11.15 showed that $\boldsymbol{z}$ is a complete sufficient statistic whose density also belongs to the exponential family. Derive a UMPU test for:
(a) $\mathrm{H}_0 : \theta_m \in [a, b]$ (with $a < b$) against $\mathrm{H}_1 : \theta_m < a$ or $\theta_m > b$;
(b) $\mathrm{H}_0 : \theta_m = a$ against $\mathrm{H}_1 : \theta_m \neq a$.
[Hint: For (a), generalize the Neyman–Pearson lemma for three values of the parameter (testing $\theta = a$ against an arbitrary additional point $\theta = c$, and $\theta = b$ against $\theta = c$), then combine the two critical regions. For (b), instead of generalizing the lemma for an additional point, consider an additional likelihood at $\theta_m = a$ based on $\psi_1(z_m)\psi_2(\boldsymbol{x}) f_{\boldsymbol{x}}(\boldsymbol{x}; \theta_m)$ for some functions ψ_1, ψ_2 not containing θ_m, which should be compared with the integrand arising from minimizing $\Pi(\theta_m)$ at $\theta_m = a$.]

Solution

By sufficiency, we can restrict our attention to the density of $\boldsymbol{z}$. Partition $\boldsymbol{z}' = (\boldsymbol{z}_1', z_m)$, with $\boldsymbol{z}_1' := (z_1, \dots, z_{m-1})$, and the realization $\boldsymbol{w}$ correspondingly. It is straightforward to show that the conditional density $f_{z_m|\boldsymbol{z}_1}(w_m)$ at $\boldsymbol{z} = \boldsymbol{w}$ is proportional to $\eta(\boldsymbol{w}) \exp(\theta_m w_m)$ (with η as defined in Exercise 11.15) and hence is also regular exponential, and that $\boldsymbol{z}_1$ is sufficient complete for $\boldsymbol{\theta}$ when fixing θ_m as we will do for the hypotheses. Thus Exercise 14.30 implies that every similar test based on this exponential setup will have a Neyman structure with respect to $\boldsymbol{z}_1$ on the boundary points of the hypotheses. Since the regular exponential-family density is continuous in $\boldsymbol{\theta}$, unbiased tests will be similar of some size α on these points, so a UMP among the class of similar tests of size α will be UMPU of size α. It remains for us to find a UMP test within this restricted class.

(a) We generalize the Neyman–Pearson lemma for three possible parameter values (instead of two), these being an arbitrary point c ($c \neq a, b$) and boundary points a, b, with the associated likelihoods L_c, L_a, L_b, respectively. Since this UMP test requires a critical region satisfying both $L_c/L_a > \gamma_a^{-1}$ and $L_c/L_b > \gamma_b^{-1}$, we can write instead the combined condition

$$L_c > \delta_1 L_a + \delta_2 L_b,$$

for some arbitrary δ_1, δ_2 to be specified further below. From substituting into this inequality $f_{z_m|\boldsymbol{z}_1}(z_m) \propto \eta(\boldsymbol{z}) \exp(\theta_m z_m)$, the critical region is of the form

$$1 > d_1 \mathrm{e}^{(a-c)z_m} + d_2 \mathrm{e}^{(b-c)z_m}.$$

Clearly, we cannot have both $d_1 \leqslant 0$ and $d_2 \leqslant 0$ because then all observations would fall in the critical region, so we exclude $d_1, d_2 \leqslant 0$ in part (a). Abstracting temporarily from the setup of H_0 and H_1 in the question, if $c \in (a, b)$, then $\operatorname{sgn}(a - c) = -\operatorname{sgn}(b - c)$ and the right-hand side of the displayed inequality is monotone unless $d_1, d_2 > 0$, with a monotone LR implying a biased test here (for example, see Figure 14.2). Hence, we require $d_1, d_2 > 0$ and, as a result, $d_1 \mathrm{e}^{(a-c)z_m} + d_2 \mathrm{e}^{(b-c)z_m}$ is a convex function and the required region can be written as the convex set

$$w_{\mathrm{l}} < z_m < w_{\mathrm{u}}.$$

If $c \notin [a, b]$, meaning that if the question's H_1 holds, the critical region is $z_m \notin [w_{\mathrm{l}}, w_{\mathrm{u}}]$, which is then the MPR C_α mentioned in the previous paragraph. That this MPR does not depend on c follows by the determination of α by a, b in the Neyman–Pearson lemma; hence the result applies uniformly for all $\theta_m \in \Theta_1$. Therefore, if we have a critical region $z_m \notin [w_{\mathrm{l}}, w_{\mathrm{u}}]$ of size α, it is a uniformly MPR and z_m is a UMPU test.

Note that the same approach can be used to obtain a UMPU test for other null hypotheses that contain intervals of positive lengths for θ_m, another example being $\mathrm{H}_0 : \theta_m \leqslant a$ or $\theta_m \geqslant b$ against $\mathrm{H}_1 : \theta_m \in (a, b)$, but the best critical region would be the complement of the region that we have used so far in rejecting H_0. Note also that the interval in $\mathrm{H}_0 : \theta_m \in [a, b]$ is about the *natural* parameter θ_m itself, which is a combination of the original

parameters, as we have seen before and will illustrate again in Exercise 14.34. Care must be exercised in translating intervals for θ_m to corresponding sets for the original parameters; see also the discussion surrounding (7.1) for an illustration of the difficulties.
(b) This is a case where $a = b$ compared with (a), but the derivations are not quite the same as in (a). We need the additional requirement that $\mathrm{d}\Pi(\theta_m; z_1)/\,\mathrm{d}\theta_m = 0$ a.s. at $\theta_m = a$, an example of which has already been encountered in Exercise 14.29(b). (In the case where Θ_0 is an interval, as in (a), there is no need to take this derivative because $\Pi(\theta_m)$ is allowed to dip below α in the interior of Θ_0.) Using the conditional density of z_m, the additional condition is

$$0 = \frac{\mathrm{d}\Pr_a(z_m \in C_\alpha \mid \boldsymbol{z}_1 = \boldsymbol{w}_1)}{\mathrm{d}a} \equiv \frac{\mathrm{d}}{\mathrm{d}a}\int_{w_m \in C_\alpha} m_1(a)\eta(\boldsymbol{w})\exp(aw_m)\,\mathrm{d}w_m,$$

where we use the shorthand

$$m_1(a) := \left(\int_{w_m \in \mathcal{Z}_m} \eta(\boldsymbol{w})\exp(aw_m)\,\mathrm{d}w_m\right)^{-1}$$

to write the factor of proportionality of the density (sums replace integrals in the discrete case), a notation which hides the dependence of this factor on other quantities that will not affect our subsequent operations. Exchanging integration and differentiation is allowed by the assumed regularity of the exponential family, so the condition becomes

$$\begin{aligned}0 &= \int_{w_m \in C_\alpha}\left(\frac{m_1'(a)}{m_1(a)} + w_m\right) m_1(a)\eta(\boldsymbol{w})\exp(aw_m)\,\mathrm{d}w_m \\ &= \mathrm{E}_{z_m|\boldsymbol{z}_1=\boldsymbol{w}_1}\left(1_{z_m \in C_\alpha}\left(\frac{m_1'(a)}{m_1(a)} + z_m\right)\right) \\ &\equiv \alpha\frac{m_1'(a)}{m_1(a)} + \mathrm{E}_{z_m|\boldsymbol{z}_1=\boldsymbol{w}_1}(z_m 1_{z_m \in C_\alpha}),\end{aligned}$$

where the expectation is taken under $\theta_m = a$. Since the definition of m_1 leads to

$$\frac{m_1'(a)}{m_1(a)} = \frac{\mathrm{d}\log m_1(a)}{\mathrm{d}a} = \frac{-\int_{w_m \in \mathcal{Z}_m} w_m\eta(\boldsymbol{w})\exp(aw_m)\,\mathrm{d}w_m}{\int_{w_m \in \mathcal{Z}_m}\eta(\boldsymbol{w})\exp(aw_m)\,\mathrm{d}w_m} = -\mathrm{E}_{z_m|\boldsymbol{z}_1=\boldsymbol{w}_1}(z_m)$$

(compare with Exercise 11.15(b)), the condition becomes

$$\mathrm{E}_{z_m|\boldsymbol{z}_1=\boldsymbol{w}_1}(z_m(1_{z_m \in C_\alpha} - \alpha)) = 0.$$

It differs from and is additional to the usual condition $\mathrm{E}_{z_m|\boldsymbol{z}_1=\boldsymbol{w}_1}(1_{z_m \in C_\alpha} - \alpha) = 0$ that fixes the size to α for a similar test based on z_m, similarity implying that $\mathrm{E}_{z_m|\boldsymbol{z}_1}(1_{z_m \in C_\alpha})$ does not depend on $\boldsymbol{z}_1$ almost surely.

If we were dealing with a symmetric z_m, then we would be all but done, as in the proof of Exercise 14.29(b). But, for the general case, we need an extra step that generalizes the Neyman–Pearson lemma again, which we will derive for $m = 1$ omitting the conditioning on $\boldsymbol{z}_1$ for ease of exposition. This time, instead of considering an additional point b, we need to consider a different likelihood at a. We now have the additional restriction $\alpha\,\mathrm{E}(z_m) =$

$\mathrm{E}(z_m 1_{z_m \in C_\alpha})$, which can be rewritten as

$$\alpha \,\mathrm{E}(z_m) = \mathrm{E}(z_m\,(\boldsymbol{x})\,1_{\boldsymbol{x}\in C_\alpha}) \equiv \int_{\boldsymbol{w_x}\in C_\alpha} z_m(\boldsymbol{w_x}) f_{\boldsymbol{x}}(\boldsymbol{w_x})\,\mathrm{d}\boldsymbol{w_x},$$

where we stress that z_m is a function of the data and use $\boldsymbol{x} \in C_\alpha$ to signify the values of $\boldsymbol{x}$ leading to $z_m \in C_\alpha$ (see Exercise 11.16 for the partitioning of the sample space implied by $z_m = w_m$). This integral is reminiscent of equations determining Type I errors α, and we can scale it by a constant ψ such that it equals a size $\in (0,1)$, where ψ does not depend on $\boldsymbol{x}$ because it has been integrated out in both expectations. To do so, consider the wider class of likelihoods of the form given in the hint,

$$\widetilde{L}_a := \psi_1(z_m)\psi_2(\boldsymbol{x})L_a,$$

for some functions ψ_1, ψ_2 such that $\psi_1(z_m)\psi_2(\boldsymbol{x}) \geqslant 0$ and $\widetilde{L}_a$ is a proper likelihood. Then, the size of C_α under $\widetilde{L}_a$ is obtained as

$$\widetilde{\alpha} := \int_{\boldsymbol{w_x}\in C_\alpha} \psi_1(w_m)\psi_2(\boldsymbol{w_x}) f_{\boldsymbol{x}}(\boldsymbol{w_x})\,\mathrm{d}\boldsymbol{w_x} = \mathrm{E}(\psi_1(z_m)\psi_2(\boldsymbol{x})1_{\boldsymbol{x}\in C_\alpha})$$

and is again calculated under $\theta_m = a$. The special case of $\widetilde{L}$ seen in the integral equation displayed at the start of this paragraph requires $\psi_1(z_m)\psi_2(\boldsymbol{x}) = \psi z_m$. Then the Neyman–Pearson lemma yields a critical region satisfying $L_c/\widetilde{L}_a > \widetilde{\gamma}_a^{-1}$, in addition to $L_c/L_a > \gamma_a^{-1}$. Using the definition of $\widetilde{L}_a$, we can write the combined Neyman–Pearson condition for z_m as

$$L_c > (\delta_1 + \delta_2 z_m)\, L_a,$$

for some arbitrary δ_1, δ_2 where ψ has been absorbed. Recalling that $f_{z_m|\boldsymbol{z}_1}(z_m)$ is proportional to $\eta(\boldsymbol{z})\exp(\theta_m z_m)$, this critical region is of the form

$$\mathrm{e}^{(c-a)z_m} > d_1 + d_2 z_m.$$

Since $\mathrm{e}^v \geqslant 1 + v$, with equality achieved at $v = 0$, the implied critical region can be either one-sided or two-sided, depending on the parameters. It should not be one-sided because the MLR property implies that then the test would be biased on one of the two sides of H_1. It is therefore the two-sided $z_m \notin [w_\mathrm{l}, w_\mathrm{u}]$ produced by adjusting d_1, d_2 to make the line $d_1 + d_2 z_m$ intersect the exponential $\mathrm{e}^{(c-a)z_m}$. That this MPR does not depend on c follows from the determination of α by a in the Neyman–Pearson lemma; hence the result applies uniformly for all $\theta_m \in \Theta_1$. In conclusion, as in (a), if we have a critical region $z_m \notin [w_\mathrm{l}, w_\mathrm{u}]$ of size α, then it is a uniformly MPR and z_m is a UMPU test.

Exercise 14.33 (Exponential family's UMPU: functions of sufficient statistic) Continuing with the setup of Exercise 14.32, suppose that we have a statistic τ that is a function of two components of the sufficient statistic $\boldsymbol{z}$, say

$$\tau := \psi(z_1, z_2).$$

Suppose further that τ is independent of z_1 when the parameter of interest equals a partic-

ular fixed value, say $\theta = \nu$, and that Θ_1 is the complement of Θ_0 in $\mathbb{R}$. Obtain a UMPU test for:
(a) $\mathrm{H}_0 : \theta \in [a, b]$ (with $a < b$), if ψ is increasing in z_2 for each given z_1;
(b) $\mathrm{H}_0 : \theta = a$, if ψ is linear and increasing in z_2 for each given z_1.

Solution
(a) For $\mathrm{H}_0 : \theta \in [a, b]$, let $\nu = a, b$; in other words, we need the independence of τ and z_1 to hold at the two boundary points and then we can apply the same derivations as in Exercise 14.32(a) which relied on the Neyman structure with respect to $\boldsymbol{z}_1$ there. Therefore, as ψ is increasing in z_2, the critical region $\tau \notin [w_1, w_u]$ of size α is a uniformly MPR and τ is a UMPU test. Note that simpler but comparable derivations hold for $\mathrm{H}_0 : \theta \leqslant a$ with a one-sided critical region.
(b) Write

$$\psi(z_1, z_2) = z_2\psi_1(z_1) + \psi_2(z_1),$$

where $\psi_1 > 0$ for each value of z_1. Then, the condition on $\Pi'(a)$ in Exercise 14.32(b) becomes (writing z_2 for z_m)

$$\alpha \,\mathrm{E}_{z_2|z_1}\left(\frac{\psi(z_1, z_2) - \psi_2(z_1)}{\psi_1(z_1)}\right) = \mathrm{E}_{z_2|z_1}\left(\frac{\psi(z_1, z_2) - \psi_2(z_1)}{\psi_1(z_1)} 1_{z_2 \in C_\alpha}\right)$$

or, multiplying throughout by $\psi_1(z_1)$ which is a constant since we conditioned on z_1,

$$\alpha \,\mathrm{E}_{z_2|z_1}\left(\psi(z_1, z_2)\right) - \alpha\psi_2(z_1) = \mathrm{E}_{z_2|z_1}\left(\psi(z_1, z_2) 1_{z_2 \in C_\alpha}\right) - \psi_2(z_1)\,\mathrm{E}_{z_2|z_1}\left(1_{z_2 \in C_\alpha}\right);$$

then $\mathrm{E}_{z_2|z_1}\left(1_{z_2 \in C_\alpha}\right) = \alpha$ reduces the condition to

$$\alpha \,\mathrm{E}_{z_2|z_1}(\tau) = \mathrm{E}_{z_2|z_1}\left(\tau 1_{z_2 \in C_\alpha}\right)$$

by $\tau := \psi(z_1, z_2)$. Since τ is independent of z_1 in $\mathrm{H}_0 : \theta = a$, we are back to the same derivations as in Exercise 14.32(b), which yielded an optimal critical region of the form $\tau \notin [w_1, w_u]$. The linearity of ψ allows our condition here to be reduced to what we had in Exercise 14.32(b).

Exercise 14.34 (t-ratio is UMPU test for the normal's mean) Continuing with the setup of Exercise 14.32, show that the t-ratio is UMPU for testing $\mathrm{H}_0 : \mu = \mu_0$ against $\mathrm{H}_1 : \mu \neq \mu_0$ in a random sample from $x \sim \mathrm{N}(\mu, \sigma^2)$ with the positive σ^2 unknown. [Hint: Give two solutions, the first using Exercise 14.32(b) and an orthogonal transformation of the parameters and sufficient statistic, the second applying Exercise 14.33(b).]

Solution
In Exercise 14.32, we used the natural-parameter formulation in the exponential, which applies to the normal case as follows:

$$f_{\boldsymbol{x}}(\boldsymbol{x}) = m_0\left(\mu, \sigma^2\right) \exp\left(\frac{\mu}{\sigma^2} \sum_{i=1}^{n} x_i - \frac{1}{2\sigma^2} \sum_{i=1}^{n} x_i^2\right)$$

and $(\theta_1, \theta_2) = (\mu/\sigma^2, -1/(2\sigma^2))$, with $(z_1, z_2) = (n\overline{x}, \sum_{i=1}^n x_i^2)$. As seen in the proof of that exercise, the argument of the exponential was all that mattered in determining the shape of the MPR. It is unaltered if we were to use an orthogonal matrix $\boldsymbol{A}$ to write

$$\exp\left(\boldsymbol{\theta}'\boldsymbol{z}\right) = \exp\left((\boldsymbol{A\theta})'\,\boldsymbol{Az}\right)$$

since $\boldsymbol{A}'\boldsymbol{A} = \boldsymbol{I}_m$, an idea illustrated earlier in Exercise 7.16 with Helmert's transformation. We are making this transformation because the θ_m of interest (in the notation of Exercise 14.32) is μ, which is neither θ_1 nor θ_2 here but rather the m-th component of a new vector $\boldsymbol{\theta}^\dagger := \boldsymbol{A\theta}$, to be determined now. Then, we can apply the results of Exercise 14.32 to $\theta_m^\dagger$. To this end, recall that a two-dimensional orthogonal matrix can be written as

$$\boldsymbol{A} = \begin{pmatrix} \cos\omega & \sin\omega \\ -\sin\omega & \cos\omega \end{pmatrix} = \begin{pmatrix} a_1 & a_2 \\ -a_2 & a_1 \end{pmatrix} \qquad (a_1^2 + a_2^2 = 1)$$

and that we are interested here in $\mathrm{H}_0 : \theta_1 + 2\mu_0\theta_2 = 0$, which we can write in terms of the second element of

$$\boldsymbol{A\theta} = \frac{1}{\sqrt{1+4\mu_0^2}} \begin{pmatrix} 2\mu_0 & -1 \\ 1 & 2\mu_0 \end{pmatrix} \begin{pmatrix} \theta_1 \\ \theta_2 \end{pmatrix}$$

as $\mathrm{H}_0 : \theta_2^\dagger = 0$. Exercise 14.32 tells us to base the desired UMPU test on the second component of $\boldsymbol{Az}$ while conditioning on its first component. Applied here, we obtain

$$\begin{aligned} \boldsymbol{Az} &= \frac{1}{\sqrt{1+4\mu_0^2}} \begin{pmatrix} 2\mu_0 & -1 \\ 1 & 2\mu_0 \end{pmatrix} \begin{pmatrix} n\overline{x} \\ \sum_{i=1}^n x_i^2 \end{pmatrix} \\ &= \frac{1}{\sqrt{1+4\mu_0^2}} \begin{pmatrix} 2n\mu_0\overline{x} - \sum_{i=1}^n x_i^2 \\ n\overline{x} + 2\mu_0 \sum_{i=1}^n x_i^2 \end{pmatrix} = \frac{1}{\sqrt{1+4\mu_0^2}} \begin{pmatrix} n\mu_0^2 - \sum_{i=1}^n (x_i - \mu_0)^2 \\ n\overline{x} + 2\mu_0 \sum_{i=1}^n x_i^2 \end{pmatrix}, \end{aligned}$$

where the second component contains $\overline{x}$ and $\sum_{i=1}^n x_i^2$. The test has to be valid for any μ_0, including $\mu_0 = 0$. But, in the second component on which the test is to be based, $\mu_0 = 0$ makes $\sum_{i=1}^n x_i^2$ vanish. We therefore need to base our test on $\overline{x}$ instead, given any $\sum_{i=1}^n (x_i - \mu_0)^2$ (the random part of the first element of $\boldsymbol{Az}$); this leads to the t-ratio $t := \sqrt{n}\,(\overline{x} - \mu_0)/s$ seen earlier. Note that a rejection region based on $t^2 > (n-1)\,\delta$ is

$$\delta < \frac{n\,(\overline{x} - \mu_0)^2}{\sum_{i=1}^n (x_i - \overline{x})^2} = \frac{n\,(\overline{x} - \mu_0)^2}{\sum_{i=1}^n (x_i - \mu_0)^2 - n\,(\overline{x} - \mu_0)^2},$$

and hence is equivalent to one based on

$$\frac{\delta}{1+\delta} < \frac{t_0^2}{n}, \quad \text{with} \quad t_0 := \frac{\sqrt{n}\,(\overline{x} - \mu_0)}{\sqrt{n^{-1}\sum_{i=1}^n (x_i - \mu_0)^2}},$$

where the critical values of t and t_0, though not the same, are related by this invertible transformation. This t_0 is a test using the restricted MLE $\widetilde{\sigma}^2 := n^{-1}\sum_{i=1}^n (x_i - \mu_0)^2$ in the denominator instead of s^2.

To apply Exercise 14.33(b), the sufficient statistic can be reformulated as $(z_1, z_2) = (\sum_{i=1}^n (x_i - \mu_0)^2, \overline{x})$. Now t and t_0 are linear in $\overline{x}$, with the required positive slope. Also, they do not depend on σ under $\mathrm{H}_0 : \mu = \mu_0$ because the sequence $\{(x_n - \mu_0)/\sigma\}$ has an $\mathrm{N}(0,1)$ distribution which is free of σ, and the same applies to any statistic based on this sequence (such as t_0 and t). Furthermore, the joint density of this sequence implies that, for any given $\mu = \mu_0$, the statistic $\sum_{i=1}^n (x_i - \mu_0)^2$ is complete sufficient for the remaining unknown parameter σ. Then, Basu's theorem tells us that t_0 and t are independent of $\sum_{i=1}^n (x_i - \mu_0)^2$, which establishes them as UMPU by Exercise 14.33(b).

Exercise 14.35 (Sample correlation is UMPU for testing independence in bivariate normal) Suppose that we have a random sample of size $n > 2$ for $(x, y)' \sim \mathrm{N}(\boldsymbol{\mu}, \boldsymbol{\Sigma})$ with $\boldsymbol{\Sigma}$ nonsingular (hence $\rho^2 < 1$). Show that testing $\mathrm{H}_0 : \rho = 0$ against $\mathrm{H}_1 : \rho \neq 0$ leads to the sample correlation $\widehat{\rho}$ being UMPU. What if the alternative were one-sided?

Solution

We start by remarking that the bivariate setup is not as restrictive as it may seem: the same can be done for a pair of variates within a general multivariate normal. The bivariate normal is a five-parameter member of the regular exponential family; see, for example, Exercises 6.1 and 11.15. Even though the density here is bivariate while the setup of Exercise 14.32 concerns a univariate density, the dimension of the data played no direct part in those derivations and they carry through to the general case. Note also that one condition from the proof of Exercise 11.15(b), which would be $n \geqslant 5$ in a 5-parameter univariate case, translates into $n > 2$ (more than 4 variates in the data matrix $\boldsymbol{X}$) in the case of a bivariate normal; see also Section 9.2 for the explicit distributional results.

From

$$f(x,y) = \frac{1}{2\pi\sigma_1\sigma_2\sqrt{1-\rho^2}} \exp\left(\frac{-\sigma_2^2 (x-\mu_1)^2 + 2\rho\sigma_1\sigma_2 (x-\mu_1)(y-\mu_2) - \sigma_1^2 (y-\mu_2)^2}{2\sigma_1^2\sigma_2^2 (1-\rho^2)}\right)$$

we have the sufficient complete $\sum_{i=1}^n \left(x_i, x_i^2, y_i, y_i^2, x_i y_i\right)$ and corresponding

$$\boldsymbol{\theta} = \left(\frac{\mu_1\sigma_2 - \rho\mu_2\sigma_1}{\sigma_1^2(1-\rho^2)\sigma_2}, \frac{-1}{2\sigma_1^2(1-\rho^2)}, \frac{\mu_2\sigma_1 - \rho\mu_1\sigma_2}{\sigma_2^2(1-\rho^2)\sigma_1}, \frac{-1}{2\sigma_2^2(1-\rho^2)}, \frac{\rho}{\sigma_1\sigma_2(1-\rho^2)}\right)'.$$

Since $\mathrm{H}_0 : \rho = 0$ is equivalent to $\mathrm{H}_0 : \theta_5 = 0$ in the natural parameterization, Exercise 14.33(b) implies that we should find a statistic that is linear increasing in $\sum_{i=1}^n x_i y_i$ for each given $\sum_{i=1}^n \left(x_i, x_i^2, y_i, y_i^2\right)$ *and* that this statistic be independent of $\sum_{i=1}^n \left(x_i, x_i^2, y_i, y_i^2\right)$ under H_0. One such statistic is the sample correlation

$$\widehat{\rho} := \frac{\sum_{i=1}^n (x_i - \overline{x})(y_i - \overline{y})}{\sqrt{\sum_{i=1}^n (x_i - \overline{x})^2 \sum_{i=1}^n (y_i - \overline{y})^2}} = \frac{\sum_{i=1}^n x_i y_i - n\overline{x}\,\overline{y}}{\sqrt{\sum_{i=1}^n (x_i - \overline{x})^2 \sum_{i=1}^n (y_i - \overline{y})^2}}$$

which is linear in $\sum_{i=1}^n x_i y_i$. It is also ancillary for $\theta_1, \theta_2, \theta_3, \theta_4$ when $\rho = 0$ (since then $\theta_1, \theta_2, \theta_3, \theta_4$ become functions of $\mu_1, \mu_2, \sigma_1, \sigma_2$ only, and $\widehat{\rho}$ is invariant to location and scale), and hence is independent of $\sum_{i=1}^n \left(x_i, x_i^2, y_i, y_i^2\right)$ by Basu's theorem. This establishes $\widehat{\rho}$ as UMPU for testing $\mathrm{H}_0 : \rho = 0$ against $\mathrm{H}_1 : \rho \neq 0$. In the case of a one-sided alternative, we note in addition that $\rho > 0$ is equivalent to $\theta_5 > 0$, and the result follows.

Exercise 14.36 (No UMP, no UMPU: two normals) Take a random sample of size n from $\mathrm{N}(\boldsymbol{\mu}, \boldsymbol{I}_2)$. For $\mathrm{H}_0 : \boldsymbol{\mu} = \mathbf{0}$ against $\mathrm{H}_1 : \boldsymbol{\mu} \neq \mathbf{0}$, show that no UMP or UMPU exists.

Solution
Let the two elements of $\boldsymbol{\mu}$ be μ_x, μ_y. Take the simple alternative $\mathrm{H}_1' : (\mu_x, \mu_y) = (c_x, c_y)$ and apply the Neyman–Pearson lemma to the simple hypotheses H_0 and H_1'. Then

$$\begin{aligned} \wp &= \frac{\exp\left(-\frac{1}{2}\sum_{i=1}^n x_i^2 - \frac{1}{2}\sum_{i=1}^n y_i^2\right)}{\exp\left(-\frac{1}{2}\sum_{i=1}^n (x_i - c_x)^2 - \frac{1}{2}\sum_{i=1}^n (y_i - c_y)^2\right)} \\ &= \exp\left(-n\left(c_x\overline{x} + c_y\overline{y}\right) + \frac{n}{2}\left(c_x^2 + c_y^2\right)\right) \end{aligned}$$

and rejecting H_0 if $\wp < \gamma$ gives the MPR:

$$-\sqrt{n}\left(c_x\overline{x} + c_y\overline{y}\right) < \frac{\log(\gamma) - \frac{n}{2}\left(c_x^2 + c_y^2\right)}{\sqrt{n}}.$$

Unlike in the single-parameter case considered before, the left-hand side "statistic" now depends on the values under the alternative, which are known under H_1' but not under H_1. The optimal test is different when we choose different alternatives; for example, it is $(\overline{x} + \overline{y})\operatorname{sgn}(\mu_x)$ when $\mu_y = \mu_x \neq 0$ under H_1, but $(\overline{x} + 2\overline{y})\operatorname{sgn}(\mu_x)$ when $\mu_y = 2\mu_x \neq 0$ under H_1. Unbiasedness does not help here, because we would still have the same problem with $\overline{x} + \overline{y}$ versus $\overline{x} + 2\overline{y}$, without the sign of μ_x. There is no *uniformly* most powerful region or test, even in this simple setup, unless we restrict the class of tests by (say) invariance. We will see in the next exercise that invariance to switching (or, more generally, to nonsingular linear combinations) of the $\overline{x}$ and $\overline{y}$ components will circumvent this problem and lead to a UMPI test that is also unbiased.

***Exercise 14.37 (Hotelling's T^2 is UMP invariant to nonsingular linear combinations)** Let $\boldsymbol{x}_1, \dots, \boldsymbol{x}_n$ be a random sample from $\boldsymbol{x} \sim \mathrm{N}_k(\boldsymbol{\mu}, \boldsymbol{\Sigma})$, where $\boldsymbol{\Sigma}$ is nonsingular and $n > k$. Show that, within the class of tests that are invariant to the transformation $\boldsymbol{y} := \boldsymbol{A}\boldsymbol{x}$ with $\boldsymbol{A}$ nonsingular, Hotelling's T^2 is the UMP test for $\mathrm{H}_0 : \boldsymbol{\mu} = \mathbf{0}$ against $\mathrm{H}_1 : \boldsymbol{\mu} \neq \mathbf{0}$. Comment on the further applicability of this result. [Hint: Restricting attention to tests based on the sufficient statistic, show that T^2 (or a one-to-one transformation thereof) is the only invariant function of it; then use Exercises 9.24 and 4.32 to apply the Neyman–Pearson lemma pointwise.]

Solution
As seen in Exercise 14.13, T^2 is one-to-one with the GLR from a normal sample, and hypotheses regarding other values of $\boldsymbol{\mu}$ can be dealt with in the same way. Here, we addi-

tionally consider the class of transformations

$$\boldsymbol{y} := \boldsymbol{A}\boldsymbol{x} \sim \mathrm{N}_k\left(\boldsymbol{A}\boldsymbol{\mu}, \boldsymbol{A}\boldsymbol{\Sigma}\boldsymbol{A}'\right),$$

where $\boldsymbol{A}$ is nonsingular (hence square) and the hypotheses are invariant to the data transformation because the transformed mean $\boldsymbol{A}\boldsymbol{\mu}$ is zero under the null and nonzero otherwise. Note, however, that transformations of the type $\boldsymbol{c} + \boldsymbol{A}\boldsymbol{x}$ would have altered the hypotheses for $\boldsymbol{c} \neq \boldsymbol{0}$, which is why they are not considered in this exercise.

In our search for UMPI tests, we start by restricting attention to tests based on the sufficient $\overline{\boldsymbol{x}}$ and $\boldsymbol{S} := \frac{1}{n-1}\sum_{i=1}^{n}(\boldsymbol{x}_i - \overline{\boldsymbol{x}})(\boldsymbol{x}_i - \overline{\boldsymbol{x}})'$, in light of Exercise 14.23. First, we need to find a function of $\overline{\boldsymbol{x}}, \boldsymbol{S}$ that is unaffected by $\boldsymbol{A}$. Here, T^2 is invariant to our class of transformations because basing T^2 on the transformed data $\boldsymbol{y}$ is the same as basing it on $\boldsymbol{x}$:

$$\begin{aligned} T_{\boldsymbol{y}}^2 &:= n\overline{\boldsymbol{y}}'\left(\frac{1}{n-1}\sum_{i=1}^{n}(\boldsymbol{y}_i - \overline{\boldsymbol{y}})(\boldsymbol{y}_i - \overline{\boldsymbol{y}})'\right)^{-1}\overline{\boldsymbol{y}} \\ &= n\overline{\boldsymbol{x}}'\boldsymbol{A}'\left(\frac{1}{n-1}\sum_{i=1}^{n}\boldsymbol{A}(\boldsymbol{x}_i - \overline{\boldsymbol{x}})(\boldsymbol{x}_i - \overline{\boldsymbol{x}})'\boldsymbol{A}'\right)^{-1}\boldsymbol{A}\overline{\boldsymbol{x}} = n\overline{\boldsymbol{x}}'\boldsymbol{S}^{-1}\overline{\boldsymbol{x}} \equiv T^2. \end{aligned}$$

Defining $\boldsymbol{z} := \boldsymbol{S}^{-1/2}\overline{\boldsymbol{x}}$, we find that $T^2 = n\left\|\boldsymbol{z}\right\|^2$ is a function of the norm (distance from the origin) of this vector, whatever the values of $\overline{\boldsymbol{x}}$ and $\boldsymbol{S}$. Since vector norms are invariant to rotations and to permutations of the axes, that is, invariant to orthogonal transformations of $\boldsymbol{z}$ (see the formulation of any vector in Exercise 7.28(a), for example), we can take

$$\boldsymbol{z}' = \left(\sqrt{\overline{\boldsymbol{x}}'\boldsymbol{S}^{-1}\overline{\boldsymbol{x}}}, \boldsymbol{0}_{k-1}'\right) = \left(\sqrt{T^2/n}, \boldsymbol{0}_{k-1}'\right)$$

without loss of generality. Any function of $\boldsymbol{z}$ will therefore depend on the only nontrivial component z_1 of the vector, that is, T^2.

Having shown that invariant tests are based on T^2, it remains for us to use the Neyman–Pearson lemma pointwise to show that T^2 is UMP within the class of invariant tests. Exercise 9.24 yields

$$\zeta := \frac{n-k}{(n-1)k}T^2 \sim \mathrm{F}(k, n-k, \delta)$$

with $\delta := n\boldsymbol{\mu}'\boldsymbol{\Sigma}^{-1}\boldsymbol{\mu}$, and we can reformulate the hypotheses as $\mathrm{H}_0 : \delta = 0$ against $\mathrm{H}_1 : \delta > 0$ or, pointwise, $\mathrm{H}_1' : \delta = \delta_1 > 0$. (Alternatively, use the MLR property of F in Exercise 14.28.) Table 4.2 or Exercise 4.32 give the p.d.f. of a noncentral $\mathrm{F}(k, n-k, \delta)$ as

$$\begin{aligned} f_{\mathrm{F}(k,n-k,\delta)}(\zeta) &= \mathrm{e}^{-\delta/2}\sum_{j=0}^{\infty}\frac{(\delta/2)^j}{j!}\frac{k}{2j+k}f_{\mathrm{F}(2j+k,n-k)}\left(\frac{k\zeta}{2j+k}\right) \\ &= \mathrm{e}^{-\delta/2}\sum_{j=0}^{\infty}\frac{(\delta/2)^j}{j!}\frac{\frac{k}{n-k}\left(\frac{k\zeta}{n-k}\right)^{\frac{2j+k}{2}-1}}{B\left(\frac{2j+k}{2},\frac{n-k}{2}\right)\left(1+\frac{k\zeta}{n-k}\right)^{\frac{2j+n}{2}}}, \end{aligned}$$

and the Neyman–Pearson lemma applied to H_0 and H_1' gives an MPR of the form

$$\gamma^{-1} < \frac{\mathrm{e}^{-\delta/2} \sum_{j=0}^{\infty} \frac{(\delta/2)^j}{j!} \frac{k}{2j+k} f_{\mathrm{F}(2j+k,n-k)}\left(\frac{k\zeta}{2j+k}\right)}{f_{\mathrm{F}(k,n-k)}(\zeta)}$$

$$= \mathrm{e}^{-\delta/2} \sum_{j=0}^{\infty} \frac{(\delta/2)^j B\left(\frac{k}{2}, \frac{n-k}{2}\right)}{j! B\left(\frac{2j+k}{2}, \frac{n-k}{2}\right)} \left(\frac{\frac{k\zeta}{n-k}}{1+\frac{k\zeta}{n-k}}\right)^j.$$

Each term in the sum is positive and increasing in ζ (for $\zeta \in \mathbb{R}_+$), implying an MPR of the form $T^2 > c$ for a critical value c chosen under H_0 hence independent of H_1' and δ_1. The test is therefore UMPI for all points in H_1.

We make the following remarks on the further applicability of these results. First, the same result applies to testing hypotheses in the linear model considered in the previous section. Second, when the hypotheses concern a subset of the parameter vector, projections can be used as in Exercise 12.39 to neutralize the remaining parameters. Note that, in Exercise 12.39(f), we mentioned that R^2 cannot be decreased (it increases almost surely) by adding variables, but that these extra variables need not be significant which we can now detect by means of the tests that we have introduced; see also Exercise 14.28(d). Third, we have used the assumption of normality for the sufficiency reduction and for obtaining the $\mathrm{F}(k, n-k, \delta)$ distribution. However, we have seen that the latter result applies more generally to the class of spherical distributions (hence elliptical for $\boldsymbol{x}$ and $\boldsymbol{y}$), a robustness property seen in Exercises 7.30 and 8.37, for example. Note that Exercise 10.32(d) implies that $T^2 \overset{a}{\sim} \chi^2(k)$ under H_0, which is comparable with the tests analyzed earlier in this chapter.

***Exercise 14.38 (Sample correlation is UMP invariant to increasing linear transformations)** Continuing with the setup of Exercise 14.35, suppose that we have a random sample of size $n > 2$ for $(x, y)' \sim \mathrm{N}(\boldsymbol{\mu}, \boldsymbol{\Sigma})$ with $\boldsymbol{\Sigma}$ nonsingular. Show that testing $\mathrm{H}_0 : \rho = \rho_0$ (or $\rho \leqslant \rho_0$) against $\mathrm{H}_1 : \rho > \rho_0$ leads to the sample correlation $\widehat{\rho}$ being UMP invariant to increasing linear transformations. [Hint: Prove the MLR property $\partial^2 \log f_{\widehat{\rho}}(u) / \partial\rho\partial u \geqslant 0$ for the second formula of $f_{\widehat{\rho}}(u)$ in Exercise 9.25. This will involve symmetrizing a double sum with respect to the two indices, say j, k, then splitting it into sums over $j = k, j < k$, and $j > k$, the latter two being equal and nonnegative.]

Solution

We first remark that the UMPU of Exercise 14.35 and this UMPI give the same answer when $\rho = 0$, which also coincides with the GLR of Exercise 14.15.

Correlations $\widehat{\rho}, \rho$ are invariant to transformations of location and scale, so we consider the transformation of $\boldsymbol{z} := (x, y)'$ into $\boldsymbol{D}\boldsymbol{z} + \boldsymbol{c}$ with

$$\boldsymbol{D} := \operatorname{diag}(d_1, d_2) \qquad (d_1, d_2 > 0).$$

Compared with Exercise 14.37, here $\boldsymbol{c} \neq \mathbf{0}_2$ is allowed but $\boldsymbol{D}$ is more restrictive because combining the variates alters the correlation. Recalling Exercise 14.35, $\widehat{\rho}$ is essentially the only function of the sufficient statistic that is invariant to such transformations, and its distribution depends on ρ only. In Exercise 9.25, the density of $\widehat{\rho}$ was obtained as

$$f_{\widehat{\rho}}(u) = (n-2)\frac{(n-2)!\left(1-\rho^2\right)^{\frac{n-1}{2}}\left(1-u^2\right)^{\frac{n}{2}-2}}{\sqrt{2\pi}\left(\Gamma\left(\frac{1}{2}\right)\right)^2(1-\rho u)^{n-\frac{3}{2}}}h(w)$$

for $n > 2$, where $h(w) := \sum_{j=0}^{\infty} a_j(\frac{1}{2}+w)^j \geqslant 0$, with

$$a_j := \frac{\left(\Gamma\left(j+\frac{1}{2}\right)\right)^2}{j!\Gamma\left(j+n-\frac{1}{2}\right)} > 0 \quad \text{and} \quad w := \frac{\rho u}{2}.$$

To show that it satisfies the MLR property, hence establishing the result by the Karlin–Rubin theorem, it is enough for us to show that

$$\frac{\partial^2 \log f_{\widehat{\rho}}(u)}{\partial\rho\partial u} \geqslant 0$$

for all $\rho, u \in (-1,1)$ (since $\rho^2 = 1$ is excluded by the assumption that $\boldsymbol{\Sigma}$ is nonsingular) and hence for all $w \in (-\frac{1}{2},\frac{1}{2})$. Differentiating with respect to ρ, we obtain

$$\begin{aligned}\frac{\partial \log f_{\widehat{\rho}}(u)}{\partial\rho} &= \frac{n-1}{2}\frac{\partial\log\left(1-\rho^2\right)}{\partial\rho} - \left(n-\frac{3}{2}\right)\frac{\partial\log(1-\rho u)}{\partial\rho} + \frac{\partial\log h(w)}{\partial\rho}\\ &= -\rho\frac{n-1}{1-\rho^2} + \left(n-\frac{3}{2}\right)\frac{u}{1-\rho u} + \frac{\partial h(w)/\partial\rho}{h(w)}.\end{aligned}$$

Since $\partial h(w)/\partial\rho = \frac{1}{2}uh'(w)$ by the chain rule, and similarly for ∂u (with u and ρ interchanged),

$$\begin{aligned}\frac{\partial^2 \log f_{\widehat{\rho}}(u)}{\partial\rho\partial u} &= \frac{\partial}{\partial u}\left(\left(n-\frac{3}{2}\right)\frac{u}{1-\rho u} + \frac{uh'(w)}{2h(w)}\right)\\ &= \frac{n-\frac{3}{2}}{(1-\rho u)^2} + \frac{h(w)h'(w) + wh(w)h''(w) - w\left(h'(w)\right)^2}{2\left(h(w)\right)^2}.\end{aligned}$$

The first term is positive, and we need to show that the numerator of the subsequent fraction, say $h_1(w)$, is nonnegative. Substituting for h and differentiating,

$$\begin{aligned}h_1(w) = &\sum_{j=0}^{\infty} a_j\left(\frac{1}{2}+w\right)^j \sum_{k=0}^{\infty} ka_k\left(\frac{1}{2}+w\right)^{k-1}\\ &+ w\sum_{j=0}^{\infty} a_j\left(\frac{1}{2}+w\right)^j \sum_{k=0}^{\infty} k(k-1)a_k\left(\frac{1}{2}+w\right)^{k-2}\\ &- w\sum_{j=0}^{\infty} ja_j\left(\frac{1}{2}+w\right)^{j-1} \sum_{k=0}^{\infty} ka_k\left(\frac{1}{2}+w\right)^{k-1}.\end{aligned}$$

Collecting terms,

$$h_1(w) = \sum_{j=0}^{\infty}\sum_{k=0}^{\infty} a_j a_k \left(\frac{1}{2}+w\right)^{j+k-2} k\left(\left(\frac{1}{2}+w\right)+(k-1)w - jw\right)$$

$$= \sum_{j=0}^{\infty}\sum_{k=0}^{\infty} a_j a_k \left(\frac{1}{2}+w\right)^{j+k-2} \left(\frac{k}{2}+k(k-j)w\right).$$

This form is equivalent to

$$h_1(w) = \sum_{j=0}^{\infty}\sum_{k=0}^{\infty} a_j a_k \left(\frac{1}{2}+w\right)^{j+k-2} \left(\frac{j}{2}-j(k-j)w\right),$$

where we have switched the roles of j, k. It can be used to symmetrize the expression for $h_1(w)$ by taking the average of the two forms to be $h_1(w) = \frac{1}{2}\sum_{j=0}^{\infty}\sum_{k=0}^{\infty} b_{j,k}$ with

$$b_{j,k} := a_j a_k \left(\frac{1}{2}+w\right)^{j+k-2} \left(\frac{j+k}{2}+(k-j)^2 w\right) = b_{k,j},$$

so that we can rewrite the double sum as

$$\sum_{j=0}^{\infty}\sum_{k=0}^{\infty} b_{j,k} = \sum_{j=0}^{\infty}\sum_{k>j} b_{j,k} + \sum_{j=0}^{\infty}\sum_{k<j} b_{j,k} + \sum_{j=0}^{\infty} b_{j,j}.$$

We have $b_{j,j} \geqslant 0$ since $\frac{1}{2}+w \in (0,1)$ and $(j-j)^2 w = 0$. Also, the case for $k > j$ gives the same *double* sum as that of $k < j$. (This can be visualized by the symmetry of the elements above and below the leading diagonal in the array of Section A.3.5, since $b_{j,k} = b_{k,j}$, one double sum being the triangle above the diagonal and the other being the triangle below it.) Hence

$$h_1(w) \geqslant \sum_{j=0}^{\infty}\sum_{k>j} a_j a_k \left(\frac{1}{2}+w\right)^{j+k-2} \left(\frac{j+k}{2} - \frac{(k-j)^2}{2} + \frac{(k-j)^2}{2} + (k-j)^2 w\right)$$

$$= \sum_{j=0}^{\infty} a_j \left(\frac{1}{2}+w\right)^{j-2}$$

$$\times \left[\sum_{k>j} a_k \frac{j+k-(k-j)^2}{2}\left(\frac{1}{2}+w\right)^{k} + \sum_{k>j} a_k (k-j)^2 \left(\frac{1}{2}+w\right)^{k+1}\right]$$

$$= \sum_{j=0}^{\infty} a_j \left(\frac{1}{2}+w\right)^{j-2} \sum_{k=j+1}^{\infty} c_k \left(\frac{1}{2}+w\right)^{k},$$

where c_k is obtained by collecting terms with the same power of $\left(\frac{1}{2}+w\right)$ from each of the two sums in the square bracket, which gives

$$c_k := a_k \frac{j+k-(k-j)^2}{2} + a_{k-1}\left((k-1)-j\right)^2 \qquad \text{for } k > j+1$$

and $c_{j+1} := ja_{j+1} \geqslant 0$. We will show that $c_k > 0$ for $k > j+1$, implying that $h_1(w) \geqslant 0$ as required. Substituting from the definition of a. and using $\nu\Gamma(\nu) = \Gamma(\nu+1)$, we obtain

$$\begin{aligned} c_k &= \frac{\left(\Gamma\left(k+\frac{1}{2}\right)\right)^2}{k!\Gamma\left(k+n-\frac{1}{2}\right)} \frac{j+k-(k-j)^2}{2} + \frac{\left(\Gamma\left(k-\frac{1}{2}\right)\right)^2}{(k-1)!\Gamma\left(k+n-\frac{3}{2}\right)}(k-j-1)^2 \\ &= \frac{\left(\Gamma\left(k+\frac{1}{2}\right)\right)^2}{k!\Gamma\left(k+n-\frac{1}{2}\right)}\left(\frac{j+k-(k-j)^2}{2} + \frac{k\left(k+n-\frac{3}{2}\right)}{\left(k-\frac{1}{2}\right)^2}(k-j-1)^2\right) \\ &> \frac{\left(\Gamma\left(k+\frac{1}{2}\right)\right)^2}{k!\Gamma\left(k+n-\frac{1}{2}\right)}\left(\frac{j+k-(k-j)^2}{2} + (k-j-1)^2\right) \end{aligned}$$

since $n > 2$. Writing $l := k-j-1 \geqslant 1$,

$$\frac{2j+l+1-(l+1)^2}{2} + l^2 = j + \frac{l(l-1)}{2} \geqslant 0$$

as required.

Exercise 14.39 (Comparison of tests: Pitman's ARE) Suppose that we wish to compare the powers of two consistent tests τ_1, τ_2 of $\mathrm{H}_0 : \theta = \theta_0$. As seen in the introduction to this chapter, their power functions depend on both the sample size n and the true parameter value θ. One simplification is to let $n \to \infty$ and compare them, but both power functions will tend to 1 by the consistency of the tests. We have encountered the concept of the relative efficiency of estimators in Chapter 11, and we now define it for tests. If the τ_j ($j = 1, 2$) are of size $\alpha \in (0, 1)$ and, as $n \to \infty$, we define a sequence of local alternatives (compare Exercise 14.16(d))

$$\mathrm{H}_1 : \theta = \theta_1 := \theta_0 + c_j/n^d \qquad (d > 0)$$

such that $\lim_{n\to\infty} \Pi_{\tau_j} \in [\alpha, 1)$ and $n_j := \inf\{n : \Pi_{\tau_j} \geqslant p\}$ for some $p \in [\alpha, 1)$, then *Pitman's asymptotic efficiency of* τ_1 *relative to* τ_2 (or *Pitman's ARE of* τ_1 *versus* τ_2) is

$$A_{1,2} := \lim_{n\to\infty} \frac{n_2}{n_1},$$

implying that the test that achieves a given power p faster than the other one is more efficient. Assume the existence of

$$\mu_j^{(k)}(\theta_l) := \left.\frac{\partial^k \mathrm{E}(\tau_j)}{\partial\theta^k}\right|_{\theta=\theta_l} \qquad \text{and} \qquad \sigma_j^2(\theta_l) := \mathrm{var}(\tau_j)|_{\theta=\theta_l}$$

for the two hypotheses ($l = 0, 1$) and for the first natural number k such that $\mu_j^{(k)}(\theta_0) \neq 0$. For $c_j > 0$, let τ_j reject H_0 when

$$\tau_j > \mu_j(\theta_0) + \gamma_j\sigma_j(\theta_0)$$

for some standardized quantile γ_j, with the inequality reversed for $c_j < 0$. Assume further that:

(i) τ_1, τ_2 have asymptotically the same type of distribution (for example, both are χ^2);

(ii) $\lim_{n\to\infty} n^{-kd}\mu_j^{(k)}(\theta_0)/\sigma_j(\theta_0) = b_j > 0$;
(iii) $\lim_{n\to\infty} \mu_j^{(k)}(\theta_1)/\mu_j^{(k)}(\theta_0) = 1$;
(iv) $\lim_{n\to\infty} \sigma_j(\theta_1)/\sigma_j(\theta_0) = 1$.
Then, show the following:
(a) For all $c_j > 0$ (implying one-sided H_1),

$$A_{1,2} = \left(\frac{b_1}{b_2}\right)^{1/(kd)} = \lim_{n\to\infty}\left(\frac{\mu_1^{(k)}(\theta_0)/\sigma_1(\theta_0)}{\mu_2^{(k)}(\theta_0)/\sigma_2(\theta_0)}\right)^{1/(kd)}.$$

[Hint: Taylor-expand $\mu_j(\theta_1)$ in the argument of Π_{τ_j}, then equate the two power functions at any θ_1.]
(b) For all $c_j \neq 0$ (implying a two-sided H_1), we get the same $A_{1,2}$ as in (a).
(c) For the setup of Exercise 11.3 comparing the median $\widetilde{x}$ and mean $\overline{x}$, show that basing tests on these estimators gives $A_{\widetilde{x},\overline{x}} = 2/\pi$ when the data are normally distributed (a case where the test based on $\overline{x}$ is asymptotically optimal). Comment on the result.

Solution
(a) Assumption (i) implies that asymptotically $\gamma_1 = \gamma_2 = \gamma$ (say). For $c_j > 0$, we reject H_0 when

$$\tau_j > \mu_j(\theta_0) + \gamma\sigma_j(\theta_0).$$

Since the two asymptotic power functions share the same functional form, we can write them in terms of their common standardized c.d.f. H as

$$\begin{aligned}\Pi_{\tau_j}(\theta_1) &\equiv \Pr{}_{\theta_1}(\tau_j > \mu_j(\theta_0) + \gamma\sigma_j(\theta_0)) \\ &\equiv \Pr{}_{\theta_1}\left(\frac{\tau_j - \mu_j(\theta_1)}{\sigma_j(\theta_1)} > \frac{\mu_j(\theta_0) + \gamma\sigma_j(\theta_0) - \mu_j(\theta_1)}{\sigma_j(\theta_1)}\right) \\ &\equiv 1 - H\left(\frac{\mu_j(\theta_0) + \gamma\sigma_j(\theta_0) - \mu_j(\theta_1)}{\sigma_j(\theta_1)}\right);\end{aligned}$$

examples of this were seen in (14.10) with $H = \Phi$ (see also Exercise 3.16). Taylor-expanding $\mu_j(\theta_1) - \mu_j(\theta_0)$ around θ_0 in the argument of H, we get

$$D_j := \frac{-(\mu_j(\theta_1) - \mu_j(\theta_0)) + \gamma\sigma_j(\theta_0)}{\sigma_j(\theta_1)} = \frac{-\mu_j^{(k)}(\overline{\theta})(\theta_1 - \theta_0)^k/k! + \gamma\sigma_j(\theta_0)}{\sigma_j(\theta_1)}$$

with $\theta_0 < \overline{\theta} < \theta_1$ and $\overline{\theta} \to \theta_0$ since $\theta_1 \to \theta_0$. By Assumption (iii), we can replace $\mu_j^{(k)}(\overline{\theta})$ by $\mu_j^{(k)}(\theta_0)$ in the limit; then the remaining assumptions and $\theta_1 := \theta_0 + c_j/n^d$ imply that

$$D_j \to -b_j c_j^k/k! + \gamma.$$

For the two asymptotic powers to be equal, we require $D_1 = D_2$, hence $b_1 c_1^k = b_2 c_2^k$ or

$$\frac{c_2}{c_1} = \left(\frac{b_1}{b_2}\right)^{1/k}.$$

Furthermore, we require the two power functions to be evaluated at the same θ_1, so we also need $c_1/n_1^d = c_2/n_2^d$; hence

$$A_{1,2} := \lim_{n\to\infty} \frac{n_2}{n_1} = \left(\frac{c_2}{c_1}\right)^{1/d} = \left(\frac{b_1}{b_2}\right)^{1/(kd)},$$

and the result follows.

(b) For $c_j \neq 0$, we reject H_0 when

$$\tau_j < \mu_j(\theta_0) + \gamma_l \sigma_j(\theta_0) \qquad \text{or} \qquad \tau_j > \mu_j(\theta_0) + \gamma_u \sigma_j(\theta_0),$$

where γ_l and γ_u are the lower and upper quantiles, respectively. As illustrated in (14.11), we write

$$\begin{aligned}\Pi_{\tau_j}(\theta_1) &= \Pr_{\theta_1}(\tau_j < \mu_j(\theta_0) + \gamma_l \sigma_j(\theta_0)) + \Pr_{\theta_1}(\tau_j > \mu_j(\theta_0) + \gamma_u \sigma_j(\theta_0)) \\ &= H\left(\frac{(\mu_j(\theta_0) + \gamma_l \sigma_j(\theta_0)) - \mu_j(\theta_1)}{\sigma_j(\theta_1)}\right) \\ &\quad + 1 - H\left(\frac{(\mu_j(\theta_0) + \gamma_u \sigma_j(\theta_0)) - \mu_j(\theta_1)}{\sigma_j(\theta_1)}\right).\end{aligned}$$

Strictly speaking, the first H should have its argument evaluated at the displayed argument minus ϵ, as $\epsilon \to 0^+$, but this applies to both tests and has no impact on the comparison. The rest of the proof follows the same lines as in (a).

(c) This follows from the limiting distributions in Exercise 11.3(a), namely $\overline{x} \overset{a}{\sim} \mathrm{N}(\mu, \sigma^2/n)$ and $\widetilde{x} \overset{a}{\sim} \mathrm{N}(\mu, \sigma^2\pi/(2n))$ for f_x normal, giving $\mu'_{\widetilde{x}} = \mu'_{\overline{x}} = 1$ (hence $k = 1$) and $b_j = \lim_{n\to\infty} n^{-d}/\sigma_j$ which implies that $d = \frac{1}{2}$ (or the estimators' consistency rate $\sqrt{n}$). Therefore,

$$A_{\widetilde{x},\overline{x}} = \frac{\sigma_{\overline{x}}^2}{\sigma_{\widetilde{x}}^2} = \frac{2}{\pi} \approx 0.637.$$

First, this shows that the tests' ARE $A_{\widetilde{x},\overline{x}}$ reduces to the *estimators'* ARE here. It turns out that, subject to further regularity conditions, this relation extends beyond this exercise. Second, the normality of x implies that LS and ML coincide, and we know from Chapter 12 that the MLE is best asymptotically normal (BAN), so it does not come as a surprise that it has better efficiency than the LAD estimator. (A similar comment can be made about using less efficient estimators than the MLE in constructing Wald statistics and about the resulting effect on the power.) However, this result is derived under the assumption of the normality of x, which may not be the case in practice. The robustness of LAD was illustrated in Exercise 11.3(b) and the corresponding potential for unlimited efficiency gains were illustrated there. We will return to robust procedures in the next section.

14.4 Distribution-free methods: nonparametric and goodness-of-fit tests

Exercise 14.40 (Testing independence: Spearman's ρ) Suppose that we observe the pairs $(x_1, y_1), \dots, (x_n, y_n)$, assumed to be drawn randomly from a continuous nonsingular bivariate distribution with finite variances. Spearman's ρ and Kendall's τ, introduced in Exercise 9.29, can be used to test the independence of the variates x and y, not just the lack of linear dependence (measured by correlation); recall that ranks are invariant to any increasing transformation of the data, linear or otherwise. Consider the null hypothesis of the independence of x, y.
(a) Derive $\mathrm{E}(\widehat{\rho}_S)$ under H_0.
(b) Derive $\mathrm{var}(\widehat{\rho}_S)$ under H_0. [Hint: When calculating the variance under the independence of x, y, reorder the i.i.d. data over $i = 1, \dots, n$ such that $\mathrm{r}(y_i) = i$.]
(c) Assuming the bivariate normality of x, y, compute the ARE (defined in Exercise 14.39) of this test of independence relative to the usual sample correlation $\widehat{\rho}$. [Hint: The normalized ranks converge to the marginal c.d.f.s, and $\widehat{\rho}_S$ is asymptotically the correlation of these marginals; see Exercise 9.30. Also, for the centered and normalized bivariate normal

$$f(u, v) = \frac{1}{2\pi\sqrt{1-\rho^2}} \exp\left(\frac{-u^2 + 2\rho uv - v^2}{2(1-\rho^2)}\right)$$

from Exercise 6.1, use $\partial f(u, v)/\partial \rho = \partial^2 f(u, v)/(\partial u \partial v)$ seen in Exercise 8.22.]

Solution

(a) For a continuous nonsingular distribution, the probability of ties is zero, hence we omit ties from the calculation of population moments and consider instead the simplified formula

$$\widehat{\rho}_S = 12 \frac{\sum_{i=1}^n \left(\mathrm{r}(x_i) - \frac{n+1}{2}\right)\left(\mathrm{r}(y_i) - \frac{n+1}{2}\right)}{n(n^2-1)},$$

by $\bar{\mathrm{r}}(x) = \bar{\mathrm{r}}(y) = (n+1)/2$. By the independence of x, y,

$$\mathrm{E}(\widehat{\rho}_S) = 12 \frac{\sum_{i=1}^n \mathrm{E}(\mathrm{r}(x_i) - \frac{n+1}{2})\, \mathrm{E}(\mathrm{r}(y_i) - \frac{n+1}{2})}{n(n^2-1)}.$$

Whatever the continuous x, the ranks $\mathrm{r}(x_i)$ are uniformly distributed over $\{1, \dots, n\}$ (but not independently distributed when n is finite) and have $\mathrm{E}(\mathrm{r}(x_i)) = \frac{n+1}{2}$, hence $\mathrm{E}(\widehat{\rho}_S) = 0$.

(b) For the variance, the denominator of $\widehat{\rho}_S$ is the nonrandom quantity seen above, and this will simplify the calculations. By the independence of x, y, let $\mathrm{r}(y_i) = i$ by reordering the i.i.d. elements y_i (and moving the corresponding x_i) in the sum appearing in $\mathrm{var}(\widehat{\rho}_S)$:

$$\begin{aligned}\mathrm{var}(\widehat{\rho}_S) &= \mathrm{var}\left(12 \frac{\sum_{i=1}^n \left(i - \frac{n+1}{2}\right)\left(\mathrm{r}(x_i) - \frac{n+1}{2}\right)}{n(n^2-1)}\right) \\ &= \left(\frac{12}{n(n^2-1)}\right)^2 \mathrm{var}\left(\sum_{i=1}^n \left(i - \frac{n+1}{2}\right) \mathrm{r}(x_i)\right)\end{aligned}$$

because additive constants do not affect the variance. Expanding the variance of the sum,

$$\operatorname{var}(\widehat{\rho}_{\mathrm{S}}) = \frac{\sum_{i=1}^{n}\left(i-\frac{n+1}{2}\right)^2 \operatorname{var}(\mathrm{r}(x_i)) + \sum_{i\neq j}\left(i-\frac{n+1}{2}\right)\left(j-\frac{n+1}{2}\right)\operatorname{cov}(\mathrm{r}(x_i),\mathrm{r}(x_j))}{\left(n\left(n^2-1\right)/12\right)^2}.$$

Since the ranks $\mathrm{r}(x_i)$ are uniformly distributed over $\{1,\dots,n\}$, Table 4.1 gives $\operatorname{var}(\mathrm{r}(x_i)) = \left(n^2-1\right)/12$, which does not depend on i. Also, $\operatorname{cov}(\mathrm{r}(x_i),\mathrm{r}(x_j))$ does not depend on i, j $(i \neq j)$ because of the i.i.d. assumption on the x's. Using

$$\sum_{i=1}^{n}\left(i-\frac{n+1}{2}\right)^2 = n\operatorname{var}(\mathrm{r}(y_i))$$

and

$$\sum_{i\neq j}\left(i-\frac{n+1}{2}\right)\left(j-\frac{n+1}{2}\right) = n(n-1)\operatorname{cov}(\mathrm{r}(y_i),\mathrm{r}(y_j)),$$

we can rewrite $\operatorname{var}(\widehat{\rho}_{\mathrm{S}})$ as

$$\begin{aligned}\operatorname{var}(\widehat{\rho}_{\mathrm{S}}) &= \frac{n\operatorname{var}(\mathrm{r}(y_i))\operatorname{var}(\mathrm{r}(x_i)) + n(n-1)\operatorname{cov}(\mathrm{r}(y_i),\mathrm{r}(y_j))\operatorname{cov}(\mathrm{r}(x_i),\mathrm{r}(x_j))}{\left(n\left(n^2-1\right)/12\right)^2} \\ &= \frac{\operatorname{var}(\mathrm{r}(y_i))^2 + (n-1)\operatorname{cov}(\mathrm{r}(y_i),\mathrm{r}(y_j))^2}{n\left(\left(n^2-1\right)/12\right)^2} \qquad (i \neq j)\end{aligned}$$

since the marginal distributions of $\mathrm{r}(x)$ and $\mathrm{r}(y)$ are the same (uniform). To work out the covariance in the last fraction, consider

$$\begin{aligned}\operatorname{cov}(\mathrm{r}(y_i),\mathrm{r}(y_j)) &= \frac{\sum_{i\neq j}\left(i-\frac{n+1}{2}\right)\left(j-\frac{n+1}{2}\right)}{n(n-1)} \\ &= \frac{\left(\sum_i\left(i-\frac{n+1}{2}\right)\right)^2 - \sum_i\left(i-\frac{n+1}{2}\right)^2}{n(n-1)} \\ &= \frac{0^2 - n\operatorname{var}(\mathrm{r}(y_i))}{n(n-1)} = -\frac{\operatorname{var}(\mathrm{r}(y_i))}{n-1}\end{aligned}$$

by $\overline{\mathrm{r}}(y) = (n+1)/2$; hence

$$\begin{aligned}\operatorname{var}(\widehat{\rho}_{\mathrm{S}}) &= \frac{\operatorname{var}(\mathrm{r}(y_i))^2 + \frac{1}{n-1}\operatorname{var}(\mathrm{r}(y_i))^2}{n\left(\left(n^2-1\right)/12\right)^2} = \left(\frac{n^2-1}{12}\right)^2 \frac{1+\frac{1}{n-1}}{n\left(\left(n^2-1\right)/12\right)^2} \\ &= \frac{1}{n-1}\end{aligned}$$

which is independent of the parameters of the distribution of x, y.

(c) Under normality and $\rho = 0$, Exercise 9.7 tells us that $\widehat{\rho}^2 \sim \operatorname{Beta}(\frac{1}{2}, \frac{n}{2}-1)$ and $\mathrm{E}(\widehat{\rho}) = 0$, hence

$$\operatorname{var}(\widehat{\rho}) = \mathrm{E}(\widehat{\rho}^2) = \frac{\frac{1}{2}}{\frac{n-1}{2}} = \frac{1}{n-1}$$

from the mean of the standard beta in Table 4.2; see also Exercise 10.35, which gives $\sqrt{n}(\widehat{\rho}-\rho) \overset{a}{\sim} \mathrm{N}(0,(1-\rho^2)^2)$ more generally and $\lim_{n\to\infty} \partial\,\mathrm{E}(\widehat{\rho})/\partial\rho = 1$ (the dominated convergence of Section A.4.3 applies here since $\widehat{\rho}$ is bounded), which we need for the ARE. Since $\mathrm{var}(\widehat{\rho})$ is the same as $\mathrm{var}(\widehat{\rho}_{\mathrm{S}})$, the formula from Exercise 14.39 (with $k=1$ and $d=\frac{1}{2}$) for the ARE simplifies to

$$A_{\widehat{\rho}_{\mathrm{S}},\widehat{\rho}} = \lim_{n\to\infty}\left(\left.\frac{\partial\,\mathrm{E}(\widehat{\rho}_{\mathrm{S}})}{\partial\rho}\right|_{\rho=0} \Bigg/ \left.\frac{\partial\,\mathrm{E}(\widehat{\rho})}{\partial\rho}\right|_{\rho=0} \right)^2 = \left(\left.\frac{\partial \lim_{n\to\infty}\mathrm{E}(\widehat{\rho}_{\mathrm{S}})}{\partial\rho}\right|_{\rho=0} \right)^2.$$

Correlations are invariant to location and scale, so we can simplify x, y to have the density $f(u,v)$ given earlier in the hint. Asymptotically, the $\{n^{-1}\mathrm{r}(x_n)\}$ are drawn independently from a continuous standard uniform distribution, and similarly for the $\{n^{-1}\mathrm{r}(y_n)\}$, with $\widehat{\rho}_{\mathrm{S}}$ the correlation between them; its limit is, from Exercise 9.30,

$$\rho_{\mathrm{S}} = 12\int_{-\infty}^{\infty}\int_{-\infty}^{\infty} \Phi(u)\,\Phi(v)\, f(u,v)\,\mathrm{d}u\,\mathrm{d}v - 3,$$

where we have used Φ for the standard normal marginals. Using

$$\frac{\partial}{\partial\rho} f(u,v) = \frac{\partial^2}{\partial u\partial v} f(u,v)$$

from the hint, then integration by parts, we obtain

$$\begin{aligned}
\frac{\partial\rho_{\mathrm{S}}}{\partial\rho} &= 12\int_{-\infty}^{\infty}\int_{-\infty}^{\infty} \Phi(u)\,\Phi(v)\,\frac{\partial}{\partial\rho} f(u,v)\,\mathrm{d}u\,\mathrm{d}v \\
&= 12\int_{-\infty}^{\infty}\int_{-\infty}^{\infty} \Phi(u)\,\Phi(v)\,\frac{\partial^2}{\partial u\partial v} f(u,v)\,\mathrm{d}u\,\mathrm{d}v \\
&= 12\int_{-\infty}^{\infty}\int_{-\infty}^{\infty} \frac{\mathrm{d}\Phi(u)}{\mathrm{d}u}\frac{\mathrm{d}\Phi(v)}{\mathrm{d}v} f(u,v)\,\mathrm{d}u\,\mathrm{d}v,
\end{aligned}$$

since $f(u,v)=0$ when u,v tend to $\pm\infty$. By $\mathrm{d}\Phi(u)/\mathrm{d}u \equiv \phi(u)$ and $f(u,v)|_{\rho=0} = \phi(u)\phi(v)$, we get

$$\begin{aligned}
\left.\frac{\partial\rho_{\mathrm{S}}}{\partial\rho}\right|_{\rho=0} &= 12\left(\int_{-\infty}^{\infty}\phi(u)^2\,\mathrm{d}u\right)\left(\int_{-\infty}^{\infty}\phi(v)^2\,\mathrm{d}v\right) = 12\left(\int_{-\infty}^{\infty}\phi(u)^2\,\mathrm{d}u\right)^2 \\
&= 12\left(\int_{-\infty}^{\infty}\frac{\exp(-u^2)}{2\pi}\,\mathrm{d}u\right)^2 = 12\left(\frac{1}{2\sqrt{\pi}}\int_{-\infty}^{\infty}\frac{\exp(-w^2/2)}{\sqrt{2\pi}}\,\mathrm{d}w\right)^2 \\
&= 12\left(\frac{1}{2\sqrt{\pi}}\right)^2 = \frac{3}{\pi}
\end{aligned}$$

by the change of variable $w = u\sqrt{2}$ and using the integral of the standard normal density. Hence,

$$A_{\widehat{\rho}_{\mathrm{S}},\widehat{\rho}} = \frac{9}{\pi^2} \approx 0.912.$$

This is remarkable: when the data are normally distributed and $\widehat{\rho}$ is optimal for the setup of Exercise 14.35, using $\widehat{\rho}_S$ implies a loss of asymptotic efficiency of less than 9% in relative terms (the variances of $\widehat{\rho}_S, \widehat{\rho}$ both go to zero in absolute terms as $n \to \infty$), which is not much in return for the robustness of $\widehat{\rho}_S$ to the possible nonnormality of the variates. If the normality assumption is violated, $\widehat{\rho}_S$ may have better power than $\widehat{\rho}$. Remember that $\widehat{\rho}$ measures only the linear relation between the variates, which summarizes the relation between x, y in the case of nonsingular bivariate normality (where independence coincides with $\rho = 0$) but not necessarily otherwise; see, for example, Exercises 6.14, 8.9, and 8.10.

***Exercise 14.41 (Testing independence: Kendall's τ)** Assume the setup of Exercise 14.40.
(a) Derive $\mathrm{E}(\widehat{\tau})$ under H_0.
(b) Assuming no ties, rewrite $\widehat{\tau}$ as

$$\widehat{\tau} = 1 - \frac{4\widehat{\eta}}{n(n-1)},$$

where $\widehat{\eta} \in \{0, 1, \dots, \frac{1}{2}n(n-1)\}$ is the number of pairwise inversions of rankings needed to bring the x's into ascending order when we take $\mathrm{r}(y_i) = i$ as in Exercise 14.40(b).
(c) Derive $\mathrm{var}(\widehat{\tau})$ under H_0. [Hint: $\sum_{j=1}^{n} j^2 = \frac{1}{6}n(n+1)(2n+1)$ from Section A.4.1.]
(d) Assuming the bivariate normality of x, y, compute the ARE of this test of independence relative to $\widehat{\rho}$. [Hint: Use $\mathrm{sgn}(a) = (\pi \mathrm{i})^{-1} \int_{-\infty}^{\infty} s^{-1} \exp(\mathrm{i}as)\, \mathrm{d}s$.]

Solution
(a) As in Exercise 14.40, we omit ties from the calculation of population moments and consider instead the simplified expression

$$\widehat{\tau} = \frac{\sum_{i=1}^{n} \sum_{j=1}^{n} \mathrm{sgn}(x_i - x_j)\, \mathrm{sgn}(y_i - y_j)}{n(n-1)}.$$

By the independence of x, y,

$$\mathrm{E}(\widehat{\tau}) = \frac{\sum_{i=1}^{n} \sum_{j=1}^{n} \mathrm{E}(\mathrm{sgn}(x_i - x_j))\, \mathrm{E}(\mathrm{sgn}(y_i - y_j))}{n(n-1)}$$

and the i.i.d. assumption gives $\mathrm{E}(\mathrm{sgn}(x_i - x_j)) = \mathrm{E}(\mathrm{sgn}(x_j - x_i))$, an equality of the form $a = -a$, implying that $a = 0$, hence $\mathrm{E}(\widehat{\tau}) = 0$. This is not surprising, since both $\widehat{\rho}_S$ and $\widehat{\tau}$ can be written as correlations between variates that are independent under H_0; see Exercise 9.29. The method used here to show that $\mathrm{E}(\widehat{\tau}) = 0$ can be used there too, to obtain the more general result $\mathrm{E}(\widehat{\theta}) = 0$.
(b) Assume that the n i.i.d. pairs $(x_1, y_1), \dots, (x_n, y_n)$ have been reordered such that the y's are in ascending order and the corresponding x's are labeled $\{x_i\}_{i=1}^{n}$. We start by illustrating the inversions before establishing the relation between $\widehat{\tau}$ and $\widehat{\eta}$. For example, if $n = 3$ and the resulting $\mathrm{r}(x_i)$ are $3, 2, 1$, then we need to: swap the first two to get $2, 3, 1$; then swap the last two to get $2, 1, 3$; finally swap the first two to get the ordered sequence $1, 2, 3$, resulting in a total of three pairwise inversions. In general, we cannot have fewer than zero inversions (when all x's are already in order) and we cannot have

more than $\binom{n}{2} = \frac{1}{2}n(n-1)$ inversions (when the whole sequence is to be inverted, as in our example, requiring all possible combinations of two elements from n). Hence, $\widehat{\eta} \in \{0, 1, \dots, \frac{1}{2}n(n-1)\}$ and $-1 \leqslant \widehat{\tau} \leqslant 1$.

As usual, we write variates based on counting in terms of indicator functions. Let

$$z_{ij} := 1_{\mathrm{r}(x_i) > \mathrm{r}(x_j)} = 1_{x_i > x_j}.$$

Then we have $\widehat{\eta} = \sum_{j>i} z_{ij}$, where this is shorthand for the double sum $\sum_{i=1}^{n-1} \sum_{j=i+1}^{n}$. Since $y_1 < \dots < y_n$, then $\operatorname{sgn}(y_i - y_j) = -1$ when $j > i$ and

$$z_{ij} = \frac{1}{2}\left(1 - \operatorname{sgn}(x_i - x_j)\operatorname{sgn}(y_i - y_j)\right);$$

hence

$$\widehat{\eta} = \frac{1}{2}\sum_{j>i}\left(1 - \operatorname{sgn}(x_i - x_j)\operatorname{sgn}(y_i - y_j)\right).$$

Since $\operatorname{sgn}(a) = -\operatorname{sgn}(-a)$,

$$\widehat{\eta} = \frac{1}{2}\sum_{j>i}\left(1 - \operatorname{sgn}(x_j - x_i)\operatorname{sgn}(y_j - y_i)\right) = \frac{1}{2}\sum_{i>j}\left(1 - \operatorname{sgn}(x_i - x_j)\operatorname{sgn}(y_i - y_j)\right)$$

where the last step entails only swapping the labels i, j (notice the inequality under the summation signs). Combining the last two equations, say $\widehat{\eta} = b_1$ and $\widehat{\eta} = b_2$ into $\widehat{\eta} = (b_1 + b_2)/2$, we obtain

$$\begin{aligned}
4\widehat{\eta} &= \sum_{j>i}\left(1 - \operatorname{sgn}(x_i - x_j)\operatorname{sgn}(y_i - y_j)\right) + \sum_{i>j}\left(1 - \operatorname{sgn}(x_i - x_j)\operatorname{sgn}(y_i - y_j)\right) \\
&= \sum_{i,j}\left(1 - \operatorname{sgn}(x_i - x_j)\operatorname{sgn}(y_i - y_j)\right) - \sum_{i=j}\left(1 - \operatorname{sgn}(x_i - x_j)\operatorname{sgn}(y_i - y_j)\right) \\
&= \sum_{i,j} 1 - \sum_{i,j}\operatorname{sgn}(x_i - x_j)\operatorname{sgn}(y_i - y_j) - \sum_{i=j} 1 \\
&= n^2 - n - \sum_{i,j}\operatorname{sgn}(x_i - x_j)\operatorname{sgn}(y_i - y_j) \equiv n(n-1) - n(n-1)\widehat{\tau}
\end{aligned}$$

by the definition of $\widehat{\tau}$.

(c) From (b),

$$\operatorname{var}(\widehat{\tau}) = \operatorname{var}\left(1 - \frac{4\widehat{\eta}}{n(n-1)}\right) = \frac{16}{n^2(n-1)^2}\operatorname{var}(\widehat{\eta}) = \frac{16}{n^2(n-1)^2}\operatorname{var}\left(\sum_{i=1}^{n-1}\zeta_i\right),$$

where $\zeta_i := \sum_{j=i+1}^{n} z_{ij} \in \{0, 1, \dots, n-i\}$ is the number of times we have $x_i > x_j$ for $j > i$. All the outcomes for ζ_i are equally likely, since the sequence of x's is random. Therefore, $\zeta_i \sim \mathrm{U}_{\{0,1,\dots,n-i\}}$ and Table 4.1 gives $\operatorname{var}(\zeta_i) = ((n-i+1)^2 - 1)/12$. The sequence $\{\zeta_{n-1}\}$ is therefore not identically distributed, since its variance changes. However, it is independently distributed because, as i increases to $i+1$, the number of times we now have $x_{i+1} > x_j$ for $j > i+1$ does not depend on the preceding x_i (the sequence of x's is independent). Therefore,

$$\operatorname{var}(\hat{\tau}) = \frac{16}{n^2(n-1)^2}\sum_{i=1}^{n-1}\operatorname{var}(\zeta_i) = \frac{16}{12n^2(n-1)^2}\sum_{i=1}^{n-1}\left((n-i+1)^2-1\right)$$

and, reversing the sum in i by taking $j = n - i + 1$,

$$\begin{aligned}\operatorname{var}(\hat{\tau}) &= \frac{4}{3n^2(n-1)^2}\left(\left(\sum_{j=2}^{n} j^2\right) - (n-1)\right)\\ &= \frac{4}{3n^2(n-1)^2}\left(\frac{n(n+1)(2n+1)}{6} - 1 - (n-1)\right)\end{aligned}$$

using the sum given in the hint, after removing $j = 1$. Hence,

$$\operatorname{var}(\hat{\tau}) = \frac{4}{3n(n-1)^2}\left(\frac{(n+1)(2n+1)}{6} - 1\right) = \frac{2\left(2n^2+3n+1-6\right)}{9n(n-1)^2} = \frac{2(2n+5)}{9n(n-1)}.$$

Notice that writing $\hat{\eta}$ in terms of $\sum_{i=1}^{n-1}\zeta_i$ implies the asymptotic normality of $\hat{\eta}$ (hence also of $\hat{\tau}$) by the Lindeberg–Feller CLT of Exercise 10.37.

(d) As in Exercise 14.40(c), $\operatorname{var}(\hat{\rho}) = 1/(n-1)$ and $\lim_{n\to\infty} \partial\operatorname{E}(\hat{\rho})/\partial\rho = 1$, so

$$A_{\hat{\tau},\hat{\rho}} = \frac{9}{4}\lim_{n\to\infty}\left(\left.\frac{\partial\operatorname{E}(\hat{\tau})}{\partial\rho}\right|_{\rho=0}\right)^2$$

by $\operatorname{var}(\hat{\rho})/\operatorname{var}(\hat{\tau}) \to 9/4$. Again, by $\operatorname{sgn}(x_i - x_i) = 0$,

$$\operatorname{E}(\hat{\tau}) = \frac{\sum_{i\neq j}\operatorname{E}(\operatorname{sgn}(x_i-x_j)\operatorname{sgn}(y_i-y_j))}{n(n-1)}$$

and the i.i.d. assumption implies that $\operatorname{E}(\hat{\tau}) = \operatorname{E}(\operatorname{sgn}(x_i-x_j)\operatorname{sgn}(y_i-y_j))$ with $i \neq j$. Since $x_i - x_j$ is normally distributed and has correlation ρ with $y_i - y_j$ (see Exercise 6.11), and since the correlation $\hat{\tau}$ is scale-invariant, we have $\operatorname{E}(\hat{\tau}) = \operatorname{E}(\operatorname{sgn}(\xi_1)\operatorname{sgn}(\xi_2))$ whose ξ_1, ξ_2 have the bivariate normal density

$$f(u,v) = \frac{1}{2\pi\sqrt{1-\rho^2}}\exp\left(\frac{-u^2+2\rho uv-v^2}{2(1-\rho^2)}\right),$$

hence

$$\operatorname{E}(\hat{\tau}) = \int_{\mathbb{R}^2}\operatorname{sgn}(u)\operatorname{sgn}(v)f(u,v)\,\mathrm{d}u\,\mathrm{d}v.$$

By the hint in the question,

$$\begin{aligned}\operatorname{E}(\hat{\tau}) &= -\frac{1}{\pi^2}\int_{\mathbb{R}^4}\frac{\exp(\mathrm{i}us+\mathrm{i}vt)}{st}f(u,v)\,\mathrm{d}s\,\mathrm{d}t\,\mathrm{d}u\,\mathrm{d}v\\ &\equiv -\frac{1}{\pi^2}\int_{\mathbb{R}^2}\frac{\operatorname{E}(\exp(\mathrm{i}\xi_1 s+\mathrm{i}\xi_2 t))}{st}\,\mathrm{d}s\,\mathrm{d}t,\end{aligned}$$

where the expectation is the joint c.f. of the bivariate normal; see, for example, the introduction to Chapter 8. Therefore,

$$\mathrm{E}(\widehat{\tau}) = -\frac{1}{\pi^2}\int_{\mathbb{R}^2} \frac{\exp\left(-\frac{1}{2}\left(s^2+2\rho st+t^2\right)\right)}{st}\,\mathrm{d}s\,\mathrm{d}t$$

and

$$\frac{\partial\,\mathrm{E}(\widehat{\tau})}{\partial\rho} = \frac{1}{\pi^2}\int_{\mathbb{R}^2} \exp\left(-\frac{1}{2}\left(s^2+2\rho st+t^2\right)\right)\mathrm{d}s\,\mathrm{d}t.$$

Evaluating at $\rho = 0$ then integrating by means of the standard normal density,

$$\left.\frac{\partial\,\mathrm{E}(\widehat{\tau})}{\partial\rho}\right|_{\rho=0} = \left(\frac{1}{\pi}\int_{\mathbb{R}} \exp\left(-\frac{s^2}{2}\right)\mathrm{d}s\right)\left(\frac{1}{\pi}\int_{\mathbb{R}} \exp\left(-\frac{t^2}{2}\right)\mathrm{d}t\right) = \left(\frac{\sqrt{2\pi}}{\pi}\right)^2 = \frac{2}{\pi}$$

and $A_{\widehat{\tau},\widehat{\rho}} = 9/\pi^2$. This is the same ARE as in Exercise 14.40, which is unsurprising given the asymptotic proportionality of $\widehat{\tau}$ and $\widehat{\rho}_{\mathrm{S}}$ under H_0; see also the discussion in the Notes to Chapter 9.

Exercise 14.42 (Equality of two distributions: sign test) Suppose that we observe the pairs $(x_1, y_1), \dots, (x_n, y_n)$, where $\{x_n\}$ and $\{y_n\}$ are random samples drawn independently from F_x and F_y, respectively, both continuous distributions. We wish to test $\mathrm{H}_0 : F_x(u) = F_y(u)$ for all u, against $\mathrm{H}_1 : F_x(u) \neq F_y(u)$ for some u. Use $1_{x_i > y_i}$ (with $i = 1, \dots, n$) to find an appropriate test.

Solution

Since the variates are continuous, we have $\Pr(x = y) = 0$ by Exercise 5.16. Under H_0, we have $\Pr(x < y) = \Pr(x > y)$, so $\Pr(x = y) = 0$ implies that $\Pr(x > y) = \frac{1}{2}$. Hence, $1_{x_i > y_i} \sim \mathrm{Ber}(\frac{1}{2})$ and $z := \sum_{i=1}^n 1_{x_i > y_i} \sim \mathrm{Bin}(n, \frac{1}{2})$ with $\mathrm{E}(z) = \frac{1}{2}n$; see Exercise 4.3. A test based on z rejects H_0 if $\sum_{i=1}^n 1_{x_i > y_i}$ is significantly different from its expectation under H_0 (as the t-ratios did earlier), namely if $|z - \frac{1}{2}n| > \gamma$, where γ is obtained from the $\mathrm{Bin}(n, \frac{1}{2})$ distribution; see Exercise 14.1 for an approximation, which also follows because z is the sum of an i.i.d. sequence to which a CLT applies. The name *sign test* is used because the test is based on counting the number of times that the sign of $x_i - y_i$ is positive, each occurrence being a Bernoulli event.

Exercise 14.43 (Equality of two distributions: Wilcoxon's rank-sum test) Consider two independent random samples $x_1, \dots, x_m$ and $y_1, \dots, y_n$. We wish to test $\mathrm{H}_0 : F_x(u) = F_y(u)$ for all u, where both distributions are assumed to be continuous. We use the following procedure. Combine the two samples and arrange the elements in ascending order, as we did for order statistics. Then, replace each element with its rank and define

$$r := \text{sum of the ranks of the } x\text{'s}$$

and

$$z := \text{number of times a } y \text{ value precedes an } x \text{ value.}$$

For example, if $m = 4$ and $n = 5$ we could have the ranked sequence $\{xxxxyyyyy\}$ with $r = 10$ and $z = 0$, or $\{xxyxxyyyy\}$ with $r = 12$ and $z = 2$.
(a) Show that $r = \frac{1}{2}m(m+1) + z$.
(b) Show that $\mathrm{E}(z) = \frac{1}{2}mn$ under H_0.
(c) Show that $\mathrm{var}(z) = \frac{1}{12}mn(m+n+1)$ under H_0.
(d) How would you base a test on r or, equivalently, z?

Solution

(a) Note that the minimal value that r can attain is $\frac{1}{2}m(m+1)$, the sum of the first m natural numbers, and that in this case $z = 0$. If exactly one y precedes one x, then $r = \frac{1}{2}m(m+1) + 1$ and $z = 1$. Each time a y precedes one more x, we raise r by 1. Hence, $r = \frac{1}{2}m(m+1) + z$.
(b) Letting

$$\zeta_{ij} := 1_{x_i > y_j},$$

we have $z = \sum_{i=1}^m \sum_{j=1}^n \zeta_{ij}$ and, under H_0,

$$\mathrm{E}(\zeta_{ij}) = 1 \times \Pr(x_i > y_j) + 0 \times \Pr(x_i \leqslant y_j) = \frac{1}{2}$$

as in Exercise 14.42. Hence, $\mathrm{E}(z) = \sum_{i=1}^m \sum_{j=1}^n \mathrm{E}(\zeta_{ij}) = \frac{1}{2}mn$.
(c) We have

$$\begin{aligned}\mathrm{E}(z^2) &= \mathrm{E}\left(\left(\sum_{i=1}^m \sum_{j=1}^n \zeta_{ij}\right)\left(\sum_{k=1}^m \sum_{l=1}^n \zeta_{kl}\right)\right)\\ &= \mathrm{E}\left(\sum_{i=1}^m \sum_{j=1}^n \zeta_{ij}^2 + \sum_{i=1}^m \sum_{j\neq l} \zeta_{ij}\zeta_{il} + \sum_{i\neq k} \sum_{j=1}^n \zeta_{ij}\zeta_{kj} + \sum_{i\neq k, j\neq l} \zeta_{ij}\zeta_{kl}\right).\end{aligned}$$

Under H_0, we have the following expectations. First, $\mathrm{E}(\zeta_{ij}^2) = 1^2 \times \Pr(x_i > y_j) + 0 = \frac{1}{2}$. Second, for $j \neq l$,

$$\mathrm{E}(\zeta_{ij}\zeta_{il}) = \Pr(x_i > y_j, x_i > y_l) = \frac{2}{3!} = \frac{1}{3}$$

because, out of the 3! possible rankings of x_i, y_j, y_l, only two satisfy $x_i > y_j$ and $x_i > y_l$. Third, the same holds for $\mathrm{E}(\zeta_{ij}\zeta_{kj}) = \frac{1}{3}$ when $i \neq k$. Fourth, when all the indices are different,

$$\mathrm{E}(\zeta_{ij}\zeta_{kl}) = \Pr(x_i > y_j, x_k > y_l) = \Pr(x_i > y_j)\Pr(x_k > y_l) = \frac{1}{2} \times \frac{1}{2} = \frac{1}{4}$$

by the independence assumption. Putting these together and recalling that $\sum_{j\neq l}$ means a double sum with $n \times (n-1)$ terms, and similarly for $\sum_{i\neq k}$ containing $m \times (m-1)$ terms, we get

$$\begin{aligned}
\mathrm{E}(z^2) &= \frac{mn}{2} + \frac{mn(n-1)}{3} + \frac{m(m-1)n}{3} + \frac{m(m-1)n(n-1)}{4} \\
&= \frac{mn}{12}\left(6 + 4(n-1) + 4(m-1) + 3(m-1)(n-1)\right) \\
&= \frac{mn}{12}(1 + m + n + 3mn) = \frac{mn}{12}(1 + m + n) + \frac{m^2 n^2}{4}
\end{aligned}$$

and the result follows by subtracting $(\mathrm{E}(z))^2$.

(d) The statistics r and z differ only by a location constant which is known, so inferences based on them are equivalent. As in Exercise 14.42, we can base a test on how far z is from $\mathrm{E}(z)$ under the null hypothesis. A simple CLT applies to z, given that it is expressible as a sum of i.i.d. components with finite mean and variance, and this provides an approximation in terms of the normal distribution.

In small samples, we can use the following procedure based on r for $\mathrm{H}_1 : F_x(u) \neq F_y(u)$ for some u. Write the sum of the m ranks of the x's in the ranked sequence of x's and y's as

$$r \equiv r_1 + \cdots + r_m,$$

with $r_1 < \cdots < r_m$; the i-th index of r now refers to the i-th smallest x (not to x_i). Under H_0, all the values that can be taken by the vector $\boldsymbol{r} := (r_1, \ldots, r_m)'$ are equally probable, and there are

$$c := \binom{m+n}{m}$$

possible values since $r_1, \ldots, r_m$ are already arranged in ascending order (which makes permutations of the data irrelevant). The probability of any value of $\boldsymbol{r}$ is therefore $1/c$. A critical region would consist of the smallest and largest possible values of r, the next smallest and next largest, and so on k times until we have $2k$ of these c values. The size of this critical region is $\alpha = 2k/c$.

Exercise 14.44 (ARE of rank-sum test against t-ratio for location shifts) We continue with the setup of Exercise 14.43. If H_0 is violated and the two distributions are not equal, consider the alternative that they differ only by a location-shift parameter, namely $\mathrm{H}_1 : F_y(v) = F_x(v - \theta)$ for all v (hence $\mathrm{H}_0 : \theta = 0$), with $F_x(u)$ not dependent on θ. Assume that F_x is continuous and that $\mathrm{var}(x) < \infty$.

(a) Calculate the ARE of the test z that is based on the sum of ranks, relative to the usual t-ratio.

(b) What is the value of this ARE in the case where F_x is a normal distribution?

(c) Calculate the worst (over all F_x) ARE that z can achieve relative to the t-ratio.

Solution

(a) By the existence of the first two moments from F_x, we know that a CLT will apply to the

t-ratio and, as seen in Exercise 14.10(a), the statistic is asymptotically equivalent to $\overline{x} - \overline{y}$ with asymptotic (as $m, n \to \infty$) mean and variance $-\theta$ and $\sigma^2(m^{-1} + n^{-1})$, respectively; see Exercise 3.16(a) for the location-shift effect on the mean, or consider $x = y - \theta$. Hence, asymptotically,

$$\left.\frac{(\partial \,\mathrm{E}(\overline{x} - \overline{y})/\partial\theta)^2}{\mathrm{var}(\overline{x} - \overline{y})}\right|_{\theta=0} = \frac{1}{\sigma^2\left(m^{-1} + n^{-1}\right)} = \frac{mn}{\sigma^2\left(m + n\right)}.$$

For z, the derivations in Exercise 14.43(b) imply that, in general (for H_0 and H_1),

$$\mathrm{E}(z) = mn \Pr(x > y) = mn \Pr(x \geqslant y)$$

by $\Pr(x = y) = 0$ for x, y independent continuous variates (see Exercise 5.16), while Exercise 14.43(c) gives $\mathrm{var}(z) = mn(m + n + 1)/12$ at $\theta = 0$. By the usual mixing argument, used for example in Exercise 5.16,

$$\Pr(y \leqslant x) = \int_{-\infty}^{\infty} F_y(u) \,\mathrm{d}F_x(u) = \mathrm{E}_x(F_y(x)).$$

Since $F_y(x) = F_x(x - \theta)$, differentiating with respect to θ gives

$$\begin{aligned}\left.\frac{\partial \,\mathrm{E}(z)}{\partial\theta}\right|_{\theta=0} &= mn \,\mathrm{E}_x\left(\left.\frac{\partial}{\partial\theta} F_x(x - \theta)\right|_{\theta=0}\right) \\ &= -mn \,\mathrm{E}_x(f_x(x - \theta)|_{\theta=0}) = -mn \,\mathrm{E}_x(f_x(x)),\end{aligned}$$

where interchange of the expectation (or the integral above) with the derivative is allowed as $F_x(u)$ does not depend on θ. This gives

$$A_{z,t} = \lim_{m,n\to\infty} \frac{12\sigma^2\left(m + n\right)\left(\mathrm{E}_x\left(f_x(x)\right)\right)^2}{(m + n + 1)} = 12\sigma^2\left(\mathrm{E}_x\left(f_x(x)\right)\right)^2.$$

(b) The expectation $\mathrm{E}_x(f_x(x))$ has already been worked out in Exercise 13.16(a) as $(2\sqrt{\pi})^{-1}$ for $f_x = \phi$; see also the proof of Exercise 14.40(c). More generally for any $\mathrm{N}(\mu, \sigma^2)$,

$$\int_{-\infty}^{\infty} \frac{\exp(-(s - \mu)^2/\sigma^2)}{2\pi\sigma^2} \,\mathrm{d}s = \frac{1}{2\sigma\sqrt{\pi}} \int_{-\infty}^{\infty} \frac{\exp(-u^2/2)}{\sqrt{2\pi}} \,\mathrm{d}u = \frac{1}{2\sigma\sqrt{\pi}}$$

and

$$A_{z,t} = \frac{3}{\pi} \approx 0.955,$$

which shows that the relative efficiency loss of using z is asymptotically less than 5% when the true density is normal and the t-ratio is the one which is optimal.

(c) In part (b), we already hinted at Exercise 13.16(a), where this general result can be found. The quadratic density (the Epanechnikov) is the one minimizing $\mathrm{E}_x(f_x(x))$ and resulting in

$$\inf_f A_{z,t} = 12\left(\frac{3}{5\sqrt{5}}\right)^2 = \frac{108}{125} = 0.864.$$

It is truly astonishing that the *maximal* loss of relative efficiency from using z is only

13.6% asymptotically. Recall from Exercise 11.3(b), for example, that there are densities for which $A_{z,t}$ will exceed 1 and can even be unbounded. Since f is unknown in practice, the 13.6% maximum price that *may* have to be paid in some circumstances (for some f) is not much in return for the reassurance that we have a robust test that does well for a variety of densities.

Exercise 14.45 (Goodness-of-fit tests) Consider $\mathrm{H}_0 : F = F_0$ for some variate x whose distribution F is continuous. Let

$$D_n := \int_{-\infty}^{\infty} (\widehat{F}_n(u) - F_0(u))^2 w(u) \, \mathrm{d}F_0(u),$$

where $\widehat{F}_n$ is the EDF from a random sample and the weighting function $w(u)$ is nonrandom. Define two such functions, $w_1(u) := 1$ and

$$w_2(u) := \frac{1}{F_0(u)\,(1 - F_0(u))}.$$

(a) Work out $\mathrm{E}(D_n)$ under H_0 for w_1 and w_2.
(b) Work out $\mathrm{var}(D_n)$ under H_0 for w_1 and w_2, as $n \to \infty$. [Hint: Use the two integral equalities $\int_0^1 r^{-1} \log(1-r) \, \mathrm{d}r = -\pi^2/6$ and $\int_0^1 \log(1-r) \, \mathrm{d}r = -1$.]
(c) For any n and regardless of which hypothesis holds, show that the distribution of D_n does not depend on F_0 if we can write $w(u) = h(F_0(u))$ with $h(v)$ some function not depending on F_0.

Solution
(a) We refer back to Exercise 9.26 for the exact distribution $n\widehat{F}_n(u) \sim \mathrm{Bin}(n, F(u))$ with

$$\mathrm{E}(\widehat{F}_n(u)) = F(u) \quad \text{and} \quad \mathrm{var}(\widehat{F}_n(u)) = \frac{F(u)(1 - F(u))}{n}.$$

Then

$$\mathrm{E}(D_n) = \int_{-\infty}^{\infty} \mathrm{E}(\widehat{F}_n(u) - F_0(u))^2 w(u) \, \mathrm{d}F_0(u) = \int_{-\infty}^{\infty} \mathrm{var}(\widehat{F}_n(u)) w(u) \, \mathrm{d}F_0(u)$$

under H_0. Substituting for $\mathrm{var}(\widehat{F}_n(u))$, we get

$$\mathrm{E}(D_n) = \int_{-\infty}^{\infty} \frac{F_0(u)(1 - F_0(u))}{n} w(u) \, \mathrm{d}F_0(u).$$

For w_1,

$$\mathrm{E}(D_n) = \int_{-\infty}^{\infty} \frac{F_0(u)(1 - F_0(u))}{n} \, \mathrm{d}F_0(u) = \int_0^1 \frac{v(1-v)}{n} \, \mathrm{d}v$$

by the transformation $v = F_0(u) \in [0, 1]$; then the integral of the Beta(2, 2) density gives

$$\mathrm{E}(D_n) = \frac{B(2,2)}{n} = \frac{\Gamma(2)\Gamma(2)}{n\Gamma(4)} = \frac{1}{6n}.$$

For w_2,

$$\mathrm{E}(D_n) = \int_{-\infty}^{\infty} \frac{1}{n}\,\mathrm{d}F_0(u) = \frac{1}{n}.$$

(b) We have $\mathrm{var}(D_n) = \mathrm{E}(D_n^2) - (\mathrm{E}(D_n))^2$ and, defining

$$\zeta(u) := \widehat{F}_n(u) - F_0(u),$$

we need

$$\mathrm{E}(D_n^2) = \int_{\mathbb{R}^2} \mathrm{E}(\zeta(u)^2\zeta(v)^2)w(u)w(v)\,\mathrm{d}F_0(u)\,\mathrm{d}F_0(v).$$

Exercise 10.30(c) gives $\zeta(u), \zeta(v)$ as asymptotically bivariate normal with means 0 and covariance function $F_0(s)\,(1 - F_0(t))\,/n$ for $t \geqslant s$. From Exercise 8.19(d),

$$n^2\,\mathrm{E}(\zeta(u)^2\zeta(v)^2) \to 2F_0(s)^2\,(1 - F_0(t))^2 + F_0(u)\,(1 - F_0(u))\,F_0(v)\,(1 - F_0(v))$$

with $s = \min\{u, v\}$ and $t = \max\{u, v\}$; hence

$$n^2\,\mathrm{E}(D_n^2) \to \int_{\mathbb{R}^2} 2F_0(s)^2\,(1 - F_0(t))^2\,w(u)w(v)\,\mathrm{d}F_0(u)\,\mathrm{d}F_0(v) + (n\,\mathrm{E}(D_n))^2,$$

from the formula for $\mathrm{E}(D_n)$ in (a). For w_1, transforming the variables of integration to $F_0(u) \in [0, 1]$ and $F_0(v) \in [0, 1]$ as in (a), with economy of notation (calling the new variables u, v instead of using new labels, and calling s, t their min, max, respectively),

$$\begin{aligned}
n^2\,\mathrm{var}(D_n) &\to \int_0^1 \int_0^1 2s^2\,(1-t)^2\,\mathrm{d}u\,\mathrm{d}v \\
&= \int_0^1 \int_0^v 2u^2\,(1-v)^2\,\mathrm{d}u\,\mathrm{d}v + \int_0^1 \int_v^1 2v^2\,(1-u)^2\,\mathrm{d}u\,\mathrm{d}v \\
&= \int_0^1 \left[\frac{2u^3}{3}\right]_0^v (1-v)^2\,\mathrm{d}v - \int_0^1 2v^2 \left[\frac{(1-u)^3}{3}\right]_v^1 \mathrm{d}v \\
&= \frac{2}{3}\left(\int_0^1 v^3\,(1-v)^2\,\mathrm{d}v + \int_0^1 v^2\,(1-v)^3\,\mathrm{d}v\right) \\
&= \frac{2}{3}\,(B(4,3) + B(3,4)) = \frac{4}{3}\frac{\Gamma(3)\Gamma(4)}{\Gamma(7)} = \frac{1}{45},
\end{aligned}$$

using the integral of the standard beta density. For w_2,

$$\begin{aligned}
n^2\,\mathrm{var}(D_n) &\to \int_0^1 \int_0^1 \frac{2s^2\,(1-t)^2}{u\,(1-u)\,v\,(1-v)}\,\mathrm{d}u\,\mathrm{d}v \\
&= \int_0^1 \int_0^v \frac{2u\,(1-v)}{(1-u)\,v}\,\mathrm{d}u\,\mathrm{d}v + \int_0^1 \int_v^1 \frac{2v\,(1-u)}{u\,(1-v)}\,\mathrm{d}u\,\mathrm{d}v \\
&= \int_0^1 \frac{2\,(1-v)}{v} \int_0^v \frac{u}{1-u}\,\mathrm{d}u\,\mathrm{d}v + \int_0^1 \frac{2v}{1-v} \int_v^1 \frac{1-u}{u}\,\mathrm{d}u\,\mathrm{d}v.
\end{aligned}$$

Since

$$\int_0^v \frac{u}{1-u}\,\mathrm{d}u = \int_{1-v}^1 \frac{1-r}{r}\,\mathrm{d}r = \int_{1-v}^1 \left(\frac{1}{r}-1\right)\mathrm{d}r = [\log(r) - r]_{1-v}^1$$
$$= -\log(1-v) - v$$

and

$$\int_v^1 \left(\frac{1}{u}-1\right)\mathrm{d}u = [\log(u) - u]_v^1 = v - 1 - \log(v),$$

we have

$$n^2 \operatorname{var}(D_n) \to -2\int_0^1 \frac{1-v}{v}(\log(1-v)+v)\,\mathrm{d}v + 2\int_0^1 \frac{v}{1-v}(v-1-\log(v))\,\mathrm{d}v$$
$$= -2\int_0^1 \frac{1-v}{v}(\log(1-v)+v)\,\mathrm{d}v - 2\int_0^1 \frac{1-r}{r}(r+\log(1-r))\,\mathrm{d}r$$
$$= -4\int_0^1 \frac{1-r}{r}(\log(1-r)+r)\,\mathrm{d}r,$$

by the change of variable $r = 1-v$ which shows that the two integrals are the same. Then,

$$n^2 \operatorname{var}(D_n) \to -4\int_0^1 \left(\frac{1}{r}-1\right)\log(1-r)\,\mathrm{d}r - 4\int_0^1 (1-r)\,\mathrm{d}r$$
$$= -4\int_0^1 \frac{\log(1-r)}{r}\,\mathrm{d}r + 4\int_0^1 \log(1-r)\,\mathrm{d}r + 2\left[(1-r)^2\right]_0^1$$
$$= \frac{2\pi^2}{3} - 4 - 2 = \frac{2\pi^2}{3} - 6$$

using the hint.

(c) Before we establish the result, we note that it holds for *any* n, not just asymptotically. Also, the specification of the function h is satisfied by both w_1 and w_2. Consider

$$D_n = \int_{-\infty}^{\infty} \left(\frac{1}{n}\sum\nolimits_{i=1}^n 1_{x_i \leqslant u} - F_0(u)\right)^2 h(F_0(u))\,\mathrm{d}F_0(u),$$

where we have substituted the definition of $\widehat{F}_n$. By the change of variable seen earlier in this exercise, $v = F_0(u) \in [0,1]$, the statistic becomes

$$D_n = \int_0^1 \left(\frac{1}{n}\sum\nolimits_{i=1}^n 1_{F_0(x_i)\leqslant v} - v\right)^2 h(v)\,\mathrm{d}v,$$

where we see that the only random variable is $F_0(x_i)$, which has the same $\mathrm{U}_{(0,1)}$ distribution for *any* continuous F_0, by the PIT in Exercise 7.38. The distribution of D_n is therefore unaffected by the choice of any continuous F_0. Note that we can interpret D_n as measuring the total squared deviation (weighted by h) of an F_0-standardized variate's EDF from the c.d.f. $F(v) = v$ of a standard uniform.

Notes

Additional general references for this chapter include Gouriéroux and Monfort (1995, vol. 2), Kendall and Stuart (1979), Lehmann (1986), and Silvey (1975). The subject matter of this chapter is large. Because of the focus of this Series, our selection for this chapter was influenced by the procedures that are most commonly used in econometrics. One absent example is the *analysis of variance* (ANOVA) usually found in statistics textbooks, which can be applied here as testing in a regression with dummy variables (recall the variance decompositions in Exercise 12.35 and subsequently). Another is the generalization of Exercise 14.10(a) to unequal (and unknown) variances, leading to the *Behrens–Fisher problem*, which has been widely debated and for which accurate approximate solutions exist. Sequential tests (with stopping rules for an increasing sample size) are also absent, as n is usually given in economics; see Mood, Graybill, and Boes (1974).

The Neyman–Pearson lemma also holds as an equivalence, a UMP test existing if and only if the displayed conditions are satisfied except for a set of probability-measure 0; this can be seen from the proof in Exercise 14.7. Similarly for the Karlin–Rubin theorem. To write either statement as an equivalence, one would need to introduce the concept of *randomization* (assigning randomly the borderline cases to either C_α or C_α^c in order to achieve any α exactly) to get the statement to apply to all $\alpha \in (0, 1)$, as opposed to choosing a specific level α for which randomization is not needed.

The indicator function $1_{\tau \in C_\alpha}$ is called a *test function*. It was used in Exercises 14.29, 14.32, and 14.33. Some authors use it to state the Neyman–Pearson lemma, but we used an easier formulation that does not require it.

The Karlin–Rubin theorem makes it straightforward to establish that a single-parameter exponential family implies the existence of a UMP test against one-sided alternatives, for all levels α. A more difficult result is the converse of Pfanzagl (1968): if there exists a UMP test for *one* level $\alpha \in (0, 1)$, then we are dealing with an exponential family.

For more general results on the inequality in Exercise 14.16(b), see Evans and Savin (1982). See also Godfrey (1988). For more on Exercise 14.20, see Dagenais and Dufour (1991). The W test can have some unpleasant features, such as lack of invariance; see the differential-geometric interpretations in Critchley, Marriott, and Salmon (1996) for W based on $\mathcal{I}$ (but not on $\mathcal{H}$), and the impossibility theorems in Dufour (1997).

The limiting distributions of test statistics can be quite different from their small-sample distributions, as we saw as early as in Chapter 10. Improvements based on approximations for exact distributions were introduced in the context of the p^* formula and others in the Notes to Chapter 12, and are used for refined inference. Bartlett corrections for LR (or χ^2), Edgeworth expansions, and saddlepoint approximations are other prominent approaches in the field; see Reid (1988), Ghosh (1994), and Ullah (2004) for introductions.

In the solution to Exercise 14.19(d), we pointed out that using $-\mathcal{H}$ or $\mathcal{I}$ leads to different results. An illustration mentioned earlier can be found in Evans and Savin (1981), Abadir (1993b), and Magdalinos (2007). This point is valid more generally. Also, in the i.i.d. case, one can use estimators based on $\frac{1}{n}\sum_{i=1}^{n} \boldsymbol{q}\boldsymbol{q}'$ (for estimating $\mathrm{E}(\boldsymbol{q}\boldsymbol{q}')$) and other *sandwich estimators* based on further products surrounding this sum. There is a large literature on whether to use estimates of $-\mathcal{H}$ (the "observed information") or estimates of $\mathcal{I}$; see, for example, Lindsay and Li (1997) and recall that, in Chapter 12, the modified profile likelihood is in terms of $\mathcal{H}$ not $\mathcal{I}$. See also Cox and Hinkley (1974), Evans, Fraser, and Monette (1986), Reid (1995), Sundberg (2003), and Mayo and Spanos (2010) on the general question of conditioning, sufficiency, and the likelihood principle in inference, as well as their relation to one another under the heading of *Birnbaum's theorem*. A compelling case for conditioning is the following famous example from Cox and Hinkley (1974, pp. 38–39), with a slight change of notation. Suppose that a physical measurement $y \in \{1, 2\}$ of an unknown $\theta \in \{\theta_1, \theta_2\}$ can be made by two instruments $M \in \{M_1, M_2\}$:

$$\text{under } M_1 : \quad \Pr(y = 1 \mid M_1, \theta_1) = \Pr(y = 2 \mid M_1, \theta_2) = 1,$$

$$\text{under } M_2 : \quad \Pr(y = 1 \mid M_2, \theta_1) = \Pr(y = 2 \mid M_2, \theta_2) = 0.01,$$

and that we choose M at random, with $\Pr(M = M_1) = 0.9$, but it is known which M ends up being selected. The probabilities, unconditionally with respect to M, are

$$\Pr(y = 1 \mid \theta_1) = 0.9 \times 1 + 0.1 \times 0.01 = 0.901 \quad (\text{same also for } \Pr(y = 2 \mid \theta_2)),$$

$$\Pr(y = 1 \mid \theta_2) = 1 - \Pr(y = 2 \mid \theta_2) = 0.099\,.$$

On the basis of these unconditional probabilities, a value of $y = 1$ indicates that $\theta = \theta_1$ is highly likely, regardless of which M was used. Now M is ancillary for θ, since its p.d.f. does not depend on θ. Furthermore, we know which M has been used. If we chose $M = M_2$, conditioning on this information gives $\Pr(y = 1 \mid M_2, \theta_1) = 0.01$, which indicates that $\theta = \theta_2$ is much more likely. In the unconditional inference case, we take into account what M might have been, whereas in the conditional case, we use only the M that has actually been selected. Similar reasoning holds for maximizing the expected power (unconditional expectation) as opposed to the conditional approach which is less powerful unconditionally; see Cox and Hinkley (1974, p. 96), Fraser (2004, pp. 335–336). Recall from Exercises 11.16–11.18 that conditioning implies the partitioning of the sample space; see also Reid (1995, p. 154) for a discussion of the impact on powers of shrinking the sample space.

Two variants of Rao's 1948 score test were published in 1959, though originally they were not acknowledged as such. They are Silvey's LM and Neyman's $C(\alpha)$ dealing with nuisance parameters by consistent estimators that are not necessarily MLEs; see Bera and Bilias (2001). See also Davies (1977, 1987) for modifications in the case where one of the parameters disappears from the model under H_0. Two other general tests are commonly used in econometrics. One is White's (1982) information-matrix test, measuring the distance between the two sides of the information-matrix equivalence (see Chapter 12); these differ when there is a misspecification of the model. The other is the Durbin–Wu–Hausman test (applied in Exercise 14.21(d)), measuring the difference between two estimators: one that is always consistent and another that is consistent only under H_0. The distribution of the LR test in Exercise 14.21 is called a chi-bar-squared and is denoted by $\overline{\chi}^2$. Its c.d.f., for general noncentrality, is derived explicitly in Conaway, Pillers, Robertson, and Sconing (1990). An alternative way of combining tests is the *multiple test* approach, which produces joint confidence intervals (for example, rectangular or elliptical), typically when the components are independent. *Union–intersection* and *intersection–union* tests have also been used, depending on the formulation of the joint hypothesis as an intersection or union of the components, respectively, the rejection regions being the other type (the complement). Results on the admissibility of methods of combining tests can be found in Koziol and Perlman (1978) and Marden (1982).

In Exercise 14.22 on the Cox test, the null hypothesis is taken to be H_g, but we can get different conclusions if we take H_h instead. Vuong (1989) solved this problem by taking the null to be that both nonnested models are equally good, then normalizing as follows:

$$V := \frac{LR}{\sqrt{\widehat{\operatorname{var}}(LR)}},$$

where

$$LR = 2(\ell_h(\widehat{\boldsymbol{\beta}}) - \ell_g(\widehat{\boldsymbol{\alpha}})) \quad \text{and} \quad \widehat{\operatorname{var}}(LR) \stackrel{a}{=} 4n\,\widehat{\operatorname{var}}(\log(h/g)),$$

using the notation of Exercise 14.22 and $\widehat{\operatorname{var}}$ denoting the sample variance. We have $V \stackrel{a}{\sim} \mathrm{N}(0,1)$ if both models are equally good; otherwise, $V \to -\infty$ if g is better and $V \to \infty$ if h is better. Vuong also suggested modifying the statistic's numerator with an additional term that is linear in the difference between the dimensions of $\boldsymbol{\alpha}$ and $\boldsymbol{\beta}$, similar to the information criterion of Schwarz (1978), but this modification is asymptotically negligible.

This brings us to another limitation: what if we need to compare more than two nonnested models? One can minimize Akaike's (1974) information criterion, $-2\ell(\widehat{\boldsymbol{\theta}}) + 2m$, where there is a penalty (arising from a bias-correction of the sample estimate of the KLIC divergence between the data-generating process and the model) based on the dimension of the model m. However, Nishii (1988) proved that the criterion is inconsistent. Alternative, consistent, criteria include that of Schwarz (1978) $-2\ell(\widehat{\boldsymbol{\theta}}) + m\log(n)$ which was also obtained in Rissanen (1978), or that of Hannan and Quinn (1979) for time series models where the data are dependent and, the "effective" sample size being smaller than n, the criterion is $-2\ell(\widehat{\boldsymbol{\theta}}) + 2m\log(\log(n))$. Each approach gives a *ranking* of models according to how large the criterion is, but the difference may or may not be statistically significant; this point is addressed in Sin and White (1996).

It is also possible to do pairwise comparisons of models with the maintained model, then combine the result. By Bonferroni's inequality (Chapters 1 and 13),

$$\Pr(A_1, \dots, A_p) \geqslant 1 - \sum_{j=1}^{p} \Pr\left(A_j^c\right),$$

so that the probability of a Type I error in testing a model against p others is bounded above by p times the Type I error α of each test. (Here, we use A_j for "accept Model 0 when it is better than Model j".) But this bound can be too large if p is large. Holm's (1979) method provides an improvement by ranking the $\Pr(A_j^c)$ in order, and proceeding recursively with $p+1-j$ Bonferroni-type bounds. See also Hommel (1988), Hochberg (1988), and Benjamini and Hochberg (1995). Clearly, this method is also directly applicable to the multiple-test problem mentioned earlier.

The innovative statistical shortcut used in the proof of Exercise 14.28 is due to Das Gupta and Perlman (1974). Their Lemma 2.3 is applicable to the specific X, Y that they define in their proof, containing their U, V in common (the simplification of the ratio of χ^2's need not apply more generally). The final exercises of our Section 14.3 use invariance ideas that should be more formally introduced in terms of the mathematical topic of group theory. We have avoided doing so because the extra machinery needed is not justified by the few exercises that use it implicitly. For a more rigorous approach, we refer the reader to Lehmann (1986), Muirhead (1982), and Eaton (1989).

Exercise 14.39 assesses AREs $A_{1,2}$ in the context of tests. Under some further regularity conditions, $A_{1,2}$ is directly related to the ratio of powers and to the estimator's AREs; see Chapter 25 of Kendall and Stuart (1979). In Exercise 14.39, we omitted the case of different consistency rates n^{-d} of the estimators, leading to $A_{1,2} = 0$ or $A_{1,2} = \infty$. We also omitted the case of different k, which arises when comparing one-sided and two-sided tests for the *same* H_1, as it is obvious from the earlier discussion that we should not use a two-sided test for a one-sided alternative; see, for example, Figure 14.2 and the exercises in Section 14.3.

As the sample size increases, one should redress the imbalance between the Type I and II errors, instead of just keeping the former fixed while the latter go to zero. As a result, one could require a lower p-value (or lower α) as n increases. A sequence of Pitman alternatives was used in Exercise 14.39 to compare the powers for a given size. But this can be complemented by reversing the roles of the Type I and II errors, an approach due to Bahadur and summarized in Section 23.2 of Gouriéroux and Monfort (1995, vol. 2). Because the power function is increasing in α, we can also write n_j of Exercise 14.39 as $n_j = \inf\{n : \alpha_{\tau_j} \leqslant \alpha\}$ for some fixed $\Pi \in [\alpha, 1)$. *Bahadur's ARE* is $\lim_{n\to\infty} \log(\alpha_{\tau_1}) / \log(\alpha_{\tau_2})$ or $\lim_{\alpha\to 0} n_2/n_1$.

There are other local approaches to evaluating powers and/or selecting tests with locally optimal properties, such as locally most powerful (LMP) tests. Tests can also be compared with the best that can be achieved pointwise in Θ_1, known as the *envelope power function* and obtained as $\sup_\tau \Pi_\tau(\boldsymbol{\theta})$ over all size-α tests τ, for any given $\boldsymbol{\theta} \in \Theta_1$. At any point in Θ_1, the *shortcoming* of a test is the distance from the power envelope, and its *deficiency* is the number of additional observations needed for this test to achieve the power of a most powerful test (compare this with AREs). For approximating powers in general contexts, see Le Cam's local asymptotic (mixed) normality (LA(M)N) approach and the related optimality results.

It is possible also to adopt a decision-theoretic approach (see Chapter 11), assigning loss functions and hence the costs of wrong decisions for errors of Types I and II, with associated risk functions calculated as expected losses. Decision-theoretic considerations could include: *minimax* tests that minimize the maximum risk (clearly $\wp$ is minimax in the simple setting of the Neyman–Pearson lemma); robustness (minimax is a special case);

most stringent tests that minimize the maximum distance from the power envelope. The general references at the start of this chapter's Notes give more details on these topics and those in the previous paragraph.

In connection with Exercise 14.43, the study of Wilcoxon's r was followed by Mann and Whitney's z. Improvements over these tests' AREs against F_x being normal, in Exercise 14.44(b), are possible. They can achieve an ARE of 1 (no loss of efficiency) under normality, if *normal scores* are used; these are defined as the expected values of order statistics from a normal sample. For example, see Kendall and Stuart (1979). Both z and t are consistent for $\theta \neq 0$, as long as $m, n \to \infty$ such that neither m/n nor n/m tend to zero. However, consistency need not hold in the case of the tests of independence seen before this in Section 14.4, whether parametric or nonparametric: we showed that there are many bivariate densities where $\rho = 0$ but the variates are *not* independent; for example, see Exercise 8.10. To obtain consistency for the alternative hypothesis of dependence, we therefore have to exclude from H_1 the case $\rho = 0$, a related point having been made in the introduction to this chapter when we stated that $\Theta_0 \cap \Theta_1 = \varnothing$. Note that, as in the case of the parametric tests described in the introduction, z is unbiased if we restrict the sign of θ but not otherwise. In general, z is unbiased for $\mathrm{H}_1 : F_y(v) > F_x(v)$ (for all v), but not for $\mathrm{H}_1 : F_y(v) \neq F_x(v)$; and z is consistent for alternatives where F_x and F_y imply different mean ranks or, equivalently, if $\Pr_{\mathrm{H}_1}(x > y) \neq \frac{1}{2}$.

Permutation tests are used when the distribution is invariant to permutation under H_0 but not under H_1; then the effect of permutation (for example, on the resulting mean under H_1) can be investigated. We briefly touched on this topic in Exercise 9.29 and in the corresponding Note on Daniels (1944). Permutation ideas also underly the more modern resampling techniques seen, for example, in Exercise 11.9.

The distribution of D_n of Exercise 14.45 is nonnormal, even in the limit. Furthermore, it is affected if the parameters of F_0 are to be estimated and are not known in advance, as when specifying the type of F_0 without knowing its mean or variance a priori. See D'Agostino and Stephens (1986) for details. Note that *minimum-distance estimators* are obtained by minimizing a functional such as D_n empirically. We have seen other measures of divergence, including KLIC, Hellinger's, and the generalized entropies in (4.8) and subsequently.

A famous goodness-of-fit test is Pearson's $\chi^2(m-1)$ test $\sum_{j=1}^{m} (x_j - e_j)^2 / e_j$, where the domain is split into m intervals or groups, with x_j and e_j denoting the observed and expected frequencies, respectively; the expected frequencies are obtained from $\mathrm{H}_0 : F_x = F_0$ by using $\Pr(u_i < x \leqslant u_{i+1}) = F_x(u_{i+1}) - F_x(u_i)$. The test is an estimate of $\mathrm{E}\left((x/e - 1)^2\right)$ under the expected frequencies. However, because of the grouping, it discards information about ranks within each interval, unlike rank tests. Recall that ranks preserve much of the sample information relevant to tests on F_x, since ranks are a monotone transformation of the EDF. Generalizing Pearson's χ^2 and other measures, Cressie and

Read (1984) introduced the *power divergence*

$$D(\lambda) := \frac{2}{\lambda(\lambda+1)} \sum_{j=1}^{m} x_j \left(\left(\frac{x_j}{e_j} \right)^{\lambda} - 1 \right),$$

yielding Pearson's χ^2 when $\lambda = 1$ and the data are grouped, the empirical LR (see the empirical likelihood introduced in Chapter 12) for $\lambda \to 0$, and the empirical KLIC for $\lambda \to -1$.

Appendix A Some mathematical tools

This appendix collects mathematical tools that are needed in the main text. In addition, it gives a brief description of some essential background topics. It is assumed that the reader knows elementary calculus. The topics are grouped in four sections. First, we consider some useful methods of indirect proof. Second, we introduce elementary results for complex numbers and polynomials. The third topic concerns series expansions. Finally, some further calculus is presented. This last section provides the main difference from Appendix A in Abadir and Magnus (2005).

In this appendix, we use $f(x)$ for a generic function. We do not use f to refer to a density function, nor x to indicate a random variable. The two exceptions are (A.4), and the discussion in between (A.8) and (A.9) where we use subscripts to distinguish the p.d.f. $f_x(u)$ from other functions $f(u)$.

A.1 Some methods of indirect proof

Perhaps the most fundamental of all mathematical tools is the construction of a proof. When a direct proof is hard to obtain, there are indirect methods that can often help. In this section, we will denote a statement by p (such as "I like this book"), and another by q (such as "I like the book on matrix algebra in this Series"). The negation of p will be denoted by $\neg p$. The statement "p and q" is denoted by $p \wedge q$, and the statement "p or q (or both)" is denoted by $p \vee q$. The statements $\neg(p \vee q)$ and $\neg p \wedge \neg q$ are equivalent: the negation transforms p, q into $\neg p, \neg q$ and $\vee$ into $\wedge$. This is the equivalent of *De Morgan's law* for sets, where p and q would be sets, $\neg p$ the complement of p, $p \vee q$ the union of the sets, and $p \wedge q$ their intersection. Clearly, $\neg(\neg p)$ is the same as p, and the operation $\vee$ is commutative (hence $\wedge$ is too) so that $p \vee q$ is equivalent to $q \vee p$.

We will explore equivalent ways of formulating that p implies q, denoted by $p \implies q$, meaning that if statement p holds then q will hold too: p is therefore *sufficient* for q ("if p

then q"). The truth of $p \implies q$ is equivalent to the truth of $\neg p \vee q$: the claim $p \implies q$ is violated if and only if we have $p \wedge \neg q$.

The first alternative formulation of $p \implies q$ is $\neg q \implies \neg p$, meaning that if statement q does not hold then p will not hold either: q is therefore *necessary* for p ("p only if q"). A proof that starts by presuming $\neg q$, and then shows that it leads to $\neg p$, is called a *proof by contrapositive*.

The second way of establishing that $p \implies q$ is through a *proof by contradiction*. It proceeds by showing that if one were to assume $\neg q$ and p simultaneously, a contradiction would occur; for example, $s \wedge \neg s$ where s is some statement. Therefore $\neg q \wedge p$ is false, and its negation $q \vee \neg p$ holds, which is precisely the required $p \implies q$. Notice the difference from the previous method of proof, where no contradictory statements ever arise.

The third method of indirect proof is of a different nature, and can sometimes lead to errors if not treated carefully. The previous two methods are examples of *proofs by deduction*. A *proof by induction* is one that takes the following structure. Suppose that $n \in \mathbb{N}$, and that we wish to prove a statement s_n (such as $p \implies q$) for all $n \in \mathbb{N}$. If s_1 is true and if we can show that $s_n \implies s_{n+1}$, then s_n holds for all $n \in \mathbb{N}$. Caution should be exercised in defining what n stands for, so that s_1 is not a trivial or empty statement.

Finally, we have used the terms "p is equivalent to q" and "p if and only if q". These can be abbreviated by $p \iff q$, which happens when we have $q \implies p$ and its *converse* $p \implies q$ simultaneously: p is necessary *and* sufficient for q.

A.2 Primer on complex numbers and polynomials

A number u is said to be *complex* if it can be expressed in the *rectangular (Cartesian) form*

$$u = a + \mathrm{i}b,$$

where i is the imaginary unit satisfying $\mathrm{i}^2 = -1$, $\mathrm{Re}(u) := a \in \mathbb{R}$ is the *real part* of u, and $\mathrm{Im}(u) := b \in \mathbb{R}$ is the *imaginary part* of u. An alternative expression for this complex number $u \in \mathbb{C}$ is the *polar form*

$$u = |u| (\cos(\theta) + \mathrm{i} \sin(\theta)),$$

where the *modulus* (or *absolute value*) of u, denoted by $|u|$, is defined as the nonnegative square root of $a^2 + b^2$, and $\arg(u) := \theta = \tan^{-1}(b/a)$ is the *argument* of u.

Euler's formula, $\exp(\mathrm{i}\theta) = \cos(\theta) + \mathrm{i}\sin(\theta)$, allows us to rewrite the polar form as

$$u = |u| \mathrm{e}^{\mathrm{i}\theta},$$

where e^x is understood to refer to the *exponential function* $\exp(x) := \sum_{j=0}^{\infty} x^j / j!$ and

$$j! := \prod_{k=1}^{j} k = 1 \times 2 \times \cdots \times j$$

is the *factorial function*. Empty products such as $\prod_{k=1}^{0} k$ are equal to 1 by convention; hence $0! = 1$. A similar formulation applies to matrices, and is known as the *polar decom-*

position.

Any complex number $u = a + ib = |u|\,\mathrm{e}^{\mathrm{i}\theta}$ can be represented graphically on the *complex plane*, depicted in Figure A.1. The Cartesian coordinates of the point representing u are

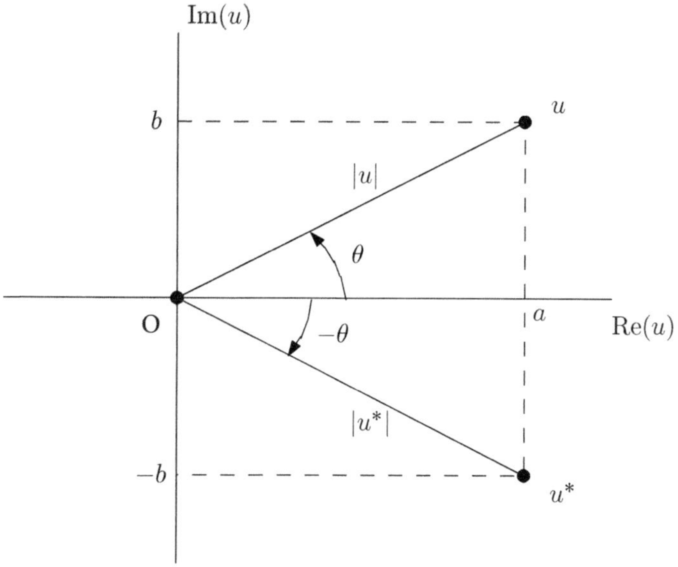

Figure A.1. Rectangular and polar coordinates of a complex number and its conjugate.

(a, b), with the horizontal and vertical axes measuring the real and imaginary parts of u, respectively. A complex number can therefore be thought of as a two-dimensional vector of real numbers. The polar coordinates representing u are $(|u|, \theta)$, respectively the length and angle of a ray joining the point u to the origin. Positive values of θ are conventionally measured anticlockwise from the positive horizontal axis, and negative values clockwise. We also see that $\tan(\theta) = b/a$. The *complex conjugate* of the number u is $u^* = a - ib = |u|\,\mathrm{e}^{-\mathrm{i}\theta}$, the reflection of point u across the horizontal axis. The product of the conjugate pair,

$$u \times u^* = |u|\,\mathrm{e}^{\mathrm{i}\theta}\,|u|\,\mathrm{e}^{-\mathrm{i}\theta} = |u|^2 = a^2 + b^2,$$

is always nonnegative.

Euler's formula clarifies and provides a simple proof of *de Moivre's theorem*, which states that

$$u^\nu - \left(|u|\left(\cos(\theta) + \mathrm{i}\sin(\theta)\right)\right)^\nu = |u|^\nu\left(\cos(\nu\theta) + \mathrm{i}\sin(\nu\theta)\right)$$

for any complex ν. A direct consequence of this theorem and Euler's formula is that the equation $x^2 = u$ (where $u = |u|\,\mathrm{e}^{\mathrm{i}\theta}$ is a complex number and x is a *complex variable*) has the two solutions

$$x_1 = \sqrt{|u|}e^{i\theta/2} \quad \text{and} \quad x_2 = -\sqrt{|u|}e^{i\theta/2} = \sqrt{|u|}e^{i(\pi+\theta/2)},$$

using the fact that $e^{i\pi} = -1$. These are shown in Figure A.2. The square-root func-

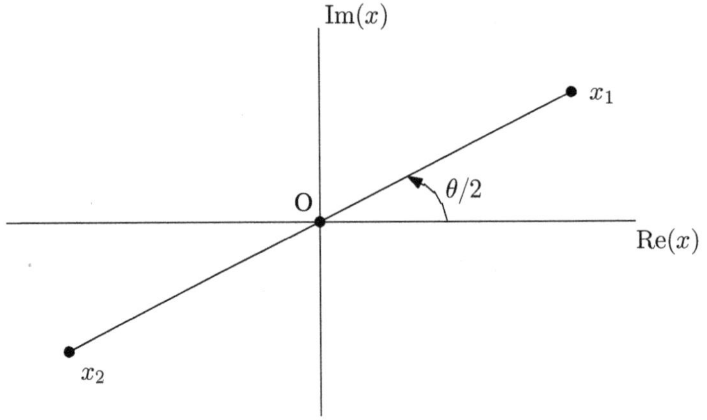

Figure A.2. The two solutions to $x^2 = u$.

tion is *multiple-valued*. In fact, there are infinitely many solutions of the form $x_{j+1} = \sqrt{|u|}e^{i(\pi j+\theta/2)}$, $j = 0, 1, \ldots$, but they have the same rectangular coordinates as either x_1 or x_2. Therefore, we restrict our attention to solutions having $0 \leqslant \arg(x) < 2\pi$. The solution x_1 is called the *principal value* of this multiple-valued function. Note that when $\theta = 0$, we have $u = u^* = |u|$ and $x = \pm\sqrt{|u|}$, with the positive square root x_1 as the principal value. Similarly, when $\theta = \pi$, we have $u = u^* = -|u|$ and $x = \pm i\sqrt{|u|}$. If, in addition, $|u| = 1$, the principal value of $\sqrt{-1}$ is i.

Similarly, the n *roots of unity*, which solve the equation $x^n = 1$, are given by $x_{j+1} = e^{2ij\pi/n}$, where $n \in \mathbb{N}$ and $j = 0, 1, \ldots, n-1$. For $n = 6$, these roots are depicted by the points on the unit circle of Figure A.3. These points are the vertices of the symmetric hexagon in the figure. The displayed circle of radius 1, which is centered around the origin, is called *the unit circle*. More generally, a circle of unit radius centered around some point (not necessarily the origin) is called *a unit circle*.

The two equations in x that we have just considered are examples of a polynomial equation. A function of the form

$$P_n(x) := \sum_{j=0}^{n} p_j x^j = p_0 + p_1 x + \cdots + p_n x^n$$

is called a *polynomial of degree* (or *order*) n in the variable x, when $p_n \neq 0$ and the p_j are all finite constants. When $p_n = 1$, we have a *monic* polynomial, an example of this being the characteristic polynomial of a matrix. Polynomials of degrees n_1 and n_2 can be

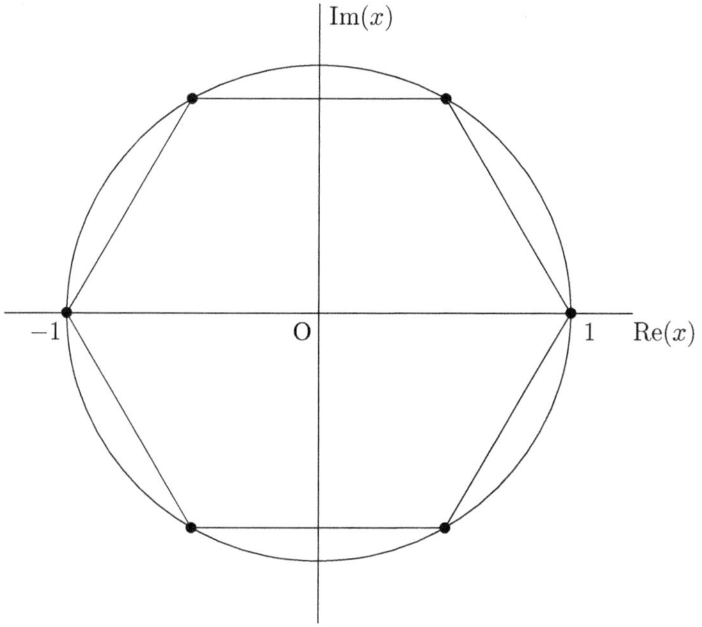

Figure A.3. The six solutions to $x^6 = 1$.

multiplied with one another, yielding a polynomial of degree $n_1 + n_2$. For example,

$$(1 + x)\left(1 - x^2\right) = 1 + x - x^2 - x^3.$$

If a polynomial does not vanish identically (that is, if $P_n(x) \neq 0$ for at least one x), then it can divide another polynomial, such as in the following example:

$$\frac{2 + x - x^2 - x^3}{1 - x^2} = \frac{1}{1 - x^2} + \frac{1 + x - x^2 - x^3}{1 - x^2} = \frac{1}{1 - x^2} + 1 + x.$$

The fraction $1/(1 - x^2)$ is called the *remainder of the division*. The *fundamental theorem of algebra* states that $P_n(x) := \sum_{j=0}^{n} p_j x^j$ can always be factored as a product of linear polynomials,

$$P_n(x) = p_n \prod_{i=1}^{n} (x - \lambda_i) = p_n (x - \lambda_1) \ldots (x - \lambda_n),$$

where the $\lambda_i \in \mathbb{C}$ are the constants that solve the equation $P_n(x) = 0$, and are known as the *roots* of this equation. Notice two features. First, there are no remainders from the division of $P_n(x)$ by any of its factors. Second, the equation has exactly n roots, when the λ_i are allowed to be complex; see the example of $x^n - 1 = 0$ in the previous paragraph. *Repeated* (or *multiple*) *roots* occur when two or more of the roots λ_i are equal; these are included in the count of the n roots. If λ_i is not repeated, then it is a *simple root*. For example,

$$1 + x - x^2 - x^3 = -(x - 1)(x + 1)^2$$

has the repeated root -1 (twice), and the simple root 1. Finally, let $f(x)$ be a continuous but otherwise unspecified function. The only functional solution to $f(x) + f(y) = f(x+y)$, called *Hamel's equation*, is $f(x) = px$ where p is a constant.

A.3 Series expansions

Polynomials were defined in the previous section. Not all functions are, however, expressible as polynomials of a finite order n. If, by allowing $n \to \infty$, we are able to express a function $f(x)$ as

$$f(x) = \sum_{j=0}^{\infty} a_j (x-b)^j,$$

then we obtain what is known as a *power series* representation of $f(x)$ about the point $x = b$. More generally, an *infinite series* representation of $f(x)$ is a sum of the type

$$f(x) = \sum_{j=0}^{\infty} g_j(x),$$

where $g_j(x)$ is a sequence of functions for $j = 0, 1, \ldots$, and $S_n(x) := \sum_{j=0}^{n-1} g_j(x)$ is known as the *partial sum* of the first n terms of the series.

Before we consider $n \to \infty$, we briefly discuss sequences and limits. Then, we consider infinite series and their properties: types of convergence, special series, expansions of functions, and multiple series.

A.3.1 Sequences and limits

The *maximum* of a set of real numbers $\{x_1, x_2 \ldots\}$ is denoted by $\max_i \{x_i\}$ and is the largest element in this set, which may not be unique. If the sequence is infinitely long, the maximum may not exist; and similarly for the smallest element, the *minimum* $\min_i \{x_i\}$. The *supremum* $\sup_{x \in A} \{x\}$ (or simply $\sup\{x\}$) is the smallest upper bound on the values $x \in A$, and may not be a member of this set. It is unique, when it exists. For example, $x \in [0, 1)$ has no maximum but has $\sup\{x\} = 1$, while the *infimum* is $\inf\{x\} = 0 = \min\{x\}$ here. In general,

$$\sup\{a+bx\} = \begin{cases} a + b\inf\{x\} & (b \leqslant 0), \\ a + b\sup\{x\} & (b \geqslant 0), \end{cases}$$

for $a, b \in \mathbb{R}$.

We briefly consider sets. A collection $\mathcal{A}$ of sets is said to *cover* a set B when $B \subset \bigcup_{A \in \mathcal{A}} A$. When this collection contains only a finite number of sets, we denote it by $\mathcal{A}_\varphi$. Let B be a set made up of some real numbers, and suppose that each collection $\mathcal{A}$ of open sets covering B has a finite subcollection $\mathcal{A}_\varphi$ able to cover B. Then B is said to be *compact*.

A sequence of real numbers is *bounded* if $\inf\{x\} > -\infty$ and $\sup\{x\} < \infty$. These finite bounds are members of the sequence if and only if it is compact. This is a variant of the

Heine–Borel theorem. An implication is the *Bolzano–Weierstrass* theorem, which states that every bounded sequence in $\mathbb{R}$ contains a convergent subsequence.

A possibly surprising result is that there always exists a rational number q between any two real numbers x and y. The rationals are therefore said to be *dense* in the reals. This implies that one can represent any real number as the limit of a sequence of rationals.

Let $\{x_i\}_{i=1}^{\infty}$ be an infinite sequence of numbers. If it converges, say to x, then its terms must ultimately become close to x and hence close to each other. More precisely, if for every $\epsilon > 0$ there exists a constant $n_\epsilon > 0$ such that

$$|x_n - x_m| < \epsilon \quad \text{for all } m, n > n_\epsilon,$$

then $\{x_i\}_{i=1}^{\infty}$ is called a *Cauchy sequence*. If $x_i \in \mathbb{R}$, then a sequence $\{x_i\}_{i=1}^{\infty}$ converges if and only if it is a Cauchy sequence, and the condition for convergence is known as *Cauchy's criterion*. The set $\mathbb{R}$ is then said to be *complete*. If $x_i \in \mathbb{Q}$, the equivalence breaks down: a Cauchy sequence of rationals may not be converging to a rational number, as seen in the previous paragraph. The set $\mathbb{Q}$ is *incomplete*.

A.3.2 Convergence of series

We can now analyze the convergence of series of complex numbers. It suffices to consider series of real numbers, since $\sum_{j=0}^{\infty} (a_j + ib_j)$ converges if and only if both of the real series $\sum_{j=0}^{\infty} a_j$ and $\sum_{j=0}^{\infty} b_j$ converge.

An infinite series *converges* if the limit of its partial sums exists and is finite, that is, if $\lim_{n\to\infty} S_n(x) = S_\infty(x)$ where $|S_\infty(x)| < \infty$. Otherwise, the series is *nonconvergent*. If convergence occurs only for some values of x, then this set of values is called the *convergence region* of the series. A series $\sum_{j=0}^{\infty} g_j(x)$ is *absolutely convergent* if $\sum_{j=0}^{\infty} |g_j(x)|$ converges. If $\sum_{j=0}^{\infty} g_j(x)$ converges but $\sum_{j=0}^{\infty} |g_j(x)|$ does not, then the series is *conditionally convergent*. For example, the *logarithmic series*

$$\log(1+x) = x \sum_{j=0}^{\infty} \frac{(-x)^j}{j+1} = x - \frac{x^2}{2} + \frac{x^3}{3} - \dots$$

converges to $\log 2$ for $x = 1$, but not absolutely so:

$$\lim_{x\to 1^-} \sum_{j=0}^{\infty} \frac{|-1|^j}{j+1} \left|x^{j+1}\right| = \lim_{x\to 1^-} x \sum_{j=0}^{\infty} \frac{x^j}{j+1} = \lim_{x\to 1^-} (-\log(1-x)) = \infty.$$

The unpleasant feature of conditionally convergent series is that the *sequence* of cancelling terms is important, and terms cannot be rearranged *ad infinitum* without changing the value of the sum. This failure of the commutative property of addition for these series can be illustrated by means of our example again:

$$\begin{aligned} \log(2) &= \log(1+1) \\ &= 1 - \frac{1}{2} + \frac{1}{3} - \frac{1}{4} + \frac{1}{5} - \frac{1}{6} + \frac{1}{7} - \frac{1}{8} + \frac{1}{9} - \frac{1}{10} + \frac{1}{11} - \dots =: S. \quad \text{(A.1)} \end{aligned}$$

If this *sequence* is rearranged to another where a negative term follows two consecutive positive terms, the resulting series is equal to

$$1+\frac{1}{3}-\frac{1}{2}+\frac{1}{5}+\frac{1}{7}-\frac{1}{4}+\frac{1}{9}+\frac{1}{11}-\frac{1}{6}+\cdots=\frac{3}{2}S$$

which can be obtained by adding S from (A.1) to

$$0+\frac{1}{2}+0-\frac{1}{4}+0+\frac{1}{6}+\cdots=\frac{1}{2}S.$$

More generally, it can be shown that conditionally convergent series can always be rearranged to give an arbitrary sum.

This example illustrates some key properties. A necessary (but not always sufficient) condition for the convergence of $\sum_{j=0}^{\infty} g_j(x)$ is that $\lim_{j\to\infty} g_j(x) = 0$. It is also a sufficient condition for the convergence of *alternating series* defined by

$$\sum_{j=0}^{\infty} (-1)^j g_j(x),$$

where $g_j(x) \geqslant 0$. When $g_j(x) \geqslant g_{j+1}(x) \geqslant 0$ and $\lim_{j\to\infty} g_j(x) = 0$, the convergence of alternating series can be seen from calculating the partial sums of $(-1)^j g_j(x)$. In general, a sufficient condition for the absolute convergence of $\sum_{j=0}^{\infty} g_j(x)$ is that there is a $\delta > 0$ such that $j^{1+\delta} g_j(x)$ has a finite limit as $j \to \infty$, meaning that the terms $g_j(x)$ decline at least as fast as $1/j^{1+\delta}$.

If the power series $f(x) := \sum_{j=0}^{\infty} a_j (x-b)^j$ converges for all $|x-b| < r$ (that is, within a circle of radius r centered around the point $x = b$ in the complex plane), and r is the largest value for which this convergence holds, then r is called the *radius of convergence*. Power series have the pleasant property that they converge *absolutely* within (but not on) their radius of convergence. The same convergence also holds for their term-by-term or *termwise* derivative, and $\sum_{j=1}^{\infty} j a_j (x-b)^{j-1}$ is the derivative of the function represented by the original series. The same is true for their termwise integrals.

An infinite series may be nonconvergent but nonetheless *summable*, meaning that it represents a finite function. Such series are often encountered in econometrics and statistics, for example in the form of Edgeworth expansions of distribution functions or, more generally, asymptotic expansions to be considered in Section A.3.4 below. One method for working out the sum of a nonconvergent series is as follows. If the average of the partial sums,

$$S_{n,1} := \frac{1}{n}\sum_{i=1}^{n} S_i, \quad n = 1, 2, \ldots,$$

converges to $S_{\infty,1}$ then the original series $S_\infty := \sum_{j=0}^{\infty} g_j(x)$ is *Cesàro-summable-1* (C-1) to $S_{\infty,1}$. (The reason for using C-1, rather than just C, is that the process can be repeated by defining $S_{n,m} := \frac{1}{n}\sum_{i=1}^{n} S_{i,m-1}$ for $m = 2, 3, \ldots$ if $\lim_{n\to\infty} S_{n,m-1}$ does not exist.)

A simple example is

$$\frac{1}{2} = \frac{1}{1+1} = 1 - 1 + 1 - 1 + \cdots,$$

where

$$S_n = \begin{cases} 1 & (n \text{ odd}), \\ 0 & (n \text{ even}), \end{cases} \implies S_{n,1} = \begin{cases} \dfrac{n+1}{2n} & (n \text{ odd}), \\ \dfrac{1}{2} & (n \text{ even}), \end{cases}$$

hence converging to $\frac{1}{2}$ as expected. To be applicable, Cesàro-summability requires a *consistency condition*, namely that the method of summation leads to the same result as $\lim_{n\to\infty} \sum_{j=0}^{n} g_j(x)$ when this series is convergent. In our example, this condition is satisfied because the *geometric progression* $\sum_{j=0}^{\infty}(-x)^j$ converges to $(1+x)^{-1}$ when $|x| < 1$.

Knowing that a series is summable can lead to a relaxation of the sufficient condition for convergence seen earlier. *Hardy's convergence theorem* states that a sufficient condition for the convergence of a C-1 summable series $\sum_{j=0}^{\infty} g_j(x)$ is that $\lim_{j\to\infty} j g_j(x) = c$ (a finite constant), that is, the terms need only decline as fast as $1/j$. Notice that the convergence may not be absolute, as the example of log 2 has illustrated.

A.3.3 Special series

We next discuss some prominent functions whose series expansions are commonly encountered. The stated radii of convergence for these power series follow from the previous section. All the series considered here can be regarded as a generalization of the exponential series introduced in Section A.2, $\mathrm{e}^x = \sum_{j=0}^{\infty} x^j/j!$, which converges absolutely for all $|x| < \infty$. In this appendix, we adopt the alternative approach of defining new series by taking the exponential as the first building block and then adding in some gamma-type function of the index j. Before we tackle these other series, we define the *gamma* (or *generalized factorial*) *function*

$$\Gamma(\nu) := \int_0^{\infty} t^{\nu-1} \mathrm{e}^{-t}\, \mathrm{d}t, \quad \nu \in \mathbb{R}_+.$$

Integrating by parts leads to the recursion $\Gamma(\nu) = (\nu - 1)\Gamma(\nu - 1)$, with $\Gamma(1) = 1$. This recursion is used to extend the definition to any real ν, except $0, -1, \ldots$ for which the limit of $|\Gamma(\nu)|$ is ∞. When the argument of the function is a natural number, this is just the factorial function seen earlier,

$$\Gamma(n) = (n-1)(n-2)\cdots 1 = (n-1)!$$

with $0! = 1$. The *binomial coefficients* can be written as

$$\binom{\nu}{j} := \frac{(\nu)(\nu-1)\cdots(\nu-j+1)}{j!} = \frac{\Gamma(\nu+1)}{\Gamma(\nu-j+1)\, j!}$$

where the definition (the first of the two equalities) is valid for $j = 0, 1, \ldots$ and $\nu \in \mathbb{R}$. When ν takes the values $-1, -2, \ldots$, that is, when $-\nu \in \mathbb{N}$, the ratio of gamma functions is understood to denote the limit obtained by using the recursion $\Gamma(\nu+1) = \nu\Gamma(\nu)$ repeatedly j times. The binomial coefficient is sometimes also written as the *combination symbol* C_j^ν, which is related to the *permutation symbol* P_j^ν by

$$\binom{\nu}{j} \equiv \mathrm{C}_j^\nu \equiv \frac{\mathrm{P}_j^\nu}{j!}.$$

We now introduce various generalizations of the exponential series.

First, for $\nu \in \mathbb{R}$, the *binomial series*

$$(1+x)^\nu = \sum_{j=0}^{\infty} \binom{\nu}{j} x^j = \sum_{j=0}^{\infty} \frac{\Gamma(\nu+1)}{\Gamma(\nu-j+1)} \times \frac{x^j}{j!}$$

converges absolutely for $|x| < 1$. It also converges absolutely when $|x| = 1$ and $\nu \in \mathbb{R}_+$. The series is summable for all $x \in \mathbb{C}\backslash\{-1\}$ when $\nu \in \mathbb{R}_-$ (an illustration is to be found in the previous section), and for all $x \in \mathbb{C}$ when $\nu \in \mathbb{R}_+$. Note that in the excluded case of $x = -1$ when $\nu \in \mathbb{R}_-$, the signs of the terms in the binomial series do *not* alternate as $j \to \infty$.

The second generalization is the logarithmic series introduced in Section A.3.2,

$$\log(1+x) = x \sum_{j=0}^{\infty} \frac{(-x)^j}{j+1} = x \sum_{j=0}^{\infty} \frac{j!j!}{(j+1)!} \times \frac{(-x)^j}{j!},$$

which converges absolutely for $|x| < 1$. It also converges conditionally for $x = 1$, but not for $x = -1$. The *logarithmic function* is defined more generally by $\log(\mathrm{e}^x) := x$, so that it is the inverse of the exponential function, and is multiple-valued. This is so because $x = x\mathrm{e}^{2\mathrm{i}\pi j}$ for $j = 0, 1, \ldots$, implying that

$$\log(x) = \log\left(x\mathrm{e}^{2\mathrm{i}\pi j}\right) \equiv \log\left(|x|\,\mathrm{e}^{\mathrm{i}(\theta+2\pi j)}\right) \equiv \log|x| + \mathrm{i}(\theta + 2\pi j),$$

which is the rectangular (Cartesian) form of the complex function. We restrict our attention to the principal value of the function, which is conventionally taken to be $\log|x| + \mathrm{i}\theta$.

Now define the *hyperbolic functions*

$$\cosh(x) := \frac{\mathrm{e}^x + \mathrm{e}^{-x}}{2}, \quad \sinh(x) := \frac{\mathrm{e}^x - \mathrm{e}^{-x}}{2},$$

$$\tanh(x) := \frac{\sinh(x)}{\cosh(x)} = 1 - \frac{2\mathrm{e}^{-2x}}{1+\mathrm{e}^{-2x}},$$

and the corresponding *trigonometric functions*

$$\cos(x) := \cosh(\mathrm{i}x), \quad \sin(x) := \frac{\sinh(\mathrm{i}x)}{\mathrm{i}},$$

$$\tan(x) := \frac{\sin(x)}{\cos(x)}.$$

Important properties follow from these definitions. First, it is easy to see that $\mathrm{d}\sinh(x)/\mathrm{d}x$

$= \cosh(x)$. Also, simple addition yields

$$\cos(x) + \mathrm{i}\sin(x) = \mathrm{e}^{\mathrm{i}x},$$

which is Euler's formula, stated earlier in Section A.2. From the definition in terms of e^x, we also see that the cosine is an *even function* (that is, it satisfies $f(-x) = f(x)$ for all x) whereas the sine is an *odd function* (that is, it satisfies $f(-x) = -f(x)$ for all x). These functions also have series expansions that are inherited from e^x. For example,

$$\begin{aligned}\cosh(x) &= \sum_{j=0}^{\infty} \frac{\frac{1}{2}\left(x^j + (-x)^j\right)}{j!} \\ &= \sum_{k=0}^{\infty} \frac{\frac{1}{2}\left(x^{2k} + (-x)^{2k}\right)}{(2k)!} + \sum_{k=0}^{\infty} \frac{\frac{1}{2}\left(x^{2k+1} + (-x)^{2k+1}\right)}{(2k+1)!} \\ &= \sum_{k=0}^{\infty} \frac{x^{2k}}{(2k)!}\end{aligned}$$

by splitting the series into two: one where the power of x is even ($2k$) and another where it is odd ($2k+1$). Similarly,

$$\sinh(x) = \sum_{j=0}^{\infty} \frac{\frac{1}{2}\left(x^j - (-x)^j\right)}{j!} = \sum_{k=0}^{\infty} \frac{x^{2k+1}}{(2k+1)!}.$$

Both the $\sinh(x)$ series and the $\cosh(x)$ series converge absolutely for all $|x| < \infty$. Merging and/or splitting series is allowed for series that are absolutely convergent, but not for series that are conditionally convergent, as seen in the previous section.

Finally, *inverse hyperbolic functions* can be defined in terms of the inverse of the exponential, namely the logarithmic function. We have

$$\cosh^{-1}(x) := \log\left(x + \sqrt{x^2 - 1}\right), \quad \sinh^{-1}(x) := \log\left(x + \sqrt{x^2 + 1}\right),$$

$$\tanh^{-1}(x) := \frac{1}{2}\log\left(\frac{1+x}{1-x}\right) = \frac{1}{2}\log\left(1 + \frac{2x}{1-x}\right).$$

One may check this by verifying that $\cosh\left(\log\left(x + \sqrt{x^2 - 1}\right)\right) = x$, using the definition of hyperbolic functions. Because of the logarithmic series, the convergence of the expansions of these inverse hyperbolic functions will depend on the magnitude of x. For example, the equality after the definition of $\tanh^{-1}(x)$ suggests two different expansions, the first one being

$$\tanh^{-1}(x) = \frac{\log(1+x) - \log(1-x)}{2} = \sum_{k=0}^{\infty} \frac{x^{2k+1}}{2k+1},$$

which converges absolutely for $|x| < 1$. Similar relations apply to inverse trigonometric functions.

A.3.4 Expansions of functions

An important question was hinted at in the previous section: does each function have a single series representation? We saw that in general the answer is no, the exponential (and hence hyperbolic) being a rare exception. Not only can one expand functions in different power series $f(x) = \sum_{j=0}^{\infty} a_j (x-b)^j$ centered around a variety of values of b (see Taylor series later), but there are also *asymptotic expansions* that are valid for, say, real $x \to \infty$ (different expansions usually apply for $x \to -\infty$, and some more if we allow x to be complex). These take the form $f(x) = \sum_{j=0}^{\infty} g_j(x)$ where, for $k \in \mathbb{N}$, the ratio $g_{j+k}(x)/g_j(x)$ is decreasing in x as $x \to \infty$. For example,

$$(1+x)^{\nu} = x^{\nu} \sum_{j=0}^{\infty} \binom{\nu}{j} \frac{1}{x^j}$$

is the asymptotic expansion of the left-hand side function. Before we can tackle the specifics of the different expansions of functions, we need to introduce some tools.

We say that a function $f(x)$ is *of order smaller than* x^{α}, written as $f(x) = o(x^{\alpha})$, if $\lim_{x\to\infty} f(x)/x^{\alpha} = 0$, where α is a constant. This definition gives a strict upper bound; a weaker upper bound is given by the following definition. We say that a function $f(x)$ is *at most of order* x^{α}, written as $f(x) = O(x^{\alpha})$, if $f(x)/x^{\alpha}$ is bounded as $x \to \infty$; that is, if for all $x > b$ (a constant) there exists a finite constant c such that

$$\left| \frac{f(x)}{x^{\alpha}} \right| \leqslant c.$$

It should be borne in mind that orders of magnitude are inequality (not equivalence) relations. For example, if $f(x) = o(x^{\alpha})$, then it is also $o\left(x^{\alpha+\delta}\right)$ for any $\delta > 0$. The following relations hold:

- $f(x) = o(x^{\alpha})$ implies (but is not implied by) $f(x) = O(x^{\alpha})$;
- if $f(x) = O(x^{\alpha})$ and $g(x) = O\left(x^{\beta}\right)$, then $f(x)g(x) = O\left(x^{\alpha+\beta}\right)$ and $f(x) + g(x) = O(x^{\max\{\alpha,\beta\}})$, and similarly when O is replaced by o throughout;
- if $f(x) = o(x^{\alpha})$ and $g(x) = O\left(x^{\beta}\right)$, then $f(x)g(x) = o\left(x^{\alpha+\beta}\right)$;
- if $f(x) = o(x^{\alpha})$ and $g(x) = O(x^{\alpha})$, then $f(x) + g(x) = O(x^{\alpha})$.

These relations can be illustrated with simple functions like $f(x) = 3x^2 + x$. Note that $\log(x) \to \infty$ as $x \to \infty$ but $\log(x) = o\left(x^{\delta}\right)$ for any $\delta > 0$, that is, $\log(x)$ is dominated by any positive power of x.

Integrating both sides of an order relation is allowed; for example, $f(x) = O(x^{\alpha})$ implies that $\int f(x)\,\mathrm{d}x = O\left(x^{\alpha+1}\right)$ for $\alpha \neq -1$. However, differentiating requires additional conditions on f, as the following counterexample shows: $f(x) = x^{1.5} + x\cos(x) = O\left(x^{1.5}\right)$ but

$$f'(x) = 1.5x^{0.5} + \cos(x) - x\sin(x) \neq O\left(x^{0.5}\right).$$

The asymptotic monotonicity of f as $x \to \infty$ would have been sufficient to rule out such a counterexample.

Sometimes, the expression $f(x) = O(x^\alpha)$ is not sufficiently precise for the required purpose, since it is actually an inequality relation. The mathematical (not statistical) symbol $\sim$ denotes the *asymptotic equivalence* of the two sides of $f(x) \sim g(x)$, that is, $f(x)/g(x) \to 1$ as $x \to \infty$. The first term of a series expansion, arranged by declining orders of magnitude, is called its *leading term*. In the previous example, we have $f(x) = 3x^2 + x \sim 3x^2$, so that $3x^2$ is the leading term as $x \to \infty$. This could have been written as $f(x) = O(x^2)$ without reference to the constant 3, which is less informative, though often adequate. As an example of a useful asymptotic expansion, we have *Stirling's series*,

$$\Gamma(x) = \sqrt{2\pi}\mathrm{e}^{-x+(x-1/2)\log(x)}\left(1 + \frac{1}{12x} + \frac{1}{288x^2} + O\left(\frac{1}{x^3}\right)\right)$$

for $x \to \infty$ (see Exercise 10.39 for a proof when $x \in \mathbb{N}$), implying that

$$\frac{\Gamma(x+a)}{\Gamma(x+b)} = x^{a-b}\left(1 + \frac{(a-b)(a+b-1)}{2x} + O\left(\frac{1}{x^2}\right)\right) \sim x^{a-b}.$$

These formulae facilitate the derivation of the convergence radii stated in the previous section.

All these concepts can be generalized to expansions around any point other than ∞. For example, the leading term of $f(x) = 3x^2 + x$ as $x \to 0$ becomes the latter term, since $f(x)/x \to 1$ as $x \to 0$, and therefore $f(x) = O(x)$ as $x \to 0$.

If a function $f(x)$ is differentiable an infinite number of times in an open neighborhood of a point b, then it has the *Taylor series* representation

$$f(x) = \sum_{j=0}^{\infty} f^{(j)}(b)\frac{(x-b)^j}{j!},$$

where $f^{(j)}(b)$ is the j-th derivative of $f(x)$ evaluated at $x = b$. *Maclaurin's expansion* is the special case obtained by choosing the point $x = 0$. Taylor's series implies that we can write

$$f(x) = \sum_{j=0}^{n-1} f^{(j)}(b)\frac{(x-b)^j}{j!} + O\left((x-b)^n\right).$$

Taylor's theorem states that for a real-valued function to have this latter representation, it need only be continuously differentiable n times in the closed interval between x and b. The *Lagrange form* of the $O((x-b)^n)$ remainder term is $f^{(n)}(c)(x-b)^n/n!$ for some point c in between x and b. (There exist other forms for the remainder.) The expansion is said to be up to order $n-1$, and the remainder follows from the *mean-value theorem*: a real-valued function $f(x)$, continuous over $[a,b]$ and differentiable over (a,b), will have at least one point $c \in (a,b)$ such that $f'(c) = (f(b) - f(a))/(b-a)$, meaning that $f'(c)$ equals the slope of the chord joining $f(b)$ to $f(a)$.

One important implication is a method of calculating $\lim_{x\to b} g(x)/h(x)$ when $g(b) =$

$h(b) = 0$, known as *l'Hôpital's rule*. It states that if $g(x)$ and $h(x)$ are differentiable in an open neighborhood of $x = b$, then

$$\lim_{x \to b} \frac{g(x)}{h(x)} = \lim_{x \to b} \frac{g'(x)}{h'(x)}.$$

If $g'(b) = h'(b) = 0$, then the process can be repeated with further derivatives. It is assumed that the first nonzero derivative $g^{(j)}(b) \neq 0$ corresponds to $h^{(j)}(b) \neq 0$. The rule would also apply if we had $\lim_{x \to b} |g(x)| = \lim_{x \to b} |h(x)| = \infty$, by working with the reciprocal of these functions (since $\lim_{x \to b} 1/g(x) = \lim_{x \to b} 1/h(x) = 0$). This also shows that it is not necessary for $g(x)$ and $h(x)$ to be differentiable at the point $x = b$, so long as they are differentiable around it.

A.3.5 Multiple series, products, and their relation

Suppose we have a sum over more than one index, called a *multiple series*. If this sum is absolutely convergent, then any two sums in this series may be exchanged. This is a manifestation of a more general result due to Fubini (for integrals) and Tonelli (for measures). Convergent multiple series are a recursive generalization of double series, so that the latter provide a convenient standard form. Rearrange the summand terms of the absolutely convergent $\sum_{j=0}^{\infty} \sum_{k=0}^{\infty} g_{j,k}(x)$ into the array

$$\begin{array}{ccc} g_{0,0}(x) & g_{0,1}(x) & \cdots \\ g_{1,0}(x) & g_{1,1}(x) & \cdots \\ \vdots & \vdots & \end{array}$$

These infinite double sums may be transformed into the infinite sum of a finite series. The former representation consists of summing over the successive rows of the array, whereas the latter calculates the sum diagonally. For example, using a southwest to northeast diagonal, we have

$$\sum_{j=0}^{\infty} \sum_{k=0}^{\infty} g_{j,k}(x) = \sum_{j=0}^{\infty} \sum_{k=0}^{j} g_{j-k,k}(x),$$

which is one way of rewriting the double sum.

Infinite products are related to infinite series. The infinite product $\prod_{j=0}^{\infty}(1 + g_j(x))$ converges absolutely if and only if $\sum_{j=0}^{\infty} g_j(x)$ converges absolutely. However, further care is needed in handling multiple products. For example, $\sum_i \sum_j f_i g_j = \sum_i f_i \sum_j g_j$, but

$$\prod_{i=1}^{m} \prod_{j=1}^{n} (f_i g_j) = \left(\prod_{i=1}^{m} f_i^n \right) \prod_{j=1}^{n} g_j \neq \left(\prod_{i=1}^{m} f_i \right) \prod_{j=1}^{n} g_j$$

for $n \neq 1$. In the case of products, parentheses are needed to avoid ambiguity.

A.4 Further calculus

This section contains some further results on calculus: difference calculus, linear difference equations, Stieltjes integrals, convexity, and constrained optimization. In addition, we just state *Leibniz' rule for differentiating integrals*:

$$\frac{\mathrm{d}}{\mathrm{d}y}\int_{a(y)}^{b(y)} f(x,y)\,\mathrm{d}x = \int_{a(y)}^{b(y)} \frac{\partial f(x,y)}{\partial y}\,\mathrm{d}x + f(b(y),y)\frac{\mathrm{d}b(y)}{\mathrm{d}y} - f(a(y),y)\frac{\mathrm{d}a(y)}{\mathrm{d}y},$$

where a, b, f are differentiable functions of y. We also recall from our companion volume, Abadir and Magnus (2005), the following results for an $m \times 1$ vector $\boldsymbol{x}$. The reader should note the difference between transpose and derivative, as we write $\boldsymbol{f}'(\boldsymbol{x})$ for the derivative of $\boldsymbol{f}$ and $\boldsymbol{f}(\boldsymbol{x})'$ for its transpose. Defining

$$\frac{\partial f(\boldsymbol{x})}{\partial \boldsymbol{x}'} := \left(\frac{\partial f(\boldsymbol{x})}{\partial x_1}, \dots, \frac{\partial f(\boldsymbol{x})}{\partial x_m}\right),$$

$$\frac{\partial^2 f(\boldsymbol{x})}{\partial \boldsymbol{x}\partial \boldsymbol{x}'} := \begin{pmatrix} \partial^2 f(\boldsymbol{x})/\partial x_1^2 & \dots & \partial^2 f(\boldsymbol{x})/\partial x_1 \partial x_m \\ \vdots & & \vdots \\ \partial^2 f(\boldsymbol{x})/\partial x_m \partial x_1 & \dots & \partial^2 f(\boldsymbol{x})/\partial x_m^2 \end{pmatrix},$$

we have the following important examples of derivatives of linear and quadratic forms:

$$\frac{\partial \boldsymbol{x}'\boldsymbol{a}}{\partial \boldsymbol{x}'} = \frac{\partial \boldsymbol{a}'\boldsymbol{x}}{\partial \boldsymbol{x}'} = \boldsymbol{a}' \quad \text{and} \quad \frac{\partial \boldsymbol{x}'\boldsymbol{A}\boldsymbol{x}}{\partial \boldsymbol{x}'} = \boldsymbol{x}'(\boldsymbol{A}+\boldsymbol{A}'), \tag{A.2}$$

for $\boldsymbol{a}$ and $\boldsymbol{A}$ not functions of $\boldsymbol{x}$. (Notice and compare the dimensions on either side of each equation.) We also have, for $\boldsymbol{b}$ in a small neighborhood of $\boldsymbol{x}$,

$$f(\boldsymbol{x}) = f(\boldsymbol{b}) + \left.\frac{\partial f(\boldsymbol{x})}{\partial \boldsymbol{x}'}\right|_{\boldsymbol{x}=\boldsymbol{b}} (\boldsymbol{x}-\boldsymbol{b}) + \frac{1}{2}(\boldsymbol{x}-\boldsymbol{b})' \left.\frac{\partial^2 f(\boldsymbol{x})}{\partial \boldsymbol{x}\partial \boldsymbol{x}'}\right|_{\boldsymbol{x}=\boldsymbol{b}} (\boldsymbol{x}-\boldsymbol{b}) + o\left(\|\boldsymbol{x}-\boldsymbol{b}\|^2\right), \tag{A.3}$$

where f is twice differentiable in an open *hyperrectangle* bounded by $\boldsymbol{x}$ and $\boldsymbol{b}$ (that is, m open intervals bounded by x_i and b_i for $i = 1, \dots, m$). This last equation is Taylor's theorem, to second order. The approximation of f as a quadratic function of $\boldsymbol{x}$ is directly verified by calculating the first two derivatives of (A.3) by means of (A.2): both sides of (A.3) when differentiated will be equal at $\boldsymbol{x} = \boldsymbol{b}$. Notice that for f to be differentiable, it is necessary that the partial derivatives exist. The converse does not hold, as the usual example

$$f(x,y) := \begin{cases} 0 & (x=0, y=0), \\ \dfrac{xy}{x^2+y^2} & \text{(otherwise)}, \end{cases}$$

illustrates: both partials exist ($\partial f/\partial x$ for any fixed y, and $\partial f/\partial y$ for any fixed x), but the function is not even continuous at the origin (for example, take $\lim_{x\to 0} f(x,x)$).

The mean-value theorem applies to a scalar function of a vector; for example,

$$f(\boldsymbol{x}) = f(\boldsymbol{b}) + \left.\frac{\partial f(\boldsymbol{x})}{\partial \boldsymbol{x}'}\right|_{\boldsymbol{x}=\boldsymbol{c}} (\boldsymbol{x}-\boldsymbol{b})$$

for $\boldsymbol{c} := \alpha \boldsymbol{b} + (1-\alpha)\boldsymbol{x}$ with $\alpha \in (0,1)$. The same, however, does not apply to a $k \times 1$ vector function $\boldsymbol{f}(\boldsymbol{x})$; in this case the theorem should be applied to each component $f_j(\boldsymbol{x})$ ($j = 1, \ldots, k$) since $\boldsymbol{c}_j := \alpha_j \boldsymbol{b} + (1-\alpha_j)\boldsymbol{x}$ will differ in general for each j.

Another result which we use frequently from Abadir and Magnus (2005) is the formula for the inverse of a partitioned matrix. Let

$$\boldsymbol{A} := \begin{pmatrix} \boldsymbol{A}_{11} & \boldsymbol{A}_{12} \\ \boldsymbol{A}_{21} & \boldsymbol{A}_{22} \end{pmatrix}.$$

If $\boldsymbol{A}_{11}$ is nonsingular, then the *Schur complement* of $\boldsymbol{A}_{11}$ is $\boldsymbol{A}_{22|1} := \boldsymbol{A}_{22} - \boldsymbol{A}_{21}\boldsymbol{A}_{11}^{-1}\boldsymbol{A}_{12}$ (notice the sequence of subscripts), which has the alternative notation $\boldsymbol{A}_{22\cdot 1}$. Then,

$$\begin{vmatrix} \boldsymbol{A}_{11} & \boldsymbol{A}_{12} \\ \boldsymbol{A}_{21} & \boldsymbol{A}_{22} \end{vmatrix} = |\boldsymbol{A}_{11}| \times |\boldsymbol{A}_{22|1}|.$$

If both $\boldsymbol{A}_{11}$ and $\boldsymbol{A}_{22|1}$ are nonsingular, then

$$\begin{pmatrix} \boldsymbol{A}_{11} & \boldsymbol{A}_{12} \\ \boldsymbol{A}_{21} & \boldsymbol{A}_{22} \end{pmatrix}^{-1} = \begin{pmatrix} \boldsymbol{A}_{11}^{-1} + \boldsymbol{A}_{11}^{-1}\boldsymbol{A}_{12}\boldsymbol{A}_{22|1}^{-1}\boldsymbol{A}_{21}\boldsymbol{A}_{11}^{-1} & -\boldsymbol{A}_{11}^{-1}\boldsymbol{A}_{12}\boldsymbol{A}_{22|1}^{-1} \\ -\boldsymbol{A}_{22|1}^{-1}\boldsymbol{A}_{21}\boldsymbol{A}_{11}^{-1} & \boldsymbol{A}_{22|1}^{-1} \end{pmatrix}.$$

A.4.1 Difference calculus

Before we define the requisite tools for difference calculus, we remind the reader of the definition of the derivative of a function $f(x)$ as

$$f'(x) := \lim_{h\to 0} \frac{f(x+h) - f(x)}{h}.$$

The quantity $f(x+h)$ is the *forward shift* by h of the function $f(x)$, and this can be written in terms of the *forward shift operator* F_h as $\mathrm{F}_h f(x) := f(x+h)$. Clearly, we also have

$$\mathrm{F}_h^2 f(x) = \mathrm{F}_h f(x+h) = f(x+2h)$$

and, more generally, $\mathrm{F}_h^j f(x) = f(x+jh)$ for $j = 0, 1, \ldots$. For negative values of j, we can use instead the *backward shift* (or *lag*) *operator* B_h (or L_h), which can be written similarly as $\mathrm{B}_h f(x) := f(x-h)$; in other words, $\mathrm{B}_h := \mathrm{F}_h^{-1} = \mathrm{F}_{-h}$. The *forward difference operator* is $\Delta_{\mathrm{f},h} := \mathrm{F}_h - 1$, such that $\Delta_{\mathrm{f},h} f(x) = f(x+h) - f(x)$ and $f'(x) := \lim_{h\to 0} \Delta_{\mathrm{f},h} f(x)/h$; the *backward difference operator* is $\Delta_{\mathrm{b},h} := 1 - \mathrm{B}_h$, such that $\Delta_{\mathrm{b},h} f(x) = f(x) - f(x-h)$. Some or all of the subscripts of these operators can be dropped when it is obvious which one is being referred to.

The derivatives inherit well-known properties which are actually obtained from the forward difference, which we shall write simply as Δ henceforth. In particular, we mention:

- $\Delta(cf(x)) = c\Delta f(x)$, where c does not depend on x, and also $\Delta(f(x) + g(x)) = \Delta f(x) + \Delta g(x)$ (*linearity*);
- $\Delta(f(x)g(x)) = f(x)(\Delta g(x)) + (\Delta f(x))g(x) + (\Delta f(x))(\Delta g(x))$ (*product rule*).

The latter relation can be verified by direct substitution of the definition of Δ. Carrying the relation with derivatives further, define the *generalized factorial*

$$x^{(j,h)} := x(x-h)\cdots(x-(j-1)h) = \prod_{i=0}^{j-1}(x-ih) = \frac{h^j\Gamma\left(\frac{x}{h}+1\right)}{\Gamma\left(\frac{x}{h}-j+1\right)}$$

for $j = 0, 1, \ldots$, where empty products are 1 by convention so that $x^{(0,h)} = 1$. There are three comparisons to make here. First, as seen in Chapter 1, the gamma function $\Gamma(x)$ is conventionally called the generalized factorial *function* of x, to distinguish it from the generalized factorial of x, although *generalized permutation* might have been a more appropriate term for the latter (with possible notation $\mathrm{P}^x_{j,h}$). Second, recall from Chapter 3 the j-th factorial moment of x, particularly useful for discrete random variables, which can now be written more concisely as

$$\mathrm{E}\left(x(x-1)\cdots(x-j+1)\right) = \mathrm{E}\left(x^{(j,1)}\right). \tag{A.4}$$

Notice that the notation is slightly different from (but related to) the notation for the j-th moments introduced in Chapter 3, $\mu^{(j)}$ and $\sigma^{(j)}$. When $h = 1$, we write $x^{[j]}$ for short (or P^x_j in terms of permutations). Third,

$$\Delta x^{(j,h)} = jhx^{(j-1,h)},$$

where differencing reduces the order j by 1. For $h = 1$ (to be used later in calculating sums whose index increments by 1), this is the discrete counterpart of the derivative of a power function x^j.

Just as differentiation has integration as its inverse operation, differencing has summing as its inverse. The *sum operator* $\sum$ is defined, up to an arbitrary constant, by $\sum := \Delta^{-1}$ (where it is understood that the summing is done with respect to x, by increments of h) and satisfies:

- $\sum(cf(x)) = c\sum f(x)$, where c does not depend on x, and $\sum(f(x)+g(x)) = \sum f(x) + \sum g(x)$ (*linearity*);
- $\sum(f(x)\Delta g(x)) = f(x)g(x) - \sum(\Delta f(x))g(x+h)$ (*summation by parts*).

The latter formula is the counterpart of integration by parts in differential calculus, and it follows directly by substituting for Δ from its definition, then collecting terms. The reason why the last term is $g(x+h)$, rather than $g(x)$, can be seen from the product rule given earlier. The *fundamental theorem of sum calculus* mirrors that for integrals; it specifies what happens when we have a *definite sum*, one where the upper and lower limits of the sum over x are stated (the previous sums in this paragraph were *indefinite* sums):

$$f(a) + f(a+h) + \cdots + f(a+(n-1)h) = \left[\Delta^{-1}f(x)\right]_a^{a+nh}, \tag{A.5}$$

where $[F(x)]_a^{a+nh} := F(a+nh) - F(a)$ and there is no need for arbitrary constants. Equation (A.5) can be verified by forward-differencing the left-hand side and simplifying it as

$$
\begin{aligned}
&\Delta f(a) + \Delta f(a+h) + \cdots + \Delta f(a+(n-1)h) \\
&\quad = \big(-f(a) + f(a+h)\big) + \big(-f(a+h) + f(a+2h)\big) + \cdots \\
&\qquad + \big(-f(a+(n-1)h) + f(a+nh)\big) \\
&\quad = -f(a) + f(a+nh) = \Delta\left(\Delta^{-1} f(a+nh) - \Delta^{-1} f(a)\right) = \Delta\left[\Delta^{-1} f(x)\right]_a^{a+nh},
\end{aligned}
$$

which is the forward difference of the right-hand side of (A.5).

Students often wonder how the useful formulae

$$
\sum_{x=1}^{n} x = \frac{n(n+1)}{2}, \quad \sum_{x=1}^{n} x^2 = \frac{n(n+1)(2n+1)}{6}, \quad \sum_{x=1}^{n} x^3 = \frac{n^2(n+1)^2}{4}
$$

can be obtained in a constructive way, rather than by the usual method of induction which provides a confirmation only. The answer is: difference calculus! In this case, the increment of the index x is $h = 1$, and we recall that $jx^{[j-1]} = \Delta x^{[j]}$, or equivalently $\Delta^{-1} x^{[j-1]} = j^{-1} x^{[j]}$. For the first sum,

$$
\sum_{x=1}^{n} x = \sum_{x=1}^{n} x^{[1]} = \left[\Delta^{-1} x^{[1]}\right]_1^{1+n} = \left[\frac{x^{[2]}}{2}\right]_1^{1+n} = \left[\frac{x(x-1)}{2}\right]_1^{1+n} = \frac{(n+1)n}{2}.
$$

For the sum of squares, we use $x^2 = x(x-1) + x = x^{[2]} + x^{[1]}$. For the sum of cubes, the result follows from

$$
x^3 = x(x-1)(x-2) + 3x(x-1) + x = x^{[3]} + 3x^{[2]} + x^{[1]},
$$

whose sum is

$$
\begin{aligned}
\left[\Delta^{-1} x^3\right]_1^{1+n} &= \left[\frac{x^{[4]}}{4} + x^{[3]} + \frac{x^{[2]}}{2}\right]_1^{1+n} \\
&= \frac{(n+1)n(n-1)(n-2)}{4} + (n+1)n(n-1) + \frac{(n+1)n}{2} \\
&= \frac{(n+1)n}{4}\left((n-1)(n-2) + 4(n-1) + 2\right) \\
&= \frac{(n+1)n}{4}\left(n^2 + n\right) \\
&= \left(\frac{(n+1)n}{2}\right)^2.
\end{aligned}
$$

Notice that in all three cases, $\sum_{x=1}^{n} x^{p-1} = p^{-1} n^p + o(n^p)$, as expected from the relation between sums and integrals.

A.4.2 Linear difference equations

Let $\{x_1, \ldots, x_n\}$ be a sequence of variables. Suppose that they are related by the *linear difference equation*

$$x_i = c + a_1 x_{i-1} + \cdots + a_p x_{i-p} \quad (i = p+1, \ldots, n),$$

where $p < n$ and p is the *order* of this equation. We assume that the coefficients, the a's and c, do not depend on x. The values $\{x_1, \ldots, x_p\}$ are called the *initial values* (or *boundary conditions*), because they initialize the sequence and allow the recursive calculation of x_{p+1}, followed by x_{p+2}, and so on. Given the initial values, one can solve explicitly for the complete sequence. We now show this by means of matrix algebra.

Define

$$\boldsymbol{y}_i := \begin{pmatrix} x_{i-p+1} \\ \vdots \\ x_i \end{pmatrix}, \quad \boldsymbol{A} := \begin{pmatrix} 0 & 1 & 0 & \ldots & 0 & 0 \\ 0 & 0 & 1 & \ldots & 0 & 0 \\ 0 & 0 & 0 & \ldots & 0 & 0 \\ \vdots & \vdots & \vdots & & \vdots & \vdots \\ 0 & 0 & 0 & \ldots & 0 & 1 \\ a_p & a_{p-1} & a_{p-2} & \ldots & a_2 & a_1 \end{pmatrix}, \quad \boldsymbol{c} := \begin{pmatrix} 0 \\ \vdots \\ 0 \\ c \end{pmatrix},$$

so that the p-th order difference equation can be written as $\boldsymbol{y}_i = \boldsymbol{c} + \boldsymbol{A}\boldsymbol{y}_{i-1}$, which is a first-order difference equation in the vector $\boldsymbol{y}_i$. Repeated substitution gives the solution

$$\boldsymbol{y}_i = \boldsymbol{c} + \boldsymbol{A}\left(\boldsymbol{c} + \boldsymbol{A}\boldsymbol{y}_{i-2}\right) = \cdots = \left(\sum_{j=0}^{i-p-1} \boldsymbol{A}^j\right)\boldsymbol{c} + \boldsymbol{A}^{i-p}\boldsymbol{y}_p$$

in terms of the vector of initial values $\boldsymbol{y}_p$. The square matrix $\boldsymbol{A}$ is known as the *companion matrix* for the *characteristic equation*

$$\lambda^p - a_1\lambda^{p-1} - \cdots - a_p = 0,$$

whose coefficients arise from the right-hand side of the reformulated difference equation:

$$c = x_i - a_1 x_{i-1} - \cdots - a_p x_{i-p} \equiv \left(\mathrm{F}^p - a_1\mathrm{F}^{p-1} - \cdots - a_p\right) x_{i-p},$$

where F is the forward shift operator introduced in Section A.4.1. The eigenvalues of $\boldsymbol{A}$ and the roots of the characteristic equation coincide, and they can be used to decompose powers of $\boldsymbol{A}$ explicitly, for example by a Jordan decomposition of $\boldsymbol{A}$.

A.4.3 Stieltjes integrals

When it exists, the usual *Riemann integral* is defined by

$$\int_a^b g(x)\,\mathrm{d}x := \lim_{\sup\{x_i - x_{i-1}\}\to 0} \sum_{i=1}^m g(c_i)\left(x_i - x_{i-1}\right),$$

with $x_0 := a$, $x_m := b \geqslant a$, and c_i an arbitrary point satisfying $x_{i-1} \leqslant c_i \leqslant x_i$. The *Riemann–Stieltjes* (or *Stieltjes*) *integral* of $g(x)$ with respect to $F(x)$ is defined similarly by replacing x by a function $F(x)$ which is right-continuous and nondecreasing over $[a, b]$:

$$\int_a^b g(x)\,\mathrm{d}F(x) := \lim_{\sup\{x_i - x_{i-1}\}\to 0} \sum_{i=1}^{m} g(c_i)\,(F(x_i) - F(x_{i-1}))\,. \tag{A.6}$$

If $F(x_{i-1}) = F(x_i)$, so that $F(x)$ is not *strictly* increasing over the interval $[x_{i-1}, x_i]$, we take $g(c_i)(F(x_i) - F(x_{i-1})) = 0$ regardless of the value of $g(c_i)$. The definition of the integral can be extended to the case where the function is decreasing by defining $-F(x)$ instead of $F(x)$, which implies that $\int_a^b = -\int_b^a$. It can also be relaxed to the case where $F(x)$ is of bounded variation, subject to some conditions on $g(x)$, but this is only covered at the end of this section.

Clearly, if $F(x)$ is continuously differentiable, then $\mathrm{d}F(x) = f(x)\,\mathrm{d}x$ where $f(x) = \mathrm{d}F(x)/\mathrm{d}x$, and we are back to the simpler Riemann integral of $g(x)f(x)$. If $F(x)$ is differentiable except at certain points, the existence of the integral will depend on the behavior of $g(x)$ at these points. For example, the integral $\int_a^b g(x)\,\mathrm{d}F(x)$ exists if $g(x)$ is continuous on an interval $[a, b]$ of finite length. It also exists if $g(x)$ is bounded and is only discontinuous at a finite number of points, $F(x)$ being continuous at precisely those points. We now list some rules of Stieltjes integration:

- if $\int_a^b g_1(x)\,\mathrm{d}F(x)$ and $\int_a^b g_2(x)\,\mathrm{d}F(x)$ exist, then

$$c\int_a^b g_1(x)\,\mathrm{d}F(x) = \int_a^b c g_1(x)\,\mathrm{d}F(x)\,, \qquad c \text{ constant},$$

$$\int_a^b g_1(x)\,\mathrm{d}F(x) + \int_a^b g_2(x)\,\mathrm{d}F(x) = \int_a^b (g_1(x) + g_2(x))\,\mathrm{d}F(x)\,,$$

  and the right-hand side integrals exist (*linearity with respect to* g);
- if $\int_a^b g(x)\,\mathrm{d}F_1(x)$ and $\int_a^b g(x)\,\mathrm{d}F_2(x)$ exist, then

$$c\int_a^b g(x)\,\mathrm{d}F_1(x) = \int_a^b g(x)\,\mathrm{d}(cF_1(x))\,, \qquad c \text{ constant},$$

$$\int_a^b g(x)\,\mathrm{d}F_1(x) + \int_a^b g(x)\,\mathrm{d}F_2(x) = \int_a^b g(x)\,\mathrm{d}(F_1(x) + F_2(x))\,,$$

  and the right-hand side integrals exist (*linearity with respect to* F);
- if $\int_a^b g(x)\,\mathrm{d}F(x)$ exists and $a < c < b$, then

$$\int_a^b g(x)\,\mathrm{d}F(x) = \int_a^c g(x)\,\mathrm{d}F(x) + \int_c^b g(x)\,\mathrm{d}F(x)\,,$$

  and the right-hand side integrals exist (*interval splitting*);
- if $\int_a^b g(x)\,\mathrm{d}F(x)$ exists, then $\int_a^b F(x)\,\mathrm{d}g(x)$ exists and

$$\int_a^b g(x)\,\mathrm{d}F(x) = [g(x)F(x)]_a^b - \int_a^b F(x)\,\mathrm{d}g(x)\,,$$

  where $[g(x)F(x)]_a^b = g(b)F(b) - g(a)F(a)$ (*integration by parts*);

- if $x = h(y)$ is a strictly increasing and continuous function with inverse $y = h^{-1}(x)$, then

$$\int_a^b g(x)\,\mathrm{d}F(x) = \int_{h^{-1}(a)}^{h^{-1}(b)} g(h(y))\,\mathrm{d}F(h(y)),$$

and the right-hand side integral exists (*change of variables*).

Two of these properties need further consideration.

First, one should be careful in interpreting the property of interval splitting, as the converse of that property is not true in general: the right-hand side integrals may exist without the left-hand side existing. For example, let

$$g(x) = \begin{cases} 1 & (x \leqslant 1), \\ 0 & (x > 1), \end{cases} \quad \text{and} \quad F(x) = \begin{cases} 0 & (x < 1), \\ 1 & (x \geqslant 1). \end{cases}$$

Then $\int_0^1$ and $\int_1^2$ both exist and are obtained from (A.6) as

$$\begin{aligned}\int_0^1 g(x)\,\mathrm{d}F(x) = \int_0^1 \mathrm{d}F(x) &= \lim_{\sup\{x_i - x_{i-1}\}\to 0} \sum_{i=1}^m (F(x_i) - F(x_{i-1})) \\ &= F(1) - F(0) = 1 \end{aligned} \tag{A.7}$$

and $\int_1^2 g(x)\,\mathrm{d}F(x) = 0$. However, $\int_0^2$ does not exist because the sum in (A.6) has no limit: the sum has different values depending on whether we take $c_i = 1$ or $c_i = 1^+$ for some i. The continuity of $g(x)$ at $x = 1$ would have remedied such a problem.

Second, the property of integration by parts applies directly as a result of the property of summation by parts from difference calculus, subject to one of the integrals existing as the limits of the sums are taken, and it applies even if g is not monotone (an example of an integral $\int_a^b F(x)\,\mathrm{d}g(x)$ with nonmonotone g will follow in the discussion of bounded variation below). This leads us to an important feature of this property by letting $g(x) = 1$ over $[a, b]$, and

$$\int_a^b \mathrm{d}F(x) = [F(x)]_a^b - \int_a^b F(x)\,\mathrm{d}g(x) = [F(x)]_a^b = F(b) - F(a);$$

this also follows directly from the definition in (A.6), as applied in (A.7). This is in accordance with (A.5) of the fundamental theorem of sum calculus, which also indicates that when $F(x)$ is a function made up purely of jumps, the lower point of integration a is included in these sums but the upper point b is not. This prevents double counting when splitting an interval is feasible, for example as $\int_0^2 = \int_0^1 + \int_1^2$. It also shows the following subtlety when x is a random variable that has a discrete component. For discrete variates, the p.d.f. is

$$f_x(u) := \Pr(x = u) = F_x(u) - F_x(u^-) = \lim_{h\to 0^+} \Delta_{\mathrm{b},h} F_x(u), \tag{A.8}$$

where the backward difference is used with $h \to 0^+$, rather than the usual $h \to 0$ used to define the derivative of continuous functions. Notice the subscript x of f_x to denote the p.d.f. of the variate, rather than the difference function f implied by the fundamental theorem of sum calculus in (A.5). From (A.5), $F_x(u) - F_x(u^-)$ defines the difference function $f(u^-)$, and so we have the correspondence $f_x(u) = f(u^-)$ rather than $f_x(u) = f(u)$. For example, if the integral exists,

$$\int_{-\infty}^{\infty} u \, \mathrm{d}F_x(u) = \sum_{u \in \mathcal{X}} uf(u^-) = \sum_{u \in \mathcal{X}} uf_x(u) \equiv \mathrm{E}(x). \tag{A.9}$$

Using $f_x(u^-)$ would have given 0 instead of $\mathrm{E}(x)$, since $f_x(u^-) = f_x(u^+) = 0$ for a discrete variate.

Finally, we consider in more detail the existence of the Stieltjes integral for special cases, assuming that $[a, b]$ is an interval of finite length. We have:

- if $I := \int_a^b g(x) \, \mathrm{d}F(x)$ exists, then $\int_a^b |g(x)| \, \mathrm{d}F(x)$ exists and is at least as large as $|I|$ (*absolute integrability*);
- if $g(x)$ is continuous on $[a, b]$ and $\{F_n(x)\}$ is a bounded sequence which satisfies $\lim_{n \to \infty} F_n(x) = F(x)$, and for which each $F_n(x)$ (not necessarily nondecreasing here) is of *bounded variation* on $[a, b]$, that is,

$$\sup_{m, \{x_i\}} \sum_{i=1}^{m} |F_n(x_i) - F_n(x_{i-1})| < \infty, \quad (x_0 := a, \; x_m := b),$$

  then $\int_a^b g(x) \, \mathrm{d}F_n(x) \to \int_a^b g(x) \, \mathrm{d}F(x)$ (*convergence*).

The latter property is especially useful when F_n is a distribution function, hence nondecreasing and of bounded variation. It can also be extended to allow $\lim_{n \to \infty} F_n(x) \neq F(x)$ at the points of discontinuity of F (as is allowed by convergence in distribution), so long as a and b are continuity points of F. This can be seen by using integration by parts, then the continuity of g to discard the points of discontinuity (recall the sentence after (A.6)), and then integration by parts again.

Bounded variation is closely related to a property that we introduced in Chapter 2, in connection with Lebesgue's decomposition. A function $F(x)$ is said to be *absolutely continuous* on $[a, b]$ if, for all $\epsilon > 0$, there exists $\delta_\epsilon > 0$ such that

$$\sum_{i=1}^{m} |b_i - a_i| < \delta_\epsilon \implies \sum_{i=1}^{m} |F(b_i) - F(a_i)| < \epsilon$$

for m arbitrary and (a_i, b_i) nonoverlapping subintervals of $[a, b]$. If F is absolutely continuous on $[a, b]$, then:

- F is also of bounded variation on $[a, b]$; and
- F has a derivative f almost everywhere in $[a, b]$, with f integrable on $[a, b]$ and $\int_a^b g(x) \, \mathrm{d}F(x) = \int_a^b g(x) f(x) \, \mathrm{d}x$.

Note that absolute continuity disposes of the sufficient condition (mentioned at the start of this section) that F be everywhere continuously differentiable for the Stieltjes and Riemann integrals, appearing in the last expression, to give the same result.

The convergence property given earlier should not be confused with the *dominated convergence theorem*, where the integrand is the one that depends on n: if $\lim_n g_n(x)$ exists for all but a countable set of x-values, and we can find an integrable G such that $|g_n(x)| < G(x)$ for all n, then $\lim_n \int g_n(x)\,dx = \int \lim_n g_n(x)\,dx$. The latter theorem can be extended to Stieltjes integrals when the countable set does not include any of the jump points of F. Dominated convergence is sometimes a strong requirement, in which case uniform (in n) integrability is used instead. We shall not cover this latter mode of convergence here; see the corresponding Note to Chapter 10.

A.4.4 Convexity

A *linear combination* of the elements of $\{x_1, \ldots, x_n\}$ is written as $\sum_{i=1}^n a_i x_i$, where the a_i are constants. If $\sum_{i=1}^n a_i = 1$, we call this linear combination a *weighted average*. If, furthermore, $a_i \geqslant 0$ for all i, and hence $a_i \in [0, 1]$, we have a *convex combination*. Similar definitions apply to integrals such as $\int_b^c a(t)x(t)\,dt$.

A real-valued function $f(x)$ defined on an interval is said to be *convex* if

$$f(ax_1 + (1-a)x_2) \leqslant af(x_1) + (1-a)f(x_2)$$

for every $a \in (0, 1)$ and every pair of distinct points x_1 and x_2 in that interval. The function is *strictly convex* if the inequality holds strictly. If $f(x)$ is twice differentiable on an open interval I, then $f(x)$ is convex if and only if $f''(x) \geqslant 0$ for every $x \in I$. A function $f(x)$ is (strictly) *concave* if and only if $-f(x)$ is (strictly) convex.

A.4.5 Constrained optimization

Suppose that a real-valued function $f(x)$ is being minimized over a compact space S. Then, we write $\operatorname{argmin}_{x\in S} f(x) = \widehat{x}$ (or occasionally $\widetilde{x}$) for the points at which the minimum of the function occurs, and $\min_{x\in S} f(x) = f(\widehat{x})$ for the *global* minimum of the function. This global minimum is *strict* if there is only one such point $\widehat{x}$. If the space is not compact, then one should use inf instead of min.

We now consider the problem of optimizing a function subject to restrictions, both differentiable. Let f be a real-valued function defined on a set S in $\mathbb{R}^n$. We consider the minimization of $f(\boldsymbol{x})$ subject to m constraints, say $g_1(\boldsymbol{x}) = 0, \ldots, g_m(\boldsymbol{x}) = 0$, and we write:

$$\begin{aligned} &\text{minimize} \quad f(\boldsymbol{x}) \\ &\text{subject to} \quad \boldsymbol{g}(\boldsymbol{x}) = \mathbf{0}, \end{aligned}$$

where $\boldsymbol{g} := (g_1, g_2, \ldots, g_m)'$ and $\boldsymbol{x} := (x_1, x_2, \ldots, x_n)'$. This is known as a *constrained minimization problem*, and the most convenient way of solving it is, in general, to use the *Lagrange multiplier theory*. Let Γ denote the subset of S on which $\boldsymbol{g}$ vanishes, that is, $\Gamma = \{\boldsymbol{x} : \boldsymbol{x} \in S,\ \boldsymbol{g}(\boldsymbol{x}) = \mathbf{0}\}$, and let $\boldsymbol{c}$ be a point of Γ. We say that:

- f has a local minimum at $\boldsymbol{c}$ under the constraint $\boldsymbol{g}(\boldsymbol{x}) = \mathbf{0}$, if there exists a neighborhood $B(\boldsymbol{c})$ of the point $\boldsymbol{c}$ such that $f(\boldsymbol{x}) \geqslant f(\boldsymbol{c})$ for all $\boldsymbol{x} \in \Gamma \cap B(\boldsymbol{c})$;
- f has a strict local minimum at $\boldsymbol{c}$ under the constraint $\boldsymbol{g}(\boldsymbol{x}) = \mathbf{0}$, if we can choose $B(\boldsymbol{c})$ such that $f(\boldsymbol{x}) > f(\boldsymbol{c})$ for all $\boldsymbol{x} \in \Gamma \cap B(\boldsymbol{c}), \boldsymbol{x} \neq \boldsymbol{c}$;
- f has a global minimum at $\boldsymbol{c}$ under the constraint $\boldsymbol{g}(\boldsymbol{x}) = \mathbf{0}$, if $f(\boldsymbol{x}) \geqslant f(\boldsymbol{c})$ for all $\boldsymbol{x} \in \Gamma$;
- f has a strict global minimum at $\boldsymbol{c}$ under the constraint $\boldsymbol{g}(\boldsymbol{x}) = \mathbf{0}$, if $f(\boldsymbol{x}) > f(\boldsymbol{c})$ for all $\boldsymbol{x} \in \Gamma, \boldsymbol{x} \neq \boldsymbol{c}$.

Lagrange's theorem gives a necessary condition for a constrained minimum to occur at a given point, and establishes the validity of the following formal method ("Lagrange's multiplier method") for obtaining *necessary* conditions for an extremum subject to equality constraints. We first define the *Lagrangian function* ψ by

$$\psi(\boldsymbol{x}) := f(\boldsymbol{x}) - \boldsymbol{\lambda}'\boldsymbol{g}(\boldsymbol{x}),$$

where $\boldsymbol{\lambda}$ is an $m \times 1$ vector of constants $\lambda_1, \dots, \lambda_m$, called the *Lagrange multipliers*; one multiplier is introduced for each constraint. Next we differentiate ψ with respect to $\boldsymbol{x}$ and set the result equal to zero. Together with the m constraints we thus obtain the following system of $n + m$ equations (the *first-order conditions*):

$$\mathrm{d}\psi(\boldsymbol{x}) = 0 \quad \text{for every } \mathrm{d}\boldsymbol{x},$$

$$\boldsymbol{g}(\boldsymbol{x}) = \mathbf{0}.$$

We then try to solve this system of $n + m$ equations in $n + m$ unknowns, and we write the solutions as $\widehat{\lambda}_1, \dots, \widehat{\lambda}_m$ and $\widehat{x}_1, \dots, \widehat{x}_n$. The points $\widehat{\boldsymbol{x}} := (\widehat{x}_1, \dots, \widehat{x}_n)'$ obtained in this way are called *critical points*, and among them are any points of S at which constrained minima or maxima occur.

As a simple example, consider the case where $n = 2$ and $m = 1$:

$$\text{minimize} \quad f(x, y)$$

$$\text{subject to} \quad g(x, y) = 0.$$

We form the Lagrangian function

$$\psi(x, y) := f(x, y) - \lambda g(x, y),$$

and differentiate ψ with respect to x and y. This gives

$$\begin{aligned}\mathrm{d}\psi &= \left(\frac{\partial f}{\partial x}\,\mathrm{d}x + \frac{\partial f}{\partial y}\,\mathrm{d}y\right) - \lambda\left(\frac{\partial g}{\partial x}\,\mathrm{d}x + \frac{\partial g}{\partial y}\,\mathrm{d}y\right)\\ &= \left(\frac{\partial f}{\partial x} - \lambda\frac{\partial g}{\partial x}\right)\mathrm{d}x + \left(\frac{\partial f}{\partial y} - \lambda\frac{\partial g}{\partial y}\right)\mathrm{d}y,\end{aligned}$$

leading to the first-order conditions

$$\frac{\partial f}{\partial x} = \lambda\frac{\partial g}{\partial x}, \quad \frac{\partial f}{\partial y} = \lambda\frac{\partial g}{\partial y}, \quad g(x, y) = 0$$

at the optimum, which can be conveniently rewritten as

$$\frac{\partial f/\partial x}{\partial g/\partial x} = \frac{\partial f/\partial y}{\partial g/\partial y} = \widehat{\lambda}, \quad g(\widehat{x}, \widehat{y}) = 0.$$

The Lagrange multiplier $\widehat{\lambda}$ measures the rate at which the optimal value of the objective function f changes with respect to a small change in the value of the constraint g.

Of course, the question remains whether a given critical point actually yields a minimum, maximum, or neither. To investigate the nature of a given critical point, it is often practical to proceed on an ad hoc basis. If this fails, the following criterion provides sufficient conditions to ensure the existence of a constrained minimum or maximum at a critical point.

Bordered determinantal criterion. Let $\boldsymbol{c}$ be an interior point of S, such that f and $\boldsymbol{g}$ are twice differentiable at $\boldsymbol{c}$, and the $m \times n$ Jacobian matrix $\mathrm{D}\boldsymbol{g}(\boldsymbol{c})$ has full row rank m. Assume that the first-order conditions,

$$\mathrm{d}\psi(\boldsymbol{c}) = 0 \quad \text{for every } \mathrm{d}\boldsymbol{x},$$

$$\boldsymbol{g}(\boldsymbol{c}) = \mathbf{0},$$

hold, and let $\boldsymbol{\Delta}_r$ be the symmetric $(m + r) \times (m + r)$ matrix

$$\boldsymbol{\Delta}_r := \begin{pmatrix} \mathbf{O} & \boldsymbol{B}_r \\ \boldsymbol{B}_r' & \boldsymbol{A}_{rr} \end{pmatrix} \quad (r = 1, \dots, n),$$

where $\boldsymbol{A}_{rr}$ is the $r \times r$ matrix in the northwest corner of

$$\boldsymbol{A} := \mathrm{H}f(\boldsymbol{c}) - \sum_{i=1}^{m} \lambda_i \mathrm{H}g_i(\boldsymbol{c}),$$

the matrices $\mathrm{H}f(\boldsymbol{c})$ and $\mathrm{H}g_i(\boldsymbol{c})$ denote Hessian matrices (second derivatives), and $\boldsymbol{B}_r$ is the $m \times r$ matrix whose columns are the first r columns of $\boldsymbol{B} := \mathrm{D}\boldsymbol{g}(\boldsymbol{c})$. Assume that $|\boldsymbol{B}_m| \neq 0$. (This can always be achieved by renumbering the variables, if necessary.) If

$$(-1)^m |\boldsymbol{\Delta}_r| > 0 \quad (r = m + 1, \dots, n),$$

then f has a strict local minimum at $\boldsymbol{c}$ under the constraint $\boldsymbol{g}(\boldsymbol{x}) = \mathbf{0}$; if

$$(-1)^r |\boldsymbol{\Delta}_r| > 0 \quad (r = m + 1, \dots, n),$$

then f has a strict local maximum at $\boldsymbol{c}$ under the constraint $\boldsymbol{g}(\boldsymbol{x}) = \mathbf{0}$.

Lagrange's theorem gives *necessary* conditions for a local (and hence also for a global) constrained extremum to occur at a given point. The bordered determinantal criterion gives *sufficient* conditions for a local constrained extremum. To find sufficient conditions for a global constrained extremum, it is often convenient to impose appropriate convexity (concavity) conditions.

Criterion under convexity. If the first-order conditions are satisfied, that is,

$$\mathrm{d}\psi(\boldsymbol{c}) = 0 \quad \text{for every } \mathrm{d}\boldsymbol{x},$$

$$\boldsymbol{g}(\boldsymbol{c}) = \boldsymbol{0},$$

and ψ is (strictly) convex on S, then $\boldsymbol{f}$ has a (strict) global minimum at $\boldsymbol{c}$ under the constraint $\boldsymbol{g}(\boldsymbol{x}) = \boldsymbol{0}$. (Of course, if ψ is (strictly) concave on S, then f has a (strict) global maximum at $\boldsymbol{c}$ under the constraint.)

To prove that the Lagrangian function ψ is (strictly) convex or (strictly) concave, several criteria exist. In particular, if the constraints $g_1(\boldsymbol{x}), \dots, g_m(\boldsymbol{x})$ are all linear, and $f(\boldsymbol{x})$ is (strictly) convex, then $\psi(\boldsymbol{x})$ is (strictly) convex. More generally, if the functions $\widehat{\lambda}_1 g_1(\boldsymbol{x}), \dots, \widehat{\lambda}_m g_m(\boldsymbol{x})$ are all concave (that is, for $i = 1, 2, \dots, m$, either $g_i(\boldsymbol{x})$ is concave and $\widehat{\lambda}_i \geqslant 0$, or $g_i(\boldsymbol{x})$ is convex and $\widehat{\lambda}_i \leqslant 0$), and if $f(\boldsymbol{x})$ is convex, then $\psi(\boldsymbol{x})$ is convex; furthermore, if at least one of these $m+1$ conditions is *strict*, then $\psi(\boldsymbol{x})$ is strictly convex.

Finally, suppose that the constraints are $\boldsymbol{g}(\boldsymbol{x}) \geqslant \boldsymbol{0}$ instead of $\boldsymbol{g}(\boldsymbol{x}) = \boldsymbol{0}$. Then, the same function

$$\psi(\boldsymbol{x}) := f(\boldsymbol{x}) - \boldsymbol{\lambda}'\boldsymbol{g}(\boldsymbol{x})$$

leads to the first-order conditions

$$\mathrm{d}\psi(\boldsymbol{x}) = 0 \quad \text{for every } \mathrm{d}\boldsymbol{x},$$

$$\boldsymbol{g}(\boldsymbol{x}) \geqslant \boldsymbol{0} \quad \text{and} \quad \boldsymbol{\lambda} \geqslant \boldsymbol{0},$$

$$g_i(\boldsymbol{x})\lambda_i = 0 \quad \text{for all } i = 1, \dots, m.$$

(This can be checked by introducing artificial variables z_i and writing the constraints as $g_i(\boldsymbol{x}) - z_i^2 = 0$, optimizing as before but now also with respect to the *slack variables* $z_1, \dots, z_m$.) The above conditions are known as the *Kuhn–Tucker conditions* and lead to a constrained minimum for f under certain regularity conditions called constraint qualifications. The additional sign constraints at the optimum, $\widehat{\boldsymbol{\lambda}} \geqslant \boldsymbol{0}$, arise as follows. Suppose that we had the constraint

$$g_i(\boldsymbol{x}) \geqslant a_i,$$

where a_i does not depend on $\boldsymbol{x}$. As a_i is increased, the *inequality* constraint becomes more stringent and the optimum value of the function f to be minimized cannot improve, that is, it increases or stays the same. Recalling that $\widehat{\lambda}_i$ measures the rate at which the optimal value of f changes as g_i changes, the effect of increasing a_i (and hence g_i where the constraint is binding) is that the minimal value of f increases or stays the same. Therefore, this derivative is $\widehat{\lambda}_i \geqslant 0$; it can then be interpreted as the *marginal cost* of the constraint, meaning the loss in the optimal value of f as a_i increases marginally (infinitesimally). If f were being maximized instead of minimized, with the definition of ψ unchanged, then $\widehat{\boldsymbol{\lambda}} \leqslant \boldsymbol{0}$

instead. The final additional restriction at the optimum, $g_i(\widehat{\boldsymbol{x}})\widehat{\lambda}_i = 0$, is a *complementary slackness* condition arising because either the constraint is binding (hence $g_i(\widehat{\boldsymbol{x}}) = 0$) or it has no effect (hence $\widehat{\lambda}_i = 0$).

Notes

In Section A.1, we did not introduce truth tables, which can be used to establish the validity of the rules of indirect proof. Further material on this section can be found in Binmore (1980).

Analysis (typically complex analysis) is a branch of mathematics that has evolved out of calculus. Most of the material covered in Sections A.2 and A.3 can be found in more depth in Whittaker and Watson (1996). Section A.3.1 requires some extra results, which are in Binmore (1981). All the series considered as generalizations of e^x in Section A.3.3 are special cases of the generalized hypergeometric series; see (4.13) in the Notes to Chapter 4 for a definition, and Whittaker and Watson (1996) or Abadir (1999) for a brief introduction.

In Section A.3.4, we did not dwell on differentiability in the case of complex-valued functions. A complex function that is differentiable is called *analytic*. It satisfies the *Cauchy–Riemann equations*, which ensure that differentiating $f(x)$ with respect to $\mathrm{Re}\,(x)$, then with respect to $\mathrm{Im}\,(x)$, will yield the same result as when the derivatives are performed in the reverse order. As a result of these equations, a complex function that is differentiable once will be differentiable an infinite number of times. This is why we defined Taylor's infinite series for complex functions, but switched to real functions when we considered a function that is differentiable only up to order n.

A function defined by a series, which is convergent and analytic in some domain, may have its definition extended to some further domain by a process called analytic continuation. This can provide an alternative proof to the result, stated in Section A.3.3, that the binomial series is summable for all $x \in \mathbb{C}\backslash\{-1\}$.

Finally, we give some references for Section A.4. Difference calculus and difference equations can be found in Spiegel (1971), Stieltjes integrals in Rudin (1976) and Riesz and Sz.-Nagy (1955), and convexity and optimization in Magnus and Neudecker (2019).

Appendix B Notation

Abadir and Magnus (2002) proposed a standard for notation in econometrics. The consistent use of the proposed notation in our volumes shows that it is in fact practical. The notational conventions described below mainly apply to the material covered in this volume. Further notation will be introduced, as needed, as the Series develops.

B.1 Vectors and matrices

Vectors are given in lowercase and matrices in uppercase symbols. Moreover, both vectors and matrices are written in bold-italic. Thus, $\boldsymbol{a}, \boldsymbol{b}, \dots, \boldsymbol{z}$ denote (column) vectors and $\boldsymbol{A}, \boldsymbol{B}, \dots, \boldsymbol{Z}$ denote matrices. Vectors can also be denoted by Greek lowercase letters: $\boldsymbol{\alpha}, \dots, \boldsymbol{\omega}$, and matrices by Greek uppercase letters, such as $\boldsymbol{\Gamma}$, $\boldsymbol{\Theta}$, or $\boldsymbol{\Omega}$. We write

$$\boldsymbol{a} = \begin{pmatrix} a_1 \\ a_2 \\ \vdots \\ a_n \end{pmatrix} \quad \text{and} \quad \boldsymbol{A} = \begin{pmatrix} a_{11} & a_{12} & \dots & a_{1n} \\ a_{21} & a_{22} & \dots & a_{2n} \\ \vdots & \vdots & & \vdots \\ a_{m1} & a_{m2} & \dots & a_{mn} \end{pmatrix}$$

for an $n \times 1$ vector $\boldsymbol{a}$ and an $m \times n$ matrix $\boldsymbol{A}$. When we have a choice, we define a matrix in such a way that the number of rows (m) exceeds or equals the number of columns (n).

We write $\boldsymbol{A} = (a_{ij})$ or $\boldsymbol{A} = (\boldsymbol{A})_{ij}$ to denote a typical element of the matrix $\boldsymbol{A}$. The n columns of $\boldsymbol{A}$ are denoted by $\boldsymbol{a}_{\bullet 1}, \boldsymbol{a}_{\bullet 2}, \dots, \boldsymbol{a}_{\bullet n}$, and the m rows by $\boldsymbol{a}'_{1\bullet}, \boldsymbol{a}'_{2\bullet}, \dots, \boldsymbol{a}'_{m\bullet}$, where a transpose is denoted by a prime. Hence,

$$\boldsymbol{A} = (\boldsymbol{a}_{\bullet 1}, \boldsymbol{a}_{\bullet 2}, \dots, \boldsymbol{a}_{\bullet n}) \quad \text{and} \quad \boldsymbol{A}' = (\boldsymbol{a}_{1\bullet}, \boldsymbol{a}_{2\bullet}, \dots, \boldsymbol{a}_{m\bullet}).$$

However, we write simply $\boldsymbol{A} = (\boldsymbol{a}_1, \boldsymbol{a}_2, \dots, \boldsymbol{a}_n)$, and occasionally $\boldsymbol{A}' = (\boldsymbol{a}_1, \boldsymbol{a}_2, \dots, \boldsymbol{a}_m)$, when there is no possibility of confusion. A vector $\boldsymbol{a}$ denotes a column and $\boldsymbol{a}'$ denotes a row. We denote a general submatrix by $\boldsymbol{A}_{ij}$, so that we can write

$$\boldsymbol{A} := \begin{pmatrix} \boldsymbol{A}_{11} & \boldsymbol{A}_{12} \\ \boldsymbol{A}_{21} & \boldsymbol{A}_{22} \end{pmatrix}.$$

If $\boldsymbol{A}_{11}$ is square and nonsingular, we denote the Schur complement of $\boldsymbol{A}_{11}$ by $\boldsymbol{A}_{22|1} := \boldsymbol{A}_{22} - \boldsymbol{A}_{21}\boldsymbol{A}_{11}^{-1}\boldsymbol{A}_{12}$.

Special vectors and matrices. Some special vectors are:

$\mathbf{0}, \mathbf{0}_n$	null vector $(0, 0, \dots, 0)'$ of order $n \times 1$
$\boldsymbol{\imath}, \boldsymbol{\imath}_n$	sum vector $(1, 1, \dots, 1)'$ of order $n \times 1$
$\boldsymbol{e}_i$	elementary or unit vector, i-th column of identity matrix $\boldsymbol{I}$.

Special matrices are:

$\mathbf{O}, \mathbf{O}_{mn}, \mathbf{O}_{m,n}$	null matrix of order $m \times n$
$\boldsymbol{I}, \boldsymbol{I}_n$	identity matrix of order $n \times n$
$\boldsymbol{K}_{mn}$	commutation matrix
$\boldsymbol{K}_n$	$\boldsymbol{K}_{nn}$
$\boldsymbol{N}_n$	symmetrizer matrix, $\frac{1}{2}(\boldsymbol{I}_{n^2} + \boldsymbol{K}_n)$
$\boldsymbol{D}_n$	duplication matrix
$\boldsymbol{J}_k(\lambda)$	Jordan block of order $k \times k$.

Note that the null vector $\mathbf{0}$ is smaller in appearance than the null matrix $\mathbf{O}$.

Ordering of eigenvalues. If an $n \times n$ matrix $\boldsymbol{A}$ is symmetric, then its eigenvalues are real and can be ordered. We shall order the eigenvalues as

$$\lambda_1 \geqslant \lambda_2 \geqslant \cdots \geqslant \lambda_n,$$

since there are many cases where it is desirable that λ_1 denotes the largest eigenvalue. If $\boldsymbol{A}$ is not symmetric, its eigenvalues are in general complex. The moduli $|\lambda_1|, \dots, |\lambda_n|$ are, however, real. The largest of these is called the *spectral radius* of $\boldsymbol{A}$, denoted $\varrho(\boldsymbol{A})$.

Operations on matrix $\boldsymbol{A}$ and vector $\boldsymbol{a}$. The following standard operations are used:

$\boldsymbol{A}'$	transpose
$\boldsymbol{A}_{\mathrm{s}}$	$\frac{1}{2}(\boldsymbol{A} + \boldsymbol{A}')$, symmetric part of $\boldsymbol{A}$
$\boldsymbol{A}_{\mathrm{a}}$	$\frac{1}{2}(\boldsymbol{A} - \boldsymbol{A}')$, skew-symmetric (anti-symmetric) part of $\boldsymbol{A}$
$\boldsymbol{A}^{-1}$	inverse
$\boldsymbol{A}^{+}$	Moore–Penrose inverse
$\boldsymbol{A}^{-}$	generalized inverse (satisfying only $\boldsymbol{A}\boldsymbol{A}^{-}\boldsymbol{A} = \boldsymbol{A}$)
$\operatorname{dg} \boldsymbol{A}, \operatorname{dg}(\boldsymbol{A})$	diagonal matrix containing the diagonal elements of $\boldsymbol{A}$
$\operatorname{diag}(a_1, \dots, a_n)$	diagonal matrix with $a_1, \dots, a_n$ on the diagonal
$\operatorname{diag}(\boldsymbol{A}_1, \dots, \boldsymbol{A}_n)$	block-diagonal matrix with $\boldsymbol{A}_1, \dots, \boldsymbol{A}_n$ on the diagonal
$\boldsymbol{A}^2$	$\boldsymbol{A}\boldsymbol{A}$

$\boldsymbol{A}^p$	p-th power
$\boldsymbol{A}^{1/2}$	(unique) positive semidefinite square root of $\boldsymbol{A} \geqslant \mathbf{O}$
$\boldsymbol{A}^{\#}$	adjoint (matrix)
$\boldsymbol{A}^*$	conjugate transpose
$\boldsymbol{A}_{ij}$	submatrix
$\boldsymbol{A}_{(k)}$	leading principal submatrix of order $k \times k$
$(\boldsymbol{A}, \boldsymbol{B}), (\boldsymbol{A} : \boldsymbol{B})$	partitioned matrix
$\operatorname{vec} \boldsymbol{A}, \operatorname{vec}(\boldsymbol{A})$	vec operator
$\operatorname{vech} \boldsymbol{A}, \operatorname{vech}(\boldsymbol{A})$	half-vec containing a_{ij} $(i \geqslant j)$
$\operatorname{rk}(\boldsymbol{A})$	rank
$\lambda_i, \lambda_i(\boldsymbol{A})$	i-th eigenvalue (of $\boldsymbol{A}$)
$\operatorname{tr} \boldsymbol{A}, \operatorname{tr}(\boldsymbol{A})$	trace
$\operatorname{etr} \boldsymbol{A}, \operatorname{etr}(\boldsymbol{A})$	$\exp(\operatorname{tr} \boldsymbol{A})$
$\lvert\boldsymbol{A}\rvert, \det \boldsymbol{A}, \det(\boldsymbol{A})$	determinant
$\lVert\boldsymbol{A}\rVert$	norm of matrix $(\sqrt{(\operatorname{tr} \boldsymbol{A}^*\boldsymbol{A})})$
$\lVert\boldsymbol{a}\rVert$	norm of vector $(\sqrt{(\boldsymbol{a}^*\boldsymbol{a})})$
$\boldsymbol{a}_\circ$	normalization of $\boldsymbol{a}$ (such that $\lVert\boldsymbol{a}_\circ\rVert = 1$)
$\boldsymbol{a} \geqslant \boldsymbol{b},\ \boldsymbol{b} \leqslant \boldsymbol{a}$	$a_i \geqslant b_i$ for all i
$\boldsymbol{a} > \boldsymbol{b},\ \boldsymbol{b} < \boldsymbol{a}$	$a_i > b_i$ for all i
$\boldsymbol{A} \geqslant \boldsymbol{B},\ \boldsymbol{B} \leqslant \boldsymbol{A}$	$\boldsymbol{A} - \boldsymbol{B}$ positive semidefinite
$\boldsymbol{A} > \boldsymbol{B},\ \boldsymbol{B} < \boldsymbol{A}$	$\boldsymbol{A} - \boldsymbol{B}$ positive definite
$\boldsymbol{A} \otimes \boldsymbol{B}$	Kronecker product
$\boldsymbol{A} \odot \boldsymbol{B}$	Hadamard product.

A few words of explanation on some of the symbols is required. First, the square root of a positive semidefinite matrix $\boldsymbol{A} = \boldsymbol{S}\boldsymbol{\Lambda}\boldsymbol{S}'$ ($\boldsymbol{S}$ orthogonal, $\boldsymbol{\Lambda}$ diagonal) is defined here as the unique matrix $\boldsymbol{A}^{1/2} = \boldsymbol{S}\boldsymbol{\Lambda}^{1/2}\boldsymbol{S}'$. Next, the conjugate transpose of a complex-valued matrix $\boldsymbol{A} := \boldsymbol{A}_1 + \mathrm{i}\boldsymbol{A}_2$ ($\boldsymbol{A}_1$ and $\boldsymbol{A}_2$ real) is thus given by $\boldsymbol{A}^* = \boldsymbol{A}_1' - \mathrm{i}\boldsymbol{A}_2'$. Then, ambiguity can arise between the symbol $\lvert \cdot \rvert$ for a determinant and the same symbol for an absolute value, for example in the calculation of Jacobians or in the multivariate transformation theorem. This ambiguity can be avoided by writing $\lvert \det \boldsymbol{A}\rvert$ for the absolute value of a determinant. Finally, possible confusion could arise between the notation $\boldsymbol{a} > \mathbf{0}$ and $\boldsymbol{A} > \mathbf{O}$. The first means that each element of $\boldsymbol{a}$ is positive, while the second does *not* mean that each element of $\boldsymbol{A}$ is positive, but rather that $\boldsymbol{A}$ is positive definite.

B.2 Mathematical symbols, functions, and operators

Definitions and implications. We denote definitions, implications, convergence, and transformations as follows:

$\equiv$	identity, equivalence
$a := b, \quad b =: a$	defines a in terms of b
$\Longrightarrow$	implies
$\Longleftrightarrow$	if and only if
$\to, \quad \longrightarrow$	converges to
$x \to c^+, \quad x \downarrow c$	x converges to c from above
$x \to c^-, \quad x \uparrow c$	x converges to c from below
$x \mapsto y$	transformation from x to y.

When dealing with limits of vectors, we use the same notation, writing $\boldsymbol{x} \to \boldsymbol{c}^+$ and $\boldsymbol{x} \to \boldsymbol{c}^-$ for element-by-element convergence from above and below, respectively. This is the context that is predominant in this volume, so it is the default meaning of the notations $\boldsymbol{c}^+$ and $\boldsymbol{c}^-$. Otherwise, we state it explicitly when we mean instead that $\boldsymbol{c}^+$ and $\boldsymbol{c}^-$ are Moore–Penrose or generalized inverses of $\boldsymbol{c}$.

We write $f(x) \approx g(x)$ if the two functions are approximately equal in some sense depending on the context. If $f(x)$ is proportional to $g(x)$, we write $f(x) \propto g(x)$. We say that "$f(x)$ is at most of order $g(x)$" and write $f(x) = O(g(x))$, if $|f(x)/g(x)|$ is bounded above in some neighborhood of $x = c$ (possibly $c = \pm\infty$), and we say that "$f(x)$ is of order less than $g(x)$" and write $f(x) = o(g(x))$, if $f(x)/g(x) \to 0$ when $x \to c$. Finally, we write $f(x) \sim g(x)$ if $f(x)/g(x) \to 1$ when $x \to c$. The two functions are then said to be *asymptotically equal*. Notice that if $f(x)$ and $g(x)$ are asymptotically equal, then $f(x) \approx g(x)$ and also $f(x) = O(g(x))$, but not vice versa. Notice also that O and o denote inequality (not equivalence) relations.

Sets. The usual sets are denoted as follows:

$\mathbb{N}$	natural numbers $1, 2, \ldots$
$\mathbb{Z}$	integers $\ldots, -2, -1, 0, 1, 2, \ldots$
$\mathbb{Q}$	rational numbers
$\mathbb{R}$	real numbers
$\mathbb{C}$	complex numbers.

Superscripts denote the dimension and subscripts the relevant subset. For example, $\mathbb{R}^2 = \mathbb{R} \times \mathbb{R}$ denotes the real plane, $\mathbb{R}^n$ the set of real $n \times 1$ vectors, and $\mathbb{R}^{m \times n}$ the set of real $m \times n$ matrices. The set $\mathbb{R}^n_+$ denotes the positive orthant of $\mathbb{R}^n$, while $\mathbb{Z}_+$ denotes the set of positive integers (hence, $\mathbb{Z}_+ = \mathbb{N}$) and $\mathbb{Z}_{0,+}$ denotes the nonnegative integers. The set $\mathbb{C}^{n \times n}$ denotes the complex $n \times n$ matrices.

Set differences are denoted by a backslash. For example, $\mathbb{N} = \mathbb{Z}_{0,+} \backslash \{0\}$. Real-line intervals defined for x in $a < x \leqslant b$ are denoted by $(a, b]$. Keep in mind the distinction between (a, b) and $(a, b - \epsilon]$, where $\epsilon > 0$ and small. The latter is said to be an interval that is *bounded away* from b. Occasionally it might be unclear whether (a, b) indicates a real-line interval or a point in $\mathbb{R}^2$. In that case the interval $a < x < b$ can alternatively be written as $]a, b[$.

Sequences are special ordered sets and are delimited, as usual, by braces (curly brackets). It is often convenient to write $\{\boldsymbol{Z}_j\}_{j=m}^n$ for the sequence of matrices $\boldsymbol{Z}_m, \boldsymbol{Z}_{m+1}, \dots, \boldsymbol{Z}_n$, or $\{\boldsymbol{Z}_n\}$ for $\{\boldsymbol{Z}_j\}_{j=1}^n$ where we drop the index j (which conveys no additional information in this case) unless this leads to ambiguity.

Let $p \in \mathbb{R}_+$. The space l_p consists of real (or complex) sequences $(x_1, x_2, \dots)$ satisfying $\sum_{i=1}^\infty |x_i|^p < \infty$, while the space L_p contains all real (or complex) variables x satisfying $\int |x(t)|^p \,\mathrm{d}t < \infty$.

Other set-related symbols are:

$\in$	belongs to
$\notin$	does not belong to
$\{x : x \in S, x \text{ satisfies } \mathcal{P}\}$	set of all elements of S with property $\mathcal{P}$
$\forall$	for all
$\exists, \nexists$	there exists, there does not exist
$A \subseteq B, B \supseteq A$	A is a subset of B
$A \subset B, B \supset A$	A is a proper subset of B
$A_1 \bigcup A_2, \bigcup_{i=1}^n A_i$	union of the sets A.
$A_1 \bigcap A_2, \bigcap_{i=1}^n A_i$	intersection of the sets A.
$\varnothing$	empty set
Ω	universal set, sample space
A^c	complement of A
$B \backslash A$	$B \cap A^c$.

Functions. We denote functions by:

$f : S \to T$	function defined on S with values in T
$f, g, \varphi, \psi, \vartheta$	scalar-valued function
$\boldsymbol{f}, \boldsymbol{g}$	vector-valued function
$\boldsymbol{F}, \boldsymbol{G}$	matrix-valued function
$\boldsymbol{g} \circ \boldsymbol{f}, \boldsymbol{G} \circ \boldsymbol{F}$	composite function
$g * f$	convolution, $(g * f)(x) := \int_{-\infty}^{\infty} g(y) f(x - y) \,\mathrm{d}y$.

Calculus. The treatment of lowercase single-letter constants is somewhat controversial. For example, the base of natural logarithms e and the imaginary unit i are often written as e and i. The same applies to operators (such as the differential operator d, often written as d). We recommend the use of roman letters in order to avoid potential confusion with variables (such as the index i in $i = 1, \dots, n$ or the distance $d(\cdot, \cdot)$). Thus, we write:

d	differential
d^n	n-th order differential
$\mathrm{D}_j \varphi(\boldsymbol{x})$	partial derivative, $\partial \varphi(\boldsymbol{x}) / \partial x_j$
$\mathrm{D}_j f_i(\boldsymbol{x})$	partial derivative, $\partial f_i(\boldsymbol{x}) / \partial x_j$

$\mathrm{D}^2_{kj}\varphi(\boldsymbol{x})$	second-order partial derivative, $\partial \mathrm{D}_j\varphi(\boldsymbol{x})/\partial x_k$
$\mathrm{D}^2_{kj}f_i(\boldsymbol{x})$	second-order partial derivative, $\partial \mathrm{D}_j f_i(\boldsymbol{x})/\partial x_k$
$\varphi^{(n)}(x)$	n-th order derivative of $\varphi(x)$
$\mathrm{D}\varphi(\boldsymbol{x}), \partial\varphi(\boldsymbol{x})/\partial\boldsymbol{x}'$	derivative of $\varphi(\boldsymbol{x})$
$\mathrm{D}\boldsymbol{f}(\boldsymbol{x}), \partial\boldsymbol{f}(\boldsymbol{x})/\partial\boldsymbol{x}'$	derivative (Jacobian matrix) of $\boldsymbol{f}(\boldsymbol{x})$
$\mathrm{D}\boldsymbol{F}(\boldsymbol{X})$	derivative (Jacobian matrix) of $\boldsymbol{F}(\boldsymbol{X})$
$\partial \operatorname{vec} \boldsymbol{F}(\boldsymbol{X})/\partial(\operatorname{vec}\boldsymbol{X})'$	derivative of $\boldsymbol{F}(\boldsymbol{X})$, alternative notation
$\nabla\varphi, \nabla\boldsymbol{f}, \nabla\boldsymbol{F}$	gradient (transpose of derivative)
$\mathrm{H}\varphi(\boldsymbol{x}), \partial^2\varphi(\boldsymbol{x})/\partial\boldsymbol{x}\partial\boldsymbol{x}'$	second derivative (Hessian matrix) of $\varphi(\boldsymbol{x})$
F_h	forward shift operator, $\mathrm{F}_h f(x) := f(x+h)$
$\mathrm{B}_h, \mathrm{L}_h$	backward shift (or lag) operator, $\mathrm{B}_h f(x) := f(x-h)$ or $\mathrm{B}_h := \mathrm{F}_h^{-1} = \mathrm{F}_{-h}$
$\Delta_{\mathrm{f},h}$	forward difference operator, $\Delta_{\mathrm{f},h} := \mathrm{F}_h - 1$
$\Delta_{\mathrm{b},h}$	backward difference operator, $\Delta_{\mathrm{b},h} := 1 - \mathrm{B}_h$
$[f(x)]_a^b,\ f(x)\|_a^b$	$f(b) - f(a)$
$f(x)\|_{x=a}$	$f(a)$.

Some or all of the subscripts of the operators of difference calculus can be dropped when it is obvious which one is being referred to. Also, instead of $\varphi^{(1)}(x)$ and $\varphi^{(2)}(x)$, we may write the more common $\varphi'(x)$ and $\varphi''(x)$, but otherwise we prefer to reserve the prime for matrix transposes rather than derivatives. To emphasize the difference between transpose and derivative, we write $\boldsymbol{f}'(\boldsymbol{x})$ for the derivative of $\boldsymbol{f}$ and $\boldsymbol{f}(\boldsymbol{x})'$ for the transpose.

The Stieltjes (or Riemann–Stieltjes) integral of a function ψ with respect to F is denoted by $\int_{\mathbb{R}^m} \psi(\boldsymbol{x})\,\mathrm{d}F(\boldsymbol{x})$ for $\boldsymbol{x} \in \mathbb{R}^m$, where $\mathrm{d}F(\boldsymbol{x})$ is interpreted as $\partial_{x_1}\dots\partial_{x_m}F(\boldsymbol{x})$. The subscript of the partial differentials denotes the variable that is changing while the others are kept fixed; for instance, we have $f(\boldsymbol{x})\,\mathrm{d}x_m\dots\mathrm{d}x_1$ in the case where F is absolutely continuous. This is the notation commonly used in statistics, though it is not ideal from a mathematical point of view: our $\mathrm{d}F(\boldsymbol{x})$ should not be confused with the total differential $\sum_{j=1}^m(\partial F(\boldsymbol{x})/\partial x_j)\,\mathrm{d}x_j$.

The Fourier transform of $f(x)$ is denoted by $\mathcal{F}_\tau\{f(x)\}$, where the subscript τ indicates the parameter of the transformation. This transform operator possesses an inverse given by $\mathcal{F}_x^{-1}\{\varphi(\tau)\}$, where x is now the parameter of the inverse Fourier transform of the function $\varphi(\tau)$. There is little scope for confusing the Fourier operator with a sigma-algebra or sigma-field $\mathcal{F}$.

Other mathematical symbols and functions. We also use:

i	imaginary unit
$\|x\|$	absolute value (modulus) of scalar $x \in \mathbb{C}$
x^*	complex conjugate of scalar $x \in \mathbb{C}$
$\mathrm{Re}(x)$	real part of x
$\mathrm{Im}(x)$	imaginary part of x

e, exp	exponential
$\arg(x)$	argument of $x \in \mathbb{C}$
!	factorial
P_j^ν	permutation symbol
C_j^ν, $\binom{\nu}{j}$	combination symbol, binomial coefficient
$\Gamma(x), \Gamma(\nu, x)$	gamma (generalized factorial) and incomplete gamma functions
$x^{(j,h)}$	generalized factorial, $h^j \Gamma(\frac{x}{h}+1)/\Gamma(\frac{x}{h}-j+1)$ or $\prod_{i=0}^{j-1}(x-ih)$ for $j=0,1,\ldots$
$B(x,y), I_v(x,y)$	beta and incomplete beta functions
ϕ, Φ	normal density and distribution functions
log	natural logarithm
$\log_a$	logarithm to the base a
cos, sin, tan, cot	trigonometric functions
cosh, sinh, tanh, coth	hyperbolic functions
δ_{ij}	Kronecker delta: equals 1 if $i=j$, 0 otherwise
$\operatorname{sgn}(x)$	sign of x
$\lfloor x \rfloor, \operatorname{int}(x)$	integer part of x, that is, largest integer $\leqslant x$
$1_{\mathcal{K}}$	indicator function (1, not I): equals 1 if condition $\mathcal{K}$ is satisfied, 0 otherwise
$B(\boldsymbol{c})$	neighborhood (ball) with center $\boldsymbol{c}$
$\max\{\ldots\}, \sup\{\ldots\}$	maximum, supremum of a set of elements
$\min\{\ldots\}, \inf\{\ldots\}$	minimum, infimum of a set of elements
$\operatorname{argsup} f(x), \operatorname{arginf} f(x)$	value of x that optimizes a function $f(x)$.

Note that $\Gamma(x)$ is conventionally called the generalized factorial *function* of x, to distinguish it from $x^{(j,h)}$ which is the generalized factorial of x, although *generalized permutation* might have been a more appropriate term for the latter (with possible notation $\mathrm{P}_{j,h}^x$). Notice the slightly different (but related) notation $m^{(j)}(t)$ for the j-th derivative of a function $m(t)$. When $h=1$, we write $x^{[j]}$ for short (or P_j^x in terms of permutations).

We have used $\{x_i\}_{i=1}^n$ or $\{x_n\}$ to summarize a sequence of x's. However, when optimizing over (or, more generally, selecting from) this sequence, we use $\{x_i\}$ not $\{x_n\}$; for example, we write $\max_i\{x_i\}$ where, if necessary, we can be more explicit about the range of the index such as in $\max_{i \leqslant n}\{x_i\}$. See the u.a.n. in Exercise 10.37 for an illustration, which also shows that using $\{x_n\}$ instead of $\{x_i\}$ would have led to an ambiguity because of the presence of λ_n as well as x_i inside the sequence.

We write $x = f^{-1}(y)$ to denote the *inverse* function; for example, $x = \tanh^{-1}(y)$ means that $y = \tanh(x)$. For the *reciprocal* of a function, we write $y = f(x)^{-1} = 1/f(x)$.

B.3 Statistical symbols, functions, operators, distributions, and abbreviations

In this section of the appendices, we revert to the convention about f and x that was used before Appendix A. We use x to denote a random variable, u its realization, $\mathcal{X}$ its support, and $f_x(u)$ and $F_x(u)$ its density and distribution functions. When no ambiguity arises about the variate in question, we drop the subscript x. When we have up to three variates, they are denoted by x, y, z with realizations u, v, w and supports $\mathcal{X}, \mathcal{Y}, \mathcal{Z}$, respectively.

Let $\boldsymbol{x}$ be a random vector with support $\mathcal{X}$. Its realization is denoted by $\boldsymbol{w}$. We reserve boldface $\boldsymbol{u}$ and $\boldsymbol{v}$ for their traditional use in regression analysis (for example in Chapter 13); hence the choice of $\boldsymbol{w}$ as the realization of $\boldsymbol{x}$. With m up to 3, we can write $\boldsymbol{w} := (u, v, w)'$ as the realization of $\boldsymbol{x} := (x, y, z)'$ to avoid unnecessary subscripts. If some ambiguity arises when using $\mathcal{X}$ for the support of $\boldsymbol{x}$ as well as that of x, we can avoid this by subscripting the support with the relevant variable. If we have n random vectors, we use $\boldsymbol{x}_i$ and $\boldsymbol{w}_i$, with $i = 1, \dots, n$. With n up to 3, we write $\boldsymbol{x}, \boldsymbol{y}, \boldsymbol{z}$ with realizations $\boldsymbol{w}_{\boldsymbol{x}}, \boldsymbol{w}_{\boldsymbol{y}}, \boldsymbol{w}_{\boldsymbol{z}}$, in which case the elements of $\boldsymbol{x}$ must now be denoted by $x_1, x_2, \dots$, even if $m \leqslant 3$, and likewise for $\boldsymbol{y}$ and $\boldsymbol{z}$. For variates having special names, such as the sample mean $\overline{\boldsymbol{x}}$, we write $\boldsymbol{w}_{\overline{\boldsymbol{x}}}$ for the realization. Note that the sample mean $\overline{\boldsymbol{x}}$ is random, just like the $\boldsymbol{x}_1, \dots, \boldsymbol{x}_n$ on which it is based.

The (raw) moments of a variate are denoted by $\mu^{(j)}$, where j is the order of the moment, and we write $\mu := \mu^{(1)}$ for the expectation of this variate. The central moments are denoted by $\sigma^{(j)}$, and we write $\sigma^2 := \sigma^{(2)}$ for the variance of this variate. We use $\boldsymbol{\mu} = (\mu_i)$ to denote the expectation of a vector variate and $\boldsymbol{\Sigma} = (\sigma_{ij})$ to denote its variance matrix (with $\sigma_i^2 := \sigma_{ii}$ for the diagonal). This does not conflict with the notation we use for the j-th raw moment of component x_i, written as $\mu_i^{(j)}$.

A parameter vector is denoted by $\boldsymbol{\theta}$. If this vector is allowed to vary, we denote it by $\boldsymbol{\vartheta}$. We also use the following:

$\sim$	distributed as
$\overset{a}{\sim}$	asymptotically distributed as
$\Pr(\cdot), \Pr(\cdot \mid \cdot)$	probability, conditional probability
$\Pr_F, \Pr_{\boldsymbol{\theta}}, \Pr_{\mathrm{H}}$	probability under some distribution F, or its parameters $\boldsymbol{\theta}$, or a hypothesis H
q_α, q	the α quantile of x, with $q_{1/2}$ or $\operatorname{med}(x)$ denoting the median
$Q_x(\alpha)$	quantile function
u_{M}	mode of x
$\mathrm{E}(\cdot), \mathrm{E}_x(\cdot)$	expectation, expectation taken with respect to x
$\mathrm{E}(\cdot \mid y), \mathrm{E}_{x\mid y}(\cdot)$	conditional expectation (given y)
$\operatorname{var}(\cdot), \operatorname{cov}(\cdot, \cdot)$	variance, covariance
$\operatorname{var}(\cdot \mid y), \operatorname{var}_{x\mid y}(\cdot)$	conditional variance
$\operatorname{corr}(\cdot, \cdot), \rho_{\cdot,\cdot}, \rho$	correlation
$\operatorname{corr}(x, z \mid y), \rho_{x,z\mid y}$	conditional (on y) correlation of x and z
$\operatorname{corr}(x, z \cdot y), \rho_{x,z\cdot y}$	partial correlation of x and z

$\rho^{\max}_{x_1,\boldsymbol{x}_2}, \overline{\rho}_{x_1,\boldsymbol{x}_2}$	canonical correlation coefficient between x_1 and $\boldsymbol{x}_2$: equals $(\boldsymbol{\sigma}'_{21}\boldsymbol{\Sigma}^{-1}_{22}\boldsymbol{\sigma}_{21}/\sigma_{11})^{1/2}$, the multiple correlation coefficient
$m(t)$	moment-generating function
$\varkappa(t)$	cumulant-generating function (cumulants are denoted by κ_j and excess kurtosis by κ)
$\varpi(\tau)$	factorial-moment-generating function, or probability-generating function if the variate is discrete
$\varphi(\tau)$	characteristic function
$C(F_1(w_1), \dots, F_m(w_m))$	copula function
$\mathrm{H}(f_z, f_x)$	Hellinger distance between f_z and f_x
$\mathrm{KL}(f_z, f_x)$	Kullback–Leibler divergence or information criterion
$\mathrm{KL}_{1\mid 2}(f_{x_1\mid x_2=u}, f_{y_1\mid y_2=u})$	conditional Kullback–Leibler divergence between conditionals
$\mathrm{KL}(f_{x_1\mid x_2}, f_{y_1\mid y_2=x_2})$	Kullback–Leibler divergence between conditionals, $\mathrm{KL}(f_{x_1\mid x_2}, f_{y_1\mid y_2=x_2}) := \mathrm{E}_{x_2}(\mathrm{KL}_{1\mid 2}(f_{x_1\mid x_2}, f_{y_1\mid y_2=x_2}))$
$\to, \longrightarrow$	converges almost surely
$\xrightarrow{p}$	converges in probability
$\xrightarrow{d}$	converges in distribution
plim	probability limit
$O_p(g(x))$	at most of probabilistic order $g(x)$
$o_p(g(x))$	of probabilistic order less than $g(x)$
$\overline{x}, \overline{\boldsymbol{x}}$	sample mean
$s^2, \boldsymbol{S}$	sample variance
R	sample multiple correlation coefficient
R^2	coefficient of determination
t, T^2	t-ratio (or t-statistic), Hotelling's T^2
$L(\boldsymbol{\theta})$	likelihood function
$L_{\mathrm{p}}(\boldsymbol{\theta}_1)$	profile likelihood for the parameter subset $\boldsymbol{\theta}_1$
$L_{\mathrm{m}}(\boldsymbol{\theta}_1)$	(Barndorff-Nielsen's) modified profile likelihood for $\boldsymbol{\theta}_1$
$\ell(\boldsymbol{\theta})$	log-likelihood function
$\boldsymbol{q}(\boldsymbol{\theta})$	score vector
$\boldsymbol{\mathcal{H}}(\boldsymbol{\theta})$	Hessian matrix
$\boldsymbol{\mathcal{I}}(\boldsymbol{\theta})$	(Fisher) information matrix
$\mathrm{eff}_n(\cdot, \cdot)$	relative efficiency of two estimators based on a sample of size n (Pitman's ARE of two tests is denoted by $A_{\cdot,\cdot}$)
$\mathrm{bias}(\widehat{\boldsymbol{\theta}})$	bias of $\widehat{\boldsymbol{\theta}}$
$\mathrm{MSE}(\widehat{\boldsymbol{\theta}})$	mean squared error of $\widehat{\boldsymbol{\theta}}$
$C(\widehat{\boldsymbol{\theta}})$	loss (cost) function for $\widehat{\boldsymbol{\theta}}$
$\mathrm{risk}(\widehat{\boldsymbol{\theta}}), \mathrm{risk}_{\mathrm{b}}(\widehat{\boldsymbol{\theta}}), \mathrm{risk}_{\mathrm{p}}(\widehat{\boldsymbol{\theta}})$	frequentist, Bayesian, and posterior risks of $\widehat{\boldsymbol{\theta}}$
$K(\cdot), K_{\mathrm{e}}(\cdot), K_{\mathrm{n}}(\cdot)$	kernel function, Epanechnikov kernel, normal kernel
α, β, Π or $\Pi_\tau(\boldsymbol{\theta})$	Type I error (size), Type II error, power of test τ as a function of $\boldsymbol{\theta}$ (with $\Pi \equiv 1 - \beta$)

C_α	critical region of size α
$\wp, LR, LM_q, LM_\lambda, W$	test statistics: GLR, LR, LM using the score $\boldsymbol{q}$, LM using Lagrange multipliers $\boldsymbol{\lambda}$, Wald (see the list of abbreviations at the end of this section)
$\tau_1 \overset{a}{=} \tau_2$	asymptotic equality of two statistics, τ_1 and τ_2.

Notice that the symbol $\to$ indicates both deterministic convergence and a.s. convergence (since it is typically clear whether the context is one of randomness or not), and that C is used for copulas (multiple arguments of the C function) and for loss functions (single argument). Notice also that the t-ratio is not necessarily t-distributed; the former is denoted by italics to distinguish it from the latter. Finally, for a sample $x_1, \dots, x_n$, we write the order statistics as $y_1, \dots, y_n$, instead of the more elaborate $x_{(1)}, \dots, x_{(n)}$, which could be used if there is scope for misunderstandings.

An estimator of $\boldsymbol{\theta}$ is denoted $\widehat{\boldsymbol{\theta}}$ and, if there is a second estimator, by $\widetilde{\boldsymbol{\theta}}$. Notable exceptions include the well-established $\overline{x}, s^2$, and the occasional uses of $\widetilde{x}$ and r for the sample median and correlation, respectively. Estimators are also denoted by hats for operators, such as $\widehat{\mathrm{var}}, \widehat{\mathrm{cov}}, \widehat{\mathrm{corr}}, \widehat{\mathrm{med}}$. Predictors are like estimators, except that they say something about a random variable. They are also denoted by hats ($\widehat{\boldsymbol{y}}, \widehat{\boldsymbol{\varepsilon}}$) or tildes ($\widetilde{\boldsymbol{y}}, \widetilde{\boldsymbol{\varepsilon}}$). The realization of a predictor is called a prediction. Notice the notation $\boldsymbol{\varepsilon}$ for disturbances (or errors); it is random and its notation differs from the ϵ seen in Section B.2 for deterministic small deviations. Notice also that we use $\boldsymbol{\varepsilon}$ if the errors are spherically distributed; otherwise we denote them by $\boldsymbol{u}$.

We denote a null hypothesis by H_0 and the alternative to it by H_1. If there exist r restrictions on $\boldsymbol{\theta}$ we write these as $\boldsymbol{h}(\boldsymbol{\theta}) = \mathbf{0}_r$ or, in the case of one restriction, as $h(\boldsymbol{\theta}) = 0$. The derivative of $\boldsymbol{h}(\boldsymbol{\theta})$ is an $r \times m$ matrix $\boldsymbol{R}(\boldsymbol{\theta})' := \partial \boldsymbol{h}(\boldsymbol{\theta})/\partial \boldsymbol{\theta}'$, specializing to a $1 \times m$ row vector $\boldsymbol{r}(\boldsymbol{\theta})'$ in the case $r = 1$. This special case also clarifies why we tend not to use $\boldsymbol{H}$ for the matrix of derivatives of $\boldsymbol{h}$, as the reduction of dimensions when $r = 1$ would lead to conflicting notation (h for both the constraint and its derivative). We use $\boldsymbol{R}(\boldsymbol{\theta})$ for the transpose of $\boldsymbol{R}(\boldsymbol{\theta})'$.

The notation is chosen so that it corresponds to the linear case, where we write the constraint as $\boldsymbol{R}'\boldsymbol{\theta} = \boldsymbol{c}$ for $\boldsymbol{R}$ a matrix of constants. The statement of H_0 as $\boldsymbol{R}'\boldsymbol{\theta} = \boldsymbol{c}$ is preferred to $\boldsymbol{R\theta} = \boldsymbol{r}$. In the latter formulation, the single-hypothesis case is usually written as $\boldsymbol{r}'\boldsymbol{\theta} = r$, which is not ideal. However, if one writes $\boldsymbol{R}'\boldsymbol{\theta} = \boldsymbol{c}$, this specializes to $\boldsymbol{r}'\boldsymbol{\theta} = c$ in the case of one constraint. This has the additional advantage that we can use r to denote the number of restrictions (the order of $\boldsymbol{c}$). In the special case where $\boldsymbol{R} = \boldsymbol{I}_r$ (or where $\boldsymbol{R}$ is square and invertible, called "linear invertible"), we usually write $\boldsymbol{\theta} = \boldsymbol{\theta}_0$ rather than $\boldsymbol{\theta} = \boldsymbol{c}$. In contrast with the constant $\boldsymbol{\theta}_0$ used in the case of $\boldsymbol{\theta}$ being fully specified by H_0, we write estimators that are restricted by H_0 but not fully specified by it as $\widetilde{\boldsymbol{\theta}}$.

Distributions. We denote by $x \sim \mathrm{D}_{\mathcal{X}}(\boldsymbol{\theta})$ a random variable $x \in \mathcal{X}$ varying according to some distribution (or law) D which depends on a vector of parameters $\boldsymbol{\theta}$. When the support is unambiguous and/or standardized, the subscript $\mathcal{X}$ is dropped. We sometimes also require the use of a subscript for the distribution when denoting its quantile; for example, $\mathrm{D}_{0.05}$ represents the 5% quantile of distribution D. Thus, the 5% quantile of the normal is $\mathrm{N}_{0.05} \approx -1.645$ (exact to three decimal places), because $\Pr(x < -1.645) \approx 5\%$ for a normal distribution. The first type of subscript is a set, whereas the latter is a real number from the interval $[0, 1]$, so no ambiguities arise. Multivariate distributions may also require the use of subscripts to denote the dimension of the variate, which is a natural number, hence there is still no scope for ambiguities; for example, N_m denotes the m-dimensional normal distribution.

A random sample is denoted by $x_i \sim \mathrm{IID}_{\mathcal{X}}(\boldsymbol{\theta})$, where $i = 1, \ldots, n$, and this is the abbreviation of "the x_i's are independently and identically distributed (or i.i.d.) as $\mathrm{D}_{\mathcal{X}}(\boldsymbol{\theta})$". There is some redundancy in this notation, in the sense that the distributions are clearly identical over i whenever $\mathcal{X}$ and $\boldsymbol{\theta}$ do not vary with i. For this reason, when drawing from $\mathrm{N}(\mu, \sigma^2)$, we write $x_i \sim \mathrm{IN}(\mu, \sigma^2)$, where $i = 1, \ldots, n$, dropping the "identical" from $\mathrm{IIN}(\mu, \sigma^2)$. We denote sequences, which are ordered sets, just as we denoted sets: with braces (curly brackets). We therefore also use the shorthand notation $\{x_n\} \sim \mathrm{IID}_{\mathcal{X}}(\boldsymbol{\theta})$.

In the following list, we use p for probability in the discrete case, but p for power in the continuous case where we also use α, β for location, δ for noncentrality, λ for scaling, and ν (or n, m) for the shape (or degrees of freedom) of the density:

$\mathrm{U}_{\{n,m\}}$	discrete uniform
$\mathrm{Bin}(n, p)$	binomial
$\mathrm{Ber}(p)$	Bernoulli
$\mathrm{Nbin}(\nu, p)$	negative binomial
$\mathrm{Geo}(p)$	geometric
$\mathrm{Hyp}(m, k, n)$	hypergeometric, negative hypergeometric
$\mathrm{Poi}(\lambda)$	Poisson
$\mathrm{Beta}_{(\alpha,\beta)}(p, q)$, $\mathrm{Beta}(p, q)$	beta, standard ($x \in (0, 1)$) beta
$\mathrm{U}_{(\alpha,\beta)}$, U	continuous uniform, standard ($x \in (0, 1)$) continuous uniform
$\mathrm{N}(\mu, \sigma^2)$	normal (or Gaussian)
$\mathrm{IG}(\mu, \sigma^2)$	inverse Gaussian
$\mathrm{LN}(\alpha, \lambda^2)$	log-normal
$\mathrm{Gum}(\alpha, \lambda)$	Gumbel
$\mathrm{GG}(\nu, p, \lambda)$, $\mathrm{Gam}(\nu, \lambda)$	generalized gamma, gamma
$\mathrm{Wei}(p, \lambda)$	Weibull
$\chi^2(n, \delta)$, $\chi^2(n)$	noncentral chi-squared, (central) chi-squared
$\mathrm{Expo}(\lambda)$	exponential
$\mathrm{Lap}(\mu, \lambda)$	Laplace
$\mathrm{Lgst}(\mu, \sigma^2)$	logistic
$\mathrm{F}(m, n, \delta)$, $\mathrm{F}(m, n)$	noncentral F, Fisher–Snedecor (central) F
$\mathrm{t}(n, \delta)$, $\mathrm{t}(n)$	noncentral t, Student's (central) t
$\mathrm{Cau}(\alpha, \lambda)$	Cauchy
$\mathrm{Par}_{(\alpha,\infty)}(p)$	Pareto

$S^p(\alpha, \lambda, \nu)$	stable (or Lévy–Khinchine)
$EC_m(\boldsymbol{c}, \boldsymbol{A})$	elliptical (elliptically contoured)
$N_m(\boldsymbol{\mu}, \boldsymbol{\Sigma})$	multivariate normal
$W_m(\nu, \boldsymbol{\Sigma}, \boldsymbol{\Delta})$	noncentral Wishart, with $W_1(\nu, \sigma^2, \delta) \equiv \sigma^2 \cdot \chi^2(\nu, \delta/\sigma^2)$
$W_m(\nu, \boldsymbol{\Sigma})$	(central) Wishart.

Abbreviations and acronyms. We list these in a logical rather than alphabetical sequence, and divide them into a handful of loose categories. The listing is close to the order in which they arise in the main text:

r.v.	random variable
c.d.f.	cumulative distribution function
p.d.f.	probability density function
[f.]m.g.f.	[factorial-]moment-generating function
p.g.f.	probability-generating function
c.g.f.	cumulant-generating function
c.f.	characteristic function
KLIC	Kullback–Leibler information criterion
PIT	probability integral transform
LIE	law of iterated expectations

i.i.d.	independent and identically distributed
$\text{IID}(\boldsymbol{\theta})$	independent and identical drawings from $D(\boldsymbol{\theta})$
a.s.	almost surely
i.o.	infinitely often
u.a.n.	uniform asymptotic negligibility (condition)
CMT	continuous mapping theorem
[S]LLN, [W]LLN	[strong], [weak] law of large numbers
[F]CLT	[functional] central limit theorem
SLT	stable limit theorem
LIL	law of the iterated logarithm
EVT	extreme value theory
GEV	generalized extreme value (distribution)

ARE	asymptotic relative efficiency
BAN	best asymptotically normal
B[L]UE	best [linear] unbiased estimator
UMVUE	uniformly minimum variance estimator (same as BUE)
CRLB	Cramér–Rao lower bound
[A][I]MSE	[asymptotic] [integrated] mean squared error
ISE	integrated squared error

DGP	data-generating process
GLM	generalized linear model
AR(p)	auto-regressive process of order p
MM, MOM	method of moments
[E]MM, [G]MM	[efficient], [generalized] method of moments
LAD	least absolute deviations
[C]LS, [G]LS, [O]LS	[constrained], [generalized], [ordinary] least squares
ML	maximum likelihood
EDF	empirical distribution function
EL	empirical likelihood
EM	estimation-maximization (algorithm)
NP	nonparametric
[LS]CV	[LS] cross validation
CI	confidence interval
HPD	highest posterior density (region)
MPR	most powerful region
UMP[U][I]	uniformly most powerful [unbiased] [invariant]
LM	Lagrange multiplier
[G]LR	[generalized] likelihood ratio
MLR	monotone likelihood ratio.

Estimation methods can be suffixed by E to denote an estimator; for example, MLE denotes a maximum-likelihood estimator. Notice the difference in font between LR in this table (the abbreviation) and LR (the test statistic) at the end of the first table in this section.

Bibliography

Abadir, K. M. (1993a). The limiting distribution of the autocorrelation coefficient under a unit root, *Annals of Statistics*, 21, 1058–1070.

Abadir, K. M. (1993b). On the asymptotic power of unit root tests, *Econometric Theory*, 9, 189–221. [See also https://rebrand.ly/UnitRt]

Abadir, K. M. (1995). The limiting distribution of the t ratio under a unit root, *Econometric Theory*, 11, 775–793.

Abadir, K. M. (1999). An introduction to hypergeometric functions for economists, *Econometric Reviews*, 18, 287–330.

Abadir, K. M. (2005). The mean–median–mode inequality: counterexamples, *Econometric Theory*, 21, 477–482.

Abadir, K. M. and A. Cornea-Madeira (2018). Link of moments before and after transformations, with an application to resampling from fat-tailed distributions, *Econometric Theory*, forthcoming.

Abadir, K. M. and S. Lawford (2004). Optimal asymmetric kernels, *Economics Letters*, 83, 61–68.

Abadir, K. M. and M. Lubrano (2016). Explicit solution for the asymptotically-optimal bandwidth in cross validation, mimeo.

Abadir, K. M. and T. Magdalinos (2002). The characteristic function from a family of truncated normal distributions, *Econometric Theory*, 18, 1276–1287. (Extended solution to problem posed by Horrace and Hernandez, 2001.)

Abadir, K. M. and J. R. Magnus (2002). Notation in econometrics: a proposal for a standard, *Econometrics Journal*, 5, 76–90.

Abadir, K. M. and J. R. Magnus (2004a). Normal's deconvolution and the independence of sample mean and variance, *Econometric Theory*, 20, 805–807.

Abadir, K. M. and J. R. Magnus (2004b). The central limit theorem for Student's distribution, *Econometric Theory*, 20, 1261–1263.

Abadir, K. M. and J. R. Magnus (2005). *Matrix Algebra*, Econometric Exercises, Cambridge University Press, Cambridge. [See also https://rebrand.ly/EctExe1]

Abadir, K. M. and J. R. Magnus (2007). A statistical proof of the transformation theorem, in *The Refinement of Econometric Estimation and Test Procedures: Finite Sample and Asymptotic Analysis* (eds. G. D. A. Phillips and E. Tzavalis), 319–325, Cambridge University Press, Cambridge.

Akaike, H. (1974). A new look at the statistical model identification, *IEEE Transactions on Automatic Control*, 19, 716–723.

Anderson, T. W. (1984). *An Introduction to Multivariate Statistical Analysis*, 2nd edition, John Wiley & Sons, New York.

Baba, K., R. Shibata and M. Sibuya (2004). Partial correlation and conditional correlation as measures of conditional independence, *Australian & New Zealand Journal of Statistics*, 46, 657–664.

Bain, L. J. and M. Engelhardt (1992). *Introduction to Probability and Mathematical Statistics*, 2nd edition, Duxbury Press, Belmont, CA.

Barndorff-Nielsen, O. E. (1980). Conditionality resolutions, *Biometrika*, 67, 293–310.

Barndorff-Nielsen, O. E. and D. R. Cox (1989). *Asymptotic Techniques for Use in Statistics*, Chapman & Hall/CRC, FL.

Barndorff-Nielsen, O. E., R. D. Gill and P. E. Jupp (2003). On quantum statistical inference, (with discussion), *Journal of the Royal Statistical Society, B*, 65, 775–816.

Benjamini, Y. and Y. Hochberg (1995). Controlling the false discovery rate: a practical and powerful approach to multiple testing, *Journal of the Royal Statistical Society, B*, 57, 289–300.

Bera, A. K. and Y. Bilias (2001). Rao's score, Neyman's $C(\alpha)$ and Silvey's LM tests: an essay on historical developments and some new results, *Journal of Statistical Planning and Inference*, 97, 9–44.

Beran, R. (1977). Minimum Hellinger distance estimates for parametric models, *Annals of Statistics*, 5, 445–463.

Berger, J. O. (1982). Selecting a minimax estimator of a multivariate normal mean, *Annals of Statistics*, 10, 81–92.

Bernardo, J. M. and A. F. M. Smith (2000). *Bayesian Theory*, John Wiley & Sons, Chichester.

Billingsley, P. (1995). *Probability and Measure*, 3rd edition, John Wiley & Sons, New York.

Billingsley, P. (1999). *Convergence of Probability Measures*, 2nd edition, John Wiley & Sons, New York.

Binmore, K. G. (1980). *Logic, Sets and Numbers*, Cambridge University Press, Cambridge.

Binmore, K. G. (1981). *Topological Ideas*, Cambridge University Press, Cambridge.

Breiman, L. (1992). *Probability*, Classics in Applied Mathematics, SIAM, Philadelphia.

Brown, L. D. (1990). An ancillarity paradox which appears in multiple linear regression, (with discussion), *Annals of Statistics*, 18, 471–538.

Casella, G. and R. L. Berger (2002). *Statistical Inference*, 2nd edition, Duxbury Press, Belmont, CA.

Casella, G. and J. T. Hwang (2012). Shrinkage confidence procedures, *Statistical Science*, 27, 51–60.

Catchpole, E. A. and B. J. T. Morgan (1997). Detecting parameter redundancy, *Biometrika*, 84, 187–196.

Černý, A. (2004). *Mathematical Techniques in Finance: Tools for Incomplete Markets*, Princeton University Press, Princeton.

Chan, N. H. and C. Z. Wei (1987). Asymptotic inference for nearly nonstationary AR(1) processes, *Annals of Statistics*, 15, 1050–1063.

Chung, K. L. (1974). *A Course in Probability Theory*, Academic Press, San Diego.

Cleveland, W. S. (1979). Robust locally weighted regression and smoothing scatterplots, *Journal of the American Statistical Association*, 74, 829–836.

Cline, D. B. H. (1988). Admissible kernel estimators of a multivariate density, *Annals of Statistics*, 16, 1421–1427.

Cochran, W. G. (1977). *Sampling Techniques*, 3rd edition, John Wiley & Sons, New York.

Conaway, M., C. Pillers, T. Robertson and J. Sconing (1990). The power of the circular cone test: a noncentral chi-bar-squared distribution, *Canadian Journal of Statistics*, 18, 63–70.

Cook, R. D. and S. Weisberg (1982). *Residuals and Influence in Regression*, Chapman & Hall, London.

Cox, D. R. (1970). The continuity correction, *Biometrika*, 57, 217–219.

Cox, D. R. and D. V. Hinkley (1974). *Theoretical Statistics*, Chapman & Hall, London.

Cox, D. R. and N. Reid (1987). Parameter orthogonality and approximate conditional inference, *Journal of the Royal Statistical Society, B*, 49, 1–39.

Cox, D. R. and N. Wermuth (2003). A general condition for avoiding effect reversal after marginalization, *Journal of the Royal Statistical Society, B*, 65, 937–941.

Craig, C. C. (1936). On the frequency function of xy, *Annals of Mathematical Statistics*, 7, 1–15.

Cressie, N. and T. R. C. Read (1984). Multinomial goodness-of-fit tests, *Journal of the Royal Statistical Society, B*, 46, 440–464.

Critchley, F., P. Marriott and M. Salmon (1996). On the differential geometry of the Wald test with nonlinear restrictions, *Econometrica*, 64, 1213–1222.

Curtiss, J. H. (1942). A note on the theory of moment generating functions, *Annals of Mathematical Statistics*, 13, 430–433.

Dagenais, M. G. and J.-M. Dufour (1991). Invariance, nonlinear models, and asymptotic tests, *Econometrica*, 59, 1601–1615.

D'Agostino, R. B. and M. A. Stephens (eds.) (1986). *Goodness-of-Fit Techniques*, Marcel Dekker, New York.

Daniels, H. E. (1944). The relation between measures of correlation in the universe of sample permutations, *Biometrika*, 33, 129–135.

Das Gupta, S. and M. D. Perlman (1974). Power of the noncentral F-test: effect of additional variates on Hotelling's T^2-test, *Journal of the American Statistical Association*, 69, 174–180.

Davidson, R. and J. G. MacKinnon (2004). *Econometric Theory and Methods*, Oxford University Press, New York.

Davies, R. B. (1977). Hypothesis testing when a nuisance parameter is present only under the alternative, *Biometrika*, 64, 247–254.

Davies, R. B. (1987). Hypothesis testing when a nuisance parameter is present only under the alternative, *Biometrika*, 74, 33–43.

Dempster, A. P., N. M. Laird and D. B. Rubin (1977). Maximum likelihood from incomplete data via the EM algorithm, (with discussion), *Journal of the Royal Statistical Society, B*, 39, 1–38.

Denny, J. L. (1969). Note on a theorem of Dynkin on the dimension of sufficient statistics, *Annals of Mathematical Statistics*, 40, 1474–1476.

Denny, J. L. (1972). Sufficient statistics and discrete exponential families, *Annals of Mathematical Statistics*, 43, 1320–1322.

Diaconis, P. and D. Ylvisaker (1979). Conjugate priors for exponential families, *Annals of Statistics*, 7, 269–281.

Dickey, D. A. and W. A. Fuller (1979). Distribution of the estimators for autoregressive time series with a unit root, *Journal of the American Statistical Association*, 74, 427–431.

Dufour, J.-M. (1997). Some impossibility theorems in econometrics with applications to structural and dynamic models, *Econometrica*, 65, 1365–1387.

Durbin, J. (1960). Estimation of parameters in time-series regression models, *Journal of the Royal Statistical Society, B*, 22, 139–153.

Durbin, J. (1980). Approximations for densities of sufficient estimators, *Biometrika*, 67, 311–333.

Dynkin, E. B. (1951). Necessary and sufficient statistics for a family of probability distributions, *Uspekhi Matematicheskikh Nauk*, 6, 68–90. (Translated, 1961, in *Selected Translations in Mathematical Statistics and Probability*, 1, 17–40.)

Eaton, M. L. (1989). *Group Invariance Applications in Statistics*, Regional Conference Series in Probability and Statistics, vol. 1, Institute of Mathematical Statistics and American Statistical Association, Hayward and Alexandria.

Efron, B. (1979). Bootstrap methods: another look at the jackknife, *Annals of Statistics*, 7, 1–26.

Efron, B. (2006). Minimum volume confidence regions for a multivariate normal mean vector, *Journal of the Royal Statistical Society, B*, 68, 655–670.

Efron, B. and C. Stein (1981). The jackknife estimate of variance, *Annals of Statistics*, 9, 586–596.

Embrechts, P., C. Klüppelberg and T. Mikosch (1997). *Modelling Extremal Events*, Springer-Verlag, Berlin.

Erdélyi, A. (ed.) (1953). *Higher Transcendental Functions*, vols. 1 and 2, McGraw-Hill,

New York.

Erdélyi, A. (ed.) (1955). *Higher Transcendental Functions*, vol. 3, McGraw-Hill, New York.

Etheridge, A. (2002). *A Course in Financial Calculus*, Cambridge University Press, Cambridge.

Evans, G. B. A. and N. E. Savin (1981). Testing for unit roots: 1, *Econometrica*, 49, 753–779.

Evans, G. B. A. and N. E. Savin (1982). Conflict among the criteria revisited; the W, LR and LM tests, *Econometrica*, 50, 737–748.

Evans, M. J., D. A. S. Fraser and G. Monette (1986). On principles and arguments to likelihood, (with discussion), *Canadian Journal of Statistics*, 14, 181–199.

Fan, J. and J. S. Marron (1992). Best possible constant for bandwidth selection, *Annals of Statistics*, 20, 2057–2070.

Feller, W. (1968). *An Introduction to Probability Theory and its Applications*, vol. 1, 3rd edition, John Wiley & Sons, New York.

Feller, W. (1971). *An Introduction to Probability Theory and its Applications*, vol. 2, 2nd edition, John Wiley & Sons, New York.

Ferguson, T. S. (1989). Who solved the secretary problem? (with discussion), *Statistical Science*, 4, 282–296.

Flemming, J. S. (1973). The consumption function when capital markets are imperfect: the permanent income hypothesis reconsidered, *Oxford Economic Papers*, 25, 160–172.

Fraser, D. A. S. (2004). Ancillaries and conditional inference, *Statistical Science*, 19, 333–369.

Frisch, R. and F. V. Waugh (1933). Partial time regressions as compared with individual trends, *Econometrica*, 1, 387–401.

Gallant, A. R. and G. Tauchen (1996). Which moments to match? *Econometric Theory*, 12, 657–681.

Ghazal G. A. (1994). Moments of the ratio of two dependent quadratic forms, *Statistics & Probability Letters*, 20, 313–319.

Ghosh, J. K. (1994). *Higher Order Asymptotics*, NSF-CBMS Regional Conference Series in Probability and Statistics, vol. 4, Institute of Mathematical Statistics and American Statistical Association, Hayward and Alexandria.

Gilchrist, W. (2000). *Statistical Modelling with Quantile Functions*, Chapman & Hall/ CRC, FL.

Godambe, V. P. (1960). An optimum property of regular maximum likelihood estimation, *Annals of Mathematical Statistics*, 31, 1208–1211.

Godfrey, L. G. (1988). *Misspecification Tests in Econometrics: The Lagrange Multiplier Principle and Other Approaches*, Cambridge University Press, Cambridge.

Goldberger, A. S. (1991). *A Course in Econometrics*, Harvard University Press, Harvard.

Gordon, L. (1994). A stochastic approach to the gamma function, *American Mathematical Monthly*, 101, 858–865.

Gouriéroux, C. and A. Monfort (1995). *Statistics and Econometric Models*, vols. 1 and 2,

Cambridge University Press, Cambridge.

Gouriéroux, C., A. Monfort and A. Trognon (1984). Pseudo maximum likelihood methods: theory, *Econometrica*, 52, 681–700.

Graybill, F. A. and G. Marsaglia (1957). Idempotent matrices and quadratic forms in the general linear hypothesis, *Annals of Mathematical Statistics*, 28, 678–686.

Grimmett, G. and D. Stirzaker (2001). *Probability and Random Processes*, 3rd edition, Oxford University Press, Oxford.

Hahn, J. and W. Newey (2004). Jackknife and analytical bias reduction for nonlinear panel models, *Econometrica*, 72, 1295–1319.

Hald, A. (1998). *A History of Mathematical Statistics from 1750 to 1930*, John Wiley, New York.

Hall, P. (1994). Methodology and theory for the bootstrap, in *Handbook of Econometrics*, vol. 4 (eds. R. F. Engle and D. L. McFadden), 2341–2381, Elsevier Science, Amsterdam.

Hall, P., S. N. Lahiri and Y. K. Truong (1995). On bandwidth choice for density estimation with dependent data, *Annals of Statistics*, 23, 2241–2263.

Hallin, M., D. Paindaveine and M. Šiman (2010). Multivariate quantiles and multiple-output regression quantiles: from L_1 optimization to halfspace depth, (with discussion), *Annals of Statistics*, 38, 635–703.

Hamburger, H. (1920). Über eine erweiterung des Stieltjesschen momentproblems, *Mathematische Zeitschrift*, 7, 235–319.

Hampel, F. R., E. M. Ronchetti, P. J. Rousseeuw and W. A. Stahel (1986). *Robust Statistics: The Approach Based on Influence Functions*, John Wiley & Sons, New York.

Hannan, E. J. and B. G. Quinn (1979). The determination of the order of an autoregression, *Journal of the Royal Statistical Society, B*, 41, 190–195.

Hansen, B. E. (2005). Exact mean integrated squared error of higher order kernel estimators, *Econometric Theory*, 21, 1031–1057.

Hansen, L. P. (1982). Large sample properties of generalized method of moments estimators, *Econometrica*, 50, 1029–1054.

Hardin, C. D. (1982). On the linearity of regression, *Zeitschrift für Wahrscheinlichkeitstheorie und verwandte Gebiete*, 61, 293–302.

Härdle, W., G. Kerkyacharian, D. Picard and A. Tsybakov (1998). *Wavelets, Approximation, and Statistical Applications*, Springer-Verlag, New York.

Härdle, W. and O. Linton (1994). Applied nonparametric methods, in *Handbook of Econometrics*, vol. 4 (eds. R. F. Engle and D. L. McFadden), 2295–2339, Elsevier Science, Amsterdam.

Hart, J. D. and P. Vieu (1990). Data-driven bandwidth choice for density estimation based on dependent data, *Annals of Statistics*, 18, 873–890.

Hartigan, J. A. (1998). The maximum likelihood prior, *Annals of Statistics*, 26, 2083–2103.

Hastie, T. and R. Tibshirani (1986). Generalized additive models, (with discussion), *Statistical Science*, 1, 297–318.

Heijmans, R. D. H. and J. R. Magnus (1986a). Consistent maximum-likelihood estimation with dependent observations: the general (non-normal) case and the normal case, *Journal of Econometrics*, 32, 253–285. [See also (1987) 35, 395.]

Heijmans, R. D. H. and J. R. Magnus (1986b). On the first-order efficiency and asymptotic normality of maximum likelihood estimators obtained from dependent observations, *Statistica Neerlandica*, 40, 169–188.

Hendry, D. F. (1976). The structure of simultaneous equations estimators, *Journal of Econometrics*, 4, 51–88.

Hill, T. P. (1995). A statistical derivation of the significant-digit law, *Statistical Science*, 10, 354–363.

Hochberg, Y. (1988). A sharper Bonferroni procedure for multiple tests of significance, *Biometrika*, 75, 800–802.

Hoeffding, W. (1948). A class of statistics with asymptotically normal distribution, *Annals of Mathematical Statistics*, 19, 293–325.

Hoffmann-Jørgensen, J. (1994). *Probability with a View Toward Statistics*, vol. 1, Chapman & Hall, London.

Hogg, R. V. and A. T. Craig (1989). *Introduction to Mathematical Statistics*, 4th edition, Macmillan, New York.

Holm, S. (1979). A simple sequentially rejective multiple test procedure, *Scandinavian Journal of Statistics*, 6, 65–70.

Hommel, G. (1988). A stagewise rejective multiple test procedure based on a modified Bonferroni test, *Biometrika*, 75, 383–386.

Horrace, W. C. and C. Hernandez (2001). The characteristic function from a family of truncated normal distributions, *Econometric Theory*, 17, 1026.

Hu, T.-C. (1988). A statistical method of approach to Stirling's formula, *American Statistician*, 42, 204–205.

Huber, P. J. (1981). *Robust Statistics*, John Wiley & Sons, New York.

Huber, P. J. (1985). Projection pursuit, (with discussion), *Annals of Statistics*, 13, 435–525.

Hull, J. (1989). *Options, Futures, and Other Derivative Securities*, Prentice-Hall, New Jersey.

Hwang, J. T. and A. Ullah (1994). Confidence sets centered at James–Stein estimators: a surprise concerning the unknown-variance case, *Journal of Econometrics*, 60, 145–156.

Ibragimov, M., R. Ibragimov and J. Walden (2015). *Heavy-Tailed Distributions and Robustness in Economics and Finance*, Springer-Verlag, Berlin.

Joe, H. (1997). *Multivariate Models and Dependence Concepts*, Chapman & Hall/CRC, FL.

Johnson, N. L., S. Kotz and N. Balakrishnan (1994). *Continuous Univariate Distributions*, vol. 1, 2nd edition, John Wiley & Sons, New York.

Johnson, N. L., S. Kotz and N. Balakrishnan (1995). *Continuous Univariate Distributions*, vol. 2, 2nd edition, John Wiley & Sons, New York.

Johnson, N. L., S. Kotz and N. Balakrishnan (1997). *Discrete Multivariate Distributions*,

John Wiley & Sons, New York.

Johnson, N. L., S. Kotz and A. W. Kemp (1993). *Univariate Discrete Distributions*, 2nd edition, John Wiley & Sons, New York.

Jones, M. C. (1991). The roles of ISE and MISE in density estimation, *Statistics and Probability Letters*, 12, 51–56.

Jones, M. C., J. S. Marron and B. U. Park (1991). A simple root-n bandwidth selector, *Annals of Statistics*, 19, 1919–1932.

Kaplan. E. L. and P. Meier (1958). Nonparametric estimation from incomplete observations, *Journal of the American Statistical Association*, 53, 457–481.

Kass, R. E. (1989). The geometry of asymptotic inference, (with discussion), *Statistical Science*, 4, 188–234. [See also (1990) 5, 370.]

Kendall, M. G. (1954). Note on bias in the estimation of autocorrelation, *Biometrika*, 41, 403–404.

Kendall, M. and A. Stuart (1977). *The Advanced Theory of Statistics*, vol. 1, 4th edition, Charles Griffin & Co., London.

Kendall, M. and A. Stuart (1979). *The Advanced Theory of Statistics*, vol. 2, 4th edition, Charles Griffin & Co., London.

Kendall, M., A. Stuart and J. K. Ord (1983). *The Advanced Theory of Statistics*, vol. 3, 4th edition, Charles Griffin & Co., London.

Kitamura, Y. and M. Stutzer (1997). An information-theoretic alternative to generalized method of moments estimation, *Econometrica*, 65, 861–874.

Koenker, R. and G. Bassett Jr. (1978). Regression quantiles, *Econometrica*, 46, 33–50.

Koop, G., D. J. Poirier and J. L. Tobias (2007). *Bayesian Econometrics*, Econometric Exercises, Cambridge University Press, Cambridge.

Kotz, S., N. Balakrishnan and N. L. Johnson (2000). *Continous Multivariate Distributions*, vol. 1, 2nd edition, John Wiley & Sons, New York.

Koziol, J. A. and M. D. Perlman (1978). Combining independent chi-squared tests, *Journal of the American Statistical Association*, 73, 753–763.

Kuan, C.-M. and H. White (1994). Artificial neural networks: an econometric perspective, (with discussion), *Econometric Reviews*, 13, 1–143.

Kullback, S. (1959). *Statistics and Information Theory*, John Wiley & Sons, New York.

Lai, T. L. and D. Siegmund (1983). Fixed accuracy estimation of an autoregressive parameter, *Annals of Statistics*, 11, 478–485.

Larsson, R. (1995). The asymptotic distributions of some test statistics in near-integrated AR processes, *Econometric Theory*, 11, 306–330.

Le Cam, L. (1952). On sets of parameter points where it is possible to achieve superefficiency of estimates, (abstract), *Annals of Mathematical Statistics*, 23, 148.

Le Cam, L. (1953). On some asymptotic properties of maximum likelihood estimates and related Bayes' estimates, *University of California Publications in Statistics*, 1, 277–330.

Lee, P. M. (2004). *Bayesian Statistics: An Introduction*, 3rd edition, Hodder Headline, London.

Lehmann, E. L. (1986). *Testing Statistical Hypotheses*, 2nd edition, John Wiley & Sons,

New York.

Lehmann, E. L. and G. Casella (1998). *Theory of Point Estimation*, 2nd edition, Springer-Verlag, Berlin.

Li, K.-C. (1991). Sliced inverse regression for dimension reduction, (with discussion), *Journal of the American Statistical Association*, 86, 316–342.

Li, Q. and J. S. Racine (2006). *Nonparametric Econometrics: Theory and Practice*, Princeton University Press, Princeton.

Lindsay, B. G. and B. Li (1997). On second-order optimality of the observed Fisher information, *Annals of Statistics*, 25, 2172–2199.

Loève, M. (1977). *Probability Theory*, vol. 1, 4th edition, Springer-Verlag, Berlin.

Mack, Y. P. and M. Rosenblatt (1979). Multivariate k-nearest neighbor density estimates, *Journal of Multivariate Analysis*, 9, 1–15.

Magdalinos, T. (2007). On the inconsistency of the unrestricted estimator of the information matrix near a unit root, *Econometrics Journal*, 10, 245–262.

Magnus, J. R. (1999). The traditional pretest estimator, *Theory of Probability and Its Applications*, 44, 293–308.

Magnus, J. R. and H. Neudecker (2019). *Matrix Differential Calculus with Applications in Statistics and Econometrics*, third edition, John Wiley & Sons, Chichester.

Malley, J. D. and J. Hornstein (1993). Quantum statistical inference, *Statistical Science*, 8, 433–457.

Marden, J. I. (1982). Combining independent noncentral chi squared or F tests, *Annals of Statistics*, 10, 266–277.

Mardia, K. V., J. T. Kent and J. M. Bibby (1979). *Multivariate Analysis*, Academic Press, San Diego.

Marron, J. S. and D. Nolan (1989). Canonical kernels for density estimation, *Statistics & Probability Letters*, 7, 195–199.

Mayo, D. G. and A. Spanos (eds.) (2010). *Error and Inference: Recent Exchanges on Experimental Reasoning, Reliability and the Objectivity and Rationality of Science*, Cambridge University Press, Cambridge.

McCullagh, P. (1987). *Tensor Methods in Statistics*, Chapman & Hall/CRC, FL.

McCullagh, P. and R. Tibshirani (1990). A simple method for the adjustment of profile likelihoods, *Journal of the Royal Statistical Society, B*, 52, 325–344.

Meng, X.-L. (2005). From unit root to Stein's estimator to Fisher's k statistics: if you have a moment, I can tell you more, *Statistical Science*, 20, 141–162.

Mood, A. M., F. A. Graybill and D. Boes (1974). *Introduction to the Theory of Statistics*, 3rd edition, McGraw-Hill, New York.

Muirhead, R. J. (1982). *Aspects of Multivariate Statistical Theory*, John Wiley & Sons, New York.

Mukhopadhyay, N. (2000). *Probability and Statistical Inference*, Marcel Dekker, New York.

Nelsen, R. B. (1999). *An Introduction to Copulas*, Springer-Verlag, Berlin.

Neyman, J. and E. L. Scott (1948). Consistent estimates based on partially consistent

observations, *Econometrica*, 16, 1–32.
Nimmo-Smith, I. (1979). Linear regressions and sphericity, *Biometrika*, 66, 390–392.
Nishii, R. (1988). Maximum likelihood principle and model selection when the true model is unspecified, *Journal of Multivariate Analysis*, 27, 392–403.
Owen, A. B. (2001). *Empirical Likelihood*, Chapman & Hall/CRC, FL.
Paruolo, P. (2019). *Econometric Theory, I*, Econometric Exercises, Cambridge University Press, Cambridge, forthcoming.
Peracchi, F. (2001). *Econometrics*, John Wiley & Sons, Chichester.
Perlman, M. D. and S. Chaudhuri (2012). Reversing the Stein effect, *Statistical Science*, 27, 135–143.
Perron, P. (1991). A continuous time approximation to the unstable first-order autoregressive process: the case without an intercept, *Econometrica*, 59, 211–236.
Pfanzagl, J. (1968). A characterization of the one parameter exponential family by existence of uniformly most powerful tests, *Sankhyā, A*, 30, 147–156.
Phillips, P. C. B. (1987). Towards a unified asymptotic theory for autoregression, *Biometrika*, 74, 535–547.
Pierce, D. A. (1982). The asymptotic effect of substituting estimators for parameters in certain types of statistics, *Annals of Statistics*, 10, 475–478.
Rao, C. R. (1973). *Linear Statistical Inference and its Applications*, 2nd edition, John Wiley & Sons, New York.
Reid, N. (1988). Saddlepoint methods and statistical inference, (with discussion), *Statistical Science*, 3, 213–238.
Reid, N. (1995). The roles of conditioning in inference, *Statistical Science*, 10, 138–157.
Riesz, F. and B. Sz.-Nagy (1955). *Functional Analysis*, 2nd edition (translated by L. F. Boron), Blackie & son, London and Glasgow.
Rissanen, J. (1978). Modeling by shortest data description, *Automatica*, 14, 465–471.
Romano, J. P. and A. F. Siegel (1986). *Counterexamples in Probability and Statistics*, Wadsworth & Brooks, Monterey, CA.
Rothenberg, T. J. (1971). Identification in parametric models, *Econometrica*, 39, 577–591.
Rudin, W. (1976). *Principles of Mathematical Analysis*, 3rd edition, McGraw-Hill, New York.
Schwarz, G. E. (1978). Estimating the dimension of a model, *Annals of Statistics*, 6, 461–464.
Schweizer, B. and A. Sklar (1983). *Probabilistic Metric Spaces*, North-Holland, Amsterdam.
Severini, T. A. (2000). *Likelihood Methods in Statistics*, Oxford University Press, Oxford.
Sheather, S. J. and J. S. Marron (1990). Kernel quantile estimators, *Journal of the American Statistical Association*, 85, 410–416.
Shenton, L. R. and W. L. Johnson (1965). Moments of a serial correlation coefficient, *Journal of the Royal Statistical Society, B*, 27, 308–320.
Silverman, B. W. (1986). *Density Estimation for Statistics and Data Analysis*, Chapman

& Hall/CRC, FL.

Silvey, S. D. (1975). *Statistical Inference*, Chapman & Hall/CRC, London.

Sin, C.-Y. and H. White (1996). Information criteria for selecting possibly misspecified parametric models, *Journal of Econometrics*, 71, 207–225.

Spanos, A. (1986). *Statistical Foundations of Econometric Modelling*, Cambridge University Press, Cambridge.

Spiegel, M. R. (1965). *Laplace Transforms*, Schaum's Outline Series, McGraw-Hill, New York.

Spiegel, M. R. (1971). *Calculus of Finite Differences and Difference Equations*, Schaum's Outline Series, McGraw-Hill, New York.

Stigler, S. M. (1986). *The History of Statistics: The Measurement of Uncertainty before 1900*, Harvard University Press, Cambridge, MA.

Stigler, S. M. (1990). A Galtonian perspective on shrinkage estimators, *Statistical Science*, 5, 147–155.

Stirzaker, D. (1994). *Elementary Probability*, Cambridge University Press, Cambridge.

Stoker, T. M. (1986). Consistent estimation of scaled coefficients, *Econometrica*, 54, 1461–1481.

Stone, C. J. (1984). An asymptotically optimal window selection rule for kernel density estimates, *Annals of Statistics*, 12, 1285–1297.

Stoyanov, J. M. (1997). *Counterexamples in Probability*, 2nd edition, John Wiley & Sons, New York.

Sundberg, R. (2003). Conditional statistical inference and quantification of relevance, *Journal of the Royal Statistical Society, B*, 65, 299–315.

Tibshirani, R. (1996). Regression shrinkage and selection via the lasso, *Journal of the Royal Statistical Society, B*, 58, 267–288.

Ullah, A. (2004). *Finite Sample Econometrics*, Oxford University Press, Oxford.

Vuong, Q. H. (1989). Likelihood ratio tests for model selection and non-nested hypotheses, *Econometrica*, 57, 307–333.

White, H. (1982). Maximum likelihood estimation of misspecified models, *Econometrica*, 50, 1–26.

White, J. S. (1958). The limiting distribution of the serial correlation coefficient in the explosive case, *Annals of Mathematical Statistics*, 29, 1188–1197.

White, J. S. (1959). The limiting distribution of the serial correlation coefficient in the explosive case II, *Annals of Mathematical Statistics*, 30, 831–834.

White, J. S. (1961). Asymptotic expansions for the mean and variance of the serial correlation coefficient, *Biometrika*, 48, 85–94.

Whittaker, E. T. and G. N. Watson (1996). *A Course of Modern Analysis*, 4th edition, Cambridge University Press, Cambridge.

Wise, G. L. and E. B. Hall (1993). *Counterexamples in Probability and Real Analysis*, Oxford University Press, Oxford.

Zaman, A. (1996). *Statistical Foundations for Econometric Techniques*, Academic Press, San Diego.

Zinger, A. A. (1958). Independence of quasi-polynomial statistics and analytical properties of distributions, *Theory of Probability and Its Applications*, 3, 247–265.

Index